RELIGIONS OF THE ANCIENT WORLD

HARVARD
UNIVERSITY
PRESS
REFERENCE
LIBRARY

RELIGIONS OF THE
ANCIENT WORLD
a guide

SARAH ILES JOHNSTON

general editor

The Belknap Press of Harvard University Press

Cambridge, Massachusetts, and London, England

2004

Library of Congress Cataloging-in-Publication Data

Religions of the ancient world : a guide / Sarah Iles Johnston, general editor.
p.   cm.—(Harvard University Press reference library)
Includes bibliographical references and index.
ISBN 0-674-01517-7 (cloth: alk. paper)
1. Mediterranean Region—Religion.   I. Johnston, Sarah Iles, 1957–   II. Series.

BL687.R47 2004
200'.93—dc22   2004054570

Contents

CONTENTS

Introduction

Sarah Iles Johnston

When Croesus, the king of Lydia, was debating about whether to attack the Persian Empire, he decided to seek advice from the gods. Being a cautious man, however, he decided first to determine which source of divine advice was the most reliable. He sent envoys to each of the famous oracles in the ancient world (which happened to be in Greece and Libya) and instructed them to ask the gods what he was doing in faraway Lydia one hundred days after the envoys had left his court. He then devised an activity that he was confident no one could guess: he boiled the meat of a tortoise and the flesh of a rabbit together in a bronze cauldron, covered by a bronze lid. When the envoys returned with written records of what each oracle's god had said, Croesus discovered that only two of them—Delphic Apollo and Amphiaraus—had correctly described his strange culinary experiment. He proceeded to make enormously rich offerings to Apollo (and lesser offerings to Amphiaraus, whose oracle was not as prestigious) and then asked Apollo's advice. Upon receiving it, Croesus attacked Persia (Herodotus 1.46ff).

Croesus's experiment serves as an apt parable for this Guide because it is one of the earliest examples of what might be called religious comparison shopping: rather than simply asking his own experts to obtain the gods' advice, Croesus checked out all the divine resources within his reach and staked his future on the one that looked best. The general concept should be familiar enough to readers who live in America or western Europe, where religious plurality offers a spectrum of deities, practices, and beliefs to which one might pledge allegiance. Our immediate environments (in sad contrast to more distant parts of our world, including some where Croesus once walked) offer us easy access to numerous variations of Christianity, Judaism, Islam, Hinduism, and Buddhism, as well as a plethora of newer religions such as Wicca and Scientology. Some of these are imports from other cultures; others are combinations of previously existing religions.

Only relatively recently, however, have scholars recognized the extent to which ancient peoples, as well, were exposed to a diversity of religions, both indigenous and imported—or even, indeed, acknowledged that ancient peoples were exposed to a diversity of cultural influences of any kind. The historical reasons for this failure are political and ideological, as well as intellectual, among which three are especially interesting, as Walter Burkert and other scholars have shown (see esp. Burkert, *The Orientalizing Revolution*). First, in the late 18th and early 19th centuries, following a long period during which scholars of the Bible and of classical antiquity had taken cultural interaction in the ancient Mediterranean for granted, the boundaries between academic fields were redrawn in universities, and what we now call classics and theology strove to assert themselves as independent entities. As they did so, each one naturally stressed the grandeur and achievements of the cultures it represented—respectively, ancient Greece and Rome, and the ancient Near East. Second, at about the same time, Romantic nationalism developed. In their desire to show that particular myths, literatures, and forms of religion could be tied to particular ancient cultures that served as models for contemporary nation-states, Romantic nationalists not only discouraged any assumption of cross-cultural influences within the ancient Mediterranean, but also brought new energy to the old quest of tracking the specific, discrete origins of each culture's practices and ideas. Finally, and also at about the same time, notions about a lost "pre-language," shared by the Greeks, Romans, Germans, and other "Aryan" peoples—but not by the Semites—crystallized into the proposal for the language we now call "Indo-European." Linguistics provided another reason for separating the (Indo-European) western Mediterranean from the (non–Indo-European) eastern regions.

One might have expected the scholarly barrier between east and west to erode during the later 19th and early 20th centuries, which brought such advancements as the deciphering of hieroglyphs and cuneiform writing and of the Hittite language (an Indo-European language attached to an "oriental" culture), along with the discovery of Mycenaean civilizations and of orientalizing elements in Greek art. Some erosion did in fact begin to occur, especially in the fields of art history, ancient history, and the study of ancient magic (a field that was itself only in its infancy). Yet during the period between World War I and World War II, scholars, particularly in Germany, once again sought to assert the unique character of each Mediterranean culture. In 1946, publication of the Hittite creation myth, which offered significant thematic parallels to Hesiod's *Theogony*, reopened consideration of the question of cultural exchange in the ancient world. Slowly but surely, a new consensus emerged: the Mediterranean Sea had been not a barrier between disparate cultures after all, but rather a conduit, through which both material goods and ideas were easily transported. No ancient culture was left untouched by its neighbors. In the mid-1960s, scholarly publications based on this now widely accepted understanding began to appear, and have continued ever since.

Religious beliefs and practices, which permeated all aspects of human life in antiquity, were inevitably transmitted throughout the Mediterranean along with everything else: itinerant charismatic practitioners journeyed from place to place, selling their skills as healers, purifiers, cursers, and initiators; vessels decorated with illustrations of myths traveled along with the goods they contained; new gods were encountered in foreign lands by merchants and conquerors and, when useful, were taken home to be adapted and adopted. Many books and articles have elucidated the ways in which this happened with regard to specific cults, gods, and ritual practices.

Yet there has not been a basic reference work that both collects information about religions in the ancient world and organizes it to encourage readers to investigate those religions within the comparative framework that is now considered essential for their comprehension. This volume attempts to do both. By steering away from an encyclopedic format, and instead presenting material from the ten cultures and traditions that it investigates side-by-side, the three parts of this Guide strive to inform its readers and generate comparative thought in complementary ways.

The first part, "Encountering Ancient Religions," consists of eleven essays whose topics cut across cultural boundaries, such as Cosmology, Myth, and Law and Ethics. The authors of these essays were charged with stepping back from the particular cultures on which their own scholarship usually focuses and taking a broader look at the given phenomena as they were found throughout the Mediterranean: What remains consistent as we cross from one culture or tradition to another? What changes, and why? What, if anything, can we say about the core functions and expressive modes that the phenomena manifest across several millennia of ancient Mediterranean history? The authors also were asked to consider what essential theoretical or methodological problems confront us as we approach these topics: How can we define "magic" in contrast to "religion," for example—or should we even try to do so? How does the transition from an orally based religious culture to one that is scripturally based affect not only the practices and beliefs themselves, but also our approach to the evidence for them? The first essay in this part asks a question that stands behind all the others: What counts as "Mediterranean religion" anyway? Or to put it otherwise: In spite of the long history of Mediterranean cultural interaction that scholars now accept, what aspects of the disparate religions most closely coalesced to form a sort of *koinē,* or common language, that could have been understood by anyone traveling through the ancient landscape?

The second part, "Histories," includes essays that trace the histories of religions in each of the cultures and traditions on which the Guide focuses between about the 3rd millennium BCE and the 5th century CE. In addition to offering accounts of how each of the cultures and its political, social, artistic, and religious institutions changed over time, these essays provide the basic information that will help to clarify unfamiliar topics mentioned elsewhere in the Guide. Here readers will find, for example, a description of the Greek polis system and its effect on civic religion, a discussion of the centrality of *ma'at* (justice, order) within Egyptian thought, a description of how Zoroastrianism developed within earlier Iranian religions, and a discussion of literary sources for

Ugaritic religion. Readers will benefit from referring to these essays as necessary as they read other portions of the Guide.

The final and longest part, "Key Topics," consists of twenty chapters that focus on single topics or sets of closely related topics: divination, religious personnel, or rites of passage, for example. Each of these chapters comprises sections that discuss the ways in which the topic manifested itself in individual cultures or traditions. (In some cases, discussions of a topic in Greece and Rome, or in Greece, Rome, and Etruria, are combined into a single essay; in others, a single culture merits two essays, divided chronologically or thematically; and in yet other cases, a topic is not discussed for a particular culture because the evidence is too limited.) Each essay concentrates on the culture or tradition at hand, but by juxtaposing the treatment of, for instance, myths and sacred narratives in Israelite religions alongside treatments of myths and sacred narratives in other cultures, we encourage the reader who consults the first to look at the others as well. To further promote comparative reading, most of the chapters are headed by a short introduction that synthesizes the individual essays, notes common concerns, and, in some cases, raises theoretical issues that apply to all. (Two chapters in this section, Ethics and Law Codes, and Myth and Sacred Narratives, do not have separate Introduction sections; the essays in the first part on Law and Ethics and on Myth, respectively, serve that purpose.)

The Guide is designed so that readers can either dip into it to consult specific entries, or read panoramically. For either type of reader, the Epilogue that finishes the Guide is an important complement to the three other parts. It poses and begins to answer questions that earlier essays, which focused on discrete topics, were unable to tackle. By asking what the phrase "ancient world" signifies, for example, the Epilogue compels us to recognize another aspect of the concern with definitions that first was broached in "What is Ancient Mediterranean Religion?": once we have arrived at a working definition of Mediterranean religions and have investigated them as fully as possible, what can we then say about the way they differed from religions of later periods? Are the common assumptions that we make about ancient religions serviceable or misleading in understanding the transition? And was there a definitive transition at all—can we even identify behaviors that are more characteristic of ancient religions than post-ancient?

Approximately 140 scholars contributed to this volume, and each brought his or her own methodology, style, and interests to the topics assigned. Rather than attempt to impose an artificial consistency on their contributions, the book's editors left them alone as much as possible. Thus, some essays concentrate primarily on conveying facts, whereas others produce a synoptic view of the topic at hand, adducing facts only as necessary.

To some degree, these variations reflect differences in the state of research among the fields: most of the texts and many of the archeological remains of

Greece and Rome have been available for two millennia; the texts of biblical religion have been around for about the same length of time, while its monuments have come to light more slowly; both the texts and the monuments of other Near Eastern cultures were almost completely hidden until recently. Egypt stands somewhere in the middle: its monuments have always loomed on the landscape, but the languages of Pharaonic Egypt were unreadable until about two hundred years ago. Fashions in scholarship and ideological agendas also helped to condemn some cultures and their religions to near-obscurity for most of the modern era. Some fields have been more eager than others, too, to embrace new theoretical methods of study—to their benefit or sometimes their detriment. Although the editors have worked to ensure that each essay presents the basic facts that are salient to its topic, we have left the overall design and approach of discussions to individual authors. We have even allowed occasional disagreements between authors to stand, as indications of ongoing debate within the larger scholarly community: readers will find, for example, that different dates are given for Zarathustra in different essays.

When Croesus asked Apollo whether he should attack Persia, the god answered that if he did, "a great empire would fall." Assuming this meant the Persian Empire, Croesus attacked. But Apollo really meant the Lydian Empire, and so Croesus eventually found himself standing on a pyre in front of Cyrus, the Persian king, condemned to be burned alive.

Interpreting what someone else says is always a risky business, even if the speaker is not a god famous for enigmatic pronouncements. Comparative work is particularly fraught with risks because, try as we might, those of us who are not trained in the languages and history of a given culture can never quite understand its complexities or catch its nuances. We are apt to make innocent but grievous errors, assuming, for instance, that the sacrificial act in Egypt had the same resonance as it did in Greece, or that the professional priesthoods found in many ancient Mediterranean cultures had correlates in the rest. To carry off a project such as this volume requires a team of people who are not only excellent scholars but also excellent communicators.

The contents and design of the present volume testify to the editors' excellence as both. This book has been very much a collaborative effort conceptually, as well as in terms of its production. It is also a volume that was designed with the individual characters of the different religions in mind, as well as their areas of overlap. As the editors worked through the myriad possible topics for this Guide, they realized that many concepts that are germane to some Mediterranean religions, such as "holy man," do not translate easily across every cultural border. The specific topics that now make up the first and third parts of the book have been honed so as both to be broad enough to include, in most cases, material drawn from each of our ten cultures and traditions, but not so broad as to be meaningless. Once these topics were in place, we were able to include under one or more of their umbrellas almost all of the subtopics that had interested us (thus, for example, holy men and holy women now appear in several of the essays on Religious Personnel, alongside priests, priestesses, and others, and occasionally appear in other chapters as well). The Index will help readers trace subjects that do not have a chapter or essay to themselves.

Throughout the book's development, the exchange of ideas was vital, and I could not have asked for better colleagues in this respect than the members of the Editorial Board. Members of the Board of Advisors—Elizabeth Clark, David Frankfurter, Albert Henrichs, Gregory Nagy, John Scheid, and Claus Wilcke—were crucial to this process as well; all of them have contributed their expertise to the project and some of them were called on frequently. The contributors, some of whom wrote more than one essay, are to be thanked both for their scholarly efforts and for their patience: the most efficient of them, who turned in their essays on time, have waited several years to see them in print; others have tolerantly revised their material in response to our requests.

I cannot leave Croesus on his pyre. Just as the flames were licking at its edges, Cyrus engaged Croesus in a debate about the meaning of happiness. Impressed with his captive's answer—Croesus held to a dictum he had learned from the Greek statesman Solon, according to which no human life could be counted as happy until one saw how it ended—Cyrus ordered that the pyre be extinguished. It was too late, however, for human intervention to quench the flames; only through Croesus's earnest prayers to Apollo did help arrive, in the form of a sudden rain shower. Stepping down from the pyre, Croesus went on to become Cyrus's staunch friend and advisor.

And so ended Croesus's experiment in religious comparison shopping. Led astray through his misinterpretation of a Greek god's advice, saved when he adduced the words of a Greek sage and prayed once again to the Greek god, Croesus the Lydian finished out his life helping Cyrus (who was himself half Mede and half Persian) carry Persian rule throughout much of the ancient world: Croesus became a true Mediterranean cosmopolite. May the present experiment in religious comparison prove to be just as inclusive in its embrace and just as fortunate in its fate.

Note on Translation and Transliteration

Personal, divine, and geographical names are given throughout in familiar or simplified forms, using no diacritical marks or special characters (Astarte, Nike, Zarathustra). Transliteration of special terms follows standard scholarly practice for the discipline involved *(nawrūz, eschatiē, pesaḥ)*.

Greek names are given in their Latinate form, except for those that are best known in their Greek forms (such as Knossos) and cultic terms or epithets (such as Hekatombaia and Zeus Ktesios).

Quotations from the Hebrew Bible and the New Testament follow the Revised Standard Version.

Translations of passages from other works, unless credited to a published source, may be assumed to be by the article's author.

Abbreviations

ANET   J. B. Pritchard (ed.), *Ancient Near Eastern Texts Relating to the Old Testament* (3rd ed.; Princeton: Princeton University Press, 1969)

CAT   M. Dietrich, O. Loretz, and J. Sanmartín, *The Cuneiform Alphabetic Texts from Ugarit, Ras Ibn Hani, and Other Places* (Münster: Ugarit-Verlag, 1995) (− second edition of *KTU*)

CIL   *Corpus Inscriptionum Latinarum*

CTH   Emmanuel Laroche, *Catalogue des textes hittites* (Études et commentaires 75; Paris: Klincksieck, 1971)

FGrH   F. Jacoby (ed.), *Die Fragmente der griechischen Historiker* (Leiden: Brill, 1923–)

IG   *Inscriptiones Graecae*

ILS   *Inscriptiones Latinae Selectae*

KAI   H. Donner and W. Röllig, *Kanaänaische und aramäische Inschriften* (3rd ed.; 3 vols.; Wiesbaden: Harrassowitz, 1971–76)

KAR   *Keilschrifttexte aus Assur religiösen Inhalts*

KBo   Keilschrifttexte aus Boghazköi (1916–)

KTU   M. Dietrich, O. Loretz, and J. Sanmartín, *Die keilsalphabetischen Texte aus Ugarit* (Alter Orient und Altes Testament 24.1; Kevelaer: Butzon & Bercker/ Neukirchen-Vluyn: Neukirchener Verlag, 1976)

KUB   Keilschrifturkunden aus Boghazköi (1921–)

PDM   *Papyri Demoticae Magicae*

PGM   K. Preisendanz (ed.), *Papyri Graecae Magicae: Die griechischen Zauberpapyri* (Berlin, 1928); 2nd ed., 2 vols., ed. A. Henrichs (Berlin, 1973–1974)

SEG   *Supplementum Epigraphicum Graecum*

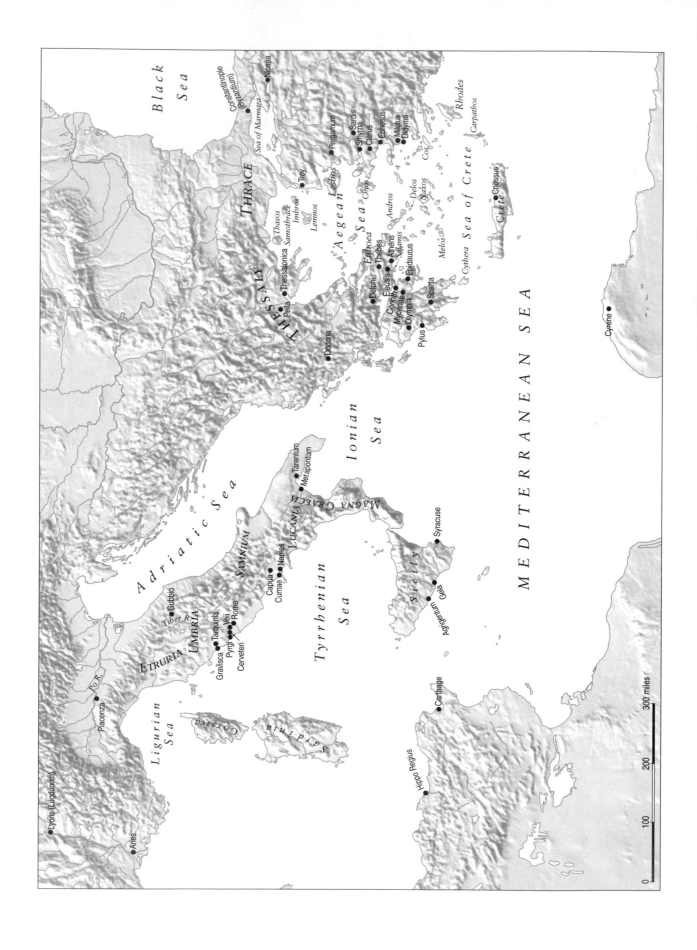

Black Sea

Nicaea
Constantinople (Byzantium)
Sea of Marmara

THRACE
Troy
Pergamum
Sardis
Smyrna
Clarus
Ephesus
Miletus
Didyma
Cos
Rhodes
Carpathos

Lesbos
Chios

Thasos
Samothrace
Imbros
Lemnos

THESSALY
Pella
Thessalonica

Aegean Sea
Euboea
Thebes
Delphi
Eleusis
Corinth
Mycenae
Olympia
Epidaurus
Sparta
Pylus
Athens
Andros
Delos
Naxos
Melos
Cythera

Sea of Crete
Crete
Cnossus

Dodona

Adriatic Sea

Ionian Sea

MEDITERRANEAN SEA

Cyrene

Tarentum
Metapontum

MAGNA GRAECA
LUCANIA

Capua
Cumae
Naples
SAMNIUM

Syracuse
Sicily
Gela
Agrigentum

Tyrrhenian Sea

Gubbio
Tiber R.
UMBRIA
Tarquinia
Veli
Rome
Pyrgi
Cerveteri
Gravisca
ETRURIA

Po R.
Piacenza

Ligurian Sea

Corsica
Sardinia

Lyons (Lugdunum)
Arles

Carthage

Hippo Regius

0   100   200   300 miles

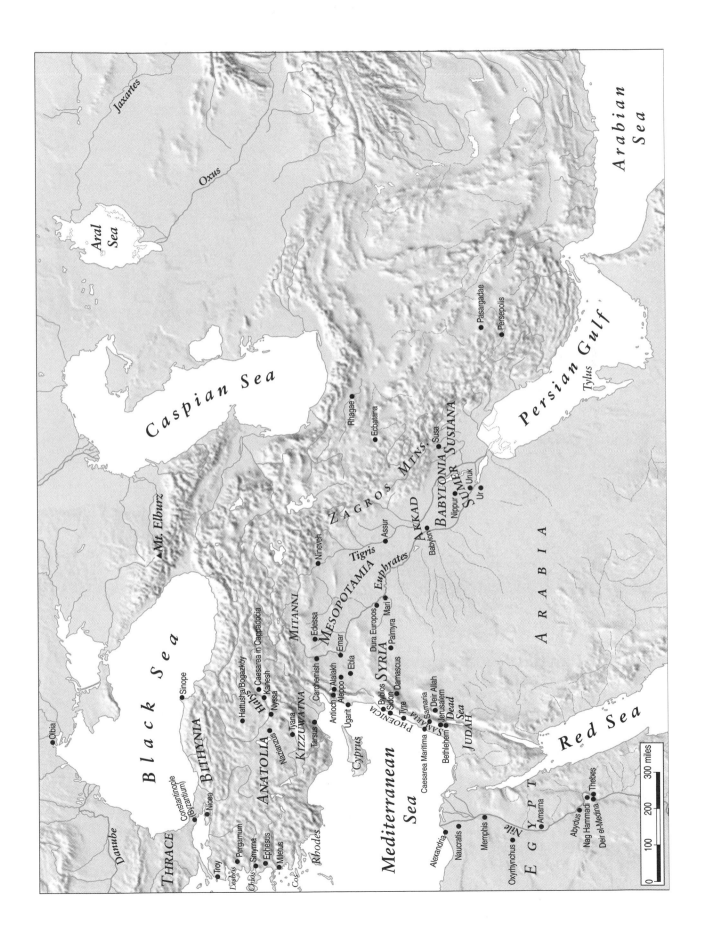

Jaxartes

Oxus

Aral Sea

Arabian Sea

Caspian Sea

● Pasargadae

● Persepolis

Persian Gulf

Tylus

● Rhagae

● Ecbatana

Z A G R O S   M T N S.

● Susa

SUSIANA

BABYLONIA   SUMER

● Nineveh

ASSUR ● Assur

Tigris

AKKAD

Nippur ● ● Uruk

● Babylon

Babylon ●

Euphrates

ARABIA

A R A B I A

● Ur

Mt. Elburz

B l a c k   S e a

● Olbia

● Sinope

THRACE

BITHYNIA

Constantinople
(Byzantium)
Nicea ●

Danube

● Pergamum

Troy ●

Lesbos

Smyrna ●

Ephesus ●

Miletus ●

Chios

Cos

Rhodes

ANATOLIA

Nazianzus ●

Tyana ●

KIZZUWATNA

Caesarea in Cappadocia ●

Hattusha/Bogazköy ●

Halys

Kadesh ●

MITANNI

Tarsus ●

Carchemish ●

Edessa ●

MESOPOTAMIA

Antioch ●

Alalakh ●

Aleppo ●

Ebla ●

Ugarit ●

Emar ●

Dura Europos ●

Mari ●

Palmyra ●

SYRIA

Byblos ●

Sidon ●

Damascus ●

Tyre ●

PHOENICIA

Cyprus

Caesarea Maritima ●

Samaria ●

SAMARIA

Deir Allah ●

Jerusalem ●

Bethlehem ●

JUDAH

Dead Sea

*M e d i t e r r a n e a n
S e a*

R e d   S e a

Alexandria ●

Naucratis ●

Memphis ●

Oxyrhynchus ●

Nile

E G Y P T

Abydos ●

Nag Hammadi ●

Thebes ●

Deir el-Medina ●

Amarna ●

| 0 | 100 | 200 | 300 miles |

ENCOUNTERING
ANCIENT RELIGIONS

What Is Ancient Mediterranean Religion?

Fritz Graf

*I*n the darkest hour of his life, Lucius, the human-turned-donkey in Apuleius's novel *The Golden Ass,* is sleeping in the sand of a Mediterranean beach. He has barely escaped from yet another humiliation, public copulation with a woman in Corinth's circus, and he is at the very end of his considerable wits. He awakens to a brilliant full moon rising over the dark waters of the Corinthian Gulf. He addresses a prayer to the moon and its goddess. And lo and behold! a beautiful woman rises out of the silvery path on the water; she consoles Lucius and introduces her astonishingly multiple personality: "The Phrygians, earliest of humans, call me the Pessinuntian Mother of the Gods; the Athenians, sprung from their own soil, call me Cecropian Minerva; the sea-tossed Cyprians call me Venus of Paphus, the arrow-bearing Cretans Dictynna, the trilingual Sicilians Ortygian Proserpina; to the Eleusinians I am the ancient goddess Ceres, to others Juno, to yet others Bellona, Hecate, or the Rhamnusian Goddess; and the Ethiopians who are illuminated by the first rays of the sun, the Africans, and the Egyptians full of ancient lore and wisdom honor me with the true rites and call me with the true name: Isis" (*Golden Ass* 11.1–5). When making these claims in Apuleius's novel, Isis is well aware of the discordant unity of Mediterranean religions. She identifies herself with most of the great goddesses of pagan antiquity, from Rome and Sicily to Cyprus and Phrygia: despite different local names and different local rituals, all people worship the same divinity. Soon enough, the Virgin Mary would top—and topple—them all.

When Apuleius wrote these lines in the latter part of the 2nd century CE, most of the geographical area we assign to the religions of the ancient Mediterranean was united as part of the *Imperium Romanum* that stretched from the Rhine to the Euphrates and from Britain to Libya and Upper Egypt; the lands east of the Euphrates—Mesopotamia, Persia, Arabia—belonged to the

Parthians, who alternated between war and diplomacy with Rome. Many inhabitants of the empire were aware of its diverse and rich religious traditions, and an exchange among these traditions had been going on for some time already. Although mountains and deserts divided the land around the Mediterranean Sea into many small and distinct units (which accounted for the astounding variety of local cultures), the sea connected rather than separated the cultures along its shore; each river valley was a unit that was open to the sea as a common interface (see Peregrine and Purcell 2000).

The imperial capital itself attracted not only countless immigrants, but also their gods. Roman colonists in their turn carried Jupiter, Juno, and Minerva far east—Gaza in the corner between Palestine and Egypt even celebrated the Consualia, with its horse races in honor of the old and shadowy Roman god Consus (Jerome, *Life of Hilarion* 11). The Celtic goddess of horses, Epona, spread as far south as African Mauretania and as far east as Greek Corinth (Apuleius, *Golden Ass* 3.27); the Egyptian Isis had sanctuaries in Italy, Gaul, and Britain; and a recently invented mystery cult that borrowed elements from the myth and cult of Persian Mitra/Varuna spread all over the empire. More was to come. A small Jewish messianic sect that claimed one Christus as its founder was slowly conquering the empire, to be seriously challenged only by the followers of an Arabian merchant-turned-prophet from Mecca. If this cross-fertilization of religious traditions in the ancient Mediterranean is so highly visible in this period, how much further does it reach into the past?

The kaleidoscope of power

History helps to understand the area's character. The Mediterranean was not the only connecting factor: empire building had been going on for a long time already, and empires, even unloved ones, facilitate communication. Going backward in time, the Roman and Parthian empires appear as the heirs to the Hellenistic kingdoms that were carved out of Alexander's conquest—the kingdoms of the Ptolemies, the Seleucids, the Attalids of Pergamum—and that allowed Macedonian troops and Greek artists to dominate almost the entire region associated with the religions discussed in this volume. Before Alexander, the vast eastern regions, from Anatolia to Iran, Afghanistan, and Egypt, had been part of the Persian Empire, founded by Cyrus the Great. Cyrus had wrested it away from the Assyrians, whose empire had risen in the 9th and early 8th centuries, to embrace the entire region between Persia and the Mediterranean and even, for some time, Egypt. In the centuries immediately preceding the rise of the Assyrians—the "Dark Age" that separated the Bronze Age from the Iron Age—this space had been fragmented, with the sole exception of Egypt: at the very end of the Bronze Age, natural catastrophes and invaders (the somewhat enigmatic Sea Peoples) had destroyed the seemingly stable power structure of the Late Bronze Age. The city-states of Mesopotamia and the Levantine coast—not the least those of Phoenicia, the Neo-Hittite kingdoms along the modern border between Syria and Turkey, the small towns of mainland Greece, and the kingdoms of Phrygia and Urartu in central and eastern Anatolia—all led a more-or-less independent existence during these centuries. The 2nd millennium, "centuries of unity" in Braudel's words, owed its unity and stability to a few large powers. Earlier in the millennium, the Babylonians had ruled in Mesopotamia and the adjacent areas, the Hittites in central Anatolia, while Egypt kept inside the Nile Valley; after about 1400 BCE, the Hittites pushed south toward Syria and Palestine and the Egyptians came north to meet them in the Battle of Carchemish, which settled the balance of power for a while. Smaller western Asiatic states such as Ugarit flourished, owing changing allegiances to the current dominant power, and the Minoan and Mycenaean kinglets in Greece kept their political independence at the margins of the larger powers, all the while eagerly absorbing their dazzling cultural achievements. Only Persia—the Empire of Elam in the hills east of the Tigris—was relatively isolated; its time would come later. The picture is somewhat hazier before that; the 3rd millennium was dominated by the splendor of Egypt's Old Kingdom and the many thriving and rival cities of the Sumerians and Akkadians between the Tigris and the Euphrates.

The one and the many

Political geography is not irrelevant for the history of religion. The existence of large, more-or-less unified regions, which characterized the eastern Mediterranean from the late 3rd millennium onward, made inland communication relatively easy long before the Persians used the famous Royal Road that led from the western shore of Turkey well beyond Mesopotamia. The coasts had always been in easy communication with each other: the Mediterranean encouraged travel and contact, either along the shore or, hopping from island to island, over vaster bodies of water, even from the south coast of Crete to the Nile Delta or from Sicily and Sardinia to Spain. The epochs during which communication was slow in the eastern Mediterranean were short and transitory, and relatively intensive communication must be at least as old as the 7th and 6th millennia, when agriculture and urban structures rapidly spread throughout the entire Fertile Crescent. This argues for a relative homogeneity—or at least an osmotic similarity—of cultural space, which has an important consequence for historical methodology: whenever we spot parallels and agreements in ritual and mythology, diffusion, however complex, is as likely an explanation as is parallel origin.

The means of transmission, however, are numerous and not always clear. Commerce, diplomacy, and exile led individuals to travel or live abroad. "Send this boy to Yamhad or to Qatna, as you see fit," ordered Hammurabi, according to a letter from Mari; and the Egyptian Sinuhe was living quite comfortably as a local dignitary among the Asians before the pharaoh recalled him; we are not told whether he took a god back with him. Sometimes, however, even gods paid diplomatic visits, as did Shaushka "of Nineveh, mistress of all land," who visited Amunhotep IV after 1350 BCE. Foreign wives were another matter. Dynastic marriages were common among the elite of the ancient Near East, as not only the Amarna Letters demonstrate. "The LORD was angry with Solomon" because he not only married many foreign wives (bad in itself) but because he followed their gods—"Ashtoreth [Astarte] the goddess of the Sidonians, . . . Milcom the loathsome god of the Ammonites, . . . Chemosh the loathsome god of Moab"—and even built shrines for them (1 Kings 11.5–9). Much later, the empress Julia Domna still favored her local Syrian gods while in Rome. There is no way of telling how transitory an influence the gods and cults had that these wives brought with them; the Syrian gods, however, backed by an immigrant community, did last some time. Conquerors brought gods with them, as did merchant communities and colonists. In the 2nd century CE, someone in Lydian Sardis renewed a sacred law written under the occupation of Artaxerxes II that regulated a Persian cult. The Thracian goddess Bendis, the Egyptian Isis, and the Sidonian Astarte arrived in Athens with the community of foreign traders that established itself in Piraeus.

The ease of communication had, from early on, worked to smooth over differences inside the wider region; and common socioeconomic conditions helped. All of the major players, even when speaking very different languages, were inhabitants of city-states, sharing a rather similar outlook on the world and comparable ideals and lifestyles. Whether ruled by a priest, a king, a group of aristocrats, or the city council and the citizens' assembly—all were living in urban centers that usually were walled, had a main temple and (when ruled by kings) a palace, with a high degree of commercial exchange and a rural hinterland controlled by the city; further outside were the nomadic pastoralists in the deserts of Syria and Judea or the mountains of Anatolia and Persia. The cities in turn had grown on the foundation of agriculture that defined the region since the Neolithic revolution and set it against the nomadic pastoralists. The city-states might be united under a powerful ruler, as they were under Egypt's god-king or the Hittite or Iranian conquering warrior caste; they might be conquered and sometimes destroyed by a powerful neighbor; or they might flourish by establishing changing coalitions: this only marginally affected their function as unities that were more-or-less self-sufficient. In religious terms, this meant that each city had its own pantheon, its own calendar of festivals, and its own mythology; alliances or political dependence on another power could express themselves in additional cultic elements that did not fundamentally alter the overall appearance of the cults.

The relative homogeneity is mirrored in the history of the writing systems. Egypt invented its own complex system and stuck to it for almost three millennia; knowledge of hieroglyphic writing petered out only during Roman imperial times, at about the time when the Copts began to develop their own alphabetic system. Throughout the Bronze Age, the rest of the region almost universally used the cuneiform system invented in Mesopotamia and now proving adaptable to all sorts of languages, including, albeit somewhat clumsily, Indo-European Hittite. Only the marginal Minoans had their own syllabic system for internal use, which they handed over to the Mycenaeans for use in yet a different language, Greek. The collapse of the Late Bronze Age empires destroyed this unity, but also opened the chance for the spread of a vastly improved system; whereas Cyprus adapted the Mycenaean syllabic systems and the late Hittite kingdoms developed their own hieroglyphs, the West Semites invented a much better alphabetic script. It adapted itself to every language, its twenty-odd signs were easily mastered, and so it spread rapidly to Greece, Anatolia, and Italy, in local variations whose vestiges are still with us today. The persistence of these variations—including Hebrew, Phoenician, and Aramaic in the east—should warn us against overrating the cultural and religious homogeneity and neglecting the force of local identities even in the 1st millennium of the Iron Age: it is a homogeneity of broad outlines, not of details.

Musical divinities

The give and take among religious traditions easily reaches back to even before the Mediterranean Bronze Age. This at least is what an emblematic case, the cult of the goddess Cybele, the "Great Mother" *(Magna Mater)* of Greeks and Romans, suggests (Borgeaud 1996; Roller 1999). Ancient worshipers and modern scholars alike agree that the goddess as we know her was Phrygian in origin. Her city, Pessinus, remained a theocracy under the archpriest of the Great Mother well into Roman times; her priests were eunuchs who had initiated themselves into the cult through self-castration. In early Iron Age Phrygia, the goddess was omnipresent. Inscriptions called her *Matar* (Mother), sometimes adding the epithet *kubileya,* which ancient Greek authors derived from the Phrygian word for "mountain."

The goddess arrived in Greece in the 8th or 7th century BCE, first on the eastern islands, but very soon as far west as southern Italy. The Greeks called her "Mountain Mother" *(Meter Oreia),* in a close translation of her Phrygian name, but also turned her epithet into the proper noun Cybele—and identified her with Rhea, the mother of Zeus, thus turning the foreigner into a native of venerable antiquity. In Phrygia and in Greece, she had cults on mountains, where her images or altars were directly sculpted from living rock. Such images in Phrygia, carved into mountain cliffs, represent her frontally and standing; the Greeks partly adopted this, but soon abandoned it in favor of showing her on a throne between two standing felines (lionesses or panthers). This image appears so often in archaic eastern Greece that it must cover a variety of local goddesses, all perceived by their worshipers as being akin to the Phrygian goddess. Eastern Greeks also called her Kybebe: as such, she had a cult in Lydian Sardis and in many cities further east. Kybebe is the Hellenization of another Anatolian divine name, Kubaba, the main goddess of Carchemish, an age-old city-state in northern Syria and the main link between Mesopotamia and Anatolia, an influential power after 1000 BCE. Kubaba's animal was the lion;

her cult in Sardis was ecstatic, like the cult of Cybele, but it lacked the eunuchs and castration that were typical of the cult of the Phrygian Lady. Although Greeks and Romans identified Cybele and Kybebe, the eastern Greeks sometimes perceived a difference and Hellenized Kybebe/Kubaba as Artemis or Aphrodite, the former identification stressing her nature as mistress of wild animals, the latter her erotic power.

Cybele's mythology was very rich. In the Pessinuntian myth that was given a Greek form in the late 4th century BCE (Arnobius, *Against the Pagans* 5.5–7), Cybele's companion is Agdistis, a goddess born from Zeus's intercourse with a rock—a story that is very close to the Hittite myth of Ullikummi from the Cycle of Kumarbi: the diorite monster Ullikummi is born from Kumarbi's intercourse with a rock and is as destructive as Agdistis. More common is the story of Cybele's love affair with the prince and shepherd Attis, which resulted in Attis's self-castration and death. Many stories narrated the terrible fate that befell a lover of the Great Goddess, beginning with the Sumerian poem of Inanna and Dumuzi and ending with the Homeric *Hymn to Aphrodite* (Inanna too, like Kybebe, was understood to be identical to Aphrodite). Gilgamesh was able to recite a long *leporello* of Ishtar's damaged lovers, in an episode that resonates in Diomedes' attack on Aphrodite in book 5 of Homer's *Iliad*. The stories thus lead back toward the Anatolian and Mesopotamian Bronze Age.

In archeology and cult, however, the Great Mother is difficult to grasp during the Bronze Age—but her iconography is already attested in late Neolithic Anatolia: a mother-goddess is highly visible in Neolithic Çatal Höyük in central Anatolia (ca. 6200–5400 BCE), represented in a statuette of an enthroned and naked motherly goddess with felines at her side, which looks tantalizingly close to the iconography of the Great Mother from early Iron Age Greece. In the same Neolithic settlement, a mother-goddess is closely associated with bulls—a symbolism that has been connected with the agricultural revolution of the region and its concomitant "revolution of symbols" (Cauvin) and that resonates, millennia later, especially in Minoan religious iconography.

This situation is complex, but typical. A neat unilinear derivation, dear to scholars, is impossible: Greek Cybele/Kybebe looks back to Pessinus and to Carchemish, and it is highly probable that the cult entered the Greek world from Anatolia from at least two sanctuaries: a sanctuary near Colophon in Ionia and another one in Cyzicus on the Hellespont are likely candidates. During the Bronze Age, the cult never really surfaces for us. This must have to do with the nature of our tradition, which is concentrated on the Hittite capital and the ritual world of the court: Kubaba, "Queen of Carchemish," becomes highly visible as soon as the Hittite power collapses. But there were stories, traditions both in Anatolia and in Mesopotamia, that were close to her. And she made her first appearance, quite impressively, in late Neolithic times: one suspects that this, too, is connected with the nature and social function of her cult in these very first urban agricultural settlements. There must have been religious traditions as old as the Neolithic Age, tenaciously preserved and distributed throughout much of western Asia, whose visibility for us depends fundamentally on the nature of the sources that are, before the epigraphic and textual explosion of the Iron Age, very narrow windows on the past indeed.

The Phrygian Matar Kubileya is not the only migrating divinity, although her story might be more complex than many, and such migration is not confined to the 1st millennium when, among others, the Etruscans and Romans adopted Greek gods such as Apollo or Asclepius. In the late Bronze Age, some Babylonian divinities such as Ea also gained a place in the pantheon of the Hittites, at the side of original Hittite and immigrant Hurrian divinities. Anat, the female companion of Baal in Ugarit, became popular in Egypt, especially during the 19th and 20th Dynasties; her consort Baal is present from the 18th Dynasty onward. Among the casualties of war were many divine images—the Hittites, we hear, abducted the image of Shimigi from Qatna in Syria (El Amarna no. 55), and the Persian conquerors took the statues of the gods together with all kinds of cult equipment and sacred writing from Egyptian shrines. While it is not clear whether this happened for religious reasons or because those statues were made of precious materials, at least the Romans had a habit of transferring the cults of conquered neighboring cities to their own.

One consequence of this general awareness, at least among Greeks and Romans, was what scholars call, with a term borrowed from Tacitus, *interpretatio*—to treat the divine names of other religious systems as translations of one's own: a divine name, in this reading, is nothing more than a linguistic marker, different in each individual culture, for a divine entity whose existence transcends those cultures. When informing his readers about the gods of other peoples, Herodotus consistently uses the Greek names, as when he talks about the Scythians: "They adore only the following gods: mostly Hestia, then Zeus and Gaea (they have the tradition that Gaea is Zeus's wife), after them Apollo, Aphrodite Urania, Heracles, and Ares" (*Histories* 4.59). Later historians repeat the procedure: "Among the gods, they adore especially Mercurius . . . , after him Apollo, Mars, Jupiter, and Minerva," Caesar writes about the Gauls (*Gallic Wars* 6.17). This reflects the attitude of worshipers as well, from Lydians and Lycians of Herodotus's time to the inhabitants of imperial Syria or Gaul. Votive inscriptions and sacred laws use the divine name in the language they are written in, and even theophoric names are translated: the same person who is Dionysicles in a Greek document turns into Bakivalis in a Lydian one. The list of the homologues of Isis in Apuleius follows this tradition. The habit of interpretation, however, is much older: in Hesiod's *Theogony*, Uranus (Sky) corresponds to Akkadian Anu (Sky); Cronus to Hurrian Kumarbi, Sumerian Ea, and Akkadian Enki in the Babylonian succession myth. Whoever brought those stories to Greece translated the names. And he must simply have repeated what his bilingual Near Eastern informers, long accustomed to this, told him; the translating habit goes far back. The Sumerian-Akkadian bilingual lists of divine names must be the result of bureaucratic interest in a Mesopotamia where, in the 3rd millennium, the two languages coexisted. Again, it is Egypt that seems to remain somewhat isolated during the Bronze Age and gives the impression of being different even later. It is not by chance that Herodotus—who otherwise makes constant use of Greek names everywhere—uses the Egyptian names Osiris for what "the Egyptians say is Dionysus" (2.42) and Isis for she who is "Demeter in the language of the Greeks" (2.59; see Monotheism and Polytheism).

This linguistic habit, however, has consequences. Hellenistic Isis can be depicted with the attributes of Demeter, take over her epithets, such as "bringer of wealth" *(ploutodoteira)* or "lawgiver" *(thesmophoros),* and be described with qualities that come from Greece: "Among Greek cities, you love most Athens: there, you brought forth grain for the first time, and Triptolemus distributed it to the Greeks, riding a chariot drawn by your sacred snakes." This statement, from an aretalogy of Isis (i.e., a long list of her accomplishments), transfers elements of Eleusinian Demeter to the Egyptian goddess. In the Late Bronze Age, Assur, the main god of the Assyrians, was not only identified with the Akkadian Enlil, but also took over Enlil's role as the god of destiny. Canaanite Baal, present in Egypt after the 18th Dynasty as a warlike and aggressive divinity, sometimes took over the iconography of Seth: that might explain why an Egyptian myth makes Seth lust after Anat, the Ugaritic consort of Baal. In Hittite Anatolia, sun-divinities were important; scholars point out that a Hurrian and Hittite sun-god were identified and that the Akkadian Shamash lent them details of mythology and iconography, whereas the sun-goddess of Arinna was identified with Hepat, a goddess whom the Greeks later knew as Lydian Hipta, nurse of Dionysus.

Earlier scholars called all this "syncretism." More recently, this term has come under scrutiny: originally, it was a term of Christian missionary theology, censuring the admixture of native religious traditions to Christian belief and practice in a colonial setting; thus, it was a normative term. The use of similarly normative terms in the history of religion—in a project that can be only descriptive—has always created problems, most famously in the case of the term *magic,* not the least because the necessary redefinition of the term proved difficult and contentious, as the divergences in its use even in this volume show (see Magic). Thus, more recently, syncretism was replaced by the more-fashionable term *hybridity.* This term originated in colonial history and was also adopted to describe immigrant cultures; it always refers to the result of adaptations and assimilation of either native or immigrant cultures or languages to the dominant culture or language. Neither term describes accurately the processes of transfer and assimilation that have been going on in Mediterranean religions over the millennia, from the late Neolithic period to the rise of Christianity. Sometimes, a dominant culture was the origin of religious features—the Hittites were influenced by the Mesopotamian cultures, the Minoan and Mycenaeans by Egypt and the Levant, the Etruscans and Romans by the Greeks who arrived in southern Italy as colonists. Sometimes, items of a conqueror's religion were taken over by the conquered—the West Semite Hyksos brought Baal and Anat to Egypt, the Persians brought Anaitis and the fire cult to Anatolia. Sometimes, the conquerors adopted large parts of the religious system already in place—most famously the Hittites, although the evidence is so closely focused on the king that it might distort the facts: the king had political reasons for concentrating the empire's religious traditions in his own hand. In other places, the natives resisted the pressure of conquerors or colonizers: the eastern Greeks turned the Persian term for a religious functionary, *magu-*, into a term of abuse, while the Scythians on the northern shore of the Black Sea killed their king when he became infected with the cult of Dionysus in Greek Olbia (Herodotus, *Histories* 4.79). The Egyptians kept their distance from the Greek settlers in Naucratis, who continued their local cults of Athena or Dionysus; if anything, the settlers shaped details of their cult after impressive Egyptian rituals that they witnessed.

Inhabitants of the ancient Mediterranean, it seems, thus could travel wherever they wanted and almost always meet the gods they knew; sometimes, there might have been different stories attached to them—the Scythians, according to Herodotus, thought that Zeus's wife was Gaea; the Babylonians narrated, as a citizen of Ugarit might have realized with some surprise, that their Astarte, whom the Babylonians called Ishtar and the Sumerians Inanna, once had been taken prisoner by her sister, the queen of the dead. But when Hittites imagined that their Zeus, the storm-god Teshub, had been born from his father's body, some Greek traveler or merchant brought this back in a somewhat garbled form, as the story that ended with Cronus vomiting up the five siblings of Zeus together with the stone that he had swallowed instead of his youngest son.

There were, of course, exceptions, where theological centralization imprinted believers with the uniqueness of their own god—most prominent in Judaism after its turn toward monotheism and then of course in Christianity. But neither denied the existence of gods of the others—it was an ongoing concern of Israel's religious elite to prevent the cult of all those Baalim. The Christians quickly turned the many gods of the others into *daimonia* (1 Cor. 10.20–21), to be fought and exorcised. And the polytheists refused to recognize the uniqueness of the one God and, continuing their interpretative mood, turned YHWH into yet another form of Dionysus or of Baal.

Rituals and places

If, thus, travelers in the Mediterranean world found their own gods everywhere, albeit somewhat disguised at times and speaking in foreign tongues, would they also have been able to participate comfortably in another culture's cults or at least have recognized places of cult and understood most of the things they saw being performed? And, as a possible consequence of this: is the process of osmosis and assimilation that is visible with regard to the divine world also visible in the forms of rituals and their physical surroundings?

The basic forms of cult seem to have been recognizable enough. When, in an Ovidian tale, a young traveler from Greek Thebes passes an altar somewhere in Lycia, "black with soot and ashes," he imitates his local companion who is mumbling a short prayer—nothing more than "bless me"—and then wants to know "whether this altar belongs to the nymphs, to Pan, or to a local divinity" (*Metamorphoses* 6.325–30). In other words, this foreigner recognizes the altar as a marker of sacred space and a focus of the rituals connected with it, but he is unable to name the recipient of the cult. Similarly, Herodotus had no problem identifying processions, sacrifices, festivals, temples, images, and altars when traveling in Egypt—to the extent that he derived Greek religion from Egyptian, as some centuries later Dionysius of Halicarnassus derived Roman religion from Greek.

Prayer and sacrifice, but also libation, procession, and votive gift, are the elements of cult that, in manifold combinations, made up the impressive festivals of ancient cities or were performed, alone or in combination, by individuals on their own behalf; altar, temple, and image were markers of space where cult took place. These ritual and architectural forms are almost ubiquitous elements of religion—this must be the reason that a foreigner could recognize them and understand their basic message.

When thus, on this very basic level, ritual might have been understandable throughout human societies, the question begins to be much more complex once we look into transfer and assimilation, and not only because of the problem of attestation. While one's own gods certainly were part of what defined one's identity—as was one's city, one's language, and one's family—the rituals in which one participated and their very specific forms, which were learned from early youth, defined identity even more so. Changing rituals can be understood to threaten loss of identity, as the debate about reforming the Catholic liturgy after the Second Vatican Council made clear. And over and over again, religious innovation and protest resulted in new rituals—the sacrifices of Pythagoreans or Zoroastrians, the strictness of Jewish ritual rules, the specific forms of baptism or Eucharist in early Christian groups all defined in-groups against outsiders. And even outside this conscious step of distancing one's group from all the others, differentiation through behavior is vital because it is behavior—not belief—that is visible. Meuli (1975: I.336) tells the story of the German woman who attended a funeral in a neighboring village and inquired solicitously whether one should start weeping already in the funeral home or only when in the cemetery—local customs matter, and if they did even in the highly normative world of Christian ritual, all the more so in the much more diverse and much less normative world of the early Mediterranean cultures. Pausanias's guidebook, the sacred laws, and the many etiological stories can teach us how many varieties of the basic sacrificial ritual existed even in the linguistically and culturally rather uniform world of Hellenistic Greece.

Furthermore, even small differences can carry significance and express social function, which makes assimilations much harder—or makes borrowing a highly selective and conscious process. Libation, the visible pouring out of an often valuable liquid such as oil or wine, is a ritual act that some scholars have traced back to prehuman origins. Whereas in Greek and Roman cult, libations are usually part of an overall sacrificial ritual or else confined to small gestures such as the one that opened and closed the symposium, they were much more visible in the eastern monarchies; this has been seen as asserting social superiority through the royal gesture of conspicuously squandering wealth. Libation vessels with elegant long spouts thus become important items in Bronze Age Anatolia and Mesopotamia—but also, at about the same time, at the royal courts of Shang and Chou China. This should teach us how easily a similar function—to turn libation into a conspicuous act—generates a similar form.

Still, transmission and borrowing are well attested in the sphere of ritual. Not all cases are as straightforward as the case of scapegoat rituals. To drive out an animal or a person charged with all the negative forces of the community is something that West Semitic and Greek cities shared, and it seems to have drifted west in the early Iron Age; this is benignly simple (see Ritual). The case of hepatoscopy—the practice of using the liver of a sacrificial sheep to divine the future—is more intriguing. It is attested in Mesopotamia, Syria-Palestine, Anatolia, and Etruria, not the least by the existence of surprisingly similar liver models that were used to help the diviner's memory. Again, a movement from east to west is highly likely, despite the intriguing and unexplained absence of the technique in Greece, the natural interface between the Levantine east and Italy.

More complex still is sacrifice. Everywhere in the Mediterranean world, sacrifice was at the center of cult. Its ostensible purpose was to feed the gods or the dead: most often, from Ur to Rome, sacrifice was understood as a common banquet of gods and humans. Thus, as in human diet, the meat of freshly slaughtered domestic animals was the choice dish, but all other food, from bread and fruit to wine, water, and oil, was used as well. Refusal to participate in animal sacrifice is always the result of theology and, in some sense, a protest against the killing, be it the Zoroastrians' cult of pure fire or the Pythagoreans' vegetarianism, which was grounded in their eschatological beliefs in reincarnation. Beyond this very general agreement, which again goes well beyond the Mediterranean world, things become complex and diverse. To convey the food to the gods by burning—to take one of the most conspicuous traits in Greek and Roman sacrifice—was no universal practice: in the large and rich Mesopotamian and Egyptian temples, the priests of the king received the food and presented it to the gods; then, the priest and their human guests ate it themselves. This is why the ritual of "Opening the Mouth" is the fundamental ritual for installing a cultic image in Mesopotamia and Egypt: "This statue without its mouth opened cannot smell incense, cannot eat food, nor drink water," as a ritual incantation has it. But the prerogative of priests to feed on the sacrifice is widespread even where burning dominates. When the newly conscripted Delphic priests of Apollo despair about living high up on a barren mountain, the god comforts them: "Each of you, a knife in his right hand, will continuously slaughter sheep, and you will have plenty, since the mortals will bring always them to me" (Homeric *Hymn to Apollo* 535–37). West Semites, in marked difference from the Mesopotamians and Egyptians, burnt the gods' parts on their altars, as did the Greeks already in the Mycenaean age and later the Romans and Etruscans; they did not feed the images but the gods themselves. Hebrews, after all, had no cult images at all, whereas Greeks and Romans consecrated them in a different way or not at all. The sequence of burning and banquet is common to all of them, as is the presence of both "whole offering" and "shared offering," the rite of entirely burning the animal and the rite of sharing it in a banquet. Lines of transmission can be guessed at, but they are complex: while the correspondence of Hebrew *bāmâ* (high place of cult) and Greek *bōmos* (altar) seems to point to a derivation of the western rite from the West Semitic world—with perhaps Cyprus as an interface—the most conspicuous form of altar in Greece, the ever-growing heap of ashes and remains of burnt animals, has parallels in central Europe already in the Late Bronze Age. The practice of burning animals could have arrived in Greece from several sides and is perhaps an Indo-European heritage reinforced from the West Semitic east.

In other cases again, a common phenomenon does not necessarily call for an explanation of transfer and assimilation. Ecstatic or "intuitive" prophecy is known all over the globe, and it is well at home in the ancient Mediterranean. Ecstatic prophets were widely attested in Mari during the epoch of Hammurabi, and their similarity to more-recent biblical prophecy has been noted; the temporal distance, however, forbids the assumption of a simple transfer. Female ecstatics are well attested in the cult of Ishtar at Arbela in the Assyrian epoch; not much later, the Greeks have their Sibyl and the Delphic Pythia, but also the male prophet Bacis; the fame of the Sibyl survives the Christianization of the Roman Empire. While specialists like this can be imagined as itinerant and thus as easy agents of transfer, it is impossible to indicate simple lines of development, and there might be no necessity for it: suffice it to indicate, once again, a common religious matrix.

In this essay, I have regarded the religions of the ancient Mediterranean world as being in constant contact with each other—a contact that, similar to that of languages in contact, resulted both in assimilation and in dissimilation. I have not looked for specific characteristics of "the" religions of the ancient Mediterranean world, beyond their being in almost constant contact; in fact, this, to me, seems their main characteristic. This is a rather minimalist approach. I am not looking for unique characteristics, those traits that would differentiate the religions of the ancient Mediterranean from, say, the religions of Southeast Asia or of Mesoamerica. To look for such unique traits in cultural studies too often proves elusive and is motivated as often by ideological longings as by disinterested scholarly concerns. Rather, I am looking for characteristics that confirm the relative unity that would justify the enterprise of studying these different religious cultures together in one vast project. Already the political and social histories of the world between the Italian peninsula and the mountains east of the Tigris argue for a high degree of interpenetration that began well before the Late Bronze Age, and the same is true for cultural history, although here, research has barely begun. The margins, as always, might be somewhat hazy and permeable to an outsider—ancient Iran also looks toward India, Celtic northern Italy toward Gaul and Spain: there are no sharp boundaries in cultural history. But the space in itself is clearly defined.

Nor have I given in to the temptation to sketch a typology of religions according to the major sociopolitical forms, the opposition between city-states and nomadic tribes being the main divide. But while the different concerns of these groups certainly were reflected by the different functions of their divinities and their rites, any more constant and fundamental difference in the religious systems is elusive. Jewish monotheism cannot be explained by nomadic pastoralism alone, but is the result of a complex constellation of social, economical, and political forces. Many city-states such as Mari combined city dwellers and nomads or developed their sedentary city life from a former nomadic life. This double origin was easily visible in lifestyle choices, but proves considerably more elusive in religion. We lack a clear religious parallel to the exhortation of a prophet in Mari to his king "to ride in a chariot or on a mule" and not to ride a horse, to follow the example of the "Akkadians," not the nomads—both lifestyles were available, but with different values attached (*Archives Royales de Mari*, Tabl. VI.76.20). Cultural systems, furthermore, can retain (and sometimes resemanticize) elements that belong to former sociopolitical systems—the pastoralist's reed hut remains prominent in Mesopotamian rituals well into the Iron Age, and the Greek pantheon remains organized as a royal court even under Athenian democracy. No theory up to now convincingly correlates social and religious systems, and most attempts by sociologists such as Max Weber or Niklaus Luhmann have concentrated on Christianity and sometimes naively generalized Christian conceptions of religion. Other possible differences, such as the difference between the religion of a city-state and of a kingdom that unites many city-states, are even less relevant: we do not deal with different religious systems but with rituals designed to express the status of the king. These rituals are, on the king's side, rituals of his court, and, on the city's side, additions to the already existing body of rituals and beliefs, but they do not change the system.

Bibliography

Borgeaud, Philippe. *La mère des dieux: De Cybèle à la Vierge Marie.* Paris: Seuil, 1996.

Braudel, Fernand. *Les mémoires de la Méditerranée: Préhistoire et antiquité.* Paris: Fallois, 1998. English translation: *Memory and the Mediterranean.* Tr. Siân Reynolds. New York: Knopf, 2001.

Burkert, Walter. "Opfertypen und antike Gesellschaftsstruktur." In *Der Religionswandel unserer Zeit im Spiegel der Religionswissenschaft,* ed. Günther Stephenson. Darmstadt: Wissenschaftliche Buchgesellschaft, 1976.

Cauvin, Jacques. *Naissance de divinités, naissance de l'agriculture: La révolution des symboles au néolithique.* Paris: CNRS, 1998. English translation: *The Birth of the Gods and the Origins of Agriculture.* Tr. Trevor Watkins. Cambridge: Cambridge University Press, 2000.

Dick, Michael B., ed. *Born in Heaven, Made on Earth: The Making of the Cult Image in the Ancient Near East.* Winona Lake, Ind.: Eisenbrauns, 1999.

Meuli, Karl. *Gesammelte Schriften,* ed. Thomas Gelzer. Basel, 1975.

Peregrine, Horden, and Nicholas Purcell. *The Corrupting Sea: A Study of Mediterranean History.* Oxford: Blackwell, 2000.

Porter, Barbara Nevling, ed. *One God or Many? Concepts of Divinity in the Ancient World.* [Chebeague, Maine:] Casco Bay Assyriological Institute, 2000.

Ribichini, Sergio, Maria Rocchi, and Paolo Xella, eds. *La questione delle influenze vicino-orientali sulla religione greca: Stato degli studi e prospettive della ricerca.* Atti del Colloquio Internazionale, Roma, 20–22 maggio 1999. Rome: Consiglio nazionale delle ricerche, 2001.

Roller, Lynn E. *In Search of God the Mother: The Cult of Anatolian Cybele.* Berkeley: University of California Press, 1999.

Monotheism and Polytheism

Jan Assmann

What is polytheism?

"Monotheism" and "polytheism" are recent words, not older than the 17th century CE, and they have different statuses. Monotheism is a general term for religions that confess to and worship only one god. "One God!" *(Heis Theos)* or "No other gods!" (first commandment)—these are the central mottos of monotheism. The religions subsumed under the term *polytheism* cannot, however, be reduced to a single motto of opposite meaning, such as "Many gods!" or "No exclusion of other gods!" On the contrary, the unity or oneness of the divine is an important topic in Egyptian, Babylonian, Indian, Greek, and other polytheistic traditions. Polytheism is simply a less polemical substitute for what monotheistic traditions formerly called "idolatry" and "paganism" (Hebrew *ʿăbôdâ zārâ,* Arabic *shirk* or *jahiliya*). Whereas monotheism constitutes a self-description of religions subsumed under that term, no such self-description exists for polytheistic religions. Monotheism asserts its identity by opposing itself to polytheism, whereas no polytheistic religion ever asserted itself in contradistinction to monotheism, for the simple reason that polytheism is always the older or "primary" and monotheism the newer or "secondary" type of religion. Monotheism is self-description, polytheism is construction of the other. However, although polytheistic religions include a concept of divine unity, these religions undoubtedly do worship a plethora of gods, which justifies applying a word built on the element *poly* (many) to them. Unity in this case does not mean the exclusive worship of one god, but the structure and coherence of the divine world, which is not just an accumulation of deities, but a structured whole, a pantheon.

Theologia tripertita

The most cogent theory of polytheism comes from an ancient author. Varro's concept of a "tripartite theology" refers to a general structure that is perfectly well applicable not only to the Roman and Greek religions that Varro had in mind, but also to ancient Egyptian and Babylonian religions. These religions know three spheres or dimensions of divine presence and religious experience, which closely correspond to Varro's three theologies, showing that we are dealing here with a rather general structure of polytheism. His *theologia naturalis* (Greek *theologia kosmikē,* cosmic theology) corresponds to the cosmic dimension of divine manifestation; his *theologia civilis* (Greek *theologia politikē,* political theology) corresponds to the cultic dimension; and his *theologia fabularis* (Greek *theologia mythikē,* mythical or narrative theology) corresponds to the dimension of *historia divina,* the stories about the gods, their names, epithets, and genealogies (*Antiquitates rerum divinarum,* frags. 6–10 Cardauns; see also Deities and Demons).

Cosmos. The first dimension of divine presence or manifestation is the cosmos or nature. Polytheistic cosmology views the cosmos as a cooperative process: the deities cooperate in creating and maintaining the world. In Egypt, the sun-god and his daily course across the sky and the underworld beneath the earth form the center of this processual cosmology. In Babylonia and Greece, the gods seem to be less involved in maintaining the cosmic process and freer to intervene in human affairs. There, the aspect of unity and coherence is expressed above all in social and political terms, especially in the model of a royal court. However, the idea of a highest god who rules as a king over the world of gods is common to all polytheisms of the ancient world. Political philosopher Eric Voegelin has coined the term *Summo-Deism* in order to emphasize the hierarchical structure of polytheism. Typically, the highest god is also the creator (Marduk in Babylonia; Re, later Amun-Re, in Egypt; although in Greece and Rome, according to the best-known cosmologies, neither Zeus/Jupiter nor any other god creates the world; it simply develops out of Chaos on its own).

In Egypt, the highest god combines the aspects of creator, sun, and king. Here, the idea of unity seems most prominent. Before the monotheistic revolution of Akhenaten, however, the fundamental plurality of the divine world in its cosmic manifestation was never questioned. The cosmic process was viewed as an interplay of convergent and divergent powers. Two otherwise antagonistic powers, Horus, the god of royal legitimacy, and Seth, the god of anarchic violence and force, cooperated in defending the sun-god against Apopis, a water-dragon personifying chaos. The order must always be defended against a gravitation toward disorder or entropy. Order is time or movement, and it would come to an immediate standstill if the foe were definitely annihilated once and for all.

In the eyes of the Egyptians, the success of the cosmic process was always at risk. In the same way as the Mesopotamians, the Chinese, and the Romans, Egyptians were constantly occupied in watching the sky and in observing all kinds of natural phenomena with the greatest attention. But whereas in Mesopotamia, China, and Rome this attention was associated with various forms of divination that served to reveal the will of the gods and to foretell the future, in Egypt it was connected with the daily ritual that served to assist the gods in maintaining the world, supplementing divine action with ritual action. Thus, the Egyptians observed the regular and the recurrent, whereas cultures that focused on divination observed the exceptional and deviant. In the context of this task and their intellectual preoccupation with it, the Egyptians accumulated an incredible amount of knowledge, a kind of sacred cosmology, whereas the Sumerians and Babylonians, in the context of their preoccupation with divination, accumulated a similar mass of omen literature, which established connections between divine signs and historical or biographical events.

The cosmic dimension provides evidence of the gods through the natural world and its phenomena. Nobody would dream of denying the existence of the divine powers: they are overwhelmingly present in the shape of sun and moon; air, water, fire, and earth; life and death; war and peace; and so on. It is possible to neglect them, to break one of their specific taboos, to miss the correct performance of their rites, but it is impossible to either enter or leave a relationship which is always already established, into which we are born, and which is never the matter of a personal decision.

Cult and political organization. The second dimension consists of the various forms of terrestrial governance in which the gods of a polytheistic pantheon typically participate. The more important deities of a pantheon are "town-gods," and the more important urban centers of a country are a god's cities in the sense that they are strongly associated with the name of a deity whose temple is the chief temple of that town: Marduk and Babylon, Assur and the city Assur, Athena and Athens, Ptah and Memphis, and so on. The pantheon is an assembly of town lords and temple owners, headed, in some cases, by a god whose temple is in the capital and who, for this reason, rules not only his city but the whole country (e.g., Marduk and Babylon) or, in other cases, who has important cults in virtually every city, even if the city worships another divinity as its own (e.g., Zeus is prominent even in Athens). Aspects both of unity and of diversity are prominent in the political and geographical dimensions of godhead as well. The aspect of unity can be represented by the unity of a country and its hierarchical structure of center and periphery (as in Egypt) or by the periodic gathering together of different towns' citizens at centralized cult places such as Olympia (as in Greece), whereas the aspect of diversity finds its expression in the specific identity and profile of the individual towns and regions.

The political dimension of the divine world may also be called cultic, because it is in their function as town lords and ladies that the deities receive cultic worship. The cult is the service that a lord or lady requires and resembles in many respects a royal ceremonial. The feasts are typically celebrated in the form of a procession and have the clear political meaning of territorial ownership and its annual confirmation.

Myth. The third dimension may be called the personal or biographical aspect of the divine world. In a polytheistic religion, a deity cannot be spoken about without reference to other deities. The gods live, act, and display their personalities and characters in interaction, not only or even primarily with humans, but with one another, in relation to other gods, in "constellations" that find their expression in myths, genealogies, epithets, names—in short, in everything that can be said about a deity. Divine constellations reflect the fundamental order and elementary structure of human society—husband and wife, brother and sister, mother and son, mother and daughter, father and son, father and daughter, lover and beloved, lord and slave, hero and enemy, and so on. These constellations unfold in stories (myths) of equally fundamental character, founding and modeling the basic structures of human life, institutions, hopes, and experience: love and death, war and peace, identity and transformation, suffering and salvation. The relation between the divine and the human world is anthropomorphic rather than anthropocentric. The natural partner of a deity is another deity, not humanity. The gods of a polytheistic pantheon care above all for themselves, in the second place for their cities and their followers, and only exceptionally for humankind at large. But this relative distance between the divine and the human worlds is compensated for by intense analogy and a relationship of mutual modeling. The structures of the divine world and the stories about the gods reflect the fundamentals of human existence, but they function as models, and not as mirrors. The gods live and die, rule and serve, suffer and enjoy, win and are defeated: they set the norms and forms of human life, which repeats and reflects the timeless models and follows the traces of *historia divina*.

The "theologization" of history: Anthropomorphism and anthropocentrism

The tripartite structure of polytheism establishes a rather indirect relation between gods and humans. The sphere of direct encounters and interventions, which plays such an important role in Greek, Roman, and Babylonian mythology, seems to be missing. How shall we account for the widespread belief that illness and misfortune are expressions of divine wrath and that the gods intervene in various forms in human affairs? There seems to be a fourth dimension of divine manifestation and religious experience, which comprises human life and history.

In Egypt, we actually observe the emergence of history as a fourth parameter or dimension of the divine world, starting with the 18th Dynasty and gaining predominance in the Ramesside age (ca. 1300–1100 BCE). With the emergence of the dimension of history, the relationship between the divine and the human worlds changes from anthropomorphism to anthropocentrism. The gods not only maintain the cosmic process, not only dwell and rule on earth in their temples, and are not only involved in stories that take place in their own sphere among the gods—they also determine the course of human history on earth, the welfare of the state and the people; they do this by sending victories and defeats, health and illness, prosperity and disaster. In Egypt, this "theologization of history" is a new development. In Mesopotamia, however, as in Greece, Rome, and Bronze Age Anatolia, the religious meaning of history seems to have been a concept that was in place from the start. Gods supervise the observance of treaties and help to protect the integrity of their sanctuaries and cities. In Mesopotamia we also find the concept of a "personal god," which brings the worlds of gods and humans into closer relationship, while at the same time preserving the principle of plurality and diversity. Each human being has a specific personal god among the lesser gods, who cares for him or her and intercedes on his or her behalf with the greater gods.

Unlike Egypt, where any forms of historiography dealing with longer periods of the past are missing until the Greco-Roman period, Mesopotamia yields many royal inscriptions that narrate the entire extension of a reign and even texts that stretch back over a series of different reigns into the remote past. The Curse on Agade, for example, narrates the history of the rise and fall of the Sargonid Dynasty during the 23rd and 22nd centuries BCE. Among other events it relates how King Naram-Sin destroyed the temple of Enlil in Nippur and how Enlil responded to this crime by sending forth the Guteans, who put an end to the Sargonid Empire. Similarly, the fall of the Empire of Ur is traced back, in another text, to certain transgressions committed by King Shulgi. The theological and juridical concept of religious guilt and divine punishment gives meaning to history and coherence to the chain of events and sequence of dynasties. In Egypt, disaster is a manifestation of chaos and blind contingency. In Mesopotamia, however, it is read as the manifestation of the punishing will of a divinity whose anger has been stirred by the king. In yet other cultures, such as Greece, a disaster can be understood as preordained by fate *(moira),* although fate's decrees are often carried out by the gods. An event such as the Trojan War, therefore, which was viewed as historical by the Greeks, can be given meaning within a larger context of ongoing human culture.

The apex of the theologization of history is reached with biblical, especially Deuteronomistic, historiography (see Van Seters 1983). The idea of forming an alliance with God instead of only appointing certain deities as supervisors of political alliances draws God much more closely into the ups and downs of human affairs than had been the case in Mesopotamia and its neighboring civilizations. There, history was just a field of possible interventions by the gods, favorable or punitive; now it turns into *one* coherent connection of events stretching from creation until the end of the world, a sequence known as *historia sacra* in the Judeo-Christian tradition.

However, the idea of divine verdict and intervention was not totally absent even in Egypt. On the contrary, the typically Egyptian idea of a judgment after death appears as the strongest possible manifestation of the principle of divine verdict. But the concept of postmortem human immortality provides a horizon of fulfillment beyond history, whereas in Mesopotamia and Israel, where the concept of human immortality is unknown, every account has to be settled on earth. Here, the horizon of fulfillment is confined to the terrestrial world, but stretched into the future, over generations and dynasties.

In Israel, this fourth dimension of theology tends to prevail over and, in the course of time, to replace the three others. With the rise of monotheism, the cosmos ceases to appear as a manifestation of divine presence and comes to be seen merely as the creation, the work of God. The geographical and cultic dimension is reduced, after the reform of King Josiah at the end of the 7th century, to the temple at Jerusalem and no longer reflects the pluralistic identity of various centers and regions. *Historia divina,* the stories that are told about the gods and that display their characters and their vicissitudes, is turned into *historia sacra,* the story of the One God and his chosen people. *Historia sacra* is the successor of both the third or mythic dimension of narrative articulation of divine constellations and the fourth dimension in the traditional Mesopotamian sense of divine intervention in human affairs. YHWH intervenes in human affairs not only occasionally; in entering the covenant with Israel, concern with human affairs becomes YHWH's dominant trait.

Historia sacra is a dimension of divine presence that excludes the principle of plurality. There can be but one lord of history, one divine partner in a story shared by god and humans. There are, however, surprising parallels to such an extremely anthropocentric conception of the divine even in Egypt. A passage in the Instruction for Merikare speaks of the ways that God cares for humans as his cattle or herd, in terms strongly reminiscent of biblical anthropocentrism:

> Humans are well cared for,
> the livestock of god:
> he made heaven and earth for their sake,
> he pushed the greediness of the waters back
> and created the air so that their nostrils might live.
> His images are they, having come forth from his body.
>
> For their sake he rises to heaven;
> it is for them that he has made plants and animals,
> birds and fish,
> so that they might have food.
> If he killed his enemies and went against his children,
> this was only because they thought of rebellion.
>
> For their sake he causes there to be light.
> To see them he travels [the heavens].
> He established for himself a chapel at their back.
> When they weep, he hears.
> He created for them a ruler in the egg
> and a commander to strengthen the backbone of the weak.
>
> He made for them magic as a weapon
> to ward off the blow of fate,
> watching over them night and day.
> He thrashed the cowardly among them,
> as a man beats his son for the sake of his brother.
> God knows every name.

This is not only an extremely anthropocentric view of creation, it is also a monotheistic view of the divine. The text speaks of God; other gods are not mentioned. This kind of monotheism, however, is not a matter of religion, but of genre and perspective. If one looks at the world in the way that this text does, the principles of plurality and differentiation disappear, and the ultimate unity of the divine appears. This perspective is characteristic of the genre of wisdom literature, a forerunner of moral philosophy that reflects in a very general way on the fundamentals of human existence. Egyptian wisdom literature generally speaks of god instead of specific gods. This is not only a generic term, to be filled in by a specific god as the case may be (*a* god instead of *the* god), but a specific term referring to the sun-god and creator, as in the Instruction of Merikare. In the perspective of moral philosophy, this is the only god that really counts, the one god on which everything else (including the other gods) depends. Such a "monotheism of perspective" is conventionally termed henotheism to distinguish it from monolatry as a monotheism of cult, worship, and commitment, whereas the term *monotheism* is reserved for a combination of both: the transformation of a henotheistic perspective into a full-fledged religion or vice versa, the transformation of a monolatrous cult (which recognizes the existence of other gods but worships only one) into a religion adopting the henotheistic perspective in which the other gods do not exist at all.

In Egypt, the henotheistic perspective of wisdom literature and the polytheism of cult coexist without any apparent conflict. During the New Kingdom, however, the henotheistic perspective starts to affect certain domains of temple literature as well, especially hymns to Amun-Re, the god of the capital, Thebes, who becomes identified with the sun-god of Heliopolis. An early hymn to this god, dating back perhaps even before the New Kingdom, adopts the anthropocentric and henotheistic perspective of Merikare:

> Hail, Re, lord of justice,
> whose chapel is hidden, lord of the gods,
> Khepri in his boat,
> at whose command the gods emerge,
> Atum, creator of human beings,
> who differentiates them and makes them live,
> who distinguishes people by the color of their skin,
> who hears the prayers of those in distress,
> and is well disposed to those who call on him,
> who rescues the fearful from the overbearing,
> who judges between rich and poor,
> lord of perception, on whose lips is the creative word,
> it is for his sake that Hapi has come,
> lord of sweetness, great of love,
> it is to make people live that he has come.

To be sure, the gods, plural, are mentioned in this text, which is still a far cry from real monotheism and even henotheism. Yet the gods are put on a level with humans and every other creature, and the general view is clearly anthropocentric and henotheistic. Akhenaten's monotheistic Amarna revolution is the radical consequence of this shift from mythical anthropomorphism to philosophical anthropocentrism. It realizes the henotheistic perspective in terms of cult and religious institutions, turning the sun- and creator-god into the sole and only one and denying the other gods any worship and even existence. In the aftermath of this revolutionary step, the gods are readmitted into cult and general worldview; the henotheistic perspective, however, still prevails, and the gods tend now to be demoted, especially in hymns to Amun, to "names," "manifestations," "symbols," "limbs," and so on, of the One. This post-Amarna theology is closer to pantheism than to monotheism; however, the tripartite structure of divine presence—the cosmic, cultic, and mythic dimensions—is again fully expressed in the religious life of the country, and the new concept of a fourth dimension, history, does not in any way invalidate the importance of the other three.

What is monotheism?

Evolutionary monotheism

The idea of unity is not alien to polytheistic religions. On the contrary, the emphasis on the oneness or uniqueness of God or the ultimate unity of the divine world with its plethora of deities is obvious in Mesopotamian and Egyptian texts and increases over time.

Translating gods. In polytheistic religions, the deities are clearly differentiated and personalized by name, shape, and function. The great achievement of polytheism is the articulation of a common semantic universe. It is this semantic dimension that makes the names translatable—that is, makes it possible for gods from different cultures or parts of a culture to be equated with one another. Tribal religions are ethnocentric. The powers and ancestral spirits worshiped by one tribe are different from those worshiped by another tribe. In contrast, the highly differentiated members of polytheistic pantheons lend themselves easily to cross-cultural translation or "interpretation." Translation functions because the names not only have a reference, but also a meaning, namely, the god's specific character as it is unfolded in cosmological speculation, myths, hymns, rites, and so on. This character makes a deity comparable to other deities with similar traits. The similarity of gods makes their names mutually translatable. But in historical reality, this correlation has to be reversed. The practice of translating the names of the gods created a concept of similarity and produced the idea or conviction that gods are international.

The tradition of translating or interpreting foreign divine names goes back to the innumerable glossaries equating Sumerian and Akkadian words, among which appear lists of divine names in two or even three languages, such as Emesal (women's language, used as a literary dialect), Sumerian, and Akkadian. The most interesting of these sources is the explanatory list *Anu sa ameli*, which contains three columns, the first giving the Sumerian name, the second the Akkadian name, and the third the functional definition of the deity. This explanatory list gives what may be called the meaning of divine names, making explicit the principle that underlies the equation or translation of divine names. In the Kassite period of the Late Bronze Age, the lists are extended to include languages such as Amorite, Hurrian, Elamite, and Kassite in addition to Sumerian and Akkadian. In these cases, the practice of translating divine names was applied to very different cultures and religions. The origin of this practice may be identified in the field of international law. Treaties had to be sealed by solemn oaths, and the gods invoked in these oaths had to be recognized by both parties. The list of these gods conventionally closes the treaty. They necessarily had to be equivalent as to their function and in particular as to their rank. Intercultural theology became a concern of international law.

The growing political and commercial interconnectedness of the ancient world and the practice of cross-cultural translation of everything, including divine names, gradually led to the concept of a common religion. The names, iconographies, and rites—in short, the cultures—differ, but the gods are the same. This concept of religion as the common background of cultural diversity and the principle of cultural translatability eventually led to the late Hellenistic mentality, for which the names of the gods mattered little in view of the overwhelming natural evidence for their existence and presence in the world.

Hyphenating gods. Scholars conventionally refer to an Egyptian phenomenon that might be compared to the Mesopotamian technique of translating gods as syncretism. It involves the collocation of two or three different gods, leading to hyphenated names such as Amun-Re, Amun-Re-Harakhty, Ptah-Sokar-Osiris, Hathor-Tefnut, Min-Horus, Atum-Khepri, Sobek-Re, and so on. As a rule, the first name refers to the cultic/local dimension, the actual temple owner and lord of the town, whereas the second name refers to a translocal, preferably cosmic deity. Thus, Amun is the lord of Thebes, in whom the sun-god, Re, becomes manifest. Ptah is the lord of Memphis, Sokar the god of its necropolis, Osiris the god of the underworld and the dead whose Memphite representation is to be seen in Ptah-Sokar. This relationship between deities does not mean equation or fusion; the gods retain their individuality. Re does not merge into Amun or vice versa. The gods enter into a relationship of mutual determination and complementation: Re becomes the cosmic aspect of Amun, Amun the cultic and local aspect of Re; Atum refers to the nocturnal, and Khepri to the diurnal aspect of the sun-god. Hyphenation implies neither identification nor subordination; Amun has no precedence over Re, nor Re over Amun. In the course of time, however, this practice of "hyphenating" gods fosters the idea of a kind of deep structure identity.

A similar practice occurs in Greece, although with very different ramifications. A god worshiped throughout Greece, such as Artemis, may become associated with a local god whose traits are similar (thus in Arcadia we find Artemis Callisto). In these cases, however, an originally independent god—even a god who continues to be worshiped independently in some cases—is subordinated to the Panhellenic god both in the sense that the lesser god's altar is smaller than the greater god's and in the sense that myth makes the lesser god a "heroic" companion of the greater god.

"All gods are One." In Mesopotamia, the pantheon is structured by strong hierarchical relations of subordination, and this, in the long run, fosters similar ideas of deep structural identity. The creation epic, the *Enuma Elish,* ends with a hymn to the chief god, Marduk, calling him by fifty names. The gods who are subordinated to Marduk become his names, aspects of his all-encompassing essence. Another text assembles a group of major deities, identifying them with roles of Marduk:

Ninirta is Marduk of the hoe,
Nergal is Marduk of the attack,
Zababa is Marduk of the hand-to-hand fight,
Enlil is Marduk of lordship and counsel,
Nabium is Marduk of accounting,
Sin is Marduk, the illuminator of the night,
Shamash is Marduk of justice,
Adad is Marduk of rains.

A hymn of Assurbanipal addresses Marduk as carrying the identity of the three highest gods as personal properties: "You hold the Anu-ship, the Enlil-ship, the Ea-ship." The culmination of these tendencies is reached when the whole pantheon comes to be seen as just aspects of one supreme god. "All gods are three," we read in an Egyptian text (Papyrus Leiden 1.350), which moreover states that these three gods are just aspects of one god:

All gods are three:
AMUN, RE, and PTAH, whom none equals.
He who hides his name as Amun,
he appears to the face as Re,
his body is PTAH.

We easily discern here the three "dimensions" of polytheistic theology: name, cosmic appearance, and cultic "embodiment" in a statue, dwelling in a temple, ruling a city. These three dimensions, however, are encompassed and transcended by a god who is referred to as only "He." Amun is just a name screening the true and hidden name of this god, of whom another hymn states:

People fall down immediately for fear
if his name is uttered knowingly or unknowingly.
There is no god able to call him by it.

In Egypt, this concept of a Supreme Being comprising in his essence the whole pantheon goes back to the Ramesside period (13th century BCE) and seems to be a reaction to Akhenaten's monotheistic revolution. It stresses the oneness of god while retaining the multiplicity of the divine. In the last instance, all gods are but One, the immanent manifold manifestation and diversification of a hidden and transcendent unity.

Hypsistos: belief in a Supreme Being. The idea that the various nations worshiped basically the same deities but under different names and in different forms eventually led to the belief in a Supreme Being (the Greek expression is *Hypsistos,* the Highest One) comprising in its essence not only all the myriads of known and unknown deities, but above all those three or four gods who, in the context of different religions, play the role of the highest god (usually Zeus, Sarapis, Helios, and Iao = YHWH). This superdeity is addressed by appellations such as *Hypsistos* (Supreme) and the widespread "One-God" predication *Heis Theos.* Oracles typically proclaim particular gods to be one and the same together with other gods:

> One Zeus, one Hades, one Helios, one Dionysus,
> One god in all gods.
> Pseudo-Justin, *Exhortation against the Greeks* 15 = Orphic frag. 239 (Macrobius, *Saturnalia* 1.18.17 quotes the first verse)

In one of these oracles, Iao, the god of the Jews, is proclaimed to be the god of time (Olam-Aion), appearing as Hades in winter, Zeus in springtime, Helios in summer, and "Habros Iao" in autumn. (Macrobius, *Saturnalia* 1.18.20; see Peterson 1926: 243–44; Hengel 1969: 476–77; and the inscription *Heîs Zeùs Sérapis Iaó* [CIL 2 suppl. 5665 = Dunand 1975: 170]). These oracles and predications manifest a quest for the sole and supreme divine principle beyond the innumerable multitude of specific deities. This is typical of the "ecumenical age" and seems to correspond to efforts toward political unification (see Peterson 1935, 1951; Schindler 1978; Momigliano 1987; Dunand 1975; and Fowden 1993). The belief in the Supreme Being (Hypsistos) has a distinctly universalist character:

> The sons of Ogyges call me Bacchus,
> Egyptians think me Osiris,
> Mysians name me Phanaces,
> Indians regard me as Dionysus,
> Roman rites make me Liber,
> The Arab race thinks me Adoneus,
> Lucaniacus the Universal God.
> Ausonius, *Epigrammata* #48 (trans. White 1985)

This tradition of invoking the Highest God by the names given him by the various nations expresses a general conviction in late antiquity about the universality of religious truth and the relativity of religious institutions and denominations and the conventionality of divine names. According to Servius, the Stoics taught that there is only one god, whose names merely differ according to actions and offices. Varro (116–27 BCE), who knew about the Jews from Poseidonius, was unwilling to make any differentiation between Jove and YHWH because he was of the opinion that it mattered little by which name he was called as long as only the same thing was meant ("nihil interesse censens quo nomine nuncupetur, dum eadem res intelligatur"; *Antiquitates rerum divinarum*, frag. 16* Cardauns). Porphyry held the opinion that the names of the gods were purely conventional. Celsus argued that "it makes no difference whether one calls god 'Supreme' [*Hypsistos*] or Zeus or Adonai or Sabaoth or Ammon such as the Egyptians do or Papaios as the Scythians." The name does not matter when it is evident what or who is meant.

In his treatise on Isis and Osiris, Plutarch brings this general conviction to the point, stating that no one would "regard the gods as different among different nations nor as barbarian and Greek and as southern and northern. But just as the sun, moon, heaven, earth, and sea are common to all, although they are given various names by the varying nations, so it is with the one reason [*logos*] which orders these things and the one providence which has charge of them" (*On Isis and Osiris* 67.377f–378a). Seneca stressed that this conviction was based on natural evidence: "This All, which you see, which encompasses divine and human, is One, and we are but members of a great body."

Revolutionary monotheism

Negative or counterreligion. Whereas evolutionary monotheism may be seen as the final stage of polytheism, there is no evolutionary line leading from polytheism to revolutionary monotheism. This form of monotheism manifests itself in the first place as a negative or counterreligion, defining what god is *not* and how god should *not* be worshiped. Revolutionary monotheism is based on the distinction between true and false, between one true god and the rest of forbidden, false, or nonexistent gods. The introduction of this distinction into the realm of religion constitutes a radical break. Polytheistic or "primary" religions generally are not concerned with questions of what to believe, but how to act. Not the truth of the beliefs but the correctness of the ritual performances and recitations is what matters: orthopraxy instead of orthodoxy. No primary religion is concerned with the danger of worshiping "false" gods; their concern is, rather, not to neglect any gods requiring worship.

The first to establish a revolutionary monotheism was Akhenaten of Egypt (ca. 1360–1340 BCE). Here, the negative energy of monotheism manifested itself not in explicit prohibitions ("No other gods! No images!"), but in practical destruction. The temples were closed, the cults abolished, the images destroyed, the names erased. Akhenaten's monotheism was based on a physical discovery: the sun was found to generate not only light and warmth, but also time. Light and time were held to be sufficient principles to explain the whole phenomenology of existence; the traditional pantheon was simply deemed superfluous. Its abolition was the logical consequence of a new cosmology. Akhenaten's monotheism was a matter not of revelation but of natural evidence. In this respect, it is closer to polytheism and to evolutionary monotheism than to revolutionary monotheism in its biblical and postbiblical manifestations.

Biblical monotheism is based not on evidence but on revelation. It is not a matter of cognition but of commitment. It requires adherents to make a conscious decision to accept revealed truth and reject deceitful evidence. Natural evidence is debunked as seduction, as luring people away from revealed truth into the traps and pitfalls of the false gods, that is, the world. The distinction between true and false refers, in its ultimate meaning, to the distinction between god and world. Revolutionary monotheism worships an extramundane or transcendent god, whereas the deities of both polytheism and evolutionary monotheism create and animate the world from within and constitute its life. These religions may be termed "cosmotheism," because they worship the world as a divine being. Biblical monotheism is based on an extramundane truth that cannot be seen or otherwise sensually experienced but only believed "with all your heart, with all your soul, and with all your power," and so is revolutionary as well.

The negative or antagonistic energy of revolutionary monotheism finds its expression, not perhaps in (f)actual history but in textual memory, in scenes of violence such as the story of the golden calf (when 3,000 men and women were cruelly executed), Elijah's competition with the priests of Baal (when the priests were massacred), Josiah's reform (when not only the "high places" [bāmôt] were destroyed but also the priests persecuted and killed), and the forced divorce under Ezra of Israelites married to Canaanites (which was a less bloody but equally violent act). This violence is not a matter of history but of semantics. However, there were always situations when textual semantics led to political action.

Canonization. Revealed truth that cannot be reexperienced in any natural way must be codified in order to be transmittable to future generations. Revolutionary monotheism appeals to memory and transmission rather than to observation, attention, divination, and diligent maintenance. In order to transmit its revolutionary message beyond the first generations of founders and followers, it must develop a body of highly normative and canonized scripture. This applies to Judaism, Christianity, and Islam as well as to Zoroastrianism, Buddhism, Jainism, Sikhism, Confucianism, Daoism, and other religions of the East, all of which are based on a canon. The revolutionary break between cosmotheism and monotheism is everywhere dependent on the invention of writing. It is an "advance in intellectuality" as Freud called it, based on a new cultural technology.

The appeal to memory and the prohibition of forgetting usually assume the form of reading, learning, and interpreting. Remembering means a form of reactualization of the normative impulses as they are laid down in the canon. The texts have not only to be learned by heart but they have to be understood and followed. This implies both believing in the truth of what the texts say and the determination to organize the collective culture and the individual lifestyle according to the codified rules, laws, and norms of scripture.

Idolatry, sin, and the construction of paganism. In consequence of its determination to distinguish between true and false, revolutionary monotheism constructs the outside world of former and foreign religions as paganism, a concept completely alien to primary religions. The Greeks knew "barbarians" but no "pagans." However, the distinction is primarily applied within the group itself; it addresses the "pagan within" and cuts right through its own community and even through the individual heart, which now becomes the theater of inner conflicts and religious dynamics. The concept of idolatry became psychologized and turned into a new concept of sin. Among the various innovations brought into the world by revolutionary monotheism, the invention of the "inner person" is of particular importance. Religion becomes a matter of the heart and soul: "The sacrifice acceptable to God is a broken spirit; a broken and a contrite heart, O God, thou wilt not despise" (Ps. 51.19 [= 51.17 Hebrew]). "And you shall love the LORD your God with all your heart, and with all your soul, and with all your might" (Deut. 6.5).

The distinction between true and false religion has not only a cognitive, but also a moral meaning. In this early stage of monotheism, the "false gods" are conceived of as fully existent and powerful beings who constitute a constant temptation and lure the human heart into the pitfalls of idolatry. Idolatry is seen not only as an error but also as infidelity and immorality. Without the existence of other gods, the commandment to be faithful to the one god would have little meaning. The gods of polytheistic religions, in their need of social bonds, formed constellations within their own sphere and were not dependent on humanity. The god of the Bible is a "jealous god," having to count on the love and loyalty of his chosen people, which inevitably fails in fulfilling his expectations. Thus, together with counterreligion, the concept of "sin" is born as the awareness of having failed in requiting God's love and of having given in to the temptations of the false gods.

The theologization of justice. Revolutionary monotheism is a religion in which the idea of justice holds the central position. Whereas in polytheistic religions such as in Egypt, the spheres of cult and justice are carefully separated (justice is for humans, and cult is for the gods and the dead), in the Bible they are emphatically connected. God does not want sacrifice, but justice. Justice becomes the most prominent way of fulfilling the will of God. This led to the still widespread conviction that justice and morals were brought into the world only by monotheism and could not be maintained without it. The construction of paganism implies the idea of lawlessness and immorality. This is, of course, a polemical distortion. The gods, above all the sun-gods (Shamash in Mesopotamia, Re in Egypt), watched over the keeping of the laws and acted as judges. In Egypt, moreover, there is the idea of a general judgment of the dead, which constitutes a first step toward a theologization of justice. But it is true that no god other than YHWH or Allah ever acted as legislator. The idea of justice is divine, but the formulation and promulgation of specific laws is the task of the king. In Egypt, the laws were never codified, and Mesopotamia had law books but no law codes. Every new king was free to promulgate his own laws and was not bound to an existing legislation. The Torah was the first attempt at creating a real law code not to be superseded by any future legislation. This was a revolutionary step by which the law—and with it religion itself, whose center the law constituted—became independent of any political government. The ideas of divine legislation, and not only codification but also revelation and canonization, are closely connected. The law formed the content of the Sinai revelation, and its codification in the various law codes in Exodus, Leviticus, Numbers, and Deuteronomy formed the core of the evolving canon.

Bibliography

Dunand, F. "Les syncrétismes dans la religion de l'Égypte gréco-romaine." In *Les syncrétismes dans les religions de l'antiquité*, ed. F. Dunand and P. Levêque. Études préliminaires aux religions orientales dans l'empire romain 46. Leiden: Brill, 1975.

Fowden, Garth. *Empire to Commonwealth: Consequences of Monotheism in Late Antiquity*. Princeton: Princeton University Press, 1993.

Hengel, M. *Judentum und Hellenismus: Studien zu ihrer Begegnung unter besonderer Berücksichtigung Palästinas bis zur Mitte des 2. Jh. v. Chr.* Tübingen: Mohr, 1969.

Momigliano, Arnaldo. "The Disadvantages of Monotheism for a Universal State." In Momigliano, *On Pagans, Jews, and Christians*. Middletown, Conn.: Wesleyan University Press, 1987.

Peterson, E. *Heis Theos: Epigraphische, formgeschichtliche und religionsgeschichtliche Untersuchungen*. Göttingen: Vandenhoeck & Ruprecht, 1926.

———. *Monotheismus als politisches Problem*. Leipzig: Hegner, 1935.

———. *Theologische Traktate*. Munich: Kösel, 1951.

Porter, Barbara Nevling, ed. *One God or Many? Concepts of Divinity in the Ancient World*. [Chebeague, Maine:] Casco Bay Assyriological Institute, 2000.

Schindler, Alfred, ed. *Monotheismus als politisches Problem: Erik Peterson und die Kritik der politischen Theologie*. Studien zur evangelischen Ethik 14. Gütersloh: Gütersloher Verlagshaus, 1978.

Van Seters, J. *In Search of History: Historiography in the Ancient World and the Origins of Biblical History*. New Haven: Yale University Press, 1983.

White, H. G. E., ed. and trans. *Ausonius*. 2 vols. Cambridge: Harvard University Press, 1985.

Ritual

Jan Bremmer

Readers of this book would, of course, expect a chapter on ritual. Yet they may well be surprised that such expectations would not have been shared by most 19th-century readers. In fact, our modern usage of the term *ritual* is barely older than just one century. During most of the 19th century, ritual signified a text, a scenario, or even a liturgy. As such, it was regularly used in connection with the books of the Veda or the *Rituale Romanum*, the standard manual for the Roman Catholic mass. It was only toward the end of that century, around 1890, that the term started to be used in its modern meaning of repetitive, symbolic behavior. This development coincided with a general shift in anthropology and classics toward the observation of behavior instead of an interest in myth and origins.

Yet in the first decades of "the ritual turn," the main semantic content of the term remained the notion of fixity and routine, although it now was also realized that ritual need not always be religious. This gradual development of the notion of ritual is perhaps the reason that no consensus has been reached about its content. It is used for acts, such as initiation, that can last many years, but also for acts that may last only a few minutes, such as a short prayer. Moreover, as it is a modern term, there are no clear equivalents in the areas we are interested in. We have therefore always to keep in mind that our approach is a typically modern one, and not one necessarily recognized by the ancients themselves.

Recent studies increasingly show that the ancient Mediterranean and Near Eastern world was one where rituals and myths regularly traveled from one culture to the next. Yet whoever tries to survey rituals in the whole of this area will soon notice that it is impossible to work from the same basis in every area. It is fairly clear that the enormous philological challenges in the ancient Near East, such as the study of Sumerian, Akkadian, Eblaite, Ugaritic, Lycian, Luvian, Hurrian, and Hittite materials constitutes, have induced scholars to concentrate much more on the decipherment of their texts than on the application of anthropological models to their meanings. Moreover, in the case of ancient Israel and Egypt, the largely prescriptive character of their ritual texts generally prevents us from seeing how ritual worked in concrete everyday life. And our information about Roman ritual is often dependent on scattered notices of only a few authors, with the honorable exception of the *Acts* of the *fratres Arvales*. Elsewhere in Italy several longer ritual texts have turned up but, unfortunately, they are very hard to read, such as the Umbrian *Tabulae Iguvinae* from Gubbio or the even harder to read Etruscan *liber linteus* found in Croatian Zagreb.

In contrast, we are extremely well informed regarding ancient Greece. Epic and lyric, comedy and tragedy, lexicography and travelers' accounts, archeology and epigraphy—all have contributed to our knowledge of the various Greek rituals, which we can sometimes follow over many centuries. Yet even in ancient Greece we can regularly see a ritual only through a glass darkly, since public rituals received more attention in our sources than private rituals, and the tradition often concentrated on the less "normal" aspects of rituals. Still, it is especially the study of Greek ritual that has been most innovative in recent decades, with Walter Burkert leading the way. From the middle of the 1960s onward, he started an approach to ritual that in the course of time would combine a variety of approaches, such as functionalism and structuralism as well as narrative and symbolic modes of analyses—an eclectic tradition also embraced by the present author.

An immense number of rituals in our area could be studied, such as the rites of passages of the life cycle (birth, maturity, wedding, death), the seasonal rituals (New Year), or the crossing of one area into the next. Naturally it is impossible to look at all of them in the limited space at our disposal. Instead, I will concentrate on those rituals that have traveled from one culture to the next or that have given rise to comments by members of a different culture. In this way, we can see something of a shared ritual landscape between the Mediterranean and the ancient Near East. We will first look at some more-extended rituals, the so-called scapegoat rituals and the Old and New Year festivals. Subsequently, we will pay attention to the "simpler" rituals of processions and purifications, and we will conclude with some observations on the much-discussed relationship between ritual and myth.

Scapegoat rituals from Ebla to Rome

Let us start with a ritual that nicely illustrates the permeability of ancient Mediterranean and Near Eastern cultures. Although some recently published cuneiform tablets seem to suggest that the scapegoat ritual was already practiced in Ebla in the 3rd millennium BCE, it is only in Hittite texts that we can start to read a fully elaborated ritual. A fine example is the prescription of Ashella, a man of Hapalla (a city-state in southeast Anatolia), which dates to the 13th century BCE:

When evening comes, whoever the army commanders are, each of them prepares a ram—whether it is a white ram or a black ram does not matter at all. Then I twine a cord of white wool, red wool, and green wool, and the officer twists it together, and I bring a necklace, a ring, and a chalcedony stone and I hang them on the ram's neck and horns, and at night they tie them in front of the tents and say: "Whatever deity is prowling about(?), whatever deity has caused this pestilence, now I have tied up these rams for you, be appeased!" And in the morning I drive them out to the plain, and with each ram they take 1 jug of beer, 1 loaf, and 1 cup of milk(?). Then in front of the king's tent he makes a finely dressed woman sit and puts with her a jar of beer and 3 loaves. Then the officers lay their hands on the rams and say: "Whatever deity has caused this pestilence, now see! These rams are standing here and they are very fat in liver, heart, and loins. Let human flesh be hateful to him, let him be appeased by these rams." And the officers point at the rams and the king points at the decorated woman, and the rams and the woman carry the loaves and the beer through the army and they chase them out to the plain. And they go running on to the enemy's frontier without coming to any place of ours, and the people say: "Look! Whatever illness there was among men, oxen, sheep, horses, mules, and donkeys in this camp, these rams and this woman have carried it away from the camp. And the country that finds them shall take over this evil pestilence." (Trans. Gurney 1977: 49)

This is not the place to analyze the ritual in great detail, but we may note the following characteristics. First, the cause of the ritual is pestilence. Second, the ritual is not tied to a specific date in the calendar, but is executed ad hoc. Third, the means of transfer can be either an animal or a woman. Fourth, the scapegoat is not sent off without decoration, but the animal is adorned with a necklace, a ring, and a precious stone and the woman is finely dressed. Fifth, the scapegoat is sent away to the land of the enemies and offered to the hostile deity who caused the pestilence. Finally, it is the king and the army commanders who play the main roles in the ritual.

It is highly interesting to note that this ritual spread in various directions in the ancient Near East. It traveled south, where we find it in the Old Testament in Lev. 16, with its description of the Day of Atonement, which has also given us the modern term *scapegoat ritual*. According to this description, the high priest Aaron selects two goats (v. 5), the cheapest of the domesticated animals. After a lottery, one of them is assigned to YHWH, whereas the other is meant for Azazel, an obscure deity or demon (vv. 7–10). Aaron then transfers the sins of the Israelites onto the goat by laying his hands on it (v. 21). Finally, somebody (not further specified) brings the goat to the desert (v. 21). We owe a few additional details to the Mishnah, treatise *Yoma* (4.2a; 6.6a), including the goat's adornment with a crimson thread around its head.

It is not difficult to see the parallels between the Hittite and Israelite rituals. Yet at the same time, we also notice that the Israelites appropriated the ritual into their own sacrificial, theological, and calendaric system. The ritual is now supervised by the high priest, not the king; the object to be removed no longer is pestilence or another illness, but the sins of the people; the victim is only an animal, since the Israelites did not sacrifice adult humans; the mention of YHWH *and* Azazel seems to point to the earlier polytheism of the Israelites; and, last but not least, the occasion is not an incidental event, such as a pestilence, but the ritual instead is attached to a fixed point in the religious year.

Due to our poor knowledge of the prehistory of the Old Testament, we have no idea when the Israelites took over this specific sacrifice, but we are better informed regarding the Greeks. It probably was in the earlier archaic age (700 BCE?), at a time of intensive contacts with northern Syria and late Hittite states, that the Greeks appropriated the scapegoat ritual. Our best testimony derives from a passage in Harpocration, where the so-called *pharmakos* ritual is described:

> They used to lead out at Athens two men to be purifications for the city at the Thargelia, the one for the men, the other for the women. [The historian] Istros [ca. 250 BCE] has said in Book 1 of his *Epiphanies of Apollo* that the word derives from a proper name, Pharmakos [Scapegoat], and that he stole the sacred bowls of Apollo and was caught and stoned by Achilles' men and that the rites performed at the [festival of the] Thargelia are a representation of this. (Harpocration, s.v. *pharmakos* = 334 *FGrH*, frag. 50)

The very late, but reliable rhetorician Helladius (ca. 400 CE) adds:

> It was the custom at Athens to lead out two scapegoats, one for the men and the other for the women, for purification. And the men's scapegoat had black dried figs round his neck and the other had white [figs]. He (the source) says that they were called *symbakchoi*. This purification was an aversion of pestilential diseases. It took its start from Androgeos the Cretan, after whose unlawful killing a pestilential disease fell upon the Athenians, and the custom prevailed always to purify the city with scapegoats. (*Apud* Photius, *Bibliotheca* 534a Henry, trans. D. Ogden)

Other examples, such as those from the cities of Colophon, Abdera, and Massilia, help us to see that the Athenian scapegoat ritual was somewhat closer to the Hittite example than the Israelite ritual was. First, the scapegoats were human. Second, the ritual was directed against the plague. Apparently, it could be performed ad hoc, but it had also been incorporated into the calendar, as the ritual was performed yearly in early summer on the first day of a two-day festival of firstfruit offering and seasonal renewal for Apollo, the

Thargelia. Third, in the city of Colophon the scapegoat carried dried figs, bread, and cheese. Fourth, the scapegoat was led by fellow citizens out of the city in a procession, but the Greeks did not send their scapegoats into enemy country or offer them to a hostile deity. Our sources are curiously uninformative about the final fate of the historical victims, but in some cases we hear of the scapegoats being chased over the city's border or thrown down a cliff into the sea. The most important difference, however, is the Greek stress on the purification of the polis. Whereas among the Hittites the king and the army commanders play the main role in the ritual, in Greece it is the city that needs to be cleansed.

Our final example derives from Rome. Roman history tells of three members of the family Decius (father, son, and grandson) who dedicated themselves and the lives of their enemies to the gods of the netherworld in three successive battles (340, 295, and 279 BCE). This so-called *devotio* took place when the battle threatened to turn against the Romans. At those critical moments, the commander-in-chief offered his life together with that of his enemies as a ransom for the whole of the Roman army. However, the historicity of all three examples is somewhat debated, and the information given by the historian Livy (8.10.11) that a commander could offer a common soldier to die for all has much to recommend it as the usual practice. Still, throughout Roman history, the image remained prevalent that at some time in the past, army commanders did sacrifice themselves in order to save the army and with it the Roman community. It is clear that the Roman example is not only geographically but also ritually furthest removed from the Hittite example, since we no longer have to do with a plague or famine and there is no calendaric aspect to the ritual. Yet, once again the community is saved by the sending away of one element of that community.

These rituals can be approached in several different ways. We can look into their origins and work out the similarities and differences. We can also look into their functions. What did the participants expect would result from their actions? In this respect, we notice that similarity in structure need not mean similarity in meaning: for example, the sending away of an animal can imply the removal of a pestilence, but also the removal of sins. Yet the rituals are also expressions of gender and class: the Hittites send away a woman or an animal, but not a man, whereas in Greece the human scapegoat often was a male slave or a male member of the lowest classes. Moreover, we can see the varying loci of power in the respective societies. Among the Hittites the king and army commanders (as in Rome) play the leading role, but in Israel it is the high priest, and in Greece the city as a whole acts out the ritual. Finally, the ritual reflects the distinction us/them (we and the enemy), but also the opposition culture/nature (the goat is sent into the desert). Ritual thus not only communicates information about society, its values, and its power structures, but it also socializes the members of a community, since through its representations (however implicit) they learn what is important for the community as a whole.

Old and New Year festivals

Let us continue with a brief look at the rituals that accompanied the transition into a new year. Even in our own Western, ever-rationalizing world, this transition is often accompanied by ritual acts, such as the production of noise and fireworks or the organization of parades. Yet, equally, for many people the transition will hardly be noticeable, and life carries on as usual. In the ancient world, on the contrary, the transition was dramatized through some striking ritual acts. During the Sacaea, a Babylonian festival that apparently was taken over by the Persians (but the reverse cannot be excluded: our sources are too scanty to decide the matter), something rather odd took place: the masters served their slaves, a criminal acted for five days as king and even had access to the legitimate king's harem. Perhaps not surprisingly, the criminal was hanged at the end of the festival.

A comparable humiliation of the king took place at the Mesopotamian *Akitu* festival, the New Year festival that goes back to at least the middle of the 3rd millennium BCE; this strongly suggests that the Sacaea was also some kind of New Year festival. The *Akitu* festival was celebrated in the main cities of the ancient Near East, such as Uruk, Nippur, and Babylon. On the fifth day of this festival, which lasted the first eleven days (a clear indication of its importance) of the first month, Nissan, the king was led into the main temple complex of Babylon, where his regalia were taken away by the high priest. After the king had stated that he had not neglected the gods, the priest brought out his scepter, loop, mace, and crown from the cella of the god Bel/Marduk and returned them to the king. The next day the king brought the gods out of the temple to a special house (the so-called *Akitu* house) outside the city in a procession, before returning at the end of the festival. This procession was evidently so important that after the defeat of the Persian Empire the Seleucid kings continued this ritual tradition. Yet rituals are rarely kept unchanged over long periods of time, and a recently published fragment of an astronomical diary from the time of King Antiochus III (ca. 242–187 BCE) shows that the ritual had been adapted to the Hellenistic ruler cult, since on the eighth day the king performed "offerings for Ishtar of Babylon and the life of King Antiochus."

As in the Mesopotamian ritual of royal humiliation, the role reversal between slaves and masters also took place elsewhere. In 1983 a Hurrian-Hittite bilingual text (ca. 1400 BCE) was found in Hattusha that contained an Epic of Release, that is, the release of slaves and the remission of debts, such as we know from the Hebrew Jubilee festival (Lev. 25). The bilingual text does not mention the ritual itself, but only supplies the accompanying myth in which the highest god of heaven, Teshub, meets with the sun-goddess of the earth, Allani, for a meal in which the primeval gods, who had been banished to the underworld, also participate; they even sit at the right hand of Teshub. The celebration of the temporary suspension of the cosmic order surely accompanied the temporary suspension of the social order on earth. In other words, the myth about the primeval gods was associated with a ritual of reversal between masters and slaves.

Our inference of a role reversal is supported by a Greek ritual during which masters and slaves reversed roles. In a poem on Greek origins for Roman festivals, the Roman playwright Accius (ca. 170–86 BCE; frag. 3) tells us about the Athenian Kronia, a festival celebrated on the twelfth day of the first Athenian month: "In nearly all fields and towns they happily feast upon banquets, and everyone waits upon his own servants. From this has originated also our custom that the servants eat with their masters in the same place." Accius evidently wanted to give the etiology of the Roman Saturnalia, but by doing so he also related an interesting element of the Athenian Kronia, the festival in honor of Cronus, one of the Titans. As was the case with the Hurrite/Hittite festival, the Athenians clearly practiced a reversal of roles between slaves and masters; moreover, as other sources tell us, on this day the slaves had a wonderful time. Now we know that Attic comedy used expressions such as "older than Cronus" and "older than Cronus and the Titans." Evidently, the antiquity of this divine generation became proverbial at a relatively early stage of Greek tradition. Cronus and his fellow Titans thus can be legitimately compared to the "primeval" gods in the Hurrian/Hittite epic. The mention of the city of Ebla in this epic shows that the origin of this ritual of reversal has to be looked for again in northern Syria, from where it traveled to the Hittites and, in a different way, to the Israelites, as was the case with the scapegoat ritual.

The Kronia, in turn, influenced the Roman Saturnalia, in which on December 17 the god Saturnus was freed from his usual chains. The fettering of a god was not unusual in the Mediterranean world and was concomitant with a loosening of the social order, often by creating a carnivalesque atmosphere. This was also the case in Rome, where during the Saturnalia the masters waited upon the slaves, who could also put on the clothes of their masters. Moreover, during the festival all Romans wore the *pilleus,* a cap that was symbolic of manumission, thus indicating, in other words, a status raising of the slaves and a status diminishment of the owners.

Yet such a status reversal was not limited to Roman males only. During the Matronalia of March 1, the old Roman New Year, mistresses served dinner to their slaves, and perhaps on that same day the Salian maidens, the obscure pendant of the aristocratic Salii priests, performed a sacrifice, dressed with important articles of clothes of the Salii. Finally, and perhaps more clearly, during the Nonae Capratinae, a festival held on July 5, Roman handmaidens put on the clothes of their mistresses and dined in huts, while their mistresses waited upon them. Moreover, mistresses and handmaidens sacrificed together, which was normally unheard of in Roman society. Finally, handmaidens also mocked passersby (who were frequently more important) and asked them for money.

These different dates point to an important phenomenon in the ritual year of the ancient Mediterranean and ancient Near East: winter, spring, summer, and autumn all had festivals that were to some extent New Year festivals. In most cases a change from scarcity to plenty or a period of leisure after laborious efforts will have sparked this feeling of a new beginning. And evidently, in no way could the transition be better and more clearly marked than by a reversal of the normal social order. This reversal could be expressed in different ways. In the autocratic societies of the Near East the most illuminating way was the temporary deposition of the king; in the more-aristocratic and (relatively) democratic slave-owning societies of Greece and Rome, the main reversal was between masters and slaves or between mistresses and handmaidens. In the latter case and in the wearing of the *pilleus,* we noticed a change of clothes. As even today we change clothes for weddings and rituals, graduations and installations, so also in antiquity change of clothing was one of the most important ritual markers.

What was the function of such a reversal of roles? Undoubtedly, earlier generations of scholars were often too generalizing in their analysis. Against scholars' natural inclination to look for profound causes, we must always keep in mind that, in the absence of a leisure industry, rituals in antiquity were often one of the most important sources of entertainment and fun. These reversals must have provided slaves and women with a highly welcome break in their often-monotonous lives. At the same time, masters and mistresses must have played along, as they knew that the normal order would be restored at the end of these festivals and thus their place in society would be confirmed once more. The festivals will therefore have had a different meaning for the varying social actors, although our sources are totally silent about their feelings. On the other hand, the temporary reversal of roles could also tempt people to try a permanent change of social roles. The Greeks in particular noticed that festivals were often occasions for revolution and regularly guarded their cities during the festivals of Dionysus, a god particularly connected with reversals. It is not surprising, then, that the end of this period was dramatized by certain ritual exclamations or, as in the case of the Athenian Anthesteria, by the burning of the phallus that had been carried along during the main procession.

Processions and purifications

Having looked at some larger and more-complicated rituals, let us conclude with two kinds of rituals of a more-limited scope: processions and purifications (especially purification as a physical act that employs blood, water, or fumigations). Processions are a phenomenon found all over the world and a good example of a more limited ritual, which often does not last longer than a few hours. Yet it is rarely a ritual in its own right. Processions are usually "framed" (Erving Goffman's term) by a special occasion that lends them their importance and atmosphere. Just as there is an "atmospheric" difference between a wedding and a funerary procession, so also as pure show the procession of a Roman triumph was evidently far superior to a procession for a Greek sacrifice. Two aspects are particularly important in processions: (1) the spatial arrangement, which often takes the form of leaving the city or entering the city;

and (2) the ability of processions, the major ones in particular, both to serve as a means of self-definition for a community and to articulate power relations between the full members of a community and those with fewer rights.

Let us look at a few examples. Herodotus (2.58) thought that compared with the Egyptians, the Greeks had only recently introduced processions. This is hardly correct, since processions are often portrayed in Mycenaean iconography and are even mentioned on Linear B tablets, but the reason that Herodotus thinks so perhaps is (in addition to the usual claim of Egyptian priority) the unusual splendor of some of the Egyptian processions. For example, he was clearly greatly impressed by the boat procession at Bubastis (near modern Tell Basta in the eastern Delta), during which men and women arrived in separate barges in honor of the goddess Bastet. The boat procession is a good example of what Graf (1996) calls a centripetal procession—a procession toward a religious center (processions could also be centrifugal, leading away from the center, as in the case of the Babylonian New Year festival). On the boats, some women continuously clattered their castanets, whereas some men, as was usual in ancient Egypt, played flutes—an interesting gender distinction in music! Moreover, the women, when passing a town, brought their barges close to shore in order to shout abuse at other women and to lift their skirts, which indicates that this procession was framed by the atmosphere of a New Year festival with its concomitant temporary subversion of the social order. Interestingly, however, the men apparently did not participate in this kind of (sexual) banter and preserved their dignity. Could the relation between the sexes in Egypt not tolerate a mocking of the males?

The Greek term for festive procession was *pompē*, the procession that usually culminated in an important sacrifice. The most impressive example was undoubtedly the procession during the Athenian Panathenaea festival. During this procession the Athenian citizens traversed the most important points of their town, such as the commercial center, the Kerameikos, and the Agora, and finally reached the great altar of Athena on the Acropolis. The procession was mainly organized on egalitarian principles in groups according to deme and thus constituted a display of the unity of the Athenian population; those who were unable to participate undoubtedly lined the streets to admire the procession. At the same time, however, the procession demonstrated the power and status of the Athenians, since their colonies and allies had to parade a cow and panoply, whereas the daughters of metics (immigrants without citizen rights) carried parasols for the upper-class females. Yet processions could also demonstrate modesty. When, during the most important Spartan festival, the Hyacinthia, aristocratic girls rode in race-carts or carriages made in the shapes of griffins or goat-stags, the daughter of King Agesilaus traveled in a vehicle that was "no more elaborate than that of any other maiden" (Xenophon).

At some point, the Greek *pompē* was taken over by the Romans, who called many of their processions *pompae*, such as the funerary procession *(pompa funebris)*, the circus procession *(pompa circensis)*, and the triumphal procession *(pompa triumphalis)*. Yet these processions, especially the last, lacked the egalitarian character of the *pompē*, which must have struck some non-Greeks as rather special, as seen in an astronomical diary from Hellenistic Babylon: "In that month I heard as follows: King Antiochus went victoriously into the cities of Meluhha [i.e., Egypt: ca. 169 BCE], the citizens performed a *pompē* [Babylonian *pu-up-pe*] and ritual acts according to Greek custom."

Let us conclude our exploration of ritual with some examples of purification on a small scale. Even today, purity is a highly esteemed value in Judaism and Islam. They clearly continue a preoccupation with pollution that can be followed via the Qur'an and the Old Testament into the earliest-known stages of religion in the ancient Near East. Purity was also a highly important value in ancient Greece, but the Romans were clearly much less concerned with it, and their more reticent attitude in this case has been continued by Western Christianity, where, as a whole, the problems of purity and pollution have been relegated to a minor role on the religious stage.

Purification is often concerned with uncontrollable events in human life, such as birth and death, illness and bloodshed. Sex, too, is an area where purity regulations circumscribe activity. In Israel contact with a person suffering from a venereal disease meant washing one's clothes and taking a bath (Lev. 15). Water was, indeed, the most common means of purification in the ancient world, as it is still today with the ritual baths for Moslems and Jews. However, there were also other, more unusual means of purification, which apparently traveled across religious boundaries, such as the use of blood and fumigations. The Old Testament prescribed blood to purify a house that was infected with spots of green or red mold, just as purifying blood was applied to people suffering from leprosy, also a type of mold (Lev. 14). In Babylon, the blood of a suckling pig was spattered on the bed of a person possessed by an evil spirit, whereas in Greece deranged people themselves could apparently be showered with the blood of a slaughtered piglet. Perhaps we find here the idea of blood as a life-giving substance that could revive people or houses in a controlled ritual context. As with the ritual of the scapegoat, one can hardly escape the impression that ritual purification with blood also traveled from West Semitic peoples to the Greeks.

This transfer also seems to have been the case with the use of sulfur as a means of purification. In Babylon, people possessed by ghosts could be treated by fumigation with a mixture of all kinds of substances, ranging from jackal dung and human bone to sulfur, but we find the latter substance also in ancient Greece: in the *Odyssey* 22.481–94 sulfur is used to purify Odysseus's bloodstained house after the murder of the suitors, and in the Hippocratic corpus it is ritually applied to heal breathing problems and problems in the womb. Once again, Babylonian influence is probable.

With these examples we come to the end of our discussion of rituals. It seems clear that the ancient Near East was an important generator of rituals for the rest of the Mediterranean. At the same time, we also notice that Egypt remained outside the Near Eastern sphere of ritual influence. Its geographical and, perhaps, political position enabled it to remain virtually untouched by

Anatolian and Mesopotamian influence in this respect. As in other aspects of its religion, such as its fascination with the afterlife, Egypt remained very much a loner in the world of the ancient Mediterranean and Near East.

Ritual and myth

The nature of the connection between ritual and myth is a complicated problem, which has only gradually become better understood. In the 19th century, scholars concentrated virtually completely on myth, but after the "ritual turn" at the end of that century the relationship between myth and ritual became a problem that had to be explained. The first to do so seriously was British classicist Jane Harrison, who suggested several possibilities. In 1890 she stated that myth is mostly "ritual practice misunderstood"; in her *Themis*, however, she not only suggested that myth and ritual "arise *pari passu*" but also that myth "is the plot of the *drōmenon*" (the thing acted out or ritual) (1912: 16, 331). This latter statement was developed by the so-called English-Scandinavian Myth and Ritual School, which concentrated on the Old Testament and the ancient Near East. These scholars thought that myth and ritual were so closely related that one could reconstruct a ritual from a myth, even when the ritual was no longer known. Finally, the last quarter of the 20th century witnessed two new, converging approaches. Burkert claimed that initiation rituals are "demonstrative accentuations of biologically programmed crises, menstruation, defloration, pregnancy, and birth. . . . The roots of the tales go back to verbalized action, whether ritualized or not" (1979). As both myth and ritual go back to "action programs," they cannot be reduced to one another but originate *pari passu*. This suggestion was taken up by H. S. Versnel (1993: 135) and applied to seasonal festivals. From an analysis of the Kronia he inferred not only a *pari passu* origin but also a correspondence in structure and atmosphere of myth and ritual.

This stress on the correspondence and *pari passu* origin of myth and ritual rightly points out that neither symbolic process can be separated from the other. Yet as soon as we look at specific complexes of myth and ritual, it becomes clear that these claims not only go too far—we do not know anything about the actual beginning of the myth and ritual of the Kronia—but also neglect to isolate important differences between myth and ritual, of which I will mention three briefly.

First, myth is never a complete reflection of ritual but only selectively focuses on certain parts of it. During the Babylonian New Year ritual, when the king was temporarily dethroned, a version of the *Enuma Elish*, the epic of creation, was recited, telling of how Marduk, the supreme god of Babylon, was imprisoned, beaten, and wounded. Clearly, the myth does not mention the details of the ritual, neither does its structure completely correspond with the much-longer ritual. Yet the myth corresponds in mood with the ritual, highlights its most dramatic part (the dethronement of the king), and gives it added meaning by closely identifying the king with Marduk.

Second, the myths of the scapegoat ritual in Greece usually speak about the death of a scapegoat, whereas the ritual enacted only its expulsion from the community: what is symbolic and reversible in ritual often becomes realistic and irreversible in myth.

Finally, myths are more mobile than rituals. Although we have seen several migrating rituals, it is clear that myths can travel much more easily than rituals. A good example is the Sumerian myth of the flood, which not only was appropriated by the Greeks and Israelites but even traveled to India, before being spread all over the world by Christianity. One myth can even be attached to several rituals. In ancient Greece the myth of the conveyance by Orestes and Iphigeneia of a very ancient statue of Artemis was told in places as far apart as mainland Greece, Sicily, and Latium. In all of these cases, the myths also become attached to preexisting rituals. In fact, despite claims made to the contrary, myths virtually always appear to be later than the rituals they are connected with, wherever we have sufficient evidence to determine their priority (further see Myth).

Bibliography

Auffarth, C. *Der drohende Untergang.* Berlin: de Gruyter, 1991.

Bremmer, J. N. *Greek Religion.* 2nd edition. Oxford: Oxford University Press, 1994.

———. "'Religion,' 'Ritual' and the Opposition 'Sacred vs. Profane': Notes Towards a Terminological 'Genealogy.'" In *Ansichten griechischer Rituale: Festschrift für Walter Burkert,* ed. F. Graf. Stuttgart and Leipzig: Teubner, 1998.

———. "The Scapegoat between Hittites, Greeks, Israelites and Christians." In *Kult, Konflikt und Versöhnung,* ed. R. Albertz. Münster: Ugarit-Verlag, 2001.

Burkert, W. *Homo necans.* Berkeley: University of California Press, 1983.

———. *Structure and History in Greek Mythology and Ritual.* Berkeley: University of California Press, 1979.

Graf, F. *Nordionische Kulte.* Rome: Institut Suisse de Rome, 1985.

———. "*Pompai* in Greece: Some Considerations about Space and Ritual in the Greek Polis." In *The Role of Religion in the Early Greek Polis: Proceedings of the Third International Seminar on Ancient Greek Cult,* ed. R. Hägg. Swedish Institute at Athens. Stockholm: Paul Ånströms Förlag, 1996.

Gurney, O. R. *Some Aspects of Hittite Religion.* Schweich Lectures 1976. Oxford: Oxford University Press for the British Academy, 1977.

Harrison, Jane Ellen. *Mythology and Monuments of Ancient Athens.* London and New York: Macmillan, 1890.

———. *Themis: A Study of the Social Origins of Greek Religion,* 1912. 2nd ed., Cambridge: Cambridge University Press, 1927. Rept., Cleveland, Ohio: World Publishing Company, 1962.

Helck, W., and E. Otto, eds. *Lexikon der Ägyptologie.* 7 vols. Wiesbaden: Harrassowitz, 1972–92.

Hoessly, F. *Katharsis: Reinigung als Heilsverfahren.* Göttingen: Vandenhoeck & Ruprecht, 2001.

Linssen, M. J. H. "The Cults of Uruk and Babylon." Diss., University of Amsterdam, 2002.

Parker, Robert. *Miasma: Pollution and Purification in Early Greek Religion.* Oxford: Clarendon, 1983.

Pongratz-Leisten, B. *Ina sulmi irub: Die kulttopographische und ideologische Programmatik der* akītu-*Prozession in Babylonien und Assyrien im 1. Jahrtausend v. Chr.* Mainz: Zabern, 1994.

Rix, H. *Kleine Schriften.* Bremen: Hempen, 2001.

Versnel, H. S. *Inconsistencies in Greek and Roman Religion,* II: *Transition and Reversal in Myth and Ritual.* Studies in Greek and Roman Religion 6.2. Leiden: Brill, 1993.

Myth

Fritz Graf

M yth is, at a first glance, the English derivative of a Greek word, *mythos* (word, utterance)—yet another legacy from the classical world, or so it seems. This often has made Greek mythology not simply paradigmatic, but even normative as to what myth is: whatever stories from a growing range of cultures came into scholarly consciousness between the Renaissance and the early 20th century were measured and classified against this background. But things are not as simple as this. Applied to narratives, the Greek word as used in the late 5th century BCE most often denoted invented, fictional stories. Plato opposed these stories to the truth, which could be verified or falsified by logic. This became the dominant meaning: rhetorical theorists turned it into their term for "fiction that lacks any resemblance to empirical reality," and Roman theory translated it as *fabula;* this became the term current in most European languages until the 18th century. It is immediately clear that this ancient meaning of the word is not ours: whatever our definition of myth—and there are more than we would wish or care for (Doty 1986: 9–10)—we understand myths as relevant and, in some deeper sense, true stories. Most scholarly attempts to understand myth try to filter this truth, be it historical, psychological, religious, ritualistic, scientific, or even biological, from the stories in an operation first described by the Greek philosopher and essayist Plutarch of Chaeronea (ca. 50–120 CE): "Our aim is to purify the mythic, making it yield to reason" (*Life of Theseus* 1; cf. Detienne 1981). This considerable semantic gap between ancient and modern meaning is easily explained: myth is a term of modern scholarship, invented by 18th-century German Hellenist Gottlieb Christian Heyne, who latinized the Greek word to *mythus* and radically changed its semantics.

The western Asiatic mythological *koinē*

When, in 1764, Heyne created our term, Greek mythology was the only known mythology of any Mediterranean culture: in this respect, it was the paradigm and norm for what myth was understood to be. The process that culminated in Heyne's new terminology and its concomitant radical reevaluation of mythical narrative had started with the confrontation of Greek myths with the traditional stories of newly discovered ethnological cultures, and it had found its first result in the rejection of Greek myths as "a heap of chimeras, dreams, and absurdities" ("un amas de chimères, de rêveries et d'absurdités"; Fontenelle 1724: 187). Heyne reacted to this by giving these same narratives a radically different status—no more absurd inventions *(fabulae),* but the result of primeval human thinking about the world and the container of age-old human memories *(mythi).* His contemporary Johann Gottfried Herder made the specific mythology into one of the defining characteristics of each ethnic group *(Volk)* and moved away from Greek mythology to his native Germans. All three—Fontenelle, Heyne, Herder—are exponents of the modernization of Europe that came with the Enlightenment, its trust in reason as the highest authority, and its struggle against a culture that was dominated by religion. The labeling of mythical narratives as fiction in later antiquity had successfully neutralized the stories of the pagan gods in the new Christian world, where there was only one story that dealt with the divine, and that was revealed truth. Fontenelle's rejection was the rational reaction to such stories; Heyne's reevaluation turned myths into a new sort of truth, not revealed by God but formulated by the budding reason of early humans, and it invested myth with the dignity of an ancestral heirloom; Herder's move clad them with the halo of being a nation's autochthonous truth, starting mythology on a pernicious path the led to the synthetic national mythologies of the 20th century. The romantics discovered and promoted Indian mythology as yet another and much-older mythology than the Greek. Greek mythology, however, remained in its splendid isolation; whoever believed, as did Herder and the German romantics, that mythology was the creation of the *Volksgeist* did not care about diffusion and influences anyway. With the exceptions of Creuzer's easily and quickly refuted theories of an Indian missionary movement and of some diffusionist theories in the 18th century, scholars did not try to connect Greek myths with other mythologies, not the least because the mythical narratives of the neighboring Bronze Age Near East were still unknown and the Old Testament was still read as history. With the quasi-simultaneous publication of Max Müller's and Adalbert Kuhn's essays on comparative mythology in the mid-1850s, the Indo-European hypothesis—the derivation of most Western languages, from Indian Sanskrit to Irish, from a common ancestor, the hypothetical "Old Indo-European"—began to move Greek mythology out of its historical isolation: Greek myths were read as related to the myths of other Old Indo-European cultures, such as Vedic India or the Iran of the Avesta. Whereas the symbolistic interpretations of Müller and Kuhn were quickly dismissed by their contemporaries, the wider assumption of Indo-European mythology was developed by scholars as different as Georges Dumézil and Jan Puhvel (Puhvel 1987), and it is still very much alive.

With the discovery of the ancient Near Eastern cultures, the decipherment of cuneiform writing, and the growing understanding of the languages involved—Akkadian and Sumerian in the 19th century, West Semitic languages and Hittite in the early 20th century—an entirely new body of texts came to be known; as a corollary, the Old Testament began to be read as yet another collection of traditional stories. But these new discoveries rarely have affected the study of myth and the normative status of the Greek stories; Egyptian mythology always stood somewhat apart—not the least because of the absence of long mythological narratives—and the Mesopotamian literary texts were of exclusive interest to biblical scholars and never to the specialists of Greek mythology. It is symptomatic that the two major collections of translations—Hugo Gressmann's (1909) and James B. Pritchard's (1950)—presented those texts as relevant for the study of the Old Testament only. Only after it became clear, through Hrozný's decipherment in the 1920s, that Hittite, the language of the Late Bronze Age rulers of Anatolia, was an Indo-European language did Hittite mythological texts begin to become visible outside their narrow discipline, and this in turn has kindled interest in the other west Asiatic mythologies. The decisive step was when Hans Gustav Güterbock published the narration about Kumarbi, whom he provocatively named "the Hurrian Cronus" (Güterbock 1946): this alerted some students of Hesiod to Near Eastern mythology (it certainly helped somewhat that, after all, the Hittites were Indo-Europeans). In the half century since then, insight has been growing that Late Bronze Age and early Iron Age Greece participated at the margins of the great ancient Near Eastern cultures (most impressively West 1997); in the last couple of years, serious research into this field finally has begun.

West Asiatic mythology crystallized into often impressively long written texts: narratives from Sumerian and Akkadian Mesopotamia, turned classics and preserved, among other places, in the splendid library of Assurbanipal at Nineveh, with the Gilgamesh Epic as the most brilliant example; Hurrian and Hittite texts, among them the Cycle of Kumarbi, from the Hittite capital Bogazköy (ancient Hattusha), but also a much-earlier version of Gilgamesh; the Baal cycle and other narratives from Ugarit; and finally the Greek texts of Homer and Hesiod, not to mention other lost epic poems from archaic Greece. They form a significant and still-growing body of texts. They share not only themes, scenes, and often enough structures, but also, on a more elementary level, the fact that behind these written texts there must be a vast continent of formalized oral storytelling—an insight less important because, in the understanding of many scholars since Heyne and Herder, myth is a mainly oral phenomenon than because oral transmission between the cultures and language groups best explains the wide diffusion of and the somewhat fuzzy correspondences between these stories.

Whereas it is firmly established that there was a long oral tradition immediately behind the poems of Homer and Hesiod, whatever their exact origin, the oral background of western Asiatic narrative texts is less well researched. But some Hurrian texts set out with the singer's announcement "I (will) sing" (Schuol 2002), as do a few Akkadian texts (Dalley 1989: 204), while the standard version of Gilgamesh opens with the promise of the singer: "I shall tell . . . , I shall teach. . . ." Although this does not necessarily point to a contemporary oral culture, as the opening of Vergil's *Aeneid* teaches us, in this case it might do just that: in all the west Asiatic cultures, literacy was not widespread enough to serve as a vehicle of diffusion for these stories. Another Akkadian text opens with a dialogue between the singer and audience in which the bard offers a choice of themes for selection (Wilcke 1977). This looks even more like the literarization of a common oral situation—which is not to deny the strongly scribal character of many of the texts that have been handed down from scribe to scribe and that contain that archetypical scribal phenomenon, the list, as does the long conclusion of the *Enuma Elish*.

Not all similarities between the stories inside this narrative *koinē*, however, need to be explained by diffusion. The Mesopotamian primeval deity Tiamat is split in two to create sky and earth; Egyptian Nut (Sky) is lifted high above her consort Geb (Earth); Hesiod's Uranus (Sky) is violently separated from his wife Gaea (Earth): these are local variations of the much more widely attested theme of separation of earth and sky (Staudacher 1942), and the local variations are widely different from each other. This, then, is a certain example of a nearly universal motif; less certain is another one, the flood story. Although attested in widely different cultures (Dundes 1988), the extant stories in Mesopotamia (Atrahasis, the Nineveh version of Gilgamesh), the Old Testament (Gen. 6–9), Syria (Berossus, *FGrH* 680; Lucian, *On the Syrian Goddess* 12–13), Anatolia (Ovid, *Metamorphoses* 8.624–700), and Greece (Caduff 1986; no trace in Homer or Hesiod) share so many details that diffusion is a more economical hypothesis, despite the marked local variations.

Even less doubtful is the closeness between versions of what is called the Succession Myth, which is present in the Hurrian Kumarbi Cycle, several Mesopotamian stories (the best known being the Babylonian creation epic, *Enuma Elish*), narrations about Baal in Ugarit and other West Semitic cultures, and several Greek narrations, most prominently Hesiod's *Theogony*. In Hesiod's familiar version, primordial Chaos (Void) is succeeded by Gaea (Earth). Chaos becomes the parent of Erebus (Deep Underworld) and Night, the dark roots of the cosmos; Gaea gives birth to Sea, Mountains, Nymphs, and Uranus (Sky, the upper levels of the cosmos). Gaea makes Uranus her consort, but when he begins to prevent their offspring from leaving her womb, she persuades her youngest son, Cronus, to castrate his father. Cronus takes over the kingship; in order to stay in power, he swallows all the children that his wife Rhea bears him, until Rhea, frustrated, feeds him a stone disguised as a baby in swaddling clothes and secretly gives birth to Zeus. Again, the youngest son deposes his father and, together with his siblings, takes over the world. But before establishing his own kingship, Zeus is challenged by the Titans, his father's siblings, and by Typhon, a monster created by Gaea herself and sent against her grandson (whom she previously had helped in his fight against the Titans). Both times, Zeus is victorious and then proceeds to "attribute the honors to the gods." (It is likely that the battle with Typhon is an addition to Hesiod's story, and in later accounts Zeus is also attacked by the Giants, other sons of Gaea, before he is able to establish his own rule.)

In the Cycle of Kumarbi (Hoffner 1998: 40–42) the generation of gods who are ruling under their king, who is the supreme god of the actual pantheon, is preceded by several earlier generations of heavenly kings; the succession of these kings was often violent, and the rule of the present supreme god has to be defended against attackers: the Succession Myth narrates how the present order of things came into being and notes that this order did not go unchallenged. In the Hittite Song of Kumarbi, the primeval King Alalu is deposed by Anu (Sky), his vizier; Anu's son and vizier, Kumarbi, then deposes Anu. During the struggle with Anu, Kumarbi bites off Anu's testicles and swallows them, thus impregnating himself; in a complex action that is only partially understood, he gives birth to Teshub (the storm-god), Teshub's vizier Tasmisu, the Aranzah River, and several other gods. From that moment on, the rivalry between the ruling Kumarbi and the pretender Teshub dominates the song cycle. Kumarbi seems to have tried to swallow Teshub again but was tricked into eating an object, perhaps a stone. Teshub might have become king already in the Song of Kumarbi, but in other narratives, Kumarbi challenges him through several intermediaries, among them the monstrous sea serpent Hedammu (Song of Hedammu) and the stone giant Ullikummi, fathered by Kumarbi through intercourse with a huge rock.

There are other succession stories as well. The Hellenistic author Philo of Byblos told a complex Phoenician version, allegedly translated from the Phoenician, which leads from Elioun and Beruth to Gaea and Uranus, whose son El deposes him, to be succeeded (not necessarily violently) by a triad of gods who dominated the actual pantheon, Astarte, Zeus Demaros, and Adodos (Hadad/Baal) (Eusebius, *Preparation for the Gospel* 1.10). Hellenization is obvious, although its exact extent is difficult to determine. The Ugaritic Baal Cycle knows at least the last two generations: El and Baal enter into a violent conflict, and Baal fights and kills Yamm (Sea), El's ally. Baal fights other monsters as well, among them Mot (Death); this fight seems to end in a tie (Wyatt 1998: 34–146). Zeus's battles echo these fights, but they resonate also with the Babylonian creation epic that pits Marduk, the Lord of Babylon, against Tiamat, at the end of a succession of several divine kings (Dalley 1989: 228–77). Some of these fights—Marduk against Tiamat, Baal against a dragon, Teshub against Illuyanka, Zeus against Typhon, YHWH against Leviathan—make use of yet another story pattern, the fight against a dragonlike monster. This motif has also an Indo-European pedigree, but is more universal.

The complexity of this web of mythological narratives is obvious; no simple explanation will do. But it is also obvious that it can be the result of only a very long and very intricate process of communication—of stories heard in marketplaces, in caravanserais, in royal courts and the wide spaces around the temples, which were adapted by their singers to ever-new conditions and then more-or-less accurately remembered by travelers and merchants, brought home and fed into yet another local network of storytelling, with its own pressures and laws.

It was not only the contingencies of human memory and linguistic competence that shaped those stories. They had to respond to their societies' needs and values. Noah "was a righteous man," and he "walked with God" (Gen. 6.9), and Atrahasis was one "whose ear was open to his god Enki, he would speak with his god and his god would speak with him" (Atrahasis 4.18–20): both theocratic Babylon and priestly Israel focused on the hero's piety. In Ovid's Rome, however, Deucalion is a lover of justice, and piety in the sense of punctual ritualism ("god-fearing"; *Metamorphoses* 1.322) is reserved for his wife, Pyrrha. The *Enuma Elish* puts much emphasis on Marduk, his temple, his cult, and all the honors that the gods decree for him, and its narrative is more interested in diplomacy among the gods than in the battle: the poem was recited during the annual festival of Marduk in Babylon, and the urban audience had little interest in deeds of war—in marked contrast to Gilgamesh. Hesiod's *Theogony*, on the other hand, avoids any reference to specific cults, puts heavy emphasis on the systematic construction of the world through the relevant genealogies, and describes in detail how Cronus castrated Uranus and how Zeus fought Typhon: its intended audience must have varied, but shared an interest in battle scenes, as did the audience of the *Iliad*. If a traditional tale were to survive, it either had to be tied to a very specific, recurrent occasion, such as a festival, or it had to adapt to ever-new conditions; presumably, it was not the most successfully adapted stories that made it into the frozen state of a written text, but rather those that offered enough semantic gaps for new interpretations that aimed at opening up the now-unchangeable story to its new audience.

The way that these stories are conditioned by their societies is even more visible in anthropogonical myths, stories about how humans came into being; after all, these mythical narratives aimed at explaining the *condition humaine* in a given society at a given time. In the priestly account of Genesis, God created humans "in our image, after our likeness, to have dominion" over all other living beings (Gen. 1.26), or God created man "from the dust of the ground" and put him in paradise, where the first couple swiftly transgressed limits and was sent out to suffer toils and death (2): whether guilty or not, humans are very close to God. In both the Babylonian Atrahasis story and the *Enuma Elish*, humans are created from clay and "flesh and blood" of a slaughtered god (Qingu, Tiamat's evil vizier, in the *Enuma Elish*) in order to "bear the load of the gods." In the theocratic state, humans, although by their nature akin to the gods, are supposed to be their servants and slaves. In Hesiod's *Theogony*, humans simply appear at some point, break away from the gods, and challenge Zeus through the trickster Prometheus. Zeus, however, creates woman, "the evil good" without whom man cannot live: humans, although deeply indebted to Zeus for their paradoxical stand in life, keep their distance and take a proud stance against the gods. In the late 5th century BCE, we begin to hear that Prometheus shaped humans from clay: although now the Greek trickster follows even more closely the paradigm of Mesopotamian Ea/Enki, humans owe their existence not to Zeus, but to his cunning adversary (see Cosmology, Time, and History).

Myth and ritual

The Babylonian creation epic was recited (or even enacted) at least once during the New Year festival: on a surface level, the myth talks about the foundation of the temple in which the audience was assembled—as the Homeric *Hymn to Apollo* narrates the foundation of Apollo's temples on Delos and in Delphi (it presumably was composed from two hymns, one addressed to an audience on the island of Delos, a second one in Delphi). The Delphic myth also explains the lavish sacrifices connected with the performance of the oracle: Apollo instituted them in order to feed his priests. Somewhat more complex is the ritual connection of the Hittite myth of Telipinu (Hoffner 1998: 15–20). For some unknown reason, Telipinu disappeared and "removed grain, animal, fecundity, luxuriance, growth, and abundance." A catastrophe ensues: "Humans and gods are dying of hunger." The gods search for him, finally find him, and seem to perform a rite to make him come back ("I have just sprinkled your paths with sweet oil"). Telipinu returns, seething with anger: a second ritual is needed to banish his anger into bronze vats in the underworld: "That which goes into them doesn't come up again." Finally, prosperity and peace return, and Telipinu again "looks after the king and the queen." The text ends with what looks like a further description of ritual: before the god stands a pole or tree on which a sheepskin bag is suspended; it contains every desirable thing, from "animal fecundity and wine" to "plenty, abundance, and satiety." We lack information as to the circumstances in which the text was recited, but it seems obvious that it gives a divine history to a set of rituals performed in connection with the royal couple.

In all these cases, as in many others, myth provides ritual with a divine foundation: the ritual is explained, legitimated, and removed from human influence. In some cases, such as the Delphic part of the *Hymn to Apollo*, the mythical narration is etiological, giving what Malinowski memorably called a charter. But this is not what the "Myth-and-Ritual School" meant to do (and Malinowski had developed his insight in reaction to this school): Frazer and his Cambridge colleagues and followers who were later designated by that nickname went considerably further. In their reading, every myth was generated and shaped by a ritual; furthermore, as Frazer and, in his wake, the biblical scholar Samuel H. Hooke theorized, the ritual in turn reacted to early human preoccupation with fertility of fields, animals, and humans and intended to promote it (Hooke 1933). The Babylonian creation myth was not only generated by the Babylonian New Year ritual; the ritual intended to preserve nature's fertility through the crisis of the year's end. Fertility as sole and only horizon of ritual and myth was questioned rather quickly, and Jane Ellen Harrison, whose first book (1903/1922) on Greek ritual had firmly adhered to Frazer's paradigm, replaced this in her second book (1911/1927) with Durkheimian society and its collective concerns of cohesion and continuity. The link between ritual and myth, however, remained, although its theoretization became more and more complex (Versnel 1993).

Some facts, however, seem undisputed. Rituals and myths often are connected: countless etiological stories explain the origin of a ritual or a festival. Storytelling, however, follows very different rules from ritual performance, and both motifs and entire stories migrate from culture to culture, seemingly without any ritual, and they can attach themselves to new rituals in other cultures. This, then, argues against any genetic connection between myth and ritual; if ever there was one, this was so far distant in prehistory that we cannot even guess at it. But attach to each other they do, and often such myths follow a narrative structure that is comparable to the ritual structure: the recombination of myth and ritual does not seem entirely arbitrary. A handful of structural patterns seem to dominate most rituals as well as most myths, such as the Quest Pattern (Propp 1928). The explanation that makes such structures genetically independent from each other and sees them as basic structures of human experience (Burkert 1979) is as good as any other and elegantly moves the question away from any genetic relationship between myth and ritual.

The ritual performance of the Babylonian creation myth during the New Year festival has always been crucially important for any myth-and-ritual theory. This performance dramatizes the implications of the ritual cycle in which it was embedded. The beginning of the new annual cycle is marked by a ritual process that moves from the dissolution of the old order to the onset of the new one: the mythical narrative turns this into a beginning on a cosmic scale that is not only felt as the success of creation but as the euphoria of "catastrophe survived": the Babylonian narration highlights Marduk's victory, not the coming-into-being of the cosmos. The Athenian festival cycle that surrounds the beginning of the year expresses a similar transition, although in a more complex way. Two of its festivals, the Kronia and the Panathenaia, focus on Cronus, the god whom Zeus deposed and who ruled in the Golden Age, before culture, work, and society; and on Athena, the goddess who gained Athens (thanks to her benefactions) and who will forever protect her city. In this instance, there is no public performance of mythical narration comparable to that in Babylon, but Athena's winning of the city is represented on the west pediment of the Parthenon and thus was visible as soon as the festive procession entered the sacred precinct. This procession prominently displayed and carried up to the goddess a sacred tapestry *(peplos)* embroidered with an image of Zeus's victory over the Giants, a battle nearly as decisive for Zeus's reign as Marduk's against Tiamat was for his, and one in which Athena played a prominent part at the side of her father. In yet another way, the Israelite Sukkot festival combines the specific ritual forms of inversion and dissolution at the turn of the year (Exod. 34.22)—erecting temporary twig huts, dancing, and wine drinking—and the agricultural horizon of harvesting ("when you gather in from the field the fruit of your labor"; 23.16) with the narration of Israel's stay in the desert during the return from Egypt: a detail of the foundation story of Israel serves as explanation and legitimation of the rite and, at the same time, puts it into the wider horizon of a fundamental new beginning. The Roman Parilia, yet another festival where ritual inversion and a focus on agrarian life are dominant (this time the purification of the sheep), is explained with the story of how Romulus founded Rome.

In a more performative reading, the recitation of the creation myth during the New Year ritual makes the renewal happen, as it does in certain ("magical") healing rites. An Akkadian incantation against toothache starts with a long narrative of creation, and many Egyptian and Greco-Egyptian spells make use of either a known or an otherwise unknown mythical story that serves as the powerful antecedent and parallel to the problem in hand: the narration of the one paradigmatic past event, when the gods easily solved the problem at hand, once again will solve it. The memory of a powerful past event carries its own performative power (see further Ritual and Magic).

Myth, history, and memory

In the cases of Israelite Sukkot and Roman Parilia, the myth that accompanies the rite is no cosmogonical myth—the creation myth will become important only for Rosh Hashanah, a New Year festival in postexilic Israel—but an event that is, at least in its indigenous reading, part of Israel's and Rome's histories: the exodus from Egypt and the foundation of the *urbs*.

Mythical narratives were often supposed to be closely connected with historical events. In the view of many indigenous cultures, what we call myth is really history: the Muses, patrons of storytelling, are daughters of Mnemosyne (Memory), after all. In the view of many interpreters of myth, whether native or not, mythical stories contain memories of historical events, albeit in a very distorted form, and it was seen as the task of interpretation to formulate general laws that would undo the distortion. This view is as old as Greek historiography (Hecataeus, *FGrH* 1F1), and the methods of turning myth into history varied widely, from simple rationalization to complex symbolical operations.

In monotheistic Israel, every intervention of God in the visible world—from the creation to the ongoing protection of God's people—is understood as history: where God reveals the past, there is no place for myth. In contrast to this, the surrounding polytheistic cultures knew stories that were similar to Greek myths of gods and heroes: narratives featuring the gods only—such as the Babylonian creation myth and the *Theogony* of Hesiod, the Kumarbi or Baal cycles, or the Egyptian narrative of Isis and Osiris—and narratives that show humans, often as protagonists, interacting with the gods—such as the Gilgamesh poem in Mesopotamia, the story of Keret in Ugarit, the tale of Appu in Anatolia, and the *Iliad* and *Odyssey* in early Greece. This is a function of the fundamental dichotomy between immortal gods and mortal humans, and in the figures of both Gilgamesh and Homer's Achilles human mortality is explicitly problematized. In many narratives, the human protagonists are kings of old or otherwise powerful people: only past humans of high distinction were worthy of being retained in memory. Gilgamesh, "son of Lugulbanda, perfect in strength," is the king who built Uruk's walls; the names of Lugulbanda and Gilgamesh appear in the Sumerian King List of Uruk (although separated by another name), and Gilgamesh is given a different father there, a high priest: whatever the historical facts, already the Sumerians regarded Gilgamesh as king of old (Dalley 1989: 40). Keret in the story from Ugarit is king of Khabur and seen as an ancestor of the ruling dynasty of Ugarit (Wyatt 1998: 177), as perhaps is Danel in the story of Aqhat. Priam is king of Troy; Agamemnon is king of Mycenae, and his contingents are led by a host of local kings; Theseus is king of Athens. Romulus, Numa, and Servius Tullius are kings in Rome, and it reflects the insistence of the Romans that historians still believe in their histo-ricity, not on the basis of any factual evidence—Plutarch, at least, made no dif-ference between Theseus and Romulus. Only the Hittite narration of Appu has a protagonist who is an ordinary citizen, albeit a very wealthy one. All these protagonists directly interact with the gods: Gilgamesh resists being seduced by Ishtar and suffers punishment for his temerity; Aqhat refuses to give his bow to the terrible goddess Anat and also suffers; Keret is personally protected and helped by El, who even creates a healing-goddess for him; the Trojan Paris is rewarded by Aphrodite for his judgment; and the Olympians all take parts for or against King Priam and his city. Romulus has a divine father; King Numa has a divine lover, and he does not hesitate to interact with Faunus, Picus, and even Jupiter in a battle of wits that he wins (Ovid, *Fasti* 3.275–344).

With these narratives, scholars sometimes felt at a loss about nomenclature: were they dealing with "myths," "legends," or "epic poems"? The question is irrelevant at best, misleading at worst: it is a matter of our own categories, and there is no scholarly consensus as to what these categories mean. Legend is as modern a term as myth, and it is often used for Christian stories, such as saints' lives, or for stories that claim a historical background (*Sagen* in the ter-minology of the Grimm brothers); neither of these associations is desirable. If myth, furthermore, is seen not as a specific narrative but as the plot structure that transcends individual narratives—a meaning that takes account of the many variations, spoken and written, of a given story—and if myth and epic poem are not mutually exclusive categories, then an epic poem is one specific concretization of a myth or of an entire cluster of myths, as is the case with Gilgamesh and the *Iliad,* compositions in the prehistory of which shorter indi-vidual songs *(Einzellieder)* are still preserved or recoverable. The difference between myth and epic poem, then, is the result of the creative power with which the individual narrator reacted to his myths and the pressures of the performative situation. In other words: both the Middle High German *Nibelungenlied* and Wagner's Ring Cycle are concretizations of the same myth. Whether any myth contained historical memories or was generated by a spe-cific historical event—as the *Nibelungenlied* contained memories of the situation of central Europe at the time of the Big Migrations or as the *Chanson de Roland* had as an origin a specific event during a campaign of Charlemagne— is very much a matter of scholarly research and debate, and recent examples also show that such a historical core does not explain much of the narrative. It would be as futile to reconstruct the history of early Sumerian kingship from Gilgamesh as it proved futile to reconstruct the Trojan War from the *Iliad*, despite our growing awareness of Troy as a historical city-state at the margins of the Hittite Empire. Mythical narratives are no faithful memories of things past; they are construed according to the memory that every generation believes it needs for its own purposes.

Triumph and demise of mythology

Some narratives had a larger impact than others and traveled from one culture to another—not just as story patterns, but as story plots that included both specific actions and specific actors. Versions of Gilgamesh were widespread around Mesopotamia; Akkadian, Hurrite, and Hittite versions were kept in the Hittite capital Hattusha-Bogazköy in the later 2nd millennium, and the best-known version belonged to Assurbanipal's library in Nineveh. Another story, Nergal and Ereshkigal, was found in widely different versions in Akhenaten's Egyptian capital (modern Tell el-Amarna) and, several centuries younger, in Mesopotamia. We might be tempted, in these cases, to talk about literature, not mythology, and compare the fate of Homer's poems: copies of the *Iliad* and the *Odyssey* made their way to Alexandria and Rome, with the Latin translation of the *Odyssey* being the first Latin literary text, the *Odusia* of Livius Andronicus (ca. 240 BCE); and we could point out that most modern libraries have copies and translations of all three epics. But the distinction between mythology and literature is tenuous and somewhat arbitrary: modern writers still generate versions of these stories, following once again the story plot (or myth) that transcends an individual version. And while most modern versions never attain long-standing societal relevance, some achieve at least a short-lived relevance, such as Christa Wolf's *Cassandra* or Joyce's *Ulysses*.

But this only, once again, points to the transitory character of most scholarly categories. More urgent, in the present context, is another phenomenon: the migration and wholesale acceptance not of a single story, but of an entire body of stories, a mythology. The archives of Hattusha not only contained the different versions and translations of Gilgamesh, they presented an extraordinary collection of mythical texts written in Hittite, Hurrian, and Akkadian and concerning divinities who were Hittite (such as Telipinu), Hurrian (such as Kumarbi), Mesopotamian (such as Anu or Enki/Ea), and Ugaritic (such as Baal or Anat). One reason for this variety seems to lie in the character of Hittite domination: the empire was multicultural, and the cults that the king attended to were not just his own ancestral cults, they comprised the worship of various divinities all over his kingdom. Myths were indispensable for the performance of cult—hence their presence in the royal archives. Not that this explains everything; the versions of the Gilgamesh story, for example, must have been collected for reasons not very different from those that make the story still worth reading and thinking about some millennia later: the story has no connection whatsoever with cult but talks about general themes—the quest for friendship and the urge to overcome mortality.

The surprising western expansion of Greek mythology had different reasons. Not much after 800 BCE, the first Greek settlers arrived on Ischia, off the coast of Campania, and in the next two centuries they built their cities around the southern coast of the Italian mainland and on Sicily. The colonists exploited Italy's fertile soil and rich metal deposits; merchants must have preceded the colonists. The first images of Greek myths appear not much later, as do the first examples of writing. Before 500 BCE, Etruscan cities had taken over Greek gods such as Apollo, both his name and his iconography; the Romans had built a temple to the Dioscuri, the Castores, in their Forum, adorned another temple with pedimental sculptures presenting Athena and Heracles, and equated their Volcanus with the Greek Hephaestus: the fragment of a vase image showing how Hephaestus introduced the drunken Dionysus to Olympus was found on the Forum next to the Volcanal, Volcanus's cult site. By 300, Etruscan bronze mirrors depict countless scenes from Greek mythology, often with the names of the persons added, in native alphabet and native spelling: gods and heroes of the Greeks had become a firm part of the Etruscan imaginary world, and scenes that depict not a Greek but a (presumably) Etruscan myth are rare indeed. When Roman literacy sets in, the staggering extent of the takeover becomes visible. Whereas many Roman gods retain their Latin names—in Ennius's famous list of the twelve Olympians (*Annales* 62–63), only Apollo is Greek—their iconography and their stories derive from Greece. Roman mythology presents itself mainly in the accounts of the historians: Romans read their nondivine myths as easily in a historical key as their Hellenistic Greek contemporaries did with their epic poetry. The quality of the images and the stories must have had an important hand in this expansion, as had the lifestyle of the Greeks, their architecture and technology; temple building, the symposium on couches, the writing system were adapted, as well as stories and images. The *Iliad* and the *Odyssey*, the Theban epics, and the feats of Heracles fascinated Etruscans and Romans in the same way that the Gilgamesh story had fascinated listeners in western Asia (and Gilgamesh, too, belonged to a culture that set standards for life and technology), and many stories that arrived in the West were far removed from any anchoring in cult and ritual. But they in turn could be put to use for new etiologies or serve as models for new stories: the Roman rite of praying with a covered head is explained by a story from the mythology connected with Aeneas (Dionysius Halicarnassus, *Roman Antiquities* 12.16.1), and the story of Numa, Faunus, and Picus is manifestly influenced by Greek narratives. Scholars have argued that such stories were "literary" and "poetic inventions" and therefore not "real" myths; but this argument rests on the romantic definition of myth as a story of hoary antiquity and falls flat as soon as tradition and relevance, not age, are made the main criteria.

The final test of Greek myth's resilience came with the expansion of Christianity. Confronted with the one living and revealed God, the gods of the Gentiles became demons (1 Cor. 10.20–21), and their stories were turned into exhibits in the court of public opinion: the easy life of the Greek gods, their sexual appetites, and their sometimes negligent cruelty were ready proofs of their bad character and of the satanic inspiration behind their cult. The Christians treated the mythological narratives no differently from the way they treated the Gospels: true accounts of life and exploits of the divine and human actors. Such accusations were not exactly new: moralizing Greek philosophers had condemned these same stories, from Xenophanes of Colophon and Heraclitus of Ephesus onward (late 6th century BCE). Plato joined them, advocated heavy censorship of storytelling, and created his own philosophical myths, as had well-meaning sophists. But immediately, interpretation came to the defense of the traditional stories: what counted was not so much the surface reading but an underlying philosophical or moral meaning; truth could be distilled from the myths, if only they were read in the proper way. Generations of philosophers developed allegorical readings, and by Hellenistic times, the system was well in place (Dawson 1992); it was easily turned against the Christian accusations. And once Christianity had changed from the small world of marginal sectarians into a movement ready to convert entire cities and provinces, positions were swapped once again. Mythical narratives were too well embedded in the fabric of ancient culture and daily life to be excised or exorcised, and Christian teachers used these same instruments of allegory in order to tame the pagan stories for their own use. Seemingly without effort, the mythical narratives could be made to teach the Christian message.

Bibliography

Burkert, Walter. *Structure and History in Greek Mythology and Ritual.* Berkeley: University of California Press, 1979.

Caduff, Gian Andrea. *Antike Sintflugsagen. Hypomnemata* 82. Göttingen: Vandenhoeck & Ruprecht, 1986.

Dalley, Stephanie. *Myths from Mesopotamia: Creation, the Flood, Gilgamesh, and Others.* Oxford: Clarendon, 1989.

Dawson, David. *Allegorical Readers and Cultural Revision in Ancient Alexandria.* Berkeley: University of California Press, 1992.

Detienne, Marcel. *L'invention de la mythologie.* Paris: Gallimard, 1981. English translation: *The Creation of Mythology.* Chicago: University of Chicago Press, 1986.

Doty, William G. *Mythography: The Study of Myths and Rituals.* Tuscaloosa: University of Alabama Press, 1986.

Dundes, Alan, ed. *The Flood Myth.* Berkeley: University of California Press, 1988.

Fontenelle, Bernard de. "De l'origine des fables." In *Oeuvres complètes,* ed. Alain Niderst, vol. 3. Paris: Fayard, 1989 (orig. 1724).

Gressmann, Hans. *Altorientalische Texte zum Alten Testament.* 2nd ed. Berlin: De Gruyter, 1926 (orig. 1909).

Güterbock, Hans Gustav. *Kumarbi: Mythen vom churritischen Kronos aus den hethitischen Fragmenten zusammengestellt.* Zürich: Rhein, 1946.

Harrison, Jane Ellen. *Mythology and Monuments of Ancient Athens.* London and New York: Macmillan, 1890.

———. *Prolegomena to the Study of Greek Religion,* 3rd ed. Cambridge: Cambridge University Press, 1922 (orig. 1903). Rpt. Princeton: Princeton University Press, 1991.

Hesiod. *Theogony,* ed. and commentary M. L. West. Oxford: Clarendon, 1966.

Hoffner, Harry A., Jr. *Hittite Myths.* 2nd ed. Writings from the Ancient World 2. Atlanta: Scholars Press, 1998.

Hooke, Samuel Henry, ed. *Myth and Ritual: Essays on the Myth and Ritual of the Hebrews in Relation to the Culture Pattern of the Ancient East.* London: Oxford University Press, 1933.

Malinowski, Bronislaw. *Myth in Primitive Psychology.* London: W. W. Norton, 1926.

Pritchard, James B., ed. *Ancient Near Eastern Texts Relating to the Old Testament.* 3rd ed. Princeton: Princeton University Press, 1969 (orig. 1950).

Propp, Vladimir. *Morfologiia skazki,* 1928. English translation: *The Morphology of the Folktale.* Tr. Laurence Scott and Louis A. Wagner. Austin: University of Texas Press, 1968.

Puhvel, Jan. *Comparative Mythology.* Baltimore: Johns Hopkins University Press, 1987.

Schuol, Monika. "Zur Überlieferung homerischer Epen vor dem Hintergrund altanatolischer Traditionen." In *Grenzüberschreitungen: Formen des Kontakts zwischen Orient und Okzident im Altertum,* ed. Monika Schuol, Udo Hartmann, and Andreas Luther. Oriens et Occidens 3. Stuttgart: Steiner, 2002.

Staudacher, Willibald. *Die Trennung von Himmel und Erde: Ein vorgriechischer Schöpfungsmythos bei Hesiod und den Vorsokratikern.* Tübingen, 1942. Rpt. Darmstadt: Wissenschaftliche Buchgesellschaft, 1968.

Versnel, Hendrik S. "What Is Sauce for the Goose Is Sauce for the Gander: Myth and Ritual, Old and New." In *Inconsistencies in Greek and Roman Religion,* vol. 2: *Transition and Reversal in Myth and Ritual,* pp. 16–89. Studies in Greek and Roman Religion 6.2. Leiden: Brill, 1993.

West, M. L. *The East Face of Helicon: West Asiatic Elements in Greek Poetry and Myth.* Oxford and New York: Oxford University Press, 1997.

Wilcke, C. "Die Anfänge der akkadischen Epen." *Zeitschrift für Assyriologie* 67 (1977): 153–216.

Wyatt, N. *Religious Texts from Ugarit.* 2nd ed. Biblical Seminar 53. London: Sheffield Academic Press, 2002 (orig. 1998).

Cosmology: Time and History

John J. Collins

According to Greek tradition, Pythagoras "was the first to call the sum of the whole by the name of the cosmos, because of the order which it displayed" (Aetius 2.1.1). Cosmology, strictly speaking, is the rational discussion of the cosmos, which developed in Greece from the 6th century BCE onward. The word is used more loosely to refer to any discussion of the nature and coherence of the world. Such discussion can be found long before the beginnings of Greek science and philosophy in the myths of the ancient Near East, especially those that dealt with cosmogony or creation.

Creation myths

It is important to bear in mind that ancient religion was not dogmatic or systematic in the manner of later Western faiths. There were no creeds to which everyone subscribed. There were several creation myths in ancient Egypt. Each city that rose to power formulated its own myth of creation. In the cosmogony of Heliopolis, the creator-god was Atum; in Memphis, Ptah; in Hermopolis and Thebes, Amun. Each cosmogony, however, had only one creator-god, and he was credited with giving life to the gods as well as to humanity. The sun-god Re appears in almost every creation account, and his name is often joined with that of other creators (Amun-Re, Re-Atum). The actual process of creation was conceived by human analogy. One model supposed that the origin of life came from the creator's semen. In the Heliopolitan cosmogony, Atum generated the first divine couple from himself, either by masturbation or by spitting. Another model associated the creative power with the utterance of a word. In the Memphite Theology, Ptah creates "through what the heart plans and the tongue commands." A third model, based on the work of an artisan, was exemplified by the potter-god Khnum. Life was often thought to have originated on a primeval mound, which emerged when the primeval flood receded.

These Egyptian creation myths are remarkable for the lack of conflict in the process. Egyptian history did not lack conflict, but the myths projected a sense of stability and permanence. This stability was expressed in the concept of *ma'at,* an all-embracing principle of order that governed all aspects of nature and society. A creator-god such as Ptah and Atum was "lord of *ma'at.*" Ma'at was sometimes portrayed as a goddess, Maat, the daughter of the sun-god Re, who accompanied him as he sailed across the sky. The sovereignty of the creator-god had its counterpart on earth in the rule of the pharaoh. The conflict often encountered by the monarchy was acknowledged in the myth of Osiris and Seth, but this myth too ended in stability. The evil Seth was defeated by Horus, the posthumous heir of Osiris, who then became king on earth. The living pharaoh was the embodiment of Horus, while the dead king, Osiris, was ruler of the netherworld.

In contrast to the Egyptian creation myths, those of the Semitic world were stories of conflict. The best known of these myths is the Babylonian *Enuma Elish,* which casts Marduk, god of Babylon, in the role of creator. More precisely, it distinguishes two stages in creation. In the beginning was a primordial couple, Apsu and Tiamat, often understood to represent freshwater and saltwater respectively, although this distinction is not explicit in the myth. The mingling of their waters produces the other gods. The creation of the world is a separate process. The young gods kill their father Apsu, but are then endangered by the wrath of Tiamat. Marduk is the hero who does single combat with Tiamat and kills her. In return, he is made king of the gods. From the carcass of Tiamat he creates the world: He split her like a shellfish into two parts. Half of her he set up as a sky and posted guards to make sure that her waters did not escape. He further fixed the astral likenesses of the gods in the sky and determined the months and the year. Finally he made humanity, from the blood of Qingu, an ally of Tiamat, to serve the gods. Another Mesopotamian myth, Atrahasis, describes a different occasion and process for the creation of humanity, involving a mixture of the blood of a god with clay. The political overtones of the Babylonian myth are transparent. If the gods need a strong monarchy in order to ward off danger, so too does Babylon.

We do not have a story of the creation of the world from Syria or Canaan. The god El is called father and is said to have begotten other deities. We might infer that creation was conceived as a form of procreation. The closest analogues to *Enuma Elish* in the Ugaritic literature are found in the myths of Baal. These myths describe combat between Baal and Yamm (Sea) in one episode and between Baal and Mot (Death) in another. What is at stake is the kingship of the gods, under El. These myths are often viewed as cosmogonic, on the grounds that they establish order in the universe. Support for this view comes not only from the analogy with the *Enuma Elish* but from the frequent association of creation with the defeat of a monster in biblical poetry (e.g., Job 26; Ps. 89.10 [= 89.11 Hebrew]). These combat myths suggest that creation, or the order of the cosmos, is fragile and has to be reestablished periodically in the face of recurring dangers.

The canonical account of creation in the Bible (Gen. 1) is closer in spirit to the Egyptian myths where a sovereign creator creates by his word, unhindered by any opposition. (This is not necessarily to posit Egyptian influence. There is some evidence that the biblical writers were deliberately rejecting the Babylonian account of creation, as they use the word *těhôm*, cognate of Tiamat, to refer to the deep without personification.)

Tales of primeval conflict are also found in Hittite (Anatolian) mythology (*ANET* 120–28). One such myth tells how Kumarbi attacked the king of heaven (Anu) and bit off and swallowed his "manhood." As a result he became pregnant with three dreadful gods, including the storm-god. The end of the myth is fragmentary, but it is likely that Kumarbi was eventually challenged for the kingship by the storm-god. In another myth, the Song of Ullikummi, Kumarbi rebels against Teshub, the storm-god. In this myth, Kumarbi impregnates a rock and fathers a giant, Ullikummi, who wreaks havoc on heaven and on earth. Eventually, the giant is crippled by the god Ea. This myth tells us incidentally that the gods severed heaven from earth with a cleaver. Yet another Hittite myth tells of a battle between the storm-god and a dragon, Illuyanka.

Greek mythology provides no comprehensive creation myth such as we have in the *Enuma Elish*. Hesiod synthesizes a range of mythological traditions in his *Theogony*. In the beginning was Chaos (a yawning void). Then came Earth, Tartarus (a terrible place beneath Hades), and Eros. From Chaos came Erebus (a dark region between Earth and the netherworld) and Night. Of Night were born Aether and Day. Then Earth brought forth Heaven and the Sea. Then she lay with Heaven and bore numerous gods. In contrast to Near Eastern mythologies, Earth is begotten, not made. While it is not clear how Earth, Tartarus, and Eros emerge from Chaos, the later stages of creation are explicitly sexual. While Heaven and Earth are not absolutely primordial, they are the progenitors of the great majority of the gods. Heaven (Uranus) is father of Cronus, who in turn is father of Zeus, the eventual supreme god. Hesiod has his own combat myth: the conflict between Zeus and the Titans and Typhon, which ends with Zeus's confirmation as king of the gods. This conflict is not related to the creation of the world, however (see further Myth). The primeval character of Earth in Hesiod is consonant with the view of later Greek philosophers such as Aristotle that the world is eternal. This view was sharply at variance with the prevalent belief in creation in the ancient Near East. According to Hesiod's *Works and Days*, the gods made the first human beings in the time of Cronus.

A quite different account of the origin of the world was proposed by Plato in his dialogue the *Timaeus*. Plato reasoned that the world must be created since it is visible and tangible, and all sensible things are in a process of change. The creator, whom he calls simply "god," desired that all things should be good and nothing bad and therefore made the world as perfect as possible. Accordingly, the cosmos became a living creature, endowed with soul and intelligence, and may even be called a god itself. Because of its perfection, it was imperishable. The emphasis on the goodness of creation is reminiscent of the biblical account in Gen. 1 and made the *Timaeus* attractive to later Jewish and Christian philosophers. Plato's creator is a craftsman, a *dēmiourgos,* like many of the creator-gods of the Near East. As in the myths, creation is not fashioned out of nothing. Where the myths began with unformed matter, or the biblical "waste and void," Plato posited invisible and formless space. Plato's idea of creation, however, was exceptional in the Greek world. Aristotle was more typical in regarding the cosmos as a self-contained whole, ungenerated and imperishable. Moreover, there is always some question as to how Plato intended his myths to be understood.

Plato's view that the initial creation was good was fully in keeping with the ancient creation myths. Hesiod provides several explanations for evil in the course of his *Theogony* and *Works and Days* (e.g., Pandora's jar). Only the Persian Zoroastrians, however, attempted to account for evil in the cosmogony itself. In their account, two opposing cosmic entities existed from the beginning: Ahura Mazda (Ohrmazd), the wise lord who was god of light, and Angra Mainyu (Ahriman), the god of darkness. These gods struggled throughout history. In a variant of this myth, the opposing gods were twin offspring of one supreme good god. The idea of a devil or Satan, which appears in Judaism in the Hellenistic period and became very influential in Christianity, was probably of Persian origin. The influence of the Persian myth can also be seen in the Jewish Dead Sea Scrolls, which say that God created two spirits to govern humanity, one of light and one of darkness.

The view of the world

Throughout the eastern Mediterranean world and Near East, the basic view of the world in the earliest literature is tripartite, distinguishing heaven, earth, and netherworld. The Egyptians variously described the heavenly realm as a bird, a cow, a woman (the goddess Nut, balancing on her feet and hands), or a flat plane held up by pillars. The sun-god Re was thought to traverse the heaven by day and then journey back to the east through the netherworld at night. After death, the soul or spirit had to encounter various dangers in the netherworld, but the righteous person might hope to ascend to a blessed life, either on earth or in heaven. The blessed abode of the dead is often called the Field of Rushes or Field of Offerings. It is far removed from everyday human life, but different texts seem to imply a location in the heavens or at the ends of the earth. The hope of the righteous was also expressed in terms of joining the stars and mingling with the gods in heaven.

In Mesopotamia, too, heaven was the abode of the gods (there were also gods of the netherworld). Human beings, however, were restricted to the netherworld after death, and this was a gloomy place. The futility of the quest for immortality is the theme of the Epic of Gilgamesh. The quest takes the hero to the ends of the earth to the abode of Utnapishtim, the flood hero, who had been granted eternal life. The myth of Adapa, in contrast, tells of the ascent of its hero to heaven, where he is offered eternal life, but rejects it because of the advice given him by the god Ea. The legend of Etana also tells of an attempt to ascend to heaven, which apparently ended in failure. The general principle held true: heaven was for the gods, humanity lived on earth and descended to the netherworld after death. There is also some evidence in Mesopotamian traditions for multiple heavens, but these had no effect on human destiny.

The most important Mesopotamian contribution to the study of the cosmos was in the areas of astrology and astronomy. The Babylonians looked to the stars for clues to the intentions of the gods. The practice of astrology implied that the movements of the stars and human affairs were interconnected, as indeed were other phenomena on earth, such as the flight of birds. But the Babylonians also developed more-scientific forms of astronomy, both by observation and by mathematical calculation. There was no clear distinction between astrology and astronomy. The movements of the stars were thought to be significant for events on earth. The term *Chaldean*, which originally referred to a tribe that rose to power in Babylon, was used to designate astrologers in the Hellenistic and Roman periods.

Neither Syria nor Israel contributed much to the study of the stars. Astrology was discouraged in biblical tradition because of the temptation to worship the host of heaven, although there is evidence that some Jews practiced astrology in the Hellenistic and Roman periods. Here again the world was usually seen as tripartite. In both Canaan and Israel, heaven was the abode of the heavenly host, while dead human beings descended to a gloomy netherworld. There is some evidence that exceptional individuals, including kings, might hope for immortal life with the gods. The Bible allowed that a few individuals (Enoch, Elijah) had been taken up alive to heaven. But such cases were exceptional. The stars were the heavenly host, divine or angelic beings, who were sometimes thought to intervene in human affairs.

The earliest Greek conceptions of the cosmos were very much like those of the ancient Near East. The earth was a flat circular surface, surrounded by the river Oceanus. The sky was a disk of comparable size above it, held up by pillars guarded by Atlas (so Homer) or by Atlas himself (Hesiod). The gods were variously said to live on Mount Olympus or in the aether above the sky. The dead went down to Hades, beneath the depths of the earth, where there was no joy.

Beginning in the 6th century, however, Greek cosmology was transformed by several developments that would have long-lasting consequences far beyond the borders of Greece.

First of these was the rise of a new approach to cosmology, pioneered by the pre-Socratic philosophers. This approach favored explanations in terms of matter, without positing divine interventions. Even when the philosophers spoke of gods, they were not anthropomorphic in the manner of the myths, but rather represented aspects of the cosmos. Of course the demise of the gods was neither immediate nor complete, even in the domain of Greek philosophy, as can be seen from the *Timaeus* of Plato. Plato not only defended the idea of a creator, but argued that the world had a soul and bitterly attacked the materialistic view of the universe put forward by some philosophers. Other Greek thinkers, such as the Stoics, dispensed with the creator and regarded the universe itself as divine. The Stoics supposed that the universe was animated by Pneuma (Spirit) or Logos (Reason), a fine fiery substance that represented the active element in humanity as well as in nature. These Hellenistic concepts provided a way of reconceiving older Near Eastern ideas. Egyptian *ma'at* and Israelite wisdom were traditional concepts of cosmic order. Jewish Hellenistic writings such as those of Philo show how such concepts could be given Platonic or Stoic overtones in the Hellenistic period. Even those such as Jews and Christians, who insisted on a creator-god and therefore found Plato more congenial than they found the Stoics, reconceived their understanding of deity in terms that were more cosmological and less anthropomorphic. In Hellenistic Judaism, wisdom or spirit was considered to be the divine element in the universe, which pointed beyond itself to a creator. In Stoic theology, the cosmos, animated by spirit, was itself the deity.

The development of Greek astronomy led to a new view of the universe, significantly more complex than the old three-tiered model. Pythagoras held that the earth and the heavenly bodies were spheres moving in harmony. Plato accepted the idea that the earth was a sphere and supposed that the moon, sun, planets, and fixed stars revolved around it in their own orbits (*Republic* 10. 616–17; cf. *Timaeus* 36–39). With some variations, this model became widespread in the Hellenistic period and later. Cicero, in the *Dream of Scipio,* posited nine spheres. The outermost, the starry heaven, contains the whole and is itself the supreme god. Beneath it are seven other spheres: Saturn, Jupiter, Mars, Sun, Venus, Mercury, and Moon. The ninth and central sphere, the earth, is immovable and lowest of all. The model of the geocentric universe, with various refinements, was given its classical expression by Claudius Ptolemy of Alexandria in the 2nd century CE. The attempt of Aristarchus of Samos in the 3rd century BCE to argue for a heliocentric universe had little impact.

This new view of the universe is reflected in the Near Eastern cultures in various ways, primarily in the belief in multiple heavens. An Egyptian depiction of the cosmos from the Ptolemaic era shows the goddess Nut bending over the world not once but twice. Jewish and later Christian apocalypses tell of visionaries ascending through multiple heavens, typically seven, but sometimes three and occasionally other numbers. These visionary texts are not concerned with scientific cosmology, but they reflect the assumptions of their time about the general shape of the universe.

Related to the interest in multiple heavens was the belief that the righteous dead lived on in heaven with the stars. The epitaph of soldiers fallen at the Battle of Potidaea in 432 BCE says that the aether had received their souls, the earth their bodies (*IG* I³ 1179). The idea of heavenly immortality was given philosophical nuance by Hellenistic philosophers, who associated the aether, or upper heavenly regions, with the finest, most divine substance. Eastern peoples related it to their own traditional beliefs. In Jewish apocalypses, astral immortality meant joining the host of heaven or the angels. In the Hellenistic period, even Hades was often located in the heavens. The new view of the world had no logical place for an underworld, although the old beliefs lived on in popular religion. Plato's pupil, Heracleides Ponticus, is said to have claimed that the Milky Way was the path of souls passing through Hades in the heaven. Jewish and Christian apocalypses located the torments of the damned as well as the joy of the blessed in the heavenly regions.

Celestial eschatology tended to imply a negative view of the earthly regions. The soul was weighed down by bodily existence and was liberated to rise up after death. This tendency was taken to an extreme conclusion in late antiquity in the gnostic cosmologies that saw the creator or demiurge as an evil figure and that represented the creation of the material world as a fall. The material world was then viewed as an evil place from which souls had to be saved by enlightenment and ascent to the realm of spirit. This late antique view of the world had come full circle from the insistence of the Bible and of Plato that both the creator and the creation were very good.

Time and history

The ancient creation myths had implications for the understanding of time and history, although they did not devote much explicit reflection to them. The heavenly bodies were seen to regulate time. When Marduk fixed the stars in the *Enuma Elish,* he established the months and the years. In the biblical account, the world was created in six days so that God could rest on the Sabbath, completing the week. According to Plato, who was vastly more systematic in his reflections, time and the heaven came into being at the same instant. The sun, moon, and planets were created in order to distinguish and preserve the numbers of time. The myths generally implied a cyclic view of history. They described not only the beginning of things, but paradigmatic events that could be reenacted over and over. For the Egyptians, each sunrise recapitulated the establishment of *ma'at.* For the Israelites, historical events such as the Exodus or the return from the Babylonian Exile were reenactments of the victory of the creator over the chaos dragon. From early times, Egyptians and Babylonians were aware that all the planets revolved. Plato formalized the idea of a Great Year—the period of time that it takes for the sun, moon, and five planets to complete their rotations and return simultaneously to the same positions in relation to the fixed stars. Plato suggested that the revolving Great Years were punctuated by periodic disasters of fire and flood, which were reflected in Greek mythology in the stories of the fall of Phaethon while driving the chariot of the sun and the myth of Deucalion. The Stoic doctrine of *ekpyrōsis* (conflagration) also involved the periodic return of all things to the primal substance and their subsequent renewal.

It was axiomatic in the ancient world that gods could intervene in human affairs and implement their plans in history. Mesopotamian rulers often attributed their rise to power to the plan of their patron deity. Homer's gods acted purposefully, even if they were often at odds with each other. In most cases, these divine plans concerned limited episodes. The biblical accounts of the role of YHWH in the history of Israel are exceptional in their scope, spanning several generations. Moreover, the opening chapters of Genesis provide an account of early universal history, which forms a backdrop for the emergence of Israel. Nonetheless, the biblical story of Israel stops well short of providing a comprehensive view of all history. Such a view emerges only in the apocalyptic writings of the Hellenistic period. In the Greco-Roman world, the best analogue to the early biblical history is found in Vergil's *Aeneid*, which describes the emergence of Rome as the culmination of an epic history under divine guidance.

Hesiod's myth of the successive ages of humanity, in his *Works and Days*, is important for the emergence of a concept of universal history. It is quite possible that the poet is adapting a myth of Median or Persian origin, but this is difficult to establish because of the notorious difficulty of dating the Persian sources. Hesiod (*Works and Days* 109–196) enumerates five ages: first the golden, then the silver, then the bronze. The fourth is not defined by a metal, but is that of "the godlike race of heroes who are called demigods, the race before our own." The fifth age is that of iron, of which Hesiod says that he wishes he had either died before or been born afterward. Since he allows that something will come afterward, some people have supposed that he expected a return to the golden age, but Hesiod does not say this. He leaves the future open. The return to a golden age is suggested much later in Vergil's Fourth *Eclogue*, which refers to a "last age" predicted by the Cumean Sibyl.

The division of history into epochs or *saecula* was developed by the Etruscans and taken over by the Romans. A natural *saeculum* was the highest age a human being could attain (approximately one hundred years). A civil *saeculum* began with the founding of a city or state and lasted as long as any member of the founding generation lived. The end of a *saeculum*, however, was not always obvious and had to be inferred from signs given by the gods. Ten *saecula* were allotted to the Etruscan people, after which they would disappear. In the mid-1st century BCE there was speculation about what point in the process had been reached. On one interpretation, a comet that appeared after the murder of Julius Caesar marked the end of the ninth *saeculum* and the beginning of the tenth. The grammarian Servius (4th century CE) said that the "last age" of Vergil's Fourth *Eclogue* was the tenth. Whether this final age should be understood in the context of Etruscan speculation is disputed.

The most elaborate division of history into periods in antiquity was that of the Zoroastrians. The classic form of their theology of history is found in the Middle Persian *Bundahishn*. According to this theology, the two opposing primordial spirits, Ahura Mazda and Ahriman, coexisted for three thousand years before the creation of the world in its physical state. Thereafter world history would last for nine thousand years, divided into three periods of three thousand years each. The first three thousand would pass according to the will of Ahura Mazda, and the second three thousand would be a mixture, governed by both gods. The third period is divided into three distinct millennia. The end of each millennium is marked by tribulations and disasters, followed by the coming of a new savior. The final battle would be fought at the end of the third period. The final millennium is further divided into periods. The *Bahman Yasht* reports a vision by Zarathustra of a tree with four metallic branches, gold, silver, steel, and mixed iron. These are interpreted as representing four historical periods. A variant of this vision, also in the *Bahman Yasht,* lists the ages as seven in number.

The Persian texts are preserved in Pahlavi manuscripts from the 6th to 9th centuries CE, but the division of history into periods is certainly much older than this. Plutarch, writing around the late 1st or early 2nd century CE, gives an elliptical account of the myth, which he derived from Theopompus (early 4th century BCE). One god would dominate the other and be dominated for three thousand years. For another three thousand they would fight and make war. In the end the evil power would be destroyed. It is not clear whether this is a somewhat garbled form of the myth known from later sources or whether it represents a different division of history. It is clear in any case that the division of history into millennia was known in Persian tradition before the Hellenistic age. Some scholars have supposed that the Persian tradition of four ages symbolized by metals, attested in the *Bahman Yasht,* underlies Hesiod's schema of four declining ages. Such a proposal is difficult to verify because of the late date of the Persian sources, but this kind of periodization is an integral part of Persian cosmology, while it is exceptional in Greek tradition.

In Jewish apocalyptic writings of the Hellenistic period, history is sometimes divided into ten generations, a schema most probably derived from the Persian millennium. This division is frequently found in the Jewish and Christian Sibylline Oracles. So, for example, in Sibylline Oracles books 1–2 history is divided into ten generations, punctuated by the flood in the fifth generation and culminating with a conflagration. These oracles sometimes incorporated the work of pagan Sibyls, and so the question arises whether the tenfold division of history was a feature of the Sibylline genre outside Judaism. The only evidence for this, however, is Servius's interpretation of Vergil's last age as the tenth, in the 4th century CE. The evidence suggests that the use of Sibylline Oracles to provide a comprehensive overview of history was a Jewish adaptation of the genre.

Other schematizations of history were also popular in Jewish and Christian tradition, notably the sevenfold division derived from the days of creation or from the idea of a sabbath. Christian writers such as Lactantius in the early 4th century CE held that the world was in the 6th and final millennium of its history. Lactantius drew on a wide range of ancient philosophical and mythical speculations about the cosmos, including the late Persian Oracle of Hystaspes, a work that has sometimes been regarded as Jewish. The syncretistic character of late antiquity is shown by the difficulty of distinguishing Persian, Jewish, and other traditions in texts such as this.

Cosmic eschatology

The periodization of history is closely related to the expectation of an end of history or of the world. Ancient Near Eastern myths, such as the *Enuma Elish*, saw the establishment of kingship as the end of a process. Insofar as one might speak of a goal in history, it was the establishment of a definitive, lasting kingship. In the Bible, this was provided by the Davidic dynasty, which was supposed to last forever. When the Judean monarchy was dissolved by the Babylonians in the 6th century, hopes for the future focused on the restoration of the Davidic line. Sometimes this was expected to usher in a virtual golden age (e.g., Isa. 11.6: "The wolf shall dwell with the lamb"). A Babylonian prophecy from the 6th century BCE speaks of a king who would rule the entire world and whose dynasty would stand forever and exercise authority like the gods. Later, Vergil's *Aeneid* promised Rome an *imperium* without end, and the Fourth *Eclogue* described the transformation of the earth.

One widespread motif relating to the hope for definitive kingship envisioned a sequence of four kingdoms and a fifth. Herodotus noted a sequence of empires in Asia: Assyrians, Medes, Persians. Since the Medes never ruled in the West, this sequence is probably of Persian origin and viewed the Persians as the final, definitive empire. In the Hellenistic era, the sequence was extended to include Macedonia and finally Rome. This schema could be used in the interests of imperial propaganda, but it could also be used for subversive purposes. In the *Bahman Yasht*, the fourth kingdom is identified as "the *divs* with disheveled hair," an unflattering reference to the Greeks. The implication of the vision is that this kingdom will be overthrown at the end of the millennium. The Jewish Book of Daniel is more explicit. Daniel sees a statue made of different metals representing a declining series of kingdoms. (This vision is closer to the *Bahman Yasht* than to Hesiod, insofar as the final kingdom is a mixture of iron and clay.) In the end, the statue is destroyed by a stone representing the Kingdom of God, which presumably would be represented on earth by a Jewish kingdom.

The classic expressions of cosmic eschatology are found in Jewish and Christian apocalypses. The Hebrew prophets had spoken metaphorically of the end of the world in describing the destruction of specific places. Beginning in the 2nd century BCE, however, such language is used more literally. The Apocalypse of Weeks in *1 Enoch* says that at a fixed point in the future the world will be written down for destruction, and the old heaven will be taken away and replaced with a new one. The apocalypse of *4 Ezra*, written at the end of the 1st century CE, provides for a period of primeval silence between the destruction of the old world and the new creation and resurrection of the dead. The Book of Revelation in the New Testament also predicts the destruction of this world and the creation of a new one. Revelation provides for a thousand-year reign on earth for the just before the new creation. The popular use of the word *millennialism* is derived from this motif in Revelation. The motif of a final millennium in history, however, had older roots in Persian tradition.

The final conflict in apocalypses such as Daniel and Revelation has much in common with the old creation myths of the ancient Near East. In Revelation, the angel Michael casts a dragon down from heaven, and there are also beasts on land and sea. In the new creation, the sea (which was personified in the old Canaanite myths) is no more. In these texts, imagery that was used in the myths to describe the beginnings of the cosmos are projected into the future, to describe its consummation. It is likely, however, that the apocalyptic view of history is also influenced by Persian tradition. In the Zoroastrian myth, each of the last three millennia is characterized by tribulations and disasters, followed by the coming of a new savior. At the end of the final millennium, those who are still alive will not die, and those who are dead will be raised in a general resurrection. The wicked are purified in streams of fire as part of the purification of the world. After the conflagration, all things will be made new.

The hope for resurrection at the end of a predetermined historical sequence first appears in Jewish tradition in the apocalypses of Enoch and Daniel in the Hellenistic period. The Zoroastrian myth was certainly current before this time. The most complete reflection of the Persian account of the last things in Jewish or Christian tradition is found in the Christian author Lactantius in the 4th century CE. Lactantius synthesized various traditions in his writings and incorporated lengthy passages from the Oracle of Hystaspes.

Greek tradition usually viewed the world as imperishable, despite periodic destructions by fire and water. This was true even for Plato, despite his affirmation of creation. Even Hellenized Jews, most notably Philo of Alexandria, allowed that the world may be made immortal by the providence of God, even though it is by nature destructible. The notion of cosmic conflagration *(ekpyrōsis)* held a prominent but controversial place in Stoic thought. The *ekpyrōsis* would purify the cosmos, but would not entail a judgment. Stoics disputed among themselves whether it would be followed by *palingenesia,* renewed birth and repetition of all things. The Roman Seneca, writing in the 1st century CE, spoke of the time when the world would extinguish itself in order to renew itself again. Stars would collide, and all matter would burn with a single fire. Seneca claimed support for these ideas from Berossus, a Babylonian priest who presented Babylonian tradition in Greek in the early Hellenistic period. According to Seneca, Berossus said that these things would happen in accordance with the course of the stars and even predicted the time of the conflagration. The idea of cosmic conflagration is not attested in Akkadian sources, however, and seems to have no basis in Babylonian tradition.

A rare example of cosmic eschatology in the Egyptian tradition is found in the late Apocalypse of Asclepius, which is written in Greek and associated with the Hermetic corpus. This apocalypse retains some of the characteristics of political oracles. An evil age is caused by the invasion of foreigners, and this is followed by a radical transformation of the earth. It differs from earlier Egyptian tradition by envisioning a destruction of the world by fire and flood and then its restitution to its pristine state. It reflects the syncretism of late antiquity, where ideas circulated widely and the coherence of cosmos and history was widely assumed.

Bibliography

Clifford, R. J. *Creation Accounts in the Ancient Near East and in the Bible.* Washington, D.C.: Catholic Biblical Association, 1994.

Cohn, N. *Cosmos, Chaos, and the World to Come: The Ancient Roots of Apocalyptic Faith.* New Haven: Yale University Press, 1993.

Collins, J. J., ed. *The Encyclopedia of Apocalypticism,* vol. 1: *The Origins of Apocalypticism in Judaism and Christianity.* New York: Continuum, 1998 (esp. essays by A. Hultgård and H. Cancik on Persian and Greco-Roman traditions).

Couliano (Culianu), I. P. *Expériences de l'extase: Extase, ascension et récit visionnaire de l'hellénisme au moyen âge.* Paris: Payot, 1984.

Wright, J. E. *The Early History of Heaven.* New York: Oxford University Press, 2000.

Wright, M. R. *Cosmology in Antiquity.* London: Routledge, 1995.

Pollution, Sin, Atonement, Salvation

Harold W. Attridge

$\mathcal{A}$ncient societies, like all human groupings, set boundaries on human behavior, defining actions that disrupted human relations in various ways as wrong. Some actions such as murder, incest, or theft were almost universally condemned, although what counted as truly unjustifiable homicide or illicit sex might vary and the boundaries of the moral community within which such actions were prohibited might vary. Other actions could easily accrue to a list of wrongful acts, from the trivial (making others sad, as in Egypt) to the profound (rebellion against God, as in Israel). Whatever the faults, people of all societies found ways of committing them, either inadvertently or maliciously. Religious systems, understood here to be the complex of rituals and stories that provided a symbolic matrix for social institutions, provided mechanisms for dealing with these actions and eliminating their results. Ritual and story, however, were not the only mechanisms for dealing with wrongful acts. Legal systems also defined crimes and specified forms of punishment and restitution. Legal systems intersected with the religious at significant points in some traditions.

Within the religious sphere, the mechanisms for dealing with "sin" involve two major conceptual schemes. Sin may be conceived as an objective defilement, a form of pollution that infects the sinner and the people and places with which the sinner might come in contact. To deal with the danger presented by the sinner, mechanisms usually involve some effort to remove the pollution or the polluting agent. Alternatively, sin may be understood in more-personal terms as an insult or offense to divine power. In that case, mechanisms for dealing with the sinner may involve appeasement of the offended power, either through cultic action or repentant behavior, restitution, and reconciliation. The logic of sin as an offense against a deity leads to suffering being construed as divine punishment and the possibility of vicarious suffering as a mechanism for atonement.

Each of these somewhat conceptual schemes for dealing with sin may be seen as an "ideal type," useful for heuristic purposes but seldom at work independently. Both are often at play in cultic traditions, and the logic of both will inspire attempts to develop moralizing critiques of traditional practice and, later, theologies of sin and atonement in the monotheistic religions of late antiquity.

Pollution

Pollution was a particularly weighted form of generic uncleanness. Even this category could be construed differently in different cultural systems, since "dirt" is simply matter out of place and the boundaries of "clean" places are culturally determined. Mud on a farmer's foot in the field need not be dirt; mud on the floor of the farmer's hut could be. Pollution was that form of "dirt" that prevented participation in the realm of the sacred; impurity at any level was simply incompatible with sanctity. It was necessary to be pure in order to enter a temple or engage in a ritual, although being pure might not be a sufficient condition to allow participation, which could be limited to people of a certain age, sex, or status. The requirement to maintain purity was thus more incumbent upon participants in religious rituals than it would be on nonparticipants. In cultures with a permanent priestly class, the requirements for purity would weigh more heavily on them than on the laity.

Many things could cause pollution, but the primary sources of pollution were natural substances: blood, spittle, semen, decaying flesh. Many polluting acts involved contact, willing or unwilling, with such substances, but the material stuff of polluting dirt was the paradigmatic source of pollution. Ancient Israel's extensively documented purity system defined sources of pollution, including diseases of the skin (Lev. 14); bodily discharges, such as semen or menstrual blood (Lev. 15); and corpses (Num. 19.11–16). Similar sources of pollution are attested in ancient Mesopotamian sources (van der Toorn 1985: 30–31). Birth, sex, and death are also major sources of cultic pollution in Greece. Bits of flesh from the corpse of Polynices polluted the altars of the gods (Sophocles, *Antigone* 999–1047). It was not right *(themis)* for the goddess Artemis to look upon her dead devotee (Euripides, *Hippolytus* 1437). The sacred island of Delos was kept free of pregnant women and the mortally ill. (Abundant examples may be found in Parker 1983.) In addition to such common sources of pollution, particular animals might be unclean for certain temples, as in Egypt or for a people as a whole (Lev. 11.24–47).

To encounter simple forms of impurity was thus unavoidable for most people much of the time. In fact, in some systems, such as that of ancient Israel, some ritual impurity was required. Thus, the act of sexual intercourse, required to fulfill the divine commandment to be fruitful and multiply (Gen. 1.28), would render husband and wife ritually impure. Similarly, to bury dead relatives was required even of Israelite priests (Lev. 21.1–3; Ezek. 44.25), though the act was defiling.

The paradigmatic case of pollution is contact with an offensive substance that renders a person "unclean" and not suitable for participation in cult. Sources from many different cultural traditions treat various wrongful acts under the same general rubric. Thus a Mesopotamian incantation seeks absolution for both the ritual infraction of "eat[ing] what is taboo to [a] god [or] . . . goddess" and also a wide variety of social transgressions, such as "oppress[ing] the weak woman," "estrang[ing] companion from companion," "[taking] money . . . not due," and so on (Reiner apud Milgrom 1991: 22–23). Similarly the Egyptian Book of the Dead (125) involves a negative confession, a denial that the deceased was guilty of various negative actions ("stopping a god in his procession," "eating what is *bwt*," or "making anyone weep") and transgressions (stealing, murder, adultery). The Israelite priestly manifesto demanding holiness of the people, Lev. 19, combines the moral injunctions to revere parents and avoid theft and sexual immorality with instructions about the proper eating of sacrificial food and appropriate hair trimming and body decoration. Modern categories of cultic, social, and moral infractions were simply not part of the conceptual scene at the earliest stages of the religious traditions of antiquity. Hence the use of the term *pollution* for serious moral offenses is readily understandable.

Another impetus for the understanding of serious moral infractions as polluting may have to do with the involvement of blood in some of them, at least homicide and illicit sexual activity. Murder was a special source of pollution in many cultural contexts. Even gods were required to wash themselves after killing (*Atrahasis* 1.206–7; van der Toorn 1985: 16). Mesopotamian sources consider bloodshed an abomination (Annals of Assurbanipal: *asakku*) or an offense that brings a divine curse (*Surpu* 2.49). In Israel, major infractions such as bloodshed (Num. 35.33), sexual infractions (Lev. 18.24–30), and idolatry (20.1–5; Ps. 106.34–41) polluted either the sinner (Lev. 18.24), the sanctuary (20.3; Ezek. 5.11), or the land as a whole (Lev. 18.28; Ezek. 36.19). Early Greek law codes (Draco, 7th century BCE) could invoke the category of pollution in connection with murder. This was probably not an innovation, but a vestige of a long-established cultural form. Dramatists of the 5th and 4th centuries wove concern with pollution in objective or personified (Erinyes) form into their plays. Heinous crimes such as patricide (Oedipus) or matricide (Orestes: Aeschylus, *Choephoroi* 269–96; Euripides, *Orestes* 580–84) could produce *miasma,* an objective state of pollution that isolated the perpetrator (Plato, *Euthyphro* 4c) and prevented participation in ritual (Euripides, *Orestes* 1600–1604). Such pollution had more-serious consequences, bringing destruction to nature and culture (Aeschylus, *Agamemnon* 1644–45).

Sexual offenses could be equally polluting. Sumerian law declared that a man who raped a girl publicly became impure (van der Toorn 1985: 17). Even a god such as Nergal remained impure, despite bathing, after an affair with the queen of the netherworld. In Israel, the priestly sources of Israel viewed various illicit sexual unions as abominations (tôʿēbôt; Lev. 18).

Offended deities

The appeal to the divine as the sanction of the moral order was a powerful tool of social control. Yet in many traditions, fickle and impetuous deities could be offended at various minor slights. In the ancient Near Eastern myths of Atrahasis (ANET 104–6), the god Enlil is enraged at noisy humans and decides to obliterate them in a flood. In Egypt the goddess Hathor/Sekhmet (ANET 10–11) lusts for human blood. The Greek Artemis, after having been forgotten at a sacrifice, sends the scourge of the Calydonian boar. The Roman authorities blamed the defeat of their army by Hannibal at Trasimene on the neglect of religious ceremonies, at least according to Livy (22.9).

Gods could be offended by more-serious slights. The Iliad opens with a scene of plague besetting the Achaean army at Troy because Agamemnon has incurred the wrath of Apollo by carrying off the daughter of his priest (Iliad 1.8–52). More serious still was the direct affront to the dignity of a god caused by sacrilege, the transgression of the places and things sacred to the deity, a concern widely attested in ancient sources. What counted as sacrilege included purely cultic issues: the misuse of sacrificial animals, improper disposition of sacred implements or foods, or introducing pollution into sacred spaces. Thus, in the defense of the sacred, the two conceptual realms of objective pollution and divine human relation merge.

The affront of a sacrilegious act was particularly apparent when the deity's name was invoked in vain. Ancient Near Eastern political treaties or covenants often involve oaths invoking divine guarantors of the treaties and threatening severe punishments for those who do not abide by the oaths. The Tukulti-Ninurta Epic of the 13th century BCE describes the anger of the Babylonian deities caused by the king's treaty violations. Either by defiling the deity's sacred space or by dishonoring the deity's name or status, the sacrilegious transgression evoked a divine sanction. In the epic just mentioned, the result was the offended deities' defection to Assyria, which conquered Babylon. The Mesha Stele from 9th-century Moab (ANET 320–21) describes a similar situation, in which the god Chemosh delivered Moab into Israelite control for a time. Homer, too, knows that Zeus punishes perjury (Iliad 4.160–62).

Gods may have felt abhorrence at the fact of moral pollution, their honor may have been compromised, or they may have been offended by the rebellious and ungrateful character of their subjects. In any case, their wrath manifested itself in fearsome responses. Israel's God can be as fierce as other ancient deities (Deut. 32.34–43; Ezek. 36.16–19), but his wrath is not arbitrary; rather, it is focused on transgressors, on the people in covenant with him who forget their obligations (Exod. 22.21–24 [= 22.20–23 Hebrew]), particularly by committing idolatry (32:7–10; Ps. 106.37–42). This wrath at the violation of the covenant leads, in the judgment of the prophets, to national destruction (Isa. 22:1–14) and exile (27.1–11). Expectations of a major day of divine wrath, in which YHWH would wreak vengeance on his foes, developed in Israel (Amos 5.18–20). In early Christian hands, the eschatological wrath of God against the universal reality of sin forms the background for the news of salvation (Rom. 1.18; Rev. 15.7).

While the threat of divine sanction could undergird moral and legal obligations, the understanding that the divine punished transgression provided a way of interpreting human history. Human suffering in the form of plagues, droughts, or military defeats was *prima facie* evidence for sin and divine wrath. The plague that visits Thebes due to Oedipus's actions stimulates a search for the guilty party, and a storm at sea leads to the search for the sinful prophet Jonah. The prophets of Israel, and the historical works they inspired, thus often appealed to the covenant formulas as the basis for their theological assessment of history. The theology of providential divine retribution at work in history was hardly confined to Israel, but also appears in Greek (Polybius, Dionysius of Halicarnassus) and Roman (Livy) historians.

Eliminating pollution and sin

For the simple and unavoidable or required forms of pollution, there were ready remedies. Things that caused impurities could be disposed of in various ways: by being burned, buried, or simply washed away. Simple procedures—such as a ritual bath, use of special substances (natron in Egypt; wine, clay, various plants, flours, salts in Hittite sources; the ashes of a red heifer in Israel [Num. 19]), periods of abstention from social contact (e.g., for new mothers or mourners) or from contact with the realm of the sacred—would restore the polluted person to a state of purity. The impurity removed, the individual could once again cross the boundary from profane to sacred and participate in cult. Homer's heroes must wash or purify themselves before sacrifice (*Iliad* 6.266–68), and all Athenian citizens had to purify themselves before entering the sacred space of the assembly. Israelite women were excluded from touching *sacra* after menstruation or birth, for varying periods of time: seven days for a son, two weeks for a daughter (Lev. 12.1–8).

Pollution could affect larger social units and thereby require more-extensive treatment. Ancient Mesopotamian (9th-century BCE Assyria under Assurnasirpal: REVIA 2.218.85; 226.26/27; and Salmanasar: RMA 3.15.26; 3.66.70) and Hittite sources report rituals for purifying armies. Places as well as people could become polluted. But cleansing was readily available through washing or "wiping" rites, such as the ancient Akkadian *kuppuru* (Wright 1987: 291). In Israel, houses as well as people could be affected with a skin disease and require extensive purification (Lev. 14). Greeks of the archaic and classical periods knew of *katharmoi* (rituals for washing, wiping, rubbing, fumigating) and professional purifiers, forebears of both magicians and physicians.

A frequent way of dealing with pollution and other undesirable substances such as disease was through rites of disposal. Such rites could involve various mechanisms for transferring the offensive pollution to a bearer of impurity, by spitting, touching, or passing through special gates. Or the pollution could be symbolically concretized through colored threads placed on a victim and then removed. The bearer of the pollution could then be either banished or destroyed. Such rituals are found in materials from ancient Ebla, 13th-century BCE Hittite texts (the Pulisa and Ashella rituals for removing plagues), the Israelite scapegoat ritual, and in various *pharmakos* rituals in Greek cities such as Abdera, Massilia, and Athens. Israel had its equivalents in the ritual for cleansing a leper, which involved the sacrifice of one bird and the expulsion of another (Lev. 14.2–7, 48–53), and above all in the scapegoat procedure, part of the ritual of the annual Day of Atonement. Part of the procedure involved sacrifice of one goat while another decorated goat was sent to the desert, to the mysterious "Azazel," bearing all the iniquities, sins, and transgressions confessed by the people (16.21). This complex ritual has given its name to the whole class of such ritual actions. The relationship among these scapegoat rituals and the differences among them have been the subject of considerable scholarly study. Although there are significant formal cross-cultural similarities, such as the use of decorated animals or human beings, specifics of goals and procedures vary considerably (see Ritual).

The manipulation of blood was frequently part of rituals designed to eliminate pollution. Actions involving blood would be particularly understandable in the case of the severe pollution caused by the shedding of blood, on the assumption that only blood, the locus of life itself (Lev. 7.26–27, 17.14), could purify the pollution caused by blood (explicitly at Num. 35.33; cf. the rite for dealing with bloodguilt when the murderer was unknown, Deut. 21.1–9). Israel's priestly code contains provisions for sacrifices connected with other purification rituals (e.g., Lev. 15.29, for an irregular discharge of blood), but there are two major blood sacrifices explicitly designed to deal with transgressions: the "purification sacrifice" (*ḥaṭṭā't;* Lev. 4) and the "reparation sacrifice" (*'āšām;* 5.14–6.7 [= 5.14–26 Hebrew]). Both are designed in order to "make expiation" *(kpr)*. The animal used for a "sin offering" varied with the status of the offerer, and its blood would be sprinkled at various sacred locations (4.5–6, 18, 25, 30, 34; 7.2). The relationship between these sacrifices and their underlying logic are unclear. The blood of these sacrifices may have been understood as a powerful cleansing agent, removing from sacred space the stain of the sin's pollution. Similarly, the blood of the sin offering of a bull on the Day of Atonement was to "make atonement for the holy place, because of the uncleannesses of the people of Israel" (16.16). The *'āšām* is distinctive in that a monetary offering could be substituted (5.15) and in that it required restitution (5.16; 6.5 [= 5.24 Hebrew]). The latter requirement indicates that, for some priestly circles, atonement involved more than ritual. In their current literary setting, both sacrifices deal with "inadvertent" sins (4.2; 5.14), although the *'āšām* also applies to swearing falsely, suggesting a broader scope.

Appeasing divine wrath

Although divine wrath may be distinguished from sinful pollution for heuristic purposes, they often appear to be intimately linked. Thus in the Hittite scapegoat rituals, gods are asked to "be appeased" by the human offerings (Wright 1987: 46, 50). But while apotropaic rituals might avert divine wrath, an offended deity might be treated as an offended human being.

Torts could be repaired by acts of restitution or the payment of a ransom. Stolen property could be restored, with an added penalty perhaps (Exod. 22:1 [= 21.37 Hebrew]), or one could pay for a gored ox (21.35–36). Serious crimes such as bloodshed required vengeance, the death of the murderer (21.12) at the hands of an "avenger of blood" (gō'ēl haddām; Num. 35.19). The Israelite legal tradition rejects the possibility that those responsible for the wrongful death of another could avoid the death penalty by payment of a ransom (Exod. 21.30; Num. 35.31), but the condemnation suggests the existence of the practice. Interestingly, the term for "ransom" (kōper; Greek lytron) derives from the same root as that used of cultic "expiation." The language of ransom was used in Israel for the sanctuary tax paid by the people (Exod. 30.12). Although they knew the mechanism, Israelite literature does not extensively exploit notions of ransom as ways of dealing with divine wrath. A stark alternative is provided in the Roman tradition of devotio, according to which a general could snatch victory from the jaws of defeat by vowing himself to the infernal gods (Livy 8.9.1–11.1; 10.28.12–29.7).

Wrongs against others could require propitiation and appeasement of the offended party. Insofar as a deity may have been involved, atonement usually included some sort of ritual of appeasement, perhaps a sacrifice or other offering to the offended deity, but also a direct appeal, in which the offending human being confessed guilt and sought reconciliation. Such appeals are found in hymns from the 2nd millennium BCE, such as one to Marduk found at Ugarit (Ras Shamra 25.460) or to Ishtar in ancient Babylonian (Iraq Museum 58424).

The notion of moral wrong as an act of rebellion (pš') against the divine lawgiver is characteristic of ancient Israel, forming the heart of the prophetic summons to repentance and renewed fidelity to the covenant relationship. The Torah (Lev. 26.40) recognizes the need for repentance and confession. The prophetic movement that achieved written form in the 8th century insists on confession and repentance (Jer. 3.11–14; 4.1–2). The pattern of confession continues with renewed vigor in the Second Temple period (Ezra 9; Dan. 9.4–19) and provided the framework for much early Christian treatment of sin and atonement.

Confessions of sinfulness and penitent appeals to divine mercy are not incompatible with notions of purification from sin's pollution. Striking versions of the pattern are found in Israel's lament psalms. Psalm 51 combines many of the metaphors, asking YHWH for mercy, for cleansing (vv. 2, 7 [= vv. 4, 9 Hebrew]) from sin, for purging from interior guilt (v. 6 [8]), leading to moral renewal (v. 7 [9])—all of which is made a condition of effective sacrificial offering (v. 16 [18]). Similarly Ezekiel, in the 6th century, proclaiming a hopeful vision for Israel's future, portrays YHWH as promising Israel purification from the uncleanness of idolatry and interior transformation with a new heart and spirit (Ezek. 36.22–33), all of which prepares for a renewed sanctuary (40–48).

Emphasizing the interpersonal character of sin, atonement could also involve the intercession of a mediator, one who, as the Hebrew tradition says, "stands in the breech," pleading for transgressors, such as Moses (Exod. 32.11–14, 30–34; Ps. 106.23), kings such as Hezekiah (2 Chron. 30.18–20), priests in general (Num. 8.19), specific priests such as Aaron (16.47 [= 17.12]) and Phineas (Ps. 106.30), or an angel (Job 33.24). A trusted mediator could avert divine wrath, as could an innocent representative of a people, whose suffering for others' transgressions brought healing (Isa. 52.13–53.12).

Criticism and resignification

Ancient rituals of purification from pollution, either ritual or moral, as well as cultic mechanisms either for dealing with the objective results of sin (expiation) or for appeasing the wrath of offended deities (propitiation), were subject to moralizing or rationalist criticism.

Israel's prophets, while calling for repentance, denounced a reliance on the mechanics of cult (1 Sam. 15.22–23; Amos 5.21–23; Isa. 1.10–15; Mic. 6.6–9), although that critique did not entail the total rejection of cult. (A similar critique seems to underlie the Zoroastrian revolution in ancient Persian religion.) Combining ritual and moral behavior was not unique to Israel. Thus Xenophon, leading his fractious Greek army, calls for both repentance and purification after some of his troops murdered local ambassadors (*Anabasis* 5.7.13–35).

Important for later developments were the admonitions of Israel's teachers of wisdom, who advocated various personal moral practices to expiate sin. Proverbs 16.6 highlights works of compassion; texts from the Second Temple or Hellenistic period suggest such things as virtuous obedience to parents (Sir. 3.3), almsgiving (3.30), and fasting (34.30–31; *Psalms of Solomon* 3.8; *Testament of Reuben* 1.10) as expiations.

In the Greek world, two significant developments occurred at the beginning of the classical period: a rationalist criticism of traditional purification rites and an insistence that moral purification was required for "salvation." Greek philosophers ridiculed purification rites—for example, Heraclitus decreed the foolishness of "trying to wipe off mud with mud" (frag. B 5). Later, Aristotle's pupil Theophrastus described those obsessed with such practices as "superstitious" (*deisidaimōn*, literally being excessively afraid of the divine world and its powers; *Characters* 16). Equally open to criticism was the notion that gods needed propitiation from human worshipers. No, argued philosophers, deity needed nothing, least of all human sacrificial gestures.

While rationalists ridiculed rites, some groups of the 5th and 4th centuries BCE, particularly Pythagoreans and those who followed teachings attributed to Orpheus, transformed purification rituals from cult-related practices to boundary markers of their own groups. Plato denounced the rituals and the books connected with Orpheus as trickery (*Republic* 364b–65a), yet appropriated their insistence that purity of the soul was a precondition for blessed immortality. Such beliefs find striking attestation in gold leaves from four 4th-century BCE burials at Thurii in southern Italy, which speak of the deceased as coming "pure from the pure" and as members of the race of blessed immortals; two of the leaves say that the deceased has done "penance for works unjust" (see Mysteries).

Plato could criticize popular purifiers yet retain vestiges of traditional notions of pollution, as in the *Laws* (9.831–73), which indicates degrees of pollution deriving from bloodshed. More importantly, his depiction in the *Phaedo* of Socrates' last hours is replete with language of purification. The soul, says Socrates, can attain to the realm of truth only if it distances itself from the contaminating imperfections of the body, with its "loves, desires, fears, and fancies." Only that which is pure *(katharon)* can attain the realm of the pure (*Phaedo* 66b–67b; 80d–81d). Plato's distinctly religious language here, as often, provides emotional support for a complex epistemological, aesthetic, and moral vision. Purification from pollution is not a ritual matter, but a distancing of the true self from the realm of physical passion. This reorientation has ultimate salvific consequences, and the combination will appeal to many later religious Neoplatonists, both pagan (Porphyry, Iamblichus, *Life of Pythagoras*) and Christian (Origen, Augustine).

Ancient notions of pollution found new homes in other spheres. Hippocratic physicians focused much of their treatment on the *katharsis* of unbalanced and hence polluting elements (Parker 1983: 213). Aristotle, perhaps inspired by the Hippocratics, applied the same notion to the effects of tragedy (*Poetics* 6.1449b28).

Heirs of the Israelite tradition in the Hellenistic period, influenced by such Greek rationalism and their own native sapiential tradition, reduced the ritual elements of their tradition to symbols of the moral (the 2nd-century BCE *Letter of Aristeas*). The Jewish philosopher of 1st-century Alexandria, Philo, who read his scriptures through Platonic lenses, insisted on the observance of ancient Israelite purification rules, but found in them Platonic ideals. Souls, that is, must be made pure before bodies can be cleansed (*Special Laws* 1.263–69), and, while eliminating the impurity of the corpse, one engages in contemplation (*On Dreams* 1.209–12).

The cosmic power of sin

As general social practice and ritual observance dealt with undesirable conditions and actions in concrete practical ways, some religious systems developed large conceptual frameworks for dealing with the realm of the undesirable in all its complexity. Ancient Egyptian sources delineated a negative realm that opposed the realm of *ma'at,* the realm of goodness, order, and sufficiency. Zoroastrian sources in 5th-century Persia, in an influential move, posited, as part of a comprehensive theodicy, an opposition of two fundamental forces, personified as the deities Ahura Mazda and Ahriman. Perhaps inspired by such dualism, Jewish sectarians of the Second Temple period envisioned a world divided into two spheres, one guided by a Spirit of Light, the other by a Spirit of Darkness, responsible for all evil. The Dead Sea Scrolls provide the primary testimony to this scheme (e.g., *Rule of the Community,* also known as 1QS or *Serek ha-Yahad*). Jewish apocalypses of the period, such as the 1st-century CE *4 Ezra,* also decry the pervasive power of sin. Other works provide explanations for that power. Perhaps the most colorful is the tale in the 3rd-century BCE *Book of Enoch.* On the basis of Gen. 6, this Jewish apocalypse recounts the myth of the Watchers, heavenly beings who became enamored of human women, had intercourse with them, and induced them to sin (*1 Enoch* 6–9). In such a context, moral transgression became not simply a matter of an individual's failing, but part of cosmic phenomenon, a manifestation of a universally pervasive sin.

Cosmic sin required a cosmic response. Jewish sources of the Second Temple period envisioned a decisive intervention by God into human history to restore Israel, often at the hands of an anointed (hence Messiah) royal or priestly figure, either human or angelic. This action could involve the elimination of political oppression (Daniel, *Psalms of Solomon*) or the elimination of sin through the action of an angelic priest such as Michael (Dan. 12) or Melchizedek (*Melchizedek* [11Q13] from Qumran). Such apocalyptic hope resolved problems with sin and sins in a rosy eschatological future.

Along with an increasing sense of the power of sin, sectarian Jewish sources also extended the category of pollution to serve as a general description for all sin (e.g., at Qumran, the *Thanksgiving Scroll* [1QH] 19[11].10–11).

The rabbinic movement, which came to dominate Israel's religious life after the destruction of the temple in Jerusalem in 70 CE, marks a shift. Continuing the critical stance of the Jewish wisdom literature, the rabbis agree that the means of expiating sin are to be found in the moral order. In a famous anecdote, Rabbi Jochanan ben Zakkai (late 1st century CE) responded to a colleague's lament for the devastated temple by noting that expiation was possible through almsgiving (*Avot of Rabbi Nathan* 1.5.4). Other rabbis noted the power of suffering and death to effect forgiveness of sin (Tosefta, tractate *Yoma* 5.6). At the same time, the rabbis insisted on repentance as the key to finding forgiveness for sins.

The rabbis also found their own way of treating the category of pollution and the mechanisms for dealing with it. Instead of expanding the category to cover the whole of the moral order, as did earlier sectarian Jews, or finding in it a metaphorical scheme for comprehending the destiny of the soul, as did the Platonic tradition, they concentrated on the details of ritual pollution in the Torah and developed a detailed logic of the rules of purity. In doing so, they demarcated a realm of behavior for the renewed people of Israel and focused on their obedience to the divine command and their common identity.

While the rabbis constrained the realm of pollution, they also avoided the cosmic power of sin. Their equivalent to the notion of the two cosmic spirits found in the Dead Sea Scrolls is a simple psychological model. In each human heart there are two roots *(yēṣer),* one good, one evil (e.g., Jerusalem Talmud, tractate *Ta'anit* 66c; Babylonian Talmud, tractate *Sukkah* 52b; *Sifre Deuteronomy* 45 on Deut. 11.18). The individual is not a pawn of cosmic powers, but a moral agent capable of choosing good and avoiding evil.

Early Christians inherited both the Jewish scriptures and the traditions that interpreted them. The claims that Jesus was the designated Messiah, assigned to effect that eschatological salvation (Rom. 1.3), appropriated the apocalyptic hopes of contemporary Jews. Some of his followers viewed salvation more in political and social terms (Luke 1, the *Magnificat*). Others focused on how Jesus provided salvation from sin, either by declaring sins forgiven (Matt. 9.2; Mark 2.5; Luke 5.20; 7.47) or by empowering his disciples to do likewise (John 20.23). Some followers used cultic imagery to rationalize his death. In their eyes it was a sacrifice, which provided expiation for sins (Mark 14.24; Rom. 3.25; 1 Cor. 15.3; Heb. 9–10). Jesus was thus the "Lamb of God who takes away the sins of the world" (John 1.29). Such imagery was probably based on Jewish martyrological traditions and perhaps reflected the influence of Isa. 52.13–53.12 and its vision of vicarious suffering as sacrificial expiation.

Most fruitful for later Christian notions was the theology of Paul, who combined a sacrificial understanding of Jesus's death with a cosmic notion of sin as a force so pervasive that it could even disable the revealed Torah and master human hearts (*Rom.* 7.7–25). Like the apocalyptic Jewish tradition from which he emerged, Paul understood that such a cosmic force required a cosmic response. Although he hoped for a future in which all such cosmic enemies would be finally overcome and salvation thus achieved (1 Cor. 15.54–55), he felt the salvific effects already in his own experience. He rationalized the effects of Jesus's death as the provision of a new "spirit" that transforms human hearts and liberates them from the power of sin (Rom. 8). Similarly, the Epistle to the Hebrews envisions the death of Jesus as a new Day of Atonement sacrifice, which expiates the stain of guilt not on altars, but on human consciences (Heb. 9.14) and works its liberating power by providing an example of fidelity to God for followers to emulate (Heb. 10, 12). Hebrews also employs the notion of Christ as an intercessor (7.25) or mediator (8.6), evoking figures such as Moses and Melchizedek.

Early Christians did not, however, confine themselves to a single image for describing the effects of the salvation wrought by Christ. His death was also viewed as a "ransom" (Mark 10.45) or "redemption" that purchased freedom from sin at the price of his blood (1 Cor. 6.20; Eph. 1.7; 1 Pet. 1.18–19). Such language combines ancient notions of the ransom for bloodguilt with contemporary images of purchase from slavery. Alternatively, the mythic imagination of early Christians could conceive of the death of Christ as a battle against the hostile power of sin, or its personification in Satan. Christ, then, achieved salvation as the victorious warrior over the powers of evil (Col. 2.15; Heb. 2.14–15; Rev. 19.11–16). In more personal terms Christians, particularly Paul, drawing upon language of Hellenistic diplomacy, focused on the effect of reconciliation that took place between God and humankind through the death of God's son (2 Cor. 5.17–19; Rom. 5.1–11).

Later Christian authors were generally content to follow the lead of the New Testament, understanding salvation primarily in terms of a deliverance from sin effected by Christ's sacrificial death and the power of the divine spirit. This vision implied the problematic assumption that spiritually transformed human beings would no longer be subject to sin, or at least would not commit serious sins, a notion resisted in 1 John 1.8. A corollary held that for those who did sin or commit apostasy from the group forgiveness was impossible (Heb. 6.4–8). Such rigorism continued in the 2nd and 3rd centuries with Tertullian in North Africa and Hippolytus and Novatian in Rome. A more realistic attitude toward the continuing reality of sin led to the development of a penitential system.

Persecutions of the mid-3rd and early 4th centuries were a particularly important catalyst, as the church had to deal with weaker Christians who had not found the courage to embrace martyrdom and had betrayed their commitment. After the Decian persecution, Cyprian, the bishop of Carthage in North Africa, in his work *On the Lapsed*, insisted against rigorists that even such extreme sinners could find reconciliation with the church, but only under the direction of the bishop.

While some Christians wrestled with the social consequences of sinning by members of the church, others, particularly 2nd-century groups, such as the Marcionites and those labeled by their opponents as gnostic, dealt with the topic in a more theoretical way. Inspired perhaps by early Christian rigorism and by an emphasis on Jesus as revealer of esoteric wisdom, they developed a notion of cosmic sin as ignorance of the transcendent deity. A typical expression of the notion is the 2nd-century *Gospel of Truth*, a work associated with the Valentinian school, which proclaims the rule of error caused by ignorance of God. Jesus remedied that problem and "took away the sin of the world" by revealing the hidden godhead (cf. also the 3rd-century Valentinian *Tripartite Tractate*). For such thinkers, the personal notions of propitiation of an angry deity or expiation of an objective polluting stain were not relevant. As Jewish interpreters had done for their cultic and ritual traditions in the Hellenistic world, these "knowing" Christians reinterpreted traditional moral and cultic categories in their own intellectual terms.

One late-antique religious movement akin to Gnosticism that did take seriously the category of pollution was Manicheism. In a system that recalls the combination of ascetic practice and interior purification encountered in early Pythagorean circles, this 3rd-century CE system advocated, particularly for its "elect" members, a strict dietary regimen that supported the moral purification of the soul, enabling its final return to a heavenly home.

Augustine, a sometime follower of Mani, in the early 5th century brought to its culmination the ancient Christian reflection on sin. Starting from Paul's Epistle to the Romans and its notion of the cosmic power of sin, Augustine developed his own understanding of how sin worked its ways. Where Paul had pointed to the narrative of the fall in Genesis as an example by virtue of which all human beings sinned, Augustine, relying on the Latin translation of Paul's text, found a doctrine of original sin, transmitted to successive generations of humankind by the very physical act of sexual reproduction.

Bibliography

Albertz, Rainer, ed. *Kult, Konflikt und Versöhnung: Beiträge zur kultischen Sühne in religiosen, sozialen und politischen Auseinandersetzungen des antiken Mittelmeerraumes.* Alter Orient und Altes Testament 285. Münster: Ugarit-Verlag, 2001.

Breytenbach, Cilliers. *Versöhnung: Eine Studie zur paulinischen Soteriologie.* Wissenschaftliche Monographien zum Alten und Neuen Testament 60. Neukirchen: Neukirchener Verlag, 1989.

Janowski, Bernd. *Sühne als Heilsgeschehen: Traditions- und religionsgeschichtliche Studien zur Sühneteologie der Priesterschrift.* 2nd ed. Neukirchen: Neukirchener Verlag, 2000.

Milgrom, Jacob. *Cult and Conscience: The Asham and the Priestly Doctrine of Repentance.* Studies in Judaism in Late Antiquity 18. Leiden: Brill, 1976.

———. *Leviticus.* Anchor Bible 3. Garden City, N.Y.: Doubleday, 1991–.

Miller, Patrick. *Sin and Judgment in the Prophets.* Society of Biblical Literature Monograph Series 27. Chico, Calif.: Scholars Press, 1982.

Neusner, Jacob. *The Idea of Purity in Ancient Judaism.* Studies in Judaism in Late Antiquity 1. Leiden: Brill, 1976.

Parker, Robert. *Miasma: Pollution and Purification in Early Greek Religion.* Oxford: Clarendon, 1983.

Sanders, E. P. *Jewish Law from Jesus to the Mishnah: Five Studies.* London: SCM/Philadelphia: Trinity, 1990.

———. *Judaism: Practice and Belief.* London: SCM/Philadelphia: Trinity, 1992.

van der Toorn, K. *Sin and Sanction in Israel and Mesopotamia.* Studia Semitica Neerlandica 22. Assen: van Gorcum, 1985.

Wright, D. P. *The Disposal of Impurity: Elimination Rites in the Bible and in Hittite and Mesopotamian Literatures.* Society of Biblical Literature Dissertation Series 101. Atlanta: Scholars Press, 1987.

Law and Ethics

Eckart Otto

Anthropological foundations of morality in ancient culture

Ethics as a theory of morals considers maxims of conduct from the point of view of the normative good, seeking its philosophical foundations and the consequences of good action. It brings to awareness aspects that implicitly govern action, to the extent that action is morally qualifiable. In the ancient world of the eastern Mediterranean, moral action is characterized by a synthetic view of life, which assumes a correspondence between the way that people fare in life and their deeds. The distinction between "what is" and "what ought to be" is foreign to antiquity, as is any distinction between moral duty and one's fate in life. In the ancient way of thinking, people consist of their actions, so that their existence is determined by fulfilling their obligations.

In the ancient world of the eastern Mediterranean, the moral quality of an action is measured by the extent to which it is in accord with the community's values and maxims; this accord is expressed by the way that justice is defined. The West Semitic root *ṣdq* does not mean justice in the sense of a *iustitia distributiva,* but rather solidarity and loyalty to the community in one's actions, so that the noun *ṣdqh* can be formed in the plural. The Egyptian term *ma'at* also denotes a *iustitia connectiva* of active solidarity and reciprocity of action. An act in accord with *ma'at* toward a person in need is stored in the collective memory of the community and recalled when someone who displayed solidarity needs assistance; the opposite term, *'wn-yb* (greed in one's heart, avarice) denotes egotism. In the Egyptian Lament of the Farmer, this notion of reciprocity is elevated to a moral requirement: "Act for the one who acts for you." The Greek philosopher Democritus observes that a person who loves no one is loved by no one and that the person who commits an evil act against another is unhappier than the victim. In ancient shame cultures, the collective memory of society not only directs the deed reciprocally against the perpetrator, but grants an honorable reputation to those loyal to the community, while humiliating the evildoer. The gods' first task, then, is simply to guarantee a correspondence between a person's deeds and a person's fate.

In a polytheistic pantheon the function of maintaining the world order implied by this correspondence falls not only to the highest god, such as the West Semitic El or the Greek Zeus, but also to special gods such as Shamash, the sun-god of Mesopotamia; Maat, the Egyptian goddess who embodies order in the world; or Dikē, the Greek goddess whose function is to see that laws are enforced. In monolatrous and monotheistic religions such as that of the god YHWH, this function of the sun-god can be either integrated into the god's character (as in Ps. 72) or separated and personified as a substitute figure such as Wisdom (Prov. 1.20–33; 8.1–36). Only when experience runs counter to the synthetic view of a correspondence between the quality of one's deeds and one's life, and the insight gains ground that this correspondence is precarious, are gods put to use as a higher authority for direct retribution. With this development, a motif stemming from sacred law and the law of contracts, in which the divinity directly punishes infringements of sacred duties or of clauses in a sworn contract, is transferred to the broad field of moral action.

At the same time, divine intervention in the world of humans acquires a moral dimension. The arbitrary will of the gods, whose intentions human beings seek to understand through divination, is domesticated by means of its attachment to the moral standards of human action. Thus, the ancients were familiar with numerous stories in which a divinity miraculously intervened in order to rescue a good person (Lycurgus, *Lament of Leocrates* 95–96). But since the idea of divine intervention on behalf of the morally good person is not consistently verified by experience, the link between deed and life can be extended over several generations, to make it mesh better with experience. In the early 6th century, Solon taught that while divine retribution could strike evildoers quickly, it might also be delayed and strike their descendants many years later. In approximately the same period, the Decalogue of the Hebrew Bible postponed divine retribution until the third or fourth generation, to keep the possibility of reform open (Exod. 20.5). Since experience also fails to confirm these theories in every case, divine retribution can be interpreted as a judgment imposed on the dead in an afterlife as well. The notion cropped up first in Egypt during the 12th Dynasty (Merikare, Papyrus Petersburg, lines 53–57) and found its classic expression in the Egyptian Book of the Dead around 1500 BCE. It made its way to Greece by at least the first half of the 5th century (Pindar, *Olympian* 2.58–83) and in the 2nd century BCE reached the Hebrew Bible on the periphery of the canon (Dan. 12.1–3).

For ancient peoples, what counted as "the good" before all ethical theory was traditional conduct in the sense of what was customary and therefore "normal." As a concept of the morally good, the Akkadian word *išaru(m)* (Hebrew *yšr*)—meaning "normal, right, appropriate" and, in connection with the synthetic view of life, also "fortunate, favorable"—expresses the traditional character of ancient value systems. *Išaru(m)* is based on the verb *ešeru(m)* (to be straight, to go straight ahead), from which the abstract noun *mišaru(m)* (justice) also derives, containing the aspect of correcting or straightening out what deviates from the normal. The word *kittu(m)*, which often forms a hendiadys with *mišaru(m)* and derives from the verb *kânu(m)* (to be firm, lasting), also gives expression to the traditional character of the Mesopotamian value system, which guarantees the stability of expected behavior through the traditional nature of ethical and legal norms. In Mesopotamia the promotion of social cohesion was inseparably linked to the concept of justice, as is shown by the *mišaru(m)* and *(an)durāru(m)* edicts of Babylonian and Assyrian kings in the 2nd and 1st millennia BCE, which served to reduce social tensions by forgiving debts and freeing slaves. But they also confirm the traditional character of the ancient Near Eastern concept of justice, which in this respect is paradigmatic for the whole value system of the ancient world. *Mišaru(m)* does not imply the idea of justice in the sense of social equality, so that the *mišaru(m)* edicts were not promulgated with the intention of ending social inequality. Rather, they were designed to prevent expropriation as a result of debt that would drive families out of the hereditary social class. The traditional character of this mentality is underscored by a Sumerian proverb: "The man who sows crops should sow crops; the man who harvests barley should harvest barley." Thus, the good as that which is just is what has always been realized in human action, not an "ought" or obligation, separated from what is, but rather the realized ethical substance of society since time immemorial. There the "ought" is in a state of tension with the possible action and becomes an independent entity when actions deviate from what counts as normal in society. At this point, morality meshes with law, insofar as both judicial practice and the social *mišaru(m)* edicts of the king were understood as correctives or a "straightening out" (*šutēšru[m]*; causative form of the verb *ešēru[m]*) that restored normal, that is, good, conditions as the epitome of just conditions.

The values intended to guide moral action propagated in the memorial inscriptions of the dead and in the educational literature of ancient oriental and biblical wisdom literature are correspondingly traditional. They demand neither great feats nor ascetic self-denial nor martial heroics, but rather are the values of an average bourgeois morality in the modern sense, to which belong diligence, self-control, discretion, honesty, obedience to parents, teachers, and superiors, but also generosity toward inferiors and those with a low position in society, as well as patience—that is to say, above all, an awareness of one's own limitations and the need to rely on fellow human beings and the gods. From such recognition follows a proper measure in all things. In this respect, the Egyptian teaching of Ptahhotep from the first half of the 2nd millennium should be compared with the maxims in chapters 10–30 of the biblical Book of Proverbs, the core of which dates from the first half of the 1st millennium.

The canon of values reflected in memorial and wisdom literature of the ancient eastern Mediterranean remained stable from the 3rd to the 1st millennium, and particular accents were set solely with regard to the literature's function. Thus the teachings of Ptahhotep, which served to educate officials, laid stress on the virtues important for dealing with one's superiors and inferiors, whereas the biblical proverbs were not oriented toward a specific profession and sought to educate in a more general and comprehensive manner. The bourgeois character of this eastern Mediterranean value system, which propagated an ethos of compassion derived from awareness of one's own limits and need for help, had a cultural and historical foundation; in contrast to value formulations of the western Mediterranean, it did not grow out of an aristocratic ethos. Instead, an intellectual caste of priests and sages drew on proverbs based on popular morals to formulate their value system. If the values, taken by themselves, possessed an astonishing similarity from Mesopotamia to Egypt (which derives less from processes of reception than from a socially and anthropologically based fundamental morality or from the peasant and bourgeois majority in the populations of these lands), nevertheless they occupied very different positions in their respective religious systems and in the anthropologies connected with them, which gave expression to different historical experiences and the sense of life. The Middle Babylonian creation epic *Enuma Elish* dates from the close of the 2nd millennium and from at least the 8th century on was recited regularly on the fourth day of the New Year festival in Esangila, temple of Marduk in Babylon; tablet 6.31–40 describes how Marduk, the god of the Babylonian Empire, killed Tiamat, the creature of chaos who embodied everything that causes life to fail, and made the world out of her corpse. Marduk then created humanity from the blood of Qingu, Tiamat's general, as servants for the gods and to free the gods from the guilt they bore for not opposing Tiamat's claim to rule. Thus, the fate of human beings was to work off the guilt of the gods. If they were created from the material of chaos, in the form of Qingu's blood, then it becomes easy to understand why human beings are not only mortal but also grow feeble with increasing age. The myth concludes with the gods building the imperial temple Esangila out of gratitude to Marduk.

In this system, a person could lead a successful life only by following Marduk, god of the empire, who conquered chaos and was represented on earth by the king of Babylon. For a fulfilled life, it was therefore necessary to obey the laws of the Babylonian state or, in the Assyrian version, to obey the laws of the Assyrian ruler, who represented the god of that empire, Assur. An Assyrian myth about the creation of human beings and the king from the first half of the 1st millennium makes a distinction between the creation of human beings *(lullû-amēlū),* who are supposed to relieve gods of the toil of cultivating the land, and the creation of the king as a "human being who by virtue of his superiority makes decisions [*malīku amēlū*]"—to the king is granted rule over people and the power to wage war following the gods' instructions. This synthetic view of life, in which good actions correspond to success, is linked with loyalty to the state; it is valid only in the context of state rule and is limited even there, since from the time of its creation humankind was ordained to deprivation and toil for the benefit of the gods and the state as embodied by the king.

The Hebrew Bible endorses the contrary anthropological view, which originated in Judah in the 8th century. The writing of the Aaronic priests, conceived in the time of exile as a response to the *Enuma Elish,* similarly ends with the construction of a holy shrine (here the tent of the encounter in the Sinai). It does not, however, recount the story of the creation of the world and human beings as the conclusion of a complex cosmogony and theomachy; rather it places the creation of the world and humans, in accordance with a monotheistic concept of God, at the very beginning. Humans, in this view, were not created to labor in atonement for the sins of the gods, but to give shape to the world as God's representatives. In Mesopotamian royal ideology, the motif of humanity made in the image of god *(soeloem)* was reserved for the king as god's representative *(salum);* in the Israelite version, the priesthood opposed the negative anthropology in Mesopotamian ideology, which bound humankind to the state legitimated by God, by applying the motif to every individual and democratizing the royal ideology. Already, in the late preexilic era, the writer of Deuteronomy set absolute loyalty to the Jewish god YHWH against the Assyrian demand of absolute loyalty to the state, by subversively transferring the oath of loyalty to King Asarhaddon to YHWH in Deut. 13 and Deut. 28. In this manner, the Deuteronomist imposed limits on demands for loyalty to the state and also deprived the state, in the form of king, of its function as a channel of divine grace. For the first time in the cultural history of the ancient orient, ethical values were disengaged from loyalty to the ruler. Correspondingly, biblical wisdom could formulate criticism of rulers that fit the kingdom of Judah, which was connected with Assyria, by attacking it on the basis of observation of nature: "The locusts have no king, / yet go they forth all of them by bands" (Prov. 30.27). The emancipation of ethical thinking from the state, which was initiated by small circles of intellectuals in Judah, prevailed when the kingdom came to an end during the late Babylonian and Persian era in Judah and consequently prevailed in the Hebrew Bible as well.

This emancipation also ran counter to Egyptian ideology of the state, which still linked the possibility of overcoming the barrier of death to an individual's loyalty to the state, without resorting to the crass negative anthropology that characterizes the Mesopotamian myths of human creation. In Egypt it was held that all human beings owed their ability to breathe—their lives—to the goddess Maat, who provided order and regularity to the cosmos as she guided the course of the sun-god. However, her protective power was directed particularly toward the king, the son of the sun-god and Maat's own brother. Just as the sun-god defeated chaos on a cosmic scale as he crossed the skies and, guided by Maat, enabled *ma'at* (justice) to prevail, so the king embodied this principle in the human sphere. State rule was, thus, the prerequisite for an individual's ability to lead a just life in terms of community solidarity, the sole standard of just behavior that would permit one to pass the test on the day of judgment. But unless the king, deified as Osiris, overcame the barrier of death, an individual had no path into the afterlife. Part of the royal practice of *ma'at* consisted of rewarding subjects for conduct that conformed to it, but it also consisted of using the law courts to resolve conflict and eliminate conduct likely to cause harm *(isfet).* The state played an indispensable role, because human actions were by their very nature not in accord with *ma'at;* the human heart followed the law of the stronger *(isfet),* that is, egotism that endangers society. *Ma'at* could reach human hearts only through the medium of the king. In Jerusalem, too, people knew that human beings could not realize "loyalty to the community" in their own actions, through their own power alone. Despite a positive theology of creation (Ps. 8), loyalty was not granted to humankind by nature; instead, a sense of loyalty to the community, and with it the ability to act for the benefit of the community, was conveyed through a sacrifice (Deut. 33.19; Ps. 4.5 [= 4.6 Hebrew]) with YHWH's blessing (24.5; 89.14–16 [= 89.15–17 Hebrew]; 99.4; Isa. 1.21–27; 33.5). In comparison with Egypt and Mesopotamia, the king in Judah was relegated to the background in the process of granting loyalty.

The ancient western Mediterranean value system differed from the eastern in being based primarily on an aristocratic ethos rather than an everyday morality of peasants and the middle classes. The aristocratic ethos was not primarily concerned with social cohesion, but rather stressed agonistic values of combat, placing defense of personal honor *(timē)* before justice (in the sense of actions that further a sense of community). The twenty-second book of the *Odyssey,* in which the poet shows Odysseus killing 108 young men who sought the hand of his wife, Penelope, during his long absence, glorifies behavior that attaches higher value to the renown of a great feat in the eyes of an aristocratic audience—even if it consists of mass murder—than to peace in the community. Hesiod, by contrast, who at about the same time questioned this traditional glorification of honor and combat, made justice *(dikaiosynē)* the core concept of his value system, in a reversion to ancient Middle Eastern wisdom literature. An ethos that declares victory in battle as the highest value was branded as unjust hubris, which the gods would avenge, and in accordance with this the nature of the gods themselves, particularly Zeus, was recast in ethical terms. Aristocrats, as judges, were made responsible for ensuring that justice prevailed, with justice being limited to punishment of injustice. The aspect of social cohesion and solidarity, which colored the concept of justice in the eastern Mediterranean, was largely absent in Greece.

Nevertheless *dikaiosynē* in Hesiod implies that peace and the well-being of the community are valued more highly than a hero's fame. It exhorts people who feel they have been wronged to resist boundless revenge and instead accept payments from the wrongdoers; thus will conflicts end. Only if the wrongdoer refuses to cooperate should one wait for an opportune moment and strike back. In contrast to ancient Middle Eastern wisdom literature, Hesiod neither required the wronged person to forgo retaliation entirely nor adopted the *lex talionis.* This role existed in ancient Babylonian law only to protect free citizens from physical injury and was limited in the biblical law of the book of the covenant (Exodus) to murder or manslaughter; in all other cases it was replaced by reparation in some form. Where Hesiod considered it appropriate to take revenge by inflicting double the injury suffered, he was taking into account the aristocratic ethos of defending one's honor. The notion of boundless revenge did remain a theme of Greek literature well into the classical period but, as the tragedies of Aeschylus and Sophocles show, this was done in order to criticize it, for one could set limits on revenge only when values higher than honor existed. Not until Plato's *Gorgias* and *Republic* was the concept of honor finally dismantled in favor of *dikaiosynē* and was it declared better to suffer injustice than to commit it.

The negative anthropology found in Mesopotamian mythology, which bound people to the state, which in turn served as mediator between them and the world of gods, was alien to Greek thought; from the archaic epoch of aristocratic rule to that of the citizen polis, Greece did not develop total subordination of every individual under the state as in the orient. In the orient, the view of chaos and order as opposites found expression in the motif of the battle against chaos, which originated in the West Semitic region and spread from there to Mesopotamia and also in Egypt in a rudimentary form. This opposition served to justify a policy of military aggression, given that the antithesis of war was not peace but chaos. In Greece the opposition between order and chaos did not lead to an expansionist imperial policy; instead it took the form of a cultural antagonism between Greeks and non-Greeks, who were labeled barbarians. It gave expression to the self-esteem of people in the region, based on culture, which could also take the form of moral superiority. In the early 5th century, a consciousness of moral superiority over the barbarians was strengthened by the successful repulsion of Xerxes' invasion. However, moral standards became differentiated within Greek culture as well. Isocrates created a moral pyramid in which Athenians stood at the top, above first the other Greeks, and then the barbarians; and Euripides alleged that barbarians commonly practiced incest and murdered relatives (*Andromache* 173–76). He also asserted that gratitude and friendship were unknown to them (*Helen* 501–2) and that this dissimilarity between Greeks and barbarians was due not to nature *(physis)* but to *nomos* (custom) and *sophia* (intelligence), that is, it represented a cultural difference.

Distinctions were also made within Greek culture. Athenians saw themselves as honest and friendly (Demosthenes, *Against Leptines* 109), but considered the Spartans treacherous (Aristophanes, *Peace* 1066–68, 1083), while the inhabitants of Phasalus were supposed to be dishonest in business dealings (Demosthenes, *Against Lacritus* 1–2). On the other hand, a Panhellenic value system was applied when Greeks distinguished themselves from barbarians. As grave inscriptions show, its central values were courage *(aretē)* and avoidance of harmful behavior *(sōphrosynē)*. The lines of demarcation separating Greek communities from the outside world arose not, as in the political theologies of the ancient Near East, from the identification of strangers with the mythical power of chaos that has to be suppressed by the political authorities, but from the Greeks' perception of their own cultural and moral superiority. As a result, Greek policies were more defensive, but there were no powerful religious impulses at work driving the creation of a large empire. They had to be borrowed from the Orient through Macedonia. But as a result, religious impulses to rationalize ethics were also lacking in Greece; they could emerge only from a philosophy that had begun to emancipate itself from traditional religion.

The realm of the gods and morality in ancient cultures

The degree of connection between human ethos and divine behavior varied in ancient cultures. The biblical world of Israel and Judah lay at one extreme and Greek culture at the other, with Mesopotamia, Syria, Egypt, and Anatolia occupying intermediate positions. In both Greek and ancient Near Eastern thinking, the key difference between human and divine beings was that the latter were immortal. But in moral terms the Greeks considered the difference between mortals and gods to be small, since their gods, unlike humans, were not morally infallible *(anarmatētos)*. Greek gods could be seduced by Eros; they were sensitive about their own honor and could feel jealousy like human beings. In both the archaic and classical periods, the most important gods could be described as indifferent to the social norms of human interaction. At the root of this religious thinking lay the archaic ethos of the aristocracy, which permitted a hero to have a direct relationship with a protective divinity, which could rupture human ties. The logic of reciprocity in dealings between mortals and gods was the same as in relationships between friends in the aristocratic ethos, so that a divinity would support human protégés even when they violated the norms of a human community, as long as they were defending their honor. Norms that furthered the cohesion of a community through solidarity of action and pursuit of conflict resolution were thus of exactly the wrong kind to be strengthened or promoted by religious impulses. Greece had no class of intellectual religious specialists to support ethical rationalization. Greek religion was a religion of sacrifices; it required the performance of sacrificial duties from everyone and thus allowed no independent caste of priests to develop alongside the political leadership, which took its models from the martial ethos of the aristocracy. As a result, the city-states also lacked a class of religious intellectuals in a position to rationalize the ethics of the religious system and propel it toward socially beneficial values, enabling religion to confront politics as political theology and achieve political standing for such norms.

A way out of traditional religion became necessary as soon as the insight grew that human beings could neither protect themselves against contingencies in life through magic nor rely on divine assistance, since the gods were not bound to any norms of behavior. The political elite thus prevented an ethical rationalization of religion in Greece. In contrast, during the late period in Egypt the priests' domination of politics allowed religion to regress to a form of personal piety with no regard for the connective norms of social justice. This late form of Egyptian religion released the gods from the norms of *ma'at* and gave them instead an arbitrary freedom of action; human beings responded with a personal piety that released the norms of connective justice from the social dimension and transferred them to the individual relationship with a god. Good fortune in life was now believed to be secured not through social behavior, but by turning toward the divinity according to the *do ut des* (I give so that you will give) principle. This also held true for the Egyptian king, who became the paradigmatic pious example to his people, while the motif of divine descent was transferred from the king to a child of a god in a holy trinity. Whenever productive tension between religion and state politics disappears, the religious system loses its power to rationalize the ethics of a society, as examples from ancient Israel and Judah in the Hebrew Bible show.

In the social crises of the Judean kingdom, priestly intellectuals turned the norms of neighborly solidarity into theology, presenting them as the will of God, and constructed models of social solidarity in Exodus (21–23) and Deuteronomy (12–26), which they offered in response to the policy that had been carried out. The scriptural prophets, and the circles of intellectuals who took their cue from them, measured the behavior of the people by the standards propagated by the priests' collections of law and informed the people what the consequences for failing to comply would be. A characteristic of priestly theology was its distance from the state; implicitly theology thus became criticism of the state, which the prophets made explicit as criticism of the king. In this way, in postexilic Judaism, YHWH, the one god who behaved ethically and required ethical behavior from followers, became the objective of a thoroughgoing process of ethical rationalization for all areas of life of his clientele, which expressed itself in the elevation of the Pentateuch to the Torah (Law) and thus could develop its power to guide conduct. No magic, which in Egypt undermined the rationalizing power of the thought of a last judgment, could liberate people from the consequences of their actions. The hostility of Judaic religion to magic (combined with monotheism's closing off the possibility of ascribing any misfortune experienced in life to adverse deities and to the negative anthropology derived from it) increased the need for an ethical shaping of life, since misfortune could be the result only of human activity. The rationalization of religion was further increased by the political experience of being at the mercy of the great powers, with all the resulting consequences for the fate of the individual; it gave rise to questions about how such experience could be reconciled with a belief in YHWH as an ethical god. As a consequence, eschatological thinking became universal, which subjected the entire population of the world to the ethical will of YHWH and sought in it the solution to the problem of theodicy for Judah. The high degree to which rationalization was achieved in the Hebrew Bible permitted Judaism and its offshoot, Christianity, to survive as world religions, whereas the religions of other ancient centers of power perished.

The history of Mesopotamian religion offers a complex picture that should be divided according to literary genres. This more differentiated interpretation replaces the notion held by scholars in the past, who thought that the conception of divinity acquired an ethical dimension at the time of Hammurabi, in the first half of the 2nd millennium. In this view, the gods developed from morally fallible figures into beings possessed of a moral perfection unattainable by humankind, with the result that human misfortune could no longer be ascribed to demons and had to be traced back to unethical human behavior instead. However, Sumerian legends dating from the late 3rd and early 2nd millennia require a more differentiated interpretation. In mythic narratives the pantheon of gods serves to reconcile phenomena in the sphere of human life that appear contradictory—such as life and death, order and chaos, peace and war, fertility and infertility, man and woman—and to render them comprehensible; this is done by personifying these occurrences as deities whose behavior follows the logic of human interaction. An ethical idealization of gods would have undermined this function of myth. The function of gods in myths must be distinguished from their task in the traditions of wisdom literature and law, where they interact primarily not with one another but with human beings and direct human behavior by establishing a code of values. In Mesopotamia, this ethical link between deities and humanity was used chiefly to provide a religious foundation for the king as the font of law (see the prologue and epilogue of the Codex Hammurabi) and in the function of deities as witnesses in the law of contracts.

In both functions—foundation and witness—the official pantheon of gods worked solely through the channel of the king, the mediator of divine action in the world, to affect individual citizens, although everyone was entitled to pray to gods such as Shamash, Marduk, or Ishtar. A citizen's personal relationship to deities was focused on a tutelary god, who was believed to accompany this person during his or her lifetime and act as an intermediary with higher-ranking gods. Since the gods had ethically ambivalent relationships with one another, the pantheon of gods had only a very limited function as a model for human action. Only magical manipulation could save human beings from the urges to exact retribution that were imputed to gods in Mesopotamian religion. And since a tutelary god was expected to take the side of the human client even if that client had failed to behave ethically, religion was the source of very few impulses toward ethical rationalization. Wisdom teachings were cultivated in the state schools for scribes, and the ethical indifference of religion offered a good basis for the emancipation of these teachings from religion as secular philosophy following the Greek pattern; however, such an emancipation prevented a close connection between religion and the state, which also prevented an emancipation of priestly specialists as champions of an ethical rationalization of religion. This connects Mesopotamian religious history with that of Egypt. It is true that the ethical values of connective justice that are supposed to guide human behavior were personified in the goddess Maat, who was connected with the order of the cosmos and thereby provided with the very highest religious authority; however, the achievement of ethical rationalization of Egyptian religion was reduced by the fact that, in the synthetic view of life, the consequences of human action could be deflected through magic. The achievement of ethical rationalization of Egyptian religion was limited chiefly by its being a state ideology, in which the king embodied *ma'at*, although in contrast to Mesopotamian religion the functions of integrating contradictory experience and stabilizing human morality were united in the figure of the goddess Maat through the aspects of connective justice, until in the late period this process also broke down.

The realm of the gods and law in ancient culture

Every ancient society needed law to strengthen its internal cohesion, both in order to settle conflicts and thereby minimize violence and also to enforce sanctions against socially harmful behavior and violations of social norms. In societies organized as states, the state either carried out these functions of law or supervised them; in monarchies, the degree to which the king personified legal functions determined whether laws were codified and with what function. In Egypt, the king's personification of law as Maat's representative meant that no restrictions could be placed on his right to decide litigation; in theory the king handed down judgments without being bound to codified norms, although in practice this occurred only in specific instances of capital crimes. Thus no laws of the king are documented from predemotic times, only a decree of King Haremheb (18th Dynasty) along with decrees to officials that regulated privileges and instructions about how to carry out their duties. In Mesopotamia, the king was regarded as having received a mandate from the gods to enforce the law; he could delegate this task to officers of the state government. In this system, legal principles as descriptions of legal practice could be codified for teaching purposes, used to give religious legitimation to the king's juridical function, or presented to the public for propagandistic purposes, as in the case of the Code of Hammurabi.

Collections of laws could also either advertise judicial reforms, as in the case of the Middle Assyrian laws, or document such a reform, as did the Hittite laws. In the legal system of the Achaemenids, judgments handed down by the king acquired the status of unalterable law for the courts. When the Persians conquered a province, imperial policy for maintaining order was to enforce any codified indigenous laws. A first step toward making the law independent of the state occurred in Anatolia in the 2nd millennium. According to early Hittite royal ideology, the king was not the font of law, but required a divine model in order to obey the law. Then, as a result of influences from Mesopotamian and Egyptian ideology, the king in the Hittite Empire came to be regarded as the earthly representative of the weather-god and as such functioned as lawgiver and supreme judge. Only in Judea and Greece, where in the long run the legal systems were separate from the king, was the law—either granted by YHWH or voted by the citizens of a city-state—able to take an independent stand vis-à-vis the state. Whereas the laws of cuneiform justice primarily described and documented the judgments that had in fact been handed down and prescriptive legal functions remained a royal prerogative, in Judea and Greece the laws exercised this prescriptive royal function themselves (*nomos ho pantōn basileus*, custom is king of everyone; Pindar, frag. 169). In the

Torah, the law is declared to have originated as divine revelation received on a sacred mountain in the desert; the circumstance prevented it from being reduced to an instrument of political power. In classical Greece, the people could become the font of laws; the gods simply confirmed them. In Judea, the theory that law emanated from divine revelation, which was broadly developed in the Pentateuch from the exilic period on, prevented a similar process of democratization in formulating laws, since a class of scribes, who derived their norms from interpreting and extending the Torah, assumed an increasingly dominant intellectual leadership in Achaemenid and Hellenistic Judea. Through its consistent presentation of law in theological terms, the Hebrew Bible made the Torah into an independent counterweight to every state that became subject to Jewish law. The followers of Alexander, on the other hand, came under the influence of ancient royal ideologies; their kingdoms took on a more-oriental character, and the king came to embody the law as *nomos empsychos* (living law) in a development that aroused fierce resistance among Jews in the population.

The emancipation of ethics from traditional religion in Greek philosophy

Greece had no intellectual class of religious specialists who could rationalize traditional religion and make it able to address the need for salvation, who could develop comprehensive theories to explain the experiences of negative contingency that impeded satisfaction of this need, and who could then impart them to their clientele in combination with moral precepts in a manner that furthered social solidarity. Thus from the 6th century, new ways to satisfy these needs arose along the margins of Greek culture, such as Asia Minor (Miletus), and then also affected traditional religion in its centers (Athens). Xenophanes (570–480 BCE) took a critical stand against traditional Greek religion, declaring, "Homer and Hesiod attributed behavior to the gods that human beings consider shameful and scandalous, such as theft, adultery, and deceitful dealings" (DK 21B11). When people wished to protect themselves from the will of the gods, which they understood to be amoral and arbitrary, they called upon the synthetic view of life, as *Odyssey* 1.32–34 already put it: "All evil, men proclaim, comes from the gods, yet nevertheless these fools ignore fate and divine warnings, and cause their own ruin." In this view the gods are anthropomorphic figures and only a mirror image of limited human imagination. While Xenophanes deduced the existence of a transcendent god from this—a problematic deduction because different *nomoi* among the human cultures had then to be traced back to differences in the world of the gods—skepticism prevailed among the Sophists. Rhetorical arguments and matters of content diverged, so that different moral judgments could coexist side by side. Increased knowledge about non-Greek peoples and their laws and customs in the 5th century led to a more relative view, in which laws were thought to be mutable rather than unchanging. The Greeks learned to distinguish between what existed in nature *(physis)* and what had been established by human beings *(nomos)*. A debate then followed over whether people ought to follow their natural instincts or act in accordance with the laws and conventions of their community. Traditional *nomos* thus became open to alteration.

In the 4th century, Plato, in a debate with the Sophists, developed a concept of *nomos* that was based on new epistemological and ontological reasoning and that did not draw on existing laws. He placed *nomos* in a world of ideas from which the material world of sensory experience was derived; human beings could approach this world by means of their powers of reasoning. A lifelong striving for knowledge became the principle of moral behavior. Since the rational human soul stemmed from the intangible world of ideas before it was implanted in the body, every grasp or comprehension of an idea was held to be a memory. And since a person's worth consisted of one's soul, one acted well and justly in improving the condition of one's soul and the souls of others. Ethics became a doctrine of happiness that reformulated the popular connection between one's deeds and one's fortune in life, for justice now numbered among the things "that must be loved for their own sake and for the consequences resulting from them by everyone who wishes to be happy [*eudaimōn*]" (*Republic* 358a). Justice could be secured permanently and human happiness realized only in the framework of the polis. Concrete ethical norms were determined by membership in one of the city-state's social classes and by the condition of one's soul. Aristotelian ethics, taking this as its starting point, is a theory of human happiness *(eudaimonia)*. Since human beings are disposed by nature to live in communities, ultimately the goal of happiness could be attained only in the polis, so that ethics became one part of political theory. For Aristotle, happiness consisted in virtue *(aretē)* as a reasonable, self-controlled life and in the possession of external goods (*Nicomachean Ethics* 1099a–b), so that human happiness was not completely under human control, but remained a "gift of the gods."

The Hellenistic schools of Stoicism, Epicureanism, and Pyrrhonian skepticism sought to point out ways by which *eudaimonia,* understood as the highest goal *(telos)* of human life, could be detached from its connections with the polis and the gods and thereby brought entirely under human control. These philosophers removed from the definition of happiness all material goods that might not be available at certain times, so that the greatest good in Stoicism was virtue, and in Epicureanism it was happiness *(hēdonē);* both terms included an attitude of indifference *(apatheia/ataraxia)* toward the material sphere. The Christian ethics of antiquity held this philosophy, which sought to attain happiness through one's own efforts, to be a way of suppressing one's experience of evil and a form of arrogance. True virtue was associated with piety and hope: "For we are encompassed with evils, which we ought patiently to endure, until we come to the ineffable enjoyment of unmixed good; for there shall be no longer anything to endure. Salvation, such as it shall be in the world to come, shall itself be our final happiness" (Augustine, *City of God* 19.4).

Bibliography

Assmann, Jan. *Ma'at: Gerechtigkeit und Unsterblichkeit im Alten Ägypten*. Munich, 1990.
Dover, K. J. *Greek Popular Morality in the Time of Plato and Aristotle*. Oxford, 1974.
Ferguson, John. *Moral Values in the Ancient World*. London, 1958.
Lambert, W. G. *Babylonian Wisdom Literature*. Oxford, 1960.
Lévy, Edmond, ed. *La codification des lois dans l'antiquité*. Paris, 2000.
Otto, Eckart. *Theologische Ethik des Alten Testaments*. Stuttgart, 1994.

Mysteries

Sarah Iles Johnston

No aspect of ancient religions has evoked greater interest—and a greater range of interests—than that of mystery cults. Scholars have repeatedly combed textual and archeological evidence in attempts to uncover their secrets (what was done? by whom? to whom?), and a variety of people from outside of academia have invoked and adapted the cults for their own uses. Mozart's *Magic Flute,* which draws on 18th-century Masonic perceptions of the mystery cult of Isis, is a well-known example; today, neopagan religious groups worship the gods of mystery cults in what they believe is the way that ancient initiates did.

In the latter part of this essay, we may gain some insights as to why mystery cults are of perennial interest. But I will begin with a summary of what scholars think we can say with certainty about the most prominent cults. In the short run, this means emphasizing Greece and Rome, the homes of mystery cults in the strictest sense of the term. This eventually leads us, however, into other cultures of the ancient Mediterranean, first through a contextualization of the Greek and Roman mystery cults within a range of religious phenomena with which they share salient characteristics, notably a promise of personal transformation and a demand for secrecy; and then through examining how later religious and philosophical systems, including Christianity, adapted the word *mystery.*

Overview

Any model of mystery cults will be imperfect, both because there were variations among individual cults in antiquity and because there remain disagreements of definition among scholars. But we must start from at least a provisional model; and so before discussing the cults themselves, I first list five criteria that many cults shared:

- Mystery cults demanded secrecy; initiates were forbidden to divulge what they had experienced ("mystery" comes from Greek *myein* [to close]).
- Mystery cults promised to improve initiates' situations in the present life and/or after death.
- Initiates garnered these advantages by establishing a special relationship with divinities during initiation.
- Mystery cults were optional supplements to civic religion, rather than competing alternatives (this is why we call them "cults," rather than "religions").
- Myths were associated with the cults, which narrated tales of the cults' divinities.

Space allows detailed discussion of only two cults here; four others are sketched more briefly, and there were other, "lesser" mysteries in antiquity as well.

The Eleusinian mysteries

The myth of Demeter and her daughter, who is called both Kore (Maiden) and Persephone, was associated already in antiquity with mysteries held in Eleusis, a town fourteen miles west of Athens. The myth appears in several, slightly different versions, of which the best known is the Homeric *Hymn to Demeter*. Hades, king of the underworld, snatched Persephone away to be his wife. Demeter searched desperately for her missing daughter and, having discovered Persephone's fate, retreated in grief from the gods' company, disguised herself as an old woman, and took work as a nursemaid in the royal Eleusinian family. When her secret attempt to immortalize the family's son was interrupted, however, Demeter became angry and, throwing off her disguise, cast the earth into famine. Under pressure, Zeus compelled Hades to return Persephone to her mother, but Hades first gave Persephone pomegranate seeds to eat, which obligated her to return to the underworld for part of each year thereafter. Hades promised Persephone that as his wife, she would have power over "everything that lives and moves" and the ability to punish those who displeased her. Demeter, reunited with her daughter, restored fertility to the fields and instructed the Eleusinians in her mysteries, promising blessings to initiates both during life and after death and warning that the uninitiated would face an afterlife in dank darkness.

Ancient sources make clear the connections between this myth and the Eleusinian mysteries. But it must be emphasized that the *Hymn to Demeter* is a literary work and probably was composed for recitation in a public context. It was not the sacred text of a cult that prized secrecy as highly as the mysteries did, and we cannot assume that all the actions it narrates signify what initiates actually did within the walls of the Eleusinian precinct. The *Hymn* can be used, however, in combination with other ancient information to paint a picture of the mysteries in broad strokes. It is likely, for example, that individuals somehow imitated Demeter's experiences during initiation and in doing so passed from grief to joy (ancient sources mention such a transition)—we know that they drank a mixture called the *kykeōn*, which Demeter also is said to have drunk in the *Hymn*, and that in doing so, like Demeter, they broke a fast. It is possible that they watched a dramatic reenactment of Persephone's kidnapping and return (a cave on the site looks like a probable setting for the kidnapping, and we are told that a bronze gong was rung during the mysteries to signify Persephone's return). Some sort of ritual probably took place around a special well in the precinct, which is echoed in the *Hymn* by Demeter's encounter at a well with daughters of the Eleusinian king. Thematically, too, the *Hymn* resonates with concerns addressed in the mysteries, most prominently the hope that a special relationship with Demeter and Persephone would protect one from the direst aspects of the mortal lot.

Other pieces of information take us further. Athens controlled the mysteries (many of its priesthoods were in the hands of two Athenian families), and thus the public parts of the ceremony were held each year in Athens, after certain secret objects had been carried from Eleusis to Athens under close guard. An Athenian official called an assembly in which the opening of the mysteries was announced. The next day, at the Athenian harbor, each initiate bathed himself or herself and a piglet, which would later be sacrificed, perhaps on the third day. The fourth day was given over to latecomers who had to catch up with what they had missed. On the fifth day, initiates walked from Athens to Eleusis wearing white garments and carrying torches. At a certain point during this journey, yellow ribbons were tied on their right hands and left legs, and at another point, as they crossed the Cephisus River, insults were cast at them by former initiates (we are not sure why). The secret objects that previously had been carried from Eleusis to Athens were carried back again on this same journey.

Upon arrival at Eleusis, initiates entered a walled precinct—and it is here that our certain information dwindles; under threat of death, initiates kept their secrets well. We do know that whatever happened inside the precinct consumed three days and that it culminated at night inside a hall called the Telesterion—literally, the place of "completion" or "initiation." Something highly significant was shown to the initiates in a sudden burst of torch light (one ancient source that many scholars judge trustworthy claims that it was "just a sheaf of wheat"; the significance of the object, whatever it was, may have been largely symbolic). We know that each initiate had to have his or her own *mystagōgos*—a guide who had already been initiated and thus could ensure that the initiate completed the process correctly. We know that initiates heard and said special things and felt that they had personal contact with Demeter and Persephone. We know that, toward the end of the process, initiates poured libations to the dead. And we know that it was possible to be initiated a second time at Eleusis, into a higher level of the mysteries. But beyond this, all is conjecture. Whatever happened at Eleusis must have been highly appealing, however: the mysteries drew initiates from all over the ancient Mediterranean and operated from the archaic into the late imperial period.

The Samothracian mysteries

The Greek word *mystēria* (mysteries) properly applies only to the Eleusinian festival, but *mystēria* was also used to refer to other, similar cults, and modern scholars have followed suit. Herodotus provides our first example, in the 5th century BCE, when he describes a cult on the island of Samothrace as *mystēria* (2.51).

The Samothracian mysteries were almost as long-lived and popular as the Eleusinian (they continued till the reign of Constantine), but we know less about them. They centered on gods whose names were secret and whom ancient authors associated with a variety of other gods, including (perhaps in imitation of Eleusis) Demeter, Persephone, and Hades; other evidence, however, suggests a central goddess and two male attendants. We know only three details of Samothrace's nocturnal initiation rite: initiates had to wear purple sashes, to tell the priest what the worst deeds were that they had ever committed, and to wear iron rings once they were initiated. Protection against dangers at sea was the most famous benefit of initiation; we hear nothing about post-mortem benefits and have only fragments of myths associated with the cult. In contrast to Eleusis, individuals could be initiated not only during an annual festival, but at any time.

The Bacchic mysteries

Unlike the Eleusinian and Samothracian mysteries, initiations associated with Dionysus (or Bacchus) could be performed anywhere—in fact, some Bacchic priests made their livings by wandering from place to place, performing "initiations" (*teletai;* cf. the Eleusinian Telesterion). The ability to initiate was considered a special craft, and many priests claimed inclusion in a chain of teachers and students stretching back to mythic priests of Dionysus. In spite of this, techniques of initiation varied. From Herodotus we hear about a *thiasos* (group) of Dionysiac initiates raving through the night in a sort of maddened, ecstatic release (4.79). We hear elsewhere about initiates, especially female, ascending mountains to participate in initiations that included nocturnal dancing. The phallus, symbol of generative power and sexuality, appears often in Dionysiac iconography.

Such practices and images have fueled imaginations. In Euripides' *Bacchae,* female worshipers tear apart live animals and, eventually, the king of their city. A famous Roman repression of Bacchic cults in 186 BCE followed accusations that they were fronts for murder, sodomy, and other crimes. We have no evidence that such extremes were reached by real initiates, but the note of wild abandon that such stories strike does reflect a genuine element of Dionysiac cult: Dionysus released worshipers from everyday concerns and limits. Less wild, perhaps, were initiations connected with the gold tablets, which centered on learning the story of Dionysus's birth and sufferings. The variegated picture of initiation rites is complicated further because the goals of initiation varied. In some cases, ecstatic communion with the god was foremost, with little or no thought for the afterlife. Other rites assuaged the wrath of the dead and thus protected the living from their attacks. Still others sought to ensure the initiate's own happiness in the next world. Also open to question is how many of these cults were formally called or considered mysteries.

Here I will focus on the rites involving the gold tablets, as they both align most closely with my working model of mystery cults, and use the word *mystēs,* which refers to an initiate of a mystery. The tablets, which have been found in Greek and Italian graves dating from the 5th century BCE to the 2nd century CE, are small sheets of gold inscribed with instructions that guide the soul of the dead through the underworld and ensure that it receives preferential treatment from underworld deities. They also incorporate fragments of hexameter poetry derived from poems attributed to the mythic poet Orpheus, which narrated the story of Dionysus and Persephone (see Sacred Texts and Canonicity). Fritz Graf suggests that these texts were also read aloud during initiations, which supports the idea that the tablets served to remind the soul (which was expected to be confused after death) of what it had already learned while alive. Some tablets were placed in the corpses' mouths, as if to actually "speak" on their behalf.

The instructions on the tablets include admonitions to avoid certain paths in the underworld and to drink from waters of Memory instead of those of Forgetfulness; this probably refers to the need to remember mistakes made during the last life lest one repeat them in the next (reincarnation also is implied by mention of a "circle of grief" from which the initiate will eventually escape). The tablets also remind the soul of declarations that it must make to Persephone, stating that it is pure, that it belongs to the divine race, that it has paid the penalty for "unrighteous deeds," and that "the Bacchic one himself [Dionysus] has released" it. The reward for doing and saying everything correctly, according to the tablets, is to join other *mystai* (initiates) and *bacchoi* who feast and drink in a pleasant part of the underworld. Similar declarations must be made to guardians who otherwise would prevent access to the waters of Memory. A late-4th-century BCE funerary vase from southern Italy, now in the Toledo (Ohio) Museum of Art, illustrates the reward: at the center of the scene, Dionysus shakes hands with Hades as Persephone looks on with approval; to his side are figures who represent the joyous afterlife that Bacchic initiates win, and separated from him, cut off from pleasure, are famous mythic figures who failed to accept Dionysus (see color plates).

The declarations concerning unrighteous deeds and atonement on the tablets can be explained by reference to the myth of Dionysus and Persephone. Dionysus was the son of Zeus and Persephone. While a child, he was lured away by jealous gods called Titans, who killed and consumed most of him.

Athena salvaged his heart, which Zeus fed to his lover Semele in order that Dionysus might be reconceived. In due course the god was (re)born, although Persephone continued to mourn her loss. Meanwhile, Zeus incinerated the Titans and created humanity from their remains. Thus human nature is predominantly wicked. Humans must strive both to overcome this and to atone to Persephone for the Titans' crime through initiation into the Bacchic mysteries; otherwise they will suffer after death.

The cult of Meter

Meter (Mother) referred to a variety of goddesses who were either at home in Greece or imported from Anatolia (e.g., Cybele). Their worship included ecstatic dancing that induced insensitivity to pain; most extremely, some male worshipers castrated themselves while in this state, dedicating their virility to the goddess and serving her thereafter as eunuch priests. A mythic exemplar of self-castration developed during the late Hellenistic period: Cybele maddened her mortal consort, Attis, because he had betrayed her; he castrated himself and bled to death. Whether such acts were always considered part of mystery initiations is unclear, but we do hear about eunuchs and other priests of these goddesses who, like Bacchic priests, wandered around performing initiations. Benefits were expected to accrue during life and perhaps after death.

Cybele officially entered Rome in 205/204 BCE under the name of Magna Mater (Great Mother), at the suggestion of the Sibylline Books. It is later, during the imperial period, that we first hear about one of the cult's most striking features, the *taurobolium* (bull slaughtering), although something called the *taurobolium* had also been practiced earlier in Anatolia. Our evidence for the Roman *taurobolium* is incomplete, but Philippe Borgeaud has convincingly suggested that it involved sprinkling initiates with blood from the testicles of a freshly castrated bull. Thus, men who did not wish to castrate themselves (and women) could partake of the goddess's benefits. Initiation could be renewed after a number of years by repeating the *taurobolium*. The Christian author Prudentius exemplifies the polemics directed against mysteries in later ages when he invents a far bloodier *taurobolium* (*Peristephanon* 10.1011–50): a bull is slaughtered atop a grate; an initiate crouches underneath in a pit, waiting to be drenched in fresh blood—but this is unlikely to reflect real practices.

The cult of Mithras

Mithra was an old Indo-Iranian sun-god concerned with the making of alliances who was transformed into Mithras by Roman men in the 1st century CE into a god of mysteries. His mysteries particularly attracted soldiers and emphasized bonds of brotherhood. This was enhanced by the small size of individual Mithraic cults, which spread throughout the Roman Empire even as far as Britain.

Initiates met in *Mithraea,* real or artificial caves that were decorated with frescos and reliefs to serve as models of the cosmos; in some intellectualized forms of Mithraism, this is reflected in the initiates' goal of causing their souls to ascend through the heavens, but most initiates were probably more concerned with the benefits that Mithras offered in the here-and-now, and it is difficult to know what such cosmic representations meant to them. (There is evidence that Mithraic worshipers were interested in astrology, too, but we do not know why.)

On either side of a central aisle in *Mithraea* were benches on which initiates reclined to dine, imitating the meal shared by Mithras and the sun-god (who sometimes appears as a separate entity in Mithraism). We know that there were seven grades of initiation—raven, bride, soldier, lion, Persian, sun-runner, and father—but little about what they signified or required. *Tauroctony* (killing of a bull) is central to the cult: numerous altarpieces show Mithras engaged in such an act, and we can guess that it was repeated by initiates. An inscription from one Mithraeum, "you saved us with the outpouring blood," is taken to refer to Mithras's *tauroctony,* which often is supplemented in artistic representations by symbols of fertility (e.g., a sheaf of wheat springs from the dying bull's tail). We have no textual traces of Mithraic myths, which makes interpretation of these representations difficult.

The mysteries of Isis

The Greeks knew about the Egyptian goddess Isis from at least the time of Herodotus and believed that Egyptian worship of Isis and her husband Osiris was similar to that of their own mysteries. But the first clear traces of a Greek mystery cult for Isis appear in an aretology that was inscribed and displayed in Isiac sanctuaries during the last two centuries BCE (the aretology itself may be older). In it, Isis declares that she has brought agriculture, good laws, and other benefits to the human race and that she has shown humans how to perform mystery initiations; probably she is here identified with Demeter, as she often was elsewhere, and the mysteries she claims to have bestowed on humanity are those of Eleusis (Merkelbach 1995: 113–19).

Information on initiation into Isiac mysteries in the proper sense becomes available only during the imperial period; they took place either at Isiac temples or private houses. The fullest account is found in the final chapter of a 2nd-century CE novel, Apuleius's *Golden Ass.* Lucius, the hero, although eager to be initiated and frequently visited by Isis in dreams, must wait until the goddess signifies that the time is right (not all initiates had to wait to be "called"; other evidence indicates that initiation was usually available on request). He abstains from forbidden foods, bathes, and purifies himself. Secrets of the cult's holy books are explained to him, and yet further secrets narrated to him. He fasts for ten days, dons linen clothes (wool was prohibited in the cult), and at night is taken into the innermost part of her temple in Corinth. There he undergoes a process that, he claims, involves a journey to the underworld, "trial by the elements" (probably water, fire, and air), and an introduction to all the gods. The following morning he is given a new and splendid cloak, a torch, and a garland of flowers and is displayed publicly to all worshipers of Isis. After he has celebrated for several days, Isis tells him to return home, but she and Osiris subsequently instruct him in dreams to seek initiation into the mystery cult of Osiris in Rome. Eventually, he is further initiated into the *pastophoroi*, a group of priests who serve Isis and Osiris (we are told elsewhere that at least some Isiac priests, in any given place, had to be Egyptian in order for the cult to be properly conducted). The blessings that the gods confer on Lucius include not only eschatological promises but an enhanced ability to earn money as a lawyer.

The myth connected with Isiac mysteries comes to us only in the 1st centuries BCE and CE and closely mimics that of Eleusinian Demeter (Diodorus Siculus 1.21–25; Plutarch, *On Isis and Osiris* 12–19). That Isis seeks and then mourns her husband Osiris, rather than her child, underscores the close link between the two spouses, which was already important in Egypt. Other Egyptian deities, such as Horus, the son of Isis and Osiris, were also adopted by Greeks and Romans, but Isis remained the central figure in her mysteries.

Interpretations

So much for the basic facts about mystery cults, such as they are. What can be said about how the cults functioned and how they fit into the larger religious and societal climates of not only Greece and Rome but more broadly the ancient Mediterranean?

Initiation as a process

Several ancient authors emphasize that initiates into mysteries not only *did* and *said* things as part of their initiation, but *experienced* things. In other words, there was a passive aspect to initiation. This is borne out by the passive participles that are sometimes used to describe initiates: those initiated into the cult of Meter, for example, are described as *tauroboliati* (they have been "tauroboliated," to coin a word) and those in the cult of Dionysus are said to be *bebaccheumenoi* (they have been "bacchiated"). Initiates do not simply go through required motions and gain promised rewards, they are "processed" by what they experience in the mysteries and emerge as something new.

In this respect, mystery initiation has a great deal in common with Mediterranean rites of passage. The adolescent undergoes a rite from which he or she emerges as an adult; the unmarried woman emerges from the wedding ceremony not only as a married woman in the sense of having a husband, but in the sense of being, in the eyes of her society, a different sort of woman altogether, with new responsibilities and rights. Some scholars have even suggested that the Eleusinian mysteries, and perhaps other early Greek mysteries, developed out of clan-based adolescent initiation rites: the Eleusinian priesthood was controlled by two Athenian clans, the Eumolpidai and the Kerykes, and in the myths connected with some mysteries, an adolescent or child (Persephone, Dionysus) experiences the sorts of transitions that are often associated with rites of passage in myth, such as death, marriage, and rebirth. Iconography and myth, moreover, associate Demeter (and sometimes Persephone) with the care and maturation of children, both at Eleusis and elsewhere.

But the mysteries' broader similarity to rites of passage, as procedures that process individuals and enable them to emerge as something new, prompts another observation: most parts of Greece (including Athens, home of the Eleusinian mysteries) had no rites of passage that formally and explicitly changed adolescents into adults, at least during historical times; what we find instead in some places are optional rites that *celebrate* the maturation of a few individuals (which usually meant the children of the noble and the wealthy). Why earlier, more-widespread rites of passage died out (if they ever existed at all) is a question we cannot consider here, but we can at least ponder the striking correlation: it was precisely in a culture from which rites of passage were missing that mysteries developed. Rome, which eagerly adopted Greek mystery cults and then went on to create some of its own, similarly shows few traces of adolescent rites of passage after the 3rd century BCE. It is tempting to see mysteries, which promised to "complete" or "perfect" *(telein)* individuals, as developing to fill a gap.

Initiation and community

Another sort of ritual in which individuals undergo experiences and then emerge with a new status are initiations into professions, such as blacksmithing, or into roles, such as priest or king. Egyptian artisans of many sorts were initiated into their professions, and Mesopotamian priests were initiated into the priesthoods of Nanna and of Enlil and Ninlil, for example. Like adolescent rites of passage, these sorts of rituals can be glimpsed behind some mysteries. The Samothracian mysteries preserve traces of blacksmiths' guild initiations (e.g., the iron rings that initiates wear and the worship of artisan divinities called Kabeiroi). The predilection of soldiers for the Mithraic mysteries may also point toward a group with guildlike bonds, and the seven grades of Mithraic initiation suggest an interest in delineation and assumption of hierarchical roles. One possible link between guild initiations and mysteries is that both promise to let the individual in on valuable secrets—secrets that will enable them, in the case of guilds, to prosper in their profession and, in the case of mysteries, to prosper in life more generally—or prosper after death. Not so long ago, indeed, the English word *mystery* could be used to refer to one's trade or occupation. Although linguists tell us that this use really derives from the Latin word *ministerium* (service, work), its development was influenced by the Greek *mystēria* and its connotations: an apprentice was understood to be initiated into the secrets of his craft by his master. Masonic mysteries straddle the two significations.

Even when contextualized within these other forms of initiations, however, one strikingly unusual characteristic of the mysteries still sets them apart: they were not mutually exclusive. One could be initiated into as many mystery cults as one desired and could afford; during the imperial period, wealthy individuals made a "grand tour" of them. Into some mysteries, moreover, one might be initiated more than once. This is different from adolescent initiations, for example, in which the transition from child to adult is singular, irreversible, and without any need (or, usually, possibility) of supplementation. It is also different from initiation into guilds insofar as individuals seldom had more than one profession and therefore more than one guild membership. By the same token, mystery initiation is different from initiation into a position such as kingship, which usually is held exclusively of other such positions.

One reason that mystery cults may have tolerated and even supported multiple memberships among initiates was that the benefits they promised were garnered not so much by entering into a community of people who would support one another (as in the case of an adolescent entering the adult community or an apprentice entering a guild) as by making the personal acquaintance of one or more gods. In a polytheistic system, the more gods one knew, the better, and particularly in a polytheistic system such as the Greeks had, where there was no concept of dualism or of orthodoxy and heresy, there was no need to avoid one god in order to please another.

Mystery initiations, then, in contrast to other forms of initiation, focused more closely on the individual as an individual than they did on the individual as a new member of a group. Even at Eleusis, where hundreds or thousands were initiated on the same night, each initiate had to have his or her own *mystagōgos* who performed the salient acts constituting initiation, whatever they were. Other mysteries, such as those of Dionysus or Meter, were promulgated partly by independent practitioners who initiated one or a few people at a time. If we believe Apuleius's account, Isiac initiation was individualized as well.

This is not to say that there was no concept of community at all among initiates: Dionysiac initiates might celebrate the god within a *thiasos* of participants that remained the same and called each other *symmystai* (fellow initiates). At some point during many mysteries, there was communal feasting—most notably in the cult of Mithras, whose places of worship included dining couches—and after death, initiates might expect to continue feasting and rejoicing with others of their kind. There is evidence for Dionysiac initiates helping to ensure that their fellows were properly buried and that the celebrations of the *thiasos* were well funded. But by and large, we lack indications that initiates felt an obligation to one another; the bond forged among them was not one of codependence, but rather of shared privilege. Plato mentions that common initiation into mysteries contributed to building a friendship, but he also makes it clear that this was just one among many other social ties that the two friends shared—it was the sort of thing that men of their stature did (*Letters* 7.333e).

The rewards of secrecy

Secrecy is the most famous and constant characteristic of mystery cults, from which the modern meaning of the word *mystery* develops.

But secrecy was not characteristic of mystery cults alone in the ancient world. The details of some adolescent rites of passage and many other gender-specific rites were kept secret both from the young people who had not yet been initiated and from all members of the opposite sex. In ancient Sparta, in fact, the name for male rites of passage was Krypteia (The Hidden [Ritual]). Guild initiations were kept secret as well. Moving outside of these two phenomena, we find plenty of others: in some societies, only the king or a certain priest might know, for example, where a particular sacred place was situated and how to tend it, or how to use and interpret the secrets in a sacred book. In Egypt, for instance, the priestly "overseer of secrets" alone knew where certain figurines were buried, and only the pharaoh, in his role as chief priest of the sun-god, had access to certain mortuary texts. In Athens, only one family, the Gephyraioi, had access to a special temple of Demeter Achaia. In Mesopotamia, the crafts of writing and reading—and therefore access to sacred documents—were closely guarded not only by limiting access to the academy but by employing cryptographic writing in some cases. Throughout the Mediterranean, practitioners of magic possessed secret methods of accomplishing remarkable things and guarded them well.

But all forms of secrecy are not the same. We must distinguish between "absolute" secrecy—that is, a situation in which the very existence of something is unknown to outsiders—and "relative" secrecy—a situation in which outsiders know that something exists but do not know all of its details (mysteries are an example of the latter). Absolute secrecy, in fact, is uncommon in religious systems that do not embrace concepts of orthodoxy and heresy for two reasons.

First, absolute secrecy is uncommon because unless a given practice or belief is outlawed, there is no need to hide it. Outside of Christianity and Judaism, concepts of orthodoxy and heresy were virtually unknown in ancient religions and so, therefore, was the need for absolute secrecy. A partial exception is the covert practice, for strategic or social reasons, of acts that are otherwise well known and accepted. For example, *silent* prayer was unusual in the ancient Mediterranean; when people prayed silently, this usually meant that they were asking for something they did not want others to know about. A charioteer might pray silently when asking a god to hobble his opponent's horses so that the opponent would not hear the prayer and counteract it with one of his own. The would-be adulterer might pray silently for help in seducing a married woman. The technique (prayer) is socially accepted even if the ends to which it is directed must be hidden.

Second, absolute secrecy is uncommon because religious systems, or cults within religious systems, need to advertise themselves and their advantages, both in order to gain converts or initiates and in order to win prestige (the two goals are closely linked). And here, ironically, secrecy helps: nothing appeals to human nature more than something that is described as secret, as contemporary advertisers know well. The appeal lies partially in the promise that those who join will garner special advantages (i.e., that the secrets are valuable) but partially in the sheer fact that in learning them one becomes part of a special group, be it the group of Bacchic initiates, adult men, stonecutters, caretakers of the hero's secret cult, or something else.

Of course, these remarks look at matters from the outside; members of secret groups have other explanations for their secrecy, such as the need to protect gender-exclusive knowledge from the potentially ruinous interference of the other gender or the need to shield a divinity's benefits from those who had not been properly prepared to receive them. Hekhalot mystics, for example, avoided discussing what they knew outside of their own circle, claiming that it could cause damage in the hands of the uninitiated; mystics in Egypt and Mesopotamia made similar statements. But this is not to say that all ancient individuals looked at mysteries from the inside; Plato and others remarked on the way in which itinerant priests of the mysteries used their claims of secret knowledge to line their own pockets. Other ancient outsiders, particularly the early Christian writers, attacked the mysteries' claim to secrecy from a different direction, charging that it cloaked behavior that was not only heretical by Christian standards, but illegal and inhuman, such as cannibalism and human sacrifice; the Romans who opposed the Bacchanalia in 186 BCE used a similar argument. This is an old trick, but a perennially effective one: those who share a secret that has been attacked cannot defend it without betraying it.

A final observation about secrecy in mystery cults takes us back to the issue of community. Most groups that share secrets share other characteristics as well: adolescents who undergo a rite of passage share not only the secrets they learn in the process but the preexisting fact that they are male (or female) and of a certain age. Guild initiates share their intention to pursue a certain craft and, typically, also share membership in the same socioeconomic class. Most mystery cults, in contrast, drew initiates from a broad socioeconomic spectrum, from both genders, and from all age groups. Mithraism is an exception, insofar as it was restricted to males. The Eleusinian mysteries are another partial exception, insofar as they did not allow the initiation of children (except for one special child initiated each year on behalf of the city), but otherwise they were markedly catholic: so long as a person had the ability to understand Greek and did not carry the stain of murder on his or her hands, he or she was welcome at Eleusis. The lack of other unifying characteristics among initiates in most mystery cults makes the demand for secrecy—and whatever it was that the demand for secrecy shielded—all the more important in defining the initiates' identities as members of the cult. This identity did not extend very far into life outside of the cult, but the very pledge that initiates gave to guard the secret for the rest of their lives (and, as far as we can tell, almost all initiates kept to this promise) would have worked to remind them thereafter of the group that they had joined and what they had gained in doing so.

Later developments

Already in the classical period, *mystēria* and cognates such as *mystēs* (initiate) could be used metaphorically to refer to matters that were difficult to grasp but important for a person's welfare. Plato, for example, often uses them to describe the process of learning philosophy (e.g., *Menexenus* 76e). Philosophical metaphor became reality in later antiquity, however, when some Platonists used *mystēria, mystēs,* and other terms to refer both to varieties of Platonic philosophy that emphasized spiritual development through the acquisition of esoteric knowledge and to rituals that brought the philosophers into close contact with the gods (*Chaldaean Oracles,* frag. 132). Interaction with the gods was expected to purify the philosopher's soul, enabling it to ascend into the divine realm and eventually, after death, escape the circle of reincarnation to which other souls were condemned.

Meanwhile, a singular form of the word *mystēria (mystērion)* came to denote simply a secret in the sense of something an individual wanted to keep hidden from others; we encounter this meaning frequently in the Jewish Apocrypha (e.g., Jdt. 2.2, Sir. 27.17). Partaking of all these meanings were ancient magicians' uses of the words: a "mystery" could be a special tool or technique that a magician might wish to keep hidden from other magicians in order to preserve his competitive edge; a technique that the gods had given the magician; a procedure into which one magician had to initiate another—or several of these things at the same time, as a single spell from a single magical papyrus demonstrates (*PGM* IV.723, 732–50, 794). Lingering behind some of these uses, both philosophical and magical, was the concept of ineffability—that is, the idea that something remained hidden because its divine nature simply could not be expressed by human words. To understand a mystery, one had to experience it oneself or learn it directly from the gods.

Some early Christian uses of mystery align with the developments that we have just reviewed: for instance, God's mysteries were made known to humans by divine revelation (Eph. 3.3) or by special instructions that only an inner circle would understand (Matt. 13.11); God's mysteries promised salvation to the individual soul, particularly eschatological salvation; certain aspects of God's plan for humans were ineffable mysteries (Col. 1.27). But the word developed in an interesting new direction as well and took the idea of mystery religions along with it. Christ's disciples proclaimed themselves to be eager to reveal God's mysteries to anyone who would listen; they erased any division between initiate and noninitiate and rejected the need to undergo special rituals before receiving valuable information (1 Cor. 15.51; Eph. 3.9). As Paul and Timothy said: "pray for us also, that God may open to us a door for the word, to declare the mystery of Christ . . . that I [Paul] may make it clear" (Col. 4.3–4). The use of mystery to mean a secret that must be kept, as we see it used in the Jewish Apocrypha, for example, is absent. As a proselytizing religion that aimed to build the largest possible community as quickly as possible, Christianity used the lure implicit in the word *mystery* more boldly than anyone previously had and in doing so turned one of the best-known qualities of mystery religions—privilege through exclusivity—upside down.

It is in part their air of exclusivity—and correlatively, the tantalizing chance that we might conquer exclusivity and seize knowledge that the Greeks and Romans (unlike Paul and Timothy) strove to keep hidden—that makes ancient mystery religions so attractive even now. For some, attaining that knowledge promises the same sort of spiritual benefits that it promised two thousand years ago, as a search of "mysteries" on the internet will demonstrate: throughout the world, neopagan groups busily process new initiates. For others, it promises the same sort of satisfaction that one gets from solving other scholarly puzzles, only more so—after all, knowledge of the ancient mysteries has been occluded not only by the same intervening centuries that dim our knowledge of all aspects of ancient cultures, but also by deliberate concealment. Any scholar who turns up a new bit of evidence or provides a persuasive new interpretation shares the feeling of a master cryptographer who has cracked an enemy code. And this leaves us with an interesting question: if, some day, scholarship miraculously were to reveal all of the mysteries' secrets, would they still fascinate us? Luckily, perhaps, it is a situation that we are very unlikely to confront.

Bibliography

Beck, Roger. "The Mysteries of Mithras: A New Account of Their Genesis." *Journal of Roman Studies* 88 (1998): 115–28.

Borgeaud, Philippe. *La mère des dieux: De Cybèle à la Vierge Marie.* Seuil, 1996.

Burkert, Walter. *Ancient Mystery Cults.* Harvard University Press, 1987.

Cole, Susan Guettel. *Theoi Megaloi: The Cult of the Great Gods of Samothrace.* Études préliminaires aux religions orientales dans l'empire romain 96. Brill, 1984.

Graf, Fritz. "Dionysian and Orphic Eschatology: New Texts and Old Questions of Interpretation." In *Masks of Dionysus,* ed. T. H. Carpenter and C. A. Faraone. Cornell University Press, 1993.

Kerényi, Carl. *Eleusis: Archetypical Image of Mother and Daughter.* Tr. Ralph Mannheim. Princeton University Press, 1967 (orig. 1960).

Merkelbach, Reinhold. *Isis Regina—Zeus Sarapis.* Teubner, 1995.

Religions in Contact

John Scheid

*C*ontact among different religions and gods was a constant in the ancient world. Ancient Rome, for example, always had more than one religion, and it was only during the last period of its history that it saw the spread of exclusively monotheistic religions. The public religion of Rome involved all Roman citizens as such, but this religion was not the only one they had to deal with. In Rome itself, every citizen belonged to several other religious communities, starting with the household religion, which was autonomous with respect to the public religion; the associations or social groups to which a citizen could belong—colleges of merchants or artisans, neighborhood groups, or military units—each of which had its own religion; and, finally, specific forms of religious practice, such as those involving sorcery, magic, and divination, which continued to flourish despite occasional persecution. Moreover, citizens of a Roman colony had religious obligations within the public religion of that colony. The gradual diffusion of Christianity did not suppress this pluralism, since the various Christian communities, divided and resistant to central authority, coexisted for a long time and shared the field with the two other religions "of the book," Judaism and, eventually, Islam. In this way, the religious life of the ancient world was shaped by a plurality of overlapping religious obligations that were not mutually exclusive, but among which certain ones had precedence.

What was true inside Rome and the city-states that surrounded it was equally true outside of that circle. Because these city-states were relatively small, they themselves were surrounded by other small states in fairly close proximity, whose religious systems were nonetheless different, despite significant structural resemblances. Rome was bordered on the north by Etruscan city-states, on the south and southeast by Latin-speaking and, more generally, Italic populations. These cities and peoples had their own religions, with which their neighbors had become familiar and with which they had learned to get along. In fact, in the archaic period, influential families moved back and forth between the various city-states, and they seem to have adapted, without too much difficulty, to local religions. Etruscan families are known to have lived in Rome; there is also the story of the arrival in Rome of the Sabine Attus Clausus, ancestor of the Claudii clan, with five thousand followers who assimilated into the Roman populace.

At another level, Rome was part of the Latin League that united thirty communities; the annual foundational act of this league was a common sacrifice to Jupiter on Monte Cavo. It would be interesting to know how this sacrifice was conducted and how it was perceived by representatives of the thirty groups, whose religious customs differed significantly, despite their kinship. But the literary tradition never mentions issues of this sort—perhaps owing to the absence of consistent source material from this period and this particular religious practice and perhaps especially because, by the very nature of their religious systems, these separate groups were accustomed to practicing religious cohabitation: it was what they did every day in their homes.

Furthermore, none of these religions proselytized. A person belonged to a religious community by virtue of birth or social position, and a notion such as conversion made no sense at all. Belonging to a religion was part and parcel of having a social position, and one's ritual obligations concerned life in this world; religion did not demand an act of faith and personal conversion as a preliminary condition of membership in the body of those "faithful" to a deity, even in the mystery cults, for which initiation was required. Depending on his social situation, a citizen was subject to some kind of religious obligation, whether he liked it or not. Participation in mystery cults was, of course, a matter of choice, but, in fact, a citizen's social situation was more often the central factor, because it opened up the possibility of choice. Thus, initiates of the cult of Mithras were recruited among mid-level Roman military and administrative personnel. Taking into account, too, that all these religions were polytheistic, ritualistic, and nonexclusive, one can understand the ease with which contacts were made between adherents to the various systems of religious obligations, which overlapped and complemented one another but were not in opposition. The precise distinctions that scholars establish between public, semipublic, and domestic cults, for clarity's sake, are justified because they correspond to legal reality, but in daily life, the citizen perceived no such distinction, since everything came together for him in a set of more-or-less important and constraining religious obligations, to which he was subject depending on the time or place.

The situation was hardly any different for what gradually became the Roman world. The religious systems of Greek city-states functioned in roughly the same manner as those of Rome and Italy. And even in the Jewish nation, which practiced a monotheistic religion, the presence of "Greek" groups and city-states with their polytheistic cults was a historical and political fact that was never systematically questioned, despite the stricter conception of purity in Jewish traditions. A similar situation developed in Egypt, where the ancestral religion of the Egyptians—governed by a pharaoh whose origins were Greek, then by a Roman, the emperor—existed alongside Greek cults. In Alexandria, the powerful Jewish community and the Greek community occupying the same neighborhoods—a characteristic of Alexandrian identity—led to sporadic pogroms and conflicts, particularly in the period of Jewish uprisings; these were triggered more by rivalry, however, than by radical religious opposition.

Initially limited to areas of immediate overlap, contacts and exchanges between religions were a fundamental fact of religious life in the entire Mediterranean world. Contacts did not stop expanding even with the Macedonian and Roman conquests. Whether out of cultural inclination or as a matter of convenience, today's observer views different religions as isolated communities or else as categorically opposed. Such an approach is misleading when applied to antiquity because, with the exception of particular situations circumscribed by the historical moment, the religions of the Mediterranean world have never been isolated. Contacts and interpenetrations have never stopped taking place.

Such a religious universe could not be radically affected by changes owing to Hellenistic and Roman imperialism, at least as long as religious values were compatible, because relations with the religions and gods of others, as well as the assimilation of new gods and religious modes, constituted part of Roman religious behavior. Contacts were not always peaceful, however.

Conflicts and resistance

In the case of political or military conflict, any religion could become the evil enemy, even if it was to shed that designation once peace was reestablished. So, for the Romans, during the Third Samnite War (295 BCE), the rites of the Samnites were deemed barbarous, a judgment that had never been made before and one that was of course abandoned when the Samnites were integrated into the Roman city-state. The situation was no different in the Hellenistic world or in Syria or Egypt. Depending on the fluctuations of conflicts and truces, religions could be the object of accusations and repressions, but for political and military rather than religious motives. While the Alexandrian Greeks and Jews exchanged mutual accusations, their aim was to do the other group harm, not to destroy its practices and beliefs; for the most part, each side managed to accommodate the other's form of religion. In spite of the catastrophe attributed to the Jewish Wars (66–70, 135 CE) and the religious consequences brought on by the destruction of the temple and the Hasmonean kingdom, once peace had returned, there was no longer any fundamental enmity between Jews and Romans in the greater part of the Roman world. After the Jewish Wars, when Greek and Roman presence increased in Judea, the rabbinic schools developed rules that allowed Jews to live in the same community as non-Jews, instead of radically prohibiting such cohabitation. So, in spite of the profound changes in Judaism provoked by the destruction of the temple, the period afterward was a relatively calm and prosperous one for Jewish communities, particularly in Asia Minor and Rome.

In Rome, some cults or ritual practices, such as those of Isis and Bacchus or those of various philosophers and seers, were persecuted from time to time, but never permanently and for their own sake. The sole prevailing issue was what passed for public order, that is, the political situation. The well-known suppression of the Bacchanalia (186 BCE) reveals the Roman desire to preserve strict control over religious developments in Rome and in Italy and over the admission of new religious practices into Rome. This repression aimed at putting an end to a new form of the cult of Bacchus, imported from Campania. The Bacchic communities did not belong to the public religion, but rightly or wrongly, their sudden proselytizing, combined with other practices viewed as disruptive to the public order, seemed to reveal a desire to create an organization encompassing all of Italy; in other words, the *thiasoi* (groups of worshipers) were thought to mask a vast conspiracy. These accusations and suspicions forced the intervention of magistrates, who severely curtailed the Bacchic movement and reduced the cult to what it had been before its expansion (Pailler 1988). This incident shows that Roman society and its authorities did not always react with tolerance to the introduction of new religious practices, even where cults with private status were concerned. The state sought to exert control over the population and repressed even the slightest attempt on the part of the populace to organize outside of public structures.

Some cults offered the possibility of this kind of organization, hence the hostility of the authorities, if the political context alerted them. There is no need to dwell on the subject of the wars that sprang out of Jewish resistance to the gradual Hellenization in Judea, brought about first by the Seleucids, then by the Romans. The policy of assimilation followed, in early imperial times, by the Hasmonean kings, a policy that reflected a much more conciliatory position, could not prevent the complete rejection of Roman influence by radical groups. The Jewish Wars offer a well-documented example of insurrection against the Romans, in which motives of a religious order played a central role and constituted the basis for the rebellion. During another Jewish revolt, in 116–17 CE, pagan temples seem to have been destroyed, notably in Cyrenaica. The pogrom incited in Egypt by this revolt characterized Jews in part as enemies of the Egyptian gods (Frankfurter 1992). Furthermore, the Greeks of Alexandria, protesting against Roman tyranny, also invoked the local Sarapis cult; more generally, in Egypt, Thrace, and Gaul, indigenous priests often played a role in insurrections (Beard, North, and Price 1998: 347). At the time of such rebellions in Germany, Gaul, and Brittany, for example, Roman temples were destroyed and participation in Roman religions was terminated. We should note, however, that local cults were generally integrated into the local Roman religion and that their priests were often members of the local elite. All this tends to show that the insurgents were rejecting the Romans rather than their gods and that religions themselves changed direction depending on political events: during such conflicts, the religious practices and the gods that had once symbolized integration into the Roman world became symbols of submission or, in the case of indigenous cults, symbols of freedom.

Contacts and exchanges

In the course of antiquity, and especially under the Roman Empire, contact among peoples, ethnic groups, and religious communities gave rise to lively and lasting exchanges, leaving aside occasional revolts, wars, or pogroms. From the earliest period about which we have information, Athens, Rome, or Carthage welcomed traditions and deities whose names revealed their foreign origins.

Let us take Rome as an example: its expansion was the most spectacular of all, and it allows us to study the process of "acculturation" in detail. The religious architecture of the 6th century BCE—that of the Capitol, for example—was in large part borrowed from the Etruscans. Tradition even attributes it, along with the Capitoline triad housed in the temple, to kings and artisans from Etruria. This same tradition holds that Roman rites of divination, such as the technique of interpreting auspices and even the practice of triumphal processions, were derived from Etruscan practices, and it situates the origins of the Sibylline Books, introduced by an Etruscan king, in Campania. Whatever the value of these traditions, it is clear that the Romans were not scandalized that central elements of their religious rites came from neighboring peoples. Early-20th-century historians clearly had more difficulty understanding this openness to outsiders; Georg Wissowa expressed astonishment at the idea that the most important gods of the Roman state, Jupiter, Juno, and Minerva, were of foreign origin (1912: 40–43). The vestiges of the archaic period likewise reveal an early Hellenism, by way of the Etruscans and neighboring Italic city-states. Statues from the archaic temples of Saint Omobono are clearly derived from contemporary Greek art, as is the decor on the temple of Castor and Pollux in the Roman Forum. Furthermore, it was during this early period that Hercules, Apollo, and Castor and Pollux themselves were installed in Rome. These deities owe more to relations with the Italic city-states (Tibur, Tusculum) than to direct contacts on the part of the Romans with Magna Graecia (the parts of Italy that the Greeks had colonized), and they show in any case the extent to which all the peoples of ancient Italy were open to other religious traditions. Archeological digs show that the Carthaginians, with the Etruscans, worshiped Uni-Astarte in her temple at Pyrgi (Cerveteri), and of course it is well known that emissaries from the Italian city-states consulted the oracle at Delphi.

These cults and gods attest to cultural and political exchanges and probably to migrations of social groups. A historical example offers some information about the integration of foreign deities. During the siege of Veii (396 BCE), the Romans used the rite called *evocatio* to adopt the local goddess Juno Regina as a Roman deity; after the taking of the city, the goddess was solemnly transported to Rome, where she was given a temple and a public ceremony on the Aventine. The Carthaginian goddess Juno Caelestis was believed to have been "evoked" when Carthage was taken in 146 BCE. As Roman colonies were established in North Africa, many local Punic cults were taken up by these Roman city-states. More generally, even if a war was not going on, deities were simply invited to Rome and established there without regard to their origin. The uninterrupted series of such deities reflects the Roman expansion, first in Italy and then in the Mediterranean: Diana, Feronia, Juno Sospita, Dis Pater and Persephone, then Aesculapius, Venus Erycina, and Magna Mater—and a little later, of course, the importing of deities was not restricted to Rome. In the 4th century BCE, the Carthaginians introduced the cult of Demeter and Persephone into the city to atone for the devastation of their sanctuary in the area around Syracuse. In Athens, the Thracian deity Bendis played a role in civic cults starting in the 5th century BCE, and Isis was introduced into the city at the beginning of the 4th century BCE.

Influences and "acculturation"

The integration of these cults came about without difficulty, according to a complex system. As far as we can tell, in Rome, for example, public ceremonies were celebrated either in the Roman style or according to a "foreign" mode, and this had been true for a long time. The Capitoline triad and Castor and Pollux seem always to have been honored according to Roman rituals, while the Hercules of the Ara Maxima was honored according to different, rather more "Greek" modalities. At the beginning of the 4th century, the first celebration of a *lectisternium* (a banquet for gods) harkened back likewise to the Greek tradition of *theoxenia* (entertaining gods at a meal). Nothing is known, of course, about the domestic practices of this period, except for the slow transformation of funerary rites; we can follow their evolution throughout Italy under the influence of aristocratic traditions coming from Greece and Magna Graecia. During the historical period, the situation was much the same, although it responds to different imperatives that were at work then. From the Punic Wars on, Rome entered into direct contact with the Mediterranean world and, at the beginning of the 2nd century BCE, with the countries of Greece. The introduction of gods and religions belonging to other religious cultures, and probably new representations of Rome's relation to the rest of the world as well, shaped the evolution of Rome's relation to the gods and cults of others. The more general concept of the "cult according to the Greek ritual" was created in Rome in this context, although this type of practice was not limited to Rome. The cult of Demeter and Persephone in 4th-century BCE Carthage must have been celebrated by Greeks living in Carthage who followed the Greek rite. About the same time, a priestess of Greek origin presided over the new "Greek" cults of Ceres that had been introduced in Rome.

The concept of the "Greek rite" was not an old one, although evidence for the practice itself was already present from the beginning of the 4th century with the introduction of *lectisternia,* with their clear reference to the Greek *theoxenia.* The very term *ritus Graecus* (Greek cultic mode) appears for the first time in the 2nd century BCE in a text of Cato the Censor (*Orationum,* frag. 77 Malcovati); it remained relatively rare and somewhat surprising. If the

Romans put "ceremonies according to the Greek rite" *(sacra Graeco ritu)* or "Greek cults" *(Graeca sacra)* in this category, this does not mean that the cults of all Greek deities fell under the same rubric. The rites of the cults of Hercules, Apollo, and Saturn were "Greek," for example, but not those of the cults of Aesculapius, Bacchus, Hecate, Nemesis, or Magna Mater. The cult of Castor and Pollux could have been classified under the Greek mode, especially since Demetrius Poliorcetes cited the cult of the Castores as proof of the Romans' and the Greeks' common parentage (Strabo 5.232); but the Romans apparently never categorized it that way. On the contrary, the twins were patrons of the Roman cavalry, that is, patrons of the elite and therefore of a constitutive element of Roman identity. And this is not because they were perceived as being less Greek than, for example, Hercules, because an ancient inscription from Lavinium called them *quroi* (= Greek *kouroi*, a term often used to describe them in Greece; Degrassi 1957–63: no. 1271a). On the other hand, Hercules came from Tibur (Tivoli) and the Castores came to Rome from Tusculum, rather than from any of the Greek city-states.

The Romans classified certain festivals and one of the modalities of Roman sacrifice as being of Greek origin. In Livy, cults founded by Romulus were celebrated according to the Alban rite (from Alba Longa, the twins' homeland), but the cult of Hercules corresponded to the Greek rite because it had been founded by Evander, who came from Greek Arcadia (Livy 1.7.3). Cato asserts that the Saturnalia, the festival of Saturn, was celebrated according to the Greek rite. The cult of Apollo was viewed as the best illustration of the Roman Greek-rite cult. Early in the 2nd century BCE, part of the cult of Ceres fell into the same category. A Sibylline oracle of 125 BCE prescribed a religious service that had to be celebrated by children according to the Achaean rite; other, still older Sibylline oracles advised processions and celebrations according to the Greek rite (see, e.g., Livy 25.12.10, 13). Finally, the protocols of the Secular Games at the beginning of the empire specified that the sacrifices be celebrated "according to the Greek rite" *(Graeco Achivo ritu)*. In other words, the category was complex; it was not simply limited to all the religious services concerning a deity originating in the Greek world or to all the rites belonging to the cult of these deities.

If we look closely at the literary texts, two additional phenomena stand out. In the first place, the concept of the Greek rite refers to an ethnic group (the Greeks) and not, as with the Alban rite, the Roman rite, or the *cinctus Gabinus* (the manner of draping the toga practiced by the Gabinians during the Roman-style cult), to a city-state such as Alba, Rome, or Gabii. This distinction denotes an opposition between a ritual mode belonging to a smaller group, or even to a city-state integrated within the Roman state, and a broader, less distinct group that extends well beyond any given city-state. In the second case, a different category is involved, one that is no longer institutional but almost geographic or cultural—in any event, it is quite vague. It would be interesting in this regard to know when the Romans themselves characterized certain of their rites as "Roman." At first glance, this classification makes sense only if it is contrasted to another cultic category—to the Greek-rite cults, for example.

In other words, the ritual concept of the Greek mode, invented around the time of the Second Punic War, is a good illustration of the open but complex relationship between the Romans and foreign cults and gods. In the 2nd century BCE, the major point of reference was Greece (or what passed for Greece in the Romans' eyes). This reference corresponds, on the one hand, to the second Hellenization of Rome, which was much more profound than the diffuse Greek influence of the archaic period; it transformed Roman culture. On the other hand, the reference reveals that Hellenization was actually a Roman phenomenon. From this viewpoint, the Hellenization of Rome and its religion perfectly illustrates the results of intercultural relations. When they had direct contact with the Greeks, the Romans had continuing access to the high culture of the period. From then on, it was no longer possible to think of Roman culture and institutions in a non-Greek manner. A cultivated Roman thought in ways defined by Greek philosophy, and Rome's national literature—its mythology in particular—could not help but be incorporated within the framework of a continuation of Greek literature. On the religious level, this intellectual broadening took a certain number of old or recent phenomena that were or appeared to be Greek and translated them into a cultic category. The cults themselves nevertheless unquestionably remained Roman and were not simple transpositions of Greek rites (Greek being a highly artificial category in this instance). The Greek-rite cults were much more a way for the Romans to affirm that they belonged to the Greek world, a justification for their imperialism or at least for their quest for alliances. The construction of a notion such as the Greek mode of venerating the gods was a completely Roman phenomenon, produced with no outside assistance. It is, in a manner of speaking, a fine example of self-acculturation. One can see in it, of course, a certain degree of fascination.

If admiration for Greek literature, art, and science could sufficiently justify the Hellenization of Roman culture, the same was not true for the Hellenization of Roman religion. In the latter context, it is more appropriate to speak of the way in which the Romans thought of themselves from then on. Not only did they introduce rites, such as the Matronal rites of Ceres, that created the (Greek) Eleusinian rites in Rome, in a way, but they also retrospectively Hellenized a part of their religious patrimony: at least by the time of Dionysius of Halicarnassus (1st century BCE), they discovered that they were in fact Greeks and thought of themselves as belonging to the Greek world. With this outlook, they made their own culture eminent and respectable, but they also justified their imperial ambitions. To the extent that Hellenism was thought to be the highest form of culture, whose mission was to dominate the world, Roman Hellenism could maintain uncomplicated aspirations to hegemony. A rather striking illustration of this attitude is found in the decoration of the temple dedicated to Hercules and the Muses (179 BCE), which was built by

Fulvius Nobilior beside the *via triumphalis* to celebrate his victory over the Aetolians, a rather bloody victory that verged on violating human rights. On this monument of Roman Hellenism, probably realized under the guidance of the poet Quintus Ennius, the unusual association of the hero with the Muses, as attested at the Asklepieion in Messana (Pausanius 4.31.10) and by Isocrates (*Philippus* 109–10), refers to a new type of domination to be exercised henceforth on the cultural level by the triumphant Romans, and it recalls the civilizing mission carried out by Hercules at the beginning of Roman times. In this temple, the most ancient period of Rome's past was associated with symbols of the highest knowledge, notably from the Pythagorean traditions, so as to express the superiority of Rome over the Greeks, thanks to a Herculean *imperator* in his invincibility and his culture.

Expansions

Following the end of the Social War and the integration of the Italics (inhabitants of Italy whose language was related to Latin) into the Roman city-state during the 1st century BCE, religious issues took on new dimensions. Not only did the Italics become members of the public religious community of Rome in this way, but their city-states were increasingly transformed following the Roman model. This evolution continued throughout the empire, until the moment when all free men became Roman citizens (213 CE). The expansion of the Roman city-state, combined with the continuous creation of Roman-style city-states elsewhere, profoundly changed the religious landscape of Rome and the Roman world.

Both as occasional allies and through the Latin or Roman colonies that were gradually created across Italy, the Italic peoples had long been familiar with Roman religion. Similarly, the Roman city-states that were established in Italy came into contact with other cults and gods, so that at the local level their religions functioned in the way that Rome functioned in the administrative center of the Roman state. They integrated local and public deities by taking up the particular cult practices attached to the former or by Romanizing them. For example, from the very beginning of the empire if not earlier, the city of Potentia included in its pantheon Mefitis Utiana, the patron goddess of a neighboring place of cult worship (Rossano di Vaglio), and under Augustus the colony of Hispellum became owner and manager of the old temple of Clitumnus, at the headwaters of the river with the same name. The principal deity of the colony of Lucus Feroniae was the local goddess Feronia. Nowhere was there any question of despising or destroying earlier religious forms. In turn, the Italic city-states were subject to Roman influence. Thus, in the Iguvine Tables, one can note the appearance of Roman institutional terms over the course of the 3rd century BCE. Other Italian cities, after their conquest, even had to merge their principal cult with Rome. Such was the case, for example, with Lanuvium, where the cult of Juno Sospita was celebrated in common with the Roman state from 338 BCE.

The consequence of this gradual fusion, in the context of the city-states of Roman Italy, was the gradual arrival of local Italic cults in Rome itself. At various historical moments, Diana, Juno Sospita, Feronia, and Angerona were given temples and cults in Rome. Conversely, an increasing number of Roman citizens living in Italy never went to Rome. Their lives unfolded in the "little homeland" of their city or colony, and their belonging to the Roman state was primarily a legal matter. As Roman citizens, they were all subject to the obligations of the public religion of Rome, and they profited from the benevolence of the Roman gods. But as they no longer participated in Roman institutional life, Rome became for them mainly a common reference point that they would encounter in literature or in the legends depicted on the various coins of the realm. This was clearly also true for the public religion of Rome. There was never any celebration of Roman religion at the level of the entire Roman citizenry, in a sort of religion of the empire, but it is undeniable that the cult celebrated by the magistrates and priests in Rome established a constant spiritual connection among all those who benefited from Roman citizenship. At the same time, the numerous Roman cities existing in the world, each with its own civic religion independent of Rome's, gave a diversified and still more pluralist picture of what foreigners might call Roman religion.

The golden age of religious pluralism

The peace that followed the Roman conquest of the world and the civil wars extended and accelerated the integration of peoples and city-states into the Roman world. The displacement of individuals also contributed to a mix of cultures and religions that was more intense than ever. In Rome itself and in other large cities, the flow of people from the entire world was manifest in the regular arrival of new cults and religions. But contact between them began to take place on a different level. Few new gods came into Roman public religion after the end of the Republic. The deities Isis and Sarapis, who had become public gods in the 1st century CE, were the last important foreign gods to become Roman, before the short-lived experience of Sol Elagabalus (218); then Aurelian's Sol Invictus (3rd century), likewise a god of Syrian origin; and finally, in the 4th century, the Christian god. No deities of Celtic or German origins were admitted into the religion of Rome; their integration took place on the local level, in the colonies and cities, in keeping with the overall evolution of religious practices: new cults spread at the subordinate or local level.

On the domestic and private level, a large number of new deities came into Rome, starting in the 1st century CE, at times enjoying fairly important places of worship: Jupiter Heliopolis, the Palmyrene gods, Jupiter Dolichenus, Mithras, the Jewish god, and the Christian god. Bringing together smaller or larger communities of Romans and non-Romans, these cults existed side by side in general harmony. Most of them were even established in communal sites where the collective cults of the Roman neighborhoods were practiced. Heliopolitan cults were set up in the old sacred wood of Furrina on the Janiculum, that of the Palmyrene gods in the Gardens of Caesar alongside other Roman and non-Roman cults (the sanctuary of Fors Fortuna, Hercules, Jupiter Beheleparus), and that of Jupiter Dolichenus and Mithras in some *vicus* (village or neighborhood) shrines (e.g., the famous Dolichenum of the Aventine and the Mithraeum near the *vicus* of the *Via Marmorata*).

In other words, in the various collective sanctuaries of Rome's neighborhoods, ancestral cults and new cults often came into contact, meaning that their celebrations became collective events. And as far as we know, Jewish prayer sites, like Jewish cemeteries, were not excluded from the collectivity. They belonged to the life of the neighborhood, just as other religious sites did, to the extent that, in Rome, a synagogue might serve as a topographical reference point (CIL 6.9821). Consequently, conditions were ripe for a broadening of religious experiences to include, in particular, religions whose practices differed from the ancestral ritualism. Proximity could encourage association with Jewish families and synagogues, all the more easily in that Jews could participate in the festive life of the neighborhood, in marriages and banquets, as long as they could observe the dietary rules drawn up in the 2nd century BCE by rabbinic schools; a place was likewise made for Romans who wished to pray to the god of the Jews. During periods of relative calm, Christian sanctuaries, which were more discreetly established in private domains since they were the object of latent hostility, might also attract "pagans." In the 3rd century, in any event, Christian churches were known, since their goods could be confiscated by the emperor Valerian.

The unification of the world

The unification of the world under Roman dominion also transformed the conditions of religious life in the provinces of the empire, especially in areas relatively exempt from urbanization. In the East, in Egypt, and in Africa, traditional religious life went on without much change, except that the finances of the large sanctuaries were more strictly controlled (at Ephesus, for example). Under the Republic, Greek city-states had already taken into account the eruption of Roman power in their world by creating cults dedicated to the goddess Roma or by honoring some particular Roman governor. Beginning with the empire, these provinces and city-states created cults dedicated to Roma and Augustus, in keeping with traditions going back to the Hellenistic period. In Egypt, with the exception of the cult of the emperor, Greco-Egyptian religious life continued to develop along its own lines. But from that point on, the Roman administration, following a tendency already evident in the Ptolemaic period, exercised tighter control over temple revenues and personnel. Similarly, in Jerusalem, the Romans controlled the election of the high priest, oversaw the financial matters of the temple, and restricted the functions of the Sanhedrin. In other respects, the cult continued as before, and the temple was granted the privilege of collecting the annual tax from the Jews. After the war of 66–70, this tax was allocated to the reconstruction of the temple of Jupiter on the Capitoline in Rome. This measure, intended to humiliate the Jews, actually exercised a decisive influence on the definition of Jewish identity.

In Africa, except for the prohibition against the sacrifice—real or imaginary—of children, nothing arose to disturb the religious life of the free city-states. But in Africa, more than in the Greek-speaking provinces, the creation of colonies and cities exerted an influence over the evolution of religious life. Local cults were revived within the framework of the colonies and were celebrated in Latin; but we cannot tell to what extent the cult remained in conformity with Punic traditions. The new colony of Carthage, in particular, assimilated local deities such as the Cereres (the Roman version of the Greek goddesses Demeter and Persephone), Aesculapius, Saturn, and Juno Caelestis at the end of the 1st century BCE. Along with specifically Roman deities, these gods of Punic origin from then on typified the religions of the metropolis of Roman Africa, which comprised an original mix of gods and cults. Thus both the local religions and the Roman religions became still richer and more complex. And, of course, with the opening of the world, Eastern religions, Judaism, and Christianity also took hold in Africa.

It was in the less urbanized provinces of western Europe, however, that the most significant mutations came about. Iberia had already known Greek and Punic colonization and, after centuries of fierce resistance, had adapted itself to the Roman mold. At the time of the conquest, Gaul, Germania, and the countries of the Danube were occupied by different ethnic groups that may have belonged to a single culture but that had virtually never known unity and organization into city-states of the Mediterranean type. One of the first results of the Roman conquest was to unify these different peoples and to inspire an idea of identity transcending that of clan. This was accomplished both at the level of the city-states, which were often created by the occupying Roman presence with the help of local elites, and at the level of the provinces (e.g., the altars to Augustus in Lyon, Narbonne, and Tarragon). Thanks to the process of urbanization following the model of the Mediterranean city-states, some of these groups acquired a self-awareness that they had never known before. This phenomenon became increasingly pronounced, starting with the beginning of the empire, when the Romans took peoples who had up to that point been living in small, fragmented units and regrouped them into city-states. The municipal laws discovered in Baetica make it clear that the creation of Latin or Roman cities and colonies transformed the religious life of these communities. The populations involved were often led to combine the entire set of religious practices and traditions that they viewed as collective and characteristic of their people into a single public religion, that of their city or colony. As the city-states in question were often Latin or Roman colonies, they had to conform to the common rules of Roman religious law. Unfortunately the sources currently available are of little help in showing how and to what extent older rites were integrated within the framework of local public cults.

With the exception of the prohibition against human sacrifice and druidic practices—about which we know very little—and the establishment of provincial cults, the Romans rarely intervened in this process of integration, except as advisers. Some of the local elites, in any case, had done military service with auxiliary troops of the Roman army and were thus familiar with the universe of city-states and civic religions, so they were in a position to accelerate the institutional development of their peoples. And just as the Romans themselves had reacted to their discovery of high Greek culture, these communities also aspired to their own participation in the Roman world. A large number among them gradually came to think of themselves as Roman. In this way, many Iberian, Gallic, and Dalmatian communities laid down the foundations for original local religions, which had never before had such scope. Once their opposition to Roman occupation had been surmounted, the local elites of these provinces may be said to have (re)invented their own cultures and religions under the pressure of Roman urbanization and within its formal framework.

Given that the cultural language of this new construction was Roman, it is very hard to tell to what extent the gods and cults of the northern provinces masked indigenous gods and rituals. The example of the Hellenization of the Romans can serve as a model, but it must be emphasized that the experience of military victors and rulers is different from that of defeated and subjugated peoples. On a different level, the deep transformation of Judaism resulting from the destruction of the temple provides a clear illustration of the second experience. After the Hellenizing evolution of the Jews, the catastrophe of 70 CE profoundly modified the Jewish religion.

The impetus toward interreligious exchanges prompted by the unification of the world is undeniable. The relative tolerance of the Romans and the people of the ancient world explains how religions and gods that came from all over were able to establish themselves in all the provinces without major conflict. As we have seen, plurality was the rule. With the exception of certain followers of Isis, Judaism, and Christianity, no religious group defined itself by a particular name. Furthermore, the term *Isiac* was rare, and the designation *Jew* was as much ethnic as religious. Only the label *Christian* came close to the term as it is used today. For the Jews, who never had any central authority, it was more the Jewish tax of 70 CE than ritual traditions and common memory that raised the question of Jewish identity. Without undertaking any active proselytizing, Jewish communities were open to converts who lived according to Jewish law and to "God-fearing" individuals who adhered to only some of the prescriptions.

The only lasting conflict with a religious community involved the Christians. Despite long periods of tolerance that allowed many people, especially in the cities, to associate with Christian communities and to blend certain Christian beliefs and rituals into their own domestic religions, the risk of repression was undeniably omnipresent. Before the middle of the 3rd century, the reasons for the hostility of the authorities stemmed more from concerns about disturbances of the public order than from a struggle against a religion as such. On the Christian side, hostility toward the Roman state, Roman cities, paganism, and Judaism was motivated by the Christian rejection of polytheism and the existing religions. Decidedly given to proselytizing, Christian communities tried to attract their neighbors to their religion, at least if the Christian sources are to be believed. For "pagans," this phenomenon of attraction was inscribed in the order of things from the moment they accepted the proximity of Christians in their neighborhoods or, for example, in professional associations. The Christians were able to attract the pagans because of the kinship between their religious doctrines and the issues known from pagan philosophical instruction. For many, however, their experience led not to the abandonment of their ancestral traditions but rather to an ultimately traditional practice of religion that was open to the religious practices of neighbors and social partners. Even apart from the Christians, who remained close to the Jews, a sign of such tolerance can be seen in what Christian apologetics calls *lapsi,* individuals who were not so much lukewarm Christians as people who had adopted a certain number of Christian practices and representations and made them part of their personal religion, but without wishing to belong to the Christian community in the strict sense. Another example can be found in the Naassenes, whom Hippolytus condemned and who combined, to a certain extent, Christianity with the mysteries of Magna Mater. If they were in any danger, the Naassenes abandoned the incriminating practices, as they did not see these as representing the central core of their religious experience.

The situation seems to have changed when Constantine and his sons raised Christianity to the level of a public religion. The rapidity and depth of the evolution must not be exaggerated, however. Non-Christian ancestral cults continued to be practiced for a long time at the local and domestic levels. Nor did the Christians abandon certain older practices; in the 5th century, Christians still carried out sacrifices and made vows before an image of Constantine (Philostorgius, *Ecclesiastical History* 2.17), in spite of repeated interdictions. Religious pluralism was not forcefully suppressed from one day to the next, either. Leaving aside the old cults and Judaism, let us note that Christians themselves were divided into regional and provincial communities, often far removed from one another, if we are to believe the history of heresies and doctrinal quarrels. The fact remains that this evolution ended up completely transforming the religious landscape of the Mediterranean world. From this point on, pluralism came increasingly to involve the religions of the book: Judaism, Christianity, and, as of the 7th century, Islam.

Bibliography

Beard, Mary, John North, and Simon Price. *Religions of Rome.* 2 vols. Cambridge, 1998.
Degrassi, Attilio. *Inscriptiones latinae liberae rei publicae.* 2 vols. Biblioteca di Studi Superiori 23 and 40. Florence, 1957–63.
Frankfurter, David. "Lest Egypt's City Be Deserted: Religion and Ideology in the Egyp-

tian Response to the Jewish Revolt (116–117 CE)." *Journal of Jewish Studies* 43 (1992): 203–20.

North, John. "Conservatism and Change in Roman Religion." *Papers of the British School in Rome* 44 (1974): 1–12.

———. "Religious Toleration in Republican Rome." *Proceedings of the Cambridge Philological Society* 25 (1979): 85–103.

Pailler, Jean-Marie. *Bacchanalia: La répression de 186 av. J.C. à Rome et en Italie: Vestiges, images, traditions.* Bibliothèque des Écoles Françaises d'Athènes et de Rome 270. Rome, 1988.

Scheid, John. "Aspects religieux de la municipalisation: Quelques réflexions générales." In *Cités, municipes, colonies: Les processus de municipalisation en Gaule et en Germanie sous le haut-empire romain,* ed. Monique Dondin-Payre and Marie-Thérèse Raepsaet-Charlier. Paris, 1999.

———. "Graeco Ritu: A Typically Roman Way of Honouring the Gods." *Harvard Studies in Classical Philology* 97 (1995): 15–31.

Wissowa, Georg. *Religion und Kultus der Romer.* Munich, 1912.

Writing and Religion

Mary Beard

*I*n 304 BCE, or not long before, a man by the name of Cnaeus Flavius displayed in the Forum at Rome, for the first time, the official calendar of religious festivals. Or so several Roman writers assure us. It was a revolutionary act. For up to that point, the calendar of festivals and all kinds of information that went with it (including various legal rules and formulas and details of the days on which one was allowed to bring cases) had been in the hands of a small group of priests: "hidden away in the storeroom of the *pontifices*" as the historian Livy puts it (*From the Foundation of the City* 9.46.5) and making the people as a whole dependent on secret priestly knowledge. The ancient writers disagree about exactly at which stage of his career Flavius did this. Was it while he held the office of *aedile* (a middle-ranking elected magistracy in the city)? Or was it earlier, while he was still a government clerk *(scriba)*? Cicero even debated this problem in 50 BCE, in a letter to his friend Atticus (*To Atticus* 6.1), who had raised the awkward possibility that the calendar had actually been made public more than a century before Flavius's intervention. But, details apart, this action was clearly seen as a blow against the power of the traditional priestly and governing class at Rome—Flavius himself being (in Livy's words again) "of humble birth" or, more precisely, the son of an ex-slave.

How accurate this anecdote is, we simply do not know. But, accurate or not, it brings into view some of the most important aspects of the interaction between religion and writing, not just in Rome but throughout the ancient Mediterranean world—and, indeed, more widely. First, the apparent complexity of the written document that Flavius is supposed to have revealed: an established, annual calendar of rituals, linked into a whole series of regulations about the use of different days in the year and other procedures of civil law. This kind of elaborate religious codification, with its fixed and complex rules of proper behavior, is scarcely conceivable without the resource of writing. Second, the contested political dimension. This story presents two alternative models of how written religious knowledge might be deployed: on the one hand, as the private text of an exclusive, literate priestly group, and so a formidable weapon in the armory of priestly control; on the other, as a potentially public piece of information, and so—as Flavius was to demonstrate by his posting of the calendar in the Forum—a weapon in the democratization of religious power. Third, the controversy between the ancient writers on the precise version of events is itself ultimately a product of writing. For the *history* of religion in the strictest sense, the very idea that religious history could be a subject of study and debate, separate from practice and tradition, largely depends on the "reification of the past" that comes with *written records*. We ourselves, of course, are beneficiaries of those same records; for in the absence of Roman writing, we would now know nothing of Flavius and his calendar, still less be able to explore its significance.

This chapter will reflect on the issues raised by Flavius's story, among other facets of the interaction of religion and writing in the ancient Mediterranean world. It will attempt to set these in the context of more-general, theoretical, and anthropological studies of the role of written texts within cultural systems and the contested interface between traditions of "literacy" and "orality" that, since the invention of writing itself, have characterized every culture, whether ancient or modern. A particular point of reflection will be the idea of the "religion of the book." How far are ancient Judaism and Christianity, with their apparent reliance on a defining body of doctrinal texts, to be set apart from the other religions discussed in this volume?

The implications of writing

Over the last fifty years or so, the disciplines of both history and anthropology have focused intensely on the cultural history of reading and writing. For ancient historians one obvious question has been: how many people in any given ancient society were literate? It is a question that is, of course, easier to pose than to answer. Even in modern societies, with all their resources of mass survey and testing, literacy rates are notoriously hard to pin down; and they fluctuate according to the definition of literacy deployed (many more people can read than can write, many more can sign their name than can transmit even a simple message in writing). From antiquity, we have no statistical data. Our conclusions must be based on deduction from hints in ancient literature and documents, on comparison with the slightly clearer evidence from more-recent premodern societies, and, frankly, on a good deal of guesswork. For all these uncertainties, however, most scholars would now agree that throughout the ancient Mediterranean adult male literacy—in the sense of the ability to send and understand a simple written message—generally remained below 20 percent. There may have been a few, short-lived exceptions to that rule in particular communities in the ancient world. But even the apparently literate culture of the classical Greek city-states or of early imperial Rome was not founded on the mass ability to read and write. And in many societies the rate of literacy would have been considerably lower than 20 percent. A recent estimate for ancient Egypt, for example, suggests that at most periods less than 1 percent of the total population was literate. For obvious social, cultural, and political reasons, far fewer women than men could ever read and write.

Some of the consequences of this are clear and hold good for all ancient societies. Crucially for any understanding of ancient religion, the vast majority of people experienced religion orally. This is true, to some extent, even today. At least, no religious system is, or has ever been, mediated entirely in writing; oral communication, performance, and reaffirmation are always significant components of religious practice. Nonetheless in antiquity, unlike in the modern West, most of the population had access to the language of religion (whether doctrine, the word of the divine, exegesis, administration, or dissent) only orally. Modern scrutiny of the written traces of ancient religions (and—notwithstanding the importance of visual images—the history of religion is heavily dependent on written evidence) must always bear in mind the wider oral context of that writing, the interface between oral and written traditions.

Beyond that, however, the particular ramifications of restricted literacy are varied in different societies, religions, and social groups. The map of ancient illiteracy is much subtler than any raw percentage might suggest. It is linked to different political and social structures: a democratic system of government might prompt a different spread of literacy from a palace bureaucracy; while urban life was everywhere strikingly more literate than was rural life. But it may also be linked to the character of the writing system involved: syllabic or pictographic scripts often entail different patterns of literacy from alphabetic systems. In Egypt, for example, hieroglyphs—known as "the god's words"—were not only different in function from the simpler, so-called Demotic script (hieroglyphs were used predominantly in official, public inscriptions, very commonly in temples) but competence in hieroglyphic writing was confined to a much-smaller scribal or priestly group. There is no clear division between those with and those without access to the written word that operates across the religions of the Mediterranean world.

But the impact of writing on a religious system does not depend solely on the rates of literacy within any given religious community. Nor is that impact restricted to the literate minority—leaving the illiterate majority in an entirely oral culture unaffected by the strategies and conventions of literacy to which they have no direct access themselves. It is now well recognized that the existence of writing within a society (even if it is a tool that can actively be deployed by only a tiny few) can have wide cultural consequences that affect illiterate and literate alike. Quite simply, writing almost always (and, some would say, necessarily) changes the ways that societies operate and think about themselves—in religion as much as in any other sphere.

Many of the recent studies of this cultural aspect of writing owe their intellectual origins to a famous article by Jack Goody and Ian Watt entitled "The Consequences of Literacy," first published in 1963. In this theoretical essay, which took archaic and classical Greece as its prime example, Goody and Watt emphasized the intellectual and cognitive consequences of the spread of alphabetic writing systems. Part of their argument rested on the sheer permanency of writing. For them, entirely oral cultures were marked by the "unconscious operation of memory" and forgetfulness ("social amnesia"): where there is no written record, myths and traditions that no longer seem useful or appropriate are simply forgotten and pass out of the cultural memory. Practices continue in what is thought to be the traditional way ("as our ancestors did it"), but in fact are constantly adjusted—albeit tacitly and unconsciously—to new circumstances and ideas. But once writing is employed as a recording device, later generations will be faced with the written evidence of their earlier customs and thought and will need consciously to align their own behavior to it—whether in the form of rigid conservatism, explicit rejection of tradition, or self-consciously critical "historical" analysis. To take one of Goody and Watt's key examples, "once the poems of Homer and Hesiod, which contained much of the earlier history, religion and cosmology of the Greeks, had been written down, succeeding generations were faced with old distinctions in sharply exaggerated form: how far was the information about the gods and heroes literally true? How could its patent inconsistencies be explained? And how could the beliefs and attitudes implied be brought into line with those of the present?" (1963).

Similar factors lie behind the development of explicitly skeptical traditions. Every society includes men and women with unorthodox ideas, people who adopt a radically dissenting attitude to generally accepted views on religion, politics, and social order. But in an entirely oral culture, skepticism tends to die with the individual skeptic. Once the skeptic commits his or her views to the permanency of writing, however, the possibility opens of a whole *tradition* of skepticism, an alternative counterculture, parallel to society's orthodox norms. This is obviously of particular importance in the history of religion and in the development of radical, skeptical inquiry into traditional religious "truths." Goody and Watt cite the example of the Greek thinker Xenophanes in the 6th century BCE, whose surviving work includes criticism of the then-standard views on the anthropomorphic form of the gods: "If horses were able to draw, they would draw the forms of the gods like horses" (DK 21 B15). Xenophanes, we may add, in confirmation of their point, was still being read and quoted at the end of antiquity, more than a millennium later.

Goody and Watt also stress the influence of writing on the potential complexity of any organization, whether political, social, or religious. As Goody argues at greater length in his later book, *The Domestication of the Savage Mind* (1977), the ability to transcend oral memory by the apparently simple device of a written list opens up a whole series of intellectual possibilities— from the detailed classification of property (furniture, animals, or agricultural produce can be listed by type, weight, location, and so forth) to the intricate definition of calendrical time, dividing the year according to months and days and the religious obligations appropriate to each occasion (as in the calendar "published" by Cnaeus Flavius). At its most ambitious, Goody and Watt's scheme follows some earlier theorists in suggesting that the invention of writing drives a cognitive revolution, enabling for the first time certain forms of what we might call logical thinking—from the simple syllogism (if *a* then *b*, etc.) to other more-complicated forms of algebraic logic.

This work has prompted considerable reaction, both favorable and—in some specific respects—dissenting. Goody himself, in response to those who objected that the phrase *consequences of literacy* appeared to suggest a too-rigid schema (in which literacy was always and necessarily followed by various social and intellectual developments) now prefers the phrase "the implications of literacy." It also remains very much an open question what level of literacy in a society, and what form of literacy, would entail the implications (or consequences) proposed. In their first article, Goody and Watt envisaged "widespread" and "alphabetic" literacy, stressing the democratic and revolutionary intellectual power of the Greek system of writing as against the scribal, narrowly restricted literacy of the syllabic or pictographic systems of ancient Babylonia or Egypt. But in his later work on lists, Goody drew as much on ancient Near Eastern material as on Greco-Roman examples (including lists and hierarchical rankings of deities from Babylonia and Egypt). In general, although the range and spread of writing differed significantly in different ancient Mediterranean societies, we can trace at least some of Goody and Watt's implications in all the (partially) literate communities covered by this volume.

Certainly, the impact of writing on ancient Mediterranean religion is evident far beyond the culture of ancient Greece, on which Goody and Watt principally drew. We have already noted the existence of a Roman calendar of festivals, whose complex and elaborately codified information would have been unthinkable without the resource of writing: in the most detailed examples of these calendars, the written data laid out include the legal and religious status of each day of the year, the divisions into months (and the main divisions within months), the traditional roster of public holidays and more-recent additions to this set of festivals, plus some information on the festival concerned (the principal deity attached, the place of celebration, or the reason for its foundation). Other aspects of religion also illuminate (and are illuminated by) the Goody-Watt hypothesis. The logic of Mesopotamian divination, for example, has been linked to the particular conventions of pictographic script in which it was recorded, while in Roman cult, one of the most striking features was the preservation of archaic and apparently obsolete religious lore. By the 1st century CE, the ancient hymn sung by the Salii at their regular ritual "dance" through the streets of Rome was incomprehensible—it is reported by one Roman writer—even to the priests themselves. Likewise the hymn chanted by the Arval Brethren and recorded on one of the inscriptions documenting this priesthood's ritual activity in their sacred grove a few miles outside the city of Rome appears now (as it must have appeared to most Romans for most of their history) to be bafflingly archaic mumbo jumbo; it makes (and made) sense, if at all, only to a few specialists in the earliest form of Latin. The preservation of these ancient religious texts would have been impossible without written documents; and indeed the inscriptions from the Arval grove explicitly refer to written copies of the hymn used by the priests in their chanting.

But Goody and Watt's implications go further than that (as Gordon has argued in his 1990 study of Roman religion in the light of Goody and Watt's work). First, the incomprehensibility of these texts itself stimulated further writing, in learned commentaries that (often equally obscurely) attempted to interpret and explain their meaning. A commentary on the Salian hymn existed already in the 1st century BCE, and one of the most distinctive parts of Roman religious discourse from that time on was a whole series of specialized treatises that offered exegesis on arcane aspects of cult and cult history (e.g., *On Religious Formulas* or *On the Derivation of the Names of the Gods*). Writing, in other words, stimulated more writing. Second are the implications for religious power and control that follow from the obscurantism enshrined in this writing. For unintelligibility (which, in Gellner's words, "leaves the disciple with a secret guilt of not understanding") could be an important defense of priestly or other expert religious power. The public display of written mumbo jumbo, and the importance vested in it as hallowed tradition, was almost bound to enhance the authority of those who could claim to understand, while disadvantaging those who could not and were reliant on the interpretative skills of others. If the story of Flavius offered a popular, democratic parable of writing, other written forms offer the directly opposite message.

Influential and instructive as they are, Goody and Watt's theories can, however, be misleading if applied too rigidly, particularly in the sphere of religion. The dangers are most clearly seen in the fundamental issue of the *function* of writing. For Goody and Watt, writing is an essentially utilitarian activity. It is there to be read and to be acted on as appropriate. So, for instance, written records of procedures establish precedent and encourage conservative practice precisely because they are consulted and their example followed. But a significant part of religious writing is not utilitarian in this way. With its functions classified under the admittedly rather vague rubric of "symbolic," it may act to display, to memorialize, to reify and make permanent a variety of legitimate and illegitimate religious claims and actions—not necessarily to be read and used, at least not within the community of living mortals. The most extreme case of this is the use of writing within the varied group of religious practices we now know as magic. Spells and curses, written on lead or papyrus and deposited in tombs or wells, may well have been thought to preserve the magician's oral utterance and to take it as close as possible to the dead or chthonic powers who would mediate or bring about the desired result (see Prayers, Hymns, Incantations, and Curses: Greece). More than that, the transgressive forms of writing commonly adopted in curses (e.g., words written back to front, varieties of nonsense script) served to reify the transgressions implicit in the curse itself. One Athenian spell, from the 4th century BCE, makes this link explicit. It is written backward, from right to left, and reads: "In the same way that this is cold and 'out of true,' let the words of Krates be cold and 'out of true' in the same way, his as well as those of the accusers and lawyers who accompany him" (Wünsch 1897: appendix no. 67). But even outside the particular area of "magical" practices, ancient religious writing was often not principally intended for a reader, and even some of the most extensive and detailed religious records were not systematically consulted as a guide to precedent. The records of ritual procedures made by the Arval Brethren and inscribed on stone in their sacred grove did not consistently dictate the future conduct of ritual—as the numerous changes in procedure that the texts document make clear. The inscription memorialized the rituals carried out, rather than providing a reference guide for how to act in the future. Likewise the vast majority of the many thousands of Roman inscriptions detailing vows and the performance of sacrifices can hardly have been widely consulted—or intended to be so; instead they instantiated and made permanent the ritual act itself. Writing, in other words, could be as much an integral part of religious symbolism as an external record of it.

Religions of the book?

It is conventional to draw a sharp distinction in terms of the role of writing between Judaism and Christianity on the one hand and the rest of the religions covered by this volume on the other. In Judaism and Christianity, doctrine and the word of God was defined in writing; they were—and still are—"religions of the book." This was not the case anywhere else, from Babylonia to Roman Italy; and in these other religions, so it follows, writing played a less important (or, at least, a less structurally central) part. How useful a distinction is this? Precisely how sharp should we make it?

There is no doubt at all that writing (and reading) had a particularly loaded role to play in the ancient Judeo-Christian tradition. It was not simply a question of the textual basis of religious doctrine. Writing was invested with even greater power and authority than that. So, for example, the Book of Exodus makes the radical claim that the tablets given to Moses on Sinai carried texts that were not merely the word of God in the sense of being divinely *inspired*, they were actually divinely *written*: "And he gave to Moses, when he had made an end of speaking with him upon Mount Sinai, the two tables of the testimony, tables of stone, written with the finger of God . . . And the tables were the work of God, and the writing was the writing of God, graven upon the tables" (Exod. 31.18; 32.16). And it is well known that Jews accorded considerable veneration to the physical form of their sacred texts, as if (in the words of Goodman) "religious power was enshrined within the physical object on which the divine teachings were inscribed." Torah scrolls were written according to strict rules, in carefully prescribed lettering, in ink and on the best parchment. Josephus—the Jewish priest and historian who eventually sided with the Romans in the Jewish revolt that ended in 70 CE—was well placed to observe that the destruction of a Jewish text by a Roman soldier ended in a riot (*Jewish War* 2.229–31) and that Vespasian and Titus had a scroll of the Torah carried in their triumphal procession through Rome in 71 (7.150); the scroll itself, among the other booty on show, was a powerful symbol of Roman victory over the Jews. Not surprisingly perhaps, these texts sometimes filled the symbolic role of writing that we have already noted. As Goodman and others have pointed out, the miniature texts used in phylacteries (pouches for Torah texts, bound onto the arms or forehead) "were encased in leather in such a way that they usually could not be read at all."

In early Christianity, too, the importance of writing went well beyond the existence of scripture (a word that is directly derived from the Latin for "writing": *scriptura*). The divergences between different groups of early Christians (divergences sometimes cast as the struggle of "orthodoxy" against the "heretics") were often cast in terms of the competing authority of different written texts, as well as different interpretation of the canonical Gospels. One 7th-century Christian theologian, for example, could refer to the "foul, loathsome, and unclean writings of the accursed Manicheans, gnostics, and the rest of the heretics" (John of Damascus, *Orations* 2.10). Written texts were also crucial in such cohesion as the early church could obtain. The scattered communities of early Christians depended, very largely, on written communication for any sense of group identity; the letters of Paul from the 50s and 60s CE are only the start of a tradition of epistolary exchange that aimed to reinforce and define the Christian community. And, in general, the symbolism of writing pervaded Christian discourse and visual representation. Jesus, for example, appears in early Christian sculpture displaying a book roll as his major attribute. One vivid image of heavenly power comes in the form of the "book of life," into which angels transcribe the names of good Christians for ultimate reward, while the names of sinners are listed with equal rigor elsewhere. Lane-Fox has aptly referred to these recording angels as "a literate police force, active above early Christian saints and sinners." Another image, in both Christianity and Judaism, pictures the prophet as a man who has literally consumed the written word of God. In John's visionary account in the Book of Revelation, "I took the little scroll from the hand of the angel and ate it; it was as sweet as honey in my mouth . . . And I was told, 'You must again prophesy' (Rev. 10.10–11); or as God said to Ezekiel, "Eat this scroll, and go, speak" (Ezek. 3.1).

Yet it is not quite so simple as it might seem. For a start, on the basis of what we can infer about levels of literacy throughout antiquity, most people, even in these apparently "textual" religious communities, must have had their texts mediated orally. In fact, one conservative—though not implausible—recent estimate puts the total number of Christians who were fluently literate at the end of the 1st century CE as no more than fifty at any one moment. But, even more significant than any low rate of literacy, both Judaism and Christianity embraced alternative traditions that appear to have vested as much authority in oral as in written discourse. In Judaism, for example, there was a powerful view that Moses was given the oral law, as well as written texts, on Mount Sinai; and the Mishnah, although it was authoritatively codified in writing around 200 CE, parades in form and style its oral origins as the sayings of rabbis. In Christianity, by contrast, the claims of oral authority were upheld by the simple fact that Jesus himself wrote nothing. And, for all the textual obsessions of the early church, there was an influential strand of Christian thought that positively glorified illiterate simplicity, while stressing that the Christian faithful did not need a learned (which often, in effect, meant a "pagan") education. Some early Christian saints were praised precisely because they were *sine litteris* (illiterate), as were Jesus's own disciples. John and Peter, for example, are dubbed "illiterate" *(aggrammatoi)* in the Acts of the Apostles (4.13). Predictably, perhaps, "pagan" intellectual critics of Christianity seem to have found such "holy ignorance" a further ground for mistrust of the new religion.

The picture becomes even more complicated if we start to compare the role of writing in the Judeo-Christian tradition with other religions covered in this volume. It is certainly the case that no other ancient belief system was so reliant on a group of doctrinal written texts. And it is partly for this reason—because we do not find writing where, as heirs of the Judeo-Christian tradition, we *expect* to find it—that scholars have tended to suggest that the practice of religious writing was less significant in ancient religions outside Judaism and Christianity. In fact, although there are clear differences, they are not so stark as they might appear at first sight. We have already noted the Egyptian term for hieroglyphs as "the god's words" and observed the central role of writing in those religious practices that go by the name of magic. The world of Greco-Roman "paganism" offers an even wider range of the uses of writing in cult and belief. Although the official state cults of Rome and the Greek cities were not generally founded on divinely inspired or divinely written texts, in some noncivic cults—such as those of Orpheus and the Egyptian Hermes—the word of the god, as inscribed in sacred texts, did hold a central place. At Rome itself, the major state collection of oracular texts, the Sibylline Oracles, owed its origin and its authority to the figure of the Sibyl of Cumae—a divinely inspired prophetess. The Sibylline Oracles were regularly consulted at times of danger and trouble for the city, and they were, in a sense, the word of god; they were preserved and recopied (even if conveniently amended in the process) with the full panoply of religious care. Other ancient oracles worked entirely through writing, without the involvement of even an original oral prophecy: the oracle at Praeneste (near Rome), for example, was based on the consultation of written wooden tablets, which had been discovered miraculously—already inscribed—inside a nearby rock. Although modern scholarship has tended to privilege the oral consultation of an oracle (as at the famous oracle of Apollo at Delphi), Greco-Roman gods regularly communicated in writing.

But writing pervaded the religious world of Rome in other senses. The priestly colleges were associated with so-called priestly books. Although these do not survive beyond the occasional fragmentary quotation and their exact content is still disputed, it seems very likely that they recorded details of religious formulas and procedure (or, in the case of the document that Flavius published, calendrical and legal information). More striking still, however, is the role of writing in dedications and vows in temples and sanctuaries. When Pliny the Younger visited the sanctuary of Clitumnus near modern Spoleto in the early 2nd century CE, he found a site full of the written word: "Everything there will delight you," he wrote to a friend, "and you can also find something to read. You can study the numerous inscriptions in honor of the spring [*fons*] and of the god, which many hands have written on every pillar and wall" (*Letters* 8.8.7). Even today, when almost everything inscribed on perishable material has disappeared, many Greco-Roman sanctuaries still preserve the written traces of their worshipers' activities and expressions of piety or gratitude. Although Pliny suggests that the elite visitor might find plenty to read (and, he goes on, to laugh at) in such a sanctuary, the reading visitor can hardly have been uppermost in the mind of most of those commissioning these inscriptions. Much more likely, the intention of the writing was to memorialize, or give permanence to, the ritual act commemorated. More generally, in a religion in which there were no clear articles of faith, no formal badge of belonging or ceremony of initiation, memorializing religious action in an inscription was a way of "writing oneself in" to "membership" of the religious community. This sense of "writing as belonging" took a notable twist in the conflicts between Christianity and traditional civic cults in the Roman Empire during the 3rd century CE. The emperor Decius ordered that everyone should sacrifice to the gods to prove that they were not Christian. But not just that. Once they had sacrificed in the presence of two official witnesses, they could be issued with a written certificate to authenticate their action—and, no doubt, to produce if challenged again. A few of these certificates still survive from Roman Egypt (e.g., Mitteis and Wilcken 1912: no. 124).

What underlies these different manifestations of the written word in ancient religions is not a simple clash between "religions of the book" and the rest. It is rather a series of questions about the mediation of divine power that all religions must accommodate, if not answer. What forms of communication—written or oral—carry most authority? How do you weigh the immediacy of orality against the permanency of writing? How does religious speech relate to religious text? Different religions offer different answers to these questions—and different answers at different periods and in different circumstances. In studying ancient religious systems, it is much more helpful to concentrate on that constant play-off between oral and written traditions, in all its different varieties and with all its different emphases—rather than to use the role of writing as a fixed standard against which to classify or hierarchize the different religions. This sense of religious dialectic is brilliantly captured in a Jewish story from the 6th-century CE Babylonian Talmud (tractate *Bava Metzi'a* 59a–b). In a dispute between a group of rabbis set in the 2nd century, different forms of authority were claimed for their different interpretations. One, Rabbi Eliezer, after performing a variety of miracles to support his own position, finally—in the face of continuing disagreement from his colleagues—called on heaven itself to prove his point. A supporting divine voice indeed came: "The law accords with what he says." But even this was not enough. One rabbi claimed that the voice did not really come from heaven; another claimed that, even if divine, the voice did not carry the day, for the written law must hold: "Since the Torah has already been given from Mount Sinai, we do not pay attention to heavenly voices, for You have written already at Mount Sinai"; and he went on to advise God to vote with the majority. And God's reaction to this dispute? "He laughed and said, 'My children have defeated me.'"

The religion of writing

So far I have discussed the role of writing in ancient culture and religion as if it were a topic of interest to modern anthropologists and historians of religion; and I have largely referred to writing as if it were a practice that reacted with, but was essentially separate from, religion. That is, of course, part of the story; but only a part. Writing could also be very much an integral part of religion and ritual, not simply an external influence on it. I have already mentioned briefly the symbolic role of writing within various cult practices, including magic. This should prompt us to see writing itself, potentially at least, as a ritual activity. This was certainly the case in the Arval Grove, where the inscriptions themselves document some of the rituals associated with their inscribing (iron was a prohibited substance in the grove, so the introduction of the iron tools had to be accompanied by expiatory sacrifices). In Greece the formal inscription and preservation of oaths and treaties was often similarly ritualized. In Plato's *Critias*, written in the 4th century BCE, he envisages a sacrifice in the mythical Atlantis, where the blood of a sacrificial animal is made to wash over, literally, the texts of preserved laws (119c–20c). And, as Steiner has observed (1994), the 5th-century BCE historian Herodotus projects a similar concern with ritual inscription onto illiterate barbarians. If barbarians do not use alphabetic writing, at least they "inscribe" their oaths as scars on the body of the oath taker (3.8; 4.70).

No less important is the incorporation of writing into ancient cultural commentary and myth. Plato, for example, in his dialogue *Phaedrus* has the character of Socrates argue that the invention of writing was culturally deleterious, among other reasons because it weakened the human memory (why bother to remember when you can refer to a written text?) and because it was indiscriminate in those it addressed (unlike an oral philosopher, who could choose his audience). And many ancient cultures attributed the origin of writing to divine (or heroic) invention. Egyptian hieroglyphs were said to be the brainchild of the god Thoth. Greek myths ascribed writing variously to (among others) the god Hermes, the mythical Palamedes, or the semidivine Prometheus, who brought writing to mortals as part of his civilizing mission, which also included the gift of fire. Others, however, would have backed the claims of Orpheus, legendary poet, musician, and mystic. He originated, it was said, from Thrace (in the far north of Greece), and different mythical accounts accorded him a quite different role in the history of writing: one tradition makes him its inventor; another claims that, as the Thracians were well known to be illiterate, he could not possibly be writing's ancestor. But more influential still was the idea that after his death his decapitated head continued to sing, and the words were either directly and miraculously transcribed on tablets or else copied down by faithful secretaries. "Orphic texts" (versions of which circulated widely in Greece) were thought to hold healing properties and to offer, to those who read them, the hope of life after death.

The myth of the talking head of Orpheus and the miraculous properties of Orphic texts might seem a world away from the story of Cnaeus Flavius and his practical assault on the priestly monopoly of knowledge in early Rome. But that indeed must be the range spanned by any study of religion and writing in the ancient world: from mundane record keeping to the "words of god"; from academic exegesis to magical mumbo jumbo; from writing in blood to writing in stone.

Bibliography

Baines, J. "Literacy in Ancient Egyptian Society." *Man* 18 (1983): 572–99.

Beard, M. "Writing and Religion: Ancient Literacy and the Function of the Written Word in Roman Religion." In *Literacy in the Roman World,* ed. M. Beard et al. Journal of Roman Archaeology Supplement 3. Ann Arbor, 1991.

———. "Writing and Ritual: A Study of Diversity and Expansion in the Arval Acta." *Papers of the British School at Rome* 53 (1981): 114–62.

Bottéro, J., C. Herrenschmidt, and J.-P. Vernant. *Ancestor of the West: Writing, Reasoning, and Religion in Mesopotamia, Elam, and Greece.* Chicago, 2000.

Bowman, A. K., and G. Woolf, eds. *Literacy and Power in the Ancient World.* Cambridge, 1994 (see esp. essays by M. D. Goodman and R. Lane Fox).

Goody, J. *The Domestication of the Savage Mind.* Cambridge, 1977.

Goody, J., and I. Watt. "The Consequences of Literacy." In *Comparative Studies in Society and History* 5 (1963): 304–45; reprinted in *Literacy in Traditional Societies,* ed. J. Goody. Cambridge, 1968.

Gordon, R. L. "From Republic to Principate: Priesthood, Religion, and Ideology." In *Pagan Priests,* ed. M. Beard and J. North. London, 1990.

Harris, W. V. *Ancient Literacy.* Cambridge, Mass., 1989.

Hopkins, K. *A World Full of Gods: Pagans, Jews, and Christians in the Roman Empire.* London, 1999.

Mitteis, L., and U. Wilcken. *Grundzüge und Chrestomathie der Papyruskunde,* vol. 1.2. Leipzig: Teubner, 1912.

Sawyer, J. F. A. *Sacred Languages and Sacred Texts: Religion in the First Christian Centuries.* London, 1999.

Steiner, D. Tarn. *The Tyrant's Writ: Myths and Images of Writing in Ancient Greece.* Princeton, 1994.

Wünsch, R. "Appendix continens defixionum tabellas in Attica regione repertas." In *Inscriptiones Graecae,* vol. II/III, *Corpus Inscriptionum Atticarum.* Berlin: Reimer, 1897.

Magic

Sarah Iles Johnston

A problem of definition

It was to be the greatest temple of all time—built to the glory of YHWH by King Solomon, in fulfillment of a promise that his father, King David, had made. Enormous and splendid, the temple would provide a place where the ark of the covenant could safely be stored and where all of Israel could worship.

But in the course of its construction, a problem arose. Solomon's favorite workman was attacked each night by Ornias, a vampirelike demon who stole the workman's vitality by sucking on his thumb. Solomon prayed to YHWH for help, and YHWH sent a ring to Solomon via the angel Michael. This ring, on which was engraved a device that came to be known as the "Seal of Solomon," could be used to control all the demons of the world. With help from the angel Ouriel, Solomon used the seal to stop Ornias from attacking his workman and then to order Ornias to invoke Beelzeboul, a more powerful demon who in turn invoked all the other demons. By interrogating them, Solomon learned what their names were and which plants, stones, and animal parts could be used to avert each one of them.

Solomon compelled the conquered demons to finish building the temple and afterward drove them into bottles, which he sealed shut with his ring. He buried the bottles under the temple, where they remained until the Babylonians pillaged Jerusalem many years later. Assuming that the bottles contained gold, the greedy invaders broke them open and once again let loose upon the world a host of demonic ills. Henceforth ordinary people, lacking Solomon's power to imprison the demons, could keep them at bay only by wearing amulets engraved with his seal or by using the techniques that Solomon had learned from the demons themselves. It was because he had foreseen the demons' eventual release, indeed, that Solomon had recorded the means of averting each one so carefully.

This story of Solomon and the demons, which is taken from a narrative called the *Testament of Solomon* that dates back to at least the 2nd century CE, is an apt introduction to an essay on magic, for it implicitly raises an issue that looms large in scholarly studies of the topic: namely, how can we distinguish between "magic" and "religion"? Using a special seal and other techniques to control demons makes Solomon look like what many would call a magician. This accords with other ancient portraits, where he is presented as an expert in incantations, astrology, alchemy, and other arts commonly gathered under the rubric and appears on amulets against illness and the Evil Eye (see ill. on p. 468). And yet, it could also be argued that several elements in the story situate Solomon within the realm of religion: the fact that the seal was a gift from YHWH, Michael and Ouriel's assistance in its delivery and deployment, and Solomon's use of the conquered demons to build YHWH's temple.

The story itself concedes nothing to this problem; the cultures in which it originated and developed simply armed Solomon with the tools that they revered as efficacious against demons and legitimated both him and those tools by linking them closely to YHWH and his angels. Nor was Solomon unusual among YHWH's devotees: Moses and Aaron performed deeds that we might call magical—not only did they turn a staff into a snake (Exod. 7.8–12) but they also devised such things as love charms and invisibility spells (*PGM* VII.619–27). Christ raised the dead and exorcised demons, feats often credited to magicians in antiquity; his name, as well as that of Iao (a variation of YHWH), empowered such things as memory charms and divinatory spells and appeared in ancient grimoires side by side with, for example, instructions for engraving silver tablets and creating (and later eating) female dolls made of bread dough (*PGM* III.410–66). The Greek hero Jason received the first *iynx* (a tool for making people fall in love) from the goddess Aphrodite (Pindar, *Pythian* 4.213–19). And on the Metternich Stele, the goddess Isis proudly claimed to teach *heka* (an Egyptian word that the ancient Greeks translated as "*mageia*" [magic]) to her favorite mortals. In other words, pagan divinities and heroes no more repudiated what we might call magic than did YHWH and his followers. In fact, far from rejecting such practices, ancient peoples enhanced their gods' and heroes' reputations by boasting that they knew more about such practices than did other cultures' gods and heroes.

And yet the modern scholarly quest to establish a division between magic and religion does have some roots in antiquity, insofar as both ancient and modern discussions hinge on terminology: what one chooses to call any particular activity (and, it follows, who is doing the choosing) determines whether the activity is understood as acceptable or discredited, pious or blasphemous, religion or magic. In antiquity, *magic* (a term that I use as a shorthand way of referring to a variety of ancient Mediterranean words) almost always referred to someone else's religious practices; it was a term that distanced those practices from the norm—that is, from one's own practices, which constituted religion. Among magicians themselves, distance could lend glamour and authority—for instance, Greek magicians claimed to one another that their spells had been invented by legendary Egyptian, Persian, or Jewish magicians—but to nonmagicians, distance usually implied charlatanry, alliances with dark gods and demons, and coercion of gods to whom other, properly reverent people prayed. Thus, in later antiquity, outsiders who feared and derided Judaism and Christianity called both Christ and Moses *goētes,* a term that had come to mean, by this time, charismatic quacks who lured their followers into illegal and immoral activities and who claimed to command armies of demons. Centuries earlier, Sophocles' Oedipus insulted Teiresias, a priest and prophet whom he no longer trusted, by calling him a "scheming *magos*" (*Oedipus Tyrannus* 387).

Thus, magic was almost always a normative, rather than a straightforwardly descriptive, term, and looking at the ancient world from our own vantage point, we can make no clean division between it and religion. Not only were many gods and religious leaders reputed to employ techniques that we might call magical (in Egypt, Persia, Mesopotamia, and Anatolia, in fact, some forms of what we call magic were in the purview of official priests), but when we examine the techniques themselves, we discover that they differ from other religious practices more in details than in substance or attitude. For example, the structure of "magical" prayers was identical to that of "religious" prayers in most Mediterranean cultures, and in cultures where sacrifice was an important part of religious practice, it stood at the center of magical practices as well. Amulets against illness and other crises invoke the aid of the same saints and holy men whom we meet in religious texts.

As for the details, we can explain many differences between magical and religious practices by noting (as some ancient authors already did) that the magician was a "technician of the sacred," someone who knew more about how to approach the superhuman world than ordinary people did. This gave him the means to innovate and improvise on established techniques. The fact that in some cultures, magicians made their livings by freelancing their skills and in others used them to supplement the incomes they earned as temple priests gave them the impetus to innovate and improvise, for the most successful practitioners would be those who confidently boasted an extensive and varied repertoire, adaptable to all occasions.

The scholarly quest to divide magic from religion, which began in earnest in the late 19th century with Sir E. B. Tylor's *Primitive Culture* and Sir James Frazer's *Golden Bough,* stems from a similar desire to divide the unacceptable from the acceptable, which in their post-Darwinian world meant not only the impious from the pious, but also the unevolved from the evolved—that is, the "primitive" from the "advanced" means of understanding the cosmos and attempting to affect it (often, "science" was brought in as a third entity to be distinguished from both magic and religion). Thus, Frazer argued that magicians' techniques developed out of an assumption that they could coerce gods and crude "prescientific" concepts such as contagion and sympathy, whereas religious practitioners, having advanced beyond this spiritually, focused on prayer and theology and scientists developed intellectually sounder means of investigation. Frazer and other armchair anthropologists used these neat (and implicitly Western, Christianocentric) divisions to distance European culture from the tribes in Africa, South America, and New Guinea, about whom missionaries sent back reports. Variations rang changes on Frazer's scheme; Malinowski, for instance, pitted magic and religion together against science (emotional phenomena against rational) but also pitted magic and science together against religion (pragmatic empiricism against nonempiricism). All such attempts, under the scrutiny of later scholarship, have been shown to rest on shaky dichotomies between "us" and "them." Most scholars of religion now concede that a reliable means of dividing magic and religion will never be found.

Does this mean that the endeavor to define magic has stopped, or should stop? No, it continues for several reasons. For one thing, scholars continue to try to identify the ways in which specific cultures internally defined magic. Although this emic approach can never be carried out perfectly—because we can never put ourselves completely into the mentality of another culture—attempts are nonetheless illuminating. Scholars of the ancient Mediterranean have another reason to pursue definitions of magic as well: we increasingly realize that religious practices and ideas traveled fluidly across cultural boundaries; it profits the Assyriologist to compare notes with the Hellenist, the scholar of Judaism with the Egyptologist, and so on. Having at least rough heuristic models under which we can categorize practices and ideas from all of these cultures, and thus compare them, facilitates discourse and analysis. As long as we keep in mind that our definitions of magic are provisional and beware of slipping into essentialist assumptions, definitions help us identify and better understand the salient features of magic in the ancient Mediterranean. It is in this spirit that the rest of this essay proceeds.

The power of words

Virtually all religious practices involve words, whether written, spoken aloud, or silently pronounced, because virtually all religious practices constitute attempts to communicate with other beings—gods, demons, angels, the dead, or the cosmos itself. (Only certain forms of mysticism, which typically stand at the margins of the religions from which they evolve, encourage worshipers to empty their minds of words completely and focus on something that lies utterly beyond language.) Distinctions between "religious" and "magical" uses of language are as elusive as any other distinctions between religion and magic.

Yet two comments can be made. First, those whom ancient cultures called magicians often were credited with extraordinary expertise in the use of words. In Egypt, temple priests, who also served as freelance magicians, were highly trained in both the written and oral use of words; *heka* itself was described as being "excellent of words"; and Thoth, the god of writing, was also a god of magic. Plato's Socrates—to take just one of many examples from the Greco-Roman sphere—said that the leaf of a certain plant would make a sick person well again, but only if special words were pronounced at the same time as the leaf was administered: "The leaf alone is nothing," he asserted (*Charmides* 155e5–8; cf. Pliny, *Natural History* 28.3.10–11). Second, particular ways of using words are commonly associated with magic, and the ancient magician tended to be marked by the power that his speech acts carried.

Curses

One characteristic shared by many magical uses of words is that they work automatically—that is, pronouncement or inscription of the words puts the statements they make into effect virtually immediately, either with or without accompanying ritual actions. Although this characteristic can be found across a range of speech acts, it is particularly common in curses—and curses, although not associated exclusively with magic, often appear in ancient collections of magical lore or in narrative descriptions of magic and its practitioners; they constitute one of the reasons that magicians were treated with respect born of fear (cf. Pliny, *Natural History* 23.4.19).

We can pursue the "automatic" nature of many curses by adapting a heuristic model developed by Christopher Faraone for study of one specific form of Greek and Roman curse, the *defixio*— a curse written on a small piece of lead or wax and deposited within a grave or other subterranean area. Faraone divides the speech acts found on *defixiones* into four groups, the third and fourth of which I combine here. (1) "Direct" formulas, in which the cursor uses a first-person verb to curse or restrain the victim from performing an action ("I curse so-and-so"); this is a "performative utterance" that is expected to effect what it describes without further ado. The cursor, in other words, assumes no gap between his ritualized articulation of the curse and its fulfillment. (2) Formulas in which imperative verbs direct the actions of gods, demons, and other nonhuman agents against the victim ("Restrain so-and-so!"). Although we might argue that there is no guarantee that the desire expressed by these statements will be fulfilled, the baldly imperative tone (which is less commonly found in speech acts that ancient Mediterraneans labeled "religious") leaves little doubt that the cursor presumes success. (3) "Wish" formulas, which use optative verbs ("May so-and-so fail!"). Here we begin to shade into what both ancient and modern commentators often call prayer, that is, a venue in which a deity's help is sought yet never assumed to be guaranteed; but we must keep sight of two differences: a prayer is more likely than a curse to include statements intended to persuade a god or demon to cooperate with the petitioner ("I have given you sacrifices in the past"; "I will build you a temple"; etc.), the implication being that the god or demon may not, in the end, fulfill the desire. Moreover, this type of curse often includes what Stanley Tambiah has called "persuasive analogies" ("As the corpse [with which this inscribed curse is buried] is cold and lifeless, thus may so-and-so be cold and lifeless"). Similar are the vivid metaphors used in some curses: "May your root not sprout upon the earth, may your head droop at the hands of the harvester!" (see Prayers, Hymns, Incantations, and Curses: Syria-Canaan). The use of such analogies and metaphors suggests an expectation that, if the curse is properly composed and spoken or inscribed, success will follow; although requests for divine aid are sometimes included in such curses, emphasis lies on finding the right analogies and metaphors—the right words.

I do not mean to suggest a dichotomy here, pairing magic with curses and religion with prayers (for example); nor do I mean to suggest that all curses, and only curses alone among speech acts, were understood to work automatically—although it is interesting that techniques such as persuasive analogy are found most often, outside of curses, in other speech acts associated with magic (thus a Jewish love charm, like many others from the Mediterranean, decrees, "Just as [this potsherd burns, so shall] burn the heart of so-and-so, after me"; and a Mesopotamian healing spell asks that "the illness be stripped off like these dates [are stripped from a tree]"). The pairs religion–magic and unguaranteed fulfillment–automatic fulfillment mark the end points of heuristic spectrums; if we were to plot each individual example of any type of speech act (curse, prayer, etc.) along either spectrum, we would see a spread. But the curse, a type of speech act that ancient cultures tended to place at the magic end of the first spectrum, also falls more often than other speech acts at the automatic end of the second one. The automatic nature of many curses is further demonstrated by the belief that one could instantly nullify the effects of a written curse by destroying the material on which it was written.

Secret words

Magicians frequently used special words and phrases, typically described as secret. Often, the words were understood as special names of gods or angels, names sure to catch the entity's attention; a magician who used them would not fail to gain aid. This does not necessarily represent coercion of the god or angel; although coercion is clearly intended in some cases, in others, we can better understand the use of secret names as forging a stronger bond between the magician and the addressee, as shared possession of secret knowledge typically does (see Mysteries). In yet other cases—for example, in Jewish incantations that use permutations of YHWH's name—powerful names seem to work on their own, rather than to invoke their bearers.

Notably, magicians believed that many of these secret names had been handed down from other cultures and represented other languages (which is not incorrect: Jewish names are embedded in otherwise Greek magical texts and vice versa, for example) or even the language of the gods and demons they addressed. Although the names might belong to a deity whom the magician's native language called something else, he never "translated" them—not only because they might please the god more in their original forms but also because the power of some *onomata barbara* (barbaric names) was inherent in their phonetic sounds or in the shape of the letters used to write them. Unbroken repetition of a name in some magical texts (often three, seven, or nine times, but even seventy times, in one Jewish amulet) underscores this latter point, although repetition of significant words and phrases could play other roles in magic, too. Theocritus's poetic representation of a Greek love spell includes periodic refrain of vital phrases in a manner suggesting that repetition works in the divine world just as it does in the mortal: it further guarantees divinities' cooperation (*Idyll* 2). Similarly, a spell in the Greco-Egyptian papyri tells the magician to start reciting an invocation at the seventh hour of the moon and to keep saying it until the "god hearkens to you and you make contact with him" (*PGM* II.1–64).

All of this is interesting with respect to what was said about the automatic nature of magical language above. Some magical words do work automatically insofar as they function by virtue of their inherent power alone; others can be understood as signals that immediately and unconditionally put other forces into action (what might be called the "Open Sesame" effect); but others function in the same way as ordinary speech acts among humans do, even if they have greater potential than other speech acts—that is, they may not work all of the time, or at least not immediately. One thing we can say about all of these uses of secret language is that they further demonstrate that the Mediterranean magician was someone who possessed knowledge of gods, demons, angels, and the cosmos that was deeper, more detailed, and more varied than that of the average person. It was by virtue of this knowledge, rather than by virtue of any essential difference within himself or the sorts of things he did, that he was apt to be more effective in his interactions with the supernatural entities. The magician was no Merlin, sired by a demon and thereby naturally endowed with superhuman power. Although lineage might predispose one toward magic (David, Solomon's father, was credited with exorcizing Saul of an evil spirit; Medea was the niece of Circe), most Mediterranean magicians had to be trained by their elders—Hogwarts School is just the most recent exposition of a very old idea. Even the gods' help was frequently described in terms of teaching. Aphrodite taught Jason how to use the *iynx;* and Isis taught mortals *heka* (a tradition that the satirist Lucian mocks by making his archmagician, Pancrates, spend twenty-three years under her tutelage, in secret chambers beneath the earth; *Philopseudes* 34–36).

Narrative power

Historiolae (little stories) are short narrations inserted into written or spoken spells, usually evocative of longer tales that are well known. For example, a Coptic Christian spell first sketches a story of how Jesus and the angel Michael relieved a doe's labor pains; implicit is the presumption that the patient for whom the spell is recited will similarly be relieved. The spell then goes on to sketch a tale of how Horus had stomach pains and sought the help of his mother, Isis; this is followed by explicit requests for their aid in curing the stomach pains of the child over whom the spell is recited (Meyer and Smith 1994: no. 49).

What is interesting here is not so much how easily Christianity juxtaposes itself with native Egyptian religion (Mediterranean religions were fluid, and magicians, as improvising freelancers, were more fluid than most), but rather the juxtaposition of a *historiola* whose relevance to the immediate situation is stated with one whose relevance is not. The first suggests that *historiolae* are similar to the persuasive analogies and metaphors mentioned above, insofar as the magician offers them as patterns that he wants the current situation to follow. (Some Mesopotamian examples take this idea further: they begin with a description of the patient's illness, followed by a *historiola*-type narration of a deity listening to the description and prescribing for it.) The second suggests something similar to the way in which some secret words work: power is inherent in the narration itself, and recitation calls that power into action without further ado. Again, assumptions that we tentatively made about how magical words work are challenged; again, although we can cling to some extremely broad generalizations ("ancient Mediterranean magicians were experts in using words"), we cannot go much beyond that.

Eating your words

The written word lends itself to physical manipulation and thus to methods of deployment that the oral word does not. Words inscribed on an amulet or a curse tablet remained effective as long as they physically existed, continuously averting demonic illnesses or binding enemies as if someone were speaking them over and over. What happened to a word once it had been properly inscribed, moreover, happened to what it represented as well: a Babylonian spell for eliminating an opponent prescribes writing his name on a lump of clay and casting it at midnight into a river (Abusch 1998: 63). Analogously, writing particular words down repeatedly, but each time leaving off another letter until the words disappeared completely, would make the illness that the words represented disappear. Some Greek and Latin curse tablets were inscribed with no more than the victim's name and then were folded and pierced with a nail. Although rituals were probably performed and words spoken while the tablet was pierced, the primary action, the piercing of the name, underscores how deeply the word and its referent were linked in ancient magic.

And the creativity of ancient magicians went beyond even this. Spells in the Greco-Egyptian papyri advocate writing words on natron tablets that are then dissolved in drinking water or on leaves that are subsequently licked; physically ingesting the words brings the benefits they represent. Sometimes other liquids are used to supplement the words' force: Jewish magicians spoke words over a cup of wine employed in the havdalah ceremony and then drank it (MS TS K1.117); and in a Greek spell attributed to Moses, words on a natron tablet are dissolved in a mixture of wine and the milk of a black cow (*PGM* XIII.343–646). A Hurrian physician recited incantations over oil that was to anoint the "lord of the army," his horses, chariot, and weapons before going into battle (KUB 30.42 1.8–14 = *CTH* 162).

Again we see that the power of the word is understood differently in different circumstances: sometimes as a stand-in for its referent, sometimes as carrying power in and of itself. That words could be used in a variety of (sometimes mutually exclusive) ways does not seem to have bothered magicians—they used whatever was reputed to work. Sometimes, spells even included a fallback technique ("If that doesn't work, try this instead"). This brings a further insight about ancient magic: not only did it lack an orthodoxy, as did most Mediterranean religious systems themselves, but it scarcely had anything that could be called an orthopraxy. As mentioned earlier, "magic" in a given culture typically used variations of the same main rituals used by the culture's "religion" (e.g., sacrifice, purification procedures), and if we stand back far enough, we can make certain other gross generalizations (e.g., magicians were experts in using words). But the more closely we look, the harder it is to generalize. Not only do things shift within specific cultures (Egyptian magic made greater use of written words, and Greek magic made greater use of spoken words, for instance; Frankfurter 1994), but they shift from spell to spell.

The power of images and essences

Much of what has been said about words applies to another characteristic often connected with ancient magic: the creation and manipulation of images. Thus, images (drawings, statues, etc.) often stood in for their referents. When a doll was pierced with needles by a magician, the woman whom it represented was understood to be affected as well (see illustration in Prayers, Hymns, Incantations, and Curses: Egypt). Binding the statue of a demon, ghost, or witch and carrying it into the wilderness or otherwise disempowering it was understood to disempower its referent as well (a particularly complex Mesopotamian example is offered by Abusch 1998: 56–58). The soles of pharaohs' sandals were engraved with images of enemies, allowing the pharaohs to crush them with every step. This strong connection between image and referent is underscored by the magical technique of making a god angry with one's intended victim by telling the god that the victim has abused the god's image (e.g., *PGM* III.110–12). Images, like inscribed words, continuously enacted what they portrayed: wearing an amulet engraved with a picture of Saint Sisinnius lancing a child-killing demon caused the saint to perform this act repeatedly on behalf of the wearer. We read about consumption of images, too. One example involves dolls made of bread dough (PGM III.410–66), another is a spell where images of Isis and Horus are to be drawn on the hand of an ill person, who then licks them off. Horus's healing power might also be internalized by sketching his seven eyes on natron and then dissolving them into beer (Ritner 1993: 95–96, 104).

Words and images are not mutually exclusive: many cases of manipulation involve both. Aramaic incantation bowls placed a picture of a fettered demon in the middle of concentric circles of written charms against it (examples in Lesses 2001), and some curse "tablets" were actually small, inscribed human figurines, representing their victims. But attention to images in particular raises another topic important throughout Mediterranean magic: what the Greeks called *ousia* (a participle from the Greek verb "to be"; the term might be translated as "essence"). *Ousia* comprised material taken from someone or something: hair, fingernail parings, fringe from a garment, a nail from the cross on which a criminal had been crucified, a plank from a shipwrecked vessel. *Ousia* might be understood as a special sort of image, a physical object that stood in for what was otherwise missing, making it present. In some cases, this meant the object of the spell: if you wished to curse someone or to make someone fall in love with you, it was useful to have some part of that person to manipulate. In other cases, it meant the entities on whom you relied to work the spell: nails from crucifixes and planks from fatal shipwrecks could represent the restless dead on whom magicians relied to carry out many tasks (as could actual parts of corpses). Ways of using *ousia* varied, from attaching it to an image representing the referent or to something on which the referent's name was inscribed—in both cases the *ousia* acted to connect the image or tablet more closely to the referent—to burning it, to rubbing it while you invoked the referent, or to incorporating it into an image, a statue.

Earlier generations of scholars would have called the use of *ousia* an example of sympathy: that is, what happens to the *ousia* or the object to which it has been attached happens "sympathetically" to its referent (Greek *sympatheia* literally means "experiencing [something] together"). Recent scholars have rejected this idea, along with most other Frazerian inheritances. Some of their remarks are insightful: thus Fritz Graf (1998: 137–41) emphasizes that in piercing a doll with needles a magician did not intend to make the referent feel pain in those spots, but rather feel desire. The needles should be understood as indicators of where something is to take place, rather than as miniature weapons injuring miniature flesh, and thus "sympathy" must be understood as something more complex than A:B::a:b. And yet there is no denying that sympathetic ideas were at work in antiquity. That *ousia* from a corpse could substitute for the practice of depositing or performing the spell at a grave builds on this: possession of the *ousia* brought the ghost to you instead of your going to visit the ghost. In Apuleius's story of a love spell gone wrong, a witch's house is visited by sexually aroused goatskins because her assistant gathered hairs the witch used as *ousia* from goatskins instead of from the man whom the witch desired (*Golden Ass* 3.15–18).

Late antique theorists of cosmic matters built their ideas on the same premises—although they transferred their attentions to the heavenly realms and rejected the term *magician*, calling themselves Neoplatonic philosophers, theurgists, or followers of Hermes Trismegistus instead. According to them, sympathy or *philia* (friendship, in the sense of a bond between otherwise separate entities) pervaded the cosmos, tying the higher, more-perfect, and divine realms to the lower realms of the material world, where humans dwell. *Philia* created "chains" of existence, at the top of which were particular divinities and at the bottom of which were materials—gemstones, animals, plants, and so on—that shared the divinities' natures. Learning what these materials were and how to manipulate them enabled the worshiper to contact the divinities and thus perform many of the same feats as magicians did (they rejected such things as using the restless dead and casting love charms, but engaged in divination and control of the weather, for example). The implicit idea is the same as that behind the use of *ousia:* in order to affect or make use of something that is unobtainable, obtain something that is existentially connected to it. Ironically, it was precisely this idea that survived antiquity and was embraced by Christian Neoplatonists such as Marsilio Ficino during the Renaissance. By developing the concept of sympathy—a concept that was understood by Frazer and his followers as distinguishing magic from (Western, European) religion—Ficino and his followers found ways of bringing the ancient learning they so admired into line with Christianity.

Imagination and reality: Gender

As used in the ancient Mediterranean, magic is a normative term, but scholars have sometimes fallen prey to using it to distance groups of people or practices as well. Related to, and complicating, these issues are several others. For example, some scholars have argued that Mesopotamians worried a great deal about being attacked by witchcraft (i.e., magic deployed for injurious purposes) and thus expended effort on averting it and eliminating its sources, but did not actually practice witchcraft themselves. In other words, witchcraft was all in the Mesopotamian imagination; there was no reality behind it. This is not an argument with which I agree (nor does Tzvi Abusch, an expert on Mesopotamian witchcraft), but it serves well to demonstrate the problems that our imperfect sources cause for us, for it springs from the fact that whereas plenty of information about people averting witchcraft and accusing others of witchcraft survives from Mesopotamia, virtually none survives for the practice itself. Obviously, this could be an accident of chance—for example, if curse tablets had not been made largely of lead, we might doubt that magic was practiced in classical Greece to any significant degree; and if the Egyptian climate had not been so kind to papyri, thus preserving numerous extensive, detailed examples of magician's textbooks, we might not believe what accusing Christian authors tell us about the "pagan" practice of magic in late antiquity. We are always at the mercy of our recalcitrant sources and must learn to read through, past, and around them whenever we can.

An especially challenging set of questions in this regard involves gender. In this chapter, I have consistently used male pronouns to refer to Mediterranean magicians. In most cases, this was because the text I quoted or referred to explicitly discussed men—exceptions are the (female) Hurrian physician who recited powerful words over oil used to anoint the "lord of the army," Medea and Circe, the (female) star of Theocritus's poetic love charm, and the witch in Apuleius who accidentally attracted goatskins. But what was the reality—did more men than women really practice magic in the ancient Mediterranean?

Our sources are frustratingly lacunose on this issue; particularly frustrating is that in the Greek and Roman worlds, we tend to hear more about female magicians in literary sources than in working texts—the magical "recipe books" of the papyri, for example, scarcely mention them. This may reflect, as some scholars have suggested, a situation in which women seldom practiced magic but men (who wrote almost all of the literature) nonetheless liked to portray them as doing so—because it expressed their fear of women or because it was titillating (nor are the two mutually exclusive). It may also reflect a situation in which women's magic consisted of actions that were regarded as too trivial or female-centered to record in working texts (spells to protect children, for example). And yet, we know of two real cases in classical Athens in which women were tried on charges of magic, which suggests that even in the real world, their magic could impinge upon the world of men in threatening ways (Versnel 1990: 116–18). Another consideration is that the professional magicians (on whom this essay has focused) were likelier to be male, just as other professionals were, and in Egypt, where the sorts of magic that come to our attention were predominantly the prerogative of temple priests, we should not be surprised to hear little about women in the sources. But there was plenty of "do-it-yourself" magic going on, as well, for which we do not have good records. In this venue, women may have been just as active or even more active than men.

So much for Greece, Rome, and Egypt—but the situation seems to have been different in some other Mediterranean cultures. Royal Anatolian magic involved not only the female physicians mentioned above but other women as well: one king, for example, accuses a rival of hiring female magicians to thwart him (KUB 21.17 1.9–12), and collections of magical lore were centrally compiled in the Hurrian kingdom of Kizzuwatna by female magicians (Haas 1972: 27–29; cf. 37). Witchcraft (i.e., magic deployed for injurious purposes) was more strongly attached to women than men in early Judaism: thus, "most women are witches," said the Babylonian Talmud (tractate *Sanhedrin* 67a). Here again, we must be leery of rabbinic sources because they were created by men and make women look bad—they undoubtedly exaggerate both the degree and the evil nature of women's involvement with magic. Moreover, as Rebecca Lesses shows, there is reason to think that women in Sassanian Babylonia, including some who considered themselves Jewish, were as active as men in magic that had beneficial ends: for instance, they were sometimes involved in the creation of incantation bowls, used the bowls about as often as men, and used them against some of the same problems.

In the end, we cannot answer most of our questions about gender and magic very securely. Moreover, when we do think we have secure answers, fate often confounds us by bringing new evidence to light. After several respected scholars of Greco-Roman magic had concluded that women cast love spells to win men only in literature (i.e., in the male imagination) and that in reality love spells were cast only by men to win women, a new curse tablet from 4th-century BCE Thessaly gave us a splendid example of a woman using magic to separate the man she desired from his wife (Voutiras 1998). Similarly, Robert Daniel and Franco Maltomini (1990: 132–153) provided an undeniable example of a lesbian love charm from 3rd- or 4th-century CE Egypt, which compelled us to look again at a few similar cases that had been swept under the rug.

It may seem that this essay is full of words such as "might," "could," and "although," and phrases such as "tended to"; a reader who is new to this topic may understandably feel frustrated by the paucity of unqualified statements. I have deliberately resisted the temptation to make such statements. For one thing (this should be obvious by now), most scholars of the topic have agreed to disagree—or rather have agreed that our materials make it difficult to reach so firm a state as the word *agreement* implies. All of us have our opinions on what constituted magic in the ancient cultures we study and how magic worked in those cultures, technically, socially, and intellectually. But most of us also know that the evidence we use to support our opinions is too lacunose and its sources are too biased for any opinion to remain unchallenged very long. In other words, beyond a few precepts that are so broad as to be almost useless, there is no current consensus on the topic that I could have presented.

And yet, because this lack of consensus springs from the protean, kaleidoscopic nature of magic in the ancient Mediterranean itself, my choice to reflect it will also, I hope, convey to readers the nature of the topic. If readers leave this essay with as many questions as they had when they began it, I shall not be disappointed—so long as at least some of their questions are new.

Bibliography

Abusch, Tzvi. "The Internalization of Suffering and Illness in Mesopotamia: A Development in Mesopotamian Witchcraft Literature." In *Magic in the Ancient Near East.* Studi epigrafici e linguistici sul Vicino Oriente antico 15. Verona, 1998.

———. *Mesopotamian Witchcraft: Toward a History and Understanding of Babylonian Witchcraft Beliefs and Literature.* Leiden, 2002.

Alexander, Philip S. "Incantations and Books of Magic." In Emil Schürer's *History of the Jewish People in the Age of Jesus Christ,* ed. Geza Vermes, Fergus Millar, and Martin Goodman, vol. 3.1. Edinburgh, 1986.

Daniel, Robert, and Franco Maltomini. *Supplementum magicum.* Abhandlungen der Rheinisch-Westfälischen Akademie der Wissenschaften, Sonderreihe Papyrologica Coloniensia, vols. 16.1 and 16.2. Opladen: Westdeutscher Verlag, 1990 and 1992.

Faraone, Christopher A. "The Agonistic Context of Early Greek Binding Spells." In *Magika Hiera: Ancient Greek Magic and Religion,* ed. Christopher A. Faraone and Dirk Obbink. New York, 1991.

Frankfurter, David T. M. "Narrating Power: The Theory and Practice of the Magical

Historiola in Ritual Spells." In *Ancient Magic and Ritual Power,* ed. Marvin Meyer and Paul Mirecki. Religion in the Graeco-Roman World 129. Leiden, 1995.

———. *Religion in Roman Egypt.* Princeton, 1998.

———. "The Writing of Magic and the Magic of Writing." *Helios* 21.2 (1994): 189–221.

Graf, Fritz. *Magic in the Ancient World.* Tr. Franklin Philip. Cambridge, Mass., 1997 (orig. 1994).

Haas, Volkert. *Magie und Mythen im Reich der Hethiter,* vol. 1: *Vegetationkulte und Pflanzenmagie.* Hamburg, 1972.

Johnston, Sarah Iles. *Restless Dead: Encounters between the Living and the Dead in Ancient Greece.* Berkeley, 1999.

———. "Sacrifice in the Greek Magical Papyri." In *Magic and Ritual in the Ancient World,* ed. Paul Mirecki and Marvin Meyer. Religions in the Graeco-Roman World 141. Leiden, 2002.

Lesses, Rebecca Macy. "Exe(o)rcising Power: Women as Sorceresses, Exorcists, and Demonesses in Babylonian Jewish Society of Late Antiquity." *Journal of the American Academy of Religion* 69.2 (2001): 343–75.

Meyer, Marvin, and Richard Smith, eds. *Ancient Christian Magic: Coptic Texts of Ritual Power.* San Francisco, 1994.

Ritner, Robert Kriech. *The Mechanics of Ancient Egyptian Magical Practice.* Studies in Oriental Civilization 54. Chicago, 1993.

Smith, Morton. *Jesus the Magician.* New York, 1978.

Swartz, Michael D. "Jewish Magic." In *The Cambridge History of Judaism,* vol. 4. Ed. Steven T. Katz. Cambridge, forthcoming.

Tambiah, Stanley. "Form and Meaning of Magical Acts: A Point of View." In *Modes of Thought,* ed. R. Horton and R. Finnegan. London, 1973.

Versnel, Hendrik S. *Inconsistencies in Greek and Roman Religion,* I: *Ter Unus.* Studies in Greek and Roman Religion 6.1. Leiden: Brill, 1990.

Voutiras, E. *Dionysophontos Gamoi: Marital Life and Magic in Fourth-Century Pella.* Amsterdam, 1998.

HISTORIES

Egypt

Jan Assmann and David Frankfurter

Classical period

There is no Egyptian word for "religion," but there is a text that clarifies the Egyptian concept. According to this text, the sun-god and creator, Re, placed the king on earth in order that he might establish *ma'at* (justice/truth/order) and annihilate *isfet* (injustice/lie/disorder) by judging humankind and satisfying the gods (i.e., by giving offerings to the gods and funerary offerings to the dead).

Establishing *ma'at* and annihilating *isfet:* this formula refers to a broad concept of religion, encompassing both cult and culture. Within this broad concept, the text draws a further distinction, setting off cult (satisfying the gods) from justice (judging humankind). This distinction between the spheres of justice and cult has been consciously and emphatically destroyed in biblical monotheism, where justice moves into the center of religion. In Egypt, the question of justice is dealt with not in the context of religion proper, which is concerned with satisfying the gods, but in the comparatively secular context of judging humankind. In the broader frame of establishing *ma'at*, however, justice and morals play a central role, and almost everything that the Bible has to say on these topics is inherited from its ancient Near Eastern and Egyptian neighbors.

At the center of Egyptian religion, however, was cult. The main function of cult was to establish a connection between this world and the otherworld, where not only the gods but also the transfigured spirits of the dead were supposed to live. The basic form of this connection was an exchange of goods. The living served the gods and spirits with offerings and sacrifices and received in return all kinds of support and blessing. The ultimate aim of these offerings, therefore, was not to "feed the gods," but to support this connection, and the cultic barter was only a symbolic expression of contact and communication. Every presentation of offerings, in temples and tombs, was accompanied by a spell stressing its symbolic or sacramental meaning. However, the Egyptian concept of the divine was not restricted to the sphere of the cult. The gods were believed to dwell in the otherworlds (supernal and infernal) and to take only temporary sojourn in cultic representations such as cult images, symbols, sacred animals, trees, and objects. Cult was concerned with establishing and supporting this sojourn, to make the divine descend from heaven into the image, to transfer divine actions from the celestial to the terrestrial realm. During the offering ritual, the god or the spirit was invoked to come from all parts of the world in order to partake of the offering meal; he or she was not supposed to be simply present in the temple or tomb. The gods were believed not to dwell on but only to visit earth, and this visit would irrevocably end if cult were discontinued. Withholding offerings would make the gods not starve but only retreat into their supernal or infernal abodes.

The cult with its rituals, symbols, and recitations formed only one dimension of divine presence. Another dimension was the cosmos as a sphere where the divine manifested itself. According to the Egyptians, the world or cosmos is a process rather than a space, and the idea of order is more a matter of successfully overcoming disorder and destruction than a matter of spatial structure and beautiful arrangement. Virtually all of the gods cooperate in the project of maintaining the world, of keeping the cosmic process going. The core of this process is constituted by what the ancient Egyptians conceived of as the solar circuit, the daily course of the sun across the heavens and through the netherworld. In the eyes of the Egyptians, the success of the cosmic process was far from taken for granted—it was constantly at stake. In the same way as the Mesopotamians, the Chinese, and the Romans, the ancient Egyptians were constantly occupied in watching the sky and in observing all kinds of natural phenomena with the greatest attention. Yet unlike with the Mesopotamians, Chinese, and Romans, the goal of this attention was not divination, that is, finding out the will of the gods and foretelling the future, but to assist the gods in maintaining the world and to accompany divine action with ritual action. Thus, the Egyptians observed what was regular and recurrent in the skies, whereas cultures interested in divination watched for exceptions and deviations. In the context of this task and intellectual preoccupation, the Egyptians accumulated an incredible amount of knowledge, a kind of sacred cosmology.

In the cosmic dimension of divine presence, every major Egyptian deity had a specific cosmic manifestation and played a role in the cosmic process, in the same way as, in the cultic dimension, they had a place on earth in which to exert their terrestrial rulership. In both dimensions, the principle of diversity was irreducibly relevant: the cosmic process resulted from the synergy of a multitude of different powers, and the order and structure of Egypt found its expression in the various towns and cities ruled by deities. All of the major deities are lords or ladies of a town, and all of the major towns or cities are the realms of specific deities. The institution of divine rulership served as a representation of social and political identity. The focus of social and political identification in Egypt was the temple and its lord, a specific deity. Being citizen of a town meant being a member of a festive community, participating in the feasts that were celebrated in the form of processions. The concept of civic allocation was thus invested with religious meaning. It was a kind of covenant, where the religious tasks of the citizen corresponded to the political role of the deity. But the principle of political identity and representation was not limited to the level of villages, towns, and cities. The gods Horus and Seth represented the two parts of Egypt, Lower and Upper Egypt, and later Egypt and the foreign countries. The sun-god Re, later Amun-Re, represented the unified empire. Therefore, the cultic dimension of divine presence can also be called the political dimension. Cult and political identity are simply aspects of one and the same concept of divine presence and communication.

The third dimension of divine presence is constituted by what the Egyptians understood by the term *name*. A name in the Egyptian sense is not just a name but everything that can be said and told of a person. A name is not just an identifier but a description, a linguistic representation of a person's essence. Telling the names of a deity means reciting hymns and eulogies in his or her praise. To the linguistic dimension of divine presence belong Egyptian concepts of sacred language and sacred texts, whose recitation in the appropriate context, according to the ancient Egyptians, has magical power and contributes to the maintenance of the world.

The most important realization of the linguistic dimension of divine presence is myth. Egyptian mythology is centered on three basic myths: the myths of cosmogony, of Osiris, and of the solar circuit. In Egypt, the principle of mythical thinking is the logic of establishing analogies between three discreet realms: cosmos, state, and individual destiny (especially death). Therefore, cosmology, political philosophy, and funerary beliefs may not be separated; all three levels of reality are constantly projected onto each other in Egyptian religious texts. The myth of Osiris is centered on the problem of death; however, it is also the myth of the state, because every king plays the role of Horus, the son and avenger of his predecessor; and it has a cosmological meaning, because it clarifies the relation between heaven, earth, and netherworld. The myth of the solar circuit is basically cosmological; however, it also concerns the state and human destiny (death), because the sun-god is the model of Pharaoh in establishing *ma'at* and the model of the dead in being reborn every morning. The cosmogony is about the origin of the cosmos and of the state; it tells how, after a period of symbiosis, the gods departed to heaven and the state was established in order to organize ways of communication between the now-separated worlds of the gods and the living. Thus, establishing analogies and making the three levels of reality transparent to each other constitutes the basic principle of the linguistic articulation of divine presence. The three dimensions of divine presence correspond surprisingly well to Varro's distinction between three forms of theology: political *(civilis)*, cosmic *(naturalis)*, and poetic *(fabularis)*. Yet this correspondence does not mean that we are dealing here with a universal structure. Mesopotamian and, above all, biblical religion is different in that a fourth dimension, history, becomes more and more prominent. This process has repercussions even in Egypt, and the rather eruptive emergence of history as a fourth dimension of divine presence after the Amarna experience (1320 BCE) changes the structure of Egyptian religion in a profound way. From now on, the gods are believed to intervene in the course not only of history but also of individual biography. This means the rise of personal piety as an attitude of deep confidence in and submission to the will of god.

Another line of religious evolution that led to fundamental changes in the structure of Egyptian religion is the rise of theological discourse, triggered first by the breakdown of the Old Kingdom, when the experience of distress and disorder posed the classical problems of theodicy. The central problem underlying the theological discourse of the New Kingdom is the relationship between God and gods on the one hand and between God and world, or creator and creation, on the other hand. Both of these relations are simply aspects of the same question, because the gods and their constellations and cooperations constitute the world in Egyptian thought. Theogony and cosmogony are the same. According to the cosmogony of Heliopolis, which played the role of a "great tradition," the One (Arum), the personification of preexisting Oneness, creates the world by engendering Shu and Tefnut (air and fire), who engender Geb and Nut (heaven and earth), the parents of the five children of Nut who prolong cosmic reality into the institutions of civilization and human history. This same sequence of generations corresponds also to a succession of rulers: cosmogony appears as cratogony, the emergence and evolution of power. The most important epithet of the highest god in Egypt, the quality that distinguishes the highest god from the other gods, is temporal firstness. To be the first means to be the chief.

With the New Kingdom, the imperialistic politics of the Thutmosid Dynasty brought about a new, universalistic cosmology. The order of creation did not stop at the Egyptian borders but stretched far beyond, comprising many nations with whom Egypt now entered into political relations. This new image of the world immensely enhanced the supremacy of the sun-god within the Egyptian pantheon who, from his original embeddedness in the synergetic process of maintaining the cosmic process, moved more and more into the position of sole creator and preserver vis-à-vis a world inhabited by both humans and gods. Akhenaten's monotheist revolution drew but the logical consequences in eliminating the gods altogether. His god is alone in creating and maintaining the world, producing light and warmth by his radiation and time and development by his motion. The theology of the post-Amarna period readmits the gods into the world, but it also stresses the distance and solitude of the solar creator and maintainer of the world. Now, besides creation, a new model is used to express the God-world or God-gods relationship. This is the Ba concept. Amun-Re comes to be called the "hidden Ba," whose manifestations are either the other gods or the visible cosmos itself. God remains One, relating to the world in a similar way to that in which the Ba relates to the body, an invisible animating principle. This new idea of god is not only a response to Amarna but also the origin of the Hermetic idea of god, *deus mundus,* a god whose body is the world. The Ramesside formula of "The one becoming millions" anticipates Hermetic formulations such as *hen kai pan* (one yet also many), *una quae es omnia* (you who are one and everything), and so on. The Ramesside Ba theology reaches its apex in the Late Period with the cult of the ten Bas in Thebes and El-Hibe. The idea of the world as the incorporation of a soul-like God and of God as a soul animating the world remains central in Egyptian theology even after the New Kingdom and the flourishing of the theological discourse.

BIBL.: J. Assmann, *The Search for God in Ancient Egypt* (trans. D. Lorton; Ithaca, 2001). H. Frankfort, *Ancient Egyptian Religion* (New York, 1948). E. Hornung, *The Conceptions of God in Ancient Egypt: The One and the Many* (trans. J. Baines; Ithaca, 1996). S. Quirke, *Ancient Egyptian Religion* (London, 1992). B. A. Shafer (ed.), *Religion in Ancient Egypt* (London, 1991).

J.A.

Later period

The later period of Egyptian religion, from the Greco-Roman and Coptic eras up to the Muslim conquest, involves a gradual separation and ultimate rupture between traditional Egyptian cults and foreign rulers, with consequences for cults, priestly institutions, religious literature, and popular religion. The stages of transformation can be roughly divided into the Ptolemaic period (305–30 BCE), which saw an infusion of royal patronage and the expansion of the Egyptian religious infrastructure; the early Roman period (30 BCE–early 3rd century CE), which saw the bureaucratization of Egyptian religious institutions for purposes of Roman control and taxation; the later Roman period (mid-3rd–4th century CE), which saw the economic decline of much of the Egyptian religious infrastructure and principal temple centers; and the Coptic period (late 4th–7th century CE), which saw the Christianization of Egyptian religion, involving both the persecution of traditional cults and the expansion of local forms of Egyptian Christianity.

Most of the temples visible today in Egypt—Philae, Karnak, Edfu, Kom Ombo, Kysis, and others—owe their principal expansions to Ptolemaic patronage. Ptolemaic kings styled themselves as Pharaohs according to archaic royal mythology, and they involved numerous priesthoods in the cultivation of this image. Some of this propaganda responded to a series of revolts around Thebes during the 2nd century BCE, which were sponsored and probably led by temple priests (sometimes to support a "native" Pharaoh) and in whose suppression Ptolemaic armies were often engaged. Consequently, the Ptolemaic kings were themselves presented as sons of Re and conquerors of chaos (Rosetta Stone), and they were consistently represented on temple reliefs as pious maintainers of cosmic order and fertility (Philae, Edfu).

Ptolemies also developed new cults at the center, like Sarapis (an anthropomorphic hybrid of the Apis bull and Osiris), and on the periphery, like Mandulis (based on a Nubian god). The influx of Greek language, art, and religious and philosophical ideals affected many domains of Egyptian religion. Temple scriptoria produced mythological tracts and legends in Greek, sometimes with influence from Greek literature. An already script-oriented religion absorbed Greek writing for record keeping, oracle responses, ritual spells, and even the quasi-nativist prophecies of the 2nd century BCE that paradoxically urged the expulsion of Greeks *(Oracle of the Potter)*. Encouraged by a Hellenistic romanticism of Egypt as the origin of culture and of Egyptian priests as consummate philosophers, some priests sought to convey Egyptian ideas in Greek philosophical or theosophical guise and to present their hieroglyphic systems, ritual traditions, and magical procedures as peerless in the Mediterranean world (Manetho; cf. Herodotus 2.2.5–3.1; 2.54.1–2). By the Roman period, the Egyptian wizard—an exoticized image of a lector-priest literate in hieroglyphs—would become a standard of Greek fiction, and Egypt itself would become the land of magic and mystery. Hellenistic artistic ideals influenced both domestic and public representations of gods like Isis, Amun, and Harpocrates (the Horus-child). Such representational styles—in poetry as well as art—contributed to the pantheization of certain Egyptian gods as omnipotent, Mediterranean-wide deities. Isis, for example, is hailed in inscriptions and papyri as the universal goddess, invoked in various lands by names like Aphrodite, Hecate, and Demeter. The particular center of such synthetic, multimedia activities was the new city of Alexandria, but many other cities also became centers of mixing classical and Egyptian cultures (e.g., Panopolis, Oxyrhynchus).

In none of these endeavors was Egyptian religious tradition smothered or replaced by Hellenism. Rather, Egyptian myths, deities, rites, and priestly roles were extended and developed through these various Greek expressions. As much as the god Sarapis, for example, emerged *de novo* in the 4th century BCE, he had clear Egyptian roots and had become an installation in shrines and festival calendars by the early Roman period. As much as new "foreign" gods such as Astarte, Demeter, and the Dioscuri arose as the protectors of immigrant communities, by the early Roman period they had become expressions of native gods such as Isis or Sobek, the crocodile god. Sobek himself, among the most distinctive of Egyptian deities, was the object of multiple different crocodile cults around the Fayyum region, almost all of which had thoroughly incorporated Greek language into every aspect of organization and communication.

The Roman period begins with the immediate consolidation of imperial control over priesthoods and temples. Under Augustus, the temple institutions were organized in a single bureaucracy under an imperial agent, the *Idios Logos,* their financial resources attached exclusively to imperial munificence. The annals of Egyptian religion from this period—predominantly in Greek— thus show a new determination in record keeping: priestly initiation oaths; inventories of temples, their property, and festivals; and other forms of institutional accounting, prepared for Roman supervision. Emperors continue to support Egyptian temples and priesthoods and are celebrated for it in temple reliefs; but the Roman relationship to Egyptian religion carries a distinct ambivalence. Egyptian cults have become a common feature of cities around the Mediterranean world, and Egyptian priests have grown ever more famous as court ritual experts and fictional wizards. Yet fears that such "foreign" cults might subvert political order, and fears of the revolutionary potential of indigenous priesthoods, all lead Roman officials to exert control over priestly affairs on every level: proscribing oracles, for example, in an ill-fated declaration of the late 2nd century CE.

Still, sources for this period show ever-new dimensions of Egyptian religion flourishing: a great variety of oracle shrines, producing both written and mysteriously vocal responses and attracting pilgrims' devotional graffiti; mortuary workshops in which archaic traditions of mummification and burial were extended to include gold masks (as in several oasis necropolises) or portraits of the deceased (as in Fayyum necropolises); and new forms of ancient deities, developed for local or domestic protection, such as Bes, Tutu, and Petbe, enlarging the phalanx of protector-gods that included most prominently Harpocrates-on-the-crocodiles, produced on small stone stelae to ward off dangers.

It is also at this time that the great literary syntheses of Greek and Egyptian theosophy are produced: the Hermetica (revelations of the scribal god Thoth in his Greek guise, Hermes the thrice-great) and the writings of Egyptian priests such as Chaeremon and Iamblichus. These texts articulate in Greek terms the efficacy of ritual utterance and gesture, the power of images and places, the relationship between an incomprehensible Divinity and the gods of traditional devotion, and the moral life of the one seeking communion with Divinity. The intellectual conventicles that produced such literature probably departed from temple scriptoria and took on a life of their own during the 2nd and 3rd centuries, ultimately communicating or even merging with similar scribal groups producing Christian (including gnostic) texts.

At the beginning of the 3rd century, Egyptian temples themselves were thrust officially from imperial patronage onto the diminishing financial resources of local councils; and with the declining economy of the empire over the course of the 3rd century, the infrastructure and institutions of Egyptian religion fell into decline. The sprawling precincts of Memphis, Thebes, and Edfu dwindled and were largely abandoned. Other temples, as at Douch (Kharga Oasis), Abydos, and Deir el-Bahri (Thebes), cultivated oracle cults to maintain some income; while local temples, such as those of Canopus and Menouthis near Alexandria, and peripheral complexes, like that of Isis at Philae, continued to prosper with more circumscribed catchment areas. A literature of apocalyptic decline, rooted in ancient Egyptian imagery of the liminal interregnum period (but now phrased in Greek, Hermetic, and even Christian terms), arose in the 3rd century to express utopian hopes for an eschatological kingship and the reestablishment of gods and proper worship (*Asclepius* 24–27; *Apocalypse of Elijah*). Egyptian papyri and Christian legends both record the impact of religious edicts issued by anxious 3rd-century emperors (Decius, Valerian, Diocletian) in the hope that the general decline of the empire could be averted through mass uniformity in ritual display.

The empire's official embrace of Christianity in the early 4th century touched off a series of edicts (e.g., the Theodosian Code) restricting non-Christian religion that, if not immediately repressive on traditional Egyptian piety, certainly threw some cults further onto their local-support networks. Given the centrality of image processions, shrine devotion, and divination in traditional religious expression, rather than sacrifice as the 4th-century edicts imagined heathen ritual, much active piety fell outside the edicts' scope (and was difficult to police anyway).

Traditional Egyptian religion in the 3rd and 4th centuries consequently underwent a centrifugal shift away from major temple complexes. Papyri, inscriptions, and archeological remains show the persistence of local cults to familiar avatars of Isis, Sobek, Horus, Bes, Tutu, and other deities, as well as regional pilgrimages, festivals, and oracles—all rather circumscribed expressions of communities' religious self-determination. The lives of Christian saints in the 4th through 6th centuries recall "heathen" domestic practices with ancient roots: household shrines, festival lamps, popular devotion to the Nile or a village image. From this evidence we derive less a sense of Egyptian mythology persisting than of the vitality and "place" of ancestral religious practices.

Yet among priests, such as those who collected the many spells preserved in the Greek and Demotic Magical Papyri, older myths were preserved and extended, combined with foreign names, and often directed to new types of "magic" with foreigners in mind—the priest self-styled as a wizard according to Roman expectations. These spells show the preservation of solar myths, imagery of Anubis and Thoth, and stories of the great Egyptian gods alongside Homeric verses and Syrian deities. The early forms of Coptic writing (Egyptian language transcribed in Greek letters) that appear in such texts suggest that the very writing system that Egyptian Christians would eventually appropriate began as a way for ritual experts to fix ritual pronunciation. Other priests—at the Bucheum of Armant or the Isis temple of Philae, for example—devoted themselves to more-traditional shrine duties; and it is in such places that hieroglyphic writing continued to the end of the 4th century. Well into the 4th century, one priesthood maintained an internationally renowned oracle temple of the popular fertility-god Bes at the ancient shrine of Osiris at Abydos, only to be closed when the Christian emperor feared its potential to intervene magically in imperial affairs. Egyptian priestly families remained prominent in the intellectual culture of cities such as Panopolis and Alexandria, producing poetry and philosophy and trying to maintain their priestly traditions in some form in a Christian world.

By the end of the 4th century the violent persecution of Egyptian religious places and practices seems to have reached a pitch, with bishops, monks and their abbots, village gangs, and occasionally (as at late-6th-century Philae) even armies acting to purify the landscape from a demonic heathenism. The destruction of the Sarapeum of Alexandria in 389 CE by Christian mobs and soldiers (under a bishop's direction) may itself have triggered further, local destructive acts by monks around Egypt. Most evidence for the continuation of local cults through the 5th century appears in the legends of Coptic saints, which celebrate these cults' extirpation. The 5th through 7th centuries also see the religious resettlement of Egyptian temples with churches and monasteries. Whether the archaic holiness of these structures is maintained by virtue of these acts of reconsecration or not, the temples' physical importance in the landscape certainly reemerges in Christian institutional guise; and certain graffiti, incised crosses, or image desecration in the temples suggest that the temples were still believed to carry some ambivalent power. Shrines with cults to Coptic saints of often murky historicity proliferate from the 5th century, offering Christians a new sacred landscape and sense of local religious identity through processions, the recitation of martyrs' legends, the magical services of shrine attendants, and even the development of ancient oracular services at these shrines: incubation, written responses, private consultation. In such ways many of the practical elements of Egyptian religion become reformulated in Christian idiom.

Occasionally Egyptian mythological ideas are transmitted past the 4th century as well, as in some Coptic magical texts of the 7th and 8th centuries. Coptic apocryphal texts preserved images of the underworld based on ancient mortuary traditions; and some Coptic martyrologies, read aloud at feast days, depicted a sacred geography based on the martyr's dismembered body that distantly recalled images of Egypt integrated through the body parts of Osiris. But the preservation of non-Christian ideas most publicly in the Coptic period involved Hellenistic rather than Egyptian motifs: the Greek heroes and gods on Coptic textiles, for example.

Over the Ptolemaic, Roman, and Coptic periods, then, we see the swelling and centralization of Egyptian religious institutions; then their decline from economic causes; and finally their persecution—dismantled or scattered—on Christian grounds. The elaborate priestly literary production, temple dramaturgy, and skilled artistic workshops that together supported the complex mythologies of Isis, Horus, Re, Amun, Osiris, and Seth, which we typically equate with Egyptian religion, all fell victim to historical vicissitudes. But the more-practical elements of Egyptian religious tradition—from the gestures at domestic altars to the visits made to oracle sites and even to priests' creative reformulation of ritual traditions—continued in local or regional form well after the official establishment of Christianity; and Coptic Christianity itself maintained many of these elements.

BIBL.: Roger Bagnall, *Egypt in Late Antiquity* (Princeton, 1993). Heike Behlmer, "Ancient Egyptian Survivals in Coptic Literature: An Overview," in *Ancient Egyptian Literature: History and Forms* (ed. Antonio Loprieno; Leiden, 1996), 567–90. Alan K. Bowman, *Egypt after the Pharaohs* (Berkeley, 1986). Françoise Dunand and Christiane Zivie-Coche, *Dieux et hommes en Égypte, 3000 av. J.-C.–395 apr. J.-C.: Anthropologie* religieuse (Paris, 1991). Garth Fowden, *The Egyptian Hermes: An Historical Approach to the Late Pagan Mind* (Cambridge, 1986). David Frankfurter, *Religion in Roman Egypt: Assimilation and Resistance* (Princeton, 1998). P. M. Fraser, *Ptolemaic Alexandria* (2 vols.; Oxford, 1972). Dorothy J. Thompson, *Memphis under the Ptolemies* (Princeton, 1988).

D.F.

Mesopotamia

Paul-Alain Beaulieu

The earliest detailed evidence for organized religious beliefs in the lands of southern Iraq (Sumer and Akkad, later Babylonia) comes from Eridu and Uruk. During the protohistorical period, these two sites, the earliest urban centers of Sumer, grew around cultic compounds that are already clear prototypes of later Mesopotamian temples. Created shortly after the invention of writing, the archaic texts from Uruk (ca. 3300–3100 BCE) shed light on the organization of the cult at the threshold of history. Many of them can be identified as offering lists to various forms of the goddess Inanna, including "Morning Inanna" and "Evening Inanna," the two manifestations of the planet Venus as morning and evening star. The art of the period provides compelling evidence that Uruk was ruled by a charismatic figure who acted as intermediary between the community and the city goddess. This ruler was probably a priest-king, denoted by the Sumerian word EN, which in fact appears several times in the archaic texts from Uruk.

The basic graphic and visual concepts stressing the essential nature of deities as separate from the world of mortals crystallized at a very early date. The divine determinative that precedes names of gods and goddesses in the writing system already appears in the archaic texts from Uruk and is universally used by the beginning of the 3rd millennium. Similarly, the horned headdress, which first appears in the iconography of deities during the Early Dynastic period, becomes the obligatory marker of divine status in the art by the middle of the 3rd millennium. Although Mesopotamian religion was always strongly anthropomorphic, gods could also be represented by an emblematic animal, whether real or imaginary, or a symbol, which could be a standard, a cult object, or even a completely abstract form. Some scholars espousing evolutionist views have claimed that there was a general historical tendency toward anthropomorphism from a more primitive stage of abstract or symbolic representation. The extant documentation, however, clearly indicates that all modes of divine representations existed side by side from earliest times. Indeed, during the

Uruk period purely anthropomorphic representations of Inanna existed along-side symbolic ones, including on the famous Uruk Vase, which depicts the goddess in human form, then with her standard, and possibly even with her emblematic animal, the lion. The preference for one mode of representation or the other in a particular place or period was mainly due to fashion or to the rise of new theological currents. During the Ur III period, for instance, cylinder seals attest to a strong predominance of anthropomorphic representations, while symbols and standards become more common during the ensuing Old Babylonian period and even more so during the late periods.

During the early periods, each town and village worshiped local deities—many of them fertility-goddesses—who ensured the prosperity of the community, while the most important members of the pantheon reigned supreme in the major political and cultural centers, such as the moon-god Nanna-Suen at Ur, the sun-god UTU at Larsa, the mother-goddess Ninhursag in Kesh, and the healing-goddess Nin-Isinna at Isin. The god Enlil of Nippur presided over the entire pantheon like a remote ancestral figure, owing his prominence to the role of his city as religious and cultural capital of Sumer. By the middle of the 3rd millennium, Enlil had clearly overshadowed other gods who filled a similar role, notably the sky-god An, at home in Uruk, and the god of subterranean waters Enki (later also known as Ea), the patron deity of Eridu.

Such a bewildering multiplicity of divine figures needed to be explained and ordered hierarchically. This favored the rise of theological reflection among the literate and priestly classes. The earliest such documents occur in the form of lists of gods from the site of Fara and date to the Early Dynastic I period (ca. 2900–2700 BCE). That contemporary fragments of these same lists were found at Abu Salabikh, Ur, and Uruk proves that they were not ad hoc creations reflecting the local pantheon, but compositions preserving a tradition already common to all Sumer. Their arrangement is either hierarchical or lexical. Both principles occur in the great list from Fara (SF1), which begins with An, Enlil, Inanna, Enki, and six other great gods, followed by a long list of goddesses with names formed with the initial element *nin* (lady, mistress). Lists of gods remained one of the most productive theological genres throughout the entire life span of Mesopotamian civilization. Sumerian hymns from the 3rd and early 2nd millennia are also an important theological source. Prominent in this respect is the collection of Sumerian temple hymns. The standard edition includes forty-two hymns, each of them a miniature theological treatise dedicated to one of the major temples of Sumer and Akkad. Such hymns have distant forerunners at Abu Salabikh.

Many distinctive traits developed by Mesopotamian religion during the early periods lasted until that religion's end: the concept of deities as the real rulers of the community served by a host of priestly attendants, the corresponding view of the temple as a princely residence where the divine rulers hold court, the representation of gods by anthropomorphic statues brought to life by incantations and complex rituals of animation, and the system of food offerings redistributed to the priests and temple personnel after ritual presentation to the gods. Some hymns were still sung in the temples a thousand years after their composition, and administrative documents from temple archives show that many festivals and cultic events occurred at the same time during the calendar year in 2000 BCE as they did in 500 BCE. Although new gods were occasionally introduced and the divine hierarchy reorganized, local deities generally retained the same attributes and survived the passing of centuries. Similarly the overall pantheon preserved its essential characteristics, with political changes being reflected mostly by the rise of new gods.

The most important catalyst for change was the intrusion of the political in the religious sphere. It is highly probable that the earliest rulers of the Sumerian city-states cumulated in their hands both secular and religious power. This type of kingship is represented by the EN, the Uruk priest-king of the archaic period. During the Early Dynastic period, however, a more secular concept of rulership emerged, expressed by the titles ENSI(K) (prince) and LUGAL (king), while the EN-ship and its female equivalents became purely religious offices. The ENSI(K) was basically the temporal ruler of the Sumerian city-state, where the land was viewed as the personal property of the god, the city ruler being only the administrator of those domains. The LUGAL represents a more personal and dictatorial type of leadership and is generally thought to have been at home originally in the north, where according to legend it had descended from heaven to Kish at the beginning of history, after the deluge. With the rise of large territorial states ruled by a LUGAL, such as the Sargonic and Ur III empires of the second half of the 3rd millennium, and the demotion of the ENSI(K) to the rank of city governor, nominations of princesses of the ruling family to high priestly offices in major cities of Sumer and Akkad became a tool of political control that survived well into the Isin-Larsa and Old Babylonian periods. The loss of the priestly function of the ruler and the increasing power wielded by him eventually led to the deification of kings. This was initiated by Naram-Sin of Akkad, was revived later by Shulgi, and then followed by the kings of the Isin-Larsa period until it died out during the First Dynasty of Babylon. The king's divine status was expressed mainly by the prefixing of the divine determinative to his name, the wearing of a horned headdress in art, and the composition of hymns extolling his divine parentage and supernatural powers.

Another important aspect of political intrusion in the religious sphere was the new symbolization of the state in the organization of the pantheon. With the rise of larger states, the gods of the capital, especially its patron deity, were often raised to a higher station reflecting the political prominence of their home. During the Sargonic period, for instance, the goddess Inanna/Ishtar enjoyed great prominence in the empire mainly because of her status as goddess of Akkad, the capital of Sargon and his successors, and this certainly explains why the native tradition attributed to his daughter Enheduanna two Sumerian hymns of great beauty and complexity to that goddess. Later in the Ur III period, the old city god of Ur, Nanna-Suen, was similarly exalted. He became the "firstborn son of Enlil," the head of the pantheon, in order to justify Ur's hegemony over Sumer and Akkad, and the composition of new hymns and myths was encouraged by kings Ur-Nammu and Shulgi to propagate this new theological concept. The most obvious, far-reaching, and lasting case of political intrusion occurred under the First Dynasty of Babylon (1894–1595 BCE), when the city god Marduk, previously a deity of no great importance except locally, was propelled to the summit of the pantheon and given the same powers as the god Enlil, the *Enlilūtu* (Enlil-ship).

Another important aspect of Mesopotamian religion during the early periods is the emergence of a synthesis of Sumerian and Semitic (Akkadian) religion. This process was certainly well under way even before the Sargonic period, when it comes into full view. Some Sumerian deities were syncretized with the Semitic gods who shared attributes with them. This was an easy process for astral and nature deities. In this manner the Sumerian sun-god UTU, worshiped at Larsa, was equated with the Semitic sun-god Shamash of Sippar, and Inanna of Uruk was identified with the Semitic Ishtar, also a Venus goddess worshiped primarily at Akkad. Generally speaking, however, the Semitic Akkadians adopted most of the Sumerian deities without any modification, although they occasionally Akkadianized their names. The Sumerian sky-god An became Anum and was provided with a wife named Antum, but such gods as Ningirsu, Ninurta, Nin-Isinna, Gula, and countless others were adopted as such. Conversely, some purely Semitic deities with no Sumerian equivalents entered the common Mesopotamian pantheon. In this category one may include such minor gods as Ishum, Shullat, and Hanish.

By and large it must be stressed that the basic structure and ideology of Mesopotamian religion was largely Sumerian in origin. As we move northward and westward, on the other hand, Sumerian influence wanes as the Semitic or local component becomes more prominent. One important center was the northern city of Asshur, where the local god of the same name, unknown in the south, was identified as the *numen loci* of the city. Various writings of the city and divine name in Old Assyrian documents indicate that the concepts of a city Asshur and a god Assur were interchangeable, from which it follows that the god Assur was originally the deified city or the location where it was built. In the south the prologue of the Code of Hammurabi sums up the official pantheon of Mesopotamia at the time when the Sumero-Akkadian synthesis has given birth to a distinctive Babylonian culture that will dominate Mesopotamia for the rest of its history. The gods Anu and Enlil have selected Babylon to be the seat of monarchy and "rule the four quarters" and its god Marduk, now promoted to the status of son of Enki/Ea, to lead humankind. Then follows a list of the great cult centers of Hammurabi's kingdom in a theological order which, significantly, still acknowledges Nippur and its god Enlil as preeminent, followed by Eridu and Enki/Ea (the father of Marduk), Babylon and Marduk, Ur and Nanna-Suen, and so on. The local theologies listed in this prologue will last until the late periods, with the important exception of the city of Borsippa, where the god Tutu, a form of Marduk, will be replaced by Nabu in the latter part of the 2nd millennium.

The Kassite kings, who by the middle of the 15th century BCE had unified Babylonia under their rule, appear to have especially favored the cult of the gods of Nippur, the ancient religious and cultural capital of Sumer. The religious buildings of their new capital Dur-Kurigalzu were all consecrated to Enlil and Ninlil, the ruling divine pair of Nippur, and to Ninurta and Gula, their son and daughter-in-law. It has been suggested that the aspect of Enlil as a mountain-god, which is often depicted in the iconography of that period, strongly appealed to the Kassites, who very probably originated from the Zagros Mountains east of Babylonia. With the exception of Suqamuna and Sumaliya, the protectors of their ruling house, the Kassites did little to impose the worship of their own deities.

During the Middle Babylonian period the worship of the personal god reached full maturity. The insistence on the intimate relation between worshiper and god favored the blossoming of a pervasive notion of sin, while the anxiety created by the frequent absence of divine response and support led to a growing awareness of the remoteness of the gods and unfathomableness of their will. These developments are evidenced by the proliferation of prayers in personal names (e.g., Sin-karabi-ishme, The god Sin heard my prayer) and on legends of cylinder seals and the composition of theodicies in which the figure of the pious sufferer appears in the forefront. Transcendental concepts of the divine are also reflected in the increasing popularity of symbolic representation of gods, especially on kudurrus (large polished stones, often used as boundary markers). The Middle Babylonian period witnessed important scholarly activity in the field of religion. Theological thinking is exemplified by the massive list of gods entitled An = Anum. Divination, magic, and medicine are introduced in the canon of scribal schools, while intellectual life becomes gradually dominated by specialists of these disciplines, whose outlook will shape religious expression and thought at the higher level until the end of Mesopotamian civilization.

In the middle of the 12th century, the Kassite Dynasty gave way to the Second Dynasty of Isin, whose rule culminated in the exaltation of Marduk, the city god of Babylon. The rise of Marduk began in the time of the First Dynasty of Babylon, when he was granted the *Enlilūtu* (power of Enlil [i.e., leadership]) over the gods. Under Kassite rule the cult of Marduk grew in importance, partly because of the continued political and cultural centrality of Babylon. The dramatic decline of Nippur during the transition to Isin II—evidenced by archeological surveys of the site—may have materially signaled the end of Enlil's supremacy. It was probably on the return to Babylon of the statue of Marduk—captured during a raid by Isin II monarch Nebuchadnezzar I (1125–1104 BCE) against neighboring Elam—that a theological reform was launched that resulted in the exaltation of Marduk, who assimilated the powers and attributes of Enlil and his son Ninurta. An inscription of King Simbar-Shipak (1025–1008 BCE) in which Marduk and Enlil are treated as the same god, provides evidence for the successful completion of this reform by the turn of the millennium.

By the 13th century, capturing the gods of the enemy had become a component of the process of war and conquest. Concomitantly, the belief developed that the ravages of war were caused by the anger of the gods at their own land,

and that the gods summoned the enemy to destroy it. Spoliation of the statue of the national god symbolized the anger of the deity, abandoning the land and people to their fates. The Epic of Tukulti-Ninurta I (1243–1207 BCE) already articulates this idea, depicting the wrath of all the city gods of Babylonia toward the Kassite King Kashtiliash. The literature describing the return of the statue of Marduk from Elam to Babylon during the reign of Nebuchadnezzar I represents the first full-fledged expression of this theology of divine anger and retribution.

The reign of Nebuchadnezzar I also seems the most probable historical setting for the composition of *Enuma Elish*, the Babylonian epic of creation. This long text describes the battle waged by Marduk against the primeval forces of chaos led by the female monster Tiamat, out of whose dismembered body he creates the world after his victory over her. Marduk is then crowned "king of the gods" by the divine assembly, and the epic ends with a long hymnic passage praising the god under his fifty names. Because of its methodic character, its description of the world from chaotic beginnings (creation was not *ex nihilo*) and its slow evolution through generations of primeval gods, its account of the creation of humankind, its eschatological projection into a future forever ruled by Marduk keeping Tiamat's evil forces in check, and its closing enjoinment to propagate the study of Marduk's names, *Enuma Elish* comes closer to being a systematic creed than any other text from Mesopotamia and thus constitutes a milestone in the history of religious thought.

The first three centuries of the 1st millennium are very poorly documented in Babylonia. One important text from that period is the sun-god tablet of King Nabu-apla-iddina (9th century BCE), which contains the earliest evidence for the *mīs pî* (washing of the mouth) ritual to transubstantiate the divine presence into the cultic image. The last great mythological composition, the myth of Erra and Isum, was created probably in the 8th century by the scholar Kabti-ili-Marduk. It portrays Marduk as an exhausted and powerless ruler, unable to stop the destructions wrought in his realm by the god Erra. The text is a theological reflection on the chaos into which Babylonia had sunk by the first half of the 8th century.

By the 14th century, Assyria had completed its transformation from a city-state into a territorial state, the *māt Aššur* (land of the god Assur). The king then extended his duties from vice-regent of the city Asshur to vice-regent of the land of Assyria, which he was now responsible for enlarging on behalf of the god. Repeated attempts to control Babylonia resulted in an influx of Babylonian learning, including the cult of Marduk, into Assyria. As in Babylonia we also see the emergence of a more transcendental concept of the deity, exemplified in the iconographic record by the altar of Tukulti-Ninurta I, which depicts the king twice in the same scene, standing and then kneeling in prayer before the altar and symbol of the god Nusku.

In spite of increased Babylonian influence, Assyria preserved some of its religious distinctiveness. The god Assur retained his original aspect of a mysterious and distant god—quite unlike that of the ubiquitous and solicitous Babylonian demiurge—which made him closer to the true character of Anu and Enlil, the ancient rulers of the Mesopotamian pantheon now displaced by younger gods. The palace decoration of Assurnasirpal II (883–859 BCE) and his son Shalmaneser III (858–824 BCE) at Kalhu, with its extensive and repetitive depiction of the king in various sacral functions and of the sacred tree tended by protective genii, underlines the distinctive role of the Assyrian ruler as high priest, intermediary between god and humankind, and mystical maintainer of the fertility and cosmic equilibrium of the land of Assyria.

With the gradual transformation of Assyria into a world-state during the Neo-Assyrian period, the need arose for a supreme god reflecting the unity and universalism of the empire. During the reign of Adad-nirari III (810–783 BCE), the god Nabu, who had reached great prominence in Babylonia by the 9th century, seemed to fulfill this function in some circles: "Trust in the god Nabu, do not trust in another god!" proclaims an inscription of the governor of Kalhu dedicated to the king and his mother Shammu-ramat (Semiramis). It is nevertheless the god Assur who ultimately became the focus of this imperial monolatry, which culminated in the theological reforms of Sennacherib (704–681 BCE), who equated Assur with the old primeval god Ansar, the logogram AN.ŠÁR then becoming the official writing of the god until the end of the empire in 612–610 BCE. From the reign of his son Esarhaddon (680–669 BCE) comes the most extensive evidence for the excessive popularity of divination, especially astrology, at the court. The library amassed by his grandson Assurbanipal (668–630 BCE) remains to this day our single most important source of Assyrian and Babylonian religious texts (rituals, incantations, prayers, myths) for the late periods, although other libraries from that period have also yielded rich material (Asshur, Sultantepe, Kalhu).

The Neo-Babylonian Dynasty (626–539 BCE) brought the cults of Marduk and his son Nabu into imperial prominence. The identity of the two gods is proclaimed in the coronation hymn of Nebuchadnezzar II (605–562 BCE), who launched a vast program of restoration of temples and cults all over Babylonia. In Babylon the ziggurat Etemenanki and the temple Esagil, both dedicated to Marduk, were rebuilt on a grand scale to reflect their new status as the navel of a vast empire. With Nabonidus (556–539 BCE) the need for a more impersonal and distant imperial deity arose once again, as earlier in the Neo-Assyrian period, this time focusing on the moon-god Sin. Under his reign the religious antiquarianism that characterizes this entire era reached a new climax, best exemplified by the consecration of his daughter as high priestess of the moon-god at Ur, an institution that had long fallen into oblivion.

The archives of the Eanna of Uruk, the temple of the goddess Ishtar (ca. 8,000 texts), and of the Ebabbar of Sippar, the sanctuary of the sun-god Shamash (ca. 35,000 texts), allow us to study the local pantheons of these Neo-Babylonian cities and the material aspects of their cult. Babylonian religion, emblematized in Judeo-Christian consciousness as mere irrational "idol worship," is there revealed in its daily routine. The main temple is the earthly abode of the city's tutelary gods and their retinue, all represented by anthropomorphic images served by numerous attendants, while secondary gods reside in the small sanctuaries located in the city and its satellite towns. Administrative texts detail the lavish offerings presented to the gods, the magnificence of their attire, the flurry of ritual activities surrounding them. This overwhelming evidence for the predominance of anthropomorphic worship of the gods stands in marked contrast to the iconography of that period—largely known from stamp and cylinder seals—in which deities are almost always depicted by their symbols.

With Babylon's fall to King Cyrus the Great of Persia, a new phase began with Mesopotamia as a mere province in a succession of far-flung multinational empires. Although the native religious institutions no longer benefited from royal patronage, there is ample archeological and epigraphic evidence that during most of the Achaemenid and Seleucid periods the traditional temples with their old gods and rituals remained the focus of civic and religious life and that their priesthood retained its elite status. With the Parthian conquest of Mesopotamia at the end of the 2nd century BCE, however, there is a drastic change. Cuneiform documentation disappears everywhere, except in Babylon, where the traditional religion appears to have survived somewhat longer, and as we reach the beginning of the common era archeological evidence for the abandonment of the old temples can be gathered from many sites. Religion in Mesopotamia then became increasingly syncretistic, a mixture of Assyrian, Babylonian, Persian, Greek, Aramean, and Jewish elements, and when the Sasanian Dynasty took over in the 3rd century CE the old religion was all but extinct. At the beginning of the 6th century CE, the Neoplatonist philosopher Damascius still accurately quotes the genealogy of primeval gods found at the beginning of the Babylonian epic of creation, but this was a final testimony to a now-vanished civilization.

BIBL.: Jeremy Black and Anthony Green, *Gods, Demons, and Symbols of Ancient Mesopotamia: An Illustrated Dictionary* (Austin, 1992). Jean Bottéro, *Religion in Ancient Mesopotamia* (Chicago, 2001). Édouard Dhorme, *Les religions de Babylonie et d'Assyrie* (Paris, 1945). Thorkild Jacobsen, *The Treasures of Darkness: A History of Mesopotamian Religion* (New Haven, 1976). A. Leo Oppenheim, *Ancient Mesopotamia: Portrait of a Dead Civilization* (rev. ed.; Chicago, 1977), chap. 4.

Sety I worships and gazes upon Osiris. Funerary temple of Sety I at Abydos, 19th Dynasty (13th century BCE).

Shrine with Isis and Osiris, who is wrapped and shrouded like a mummy, but with green skin perhaps symbolizing regeneration. Painted on papyrus, from Thebes, 19th Dynasty; Book of the Dead.

Painted figure of the goddess Maat in the tomb of Nefertari (19th Dynasty), Valley of the Queens, Thebes.

Glazed brick relief, one of the 120 lions along the Procession Way leading to the Ishtar Gate, Babylon, 6th century BCE. Louvre.

Silver bull calf, probably an emblem of a Canaanite god, with its pottery shrine, about 1600 BCE. Found at Ashkelon.

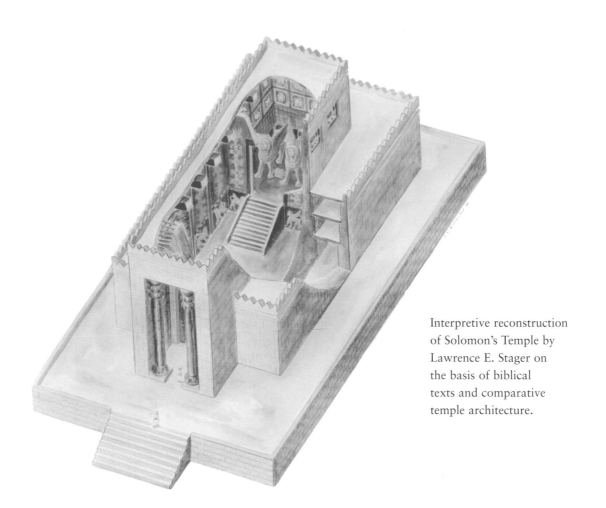

Interpretive reconstruction of Solomon's Temple by Lawrence E. Stager on the basis of biblical texts and comparative temple architecture.

Ezekiel in the Valley of the Bones. Ezekiel stands at right between tombs and body parts; the hand of God is seen reaching down from above. From the synagogue at Dura Europos, Syria.

Mosaic from the synagogue at Hammath-Tiberias with Helios encircled by signs of the zodiac as well as menorahs and the ark of the Torah.

God wearing a cone-shaped crown; Hittite gold pendant from Yozgat, near Bogazköy, Turkey, 17th century BCE. Louvre.

Sphinx gate, entrance to a Hittite fortress, about 1300 BCE. Alaca Höyük, Turkey.

Zoroastrian fire temple, Achaemenid period (end of 5th century BCE), Naqsh-i-Rustam, Iran.

Minoan ritual (left, women bring liquid offerings; right, men bear precious offerings). Panel of a sarcophagus from Haghia Triada, Crete, about 1400 BCE. Iraklion, National Museum.

Dionysus (standing) shakes hands with the enthroned Hades, in the presence of Persephone (standing, center), Hermes (leaning against a column, right), Cerberus (bottom), maenads and a satyr (left), and members of the Theban royal family (right). Red-figure volute krater from Apulia, after 340–330 BCE. Toledo Museum of Art.

Man before an altar, a painted terra-cotta panel (the Campana Panel) from the Etruscan necropolis at Cerveteri, 6th century BCE. Louvre.

Statue of Artemis of Ephesus, Roman copy in black and white marble, 2nd century CE. Museo Archeologico Nazionale, Naples.

Interior of the Etruscan Tomb of the Reliefs, Cerveteri.

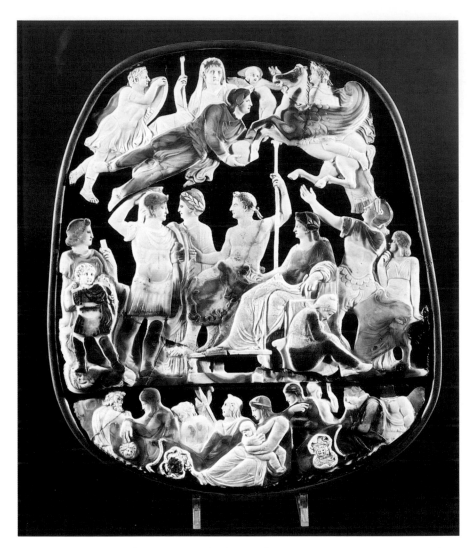

Cameo cut in Rome, about 20 CE. The divinized emperor Augustus rises to join the Roman gods while his wife, Livia: her son, the emperor Tiberius; and other mortals sit below. Bibliothèque Nationale, Paris.

Shrine of household gods: Genius flanked by two Lares. House of Vettii, Pompeii.

Wall painting of Isis ceremonies, from Herculaneum. Museo Archeologico Nazionale, Naples.

The Last Supper depicted in a mosaic at S. Apollinare Nuovo in Ravenna. A 6th-century example of a motif—the meal scene—that is found in the earliest Christian art.

A Good Shepherd in a fresco from the Catacomb of Priscilla,
Rome, 3rd century. The Good Shepherd motif is often found
in pre-Constantinian Christian art; the figure may have been
a representation specifically of Jesus.

Syria and Canaan

David P. Wright

The historical study of the religion of ancient Syria and Canaan (Syro-Canaanite, Syro-Palestinian, Northwest Semitic religion) is made difficult by the lack of documentary and material evidence from which to construct a clear and continuous image of religious ideas and practices. The textual evidence from the first three millennia BCE gives a general idea of the main ideas and their development of Northwest Semitic religion.

The earliest substantial sources pertaining to Syro-Canaanite religion come from finds at the ancient site of Ebla (modern Tell Mardikh), located halfway between the Mediterranean Sea and the Euphrates River in Syria. It was a significant city-state in the 24th century BCE. Although few of the two thousand complete or fragmentary texts discovered there pertain directly to religious matters and although the interpretation of the texts is still in flux, some basic features of Eblaite religion have emerged. About forty deities are mentioned in the tablets. A core of West Semitic deities is observable: Dagan, Hadda (the thunderer or storm-god; later Hadad), El, Belatu (the lady), Ashtar, Suinu (moon-god), UTU (sun-god), Kabkab (star), Kamish (later Chemosh), Malik, Rasap (later Rashpu/Reshep). The four city gates were named after the gods BE, Baal, Rasap, and UTU. The first two are probably to be identified as Dagan and Hadda, respectively, which shows the prominence of these deities.

The texts indicate that Ebla had several temples devoted to various gods that housed the statues of the deities. Some texts speak of the quantity of silver or gold used to make such statues. Animals as well as bread, beer, wine, and oil were offered to the gods. Objects of precious materials were also devoted to the deities. In addition, special feasts for different gods were distributed throughout the year. Some of these celebrations included processions parading the deity's statue. Besides the high liturgy of the temples and feasts, many incantations sought to bind demonic evil and to oppose serpents and scorpions.

Details about Northwest Semitic religion after the time of Ebla are lacking for almost a thousand years. Part of this gap is filled by evidence from the theophoric personal names borne by Amorites. The Amorites were pastoral groups attested at the end of the third and the beginning of the 2nd millennium BCE whose homeland appears to have been northwest of Mari along the middle Euphrates and lower Khabur rivers and in the surrounding steppe areas. While Amorite names cannot be counted on to indicate the specific religious propensity of the bearer, they can in a general way reflect the gods venerated near the time when they appear. The list of gods has resonances with the earlier Eblaite pantheon. The Amorite names from Mari around 1800 BCE, for example, show a frequent appearance of the gods Hadda, El, Dagan, and Lim (also attested earlier at Ebla). Amorite names are also found with Anat, Samas (later Shamash, the sun-god), Rasap, and perhaps Ashtar. The epithet or name Baal also appears in many names. The Ur III Amorite names from a few centuries earlier do not reflect as many West Semitic deities, but there are many with El and a few with Hadda.

Documentation of Northwest Semitic religion is much more abundant in the latter half of the 2nd millennium BCE. The major sources from this time are the texts and material finds from Ugarit (modern Ras Shamra), near the Mediterranean coast in Syria, and from surrounding areas. More than one thousand documents, dating to around the 13th century and written in Ugaritic, the native language of the region, have been unearthed. Because of the quantity of tablets, the breadth of genres, and their antiquity, this is presently the most important single corpus for the study of Northwest Semitic religion.

The main distinction in genres is between the narratives (myths and legends) and texts that describe or prescribe actual ritual practice (incantations, prayers, hymns, votive texts, god lists, festival catalogues, sacrificial lists, ritual prescriptions or descriptions). These two groups provide different kinds of information about Ugaritic religion. The longest narratives are the Baal myth cycle (*KTU* 1.1–6), a series of stories telling of Baal's rise in authority among the gods, and the stories of Aqhat (1.14–16) and Kirta (1.17–19), legends about childless patriarchal figures whom the gods bless with offspring. These stories are valuable for their insight into the context and motivation for various religious activities, such as religious feasting, sacrifice, prayer, temple building, funerary ritual, cursing, blessing, and healing. They explain the relationship between various gods, including conflicts between them, and reflect views about the gods' personalities. These texts also reflect on the nature of life, such as the importance of children, the immortality of the gods, and the mortality of humans. Because the religious practices described in the Aqhat and Kirta texts do not entirely agree with texts that describe actual ritual practice, they may reflect popular customs or customs of earlier times.

The texts pertaining to actual ritual practice reveal other dimensions of Ugaritic religion. The texts listing offerings to various gods and other lists of deities mention many more gods (probably more than one hundred) than do the narrative texts, and they show some variation in the order of the gods from one text to the next. The Sacrifice of Sapan (*CAT* 1.148) is a chief example of a royal sacrificial text. The occasion was one of about twenty "feasts of the king" (*dbú mlk*; cf. *CAT* 1.91). The text is essentially a list of sacrifices. The gods that appear at the head of the list are *ilib* (god-father, perhaps a dynastic deity), El, Dagan, and several Baal deities. Other major deities mentioned include Athirat, Sapan, Kothar, Shapsh, Yarikh, Anat, Rashp, and Yamm.

Other ritual texts are connected with the royal cult. One custom they illuminate is the revering of the dynasty's deceased kings. The kings were thought to live on as the *rapa'ūma*, associated with the underworld. They were incorporated quite fully into myth, ritual, and the standard theology of Ugarit. These dead kings were invoked alongside the main gods of the kingdom. They bring blessings to the nation and its people, and they are given offerings, with the other main gods (*KTU* 1.39, 48, 105, 106). *KTU* 1.108 may be a ritual celebrating the deification of the dead king. The beginning of the text can be read: "Lo! the *rap'u* [singular of *rapa'ūma*], the eternal king, has been established," referring to the dead king. Another text—perhaps a funeral liturgy—appears to treat the descent of the recently deceased king Niqmaddu to the netherworld (1.161). The *rapa'ūma* are invoked, offerings are made, and well-being is proclaimed for the new king and the kingdom.

Sacrifices and festivals were often for the benefit of the community or nation. A rather long text (*KTU* 1.40; cf. 1.84, 121, 122, 54) offers perspectives on sin and atonement (*npy*, sweeping away) for sin. At least two sheep and two donkeys, designated for "justification" *(mšr)*, are offered for the sins of the men and women of Ugarit, the royal couple, and others, no matter what sin they may have committed.

Apart from sacrifice, humans made contact with the deities through prayer. A liturgy for the month *ib'lt* (*KTU* 1.119) prescribes the offering of sacrifices to Baal and other gods over a number of days. At the end it prescribes a prayer when the city is under attack: "O Baal, drive away the strong one from our gates . . . O Baal, we shall consecrate a bull [to you], we shall fulfill a vow. . . . We shall ascend to Baal's sanctuary, we shall walk the paths of Baal's temple." The result is that Baal will hear the prayer and ward off the enemy. The gods spoke to humans in dreams and symbolically through divination, specifically, through features present in animal innards, birth abnormalities, and astrological phenomena. A text giving instructions about curing a sick child may indicate that a cultic official of some sort was responsible for announcing an extended oracle (*KTU* 1.124; cf. 1.104). This curing of a sick child brings to mind other incantations against various evils, such as snakebite, demons, or the Evil Eye (*KTU* 1.100, 169, 96, respectively).

Excavations at Emar, located on the west side of the Euphrates where it takes its northward bend in Syria, have produced about 400 texts pertaining to religious matters and dating between 1340 and 1190 BCE. Most of these were found in a temple supervised by a diviner (^{LÜ}HAL). This diviner apparently was a cultic overseer of the larger region, and cultic practice proceeded rather independently of the monarchy. The documents include four major festival texts. The seven-day *zukru* rite was celebrated on the year's first new moon. It was performed for Emar's chief deity Dagan, whose main center of worship was in the middle Euphrates area. A main feature is a procession in which the god was taken outside the city. He passed between sacred stones anointed with oil and blood. These stones represented deities, constituting a council of the gods, as it were. The text includes a list of Emar's gods, nearly ninety lines long. Another festival is for the installation of the NIN.DINGIR, a priestess, in the temple service of the storm-god. This rite takes nine days and includes rites that transfer the woman from her father's domain to the temple. A third festival, lasting eight days, is for the installation of the *maš'artu* (another priestess) of Ashtart of Battle. Many of the activities take place at night, and the ritual is implicitly concerned with the idea of battle. Finally, many texts deal with *kissu* festivals for various deities. The one for Dagan lasted three days. These apparently are performed to acknowledge and honor the various deities.

There is some evidence that the people at Emar revered their dead ancestors by making offerings to them. This responsibility may be spelled out in legal documents, and a liturgy in the month of Abu may describe some of the offerings made to them. There is no clear evidence, however, that these ancestors were considered gods.

The fragmentary Hittite Elkunirsa myth (Hoffner 1998: 90–92), from the 13th century BCE, likely derives from a West Semitic original. It tells how the goddess Ashertu (= Athirat) asked the storm-god (= Baal) to sleep with her. He refused and told Elkunirsa, the husband of Ashertu. Elkunirsa is a Hittite transliteration of the West Semitic epithet of El, *qōnē'arṣ-* (creator/possessor of the earth) (e.g., *KAI* A iii 18). Baal disgraces her at Elkunirsa's instigation by killing dozens of her children. After a break in the text, Elkunirsa tells Ashertu to take Baal captive, but Anat-Astarte, Baal's sister, warns Baal. Nonetheless, Baal is injured and has to be magically healed and purified.

The religious tradition of the Phoenicians, the Northwest Semitic people whose homeland was on the Lebanon coast, begins to be firmly documented early in the 1st millennium BCE, although its roots go back into the 2nd millennium. Most of the Phoenician sources are dedicatory or building inscriptions that contain little information about religion. Some later non-Phoenician sources (e.g., the Hebrew Bible and classical, Hellenistic, and Christian writers) also contain information on Phoenician religion. The texts from the different cities in the Phoenician homeland reveal that each city had its own pantheon, continuing the tradition of particular gods being associated with particular cities. Two gods, a male and female pair, headed the pantheon of each city. The chief gods of Byblos were Baal-Shamem (perhaps identifiable with earlier Baal/Hadda) and Baalat (Lady of Byblos, perhaps identifiable with Anat) (*KAI* 4–7, 10); the chief gods of Sidon were Eshmun and Astarte (biblical Ashtoreth) (13–14); and the chief gods of Tyre were Melqart (the Tyrian form of Baal) and Astarte (see Esarhaddon's treaty with Tyre; *ANET* 533–34). Later classical tradition identified these with various Greek gods (e.g., Astarte = Aphrodite; Eshmun = Asclepius). Other gods were revered in each of the cities. The texts also reflect the Syro-Canaanite belief in a collectivity or assembly of gods (*KAI* 4). Phoenician religious ideas were carried throughout the

Mediterranean area and are found in Phoenician and Punic (i.e., the Phoenician language tradition of the Carthaginian Empire from the 5th century BCE on) inscriptions on the island and coastal sites.

Religious ideas were part of the royal ideology. A king may be described as legitimate "before the holy gods" (*KAI* 4). The gods make the kings rulers (10). Some kings were also priests (13), and some queens were also priestesses (14). Kings were responsible for building or rebuilding temples (14). Inscriptions on coffins of kings or officials show a concern about proper burial and respect for the dead (1, 10, 13–14, 30). The Tabnit inscription (13) describes opening the king's coffin as "an abomination of Astarte." Curses by the gods are often invoked against one who would open a sarcophagus, remove the body, or efface the accompanying inscription. These curses involve the destruction of one's posterity, not receiving a resting place with the shades (the *rpʾm*, which are either the ghosts of all the dead or of the kings specifically, like the *rapaʾūma* at Ugarit), and not receiving proper burial. They imply a view of the afterlife where the dead are relatively inactive and where this life is the time of activity, reward, and punishment.

The tariffs speak of offerings and festivals. One text (*KAI* 37) lists expenditures for new moon festivals during two different months paid to officials and workers, such as the leader(?) of the new moon festival, masons, doorkeepers, singers, sacrificers, bakers, builders, and others. New moon and full moon festivals are mentioned in *KAI* 43. The 3rd-century BCE Marseilles Tariff (69; cf. 74–75), apparently originally made at Carthage and transported to France as ship ballast, describes animals used in different offerings in the temple of Baal-Saphon, a divine name known from Ugarit.

Many of the inscriptions are found in connection with objects devoted to the gods in fulfillment of a vow, as an offering to induce the god to bless the giver or as part of a building project. These objects include such things as statues of the giver (*KAI* 5–6, 43; Gibson 1982: 29), ornaments (*KAI* 25), maces (38), altars (43), walls (7), and various building structures (10). The gift of a throne to Astarte, flanked by two griffins (17), has been compared to the biblical ark of YHWH, mounted with two cherubim, which was considered a type of throne for that deity.

Child sacrifice was also practiced at times as part of Phoenician and Punic religion, especially at Carthage. Two inscriptions from Malta in the 6th century may be the earliest documentary evidence of the practice (*KAI* 61 A–B). The stelae were set up to Baal-Hammon (who became the chief god at Carthage; his consort was Tanit), the god generally associated with child sacrifice. This god appears to have been native to Phoenicia (*KAI* 24; Gibson 1982: 31) and later brought to Carthage, where he became the chief god (and identified with classical Cronus).

Roughly contemporary with early Phoenician texts are texts that provide data about the religion of the Arameans, the Northwest Semitic people of the area of ancient Syria. These sources are relatively meager, consisting mainly of royal building or dedicatory inscriptions from the 9th and 8th centuries BCE.

The chief deity of the Arameans was Hadad, the "thunderer" or storm-god, who can be identified with Baal (*KAI* 214, 222). Other chief deities included El, Shemesh (the sun-god), and Resheph (214). The inscription of Barhadad (201) found north of Aleppo from about 860 BCE venerates Melqart, a Phoenician deity. The inscription, in fact, follows a Phoenician model. Barhadad would have, nevertheless, officially worshiped Hadad.

The sparse inscriptions reflect the communication between deities and humans. The gods hear a king's prayer (*KAI* 201), and they communicate back to him. The Zakir (or Zakkur) Inscription describes how the king implored and received Baal-Shmayn's help against attacking enemies: "I lifted my hands to Baal-Sh[may]n; Baal-Shmay[n] answered me; Baal-Shmayn [spoke] to me by means of seers [*ḥzyn*] and prophets [*'ddn*]; Baal-Shmayn [said to me]: 'Do not fear, for I have made you [king, and I will stan]d with you, and I will deliver you.'" This presupposes a rather elaborate way of ascertaining the divine will, with prophetic specialists and interpreters.

The texts show the intertwining of theology in royal ideology. The gods are the powers that make people kings and save them from enemies (*KAI* 202, 214). They bless the kings and fulfill their requests (214–17). They call upon kings to perform certain tasks (214). They enforce treaties made by kings (222–24). Aramean religion was taken up by foreigners who came to rule in the area (214–15). The Panammu text inscribed on a statue of Hadad (214) appears to refer to the veneration of dead kings, similar to the veneration of the *rapa'ūma* at Ugarit. It says that the person who sacrifices at the statue of Hadad is to "remember the ghost [*nbš*] of Panammu with [Ha]dad" by saying, "May [the gho]st of Panammu [eat] with you [Hadad], and may the [gh]ost of Panammu dri[nk] with you." Here the dead king receives sustenance along with the chief god.

Although the Aramaic texts say little about sacrifice, the Panammu text says that sacrifice was considered a meal given to the gods. The kings also give concrete objects to the gods. For example, Barhadad gives a statue of himself as a vow offering to Melqart (*KAI* 201). Other ritual practices included the enactment of analogical curses in a treaty ceremony. The Sefire Inscriptions (222–24), partly dependent upon Mesopotamian treaty forms, list hyperbolic descriptive curses to befall one who breaks the treaty stipulations. Then it lists simile curses that indicate that they were performed by the participants. For example, one clause says, "Just as this wax is burned with fire, so shall M[atiel] be burned [with fi]re."

The religion of Israel or the Hebrew Bible is another well-documented religious tradition of the 1st millennium BCE. It is important to realize that, although several cultural influences are discernable in Israelite/biblical religion, it is in the main an outgrowth of and part of Syro-Canaanite religion. The institutions and phenomena of temple, priesthood, sacrifice, sacrificial system, and prophecy are all Northwest Semitic in character. Even monotheistic Israelite monotheism may be seen as having a foundation in West Semitic religious notions, especially that where a city or national group recognized one deity as a chief among others. The Hebrew Bible retains the notion of multiple supernatural beings subordinate to and appearing in council with the chief god (1 Kings 22.19–23; Isa. 6.1–10). The Israelite god YHWH was given the attributes of Northwest Semitic gods and was identified, for example, as El.

Other traditions are less well attested in the 1st millennium. Only two important texts and traditions require mention here. The Mesha Inscription (ca. 850 BCE) is the major source of information about Moabite religion. It may have been written to celebrate the building of a shrine (or high place, *bmt*) to the chief Moabite god Chemosh, known already at Ebla and in the place-name Carchemish. The text describes the ritual slaughter of enemies in battle (*ḥrm*) in dedication to the deity, also a biblical practice. Mesha places "before Chemosh" the "implements of YHWH" that he takes as booty. According to the Bible, Mesha sacrificed his son so that his god would save him from Israelite attack (2 Kings 3.27). Finally, the Mesha Inscription may imply an institutional means of conveying the divine word (prophecy?) when it says that Chemosh spoke to Mesha.

The other text is the difficult and fragmentary inscription from Deir Allah (about 700 BCE, found on the east side of the middle course of the Jordan River), written in a unique Northwest Semitic dialect (with similarities to Aramaic; see Hackett 1980; Levine 2000: 241–75). It tells of a vision of Balaam son of Beor, who was "seer of the gods" (cf. Num. 22–24). The gods visit Balaam at night in council, of whom El is chief. They tell him, and Balaam tells the people, that the gods will punish the land with darkness for the unnatural (i.e., socially inverted) behavior of people and animals. The second part of the text is hard to understand and may be independent of the first. It has been suggested, however, that it may deal with offering a child sacrifice in response to the gods' punishment in the first part of the text.

Syro-Canaanite religion can be best summed up as a belief in a group of deities or supernatural beings that were immanent in the natural world, although generally hidden from human view. Their powers were manifested through natural phenomena and in political and military acts of the rulers or kings whom they chose and supported. The gods and humans related in a master-servant relationship. The gods provided blessing and support to the people, and the people were expected to serve the deities, with various gifts and lavish praise. Offending the deities could anger them and bring catastrophe to humans. In large part, these religious ideas were a metaphorical construction from social and political relationships in the human world. This tradition is the heritage of modern Judaism and Christianity, whose theologies today continue to reflect aspects of Syro-Canaanite religion.

BIBL.: Mark W. Chavalas (ed.), *Emar: The History, Religion, and Culture of a Syrian Town in the Late Bronze Age* (Bethesda, Md.: CDL, 1996). J. Andrew Dearman (ed.), *Studies in the Mesha Inscription and Moab* (Society of Biblical Literature Archaeology and Biblical Studies 2; Atlanta: Scholars Press/ASOR, 1989). Daniel E. Fleming, *Time at Emar: The Cultic Calendar and the Rituals from the Diviner's House*

(Mesopotamian Civilizations 11; Winona Lake, Ind.: Eisenbrauns, 2000). Jonas Greenfield, "Aspects of Aramean Religion," in *Ancient Israelite Religion* (ed. Patrick D. Miller Jr., Paul D. Hanson, and S. Dean McBride; Philadelphia: Fortress, 1987), 67–78. Jo Ann Hackett, *Balaam Text from Deir 'Alla* (Harvard Semitic Monographs 31; Chico, Calif.: Scholars Press, 1980). Baruch Levine, *Numbers 21–36* (Anchor Bible 4A; New York: Doubleday, 2000). Glenn E. Markoe, *Phoenicians* (Peoples of the Past; Berkeley: University of California Press, 2000). Gregorio del Olmo Lete, *Canaanite Religion according to the Liturgical Texts of Ugarit* (trans. Wilfred G. E. Watson; Bethesda, Md.: CDL, 1999). Robert R. Stieglitz, "Ebla and the Gods of Canaan," in *Eblaitica: Essays on the Ebla Archives and Eblaite Language* (ed. Cyrus H. Gordon and Gary A. Rendsburg; Winona Lake, Ind.: Eisenbrauns, 1990), 2.79–89.

Israel

John J. Collins

The religion of ancient Israel is known primarily from the Hebrew Bible, but archeological discoveries, as well as critical examination of the biblical text, suggest a different history of its development.

The biblical account

According to the Bible, Abraham came from Mesopotamia at some time in the 2nd millennium BCE and lived a seminomadic life in the land later known as Israel. He built altars in various places and worshiped the god El in various manifestations. In the fourth generation, his descendants went down to Egypt and were enslaved there, but escaped miraculously in the exodus under the leadership of Moses. Moses had already encountered the god of his forefathers on a mountain in Midian, south of Israel, under a new name, YHWH. In a revelation at Mount Sinai, this god gave Moses a code of laws that became the basis of a covenant. Israel was obligated to serve YHWH alone and to obey strict ethical and ritual commandments. After the death of Moses, the Israelites invaded the land of Israel and slaughtered its Canaanite inhabitants. With the rise of a monarchy (about 1000 BCE) the Mosaic religion was contaminated with customs and cults from the surrounding peoples. When the kingdom divided in two after the death of King Solomon, pagan influence was especially strong in the northern kingdom (Israel). Various prophets railed against the worship of deities other than YHWH. After the northern kingdom was destroyed by the Assyrians (722 BCE), the southern kingdom of Judah underwent a reform in the reign of King Josiah (621 BCE) and restored the observance of the law of Moses. This kingdom was brought to an end by the Babylonians in 586 BCE, and large numbers were deported to Babylon. Some fifty years later, however, the exiles were allowed to return and restore the religion of Moses in Judah.

Critical reconstruction

The consensus of archeologists at the beginning of the 21st century is that the early Israelites evolved within the land and culture of Canaan. There is no archeological evidence that they came from either Mesopotamia or Egypt. If the story of the exodus has a historical basis, it can account for only a small segment of the Israelite population. The god El, worshiped by Abraham and later identified with YHWH, was the high god of the Canaanite pantheon. It is clear from the Bible that many Israelites worshiped the Canaanite god Baal, who was YHWH's archrival. The theophanies of YHWH in the Bible (e.g., on Mount Sinai) are described in language that is very similar to descriptions of Baal in the Ugaritic texts. The biblical insistence that Israel serve only YHWH is highly unusual in the ancient world. Some scholars have supposed that it was influenced by the example of the 14th-century Egyptian pharaoh Akhenaten, who tried to suppress the worship of deities other than the sun-god Aten. There are some points of affinity between YHWH and Aten in the Bible, most notably in Ps. 104, which has many parallels to the Egyptian Hymn to Aten. But solar imagery is relatively rare in the Bible. YHWH is far more often depicted as a storm-god, in accordance with Canaanite imagery.

The earliest depictions of YHWH in the Hebrew Bible associate him with the region of Midian south of Israel. It may be that his cult was brought northward to Israel by people who had escaped slavery in Egypt, or it may have been spread by Midianite traders. In Israel, however, YHWH was no longer worshiped primarily as a storm-god, but as the god who brought the people Israel into existence. In northern Israel, his role was celebrated chiefly in connection with the exodus from Egypt. In contrast, the exodus became central to the Jerusalem cult only in the reform of Josiah in the 7th century BCE. The Jerusalem cult centered on the kingship of YHWH, which was reflected on earth in the rule of the Davidic Dynasty. YHWH had promised David that one of his sons would always sit on the throne in Jerusalem (2 Sam. 7). The Jerusalem temple was regarded as "the holy habitation of the Most High" (Ps. 46.4 [= 46.5 Hebrew]). The presence of YHWH in his temple ensured the protection of the city.

One of the distinctive features of Israelite religion in the biblical account is the absence of goddess worship. It now appears, however, that the goddess Asherah was worshiped widely, both in Israel and in Judah. An inscription from the 8th century BCE in a tomb at Khirbet el-Qom, near Hebron, south of Jerusalem, reads, "May Uriyahu be blessed by YHWH, from his enemies he has saved him by his Asherah." Another inscription from Kuntillet Ajrud, a stopover for caravans in the Sinai desert, has a blessing formula, ending with the words "by YHWH of Samaria and his Asherah." (Samaria was the capital of the northern kingdom of Israel.) Some scholars deny that Asherah is the name of a goddess in these inscriptions, since the possessive pronoun is not usually used with a proper name. They suggest that the reference is to a wooden image of some kind, a pole or tree, that is mentioned some forty times in the Hebrew Bible. But the wooden image was a symbol of the goddess, and so the inscriptions testify to the worship of Asherah in any case. Moreover, numerous figurines of a nude female figure, presumably a fertility-goddess, have been found by archeologists all over Israel and Judah. We also know that a goddess called Anatyahu (YHWH's Anat) was worshiped by a Jewish community in Elephantine in southern Egypt in the 5th century BCE. The Bible records that "the queen of heaven" was worshiped in Judah at the time of the Babylonian crisis in the early 6th century BCE (Jer. 7.18; 44.18).

The Bible does not deny that the people of Israel and Judah worshiped deities other than YHWH, including goddesses. It represents that worship, however, as violation of a covenant that had been formulated by Moses at the beginning of Israel's history. Scholars are divided, however, as to the antiquity of the Mosaic covenant. It finds its clearest expression in the Book of Deuteronomy, which was formulated at the time of King Josiah's reform in the late 7th century BCE. The 8th-century prophets (Amos, Hosea) presuppose that the exodus was being celebrated in northern Israel. The prophets clearly assume that the delivery from Egypt entailed obligations for the Israelites, but it is clear that most people did not share that view. Whether the prophets based their preaching on ancient traditions about a covenant or contributed to the development of the covenant idea is hard to decide. In any case, it is clear that during the period of the two kingdoms (approximately 922–722 BCE) only a small minority of Israelites restricted their worship to YHWH alone.

The phenomenon of prophecy was known throughout the ancient Near East, but the corpus of biblical prophecy has no parallel in the ancient world. There were hundreds of prophets in Israel and Judah at any given time. Most of these lent their support to the policies of the kings and to popular views. The prophets whose oracles are preserved in the Bible are exceptional. Not only do they flout popular opinion by railing against the worship of deities other than YHWH, but they also hold both king and people accountable to a strict moral standard. They are particularly outspoken on the subject of social justice and the abuse of the poor. They are also scathing on what they perceive as the abuse of cultic worship. For most people, the worship of a god was expressed through prayer and the offering of sacrifices. The more valuable the offering, the greater the devotion of the worshiper was assumed to be. Human sacrifice was practiced on occasion, even by kings. The prophets argued that all such gestures were empty if they did not lead to the practice of justice. "I hate, I despise your feasts," said Amos (5.21). "For I desire steadfast love and not sacrifice," said Hosea (6.6), "the knowledge of God, rather than burnt offerings." It is not clear whether these prophets thought that there should be no sacrificial cult. Such a view would have been extraordinary in the ancient world. But at least they thought that the cult as practiced was counterproductive. It gave people illusory confidence that they were serving God when in fact they were not.

Deuteronomic reform

The religion of Israel was transformed by the reform of King Josiah in 621 BCE (2 Kings 22–23). The central element in this reform was the centralization of the cult of YHWH. Henceforth no sacrifices were to be offered outside the Jerusalem temple. Josiah's troops tore down other altars that existed around the country. The worship of Canaanite deities (Baal, Asherah) was suppressed, and the place where human sacrifices were offered was destroyed. But even legitimate offerings to YHWH were no longer allowed outside Jerusalem. This reform was authorized by a "book of the law" allegedly found in the Jerusalem temple. This book evidently corresponded to some form of the Book of Deuteronomy. (See especially Deut. 12, which demands that sacrifice be restricted to one site, which YHWH would choose.) While this book purported to contain the laws of Moses, its formulation is influenced by the language and concepts of Assyrian treaties of the 7th century BCE, and it cannot have been composed before that time.

Josiah's reform laid the basis for great changes in the worship of YHWH. If sacrifice could be offered only in Jerusalem, then people who lived at a distance from the city could make offerings only on special occasions. The Jerusalem temple retained its importance, although Deuteronomic theology downplayed the presence of YHWH by saying that he made *his name* to dwell there. Since Jerusalem was now the only place of cultic worship, the temple was arguably more important than ever. New importance, however, was attached to "the book of the law." In earlier times, law (Torah) was taught orally by priests or was passed on by judges and elders in the gates of the cities. Now it was written in a book. Consequently, scribes became very important. These were the people who could read and write and who controlled what was actually contained in the book. Modern scholars hold that the book of the law was expanded several times in the century after Josiah's reforms. Even in antiquity, however, people were aware that scribes tampered with sacred writings. Less than a generation after Josiah's reform, the prophet Jeremiah complained bitterly: "How can you say, 'We are wise, and the law of the LORD is with us'? But, behold, the false pen of the scribes has made it into a lie" (Jer. 8.8).

Josiah's reforms were not immediately successful. He himself met an early death at the hands of the Egyptians in 609 BCE. The prophets Jeremiah and Ezekiel claimed that worship of other deities was widespread during the Babylonian crisis at the beginning of the 6th century. But the long-term impact of the reforms was ensured by the Babylonian exile. The exiles could not take their temple to Babylon, but they could take the book of the law. From this time forward, large numbers of people of Judean descent lived outside their native land. (This phenomenon is called the Diaspora.) Consequently Judaism developed as a religion that was independent of its geographical location. This development was greatly facilitated by the book of the law. Eventually, the synagogue (a house of prayer and study) and other community events would replace the temple as the focus of the religious life of most Jews. This development would not be complete for several centuries, but its root was already present in the Babylonian exile.

Second Temple period

The Jerusalem temple was rebuilt approximately fifty years after its destruction. Life and religion in the period of the Second Temple, however, were different from what they had been before.

There was no longer a king in Jerusalem. Immediately after the restoration, authority was shared by a governor and the high priest. Later, the high priest was de facto ruler under the foreign overlord. While the high priests were often quite worldly, their prominence guaranteed that the temple cult was a focal point of Jewish religious life.

The concept of a normative "book of the law" had been introduced by Josiah. During the exile, or in the following century, this Torah was expanded to include the foundational traditions about the patriarchs and the exodus and also to incorporate extensive priestly traditions. The priestly code, typified by the Book of Leviticus, was concerned with ritual matters, such as regulations for sacrifices, and also with issues of purity. Many of these laws may have been quite old, but they became much more prominent in the Second Temple period. Matters that had primarily concerned priests at an earlier time were now deemed to be binding on all Jews. After the Babylonian exile, some distinctive (though not all unique) observances came increasingly to define Judaism. These included the observance of the sabbath, the circumcision of male children, dietary laws that forbade the eating of pork among other things, and the prohibition of marriage with non-Jews (Gentiles).

The impact of the priestly legislation is seen most clearly in the reform of Ezra, which should probably be dated to 458 BCE. Ezra was authorized by the Persian king to implement the law of "the God of heaven" in Jerusalem (Ezra 1.2), in accordance with a Persian policy of codifying local laws and enforcing them. (Ezra is sometimes regarded as the final editor of the Torah or Pentateuch, but this is uncertain.) He was horrified to discover that Jewish men, descendants of the exiles, had married women from outside the community, so that "the holy race has mixed itself with the peoples of the lands" (9.2). Ezra insisted that they divorce the foreign women and send them away, with their children. Underlying this action was the concern for the preservation of a pure and distinct community, which could be eroded by assimilation to the neighboring peoples. It was by such means that Judaism preserved its identity, while neighboring peoples (Moabites, Edomites, etc.) gradually disappeared from history.

Not all Judeans conformed to Ezra's strict interpretation of the Torah. Other writings of the Second Temple period (Nehemiah, Malachi) complain of lax observance and widespread abuses. Ezra represents one tendency in Second Temple Judaism that would become increasingly prominent in the Hellenistic period. But there was considerable diversity in Judaism throughout this period.

One source of diversity lay in different responses to neighboring cultures. After the conquests of Alexander the Great, Greek culture exercised a great fascination for many people in the Near East. In the 2nd century BCE, some people in Jerusalem set about promoting Greek culture in Jerusalem, with a view to breaking down the separation of Jew and Gentile. According to 2 Maccabees, this led to neglect of the temple cult, and some people even went so far as to disguise the marks of their circumcision. The motives of the reformers were not entirely idealistic. The leaders, Jason and Menelaus, outbid each other for the high priesthood and eventually engaged in civil war. At that point the king, Antiochus IV Epiphanes, intervened and attempted to suppress by force the observance of the traditional law. The religious persecution that resulted was a rare phenomenon in antiquity, and there is no consensus as to the king's motivation. The persecution led to the Maccabean revolt, which resulted in the establishment of a native Jewish kingship under the Hasmonean Dynasty, which lasted for a century. The Hasmonean kings also acted as high priests, despite severe criticism from some parties.

The conflict in the Maccabean era is often depicted as a clash between Judaism and Hellenism, as if Hellenistic customs were incompatible with Jewish religion. This is a misconception. The revolt was not provoked by the introduction of Greek customs (typified by the building of a gymnasium) but by the persecution of people who observed the Torah by having their children circumcised and refusing to eat pork. The Hasmoneans embraced Greek customs in many ways, even while forcing some conquered people to be circumcised. Moreover, while the Maccabees fought to defend the right of Jews to observe their traditional laws, they themselves were willing to make an exception to the law, by fighting on the sabbath. They were not, then, strict purists in the matter of legal observance.

After the Maccabean revolt, however, we see the rise of sectarian movements devoted to the strict observance of the Torah. The most influential of these were the Pharisees, who attached great importance to oral tradition, which specified how the law should be interpreted. The name Pharisee means "separated" and reflects their tendency to eat apart from less-observant Jews. A still-stricter form of Judaism is found in the Dead Sea Scrolls from Qumran, in writings that are usually attributed to the Essenes. These people went further than the Pharisees in separating themselves from the rest of Judaism, and they appear to have been bitter enemies of the Pharisees, although they shared many of the same concerns. Many of the reasons that led to the separation of the Essenes from the rest of Judaism had to do with purity, but they also seem to have had a different calendar, which made participation in the temple cult impossible.

Not all Jews of this era were preoccupied with purity, however. The Sadducees rejected the oral Torah, and with it the stricter interpretations of the Pharisees, and continued to observe a more-traditional form of Judaism, centered on the temple cult. Jews in the Diaspora, especially in Egypt, paid remarkably little attention to purity issues, if we may judge by the writings that have survived. These writings enter into an extensive dialogue with Greek traditions and sometimes present Judaism as a philosophical school, analogous to the Stoics or the Platonists (so especially Philo of Alexandria, in the 1st century CE). To a great degree, they emphasize the common ground shared by Jews and Gentiles, but there remain some characteristic positions that set Jews apart. Most fundamental of these is the rejection of idolatry and the insistence that only the one God should be worshiped. Jewish authors typically inveigh against homosexuality, which was widespread in the Hellenistic world. Only rarely, however, do they mention the Jewish dietary laws, and when they do they provide an allegorical interpretation to suggest that the laws are really about the practice of virtue. We know from Philo that some Jews thought it sufficient to pursue the allegorical meaning of these laws. Philo himself insisted that they should also be observed in their literal sense. These writings, however, may reflect a rather rarified, intellectual, stratum of Jewish society. Greek and Latin authors who comment on Judaism typically emphasize its distinctive aspects: circumcision, sabbath observance, the dietary laws. It is likely, then, that most Jews continued to observe the traditional practices, despite the attempts of people such as Philo to reinterpret the religion in philosophical terms.

One other aspect of Second Temple Judaism should be noted: the development of apocalypticism. The apocalyptic writings first appear in the Hellenistic period, especially around the time of the Maccabean revolt. They might be described as prophecy in a new key. They are not attributed to their actual authors, but to ancient figures such as Enoch and Daniel, who allegedly received revelations in visions or in the course of guided tours of otherworldly regions. The revelations include many mysteries of the heavenly world, but also concern the end of history and the judgment of the dead.

The apocalyptic writings are important for several reasons. It is here that we first encounter a clear belief in the judgment of the individual dead in Jewish tradition. (Another form of this belief developed separately a little later in the Greek-speaking Diaspora, in connection with the philosophical idea of the immortality of the soul.) The idea that the end of history can be predicted had long-lasting and fateful consequences in Western history and gave rise to numerous millenarian movements. Apocalyptic expectations played a major role in the development of early Christianity. In the context of Second Temple Judaism, apocalyptic writings were often associated with sectarian movements, which claimed to have a special revelation, above and beyond the Torah of Moses. The community of the Dead Sea Scrolls (the Essenes) has often been called an apocalyptic community, with considerable justification, as it too claimed to have special revelations, which concerned both the heavenly world and the end of history.

Rabbinic Judaism

Second Temple Judaism came to a disastrous end in the late 1st and early 2nd centuries CE in the course of three revolts against Roman rule. The first, in 66–70 CE, ended in the destruction of the Jerusalem temple, the great unifying symbol of Judaism, which has never been rebuilt. The second, in the years 115–18 CE, took place in Egypt and ended in the virtual annihilation of the Jewish community there. The third, in 132–35 CE, led by Bar Kochba, whom some people took for a messiah, was something of an aftershock. Any hopes that Jews might have had of regaining their independence had been dashed decisively in the earlier revolts.

The survival of Judaism as a religious way of life was due primarily to groups of rabbis in Galilee and Babylonia who devoted themselves to the study and elaboration of the scriptures. They accepted a limited canon of writings, which we now know as the Hebrew Bible. (This canon may have been held by the Pharisees before 70 CE, but the first references to a fixed number of writings come from the last decade of the 1st century CE.) The rabbinic canon included no apocalyptic writings except the Book of Daniel, although some others, such as the books of Enoch and Jubilees, appear to have enjoyed authority with the Dead Sea sect. Neither did the rabbis preserve numerous writings that survived in Greek and Latin translations and are now found in the Apocrypha, although some, such as 1 Maccabees and the Book of Ben Sira, were originally composed in Hebrew. Much of the religious diversity that characterized Second Temple Judaism was lost and survived only in translations preserved by Christians or in the scrolls hidden in caves by the Dead Sea.

The deliberations of the rabbis were eventually codified in the Mishnah (late 2nd century CE) and in the Babylonian and Jerusalem Talmuds, some centuries later. These are primarily legal expositions of the Torah, but they are not legalistic in the narrow sense. They preserve the debates among the rabbis and often include dissenting opinions. The kind of religion they represent has been well described as "covenantal nomism": the law is understood in the context of the whole relationship between God and Israel, not just as a measuring stick for individual performance. While rabbinic Judaism always has its starting point in the Torah, there is plenty of room for imagination and for the preservation of tradition in the biblical commentaries or midrashim, compiled between the 4th and 12th centuries CE. Even the mythological traditions associated with apocalyptic literature survived and reappear centuries later in the midrashim and in the mystical literature (Hekhalot). The main achievement of rabbinic Judaism, however, was to construct a body of commentary on the Torah that defined Judaism as a way of life that has endured down to the present day.

BIBL.: R. Albertz, *A History of Israelite Religion in the Old Testament Period* (2 vols.; Louisville: Westminster, 1994). F. M. Cross, *Canaanite Myth and Hebrew Epic* (Cambridge: Harvard University Press, 1973). P. D. Miller, *The Religion of Ancient Israel* (Louisville: Westminster John Knox, 2000). E. P. Sanders, *Judaism: Practice and Belief, 63 BCE–66 CE* (Philadelphia: Trinity, 1992).

Anatolia: Hittites

David P. Wright

*H*ittite religion is a blend of diverse cultural streams. While it includes features from the immigrant Indo-European peoples linguistically attested by the Hittite language, its main foundation consists of Hattian traditions, that is, of the people living in central Anatolia prior to the arrival of the Indo-Europeans. Furthermore, over time, it adopted beliefs and practices from Hurrian (the people of north Mesopotamia and Syria) as well as Akkado-Sumerian and Syrian religion. This amalgam is richly attested in the thousands of documents found at Bogazköy, Turkey, the site of Hattusha, the ancient Hittite capital. A large percentage of the six hundred plus individual works discovered pertain directly or indirectly to religious matters. The relevant genres include myths, hymns, prayers, festival prescriptions, rituals, divination texts, treaties, cultic inventories, and other administrative texts. Most of the texts date to the latest period of Hittite history (the Hittite Empire or New Kingdom, ca. 1350–1200 BCE), though there are many texts from the earlier periods (the so-called Middle Kingdom, ca. 1400–1350; and the Old Kingdom, ca. 1650–1400). This allows scholars to determine with some confidence the development of religious ideas and institutions. The textual evidence is complemented by archeological data, including the remains of temples, pictorial reliefs (especially at the Yazılıkaya shrine), seals, divine statues and symbols, and cult objects.

The Hittite pantheon grew in complexity over time, owing to the contributions from various cultural traditions. The Hittites were aware of the ethnic origin of their deities and provided them at times with worship in their native languages (Hattic, Hurrian, Luwian, Palaic, and Akkadian). The Hattian basis of the religious system is seen in the Old Hittite pantheon, which retained many Hattian deities. These include a storm-god (Taru), a sun-goddess (the "Sun-goddess of Arinna," later identified as Wurusemu), a sun-god (Estan), Inar (Hittite Inara), Telipinu (a vegetation-god), Halmasuit (a throne-goddess), Wurunkatte (a war-god), plus many other, lesser deities. The storm-god (called the Storm-god of Hatti) and the sun-goddess of Arinna presided as a divine pair over the pantheon. The prominence of a sun-goddess may be partly a reflection of a long-standing Anatolian tradition of a female fertility-goddess or mother-goddess, which is attested four millennia earlier at Çatal Höyük (south central Anatolia) and in the 1st millennium in Phrygia and Lycia. One early Hittite god was Sius, god of heaven and light, a term later used as the general Hittite word for god. This is cognate with Indo-European *diēu-s,* which is found in the Greek word *Zeus* and Latin *deus* (god).

The Hittite pantheon grew by the addition of Hurrian as well as Mesopotamian deities (sometimes in Hurrian guise), especially starting around 1400 BCE (the time of Tudkhaliya II and his wife Nikkalmati, whose name is Hurrian) and mainly as a result of the campaigns of Shuppiluliuma I (ca. 1344–1322) into southern lands under Hurrian influence, including Syria. The main imported Hurrian gods included Teshub (the chief storm-god), Hepat (consort of Teshub), Kumarbi (a grain and fertility deity, also associated with the underworld), Sauska (a Hurrian Ishtar), and Simegi (sun-god). Hurrianized Mesopotamian gods who entered the pantheon include Ea, Damkina, Anu, and Enlil. In many cases borrowing was syncretistic. For example, Teshub was equated with the Storm-god of Hatti and Hepat with the sun-goddess of Arinna. Pudukhepa, wife of Hattushili III (ca. 1267–1237) and a priestess from the Hurrian-influenced land of Kizzuwatna, south of the Hittite homeland, explicitly makes the latter identification at the beginning of a prayer: "O Sun-goddess of Arinna, you are queen of all the lands. In the land of Hatti you go by the name of the Sun-goddess of Arinna, but in the land which you made cedar, you go by the name Hepat" (*CTH* 384; KUB 21.27 1.3–6; cf. *ANET* 393).

Treaties from the time of Shuppiluliuma I onward provide the most extensive list of deities and reflect a tendency toward theological systematization. The treaties show a fixed order in the deities, starting with the sun-god of heaven and the Sun-goddess of Arinna. These are followed by various storm-gods of various cult centers (e.g., Hattusha, Nerik, Samuha), followed in turn by various other groups of gods, including Babylonian gods, local deities, netherworld deities, and natural phenomena (mountains, rivers, springs). Despite the move toward a systematic listing of the gods, it was not complete. Some significant deities are missing, including the chief Storm-god of Hatti, whom one might expect to appear at the top of the list in association with the sun-goddess of Arinna. The inclusion of local pantheons in such lists shows that their maintenance was partly responsible for the multiplication of the Hittite gods. From about this time in Hittite history we begin to see the concept of "the thousand gods of Hatti," an indication of the compound nature of the pantheon (the actual number of known divine names is just over six hundred). The complexity of the Hittite pantheon at this period can be seen in the Prayer of Muwattalli II (ca. 1295–1272; *CTH* 381; cf. Singer 1996), which contains the longest list of deities in any single text (140 gods). Further systematization of the pantheon came with the development of male and female series *(kalutis),* mainly employed in the distribution of offerings. This bifurcated series is visually attested in the parade of deities carved into rock walls of the main chamber of the Yazılıkaya shrine. The reliefs date from the time of Tudkhaliya IV (ca. 1227–1209) and reflect the highly Hurrianized form of Hittite religion. The female gods are led by Hepat, and the male gods by Teshub. These two chief deities meet face to face.

Just as the pantheon derives in large part from Hattian and Hurrian sources, so too Hittite myths mainly derive from these two cultural sources, though there is a handful of myths with Hittite origins (the Tale of Kanes and Zalpa and the Tale of Appu). Both Hattian and Hurrian myths are, in general, concerned with negative and positive effects of deities on the cosmos. But they otherwise have distinct characteristics. The Hattian myths are generally simple and less artistic than the Hurrian myths, and they have connections with ritual performances or festivals. These include the Illuyanka myth, which is connected with the spring *purulli* festival. One version of this story tells how Inara, with the help of a human named Hupasiya, defeats a serpent who had defeated the storm-god. Many other myths deal with the disappearance of deities, such as Telipinu, the storm-god, the sun-god, and the moon-god. These myths are generally part of a ritual scheme in which offerings are made, often with the accompaniment of magical motifs and techniques, in order to find, appease, and return the deities. The mythical portions of these texts often describe the destructive effects of the gods' disappearance upon the land and the felicitous consequences of their return.

The Hurrian myths became part of Hittite culture mainly as part of the influx of Hurrian religious ideas from the Middle Kingdom and afterward. These are more artistic in character than the Hattian myths and are called songs. The Kumarbi Cycle of tales includes the Song of Kumarbi (also known as the Theogony or Kingship in Heaven), Song of the god LAMMA, Song of Silver, Song of Hedammu, and Song of Ullikummi. These myths describe the struggle for divine kingship between Kumarbi and Teshub, whom Kumarbi gave birth to as the result of biting off and swallowing the testicles of Anu, his older royal adversary. The stories are similar to the Ugaritic cycle of Baal myths, which describes Baal's struggle for divine power, and the Akkadian *Enuma Elish,* which describes Marduk's struggle for supremacy among the Babylonian gods. Indeed, Hurrian tradition appears indebted to Mesopotamian tradition for the idea of a theogony with successive generations of gods. Another myth-related text is the Song of Release, which exists in Hittite translation alongside the Hurrian (the Hurrian text may go back to a Syrian original). It begins with praise of Teshub, Allani (in Hittite called the sun-goddess of the underworld), and the Syrian goddess Ishhara. It also contains a series of ethical parables in the wisdom genre, a description of a feast for Teshub in the underworld, and Teshub's ordering the release of debts in Ebla (related to the Mesopotamian and biblical custom of releasing debts).

The gods were represented by images or by symbols, such as standing stones. Their images and symbols were generally housed in numerous temples throughout the kingdom. Temples were not just religious institutions, but integral parts of the economy because they employed a large number of people and held land. Temples contained storerooms for foods, valuables, and archived documents. In the capital city Hattusha several temples, large and small, have been discovered. The largest is devoted to the storm-god and contains a dual chamber for him and his consort the Sun-goddess of Arinna. Being the abode of the deities, the temples were to be kept pure. Priests, including the king during festivals, and other visitors were required to purify themselves before entering the sacred precincts. Certain animals could pollute the temple. For example, the Instructions for Temple Officials warn, "For you, let the place of broken bread be swept and sprinkled [i.e., purified]. Let not a pig or dog cross the threshold!" (*CTH* 264; KUB 13.4 3.59–60; cf. *ANET* 207–10). A bit later it warns kitchen personnel: "If the implements of wood and implements of fired clay which you hold—if a pig or dog ever approach [them], but the kitchen official does not throw them away [and] he gives to the god to eat from an unclean [vessel], then to him the gods will give excrement and urine to eat and drink" (3.64–68). Guards were posted to keep out such animals and unauthorized individuals.

A unique type of shrine is found at Yazılıkaya, three-quarters of a mile northeast of Bogazköy. It operated as a sanctuary from before the Old Kingdom and may have been considered sacred in part because of a spring that flowed there. It gained particular prominence late in Hittite history under Tudkhaliya IV. The area consists basically of a rocky structure with crevices or open-air passages between rock walls. A temple was built in front of this natural maze. Reliefs carved on the walls of the passageways celebrate the gods as well as, implicitly, Tudkhaliya's kingship (his figure is found three times in the sculptures). The purpose of this shrine is not known, although it may have been used in the annual festivals. Some suggest that it was used specifically in new year ceremonies or that it was the mortuary temple of Tudkhaliya.

Offerings were mainly made to the gods at temples. These consisted of foods, for example, meats, breads, grain preparations, honey, oil, fermented drinks. As in most cases throughout the ancient Near East, offerings were a meal presented to the deities, to thank and praise them, to induce them to perform certain actions for the offerer's benefit, or to appease their wrath. This system operated on the analogy of feasting and offering gifts to a political superior to elicit his or her favor. The Instructions to Temple Officials make this metaphor clear: "Are the minds of man and the gods somehow different? No! Even here [in regard to their respective meals]? No! The[ir] minds are the same. When a servant stands up before his master he is washed and wears clean clothing, [then] either he gives him [the master] [something] to eat, or he gives him something to drink. Then when he, his master, eats [and] drinks, he is relieved in his mind" (KUB 13 1.21–26; *ANET* 207).

Killing the animal and manipulating its blood were generally unimportant in Hittite sacrifice, as opposed to biblical custom. Theories of sacrifice that focus on the killing of the animal as the central act or even a significant act therefore do not seem to help explain its meaning among the Hittites. Nevertheless, blood was occasionally offered to chthonic deities. Blood was also used for purification, such as to cleanse a temple and divine image (*CTH* 481; KUB 29.4 4.38–40) and apparently a new birth stool (*CTH* 476; KBo 5.1 1.25–26).

Festivals were occasions when offerings were made in great number. The importance of festivals can be partly seen in their making up the largest group of texts discovered at Bogazköy. Unfortunately we do not have a text that lays out the liturgical calendar systematically. The texts generally describe individual festivals. The main festivals were the AN.TAḪ.ŠUM (Festival of the Crocus Plant) in the spring and the *nutarriyashas* (Festival of Haste [?]) in the autumn. The former lasted thirty-eight days, and the latter lasted more than twenty-one. Other major festivals include the *purulli* (in the spring), the KI.LAM (season unknown, perhaps autumn), and the *(h)isuwas* (a late addition to the liturgy from Hurrian influence). The king, as chief priest, presided in the main festivals. Part of his responsibility included making procession to various local shrines at which ceremonies were held, as well as traveling to the several shrines in various cities to make offerings to the local gods. While the king's attention to cultic matters may appear to us to have been excessive, the purpose of the festivals was no doubt political in nature. By maintaining the various cults in the kingdom, the king shored up the unity of the kingdom and engendered support for his rule. Apart from offerings, festivals included purification rites to ensure the fitness of the king and other participants. They were also occasions for entertainment, including music and even competitive races and other athletic events. All of these activities helped secure the gods' attention, continuing presence, and favor.

The Hittite corpus contains a rather large number of rituals performed as occasion required. Several of these come from the later period and are of Hurrian and Luwian (another Indo-European people closely related to the Hittites) origin, mediated via the southern Luwian-populated province of Kizzuwatna, near Syria. The patients treated in these rites ranged from the king, queen, and the royal house down to unspecified individuals. Some of these rites were performed at the main transitions in life: birth, puberty, and death. Others sought to remove evils of various sorts, including uncleanness *(papratar)*, sorcery *(alwanzatar)*, curse *(hurtais)*, oath *(lingais)*, blood/murder *(eshar)*, evil tongue *(idalus lalas)*, sin *(wastul)*, plague, various sicknesses and infirmities, and also malevolent supernatural beings (including the ghosts of the dead).

Various means, usually symbolic, were used to remove these evils. Evils may be transferred to other objects or entities, and these may then be further disposed of or sent away in scapegoat fashion, sometimes with the accompanying notion that they are being banished to the underworld. According to one text, when a plague breaks out after a battle, one is to dress a foreign prisoner in the Hittite king's clothing and send the prisoner back to the enemy country as an "offering" to the attacking deity, to divert wrath from the Hittite country. The king or his representative says to the prisoner: "If some male god of the enemy land has caused this plague, behold, to him I have given the decorated man as a substitute. At his head this o[ne is gr]eat, at the heart this one is great, at the member this o[ne is gre]at. You, male god, be appeased with th[is dec]orated man. But to the king, the [leaders], the ar[my, and the] land of Hatti, tur[n yourself fai]thfully. . . . Let this prisoner b[ear] the plague and carry [it] ba[ck into the land of the enemy]" (*CTH* 407; KBo 15.1 1.14–21). Evils may also be placed on animals, providing interesting parallels to the biblical scapegoat ritual (Lev. 16). Other means of getting rid of evil include concretizing the evils by representing them with colored threads, certain types of clothing, or other objects. When these are removed, the evil is removed. The evils may also be purged by ritual "detergents," that is, by water, wine, clay, plants, flours, salt, blood, fire, and various mixtures.

An almost ubiquitous feature of Hittite ritual, found to some extent in other Near Eastern ritual, is the use of analogy. For example, in the ritual of Anniwiyani, which is performed to attract and appease a protecting deity, nine pebbles are heated. Anniwiyani, the female practitioner (the Old Woman), cools them off by pouring beer on them, saying: "Just as these have quenched their thirst, so you, protective god . . . , quench your thirst. For you let anger, wrath, and animosity vanish" (*CTH* 393 4.1–4). The analogy need not be dramatically enacted in every case. It may involve only reference to a natural or empirical fact that is brought to bear on the patient's situation. Analogy may be used not just to remedy evils, but also to impart blessing. An Old Woman ritual practitioner, Tunnawiya, grabs hold of the horn of a cow and says: "Sungod, my lord, just as this cow is fertile, and [is] in a fertile pen, and keeps filling the pen with bulls [and] cows, indeed, in the same way may the offerer be fertile! May she in the same way fill [her] house with sons [and] daughters" (*CTH* 409; KUB 7.53 4.8–13).

The maintenance of the many temples and the performance of the several-day and multiday festivals required an elaborate body of temple personnel. Functionally and conceptually, the highest priestly figure was the king, who presided at the main festivals and was responsible otherwise for maintaining good relations with the gods and securing their favor for the people and land at large. The primary priest was the ^{LÚ}SANGA (priest). Other priestly functionaries included the ^{LÚ}GUDU$_{12}$ ([anointed] priest) and the priestess ^{MUNUS}AMA.DINGIR (mother of the god). In addition, many cultic functionaries served at the temple: cooks, cupbearers, people who set out offerings, musicians, singers, people who cleaned, and those who cared for temple animals. The rituals of crisis performed for individuals employed a different set of practitioners. The performers of these rites are often mentioned by name. Often the performer is a female designated with the title "Old Woman" (perhaps meaning "Wise Woman"; Sumerian ^{MUNUS}U.GI = Hittite *hasawas*). Other participants in such rites include the ^{LÚ}A.ZU (physician), the ^{LÚ}HAL (seer), and the ^{LÚ}MUŠEN.DÙ (observer of birds).

Rituals of crisis may also include incantations and prayers. These spoken elements are relatively brief. The Hittite corpus also contains several texts that consist of lengthy prayers, sometimes with accompanying ritual description or prescription (*CTH* 371–89). These texts are virtually all spoken by the king or other members of the royal family and mostly date from the New Kingdom (e.g., the prayers by Queen Pudukhepa and King Muwattalli II). Another group of informative prayers is the Plague Prayers of Murshili II (ca. 1321–1295). In one prayer, the king petitions the gods to alleviate a plague that had been raging in the land since the end of the reign of his father, Shuppiluliuma I. He speaks of how his previous prayers for healing were ineffectual. He consequently inquired by oracle to find out why the gods were angry, the presupposition being that the plague was the result of divine anger. The oracles determined that offerings to a certain god had not been properly made and that a treaty oath made to the Storm-god of Hatti had been broken. Murshili promised to make proper offerings to appease the various deities angered. In addition to prayer texts, Hittite vocabulary contained its own terms for types of prayers, found in colophons or in the body of the texts themselves: *mugawar*, a petition for the god to attend to the plight of the one praying, often with an evocation ritual to attract the deity; *arkuwar*, a prayer defending against charges of wrongdoing; *walliyatar*, a hymn or prayer of praise; and *wekuwar*, a request or petition. The different genres may be mixed in any given prayer.

While humans spoke to the gods directly, the gods made their will known indirectly. A chief method was through dreams. These could come unexpectedly or be prepared for ritually or requested from the deities. In the prayer of Murshili II to relieve the plague, he asks the storm-god to send him a dream advising him of any other satisfaction he must provide to insure that he is making proper amends. External phenomena were also thought to convey the will of the gods. Heavenly occurrences, the behavior of birds or water snakes, birth defects, the drift of incense smoke, the disposition of oil on water, and the physical character of the liver, heart, gall bladder, and intestines of animals were examined and interpreted to discover divine intent. The Hittites also used a lot oracle (the KIN oracle), which may have been used in a gamelike fashion, to reveal the divine mind. As they did with respect to other cultural features, the Hittites borrowed some of their oracular techniques from the Mesopotamian world via Hurrian influence and even had their own editions of Babylonian divination texts. Since the divination techniques generally produced yes/no answers, the Hittites employed a series of oracular inquiries in order to arrive at a specific answer to a question. A good example of this is found in the text that recounts how Murshili II overcame the effects of a disability (perhaps a stroke) that resulted in his not being able to speak easily. After a dream, which may have aggravated his condition, he consulted a series of oracles to determine what he should do. The first oracle indicated that the storm-god of Manuzziya was responsible. A second oracle determined that he should give this god a substitute ox. A third oracle indicated that he should send the offering to the town of Kummanni, located just south of the main land of Hatti (*CTH* 486; see translation by Gary Beckman in Frantz-Szabó 1995: 2010).

Finally, most of what we know about the Hittite view of death concerns the king and royal family. At death the king "became a god," that is, a *sius*. This may mean that he became identified in some way, or entered into association with, the Indo-European deity Sius. One text preserves a fourteen-day funerary rite for the king (*CTH* 450; Otten 18–91; detailed summary in Haas 1995:

2024–27). The text begins by stating the circumstance for the ritual: "When a great calamity [lit., sin, *šalliš waštaiš*] occurs in Hattusha." This calamity is the king's death. On the third day the king is apparently cremated, a custom probably of Hurrian origin. On the sixth day his burned bones, which had earlier been wrapped in linen, were taken to a mausoleum or tomb called the "stone house." Offerings were presented to the deceased king and to the gods at various points. Other performances appear to symbolically outfit the dead with what he needs in the next life and to appease any anger he may have toward those who remain alive. The conception seems to be that life after death continues in a way similar to life during mortality. It is not entirely clear whether the ghost of the deceased was thought to live in the netherworld, the area under the physical earth. The netherworld figured significantly in the Hittite cosmological picture. Caves, springs, dug pits, and tombs provided passageways to the underworld. The sun traversed the sky during the day and crossed the underworld at night and therefore was the chief god of the netherworld. The netherworld (or the deep sea) was also conceptually the place where impurities were banished through elimination rituals. The ghosts of the kings could have resided here. Some have suggested that their habitation was in the west, where the sun entered the underworld.

BIBL.: Gary Beckman, *Hittite Birth Rituals* (Studien zu den Boğazköy-Texten 29; Wiesbaden: Harrassowitz, 1983). Gary Beckman, *Hittite Diplomatic Texts* (Society of Biblical Literature Writings from the Ancient World 7; Atlanta: Scholars Press, 1996). Gabriella Frantz-Szabó, "Hittite Witchcraft, Magic, and Divination," in *Civilizations of the Ancient Near East* (ed. Jack M. Sasson; New York: Scribner, 1995), 3.2007–19. O. R. Gurney, *Some Aspects of Hittite Religion* (Oxford: Oxford University Press, 1977). Volkert Haas, "Death and the Afterlife in Hittite Thought," in *Civilizations of the Ancient Near East* (ed. Jack M. Sasson; New York: Scribner, 1995), 3.2021–30. Volkert Haas and Gernot Wilhelm, *Hurritische und luwische Riten aus Kizzuwatna* (Hurritologische Studien 1; Alter Orient und Altes Testament Sonderreihe 3; Kevelaer: Butzon & Bercker/Neukirchen-Vluyn: Neukirchener Verlag, 1974). Harry A. Hoffner Jr., *Hittite Myths* (2nd ed.; Society of Biblical Literature Writings from the Ancient World 2; Atlanta: Scholars Press, 1998). Theo van den Hout, *The Purity of Kingship: An Edition of CTH 569 and Related Hittite Oracle Inquiries of Tuthaliya IV* (Documenta et monumenta orientis antiqui 25; Leiden: Brill, 1998). Alexei Kassian, Andrej Korolëv, and Andrej Sidel'tsev, *Hittite Funerary Ritual šalliš waštaiš* (Alter Orient und Altes Testament 288; Münster: Ugarit-Verlag, 2002). Jörg Klinger, *Untersuchungen zur Rekonstruktion der hattischen Kultschicht* (Studien zu den Boğazköy-Texten 37; Wiesbaden: Harrassowitz, 1996). R. Lebrun, *Hymnes et prières hittites* (Louvain-la-Neuve: Centre d'Histoire de Religions, 1980). Itamar Singer, *Muwatalli's Prayer to the Assembly of Gods through the Storm-God of Lightning (CTH 381)* (Atlanta: Scholars Press/ASOR, 1996). David P. Wright, "Analogical in Biblical and Hittite Ritual," in *Religionsgeschichtliche Beziehungen zwischen Kleinasien, Nordsyrien und dem Alten Testament* (ed. B. Janowski, K. Koch, and G. Wilhelm; Orbis biblicus et orientalis 129; Freiburg: Universitätsverlag/Göttingen: Vandenhoeck & Ruprecht, 1993), 473–506. David P. Wright, *The Disposal of Impurity: Elimination Rites in the Bible and in Hittite and Mesopotamian Literature* (Society of Biblical Literature Dissertation Series 101; Atlanta: Scholars Press, 1987).

Iran

William Malandra and Michael Stausberg

*I*n antiquity the Iranian cultural sphere extended over a large part of western Asia, far exceeding the borders of the modern state. It included the modern states of Iran, Afghanistan, western regions of Pakistan, the "republics" of the old Soviet central Asia, and areas within the Caucuses—all of them places where related dialects of the common Iranian language group were spoken and where many cultural and religious institutions were shared. Other peripheral areas came under strong Iranian influence at various times. Median, Persian, and Parthian dynasties extended their empires westward into the ancient Near East, the eastern Mediterranean, and Egypt and northward into Azerbaijan and Armenia. Commerce encouraged the expansion of Iranians along the trade routes to China. The Iranians living within such geographic diversity were not a monolithic people. The languages they spoke, although related, were often quite distinct from one another. For example, the Iranian Scythians (Saka) in central Asia spoke languages and carried out ways of life far different than Iranians living in the southwest on the borders of Mesopotamia.

Any historical study is limited by the nature and extent of the sources. This means that there are often long temporal and broad geographical gaps. There are subjects about which we would like to know more or at least something; yet the sources may be silent. Because we cannot interrogate the creators of the source material, we are frequently in the dark as to what something means. As one example, much of the collection of sacred poetry composed by Zarathustra is so obscure in its language and conceptual framework that we cannot always achieve a secure understanding of what the prophet wished to communicate. As another example, although we have the rich iconography of Achaemenid imperial art, no verbal testimony links an icon to its symbolic referent. While art and architectural remains provide some source material for religion, by far the most important sources are literary. Among the latter may be distinguished indigenous Iranian sources and foreign ones. The latter are predominantly Greek and Latin, with occasional references in Aramaic, Hebrew, and Neo-Babylonian. They all should be approached with caution. With the exception of lists of theophoric names in Elamite, all indigenous sources are in Iranian languages.

The most ancient Iranian literary sources are the inscriptions of the Achaemenid kings in Old Persian and the sacred texts of the Zoroastrian religion composed in the Avestan language. The inscriptions are easily dated to the 6th and 5th centuries BCE, to the reigns of Darius, Xerxes, and Artaxerxes. Although they serve the propagandistic ends of the rulers, they are rich in materials related to religion. The corpus of Zoroastrian texts known as the Avesta is a heterogeneous collection whose components were composed at various times and in various genres. Among them the most ancient are the five Gathas or songs attributed to Zarathustra, which comprise a total of seventeen chapters. Unfortunately no one knows when he lived. Some scholars place him at or just prior to the rise of Cyrus the Great (6th century BCE), while many prefer an earlier time between 1200 and 1000, and yet others seek an even earlier date. The large collection of hymns, the Yashts, which honor the deities, contains much material that may well be as ancient as the Gathas, yet the Yashts have been thoroughly edited by redactors who probably worked long after the fall of the Achaemenid Empire. The same may be said about the Yasna, a part of the Avesta which was, and is to this day, recited during the performance of the ritual of the same name. Another significant text is the Widewdad (Vendidad) which, for the most part, contains instruction on a variety of matters pertaining to questions of purity and pollution; parts of it seem to have been composed in the Arsacid period, as the Greek system of spatial measurement is presupposed. If we regard the Avesta as reflecting a period of antiquity that more or less ended with the conquest of Iran by Alexander of Macedon, it, together with the inscriptions, comprises almost all the source material for the most ancient forms of Iranian religion.

In the very extended period between Alexander and the 9th century CE, we have few extensive sources. Of the Sassanid inscriptions, the long inscription of the high priest Kirder is particularly important. But, apart from coin legends (especially those of the Kushans), minor inscriptions, and graffiti, nothing is preserved in significant volume until the renaissance of literary activity in the 9th century, after the coming of Islam to Iran. During this century, Zoroastrian scholars sought to preserve as much Sassanid learning as they could, and what they produced, for the most part, were digests, some very long, of older texts composed in the Pahlavi language. The main problem for the student of Iranian religion is how to sort out historical layers in these texts, for they quote extensively from Sassanid texts which themselves may be translations of lost Avestan texts or else contain more-ancient materials of unclear provenance. One could also include Manicheism in this survey, since Manichean sources in Middle Persian, Parthian, and Sogdian contain a great deal of material borrowed from Iranian (and other) religious traditions. It follows from the foregoing survey of the sources for ancient Iranian religion that the largest part of what we know is mediated by Zoroastrianism.

During the middle of the 2nd millennium BCE there was a gradual migration of nomadic or seminomadic peoples from the steppes into the eastern Mediterranean, the Near East, the Iranian plateau, and the Indian subcontinent. These peoples spoke languages belonging to the Indo-European family. Within that broad family of related languages were two closely related groups collectively identified by linguists as Indo-Iranian. As the name implies, one group settled in India (but also Anatolia and part of the Near East), the other in greater Iran. Not only in language but also in culture and religious ideology did they share a common heritage. Central to both was the sacrificial worship (Old Indic *yajñá*, Old Iranian *yasna*) of the gods (Old Indic *devá*, Avestan *daēwa*, Old Persian *daiwa*, proto-Indo-European *deiwó-s*) in which an essential element was the preparation of the sacred drink (Old Indic *sóma*, Avestan *haoma*, Old Persian *haumd*). They worshiped deities, some of whom bore the same or nearly identical names, for example, Mitra/Mithra, Vayu/Wayu, Tvastar/Thworeshtar, and some of whom represented common concepts of divine functions, for example, Indra/Werethragna (Warrior), Prthivi/Spenta Armaiti (Earth), Agni/Atar (Fire). The most ancient Indian texts, the Vedas, are extremely important for the study of Iranian religion, as they contain a volume and richness of material far beyond what survived in Iran. Nevertheless, both branches of the family exhibit such divergent evolution that they cannot simply be superimposed upon each other.

At the head of the Iranian pantheon stood Ahura Mazda. He was a creator *(dātar)* in the sense that he exercised dominion over creation in establishing order and putting *(dā-)* everything in its proper place. The actual crafting of the creation was the work of the demiurge, Thworeshtar (Craftsman). Ahura Mazda's consort was the Earth, known by the name Spenta Armaiti, although he seems to have had other wives, the Ahuranis (wives of Ahura). Ahura Mazda had a particular connection to the cosmic principle of order and truth called Rta (Avestan *aša,* Old Persian *arta*), and, like the supreme Vedic god Varuna, was a source of insight into truth for poets, the divinely inspired creators of sacred hymns. Two male deities were closely associated with Ahura Mazda. One was Rashnu (Judge), who had a limited judicial function, analogous to that exercised by Varuna, in serving as the divine judge presiding over the oaths sworn by humans. The other was Mithra. While Mithra was a complex deity, the essence of his being was that he was foremost the god Covenant. That is, he presided over all treaties between nations and covenants between people. The image of him as a mighty warrior riding in his chariot full of weapons reflects his ability to enforce the sanctity of covenants. As a warrior he shares much in common with another powerful deity: Werethragna (Victory), whose name etymologically means "the smashing of resistance." As such he embodied the ideal of the Iranian warrior who was capable of smashing the defenses of all enemies. Warriors invoked both Mithra and Werethragna as they went into battle, yet when it came to the exercise of legitimate temporal power and the success of the ruler in wielding that power, two other forces came into play. The Iranians developed a unique concept of an impersonal force called

Xʷarnah, conceived as a fiery presence that attached itself to legitimate rulers, but remained unseizable by illegitimate usurpers. Without this royal glory one could not hope to hold power. Whereas Xʷarnah was an impersonal power, victory to the legitimate ruler and righteous warrior was granted by a goddess, Aredwi Sura Anahita. Like Athena and Ishtar, she dispensed success in arms.

The cosmos was basically three-tiered, consisting of earth, atmosphere, and heaven. The earth was divided into six concentric continents *(karšwar)* surrounding the central continent, Xʷainiratha, where *aryana waējah* (the Iranian Expanse) is located. At the center of the earth was the cosmic mountain, Hara Berezaiti, the Elburz, which acted as the axis mundi. At its southern flank was the sacred Wouru-kasha sea, in the middle of which grew the Tree of Life. Over the earth and expanse of sky arched the stone vault of heaven *(asman),* beyond which was the realm of the Infinite Lights *(anagra raocah),* the heavenly abode called the Best Existence *(wahišta ahu),* and the House of Song *(garō-nmāna).* Below the earth was the realm of Infinite Darkness *(anagra temah).* The entire earth rested upon and was surrounded by the waters of chaos. Fresh water flowed down Hara in the river goddess Aredwi Sura (Strong Moist), into the Wouru-kasha, and from it the various rivers of the world flowed, accumulating pollutants in their courses to the salt sea, called Puitika (Filterer), from which the hydrological cycle repeated itself.

As far as one can reconstruct on the basis of Pahlavi sources, the temporal dimension of the cosmos was a system of four world ages, analogous to the yuga system of ancient India and the four metallic ages of Greece, with each lasting three thousand years. One can guess that there was degradation of the cosmos over the course of the ages and that a complete cycle would have ended with a cataclysm and subsequent creation that renewed the cycle, although in its present form the cycle has been thoroughly transformed into a myth of creation, a battle of good and evil, with the final triumph of the good and establishment of the eternal kingdom of God, Ohrmazd. The yearly cycle was punctuated by various sacred festivals, which probably varied from region to region. The most important was the spring festival celebrating the New Year (Pahlavi *Nōg Rōz),* preceded by a liminal time marking the return of the spirits of the dead, the *frawašis.*

The ancient Iranian cultic practices seem to have been very similar to those referred to in the Vedic literature. Men with special training were required, and, as at later periods, the priestly functions may have been hereditary. The presiding priest was the *zaotar* (Old Indic *hótar)* (the one who offers libations) and was attended by various functionaries. Another functional title, *athaurwan* (cf. Old Indic *átharvan),* became the name for the sacerdotal caste, though originally it may have designated those priests charged with the care of the sacred fire, *ātar,* both the element and a deity. Worship of the deities was ritually performed through the *yasna.* Originally this was a complex ritual that involved the offering of a victim (food) and the sacred *haoma* (drink). Modeled on rites of hospitality, the *yasna* was an elaborate festive meal to which a deity or deities were invited as honored guests. The deity was offered food and drink and was entertained through the recitation of poetry created for the occasion to magnify the divine guest(s). The poet was called a *maθrān* (cf. Old Indic *mantrín*), that is, one who creates sacred poetry *(maθra)*. The Yashts of the Avesta are collections of such poetry. Since hospitality is part of the complex social interaction of gift exchange, the *yasna* placed the deities under an obligation to present the host with a gift. Thus, beyond the general desire to maintain favorable relations with the powers controlling the world, the sacrificer could hope for specific boons.

Our picture of ancient Iranian religion is colored by the prophet Zarathustra (Zoroaster). His specific dates and place of activity are unknown, though we may say with imprecision that he lived between the 12th and 6th centuries BCE somewhere in the northeastern Iranian cultural sphere. We assume that his religious milieu was that sketched above. He was both a *zaotar* and a *mathran*. The only reliable biographical information about him is contained in his Gathas, preserved by the oral tradition, of which he was a part, for centuries and then continued to the present in oral and written priestly transmission. Zarathustra had a particularly close relationship with Ahura Mazda, from whom he received revelatory visions *(daēnā)*. His vision, expressed in the Gathas, included a radical transformation of traditional beliefs. In place of the pantheon he elevated Ahura Mazda to a position of supremacy that approaches monotheism and surrounded him with a group of abstract entities, the Amesha Spentas, all of whom perpetuate key concepts of Iranian religion as hypostases of Ahura Mazda. At the heart of the vision, however, was an ethical dualism that saw the principles of *aša* (Old Persian *arta*, Old Indic *ṛtá*), Truth, and *druj* (Old Persian *dranga*, Old Indic *dróha*), Falsehood, in fundamental opposition. In Zarathustra's thought dualism is not primordial, as it appears in later Sassanid theology, but arose out of the right and wrong choices made by twin spirits, who stand in paradigmatic relationship to human beings in the exercise of free will. As a result, the world could be divided between the followers of Truth (*ašawan-*; cf. Old Persian *artāwan*, Old Indic *ṛtā́varn*) and the followers of the Lie *(drugwant)*. His dualistic theology also led to the polarization of the traditional classes of deities, the *ahuras* and the *daēwas*. A *zaotar*, Zarathustra was concerned with proper cultic practice, especially the proscription of violence upon the sacrificial victim as carried out by the *daiwic* priests. He may have modified the *haoma* cult, but certainly did not ban it. Finally, Zarathustra articulated the kernel of the idea of a savior figure, the Saoshyant, who would arrive in the future to redeem the world. (Further on Zarathustra and his religious innovations, see the Appendix to this essay.)

The history of Iranian religion after Zarathustra is very difficult to reconstruct. In the course of his ministry in eastern Iran, he converted a local ruler *(kawi)* named Wishtaspa, who became his patron and protector. For convenience scholars call the religion of the prophet Zarathustrianism or Zoroastrianism. We can only assume that the religious community that Zarathustra founded continued and thrived after his death. With the consolidation of greater Iran under the Achaemenids, his religion, into whatever form it had evolved, made its way to western Iran. There it encountered forms of Iranian religion different not only from itself, but also from non-Zarathustrian religions of the East. In particular, there was the politically entrenched priestly caste of the Magi who, according to Herodotus (1.132), presided at all religious ceremonies, at which they recited "theogonies," presumably Yasht-like hymns. There is no consensus among scholars over the question of whether the early great kings, Cyrus, Darius, Xerxes, were influenced by Zarathustrianism. They certainly believed in the absolute supremacy of Ahura Mazda and probably in the dichotomy of *ahura/daiwa*. But, beyond that all is speculation. Neither the Achaemenids themselves nor Herodotus mention Zarathustra, and Gathic quotations that some see in the inscriptions may merely reflect phrases common to the shared (Indo-)Iranian poetic diction.

In any case, what emerges during the Achaemenid period is an eclectic Iranian religion, called by scholars Zoroastrianism, which contains elements of Zarathustrianism, apocryphal legends of the prophet, a full pantheon of deities almost entirely absent from the Gathas, an overriding concern over purity and pollution, the establishment of fire temples. Curiously, the extant Avesta remains thoroughly eastern Iranian in its geographic and linguistic orientation. One assumes that radical concessions to traditional beliefs had already taken place after Zarathustra's death and before Zoroastrianism became pan-Iranian.

After the conquest by Alexander, Iran fell under the superficial influence of Hellenism. Apart from fragmentary evidence it is difficult to formulate a cohesive history from Alexander to the foundation of the Sassanid Dynasty in the 3rd century CE. The Pahlavi books hint at a Zoroastrian revival under Vologases I (ca. 51–80 CE) in which some sort of collection and codification of the Avesta took place. Kushan coins of the same period from the northeast show a pantheon of Iranian deities. From Gandhara Mahayana, Buddhism gained strength throughout the region, traveling along the trade routes to China. Jews, Christians, and eventually Manicheans also entered the religious mix. With the founding of the Sassanid Dynasty around 224 CE under Ardashir, there was a revival of Iranian nationalism that consciously harkened back to the glory of the Old Persian Empire. Part of this was the creation of a centralized Zoroastrian ecclesiastical structure that was inseparable from the royal authority of the state. After an initial struggle over the patronage of Shapuhr I (240–72 CE), the high priest Kirder overcame his rival Mani and established Zoroastrianism *(dēn mazdēsn)* throughout the empire, while persecuting religious minorities. Zoroastrianism remained the state religion until the Arab-Islamic conquest in the latter part of the 7th century CE.

W.W.M.

Appendix: Zoroastrianism

The name Zoroastrianism is a product of modern colonial discourse. It goes back to a Greek rendering (Zoroastres) of the Iranian name Zarathustra, which refers to the key individual, the founder, or prophet of this religion. The designations of the religion found in most premodern primary sources, on the other hand, draw attention either to the (supposed) quality of the religion—the "pure/good religion"—or to the name of its dominant male divinity, Ahura Mazda. This is an ancient Iranian (Avestan) term that can be rendered either as "the Wise Lord" or as "Lord Wisdom."

Together both names—Zarathustra and Ahura Mazda—occur in the Gathas. These are five hymns that are often assumed to be part of the oldest layer of the corpus of ritual texts written in Avestan, an ancient Iranian language. Many scholars nowadays believe that the Gathas were composed by Zarathustra himself, whereas others argue that Zarathustra as a person belongs to the realm of myth. While many linguists distinguish between two or even more historical layers of the Avestan language—Old and Young Avestan—others reject that distinction, opting instead for a distinction between Gathic and Standard Avestan.

There is disagreement about virtually everything in the study of Zoroastrianism, not the least on the question of origins. There are dozens of theories, mostly mere speculative assumptions, about the homeland of the religion (or of its prophet), generally held to be somewhere east of what is modern Iran. It is not clear when Zarathustra lived (if there ever was such a person). While some scholars argue that he must have lived in remote antiquity, even going back as far as 1700 BCE, some place him in the 6th or 5th century BCE, whereas the majority puts the date around 1000 BCE. Some later Zoroastrian texts in Middle and New Persian recount "biographies" of Zarathustra. These biographies focus on his miraculous birth and childhood, his divine revelations and encounters, and his eventually successful campaign at the court of a king.

Whatever their origin, the Gathas came to be orally transmitted in ritual contexts. Although many translations of the Gathas are available, most of them disagree about fundamental issues, and the Gathas are still obscure in many ways. It is difficult to avoid the suspicion that one finds in the Gathas whatever one may be looking for. By way of example, Zoroastrian scholars have "discovered" such modern ideas as gender equality, ecology, and human rights in the Gathas. To the eyes of many modern Zoroastrians, especially in Iran and the West, the Gathas are the normative model of religious scripture, while the later (or Standard) Avestan texts containing more-straightforward material of praise to the divinities and divine prescriptions are disregarded as secondary elaborations.

The issues of monotheism and dualism are a major concern of both modern Western orientalists and Zoroastrian theologians. These often (erroneously) have been presented as an either-or argument. It can easily be understood that modern Zoroastrians living in a world dominated by Christian and Islamic patterns have insisted on their religion being regarded as a pure monotheism; and for many scholars monotheism has served as a bridge linking Zoroastrian and Jewish religious history. (Some scholars hold that Zoroastrianism had a profound influence on Jewish traditions.) In the Avestan texts, however, one can easily find support for monotheist, dualist, and polytheist interpretations. Whereas monotheism, dualism, and polytheism are different sets of classification in Western thought, no such distinctions seem to have existed in the Avestan mentality. To stretch things into a schematic pattern: Ahura Mazda—the most powerful of the gods, who set the creation into place and motion, together with the other male and female divinities and divine beings, most prominently the Amesha Spentas (Bountiful Immortals), a group that came to consist of six divinities closely allied to or created by Ahura Mazda and thought to represent moral virtues and cosmic elements (such as fire, water, earth, etc.)—is held to be actively involved in a continuous struggle against impure demons and demonic agents of varying degrees of power. Humanity is involved in this struggle in a number of ways. Ideally, humankind is expected to support the divinities by properly performing rituals and by a virtuous conduct of life implementing truth, purity, the right measure, and god-given order, the latter also containing submission to elders and gender rules. While females play an important role in that struggle, they are assumed to be more easily affected by demonic forces and thus need to be held under tight male, patriarchal control. From the Achaemenian period onward in Iran, similar forms of dualist rhetoric were also employed in order to foster political claims for legitimacy, loyalty, and empire.

According to more-systematic accounts transmitted in the Middle Persian (Pahlavi) books, the struggle between the forces of good and evil evolved out of an original opposition between Ohrmazd (i.e., Ahura Mazda) and his main adversary Ahriman (i.e., Angra Mainyu) in the early stages of the history of creation, which then had obtained two dimensions: a spiritual, invisible, meta-empirical level *(menog)* and an equally good material, tangible, empirical level *(getig)*. The Zoroastrian version of dualism, monotheism, and polytheism is thus closely linked to a vision of cosmic history. Events culminate in a process often referred to as *frašgird,* the final transfiguration of the cosmos, when the forces of evil (and hence dualism) will be eliminated. This process is instigated by the arrival of a future hero who is regarded as a posthumous son of Zarathustra.

The climax of cosmic history can be expressed in terms of a final ordeal or a final judgment. In a way, this can be regarded both as the culmination and a reversal of the eschatological judgment that each and every human being is expected to face after death. The number of merits and sins that each person has gathered in the course of his or her life are held to be decisive for the progress of the soul on its journey, which may lead to paradise, hell, or a place in between. Probably, fear of hell and the promise of heaven were major factors promoting religious commitment and ritual practice.

At least starting from the reign of the Achaemenians (6th to 4th centuries BCE), Zoroastrianism was the dominant set of religious traditions in pre-Islamic Iranian history. The link between the religion and the land of Iran has been given particular importance, especially since the Sassanian period (3rd to 7th centuries CE). Recent scholarship draws attention to many—partly local, popular, and lay—varieties of the traditions, while premodern written Zoroastrian sources as products of male, priestly, and partly local discourse draw only a partial picture of religious practices and mentalities. In the aftermath of the Arabic invasion of Iran, groups of Zoroastrians have relocated to western India, where they are known as Parsis (derived from the name Persia). Nowadays, Zoroastrianism has around 125,000 adherents, mostly in India, Iran, and North America.

M.ST.

BIBL.: Mary Boyce, *A History of Zoroastrianism* (3 vols.; Leiden, 1975–91). Albert de Jong, *Traditions of the Magi* (Leiden, 1997). *The Cambridge History of Iran* (ed. I. Gershevitch; Cambridge, 1985), 2.640–97. Michael Stausberg, *Die Religion Zarathushtras: Geschichte, Gegenwart, Rituale* (3 vols.; Stuttgart, 2002–2003).

Minoan and Mycenaean Civilizations

Nanno Marinatos

Minoan Religion

Minoan culture flourished on the island of Crete from the 3rd to the 1st millennium BCE and from the 2nd millennium onward as a palatial society. At that time, its writing system, its religious symbols, and its material culture spread beyond the boundaries of Crete to encompass most of the islands of the Aegean and the southern part of mainland Greece. Scholars debate whether this spread of Minoan art, writing, and religion was only superficial and indicates nothing more than trade connections or whether it reveals the network of an empire. Whatever the case, the ubiquity of Minoan religious symbols is certainly a result of power, perhaps even colonialism.

The basic mythology and theology of Minoan religion cannot be reconstructed on the basis of texts. Such literary documents as have been left behind, consisting of clay tablets inscribed in a language we call Linear A, are inaccessible because the writing system is only partially understood and the language itself is unknown. This leaves us with only archeological remains and images; still, they yield a great deal of information.

Contemporary ideas about the Minoans go back to Sir Arthur Evans, who excavated the palace of Knossos on Crete during the first decades of the 20th century. Many of his observations were keen and have stood the test of time; others need revision. One of the fallacies introduced by Evans into Minoan religion is the dominant role of a Great Minoan Mother Goddess, with its concomitant matriarchal society. A close scrutiny of the iconography of the numerous extant rings and seals shows that the Minoan pantheon consisted of several deities, among whom a youthful male god armed with a spear features prominently. On a ring imprint found at Chania, a god is shown towering over

Figure 1

a town (Fig. 1). The hierarchy and relationship of gods within the pantheon is difficult to decode from the images alone. On a ring impression from Knossos (Fig 2.), the dominant deity is female, flanked by lions. She faces a male who is probably a god rather than a worshiper. They may be a divine couple. On a wall painting from the island of Thera (modern Santorini), a seated goddess receives an offering of saffron from young girls.

Evans also overemphasized fertility as a central concern of Minoan cult, and he characterized Minoan religious mentality as conceptually primitive; these ideas were further developed in the middle of the 20th century by A. W. Persson and the sober and systematic M. P. Nilsson. The unfortunate consequence of this is that Minoan religion is still classified as primitive.

In reality, Minoan religion was the religion of a sophisticated and urbanized palatial culture with a complex social hierarchy. It was not dominated by fertility any more than any religion of the past or present has been, and it addressed gender identity, rites of passage, and death. It is reasonable to assume that both the organization and the rituals, even the mythology, resembled the religions of Near Eastern palatial civilizations.

The palaces seem to have been at the core of a religious system that can be termed theocratic. On the Knossos seal impression (Fig. 2), the palace is depicted behind a goddess. It is multitiered and topped by "horns of consecration." Evans recognized that the horns were a symbol of sacred authority as well as political power. The diffusion of this symbol outside Crete testifies to the function of Minoan emblems as carriers of ideology.

Figure 2

There are no temples in Minoan Crete, although buildings associated with cult have been found on mountaintops ("peak sanctuaries"). They were apparently controlled by the palaces, but the varying quality of the votives shows that common people and rural folk congregated there. Typical offerings are statuettes of humans and animals, libation vessels, and portable offering tables.

The fall of the palatial system in Crete sometime after 1400 BCE caused some changes in the archeological record of religion. Rooms with benches and statues make their appearance, which structurally resemble shrines both on mainland Greece and in Syria and Palestine. Many terra-cotta statues of goddesses date to this era; they stood on the benches, and offerings were made to them.

Mycenaean religion

The inhabitants of Greece during the 2nd millennium BCE are called Mycenaeans after the famous and impressive citadel of Mycenae, which was excavated by Heinrich Schliemann at the end of the 19th century. Many similar citadels existed in Greece, and there is enough homogeneity among them that we are justified to speak of a Mycenaean culture. Mycenaean religion shares many symbols with Minoan religion, from the period of the Shaft Graves in the 16th century BCE to the end of its existence. For example, Mycenaean palaces were also topped by horns. One generally assumes that the borrowing of symbols of authority demonstrates that the Mycenaean palaces took over the entire theocratic Minoan system and adapted it to their culture. We also suspect that there were dynastic links. After the 14th century BCE, the Mycenaean writing system, Linear B (most probably a derivative of Minoan Linear A), is also found on Crete. The decipherment of this system revealed its language as an early form of Greek; its syllabic structure, however, cannot have been intrinsic to Greek, because the numerous consonant clusters that are characteristic of Greek translate rather clumsily into Linear B.

There were other differences, as well, between the two cultures. Mycenaean palaces included a *megaron,* a large central rectangular room with a hearth in the center where offerings were made; only one palace on Crete, that of Galatas, contained a hearth. Apart from the *megaron* in the palaces, modest bench sanctuaries are found within the citadels and the towns. On the benches of these small shrines were found terra-cotta figures of varying sizes; normally there was a hearth in the center, showing that offerings took place there as well. The bench sanctuary seems to have been a prevalent type throughout the Aegean and the Levant in the 13th and 12th centuries BCE. Sanctuaries existed outside the Mycenaean palaces as well, on mountaintops (as on a hill near Epidaurus) and within settlements. Recently such a settlement sanctuary has been excavated on the peninsula of Methana (Saronic Gulf). Its main feature was a hearth and the usual benches. Typical offerings in all Mycenaean sanctuaries are terra-cotta figurines of varying sizes.

Linear B tablets of the 13th century BCE, found in Thebes and Pylos on the mainland and in Chania and Knossos on Crete, attest that the Mycenaeans had an elaborate pantheon. These tablets were clay scrapbooks that survived decomposition because they were accidentally burned when the palaces were destroyed. The tablets record offerings to various gods, the titles of religious officials, and the dispensation of various goods to diverse sanctuaries. Among the gods mentioned are Poseidon, Zeus, Dionysus (attested only on Crete), and Marineus. Goddesses named include Potnija, Ifimedia, Diwija, and Posidaeja —the latter two being the female equivalents of Zeus and Poseidon, respectively.

Many names correspond closely to those of the later Greek gods of the 1st millennium. Yet, the danger of projecting the Greek religious system backward onto the Mycenaean world must be resisted; some divine names are unattested later, while prominent Greek gods, such as Apollo and Aphrodite, seem to be absent. Minoan and Mycenaean theocracies can be understood best as a subcategory of Near Eastern theocracies. The archeological evidence suggests that the Minoan and Mycenaean religions, despite their differences, had many common elements: palace-centered cults, absence of temples, hearths, and animal bones attesting to banqueting. Neither foreshadows the Greek polis religion.

BIBL.: Robin Hägg, "Mycenaean Religion: The Helladic and the Minoan Components," in *Linear B: A 1984 Survey* (ed. Anna Morpurgo-Davies and Yves Duhoux; Louvain-la-Neuve: Peeters, 1985), 203–25. Nanno Marinatos, *Minoan Religion: Ritual, Image, and Symbol* (Columbia: University of South Carolina Press, 1993). Hélène Whittaker, *Mycenaean Cult Buildings: A Study of Their Architecture and Function in the Context of the Aegean and the Eastern Mediterranean* (Monographs from the Norwegian Institute at Athens; Bergen: Norwegian Institute at Athens, 1997).

Greece

Jon Mikalson

For the student of antiquity, Greek religion seems, like Athena from the head of Zeus, to spring forth suddenly, mature, and fully developed. And it does so in the epic poetry of Homer and Hesiod, commonly dated by scholars to the mid- to late-8th century BCE. In these poems appear most of the fundamental features of Greek religion as we know them from later sources: polytheism; anthropomorphism; the names, functions, and iconography of individual gods; the forms, language, rituals, and occasions of sacrifices, prayers, and dedications; the nature and forms of sanctuaries, altars, cult statues, and temples; the nature and role of priests and priestesses; the rituals and purposes of oath taking; divine concern with the guest/host relationship *(xenia);* and the forms and occasions of divination by seers, bird augury, omens, oracles, and dreams.

These elements of Greek religion are treated in Homeric and Hesiodic poetry with such familiarity and consistency that one may assume that they had already become conventional in this oral epic tradition. Moreover, if we view this "epic" religion retrospectively in terms of what we know of later practiced Greek religion from nonpoetic sources, it would appear that even this early epic religion had already been subjected to considerable patterning, simplification in some areas, expansion in others, and, in general terms, to a process of Panhellenization. For example, the poet-singers selected and featured a few from the hundreds of gods worshiped throughout Greece. They then largely stripped the chosen few of their local identities and of many of the epithets and peculiarities of ritual, cult, and even mythology that they would have had in the individual cities in which they were originally worshiped. And, by expansion, the poets constructed for the chosen few personal histories and an elaborate Olympian family structure—with the result best exemplified in Hesiod's *Theogony.* And it is in this sense that Herodotus, who had no notion of an oral epic tradition prior to these poets, could say that Hesiod and Homer "created a divine genealogy for Greeks, gave their epithets to the gods, distributed their offices and their skills, and marked out their outward appearances" (2.53.2).

The deities favored by the poetic tradition, now freed from limitations and particularities of their local cults, could serve—within the poetic tradition—as gods for all Greek audiences. Rituals in the epics were similarly stylized. The ritual sequence for the sacrifice of a cow is firmly set in the Homeric tradition: the gilding of the horns, the barley-corn preliminary offering, the ritual throat cutting, the butchering, the burning of the thigh pieces on the altar, the eating of the vital organs, the cooking, and the feast. But we know from later sources that many major variations were possible, depending on the occasion, the deity, and local traditions. In sacrifice, as in other rituals, the epic tradition selected or created one ritual set, generalized it, and made it into a set scene.

We must assume a period of maturation for this "epic" portrayal of Greek religion, to be measured perhaps in centuries. And that would bring us back to the Greek Dark Ages (ca. 1125 to ca. 700 BCE) at least, perhaps even to the end of the Mycenaean age. And, second, if the development of epic religion is somewhat as I have described, then the relationship of the Greek religion known from the Homeric epics to practiced religion of Homeric or later times is very complex. Homeric religion would ultimately derive from practiced cult and would preserve many of its features, but it would also differ from it in some major elements. And so the religion that springs upon us in such a full, complete, and appealing form in the 8th-century BCE epics is a religion significantly different from that practiced by the Greek peoples of that or any time. And, to further complicate the issue, the epics enjoyed such popularity among the Greeks that they, in turn, could influence local cults and certainly shaped later literary and artistic representations and philosophical discussions of what was considered to be Greek religion.

If we attempt to look beyond the Homeric period, to the prehistory of Greek religion, some isolated details emerge, enough to suggest that some defining elements of Greek religion do in fact reach back to the Mycenaean period. Zeus alone of the gods is unmistakably Indo-European, etymologically linked with the Roman Jupiter and the Dyaus pitar of the Rig Veda. Some aristocratic Greeks claimed genealogies that went back to a divine ancestor in the 16th century BCE. And the Linear B tablets from Knossos, Mycenae, Chania, and Pylos (all probably from about 1200 BCE) contain the familiar names of Zeus, Athena, Poseidon, Hera, Hermes, and Dionysus intermixed with deities unfamiliar to us. For the Dark Ages, there has been considerable speculation about what archeological finds at scattered places may or may not reveal about change or continuity in Greek religious concepts and about the social and political meaning of the placing and design of sanctuaries and the changing types of dedications. Much of this discussion attempts to place religion in the equally theoretical models for the social and political development of the early city-state. The sites are few, the interpretations of finds often uncertain, and the theories many and strongly contested.

Archeological finds do, however, indicate a sharp increase in religious buildings and dedications at the end of the Dark Ages. As one example among many possible, 10 apparently religious dedications from Olympia are dated to the 11th and 10th centuries BCE, 21 to the 9th century, and 837 to the 8th century.

Monumental temples begin to appear only in the second half of the 8th century, with that of Hera on Samos, of Apollo at Eretria, and those of Artemis and Hera on Delos. Perhaps the earliest surviving cult statues—seemingly distinct from the usual votive dedications—come from Dreros on Crete, about 700 BCE. Religion shared in the renaissance of Greek culture in the 8th century, and it is noteworthy that many of the elements appearing first in the archeological record then—temples, demarcated sanctuaries, altars, dedications, and cult statues—are also well-established features in the *Iliad* and *Odyssey*. This may suggest that what appears in the archeological record at this time had antecedents—how far back it is impossible to know—in more-perishable materials such as wood and mud-brick. But it is unmistakable that the most distinctive features of Greek religion take their definitive form—in both literature and material remains—as part of the 8th-century BCE renaissance.

Pollution and purification

The Greek concept of pollution—an impure state resulting from murder, sexual intercourse, childbirth, or contact with the dead, negatively affecting relations with the divine world and requiring purification by time or through rituals—is at best latently apparent in concerns for physical "cleanliness" before ritual activities and the exclusion of murderers from society in Homeric epic and in the injunctions of Hesiod's *Works and Days*. Ritual purification for murder is first unmistakably attested in literature in Achilles' purification in the *Aethiopis* (mid-7th century BCE[?]). The concept that the dead cause pollution of the sacred is first documented in Pisistratus's exclusion of tombs from areas even overlooking Apollo's sanctuary on Delos in the mid-6th century. Both presume preexisting traditions, and the question remains open whether purification rituals did not exist in Homeric times or were, for some reason, suppressed by the epic poets. Whenever introduced, pollution remained a live issue until the end of the Hellenistic period and beyond, with only pollution concerning murder apparently beginning to lose some of its efficacy in the 4th century BCE.

Heroes

Heroes, individuals who received public cult after their deaths, form a second class of deities in the Greek tradition, and the first cults of named heroes date to the end of the 8th century and are associated with Homeric heroes, the best examples being those of Menelaus and Helen near Sparta. Hero cults have been claimed for a few 10th- and 9th-century sites, and some scholars see traces of them in the *Iliad* (e.g., 2.546–51). But the real development of these cults is in the period 750–650 BCE, a movement perhaps influenced by the increasing spread and popularity of the Homeric epics. Many, perhaps most, such cults were not, however, devoted to Homeric heroes, and some cultic heroes and heroines even remained nameless. It is unknown whether these cults were antecedents, by-products, or parallel developments with the cults of the Homeric heroes. Some heroes were linked with Olympian deities, as Erechtheus with Athena at Athens, Hyacinthus with Apollo at Sparta, and Pelops with Zeus at Olympia, and in some cases the hero may have been established first. Hero cults were highly localized, closely bound to the presumed tomb of the hero, and a hero's cult could be moved only by the transfer of his bones. A few heroes such as Heracles and Asclepius broke local boundaries and became Panhellenic, usually in the process becoming assimilated to gods in cult and ritual. Once established, these hero cults persisted throughout antiquity. In classical times occasional individuals, such as the "tyrant slayers" Harmodius and Aristogeiton in Athens or the athlete Cleomedes of Astypalaea, were given such cults, usually for outstandingly beneficial or fearsome actions. Heroes might be benefactors, but theirs was still a cult of the dead, and about many of them, particularly the old ones, lingered an atmosphere of fear and uncanniness—well reflected in the cult that Sophocles creates for Oedipus at Athens in his *Oedipus at Colonus*.

Polis religion

It is not until the mid-6th century that we have sufficient historical, archeological, and epigraphical records to develop a sense of the underlying structure of state religion in a Greek polis, and that polis is Athens. We find cults in the urban center: that of Athena Polias, patroness of the city, associated with the hero Erechtheus in her temple on the Acropolis; that of Athena Nike with her altar, also on the Acropolis; that of Dionysus with the very beginnings of tragedy, now or soon to be situated in the Dionysus sanctuary and theater on the south slope of the Acropolis; in the "old city" southwest of the Acropolis, a sanctuary of Apollo with ties to Delphi and, under construction, a major temple of Zeus Olympios. In the developing new Agora northwest of the Acropolis was placed the altar of the twelve gods, at the imagined geographical center of Athens. In the Agora were also sanctuaries of Zeus Soter/Eleutherios and of Apollo Patroös, the putative ancestor of Athenians and all Ionian Greeks. Some cults in the rural areas of Athens were now assuming statewide importance, for example, the cult of Artemis Brauronia in the township Brauron and that of Demeter at Eleusis with its annual Mysteries, and there are indications of the state laying claim to these by building subsidiary sanctuaries of each on or near the Acropolis. And, after the establishment of democracy in 508/507 BCE, ten from one hundred local heroes were selected by the Delphic Oracle to give their names and protection to each of the ten tribes into which the Athenian polity was now divided. Part of the democratizing process was to bring into the state administrative structure the 139 individual townships (demes) that made up Athens, and later calendars and records of their sacrifices and festivals suggest that already in the 6th century rural demes had, for their residents, a rich program of religious activities. Some centered on local gods and heroes, others mirrored the cults of state deities.

Festivals

In the 6th century, statewide religious festivals *(heortai)* are introduced or elaborated in Athens. Among them, the Panathenaia for Athena and the City Dionysia included processions, sacrifices, hymns, and dances. Athena's festival featured a variety of athletic, equestrian, and musical competitions, and at the City Dionysia competitions in dithyrambic poetry, tragedy, and, later, comedy were held. Only citizens could fully participate in most such festivals, but the Panathenaia was truly Panathenian, with designated roles for male and female citizens of different ages, resident aliens, and even slaves. Such festivals, ranging over several days, combined communal worship of the deity with the pleasures of holiday feasting and the entertainment that the games offered, and they remained a feature of Greek religion throughout antiquity.

Priests

In these times and for centuries to come, most religious (in contrast to financial) matters of individual cults, even those of the state on the Acropolis, remained largely in the control of aristocratic families, with the priesthood of the cult passed from generation to generation within each family. Except at major religious centers such as Delphi and Eleusis, a Greek priest served part time, on occasions of sacrifices and festivals, with some responsibility for cult affairs, but possessing no esoteric religious knowledge and not subject to special restrictions on his daily life. In democratic Athens, priests of new cults were selected by lot for annual terms, and in several Asia Minor Greek cities priesthoods were auctioned off annually. Greek religion is distinguished by a lack of a central authority based on either a canonical text or a professional priesthood. State supervision, when it existed, consisted largely of lay committees overseeing the financial affairs of individual cults, of the legislative assembly approving the introduction of new cults, and of the courts prosecuting cases of impiety.

Diversity

We have the most knowledge about Athens, but the particular alignment of deities and their functions at Athens cannot serve as a model for all states. Epigraphical and historical evidence indicates that, in matters small and large, religion developed in various different ways in other Greek cities. On Naxos, for example, the patron deity of the state was Dionysus, not Athena, and the

Naxians would have had a quite different religious calendar featuring somewhat different kinds of festivals at different times of the year. Rare was the cult, such as that of Demeter Thesmophoros, that was practiced in much the same form by all Greeks. As ethnic, cultural, political, and economic conditions varied from city to city over the centuries reaching back to the Dark Ages, so too, in these relatively isolated little countries, the specific deities worshiped, the rituals of this worship, and the functions of these deities came to differ, or, perhaps better, original differences were maintained.

The local nature and diverse functions of Greek deities are often revealed by the epithets attached to their names. The Athenian Artemis Brauronia (of the deme Brauron) differed in major respects from Artemis Ephesia (of Ephesus) in cult, function, and appearance. In Athens, Zeus Ktesios (of the stores) was represented in the storeroom of each house as a pot wrapped in wool, but Zeus Eleutherios/Soter had a state sanctuary and statue in the Agora and protected the "freedom" of the city as a whole. Sanctuaries of Zeus Katabaites (coming down) marked spots hit by lightning, and Zeus Meilichios, a chthonic figure, was pictured as a bearded snake. Each was worshiped as a distinct deity at a separate place and time and with a separate function and ritual. How they each became associated with Zeus in Athens is unknown, but for Zeus and all Greek deities the epithet often reveals more than the Homeric name about their cults and functions.

Relationships between human and divine

To judge by prayers and dedications, what the Greeks sought from their gods, in general terms, was fertility of crops, animals, and selves; economic prosperity; good health; and safety of self, family, and country. These purposes were accomplished by establishing with the deities a relationship based on *charis*. A *charis* was a "favor" that was expected to be repaid, and the mutual exchange of favors or gifts is at the heart of successful human / divine relationships. This is a subtler and more complex relationship—based on aristocratic rather than mercantile values—than the formula *do ut des* (I give so that you may give), often used to describe this relationship, implies. The model for the relationship of a human to a god is that of a good subject to a beneficent king, a relationship in which "gifts" of very different types and values might be exchanged for a variety of purposes. The gifts that the Greek gods give are successes in those areas listed above. The gifts that humans give include sanctuaries, sacrifices, dedications, hymns, and dances. These gifts are intended to reflect the "honor" *(timē),* not "love" or "fear," in which the humans hold these deities for the power they have and for the gifts they give. The gods, in turn, "rejoice" *(chairein)* in these honoring gifts. These gifts of humans are, in addition, "adornment" *(kosmos)* for the deities and their sanctuaries, and much of the finest Greek art, architecture, and poetry results from the Greek inclination to make their gifts to the gods beautiful.

In epic and tragedy, the relationships between humans and gods are often fractured, by gross impieties on the human side or by capricious and unjust behavior on the divine side. In everyday life, however, the Greeks seem remarkably confident that a good relationship between humans and gods is the normal situation, interrupted only temporarily by occasions of pollution or minor religious oversights, both of which can be corrected by rituals or additional gifts acknowledging the worth of the deity. The foundation myths of cults usually stress two elements: the power of the deity and the specific benefit that the god, of his or her own accord, is offering to humans, for Apollo of Delphi the oracle, for Dionysus of Thebes wine, and for Eleusinian Demeter grain. And in return, the gods expect "honor" in the form of cult. Some etiological myths, as for Artemis, put more stress on the dangerous side of the deity who, when offended, demands cultic acts as appeasement. But in both cases the humans, through cult, establish and maintain with the deity a mutually beneficial relationship based on *charis* and *timē*. And, finally, a human's relationships with the deities worshiped in life are severed by death. Apart from a few mythical figures of massive impiety, individuals were neither rewarded nor punished in the afterlife for religious behavior in this life. If such rewards and punishments did not fall on individuals during their lifetimes, they fell on their descendants, if on anyone. The hundreds of surviving Greek epitaphs suggest that the Greeks expected little of the afterlife, but the concept of a blessed afterlife was known to some: initiates into the Eleusinian Mysteries were said to have "sweeter hopes concerning the end of life and all eternity," and from the 6th century on, some private cults, associated with the historical Pythagoras and the legendary Orpheus, promised to their devotees a more blessed afterlife as a reward for following prescribed behavior in this life. It is unknown, however, how widely such beliefs about the afterlife were held.

Transmission, transformation, and conservation

From about the mid-8th to the early 6th century BCE, the "old" Greek cities sent throughout the Mediterranean colonies of their own citizens, and these colonies then often sent out colonies of their own. These colonists, for example, Corinthians to Syracuse in Sicily and Therans (themselves colonists of Sparta) to Cyrene in North Africa, initially transplanted some cults and festivals from their homelands in their new cities, and this was the prime cause of the spread of Greek religion throughout the Aegean and Mediterranean areas. But in the move some elements changed. Some cults, especially those of heroes and of deities with connections to local springs and such things, could not be transferred from the motherland. In place of the hero cults of their homelands, the colonists established hero cults of their founders. The colonists also encountered in their new lands indigenous cults, some of which they brought into the pantheon of their new state, such as the hero cult of the Argonaut Idmon at Herakleia Pontika. After their own period of development, the cults of a colony would come to differ in significant ways from those of the motherland. And so we have, even at this early stage, two types of state religion: that long established in the "old" Greek cities, with a multitude of well-entrenched heroes, local cults, and Olympian deities, and that in colonies, perhaps initially with fewer cults but surely more open to innovation and integration with indigenous cults.

Once established, the religious structures, particularly in the old cities, appear remarkably resistant to change. In part, this was due to a high degree of religious conservatism, often expressed in the necessity to worship the gods "in the ancestral ways." These ancestral ways would be in part preserved by the aristocratic families that controlled these cults and, for the state, from Solon's time in Athens, in official calendars of religious activities and sacred laws, often inscribed in stone. Contributing to this stability was the characteristic that deities and cults were not closely identified with one economic or social, or political faction within the city and hence were remarkably unaffected by economic and political tribulations that most Greek cities experienced. The priests and priestesses of most cults were aristocrats, but these same cults provided benefits, not only good relations with the divine world but also banquets and games, to the whole citizenry. And the costs of these benefits were paid sometimes by the wealthy, sometimes from the state treasury. Each citizen group thus benefited in some significant way, and hence the cults remained outside the clashes among these groups.

The greatest physical danger to religious cults came from outside the city-state, from foreign invaders such as the Persians Darius and Xerxes in the early 5th century and Philip V of Macedon in the 2nd century BCE. Darius promised revenge on Greek sanctuaries for the Greek burning of the temple of Kubaba in Sardis in 498, and for the next eighteen years he and his successor Xerxes ravaged and burned all Greek sanctuaries that came under the control of their armies, including most of the sanctuaries in Asia Minor, many of those in central Greece, and, of course, all those of Athens. In 200 BCE, the Macedonian king Philip V ravaged the Athenian countryside as he had other areas in Greece, apparently destroying beyond repair the hundreds, perhaps thousands of sanctuaries there. Within two generations of the Persian Wars most of the Greek sanctuaries had been rebuilt, often with considerably greater splendor. Times were, however, much worse in 2nd century BCE Greece, and the sanctuaries destroyed by Philip V disappear from the historical and epigraphical record.

Many have seen a threat to the foundations of Greek religion in the speculations concerning religion in the late 6th and 5th centuries by the pre-Socratic philosophers such as Xenophanes and the Sophists such as Prodicus. They and their successors in philosophy offered criticisms of the gods in terms of morality, proposed euhemeristic or other theories about the origins of gods, and theorized new types of deities more abstracted from human life. One could also include here the criticisms of deities found in Athenian tragedy (as in Euripides' *Hippolytus* and *The Trojan Women*) and old comedy (e.g., Aristophanes' *Birds*). But these criticisms of both philosophy and literature were directed almost solely against the gods of Homeric epic and rarely if ever touched the gods and rites of local cult. There is no indication from the historical evidence for practiced cult in Athens that family, local, or state cults suffered any loss of attention or support as a result.

The changes we see in classical and early Hellenistic Greek religion are incremental and not revolutionary. Cities with extensive trading interests often set up small sanctuaries in other countries for their own traveling or temporarily resident citizens to use, as the Samians did of their Hera in the Egyptian trading center of Naucratis, or as the Athenians allowed the Thracians to do in Piraeus for their goddess Bendis. In the late 5th and the 4th centuries, Asclepius, who offered new and welcome means of physical healing, was imported from Epidaurus into many cities, among them Athens in 420 BCE, just five years after the end of the plague that had devastated Athens. And a few new hero cults were created, as we have seen. In a typical Greek city the pantheon thus grew, but very slightly and very slowly, without any apparent neglect of preexisting cults.

The rise and dominance of the Macedonian kings, beginning with Philip II and Alexander the Great in the mid-4th century BCE and continuing with the line of their successors in Macedonia, Anatolia, Syria, and Egypt, brought major changes to the Greek world, and religion in the Hellenistic period reflected some of these changes. These Macedonian monarchs patronized Greek religious centers and in most of the hundreds of cities under their control received divine honors, with cults, priests, statues, and often elaborate festivals in their names. Through these cults the individual cities could express their gratitude for the favors large and small that these new kings, almost greater than human to their contemporaries, bestowed. These new cults did not displace, but apparently were added to or linked to existing cults and festivals. The Ptolemies, Alexander's successors in Egypt, seem most systematically to have manipulated cult for political purposes, with the Hellenization of the indigenous Sarapis to unify their subjects of Greek, Macedonian, and Egyptian origin and then with the exportation of this deity to international centers.

Foreign cults

So long as Greek citizens were bound to their cities, religion for individuals and cities remained quite stable. But the social, economic, military, and political conditions under Macedonian and then Roman domination broke down national barriers and caused or allowed the movement and temporary or permanent relocation of many Greeks throughout the Aegean and Mediterranean areas. As traders, sailors, mercenary soldiers, governmental officials, performing artists, and refugees, Greeks were exposed to and participated in "foreign" cults, either cults of other Greek cities or, more commonly, Egyptian, Syrian, and other non-Greek cults—cults of peoples who now too were moving freely around the Mediterranean world. Delos, which became a major international trading center after 167/166 BCE, epitomizes this development. Apollo's island was soon filled with a bewildering variety of Egyptian, Syrian, Anatolian, local Greek, and Roman cults, and Delos provides extensive epigraphical evidence of Greeks of many cities now participating and officiating in Egyptian cults, Syrians in Greek cults, and Romans in cults of all nationalities. International centers such as Delos and the new cities founded by Macedonian kings with heterogeneous populations, such as Antioch, became the melting pots for Greek religion, breaking down distinctions between Greek and foreign deities and rituals and between nationalities of worshipers. In these cities Greek deities were assimilated to foreign deities (what is often called syncretism), foreign deities were given Greek names, and foreign cult structures were adopted by some Greek cults. As traveling and emigrant Greeks returned to their home cities, they brought with them their new deities, and these were gradually added to the pantheon of their homelands. Again, the "old" Greek cities of the mainland seem most resistant to the changes, but Greek cities in Asia Minor, physically closer to the homelands of these "new" foreign cults and more open to influences from indigenous peoples, appear more readily and completely to have accepted the new mix of foreign cults that came to characterize late Hellenistic and Greco-Roman religion.

BIBL.: W. Burkert, *Greek Religion* (Cambridge, Mass., 1985). F. Graf, "Religion und Mythologie im Zusammenhang mit Homer: Forschung und Ausblick," in *Zweihundert Jahre Homer-Forschung* (ed. J. Latacz; Stuttgart/Leipzig, 1991), 331–62. J. D. Mikalson, *Religion in Hellenistic Athens* (Berkeley, 1998). M. P. Nilsson, *Geschichte der griechischen Religion* (2 vols.; 2nd/3rd ed.; Munich, 1961–67).

Etruria

Olivier de Cazanove

*E*truria is, geographically, the region of Italy that lies between the Tyrrhenian Sea to the west, the Apuan Alps to the north, and the river Tiber to the east and south. On the left bank of the river lie Umbria, Sabine territory, and Latium. Within this boundary—but also, to some extent, in adjacent areas temporarily under Etruscan influence, the Po Plain and Campania—there developed, starting in the archaic period, a group of flourishing city-states. These were independent, but linked by a common cultural identity cemented among other things by a shared language. Etruscan is a non-Indo-European language whose interpretation still poses serious problems. It is clearly distinguished not only from Latin (and related dialects, such as Faliscan) but also from the three "Sabellic" languages, South Picenian, Umbrian, and Oscan. All these local languages disappeared once Italy was incorporated by Rome (between the Social War in the early 1st century BCE and the Principate of Augustus). But the military submission of Etruria (as of the rest of Italy) to Rome had been achieved long before Tarquinia, Veii, and Volsinii (Orvieto) were decisively defeated in the period 273–264 BCE, at the same time as Rome extended its power over south Italy (capture of Tarentum, 272 BCE).

The history of Etruria, and especially its religion, presents formidable problems of analysis for modern scholars. There is no surviving Etruscan literature. We are therefore dependent on Roman authors who wrote after (sometimes long after) Etruria had come under Roman control. As a result they possibly committed anachronisms or even outright errors. Their accounts were strongly influenced by various factors in Rome's relations with Etruria, among other things by the tradition of Etruscan kings of Rome. Partly as a result of this, the Romans themselves projected the origin of many of their own religious institutions onto the Etruscans, while at the same time also presenting Etruscan religion and culture as significantly different from their own. Etruscans, for example, were often assumed to have particular expertise in divination, and the Etruscan diviners known as haruspices were still being consulted by the Romans for specialized divinatory advice far into the period of the Roman Empire.

Modern studies of Etruscan religion have for a long time been dominated by the idea that it was a religion not so much "of the book," but "of books": *libri haruspicini, libri fulgurales,* and *libri rituals*—that is, books of haruspicy, which concerned the practice of divination by the examination of entrails; books concerning the religious interpretation of lightning; and books concerning religious ceremonies. This *disciplina Etrusca* (Etruscan discipline or Etruscan religious science) comprised the systematic account of techniques of divination and of the interpretation of different kinds of divine signs. It was supposed to originate from divine revelation, brought to humankind by the mythical infant Tages, who emerged from the furrow of a plowed field in the territory of the Etruscan town Tarquinia; he was preternaturally wise and, although newborn, had a paradoxically elderly appearance. However, we now possess only fragments of the *disciplina Etrusca,* mostly summaries or later elaborations given by Roman writers, and modern scholars have tried to reconstruct these books. In the past, scholars often tried to make links between them and what was known of divination in the ancient Near East, an idea based on the theory (suggested by the Greek historian Herodotus, but now largely abandoned) that the origin of the Etruscans went back to Lydia, in Asia Minor. They also tried to elucidate the fragmentary textual evidence through visual images and material objects—for example, a famous bronze mirror with an engraved design showing the prophet Chalcas (= Greek Calchas) examining the liver of an animal or the bronze model of a liver from Piacenza, which is of relatively late date (2nd to 1st century BCE) but seems to summarize the traditional knowledge of the Etruscan haruspices (one side of the model marks forty sections of the liver, each containing the name of a divinity).

This line of research, which has been intensively investigated for more than a century, does not seem likely, for the moment, to produce any radically new insights, since there is little possibility of new literary evidence. There are a few major epigraphical texts. Most significant, longest, and most frequently cited are the so-called Capua Tile and the wrapping of the Zagreb mummy: the Capua Tile comprises some sixty lines of text inscribed on terra-cotta, found at Capua in south Italy and probably dating to the first half of the 5th century BCE; the mummy wrapping, now in the collection of the Zagreb Museum, in Croatia, was made out of an Etruscan linen book *(liber linteus),* most likely of the 3rd or 2nd century BCE, which was cut into strips and reused in the 1st century BCE or CE to wrap an Egyptian mummy. Recent advances in the decipherment of the Etruscan language has helped our understanding of both these texts, but there is still no definitive interpretation. It is generally agreed that both the Capua Tile and the Zagreb mummy wrapping contain Etruscan religious calendars, including details of prescribed offerings, but there are still many uncertainties about their precise translation and significance. There is also evidence of numerous Etruscan images (relief sculptures, mirrors, tomb paintings) representing gods and myths; but these can be tricky to interpret because they appear largely to follow Greek iconographic conventions.

Future advances in our knowledge of Etruscan religion are most likely to come from archeology. There is increasing interest in the physical settings in which religious cult took place. This approach has the advantage of pinning down rituals and divinities to spatial contexts and of showing that they cannot be understood outside the city (and its territory) whose identity they helped to define. It follows from this that there is no single Etruscan religion, but a multiplicity of Etruscan religions, each one belonging to its own community: Caere, Tarquinia, Vulci, Veii, and so on. True, various "federal" cults linked the different cities, such as the sanctuary of Voltumna ("the principal deity of Etruria" according to the Roman writer Varro) in the territory of Volsinii, which also served as the setting for the annual assembly of the various Etruscan peoples (sometimes referred to as the "twelve peoples of Etruria"). And the same major divine figures were certainly to be found in various cities (Tinia [identified as the equivalent of Roman Jupiter], Uni-Juno, Turan-Venus)—the names of some clearly betraying traces of borrowing from the Greek world (Aritmi-Artemis, Charun-Charon) or from the Italic (Menrva-Minerva). But they also appear to have had a distinctive role in each of the cities where they were worshiped. Graffiti on vases, for example, refer to *Fufluns Pachies Velclthi* (Fufluns Bacchius of Vulci): these give the god Fufluns a Greek epithet, defining him as Dionysus, the master of the *thiasos;* but the reference to the city, Velclthi, also ties the god to that particular location.

Important recent work is also being carried out in the excavation or the reexamination of major sanctuaries that put a particular monumental stamp on the urban spaces of Etruria and the territories of the cities with a characteristic form of monumental religious building—notably the great "Tuscan" temples with three *cellae* (cult chambers), later codified in Vitruvius's typology of architecture. But at the same time, some of these sanctuaries were widely attended by people who came from every part of the Mediterranean world and its different religious traditions: Greeks from Ionia and Aegina at Gravisca, the Greek *emporion* (port of trade) at Gravisca, Carthaginians at Pyrgi, the *emporion* at Caere. The cultural complexity is illustrated by the Carthaginians calling the patron deity of Pyrgi "Astarte," the Etruscans "Uni," and Greek sources "Leucothea" or "Eileithyia." The archeological investigation of the sanctuaries and cemeteries of Etruria—the layout of temples, altars and associated structures, iconography, the distribution of votive offerings, analysis of bone remains—has brought advances in our understanding of public and private ritual (although the evidence has sometimes been overinterpreted).

The state of the evidence and recent directions in research are similar if we turn to the religion of the other early Italic peoples on the peninsula of Italy outside Rome. Here too there can be no question of reducing the many different systems into one single religion. Of course, there were similarities between them (especially in the case of adjacent areas where cultures were in general closely related); but they also had their own distinct and independent characteristics. A striking illustration of this independence, from the Roman perspective, is found in Rome's official refusal to consult the oracle of Fortuna at Praeneste (only twenty-three miles from Rome) until 241 BCE; that would have meant having recourse to a "foreign" oracle.

The literary sources (which are rarely earlier than the reign of the first Roman emperor Augustus, 31 BCE–14 CE) tend to reflect the distorting view of Greeks and Romans on the native cults of Italy; these writers almost always reduce indigenous religion to a series of natural curiosities—the sulfurous waters of the sanctuary of the goddess Mefitis at Ampsanctus in Hirpine country in southern Italy; or the "floating island" of Aquae Cutiliae in Sabine territory, consecrated to the deity "Victory." This represents very much the point of view of ancient travelers ("tourists" might almost be the best term) or of learned antiquarians; one thinks, for example, of the Roman poet Ovid participating in the traditional procession in honor of Juno in the country of the Falisci, between Etruria and Sabine territory (*Amores* 3.13).

Inscriptions give rather more information on rituals and the structure of local pantheons: the seven tablets from Gubbio (ancient Iguvium), commonly known as the Iguvine Tables, written in Umbrian between 200 and 70 BCE; the bronze tablet, written in Oscan, "of the enclosed garden [*hurz*])" of Kerres (Ceres) near Agnone in Samnium; the fifty-eight votive inscriptions from a cult site of Mefitis at Rossano di Vaglio in Lucania, which flourished between the mid-4th century BCE and the 1st century BCE or CE—all of these reveal hierarchized systems of divine power, in which divinities were defined, one against the other, in a complicated and sometimes obscure series of epithets. We find, for example, at Agnone a "Cererian" Hercules and at Rossano a "Mefitanian" Mamers (= Mars); presumably these two major Italic divinities, Hercules and Mamers, were here the "guests" of Ceres and Mefitis, and so in some senses subordinated to the titular deity of the sanctuary. But some formulations are even more complicated. At Gubbio, among the twenty-nine divinities cited, are two, Prestota and Torsa, defined as "Cerfian of Martian Cerfus." This expression links them to the god Cerfus and indirectly to Mars—although it is hard now to unravel what exactly this double dependence entails. The Iguvine Tables also document a set of rituals (taking the auspices, sacrifice) that took place usually at the gates of the city on behalf of either the community as a whole *(touta)* or the Brotherhood of the Atiedii (often compared to the Arval Brethren at Rome).

As in Etruria, the excavation of sanctuaries has multiplied our knowledge of the religious systems. Cult places were often open to the sky, as in the paved courtyard closed off by a long altar at Rossano di Vaglio. Major temples were built, in Samnium for example, notably at Pietrabbondante; but these were a relatively late phenomenon, occurring between the second Punic War and the Social War (late 3rd to early 1st century BCE). After the Social War, when most of Italy was incorporated within the Roman state, some elements of the cults of the erstwhile Italic allies of Rome survived in the towns *(municipia)* and colonies of Italy—although restricted and controlled both politically and religiously. "What we used to call 'municipal cults' [*municipalia sacra*]," noted the Roman writer Festus, "are those that the peoples concerned used always to practice, before receiving Roman citizenship, and which the [sc. Roman] *pontifices* wanted them to continue to observe and practice in the traditional way." It was at this price that the cults of independent Italy enjoyed a sort of survival. But in fact they had become Roman.

BIBL.: O. de Cazanove, "La penisola italiana prima della conquista romana," in *Storia dell'Italia religiosa*, vol. 1: *L'antichità e il medioevo* (ed. A. Vauchez; Rome/Bari, 1993), 9–39. G. Colonna (ed.), *Santuari d'Etruria* (Milan, 1985). F. Gaultier and D. Briquel (eds.), *Les plus religieux des hommes: État de la recheche sur la religion étrusque (Actes du colloque international, Paris 1992)* (Paris, 1997). J.-R. Jannot, *Devins, dieux et démons: Regards sur la religion de l'Étrurie antique* (Paris, 1998). A. Prosdocimi, "Le religioni degli Italici," in *Italia: Omnium terrarum parens* (Milan, 1989), 477–545. G. Radke, *Die Götter Altitaliens* (2nd ed.; Münster, 1979). H. Rix, *Sabellische Texte* (Heidelberg, 2002).

Rome

John North

Rome and the development of its empire

In the centuries before the lifetime of Julius Caesar (100–44 BCE), what we now call Italy was a patchwork of different languages, cultures, and traditions. When Rome was founded, perhaps nine centuries before Caesar's birth, the first inhabitants of the site shared a common language and cultural tradition with just a handful of similar communities (we should say villages) in part of what we now call Latium. Around them, both at the time and for at least three centuries afterward, there were more-powerful and numerous groups in central Italy: tribes speaking Oscan (a language related to Latin but distinct) to the east and south, Etruscans to the north, Greeks in new cities founded in the south and Sicily from the 8th and 7th centuries BCE onward. The history of Rome's early development and expansion was scarcely recorded at the time, and all but the barest outlines had been long forgotten when Roman history began to be written up in the 2nd century BCE, although Greek historians had noticed the rise of this new power in the west in the previous century.

We can reconstruct, with a good deal of help from the archeology of the region and from a handful of surviving documents, some of the key turning points. By the 6th century BCE, Rome was a substantial power with a developed urban center and contacts widely spread through Italy and beyond. In common with other parts of Italy, the Romans abolished their original system of kingship and by the 5th century BCE were being ruled through officials elected for annual terms of office. This is the system called "the Republic," which lasted until the 1st century BCE. It allowed all citizens to have a limited say in decision-making, although its working was dominated by an oligarchy, largely hereditary, drawn from rich and powerful family groups. By the early 3rd century BCE, the Romans had established a highly successful military system and were in control of a large Italian empire, including south and much of central Italy, though not yet the Po Valley. At this stage, they were sending colonies—newly created cities—into many parts of Italy, but other areas were still self-governing, maintaining their own traditions and obliged only to provide troops to fight in Rome's ever-increasing wars.

The Roman Empire, as we think of it today, was created in a long series of wars with Carthage in North Africa, with the great kingdoms of the Hellenistic world, and with the local peoples of Spain. By the time of Caesar's birth, Roman power, sometimes direct, sometimes indirect, was established around much of the Mediterranean and deep into Asia Minor. In an astonishing period of sustained aggression from about 70 BCE until the turn of the era, Rome came to control militarily and to impose methodical government over the whole of western, central, and eastern Europe and the Near and Middle East as far as Syria and Iraq. Three men dominated this history of expansion: Caesar's great rival Pompey, who imposed Roman rule in much of the East (66–61 BCE); Caesar himself, who campaigned in France (58–49 BCE); and his adopted son Caesar Octavianus, who took the title Augustus, whom we think of as the first emperor of Rome, and who supervised the pushing of Roman boundaries to the Rhine and the Danube.

So far, the story is one of ruthless and highly successful imperialism. For the historian of Roman religion this tale of triumph and expansion from humble beginnings creates major problems. First, our knowledge of the early stages of the history is hopelessly inadequate, since our sources of information come from hundreds of years later than the religious situation we are trying to reconstruct; second, as the empire expands from Latium to Italy and from Italy to the greater part of the ancient world, the impact on the nature of Roman society, on their cultural inheritance, and even on their identity as Romans is profound. To take the most obvious example, the population of the city of Rome evidently expanded dramatically in the last three centuries BCE; processions and rituals that once would have been known to all citizens must have been virtually inaccessible to many by the time that Rome had a million inhabitants. We can find areas of continuity and trace the sequence of changes to a limited extent. But, all too often, theories depend on an a priori decision as to what should be thought traditionally Roman and what should not, about which scholars have continuing debates and divisions.

A further complication is implied by the political transformation that accompanied the growth of the empire. The republican system was believed to have lasted since the late 6th century BCE, though much changed in the course of centuries; but the last century BCE saw not only an unprecedented rate of expansion, but also the rise of increasingly severe conflict and divisions within the ruling oligarchy. The system had always depended on the leading men accepting restraints on their ambition, but the men of the 1st century were no longer willing to limit their desire for money, power, and fame. The result was civil conflict and the emergence, in the end, of a single dominant family led by a single dominant ruler. Augustus sought to veil this dominance by operating through republican traditions and powers. But historians, both ancient and modern, have treated the result as a monarchy and have called Augustus and his successors "emperors," with the result that the word *empire* came to mean both the vast territories over whom the Romans had come to rule and the new regime in Rome that had replaced the old Republic.

The city and its gods

The gods and goddesses of Rome, like those of many other cities of the ancient world, were closely identified with the life of the city. This local divine role seems not to have been compromised in the eyes of ancient people by the existence of the worship of the same gods and goddesses in other cities near and far, sometimes by allies, sometimes by enemies. So Jupiter, Mars, and Juno were worshiped under those or similar names very widely throughout Italy; but that did not stop the Romans from treating them as their own. They participated, almost like divine citizens, in the life of the city and all its activities. They were consulted before actions; they sent messages and warnings; they received honors and sacrifices in the event of successes; they had spaces in the city devoted to them; and their images attended processions and games.

There were many channels through which communications could pass between deities and humans, and much ritual activity was determined by these channels. Some messages were sought from the gods by divination, originally from the flight of birds, later from a variety of techniques, including the study of the entrails of sacrificed animals and lightning in the sky; others came unbidden, as when extraordinary happenings were reported from Roman territory (the birth of monsters, groanings from the earth, flashings in the sky), taken as signs from the gods and dealt with regularly by ritual action on priestly advice. The authorities also sought the advice of prophetic books preserved by a special priestly college, whose task was to consult the books and recommend action, sometimes to appease established deities, sometimes to introduce new ones. Messages are passed from humans to gods by prayer (which usually goes with sacrifice) and vows, which specify ritual or gifts in return for divine support. Surviving records of dedications made in gratitude for the fulfillment of such vows leave no doubt about the enduring importance of these transactions throughout the Roman world.

In some respects at least, the religious situation of pagan Rome strikes a modern observer as familiar enough. Holy places had to be consecrated and cared for. Texts for prayers and vows had to be carefully preserved and pronounced. Processions were made through the streets, and divine images were paraded from their temples on special occasions. Prophetic texts were preserved and consulted for advice. The divine beings were conceived of as concerned about human welfare and powerful enough to intervene on behalf of their loyal worshipers. Inherited rituals were respected in the case of birth, marriage, and death within the family. Other aspects, although still practiced in some parts of the world today, would be regarded as deeply "alien" by much modern opinion: the central rite consisted of the killing of animals. This was not a simple ceremony—complex rules determined the nature of the victim for a particular god or goddess, and the sequence of events consisted of procession, sanctification of the victim, prayer, killing, and cooking, leading to a feast for the participants.

On closer examination, however, the differences from almost any modern religion seem to become more profound. The religious identity of a Roman was precisely to be a Roman and to worship the gods of Rome. There was no option of losing this identity or replacing it by becoming a member of some other religion. There were no other religions in competition for the adherence of Roman citizens, nor could they be members of anything corresponding to a "church," to which a citizen might or might not belong. There were various kinds of religious groupings, some open to particular areas or professions, many dedicated to a particular god or goddess. Individuals must have made choices according to their ranks, needs, or preferences; but such choices were within the religious life accepted by the city and caused no problem as to loyalty to the city. In other words, religion did not constitute an autonomous area with the city's life. In the same way, the priests, of whom there were many types, did not represent a rival source of authority to that of the state or its officials. It can be argued plausibly that the same institution in Rome—the Senate, whose members were all who had held annual offices in the past—was the highest authority on religious and nonreligious issues alike, although they respected the advice of the priests.

At all dates for which we have any substantial knowledge, the religious life of the Romans was deeply implicated with their political life. This is a feature of which they were themselves aware, at least in the later republican period. Cicero (the great orator and writer on politics; born 106 BCE) is even proud of it. He himself and his great contemporaries were not just politicians (and, many of them, warriors) but also priests, members of the powerful groups that supervised the different aspects of public and to some extent private religious observance. The state maintained a complicated ritual program, consisting partly of an annual fixed cycle of festivals, partly of rituals to mark specific occasions in public life, and partly of an elaborate system for the consultation of the gods and goddesses of the city before any action was taken. It followed that almost all actions, in civilian as well as in military life, were perceived as involving divine as well as human agents. The priests were responsible for the supervision of the ritual; they did not themselves carry out most of it, but characteristically they dictated the formulas, adjudicated if there were any problems, and were consulted after the event if there was any challenge to the validity.

Modern interpretations have sometimes emphasized this aspect of public life in Rome and argued, consequently, that religion had been reduced to the level of a tool in the hands of the politicians, who found it useful long after they had ceased to put their faith in its claims; during earlier periods, they imply, the Romans would have been genuinely pious and not abused religious rules in this way. In fact, there is no independent evidence for the supposed period of either piety or cynicism, and almost certainly, the whole interpretation rests on a misunderstanding of the fundamental relationships. So far as Romans were concerned, there was no question of choosing between religious objectives and political objectives, between church interests and state interests; most activities were involved with rituals of some kind, and their validity was automatically wrapped up with religious issues.

Another negative perception is that the religion described above was a public ritual system, which ignored or destroyed the needs of individuals for "real" religious experience. Previous scholars reacted to this state of affairs either by vilifying the whole religion as impoverished or by assuming that private religious needs were satisfied in private or family cults about which we know very little. The strong version of this second position is to say that all religions must cater to individual emotional needs; where there are no records of the means used, we must assume that the records are defective. There can, in fact, be little doubt that our knowledge of the religion of the Romans is partial and concentrates on the affairs of the state and public institutions. But forcing all religions into the same mold ignores the possibility that different societies can operate in profoundly different ways. "They *must* have been like us" is not a good principle for writing religious history.

Origins and development of the Roman religious system

Our understanding of the whole Roman religious system is essentially derived from information about its character in the 2nd and 1st centuries BCE and the 1st century CE, from writers of the late Republic and early imperial periods. To a limited extent, we can be confident in projecting this picture backward in time to earlier periods: the names of gods, rituals, festivals, priests, and so on were seen by the Romans as of the greatest antiquity, and we know that they were sedulous in preserving all the details they could of their religious formulas and rituals. But over the course of centuries we also know that the society of Rome and its physical appearance were radically transformed. However conservative they sought to be about the details, religion must have changed as the life of the Romans changed.

In some respects it is quite clear how such changes might have come about. Given the close connection between the religious order and the political system, it must always have been likely that political changes would produce religious consequences. Thinking along these lines, it can be seen that the religious system of the later republican period echoed the political system in having no sharply established focus of consistent authority. Religious decisions were split between the Senate and the priestly colleges; and, although the colleges had senior members, they acted in important matters as a corporation; no priest was normally in more than one college, so an accumulation of authority was difficult if not impossible. But once the position of emperor was established by Augustus and his successors, then the emperor began to acquire an irresistible concentration of religious authority; he became *pontifex maximus* (senior priest of the college of *pontifices*), held all the other priesthoods as well, and combined these with an unprecedented degree of political authority, both formal and informal. The image of the emperor sacrificing to the gods becomes the most common representation of religious action, the key expression of the relationship of humans to the divine.

When we try to go back to still earlier periods, rational speculation becomes difficult. It is a possibility, although no more, that at this early stage religion was a more separate area of life than in later periods, and consequently the religious personnel were more professionally dedicated to their religious tasks than were Caesar and his contemporaries. On the other hand, we have little understanding of the real character of the early monarchy of Rome, and it is also possible that the kings combined in themselves authority over all areas of life and that the priests were no more than their religious advisers on their particular areas of expertise. But it seems that, when the monarchy was abolished, the king's ritual role was handed on to a priest known as the King of Sacrifices *(rex sacrorum),* who was far from being a high priest. Meanwhile the various colleges of priests continued to be autonomous, keeping their own rules and records and making decisions according to their own traditions within their own defined area of concern. The state intervened only to widen their membership.

One subject on which we do have a good deal of information over the republican years is the regular practice of importing new cults and new rituals from outside the city—from elsewhere in Italy, from Greek cities, and later still from Asia Minor. The importations were triggered by a wide range of circumstances, but often by vows taken in the face of defeat or disaster or by recommendations from the priests. New cults were also sometimes created internally by recognizing as a deity what had previously been seen as a quality—Hope, Honor, Piety. For the Romans themselves, these innovations seem not to have been seen as problematic: they themselves recognized deities without number and were willing enough to worship and honor still more. The long-established custom perhaps throws light on a contentious area, namely, their willingness to add more deities still in the form of their own emperors.

Within the city of Rome itself, this custom of deification took place after the emperor's death and only when the Senate approved the transition from human to divine honors, so that emperors whom the senators disliked (Caligula, Nero, Domitian) never achieved the status at all. Outside Rome, no such reticence applied. The living emperors received temples, sacrifices, festivals, and priests exactly as the old gods and goddesses did, although their role stayed consistently in the public sphere and they never received vows or dedications from individuals, as did their divine predecessors. The cult was not standardized through the empire, though it must have been encouraged from the center. But everywhere it provided dignified roles for prominent local dignitaries, who both formed a link between Rome and the cities and also gained high status in the eyes of their fellow citizens at home.

It is important to remember that the overwhelming majority of the empire's inhabitants, not just Greeks and Romans but most of the original peoples of the whole area, were (in modern terms) polytheists, who were willing enough to accept the mutual identity of their gods and goddesses. In many ways, this provided great advantages for the empire: those who moved from one area to another found beliefs and rituals they could understand; it could be assumed that "the gods" were the patrons of all the peoples of the empire, although called by different names in different areas; the worship of the emperor could be accepted everywhere in terms of the local cult practice, without raising too much conflict. There was of course one locality that provided a famous exception: the cult violated the religious principles of the Jews.

Religions in the Roman Empire

As we turn from the story of the Romans and their city to that of the empire that the Romans created, it becomes harder still to agree on the right material for a historical analysis, let alone on the main lines of religious development. But it is at least clear that profound changes in the whole nature of religious life occurred between the lifetime of Caesar and that of Augustine in the 4th and 5th centuries CE. By this later date, individuals (sometimes with their whole family) could choose from radically different religious groups to which they might adhere: orthodox Christians, other Christians considered heretical by the orthodox, Manicheans, Jews, pagans, and so on. They could and did identify themselves by their religion as well as by their city or their family, in a way that earlier centuries would not have understood at all. In terms of religious history, it is hard to exaggerate the importance of this change in the location of religion in society and in the lives of individuals.

One effect of the change was to introduce a new level of hostility and conflict into the relationships of the adherents of the different systems. The most obvious and celebrated sign of this hostility within the Roman Empire was the persecution of Christians by the authorities both of Rome itself and of the cities of the eastern and western provinces. There had been a great deal of strife between the Greek and Jewish inhabitants of the cities of the eastern provinces in the Hellenistic period and the early years of Roman rule; but this, although it certainly had its religious aspects, was essentially intercommunal conflict within a city, not the attempt to eliminate a particular religious form. Moreover, the Jews were recognized as an ethnic group, and this explained why they would have different religious values, profoundly eccentric to pagan eyes, but at least inherited and not adopted. Christians were often pagans choosing to abandon the true religion and hence deeply suspect.

It is important, however, not to exaggerate this element of conflict. The persecutions were occasional and local, their memory being preserved for the most part by the Christians themselves in the promotion of their new cults of martyrs. General persecution throughout the empire was attempted for only two quite brief periods during the second half of the 3rd century CE. For most of the time, through most of the empire, pagans and Christians occupied the same cities peaceably enough. We know of families that included both pagan and Christian members; we find Christian and pagan places of worship close together. The official position of the emperors of the 2nd century CE was normally to take no inquisitorial action, but act only if there were complaints from pagan informers. There was no toleration in principle, but little action in practice.

There is no doubt about the importance of this process of religious change, but little agreement as to its origins, although it is clear that the existence of the empire between 200 BCE and 200 CE must have been a factor giving conditions of relative tranquility and ease of travel throughout the Mediterranean area and also deep into central Europe and the Near and Middle East. Whether it was easy to move around, it is clear that much movement of population did take place and that the cities of the whole empire came to consist not just of locally based communities, but mixtures of different kinds; in many cases, their religious cults and practices traveled together with these mobile groups. We find Greek communities in the west, Egyptian communities and Jewish communities everywhere. The Romans promoted this process themselves, first, by importing and subsequently freeing very large numbers of slaves from all over the eastern world; second, they both exported Roman citizens into the provinces and gave the rights of citizenship to members, especially influential members, of the local elites. Later still, citizenship was conferred on free people throughout the empire.

The coexistence of these different ethnic groups certainly led to a religious life of rich variety in many parts of the empire, and the evidence proves not only that a wide range of cults existed, but also that individuals joined them on the basis of religious preferences and a desire for particular kinds of experience. Thus the Egyptian cult of Isis spread far outside Egypt; the cult of Mithras, perhaps from Persia, but heavily adapted to Western tastes, became widespread in frontier areas of the empire; non-Jews attached themselves to Jewish practices although there was little encouragement from the Jewish authorities to do so. Much of this movement would have consisted of pagans joining groups within the boundaries of paganism and attracted little or no resistance from the authorities, though we do sometimes hear strong disapproval from conservative Roman commentators, particularly when women become the devotees.

These developments must have provided the context within which profound religious changes came about. The outcome is also reasonably clear: by the end of the 3rd century CE, many sharply defined religious options were in existence, which differed deeply from one another in the ideas and value systems they advocated and in their whole conception of the place of human beings in the cosmos. There were still practicing pagans throughout the Roman world, as there continued to be for many generations; but increasingly they were forced to defend their position by argument and by resistance to Christian and other rival claims. It was a struggle for which pagan religious life had given little preparation.

BIBL.: Mary Beard, John North, and Simon Price, *Religions of Rome* (2 vols.; Cambridge, 1998).

Early Christianity

Harold Attridge

A mutation in ancient religiosity, Christianity began as a revitalization movement within Judaism. The movement was inspired by the preaching of an itinerant charismatic, Jesus of Nazareth, who proclaimed the "reign of God" as a future reality anticipated by his own healing, exorcism, and provocative teaching. His claims about his own status in that reign of God remain unclear. It is highly unlikely that he claimed to be divine, as his followers would later assert. He probably did understand himself in prophetic terms, as a divine emissary, but not without irony. He may have spoken of his role allusively, with images such as "Son of Man" from the Hebrew scriptures (Dan. 7.13). His teaching utilized images from daily life in Galilee, farmers sowing, mustard seeds growing, householders entertaining, parents dealing with problem children, a Samaritan helping a stranger. Such images combined with injunctions to nonviolence, and a practice of openness with conventionally defined "sinners." The use of language of divine kingship involved at least an implicit threat to the current political and social order. When such preaching was coupled with a dramatic prophetic gesture, for example, the "cleansing" of the temple of Jerusalem (Mark 11), Roman authorities reacted forcefully.

After Jesus's crucifixion, his followers experienced him triumphant over death, raised from the netherworld, and enthroned at God's right hand. Expectations of the imminent reign of God grounded new readings of Israelite scripture and the formation of new social groups. Inspired by prophetic visions (Isa. 42.6; 43.6–9), some disciples hoped that scattered Israelites would be reassembled, in the company of people from all nations, to worship Israel's God. Followers of Jesus recruited adherents to this vision from non-Israelites throughout the eastern Mediterranean. Jesus's shameful death remained a scandal, but followers explained it as a sacrifice for the sins of humankind (Rom. 3.25), the vehicle for the inauguration of a "new covenant" between God and humanity (Heb. 8–10).

The missionary success of Saul of Tarsus, who also bore the Roman name

Paul, provoked a crisis over conditions of membership within the movement. A conference of leading disciples in Jerusalem around 49 CE confirmed Paul's essential claim that non-Israelites could join the messianic fellowship without undertaking the covenantal sign of circumcision (Acts 15; Gal. 2). The presence of Gentiles within Christianity continued to increase, until by the 2nd century they came to dominate the movement.

During the 50s, Paul and his collaborators continued evangelizing in Asia Minor, Macedonia, and Achaea and planned further work in Rome and Spain (Rom. 15.24). Paul called his new communities the *ekklēsia,* a traditional term for the popular "assembly" in a Greek polis and for the people of Israel (Deut. 4.10; 18.16). Neither political expediency nor genetic affinity united Paul's communities, but the conviction that they possessed a new *pneuma* (spirit) that transformed the present and offered a foretaste of future bliss (Rom. 8). Emissaries (2 Cor. 8–9) bearing letters knit together the scattered and sometimes fractious Christian communities. Paul's own letters, probably collected by the late 1st century, eventually formed an important part of Christian scriptures.

Despite the Jerusalem Council, controversy over entry requirements continued. Paul argued for the equality of Jews and Gentiles because both needed rescue from the power of sin, to which God responded by a gracious act of justification (Rom. 3–7). Paul strove to bridge the divide through a monetary collection from his Gentile congregants for Jerusalem's "poor" (1 Cor. 16; 2 Cor. 8–9; Rom. 15.25–27). The fate of Paul's offering is unknown, but he himself was arrested, sent to Rome, and executed under Nero in the early 60s.

At Paul's death, Christianity consisted of small, mainly urban communities, organized in the households of well-to-do patrons. Members celebrated the memory of the death and resurrection of Jesus at communal meals, enhanced with various spiritual displays (1 Cor. 12–14). Set liturgical forms and hierarchical organization were yet to emerge.

Two sets of events marked the end of the movement's first phase. The deaths of leading apostles such as Paul and Peter, who was also, according to tradition, martyred in Rome under Nero, signaled the passing of the founding generation. The Jewish revolt against Rome, begun in 66 and culminating with the destruction of Jerusalem in 70, eliminated the Christian presence in Israel's ancient symbolic center.

The late 1st century saw the emergence of new literary forms. The first apostolic generation had preached a gospel of "good news" about the new era inaugurated by Jesus's life, death, and resurrection. These traditions now coalesced into narratives combining images of Jesus as wonderworker and teacher with accounts of his noble death and divinely engineered triumph over death. Three such narratives are closely related. The Gospel according to Mark, probably composed around the time of the Jewish revolt, reflects that period's tension, while it admonishes disciples to follow Jesus's way to the cross. The Gospel according to Matthew, probably from the 80s, insists on the ongoing validity of the Torah and portrays the person of Peter as its authoritative interpreter. The Gospel according to Luke, probably written in the 90s along with the Acts of the Apostles, portrays a compassionate Jesus, preaching repentance and forgiveness. Both Matthew and Luke evidence rivalry from leaders of Jewish communities, which probably intensified in the postrevolt period. The last gospel eventually included in the Christian canon, the Gospel according to John, probably achieved its final form around the turn of the century. Even more than Matthew and Luke, it displays an extreme animosity toward Jewish rivals, while trying to inspire a deeper understanding of the significance of Jesus as the incarnate Word of God who fulfills all that temple and Torah promised.

In the late 1st and early 2nd centuries, Christians composed other forms of the "good news." These texts include collections of sayings of Jesus (such as the *Gospel of Thomas*) and apocalyptic visions (such as the canonical Book of Revelation, which tells of the ultimate defeat of satanic powers by the Lion of Judah/Slain Lamb), all of which respond to pressures being placed on followers of the Jewish Messiah in the late 1st century. This literary tradition continued in the 2nd century with *Shepherd of Hermas* and many other "revelations" of eschatological and heavenly realities. Other Christians imitated the work of the previous generation and produced didactic exercises in the names of revered apostles *(Didache)* or romances recounting the missionary adventures of various apostles *(Acts of Peter, Acts of Paul and Thecla)*.

New organizational forms accompanied the literary creativity. The loose associations of house churches of the earliest communities organized into local and regional assemblies, under various forms of leadership. Councils of elders *(presbyteroi)* were the norm in many areas in the late 1st century. By the early 2nd century, one of the elders, designated bishop or overseer *(episkopos)*, began to take on special leadership functions. The trend first becomes apparent in the letters of Ignatius of Antioch, martyred in Rome under the emperor Trajan around 110. On his way to battle the beasts, Ignatius composed a series of letters to communities in Asia Minor and Greece, emphasizing the importance of episcopal authority, as well as belief in the incarnation of Christ.

The institution of the monarchical episcopacy came more slowly to important sites such as Rome. The *First Epistle of Clement* attests to the situation of the late 1st century. Written around the end of the century from Rome to Corinth to resolve a local dispute, it appears to be the work of a Roman presbyteral council, perhaps recorded by its secretary or convener. Although not yet committed to episcopal leadership, the letter offers an early indication of the claims of the Roman community to broader leadership. It also presages later developments by describing the leadership of the Roman community in Jewish sacerdotal terms (*1 Clement* 40).

While hierarchical organization dominated in some locales, looser organizational principles obtained elsewhere. Little evidence survives from Christian communities in Egypt in the late 1st and early 2nd centuries, but later documents suggest that Christians there developed a variation on the "house church" model attested in Pauline communities. What apparently emerged, at least in the urban environment of Alexandria, were small "study circles." Under the guidance of a spiritual master, these groups, like their Platonic and Hermetic counterparts, engaged in the interpretation of texts and comparison of their own traditions with other religious and philosophical sources. Out of such groups emerged, in the mid- to late 2nd century, the phenomenon known as Gnosticism, led by charismatic teachers such as Basilides and Valentinus. Their disciples formed groups with distinctive interpretations of received traditions, both from scripture and the early stages of the Jesus movement.

Gnostics would eventually pose challenges to Christian self-definition, but the first major figure who convulsed the 2nd-century Christian world was Marcion. A successful merchant from Pontus, in the north of Asia Minor, he came to Rome in the late 130s, made a significant benefaction to the community, but was soon expelled on dogmatic grounds. Marcion advocated recognizing one authoritative source for Christian teaching, a collection of the letters of Paul and the Gospel of Luke, duly expurgated of problematic "Judaizing" additions. This first "canon" of scripture supported a theology sharply differentiating the loving God of Jesus from the merely just, and thus inferior, God of the Old Testament. The rejection of Marcion's position guaranteed that Christians would continue to revere the God of Israel as Creator and Redeemer and would continue to read Israel's scriptures as revelatory.

As Christians emerged from obscurity, they encountered opposition and occasional persecution, attested in the correspondence between Pliny the Younger and the emperor Trajan, while the former served as governor of Bithynia in northern Asia Minor. While Trajan approved Pliny's policy of executing recalcitrant Christians, the governor's testimony shows that there was not a settled official policy on the matter and that Christianity was beginning to have a larger social impact.

While governors such as Pliny took sporadic action against Christians, some members of the community offered apologetic responses. In Rome, Justin (a teacher martyred in 165), Tatian (his pupil), Theophilus of Antioch, and others published tracts refuting various charges, for example, of incest (men and women exchanging "kisses of peace" in darkened rooms by night) and cannibalism (devotees consuming Christ's "body and blood"). On the offensive, they excoriated the immorality of traditional Greek and Roman mythologies with their stories of lascivious and sensual deities.

Apologists also reveal Christian practice in the mid-2nd century. Thus Justin describes (*Apology* 1.59–61) the weekly meetings of his community with their readings of scripture and eucharistic celebrations. His report indicates that the rudiments of the central Christian ritual were in place. Yet ritual practice did not develop at the same pace in all quarters. The *Didache,* a document from Syria dating probably from the late 1st or early 2nd century, records a "eucharist" that lacks elements later considered essential: the remembrance of Christ's death and presence in the elements of the meal.

By the end of the 2nd century, Christianity had been sown from the western Mediterranean, through Gaul, Italy, North Africa, Asia Minor, Syria (including the hinterland of Edessa and Nisibis), and Mesopotamia. Christians had even traveled as far away as the Malabar coast of India, which missionaries had already visited when a teacher from Alexandria, Pantaenus, made the journey in the late 2nd century (Eusebius, *Church History* 5.10). Some of these early non-Greek Christian communities have left only scattered traces. Others were more influential. Syrian Christians, for example, composed the exuberant *Odes of Solomon* and developed a rigorously ascetical practice, evident, for instance, in the *Acts of Thomas.*

As Christianity expanded, it adapted in various ways to the ambient culture. In the process it began to deal with the reality that sin remained within the community of the saved. A 2nd-century visionary text from Rome, the *Shepherd of Hermas,* calls the community to renewed moral vigor, but holds out the promise of forgiveness, at least once, for serious sinners such as adulterers. Not all Christians were so lax. As some moved toward accommodation, movements arose to return the church to the purity of its origins. Montanism, a rekindling of apocalyptic prophecy in Asia Minor in the last half of the 2nd century, was precisely such a reaction. While hoping for a literal fulfillment of eschatological hopes, it also insisted on the moral rigor of the movement. If some Christians laid the foundations for a penitential system, others, such as the North African polemicist Tertullian, found the rigorism of the "new prophecy" of Montanism attractive and denounced lax confreres. Disputes between rigorist and accommodating forms of Christianity would mark much of the 3rd century and, in 4th-century North Africa, would lead to the division between Donatists and Catholics.

In the first two centuries, forms of organization and ritual practice exhibited considerable local variation. While Christians generally negotiated the boundaries of their communities and the requirements of membership, debates about the intellectual content of the faith continued. Troublesome questions about the nature of Jesus and his relationship to the God of Israel continued. Apologists explored ways of explaining the mediatorial role of Jesus, developing the category of the Logos (Word) found in the Fourth Gospel. Thus, as the ordinary human word has two forms, in the mind *(endiathetos)* and on the lips *(prophorikos),* so the Word of God has two forms: in the mind of God and in the person of Jesus. This description of Christ's significance dominated Christian theological discourse for the next three centuries, and theologians wrestled with the strengths and weaknesses of the image.

Equally troubling were questions about the nature of the godhead itself and the structure and fate of the cosmos. One set of answers came from the "gnostic" teachers, who explored mythical accounts of the origin of evil in divine complexity. Their work combined radically literal readings of Jewish scriptures and elaborate metaphysical schemes at least partially inspired by Platonic cosmologies. The result was a distinction between an inferior god of creation, the Demiurge, equivalent to YHWH of the Old Testament, and a transcendent spiritual entity, sometimes named the Silent Depth, from whom emanated the revealing Wisdom or Logos that briefly inhabited Jesus. Their writings, such as the Valentinian *Gospel of Truth,* which was found at Nag Hammadi in Egypt in 1945, also offered a powerful vision of what Jesus came to do, namely to awaken in all the spark of divinity sown into matter by a primordial fault in the godhead itself. Once awoken, that spark would find its way back to its transcendent source, with little need of episcopal supervision or sacramental practice. Thinkers of this sort united their metaphysics with a distinctive interpretation of scripture, particularly the cosmogony of Genesis. Their literal reading found evidence of a vengeful and ignorant deity inimical to human welfare. Salvation lay not through that Demiurge, but by escaping his realm.

The theological construal of Christianity offered by such gnostic teachers met resistance from thinkers who defended both the God of Israel, the moral law, and the contemporary ecclesiastical organization that taught it. Irenaeus of Lyons attempted a refutation of gnostic teachers in a massive heresiological work, *Against Heresies*. In addition to mocking denunciations of particular claims of Valentinians and others, Irenaeus articulated an influential vision of orthodox Christianity. For him, the normative scriptures, of both Old and New Testaments, correctly interpreted by bishops whose succession guaranteed their authority, grounded the life of faith. That episcopally guaranteed faith came to expression in creedal form, the "rule of faith."

Other heresiologists followed Irenaeus, including Hippolytus, an early-3rd-century teacher who formed a rigorist schismatic faction within the Roman church. The most significant intellectual of 3rd-century Christianity was undoubtedly Origen. Born in Alexandria in the late 2nd century, he gained prominence as a catechist preparing neophytes for baptism. After tensions arose with his bishop, he moved to Caesarea in Palestine, in 230. Enormously prolific, Origen wrote many tracts on exegetical, apologetic, and dogmatic issues, although his masterpiece was a major work of systematic theology, the *De principiis* or *On First Principles*. The work matched the comprehensive sweep of the imaginative systems of the 2nd-century gnostics, although it rejected their controversial claims about the relationship between the God of creation and the transcendent God of salvation. Like the gnostics, Origen's work was steeped in the Platonic tradition, and some of his platonizing moves, his flirting with metempsychosis, for example, would later elicit criticism.

Despite the apologists' efforts, 2nd- and 3rd-century Christians remained on the periphery of society. Accounts celebrating their heroic deaths (*Martyrdom of Polycarp*, from around 155; *Martyrdom of Perpetua and Felicitas*, early 3rd century) braced others to follow in their footsteps but also reinforced their sense of alienation. The political crisis of the mid-3rd century created more martyrs. The first empire-wide persecution under the emperor Decius (251) tried to solve the "Christian problem" by systematically suppressing the movement. Although intense, the persecution was relatively short. Subsequent sporadic attempts at suppression culminated in the persecution under Diocletian and Galerius, rulers of the eastern half of the empire in the first decade of the 4th century. Persecution ended with the death of Galerius. The subsequent Edict of Milan of 313, issued by the two Augusti, Constantine and Licinius, guaranteed the freedom of Christians to assemble and worship without fear.

Constantine's victory over Licinius in 324 inaugurated the ascendancy of the Christian church as an instrument in the administration of the empire, Shortly after his assumption of supreme authority, Constantine summoned a synod of bishops at Nicea to resolve a festering dispute over the nature of Christ. Although not immediately successful, the council laid the foundation for later orthodoxy. More importantly perhaps, it inaugurated the process of unification of political and religious forces, leading to Christianity's eventual establishment as the empire's formal religion under Theodosius (379–95).

The 4th century marked a period of consolidation, after considerable controversy, of doctrine and organizational form, the fixation of scripture, and the elaboration of liturgical expression. From that point onward Christianity was not simply one religious force among many, but the dominant religious force of the late antique world.

BIBL.: W. H. C. Frend, *The Early Church, from the Beginnings to 461* (London: SCM, 2003). Helmut Koester, *Introduction to the New Testament* (2 vols.; New York: Walter De Gruyter, 1995–2000). Ramsay MacMullen, *Christianizing the Roman Empire A.D. 100–400* (New Haven: Yale University Press, 1984).

KEY TOPICS

Sacred Times and Spaces

Introduction

Space and time are universals, dictated by the physics of terrestrial existence: our bodies are embedded in space and subjected to time. But humans (or perhaps all sentient beings) do not accept physical conditions blindly and obediently; we prefer to control them, and in order to do so, we construct mental and cultural maps. These maps then shape the ways that we experience and think about space and time. Far from being unchanging categories, firmly wired into our brains, they are modeled within our imaginations.

In a very elementary fashion, we map space by looking out from our bodies—in front and behind, above and below, right and left. More importantly for cultural studies, space is mapped by the ways in which we inhabit it and build within it, in ever-growing circles: the individual perceives his or her house as the center of the settlement, while for the group the settlement is the center of a world within other circles, the cultivated fields, the woods where cattle are grazing and deer are being hunted, then the wild and hostile areas of forest, desert, and sea. Time is more complex, since we perceive and reconstruct two contradictory movements: (1) linear time, to which all created beings are subjected, from beginning to end, birth to death, is a finite movement: it will have an end in time, as it has a beginning; and (2) the cyclical movement dictated by the sun's and the moon's circling the earth (as the ancients perceived it)—day and night, the lunar phases, the recurrence of the seasons as immediately experienced in the plant and animal life around us and confirmed by the observation of the stars—is an infinite movement that is repeated over and over; with the advent of longtime astronomical observation, even longer periods become visible.

The calendars of different Mediterranean societies deal differently with these cycles, one major problem being the incompatibility of lunar and solar years: a solar year—the sun's journey through the zodiac—reflects itself in the recurrence of the seasons and seems to be a universal measurement of time; but a solar year is somewhat longer than twelve lunar months, counted from new moon to new moon. The gap between twelve lunar months and the solar year must somehow be filled (a process called intercalation) by adding days or even another, shorter month—and yet, long after the reform of the calendar instituted by Julius Caesar for the Roman Empire, there existed no uniform solution.

Rituals help to construct the movements of both sun and moon. Some rites mark the days, that is, the arrival of morning and evening; there is a tendency, in some Mediterranean cultures, to confine these rituals to the private house rather than to the city's sanctuaries. Other rituals are monthly, structured according to the phases of the moon, and even in a calendar that utterly disregards the moon, such as the Roman calendar, the lunar cycle somehow survives (e.g., in Mediterranean cultures, the simple solar year that takes no account whatsoever of the moon is a rationalization achieved only after antiquity). Most major city festivals are annual, sometimes reflecting the seasonally changing occupations of farmers or mariners; a few are pluri-annual, binding together several years into a larger unit, as does the Greek Olympiad. Linear time concerns the life cycle and thus is marked by rites surrounding birth, maturation and marrying, and death. But even these rites can be turned into a cyclical movement: birthdays commemorate the births of individuals, and unlike birth itself, birthdays come back every year (in some cultures, even every month). Foundation days commemorate the foundations of sanctuaries and cities in annual repetition. Rites of adolescence are repeated every year by the group, the dead are remembered once a year, either collectively in a festival or individually on the days of their deaths. These rites can be repeated every year and transcend the living individual: the finality of linear time, the lifetime allotted to an individual or a city, thus is turned into the eternity of the group's survival.

Sanctuaries—which are, in their most elementary form, spaces with a place where sacrifice can be performed, be it an altar, a pit, or simply a stone marker—mark space and its divisions; both cities and the open land are dotted with sanctuaries and sacred places. Research into the question of why a specific sanctuary was placed where it was has just begun; currently, there are more questions than answers, despite reflection on the topic already in antiquity. Borders are marked by shrines, as are gates that, in an indigenous reading, are often protected by an altar or a divine image. A city typically contains, among other sanctuaries, one main sanctuary for the city gods, often lifted high above the surrounding plain, either artificially, as in the case of the ziggurat, or on a natural elevation, an acropolis, or a Capitolium. Such a sanctuary is not only the conceptual center of the city's horizontal extension but also mirrors its vertical relationship with its gods. Border sanctuaries not only mark the outer limit of a city's territory but also form points of exchange between neighbors and may develop into nodal points for a league of several cities.

Rituals belong to sanctuaries and, as such, help to construct space. Processions lead worshipers to a sanctuary, marking its relationship to the city—from outside to a city's central shrine, from a city to an outlying sanctuary—or they demarcate the territory in a circular movement around the city or the fields. Travel—of visitors, athletes, ambassadors—to a supralocal shrine and its festival constructs an even larger map of spatial relationships, as do pilgrimages by individuals or groups.

But a sanctuary in itself is not a uniformly sacred space, as opposed to the profane space outside its borders. It can contain spaces of varying degrees of accessibility—areas and rooms that are open only after a special ritual, or that are open only to the priests, or that are closed to human access altogether. Degrees of accessibility are correlated to different degrees of divine presence: the closer and more immediate the divine presence is, the more difficult it is for humans to gain access into it. This helps to construct divinity as being the "other"—as being more-or-less radically different from human worshipers. This observation calls into question our simple dichotomy between sacred and profane, holy and ordinary (which might, in the end, be a Christiano-centric conception). Most ancient religions prefer multiple gradations of space, which is mirrored by their languages' containing several words to express our notion of sacred. The same holds true for time: there is no simple opposition between sacred and profane time, festival and everyday life, Sunday and workday: some rituals are celebrated by the entire population of a city or an even larger crowd, others by smaller groups inside the city, others again are performed only by the priests or other specialists.

BIBL.: Pierre Bourdieu, *Outline of a Theory of Practice* (trans. Richard Nice; Cambridge: Cambridge University Press, 1977). Rolf Gehlen, *Welt und Ordnung: Zur soziokulturellen Dimension von Raum in frühen Gesellschaften* (Marburg: Diagonal, 1995). Alfred Gell, *The Anthropology of Time: Cultural Constructions of Temporal Maps and Images* (Providence, R.I.: Berg, 1992). Nicolas Wyatt, *Space and Time in the Religious Life of the Near East* (Sheffield: Sheffield Academic Press, 2001).

F.G.

Egypt

The Land: Sacred Geography

In papyri and temple inscriptions from Greco-Roman Egypt, the whole land of Egypt appears as a sacred space. Litanies, scenes, and writings devoted to specific nomes or provinces (e.g., Papyrus Jumilhac and Book of the Fayyum) codify the sacred structure of Egypt, enumerating the forty-two nomes with their capitals, chief deities, specific priesthoods, sacred animals, sacred trees, taboos, and the "limb" and "tomb" of the dismembered god Osiris, a huge body of cult-topographical knowledge that was also ritually enacted in the form of processions. During the Khoyak rites, which were celebrated in every nome that contained a tomb of Osiris, a "canopic procession" of priests representing the forty-two nomes carried jars with Nile water in order to "re-member" the dismembered body of Osiris, symbolizing the sacred integrity of the land of Egypt. During the classical period of Egyptian history, a similar concept was expressed in the royal rituals of coronation and jubilee (or *sed* festival). In these rites, the king acted before the assembled deities of the land, and as lords of the land, they recognized him as their representative. They embodied the land as a political unity and as a sacred space.

Cities. Just as the totality of deities embodied the political concept of Egypt, the individual local deity embodied the concept of city. Every city, therefore, was a holy city and a sacred space. However, one city always stood out as the center of holiness. This role was played by Heliopolis (*Iwnw* = Hebrew *'ōn*) during the Old and Middle Kingdoms. Later, Thebes took over, assuming in this role the name Southern Heliopolis. In the Greco-Roman era, when Alexandria played the part of secular capital, Memphis was reinvested as a sacred city. But the specific holiness of Heliopolis, Thebes, and Memphis never deprived any other towns and cities of their specific sanctity. Paraphrases such as "city of Amun" and "city of Ptah" so unequivocally designated Thebes and Memphis that the Greeks introduced names of this sort for most Egyptian cities, replacing the names of the Egyptian deities with their Greek equivalents. Hermopolis thus became the Greek name for "city of Thoth," Hermes being, according to the Greeks, another name for the god Thoth.

The sacred rank of an Egyptian city was determined by its antiquity. The holy city lay on the primeval mound that emerged from the waters at the beginning of creation:

Aerial view of the temple of Amun at Luxor. *Hirmer Fotoarchiv*

Thebes is the model for every city:
water and land were [mixed] in it at the beginning.
Sand came to measure the fields,
to make its soil come into being on the primeval
    mound,
that the land might come into being.
Papyrus Leiden 1.350

By serving as home to deities, Egyptian cities also made humans at home on earth. To live in a city meant to be in the proximity of the deity who had dominion there. In Egypt everyone had a city and a deity, whom he or she followed and who cared for him or her. An Egyptian always considered himself or herself a citizen of a city and never of the country. Citizenship was a tie between the divine and the human. Social and political belonging, in Egypt, meant membership in a sacred community, the festive community of the local deity. It was the religious feast that established and secured one's identity as Theban or Memphite. This was the focus of civic identity.

The religious feast was the one occasion on which the gods left their temples and appeared to the people at large; they normally dwelled in complete darkness and seclusion inside the sanctuaries of their temples, inaccessible to all save to the priest in service. But on the occasion of a feast these boundaries between secret and public, sacred and profane, inner and outer, were suspended. Every major Egyptian religious feast was celebrated in the form of a procession, turning the whole city into a vessel of divine presence.

Temples. As lords of the cities and proprietors of huge landed estates, the deities lived in their templelike castles. In the Egyptian language, the *pr* (divine household) is contrasted with the *Hwt-nTr* (god's house). The latter term designates the actual temple, built of stone, whereas the former also includes storehouses, workshops, and lay dwellings that were built of mud brick. In the Greco-Roman period, the same architectural concept underlies all the large temples. It was thought to have been designed by the creator-god himself at the beginning of the world. The most outstanding feature of this canonical temple type is the sequence of seven doorways leading from the most exterior portal in the outer enclosure wall to the holy of holies, separating space into zones of increasing holiness and intimacy, leading from the city into the sacred enclosure, through the business area to the temple proper, from the open court

245

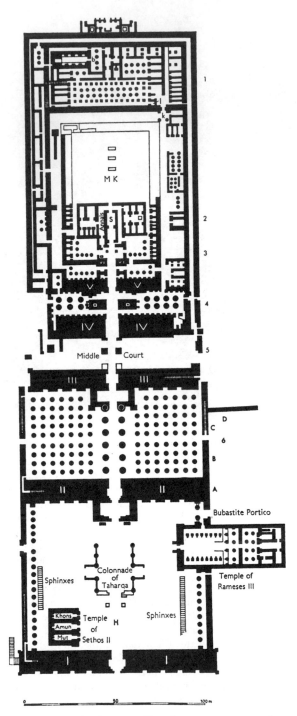

Plan of the temple of Amun at Karnak. *From Kurt Lange and Max Hirmer,* Ägypten: Architektur, Plastik, Malerei in drei Jahrtausenden *(1955)*

to the covert rooms, and so forth. From the exterior to the interior, the rooms become ever smaller, while the floor becomes higher and the ceiling lower. Corresponding to the diminution of space is an increasing darkness. The courtyard, which is flooded with light, is followed by the crepuscular Hall of Appearance. The inner rooms lie in deep darkness.

The succession of rooms, halls, and courts gave architectonic form to the processional route of the deity, which also extended beyond the temple: a sacred avenue led straight to the river; other sacred avenues made a connection with other temples and holy places that the god visited during his processions. The festival outings thus affected urban planning. In earlier periods, temples conformed more or less to the same basic idea, although in a less canonical way. Already in the New Kingdom, the processional feast makes the most important imprint on temple architecture. Especially temples belonging to oracular deities (e.g., the temple of Luxor) stressed the processional route. In Egypt, deities "spoke" through movement to make their will known. A forward movement of the divine image signified assent, a backward movement disapproval. Oracles, therefore, were fundamentally connected with processions. The festival procession was the form in which city deities exercised their de facto rule.

BIBL.: Dieter Arnold, *Die Tempel Ägyptens: Götterwohnungen, Kultstätten, Baudenkmäler* (Zurich: Artemis & Winkler, 1992). Jan Assmann, *The Search for God in Ancient Egypt* (trans. David Lorton; Ithaca: Cornell University Press, 2001), chap. 2. R. B. Finnestadt, *Image of the World and Symbol of the Creator* (Studies in Oriental Religions 10; Wiesbaden: Harrassowitz, 1985). B. E. Shafer (ed.), *Temples of Ancient Egypt* (Ithaca: Cornell University Press, 1997).   J.A.

Calendars and Festivals

Temples were often inscribed with calendars covering the daily religious activities of the residing deity or deities. Usually, they consisted of a terse, nonnarrative rendering of the key events involved. Following an introduction to the body of the text in which some historical data such as the date and the name of the king are presented, the donations made by the pharaoh were listed, as well as the dates of each celebration that took place within the 365-day civil calendar. By and large, then, these festival calendars record the date, the offerings donated, and the specific feast (if applicable). In the Greco-Roman period a few additional details referring to the time of day or the type of religious procession might be included. The offerings, however, were no longer recorded.

Most religious celebrations were fixed within the civil year, a period of 365 days that was established early in the 3rd millennium BCE for bureaucratic purposes; this replaced an earlier system based on a year composed of

Mural of Egyptian priests carrying a bier with image of the crocodile god Sobek. Copy from the temple of Pnepheros at Theadelphia. *From Evaristo Breccia,* Monuments de l'Egypte gréco-romaine *(1926)*

lunar months. The names of the months in the lunar calendar were transferred to the civil calendar without difficulty, although a time lag of one month was introduced (i.e., each name was associated with a month later than it previously had been). The Egyptian civil year was additionally divided into three seasons of four months apiece: Inundation, Emergence (the title presumably refers to the emergence of the grain), and Heat.

Later cultic calendars were associated with specific gods, such as Amun of Thebes. From these calendars we can determine whether the timing of a feast depended only on the civil calendar or, rather, was organized according to the moon (e.g., on day 6 of the new moon or day 4 of the full moon) as well. Additional lunar-based celebrations, labeled "seasonal festivals," were distinct from annual, civil-based ones. By and large, the number of feasts that were determined according to phases of the moon shrank considerably after the inauguration of the civil calendar.

The first of the standardized religious events that were labeled "annual festivals" was New Year's Day *(Wep-renpet);* this heralded both the first day of the civil calendar and general rejuvenation and rebirth. Subsequent to New Year's Day was the more somber feast of Wagy on day 18 of the first month. Eventually, however, Wagy, which was connected with the funerary rituals of Egypt, came to be associated with the festival of Thoth on day 19. In historical times, we find two separate Wagy feasts: one set according to the cycle of the moon and a later one firmly placed at day 18 of the first civil month.

The following month was dominated by the Opet festival, a rite connected with the pharaoh and his divine father Amun(-Re). This festival required the monarch to go to the temple of Luxor at Thebes in order to receive the powers of kingship. By the New Kingdom, this event became part of the official royal ideology of the state and may regularly have included coronation.

An older festival was that of Choiak or Sokar, celebrated during the fourth month. This event involved Osiris and highlighted the centrality of the city of Memphis in funerary matters. Evidence for it is first found in the private feast lists of the Old Kingdom, although the funerary deity Sokar himself predates the unification of Egypt at the beginning of the first Dynasty. Originally, Sokar encompassed only two days—days 25 and 26 of the month—with the second, key day focusing on the death of Osiris; later, the number of days that it encompassed grew considerably. Sokar brought the first season of the Egyptian year (Inundation) to a close, and so the first day of the following month saw the celebration of Neheb-kau, a festival celebrating rebirth (which thereby duplicated in theme the calendrical New Year of the first day of the first month).

Later, the festival of Min, a god of fertility, also began a new season; it was celebrated during the ninth civil month, although its specific date was determined according to the moon. The rejuvenatory elements of this festival included the pharaoh's enactment of his role as life-sustainer of his people, especially insofar as he cut the first sheaf of grain. Generally, the agricultural aspect of harvest dominated this festival.

The tenth month included the famous Valley feast, a second Theban celebration that can be traced back to the Middle Kingdom. From Karnak the statues of the god Amun, his consort Mut, and son Khonsu were carried across the Nile to Deir el-Bahri on the west bank. It was a popular event insofar as families visited the tombs of their relatives as part of the festival and celebrations ensued. Certainly by the time of the New Kingdom, there were major celebrations in which nonparticipants looked on while the god Amun processed from Karnak to Luxor or crossed the Nile westward to visit Deir el-Bahri (Valley festival) or Medinet Habu (Opet festival). Oracles could be granted to observers at these times.

Another celebration, not listed in the official festival calendars, was connected with the rejuvenation of the pharaoh himself: the Heb-Sed rite. This traditionally occurred after the first thirty years of a pharaoh's reign; we know it best from pictures and inscriptions. Its date was originally determined by the lunar calendar, as the number of years could be equated with the 30 days' length of a month. It highlighted the pharaoh's connection to rebirth, and it is significant that a separate feast, connected with some of the same events, took place soon after the death of Osiris during the feast of Sokar or Choiak.

We know little about secular festivals. One exception is the annual celebration of victory established by Rameses III in recognition of his military victory over the Meshwesh Libyans in his eleventh regnal year (ca.

1176 BCE). The annual king's coronation, of course, should be mentioned here as well.

The walls of the temples of Dendara, Edfu, Esna, Kom Ombo, and Philae provide additional information from the Greco-Roman period, which permits us better to reconstruct the events of festivals held there. Moreover, papyrus rolls, such as those found at the Middle Kingdom site of Illahun, and fragmentary biographical texts reveal the intricate details of processions; the morning, noon, and evening appearances and rites of the deity; chants; and speeches. The detailed program at Rameses III's mortuary temple of Medinet Habu casts light upon the age-old performance of the cutting of the first sheaf of barley during the Min feast, for example. Similarly, the scenes portrayed on the temple of Luxor in Thebes reveal a wealth of cultic information connected to the politically and theologically central concept of kingship during the feast of Opet.

BIBL.: Leo Depuydt, *Civil Calendar and Lunar Calendar* (Louvain: Peeters, 1997). Alfred Grimm, *Die altägyptischen Festkalender in den Tempeln der griechisch-römischen Epoche* (Wiesbaden: Harrassowitz, 1994). Harold H. Nelson and Siegfried Schott, *Work in Western Thebes, 1931–33* (Chicago: University of Chicago Press, 1934). R. Parker, *Calendars of Ancient Egypt* (Chicago: University of Chicago Press, 1950). Sherif El-Sabban, *Temple Festival Calendars of Ancient Egypt* (Liverpool: Liverpool University Press, 2000).   A.J.S.

Festivals (primarily Greco-Roman period)

Festivals in Egyptian religion carried many of the same functions as in other cultures, but they must be understood first as a ritual process surrounding the god's appearance and procession (as an image) from within the confines of the temple. According to the processional schedules often inscribed on temple walls, priests would carry the god's primary image out of the temple, often on a barque, accompanied by music and dancing, to complete an established circuit of lands and shrines with which the god had some connection. Major cult festivals sometimes included a flotilla down the Nile as an extension of the god's circuit (Herodotus 2.60).

As the god processed overland or along the Nile, priests would convey his or her fertilizing and protective power to bystanders and fields by means of gesture, chant, and pronouncement (Sauneron 1962). Many processions also incorporated oracles: as the image was held in some public space, a supplicant (or a priest on his behalf) would ask a question; and a priest would interpret the god's answer from the image's apparent movement on the bearers' shoulders. The procedure is recorded in a wall painting from the temple of Pnepheros (Theadelphia) and in the Brooklyn Oracle Papyrus (Amun temple, Karnak) and has parallels in modern African and African American cultures. Both classical sources and temple inscriptions suggest that some festival processions culminated in priestly dramas, evoking central myths of the god through song, dialogue, pantomime, or even ritualized slaughter (Herodotus 2.63; Plutarch, *On Isis and Osiris* 30, 39, 50; Fairman 1954; Sauneron 1962). References in papyri to "dog-headed" priests (= Anubis; *Sammelbuch griechischer Urkunden aus Ägypten* 5.7336; Wessely 1922: 56) and a "basket-carrying priestess" of Demeter (= Isis? Papyrus Oxyrhynchus 36.2782), as well as evidence for masks of the god Bes, all point to the ritual embodiment of gods during festival processions.

Whether local or regional, festivals revolved around the temple, priesthood, and sacred image in procession and consequently had the effect of centralizing religion in the immediate culture in several important ways. First, those festivals that included conflict dramas—the arising of Osiris, the vanquishing of Seth—rearticulated social and cosmic order through these ritual reenactments of disorder. Second, inasmuch as most festivals pertained in some way to the agricultural cycle—crops, Nile—and coordinated it with mythology, festivals had the function of sanctifying the natural cycles of the environment. Third, the festival calendar, based on temple schedules and records, coordinated the social experience of time. Fourth, festivals were occasions for the display and reassertion of symbols—divine image, barque, processional dress, songs and slogans—that traditionally defined the locale or the region. Fifth, festivals involved the dispensing of divine power for personal, domestic, and collective needs, delivered from the images themselves, from priests' gestures and prayers, and from such substances as might be scattered during procession. In all five functions we see the ritual interweaving of local, extratemple tradition with the literate, systematizing tradition of the temple priests.

But Egyptian festivals were also, as Herodotus, Plutarch, and papyri make clear, occasions for enthusiastic popular participation. Terra-cotta figurines intended for popular purchase show priestesses with musical instruments, dancers, and animals decked for procession (Dunand 1979). Various versions of hymns to the Nile reflect group festival song. Herodotus describes a festival—ostensibly for Dionysus but more probably Min—in which women go from village to village carrying ithyphallic figures (2.48). The 4th-century church father Epiphanius of Cypriot Salamis describes veritable orgies taking place at Memphis, Heliopolis, Menouthis, and elsewhere (*De fide* 12.1–4). And traditional choreographies undergirded the frivolity: along with the processions and the hymns, some communities engaged in mass hunts of animals that represented chaos (Plutarch, *On Isis and Osiris* 50), while other communities made special clamors for apotropaic effect (63). It is also likely that some ritualized interactions took place between priests masked as Bes or holding images of procreative power (Min, Bes, Isis) and onlookers desirous of such benefits. A Besia (Bes festival) held in 2nd-century CE Dendara probably celebrated human fertility and its protection through just such dramatic representations of the god (Papyrus Heidelberg inv. 1818). A quieter, more domestic form of popular participation in festivals involved the lighting of lamps. Herodotus mentions a "festival of lights" based in Sais but celebrated throughout Egypt (2.62), and the numerous terra-cotta lamps produced in Egypt throughout the Greco-Roman period and often stamped with mythic imagery attest to such observances. Even in the 5th century CE, the Christian abbot Shenoute of Atripe criticizes people who light lamps and burn incense in their homes on the day of the god Shai (in a sermon entitled "The Lord Thundered").

Festivals were occasions to interact with the gods in forms either carried or personified by temple priests and thus to derive benefits from them. These benefits could be received collectively, by touching the god for his blessing or by acquiring images of the gods or priests to evoke the powers of the festival. Terra-cotta representations of priestesses and divinities (Isis, Harpocrates, Bes, and others) in states of nudity convey not real festival attire but rather the procreative power of festival officiants (Dunand 1979). Such images were painted and sold for domestic shrines. Hence the festival was an opportunity to reaffirm the link between domestic piety and the altogether sacrosanct temple cult (Frankfurter 1998).

Documentary papyri make clear that festivals were occasions of great consumption (Perpillou-Thomas 1993). Food and drink were often consumed in ritual forms. Plutarch describes a festival to Thoth in which sweet foods are eaten while slogans are shouted (*On Isis and Osiris* 68); and numerous terra-cotta figurines of the child-god Harpocrates stirring a pot may likewise point to the ritual consumption of sweets (especially for children) in symbolic connection with the god. Other festival foods are ritually designated with stamps: of Seth as a hippopotamus in order to declare him impotent (Plutarch, *On Isis and Osiris* 50) or of Bes or other gods in order to gain intimacy with their powers. Terra-cotta jugs bearing the face of Bes probably had such a purpose in designating some liquid as festival drink.

In these various aspects of enthusiastic participation outside temple walls, festivals allowed the articulation and celebration of social identity and solidarity along traditional lines, which were established through the festival's specific myths and rituals.

Temple festival calendars changed continually over Egyptian history, especially in the larger cult complexes and especially under the influence of Ptolemaic and Roman rules and of Mediterranean cultures more generally. The Ptolemaic dynasties' intimate engagement with Egyptian royal mythology to sanction their rule expanded the importance of the royal festival as a national event, both in the main Egyptian temples and among Greek colonists. Through the Roman period, temples throughout Egypt held various kinds of festivals on behalf of kings and emperors, both a means of political propaganda and to sanctify the political order through ritual means. Outside the temples, however, these kinds of festivals were typically celebrated only by private religious associations.

Greco-Roman culture brought with it new gods with their own festivals, however, and with them new concepts of celebration. Urban festivals in Roman Egypt, whether for the Nile, the god Sarapis, or a local "Cronus," came to include Homeric recitation, gymnastic displays, comedians, and other hallmarks of Hellenistic culture; athletes took on some of the charisma of priests; and festivals came to be designated increasingly by the more secular term *panēgyris* instead of the more religious *heortai*. As elsewhere in the Roman world, the production of a spectacular *panēgyris* brought renown and authority to a city.

Greco-Roman indulgence of major Egyptian festivals included the *sēmasia* (celebration of the Nile's rise); the Sarapia (celebration of the hybrid god Sarapis, popular throughout Egypt); the Harpokrateia (celebration of Horus in his child aspect); and the various Isia and Amesysia festivals to which Hellenistic culture contributed, first, new forms of iconography (these innovations appeared in processional performance and in souvenirs, but never on temples or as major temple images). Second, Hellenistic culture developed new offices and ways to coordinate festival observance across Egypt: for example, the new processional office "high priest of the most holy Nile" (Papyrus Wisconsin 9.4), whose duties do not seem to have extended beyond festival appearances. Festivals for Greek and Roman gods, for example, Demeter, Athena, Dionysus, and the Dioscuri, also become increasingly common, if still the business primarily of local religious associations. Festivals also arose to commemorate more recent events. Among its numerous festivals to gods, the city of Oxyrhynchus was still celebrating, some eighty years later, the day of victory over the 116/117 CE Jewish revolt (Tcherikover 1957–64: 450), although the victory might by then have been mythologized as the triumph of Horus over Seth.

After the 3rd century CE, financial pressures, imperial religious edicts, Christianization, and new forms of urban conviviality such as the circus led to the decline of many of the central religious festivals, although many local forms continued throughout Egypt, maintained by communities, religious associations, and households. While the Amesysia is no longer attested after the 3rd century, festival observance of the *sēmasia* in various local forms continues through late antiquity, when the Christian abbot Pachomius recalls it as a family tradition in his youth (*Vita* 4) and another 4th-century monk tries to stop a temple procession "to ensure the flooding of the Nile" (*Historia monachorum* 8.25). By the 5th century, Egyptian religious festivals consist mostly of those surrounding Christian martyrs' shrines, which bear many of the accoutrements of the temple festivals: processions, terra-cotta souvenirs and "blessings," and popular expectations for procreative power from the saint. Still today, the festival of the Muslim saint Abu el-Haggag, patron of Luxor, culminates in the procession of his barque through the city's streets.

BIBL.: Françoise Dunand, *Religion populaire en Égypte romaine* (Leiden, 1979). H. W. Fairman, "Worship and Festivals in an Egyptian Temple," *Bulletin of the John Rylands Library* 37 (1954): 165–203. David Frankfurter, *Religion in Roman Egypt: Assimilation and Resistance* (Princeton, 1998). Françoise Perpillou-Thomas, *Fêtes d'Égypte ptolémaïque et romaine d'après la documentation papyrologique grecque* (Louvain, 1993). Serge Sauneron, *Les fêtes religieuses d'Esna aux derniers siècles du paganisme* (Cairo, 1962). V. Tcherikover, *Corpus papyrorum judaicorum* (3 vols.; Cambridge, 1957–64). C. Wessely (ed.), *Catalogus papyrorum Raineri* (Studien zur Palaeographie und Papyruskunde 22; 1922). D.F.

Mesopotamia

Sacred Times

The Mesopotamian concept of time finds its expression in two complementary models: linear progression, as in the case of a human life or in history; and cyclic, periodical return, as determined by nature, such as day and night, lunar months, and solar years. Prominent points in these cycles mark the appropriate times for religious festivals; events of historical time are not important.

A month begins with the first appearance of the crescent moon in the evening sky; consequently, nightfall marks the beginning of a new day. Twelve months usually add up to a year, which starts ideally at the vernal equinox. The difference between the 354-day lunar year and the 365-day solar year is compensated for by the occasional insertion of an extra month. This division of time (i.e., a year divided into twelve or thirteen months, each containing twenty-nine or thirty days) was used in everyday business as well as in the cult.

Months are divided into days, and a specific time of the day may be especially suited for certain religious matters. Magic rituals usually have to be performed in the early morning, before daybreak. The morning hours were also of special significance in temple rituals. A month is further divided according to lunar phases (new moon on day 1, first quarter on day 6/7, full moon on day 14/15), and thus forms the backbone of the cultic calendars of Mesopotamia. The three days already mentioned mark monthly festivals held in many temples, especially during the late 3rd and early 2nd millennia BCE. In these cases, cultic rituals and offerings are performed for the highest gods of a city, but the divine power of the moon per se is not venerated. The disappearance of the moon at the end of the month is considered a time of danger, especially for the king; mourning rites are performed (often by the queen) in order that these days may pass safely.

The days of a month are counted simply by number, but these numbers always represent a cosmic order, because each day always corresponds to a specific lunar phase. This might, to some extent, explain the importance in Mesopotamia of hemerologies or menologies (manuals that list felicitous days or months). The practical relevance of hemerologies has been tested against records of the Neo-Assyrian royal court (7th century BCE), and it turns out that extispicy reports (reports on what the organs of a sacrificed animal signify) are usually not dated to those days that are forbidden for extispicy in the hemerologies, namely, days that are related to certain phases of the lunar disc.

The agricultural year and its festivals. The agriculture of southern Mesopotamia depended on irrigation. Therefore, the agricultural year was primarily determined by the weather and to a lesser extent by the water level of the Euphrates and Tigris. The annual flooding occurred in spring (April/May). Sowing of seed, mostly barley, took place in autumn (October/November). In April/May the grain was harvested; the vegetation then dried up during summer until the rains started again in autumn.

In early Mesopotamia, the agricultural year was reflected in festival and month names. Directly linked to the farmer's work were the important festivals of Sowing the Seed and Cutting the Grain. At Ur, these so-called *Akitu* festivals were fixed respectively at the autumnal and vernal equinoxes. Interestingly, these festivals, like others, were celebrated at the very beginning of the work. Thus, the sowing season started with a ritual plowing of the first furrow. This was done by the king as a representative of the whole country; the divine blessing that followed applied to the king and to his country as well. Furthermore, the timing of the festival allowed for a certain concentration of the population within the settlements (before it dispersed into the fields); and the festive gathering also provided an appropriate beginning to collective labor. In addition to these official cults, more modest rites were required to secure the prosperity of the fields. The festivals at the end of the plowing period, and especially at harvest, only rarely surpassed those celebrated at the beginning, however.

On a more metaphorical level, the life of vegetation and its death in late spring was reflected in the Dumuzi cycle and its female celebrations in springtime (see Myth and Sacred Narratives). The dead were remembered during the festival/month of Abu (August), when the whole land dried up.

Local deities and their festivals. Each Mesopotamian city had its own, local deities, which were often conceived of as families with their own courts. Marriage between gods was also a prominent festival theme. Within the main temples the gods received offerings as their daily food, and they also figured prominently in the monthly and annual festivals. Their cult was maintained by the local ruler and his family.

The highest festival of a local deity in Sumer was his or her "New Year" (e.g., the Great Festival of Nanna at

The Procession Way at Ishtar Gate, Babylon. *Hirmer Fotoarchiv*

Ur). The festival usually featured a procession to a rural sanctuary (see also the state festivals below); here also the spatial extension of the deity's area of influence was demonstrated. It was on only this occasion that the deity left the temple and could be seen by the common people. The return of the god was a triumphal *adventus* to his chosen city and temple, which he would inhabit for another year. As represented in Sumerian hymns, the divine King Enlil decreed the particular god's good fate at such an occasion. In ritual, the bathing and dressing of the divinity's statue, which took place at this time, apparently reflected the annual renewal of the god's power.

State festivals. The king represented his country before the gods. As such he played a prominent role in the most important festivals, which were considered state festivals. Two prominent examples of such festivals are offered here.

The Tummal festival was held in Nippur under the kings of the Third Dynasty of Ur (21st century BCE). Being the city of the divine king, Enlil, Nippur held first rank among the cult places of Babylonia at that time; shortly thereafter (Isin Dynasty, 20th century BCE), it even achieved the unique position of a religious capital like later Babylon or Asshur.

The Tummal festival started at the end of the seventh month (about October) with rites at the Duku (a mound representing a cosmic locality where the primordial gods dwelled; see further Sacred Times) at the temple of Enlil at Nippur. According to later, more explicit sources, the dead forefathers of Enlil, who were apparently the source of his supreme power, were mourned. This ceremony took place at the end of the month, when no moon was visible. With the beginning of the new month, the cult statues of the divine pair Enlil and his wife Ninlil, accompanied by the other gods of Nippur and by the king, left the city by boat and journeyed to the nearby cult center of Tummal, where the elite of the country gathered. According to administrative documents, large quantities of drink and food, especially meat, were distributed to the people. After celebrations and offerings at Tummal, the gods returned to Nippur, whereupon they decreed a good fate for the king. The king also attended other festivals at Nippur and elsewhere, including the Gusisu festival, the main festival of the warrior-god Ninurta, the son of Enlil.

The most prominent festival of ancient Mesopotamia, the New Year or *Akitu* festival of Babylon, is documented by sources from the 1st millennium BCE. It took place during the first twelve days of the first month Nisannu (about April). Gods from Babylonian cities

Ziggurat (Temple Tower) at Ur, ca. 2100 BCE. *Hirmer Fotoarchiv*

visited the divine king Marduk/Bel, first among them Marduk's son Nabu, from nearby Borsippa. Marduk was called to appear, the gods gathered in the court of his temple, Esagil, and Marduk decreed the fate of the earthly king; the king had previously received his royal insignia in the cella of the god's temple. The procession left the temple, crossed the city, and finally reached the *Akitu* house, a sanctuary in the steppe. Upon his return, Marduk decreed the fate of the country.

Various aspects of this complex festival are relevant. On the mythological level, it represented Marduk's fight against the primordial ocean, his creation of the cosmos, and his subsequent exaltation as narrated in the *Enuma Elish*, which was recited on day 4. On the cultic level, it represented the festive *adventus* of Marduk to his cella, the annual reinstallation of his cult within Babylon, and the paying of respects to the divine king by the other gods. Politically significant was the re-installation of the human king and his participation in the procession (his "taking Bel by the hand") and the god's decreeing of fate for king and country. A replica of this festival was installed in Asshur during the 7th century BCE.

Cultural and social aspects of festivals. The holidays brought about by the festivals stood in contrast to normal workdays. People apparently did not have to work during festivals, but instead participated in colorful processions, which were accompanied by music and dancing. They received beverages and even meat, a luxury item, as part of the "conspicuous consumption" that marked the event. Festivals thus appealed to all the participants' senses.

Various art forms thrived in the context of festivals. Prayers to the gods and hymns to gods and rulers were composed and subsequently recited at festivals. Contest debates between cultural entities (e.g., grain and cattle) were performed for the entertainment of the audience. Our few attestations of sports (wrestling, running) from

Mesopotamia situate them within the context of festivals. Specific paraphernalia for the cult—such as a procession boat for the Tummal festival—were commissioned by the king and praised as examples of skillful workmanship. For the inauguration of such objects, hymns and inscriptions were composed. Buildings specific to festivals were erected and adorned with ornaments; the most prominent examples excavated are the *Akitu* festival house of Asshur and the Procession Way of Babylon with its reliefs of bulls, lions, and dragons.

The enormous economic expenses of a festival were covered by special contributions; such religious "taxes" are well attested for the 3rd millennium BCE. Members of the elite contributed goods such as silver, animals, or milk and cream; such goods were later distributed during the festival. This process replicated the redistribution of goods that was so important in the early ancient Near East; furthermore, the remains of offerings were distributed to particular servants of the temple. Thus the festival's social aspects became apparent to those involved. Because the fulfillment of basic needs was directly dependent on the temple and its festivals, the dates of the festivals became firmly embedded in the public consciousness.

In addition to the public festivals with their processions and excessive consumption, we know of a festival commemorating the dead ancestors during the summer heat in Abu, of festivals celebrating the harvest, and of special rites, such as the release of doves on New Year's Day.

Significant elements of festivals are the economic and social aspects of the redistribution of festival goods and the tendency of festivals to be set at times when the population can be brought together. The role of festivals in representing, preserving, and creating the right social order also becomes apparent on various occasions: the songs recited at festivals provided examples of correct order; the ruler was installed and thus validated by the main god; and the local gods, a focal point of the self-identification of cities and their hinterland, manifested themselves during the annual processions. All of these observations may help to explain why festival dates were so rigorously honored not only from the 3rd millennium to the 1st millennium—that is, within cuneiform culture—but even survived the end of that culture, until the first centuries CE.

BIBL.: Mark E. Cohen, *The Cultic Calendars of the Ancient Near East* (Bethesda, Md., 1993). Alasdair Livingstone, "The Case of Hemerologies: Official Cult, Learned Formulation, and Popular Practice," in *Official Cult and Popular Religion in the Ancient Near East* (ed. E. Matsushima; Heidelberg, 1993), 97–113. Walther Sallaberger, *Der kultische Kalender der Ur III-Zeit* (Berlin, 1993).　　　　WA.SA.

Sacred Places

In Mesopotamia, the perception and symbolic formation of space reflected both the culture's dependence on irrigation and agriculture and the political systems of the Sumerian city-states, including the later formation of empires. Humans structured their natural surroundings and composed mental maps and worldviews according to the contrast between the alluvial plains, on one hand, and mountains to the east and north and the steppes and deserts to the west, on the other. These mental maps and worldviews were mediated in different ways: through architecture, image, text, and ritual. Both archeological and written sources demonstrate the importance of the contrast, even antagonism, between center and periphery, between cultivated land/civilization and nature/steppe/wilderness, between order and anti-order, and between natural and artificial boundaries. Temples, shrines, streets, stelae, betyles, or mountains and rivers became encoded as parts of the mental map. The spatial concept of an inner and outer world was continuously reactualized and memorized by means of language and action, myth and ritual, ideology, and military activities.

Whereas the mental map was most clearly characterized by spatial relationships, the worldview was shaped by the self-image of the Mesopotamian urban elite, by their narratives about primordial times and especially about the origin and order of the world. The two systems were mutually dependent and constituted a cultural model of Mesopotamian society. The myths concerning the origin of culture, which are mostly a mixture of cosmogony, anthropogony, and cratogony (the emergence of power structures), defined the religious dimensions of the relationship between humans and nature in a cultural model that counted defense against hostile nature among the enduring achievements of civilization. Domination of hostile regions (e.g., mountains, desert, and steppe) surrounding Mesopotamia and their inhabitants (nomads, rebels, and demons) was the king's central political and religious tasks.

Perception and formation of sacred space. Space is not something that exists from the beginning, but something that must be developed through action. The supraregional irrigation system, on which Mesopotamian civilization depended, is emblematic of how that civilization worked insofar as it involved those who planned and built it in a hierarchically organized society, led by a city ruler or king. This helped to form the concept of the city god, whose main function was to guarantee fertility and protection for the city over which he or she watched.

In sources from the 1st millennium BCE, the cosmological vertical axis includes six levels, three of which are correlated with the horizons of heaven and earth respectively. In the first level, that of upper heaven, resides Anu, god of heaven; the second level, that of the middle heaven, belongs to Enlil and the Igigi, gods of heaven; the third level, that of the lower heaven, is reserved for the stars.

The fourth level, which is at the same time the first horizon of the earth, is the human realm, comprising both the area of order, that is, the city, and the area of anti-order outside the city. The core of the cosmos, situated at this level, is the temple with the Duku, the primordial mound that rises out of the freshwater ocean, the Apsu, and that is part of every temple. This concept, which is narrated in the Story of the Flood, is recalled in the Epic of Gilgamesh when the narrator uses the temple's ziggurat, a landmark in the alluvial plain visible from afar, as a metaphor to describe a mound rising out of the water after the flood.

Because of its foundation in the Apsu, the temple was imagined to be the bond between heaven and earth, including the underworld. Optically, the sacred precinct was set off from its surroundings by its monumentality and by specific architectural features, such as the wall that separated it from the rest of the city and the alternating buttresses and recesses on the exterior that marked it as a sacred precinct. Within the temple, the specific construction of the ground plan produced an intensified sacralization by means of numerous courtyards and gates—zones of passage that emphasized the transition between the temple and the outside world. In addition to these material architectural codes, symbolic actions, such as foundation rites for the construction of the temple and purification rites that preceded entry into the gods' presence, marked the temple as a sacred place. A late Babylonian ritual for the restoration of the temple refers back to cosmic origins by including the recitation of the creation epic, thus verbalizing the cosmic aspect of the temple. According to this text, nature was created to provide the materials necessary for the temple's construction and the food that guaranteed the daily cult of the gods.

The town as the symbol of actual order and power, protected by a city wall against forces of the anti-order (nomads and the demons and ghosts who on the steppe move freely between the human sphere and the underworld), fell under the control of the king, who continuously had to reestablish this order by the command of the gods.

The fifth cosmic level, which is also the middle earth horizon, consists of the freshwater ocean, Apsu, seat of the god Ea. The sixth cosmic level, which is also the third earth horizon, belongs to the gods of the underworld, the Anunnaki.

Mythologization and ritualization of sacred space. Regarding the perception of sacred space, we must distinguish between, on the one hand, the mythologizing of space and, on the other, its ritualization. Mythologization marks space by drawing mythical connotations from cosmologies and other types of myths and by deifying rivers and mountains. It also includes the association of distant regions, such as the cedar mountains in Lebanon, with monsters, such as Humbaba. Mythologization is also expressed by the ceremonial names and epithets given to cities and temples. Sumerian ceremonial names for temples reveal either a mythic or cosmogonic relationship to the divine owner, as in the case of the name of Enki's temple at Nippur, E-engurra (house of the subterranean ocean), or in the case of the name of Inanna's temple in Isin, Esigmeshedu (house, brick, worthy of the MES. (The MES are emblems of the institutions of civilization.) Temple names may also make programmatic statements, such as E-hursaggalkurkurra (house, big mountain of all the lands), the name of the Assur temple in the city of Asshur, which propagates throughout the world the domination of Assyria and its national god.

In Mesopotamia, the relationship between time and space differed, depending on the context. Whereas real itineraries tried to be very exact about individual stages of passage between places—even to the extent that we have been able to identify places with their help—mental maps tended to collapse geography as far as myth and ritual were concerned. An extreme example of this is offered by the Legend of Etana, in which an eagle carries King Etana upward and after every double hour asks him to look down. After the first double hour the earth appears as a hill, the sea as a river; after the second double hour the land resembles a garden, the sea a ditch; and after the third double hour neither earth nor sea is to be seen.

Whereas mythologization of space can take place at any time, a place is regarded as ritualized only after it has been declared sacred and segregated from the outside world through rites, such as those for temple building. Sanctification of space might occur in festivals that included ritualized movements in the form of processions, during which the gods—who normally remained inside their temples, inaccessible to the common people—were brought into public view. On such days, ordinary people had, if only briefly, direct access to a god and his worship.

This divine mobility took several forms, geographically: so-called journeys of the god, processions within the city, and processions to a festival house outside the city. Journeys of the god, in which a god of lower rank, associated with a particular city, visited a god of higher rank, associated with another city, expressed the hierarchical system of theological and political dependencies. This was reflected on the political level by the myth of Inanna and the MES, which described the journey of the goddess Inanna from her city, Uruk, to the city of Eridu in order to steal the MES from her father Enki and transfer them to the city of Uruk. The so-called Love Lyrics from the 1st millennium BCE offer a good example of a procession within the city, in which the gods sanctified several different quarters of the city of Babylon by visiting their respective temples.

The New Year festival took the god outside the city walls and into his festival house, which was situated in the steppe, the realm of anti-order, liminality, and chaos. This procession subjected an area that was perceived as unstructured on the mythological level to the ordering control of the center. In the case of Babylon, we can identify eleven stations that Marduk visited during his procession from the cella in his main city temple, Esagila, to the *Akitu* house outside the city. During this procession, spatial position was correlated with enhancement of Marduk's status, because Marduk's victorious battle against Tiamat (who represented anti-order) took place outside the city walls; it was after this battle that Marduk became the king of the gods. Theological texts related Marduk's different names to specific stations of the procession and their mythical and cultic connotations and thus stressed concrete aspects of Marduk. These texts also imparted different functions to specific cultic locations. This interplay of cultic topography and theology threw into high relief the universality of the god Marduk, simultaneously showing him as king of the gods and displaying his relationship to humanity.

In Mesopotamia, the temple centrally encoded cultural identity, crystallizing past and present and communicating with posterity by its monumental appearance. Through its symbolic system, it provided and ensured identity in the context of daily cult as well as during festivals. That is why many royal inscriptions, from all periods, record the construction and restoration of the temples at cultic centers of the empire and the king's fulfillment of his cultic duties. Ideologically, such claims centered on restoring the temple in accordance with its original ground plan. Every restoration or act of new construction was preceded by divinatory rituals, in which the gods' permission and blessing were sought. Very often, royal inscriptions claim that a temple was built following a divine command that had been conveyed, for example, in a dream message. The dream might even have conveyed the specific ground plan for the temple, as in the case of King Gudea, in whose dream such a plan was engraved on a lapis lazuli tablet. Thus, the temple was sacralized not only by ritual and monumentality but also by the ground plan's connection to cosmic origins.

BIBL.: A. R. George, *Babylonian Topographical Texts* (Louvain, 1992). Idem, *House Most High: The Temples of Ancient Mesopotamia* (Winona Lake, Ind., 1993). B. Pongratz-Leisten, *Ina šulmi īrub: Die kulttopographische und ideologische Programmatik der akîtu-Prozession in Babylonien und Assyrien im 1. Jahrtausend v. Chr.* (Mainz, 1994). Idem, "Mental Map und Weltbild in Mesopotamien," in *Die biblische Kosmologie und ihre altorientalischen Kontexte* (ed. B. Janowski and B. Ego; Frankfurt, 2001).   B.P.-L.

Syria-Canaan

In the culture of Syria and Canaan, as in almost all ancient cultures, sacred times mainly aligned with the people's experience of life and death, both seasonal and existential. Consequently, the sacred calendar was cyclical, and the cult of the dead (mainly the royal ancestors) held a very significant place—indeed, although it was part and parcel of the seasonal cycle, the cult of the dead was, in fact, preeminent among other cults. The calendar included lunar months, the main cultic subunits, arranged in a solar cycle of twelve, and feast days, which were established according to particular key days (e.g., days 1 and 15) within this lunar-solar cycle. The days of the new and full moon had special significance in this system.

Texts from Ebla, Ugarit, and Emar, dating from the 3rd and 2nd millennia BCE, and some inscriptions and external sources from the 1st millennium, provide further information. The menologies (lists of activities arranged according to months) of Ugarit are perhaps the most explicit of these and specify the ceremonies and offerings to be carried out on different days. Among them, those for the first month of the New Year (similar in many aspects to the Hebrew ritual for the New Year) and those for the month of the dead stand out. From Emar we also have menologies for at least five consecutive months.

Specific festivals frequently lasted several days within a single month. An exception seems to have been the expanded *zukru* festival at Emar, to be celebrated every seventh year during several months, in contrast to the annual version of this festival, which lasted only seven days. Among the royal festivals that lasted several weeks, notable are the ritual at Ebla connected with the succession of a new ruler to the throne and several texts from Ugarit commemorating the royal funeral. Also famous was the Melqart festival at Tyre, a New Year festival that is mentioned in Greek sources of the Hellenistic period, and the festival held at Hierapolis.

Sacred spaces in Syria and Canaan from the 3rd millennium to the 1st millennium are fairly well documented by archeological remains and documents. Only the most significant examples can be mentioned here. A remarkable complex of temples attests to the rebirth of

Cult object from a Canaanite temple, 11th century BCE (Beth Shean). Birds sit on two hoop handles and in triangular apertures; four serpents wind their way up it. *University of Pennsylvania Museum, Philadelphia (Neg. #S8-30310)*

Amorite Ebla at the beginning of the 2nd millennium; some of these temples were built on previously sacred places. Their structure is characterized by a large hall (cella), preceded by an enclosure formed by the extended walls as a sort of atrium without a façade; this was the typical way of marking the entry into a sacred space during the Syrian Middle Bronze period. The cella was the place where the sacrificial altar and other sacred furniture were located. Some cellae are unicellular, consisting of a hall and atrium, such as temples B1 and N from Ebla and those from Qara Quzaq, Megiddo, Shechem, Hazor, and Emar. Others are multicellular (hall, vestibule, atrium), such as temples D and T at Ebla, the temples at Munbaqa and Tell Fray, and possibly the so-called Syrian temple of Byblos.

Besides these urban temples, dedicated to particular deities, others were apparently connected with the pal-

Shrine model from a Canaanite temple, 11th century BCE (Beth Shean). The rounded top suggests it supported a bowl for offerings or incense. On either side is a nude human figure holding two birds and a serpent headed toward the upper level.
University of Pennsylvania Museum, Philadelphia (Neg. #S4-142012)

cultic and magical activities under the direction of specialized priests.

Phoenician and Aramean cultures of the 1st millennium BCE left behind considerable evidence of their sacred places. In Phoenicia a temple from 3rd-millennium Byblos was dedicated to its protective goddess. Some centuries later, in the 2nd millennium, a new temple, called the obelisks temple, was built on top of it. An echo of their existence and function can be heard in the Story of Wen-Amun (cf. *ANET* 25–29), about the visit of Wen-Amun, an official of the Karnak temple, to Byblos to obtain wood to build the barque of Amun-Re. In this story, the prince of Byblos makes offerings, presumably at the Byblos temple. Also from the second half of the 2nd millennium comes the temple of Kumidi, which was built near the palace. Its whole structure is more reminiscent of the multicellular type of temple.

Very few temples are preserved from 1st millennium Phoenicia, although some of them are very impressive. Nothing remains of the famous sanctuaries of Tyre, dedicated to Baal-Shamen and Melqart, but we do have sanctuaries such as the one at Amrit, dedicated to a spring. This is nothing like the sacred structures already mentioned; instead we find a temple situated in the middle of a basin surrounded by a portico. The centrality of water in this cult structure is also found in the sanctuary at Hierapolis.

The Arameans left very few remains of their sacred places. Of the famous sanctuaries of Hadad of Aleppo and Damascus, no trace remains. The same can be said of the temple of Hierapolis devoted to Atargatis. Only the tripartite temple of Deir Alla (10th century BCE) preserves the basic structure, but under Neo-Hittite influence.

At the turn between the 2nd and 1st millennia, the well-preserved temples of Nabu, Bel-Shamen, and Bel of Palmyra, especially the last named, as well as other minor sacred places, show the influence of the Hellenistic architectural style, while those from Baalbek may already be considered pure Greco-Roman sanctuaries. On the other hand, the splendid funerary monuments from Palmyra and Petra also undoubtedly had cultic importance. In Syria the Nabatean kingdom also left important remains of temples in the Hellenistic style.   G.O.L.

Israel

Abundant evidence survives for the Israelite cultic cycle of pilgrimage festivals, new moon observances, and sabbaths. The Hebrew Bible preserves several cultic calendars of varying date and provenance, and a close reading of these suggests a tendency to historicize the agriculturally oriented festivals as time went on. In addition, the calendar itself expanded over time as festivals were transformed and new observances were added. The earliest cultic calendars are preserved in Exod. 23.14–17 and 34.18, 22–23. Each of these speaks of three pilgrim-

ace and the dynastic cult. Their structure is quite different from those dedicated to gods, however, having a side entrance to the east and a double-sized central hall, surrounded by various rooms and small buildings of different sizes, with altars and podiums where royal images could stand.

From Ugarit we also have two well-preserved city temples of the Syrian tripartite structure, buildings with vestibules and large rooms situated within courts that were dedicated, it seems, to the gods Dagan and Baal. Their strong walls, as well as the remains of a staircase, suggest that these temples had towers with terraces where regular cultic actions could be carried out. The Ugaritic texts make abundant reference to such sacred places. Besides these public or official sacred spaces, excavations in Ugarit have also revealed some private sanctuaries, which seem to have been used for certain

Torah shrine from the mosaic floor of the Samaritan synagogue at Khirbet Samara, 3rd century CE. *Photo by Z. Radovan, Jerusalem*

age festivals in the year, to which every male Israelite was obligated to bring offerings: Unleavened Bread (*maṣṣôt*), a seven-day festival in the early spring, in memory of the exodus from Egypt; the late spring/early summer harvest festival (*qāṣîr*) or Weeks (*šābūʿôt*), in which the first fruits were brought to the sanctuary (34.22 specifies the first fruits of wheat); and Ingathering (*ʾasîp*), a harvest festival in the fall, at the "turn" or "the going out" of the year. Only Unleavened Bread has a historical explanation associated with it, and both calendars appear to associate the New Year with the fall festival.

The calendar of Deut. 16.1–17, very likely a product of the late monarchy (late 7th century BCE), manifests several interesting shifts and adds much detail to the two rather reticent earlier calendars. The festival of Unleavened Bread began with the sacrifice of the *pesaḥ* (either from the flock or herd) to YHWH on the eve of the first day. (The Jewish day begins at sunset.) Both the meaning and origin of the word *pesaḥ* are obscure. The *pesaḥ* sacrifice, not mentioned in the earlier calendars, was to be boiled according to this text (contrast Exod. 12.9, where it is to be roasted), unleavened bread was to be eaten throughout the festival, and all leaven was avoided. The *pesaḥ* sacrifice was to be performed at the central sanctuary—Deuteronomy's major innovation is cult centralization—and the rest of the festival was to

be observed at home. The other major shift manifested by this calendar is in the name of the fall festival, now called Booths (*sukkôt*). Although no historical explanation is given, the name change appears to reflect historicization of the festival, as it apparently alludes to the story of Israel's ancestral wanderings in the wilderness, during which the Israelites lived in booths or tents.

The most elaborate and detailed calendars are found in Lev. 23 and Num. 28–29; these also appear to be the latest in date. The most significant change to which these versions of the cultic calendar bear witness is a major augmentation of the fall festival. Where Exod. 23.16 and 34.22 speak of a fall harvest festival at year's end and Deut. 16.13–15 bears witness to a seven-day festival of Booths, Lev. 23.24–36 makes provision for a three-part observance in the seventh month: a holy convocation on day 1 of the month (later identified with Rosh Hashanah [New Year]); a holy convocation for self-affliction and purgation on day 10 of the month (Yom Kippur; see also Lev. 16); and the festival of Booths (*sukkôt*) beginning on day 15 of the month. In addition, the festival of Booths now has an explicit historical explanation: Israel was to live in booths during the festival in order to remember YHWH's saving acts at the time of the exodus and wanderings in the wilderness. The emergence of a distinct New Year's observance at the time of the fall festival is not surprising, given the older tradition, attested in Exod. 23.16 and 34.22, that this was the time of the "going forth" or "turn" of the year.

Development of the cultic calendar would continue throughout the Second Temple period (515 BCE–70 CE). By the 2nd century BCE, there is evidence that the feast of Weeks had—in some circles at least—come to be associated with the making of covenants between YHWH and humans, including the revelation at Sinai (see Jub. 1.1; 15.1–4). This association would become the norm in rabbinic circles (see Babylonian Talmud, tractate *Shabbat* 86b). Other regular observances, such as Hanukkah (1 Macc. 4.59; Josephus, *Antiquities* 12.323–26) and Purim (Esth. 9.26–28; Josephus, *Antiquities* 11.284–96), were added to the cultic calendar during the Second Temple period.

Aside from the pilgrimage festivals, biblical texts bear witness to the regular observance of the new moon and the sabbath. The new moon marked the beginning of each month in the modified lunar calendar that was widely used throughout ancient west Asia and elsewhere in antiquity. During the period of the First Temple, it was evidently a time of festive rejoicing, much like the three pilgrimage festivals. No work was to be done on the new moon (Amos 8.5), and special sacrifices were offered to YHWH (Num. 28.11–15). The new moon, like the festivals, was marked by the blowing of trumpets (10.10).

The observance of a day of rest on the seventh day of each week is attested in the earliest biblical legal collections, although the word *sabbath* does not occur in them. In Exod. 23.12, the mandatory weekly day of cessation is justified on humanitarian grounds: to provide rest and refreshment for draft animals, slaves, and resident outsiders. Exodus 34.21 adds that the day of rest remains obligatory even during planting and harvest. Deuteronomy 5.12–15 mentions the sabbath and demands its sanctification through cessation of labor. Like Exod. 23.12, the motivation for sabbath observance is humanitarian: the whole household rests, including slaves. But a historical justification has been added: the sabbath is meant to recall the bondage of Israel in Egypt and YHWH's saving acts for them. Exodus 20.8–11 gives a different reason for sabbath rest: God blessed and sanctified the seventh day and rested on it after he finished creating the world; by implication, people must also rest on the sabbath (compare Gen. 2.2–3). Other texts endow the sabbath with significance. According to the Holiness source, the sabbath is holy and a sign for all time that YHWH sanctifies Israel (Exod. 31.13). The Priestly writers refer to it as "a perpetual covenant" and "a sign for ever" in 31.16–17, making reference to creation, as they did in 20.8–11. The emphasis on the significance of the sabbath and its observance in Priestly and Holiness materials may reflect a reaction to the loss

of the temple and the land during the exile, as some scholars have argued, though this remains uncertain. In any case, texts from the Second Temple period bear witness to a continuing emphasis on sabbath observance (Neh. 13.15–22; 1 Macc. 2.29–41; Jub. 2.1, 17–33; *Damascus Document* 10.16–23).

The primary locus of worship in ancient Israel was the sanctuary, a sacred space set apart for the deity's service and often, where a temple stood, for his dwelling. (Open-air sanctuaries without dwelling places for a deity are known mainly from textual descriptions.) Until the (apparently) successful centralization of the cult in Jerusalem during the late 7th century BCE, sanctuaries of local and regional importance existed all over the country. Leading regional centers, such as Dan, Bethel, and Jerusalem, attracted pilgrims, who would come from a distance with obligatory and voluntary offerings to be processed, in conjunction with priests and other sanctuary personnel. With centralization, Jerusalem's temple became the only legitimate sanctuary in the land, drawing pilgrims from its length and breadth. Texts describe the sacrificial process. Worshipers would gain admission to the sanctuary sphere if they were unpolluted. Although the temple building was off-limits to worshipers, they were admitted to a courtyard. Animals would be slaughtered, stripped, and divided; their meat, fat, organs, and blood would then be handed on to priests for further processing at the altar as burnt offerings. Routine procedures for collecting and processing grain, wine, oil, and other offerings would be followed. In the case of offerings from which worshipers were entitled to a portion, worshipers would receive back processed foods (e.g., cooked meat) for consumption at the sanctuary, which they in turn would distribute to members of their households (see 1 Sam. 1.3–5).

The sanctuary at Arad at the southern frontier of Judah was not atypical of temple complexes during the monarchic period. Like other temples known from textual descriptions or excavations, the Arad shrine consisted of a courtyard with an altar for burnt offerings. (The altar at Arad was made of fieldstones and earth; compare Exod. 20.24–25, which speaks of an altar of earth or uncut stones.) It also contained a building—the deity's house—which followed a popular architectural pattern of a single rectangular room (the "broad room") with the entry on one of the long sides. Within the temple building, opposite the entrance, was a niche or holy of holies, approached by several steps, at the top of which stood two stone incense altars. Within the holy of holies stood two smoothed stone slabs or stelae (*maṣṣēbôt*) marking the presence of the deity and possibly, as some scholars believe, his consort. Various other accoutrements of the cult were discovered at Arad, including two stone tables and an incense stand.

The temple said to have been built by Solomon in Jerusalem during the 10th century was similar to the

Arad shrine in many respects, although we must depend on textual descriptions such as 1 Kings 6–7 to reconstruct it. Like the Arad sanctuary, Solomon's temple followed a well-known west Asian architectural pattern (the "long house"), although one that was quite different from the "broad room" at Arad. Other architecturally similar temples have been found through excavation (e.g., at Tell Tayinat, in northern Syria).

The Jerusalem temple was entered on one short side and consisted of three rooms, the innermost of which was the holy of holies. In the Jerusalem temple, YHWH's presence was not marked by a simple stele as at Arad, but by the ark of the covenant, upon which YHWH was believed to be enthroned. This object sat in the holy of holies. As was the case at Arad, the altar for burnt offerings was located in a courtyard, while incense altars were placed within the temple itself. It is probable that the Jerusalem sanctuary had two courts, rather than the single courtyard found at Arad. The outer court would have been the locus for the assembly and activity of worshipers; the inner court for priestly service.

The temple of Solomon was destroyed in 587 or 586 BCE by the Babylonians. A second (and apparently less impressive) temple was built at the same place during the period between 520 and 515. This sanctuary complex, reconstructed by Herod the Great in the late 1st century BCE, stood until 70 CE, when it was destroyed by the Romans. The Herodian temple, in contrast to its predecessors, added separate courts for women and aliens (Josephus, *Antiquities* 15.417–19).

The synagogue (from Greek *synagōgē* [place of assembly]) emerges as an important institution in Jewish religious and communal life during the period of the Second Temple. Although the origins of the synagogue as an institution remain unclear, an institution called the "place of prayer" *(proseuchē)* is first mentioned in Greek inscriptions from 3rd-century BCE Egypt. Eventually, synagogues would be found throughout much of the Mediterranean world and west Asia at sites such as Jerusalem, Masada, and Meiron in Palestine, Dura in Syria, and Sardis in Asia Minor. Dedicatory and other inscriptions in languages such as Hebrew, Aramaic, and Greek, as well as mosaics and other forms of artistic decoration, characterize many of the ancient synagogues that have been excavated. Evidence, both textual and archeological, suggests that ancient synagogues had many functions, although the reading and interpretation of scripture appear to have been of primary importance.

BIBL.: Steven Fine and Eric M. Meyers, "Synagogues," in *The Oxford Encyclopedia of Archaeology in the Near East* (ed. Eric M. Meyers; New York, 1997), 5.118–23. Beth Alpert Nakhai, "Temples: Syro-Palestinian Temples," in *The Oxford Encyclopedia of Archaeology in the Near East* (ed. Eric M. Meyers; New York, 1997), 5.169–74. R. de Vaux, *Ancient Israel*, vol. 2: *Religious Institutions* (trans. John McHugh; New York, 1965). S.M.O.

Anatolia

Sacred Times

We are very poorly informed about Hittite conceptions of time and even about the particulars of the basic calendrical system. We can say that each day included a night, itself divided into three watches, that thirty days comprised a month (lit., moon [*arma-*]), and that a year contained twelve months. The year was made up of four seasons: spring *(ḫamešḫa-)*, summer (BURUₓ-*ant-*), autumn *(zena-)*, and winter *(gimmant-)*, which were not, however, precisely defined chronological units tied to the procession of the equinox. It seems that, in early times, the Anatolian year began in the autumn, but by the period of the Hittite Empire (14th–13th centuries BCE), the Hittites followed the Babylonians in starting the annual round with the coming of spring. We do not know how the people and administrators of Hatti referred to the days and months (by name or by ordinal number?) or by what means they designated individual years.

More generally, the temporal spectrum encompassed the past *(karūiliyatt-)*, the present *(kinuntarriyala-* or *nanuntarri-)*, and the future *(appašiwatt-* [lit., after-day]). Events recounted in mythological narrative, which had occurred in the primeval past, set the pattern for the cosmos of the present and thus partook of a certain contemporaneousness. On the other hand, an eschatological conception may lie behind the wish of a Hittite magician that evil influences be bottled up until the day "when the former [divine] kings return to take account of the customary behavior of the land" (Mastigga ritual, CTH 404; ANET 351b).

In practical terms, the only sacred times that we can discuss for Hittite Anatolia are those hours, days, or weeks devoted to the worship of individual deities by the holders of particular cultic posts. For the most part, available written sources report or prescribe the activities of the members of the royal household and their servants, activities that included the performance of the state cult. Very little is known about the religious life of the common person, so we can hardly speak of national holidays or communal celebrations, which may well have existed and have exerted some influence upon the temporal perceptions and quotidian behavior of the general populace. For instance, the texts tell us that priests who officiated in the temple were required to observe standards of ritual purity while on duty. Did other people in Hatti correspondingly dress in a particular way or avoid certain foods at the time when a major festival was in progress? We simply do not know the answer.

Furthermore, even the incomplete information that we have recovered concerning official religion makes it clear that ceremonial schedules were by no means stan-

The great gallery of the Hittite rock sanctuary at Yazılıkaya, chamber A. Teshub and Hepat face each other on the back wall, right of center. *The Art Archive/ Dagli Orti (A)*

dardized for all gods and goddesses. The cultic calendar followed for a particular deity might also vary considerably among his or her sites of worship in various towns.

But there can be no doubt that festivals (EZEN) constituted the core of the state religion of Hatti. In a time of crisis, King Murshili II (mid-14th century) supported his request for divine assistance with the reminder to a god that "only in Hatti do you have festivals: the monthly festival and annual festivals, [in particular] the festivals of winter, spring, and summer, as well as those of Invocation and Bloody Sacrifice" (Prayer to Telipinu, CTH 377; ANET 397a; Singer, *Hittite Prayers,* 54–56). Indeed, most Hittite divinities enjoyed such rites at regular intervals—monthly, yearly, seasonally—or in connection with particular agricultural activities. Nearly one hundred different festivals are attested by name in Hittite cuneiform texts, several dozen of which were performed in the capital alone.

Since in theory the Hittite king's authority stemmed from his position as chief priest of all the gods, he was required to make occasional visits to the shrines of those deities whose cult centers lay outside Hattusha, his usual residence. By the time of the empire, these duties had been amalgamated into two annual cultic progresses made by the royal family through the heart of Hittite territory in Anatolia. The Crocus (AN.TAH.ŠUM) Festival lasted around forty days in the spring, and the Festival of Haste *(nuntarriyašha-)* stretched over at least fifty days in the autumn.

The preeminent festivals during Hatti's final centuries were the New Year festival, the yearly festival, the monthly festival, the *purulli* festival (a complex of New Year rites held in the town of Nerik), the (*h*)*išuwa* festival (meaning of term unknown), and the festival of the Gate Building (in which the agricultural produce of various central Anatolian cities was displayed for the monarch). Also to be noted are the festivals of the Cutting of Grapes, Grain Pile, Thunder, Rain, Grove, Stag, Hearth, Torch, Invocation, Baetyl (Divine Stele), and Pure Priest. Other festivals derived their designations from particular towns or geographic entities.

Although we are seldom able to place these rites chronologically, for the ancients it was imperative that they be carried out at the proper time. A text regulating the duties of temple employees threatens dire consequences: "If you do not perform the festivals at the [correct] time for the festivals—if you perform the festival of spring in the autumn or the festival of autumn in the spring" (Temple Officials Instructions, CTH 264; ANET 208b; Hallo, *Context of Scripture,* 1.217–221).

Sacred Places

A sacred space is a location in which contact between the human and the divine is focused and often even unavoidable. One is therefore well advised to enter such an area only when he or she is seeking to serve or communicate with a deity—and to maintain the required state of purity while doing so. Sacred space is thus distinguished from ordinary, or profane, localities, where communication with the parahuman is more intermittent and difficult to achieve. Sacred places might be constructed by humans, as with temples, shrines, or mausoleums, or they may be inherently sacred because the

A relief in the great gallery at Yazılıkaya, chamber B. *The Art Archive/Dagli Orti (A)*

gods themselves chose to frequent them. That both fabricated and natural sacred spaces were important in Hittite Anatolia is shown by a passage in a prayer of King Muwattalli II (late 14th century), who pledges to make amends if "some mountain or a constructed shrine—a holy place—has been abused" (Prayer to Teshub, CTH 382; Singer, Hittite Prayers, 84, obv. 32–39).

The erection of a new temple called for special ceremonies to demarcate the newly sacralized structure from the surrounding profane world. To the accompaniment of prayers, the Hittite priests deposited objects of precious metals and other costly goods beneath the building's foundations and sacrificed numerous cattle and sheep for the gods. Materials employed in the temple's construction had been chosen with care and with the blessing of the deities in whose charge they had been produced. When the edifice was fit for occupancy, the divine proprietor was ceremonially transported to the new dwelling in the physical form of an image or symbol or invisibly drawn there along convergent magical paths strewn with delectable foodstuffs.

The ravages of war and time have left little trace of Hittite buildings beyond their foundations, and very few religious objects that might have signaled the presence of a temple have been found in their original locations. We must therefore identify Anatolian sacred architecture on the basis of characteristic structural elements. Sometimes temples may also be recognized because spe-

cial materials, such as an unusual type of stone, had been employed in their construction. Fortunately for the archeologist, major Hittite temples display a standardized layout: a gate structure (ḫilammar) led to a large enclosed courtyard (ḫila-) open to the sky, where a small freestanding structure for purification rites was frequently located. At the rear of the courtyard a pillared hall fronted the cella or cult room. This cella was always situated along an outside wall of the temple complex so that light might enter through large windows; orientation toward a cardinal point was seemingly irrelevant to the builders. Entrance to the cult room was through a doorway located near a corner. Entering the cella, the worshiper had to turn ninety degrees to the left or right in order to face the deity. That is, the plan of Hittite temples afforded "bent-axis," rather than direct, access to the inner sanctum.

Some excavated cellae preserve a stone pedestal, on which the divine image presumably once stood, and most contain traces of one or more shallow pilasters (šarḫulli- pilasters), whose presence was a defining characteristic of Hittite sanctuaries. From written sources we learn that other, more portable temple furnishings might include a throne, an altar or offering table, a brazier, various cultic utensils, and of course an image or other representation of the deity.

The most impressive Hittite religious building recovered in the excavations at Bogazköy is Temple I of the

Procession of women. Relief from Carchemish, 1050–850 BCE. Ankara, Museum of Archaeology. *Hirmer Fotoarchiv*

Lower City, the largest single structure to be found in the Hittite capital. This giant construction featured two cult rooms, one for each member of the divine pair at the head of the pantheon—the Storm-god of Hatti and the sun-goddess of the city of Arinna. The temple itself was just one part of an immense precinct that housed its own workshop area and storage facilities, befitting the role of the Hittite temple as an economic entity as well as a religious establishment. Within the multitudinous rooms of the annex to Temple I were located at least six small chapels, presumably dedicated to minor deities in the entourage of the storm-god and sun-goddess. These cult rooms were less regular in plan than the full-fledged sanctuaries, but they reveal their function nonetheless through the placement of the distinctive *šarḫulli*.

Although all known Hittite religious structures save Temple I contain but one cella, textual evidence shows that more than one deity was worshiped in most temples. Since the usual Hittite expression for temple, *šiunaš per* (lit., house of the deity; Sumerographic É.DINGIR), could denote a single room within a complex, an independent structure, or an extensive building tract, it is difficult to determine from most contexts just how large a home was enjoyed by a particular god or goddess. Because the Hittite pantheon was very extensive, many lesser deities no doubt had to be satisfied with service within a small chapel or even within a cult room primarily dedicated to a more prominent figure. The terms *šinapši-* and *karimmi-* seem to be synonymous words for temple rather than designations of special types of religious buildings.

Not only was the temple as a whole sanctified, but many of its constituent parts were also "[holy] places." Thus elements such as the window, the door bolt, and the hearth could receive their own offerings in the course of a ritual. It remains unclear whether these architectural components were held to be sacred in themselves or were merely thought to be efficient conduits to the divine proprietor(s) of the sanctuary.

Temple I and all other cultic structures thus far discovered at Bogazköy date from the empire period. Indeed, most of them seem to be roughly contemporaneous and to have been constructed in the course of an ambitious building program carried out by King Tudkhaliya IV (late 13th century) that obliterated all earlier edifices in the area, religious or secular. Thus it is particularly unfortunate that the cella of the Old Hittite temple excavated at Inandik near Ankara (early 16th century) was not preserved, for its examination would have given us useful information on the development of classical Hittite religious architecture prior to its final century.

Recent exploration of the extensive Upper City at Hattusha reveals that this area was not a residential quarter as archeologists long believed, but rather contained a significant number of small freestanding temples. It may now be recognized that Tudkhaliya's construction efforts turned his capital into a city of the gods, accommodating at least thirty temples of varying size. Where the bulk of the city's population, whose labor supported these pious establishments, resided in this era is not yet clear.

Another impressive sacred place that must be attributed to Tudkhaliya, at least in its final form, is the rock

Procession and meeting of
Hittite gods Teshub and
Hepat, with mythological
animals, from Yazılıkaya.
Plaster cast, Vorderasiatisches
Museum, Berlin. *Erich
Lessing/Art Resource, New York*

sanctuary of Yazılıkaya (Turkish meaning "Inscribed Rock"), located several kilometers outside Bogazköy. For this shrine, the Hittite builders adapted a natural rock outcropping so as to form a complex of several cultic chambers open to the stars. In front of the natural entrance to the cluster of rock faces they erected a structure analogous to the usual temple gate building, and their sculptors carved a large number of bas-reliefs, primarily of deities, upon the expansive rock surfaces themselves.

The most significant of these visual compositions comprises two divine processions, one depicting the most prominent gods of the empire period and the other the goddesses—more than sixty figures in all. These parades converge upon a panel in larger format presenting the meeting of the storm-god and the sun-goddess. The bigger chamber A, on whose walls this magnificent sculptural program is carved, was in all probability the scene of an annual New Year celebration similar to that carried out in the extramural *Akitu* house of Babylon and other Mesopotamian cities. The smaller chamber B at Yazılıkaya is almost certainly the mausoleum, or "stone house" (É.NA₄), of Tudkhaliya IV. In this passage the deceased ruler would have received the offerings due him in his mortuary cult, in which he was treated as a minor deity.

Such mausoleums were probably built for all Hittite great kings, at least for those of the empire period, but we know of only one other possible site of such a structure, namely Gavur Kalesi (Turkish meaning "Fortress of the Infidel"), located southwest of Ankara. On and around this rock outcropping, the spotty remains of a modest walled precinct, which probably constituted the

stone house, are set within a larger circumvallation, and a relief on the living rock depicts two striding gods approaching a seated goddess. It must be admitted, however, that neither here nor at Yazılıkaya—nor indeed anywhere else—has the final resting place of a Hittite monarch been conclusively identified.

Other sacred structures mentioned in the Hittite texts include the *ḫešta* house (a shrine for the worship of chthonic deities and divinized ancestors, perhaps identical to Sumerian É.GIDIM [house of the dead]) and the purification hut *(tarnu-)*, in which the royal couple performed their ablutions and changed into ritually pure garments before entering the inner sancta of the temples, and the bathhouse.

Natural features such as mountains, rivers, and springs were by their very nature sacred in Hittite Anatolia, as shown by their inclusion among the deities summoned to witness treaties. While some mountains might themselves be personified as divinities, they could also be the location for the worship of other deities, particularly manifestations of the storm-god. In some cults a small shrine on the lower slopes of a mountain was coupled with a more substantial temple at a higher elevation.

The term *ḫegur* (rocky peak) designated the stone outcroppings so characteristic of the Cappadocian and central Anatolian landscape. A stone house or mausoleum might be built upon or within a *ḫegur*, but such crags were holy places even prior to human construction and consecration. Within mountainous terrain, rock carvings could be the focus of cult, as with the scene of the royal couple worshiping their gods at Fıraktın in Cappadocia and the image of King Muwattalli II at Sirkeli in Cilicia. Religious activity at these localities is indicated by the presence in the nearby stone of shallow cup-marks that once served as the recipients of libations.

In Hatti an outdoor cult site was customarily marked by a stele (ḫuwaši-), which might be sculpted or aniconic. Texts reveal that such stelae could be erected in groves, in the open countryside, within the passage of a rock outcropping, just outside the gate of a city, or even inside a cult room in place of an anthropomorphic image.

In parallelism with their special reverence for the storm-god, the Hittites attributed a special numinosity to water, the element essential for the increase of both crops and herds. Religious installations were often constructed at sacred springs. The most spectacular of these is that at Eflatun Pınar in Pisidia, where a good portion of the Anatolian pantheon is presented in an assemblage of sculpted blocks rising from the pool at the wellhead. Within Hattusha were situated several large artificial pools or basins, whose cultic function is evidenced by the recovery from them of miniature votive pottery and other ritual artifacts.

The bank of a river, the site of the creation of humans in primeval times, was an ideal location for communication with chthonic forces and was therefore a favored spot for the performance of purification rituals. Furthermore, clay dug from the riverside was held to have magical properties. Finally, those places where watercourses disappeared underground into the limestone landscape of central Anatolia were thought to be entrances to the underworld and were therefore sacred.

BIBL.: H. G. Güterbock, "The Hittite Temple according to Written Sources," in Le temple et le cult (ed. E. Van Donzel; Istanbul, 1975), 125–32. Idem, "Some Aspects of Hittite Festivals," in Actes de la XVIIe Rencontre assyriologique internationale (ed. A. Finet; Brussels, 1970), 175–80. William Hallo et al., Context of Scripture, vol. 1 (Leiden: Brill, 1997). K. Kohlmayer, "Felsbilder der hethitischen Zeit," Acta praehistorica et archaeologica 15 (1983): 7–154. P. Neve, Hattusa—Stadt der Götter und Tempel (Mainz, 1993). I. Singer, "A City of Many Temples: Hattusa, Capital of the Hittites; Sacred Space: Shrine, City, Land," in Proceedings of the International Conference in Memory of Joshua Prawer (ed. B. Z. Kedar and R. J. Z. Werblowsky; Jerusalem, 1998), 32–44. Idem, Hittite Prayers (Writings from the Ancient World Society of Biblical Literature; Leiden: Brill, 2002). T. van den Hout, "Tombs and Memorials: The (Divine) Stone-House and Hegur Reconsidered," in Recent Developments in Hittite Archaeology and History: Papers in Memory of Hans G. Güterbock (ed. and K. Aslihan Yener and H. A. Hoffner Jr.; Winona Lake, Ind., 2002), 73–91.   G.M.B.

Iran

Much of what we know about Zoroastrianism in ancient Iran is preserved in the living tradition of today. This section combines documented textual history from antiquity with what contemporary Zoroastrians see as

Fire altar in a Zoroastrian temple complex, Surkh Kotal, Afghanistan, 2nd century CE. Borromeo/Art Resource, New York

their ancient history, especially as it lives within their temple liturgies and public ceremonies.

Specific times and places designated as sacred by Zoroastrians first need to be understood within a theological context that regards the space-time continuum itself as sacred. Time, in Zoroastrian thought, is conceived of as both infinite and finite, and the distinction between them is often expressed in spatial terms. Space, similarly, has two fundamental dimensions, the invisible and visible, which are inextricably tied to the two conceptions of time.

Infinite time (Avestan zruvan akarana) is eternal duration, undivided into past and future, without beginning or end. As pure duration, it is absolute time, a time that endures forever without change. As such, time is the eternity of Ahura Mazda (Lord of Wisdom, or Wise Lord; Pahlavi Ohrmazd) and defines his unlimited (Pahlavi akanāraq) nature: boundless, infinite, and eternal wisdom. Infinite time is also the source of finite time. Finite time (Avestan zruvan dareghō-khvadhāta) is the first creature fashioned by Ahura Mazda and is a "segment" of infinite time. The essence of finite time is transient duration and can be divided into future and past. It is the time in which cosmic history begins, unfolds, and reaches its culmination. Finite space-time, in other words, is the good creation of Ohrmazd, sacred in its origins and also the instrument of a sacred purpose.

Of the two fundamental conceptions of space, the invisible (Pahlavi mēnōg) realm has ontological priority over the visible (Pahlavi gētīg). The mēnōg realm is invisible to the physical eye, but accessible to the eye of the mind and human spirit. It consists primarily of the universal ordering principles of all material existence, that is, the universal archetypes of Righteousness, Health, Life, Dominion, Good Mind, and Devotion. Although these Bountiful Immortals are metaphysically prior to the visible, created order, they are themselves derived from the ultimate and eternal source of all that is good, namely Ahura Mazda.

The visible spatial realm *(gētīg)* is the material universe made up of particular, changing things. It derives its existence, order, and meaning from the archetypal *mēnōg* dimension of Wisdom and consists of the finite world of humans, animals, earth, water, plants, metals, and fire (the seven creations). Metaphysically, the relation between the material world of particulars and the immaterial world of universals is so intimate that some theological commentators view the entire scheme of creation as the body or "form" (Avestan *kehrp-*) of Ahura Mazda. The four elements that make up the basis of material creation—fire, water, earth, and air—are sacred manifestations of the invisible archetypal order created by Ahura Mazda.

The entirety of space-time, in other words, in both its visible-finite forms and its invisible-infinite dimensions, is conceived of as sacred. It is in this evaluative context that one must understand specific historical times and places that are regarded as sacred. The latter are necessary and important because, according to the Zoroastrian worldview, aspects of the finite creation, both visible and invisible, have become polluted and diminished by the powers of evil and must be purified by eradicating evil.

The principle of evil (Avestan Angra Mainyu; Pahlavi Ahriman) is understood as a counterproductive power in existence, an inexplicable surd in life. This hostile force—given by some commentators a pervasiveness in space-time almost equivalent to that of Ahura Mazda—realized the existence of Ahura Mazda's creation and sought to destroy it. In the invisible realm, this hostile spirit is one of unrighteousness, falsehood, disorder, arrogance, ill health, and destruction. It epitomizes the powers opposite that of Wisdom: darkness and ignorance. This reality also manifests itself in the visible, finite realm, with the result that pure waters are sullied, the earth turns to desert, fires become mingled with smoke, the air becomes polluted, and plants, animals, and humans of the good creation suffer decay and death.

According to the Pahlavi *Bundahishn,* this mixture of good and evil in Ohrmazd's sacred creation defines the sacred purpose of cosmic history. Evil is lured out of infinite time into finite duration when the hostile power agrees to do battle with the powers of the good. By so doing, the Evil One becomes trapped in space-time for nine thousand years and his power eventually brought to an end. As an instrument of Ohrmazd, finite time is thus the "time of long dominion" (Pahlavi *zamān ī dagrand-khwādy*), for it is through Ohrmazd's dominion during this period of cosmic history that evil is eventually vanquished.

As the "connection" (Pahlavi *paywand*) between the first period of boundless time, in which Ahura Mazda's power is threatened and circumscribed by the power of evil, and the final period of separation in which his power reigns supreme, finite time-space also can be spoken of as the "continuous evolution toward the Frashegird" (Pahlavi *paywandishn ī ō Frashegird*)—that longed-for realm of endless joy and unlimited duration of happiness. Following this victory, finite time can return to boundless infinite time, the material world can once again be restored to its original sacredness, and Ohrmazd can reign in infinite, uncompromised dominion.

Thus space-time plays an absolutely decisive role in the Zoroastrian religion. It is to this cosmic task of restoring the sacredness of all dimensions of existence that humans are called. Ohrmazd's victory is not automatic; righteous human activity and the establishment of purified times and places help bring about the end of the powers of desolation and pollution. A person's every thought, word, and deed is of supreme importance, for each individual act has cosmic implications. Either it restores and strengthens the sacredness of the whole of creation or it helps manifest the destructive powers of darkness that violate all that is good.

Places of purification and the rituals conducted at specific times are thus central to Zoroastrians. Like cosmic space-time itself, fire temples and the times in which the rituals are conducted are segments of the physical-temporal world made special, lifted out of this time of mixture with evil and purified so as to manifest more fully the sacred power inherent in creation.

Hence, one of the most sacred places for Zoroastrians is a fire temple. Such temples were likely introduced in Achaemenian times, when buildings were consecrated as centers of worship and ritually purified fires were placed on raised stands in inner sanctuaries. Zoroastrian temples today are constructed in such a way that the sanctuary area is nested within the temple compound itself, and the ritual precinct is demarcated by furrows in the floor, a design that offers visible designations of invisible protective barriers against pollution.

Fires of victory (Pahlavi *ātash wahrām*) consecrated in the fire temples are especially sacred. The theological vision that informs this focus on fire is derived from the Zoroastrian conception of Ohrmazd himself. Zarathustra spoke of the radiance and glory of Ahura Mazda, whose abode is the realm of light, endless and infinite light. When Ahura Mazda created fire, he joined the radiance of this infinite light with fire "himself." He, the fire, therefore, is an epiphany of Wisdom, the "son of god" (Avestan *āthrō ahurahe mazdāo puthra*), whose essence is light and an exemplification of the cosmic principle of Righteousness. He *is* a spark of the infinite—an unsullied, visible instantiation of the animating principle of life itself that sustains the spatial and temporal universe. For these reasons, a fire of victory is a central focus (Avestan *qibla*) for the worship of Ahura Mazda.

The special ritual precinct located within each fire temple is designated the "Court of the Lord of Ritual"

(Persian *dar-i mihr*). It is in this sacred place that the high liturgy, the *yasna,* is performed daily by two qualified priests during the morning hours (Pahlavi *hāwan gāh*)—a time especially sacred and presided over by the guardian spirit Mihr. This 2.5-hour liturgy is essentially a priestly act of worship on behalf of the whole Zoroastrian community. The officiating priests know by memory the entire Avestan Yasna (seventy-two chapters) and know in detail all the ritual actions that accompany its recitation.

The service begins with a recitation that invites Ahura Mazda, the Bountiful Immortals, and all good spirit beings to be present at this liturgical celebration and asks that they receive the offering and bestow their bountiful blessings upon the world. The final purpose of this liturgy is to restore and renew, on a daily basis, the sacred realities inherent in the whole of creation. As such it is a weapon of purification in this time of cosmic struggle between the powers of light and darkness.

Furthermore, just as a consecrated fire is a specific manifestation of the sacred light, so all the other ritual items in the *yasna* service exemplify some aspect of the invisible created order. The *barsom,* a bundle of twigs or metal wires used in high liturgies and an ancient Indo-Iranian emblem of seeking the holy, serves as a conduit between the finite world of human endeavor and the invisible universal realm from which we derive our existence. The metal basin, cups, saucers, and stands, like the crystal sky, which was conceived as metallic by Zarathustra, manifest the power of Good Dominion; the earth and stone of the ritual area manifest the spirit of Devotion; milk and clarified butter and the hairs from a white bull are samples of the whole good animal kingdom and exemplify the principle of Good Mind. The *hōm* (a sacred drink; Avestan *haoma;* Pahlavi *hōm*) and pomegranate twigs exemplify the plant kingdom and the Life they bring us. Consecrated well water exemplifies all the waters of the world, which promote Health. The priests themselves strive to live righteous lives, thereby exemplifying purity and righteousness. In other words, like the enactment of the ritual itself, each consecrated ritual item, by its very presence, contributes to the increase, prosperity, and salvation of the world and effects the restoration of the cosmos.

There are also special acts of worship (Pahlavi *jashan*) for the community, including major festivals (Pahlavi *gāhāmbār*), which are conducted in any clean place outside the fire temple precincts. In a *jashan* service, a ceremony of blessings (Pahlavi *āfrīnagān*) is performed by two or more priests on behalf of the assembly of the faithful (Persian *anjoman*) and the soul of a living or deceased Zoroastrian. Frequently major community events are commemorated with *jashans,* such as the anniversary celebration of the installation of a sacred fire or the inauguration of a high priest.

The *gāhāmbār* festivals also bring people together in community observance and are ritual reaffirmations of the inherent sacredness of the whole of creation. These six seasonal festivals commemorate the six creations and occur midspring, midsummer, harvesttime, the time of bringing home the cattle, midwinter, and a specially designated time in which all the guardian spirits (Avestan *fravashis*) of the souls of the dead are invited to be present.

Finally, the Gatha days are considered the holiest of times and are named after the five Gathas of Zarathustra (there are two systems for numbering the Gathas, one of which makes them seventeen in number and the other of which, used here, makes them five). The Gatha days occur on the last five days of a Zoroastrian calendar, which is made up of 365 days divided into twelve months of thirty days each, leaving five supplementary days. The Gatha days, consequently, are commemorated in different seasons as the calendar shifts. During these times, Zoroastrians are forbidden to do secular work and endeavor to concentrate on prayers and recite the particular Gatha that names the day. They confess their sins committed the previous year and on New Year's Day (Persian *nawrūz*) vow to perform good thoughts, words, and deeds during the coming year. In this way, Zoroastrians rededicate themselves to the purification of the whole creation and resolve to contribute to the restoration of the original sacredness of infinite time and space.

BIBL.: B. T. Anklesaria (trans.), *Zand-Ākāsīh, Iranian or Greater Bundahishn* (Bombay: Rahnumae Mazdayasnan Sabha, 1957). Mary Boyce, *A History of Zoroastrianism,* vol. 2 (Leiden: Brill, 1982). Firoze M. Kotwal and James W. Boyd, *A Persian Offering: The Yasna, a Zoroastrian High Liturgy* (Paris: Association pour l'avancement des études iraniennes, 1991). J. J. Modi, *The Religious Ceremonies and Customs of the Parsees* (repr. Bombay: British India Press, 1986). E. W. West (trans.), *Pahlavi Texts* (repr. Delhi: Motilal Banarsidass, 1970). J.W.B., F.M.K.

Greece

Sacred Times

The Greek city-states regulated their year with a lunar calendar; each month started with the new moon *(noumēnia),* determined in theory by the first observation of the moon, and the days began at sunset. Differences between the solar and lunar years were corrected by rather haphazard intercalation. Normally, calendars counted the days forward until the twentieth of each month, as in our calendars, and then, unlike ours, counted backward from the end of the month (day 21 thus being called "the first of the last decade": *dekatē hystera*); the phases of the moon thus were irrelevant for the counting of days, unlike in the Roman calendar. Phases of the moon did, however, determine the ritual character of at least two days. The first day of the new cycle, "the most sacred of all days" (Plutarch, *Moralia*

828A), was marked in most Greek cities by sacrifices and was said to be sacred to Apollo; in some places, the god had the epithet Noumenios (He of the New Moon) (Philochorus, *FGrH* 328 F88). Day 7, when the moon was half-full, was again sacred to Apollo, whose festivals ordinarily were celebrated then (Hesiod, *Works and Days* 770), while his birthday was supposed to be, in the Attic and Ionian calendars, on day 7 of the month Thargelion. As a consequence of this, his twin sister Artemis was thought to have been born on Thargelion 6—a day earlier because she, being a birth-goddess, was supposed to have helped with her brother's birth (Apollodorus, *Library* 1.4.1). We detect no comparable emphasis on the day of the full moon. But in most Greek calendars, festivals are concentrated during the first half of the lunar cycle, just as in Hesiod's calendar the good days are mostly placed there (Hesiod, *Works and Days* 765–828): the waxing moon and its association with growth was seen as positive; the waning half of the lunar cycle often contained festivals with less auspicious connotations (although it is impossible to state this as an incontrovertible law). The transition between the months was marked by private gifts and sacrifices to Hecate and Hermes (Porphyry, *On Abstinence* 2.16).

Month names and festivals. No two Greek cities—with the exception of colonies, which adopted the calendars of their mother cities—had identical calendars. Names and sequences of months differed, as did the date on which the year began, a date mostly determined by pauses in the agricultural year. In Athens, for example, the year began in July/August, after the harvest and the summer solstice. Most Greek month names are derived from the names of festivals, such as the Attic/Ionian month Anthesterion from the festival called Anthesteria or the Dorian month Agrianios from the Agriania. Festival names that seem connected with a divinity—Artemision with Artemis—really owe their names to the respective festivals in honor of the god (Artemisia). This system is already attested in the Linear B texts from the Bronze Age: the Greek calendar thus goes back to Mycenaean times. This helps to explain why many months derive their names from festivals that are either shadowy or nonexistent during later times. It also explains why a series of month names is common to Athenians and Ionians on both sides of the Aegean: the underlying festivals were celebrated already by their Bronze Age ancestors; the clan festival of the Apatouria was seen as the proof of their common descent already in antiquity (Herodotus 1.147), although its date varied in different cities.

The festival calendar. From only Athens do we have enough evidence to determine how the festival calendar looked. In addition to the festivals of the state, there were festivals in the single demes (townships; i.e., the geographical subdivisions of the Athenian territory), attested by several inscribed stone calendars; festivals of the other subgroups of the population, the phratries

(brotherhoods; i.e., hereditary groups) and the clans *(gene),* such as the Apatouria; and the Hephaisteia, the festival of the most-important guilds of Athens, the potters and blacksmiths, in honor of their patron deities Hephaestus and Athena.

In some cases, the festivals were grouped into cycles. The main New Year festival of the Athenian state was the Panathenaea at the end of the first month, Hekatombaion, with its magnificent sacrifice of one hundred white cows on the altar of Athena on the Acropolis. The festival concluded a long period of transition, disintegration, and purification, centering on Athena and the Acropolis, which had begun in Thargelion, the penultimate month of the previous year. The Thargelia, which gave this month its name, was held on Thargelion 7; it was preceded, on the 6th, by a scapegoat ritual that cleansed the city of evil (see "Ritual"). At the Thargelia itself, the participants carried into the sanctuary of Apollo a pot that contained a primitive dish, cooked from all sorts of grain and understood to mimic foods from the very beginnings of civilization. At the Plynteria (Laundry festival) toward the end of this month, girls from a noble family removed gold jewelry from the old, small wooden image of Athena on the Acropolis and then disrobed and veiled it; the image was then carried in procession to the sea, washed, brought back, and newly dressed. By its anthropomorphic treatment of the goddess, as represented by her statue, the festival enacted an initial purification and a new beginning. The day, however, was also uncanny: the city's goddess was absent from her home, the people could not hold assemblies, and the participants in the rite ate a fig paste that was thought to be the first civilized dish of humanity. Early in the next month, Skirophorion, the festival of the Arrhephoria marked the end of service for the *arrhēphoroi,* two noble girls who had spent the year on the Acropolis in the service of Athena.

On Skirophorion 12, the gods markedly left the Acropolis: in a procession, the priestess of Athena, the priest of Poseidon (who had his cult in the temple complex on the Acropolis called the Erechtheum), and the priest of Helios walked from the city to a sanctuary outside the city wall. While these main state gods were absent, the women took over the city: this was the only day of the year when they could hold their own assembly, to the dismay and secret horror of the men. Two days later, at the Diipoleia (festival of the City Zeus) on the Acropolis, the Athenians enacted the Bouphonia (ox murder), the parody of a sacrifice. A plow ox, an animal not usually sacrificed, was understood to offer itself (a ritual fiction found in several cults) and was killed. The sacrifice was interpreted as murder, and in the ensuing trial, the sacrificial knife was found guilty and thrown into the sea. Afterward, the oxhide was stuffed with hay and the ox was "brought back to life." As in many cultures, then, the end of the year was marked by a carnivalesque suspension of normality, and this offered the possibility of thinking about the implications of sacrifice—just as the European Carnival opens up a space for travesty that is, at the same time, a way of thinking about society and its values.

The New Year should reinstate order and normalcy. The first-named festival of the year, the Hekatombaia, seems to confirm this: the city performed a sacrifice of one hundred animals. The recipient, however, was not Athena, the Lady of Athens, but Apollo, the Lord of the calendar: order there was, but for Athens it was still far away. It fits that the next festival again insisted on the suspension of order: the Kronia on Hekatombaion 12 recalled the golden age under Cronus that preceded the order of Zeus. The coloring, however, was no longer uncanny but cheerful: it was at this festival that the slaves were freed for one day and dined together with their masters (see further Ritual).

The turn in the moon's cycle marked the definite change. In a first move, the Synoikia (Festival of Living Together), on Hekatombaion 16, recalled how Theseus united the villages of Attica into one city-state (his disguised entry into Athens as an unknown young prince who frightened his father, King Aegeus, had been commemorated on Hekatombaion 8, earlier during the period of transition). Twelve days later, the birthday festival of Athens, the Panathenaea, closed this period of transition. In a dazzling procession from outside the city wall up to the Acropolis, the city represented itself in all its orderliness and splendor and honored its goddess with lavish sacrifices at her main altar on the Acropolis.

Some festivals covered several days, with specific stages that staked out a clear ritual progression. The Athenian Thesmophoria, the festival during which married women left their homes and stayed in makeshift huts in the sanctuary of the goddess Demeter, lasted three days: the first was anodos (going up), since Demeter's Athenian sanctuary was on the slope of the Acropolis; the second, nēsteia (fasting), named from the fasting the women underwent; the third, kalligeneia (beautiful birth)—both the main aim of the festival and the name of a divinity worshiped on this day.

The Athenian Mysteria, which led to initiation into the cult of Demeter and her daughter Kore (also called Persephone) at Eleusis, covered twelve days, including preparation and aftermath: in a first move on Boedromion 13, the Athenian ephebes (young men undergoing military training), marched out to Eleusis, a small town fourteen miles to the northwest of Athens. The next day, they escorted the priests and the sacred objects (hiera) of the Mysteries back to Athens. There, the hiera were kept in the Eleusinion, the sanctuary of the goddesses halfway up the Acropolis. Then, those who wished to be initiated into the Mysteries prepared themselves. They assembled in the Agora (on Boedromion 15), took a purificatory bath in the sea (16), and started fasting (17–18), while the city sacrificed to Demeter and Kore (17) and celebrated the god Asclepius (18), who was said to have arrived late when he was an initiate. Then, the initiates walked in a long procession out to Eleusis (19), where they arrived at nightfall for the secret rites in the sanctuary (20). A market fair (panēgyris) and the return to the city closed the festival period (22). On the day after the Mysteries (24), finally, the Athenian Council met in the Eleusinion, to review how the festival had gone. Not all of these twelve days were entirely occupied by the festival, unlike the three days of the Thesmophoria or of the Dionysiac Anthesteria, since the rites concerned only those who were to be initiated. Still, normal Athenian life was drastically suspended: on only two days out of the twelve could political business take place in the assembly.

Sacred time. Sacred time is a modern concept. Ancient Greeks seem not to have distinguished two essentially different sorts of time, sacred and secular—rather, festival times were set aside for the gods by human will and decision. The term that is closest to "sacred time" is hieromēnia (sacred month): it is the time before and after one of the major festivals in which all Greeks could participate—the Mysteria in Eleusis, the athletic contests at Olympia, Delphi, Isthmia, and Nemea. In order to allow safe travel to and from these festivals, cities agreed on suspending all warfare and sanctioned the agreement with a sacrifice. Transgression could be regarded as a crime (Thucydides 3.56.2).

Thus, there could be a conflict between daily business and time set aside for a festival. When the Persians attacked Athens in 490 BCE, the Athenians called for help. But the Spartans were celebrating their main festival, the nine-day-long Karneia, and could not go to war before its end at the full moon: they were too late to participate in the victory at Marathon (Herodotus 6.106). Ten years later, when the Persians arrived again, they had the same problem, but now they compromised and at least sent their king, Leonidas, with three hundred soldiers (Herodotus 7.206), while the Argives, in a similar quandary but in a more radical spirit, simply decided to change their calendar (Thucydides 5.54).

Festival times were not immutable: it was tradition that sanctioned them. Over time, the festival calendar of any Greek town changed. Festivals could become longer in order to enhance the splendor of the cult; during the early imperial epoch, for example, the Ephesians decided to extend their main festival, the Artemisia, for the entire month of Artemision. Festivals could disappear, especially in economically difficult times; when they were resumed, it was invariably tradition (patrios nomos) that was invoked. Hellenistic kings and Roman emperors could have their own festivals, usually on their birthdays, which could be understood as extending traditional honors to these new gods. In earlier times, major victories were celebrated by festivals, starting with those against the Persians at Marathon and Salamis. Surprisingly, the festival often did not coincide with the date of the event: the festival for Marathon was held on Boedromion 6, three weeks after the battle date, and the festival for Salamis was four and a half months too early. Both festivals concerned Artemis in her capacity as savior in warfare: traditions of her cult determined the dates, not the "real" events.

Sacred Places

Greek spatial concepts focused on the city-state. Space was tripartite: at its center was the city (*polis* or *astu*), usually determined in its spatial extension by the city walls; outside the walls stretched the fields *(agroi)* with their unfortified villages; and beyond this were the uncultivated borderlands *(eschatiē)* with their forests and mountains, used mainly by herders and patrolled by the ephebes, but also the place to which scapegoats, accursed persons, and evil demons were sent. The passage from the city to the fields through the city gates, a notoriously weak point, was often protected by specific gods, as was the passage through the house door into the street. Outside the city, the crossroads were another critical point, usually given over to the protection of Hecate.

The sanctuary. All three of these spaces—city, fields, and borderlands—could contain sanctuaries, space set aside for the cult of gods or heroes. The basic form of a sanctuary was an open space containing an altar, surrounded by a wall or by border stones *(horoi)* that proclaimed it sacred *(hieron),* often adding the name of its superhuman possessor. This was the *temenos,* the "cut out" space, set aside solely for communication between human and superhuman beings. The altar, on which the main act of communication, sacrifice, took place, served as the interface between the two worlds.

All the other possible features of a *temenos* were optional. It could contain an image of the god (*hedos* [lit., residence]), set up either in the open (sometimes protected by a canopy) or in a building, the temple (*naos* [lit., dwelling place]). It could contain other buildings: a portico *(stoa)* to give shelter from sun or rain to the visitors and a house for the priest, if he was supposed to take up residence. And it usually contained a wealth of votive gifts (*anathemata* [lit., things put up out of reach]): inscribed and sculpted monuments; statuettes of terra-cotta, bronze, or lead or more ambitious marble and bronze statues; precious objects, weapons, and objects of daily life; or whatever tradition and the intention of the donor could contrive as a gift of thanksgiving for help that the divine possessor of the *temenos* had given. The *temenos* also might contain the bare skulls of sacrificial bulls in order to commemorate a specially lavish sacrifice. Votive gifts thus proclaimed both the power of the divinity and its response, the generous piety of the human worshiper.

What was inside the *temenos* belonged to the divinity. To steal a votive gift was a sacrilege punishable by death; anecdotes told how the gods meted out punishment even

to those so powerful that human justice could not reach them. If space within a *temenos* became scarce because of the number of votive gifts, small statuettes and other objects were collected and buried inside the *temenos* (to the later delight of archeologists). Objects made of precious metals were melted down and recast as ritual vessels for the sanctuary's use; the same happened to objects that became damaged or ungainly for other reasons. When the Persian invaders of 480 BCE sacked and burned the Acropolis, the Athenians used the broken materials left behind as fill under the new structures they built; this rubble left by the Persians (*Perserschutt* in German archeological terminology) helped to establish a main criterion for dating late archaic Greek art and architecture.

Access to the *temenos* ordinarily was open to any person who wanted to sacrifice or even do some sightseeing, provided that the person was ritually pure. Ordinarily, ablution at a basin at the entrance was enough (Hippocrates, *On the Sacred Disease* 4). Because what could cause pollution varied in many places, however, sacred laws displayed at the gates of some *temenē* gave details; in a few late instances, access demanded moral as well as physical purity. Some sanctuaries went even further and completely excluded specific groups. Men were ordinarily excluded from sanctuaries of Demeter Thesmophoros, the women's own goddess, for example; the Athenian general Miltiades, who jumped the fence around the Thesmophorion on Paros, broke his leg and later died of the wound (Herodotus 6.134–36). Women could be excluded from sanctuaries of Heracles; in one case, only men and slave girls could enter a Herakleion (Pausanias 7.5.8). Other local conditions could keep away other categories of visitors.

The temple. The classical temple was not much more than a casing for the cult statue. Altar, statue, and temple formed a unity: ideally, a Greek temple had its main side facing east, with a wide door through which visual communication between the altar in front of the temple and the image in the rear of the temple was possible. Columns marked the main side or surrounded the one room of the temple (cella); originally these were wooden supports for a roof that could shelter visitors while keeping them outside the cella. Ordinarily, the cella was open for worshipers who wished to pray to or touch the image; some images that were too precious for this (such as the gold and ivory Zeus in Olympia) or attracted the fervor of too many worshipers (such as the images of the healer Asclepius) were protected by a low balustrade. Other activities were strictly forbidden; a sacred law from the Athenian Acropolis explicitly bans cooking from the interior of the temple—sacrificers were supposed to prepare the meat outside.

Some temples were more complex. In archaic Greece, some temples had a hearth in the interior, continuing the form of the Bronze Age *megaron* (king's assembly hall); they must have served as assembly houses *(andreōn)* for

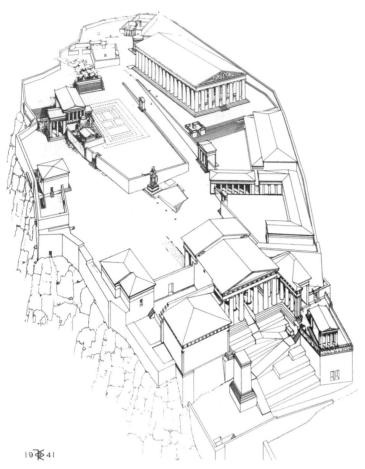

The Acropolis as it looked after the late 5th century BCE. In the foreground, above a flight of ramps and stairs, the main entrance (Propylaia) with, to the right, the small temple of (Athena) Nike. The main temple to the right is the Parthenon, with, toward the Propylaia, the *chalkotheke* and the open sanctuary of Brauronian Artemis. To the left is the complex structure of the Erechtheum (consisting of Athena's Old Temple on the far side; the Porch of Poseidon, left; and the Porch of the Maidens, right), with Athena's olive tree and the small temple of Pandrosus in front. In the very center of the open space is the monumental bronze statue of Athena Promachos by Phidias. Drawing by Gorham P. Stevens. *Courtesy American School of Classical Studies in Athens*

the adult citizens in their communities. Other temples contained an extra room at the back to which access was limited (*adyton* [that where entry is impossible]), most often to the priests, sometimes to other groups, such as nubile girls (*parthenōn*). More complex are the main buildings for the Mysteries, where different traditions and their ritual necessities dictated the shapes. The Eleusinian *telestērion* (initiation hall) started out as a rectangular hall with an *adyton* that contained an unworked rocky floor and from which, at the high point of the rite, fire burst forth. This simple building, which provided shelter and secrecy to the initiates, developed

into a vast square hall that was able to house a much larger crowd of initiates but which still contained the *adyton* in its original place. The Mysteries of Despoina in Arcadian Lycosura contained, besides the ordinary temple, what the locals called the Megaron, a rectangular structure with high walls and an open roof, where initiations took place (Pausanias 8.37.8).

In any temple, the *adyton* constituted a space even more sacred than the *temenos* and restricted to priests only. In other cases, a sanctuary contained a special space reserved for direct contact with the divinity, especially for divination and healing; again, accessibility was restricted. All of the major oracular temples contained a space restricted to the medium, through whom the god prophesied, and to the priests; the sanctuary of Apollo in Didyma admitted visitors only into the entry hall, while the huge unroofed cella was open to the priests alone. In some cases, access to such an interior space needed specific ritual preparation. In the sanctuary of Claros, the priest had his ecstatic vision in a crypt under the cella that was accessible only to him; exceptionally, visitors could "go down" into it after a special initiation rite. In all healing sanctuaries of Asclepius, the patients were advised and cured by the god in their dreams, which they had while sleeping in special incubation halls in the sanctuary; they entered these after purification rites and a special sacrifice to, among others, Mnemosyne (Memory) in order remember the dream.

Abaton. There was, thus, a gradation of sacred space, from the space of a *temenos* that was somehow a god's possession, to the space where humans and gods met in dreams and prophetic ecstasy. Even further out were spaces where a god really touched human space. This was the case where lightning, Zeus's divine form, hit the ground: this space was cut off from the rest of the ground, marked as "inaccessible" (*abaton*), and given over to Zeus Kataibates (he who comes down).

The placing of sanctuaries. Sanctuaries are not placed randomly. No Greek text formulates the rules (although the Roman architect Vitruvius gives some indications; *On Architecture* 4.5), and modern research on the topic has barely begun. Some things are obvious. There is a fundamental opposition between sanctuaries inside the town and outside it *(pro poleos)*; the opposition hinges

Temple of Hera (formerly called Temple of Neptune) at Paestum. Doric, second quarter of the 5th century BCE. *Scala/Art Resource, New York*

on the function of the respective cults. Sanctuaries of divinities intimately connected with civic life are inside the cities; sanctuaries that in some way or another are connected with cults that were viewed as opposed to the orderliness of civic life were outside. The main protector of the city, usually Athena, had her sanctuary on the Acropolis. Zeus, who guaranteed the lawful coexistence of humans in society, was established in the marketplace, which also was the place for political assemblies (Zeus Agoraios [he of the market]), as were the sanctuaries of other gods who were concerned with the political (Apollo) or commercial life (Hermes, Hephaestus in Athens as the patron of craftspeople). Artemis, more concerned with wild nature or with the young whom Greeks conceived of as part of wild nature, had her sanctuaries mainly in the outlying wilderness, as had Pan, the herder's god, and the nymphs, creatures of the wild. The same seems to be true for several south Italian sanctuaries of Hera that focused on maturing girls. Oracular and healing sanctuaries, where people sought closer contact with the divine, tended to be outside the cities as well, often enough in the *eschatiē* (Apollo in Delphi and Didyma; Asclepius in Epidaurus); the sanctuaries of Asclepius, furthermore, were associated with the running water of streams and springs, which played a role in healing rites. Demeter, associated with the fertility of wives and fields, had her sanctuaries in the fields, often halfway up a hill so as not to take up valuable agrarian space. Hilltops and mountain peaks harbored sanctuaries of Zeus as god of weather and rain;

the seashore with its highly visible promontories had sanctuaries of Poseidon.

We know virtually nothing about foundation ceremonies for Greek sanctuaries; when founding a new city—as in the colonies or in later refoundations—a general prayer and sacrifice on behalf of the new city seem to have been enough. Only rarely does archeology produce foundation deposits that indicate that the building of a new temple might have been accompanied by a sacrifice. Similarly, we lack data about what happened when the space of a sanctuary was converted back into ordinary space; in at least one case, we know that an oracle was consulted before the move (*SEG* 15 [1958]: 397), but we hear nothing about rituals of desacralization. Rather than assume a gap in our documentation, we might take this as the characteristic of a religion in which the borderline between sacred and profane was weak; we similarly lack any data about the consecration of divine images and only rare and local information on that of Greek priests.

BIBL.: Susan E. Alcock and Robin Osborne (eds.), *Placing the Gods: Sanctuaries and Sacred Space in Ancient Greece* (Oxford: Clarendon, 1994). Nanno Marinatos and Robin Hägg (eds.), *Greek Sanctuaries: New Approaches* (London: Routledge, 1993). Jon D. Mikalson, *The Sacred and Civil Calendar of the Athenian Year* (Princeton: Princeton University Press, 1975). Martin P. Nilsson, *Griechische Feste von religiöser Bedeutung mit Ausschluss der attischen* (repr. Leipzig: Teubner, 1995 [orig. 1906]).   F.G.

Etruria

Roman sources state that the Etruscans were strict observers of religious ritual and that prescriptions regarding public and private religious practice were set out in a series of *libri rituales* (books of ritual instructions). These were believed to comprise precise instructions for the repetition of complex sets of activity that divided and marked both time and space. Although no such books survive, two excerpts from Etruscan ritual calendars have been preserved: one on the so-called Capua Tile, the other on the Zagreb mummy wrappings. The fragmentary nature of these texts, as well as the difficulties of interpretation, makes the compilation of a complete calendar impossible; and it is extremely unlikely that there was any single standard calendar that operated through all the Etruscan cities and territories. Nevertheless, it is possible to build a tentative account of some aspects of their cycles of religious practice.

Etruscan religious time appears to have operated on at least four levels. The first, monthly, cycle is evident in the repetition of certain days for religious ceremonies; for instance, the Ides on day 15 (sometimes day 13) of each month. The second cycle was annual, illustrated by the practice of drawing up codified lists of festivals in the form of a calendar and more specifically by the tradition known in the city of Volsinii of hammering a bronze nail into a temple door to mark the passing of each year (Livy 7.3.7). Third, Etruscans conceived of far longer spans of time (Latin *saecula naturalia* [natural generations]), the length of which were determined by the age of the oldest survivor of all those born on the first day of the *saeculum*. Finally, according to the grammarian Censorinus writing in the early 3rd century CE but apparently drawing on the 1st-century BCE Roman antiquarian Varro (*On the Birthday* 17.6), the Etruscans predicted that their civilization would last for ten *saecula,* thus defining Etruscan civilization itself as a measure of time, with a beginning and an end point.

These different levels of temporal division were punctuated and marked by religious festivals. The ritual focus of such festivals, regardless of the deity, was sacrifice. Both the Capua Tile and the Zagreb mummy provide a wealth of detail on the practice of Etruscan sacrifice. The sacrificial offering could be food (cakes, fruit, grain), incense or perfume, animals (oxen, goats, deer), and in the earliest period perhaps humans (although this evidence is much disputed). The deposits of the remains of sacrifices found at Tarquinia are remarkably homogeneous, suggesting the particular rigor and adherence to prescriptions that Etruscan ritual entailed.

The sacrifices and the festivals of which they were a part marked the monthly and annual cycles of Etruscan conceptions of time. They also marked special beginnings, for instance, the foundation of a city. Religion was deeply embedded in Etruscan notions of time, past, present, and future. However, for the Etruscans, sacrifices and festivals involved not only temporal but also spatial differentiation. The Etruscan practices of augury (reading birds' flights) and hepatoscopy (reading animals' livers) were used not only in dealing with portents but also in the physical planning of sanctuaries and cities and the differentiation of space between sacred and profane, a differentiation that applied as much to urban as to rural environments. Although not strictly Etruscan (but from the nearby town of Gubbio, in Umbria), the Iguvine Tables give detailed prescriptions for the establishment of sacred space and the religious boundaries of the city; Etruscan procedures were most likely very similar. Thus the entire landscape of Etruria became ritually ordered. Sacrifices and festivals took place within that order, both spatially and temporally.

From the 9th century BCE until the 6th century BCE, ritual activity took place largely in sacred places within the natural landscape, for instance, mountaintops (Soracte) and lakes (Falterona); in both places, cultic activity is attested by votive deposits. Although some religious buildings existed during this time, such as those at Roselle, Cerveteri, and possibly Murlo, they cannot be clearly or definitively differentiated from buildings with domestic or other functions. By the late 6th century, however, codified sanctuary architecture signals the construction of environments specifically for religious practices; the first identifiable Etruscan temple is at Veii (ca. 600 BCE). Although the use of natural shrines often continued, the sanctuary became the new locus for festivals and sacrifices, both public and individual.

The Etruscan sanctuary consisted of one or more temple buildings with associated altars and a boundary wall. Temples were relatively simple in plan, often with their inner room divided into three subsidiary chambers (the Roman architectural writer Vitruvius saw this tripartite division as a characteristically Etruscan—or "Tuscan"—form). They were decorated with molded terra-cotta reliefs of both geometric patterns and representations of deities. A distinctive feature of some of these buildings (as, e.g., at the Portonaccio sanctuary of the goddess Menerva at Veii) were terra-cotta statues, ranged along the ridge of the roof. The architectural form was designed in a manner that seems deliberately to emphasize the separation of the sacred from the profane. The temple was set on a high podium, usually with steps allowing access only at the front (unlike the standard Greek model of steps on all sides); it was often (as at Orvieto) on high ground. As with Greek and Roman temples, the temple building itself, however, was not the prime focus of ritual activity, which centered on the open-air altar. Other features of these sanctuaries included storage facilities for offerings made to the deity (small buildings now known as "treasuries" or pits into which older offerings might be relegated) and, at Portonaccio, a complicated water system, with a large pool (of unknown—possibly healing—function) adjacent to the temple itself.

Model reconstruction of an Etruscan temple. German Archaeological Institute, Rome.

It is impossible now to reconstruct any general ideas—cosmological, political, or cultural—of which these divisions of time and space may have been a part. Some recent archeological studies attempt to define the wider "ritual landscape" of areas of Etruria, arguing, for example, that religious sites (including cemeteries) might serve to monumentalize liminal or marginal political areas (between country and city or between the territories of different cities). It also seems very likely that spatial divisions and the techniques associated with them were (as at Rome) seen as a manifestation of divine order and in some way a reflection of wider cosmology; but we can only speculate on what that cosmology might be.

BIBL.: I. E. M. Edlund, *The Gods and the Place: Location and Function of Sanctuaries in the Countryside of Etruria and Magna Graecia (700–400 BC)* (Skrifter utgivna av Svenska Institutet i Rom 43; Rome, 1987). C. Riva and S. Stoddart, "Ritual Landscapes in Archaic Etruria," in *Approaches to the Study of Ritual: Italy and the Ancient Mediterranean* (ed. J. B. Wilkins; London: Accordia Research Centre Specialist Studies, 1996), 91–109. G. Colonna (ed.), *I Santuari d'Etruria* (Milan: Electa, 1985).   V.E.I.

Rome

To understand the nature of sacred times in ancient Rome, we must grasp the basic principle that human beings shared their entire environment with the gods. In human communities, space and time formed a whole that was divided, in a variety of ways, into divine portions and human portions. This is reflected by Rome's calendar and its sacred places.

Sacred Times

Roman traditions offered two main ways of conceiving the time that human beings and gods shared in the Roman world: either according to a natural calendar set up by the gods, which was supposed to be recognized and accepted by all people, or according to a civil calendar created by magistrates. To these might be added the various different conceptualizations of times and its divisions projected by the "private" calendars of individual families in districts of the city or within nontraditional religions at Rome, such as the worship of Isis or Mithras.

Divine calendar and human calendar. The natural calendar was built around the rising and setting of the zodiac signs. Often characterized as agrarian, because it determined the timing of farmwork, this calendar had the advantage of being universal, as it was more or less identical for everyone, at least in Italy. Moreover, the course of the heavenly bodies expressed a divine law that the pious were well advised to follow, since this law appeared to govern agricultural work and the life of crops. In the historical era, this calendar was always used in the daily life of peasants as well as being a focus of learned speculation.

The second—or civil—calendar was that of magistrates and citizens. Decisions on its structure and festivals were initially established by laws or by decrees of the senate. According to the myth of its origins, the major divisions of the year and the first official calendar were the work of King Numa, the second king of Rome. Although it was overseen on an everyday basis by the priestly college of *pontifices,* the official religious calendar of Rome thus reflected only the decisions of earthly authorities. Over time, these decisions had established the structure of the months and the year, as well as the list of the regular major festivals. They had also specified the conditions under which the movable festivals and other ceremonies, sacrifices, or rituals would be determined or announced. The public calendar included only the public festivals and rites of Rome itself and made no mention of the countless feast days celebrated by any subgroups of the population—districts of the city, colleges, or families. The calendars that were painted or inscribed on marble reflected only the public calendar of Rome in the narrow sense; only the most important traditional festivals appear on these calendars, and a public deity was above all a deity who had been favored with an official festival day.

The first level of organization of the civil calendar concerned the general distribution of the days of the month. According to Varro (1st century BCE), this distribution distinguished between days set aside for the gods and days reserved for humans (*De lingua latina* 6.12; cf. Macrobius, *Saturnalia* 1.16.2–3). The roughly 235 days open to human action—judicial, military, commercial business, or work—were called *dies fasti*. Some of these were marked F on written calendars, but those specifically intended for political life (192 days in all) were marked C, standing for *dies comitiales* (assembly days). The 109 days created in honor of the gods were *dies nefasti* (N on calendars); among these, about 61 days also were characterized as public festivals *(feriae publicae*, marked NP on calendars, probably standing for *nefastus publicus)*; days that were not public festivals in the traditional sense began to be designated as *feriae* only in the 1st century CE. During the *dies nefasti*, the activities of mortals in public spaces were supposed to cease, yielding to religious ceremonies that honored the gods and put their personalities and virtues on display. From the beginning of the empire, a large number of festivals were expanded, in particular by the extension of the festive character to the days preceding and following the festival in question. In short, behind Varro's formula for dividing up the year lies the model of a festival day as one on which the gods symbolically exercised their functions, while humans honored them because the gods were carrying out these functions in the interest of all.

The *calends* (day 1 of the month) and the *ides* (day 13 or 15, depending on the month) were included among the *dies nefasti*. On the *nones* (day 5 or 7, depending on the month), the *rex sacrorum* (see Religious Personnel) published an edict announcing all the regular fixed festivals *(feriae statae sollemnes)* up to the next *calends*. This ritual was still carried out at the end of the republic. It shows that the calendar could not be decreed once and for all; it had to be instituted by an edict published every month. Moreover, the announcements made by the *rex sacrorum* included neither the movable feasts *(feriae conceptivae)*, which were announced by a magistrate (e.g., the *Compitalia*, decreed by the urban praetor), nor the religious rituals that were not major festivals; the latter were announced at the beginning of the year by the presidents of priestly colleges or other subgroups of the city.

Religious calendar. The traditional festivals that figure on painted or inscribed calendars fall into several groups. A first set appears in large letters on epigraphic calendars. These festivals, whose names occur in what is grammatically a neuter plural form, are generally con-

sidered to date from the first civil calendar, traditionally attributed to the 6th century BCE (the so-called calendar of Numa). We do not know how soon this calendar was recorded in writing; but even if that process was considerably later, we can presume that the system of festivals itself was ancient.

This calendar appears to encompass the essential activities and characteristics of the city: the organization of time, the beginning and end of the year and of each month, agricultural work, and military and political functions. In other words, this program of festivals gives the impression of being a typically political rationalization of the nature of things, substituted for the old "natural" calendar of divine origin.

Among the *feriae* of the religious calendar, the agrarian festivals offered homage to their patron divinities and so celebrated the seasonal cycle of work and obedience to the fundamental law instituted by the gods; examples include the first Vinalia (April 23), the Robigalia (April 25, the aversion of corn blight [*robigo*]), the rustic Vinalia (August 19), and the Consualia (August 21, the storage of crops after harvest). It is easy to see that these "very old" celebrations were also festivals of the cosmic calendar transcribed into the civil calendar: their antiquity corresponds to the particular status of the "natural" calendar that had been established before or apart from the city. Certain of these festivals clearly celebrated the beginning of the food cycle, others its conclusion.

This first cycle of natural festivals connected with the natural condition of mortals, that is, with the production of their food according to the law willed by the immortals, has as its counterpart a second major group of essentially civic festivals, for example, the Liberalia (March 17), the Saturnalia (December 17), the Lupercalia (February 15), the Feralia (February 21), and so on. It should be noted that the Romans had two festivals celebrating the end of the year. In fact, March 1, which more or less corresponded to the astronomical New Year, seems to have served as the civil and religious New Year until 153 BCE. After that date, the consuls began to serve their terms January 1, and for this reason a certain number of festivals connected with the winter solstice and to the opening of food stores were transformed into festivals celebrating the year's end. The most famous of these was the Saturnalia, held on December 17. In addition to the civic festivals, other festivals related to military life, such as the famous horse sacrifice (*Equus October*, October 15) or those that are thought to have celebrated the structure of time (probably the Matralia, June 11).

Most of these festivals fell on days that are odd numbered in our calendar: thus the Feralia fell on what we call February 21. They were often separated from other festivals by an interval of one day, and for the most part they came after the ides of the month in question. In general, these festival days were holidays on which people did not work. As occasions for major sacrifices, these festivals gradually became connected with picturesque rites that were viewed, by antiquarians of the early empire, as evidence of their antiquity. Thus the very popular race of the *luperci* around the Palatine, on the day of the Lupercalia, was thought to go back to Romulus and Remus. Most of the major festivals concluded with formal games at the Circus.

Starting in the 2nd century BCE, the liturgical calendar began to include the anniversaries of the temples, especially those of the new temples built in large numbers since the 3rd century. The temple anniversaries certainly celebrated the great deeds of the Roman people and their immortal protectors, but, unlike the festivals of the old calendar, they also implicitly celebrated the triumphs of the great Roman families. From the time of the dictatorship of Julius Caesar, this theme was explicit: it became customary to celebrate the anniversaries of Caesar's victories and exploits as major public festivals; later, those of Augustus and succeeding emperors were similarly celebrated. After their exploits came the emperors' birthdays and other events marking their lives, some of which continued to be celebrated after the individuals' deaths (e.g., the Augustalia, commemorating Augustus's return to Rome in 19 BCE). These honors effectively conferred on the emperors honors equal to those enjoyed by the gods.

The Roman religious calendar as a whole cannot be reduced to the documents that became known as *fasti*. No document of the complete calendar survives. Besides, the official calendar as it appears in painted or inscribed *fasti* was not a religious calendar, but a representation of civic time, based on a selection of festivals that were known to all. If we were to imagine a complete religious calendar, it would include countless public and private festivals and rituals. On the public level, there were not only the great holiday festivals and the anniversaries of the foundation of temples, games, and other rituals tied to the service of the gods, but also divination, regular vows (*vota*, offered January 1 under the republic, January 1 and 3 under the empire) or extraordinary ones, sacrifices made in thanksgiving or expiation, and prayer, as well as the rituals of family calendars, the military calendar, those of associations of shopkeepers, craftspeople, and other subgroups of the city-state. And this is not to mention the calendars of the Roman colonies and cities outside Italy, whether granted full Roman status or not. It is easy to understand why no single calendar can account for the proliferation of festivals and ritual obligations.

Something of the complexity, even within Rome itself, can be gauged from the festival of the Megalesia, celebrated for the goddess Magna Mater, who had been introduced from Asia Minor and granted an official temple on the Palatine at the end of the 3rd century BCE. One part of the goddess's festival cycle (the Megalesian Games) was included in at least one inscribed calendar; but this kernel of the festival was expanded at some point during the first two centuries CE by a series of pre-

liminary rituals starting with "The Introduction of the Reed" (*Canna Intrat,* March 15) and ending with the "Washing" (*Lavatio,* March 27). These rituals, unlike the games, were performed solely, it seems, by the attendants of the goddess. The complete cycle never figures in any written *fasti* but occupied an ambivalent position on the borders of the official calendar.

The obligations listed by the official calendars were not imposed on everyone, either in Rome or in other cities with full Roman status in Italy or abroad. Many festivals and rituals involved principally magistrates and public priests and often only certain of these. The experience of such festivals for ordinary citizens was essentially a passive one: for the length of the festival they could not participate in administering justice, conclude legally valid business, or work in public areas of the city. For the rest, they could attend the proceedings as spectators, they could try to participate in the ritual distribution of sacrificial meat, and they might watch the games conducted at the major festivals. But this was a right rather than an absolute duty for ordinary citizens. In contrast, everyone, citizens and noncitizens alike, actively celebrated the religious festivals and obligations that concerned them in the context of the domestic cult or that of the various subgroups of the city.

This typically Roman calendar cannot be transposed without adjustments to other cities. It is clear that Roman colonies and other cities with full Roman status all adopted this civil calendar and its way of dividing months and years. The cities without that status (*peregrini*) in the Greek-speaking countries, however, kept their own calendars and made only a few alterations to their prevailing rules in the names of the months or the dating of the New Year (e.g., in the reign of Augustus the province of Asia voted to start its New Year on Augustus's birthday; Dittenberger 1903–5: 458).

All the same, it is likely that at least the major Roman cities of the empire (although not the *peregrini*) adopted part of Rome's festive calendar. But this probably involved festivals and rituals connected with a particular deity or temple and new dynastic feasts, rather than the cycle of traditional Roman festivals. The old festivals, like the system of *dies fasti, dies nefasti,* and NP days, concerned Rome alone. In fact, in cities all over the Roman world, as it became progressively more integrated in the imperial period, local calendars were developed that resulted from a mix of Roman and local traditions.

Sacred Places

Just as it exercised mastery over time, the city defined and controlled the spatial environment that it shared, as it were, with the deities.

Templum. The space occupied by the city was "freed and defined verbally" *(liberatus et effatus).* During this operation, carried out by the augurs, the spaces destined for appropriation by the city were released from all divine charge upon the land. Such was the case for the

Frieze on the Ara Pacis (Altar of Peace), Rome, depicting a sacred procession, late 1st century BCE. On the left are the *flamines* with their distinctive headdresses. *Alinari/Art Resource, New York*

ancient territory of Rome *(ager Romanus antiquus),* the city *(urbs),* and the *templum.* Once liberated, these spaces could then be inaugurated *(inaugurare),* meaning that their definition was approved by consultation with the gods via the augurs. Inauguration, which constituted a space defined by the city-state with Jupiter's approval, was required for all sites where public activities took place: political assemblies, sessions of the senate, judicial activities, religious ritual, taking the auspices (see Divination and Prophecy). A site approved by augurs was a *templum.* In principle quadrangular spaces, inaugurated sites were marked with a bronze star (Festus, ed. Lindsay, p. 476), and they bore the label *augustus* (august). In his treatise on the Latin language, Varro includes a formula used by the augurs in defining a *templum*—no more comprehensible to us than it was to most Romans, we must imagine (*On the Latin Language* 7.8–10).

A *templum* was thus neither a building nor a sacred site, in the Roman sense of the term. For a *templum* to become sacred, it needed to be consecrated, entirely or in part. As many temples (in our sense of the word) were built in *templa* and often corresponded to them in surface area, they themselves were also called *templa.* In this way the term began to be applied in common parlance to a cult building.

Pomerium. A second ritual limit separated the city of

Rome *(urbs)* from its territory *(ager):* the *pomerium.* This limit was established by the official foundation ritual. It thus applied only to Rome, to the ancient cities of Latium (the region around Rome), and to the Roman colonies, and it is incorrect to use it for every Roman city during the imperial era (obviously, no peregrine city had a *pomerium*). Cities were placed within the *pomerium,* and the pomerial line itself ran between a ditch and the ridges of earth created by ritual plowing that traced the boundaries of the *urbs.*

The *urbs* was neither a *templum* nor a sacred space: the function of the *pomerium* was to mark out and protect the privileged status of the city's ground for taking the auspices and other augural activity; the rest of the city's territory, outside the *pomerium,* did not enjoy this privilege. To take the auspices, a *templum* first had to be traced within this privileged space; to install a deity there, part of the space had to be consecrated. To preserve the integrity of the space within the *pomerium,* it was forbidden to site tombs within it; the army—that is, armed soldiers—did not enter the space (except on days of triumph). The pomerial line constituted the limit between the *imperium domi* (civil power within the city) and the *imperium militiae* (unlimited power for the command of the army and the conduct of war outside Rome).

The *pomerium* of the mythical period of the kings

The temple of Portunus in the Forum Boarium, Rome: façade.
From Jean-Pierre Adam, Le Temple de Portunus au Forum Boarium

of Rome is supposed to have encompassed no more than the Palatine hill; under the republic it corresponded more or less to the much more extensive line marked by the so-called Servian wall. Because it was thought to be connected also to the territory of Rome as a whole, generals who had expanded the empire had the right to extend the *pomerium;* thus under the empire this line ended up incorporating a large part of the Campus Martius as well as the Aventine. The effect of the line on the location of sanctuaries in the city has been much discussed in recent scholarship. In principle, it seems, deities sponsoring the activities of death and destruction, such as Dis pater, Mars, and Vulcan, could not receive sanctuary within its boundary. Yet there are examples of shrines and temples that seem to break that rule. One possible explanation is that they were originally outside the *pomerium* but became caught up in its extension. This might even explain why the archaic Vulcanal could have been founded in the Forum (outside the "original" Palatine *pomerium*). Certainly when a new temple was dedicated to Vulcan, it was outside the *pomerium.* At first glance, certain deities of foreign origin too, such as Apollo, Hercules, Diana, Juno Regina, and Aesculapius, seem to have been relegated to the area outside the line. Yet, that the temple of Castor and Pollux (dedicated 484 BCE) was established in the Forum, that of Venus Erycina (dedicated 215 BCE) on the Capitol, and that of the Magna Mater (dedicated 191 BCE) on the Palatine shows that the situation was more complex.

Sacred spaces. The spaces of the city-state and the territory were divided between gods and humans: some spaces were sacred and some were not. Sacred spaces were of two types: those that mortals built and dedicated to the gods, and those that the gods chose and set up themselves, as it were—sites that human beings simply needed to recognize as sacred.

The many types of man-made sacred spaces ranged from simple enclosures for worship, furnished with an altar, to vast temples with altars in front, dominating a square, surrounded by porticos and sometimes by secondary buildings as well. In the eyes of the city, that is, from the public standpoint, only legally consecrated spaces and buildings were sacred *(sacer)*. An altar or a temple that had not been officially consecrated—that is, by a magistrate with *imperium* or one charged by law to do so—was not sacred.

This did not mean that unofficial altars or chapels, dedicated by private individuals in public spaces, were systematically banned or destroyed by the authorities. Generally speaking, these private dedications were tolerated, even if they never had the legal status that an official consecration conferred. All the offerings made by private individuals in public sanctuaries fell into this category. Numerous private sanctuaries, set up on private lands and consecrated according to private procedures, were considered by law as bound by a religious obligation and were called *religiosi*: these were protected and could not be expropriated. They fell into the same category as spaces struck by lightning or as tombs. Moreover, the categories of *sacer* and *religiosus* were originally only for Rome and the surrounding territory. After the Social War (91–87 BCE), they were extended to all Italy. Nonetheless, dedications in these places, even when they were public, were considered under the law "as if sacred" *(pro sacro)* or "as if religious" *(pro religioso)*.

Consecration. Consecration was a complex operation, possible only on a Roman territory that had been "liberated and defined" and in some cases inaugurated. After the official decision to go ahead with a consecration (called the *constitutio*), the space in question was purified, the borders of the site were marked, and the first stone was laid. Once the building was completed, it was dedicated or consecrated. The officiant grasped the doorpost (or touched the altar) and pronounced the formula of dedication *(lex dedicationis)* under the dictation of a *pontifex*: this caused the building and space to pass from the public domain into that of the deity, and from then on, the site was sacred. The *lex dedicationis* also articulated a certain number of stipulations concerning the forms of worship.

Consecrated places bore a variety of names that are often difficult to distinguish and that were probably used quite loosely in the Roman world itself. We have already seen the ambiguity of the term *templum,* which sometimes designates an inaugurated space, some-

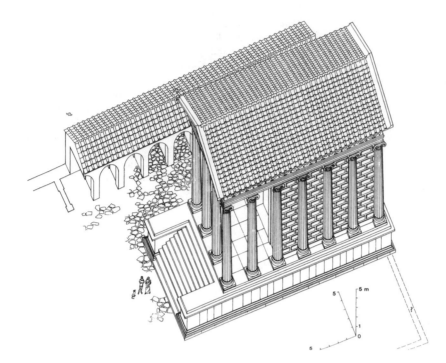

The temple of Portunus: axonometric drawing. *From Jean-Pierre Adam,* Le Temple de Portunus au Forum Boarium

times a building (generally inaugurated). *Aedes* refers to a building where a deity resides, and the term is now regularly translated "temple." It implies nothing about the technical religious status of the place concerned, and as such it can be used to refer to cult places that were not inaugurated, such as the *aedes* of Vesta, of Hercules Olivarius in the Forum Boarium, or the Pantheon on the Campus Martius. A *delubrum* was a paved area connected with a temple or an enclosure surrounded by porticos. *Fanum* has a generic sense and refers to a place of worship or to a temple in general. A *sacellum* was in principle a consecrated space that had no roof (an outdoor area with an altar; an altar with a chapel or placed before a niche), whereas a *sacrarium* was a building or a room in which sacred objects were placed.

A cult place was surrounded by a wall, a railing, or simple columns. The most important element was the altar *(ara),* which was the minimal cult requirement. When the site included a temple, the altar was always located outside the building, generally on its axis, except in the cult of Mithras, where the altar was placed in a closed space, imitating a grotto. Next to the "master altar," which belonged to the proprietary god of the temple, there were often temporary altars *(temporalis)* for "invited" deities.

A typical Roman temple was built on a raised *podium.* A stairway led to the *pronaos* of the temple, which housed open-air rites. At the rear of the *pronaos,* a gate led to the cella, which was the god's residence. Each deity had his or her own cella and an altar placed in front of the temple; thus there were three cellae (for Jupiter, Juno, and Minerva) in the main Capitoline temple at Rome, each with its own door and altar. At the rear of the cella stood the cult image of the deity. The cella often included a table for supplementary sacrificial offerings, statues of deities associated with the proprietary deity of the site, works of art, and ritual objects. In principle, one entered the cella only in connection with worship, public or private. Certain temples also included spaces about which little is known, where beds or chairs were placed for the gods' banquets; these facilities were probably located outside the temple.

In front of the temple, all around the altar and the *aedes,* there was a space *(area)* whose status varied. It was sometimes sacred, like the temple itself, and was accessible only for worship or maintenance; in other instances it was partly secular, that is, open to mortals' activities and offerings: stelae, altars, statues. The richest places of worship, or those that were isolated in rural areas, were often flanked or surrounded by porticos. Sanctuaries too far outside Rome to allow celebrants to return the same day included places to stay that were sometimes no more than simple porticos. Near the temple or in the portico there was a kitchen for preparing offerings and sacrificial banquets. Well-furnished sanctuaries included banquet halls. Since participation in cult might require repeated ablutions, sanctuaries had wells, natural or artificial pools, and, if they were isolated, even thermal baths that allowed celebrants to wash before worshiping. Certain cult places also included springs and bathing pools and sometimes also baths belonging to a water-god, with a therapeutic function. Finally, depending on the needs of the cult and the public activities that took place there, some important temples could be associated with theaters or circuses. Major rituals were concluded by plays or chariot races.

Cult places outside the traditional civic cult presented a variety of significant differences in the organization of sacred space. Temples of Mithras were not only dark, enclosed places (often known as "caves"). They were in the form of an elongated *triclinium,* to accommodate communal worship, with an altar at the rear and a relief representing the myth of the god. Sanctuaries devoted to Isis, by contrast, regularly paraded their topographical connection with Egypt itself: they could include a representation of the Nile, as well as genuine Egyptian or Egyptian-inspired sculpture (as in the magnificent furnishings of the Isaeum in the Campus Martius); the cult also was supposed to use water brought directly from the Nile for its rituals (a fact more often symbolically than literally true). Isiac establishments often had an attached residential and assembly facility for priests or temple guests *(pastophorion)* and a place for initiations. Still other types of cult space were associated with the Syrian cult of Jupiter Dolichenus and with the various facilities for the Phrygian cult in the Palatine temple of the Magna Mater. Nonetheless, despite these different arrangements in different cults, the basic Roman model for a cult place was an area with an altar, a temple, and rooms for other ritual functions.

In private homes, the size and number of cult places varied greatly. Not all houses had a niche for the Lares in masonry or wood in the *atrium,* let alone altars or secondary rooms devoted to worship, as the great aristocratic residences did; in poorer homes, without *atria* or public rooms, terra-cotta statuettes of the family "pantheon" were enclosed in cupboards, and sacrifices were made primarily on the ground or in the flames of a portable altar.

Sacred woods, grottoes, pools, and springs. Alongside the spaces that had been liberated, defined, and consecrated, there were other ritually constructed places that the ancients took to be residences established and managed by the gods themselves. These natural sites (sacred groves, vast grottoes, pools of unfathomable depth, sources of rivers, and so on) inspired fear, for each was believed to serve as home for a deity. The fright and astonishment that these places aroused signaled the divine presence. The role of mortals was restricted to identifying such places and marking their boundaries. People went there only to perform the cult and to maintain the site. Sacred groves *(luci)* in particular were privileged places for this type of divine residence. A *lucus,* properly speaking, was a clearing in a sacred grove: cult activities took place in that clearing, which was ritually created and maintained and often equipped with temples and porticos.

Sacred groves (which were also found inside cities) were not the only sanctuaries in Roman territory or that of the other cities. In addition to the suburban temples, constructed in immediate proximity to the *pomerium* and the gates, the territory included temples outside the cities. Certain of these were private and were the concern only of their owners or residents of the area. But there were also public sanctuaries outside the cities, which are not to be confused with rural places of worship intended for the inhabitants of the countryside. Through these sanctuaries located on the major roads and occasionally on the outskirts of a city, the city exercised and celebrated its hold over its territory; the city authorities with their attendants went to these sites to worship, once or twice a year. The sanctuaries of the *vici* (villages or settlements) scattered over the territory of major cities played a particular role. Although they were associated with an individual community, these cults were really tied to the collectivity of the city; for the *vicus* was not so much an independent "village" in our sense of the word as an integral part of the city— one established outside the urban center, in the city's territory. The cults of the *vicus* were thus no different from those of the regions or neighborhoods of the city itself.

BIBL.: Attilio Degrassi, *Fasti anni Numani et Iuliani* (Inscriptiones Italiae 13.2; Rome, 1963). Wilhelm Dittenberger (ed.), *Orientis graeci inscriptiones selectae* (2 vols.; Leipzig, 1903–5). Pierre Gros, *L'architecture romaine du début du IIIe siècle av. J.-C. à la fin du Haut-Empire,* vol. 1: *Les monuments publics* (Paris, 1996), 122–234. Eric M. Orlin, *Temples, Religion, and Politics in the Roman Republic* (Leiden, 1997). Jörg Rüpke, *Kalendar und Öffentlichkeit: Die Geschichte der Repräsentation und religiösen Qualifikation von Zeit in Rom* (Religionsgeschichtliche Versuche und Vorarbeiten 40; Berlin, 1995). H. H. Scullard, *Festivals and Ceremonies of the Roman Republic* (London, 1981). J.S.

Christianity

Sacred Time

At the center of early Christianity was the theological conviction that the events surrounding the life, death, and resurrection of Jesus, who was the Christ, had changed time forever. Already the ministry of Jesus had inaugurated a new age—the time was fulfilled and the kingdom of God had drawn near (Mark 1.15). With the events of, first, the resurrection and then Pentecost, the time of the Spirit or the time of the church had begun, which was regarded as a prelude to the *parousia* (second coming), when Christ would come in glory to judge the living and the dead. Thus, all time was eschatological— all humanity was living in the last era or epoch of theological significance (Rev. 22.17, 20; 1 Cor. 16.22). However, even within this broad eschatological time, certain days and hours of the day emerged as having particular significance.

First was the weekly commemoration of the resurrection. According to all the gospel accounts, Jesus was crucified on a Friday; because of the approaching sabbath, the bodies had to be taken down from the gibbets, and Jesus's body was hastily placed in a tomb. On the first day of the week (Sunday), when the sabbath was over, the women came to the tomb to anoint the body, only to discover that the tomb was empty. It seems that almost immediately the first day, or the Lord's day (Rev. 1.10), became a special time for many Christian communities. The Gospel of John and Acts of the Apostles record gatherings on the first day, and Paul mentions a collection being taken on the first day (1 Cor. 16.2). The *Didache* 14.1 (composed in the late 1st or early 2nd century CE) reminds its community, "on the Lord's day come together, break bread, and give thanks." Ca. 107 CE, Bishop Ignatius of Antioch wrote to the Christians in Magnesia mentioning those who "no longer observe sabbaths but fashion their lives after the Lord's day, on which our life also rose through him and through his death" (*Magnesians* 9.1). Justin Martyr, writing for a pagan audience around 155 CE reported that "we all hold this common gathering on Sunday since it is the first day, on which God, transforming darkness and matter, made the universe, and Jesus Christ our savior rose from the dead on the same day" (*Apology* 1.67). But in the *Epistle of Barnabas*, even this is given a further eschatological significance; Sunday is "the eighth day," the beginning of a new age, a world renewed (*Barnabas* 15.8). Some communities may have continued to observe the Jewish sabbath (Saturday) in some way or other, but in the early centuries, the first day was not regarded as a substitute Christian sabbath or day of rest.

At least according to the Acts of the Apostles, each day was sanctified by set hours of prayer. The apostles, the author asserts, were daily in the temple, and prayer at the third (Acts 2.1, 15), sixth (10.9), and ninth (3.1; 10.3, 30) hours is mentioned, as well as a night vigil (16.25). The *Didache* gives the Lord's Prayer with the command to pray three times a day, and it seems that morning and night prayer, marking the natural light and darkness, was given a Christological meaning—Christ was the true morning sun and the light of the world. The cumulative evidence of Alexandrians Clement (*Stromata* 7.7) and Origen (*On Prayer* 12.2), Tertullian from North Africa (*On Prayer* 25), and the so-called *Apostolic Tradition* 41 attributed to Hippolytus (now dated late 2nd century) suggest that ideally the day should be punctuated with prayer, although how far the ideal was realized is uncertain, and the recommended times were not uniform.

The *Didache* (8.1) also mentions days of fasting—Wednesday and Friday—and at least by the 4th century, according to the *Apostolic Constitutions* 7.23, these were given a significance related to the life of Jesus—Wednesday was the day that Judas betrayed him, and Friday was the day of his crucifixion.

At least in the 1st century, Sunday was a complex feast, celebrating the whole of Christ's life, death, and resurrection. But what of annual festivals? The events surrounding Jesus between Passover and Pentecost had changed the significance or importance of these Jewish festivals for the early Christian communities. However, it is only in the 2nd century that clear testimony emerges for observation of an annual Christian Pascha, a Passover celebration focused on the death and resurrection of Christ. The *Epistula Apostolorum,* probably written in Asia Minor in the 3rd century, includes an address from the risen Christ to the apostles, requesting them to commemorate his death at Passover (Nisan 14–15 in the Jewish calendar), although it is clear that this meant his passion, death, and resurrection (*Epistula Apostolorum* 15). The problems of correlating the Jewish lunar calendar with the Julian calendar led to the Quartodeciman controversy, a dispute between Christians who observed the Christian Pascha on the equivalent date in the Julian calendar (March 25) and those who always observed it on a Sunday. Ultimately, the Sunday observance won the day. Only in the 4th century did this combined observance develop into separate commemorative observances—Good Friday for the passion and death, Holy Saturday for the entombment, and Easter for the resurrection. Pentecost, the seventh Sunday after Christ's resurrection and traditionally the day when the Spirit descended upon the apostles, seems to have had significance for St. Paul, but it is not until the late 2nd century that we have evidence (in a reported lost work of Irenaeus and in Tertullian) that Christians celebrated Pentecost as a time of joy and festivity, bringing a conclusion to the paschal season.

The third major annual observance that developed was a combination of what we now call Epiphany and Christmas. Attempts to relate this to the Jewish festival of Sukkot have not been successful. Some scholars have seen the identification of December 25 and January 6 with Christmas and Epiphany as deliberate attempts by the church to counter pagan festivities that fell on these days—either the Roman Natalis Sol Invictus (Birth of the Unconquerable Sun) or any of several feasts of Dionysus, which tended to fall in the winter months. Others see these dates as Western and Eastern versions of a calculation, based on perfect numbers, of the birth of Jesus, assuming March 25 or April 6 as the date of his conception. Although the earliest uncontested evidence for the observance of both festivals is the 4th century, some have argued that already in the early 3rd century, December 25 was being observed by the Donatists in Africa. In the Eastern part of the empire, the focus of January 6 was the baptism of Jesus and the turning of water into wine at Cana in Galilee, with lesser emphasis on the nativity. In the West, December 25 emphasized the nativity. Gradually, East and West adopted one another's dates, and separate events were understood to be commemorated by the feasts. The Armenian church still sticks rigidly to the older Eastern tradition of celebrating the nativity, the baptism of Christ, and his first miracle of turning water into wine as a combined commemoration on January 6. Although some scholars have argued that this development of historicization represents a surrender of the earlier emphasis on eschatology, such a conclusion is not necessary; since Christianity celebrates the acts of God in history, eschatology and secular history have always been entwined.

Sacred Space

Part of the teaching of Jesus was that both Jerusalem and the temple would be destroyed. He was alleged to have said, "Destroy this temple, and in three days I will raise it"—speaking of his own body (John 2.19). It is no accident that in 1 Corinthians Paul speaks of the Christian community being the body of Christ (1 Cor. 12.27) and as a temple (3.16). Furthermore, in the Acts of the Apostles, the speech of Stephen sets forth a theology that disputes the meaning of the phrase *in this place*. The divine presence "in this place," according to this speech, is not to be located in Jerusalem and the temple, but in Jesus Christ. Thus although the Jerusalem apostles still prayed at the temple, there was a recognition that it was no longer quite the holy place that it was once thought to be. Furthermore, the gift of the Spirit on the day of Pentecost, as narrated in Acts, suggests not only a reversal of the story of the tower of Babel, but a distinct move away from emphasis on a special race and geographical location to inclusion of potentially the whole of humanity as the people of God. Thus the holy place became the body—either of the individual Christian or of the assembled group as the body of Christ (1 Cor. 3.16; 6.19).

While the final destiny of the individual in most cases was located in God's eschatological future, there was an exception for martyrs, with Stephen in Acts being the protomartyr. Just before his death, Stephen saw the Son of Man in his glory; he then "fell asleep." This combination of the noble death of martyrs and the heavenly glory they shared with the martyred Son of Man led to a special interest in the bones of the martyrs as being in some way already in heaven. Polycarp was martyred in Smyrna in 156 CE; the Christians at Smyrna wrote: "We later took up his bones, being of more value than precious stones and more esteemed than gold, and laid them apart in a convenient place. There the Lord will grant us to gather so far as may be and to celebrate with great gladness and joy the birthday of his martyrdom" (*Martyrdom of Polycarp* 18.2–3). Not only did the faithful gather at the graves of the martyrs; they also buried other departed Christians in the vicinity of the martyr, in the belief that this was one of the places where the transformation at the last judgment would begin.

Writing about 200 CE, the apologist Minucius Felix claimed that "we have no temples and no altars" (*Octavius* 32.1). Indeed, periodic persecution, poverty,

and the hostility against holiness located in a physical building precluded the idea of a holy building for worship. But the body, bone, or relic of a martyr could make a place holy, be it a shrine or a place for worship. Writing in the 4th century, Gregory of Nyssa said: "Those who behold them [i.e., relics] embrace, as it were, the living body in full flower: they bring eye, mouth, ear, all senses into play, and then, shedding tears of reverence and passion, they address to the martyr their prayers of intercession as though he were present" (*Encomium on St. Theodore* in *Patrologia graeca* 46.740B). The early Christians tended to favor two types of buildings for communal worship: private houses of suitable size and a room/hall rather like those used by the philosophical schools. But these buildings remained what they were—domestic houses or teaching halls—and were not regarded as sacred spaces. Although there is some evidence for purposely built church buildings in the 3rd century, it was finally Constantine in the early 4th century who not only funded the building of churches, but also encouraged others to fund such projects. The cathedral at Tyre was dedicated in 314; Eusebius of Caesarea preached the dedication sermon. The basilica style developed as the most popular model for places of worship, but there were also martyria (shrines enclosing some part of a martyr's body) and covered burial grounds, and certainly the two later acquired an immediate holiness because of what they housed. Davies (1952) has pointed out that in the 4th century, the terminology used of temples began to be applied to church buildings—terms such as *penetralia* and *adytum,* which refer to the holiest parts of the old pagan temples. With the vocabulary went the associated idea of especially holy places set apart for the Christian cult.

The gradual development of holy buildings was joined by the concept of holy places. Jerome could certainly argue that the church was the true temple of God; but he could also say of Bethlehem, "I know this spot is holier than the Tarpeian rock," referring to a famous monument of pagan Rome (*Epistle* 46.11). After the Romans' destruction of Jerusalem in the 1st century, Jerusalem seemed to have little importance for the church. This was to change again with Constantine, who undertook a program of historicization, building churches at certain locations believed to be the sites of events in the life of Jesus. Eusebius of Caesarea said that Palestine was chosen to benefit from this activity "since it was from that source that the river of life flowed forth to humankind" (*Praise of Constantine* 9). Jerusalem thus became a holy place with holy sites and attracted pilgrims who wished to be close to the sites. Palestine became for Christians the Holy Land. Other locations associated with saints and martyrs and miracles became holy places as well.

BIBL.: D. A. Carson (ed.), *From Sabbath to Lord's Day* (Grand Rapids, 1982). J. G. Davies, *Origin and Development of Early Christian Church Architecture* (London, 1952).

Thomas Talley, *The Origins of the Liturgical Year* (New York, 1986). John Wilkinson, *Egeria's Travels to the Holy Land* (Jerusalem, 1981).   B.D.S.

Dictionary of Religious Festivals

EGYPT

Amesysia. Held in late July or August (especially during the Roman period), celebrating the birth of the goddess Isis. Popular festivities included the lighting of lamps.

Amun Festival of the Valley (Thebes). Held in May, involving the procession of Amun's barque from its main Theban sanctuary across the Nile to the western tombs.

Besia (attested in Roman Dendara; period of celebration unknown). Celebrated the protective and fertility-god Bes. Festivities probably included processional Bes-masking and the preparation of breads and drinks in celebration of the god.

Choiak. See Sokaris

Harpocrateia. Held in January, celebrating the god Horus in his child manifestation as Harpocrates (or, in some places, Ihy), associated also with military prowess. Popular festivities included the preparation of sweet foods and possibly the exchange of gifts.

Heb-Sed. Festival rejuvenating the king's physical forces, celebrated after thirty years of reign and repeated every three years thereafter.

Isia. Held in mid-November (Egypt) or late October (Rome), involving the symbolic reenactment of the mourning and search by the goddess Isis for the dismembered body of Osiris, culminating with the discovery of the pieces. The drama, in which a gilded cow is processed before priests and water is poured over a container of earth, expresses the renewal of cultivation after the recession of the Nile surge. Popular festivities included the preparation of special cakes and breads and celebratory responses during the drama.

Khnum Festival of Esna. Paired with the festival of Raising the Heavens, held in winter (Phamenoth 1), celebrating the potter-god Khnum's acts of creating the cosmos on his wheel. Festivities included processions throughout the region, masking, protective chants, and invocations of Khnum's creative acts for human procreation.

Kronia. Variously attested in late September and mid-November, celebrating the birth of several regional Egyptian gods (especially Sobek of the Fayyum as Cronus). Festivities may have verged on the carnival-esque, since some Roman authors compared it to the Saturnalia. This festival originated in Greece.

Min. Held on I "Heat" day 1, celebrating the beginning of the harvest of grain.

Navigum Isidis. Held in early March, celebrating the reopening of river navigation but originating (probably in the Egyptian Delta) as a celebration of the role of Isis as pilot of the Osirian funerary barque. Apuleius's description of this festival in Cenchreae (Greece) includes an elaborate procession with masking, attended by great crowds, culminating in the launching from the shore of a ritual vessel representing the boat of Isis.

Nehebkau. Held on I "Emergence" day 1, another New Year's Day celebrating the rebirth of vegetation.

New Year. Celebrated in mid-July, the New Year festival included mutual gift-giving and special sacrifices in the temples.

Opet Festival of Amun of Karnak. In the second and third months of the inundation (ca. late June), the barque of Amun traveled south to the god's temple in Luxor. Festivities recorded on the walls of the Luxor temple include elaborate processions, sometimes by boat. Elements of this procession are still maintained in the festival of 12th-century CE Sheikh Abu el-Haggag of Luxor, whose commemorative boat is still carried through the streets of Luxor during his spring *moulid.*

Sarapia. Held variously around Egypt in mid-March and mid-November, celebrating this central Greco-Egyptian deity carrying royal, oracular, and military overtones. Popular festivities included wine libations, sacrifices of bulls and pigs, acts of purification, and processions with masking.

Shai Festival (attested in early-5th-century CE Panopolis; period of celebration unknown). Celebrated the Egyptian god of civic fortune and domestic protection associated with Agathos Daimon. Popular festivities included the lighting of lamps in the home.

Sokaris. Held during the second half of November to celebrate a form of Osiris associated with the promotion of fertility. Festivities included a ritualized "breaking of the earth," the formation and burial of a corn-mummy, and processions of the barque of Sokaris.

Typhonia (attested in Roman Dendara; period of celebration unknown). Honored Seth-Typhon as a protective deity.

Wagy. Celebrated on I "Inundation" day 18, a funerary feast associated with the "pilgrimage to Abydos."

MESOPOTAMIA

Abu. A festival and the name of the fifth month (about August). At the festival, families commemorated their dead ancestors venerated in shrines within their private houses. Rites took place also at the burial or memorial places of the ruler's ancestors within the palace.

Akitu (Babylon). The *Akitu* festival of Babylon, the most important festival of ancient Mesopotamia, celebrated the divine king Marduk in the first days of the first month Nisannu. *Akitu* festivals are also attested for other towns.

Akitu (Ur). Festivals of the local god of Ur, the moon-god Nanna (Suen), held twice a year at each equinox. The *Akitu* of harvest and the *Akitu* of handling of seed took place in spring (first month) and autumn (seventh month), respectively. Both festivals featured processions to the rural Akitu sanctuary.

Bridewealth. A festival in Girsu, named after the giving of the bridewealth to the goddess Bawu (or Baba) by her bridegroom Ningirsu, the state's main god. The term *bridewealth* referred to the entire ceremony of a divine marriage. In a subsequent procession by boat, Bawu reached the female chamber in her husband's temple.

Consumption of Barley or of Malt. Festivals of gods of Lagash and Girsu in 3rd-millennium Sumer, apparently named after the first ritual consumption of these cereals. The local calendar of Ur knows of festivals named similarly after the consumption of gazelles, pigs, or birds.

Dumuzi. Named for the Sumerian god linked with the birth and death of vegetation and the husband of Inanna as celebrated in numerous Sumerian songs, the Dumuzi festival in early spring was celebrated primarily by women.

Great Festival. The main festival of the Sumerian moon-god Nanna of Ur, celebrated at full moon in the tenth month (December/January), the longest moon-night of the year.

Gusisu. Festival of the divine warrior Ninurta held at Nippur in the second month (about May). It celebrated the god's victorious return from the fight against the mountains, a mythological account referring to the onrushing flood of the rivers in spring.

Harvest. While the harvest was rarely celebrated in the official cult, administrative documents attest rituals at the threshing places of the fields, celebrated by the persons who worked this specific field.

New Moon. The appearance of the lunar disc in the evening sky marked day 1 of a new month. Along with days 7 and 15, it was linked to the royal cult and celebrated monthly before the local gods; it also marked the date of an annual festival.

New Year. The New Year festival of Babylon was the *Akitu*. In Sumer, the main festival of a local god was called his or her "New Year."

Nismmu. Name of the first month, derived from the Sumerian word for "first fruits," in which "first fruit" deliveries were sent to the central sanctuary of Nippur.

Sacred Marriage. The sacred marriage of a divine couple was a common festival theme in Mesopotamia.

Some Sumerian texts of the early 2nd millennium have been interpreted as describing a "sacred marriage" between the king as Dumuzi and the goddess of love, Inanna. Scholarly opinions differ on the literal or metaphorical understanding of these texts and on the human participants of the rite (probably king and queen).

Sowing of Seeds. Like the cutting of the grain, one of the most important occasions for festivals. It celebrated the beginning of the work.

Tammuz. At the end of the month Tammuz (about July), the rarely attested wailing of Tammuz (Sumerian Dumuzi) by women took place.

Tummal. The Tummal sanctuary of Ninlil, wife of the god Enlil of Nippur, is situated near Nippur on a branch of the Euphrates. It gave its name to the main festival of the divine couple Enlil and Ninlil.

SYRIA-CANAAN

Zukru. At Emar, a seven-day rite celebrated for the god Dagan on the year's first new moon.

ISRAEL

Day of Atonement (Yom Kippur). Day of penitential observance in the fall, beginning after the Babylonian exile.

Hanukkah. Celebration of rededication of the temple by Judas Maccabee (164 BCE), in December.

New Moon. Ancient observance in Israel, before the exile.

Passover. Spring festival associated with the exodus from Egypt.

Purim. Celebration of the deliverance of the Jews described in the Book of Esther.

Rosh Hashanah. Fall New Year festival. Introduced after the Babylonian exile.

Sabbath. Weekly day of rest.

Shavuoth (Pentecost). Festival of first fruits.

Tabernacles. Fall festival of grape harvest. Sometimes called "the festival of YHWH."

Unleavened Bread. Spring festival eventually combined with Passover.

ANATOLIA

AN.TAḪ.ŠUM. Crocus Festival held in the spring and lasting around forty days. The king was a major participant and traveled to various towns in the kingdom.

(H)isuwas (meaning unknown). A late addition to the liturgy from Hurrian influence.

KI.LAM. Perhaps an autumn festival.

Nuntarryashas. Festival of Haste held in the autumn and lasting at least fifty days. The king was a major participant.

Purulli. A complex of New Year rites held in the spring at the town of Nerik.

IRAN

Ascension of Zarathustra (wihēz ī zardusht). Celebrated on day 11 (Khorshed) of the tenth month (Dae), also known as the "Death Anniversary of Zarathustra" *(Zarthōshtnō disō)* by the Parsis of India. On this day the soul of the prophet Zarathustra is honored with special prayers and ceremonies.

Feast of a Hundred Days (jashan-e sadah). Held on day 26 (Ashtad) of the ninth month (Adur), a hundred days before the New Year. It commemorates the discovery of fire by King Hoshang in prehistoric times. The light and warmth of the fire of Righteousness combat the evil forces of cold and darkness.

Feast of All Souls (frawardīgān). Held during the last ten days of the Zoroastrian calendar. Ceremonies are performed in honor of all righteous guardian spirits of departed souls. Devout Zoroastrians recite prayers and perform good deeds during this time.

Festival of Agriculturists (jashan-e burzīgarān). Falls on day 5 (Spandarmad) of the twelfth month (Spandarmad) of the Zoroastrian calendar. Prayers seek good harvests and honor Spandarmad, the divinity presiding over earth. Incantations with the power to destroy noxious creatures are pasted on front doors.

Festival of Fires (jashan-e āduragān). Celebrated on day 9 (Adur) of the ninth month (Adur). Zoroastrians keep the hearth fire continuously burning on this day and offer a litany to fire in all five watches of the day. Fragrant sandalwood is also offered to consecrated fires in fire temples.

Festival of Khordad-Sal (jashan-e khordād-sāl). Celebrated on day 6 (Khordad) of the first month (Frawardin), it commemorates the birthday of the prophet Zarathustra.

Festival of Mihr (jashan-e mihragān). Held on day 16 (Mihr) of the seventh month (Mihr) to commemorate with thanksgiving the death of the evil ruler Zohak by Faridun, who saved the lives of many innocent people in Iran.

Festival of Noonday (jashan-e rapithwin). Celebrated at noon on day 1 (Hormazd) of the first month (Frawardin). The spirit guardian Rapithwin is closely linked to the guardian of fire, Asha Vahishta, and remains on earth for the first seven months of summer and withdraws underground during the five months of winter.

Festival of Tir (jashan-e tīragān). Held on day 13 (Tir) of the fourth month (Tir). It is dedicated jointly to the star Tishtar, which dominates the eastern sky, and to Tishtar, the lord and overseer of all stars, associated with water and invoked in times of drought and famine.

Festival of Waters (jashan-e ābānagān). Celebrated on day 10 (Aban) of the eighth month (Aban) when Zoroastrians offer litanies and hymns to moving bodies of water. About two thousand Zoroastrians in Mumbai participate in this celebration every year, facing the Arabian Sea.

New (Year) Day (naw-rūz). Celebrated on day 1 (Hormazd) of the first month (Frawardin), also known as "the day of repentance" *(paētī)* by the Parsis of India. It is a day when Zoroastrians take stock of the past year and resolve to perform acts of merit during the new year.

New (Year) Day of (King) Jamshid (jamshīdi naw-rūz). Celebrated by followers of the seasonal Gregorian calendar (Faslis) on March 21. The day has no recognized place as a religious festival in the ancient Zoroastrian calendar.

GREECE

Adonia. The festival of Adonis, the consort of Aphrodite; it commemorated the death of Adonis. It was a women's summer festival, attested in many Greek cities from the early 6th century onward. The women mourned for an image of the dead god and they sowed seeds that would grow very fast and wither just as fast (gardens of Adonis). Frazer and his followers understood it as a vegetation or agricultural rite; recent interpretations stress the role of the women and its opposition to the Thesmophoria.

Agriania (often *Agrionia*). A festival of Dionysus, common to Boeotia and its colonies on the northwestern shore of Asia Minor, that in many cities gave rise to a month name. Its rituals oppose the genders to each other, often in a rather violent way; the name is connected with *agrios* (wild).

Anthesteria. A festival of Dionysus in early spring (Flower Festival), common to Athens and the cities of Ionia. Among its themes are the tasting of the new wine and the appeasing of the souls of the dead. In Athens, it lasted three days. The first was Pithoigia (opening of the wine containers); the second Choes (jugs), from the isolated and silent ritual drinking from an individual jug; the third Chytroi (pots), from the ritual food that was handed out to the ghosts in a pot, before they were chased away again.

Apatouria. A festival, common to Athens and the Ionian cities in western Asia Minor said to be colonies of Athens. The festival does not concern the city as a unit but its singular genealogical subdivisions (in Athens the phratries); the name means "festival of the common fathers."

Artemisia. The main festival of Artemis in many Greek cities; it often gave the name to a month. It was the main city festival of Ephesus with its old and famous sanctuary of Artemis, and featured, among other rites, a splendid procession.

Dionysia. The main festival of Dionysus in many Greek cities. Athens had two Dionysia, the Lesser Dionysia (or Dionysia in the Fields) and the Greater Dionysia. The Lesser Dionysia were a rustic festival in December, performed in the villages; the Greater Dionysia (in March) were the main festival of Dionysus in Athens; they were introduced under the tyrant Pisistratus (ca. 550 BCE) and featured a lavish procession that marked the entry of Dionysus into the city and, at least from the 5th century onward, dramatic contests in the theater that were imitated in most city Dionysia throughout the Greek world.

Elaphebolia. An old festival of Artemis that named a month in many Greek cities. It is unclear whether it still existed in Athens; in some mainland cities, however, its main ritual was the sacrificial burning of live animals and votive gifts. The name perhaps means "stag killing" (*elaphos* [stag] and *ballein* [to hit]). In Calydon and Patrae, a very similar festival was named Laphria, in the cult of Artemis Laphria that was widespread in the Greek northeast.

Hyakinthia. One of the two major festivals of Sparta, held in the sanctuary of Apollo and Hyacinthus in Amyclae; its celebration prohibited the Spartans from warfare. It lasted several days and featured sacrifices for the hero Hyacinthus and a procession for Apollo.

Karneia. One of the two major festivals of Sparta and a major festival of many Dorian cities; it was celebrated in honor of Apollo Karneios and gave rise to a month name. In Sparta, it lasted nine days and prohibited the Spartans from warfare during its celebration; the main organizers were the young men.

Kronia. The festival of Cronus in some Greek cities, including Athens. Like the Roman Saturnalia, which ancient commentators derived from the Athenian Kronia, it was a carnivalesque festival at the end of the year; one of its salient characteristics was the temporary freedom of the slaves.

Laphria. See Elaphebolia

Mysteria. The Athenian festival of Demeter and Kore, celebrated with a secret initiatory cult in the sanctuary of Eleusis. Its name, understood as connected with *myein* (to close [the eyes or the mouth]), was extended to comparable rites in the cult of Dionysus and on Samothrace and become a noun, denoting all related cults.

Olympia. The most prominent of the four major Panhellenic contests, held every fifth year (counting inclusively) in the sanctuary of Zeus Olympios in Pisa (southeastern Peloponnese). The festival, said to have been founded by Heracles, featured sacrifices to the hero Pelops and to Zeus Olympios, with a torch race whose winner lit the fire on Zeus's altar. The first Olympia were celebrated in 776 BCE.

Panathenaea. The main city festival of Athens, celebrated toward the end of the first month. It featured a lavish procession from one of the city gates through the marketplace up to the Acropolis. It culminated in a large sacrifice of white cows to Athena on her main altar and in the dedication of the new garment *(peplos)* for her image.

Pythia. The festival of Delphic Apollo (Apollo Pythios). The festival in Delphi developed during the archaic age into one of the four major Panhellenic athletic contests. Many other Greek cities held similar festivals and contests, after having introduced the cult of Apollo Pythios from Delphi.

Thesmophoria. The main festival of Demeter in most Greek cities, performed exclusively by the married women who, for the time of the festival, retired into the Thesmophorion, Demeter's sanctuary. In Athens, it lasted three days, during which ordinary city life was suspended; similar traits are attested in other Greek cities. The name, originally alluding to a secret rite ("to carry something deposited"), came to mean "to give laws," when Demeter was understood as having civilized humanity through the introduction of agriculture.

ROME

Augustalia (October 12). In 19 BCE, when Augustus returned from the Greek provinces to find Rome in a state of unrest, a *senatus consultum* established an altar to Fortuna redux and inaugurated a festival, the Augustalia, to commemorate the day of the emperor's return. It is remarkable that the senate named the day after Augustus, as if he were a deity. Augustus did not authorize the use of his name before his death. The Augustan Games, which were first celebrated in 11 BCE, became a fixed element of the calendar (October 5–12) after Augustus's death.

Feralia (February 21). Last day of the annual festival of the dead (*dies parentales* [Parentalia]). On that day families sacrificed to the *manes* (spirits) of the deceased and feasted at their tombs. This sacrifice marked the end of the mourning period that began on February 13.

Ludi Romani, Ludi Magni (Roman Games or Great Games; September 4–19). The Roman Games were celebrated by the *aediles curules* (magistrates elected by the patricians) in honor of Jupiter and the Capitoline triad. On September 13, the anniversary of the Capitoline temple, a great sacrificial banquet *(epulum Iovis)* brought the senators together on the Capitol, in the presence of the three deities. Chariot races in the Circus Maximus concluded the festivities. The number of race days was gradually increased to four (September 15–19); later, nine days of theatrical games (September 4–12) opened the festival. Celebrated by the plebeian *aediles*, the Plebeian Games (November 4–17) were identical to the Roman Games, but they ended a little earlier. The races for these games took place in the Circus Flaminius. The Plebeian Games were implemented later than the Roman Games.

Ludi saeculares. In 17 BCE, Augustus celebrated the Secular Games on the recommendation of a Sibylline oracle. According to a tradition that may have been reconstituted by Augustan scholars, these games dated from the beginning of the republic and were celebrated for the fifth time in 17 BCE. Consecrating the advent of a new generation (*saeculum*, roughly 110 years) and asking the support of the gods for the enterprises of the Roman people, the games consisted in a double series of sacrifices offered June 1–3. Nocturnal sacrifices were held at the northern extremity of the Campus Martius, in the sanctuary of Dis pater and Proserpina (Terentum); they were offered to the Moerae (the fates) on June 1, to the Eileithyae (goddesses of childbirth) on June 2, and to Terra Mater (Mother Earth) on June 3. The sacrifices were followed by plays. On each morning of June 1–3, on the Capitol, 110 matrons celebrated the Sellisternia in honor of Juno and Diana, while sacrifices were being offered on the Capitol to Jupiter and Juno on June 2, then on the Palatine to Apollo and Diana on June 3. The daytime sacrifices were also followed by plays. On June 2, after the sacrifice to Juno, the 110 matrons made supplications to Juno. On June 3, after the end of the plays, a hymn was sung on the Palatine and on the Capitol. Chariot races concluded the festival. The Secular Games were celebrated by the *quindecimviri* (one of the four principal groups of priests), and took place in 17 BCE, 88 CE, and 204 CE.

Lupercalia (February 15). During this festival, when the "chaos" representing the end of the year was staged, Rome was delivered up to the Luperci, a priestly brotherhood believed to go back to Romulus. After the sacrifice of a goat, the Luperci ran around the Palatine brandishing strips of ram's skin and striking those whom they encountered, women especially, with strips cut from the sacrificial animal.

Matralia (June 11). During the festival of Matuta Mater, goddess of the dawn, married women introduced a slave woman into the temple of the goddess—an exception to the usual practice—and then expelled her from the temple violently; afterward, they carried their sisters' children in their arms and treated them with respect. There is much debate over the meaning of this festival. According to Georges Dumézil, it may have involved the celebration of the return of daylight during the period in which days grew shorter after the summer solstice.

Megalesia (April 4–10). On April 4, 204 BCE, the black stone symbolizing the Magna Mater (Great Mother) was laid in the Palatine in the temple of Victory before her temple was finished. From that point on, the festival, called Megalesia, was celebrated by a sacri-

fice made by the city praetor to the Magna Mater and in the homes of aristocratic families by banquets (*mutitationes*). Starting with the dedication of the temple on April 10, 191 BCE, plays were organized at least between April 4 and 10. This festive kernel was gradually expanded by introductory festivities, celebrated solely by the *cultores* of the goddess: the Canna intrat (March 15), the Arbor intrat (March 22), the Sanguen (March 24), the Hilaria (March 25), Requ(i)etiio (March 26), and especially the Lavatio (March 27). On the day of the Lavatio, the stone symbolizing the goddess was transported by a brilliant procession to the Almo, to be bathed. With the exception of the Lavatio, none of the festivals is attested before Marcus Aurelius.

Parilia (April 21). The festival of the goddess Pales celebrating the purification of the sheep. Shepherds and their herds passed through fires fed by various purifying substances, in particular the ashes of calf embryos that had been burned during the Fordicidia (April 15), when a pregnant cow was sacrificed to Tellus. Either because the Parilia was connected with shepherds or because the goddess Pales was seen as tied to the Palatine, this festival gradually came to be taken as the anniversary of Rome.

Sacrum anniversarium Cereris. Introduced before the Battle of Cannae (216 BCE), the matronal festival of Ceres (probably around August 10) referred to the myth of the abduction of Proserpina and her marriage to Pluto. Matrons, dressed in white, abstained from all sexual activity and from eating bread. During the main ceremony, celebrated under the direction of the public priestess of Ceres, they acted out the myth of Proserpina in mime. During the ceremony, no wine was supposed to be offered. According to Cicero, the ceremony was a Roman version of the mysteries of Demeter.

Saturnalia (December 17). This very popular festival went on for seven days at the end of the republic; it was reduced to five days under the empire. Celebrating Saturn, the god of dissolution, the festival initially included a sacrifice before the temple of Saturn near the Roman Forum. In 217 BCE, the festival was transformed; according to Cato, it followed the Greek rite, at least in part. To the traditional sacrifice was added a *lectisternium* celebrated by the senators and a public banquet. The Roman people as a whole were also supposed to honor the god by daytime and nighttime revelries, staging the overturning of the established order, in particular by changes in precedence at banquets: slaves ate before masters. This very popular festival of dissolution, probably connected to the winter solstice, took on new meaning when January 1 became the public New Year.

Vinalia. Two festivals celebrated the virtues of wine. In autumn (August 19), the rural Vinalia signaled the opening of the harvest by the offering of the first bunch of grapes to Jupiter. The principal festival, the Vinalia priora (April 23), offered Jupiter the first fruits of the new wine.

Vota pro salute reipublicae/imperatoris. On New Year's Day (March 15, under the republic, and January 1 starting in 153 BCE; under the empire, January 1 and especially January 3), ritual vows for the health of the state and later also for that of the emperor were taken in the capitol by the new consuls. The celebrants offered a steer or a cow to the Capitoline triad and to "the health of the Roman people." respectively, in fulfillment of vows made the previous year by their predecessors. They then pronounced new vows. Under the empire, the sacerdotal colleges and, over time, many other public and private groups formulated and fulfilled the same vows for the emperor's health (January 3).

CHRISTIANITY

Ascension. A feast of Christ's return to heaven (Luke 24.51; Acts 1.9) is first attested in the late 4th century in Gregory of Nyssa (388) and John Chrysostom.

Christmas. The festival celebrating the birth of Christ on December 25 is attested in the 4th-century Roman list of bishops, the Philocalian Calendar, which represents Roman practice of the year 336. The festival may have competed with the Roman festival of Natalis Solis Invicti (Birth of the Invincible Sun).

Easter. The celebration of the death and resurrection of Jesus, the Christian Passover (Greek Pascha) was widespread by the 2nd century, when two divergent traditions are apparent. Rome, Alexandria, and other Christian churches celebrated the feast on the Sunday after the first full moon of spring. Other churches, particularly in Asia Minor, celebrated at the time of the Jewish Passover, which took place on Nisan 14, the date of the death of Jesus according to the Gospel of John (the Synoptic Gospels place the date on Nisan 15, after Jesus had eaten the Passover meal). Those who followed the practice of celebrating the central Christian event at the time of Passover were dubbed Quartodecimans (Fourteeners). The difference in observance was tolerated in the mid-2nd century (Eusebius, *Church History* 4.14.1, citing the 2nd-century Irenaeus), but in the late 2nd century the Roman bishop Victor threatened to excommunicate those who followed the Eastern practice (Eusebius, *Church History* 5.23.3). The Council of Nicea (325 CE) stipulated that the feast would be observed on the Sunday following the first full moon after the spring equinox. By the 4th century, the feast was prefaced by a three-day solemnity commemorating the last days of Jesus.

Epiphany. A festival around January 6 celebrating the baptism of Jesus is attested in the late 2nd century in the writings of Clement of Alexandria (*Stromata* 1.21), who notes that it was observed by the Basildeans. By the 4th century, it was widely celebrated in the Greek East. Syrian and Armenian Christians celebrated the day as the commemoration of the nativity of Jesus. Western Christians by the 4th century celebrated it as the manifestation ("epiphany") of Jesus to the Gentile magi (Matt. 2.1–12).

Lent. A period of fasting before Easter, first mentioned by Athanasius of Alexandria in 334.

Pasch or Pascha. See Easter.

Pentecost. The name derives from the Greek name of the Greek feast of Weeks (Exod. 23.14–17). In the 2nd century (Tertullian, *On Baptism* 19.2), Christians celebrated the fifty days after Easter as a period of joy, when fasting was excluded. In the 4th century, the fiftieth day itself became a festival, commemorating the descent of the Holy Spirit on the apostles (Acts 2.1–11).

Sunday. From earliest times (1 Cor. 16.2; Acts 20.7; Rev. 1.10), Christians gathered for prayer and thanksgiving, commemorating the resurrection of Christ, which took place on the first day of the week.

Religious Personnel

Introduction

This chapter reveals a vivid picture of the wide range of roles played by individuals in the service of numerous gods and goddesses in the historic societies of the ancient world. The key questions to be asked are everywhere much the same: how were these people recruited and trained? by what means and how sharply were they differentiated from the rest of society? what functions did they perform for their contemporaries? how were they rewarded for their efforts? how did the roles they played change over the long periods of time covered by this volume? The answers are never simple: the societies are themselves quite varied in organization, and the sources of information available are sometimes limited; in some cases, we have little more than lists of officials with few letters or records to define what these officials actually did. Some of the roles were not full-time or even part-time occupations, but rather parts to be played on special occasions or at particular festivals; other roles were clearly major full-time tasks of high prestige.

At a casual glance, one conception links almost all of the sections in this chapter: all of them use the words *priest*, *priesthood*, or *priestly* to describe some, although not all, of the roles they are discussing. Scholars cannot always be sure which officials were priests, which were administrators, which were mere artisans working in a religious environment. Sometimes the word *priest* is linked to an ancient title as with, for example, the *šangû* priest of the Babylonians. In all cases, however, the word *priest* is only a representation in English of a host of different words in the many languages of the different societies covered—Akkadian, Hittite, Aramaic, Egyptian, Greek, Latin, and so on. Some of these words denote priests generically, but many are the titles of particular offices. The modern decision to use *priest* implies at least some overlap between a defined role in that society and today's conceptions; but the overlap will evidently be different in different societies; and, in any case, what

is our modern conception of the priest? If it is essentially Christian, Jewish, or Muslim, then we risk deep confusion, because modern religions allocate advisory, spiritual, or comfort-bringing duties to priests that rarely arise in antiquity as part of the priestly role. Interestingly, only one ancient group of religious personnel is said to have avoided the priestly vocabulary in describing themselves: the Christians, who paradoxically enough had leaders who came closest to resembling our modern conception of the role. They avoided Greek and Latin words for priest because they were too strongly associated with pagan and Jewish priests and practices and perhaps above all with the ritual of sacrifice. Christian religious authority was to be quite different, and the words they used were intended to reflect their new ideas.

In assessing what the different groups of religious personnel signified in their own times, it is essential to relate them to the order of society in which they lived. In some cases (e.g., Egypt or the Hittites), the king and queen were themselves priests and therefore at the heart of the ritual order; in some cases (Egypt again, but also in most other early empires) many religious officials (priests or not) lived and worked in temples, which were themselves major enterprises, owning and administering great estates and employing large numbers of workers; in the later city-state societies (e.g., in Greece) priests and priestesses were often elected or chosen by lot to carry out ritual duties for a limited period and were otherwise free from special religious obligations. In republican Rome, the priests formed colleges and held office for life, but they were in no way religious specialists or professionals and in fact were the same leading citizens who also held political and military office.

It is difficult to find a common formula to cover the whole range of these situations. It seems safe, but not helpful, to say that all the people in question were concerned in one way or another with the maintenance of rituals that brought about communication between humans and the supernatural beings they believed in. Some were close to the centers of power in their own states or cities; some lived in remote areas and carried out only the humblest duties. In most of the societies in question, the priestly or other religious personnel do not seem to have constituted a separate class or interest group; they consisted of different types of people, with different degrees of involvement in religious life and often only a temporary commitment to ritual activities; often too their religious activities were embedded in court life or in the life of a great temple. It is hard to find evidence of priests acting as a self-conscious interest group, pursuing characteristically religious objectives, earlier than the priests of the Jewish people or the early Christian bishops.

So far, this introduction has concerned only the official religious institutions of the kingdoms and cities, not the many unofficial diviners, astrologers, healers, and magicians whom we know to have operated more or less everywhere in the same periods. Similarly, such people feature less prominently in this chapter than do their official contemporaries—and for good reasons: the sources that survive, particularly in the case of the earliest societies, are preserved from palaces and official or temple archives and tell us about the concerns either of states or of rich and powerful individuals. When we hear of other religious experts (or self-proclaimed experts), it is often because they attracted disapproval or condemnation from their betters; they were rivals in access to religious power and either to be feared as dangerous or despised as charlatans. It should not be forgotten that they, too, were important elements in the religious life of the period.
J.N.

Egypt

Egyptian religion is characterized by a large number of highly specialized priests. At least for the larger temples, no single priest was generally responsible for all religious duties. Instead, a multitude of different titles indicate many priests with specific tasks. (The smaller the temple was, however, the likelier that the specialists' tasks were subsumed by a few officials.) In particular instances, for example, in the cult of the deified Amunhotep, son of Hapu, administrative documents from the Ptolemaic period indicate that the same individual held the titles of prophet, priest, doorkeeper, and every other occupation, making this temple a one-person affair.

The best example of the ideal arrangement of temple staff can be gleaned from the Book of the Temple, a huge composition indicating the architectural layout of a temple and the titles and the individual duties of all temple employees. This text is attested, although unfortunately unsatisfactorily preserved, in a Middle Egyptian hieratic version, a Demotic translation, and fragments of a Greek translation. From its attestations, one can suppose that it was a standard text present in several copies at each temple library.

The highest rank in a temple was held by the governor and overseer of prophets, at least at the main temple of each nome (province). This man not only ran the temple, but was the most important authority in local civil administration. His duties in the temple were mostly of an administrative character, but he was also involved in ceremonies when the god, as represented by his or her statue, came forth from the shrine. On solemn occasions, he had to wear a panther skin (like many other priests), but the Book of the Temple makes it clear that this was not a natural skin; a linen garment, painted and set with precious stones, was used instead. The most important person in a temple, be it the governor or the prophet, was usually given an individual title characteristic of the nome and typically reflecting some mythical episode of the local god. The bulk of attestations for these titles comes from the late period.

The inner-temple administration started with the so-called prophet, a term used by the Greeks to describe a certain type of Egyptian priest. Contrary to what the title implies to modern ears, he was not understood to be divinely endowed with the ability to utter prophetic statements. Rather, his duty was to ensure the correct conduct of the daily rituals in the temple, although we might suppose that the actual officiating quite often was delegated to individuals of the minor ranks, acting as "great priests in their days [of duty]." Ideally, the king of Egypt was the one expected to make offerings to the gods. In practice, he had to delegate most of the actual officiating, and the priest who served during the offering and clothing rituals legitimated himself by declaring to the god that he was sent by the king.

Several priestly ranks had specific liturgical tasks in particular rituals. The most important were the so-called overseers of secrets and purifiers of the god. Their duties centered on the rituals in honor of the dead god Osiris. They involved the creation of small figurines out of sand and barley grains, as well as others out of earth, date pulp, pulverized minerals, and herbs. After these figurines had been used in ceremonies performed during the month of Khoyak (about December), they were either buried within the "sacred mound" or ritually thrown into the "sacred lake" or the Nile. The region of the temple ground dedicated to Osiris was carefully separated from the profane world, and access was restricted to a small group of priests. It seems that some of them held the specific title "someone authorized to enter." All others entering this prohibited area were liable to severe punishment, normally execution with subsequent incineration of the corpse. Only the overseer of secrets was present when offerings were made at the place where the figurines had been buried. He had to expel members of his retinue and keep his own face averted as he performed the ritual.

The somewhat enigmatic figure of the "god's father" seems to have been a priest mainly concerned with the cult of Osiris; we must be careful not to confuse him with the father (or father-in-law) of the reigning pharaoh, who was designated by the same term, since the pharaoh was regarded as a god.

The "lector-priest" was responsible for reciting during many rituals. Apparently, he was called on especially for ceremonies involving Osiris rather than normal offerings. This responsibility led to his further involvement in burial rites and private funerary cults. The lector-priest was one of the most important religious functionaries, present even in many smaller temples.

The "scribe of the divine book" was distinguished by a particular costume. He wore two ostrich feathers on his head, and for this reason the Greeks called him "feather bearer." He participated in execration rituals directed against the enemies of the state. Occasionally, he appeared as leader of the ceremonies in liturgies for Osiris. He also inspected the staff of the temple for skin diseases, especially leprosy. Infected people were removed from the community.

The so-called priest of Sakhmet was not priest of a specific deity but rather a kind of veterinarian. He had to confirm the good health and ritual purity of all animals that were to be slaughtered; it was forbidden to offer an animal without his approval. This included watching for external marks indicating that a particular animal was sacred and therefore not to be killed. Being connected with Sakhmet, a goddess responsible for pestilence, he also had to check the environment for indications of potential outbreaks of epidemics. Several times a year, he had to conduct rituals to appease the dangerous goddess.

Egyptian religion accepted magic as an essential part of official cult. One of the priests most responsible for its practice was called the "conjuror of scorpions"; his role was to drive off all kinds of dangerous animals, not only scorpions but also snakes, crocodiles, and lions. He also had medical skills, especially those that cured skin diseases. Surprisingly, he was also responsible for the ceremony of "throwing the Nile book" (probably a list of offerings thrown into the river), and he announced the flow of the Nile's inundation at the celebration marking the beginning of the inundation.

Another special priest was responsible for the cult paid to statues of the king placed in temples. Little is known about him, and he seems to have been active at only certain places.

The chief instructor of the temple taught the children of the priests basic knowledge of the relevant cult and proper behavior in the temple. One of the most important skills he passed along was the proper recitation of ritual formulas; additional instruction was given to children of prophets, including the study of myth, court etiquette, medicine, and astrology.

Some senior artisans concerned with the manufacture of divine statues also held priestly rank. They participated in the important ritual of "opening the mouth," which animated and activated statues and by extension also animated other fabricated objects.

Many officials described in the Book of the Temple were less concerned with cult per se than with the practical organization and maintenance of the temple as a large social and economic unity. There were many administrative scribes, supervisors of cattle and fields and so on, to say nothing of staff for policing the area and prospectors in search of precious minerals, who also formed part of the temple.

In the late period, the so-called Lesonis priest, who was responsible for the economic health of the temple, became very important. Some Greek texts translate his title as "archpriest," and in administrative documents of Egyptian temples attested at Soknopaiou Nesos, Elephantine, and elsewhere, he is always mentioned explicitly in addition to the prophet and the senior priests. This office seems to have been a temporary appointment, which had to be confirmed anew each year. Below the priests were a multitude of lower ranks and occupations. The most important and frequently attested is that of the doorkeeper (Greek *pastophoros*), whose job was to restrict access to parts of the temple.

In addition to the male personnel, there were female clergy. Some of these women were connected to cults of regions whose principal deity was female. Even in male-dominated cults, there was always one specific office for a woman, whose title varied from nome to nome; the best known of these was the "god's wife of Amun." For some time, this figure (normally the daughter of the king) had significant control over the enormous wealth of the temple of Karnak. Later, her actual power seems to have been transferred to the majordomo of the god's wife. Many wives of high-ranking officials were part of the sacred choir of the god.

Most priesthoods were hereditary, although it was possible to buy and sell priesthoods, and merit played a role in selection of a new priest as well. The chief teacher of a temple was instructed to check the writing of the sons of the priests in order to determine which were capable of assuming their fathers' duties, and during the Roman period, by imperial decree, proof of being able to read hieratic texts (probably those of traditional rituals) correctly could serve in place of a hereditary right. Even earlier, it seems to have been at least possible for newcomers to gain admission to the priestly hierarchy. In general, sons were supposed to learn from their fathers (as well as from temple schools) all the knowledge they would need to fulfill the duties as priests.

Becoming a priest included some sort of religious initiation ceremony. Our best sources for this are texts concerned with the higher staff of the Karnak temple during the Third Intermediate Period. The texts describe experiences in which initiates had direct visions of gods. It seems that, during the Greco-Roman period, at least parts of these rituals were borrowed from rituals of initiation into the mysteries of Isis.

At two points at least in his career, a priest had to swear an oath. These included declarations that he had never committed any crimes that would have made him unfit for his office, such as murder, and promises that he would not indulge in behavior that, while acceptable for ordinary people, were unacceptable for priests, such as eating prohibited food, measuring fields, or lifting a balance.

At least for the late and Greco-Roman periods, there is evidence that when a priest was installed in office he had to pay a tax to the state—unless special permission had been given for a tax-free appointment. Such grants of tax exemption are a recurrent motif in some Demotic narratives.

The material well-being of the priests was assured by regular provisions. It was usual for offerings to be distributed among all the priests, according to a fixed ratio, after the god had "satisfied himself" with them. It also was customary to endow at least the highest ranks of priests with fields. Regulations concerning the maintenance of a priest's wife and children in case of his death are, unfortunately, poorly preserved.

Because priests, at least at the higher ranks, had significant material advantages, people were eager to document their claims to priesthoods and to assure them for their progeny, by declaring them in graffiti or by setting up statues that were inscribed with all their titles. During the late period in particular, some people proudly gave genealogies running back many generations and documenting their priestly forefathers. In some cases we hear about rivalry and contention for priesthoods. The best-attested case concerns the temple of El-Hiba in Middle Egypt. There, a close relative of one of the most important civil administrators during the early Saite period managed to attain the position of prophet and received for himself alone one-fifth of all the temple's income, whereas the twenty ordinary priests of each phyle (in all, eighty priests) had to share the rest. This created great dissatisfaction, which erupted after many years in bloody violence, arson, and the bribing of high administrators in order to get rid of the offending prophet's heirs. Still, one-fifth is attested in other sources as normal revenue for a prophet.

For all temple personnel, certain rules of moral behavior and bodily perfection were established, as transmitted in the Book of the Temple:

List of people not to be initiated with the god: as for all men who are larger than all [other] men in their size, with huge limbs, . . ., small people, those with defective limbs, all . . . which men do not love to see, with totally white skin [albinos?], with totally red skin, with . . ., with distorted teeth, with . . . extremities, with pustules(?) on the body, with . . . limbs, with a jerking(?) body who are . . . like those suffering from . . ., with dripping(?) eyes, those who drink wine or beer till the heart is raging, those who tell lies as gossip, those who divulge what they have seen or heard, those who are cruel faced about possessions, . . ., those who want larger possessions than necessary for their needs, those who are loudmouthed

more than befits their position, those who are refractory against those of higher rank, those who take objects by theft, those who fornicate, and every man who is in the way of Seth, Apopis, and that god against whom the arm is stretched out in Memphis; as for every man [who is like that(?)], he is an abomination of the temple, he shall not be initiated with the god.

The priest was also expected to adhere to important standards of purity. Regular ablutions were mandatory, normally thrice a day. Their heads had to be shaven. As for clothing, only linen was permitted, while wool and leather were prohibited. Plutarch explains this by the concept that wool was imagined to be an excess outgrowth of the body (*On Isis and Osiris* 342C). Nor were all textiles, even if linen, allowed to a priest: only an apron and a girdle were permitted. They could wear white sandals, but had to remove them before entering the front hall of the temple. Before performing ritual acts or coming into contact with a statue of a god, a priest had to go through a ten-day period of special purification, abstaining from sexual contact and drinking a solution of sodium carbonate in order to purify his mouth. Similar requirements were imposed on outsiders who wanted to enter the temple to worship or work there as artisans. There were also dietary restrictions. Priests were prohibited from eating fish and some sorts of meats. Further dietary restrictions existed as well, although our sources of information about them are poorly preserved.

A priest had to be circumcised; traces of this can still be seen on mummies. When the emperor Hadrian prohibited circumcision in the Roman Empire, Egyptian priests were among the few groups who could, by application and proof of priestly descent, obtain permission to continue the practice.

Because there was no independent scholarly community in Egypt, temples became the centers of knowledge, and learning was transmitted by the priests. Actual finds from temple archives, unfortunately preserved only for the latest periods, show how much information was stored there. Besides strictly religious texts such as hymns, rituals, and mythological narratives, there are medical and magical manuscripts and mathematical, astronomical, and astrological treatises. Clement of Alexandria (*Stromata* 6.4: 35.1–37) describes how different types of books were associated with different priests in the Egyptian temple. Chaeremon's picture of the priest's life as frugal and philosophical (as transmitted by Porphyry, *De abstinentia* 4.6–8), although idealized, conforms quite well to at least the theoretical standard in late Egyptian temples.

Although a priesthood might seem like an enviable position, some ancient voices speak against this idea. The loudest come from members of the civil administration, which needed new recruits and wanted to draw gifted young men away from other possible careers;

therefore, they exaggerate and caricature the negative aspects of all other professions, including the priesthood, about which we hear: "The prophet stands there like a field cultivator, the priest does his duties only after having spent the time (and there are three daily services)—to submerge himself in the river. He does not distinguish winter from summer, even when the sky is stormy and rainy" (Papyrus Sallier 1.7.6–7).

The multitude of priests who operated within the framework of official temple procedure meant that a relatively large part of the population participated in official religion. This left rather little opportunity for unorganized private religion. But there are examples of so-called private chapels at cities such as Amarna and Deir el-Medineh, which allowed their owners the possibility of venerating their gods without having recourse to the official priesthood.

BIBL.: Hermann Kees, *Das Priestertum im ägyptischen Staat vom neuen Reich bis zur Spätzeit* (Leiden, 1953). Walter Otto, *Priester und Tempel im hellenistischen Ägypten* (Leipzig, 1905–8). Joachim Friedrich Quack, "Das Buch vom Tempel und verwandte Texte: Ein Vorbericht," *Archiv für Religionsgeschichte* 2 (2000): 1–20. Serge Sauneron, *Les prêtres de l'ancienne Égypte* (Paris, 1988).   J.F.Q.

Mesopotamia

Religious personnel occupied a central place in Mesopotamian religious life, for only they had the ability to communicate with the unseen forces that directed mortal lives, acting on behalf of the community as well as of individuals. Ritual specialists were of many types, with different religious functions, some of which changed over time, although their titles remained the same. They were differentiated from one another by certain processes of selection and by their social roles. Nevertheless, it is difficult to divide these religious personnel into distinct groups because their functions overlapped: administrative personnel could also perform ritual functions, and cultic celebrants could lead rites inside and outside various sacred spheres. Spiritual healers, diviners, and experts in magic, moreover, were not tied to any specific locality: some addressed the gods in temples, while others served the king and the people. The most noticeable division was between cultic functionaries who officiated in the worship of one specific deity and noncultic ritual specialists who operated in any setting and were not limited to the rites of a particular deity. Nevertheless, one person could hold the prebends of functionaries of different deities and thus could retain multiple offices.

Sources. Three millennia of written records from Mesopotamia yield evidence of a large number of temple offices and personnel. However, in attempting to reconstruct their functions and duties, modern scholars have few sources at their disposal. Most of our information comes from lexical lists or ancient dictionaries.

These yield hundreds of titles of religious personnel. Administrative texts document the sacrifices and offerings brought to the temple and the temple officials in charge of these items.

Priests' archives and letters help to sketch a picture of the life and functions of religious specialists. Several such documents survive from the Old Babylonian period. One fragmentary archive of 111 texts from the site of Tutub (modern Khafaje in the Diyala region) was found in the temple of the moon-god Sin, in the apartments of the *enum* priest (chief or high priest). Their contents reflect the dominant role of the temple and its functionaries in the town's economy. Another archive of 300 tablets from Ischali (Diyala region) belonged to the *šangû* priests (chief administrators of a temple) of the temple of the goddess Kittum. They concern a father and two sons who were occupied with institutional duties and include the usual receipts for items such as tools and building materials, records of loans, inventories of gifts made to the goddess, and other administrative memoranda, several legal records, and letters. Two letters from this archive, addressed directly to King Ibalpi-El, contain messages purporting to come from the goddess herself, providing evidence of prophetic practices in Old Babylonian Mesopotamia. The largest group—2,000 texts—comes from the archive of Ur-Utu, the *galamaḫ* (chief lamentation priest) of the goddess Annunitum of Sippar-Amnanum. In addition to legal and economic texts, there are also tablets recording ritual and cultic activities performed by laymen and laywomen under the supervision of a priest—activities of which we had no knowledge before this archive was excavated. The informative letters, long known to scholars, from royal priests to the Neo-Assyrian kings, record the king's questions to and answers from the astrologers, exorcists, and haruspices (diviners). Cultic and religious ceremonies, magical activities, and healing practices are also mentioned.

Literary texts shed light on religious personnel from another angle. One Sumerian poem describes the fashioning of the GALA (lamentation priest = Akkadian *kalû*): Enki, god of wisdom, creates the GALA and provides him with prayers, laments, and musical instruments to soothe the raging heart of the goddess Inanna, who was troubling heaven and earth. Another Sumerian tale, Enlil and Namzitarra, recounts how the high god Enlil, disguised as a crow, meets Namzitarra, a servant of the GUDU$_4$ priests (purification priests), going home after having completed his daily work. Namzitarra recognizes and acknowledges the power of Enlil, who rewards him by giving him a hereditary prebend in his temple. This folktale provides an explanation of how Namzitarra's humble family gained possession of a prebend, the source of the family's wealth.

The conception of priesthood as a gift of the gods to humankind is the subject of an Akkadian literary tradition recounting how the gods Shamash and Adad re-

A three-dimensional bronze sculpture depicting two nude priests performing a ceremony, interpreted as the ritual of the dawn. Altars for sacrifice, libation bowls, and sacred trees are represented. Made for an Elamite king, 12th century BCE; from Susa. Louvre. *Réunion des Musées Nationaux/Art Resource, New York*

vealed *bārû* divination lore to Enmeduranki, the antediluvian king of Sippar, and how he in turn passed it on to the citizens of Nippur, Sippar, and Babylon. Next follows a section laying down the qualifications required in such a priest, and a final section explains the mythological significance of various items used in the rites. This text reflects the conception of the *niṣirti bārûti* (secret of divination), an esoteric tradition passed down from father to son. Not only did diviners acknowledge that their traditions came from the gods, but purification priests and exorcists also recognized that the source of their knowledge was Enki of Eridu.

Temple clergy. Those who served in the temples, from lowly courtyard sweepers to high priests, belonged to various grades of the temple clergy. This broad definition of religious personnel is given by Mesopotamian word lists, ration rolls, and lists of prebends of temple offices. They list both sacerdotal and nonsacerdotal offices, including subordinate personnel such as artisans or other specialized workers.

A general term for temple clergy is *ērib bīti* (enterer of the temple), a person authorized to enter (all parts of) the temple. Such a person was involved in certain cultic duties, including the most sacred creation of the divine image. The group thus included not only those who performed the service but also expert artisans. Being an *ērib bīti* was also a prerequisite for obtaining a high administrative position in the temple hierarchy. The temple had a priestly council, called by different names through the centuries, which included all the enterers of the temple—in later periods equated with all the prebendaries of a temple organization.

There was no temple where all the members of the various priestly classes served together. Nor was there a single term designating the high priesthood. In the 3rd millennium, the apex of the clerical hierarchy was occupied by the EN, whose gender depended on that of the deity that he or she served. If the deity was female, the EN was male, and vice versa. The EN was considered the spouse of the deity, and this metaphorical relationship expressed the harmony, balance, and unity of the divine

and human worlds contained in the EN. The EN had a ceremonial station in the temple of his or her god, a separate residence called the *gipāru,* and various offices to perform. However, this cross-gender system disappeared in the mid-2nd millennium and was replaced by a system in which each temple had a collegium of priests, headed by a *šešgallu aḫu rabû* (big brother).

The most-numerous group was that of the purification specialists, charged with maintaining the holiness of the statues, the sacred objects, and the sacrosanct areas of the temples; they also offered sacrifices and libations. They were the GUDU$_4$/*pašišu* (the anointed one) and SUSBU/*ramku* (the bathed one). Some of these posts could be filled by men or women, but the majority by only men.

There were two types of liturgical priests: the NAR/*nāru* (musician, singer), who sang songs and played musical instruments, and the GALA/*kalû* (lamentation priest), who wrote the liturgical compositions that were intoned during temple, state, city, and even funerary rituals. Whereas either men or women could fill the former positions, the latter were restricted to males who seem to have had feminine traits and might have been castrati.

The functions of the various female ritual specialists are less clear. Some took an active part in temple rituals, while others played specialized roles, such as the wailing women who led funerary rites.

Certain functionaries were limited to the cults of certain divinities. The "transvestites" who carried the symbol of femininity, the spindle, and the *kurgarrû,* the cultic performer who performed a ritual of self-mutilation, took part in the cult of the goddess Inanna/Ishtar. The rites of the birth-goddess Nintu involved female celebrants, including the A-TU, who held the staff, the TU, who brought the gathered waters, and the LÀL-E-ŠÀ-GA, the midwife who sat in a holy place.

The priesthood was restricted to certain persons; admission requirements included high levels of spiritual and physical purity. Godliness—freedom from profaning influences—was essential, and criminals and liars were excluded. Physical purity was required, and the candidate was inspected from head to toe. Physical integrity and cleanliness were of acute importance in the encounter with the gods, and all those who participated in sacred ceremonies had to be physically intact—to the extent that even those with bad breath were excluded!

In addition, the individual had to belong to a family that was esteemed or priestly or had hereditary rights. Those with uncertain backgrounds, such as adoptees, were excluded from the priesthood. Certain offices were passed on from father to son from the earliest period. These hereditary offices are termed *prebends* and can be described as the right to an income from the temple in return for the performance of services connected with the cult—ranging from bread baking and the delivery of fish for the divine banquet to serving as a guardian or porter of the temple to more traditional cultic duties. Three features characterized a prebend: profession, period of service, and the deity or the temple for which the service was performed. Once a prebend belonged to a certain individual, his descendants automatically inherited it, unless it was sold to an outsider.

The hereditary priesthood must be distinguished from the vocational priesthood. There are examples of members of other professions becoming GALA priests. A divinatory process was used to choose the highest officials in the temple hierarchy, who were said to have been selected by the gods. Certain female functionaries (including the *kulmašītu, nadītu, qadištu, sekertu,* and *ugbabtu*) could be dedicated by their father to a deity.

Once the candidate was selected, he or she had to undergo an initiation process. Only one known text, from the late 2nd millennium, actually details a ritual initiation of temple personnel for the cult of Enlil and Ninlil. It describes the lengthy process of cleansing and purification, designed to ensure that everything touching the candidate was pure. He was bathed, his hair was washed, and he was then completely shaved. Haircutting as an initiation rite is also attested for other prebendary professions. Another text may refer to an initiation rite either dedicating women to divine service or cloistering them and involving a purificatory mouthwashing ceremony.

Priestly novices were either trained by their fathers or by master practitioners who took on apprentices and eventually certified their competence. After training, novices were examined by the temple assembly or a special assembly of priests. Upon the successful completion of his or her training, a priest or priestess was ceremonially inducted. The title of a lost ritual, *nišûti eni* (the enthronement of the EN priest), is known, as are references to the king performing such enthronement rites. One literary text, depicting the ordination of the EN priestess of Nanna, describes her purification rites in preparation for entering the temple, followed by her entrance and song of praise, at which point she is declared worthy of being brought into the temple. She then undergoes the purification rites of the EN-ship and is given her cultic name.

The *nadītu* was consecrated by being sprinkled with water and having a thread placed in her hand. A similar cord appeared in the ordination of the NU-ÈŠ/*nešakku* priest and NAM-ŠITA/*pašīšu* priest: Uttu, the goddess of weaving, was said to place a cord in the candidate's hand.

The praise recited by the EN priestess resembled the "positive confession" of the *nešakku* and *pašīšu* priests, who declared their purity. The GALA priests offered animals to the temple upon their entrance into office.

In the earliest period, male priests went naked, perhaps in order to display their physical wholeness to the gods. This practice disappeared by the 2nd millennium, although there are scattered later references to naked ecstatics. Generally, however, the various classes of priests were demarcated by differential special garb. Certain priests are termed "linen-clad" and others "skin-clad." For example, the consecrated lamentation priest wore a linen garment, while the unconsecrated lamentation priest wore a *šibtu* garment. In general, colors seem to have been significant, especially red. The exorcist donned a red garment and wrapped himself in a red cloak to expel illness-causing demons. Ritual specialists also wore special symbols, jewelry, headgear, and even weapons and usually carried a pail and aspergil.

The presence or absence of body hair designated various types of officiants. Shaving body hair always formed part of purification ceremonies to prepare priestly candidates and cultic celebrants. But there was a class of temple personnel with special coiffures who were described as "hairy" or with "loose hair," which implies that some individuals, at least, allowed their hair to grow back.

Most temple personnel were married, with the exception of specific groups of women, such as the *nadītu, qadištu, sekertu,* and *ugbabtu,* who were provided with a dowry and "married" to the male gods they served, thus forgoing sexual relations with human males.

Most temple personnel lived in or around the area of the temples in which they served. In the earlier periods, we know of the residence of the chief ministrant, the EN, who dwelled in a *gipāru,* a separate building, including public reception rooms, lustration and ablution rooms, private quarters, and a chapel or major temple. Female votaries in certain cities at certain times were cloistered.

Cultic functionaries served as mediators between the gods and the people. They offered expiatory sacrifices, penitential prayers, and liturgical psalms. They were also responsible for building, refurbishing, and maintaining the temples, fashioning and installing statues of the god and the king, provisioning the cult, performing the sacrifices, and carrying the divine images in procession.

The first step in any ritual was the purification of the priests in preparation for sacral functions. The NAR and GALA priests anointed themselves with oil. Often a ritual bath was taken, usually before sunrise. For instance, preceding the *mīs pî* (mouth washing) ritual for the consecration of a cult statue, the ritual performer announced: "I, the bathed one, whose mouth is washed, my hands are pure, my feet are clean." Such a statement seems to imply an overall state of purity, preparing the officiant to perform a ritual. Many rituals involved bathing in clean water and donning clean garments. Shaving to cleanse the body, along with cutting of body hair and of nails, was sometimes performed after certain rituals.

Religious personnel of the court and the community. A memorandum from Assurbanipal's reign enumerates forty-five individuals employed at the royal palace: seven astrologers, nine exorcists, five diviners, nine physicians, six lamentation chanters, three augurs, three Egyptian magicians, and three Egyptian scribes.

The *āšipu* (exorcist, magician, conjurer) was expert at healing the sick and warding off illness by magical or spiritual means, including spells, rituals, drugs, figurines, amulets, magic flour circles, libations, and anointings. His knowledge was recorded in many tomes and includes information on diagnosis and magical prescriptions (as opposed to the physician's "therapeutic" prescriptions). Since illness was thought to be caused by evil spirits, this ritual specialist also performed exorcisms to expel them.

The court exorcists are well known from their letters. Adad-shum-usur, the court exorcist of kings Esarhaddon and Assurbanipal, performed rituals to heal the royal family and researched medical tablets for the king. He performed expiatory rites as part of the substitute-king ritual, antiwitchcraft rituals for the queen mother, an earthquake ritual, rituals against retrograding Mars, and *bīt rimki* and other purification rites for the king. He also prepared for a solar eclipse, recited hand-lifting prayers, and made burnt offerings. Coming from a prominent scholarly family, he began his career as a scribe and rose to receive the rare title of purification specialist. In addition to the court exorcists, there were temple exorcists in both Assyria and Babylonia. In the Neo-Babylonian temples there was also a temple exorcist, whose office was prebendal.

The diviners, MAŠ.ŠU.GÍD.GÍD/*bārû*, were responsible for clarifying divine will. The qualifications of the diviner were recorded: he must be perfect in appearance and in his limbs; a cross-eyed man or one with chipped teeth was not allowed to approach the place of (divine) judgment. He kept his hair long and was not shaved. He had to have the correct parentage: in one text, it is stated that he had to belong to the families of Nippur, Sippar, and Babylon, be a functionary of the cult of the sun-god Shamash, and descend from a *nešakku* priest. Furthermore, if he wanted to be a master of oil divination, he had to be a descendent of Enmeduranki, the mythical antediluvian king of Sippar. His training included a thorough grounding in the scholarly literature and in

omens from sheep entrails, oil, and birds. In the 1st millennium, the diviner's art was also passed from father to son, and the *nişirti bārûti* (secret traditions of divination) became professional secrets. The exorcist's performance of extispicy (reading the liver or other internal organs of the sacrificed animal) began in the morning before sunrise, when he bathed in a special vessel with herbs and fragrant oil. He anointed himself, donned a pure garment, and purified himself. Having had no meal, he chewed cedar wood, after which he purified his hair and the fringes of his garments with cedar resin. He now could approach the place where the extispicy was to be performed and stand in the presence of the gods. He summoned the gods by burning fragrant incense and honored them with a meal and gifts, asking for a reliable answer. After the meal, the gods sat in judgment and wrote their decision into the animal's entrails. The diviner then interpreted the divine message on the basis of his scholarly knowledge of omen literature.

While there are few attestations of female diviners, there were more female than male dream interpreters. People went to the house of the dream interpreter to consult her concerning their dreams. The necromancers, who were less common than diviners or dream interpreters, offered incense to the spirits of the dead.

Last, there were ecstatics and prophets, male and female, who used different methods to learn the divine will through noninductive, inspired, direct channeling, rather than through the inductive technical divination practiced by diviners. Both of these spiritual figures underwent extraordinary experiences, although the prophet not only had a visionary experience but was conscious of being commanded by a deity to convey the revelation to a third party. These practitioners might be private citizens, temple prophets, or court prophets.

BIBL.: D. Charpin, *Le clergé d'Ur au siècle d'Hammurabi* (Hautes études orientales 22; Geneva, 1986). R. A. Henshaw, *Female and Male: The Cultic Personnel, the Bible, and the Rest of the Ancient Near East* (Allison Park, Pa., 1994). Gilbert J. P. McEwan, *Priest and Temple in Hellenistic Babylonia* (Freiburger altorientalische Studien 4; Wiesbaden, 1981). K. Watanabe (ed.), *Priests and Officials in the Ancient Near East* (Heidelberg, 1999). J.G.W.

Syria-Canaan

In Syro-Canaanite culture, as in most other ancient cultures, the first and principal cultic offerer and sacrificer was the king, together with his sons: the public cult was a royal cult. In addition, official personnel appointed for this service by the palace attended to sacred places; they were part of a strongly hierarchical system and had high political and administrative status.

Thus, for example, in Ebla, apart from the activities of the royal couple, we hear about an *abu-mul* and an *ama-mul* (father/mother of the deities) at the head of the cultic personnel and about the *lú-mal* (the man in charge of the deities). Some texts also mention the term *ensi* (= Sumerian EN.LI [female diviner]), while the expression *dam-dingir* (daughter of god or high priestess) seems to have been reserved for royal princesses. A frequent category is that of the *pāšeš*-DN (anointer of DN rather than *pašiš* [anointed]), whose many functions included purification, invocation, and recitation; he may have been identical with the GUDU₄ (anointed). They were at the service of gods and humans, kings and commoners. Other priestly classes of indeterminate function and significance were the *ses-2-eb, āpilum/āpiltum, māa-ḫu*(?), *balag-di,* and *balum,* some of which are derived from Mesopotamian sources.

At Emar, instead of the king and his family, the figure of the "diviner" (LU.ḪAL) seems to have been the overall supervisor of the cult and administrator of the town. He was also concerned with installing the different priests who were appointed for the different gods. And yet the presence of feminine personnel was also very strong in Emar. The great festivals were conducted by the high priestess (NIN.DINGIR [*ša* DN], sometimes called entu/ittu) and several other classes of priestess, both high (*mas'artu*) and low (*nugagtu, qadištu, munabbištu*) as well. The installation of the new *ittu* priestess of Hadad upon the death of her predecessor was solemnly celebrated. However, male officiants are also mentioned: butchers, singers, implorers, statue bearers, and those in charge of the consecration (*zābiḫu, bel biti, zammāru,* and "men of the *qidašu* and the *ḫussu*"). Each temple had its own personnel, under the command of a high priest, whose function passed from father to son. A temple could also be built by a private person, who in this way was able to establish a family priesthood. In fact, family cults of ancestors were established and maintained, and each family's "gods and dead" were transmitted to each new heir of the household.

At Ugarit the presence of the king, sometimes together with his sons and daughters, is frequently mentioned; in cultic texts he is almost exclusively the officiant of the rituals. These texts mention other cult personnel only incidentally: a "desacralizer" (*mḫll*), "singer" (*šr, qdš*), and perhaps "sacrificer" (*t'[y]*), possibly the king himself. According to other texts, at the head of the cultic personnel was "the high priest" (*rb khnm*), who was very important politically, just as in Israel. Curiously enough, however, "priests" (*khnm*) are not mentioned in the cultic texts, but only in the administrative ones, as functionaries with ritual and possibly divinatory functions as well, sometimes together with the "sanctifiers" (*qdšm*), who had a variety of roles (singer, soothsayer, anointer), possibly like the Eblaite "anointer" (*pāšeš*). The *khnm* constitute a "family body" (*dr khmn*), and their office seems to have been inherited. Other kinds of sacred personnel included the *rm* and the female *sib mqdšt* (water carrier) as well as general "workers" (*b'lm*) in the service of holy places. Archeology provides evidence for the existence of divinatory and cultic prac-

tices carried out in private shrines, possibly by freelance or specialized priests.

We have very meager information concerning the cultic personnel of 1st-millennium Phoenician city-states, supplemented by the Punic inscriptions. Kings and even queens continued to act as priest (*khn*) and priestess (*khnt*) of the city deity, as David and his sons did in the royal sanctuary of Jerusalem (2 Samuel 8.18). However, an official body of cultic personnel (*khnm*), both male and female, conducted the temple services in different functions and under the leadership of the high priest/priestesses (*rb khnm/khnt*). These were organized into a highly hierarchical college. A couple of tariff texts from Cyprus and Carthage preserve the salaries and allowances due to the various classes of cultic personnel and thus fill out our list of types further: "sacrificer" (*zbḥ*), "conductor of the new moon festival" (*'ln ḥdš*), "tower sentry" (*'dmm 'š 'dl*)(?), "one who has charge of the temple curtains" (*prk*), "baker" (*'p*), "scribe" (*spr*), "singer" (*šr*), "hairdresser" (*glb*), "water carrier" (*b'l mym*), and general auxiliaries (*'bd, mt*), including those devoted to sacred prostitution (*klbm, grm*), a ritual commonly carried out in Phoenician sanctuaries according to classical sources. The *zbḥ* (sacrificer) and the *mqm 'lm* (raiser of the gods) seem to have had special importance, even if the latter's function remains a matter of debate; it was perhaps connected with the "waking up/resurrection" (*egersis*) of certain deities such as Adonis and Melqart. Civil commissions seem also to have intervened in cultic affairs.

We have almost no information regarding the cultic personnel of the Old Aramean period. Here as well, the kings seem to have carried out cultic functions, according to the wording of some of the inscriptions. In only one case are the "seer" (*ḥzyn*) and the "prophet" (*'ddn*) mentioned, thus hinting at divinatory cultic activities for which Phoenician sources have preserved no evidence, apart from an allusion in the Wen-Amun story (see Sacred Times and Places). The inscriptions from Palmyra, in contrast, provide a fairly well-documented view of temple personnel. The priests (*kmry'*) were organized into collegia presided over by a high priest. It seems that the high priest of the temple of Bel was also the high priest of all the clergy of Palmyra. In the sanctuary of the spring of Efqa, the great water supply of the Palmyran oasis, dedicated to its city god Yarhibol, there was a special class of priests under the orders of the head priest of the sacred place; these were oracle priests. Other cultic personnel include "guardians" (*mdnyn*), under the orders of their respective "mayor" (*rb, 'rkwn*), whose office lasted one year and who was elected by the different tribal patrons of each sanctuary.　　G.O.L.

Israel

The priest (*kōhēn*) was the primary cultic functionary of the Jerusalem temple and, before centralization, of other Israelite sanctuaries, in every period for which there is evidence. Other, secondary cultic personnel such as the temple slave *(*natîn)* mentioned in Chronicles-Ezra-Nehemiah or the temple servitor *(lhn)* of the Elephantine papyri are occasionally attested, often only in a limited corpus of materials, and our knowledge of their functions is, in most cases, limited or nonexistent. By the period of the Second Temple (515 BCE to 70 CE), a major secondary type of cultic servant, the Levite, is widely attested in surviving texts. Levites were responsible for music, singing, gatekeeping, oversight of temple courts and chambers, and other functions of the sanctuary according to texts such as 1 Chron. 23. Two texts, 1 Sam. 2.22 and Exod. 38.8, mention women who serve at the entry of a sanctuary, but their responsibilities are not at all clear, and no other evidence survives that might tell us something about female cultic servants in ancient Israel. In contrast to surrounding cultures, no evidence suggests that women were ever priests in the cult of YHWH, although various biblical texts speak of women in other public, professional roles (e.g., as prophets, mediums, or professional mourners). The reasons for the exclusion of women from the priesthood of YHWH are unknown, and the typical explanations proffered by scholars (e.g., the duration of feminine impurities) are unconvincing. Finally, the rabbis, a group of male lay teachers, produced a huge corpus of literature, beginning with the Mishnah circa 200 CE and including the Babylonian and Jerusalem Talmuds (compilations of commentary on the Mishnah). With centers in Israel and Babylon, the rabbis claimed religious and social leadership of the Jews in a period after the Jerusalem temple had ceased to exist and provided models for Jewish practice without the temple.

The responsibilities of the priests and other cultic functionaries were varied, and surviving texts do not always offer us a consistent picture, but a coherent impression does emerge from a reading of the extant data. In general, cultic personnel were charged with the upkeep and maintenance of the sanctuary sphere, a sacred locus and—if a temple building or tent shrine stood there—the site of the deity's dwelling place. Sanctuary personnel collected, processed, and (often) redistributed obligatory and voluntary offerings of grain products, wine, oil, incense, and meat (sheep, goats, cattle, and certain birds such as the dove, turtledove, and pigeon). A portion of the inflow of goods remained in the sanctuary sphere, where it was set aside for the support of cultic functionaries and their dependents or offered to the deity himself. Several texts mention the holy and most holy offerings reserved for the priestly households (Lev. 10.12–20; 22.1–16; Num. 18.8–19); other texts mention the tithe, assigned for the upkeep of the Levites (Num. 18.21–32; Neh. 13.10–14). Fat and organs were always YHWH's portion, and YHWH sometimes received meat as well (e.g., the whole burnt offering). Sacrificial blood, brought to YHWH's altar by priests, was to be poured out or manipulated for a variety of purposes (e.g., purification).

All cultic functionaries were required to be free of pollution. Because priests approached the deity to give him offerings or to petition him on behalf of the people, they, like most offerings of sacrificial animals (Lev. 22.17–25), had to be physically unblemished as well (21.16–23). A blemished priest was disqualified from making offerings to YHWH on the altar, but could remain in the sanctuary sphere (presumably involved with other, lesser cultic activities) and continue to eat holy foods (21.22). Blemishes included blindness, lameness, genital damage, and other (mainly visible) physical defects. Priests and their minions controlled access to the cult, excluding persons who were polluted or otherwise unqualified to enter the sanctuary in order to protect its sanctity.

The priesthood also controlled the cultic activities constructed as most elite. They burned incense to the deity, an exclusive prerogative of the priesthood according to Num. 16.1–50 [= 16.1–17.15 Hebrew]; they made sacrificial offerings (including fat) and manipulated sacrificial blood on the altar of burnt offerings in the courtyard of the sanctuary (Ezek. 44.15). In addition, there is evidence that Israelite priests, like many of their peers in surrounding cultures, functioned as diviners, manipulating obscure oracular devices such as the Urim and Thummim or the ephod in order to reveal the deity's will (1 Sam. 30.7–8; see Divination and Prophecy). Priests drew upon expert knowledge to evaluate complex questions of purity (Lev. 13–14). They also had teaching responsibilities (Deut. 33.10; Mic. 3.11; Ezek. 44.23), which included the interpretation of sacred texts in later periods. Some materials suggest that priests were required to observe special behavioral restrictions (e.g., with respect to self-pollution, mourning rites, and marriage; see Lev. 21.1–5, 7; Ezek. 44.20).

The office of high priest is mentioned in a variety of texts. According to Lev. 16.17, the high priest effected purgation once a year for himself, his priestly house, and the whole congregation of Israel. Leviticus 21.10–15 provides other details concerning the activities of the high priest. In general, this text suggests that his behavior was more strictly regulated than that of other priests. For example, where the priest was allowed to pollute himself by contact with next of kin who have died, the high priest could not do so. And while certain easily reversible mourning rites such as unbinding the hair were permitted to the priest, apparently the high priest could not participate in any mourning rites whatsoever. (See Ezek. 24.16–17 on priestly mourning, as well as Lev. 21.5; the latter text forbids the priest to shave a bald spot and lacerate himself—both mourning rites—but says nothing about unbinding the hair or tearing garments—mourning rites proscribed for the high priest in 21.10.)

The history of the Israelite priesthood is complex and poorly understood by modern scholars, but can be reconstructed in broad outline. The J and E strands of the Pentateuch (the oldest narrative sources) portray male ancestors such as Noah, Abraham, and Jacob as offering sacrifices and founding sanctuaries (e.g., Gen. 8.20–22; 15.9–10; 28.18–22); "young men" assisting Moses perform sacrifices at the foot of Mount Sinai according to Exod. 24.3–8. Kings such as Jeroboam and Solomon sacrifice, apparently without priestly assistance. In short, texts from the early monarchy are not much concerned about whether professional priests perform every priestly function. Yet early texts do bear witness to the existence of a professional, priestly group: the male members of the tribe of Levi. The early Levitic priesthood, consisting of many separate clans—Num. 26.58, thought to be the oldest clan list, mentions several—was open to males of the tribe of Levi as well as to other males who might be adopted into a Levitic clan and acquire specialized priestly skills there. Samuel is an example of such an adoptee. That he was an Ephraimite by origin who was adopted into the Shiloh priestly line is indicated in 1 Sam. 1.1; that his Ephraimite genealogy was coopted and incorporated into his later Levitic genealogy is clear from 1 Chron. 6.33–38 [= 6.18–23 Hebrew]. At least one early text suggests that although any male could perform priestly functions, it was better to have a Levite perform them. In Judg. 17, a certain Micah of Ephraim sets up a cult site and installs one of his own sons as priest. Then he hires a passing Levite to work for him: "Now I know that the LORD will prosper me, because I have a Levite as priest" (17.13). Thus, the priesthood of the early monarchic period, as reflected in a variety of texts, was an elite group of male cultic specialists sharing fictive or blood kinship ties and exercising limited control over the apparatus of the cult. Although the priesthood was a hereditary elite, outsiders could join one of the many priestly families, which traced their descent from a common eponymous ancestor, Levi.

The variety of priestly clans tracing their ancestry back to Levi appear to have existed simultaneously in the land of Israel before the 6th century BCE. These priestly families—sometimes at odds, if surviving texts are any indication—included the Aaronids, who traced their descent from Aaron; the Mushites, who claimed to be descendants of Moses; and the Korahites, who traced their genealogy back to Korah. Each of these rival clans likely controlled individual sanctuaries. Texts suggest that the Aaronids controlled the northern sanctuary of Bethel, and the Mushites, the far northern sanctuary at Dan. Jerusalem, from the time of Solomon's coup d'état, was under the control of the Zadokites, a particular Aaronid line. Priestly families produced many extant polemical texts. These include Exod. 32, in which Aaron is portrayed as a sinner who makes the golden calf and the sons of Levi figure as heroes, slaughtering the calf's worshipers. Deuteronomy 9.20 on Aaron's transgression with the calf is similar in intent: it functions to embarrass the Aaronids, putting them on the defensive about their eponymous ancestor's record. A comparable polemic

from the Aaronid side is Num. 16.1–50 [=16.1–17.15], in which Korah—the ancestor of the Korahite priesthood—and his allies are slaughtered by YHWH for challenging alleged Aaronid control over the priesthood.

Over the course of the monarchic period and the exile (the 10th through 6th centuries BCE), the relatively open priesthood, populated by a variety of priestly clans, became a closed, strictly hereditary elite exercising greater control of the cult. Nonpriests lost their access to priestly activities, and adoption into priestly clans ceased, although we cannot determine when. Eventually, one priestly house, the Aaronids, became preeminent, reducing all of their rival Levitic clans to a secondary, servile status. These rivals to the Aaronids became the Levites—a group of cultic servants of inferior status to priests and under their control. We know nothing about how this reduction in status occurred, nor is it clear when it occurred. By the time of the Second Temple (515 BCE–70 CE), it is apparently an accomplished fact, as witnessed in various sources from the period (Chronicles-Ezra-Nehemiah, Qumran, Josephus). In Priestly and Holiness materials in the Pentateuch (i.e., in Leviticus and Numbers), as well as in Chronicles, the sons of Aaron are—and always have been—the only Israelite priests. Their exclusive control of the priesthood, according to the Priestly tradition, was established from the founding of the cult during the desert wanderings and it reflects YHWH's will (Num. 16.1–50 [= 16.1–17.15]). The Levites, completely under Aaronid control, perform non-elite functions in the sanctuary (3.5–10). Yet it is clear to the contemporary critic that such claims to Aaronid priestly exclusivity reflect developments in the cult, very likely during the exile of Judah's elite to Babylon during the 6th century BCE. Surviving texts are sufficient to demonstrate the variety of priestly families in Israel before the Aaronids managed to exclude all of their rivals from the priesthood. For example, Deut. 18.1–8 and Jer. 33.18, 21–22 see the priesthood as the possession of the whole tribe of Levi rather than that of a single clan, the Aaronids.

The high priesthood of the Jerusalem temple finds its origins in David's priest, Zadok, who assumed complete control of the Jerusalem cultic establishment after Solomon's coup. Until the 2nd century BCE, Zadok's descendants controlled the priesthood. The Zadokites lost the high priesthood as a result of the political struggles of the 2nd century BCE. By 152 BCE, the Hasmoneans, who were non-Zadokite Aaronids, had established themselves as high priests and remained in the office until 35 BCE, when the last of the Hasmonean high priests, Aristobulus III, was assassinated. The Hasmonean takeover of the high priestly office may have been a stimulus for the founding of the Qumran community, the group whose library is commonly referred to as the Dead Sea Scrolls.

BIBL.: Frank Moore Cross, *Canaanite Myth and Hebrew Epic* (Cambridge, Mass., 1973), 195–215.　　　S.M.O.

Anatolia

The center of Hittite state religion was the king. His religious obligations were the most important responsibilities of his kingship and were the foundation of the entire system of royal ideology. His daily schedule—indeed, his whole life—was determined by his religious duties. He and the queen were the highest priest and priestess of the national deity (the Storm-god of Hatti in the earlier period and the sun-goddess of the city of Arinna later), and as such they were in charge of ensuring that humanity worshiped the gods properly. (A significant royal title under the Hittite New Kingdom was "priest of the sun-goddess of the city of Arinna and all the gods.") Moreover, the Hittite king was often identified with the sun-god. He was addressed with the title "my/his sun-god" (usually rendered in translation as "my/his majesty") and was often depicted on reliefs in a ceremonial outfit that the sun-god also wore.

Most of the major state festivals required not only the king's and queen's presence, but their performance of parts of the festivals (although their participation could also, at times, be simply passive). Hittite King Murshili II went so far as to postpone an important military campaign to celebrate a festival in honor of the goddess Lelwani, censuring his father for having previously neglected the cultic calendar and thereby caused difficulties concerning his own accession to the throne.

The Hittite king also made sure that the gods—or rather their temples—got a share of the booty from military operations and from the regular distribution of livestock, foodstuffs, and other products. As a matter of fact, it is impossible to separate the king's concern for the temples from other types of state business that are documented in the records of the royal archives. Furthermore, according to Hittite texts, the king was not the proprietor of the land of Hatti but rather a steward, appointed and protected by the gods. In addition to serving as the gods' steward, the king represented humankind before the gods. Thus the king acted as an intermediary between the sphere of the gods and that of human beings, maintaining harmonious relations between the two.

Being in such close contact with the gods, the person of the king was subject to special standards of purity. This is well attested by regulations for palace personnel. For instance, the water carriers were instructed to be very careful with the drinking water that was presented to the king. They had to strain it, ensuring that it was not contaminated by the hair of others, for example. Purity was similarly an important consideration for everyone who served the gods, including priests and other temple officials. This included the modification of even their personal lives. For instance, in order to maintain their purity, priests were forbidden to spend the night at home with their wives and family: they had to return to the temple before the gates were closed for the night (celibacy in the strictest sense, however, was not required of priests). Priests' and attendants' daily personal care, such as cleansing or removal of body hair and fingernails, was also of great importance:

> Let those who make the daily [sacrificial] bread be clean. Let them be washed and trimmed. Let [their] hair and finger[nails] be trimmed. Let them be clothed in clean garments. . . . When the servant stands before his master, he [is] washed. He has clothed [himself] in clean [clothes]. He gives him [his master] either to eat or to drink. Since the master eats and drinks, [in] his spirit he [is] relaxed. He is favorably inclined toward him [the servant]. . . . If the servant at some point angers his master, either they kill him, or they injure his nose, eyes, [and] ears. If ever he dies, he does not die alone. His family [is] also included with him. If, however, someone angers the mind of a god, does the god seek it [revenge] only from him alone? Does he not seek it from his wife, [his children,] his descendants, his family, his male and female servants, his cattle, his sheep, and his grain? He utterly destroys him with everything. (Instructions for Temple Officials 217–221)

Temple personnel lived so close to the gods that their behavior could affect the attitude of the gods toward the temple and ultimately toward the whole state. Thus, their purity was a matter of national significance. The purity of the temple itself was also an important national concern. Everything that entered the temple—performers of rituals, cult utensils, and offerings—had to be ritually pure; sacrificial animals had to be in good condition (sometimes virginal animals were required).

The queen was the highest priestess of the national deity. She is portrayed alongside the king on reliefs, presenting offerings to the gods. The queen remained queen until death, often overlapping with her son's reign if her husband, the king, died before she did. Thus the office of queen, termed Tawananna, was inherited separately from that of king. In her role as Tawananna, the queen had certain religious responsibilities, primarily that of controlling funds and resources of temples and religious endowments. The Hittite religious calendar also included certain ceremonies that were performed by only a prince.

In addition to the king and the queen, the Hittite state maintained a well-organized religious administration, directed by the official priesthood or the temple personnel. Several terms refer to such persons (including the rather generic phrases "men [or women] of the temple," "servants of the temple," and "lords of the temple"), and it is not yet possible for scholars to distinguish each particular functions. Exacerbating this problem is the sheer number of temple personnel and the variation in their titles and functions from temple to temple and from period to period. We do know, however, that priests and assistants were perceived as a differentiated group with a strict hierarchy. The highest religious official (following the king and the queen) was the so-called ^{LÚ}SANGA (Hittite *sankunni-*), conventionally translated "priest." He was administratively responsible for the performance of festivals and in charge of a deity's daily routine, as well as of implements used in cult. His religious duties and activities also included participating in various rituals and offerings, performing purification ceremonies, conversing with the deity, reciting, and singing. The texts also mention a priestess who was his counterpart, called ^{MUNUS}SANGA, as well as a DUMU SANGA (novice or junior priest[?]). Still more difficult to translate is ^{LÚ}GUDU₁₂; it literally indicates an "anointed" person, but this does not tell us much. Other Hittite texts mention ^{LÚ}*tazzelli-* and ^{LÚ}*hamina-;* the meaning of the first is unknown, but the latter is most probably the official in charge of storehouses. Another type of priest, ^{LÚ}*patili-,* had mostly purificatory functions.

The chief priests of temples in major cities were mostly of royal descent, younger brothers or second sons of the king, who were not eligible to succeed to the throne. Priests were exempted from certain duties, such as paying taxes or performing forced labor. On the occasion of great festivals they had the privilege of receiving food and new implements. Local, more minor priests, on the other hand, were not of noble descent and occupied a relatively low rank in Hittite society.

Priestesses were rarer than priests and were usually associated with the cults of female deities. The texts mention, for instance, an important priestess with a somewhat obscure title, ^{MUNUS}AMA.DINGIR-LIM, an ideographic rendering of Hittite *siwanzanni-* (lit., mother of a god). The high rank of both the *sankunni-* and the *siwanzanni-* is manifested by the king and queen often applying these titles to themselves. Many texts also mention an "old woman" or "wise woman" (^{MUNUS}SU.GI), whose existence distinguishes Anatolia from other countries of the Near East. The Old Hittite texts place her among the palace personnel. She was mainly engaged in divination, as well as in magical proceedings. (Personnel called the "man of the storm-god" and "woman of the storm-god" also carried out various magical rituals, mainly those concerned with purification.)

In addition to celebrating festivals alongside of the king and queen, the priests and priestesses also carried out offerings to the gods and thus directly approached divinities (i.e., divinities' cultic images or attributes) in their sacred chambers. In doing so, the priests and priestesses were unique, for other people could not come so close to the gods.

The staff required to run the major temples in Bogazköy and other large cities also included augurs and other diviners, scribes (including scribes who worked on wood as opposed to clay), seers or incantation priests, magicians and exorcists, various types of singers and musicians, dancers and ritual reciters, as well as many others with occupations that were more secular in nature and who had rather subordinate tasks: kitchen personnel, literally "masters of dishes" (cooks, bakers, brewers, "men of the table," cupbearers, water carriers), "men of the spear" (serving as a kind of temple guard), gatekeepers, courtyard washers, barbers, leather workers, potters, and other artisans (carpenters, goldsmiths, silversmiths, stonecutters, engravers, weavers), herders for the temple flocks and herds, and farmers who cultivated the temple lands. Even the smallest local temples required a minimum staff of two or three.

Various supervisors oversaw the work of laborers, ranging in size from a few persons to several hundred, depending on the assigned task. Usually this was of an agricultural character: plowing and sowing the temple's lands, harvesting the crops and transporting the grain to the temple's storehouses, constructing and regularly maintaining irrigation systems. They derived the major portion of their own and their families' sustenance from the temple. Large areas of the temple's lands also were worked by community members who owed services to the temple. In addition, there was a huge group of full-time, permanent dependents of the temple household, who came from the impoverished elements within the local population, including widows and children with no other means of support, orphans, captives of war or deportees, as well as the crippled. These people relied entirely on rations allocated by the temple for their service.

The participation of musicians, singers, dancers, or other performers (jugglers, acrobats, comedians, the "wolf-man," the "bear-man," the "sword eater") was required in most cultic ceremonies, since the offerings to gods and the communal meal were usually accompanied by music or other entertainments. Festival texts often prescribe singers from a certain place, such as, for instance, singers from Kanesh (modern Kültepe) or Babylon, or singers who would perform in Hurrian or Hattian. Recitations or litanies were conducted by several cultic professionals, such as ^{LÚ}ALAN.ZU₉, ^{LÚ}*palwatalla-,* or ^{LÚ}*kita-.* The liturgy consisted of not only recitations, but also some ritual movements such as running, bowing, kneeling down, or kissing.

There were also well-defined offices for the administration of offerings and libations to the gods, which were a significant part of cultic ceremonies. The "cupbearer" oversaw the libations of wine and beer, whereas the "men of the table" saw that the appropriate altars or offering tables were provided in a timely manner. Cooks and bakers supplied the foodstuff for offerings. The cooks also sometimes participated directly in the ceremonies by butchering or carving the sacrificial animals, while the bakers baked the sacrificial loaves.

The texts also mention a functionary of a rather obscure nature, called ^{LÚ}*tahiyala-* (barber, shearer[?]), who participated in festivals by pouring out libations and supplying bread offerings, as well as by carrying out other cultic activities. Other temple functionaries included those who swept up crumbs after bread was offered or supplied various garments for use in rites, as well as attendants (male or female) who cared for various parts of the temple or cultic objects.

Other female cult functionaries attested in Hittite texts are the *hazqara*-women, *zintuhi*-women, and *katra*-women (whose professions are not very clear), prostitutes or harlots, young ladies or virgins, and female exorcists, criers, singers, musicians, and many others.

Finally, in Hittite society, certain military commanders (e.g., "the chief of the royal bodyguard") or local administrators ("provincial governors") also played important, although sometimes unclear, cultic roles. They accompanied the king and queen during cultic ceremonies, but were neither engaged in the cult proper nor listed in enumeration of temple personnel.

BIBL.: H. G. Güterbock, "The Hittite Temple according to Written Sources," in *Perspectives on Hittite Civilization: Selected Writings of H. G. Güterbock* (ed. H. A. Hoffner Jr.; Chicago, 1997), 83–85. Gregory McMahon, "Instructions to Priests and Temple Officials," in *The Context of Scripture* (ed. W. W. Hallo et al.; Leiden, 1997), 1.217–18. Idem, "Theology, Priests, and Worship in Hittite Anatolia," in *Civilizations of the Ancient Near East* (ed. J. M. Sasson et al.; New York, 1995), 3.1990–91. Franca Pecchioli-Daddi, *Mestieri, professioni e dignità nell'Anatolia ittita* (Rome, 1982), 204–435. Maciej Popko, *Religions of Asia Minor* (Warsaw, 1995), 77–80, 142–46.　　　　　　　　　　　　　H.H.

Iran

Owing both to its broad geographic limits and to its long history in antiquity, Iran produced various sorts of religious personnel, some confined to specific periods and/or places, some universal. While Zarathustra was both a *zoatar* and a *mathran*, the latter function seems not to have survived much beyond his lifetime; the former continues to this day. The *magi,* initially a Median priestly caste, became the universal priesthood through the fortunes of empire.

Zarathustra performed two priestly functions. As a sacrificial officiant he was the presiding priest called the *zaotar* (who pours the libations; cf. Vedic *hótar*). This was a traditional office inherited from Indo-Iranian times and passed on from generation to generation down to the present day. As a visionary skilled in the art of poetic composition, he was a *mathran* (composer of hymns [*mathra*]; cf. Vedic *mántra*). In contrast to the office of *zaotar,* which could be transmitted from father to son, the art of the *mathran* could be learned by only a few intellectually gifted boys. Like the men, and a few women, who created the hymns of the Vedas, Zarathustra inherited a poetic repertory, some of it with Indo-European origins. The structurally complicated, often enigmatic, yet profound Gathas (songs), which are

traditionally credited to Zarathustra, are all the more marvelous to us because they were composed without the knowledge of writing. In these hymns, Zarathustra mentions rival priests, *kawis* (cf. Vedic *kaví*), *karapans,* and *usigs* (cf. Vedic *uśíg*), about whom we know almost nothing except that they were connected with worship of the Daewas and the attendant brutalization of the Cow.

In the eclectic Zoroastrianism of the Avesta, the general term for priest, as well as for a member of the priestly caste, is *athaurwan.* Although the meaning of the term is uncertain, *athaurwan* is the same word as Old Indic *átharvan,* a class of priests especially connected with the god Agni (Fire) and Soma. The *zaotar* was the chief officiant at the daily *haoma* ritual, the *yasna.* Initially the *zaotar* was assisted by other priestly functionaries, but by Sasanid times just the *zōd* (the priest who officiated at the *yasna* ritual) and his assistant, the *raspīg,* were sufficient to perform the *yasna.* Education was administered under another class of priests called *aēthrapati* (masters of instruction) (Middle Persian *hērbed*). Practitioners of occult sciences were generally considered to be in league with Druj (Lie); sorcerers *(yātu),* witches *(pairikā),* and soothsayers *(kaēta, kayada)* are mentioned in the texts, but little is known about them.

In the ancient world, the best-known Iranian religious practitioners were the *magi* (Old Iranian *magu*) who were widely held to possess occult knowledge and magical powers. The Greek historian Herodotus identified them as one of the Median tribes. As the priestly caste, they served both Medes and Persians, presiding at sacrifices where they recited theogonies, probably hymns similar to those of the Rig Veda and of the Yashts, in praise of the gods. Herodotus also remarked that they took great pride in killing creeping animals (1.140), a well-known practice in Zoroastrianism of killing *xrafstras* (noxious creatures). They wielded considerable political power and may sometimes have come into conflict with the rulers, although Herodotus's account of the annual *magophonia* (slaying of the magi) may be inaccurate (3.76–79). Whenever it was during the Achaemenid period that Zoroastrianism became the predominant religion of the empire, the magi took over the ecclesiastical leadership and preserved the so-called Good Religion after the Macedonian conquest through the Arsacid and Sasanid periods.

Although their name appears nowhere in the extant Avesta, indicating that they were unknown in eastern Iran, the term *mowbed* is the common designation of a priest in Middle Persian and Parthian. Under the Sasanids, the *mowbedān mowbed* (priest of priests) was the head of the state religion paralleling the *šāhān šāh* (King of Kings). Prominent among the Sasanid chief priests was Kirder, who held power during much of the 3rd century and was probably responsible for the untimely death of Mani, his rival at the court of Shapur I. During the Sasanid period, another grouping of priests, the *herbeds,* played a prominent role, especially in the service of the sacred fires maintained throughout the empire. From the King of Kings to the common person, the Sasanid priesthood dominated almost every aspect of religious life.

Since the 1938 publication of H. S. Nyberg's *Die Religionen des alten Iran,* there has been controversy over the existence of shamanism in ancient Iran. Nyberg's thesis was that Zarathustra was a religious figure whose Gathas bear witness to a form of religion practiced widely in central Asia (as well as other parts of the world), in which, as part of a ritual séance with song and dance, a trained and initiated individual could fall into an ecstatic trance, during which his soul departed from his body and traveled through the various levels of the cosmos in order to combat demons, gain favors from divine beings, or obtain special knowledge, usually in the service of the social group he served. Although Nyberg's ideas about Zarathustra were refuted in 1951 to the satisfaction of many by H. B. Henning in his polemical *Zoroaster: Politician or Witch-doctor?* they have been revived in recent years and even applied to the Sasanid priest Kirder, as well as to the somewhat historically elusive figure Arda Viraz. While the supposition that people, such as the Iranians, hailing from the steppes should have practiced shamanism is reasonable, the evidence is weak or, at best, inconclusive.

In contrast to ancient India, ancient Iran never provided fertile soil for mysticism. One can point to Zarathustra's inspired religious vision *(daēnā)* or to the narcotic-induced celestial journey of Arda Viraz; and Herodotus attests to the ritual use of hemp smoke among the Scythians (a non-Zoroastrian Iranian people), which may reflect shamanism (4.75). However, there is no evidence for the sort of asceticism in which one strives to experience the absolute oneness of the universe, such as one finds in Hindu and Buddhist traditions or later in the Sufi tradition of Islamic Iran.

With the exception of witches, women seem not to have had any public or official religious office. From a ritual standpoint, the reason for the exclusion of women was the great fear of pollution from menstrual blood.   W.W.M.

Greece

The key context for our understanding of Greek religious personnel is the polis. The central religious figures of the polis are the priests responsible for particular civic cults (they differ in this respect from the most prestigious Roman religious personnel, who were generally not attached to particular cults). The image of such a priest is embedded already in the *Iliad,* which describes in some detail a Trojan procession of supplication up to Athena's temple on the citadel: "Theano of the fair cheeks opened the door for them, daughter of Cisseus, and wife of Antenor, breaker of horses, she whom the

Preparation for a sacrifice. The sacrificer (center) washes his hands over an altar in a basin offered to him by an attendant, who balances a basket on his other hand; to the left, another helper brings the victim, a ram. Attic red-figure bowl, 450–440 BCE. *Gemeentenmuseum, The Hague*

Trojans had established to be Athena's priestess" (*Iliad* 6.298–300; trans. Lattimore). Theano is clearly represented as the person responsible for this cult: it is she who places the offering on the knees of the cult statue and prays to the goddess on behalf of the community. Such figures recur throughout Greek antiquity. At Athens, priestesses were responsible for the cult of Athena Polias, while at Magnesia on the Maeander there were both priests and priestesses of Artemis Leukophryene. In the 2nd century BCE, it was decided by the city that "the *stephanēphoros* [chief magistrate] in office, together with the priest and priestess, shall from henceforth lead the procession in the month of Artemision on the twelfth day and sacrifice the designated bull" (*Inschriften von Magnesia* 98; Sokolowski 1955: 32; 197–196 BCE). Priests headed processions and presided over sacrifices to their deity, in the sanctuary or elsewhere.

Appointment and qualifications. The modes of appointment to civic priesthoods varied over time. While Theano is seen as a consensual appointment, it is obvious that in such a society only someone of her aristocratic standing would have been suitable for the principal cult of the state. By contrast, in democratic Athens, when new cults were established or old ones reorganized, the priesthoods were open to all Athenians and were filled by the democratic procedure of the lot. For example, the first priestess of the new 5th-century sanctuary of Athena Nike (a cult that went back to the 6th century BCE) was appointed by lot "from all Athenian women" (Meiggs and Lewis 1988: 44 = *IG* I³ 35; ca. 448 BCE). Appointment to religious office is parallel in procedure to appointment to political office and here implies that both religious and political competence is shared by all citizens. There were also regional variations in procedures of appointment. In western Asia Minor and the eastern Aegean islands it was common for cities to sell priesthoods to the highest bidders. The practice is widely attested, from the classical period through to the Roman period.

One category of civic priesthoods is that held by members of a particular lineage *(genos)*. At Athens, for example, the lineage of the Eteoboutadai claimed descent from Boutes, who was, according to one tradition, one of the two sons of King Pandion I, who received the priesthood of Athena Polias and Poseidon Erichtheus (his brother Erechtheus received the kingship) (Apollodorus, *Library* 3.14.8–3.15.1). The lineage continued to fill both priesthoods throughout antiquity. There is a dispute as to how these lineage cults should be seen in relation to other civic cults: are they in origin the cults of particular families that were subsequently taken over by the state, preserving the rights of the founding line? or are they cults which were from the outset civic cults, whose officials were nonetheless drawn from one lineage? We cannot decide because we have no good evidence for the period of formation of the major cults and cannot safely take as historical later traditions. In periods for which we do have better information we occasionally find cases of the civic takeover model. For example, at Pergamum, the cult of Asclepius was introduced from Epidaurus by one Archias; it was taken over in the Hellenistic period as a civic cult, whose priesthood remained in the lineage of Archias (in the 2nd or 3rd century CE one Flavius Aristomachos is honored as the priest of Asclepius, twenty-second in line from Archias). And at Athens it was believed that lineage cults could be reserved for members of that lineage. The lineage of the Gephyraioi, according to Herodotus (5.61), "have certain temples set apart for their special use, which the other Athenians are forbidden to enter; one of them is the temple of Demeter Achaia, in which secret rites are performed." But the tradition of the Eteoboutadai is of a lineage service of a public cult, and in general it is preferable to see civic cults and lineage control developing hand in hand.

The qualifications expected of a priest or priestess were formal: they had to be citizens (or even members of a particular lineage), and they had to be "healthy and whole." Priests were formally initiated by the city (specific regulations might be made for the financing of this initiation, which at Cos involved purifying the priest with a piglet and then the priest sacrificing a bovine and a sheep, with consumption of meat at the following banquet [Sokolowski 1969: 156 A 17]. Once appointed, priests commonly served for long periods or even for life. One 5th-century priestess of Hera at Argos served

for fifty-six and a half years before she accidentally burned down the temple and was deposed from office (Thucydides 2.2.1; 4.133).

Priests received remuneration for their work. Sometimes this was money, but more normally it was perquisites from animals sacrificed in the sanctuary. The new priestess of Athena Polias at Athens was to receive both: "To receive 50 drachmas, and to receive the legs and hides from public sacrifices" (Meiggs and Lewis 1988: 44 = *IG* I³ 35). However, in this case there was a bureaucratic problem: a second civic decree had to be passed some twenty-five years later (and inscribed on the reverse of the first decree), which specified a procedure for the payment of the fifty drachmas (which had perhaps not been paid in the interim). In the case of priesthoods sold to the highest bidder, the perquisites from the sacrificial animals were minutely specified and may have been of sufficient financial value to remunerate the holder of the office for the purchase price.

Priestesses. One of the most surprising characteristics of Greek religious personnel is that they consisted equally of men and women. This is true from the earliest representation of Greek religion onward. In the *Iliad*, Theano is priestess of Athena, while Chryses, "priest of him who strikes from afar, Apollo," plays a prominent role in the narrative at the start of the epic (seeking to get back his daughter). This pair of characters exemplifies later practice: women were priestesses of goddesses, while men were priests of gods. The practice is remarkable. Only men could hold political public office or indeed had political rights. While it is true that priesthoods were not quite the same as political magistracies, they were offices that were run by cities, and it might so easily have been the case that rules for magistracies were taken to apply by analogy to priesthoods. But they did not, even in the case of new cults. The explanation must lie in the perceived appropriateness, indeed power, of the analogy between the gender of the official and that of the deity. The real puzzle is therefore pushed further back, to why it was that the Greeks so emphasized both genders of their gods.

Priests and their cults. The implied gender link between official and deity raises another important issue: the general relationship between cult, officials, and city. The conventional view is that the officials were just amateur pseudomagistrates, who ran the cults in the same way as the *archontes* (chief magistrates) at Athens or the *stephanēphoros* at Magnesia on the Maeander ran the secular side of the city. There are problems with this view. Aristotle in the *Politics* (1322b18–29; cf. 1328b11–13) does treat superintendents of religion (priests and other officials) as one set of offices necessary to the functioning of a state, but he wavers as to their relation to magistracies. And there are major formal differences between magistracies and priesthoods in terms of mode of inauguration of office (ritual initiation for priests) and often in terms of duration (magistracies had by definition to rotate and could not be held for life). The gender appropriateness of the priest also lent them extra authority, in addition to that acquired from the solemnity of their ritual roles per se. When Alcibiades (inadvertently?) captured some priests and priestesses during his campaign in Asia Minor, he released them without seeking a ransom (Plutarch, *Alcibiades* 29.5).

In addition, it is possible to find religious officials standing up for the interests of their cults in cases when conflict occurred between the cult and the city. No doubt most such cases were settled internally, but in the Hellenistic and Roman periods we find the ruling power intervening in such disputes. For example, Demetrius II of Macedon was approached by priests of Heracles at Beroia (a town in Macedon) who were irate that funds properly belonging to the cult had been expropriated by the city. The king wrote as follows to the administrator of the city: "Demetrius to Harpalos, greetings. The priests of Heracles say that some of the revenues belonging to the god have been diverted to political ends. Please make sure that they are restored to the god. Farewell" (Dittenberger 1915–24: 459; Hatzopoulos 1996: no. 8, lines 4–8; 248 BCE). Such disputes and interventions show that priests cannot be treated simply as a branch of civic administration. Rather, priests were officials with a special relationship and commitment to their office and deity, who would, if necessary, seek outside support for their cult.

Other religious experts. In addition to civic priesthoods there was a wide range of other religious experts. A story in Herodotus (7.140–44; 8.51–53) depicts such people in action. Before Xerxes' invasion of Greece, fear was mounting as to the likelihood of successful Greek resistance to Persia. The Athenians sent religious envoys *(theopropoi)* to consult the oracle of Apollo at Delphi. The mouthpiece of Apollo was a woman, the Pythia (this cross-gender priesthood was perhaps felt to be appropriate because of the way that Apollo was supposed to possess the Pythia). She uttered an oracle that advised the Athenians to flee to the ends of the world. The envoys were reluctant to accept this advice and returned as supplicants to Apollo (*not* to the Pythia), asking for a more favorable outcome. They took the second oracle back to Athens and presented it at a meeting of the assembly. There then occurred much debate as to the correct meaning of the oracle: was the "wooden wall" that would protect Athens a literal wooden wall around the Acropolis, or was it (metaphorically) ships? And why was the island of Salamis called "divine"? Old men argued one thing, the *chrēsmologoi* (professional interpreters of oracles) argued another. However, the *chrēsmologoi* were not official functionaries, and it is striking that despite the authority that they must have claimed, their interpretation of the oracle was rejected by the assembly in favor of the one proposed by the politician Themistocles (ships). The Athenians therefore prepared to resist Persia and to

fight at Salamis. Some, however, stuck to a different interpretation of the oracle: stewards of the sanctuary and others died fighting to preserve the Acropolis within its wooden wall (see further Divination and Prophecy and Religion and Politics).

At a level that is less visible in our texts, there were also other itinerant figures, whose authority was disputable. According to Plato, "vagrant priests and diviners [*manteis*] go to the doors of the wealthy and, as if they possessed a power provided to them from the gods because of their sacrifices and incantations, they persuade the wealthy person that they can remedy with rejoicings and religious celebrations any injustice that the wealthy man himself or his ancestors may have committed, and if the wealthy man wishes to harm some enemy they say that at little cost they will harm a just man as easily as an unjust one with some invocations and spells (which they say they do by persuading the gods to serve them)" (*Republic* 2.364b–c). This depiction of itinerant priests and diviners is deeply hostile (part of an argument that true justice and virtue cannot be bought), but such people were sometimes considered reputable by the state (which did occasionally grant honors to a *mantis*), although more often they served private individuals. From the archaic period onward, there existed specialists in religious initiations who initiated people into various elective cults (such as those called Bacchic and Orphic). Another area where the presence of unofficial personnel was both normal and problematic was that of dream interpretation. Artemidorus, the author of the one surviving ancient Greek dream book, says: "I have rubbed shoulders for many years with the much despised diviners of the marketplace. People who assume a holier-than-thou attitude and who raise their eyebrows in a superior fashion dismiss them as beggars, charlatans, and buffoons; but I have ignored their disparagement. Rather, in the different cities and festivals of Greece, Asia, and Italy and in the largest and most populous of islands I have patiently listened to old dreams and their consequences" (1 pref.; cf. 5 pref.).

Outside the framework provided by the polis, religious personnel had a problematic status, respected by some, rejected by others as frauds and charlatans. Some sense of these debates is given, for example, by Lucian in his *Alexander or the False Prophet*. Lucian describes Alexander of Abonuteichos, the founder of a new healing cult of a sacred snake called Glycon or the "New Asclepius," as an impostor and charlatan; inscriptions, coins, and religious sculpture show that the cult made a large impact, spread far beyond its place of origin, and outlived its founder by a considerable time.

BIBL.: S. B. Aleshire, "The Demos and the Priests," in *Ritual, Finance, Politics: Democratic Accounts Presented to D. M. Lewis* (ed. R. G. Osborne and Simon Hornblower; Oxford, 1994), 325–37. Beate Dignas, *Economy of the Sacred in Hellenistic and Roman Asia Minor* (Oxford, 2002). Wilhelm Dittenberger (ed.), *Sylloge inscriptionum graecarum* (3rd ed.;

Leipzig, 1915–24). M. B. Hatzopoulos, *Macedonian Institutions under the Kings* (Athens, 1996). Uta Kron, "Priesthoods, Dedications, and Euergetism: What Part Did Religion Play in the Political and Social Status of Greek Women?" in *Religion and Power in the Ancient Greek World* (ed. Pontus Hellström and Brita Alroth; Boreas 24; Uppsala, 1996), 139–82. R. Meiggs and D. Lewis, *A Selection of Greek Historical Inscriptions to the End of the Fifth Century BC* (rev. ed.; Oxford, 1988). Robert Parker, *Athenian Religion: A History* (Oxford, 1996), 56–66, 125–27, 129. S. R. F. Price, *Religions of the Ancient Greeks* (Cambridge, 1999), 67–76, 114. F. Sokolowski, *Lois sacrées de l'Asie Mineure* (Paris, 1955). Idem, *Lois sacrées des cités grecques* (Paris, 1969).   S.R.F.P.

Etruria

Ancient sources on Etruscan priesthoods are very scarce, the sole exception being literary, epigraphical, and archeological evidence concerning the most characteristic priests of Etruria, the *haruspices* (Latin *haruspex*, Etruscan *natis* or *netśvis*). This is largely due to their importance in Roman political life. It seems that the young members of the great Etruscan aristocratic families destined to the priesthood received, while still at home, instruction in the *disciplina Etrusca,* as our sources call the corpus of the haruspical doctrines. At an unknown date, probably no earlier than the 4th century BCE, the cities belonging to the Etruscan religious league of *XII populi* (Twelve Peoples) created a *collegium LX haruspicum* (College of Sixty *Haruspices*), headed by *magistri.* This was established near the temple of the Tarquinii, the leading family of Tarquinia, perhaps where tradition placed the miraculous birth of the mythical founder of the *disciplina Etrusca,* a prodigious child named Tages. Marble fragments of the Latin calendars and lists of magistrates of the *collegium* have been discovered in the area of the temple: these possibly were carved during the reign of the emperor Claudius (41–54 CE), who tried to censure the continuance of the *collegium* following the decline of the Etruscan ruling class after the Roman conquest of Etruria (Tacitus, *Annals* 11.15). *Haruspices* were still active at the beginning of the 5th century CE, and Latin texts of haruspical doctrines were still circulating in 6th-century CE Constantinople.

Many Etruscan inscriptions (4th–2nd centuries BCE) and archeological evidence provide us with a few pieces of information on other Etruscan priesthoods. They also make it clear how difficult it is to decode Etruscan religious offices when we have no Latin sources to help us. There is general consensus that we should accept Varro's equation (1st century BCE; quoted by Servius, *ad Aeneid* 12.538) of the Etruscan office of *cepen* with the Roman office of *cupencus* (priest). *Cepen* was known also in the more complex form of *marunucva cepen,* that is, "*cepen* of the group of the *maru*": the title *maru*

An Etruscan *haruspex*. Statuette in the Vatican Museums. *Alinari/Art Resource, New York*

corresponds to the name of certain Umbrian magistrates called *maro,* whose functions were possibly identical to those of the Latin *aedilis,* thus pointing to a magistrate in charge of public works, including temples. An Etruscan inscription (Pallottino 1968: 131) discloses the existence of specialized priesthoods, such as those of *paca* and *cavqa* (Bacchus and Sol), and possibly of a female priesthood with the title *hatrencu.* Archeology suggests the existence of an Etruscan priesthood that practiced the same rites as the Roman augurs and defined the nature of sacred and nonsacred space. Finally, several imperial inscriptions by men of senatorial or equestrian rank who boasted of Etruscan origin attest to the existence of a *praetor Etruriae.* This office was probably a Roman restoration, after a long lapse, of the priestly official of the earlier league of the *XII populi,* appointed, according to the tradition, every year in the "federal" sanctuary of the *Fanum Voltumnae apud Volsinios.* Most likely, the restoration was undertaken by either Augustus or Claudius. The *praetores Etruriae* survived into the 4th century CE, performing old ceremonies in combination with new rituals of the imperial cult.

BIBL.: B. Liou, *Praetores etruriae XV populorum* (Brussels, 1969). M. Pallottino, *Testimonia linguae etruscae* (2nd ed.; Florence, 1968). F. Roncalli, "Carbasinis voluminibus implicati libri: Osservazioni sul liber linteus di Zagabria," *Jahrbuch des deutschen archäologischen Instituts* 95 (1980): 227–64. M. Torelli, *Elogia Tarquiniensia* (Florence, 1975). Idem, "Etruria principes disciplinam doceto: Il mito normativo dello specchio di Tuscania," in *Studia Tarquiniensia* (Rome, 1988), 109–18.   M.T.

Rome

Numa Pompilius, second king of Rome after Romulus, brought religious organization to Rome, according to tradition, by instituting the augurship, the pontificate, the flaminates of individual gods, the cult of Vesta, the *salii,* and a lunar calendar (Ennius, *Annals* 113–19, ed. Skutsch; Livy 1.18–20). The details are spurious (*pontifices* and *augurs* were probably Etruscan in origin; Vesta came from Alba Longa), but the picture of a miscellany is accurate. Roman religion was an amalgam of native Latin, Etruscan, and Italic elements, and its institutional organization, from the time it can first be discerned in the 3rd century BCE, reflects the diversity of its origins. Two general principles underpinned the system. Religious authority lay in the same men who controlled the chief social and political institutions: the heads of families *(patresfamilias)* and their civic counterparts, the magistrates and "enrolled fathers" *(patres conscripti)* of the Roman senate. Their main, indeed sole, religious duty was to maintain peace with the gods *(pax deorum)* on behalf of their constituents—the family and the *populus Romanus*—through the public observance of ritual.

Within the public and private spheres the distribution of authority was different. Whereas in matters of the *familia* the jurisdiction of the *paterfamilias* was all-encompassing, religious power in the public realm was compartmentalized and diffuse. Since Rome had no separate priestly caste, religious and political power became concentrated in the same hands (Cicero, *On His House* 1.1); the parceling out of specialized religious authority within the priestly magisterial class thus prevented any one person or priesthood from acquiring undue influence.

Although shared by the same men, magisterial and sacerdotal competencies were distinct. Magistrates regularly performed priestly tasks (sacrifices, vows, dedications of temples, taking of auspices), whereas priests had no executive powers (except in certain cases narrowly prescribed by their priestly *ius* [right] as with the pontifices and burial practice) and never acted as magistrates. Although regularly consulted as experts in their areas of sacred law, priests merely advised the magistrates and the senate, who alone had the authority to act for the *res publica.* Conversely, much cult activity of priests centered on rites of the archaic community that ignored the political structures of the republic. Magistrates ascended the same career ladder of short-term political offices (the *cursus honorum*) and differed from each other mainly in how far they climbed. Priests held only one major priesthood, normally for life, and enjoyed religious authority only within their specialized realms.

The republic. When the last king was expelled from Rome (ca. 510 BCE), some of the king's sacral functions devolved upon a *rex sacrorum* (king of sacred rites), who ranked first among priests in prestige (Festus, in *Glossaria Latina* 299) but who was barred from holding political office and who, like the *flamines,* was subordinate to the *pontifex maximus.* The *flamines* were anomalous in being individually tied to specific gods—three to major deities (Dumézil's archetypal Indo-European triad of Jupiter, Mars, and Quirinus), twelve to lesser gods (some agricultural, others toponymic, most obscure, two unknown; Varro, *On the Latin Language* 7.45). Other priests were attached to particular festivals (as the *luperci* to the Lupercalia) or to specific areas of competence (as the *fetiales* to treaties and declarations of war). Most were organized into colleges, within which each member exercised equal and independent authority. The pontificate was exceptional in providing for a leader *(pontifex maximus)* who held jurisdiction over other priests (the Vestal Virgins as well as the *rex sacrorum* and the *flamines*) and in including within its purview public duties, such as keeping an annual record of events, and areas of private behavior, such as adoption law, that might seem to fall outside the sphere of public religion.

Of the four "more illustrious" *(ampliora)* priesthoods, next to the pontiffs in prestige were the augurs *(augures),* who interpreted the doctrine concerning auspices. Then came the *decemviri* (ten men; originally *duoviri* [two men] and later *quindecimviri* [fifteen men]) *sacris faciundis* (concerned with sacrifices), who alone had the right to consult the Sibylline Books of oracular prophecy, and the *septemviri epulonum* (seven men concerned with feasts), in charge of ritual feasts for the gods. Originally the major priesthoods were exclusive clubs: the number of places in each college was finite, and new members were recruited by cooption. The result was a patrician monopoly on sacerdotal office until 300 BCE, when a *lex Ogulnia* opened membership in the pontificate and the augurate to plebeians.

The *pontifex maximus,* originally chosen within the college by its members, from around 250 BCE was elected by a special assembly of seventeen of the thirty-five Roman voting tribes from a slate of three candidates presented by the college. In 104/103 BCE a *lex Domitia* extended this procedure to all the major priesthoods. Within the pontifical college the *rex sacrorum, flamines,* and Vestal Virgins were neither coopted nor elected but were "taken" *(capi)* by the *pontifex maximus* from among the eligible candidates (by what process we do not know).

Beneath the four great priesthoods, several lesser "brotherhoods" *(sodalitates)* dedicated to specific cult

EX DONO · DVCIS · SFORTIAE · SFORTIAE

Tomb portrait of a *gallus,* a priest of Magna Mater, 2nd century CE. The *galli* were eunuchs, reputedly self-castrated; various features of this image (the musical instruments, the thongs for self-flagellation) allude to their ritual practices. *German Archaeological Institute, Rome*

tasks or locations continued to recruit new members by cooption well into the empire. Among them were the *salii* (two groups of twelve "leapers" associated with the Palatine and Quirinal hills in Rome), the *luperci* (two groups of unknown number named after Roman clans, celebrants of the Lupercalia in mid-February), the *fratres arvales* (twelve Arval Brethren devoted to the cult of the Dea Dia at her grove outside Rome), and the mysterious *sodales Titii.*

Etruscan *haruspices,* foreign specialists in divination (especially extispicy, the examination of entrails), were summoned from Etruria by the senate when needed to interpret prodigies and portents; by the end of the republic they constituted a formal college of sixty members (CIL 6.32439) and under the emperor Claudius came under supervision of the pontiffs (Tacitus, *Annals* 11.15).

The empire. "I was *pontifex maximus,* augur, *quindecimvir sacris faciundis, septemvir epulonum, frater arvalis, sodalis Titius,* fetialis." So were the emperor Augustus in the autobiographical account published after his death, listing his priestly offices in descending order of prestige (*Res gestae* 7.3). Elsewhere in the same document he recorded his refusal to accept the position of

pontifex maximus before the death (in 13 BCE) of its incumbent, who had usurped it thirty years earlier (10.2). Scrupulous in matters of form, the emperor was less reluctant to tamper with the substance of the traditional organization of religion. By assuming membership in all the major priestly colleges, Augustus consolidated in the office of *princeps* the religious authority that had previously been spread throughout the system. Having obtained in 29 BCE the privilege of naming candidates for election to the priestly colleges (a privilege his successors retained), he began exercising his accumulated religious power under the mantle of *pontifex maximus* in 12 BCE and thus furthered the transformation of the office, initiated by Caesar half a century earlier, into something resembling that of a high priest. By converting part of his Palatine house into public property (tradition required the *pontifex maximus* to reside in a *domus publica* [public house]) and incorporating a shrine of Vesta within it, Augustus linked the public hearth of the state and the official home of the chief priest to the emperor's residence on the Palatine. Henceforth none but the emperor could become *pontifex maximus;* all did, shortly after succession, until Gratian in (probably) 379 CE renounced the title.

Statue of a Vestal Virgin, in the Roman Forum, with characteristic Vestal hairdo. The temple of Antoninus and Faustina is in the background. *SEF/Art Resource, New York*

Although traditional priestly authority was now concentrated in the *princeps,* the system itself was opened up to wider participation by all levels of society. Competition for membership in one of the prestigious four major colleges (comprising 83 positions in all) remained intense among leading senators, but other priesthoods (some 160) were distributed between the equestrian and senatorial orders, and new urban and municipal organizations provided various opportunities for others to engage in the civic-religious enterprise.

In 7 BCE, Augustus reorganized the districts *(regiones)* and wards *(vici)* of Rome and grafted a new cult of the *lares Augusti* and the *genius Augusti* (essentially the ancestors and personal spirit of himself) onto the traditional cult maintained by block captains *(magistri vici)* at the crossroads of the city wards *(compitalicia).* Outside Rome in the towns of the western empire, local colleges (usually of six, hence *seviri*) and orders of Augustales enabled wealthy freedmen, who were legally barred from holding municipal office, to parade their civic service from a prestigious public platform. (Apparently comparable but more obscure local groups of *Mercuriales, Apollinares,* and *Minervales* in Italy and of *Cereales* in North Africa provided similar outlets for civic benefaction beneath a respectable umbrella of religion.) Despite the implications of their name, the Augustales had no special responsibilities for the imperial cult beyond those of any public official. Worship of the emperor and his deified predecessors, although a unifying feature of Roman religion across the empire,

was not propagated by any organized cult but fell rather within the general religious responsibility of the civic and military leaders and took different forms in different places.

Outside Rome, priestly authority was exercised by the chief civic and military officials (governors of provinces, commanders of legionary camps, local magistrates) and the elected leaders *(magistri)* of private associations *(collegia),* who performed the liturgy on behalf of the members. Roman colonies had *flamines divi Julii, pontifices,* and *augures* on the Roman model, with similar privileges and responsibilities (*ILS* 6087 §66), except that local pontiffs and augurs in the provinces were subject to the authority of the governor. In municipalities *(municipia)* and towns without Roman status, we find *pontifices, augures,* and *haruspices* besides local priests, but the opportunities for priestly office seem to have been fewer and less diverse than at Rome. Other cities of the empire had variously similar religious systems in which local priesthoods more often served as temporary offices in a civic career than as lifelong religious obligations.

Outside Rome. Although fundamental to the system, the republican principle of distributing religious authority among a class of male magistrate-priests was not rigidly imposed upon foreign forms of worship, once accepted by the state. Foreign gods were always marked as separate, however, and participation in their rites by Roman citizens was occasionally restricted. According to tradition, the Greek rites founded by Hercules at the Ara Maxima in the Forum Boarium (the only foreign cult supposedly adopted by Romulus) were maintained by two families, until the extinction of one (312 BCE) caused the duties to be entrusted to public slaves (Livy 1.7; 9.29). When an oracle in the Sibylline Books promised victory over Hannibal if the Idaean Mother (Cybele) were brought to Rome, the senators welcomed her with a temple on the Palatine (194 BCE) and annual games (the *ludi Megalenses;* Livy 29.10–11), but they limited the public activity of the Phrygian priests, forbade Roman citizens from participating in the rites (Dionysius of Halicarnassus, *Roman Antiquities* 2.19), and set up their own "brotherhoods" *(sodalitates)* to cultivate her worship (Cicero, *On Old Age* 45). A few years later (186 BCE), when the senate moved to suppress the ecstatic cult of Bacchus (Dionysus), the size and form of Bacchic congregations were brought under the control of the urban praetor (*ILS* 18). Similarly, the Greek priestesses who tended the temple of Ceres on the Aventine worked under the supervision of the plebeian *aediles* (Cicero, *Pro Balbo* 55).

In fact, outside civic cults, the character of priests and other religious personnel varied widely—as well as being significantly different from that of the official priests of Rome. The most striking difference is that some (though by no means all) held their religious office as a full-time profession, a marker of identity, even vocation;

some wore a distinctive religious dress. The Phrygian priests imported with the Great Mother, for example, were known as *galli;* these were eunuchs, and were often satirized in Roman writing (see, e.g., Juvenal, *Satires* 6.511–21) as wild and frenzied, effeminate, bejeweled, and sex crazed. The cult of Isis included a variety of specialized religious roles (for women as well as men); but the characteristic Isiac priest was shaven headed, dressed in white, and could play a pastoral role to members of the cult (see, e.g., Apuleius, *Golden Ass* 11.21). The majority of the priests outside civic cults were of relatively low or marginal social status. But in the 4th century CE, some senators came to fill these roles, often alongside traditional, official priesthoods.

BIBL.: Mary Beard and John North (eds.), *Pagan Priests* (Ithaca, 1990). Jerzy Linderski, *Roman Questions* (Stuttgart, 1995). John Scheid, *Religion et piété à Rome* (Paris, 1985). Georg Wissowa, *Religion und Kultus der Römer* (2nd ed.; Munich, 1912). J.B.

Christianity

The traditional debate about the origin of ordained ministers in the Christian tradition centered on whether the terms *episkopos* (bishop) and *presbyteros* (elder/presbyter) in the New Testament were simply alternative ways of speaking of the same role in early Christian communities or, rather, referred to quite distinct offices from the outset. The path to answering this question has taken scholars in several directions. At the end of the 19th century, scholars began to believe that those in charge of the churches founded by the apostle Paul would have emerged on the basis of their possession of particular spiritual gifts rather than by formal appointment to office. This led many in the 20th century to conclude that all Christian leadership was at first charismatic in character and only later superseded by a pattern of elected officials. Others, in contrast, espoused the conviction that Jewish models of synagogue governance would originally have held sway in Christian congregations, perhaps even in Pauline churches. From that model later derived a hierarchical structure with three distinct categories: bishop, elder, and deacon.

Recent scholarship, however, has begun to abandon the search for a single archetypal form and to accept that the evidence is better served by presuming the existence of varied patterns of leadership in different early Christian communities and also of different influences in bringing those patterns about, among them the disposition of officers in the pagan *collegia*, the organization of the Greco-Roman household, and the model of the Jewish synagogue. The varied forms of Christian leadership would have included those recognized as such because of their possession of particular *charismata*, especially prophecy and teaching; those who offered hospitality to the house-churches (communities of believers organized in or around a single-family dwelling);

and those elected to office by a local congregation, the latter especially when those with obvious charismatic gifts were lacking or there was dissension within the community over who should lead it. Sometimes leadership may have been shared between those from two or more of these groups, for example, the patron and several prophets. Similarly, while in some cases leadership may have been exercised by a corporate body for a considerable period of time, in other churches a single individual may have emerged as the principal leader at quite an early stage, with others functioning only in an advisory capacity.

Whether such leadership was from the first restricted to men or at least in some cases included women has been a much debated topic in recent years. An honored position was granted to widows in early Christian communities; women functioned as prophets at least in some fringe groups; and Eastern sources speak of female deacons, later called deaconesses; but it is unclear whether women exercised any greater leadership roles in the New Testament period.

The original debate about the relationship between *episkopoi* and *presbyteroi* in the New Testament has also taken a new turn in recent years. Although the dominant view has been that the two titles were at first synonyms, several scholars have suggested that presbyters originally may not have been church officers in the same sense that an *episkopos* was. Just as the terms *diakonos* and *diakonia* can be used both in a general, seemingly nontechnical sense to refer to "ministers" and "ministry" in early sources and at the same time more specifically to denote particular officials called "deacons" and the "diaconate," so too *presbyteroi* seems to be capable of several meanings: its normal Greek sense of "older people," to whom societal norms would expect respect to be paid because of their age; perhaps also a more specifically Christian sense of "those senior in the faith," that is, those who had been converted longer and therefore were deserving of respect for that reason; and a third more specific, technical sense of "elders" as a council whose opinion and judgment were respected in the Christian community.

Be that as it may, before the end of the 2nd century the transition to a threefold leadership structure in each local church of a bishop, presbyters, and deacons does seem to have been made everywhere in mainstream Christianity. At first, the presbyters clearly formed a college of advisers around the bishop, but there are signs that within the next fifty years they were regarded more as his subordinates, who might assist him in his various functions and even on occasion deputize for him. While the original role of deacons remains unclear, deacons too eventually became the bishop's officers and, influenced partly by a new attribution of their origin to the seven "Men of Spirit" described in Acts 6, were concerned chiefly with ministering to the needs of the poor and sick in the Christian congregation.

309

The 3rd century is also witness to a widespread tendency to acknowledge the bishop as a priest—a new development in the Christian tradition. With rare exceptions, Christians previously had restricted sacerdotal language to Christ himself, as the great high priest, and to the church, as God's priestly people. Presbyters also began to be thought of as sharing in the bishop's priesthood in some way, and deacons were described either as the equivalent of the Levites of the Hebrew Bible (see Religious Personnel) or as forming a third order within the priesthood. This sacerdotal imagery became standard in the 4th century.

Nevertheless, ordained ministers were not the only figures of authority in early Christianity. Although formal leadership of Christian communities may have passed into their hands at quite an early date, others continued to retain vestiges of spiritual influence over believers, which sometimes brought them into conflict with the ordained. While the episcopate attempted to subsume into itself the ministries formerly exercised by teachers and prophets, it was not always successful in this, and some Christians still tended to listen instead to others who claimed to have received divine gifts. Similarly, those who had suffered torture and imprisonment for their faith during times of persecution were held in high esteem and thought to possess various powers, and those who had been put to death were venerated as martyrs and invoked in prayer for their assistance in the lives of believers. When persecution finally ceased in the 4th century, their place as sources of spiritual teaching and authority was taken by the holy men and women who at that time went out into deserts to undertake lives of extreme asceticism.

BIBL.: Paul F. Bradshaw, Maxwell E. Johnson, and L. Edward Phillips (eds.), *The Apostolic Tradition: A Commentary* (Minneapolis, 2002). Hans von Campenhausen, *Ecclesiastical Authority and Spiritual Power in the Church of the First Three Centuries* (Stanford, 1969). Mark Edwards, "The Development of Office in the Early Church," in *The Early Christian World* (ed. Philip F. Esler; New York, 2000), 1.316–29. Richard Hanson, "Office and Concept of Office in the Early Church," in *Studies in Christian Antiquity* (ed. Richard Hanson; Edinburgh, 1985), 117–43.   P.F.B.

Religious Organizations and Bodies

Introduction

In 1924, Arthur Darby Nock drew attention to the "historical importance of cult-associations." At that time, the process of discovering papyri and inscriptions was still going on. According to Nock, these findings revealed a world of private cults alongside the public worship in temples. The members of these cults regarded themselves as a kind of family and "provided an opportunity for the evolution of new religious ideas" (Nock 1924: 105). A hitherto unknown social and religious domain of domestic/voluntary/private religions added substantially to our knowledge of the history of ancient religions, as is confirmed by recent studies (Kloppenborg and Wilson 1996; van Nijf 1997).

The types of internal organization of these associations and their external relation to the temples and priesthoods are known only by chance and are certainly not always the same. In some cases we merely hear that people were meeting in temples in order to share a sacrificial meal, as in the Syro-Canaanite culture, where these meetings were called *marzēaḥ*, known to Israelite prophets who strongly rejected them as idolatry (Amos 6.7; Jer. 16.5). In Egypt we have extensive evidence. Demotic (and Greek) papyri of the Hellenistic age record the statutes of religious associations: the election of a president for one year; dues; provisions for meetings; rules of conduct; provisions for mutual assistance in cases of lawsuits, detention, and debt slavery; regulations for funerals and fines. The statutes were adopted by the members, and the association was sanctioned by the Ptolemaic officials. In these contracts the place of meeting was a public temple (de Cenival 1972). In Greece and Asia Minor, associations mostly met in private houses. Archeology has yielded evidence that private houses were turned entirely or partly into a sacred space (documented by White 1996–97). Members of these associations often belonged to lower classes. Due only to the initiative of an owner of a house as a patron *(benefactor, euergetēs)* was an association established (Danker 1982).

A chapter in Justinian's *Digests* entitled "De collegiis et corporibus" (47.22) and composed in 533 CE transmits legal opinions and rulings on associations deriving from the writings of the pagan jurists Gaius, Aelius Marcianus, and Domitius Ulpianus from the 2nd and 3rd centuries CE. As Gaius declared in his commentary on the XII Tables in the 2nd century CE, the citizens of Greek and Roman cities were in a remarkable degree free in establishing private associations: "A statute [*lex*] gives the members of an association [*sodales*] the power to enter into any agreement [*pactio*] they like, so long as they do not contravene the public statute [*lex publica*]." Gaius added that this statute appeared to have been adopted from the law of Solon, which says: "If the people of a city or the clansmen or the members of the sacred mysteries(?) or sailors or those dining together [*syssitoi*] or those providing for their burial [*homotaphoi*] or members of the same club [*thiasotai*] or who combine to engage in some enterprise or for profit: anything that they agreed between themselves will be valid [*kyrion*] unless forbidden by public statutes [*demosia grammata*]" (*Digests* 47.22.4). This legal provision accounted for the flourishing of religious associations in the Hellenistic and Roman worlds. Here was a legal form that was available for religious communities traveling from the East to the West. Adherents of Sarapis, Isis, Mithras, Dionysus, YHWH, and other gods established corporate bodies by adopting that form. Yet the same sources also point to a restriction: the association had to comply with the public order. In the purview of the Roman law, the history of associations was often a history of conflicts.

When Dionysian rituals, the Bacchanalia, spread clandestinely in Italy, Roman officials suppressed them in 186 BCE (Livy 39.8–22). In the 1st century BCE, *collegia* were suppressed due to their involvement in civil strife. According to Suetonius, Julius Caesar (49–44

BCE) dissolved all associations "besides those that were long ago established" (42.3). Whether a special *lex Julia* on *collegia* existed, the criterion for legitimacy under Roman law was *antiquitas*. New associations had to ask for permission. A *collegium Symphoniacorum* in the 1st century CE proudly announced that "the senate has given permission to hold meetings, to be called to assembly, and to be mustered in accordance with the Julian law by authority of Augustus for the sake of the games" (Arangio-Ruiz 1968: 38). Other inscriptions contain the same formula *quibus licet ex senatus consulto* (ILS 335, 1164, 1367, 4966). But altogether, the number of official recognitions is surprisingly low. Were all associations lacking an official recognition of the senate actually forbidden? An inscription from Lanuvium from 136 CE containing the regulations of a society of Diana and Antinous points to a different solution. It refers to a *senatus consultum* sanctioning an entire category of *collegia*: "Clause from a decree of the senate of the Roman people. Who shall be permitted to assemble, to come together, and to have an association [*Quib(us coire co)venire collegiumq(ue) habere liceat*]: those who wish to make a monthly contribution for funerals may assemble in an association [*collegium*] of that description, provided that they do not assemble more than once a month under the pretext of the said association for the purpose of making contribution whereby dead persons may be buried" (Arangio-Ruiz 1968: 35).

There also existed a certain type of *collegium* that legally could be established without prior endorsement of the senate. The existence of such a type is confirmed by the lawyer Aelius Marcianus (early 3rd century CE). From his writings the opinion was extracted that "the lower orders [*tenuiores*] are allowed to pay a small monthly fee, provided that they meet only once a month, lest an unlawful association [*collegium illicitum*] be created under this guise. And the deified Severus stated in a rescript that this applies not only to Rome but also to Italy and the provinces. There is, however, no ban on assembly for religious purposes, so long as there is no contravention of the *senatus consultum*, which prohibits unlawful *collegia* [*quo illicita collegia arcentur*]" (*Digests* 47.22.1).

The contradiction that Christian associations were established with a hierarchy and property of their own in an age during which new associations were suppressed can be explained if they were regarded as associations of that type. A major witness in this regard is the church father Tertullian, who in his *Apology* defended Christians against the two main accusations: sacrilege (*crimen laesae religionis*; *Apology* 10–27) and high treason (*maiestas*; *Apology* 28–45). He emphasized that Christians were not a *factio illicita* (38.1) or a *coitio illicita* (39.20), but admits frankly: "We are a society [*corpus*] with a common religious feeling, unity of discipline, a common bond of hope" (39.1). Tertullian pre-sents the association as being like a *collegium tenuiorum*, although he does not mention a *senatus consultum*. Everybody contributes once in the month to a common chest, which is used not for banquets or drinking parties, "but to feed the poor and to bury them" (39.5–6). They call each other "brothers" and share property: "All is common among us—except our wives" (39.11). Tertullian assumed that an association described in these terms was not illicit—that indeed, Christian associations deserved to be recognized officially as part of a *religio licita* like Judaism (21.1). That recognition occurred in 313 CE, and in 380, Theodosius went a step further and recognized the church *in* the empire as the church *of* the empire.

BIBL.: Vincentius Arangio-Ruiz (ed.), *Fontes iuris romani antejustiniani* (Florence: Barbèra, 1968), 3.91–125: "Collegia." Françoise de Cenival, *Les associations religieuses en Égypte d'après les documents démotiques* (Cairo: L'institut français d'archéologie, 1972). Frederick W. Danker, *Benefactor: Epigraphic Study of a Graeco-Roman and New Testament Semantic Field* (St. Louis, Mo.: Clayton, 1982). Hermann Dessau, *Inscriptiones latinae selectae* (Berlin: Weidemann, 1892–1916), 2.2 chap. 15: "Tituli collegiorum." Wilhelm Dittenberger (ed.), *Sylloge inscriptionum graecarum* (3rd ed.; Leipzig: Hirzel, 1920), vol. 3.2.5: "Collegia et sodalitates sacrorum causa institutae." John S. Kloppenborg and Stephen G. Wilson, *Voluntary Associations in the Graeco-Roman World* (London: Routledge, 1996). Charles Michel, *Recueil d'inscriptions grecques* (Brussels: Lamertin, 1900), 757–813: "Phratries, Thiases, Corporations." Onno M. van Nijf, *The Civic World of Professional Associations in the Roman East* (Amsterdam: Gieben, 1997). Arthur Darby Nock, "The Historical Importance of Cult Associations," *Classical Review* 37 (1924): 105–9. L. Michael White, *The Social Origins of Christian Architecture,* vol. 1: *Building God's House in the Roman World: Architectural Adaptation among Pagans, Jews, and Christians;* vol. 2: *Texts and Monuments for the Christian Domus Ecclesiae in Its Environment* (Valley Forge, Pa.: Trinity, 1996–97). H.G.K.

Egypt

The Egyptian religious organization is characterized by a rather high degree of professionalism among the priesthood, accompanied by a differentiation of many specialized tasks. At the same time, professionalism and segregation of the priests were tempered by the Egyptian way of part-time employment. The priests were typically organized in so-called phyles and rotated monthly in service. This rotation was at first based on the civil calendar of thirty days each month, but it switched later (probably during the Middle Kingdom) to the lunar calendar. The probable reason for this was the wish to achieve a more equal distribution of the additional offerings associated with feasts based on the lunar phases.

During the Old Kingdom, a fine-grained separation

into five phyles, each with two subgroups, produced a complicated system with one individual serving every tenth month. Those groups also had specific names and special animal emblems. Similar names are attested in texts dealing with different parts of a ship's crew. It is still debated today whether the phyle designations developed out of the crew's working system.

Beginning with the Middle Kingdom, the Old Kingdom organization was simplified to a system of four basic phyles that were numbered (without name), so that every member of a phyle served three months a year in the temple. The ideal size of a phyle seems to have been twenty men. This system remained stable until the Ptolemaic period. Then, at the synod of Canopus (237 BCE), a fifth phyle honoring the reigning king was introduced by decree. We do not know much about what the part-time priests did the rest of the year. For some high-ranking people, membership in several phyles of a temple or at different temples is attested, which suggests that temple duties of one type or another would occupy them most of the year; but one has to presume that many of those at lower levels made a lay living for most of the year. Only some highly specialized ranks within the priestly hierarchy, normally connected with the necessity of special knowledge of restricted access, served on a nonrotating basis.

The temples were of varying size and importance, and smaller chapels were quite often subsumed under the authority of the larger institutions. During the New Kingdom, the most important temples were the temple of Amun at Karnak, the temple of Ptah at Memphis, and the temple of Re at Heliopolis. Their "households" had wide-sweeping economic importance, and many other institutions are said to be "provided for by them." Quite typically, the landholdings of the temples were not concentrated near their actual location but scattered all over the country. This had the advantage of providing access to different forms of cultivation appropriate to different ecological conditions; for example, vineyards could not tolerate the heat of southern Egypt but thrived in the Delta, so a temple producing its own wine needed some land in the Delta.

We glimpse in a few documents, mostly multilingual decrees of the Ptolemaic period, a system whereby temples themselves were hierarchically ranked. They mention a first, second, and third order of temples. Such a ranking might be dependent upon the size and importance of the temple, although it is unclear to what degree it was formalized institutionally.

At the head of the inner-temple administration in the larger temples was the governor and overseer of priests. At least during some periods of Egyptian history, the pharaoh installed a general overseer of prophets of Upper and Lower Egypt, so to speak a "secretary of religion" for the whole country. In smaller temples, the prophet, the Lesonis, and a body of the elders made the actual decisions.

Traditionally, scholars suppose that different and conflicting theological systems developed at the main religious centers. However, it is quite difficult to find actual conflicts of opinion. The general flexibility and adaptability of Egyptian religion helped to avoid clashes of a theological nature. From the beginning of historical times, the religious system of Heliopolis made a strong impact on all other centers, and it was common to identify the local gods with gods of the Heliopolitan ennead. Typically, because there were fewer local gods available than open slots in the Heliopolitan system, the local gods were often split into different cultic forms and different genealogical positions. For example, at Esna the local god Khnum in his different forms plays the roles of the Heliopolitan Re as well as the Heliopolitan Shu, son of Re. Local myths and traditions could exist side by side with Heliopolitan ones, and the two seldom really infringed upon each other. Peaceful coexistence is attested by mythological manuals that indicate the religious traditions of all nomes of Egypt without spelling out any judgments of their value. Even a document such as the so-called Monument of Memphite Theology is less a critique of the Heliopolitan system than an essay in interpreting and adapting it.

More important than possible local theological peculiarities were the specific local taboos and restrictions. Quite often, an animal sacred to people of one nome could be killed without religious problems in the neighboring one. But sometimes one nome provoked another by slaughtering its holy animals—thus instigating conflicts that could grow into small wars.

Some thought has to be given to the problem of whether the hermetic movement can be classified as a philosophical school and how it developed out of an amalgamation of Egyptian traditions and Greek popular philosophical notions. The clearest Egyptian forerunner is to be found in the so-called Book of Thoth, which features a dialogue between Thoth (the god of wisdom) and someone "loving knowledge" (a term that corresponds with Greek *philosophos*). The topics of this difficult and still largely unpublished composition are mainly centered on exhortations to learn and understand, combined with quite a bit of theology of profound complexity. It can be supposed that fusing this line of thinking with Greek popular philosophy led to the milieu that produced the Greek philosophical and theological writings known as the *Corpus Hermeticum*.

It is a long-debated point whether, in ancient Egypt, one can suppose a conflict between secular or military administration on the one hand and religious groups on the other hand. Some scholars suppose that the breakdown of the New Kingdom was brought about by the takeover of the priests. It certainly can be said that the period immediately after the end of the New Kingdom looks like the rule of priests in a theocratic system where all major decisions were made by oracles of the supreme god. The first prophets of Amun went as far as taking an abbreviated form of the royal titulary. However, this system is mostly attested for the region of Thebes, while other parts of Egypt seem to have been subject to military rule. Besides, it should not be forgotten that the ruling family of the first prophet of Amun had a military, not a religious, background, taking the title during a period of political unrest to back their power.

An interesting insight is provided by some Demotic romances (e.g., the Petubastis cycle) attested in manuscripts of Ptolemaic and Roman times but probably reflecting social reality of the late pharaonic period. There, the normal system is that the land is fractured into many small polities. Each is led by a warrior-hero. But at the same time, he also has a religious background, and his elite soldiers are explicitly designated as priests.

Cult associations are positively attested since the Saite period, although some scholars have proposed their existence in the New Kingdom. Their head is normally designated as "general," which does not imply military duties but means simply "overseer of the multitude." Membership in an association meant an obligation to deliver money, food, drinks, and aromatic resins, thus participating in the expenses for the festivals and offerings. Membership in those associations seems to have been quite mandatory for certain classes of temple associates. There was strong social pressure against people trying to avoid the membership. Among the members, a group solidarity was expected. Behaving against the established norms, for example, by calumniating a fellow associate or giving testimony in court against him, entailed punishment according to fixed rates of payment.

Besides the temple cult, private individuals had the opportunity to organize a mortuary cult. One or several persons, often members of the household, were chosen to perform the liturgies and offerings at the tomb. They were called "priests of the Ka." For their work, they were remunerated with the income from fields. Such a system was designed to ensure an ongoing service regardless of the continuity of the bloodline. In some cases, the actual contracts for this arrangement are preserved. Although the title in this form later lost popularity, similar systems persisted into the latest periods. Then, it was mostly the minor staff of the temples (especially the doorkeepers) who were active during their off-duty time, performing the service at the tombs. In this function, they were mostly called "water pourers," because libations were the most important part of the offering service for the dead.

At least for some periods of Egyptian culture, archeological evidence points to the existence of burial associations, where larger tomb structures were used by a group of people who had contributed equally to the endowment. In other times, normally during periods of more centralized political power, it was typical for high officials to provide a burial for their retainers within secondary shafts of their own tomb structure, whereas the family of the retainers went into lower-class burial grounds.

BIBL.: Françoise de Cenival, *Les associations religieuses en Égypte* (Cairo, 1972). Ben Haring, *Divine Households* (Leiden, 1997). Ann Macy Roth, *Egyptian Phyles in the Old Kingdom* (Chicago, 1991).   J.F.Q.

Mesopotamia

Personal religion and piety are subjects on which the cuneiform texts shed little light; we are forced to read between the lines of economic documents, private letters, and certain literary texts in order to catch a glimpse of their existence. The same cloud of uncertainty hangs over our knowledge of religious associations. It seems reasonable to assume that religious associations might have existed, since shared rituals create a formative experience in the structuring of the community and the maintenance of its identity. In turn, the community requires the performance of certain rituals that sustain and regularly regenerate communal reality.

Nevertheless, evidence for such rituals is lacking in the ancient literature. One problem is the result of modern Assyriological categorization, which assumes that all individuals whose duties and obligations lay within the sphere of religion must have been professional personnel. Part of the problem thus lies in the definition of basic terms. Not only were there religious specialists whose profession was intimately connected with the temple or with other religious functions, but there were also nonprofessionals who participated in temple rituals. How should we define a layperson who carried out religious rites? There seems to have been a spectrum of relationships between morals and deities. For instance, hereditary offices (i.e., prebends) could be bought and sold for profit. These endowed an individual with the right to an income from the temple in return for the performance of services connected with the cult, ranging from bread baking and the delivery of fish for the divine banquet to cultic duties.

Two institutions might be considered in a discussion of religious associations. The first comprised members of a particular religious group whose religious duties are unknown. The second consisted of lay individuals who carried out certain unknown rites in the temple, although whether they should be thought of as members of any group is uncertain.

Three letters and one administrative document refer to the first group as "sons of the god(s) and goddess(es)." Various scholars have interpreted this expression as describing the members of religious communities. These references are found in texts from the Old Babylonian period (18th–17th centuries BCE), when there is evidence of the importance of the religious practices of home and family, such as those surrounding the family (i.e., personal) god. In Akkadian, the designation *son/daughter of* does not necessarily imply any blood relationship but is a commonly used expression identifying membership in a group or profession. Two of the references say "those members [bound to him] by oath of his god" and "one [bound to me] by oath of my god." Very little can be said about these persons. They apparently dwelled outside the city, in the hinterland, for some unknown reason. It might be assumed that they had withdrawn there to live together in companionship and to build a cooperative life.

While the term *son of the god/goddess* is understood as referring to a member of a religious group, the term *daughter of the god/goddess* is interpreted as designating a priestess, as in the case of examples of this term in texts found in the city of Mari in Syria. In the 1st millennium, only traces of the female "daughters of a god" occur, usually among women known to have had some religious role. One text speaks of them as "reverent, circumspect, mindful of virtue, the daughters of the gods always." While the 1st-millennium exorcistic compendium Shurpu also mentions the "daughters of the gods" in a similar context, the commentary on that word explains the term by "his sister," apparently assuming that it is the feminine counterpart to the term *son of the god,* although this interpretation is sometimes dismissed as erroneous.

The second institution, *parṣu* (cultic office), concerned individuals who had a contractual relationship with the temple. Although documents and letters mention cultic activities performed by laypersons (in one case, a *nadītu,* a woman who, although she could be married, lived in a separate female community) in the rites of the temple, it was not until the discovery of the large archive from ancient Sippar that we learned more about these activities. The archive's documents record ritual and cultic activities performed by men and women under the supervision of a priest named Ur-Utu, who was the *galamaḫ,* the head of the GALA (lamentation priests) of the goddess Annunitum. The archive includes a group of tablets—consisting of one hundred contracts and thirty-two letters—concerned with the economic and financial implications of these cultic and ritual activities at the Annunitum temple. The texts reveal details of the administration of the *parṣu* rites, the persons involved, the income accrued, and the distribution of the profits to the temple, the palace, and the temple personnel. Contracts record the debt from the performance of the rite, the performer, and the guarantor. We know only the names of the rites performed and that they were all related to the Annunitum temple: *rēdûtum* (performed exclusively by women), *ḫarimūtum* (by men), *muqabbirūtum, mubabbilūtum, qulmû, kunukkum,* NA₄.GAL.ᵈUTU. One of these rites, *muqabbirūtum,* might be related to funerary activities. What undermines their identification as activities characteristic of a religious as-

sociation is that no performer is mentioned twice in the archive, as if an individual could participate only once in these rites. Sometimes a husband and wife perform the *parṣu* rites together. Similar cultic offices belonged to individuals in other cities. Letters from other archives provide further evidence of this practice, and one reads of complaints regarding the confiscation of cultic offices.

In the 1st millennium, cultic offices were also held by lay individuals, and complaints are voiced again when individuals are deprived of them—as with, for instance, the Babylonian Job: "They have let another take my cultic offices and appointed an outsider in my rites" (*Ludlul bēl nēmeqi* 1.103–4). In the late 1st millennium, under Hellenistic rule, the term *mār bēl parṣi* designates a "lay group of members of the ritualists," as well as "anyone who has been initiated into the mysteries of the temple rites."

In Assyria, there are other hints of similar practices, such as a layperson giving a *qerītu* (banquet) in the temple. Moreover, there seems to have been an Assyrian "mystery" religion, centered on a manifestation of the goddess Ishtar, which provides direct evidence for cult organizations. Ishtar's secret teachings are at the center of the Middle Assyrian ritual *KAR* 159, on the basis of which Oppenheim (1966) postulated the existence of these Assyrian mystery cults. The text gives the scenario for a ceremony in the *bīt eqi* sanctuary on the cultic occasion called *simunu* (right moment). The word *piriltu* (*-pirištu*) denotes the secrecy that surrounds a body of rules imparted exclusively to a particular group of worshipers of a deity. However, there is no evidence of what specific behavior was required of the members of this religious group, or of its size, or the social status of its members. It might be suggested that members participated in certain secret rites (involving otherwise inadmissible practices) or that the group's members observed food taboos or certain bodily mutilations and so on.

In conclusion, these two institutions and the mystery rites of Ishtar furnish the only clues available on the nature of popular religion and religious associations in Mesopotamia.

BIBL.: A. Leo Oppenheim, "Analysis of an Assyrian Ritual (KAR 159)," *History of Religions* 5 (1966): 250–65. M. Tanret and K. van Lergerghe, "Rituals and Profits in the Ur-Utu Archive," in *Ritual and Sacrifice in the Ancient Near East* (ed. J. Quaegebeur; Orientalia Lovaniensia Analecta 55; Louvain, 1993), 435–49.   J.G.W.

Syria-Canaan

The administrative and cultic texts of the Syro-Canaanite cultures, beginning with those of Ebla, record the various categories of cultic personnel and workers, although we know nothing about the system(s) under which they were organized. In the case of the priests and priestesses, we can easily guess that organization of some form existed, however, since they usually have a "head" (*rb* or equivalent) and different functions are mentioned, which presupposes a certain hierarchy.

But we have extraordinarily ample information for one religious body from Ebla to Palmyra: the *marzēaḥ* organization. Its echo can be heard in the Eblaite texts *(mar-za-u₉)*, although its meaning is uncertain. At Emar, also, this West Semitic institution seems to be present in the name of a month (ITI.*marzaḥanu*) and in the obscure allusion to the "men of *marzaḥu* from a certain PN" (LU.MEŠ.*mar-za-ḥu ša mi-*KI). In Ugarit, several texts, syllabic as well as alphabetic, provide explicit information on this religious association (again "the men of the *marzaḥu*"), which owns property (fields and vineyards) and can even either hire an apartment for use as a meeting place or obtain one by a royal grant. It is quite possible that this organization had a funerary function, and its connection with the consumption of wine is certain.

Mrzḥ came to signify the guild, the sacred meal, and the place where this took place, under the leadership of a *rb mrzḥ* (chief of the *marzaḥu*). Even the supreme god Il was said to have a *mrzḥ,* to which he invited his sons and at which he indulged in wine to the point of intoxication (*KTU* 1.114). There were different *mrzḥ* under the patronage of different gods and goddesses, and even the heroes of the afterlife, the *rpum,* seem to have been considered members of a *mrzḥ.* The Hebrew Bible provides evidence for the existence of the *marzēaḥ* in historical Israel, which was opposed with bitterness by the prophets as a form of pagan cult, while in Palmyra, among the Nabateans, and in the Phoenician world, they also flourished. Sacred meals or banquets seem, according to that evidence, to have been their distinctive cultic activity. In these contexts the association was well organized under the leadership of a *rb/rbwn* (chief) (as in Ugarit) and had its own clergy. In Palmyra the *marzēaḥ* was governed by precise regulations. Its members were chosen and elected to certain roles by vote; they paid fees and were obliged to attend the gatherings and guild banquets. Greek influence was felt in later times, with the result that this institution became more like the Hellenic *thiasos.* Its funerary character also became more apparent during later periods, again, perhaps, under the influence of Greek *thiasoi,* which often had funerary functions.

There were, of course, other private ritual associations, as can be easily concluded from sporadic references, for instance, to the "consecrated of Astarte" in Ugarit, "the brothers of the temple of GN(?)" in Emar, and the different groups of "servants" of deities in Phoenician inscriptions, but we do not have enough information on their organization or their relationship to the official and national cults.

BIBL.: G. del Olmo Lete, *Canaanite Religion according to the Liturgical Texts of Ugarit* (Bethesda, Md.: CDL, 1999). J.

McLaughlin, "The *Marzeah* at Ugarit: A Textual and Contextual Study," *Ugarit Forschung* 23 (1991): 266–81. G.O.L.

Israel

The religion of ancient Israel and Judah was a local cult, centered on the temples and shrines of YHWH. After the destruction of the kingdoms of Israel (722 BCE) and Judah (586 BCE), Jews were scattered throughout the Mediterranean and Middle East. Nonetheless, Jews in late antiquity achieved a remarkable level of group cohesiveness and solidarity. The major reason for this was that they all subscribed to the same broad religious culture based on the Torah of Moses, a culture that was defined and disseminated above all by two institutions, the synagogue and the school. Judaism had other institutions. The temple in Jerusalem was of immense importance while it stood. There was a developed system of Jewish law courts in Palestine and Babylonia. We know also of small religious associations *(havurot)* in which the scrupulous and ultra-observant banded together for a variety of purposes. But on the long view these all pale into insignificance when compared with the synagogues and the schools.

Schools. There were schools in Israel going back at least to the early monarchic period. They were needed to train scribes to serve the court in administration and diplomacy. However, it was not until the Second Temple period that these schools began to acquire central importance in Judaism. The national literature, known as "the holy scriptures," became the basis of an educational system in which a significant number of boys were trained from infancy to manhood. It is not easy to reconstruct in detail the organization of these schools. We can deduce something from the writings of Philo of Alexandria (ca. 20 BCE–50 CE). More information can be derived from the Dead Sea Scrolls, which reveal the existence at Qumran of a community with many of the characteristics of a school. However, the best documented and historically most significant early Jewish schools were the rabbinic academies *(bêt hammidrāš)* of the talmudic era (2nd–7th centuries CE).

These rabbinic schools were of two broad types: (1) disciple circles and (2) ecumenical yeshivot. The disciple circles were small groups of students gathered around a single teacher. They usually possessed little by way of school property: they tended to meet in public spaces, and the students sat on the ground at the teacher's feet. They were somewhat ephemeral institutions. The ecumenical yeshivot were larger and more complex, involved more than one teacher, possessed extensive school buildings, and survived for many generations. Ecumenical yeshivot were the norm in Babylonia: the two most prestigious schools there, Sura and Pumbeditha, continued for centuries into the Middle Ages. Disciple circles were the norm in Palestine, although one ecumenical yeshivah did exist there, at Tiberias.

The curriculum and methods of instruction were similar in both types of school. The Hebrew Bible continued to be studied, as in the lower educational levels, but more attention was paid to studying a body of oral tradition that Judah the Patriarch codified in the Mishnah around 210 CE. Great stress was placed on memorizing and repeating. The schools were financed by private donations from supporters and patrons. In theory, this meant that students from any social background could attend, but it is likely that most were from well-to-do families. The schools trained judges (dayyānîm) who could act as arbitrators in intracommunal disputes. But they also formed and molded their students. While at the school, the students lived a communal life, and they emerged from it imbued with the rabbinic worldview and values, which they then expected to impart to their fellow Jews.

Synagogues. One Jewish tradition carries the institution of the synagogue back to the Babylonian exile, but the earliest clear evidence for the existence of a synagogue dates from Egypt, from the reign of Ptolemy III Euergetes (246–221 BCE). In the succeeding centuries, synagogues proliferated throughout the whole Jewish world, including Palestine. They existed before the destruction of the temple in 70 CE, but after the destruction they became the sole focus of religious life for the majority of Jews. The role of the synagogue evolved, but from the earliest times it seems to have served as a place of prayer and for reading the Torah. It was never a place of sacrifice. The worshipers prayed toward Jerusalem, at times that notionally coincided with the times of sacrifice in the temple.

The synagogue seems to have been controlled by local grandees, who were able to defray the synagogue's expenses. Their patronage was rewarded by honorific inscriptions or titles such as *archisynagōgos* (leader of the synagogue). The synagogue was not in origin a rabbinic institution. A rabbi was not needed to officiate at its services (nor was a priest): any adult male of the congregation could lead, provided he was competent. From the late 1st century CE, the rabbis made a concerted effort to gain control of the synagogues, beginning with Palestine and later extending into the Diaspora. They convinced their supporters to introduce distinctively rabbinic forms of the standard synagogue prayers (such as the Amidah); they advocated the public reading of the Torah in Hebrew, even in Greek-speaking synagogues; and they claimed that the Palestinian rabbinate alone had the authority to determine the calendar and so fix when the festivals were to be celebrated. Their idea that all Israel, worldwide, should celebrate the festivals at the same time, in the same way, strongly promoted the notion that Israel was one people, united, of course, under the rabbinic aegis.

BIBL.: David Goodblatt, *Rabbinic Instruction in Sasanian Babylonia* (Leiden, 1975). Catherine Hezser, *The Social Structure of the Rabbinic Movement in Roman Palestine* (Tübingen, 1997). Lee I. Levine, *The Ancient Synagogue: The First Thousand Years* (New Haven, 2000).　　　　P.S.A.

Anatolia

When trying to reconstruct the administrative structure of Hittite religious organizations, we have to employ mainly the results of archeological excavations of ancient Anatolian settlements, as well as the Hittite economic and religious records, which, unfortunately, furnish only isolated episodes of their history. These records are represented in fragments of cuneiform texts recovered from only a few sites, mostly from central Anatolia. They provide a very uneven coverage of the recorded history of religious establishments (mostly of the later, empire period). Moreover, these texts deal primarily with rites and ceremonies performed within the precincts of a religious institution and do not document the entire range of economic and religious activities involving a specific temple during a given period.

Naturally, the temple stood as the central feature of the cult. It was the house of the god. Every city and town of any size within the Hittite domain had at least one temple, which was administered by its priesthood and staffed by cult personnel. They were also under the ultimate control of the king, who was the chief priest of Hatti. As a matter of fact, it is impossible to separate the upkeep of temples from other state business documented in the royal archives. For instance, Tudkhaliya IV organized a voluminous inventory of local cults in northern and central Anatolia. These inventory texts give a detailed account of the property of various temples, description of images of the gods maintained by those temples, and lists of religious personnel. However, only a select number of cities served as the main state cultic centers: Arinna, Nerik, Zippalanda, Shamukha, Khakmish, and Hattusha.

Large territories of land outside the cities were owned by the local temples and cultivated by temple-dependent farmers. The produce from these fields, as well as the temple livestock, supported the temple personnel and administration. The Hittite temples were powerful factors in the ancient Anatolian society and economy. The wealth and resources that they created and controlled, as well as the lives of the personnel responsible for the care of the gods and the livestock that they sustained, were essential for the prosperity and even survival of urban communities.

The vast economic resources and complex administrative organization of temples in the Hittite local communities functioned, first of all, to attend to the needs and comfort of its local patron deity, because his or her presence was conceived to be the most fundamental prerequisite for the community's prosperity. The eternal dependence on divine favor created the constant fear that the god might abandon the temple, as well as the community, with disastrous consequences for its members. Therefore, there was a hierarchy of human attendants in temples, whose most important responsibility was to attend duly to the god's needs, which involved the strictly prescribed daily ritual of awakening the deity's statue in the morning, washing, clothing, feeding, and bringing it to the cult platform for the day's duties, and then at night putting it to bed again.

The deities' needs also comprised agricultural commodities and crafted products that were produced and delivered within the framework of the temple household, which usually was autonomous and self-sustaining.

Funding for these complex religious organizations came from the donations of land or groups of people made by the Hittite king and local rulers. There were also other gifts made by them or by members of a community, ranging from precious items, divine images, and cultic objects to livestock. A major source of income for the temples was also the animal and food offerings that the community was mandated to make to the temple on a regular basis during the festivals.

BIBL.: Gary Beckman, "Royal Ideology and State Administration in Hittite Anatolia," in *Civilizations of the Ancient Near East* (ed. J. M. Sasson et al.; New York: Scribner, 1995), 1.529–43. H. G. Güterbock, "The Hittite Temple according to Written Sources," in *Perspectives on Hittite Civilization: Selected Writings of H. G. Güterbock* (ed. H. A. Hoffner Jr.; Chicago: Oriental Institute, 1997), 81–83. Maciej Popko, *Religions of Asia Minor* (Warsaw: Academic Publications Dialog, 1995), 74–76, 153–54.   H.H.

Iran

In the Achaemenian period, the religious organization was hardly known. Herodotus (1.131–32) informs us that the Persians had no established place for cult and that they offered sacrifices in the open air, without temples, images, or altars. For the western Iranians, the priest was called *magu* (or, as the word came into Greek, *magos*, and thus into our language, *magus*), a term designating a sacerdotal tribe among the Medes, which the Persians were supposed to inherit. The Greeks, who encountered them in Asia Minor, considered them to be magicians. Because the magi held a monopoly of priesthoods, they were considered to be disciples of Zarathustra. But the *magus* is unknown in the Avesta.

Religious hierarchy. Only the Sasanian period (3rd–7th centuries CE) gives a more detailed panorama of the priesthood's hierarchy and organization. The four inscriptions of the great magus Kirder in the 3rd century CE offer a wealth of historical data. This religious man, who was only a simple *herbed* under the reign of King Shapur I—a category of priests lower than the *mowbed*—ascended in his profession remarkably under the successors of that king, becoming *Ohrmazd-mowbed* under kings Ohrmazd I and Vahram I and, under Vahram II, becoming "judge of all empire" and *ayenbed* of the temple of Anahid at Staxr, a kind of keeper of records. He proclaimed himself the renewer of Zoroastrianism in Iran; claimed that on the order of the King of Kings he had built many Vahram fires, the most important category of fire temples; and claimed to have developed the magi attached to these temples. He also claimed, finally, that he had struggled against those who deviated from the "Good Religion" and against competing religions: Manicheism, Christianity, and Buddhism, even in the non-Iranian countries of the empire. There is probably some exaggeration in all of this. The alliance of this religious reformer with the King of Kings might encourage us to believe what we read in the late Pahlavi literature: that religion and kingship were united like two sisters or twins. And yet this idealization, found in later theologians, is probably no more than a literary topos, used to exaggerate the greatness of an empire that had already been destroyed.

A very hierarchized organization developed only in the 5th–6th centuries CE, when the title *Mowbedan Mowbed* was invented according to the pattern of *Shahan Shah* (King of Kings). We can distinguish an officer who served as the supreme chief of the Mazdean church, the "Great *Mowbed*," who could be the *Mowbedan Mowbed*'s substitute, although we know nothing more about his specific function; and further below him were several provincial *Mowbed*s, having jurisdiction over the various regions of the Sasanian Empire. This tripartite hierarchy apparently follows the model of that of the eastern Syrians, who were ruled by the *catholicos* or the patriarch (see Gignoux 1980). (This model can be reconstructed from the Syriac sources.)

Sasanian seal inscriptions provide a lot of information about civil and religious functions, as Gyselen (1989) shows. The *Ohrmazd-mowbed* is attested, as are the provincial *mowbed*s. The *mogan handarzbed* (councilor of the magi) is listed as a member of the high clergy; he could also be a councilor of the court, a councilor of the queen, or have a provincial status, which underlines the importance of his office. This function, however, was not in itself religious but rather chiefly juridical. Among the low clergy, the *herbed* was the highest of the priests during the Parthian period, according to Boyce (1975). There was perhaps also a *herbedan herbed* (director of the teaching priests). Judges were normally charged with judiciary functions, as attested by sentences against Christians who refuse to renounce their faith and to reembrace Mazdaism. Finally, there was a "defender and judge of the poor," attested on seals in sixteen different circumscriptions; this was a religious institution dating back to Khusrau I.

Schools. There were no religious schools for laypeople, but because the priestly status was hereditary, religious science either passed from master to disciple or, as today, was transmitted in *madressas* (seminaries), where the young from sacerdotal families were, and still are, educated for the priesthood. Apprenticeship is a matter of memorization, for it is necessary to learn by heart the texts of the religious offices (Yasna, Vendidad, and so on).

BIBL.: Mary Boyce, *A History of Zoroastrianism,* vol. 1 (Leiden, 1975). P. Gignoux, "Pour une esquisse des fonctions religieuses sous les Sassanides," *Jerusalem Studies in Arabic and Islam* 7 (1986): 93–108. Idem, "Titres et fonctions religieuses sasanides d'après les sources syriaques hagiographiques," *Acta antiqua academiae scientiarum hungaricae* 28 (1980): 191–203. R. Gyselen, *La géographie administrative de l'empire sassanide: Les témoignages sigillographiques* (Res orientales 1; Paris, 1989).   P.G.

Greece

The organization of private and public cult in ancient Greece is as multifaceted and diverse a phenomenon as the Greek communities themselves. In addition to the community of the citizens, which can be conceived of as a community of worshipers, and in addition to the extended family that presents the framework for private worship and for life-cycle rituals, as early as the archaic period one can discern organizational forms that cut across, divide, or transcend the boundaries of these groups. Various subdivisions of the citizen body were primarily concerned with cultic activities, and to a certain extent they can be conceived of as religious groups; they often owned exclusive cult places and altars or elected their sacred officials. Voluntary cult associations of various kinds and varying degrees of exclusivity and doctrinal uniformity make their first appearance in the 6th century BCE and develop into one of the most influential venues of worship during the Hellenistic period.

But beyond the community of citizens there also existed religious unions of city and tribal states (amphictyonies) that shared worship in common cult places and agreed upon the rules that governed such interstate sanctuaries; the Delphic amphictyony is the best documented and most influential, but not the only one. Within the polis, one should distinguish between the early forms of organization that are connected with citizenship, tribal membership, or heredity and religious bodies based on voluntary membership ("associations"). A general tendency in the development of religious bodies and organizational forms can be seen in the gradual rise of individuality and personal piety. A consequence of this was the strengthening of the voluntary associations. This does not, however, mean the disappearance of hereditary groups or a decline of public worship.

The principle of heredity seems predominant during the archaic period. Besides the cultic activities of real or virtual family groups (such as a phratry or a *genos*

[lineage]), the Greek communities acknowledged the priesthoods of certain deities and the performance of specific cultic duties as the exclusive privilege of specific lineages; functional names, such as "the heralds" *(kērykes)* or "the ox-yokers" *(bouzygai)* in Athens, indicate their ritual specialization. In addition to the involvement of such hereditary groups in public cult, they were also concerned with their private and exclusive rites. The reorganization of the civic communities in the archaic period, the writing down of laws (including the registration of sacred regulations), and later the diffusion of democratic institutions affected to some extent the mode of appointment of state sacred officials and, consequently, the organization of cult; but although new public religious offices were usually open to all citizens, the privileges of hereditary groups in traditional cults and rituals survived these changes, and traditional priesthoods remained, often until the imperial period, the exclusive privilege of certain families. Fourth-century inscriptions concerning the *genos* of the Salaminians and the phratries of the Demotionidai in Athens and the Labyadai of Delphi provide the fullest picture of the sacrificial calendars and the cultic activities of such groups (*IG* II² 1232, 1237; Rougemont 1977: 1.9). Their activities included the appointment of sacred officials, the administration of property, the performance of sacrifices, the participation in public cult (Salaminioi), the performance of funerary rituals (Labyadai), and the observance of rites of passage for the children (Demotionidai). We lack information about the rules of membership for other early religious groups with specific cultic responsibilities, such as the Milesian "singers" *(molpoi;* Kawerau 1914, 133). The significance of these groups for public cult survived, with only minor changes, the institutional developments of Greek states. Nonetheless, the organization of private worship underwent deep changes with the diffusion of voluntary cult associations, especially during the Hellenistic period.

The notion of a "cult association" is modern; it designates private voluntary groups, usually of mixed membership (men and women, citizens and foreigners, free persons and slaves), whose main, but not necessarily sole, aim was the worship of a particular deity or a group of deities. The Greeks had, from the 6th century onward at the latest, associations that fulfilled various purposes, including cultic activities. In a sense every association, including, say, professional colleges and banqueting clubs, was a cult association. When we speak of cult associations in a narrower sense we mean voluntary corporate bodies, whose primary activity was religious worship and the observance of customary rituals. If an Athenian law (quoted in Justinian's *Digests* 47.22.4) is correctly attributed to Solon, voluntary religious groups must have been one of the objects of archaic legislation: "Whatever the inhabitants of a district, or members of a phratry, or members of groups that perform sacred rites, or sailors, or members of groups that organize common dinners or provide for a common burial, or members of religious associations, or members of groups that engage in some enterprise for plunder or trade agree between themselves will be valid, unless forbidden by written public statutes."

The birth of philosophy and the diffusion of "apocryphal" religious teachings in the later part of the archaic period resulted in cultic activities of voluntary associations that followed specific rules and doctrines outside traditional polis religion. The best-known example is that of the "Orphics," initiates into a cult closely related to the mysteries of Dionysus Bacchus who followed a set of eschatological ideas probably contained in a sacred text *(hieros logos)* attributed to Orpheus; they hoped that initiation and observance of a pure way of life would secure them a blessed life after death. The internal organization of these groups is unknown, but one can observe a certain amount of standardization in their ritual texts. Pythagoras, who often is associated with them, was the first to establish a "philosophical school" of disciples committed to the teachings and religious observances of the founder (late 6th century).

The importance of voluntary religious associations increased during the classical period, favored both by the presence of foreigners, who organized themselves into cult associations, and by the establishment of philosophical schools, organized as communities of worship, such as Plato's Academy. When the great mobility of the Hellenistic period strengthened the desire of expatriates to create new religious bonds, private cult groups were established in almost every urban center. Other important factors for their diffusion were the popularity of mystery cults and the development of private piety connected with individual, sometimes idiosyncratic religious preferences. During the Hellenistic period, voluntary associations are ubiquitous, presenting one of the most important venues of religious practices; from Rhodes alone we know of roughly two hundred private associations that derive their names from gods or heroes. The diffusion of private associations is often regarded as a response to a crisis of the polis institutions and to a decline of public worship; this claim is not substantiated by the evidence, which rather suggests that cult associations were complementary to public cults and not an alternative to them.

There is, in our sources, a somewhat bewildering plurality of terms that designate cult associations and often refer to specific religious activities. They were usually founded upon the initiative of an individual, sometimes by testamentary provisions, such as the foundation of Epicteta in Thera; the founder's birthday was one of the association's festival days, as was Epicurus's birthday for his school long after his death. In some cases, voluntary associations evolved from family associations or other hereditary groups that accepted outside members. Foundation charters are rarely attested, but usually there were customary rites, sacrificial calendars, and written rules by which members had to abide.

Often enough, the only thing we know about a cult association is its name. Often this name refers to the divinity whom the cult worshiped (such as Apolloniastai), the epithet of a divinity (Aristobouliastai, an association honoring Artemis Aristoboule), the name of a festival (Panathenaistai), the name of their founder (Dioskouriastai Theudoteioi, an association of worshipers of the Dioskouroi founded by one Theudotos), or to all these elements (Adoniastai Apolloniastai Soteriastai Asklapiastai Aristodameioi—the joint worship of several gods was not uncommon); this, however, does not necessarily mean that the association was of a purely cultic nature. Generalizations about the choice of the divinity worshiped by an association are not permissible, but important factors were patriotism (expatriates worshiping a deity of their place of origin), the patronage a deity offered to a professional activity (traders worshiping Hermes), the expectation of personal protection (from, say, Agathos Daimon [The Good Daimon]), or eschatological ideas.

Voluntary associations usually had a rather limited number of members. The qualifications for membership often escape our knowledge, but criteria that are often attested are the membership in a family (e.g., in the family association of Epicteta in Thera), common ethnic origin, the devotion to a particular deity, initiation, and observance of certain rules (especially in the case of mystery cult associations). In some cases legal status (citizenship, freedom), occupation (the various Dionysiac associations of stage artists), and gender also played a role. Immigrant groups established associations in order to preserve a sense of identity and origin (such as, in classical Athens, the worshipers of the Thracian goddess Bendis or in Hellenistic Delos the Heraklesiastai of Tyros). Usually cult associations did not demand the exclusive allegiance of their members, although membership in a philosophical school involved the adoption of certain values and a new way of life and, therefore, might have excluded participation in another school. Most philosophical schools were organized according to the principles of cult associations; in addition to their educational and scientific activities, they were devoted to the cult of particular deities; regular banquets and rituals were a central part of the life in an Epicurean community. In some associations, such as the mystery groups of Mithras, membership was exclusively male; exclusive female associations are less common and attested mainly in the context of Demeter's cult, such as the worshipers of Demeter Thesmophoros under the leadership of Dikaio in archaic Gela (Dubois 1989, 155). Slaves are often attested as members with equal rights, but this was not a general rule. The epigraphic evidence shows that in the Hellenistic period at the latest, most associations had mixed membership with regard to legal status, social position, and gender.

In some mixed associations, such as Dionysiac associations and family clubs, women had a significant role; in others they participated as spouses of members or were welcome as donors. Although the majority of the evidence suggests that voluntary associations recruited their members primarily from the lower classes, often among freedmen who found in this venue a substitute for political activity, in many cases, notably in Rhodes, associations were supported or even founded by members of the elite. Associations were financed by member contributions, donations, and gifts of wealthy patrons.

The typical activity of a voluntary association was the monthly or annual sacrifice, combined with processions, prayers, and sacrificial banquets, in which the god was often perceived as present (theoxenia). In many cases, the members met once every month; the meeting took place on a particular day—Noumeniastai met on the noumēnia, day 1 of every month, the Dekadistai on day 10. The associations also looked after sanctuaries and made dedications, celebrated the birthdays and weddings of their members, organized their funerals, performed the funerary rites and erected funerary monuments (especially "burial societies"), honored benefactors, and listened to orations in praise of their god. Many benefactors made donations for the celebration of commemorative days (eponymoi hēmerai) to honor deceased members of their family or themselves. For these, one often chose a day that was already marked as a festive day in the calendar; for example, the commemorative day for Plato in the Academy coincided with a festival for Apollo.

Cult associations had officials, usually an annually elected president, a priest or a priestess, a scribe, a treasurer, and cult functionaries; when the association met on a monthly basis, they could be called epimēnioi (monthly officials). They owned shrines, clubhouses, and private burial grounds; when they did not own their meeting place, they could gather in the house of a patron. Cult associations were normally local organizations; in exceptional cases we observe a connection with larger networks; uniquely, the association of the Dionysiac artists spanned most of the Greek and Greco-Roman worlds.

The diffusion of voluntary cult associations was of paramount importance for Greek society and religion. In the classical period, when citizenship was still an exclusive privilege, associations gave foreign residents of a city the possibility to organize themselves, to express their own identity and compensate for their lack of political participation, to provide for funerary rites, but also to come into contact with local citizens. Even when, in the Hellenistic period, citizenship lost some of its exclusivity, the voluntary associations remained an important medium of identity. In cities with substantial trade activity (such as Athens, Rhodes, and Delos), they can be seen as part of the infrastructure that attracted foreign residents and facilitated their activities. Their corporate identity did not isolate the members of the voluntary associations. They pursued the generally accepted social ideals and adopted the predominant forms of social behavior. In the microcosmos of the association, the traditional divisions that kept citizens and foreigners apart were largely overcome, social tensions could be alleviated, and the performance of rituals according to traditions and with respect to social hierarchy contributed to the social integration of groups that might otherwise have been marginalized. In a city's cultic life, the cults of voluntary associations were, generally, complementary to public religion.

But in at least one way they permitted the innovation of religion. In a world in which the hereditary groups presented themselves as transmitters and interpreters of old traditions, some voluntary associations developed their own, in part innovative, religious norms; the founding charter of an association in Lydian Philadelphia, founded in the 1st century BCE, contains a set of strict moral rules and gives the widest definition of guilt, excluding not only persons who committed a crime or those who assisted in it, but also persons who did not attempt to prevent it (Barton and Horsley 1981). As organizational forms the cult associations probably influenced the organization of the early Christian communities.

BIBL.: S. Aneziri, Die Vereine der dionysischen Techniten im Kontext der hellenistischen Gesellschaft (Stuttgart, 2002). I. Arnaoutoglou, "Between koinon and idion: Legal and Social Dimensions of Religious Associations in Ancient Athens," in Kosmos: Essays in Order, Conflict, and Community in Classical Athens (ed. P. Cartledge, P. Millett, and S. von Reden; Cambridge, 1998), 68–83. S. C. Barton and G. H. R. Horsley, "A Hellenistic Cult Group and the New Testament Church," Jahrbuch für Antike und Christentum 24 (1981): 12–14. F. de Cenival, Les associations religieuses en Égypte d'après les documents démotiques (Cairo, 1972). L. Dubois, Inscriptions grecques dialectales de Sicile (Rome/Paris, 1989). V. Gabrielsen, "The Rhodian Associations and Economic Activity," in Hellenistic Economies (ed. Z. H. Archibald et al.; London, 2001), 215–44. N. F. Jones, The Associations of Classical Athens: The Response to Democracy (New York, 1999). G. Kawerau and A. Rehm, Das Delphinion (Milet 1:3 1914, 133). J. S. Kloppenborg and S. G. Wilson (eds.), Voluntary Associations in the Graeco-Roman World (London, 1996). S. D. Lambert, The Phratries of Attica (2nd ed.; Ann Arbor, 1998). G. Rougemont, Corpus des inscriptions de Delphes, vol. 1: Lois sacrées et règlements religieux (Paris, 1977). M. C. Taylor, Salamis and the Salaminioi: The History of an Unofficial Athenian Demos (Amsterdam, 1997). A. Wittenburg, Il testamento di Epikteta (Trieste, 1990).   A.C.

Rome

From early in the city's history, Roman society included at least certain religious groups. In the time of the kings, there were several types of priests; some of these were experts and practitioners in some defined areas of religious activity; some operated only once or twice a year, on the occasion of particular regular festivals. All of them consisted of specially selected members of the better-off classes in society. Certainly by the early republic, but perhaps earlier, these priests established a collegiate organization with its own rules. We hear later of the creation of other groups of specialists, who may well have been dedicated to the practice of a specific skill (flute players, actors) and who were under the patronage of a particular deity (e.g., the traders were under the patronage of Mercury and formed a group called the Mercuriales).

Later still, it becomes a common pattern for groups, also called colleges, although we might rather call them clubs, to draw their membership from far-wider sections of society, including ex-slaves, who are commonly listed as full members. These colleges had a leadership structure, funds administered in common, and often a specific purpose such as ensuring a decent burial for members when they died. They are surprisingly well attested in the surviving records. They normally had a priest (called a *flamen*) as well as "masters" *(magistri)*; each group was devoted to a particular deity and maintained cultic rituals to their deity. It is clear that the members of such colleges joined voluntarily, not as part of their profession or calling; there is, however, no way of knowing whether they joined because of devotion to the particular deity of the group or for some other reasons. They are widespread in the Roman world and especially common in our evidence for the late republican and early imperial periods.

In the 3rd to 2nd centuries BCE, we meet the first Italian evidence, widespread throughout Italy, of religious associations, whose members had evidently joined out of devotion to a particular form of religious belief or practice. In form they seem much like the *collegia,* with "masters," priests and priestesses, and common funds. But in this case, the groups' activities were held in secret, their devotion given to Bacchus, god of wine and ecstasy, and the revelation of the god's mystery was at the heart of their religious practice. These groups included Romans and non-Romans, men and women, and slaves, freedmen, and free people. The members of the Roman senate, proclaiming in 186 BCE that they had just discovered the existence of the cult, denounced it as a treasonable conspiracy and persecuted its adherents ruthlessly throughout Italy. The senate's decree, of which a text still survives, allowed a modified and licensed form of the cult to continue, but we have no way of knowing whether this offer was taken up (see further Controlling Religion).

This dramatic episode of suppression is isolated in our records and anticipates the persecution of the Christians two or three centuries later. Between the two persecutions, we have much evidence that the traditional *collegia* continued to operate as before and that in the imperial period their activities were regulated by the senate; but groups also continued to develop devoted to the worship of particular deities, often foreign ones, without attracting the hostile attentions of the Roman authorities. Occasionally, a religious group was expelled from the city of Rome (the Jews in 139 BCE; worshipers of Isis repeatedly in the 1st century BCE), but there is no sign of methodical action on the model of 186 BCE.

A good deal of evidence survives of the activities of various cults throughout the period of the Roman Empire: they are described in the older literature as "oriental cults," because many of them were devoted to Eastern deities, such as the Egyptian Isis, the Persian Mithras, Atargatis and Jupiter Dolichenus from Syria, Attis from Asia Minor, and so on. Part of the appeal of these cults must in fact have been to those of Eastern origin who lived far from their families' original homelands. Much of the evidence we have, however, makes it clear that the connections with the East are sometimes flimsy and that the cults themselves have been heavily adapted for worshipers far from the original base of the deity; in the case of Mithraism the most plausible current theory is that it was invented in or around Rome itself. More seriously still, many cults have at their very core the revelation of a mystery in the ritual of initiation, guarded from the noninitiates and transforming the lives of the devotees who experience it. This distinctive religious pattern (found already in the Bacchic cult suppressed in 186 BCE) can be traced back not to the East, but to Greek mysteries of the archaic period. All these religious movements were apparently joined voluntarily by devotees, but they do not involve any separation from other pagan rituals or from the traditions and festivals of the cities where devotees lived. Nor did the initiates, so far as we can tell, seek to be buried or memorialized separately from their fellow citizens.

It used to be commonly argued that the development of these cult groups was an important step toward what was often called the "triumph" of Christianity. It may be valid to see the growth of religious choices in the empire as part of a single process, through which voluntaristic groups (whether pagan or Christian) became progressively more independent, running their own affairs and controlling their membership. But the new nonpagan groups, operating outside or even against paganism, offered radically different options to potential converts, as well as more risk of official hostility: they offered different ideas of divinity, a new pattern of priesthood, new models of behavior for adherents. They asked their members to reject the gods and goddesses who had once held almost universal belief. To put the point more generally, these groups depended on the advocacy of a certain set of beliefs to which converts were asked to subscribe; the explicit making of this connection between which group to join and which religious doctrines to accept was a fundamental change leading directly to the developing of new religious identities, in a way that would have been inconceivable only a couple of centuries earlier.   J.N.

Christianity

Beginning in the 1st century CE, the organizational structure of early Christian communities was marked by small groups meeting in private homes (*domus ecclesiae* [house church]) for liturgical services and instruction. Distinctive leadership roles, most prominently the offices of overseer (bishop), elder (presbyter), and server (deacon), were in place by the 2nd century. The emergence of Christian offices was influenced both by the pattern of leadership exercised in contemporary Jewish synagogues, where councils of elders (presbyters) regulated worship and social life, and by the organizational structure of Greco-Roman private associations (*collegia* or *thiasoi*), where officials were selected largely on the basis of a willingness to bestow benefactions (patronage) on the association and its members.

The earliest Christian literature, especially the letters of Paul from the mid-1st century, reveals a fluidity of leadership roles for both men and women amid the charismatic worship of the churches (1 Cor. 11.2–16; 12.4–31). By the end of that century, texts such as Titus 1.5–9 (cf. 1 Tim. 3.1–13), Acts 20.28, and *1 Clement* 44 refer to bishops and presbyters as the same persons, apparently as part of a collective governance structure, exhorting virtues of good leadership taken largely from contemporary Greco-Roman moral philosophy. In *1 Clement* 40 is a description of the presbyter/bishop as cultic priest who performs liturgies and makes offerings—religious language and activity that would have affinities both with Christian self-identity as the restored assembly (church) of ancient Israel (Septuagint Num. 4.16; 2 Chron. 34.12) and Greco-Roman civic and religious sacrifice.

In the early years of the 2nd century, Ignatius of Antioch, in letters to several churches in Asia Minor and Rome, exhorted the churches to obedience toward a single person in the role of bishop, a person apparently to be assisted in that office by the council of presbyters and service of deacons. The fact of his special pleading, coupled with his failure to acknowledge a single bishop at Rome in his letter to that city, probably indicates that this form of church organization, sometimes referred to as monarchical episcopacy, was only gradually adopted by Christian churches throughout the first half of the 2nd century.

Yet by the mid-2nd century, in many of the more prominent Christian communities, these monarchical bishops were in a position to exercise the role of both priest and patron. Justin Martyr, in an apology for the Christian churches ostensibly directed to the emperor of Rome, describes the Christian liturgy as a gathering wherein the people bring offerings that are then offered to God by the "presider" (Justin does not use the specifically Christian term *bishop*) and subsequently distributed by the deacons to those present. Moreover, it is clear from Justin's description that the patronage of the church extended from the hand of the bishop to a wider network of those in need: it is his responsibility to take care of the orphans and widows and those in difficulty, those who are in prison, and "the strangers who are sojourning among us" (*Apology* 1.67.7 in *Patrologia graeca* 60.428–29). Hence the ordinary function of ancient priesthood—to act as mediator between human beings and the divine, to make sacrifice and incur divine blessing—is here combined with the practice of distributing extensive social charity. Such episcopal patronage developed within the broader social conventions governing patrons and clients, known to us from thousands of contemporary Greco-Roman inscriptions that describe the particular benefactions of persons who were then "elected" and honored as leaders of a myriad of private and religious associations. By ancient social convention then, church members receiving such benefactions would have been obligated to become clients of the bishop, in turn bestowing honor and loyalty on their patron.

Although the monarchical episcopate became the focal point of Christian organization throughout much of the Roman Empire, there were prominent exceptions to the general rule. The church in Alexandria, one of the very earliest Christian communities, was apparently ruled by a council of presbyters until the 3rd century. Gnostic Christian groups, prevalent throughout the empire, were organized more along the lines of ancient philosophical schools, with small groups of pupils devoted to a teacher (see, e.g., Ptolemy, *Letter to Flora*). Montanism, a prominent form of Christianity in both Asia Minor and North Africa, developed a unique form of organization. The so-called "new prophecy" featured ecstatic prophecy at the center of the cult and allowed both men and women to occupy the positions of prophet, presbyter, and deacon.

In the 3rd century, monarchical bishops in the most prominent cities of the empire—Rome, Carthage, Antioch, and Alexandria—began to solidify their influence over several churches in a region. For example, Cyprian of Carthage (bishop 250–58 CE) refers to councils of bishops held in that city earlier in the 3rd century (*Epistle* 1). Churches in Spain could appeal disciplinary decisions to the bishop of Carthage (*Epistle* 67). The records from one North African episcopal council of the mid-3rd century, *Sententiae episcoporum*, certainly demonstrate the power and influence of the bishop of Carthage.

By the 4th century and the rise of Constantine as the first emperor who openly patronized Christianity, Christian bishops throughout the empire could be called to an ecumenical or worldwide council at Nicea at the behest of the emperor to rule on issues of doctrine and discipline for churches from Spain to Syria. And it is perhaps no accident that just as bishops took council with emperors and began to be influential in matters of state, other Christians, men and women, withdrew to the desert regions of the empire, most notably in Syria and Egypt, in order to pursue more ancient religious practices of prayer and virtue, both individually and in new monastic foundations. At the end of the early Christian period (sometimes marked by the "fall" of Rome in 476 CE), these two organizational forms—a powerful regional clerical structure that could be both supportive of and in tension with the secular government and rapidly spreading monastic foundations—provided the transition to the medieval Christian church.

BIBL.: Allen Brent, *The Imperial Cult and the Development of Church Order: Concepts and Images of Authority in Paganism and Early Christianity before the Age of Cyprian* (Leiden, 1999). Peter R. L. Brown, *Authority and the Sacred Aspects of the Christianisation of the Roman World* (Cambridge, 1995). Douglas R. Edwards, *Religion and Power: Pagans, Jews, and Christians in the Greek East* (New York, 1996). J. B. Rives, *Religion and Authority in Roman Carthage from Augustus to Constantine* (Oxford, 1995). Jack T. Sanders, *Charisma, Converts, Competitors: Societal and Sociological Factors in the Success of Early Christianity* (London, 2000).   C.A.B.

Sacrifice, Offerings, and Votives

Introduction

Offerings are among the most common practices of religious practice; we may define them as actions whereby goods are transferred from mortals to transcendent recipients. The value of the goods involved bespeaks the seriousness of the transaction and importance of the addressees; there is high hope that it shall not be undertaken in vain. Whoever sacrifices signals to the addressee that the offerer wishes to make contact and expects an answer to be given or a request to be met. Typical addresses include gods, demons, and the dead; their specific characteristics, as elaborated in local tradition, help to shape the performance of the ritual.

In most languages, the basic verb used to express the act of making an offering is "to give"—a concept that spreads itself over a large and variegated landscape. Within the most basic form of giving, the offering of food, we find two elaborate systems: the Near Eastern temple economy and the Egyptian cult of the dead. The Near Eastern temple, called the Great House, is the place where the gods come to dine, as described in prayer and poetry. Gods insist on their "provisions," and they have created humans in order to care for these and have appointed kings to survey the regulations. The temples have their property, real estate, herds, and personnel, and they receive regular and irregular contributions within the ups and downs of royal government. De facto temple offerings constitute a system of taxation, with the "tenth" becoming the standard measure of contribution. They support a leisure class of priests and scribes, of intellectuals. The priests are anxious to perform the daily service of their gods, and of course the gods' leftovers—normally 100 percent—are transferred to the temple personnel. We need not believe the Jewish parody of these actions, which implies that a deceit of the public was involved. The gods, in turn, would give victory, peace, and all good things to the king and his people.

Unique in its way is the systematic elaboration of feeding the dead that developed in Egypt. It was part of the Egyptians' great attempt to deny death, also expressed by their preservations of bodies through mummification, their ceremonies of "opening the mouth" of the dead for eating and drinking, and their detailed texts describing the voyage of the dead in the wake of the sun-god toward a "new rising" in the east. There are problems as to the "real" proceedings. Who really ate the food that was left at tombs? We perceive how reality sometimes elides into symbolism. The system remained incredibly stable for three millennia.

Another form of giving may also be of immemorial age: the presentation of striking objects to mark out a divine place or a personal relationship with a deity in a permanent way. Already from prehistoric times we find natural crystals or seashells in suggestive contexts. In higher civilizations, this develops into the lavish adornment of sanctuaries through all kinds of communal or private deposits, intended to document that the giver or givers have a hold on the divine sphere. One speaks in various languages of "setting up" or "putting up high" (e.g., Greek *anathemata*). The objects given might be tokens from the giver's personal life: weapons in the case of warriors, spindles in the case of women. Or they may be garments intended for a goddess's use. In the Hittite-Luwian, northern Syrian, Anatolian, and Greek cultures, where metals were scarce and precious, huge bronze tripods—lacking any practical use—were produced and set up in sanctuaries. A text that elaborates the ideal form of such a sanctuary is the description of Solomon's temple in Jerusalem (1 Kings 6–7).

At the base of all this is the constant and multifarious practice of making gifts to the gods both publicly and privately, as motivated by individual needs and anxieties, as propagated and regulated by sanctuaries and their priests, as instrumentalized by rulers' policies. Traditional forms of doing this may be established, but the opportunity for individual innovation always remains.

One motor of change is the advent of representative art: as symbolic relations become more explicit, reality goes on the retreat. "Gods accept fictions instead of real things," as Varro says. Terra-cotta, in particular, may represent everything by means of cheaper counterfeits: we find terra-cotta representations of food (including painted representations), animals, worshipers, and even divinities themselves. Through this medium, religious practices permeate everyday life all the more.

It presupposes, of course, all kinds of explanations and justifications: teachings of the elders, lore of priests, creations of the poets, formulas of invocation, of prayer, and of thanksgiving, with descriptions of the gods, their likenesses and their likings. Local characters of gods and local pantheons will differ and still remain comparable or even translatable; Israel alone remains rigidly monotheistic.

Thoughts about practice lead to problems, questions, paradoxes: Why do we need to recirculate goods? How can the superior powers definitely be reached? One option that comes to the fore is burning, through fire that reaches to the sky. Burn holocausts for the gods, burn garments for the dead—and wait for good things to come from above or from below.

The one principle in all these transfers, proclaimed again and again and taken for granted throughout, is reciprocity: gifts elicit countergifts; they may be already part of a circle of giving by themselves, thanksgiving for what the god has granted. The principle of reciprocity seems to be a universal in anthropology, the very basis of morality and economy, even if its origin is still debated. Religious offerings are a prime example of its application, yet in a problematic setting: reciprocity is not subject to experimental proof; there may be counterexamples, yet its efficacy is emphatically postulated, and reciprocity has given rise to a whole genus of poetry of praise and thanksgiving. Offerings are a constantly renewed experiment of trust, a great postulate of sense projected into the unforeseeable ups and downs of the future, in order to make the world "divine" and thus controllable.

The offering of animals is a special case. Animals are part of food offerings, normally the most valuable type of food, but there is more to it than that. To offer animals means to deal with life, blood, and death. This is not transfer, but transformation; it may be called the "sacred act" in an emphatic sense, *sacrificium* (sacrifice). The reactions to these problems are not uniform. We find expressions of "guilt," rituals of remorse and recompensation, limitations of use: the bones shall not be destroyed, the blood belongs to the Lord of Life; or else the license to kill comes directly from the gods, as it is done for the gods and with the gods. Egyptian ideology, in contrast, makes the animal the "enemy" of the gods, to forestall—and thus to acknowledge—feelings of guilt. Religion is not managing a world of objects, but participating in a paradoxical world of life.   W.B.

Egypt

Meaning and contexts of offerings. In ancient Egypt, presenting offerings to gods (or divine beings of other kinds) forms the core activity in most rituals. Yet the background of most offerings is markedly different from that in the biblical world. Making a sacrifice, for instance, in no way carried with it the implication of a voluntary loss of wealth as a means of demonstrating religious sincerity. Sacrificial meat was not burnt for the god, but eaten by the worshiper after the ritual had ended, and ritual texts usually present offerings as a kind of economic trade. The human presents a gift in an attempt to induce the divinity to present a reward. To the extent that this perspective can also be reversed (the divinity receives a gift in return for his charitable acts), the giver and the recipient can be said to stand in a symbiotic relationship.

Given that most middle-class and lower-class Egyptians were illiterate, textual references to offerings and sacrifice and the artistic representations left on the monuments of the wealthy must be supplemented by our knowledge of votive offerings left by ordinary people at popular shrines. Unfortunately, only a few such shrines are known, and they date from a relatively short period of time, between the late predynastic period and the Old Kingdom. But shrines such as the predecessor of the Satet temple at Elephantine, the early temples at Hierakonpolis, Medamud, Coptos, and Abydos, and the one currently under excavation in Tell Ibrahim Awad in the Nile Delta have produced evidence suggesting that the deposition of votive offerings was common. This material includes a large number of crude figurines of different sorts, but also of "funny rocks": pebbles of irregular form, which for some reason seemed sufficiently important to be deposited in or near the shrines. Similar pebbles have been found in votive contexts dating to as late as the New Kingdom. Moreover, crude statuettes not dissimilar to those found in these early dynastic shrines have been found in settlement contexts dating to the late Old Kingdom (Ayn Asil), early Middle Kingdom (Tell el-Daba), and New Kingdom (Kom Rabia). In these latter cases, however, it is unfortunately impossible to tell whether their aim was religious and, if so, whether they played a part in offering rituals. Moreover, in none of the cases discussed so far is it clear who deposited the items or in the course of what kind of ritual. Nevertheless it seems likely that, in the earlier periods of pharaonic history, there existed forms of cultic offerings that were only remotely connected with the classical, truly pharaonic, elite forms of offerings.

Funerary offerings. Already in the early dynastic period, increasing numbers of tombs receive a so-called slab stele, representing the deceased seated on a chair in front of a table covered with piles of food. In many cases, there is also a list describing the quantities of

King making offering of two cakes to the god Montu. Limestone relief, 17th Dynasty (17th–16th centuries BCE). *Courtesy Gay Robins*

food, drink, and other commodities to which the deceased was entitled. Many such stelae occur in the relatively modest tombs at Helwan, which were certainly too small for the storage of large amounts of gifts. This suggests a tendency to replace real gifts by a mere statement to the effect that they should be there. The mechanism by which such statements were made effective was the performance of an offering cult. One of the most important technical terms for funerary (and divine) offerings from this time onward is *prí.tḫrw* (lit., bringing forth the voice). So the act of reading out a list of offerings was one of the mechanisms by which the deceased was provided with offerings. The ritual could be restricted to merely this act: several tomb inscriptions of the Middle Kingdom implore visitors to recite an invocation offering and remind them that such offerings cost nothing but a breath of air. But in full-blown offering rituals, the act of reading accompanied real presentations of offerings.

In the course of the Old Kingdom, the funerary cult places where these acts were performed developed a general layout that can be found both in royal pyramid temples and in the offering chapels in the tombs of the elite. The core of such offering places is formed by an offering table where the gifts could be deposited and a false door through which the *ka* of the deceased could enter the offering hall in order to collect the victuals. In some cases cult statues, that is, three-dimensional renderings of the beneficiary, also played a part. These are best known from the royal pyramid temples of the mid-4th Dynasty and later, where the offering hall is preceded by another sheltering five cult statues of the king. However, cult statues are occasionally encountered in private tombs as well.

Offering places of such an elaborate form are common in the elite and royal cemeteries of the Old Kingdom, and the layout persists in tombs of the Middle and New Kingdoms and later. They are still a common feature, for instance, of the gigantic tombs of the Theban clergy of Amun in the 26th Dynasty. However, already in the course of the New Kingdom, the importance of the offering table, the false door, and the list of offerings seems to be on the retreat, and many cases where they are still encountered may rather testify to an adherence to a time-honored architectural layout rather than to the persistence of a ritual practice in an unchanged form. In any case, these and other variations, occurring over several periods for both royal and nonroyal burials, remind us that it was always possible to vary the way in which an offering ritual took place.

Funerary and divine offerings. Apart from the small, early provincial shrines mentioned earlier, very little remains of Old Kingdom and Middle Kingdom temples. It is certain that a large temple existed at Heliopolis, and the references to local cults in the Pyramid Texts leave no room for doubt that local sanctuaries existed elsewhere in the country, too. The problem is that we know very little about the way in which the offering cults in these sanctuaries worked. By the Middle Kingdom, the picture gradually becomes less hazy, but we reach firm ground only in the New Kingdom and later, from which temples are infinitely better preserved. The core of most temples was formed by a *naos* (dwelling place) that sheltered the cult statue of the deity; an offering hall stood in front of it. Daily cult consisted of a morning ritual and an offering ritual. The morning ritual consisted of the purification and clothing of the cult statue, whereas the offering ritual provided the god with food and drink. The first well-documented and detailed evidence for offering practices in temples postdates similar evidence from mortuary contexts by many centuries. This and other considerations suggest that the daily temple cult (as well as many other forms of veneration in Egyptian temples) reproduced the most important elements of funerary or mortuary rituals. Schenkel argued that the divine cult and the private mortuary cult were variant forms of the same model. Also notable in this respect is that morning and offering rituals in Egyptian temples cast the divinity in the role of Osiris, the god of

Sacred baboon offers Eye to the Egyptian god Re. *University of Pennsylvania Museum, Philadelphia (Neg. #S5-23173)*

death, and the priest (officially the king) in the role of his son, Horus. In this way, the temple ritual mimics the funerary cult ideally carried out for a dead father by his eldest son. In short, with some caution we may combine temple and mortuary texts in order to build a coherent image of the ideology of the offering cult.

The aim of the offering. In Old Kingdom funerary chapels, the presentation of offerings is occasionally designated as *sꜣḫ*, a technical term referring to the transformation of the deceased into a person of divine status. Clearly, the administration of the offering was not merely regarded as a provision of food and drink, but as accomplishing a much higher aim.

In contemporary Pyramid Texts such as §§50–112, it becomes clear how this was achieved. As the offerings were presented, the lector-priest recited a text from a papyrus scroll in which the offering was associated with a mythological precedent. This happened in two ways.

First, the deceased was invited to accept the "eye of Horus," the latter expression being a blanket term for each of the offerings delivered. Thus, by presenting the offering to the deceased, the officiant re-created part of the Horus myth, in the course of which Horus's eye was torn out by Seth, later to be returned by other deities, including Thoth. Clearly, the ritual had the aim of typecasting the deceased as Horus at the moment of his triumph over Seth.

Second, the subsequent text established further mythological links between the offering and the mythological world. Usually, puns were employed: a pun on the name of the item linked it with a particular mythological episode. Offering texts of this type are usually quite brief, and no overall mythological picture emerges; we must assume that common knowledge filled in the background.

However, other texts (the *sꜣḫ.w* spells) are longer and more coherent, clearly aiming at a description of the metaphysical personality that the deceased hoped to assume in the netherworld. It is argued that the recitation of such texts constituted a ritual in itself, such as the presentation of offerings. However, there are reasons (such as the occurrence of the term *sꜣḫ* in offering scenes) for believing that the recital may well have accompanied the performance of the offerings.

The distinction between meat offerings and other offerings. The texts recited when offerings were presented make a marked distinction between meat offerings and other offerings (the former being usually designated "sacrifice" by Egyptologists). In the case of most kinds of food, the topic of how the food was produced and prepared is of no interest. In contrast, descriptions of meat offerings characteristically include treatment of the animal's slaughter. Innumerable depictions show how sacrificial oxen were slaughtered: their foreleg was severed while the animal was still alive. The presentation of the foreleg (and sometimes the heart) is frequently depicted as well.

Yoyotte (1980–81) convincingly discussed the remarkable fact that ritual texts regularly describe the sacrificial animal as an enemy. Thus, presenting meat to a dead person or a god implies not only the provision of food, but also the punishment or death of a hostile entity. Ritual texts concerning the sacrificial slaughter often describe in gruesome detail how the enemy is dealt with.

Several texts leave the identity of the "enemy" vague, but many others identify him with Seth, the divine enemy of Horus and Osiris. Texts of the late and Greco-Roman periods alternatively point to Apopis, the cosmic enemy of the sun-god Re, who, by that time, was in many ways considered to be identical with Seth. Accordingly, the sacrifice had a clear apotropaic function: divine evil was averted and crushed. The sacrifice also tied into royal ideology, since the king was considered the earthly embodiment of Horus, and Seth was a disruptive force that menaced the line of royal succession and thereby Egypt in general. Apopis, on the other hand, was the personification of chaos threatening the created world. In the Books of the Netherworld found in New Kingdom royal tombs, we encounter powerful images of his harmful influences. Apopis almost succeeds in stopping the journey of the sun-god through the netherworld. Apopis's defeat enables the sun-god to accomplish a new sunrise—and by extension to inaugurate a fresh episode in the eternal cycle of creation.

Slaughtering rituals, thus, establish associations between the human and divine worlds. Considerable variation was possible, however, regarding the creatures on which the rite was performed. Bulls were the most popular animals, but by no means the only ones. Because the victim represented an enemy of Egypt, various kinds of animals that were considered "un-Egyptian" were used as well; animals that dwelled in the desert—the realm of Seth—are examples. Humans classified as criminals sometimes were used, too, for their behavior placed them in league with Seth. Such criminals mostly were persons who trespassed against a sacred institution of some sort. Although such human sacrifices may have been exceptional, there is no reason to assume that the texts that describe them are exaggerating, because the remains of human sacrifices are attested archeologically.

Offering scenes in Egyptian temples. One more type of evidence must be considered to complete our picture of Egyptian offerings: the numerous ritual scenes on Egyptian temples dating between the New Kingdom and the Roman period. Characteristically, these scenes show the king—the archetypal priest—facing one or more deities during the performance of a ritual. Some of the episodes presented (e.g., the daily temple ritual) are rather involved. Other scenes give more-or-less realistic renderings of the Sokar festival in, for instance, the temple of Medinet Habu or of the festival of the annual union of Hathor of Dendara and Horus of Edfu in the Ptolemaic temple of that latter city. Numerous other instances could be cited. It is argued that the distribution of certain types of scenes is intimately linked to certain rooms of the temple. This might suggest that the ritual scenes reflect acts that really took place in the various rooms. Considering that most scenes depict the king making an offering to a deity, this could lead to the conclusion that the offering scenes are a mine of information on how offering rituals were actually carried out in the rooms where they are depicted.

We must be cautious, however. First, religious iconography in general, and the ritual iconography of temples in particular, gives more-or-less fossilized renderings of performances which, in actual practice, must have changed continually. Temple iconography can therefore be little more than an abstraction of the ritual life that once reigned in the temples.

In New Kingdom temples, moreover, these scenes are highly formal, and the texts usually provide little more than stock phrases giving only restricted information as to what the ritual was really about or the context of its performance. It is true that this changed dramatically in the late period, and particularly in the Greco-Roman period, but even then the scenes are often of little help in understanding the organization of the ritual performance. The depictions and inscriptions admittedly become more detailed and varied, but the increased

amount of information primarily concerns the theology of the temple and the religious meaning of the interaction between the officiating king and the god(s). It is quite another matter whether the scenes are reliable representations of what actually happened.

This is particularly clear in the case of apparent offerings that have no precursors in older offering rituals and which in some cases are rather unlikely to have taken place in the way that they are rendered on the walls. A clear case is that of the famous ritual of "offering the field," in which the king is shown holding the hieroglyph for "field" in his hands. Since there is no evidence that ritual objects of this form existed, the scenes must at best have been symbolic renderings of the ritual performance. But in fact we do not know whether the presentation of lands ever formed part of offering rituals. It has been suggested that, in the course of certain performances, priests read out documents listing the lands that the temple had acquired through pious donations and that the "offering of the field scenes" allude to this. Even if this is correct, the matter is not an offering in the sense of the word used in this section.

The offering of the goddess Maat, which is very frequently depicted in Egyptian temples, is a similar case. Considering the prominent locations where it is usually encountered, this scene must have been of tremendous importance. Yet Maat does not appear in the offering lists, although the expression "to present Maat" occurs from at least the Middle Kingdom on as a general expression for providing gifts to the god. Maat was the embodiment of divine order, and "presenting Maat" could apparently be used as a general expression for the correct performance of rituals. It is quite another matter whether this entailed presenting physical effigies of the goddess to the god, although we do know that such effigies were made in the course of time. (This might be regarded as a secondary and perhaps optional development.) Basically, "presenting Maat" is an abstract term referring to the sense of the act rather than to an act itself. Clearly, we are dealing with depictions of the transference of abstract properties rather than offerings.

In cases like this it seems clear that the offering scenes express the theology of the temple ritual rather than visualize actual performances. It is perhaps surprising that the theologians who designed the decoration of the temples did not opt for the more straightforward method of inscribing the walls with theological tractates. Although, for us, this would indubitably have had the advantage of clarity, this is apparently not what the decorators were after. As a matter of fact, theological treatises seem to be singularly absent from the incredible mass of religious literature left behind by the ancient Egyptians. Most theological documents, in fact, seem to have a ritual purpose or background. If this is so, the ritual aspect must have been deemed as vital as the theological one. In view of the interaction between the divine world and the officiants being fundamentally ritual in nature, the scenes depict matters as they really were, without, however, always aspiring to illustrate real ritual episodes.

This can be most clearly seen in cases where the offerings are not objects in the normal sense of the word but combinations of hieroglyphic signs with a symbolic meaning, such as the hieroglyphs for "stability," "durability," and "life." Although, in the late and Greco-Roman periods, such symbols came to be reproduced in the form of three-dimensional ritual objects, it seems clear that they first emerged within the interplay of symbolic meanings in temple iconography. They are of secondary importance for an understanding of how offerings and sacrificial rites were performed.

BIBL.: W. Barta, *Die altägyptische Opferliste von der Frühzeit bis zur griechisch-römischen Epoche* (Berlin, 1963). E. Graefe, "Die Deutung der sogenannten 'Opfergaben' der Ritualszenen ägyptischer Tempel als 'Schriftzeichen,'" in *Ritual and Sacrifice in the Ancient Near East* (ed. J. Quaegebeur; Louvain, 1993), 143–56. G. Lapp, *Die Opferformel des Alten Reiches* (Mainz am Rhein, 1986). A. Moret, *Le rituel du culte divin journalier* (Paris, 1902). J. Yoyotte, "Héra d'Héliopolis et le sacrifice humain," *Annuaire: École pratique des hautes études* (1980–81): 29–102.   H.O.W.

Mesopotamia

Let us begin by confronting a lexical difficulty. "Sacrifice," which literally means "to make [something] sacred or holy," can be used to describe offerings of all types. Offering something to the gods sanctifies it, makes it holy. But within the biblical world, sacrifice more typically connotes a specific type of offering in which blood is poured out. Connected with this, usually, is the idea that blood is endowed with a special power. Although this idea is common to most of the Semitic world, it is unknown in Mesopotamia, because sacrifices in the strict sense did not exist in Mesopotamia. In this section, therefore, we shall speak only of offerings.

Cosmology. To understand the place of offerings in Mesopotamian religion, we first must examine cosmology briefly. Two interrelated perspectives are central. The first, as expressed in the Myth of Atrahasis (the Babylonian story of the flood), presents humans as providers of food and drinks for the gods. Humans replaced the lesser gods in this role after the latter revolted against the god Enlil. Through this myth, the whole regimen of the daily offerings in the temples, which consists simply in the feeding of the gods, is justified.

According to the second perspective, the gods, because they are somehow responsible for the origin of humanity, also have control over human life and can decide human destiny. These decisions are irrevocable but can, nevertheless, be influenced by humans. Through prayers and offerings an individual can change the course of his or her destiny. The two perspectives suggest both that gods and humans exist in a master-servant relationship and that a certain contractual element is present. In the main, this section deals with offerings set into the first perspective.

Recipients of the offerings. In Mesopotamia, every being that was not of this world, except evil beings and demons (even good demons), might receive offerings because they had some power over human lives, propitious or nefarious, and, therefore, humans had to remain on good terms with them. Among the preeminent recipients were the celestial gods and the powers of the netherworld. Anything that surrounded these powers, moreover, was holy and therefore might also receive sacrifices. This included all the gods' paraphernalia—statues, thrones, chariots, garments, musical instruments.

The dead, too, received offerings. The spirits *(gidim)* of the dead kings were honored thus. As the myth of Ishtar's descent into the netherworld suggests, if the dead were not satisfied, they might leave the Land of No Return and affect the world of the living. Offerings were used to keep them in peace.

The heavenly bodies, as symbols of the divinities, also received offerings. The cycle of the moon was followed closely, and the three first quarters of the moon were occasions for special offerings. The celestial places in which the moon and the sun appear also received offerings.

Finally, the divinized kings of Ur, and later of other Mesopotamian cities, received offerings. In part, this was because the king was the mediator or "pontifex" between this world and the divine one. But he also belonged to the otherworld because he was understood to have been conceived from a divine seed, carried in the womb of a goddess, and fed at the breasts of goddesses. The king was divine and therefore had to receive offerings just as the other gods. His throne, signifying his presence, was honored in the same way. His burial, and probably also his coronation, occasioned lavish ceremonies.

Products offered. The quantities and qualities of specific offerings were proportional to the dignity of those who were to receive them. Aside from votive offerings, the most valuable offerings a person could make were the products of his herd; this followed on the idea that wealth was measured by the number of sheep. Meat was the most highly valued product that could be given to the gods, but we must remember that the Mesopotamians practiced no ritual killing or special killing of animals and no ritualized draining of blood. In other words, meat was offered in the same spirit as other agricultural products. Different animals carried different values: one ox was worth ten sheep. Other animals, such as gazelle, ibex, and similar types of *cervidae,* might also be offered, although more rarely because they were more difficult to obtain and thus more valuable. Poultry might also be offered, as well as their eggs and even their feathers (the latter probably for decora-

The sacrifice of a ram, or perhaps a divination scene, depicted in a mosaic inlay, temple of Shamash at Mari. Damascus Museum. *Erich Lessing/Art Resource, New York*

tion). Pork and fish are rarely mentioned in our texts; although fish was probably a staple food for humans, it was not considered good enough for the gods' table.

A complex classificatory system was applied to cattle, who were fattened on barley. Other animals were simply fed with grass and more often served as food for the workers. Only the best were for the gods' temples. The kitchens of the temples were quite large, and the ovens where the gods' meals were prepared roared continuously with fires.

Anything that was edible could be offered. The most important foodstuff aside from meat was flour of all kinds, which was used to make bread or cakes, but we also hear of onions, garlic, and dates.

We hear little about how the food was actually prepared. One text mentions cooking suckling lambs by roasting them, burying them in ashes, or boiling them in water. The recipes were probably quite simple because we have no evidence for sophisticated cooking pots. Salt and spices are not mentioned very often in lists of temple deliveries.

Offerers. In Mesopotamia, most high priests were of royal descent, and the king, as he often reminded people, was the bridge maker to the otherworld, the one who received the gods' orders and was responsible for the welfare of the people, ensuring an abundance of water and a harvest that only the gods could give.

Based on this, one would assume that the king was the main provider of offerings in temples, but at least during the Ur III period, probably, it was the real owners of the land, the governors of the cities, called *ensi,* who organized the deliveries of offerings in turns, according

to the affluence of their provinces. In this way, each of them provided for the needs of the palace and the major temples for about a month's time. In addition, the high officials of the kingdom were taxed according to their rank, and they paid with cows and sheep. Even the wives of some of these high officials were taxed.

Time, place, and organization. Most offerings took place in the temples of the important divinities; the palaces of the king and the governor also contained cultic installations, in which some ceremonies took place—which suggests that we should be very careful about making a clear distinction between buildings for religious and profane uses.

Like human meals, divine meals took place at fixed times, twice a day. An early service was scheduled in the cool of the dawn, and a second service took place in the evening or even at night.

Many tablets mention that the offerings took place in the presence of the king, after he had entered the temple or palace as part of a procession. A libation was made while the king held a sheep against his breast or presented a fish. Did this represent his attempt to obtain an abundance of fish or herd animals? Many statues represent the king in such a pose, and annual royal records speak of him doing this, which implies its importance. We also hear about the pouring of cold water, the offerings of bread, and the erection of stelae. The Ur III tablets mention a lustration *(a-tu-a).*

Ultimately, the offerings nourished all the attendants of the temple and therefore the needs of the divinities must always have matched the needs of the temple staff.

Votives. The term *votive (arua)* refers to an offering made of nonperishable materials, such as stone, cloth, or metal. Normally the word means an offering made after a vow, as part of a bargain with the divinity. A sick person might say, for example, "If I am healed I will give you the most precious item I possess." But in the context of Mesopotamian religion, *arua* meant, more broadly, the dedication of an object for the sole use of the divinity. It could be a precious stone, a rich garment, pearls, a seal, and so on. Because votive objects were expected to endure, they were often inscribed with the name and the purpose of the donor and the name of the divinity who received it.

Human beings given to temples were also considered to be votives. Men, women, and children could be dedicated to serve in a temple or as a kind of labor force in the mills and factories belonging to a temple. Clearly, this solved the temple's need for help quite economically, as these dedicated humans served without pay or rights. Many questions remain about this custom,

Two depictions of the king pouring libation on a stylized palm tree, a Tree of Life, before seated moon-god Nanna; relief from Ur. *University of Pennsylvania Museum, Philadelphia (Neg. #S4-140070)*

however: who made people into votive gifts, who could be votives, how were such votives replaced after death, how large was this institution?

BIBL.: Tzvi Abusch, "Sacrifice in Mesopotamia," in *Sacrifice in Religious Experience* (ed. A. I. Baumgarten; Studies in the History of Religions 93; Leiden: Brill, 2002), 39–43. Mark E. Cohen, *The Cultic Calendar of the Ancient Near East* (Bethesda, Md.: CDL, 1993). H. H. Figulla, "Offerings in the Ningal-Temple at Ur," *Iraq* 15 (1953): 88–122, 171–92. Andrew George, *House Most High: The Temples of Ancient Mesopotamia* (Mesopotamian Civilizations 5; Winona Lake, Ind.: Eisenbrauns, 1993).   M.S.

Syria-Canaan

The character of administrative records in Syro-Canaanite ritual texts provides good information about the cultic elements of offerings and sacrifices. In this section, we will consider first the sacrificial system itself, its different kinds of complex rituals, and then the materials that were offered.

In the ancient Near East, offerings were intended, in general, as a way of nourishing and entertaining the gods, who participated in the sacred meal or banquet that such offerings represented. The archives of 3rd-millennium Ebla provide only a general term (NÌ-BA, NÌD.BA) for any kind of offering presented to all the different deities. Similarly, in Emar, the offerings to the gods were above all "sacrifices" *(naqû)* in a general sense, which included offerings of any kind, animal victims, and libations. The word conveys the meaning of "provision" for both gods and humans.

The sacrificial system is described in more detail,

however, in the alphabetic cult texts from Ugarit; here we find parallels with the sacrificial system of the Hebrew Bible. The most generic term for any sort of offering rite is *dbḥ,* which properly means "sacrifice," that is, involving the slaughter of animals, but which includes various types of rite, both sacrificial and nonsacrificial in the strictest sense. Several other generic terms, both literary and ritual, in Ugaritic and in Hurrian, also refer to generic offering rites that are not easy to understand. The term *šrp* has been connected with the Hebrew "holocaust" *(ʿōlâ)* and *šlmm* (peace or communion sacrifice; *šĕlāmîm*). However, Ugaritic *šrp* did not imply a complete holocaust. Overall, our evidence for sacrificial ritual suggests that it was understood as a banquet, in which both gods and humans took part. Libations, also, might be made at times *(ntk, sgy).* Mention must also be made of the *pgr* offering, commemorated in two stelae. This may be the specific name for "funerary sacrifice" at Ugarit, which is likely connected with the Mari sacrifice *pagrāʾum.*

Our evidence for the Phoenician sacrificial system is very meager, although two late and peripheral tariff texts from Marseilles and Carthage provide some information. *Zbḥ* seems to be the general term for "offering" or "sacrifice," although there are also terms for particular types, the meaning of which is uncertain. There are also isolated references to the *zbḥ ymm* (annual or regular sacrifice) and the *zbḥ bmnḥt* (sacrifice as a *minḥâ*), which are similar to the Ugaritic and Hebrew phenomena. Archeological remains of large and small altars hint at sacrifices, libation rites, and the offering of incense and vegetables.

We have no records of the sacrificial system of the Old Aramean religion, aside from generic allusions to offerings of food and drink to the gods in some inscriptions. The situation becomes a little better in our evidence from Palmyra. Altars, various kinds of sacred vessels, and incense burners that have been found sketch the situation and hint at burnt sacrifices, libations, and offerings of incense.

As for the materials involved, the central items at any time and place were cattle and sheep, as well as other animals; there were no special taboos about which animals could be used, as in some other Mediterranean cultures. Libation liquids, above all oil and wine, also are mentioned frequently in our sources, as are vegetables and minerals (silver and gold), either in their natural state or processed into items such as textiles, clothing, ingots, vases, plates, statues, and other utensils.

At Ebla, the gods chiefly received bread and mutton

Canaanite cult stand from Taanach, 10th century BCE, with shallow basin on the top. Probably used for offerings. The images include a winged sun disk in the top level; a stylized tree, perhaps the Tree of Life, in the next level; two sphinxes in the third level; and a goddess at the base. *Photo by Z. Radovan, Jerusalem*

with several other rarer animals such as asses, geese, lambs, and kids. Burnt animal entrails, mainly offal, make for an unusual offering; this practice was also known and regulated in the Hebrew sacrificial system. Blood, in contrast, is never mentioned. Flour and bread, honey and balsam were also offered.

Our knowledge of Phoenician-Punic offerings comes from the tariff lists of Marseilles and Carthage: cattle, calves, rams, goats, lambs, kids, birds, pastries, milk, and fat. Archeology attests to the common custom of dedicating stelae above all as funerary offerings. With the move away from sacrificial religion and toward dedicatory or votive religion, as attested in later times at Palmyra and Petra, the dedication of sacred objects and even structures (columns, porticos, altars, reliefs, statues, and so on) became more common in general.

The tesserae from Palmyra provide good information on offerings in the Aramean world. The provisions, food, and drinks to be consumed and previously offered in the ritual meals are specified: bread, grain, salt, honey, fat, wine, oil, and fruit. We meet with a similar situation in our materials from Petra, although a further peculiarity, the offering of camels, also is found there.   G.O.L.

Israel

The movement of animal sacrifices and other offerings to sanctuaries and their processing and redistribution were characteristic of cult in ancient Israel, as they were of religious devotion in related civilizations. According to several early biblical legal collections, all male Israelites were obligated to bring offerings and sacrifices to cultic centers three times during the year: the early spring festival of Unleavened Bread (Passover), the late spring/early summer festival of Harvest (Weeks), and the fall festival of Ingathering (Booths) (Exod. 23.14, 15b, 17; 34.20c, 23; Deut. 16.16–17). Visits to sanctuaries occurred at other times as well, as shrines were the primary places where meat was processed and consumed (at least until the success of the Deuteronomistic effort to forbid sacrifice outside Jerusalem [Deut. 12.4–18]). Cult sites were also the locus for petitioning and thanking the deity; for the fulfillment of vows; for the correction of transgressions; and—in many instances—for the final stages of purification. A variety of texts bear witness to sanctuary pilgrimages during which heads of household and their dependents participated in the sacrificial process (they "rejoiced," in the biblical idiom; see, e.g., Deut. 16.11, 14; 1 Sam. 1.3–5).

Israelite sacrifices and offerings are described in detail in many biblical texts. They consisted of clean livestock such as sheep, goats, and cattle (ungulates with a split hoof that chew the cud); clean birds such as the dove, turtledove, and pigeon; certain products of agriculture, horticulture, and viticulture (grain in various forms [flour, parched grain, unleavened bread, pancakes], oil, wine); and other materials such as salt and

for their maintenance, both in large amounts. Cloths and precious metal objects are also mentioned, and we hear of an "offering of oil," which possibly was to be used in a cultic setting.

At Emar, the main sacrificial staples were cattle and sheep, from which some parts (e.g., the head) were singled out for special offering rites and others were allotted to the cultic personnel for their private use. The ritual texts also mention breads of various kinds, liquids (beer, wine, and oils) along with their containers, fruit, cereals (barley), and woolen garments. At Ugarit, in addition to the usual victims—cattle and sheep, sometimes in large quantities—we encounter birds and fish, along

Sacrifice of Isaac portrayed in a mosaic in the Bet Alpha synagogue; the hand of God, top center, is restraining Abraham. *Photo by Z. Radovan, Jerusalem*

incense. Later texts, such as Neh. 10.34 [= 10.35 Hebrew] and 13.31, speak also of a wood offering. Although all sacrificial animals and birds had to be clean (i.e., without pollution), not all clean animals and birds were acceptable as sacrifices. For example, although the gazelle and hart were classed as clean and edible, they were never brought to the sanctuary for sacrifice (see Deut. 12.15). In general, sacrificial animals were acceptable for cultic slaughter only if they were both clean and unblemished. Among blemishes disqualifying a sacrificial animal were asymmetrical limbs, lameness, blindness, scabs, and damaged genitals (Lev. 22.17–25; Deut. 15.21–22; 17.1).

Specific requirements for each type of sacrifice varied. Where one sacrifice might require a male animal, another might require a female; where one might be expensive, another might be more affordable. For sacrifices intended to restore purity after a period of pollution, the value of the required animals or birds varied, depending on the severity of the pollution experienced. For example, the Priestly Code in the Pentateuch requires a woman or man who has recovered from a genital discharge to bring two birds to the sanctuary (Lev. 15.14, 29); in contrast, a person who has recovered from skin disease must make a more costly contri-

bution of two male lambs, one female lamb, a grain offering mixed with oil, and a measure of oil (14.10). Texts also suggest that the social status of the sacrificer could play a role in determining the animal to be sacrificed. For example, though 4.28 demands a female goat as a purification offering from a common person, 4.23 requires a male goat from a ruler.

Sacrifices and offerings brought to sanctuaries were processed by worshipers in conjunction with cultic specialists (primarily priests): animals were slaughtered, their skins were flayed, their blood was drained, and their meat, fat, and internal organs separated for later use. Generally, fat and certain internal organs were burned on the altar as an offering to the deity; blood was manipulated by priests on the altar or elsewhere; meat was either burned to YHWH, cooked and reserved for the priests, or apportioned among worshipers, the sanctuary staff, and their dependents; skins and other refuse were discarded in predetermined, ritually acceptable ways (e.g., Lev. 4.11–12). Grain products, wine, oil, and incense were also processed and redistributed within the sanctuary. Many sources insist that blood and fat were never to be eaten under any circumstances: fat was to be burned on the altar to YHWH, and blood was either poured out or reserved for priestly manipula-

Horned altar, 10th–9th century BCE, from Megiddo. A number of altars of this type have been found at sites in Israel dating to the same general period. *Erich Lessing/Art Resource, New York*

tion (see, e.g., Lev. 3.16b–17; 7.22–27; 17.10–14; 19.26; Deut. 12.23).

Sacrifices and offerings had several purposes. First fruits, firstborn of sacrificial animals, tithes, and other obligatory contributions are best understood as taxation in kind to support the cultic establishment (including the dependents of priests and other cultic functionaries). Sacrificial and offering portions reserved for YHWH are a form of tribute to the divine overlord, intended to honor him (see Isa. 43.23). Sacrifices may function to appease an angry deity (1 Sam. 26.19). They correct sin, effect purification, communicate thanksgiving, fulfill vows, and elicit blessings for worshipers. References to feeding and smelling are present in many passages describing sacrifices. These give the impression of an anthropomorphic divinity who receives food and who delights in the scent of cooking meat and burning incense or grain (see, e.g., Gen. 8.20–22; Lev. 21.17; Num. 28.2; Deut. 33.10).

Most of the data upon which we depend for the classification of sacrifices and offerings and for the reconstruction of sacrificial rituals are found in the Priestly Code (P) and, to a lesser degree, the Holiness Code (H = Lev. 17–26). Earlier texts also bear witness to a variety of sacrificial types and sacrificial rites which do not necessarily conform to the picture projected by P or H,

and P and H themselves do not necessarily present a consistent picture. Thus, we are dependent upon a variety of biblical sources that are sometimes contradictory for our reconstruction of the sacrificial system. The richest description of biblical sacrifices and offerings occurs in Lev. 1–7, a pericope assigned mainly to P. In that block of material, we find detailed descriptions of the sacrifices as well as instructions about how these are to be performed. Among the sacrifices described in Lev. 1–7 are the whole burnt offering *('ôlâ)*, the cereal offering *(minhâ)*, the purification sacrifice *(hattā't)*, the reparation sacrifice *('āšām)*, and the well-being sacrifice *(šělāmîm)*, which is subdivided into the offering of thanksgiving *(tôdâ)*, the votive offering *(neder)*, and the freewill offering *(nědābâ)*. Other offerings of note include the tithe, the first fruits, firstlings of animals, and devoted things *(hērem)*, each discussed in Num. 18. Each offering type has a specific function or set of functions and is processed in a particular way. Where the purification offering might correct an unintentional transgression (see Lev. 4.1–31) or purge uncleanness (e.g., of the parturient woman; 12.6) and provide the sacrificing priest with meat to eat (6.26 [= 6.19]), the well-being sacrifice functions mainly as a source of meat for worshipers and, secondarily, for priests. When the whole offering is burnt in its entirety on the altar, the meat of the reparation sacrifice is reserved for the priesthood, and only the entrails and fat are burned to YHWH (7.1–6). Whereas all members of a priestly household are entitled to eat the first fruits, only priests and their sons may eat the meat of the purification and reparation sacrifices and the grain offering (Num. 18.9–10, 13).

There is vestigial evidence for child sacrifices and offerings to the dead in biblical materials, and these may well have played a more central role in Israelite cultic life than extant texts might suggest. The Hebrew Bible preserves several polemics against child sacrifice (e.g., Lev. 20.2–5; 2 Kings 21.6), including texts that associate the practice with an alleged (but not securely attested) Canaanite deity Molech. Nonetheless, some texts suggest that child sacrifices in Israel were made to YHWH himself and that the practice was legitimate in at least some Israelite circles (e.g., Gen. 22; Exod. 13.2; Judg. 11; Jer. 7.31; Ezek. 20.25–26, 30–31; Mic. 6.6–8, which all suggest that YHWH was the recipient of child sacrifices). Offerings to the dead, one element of devotion to ancestors well known from the larger west Asian cultural environment, are mentioned in biblical texts from both the First and Second Temple periods (e.g., Deut. 26.14; Ps. 106.28; Tob. 4.17; Sir. 30.18). Some texts speak specifically of placing these offerings at the gravesite (Tob. 4.17; Sir. 30.18), and texts do not necessarily express disapproval of such offerings (see, e.g., Tob. 4.17; Deut. 26.14 suggests only that the tithe not be offered to the dead; it says nothing about presenting other offerings to them). In addition to offerings made to ancestors, vestigial biblical evidence survives of other ritual elements of what might have been a widespread cult of the dead in ancient Israel (e.g., the rites of setting up a stele to an ancestor and invoking the ancestor's name, witnessed in 2 Sam. 18.18).

Two types of vow *(neder)* are attested in biblical materials: a voluntary pledge in exchange for nothing on the part of the deity, and a voluntary pledge made to the deity in exchange for the deity's fulfillment of the petitioner's request. The Nazirite vow of Num. 6—an ascetic vow of men and women—is often taken as typical of the former. In this text, the votary abstains from the products of viticulture, corpse contact, and haircutting for the period of the vow. Nothing is asked of YHWH in return. Typical of the latter is Jacob's vow at Bethel in Gen. 28.20–22: in exchange for protection, food, and clothing on his journey, Jacob declares that he will embrace YHWH as his god, establish Bethel as a sanctuary, and pay a regular tithe to YHWH. The typical vow probably consisted of a modest gift in exchange for a favor from the deity and, like all vows, had to be paid eventually. Yet people could vow themselves or their dependents to YHWH, their landed property (including their houses), or their movable property (including livestock). In 1 Sam. 1.11, Hannah vows that if YHWH will provide her with a son, she will commit him for life to YHWH's service in the sanctuary. Vows of women are discussed at length in Num. 30.

In general, the Israelite repertoire of sacrifices, offerings, and vows—including offerings to the dead and child sacrifices—was not unlike what is commonly attested for other Northwest Semitic–speaking peoples such as the population of Ugarit, Arameans, mainland Phoenicians, and Phoenician colonists in the central and western Mediterranean.

Offerings, sacrifices, and votives play a central role in the corpus of classical rabbinic literature. The earliest rabbinic legal collection, the Mishnah (compiled circa 200 CE), contains tractates that focus on animal sacrifices, cereal offerings, firstborn animals, vows, the daily offering, and the observance of the Passover festival, among other topics. This material contains extensive rabbinic discussion and debate, originally preserved orally and antedating 200 CE, concerning sacrificial and votive practice. It is supplemented in the Babylonian Talmud (and, to a lesser extent, in the Jerusalem Talmud) with commentary and elaboration from later generations of rabbis (circa 200–500 CE).

BIBL.: Gary A. Anderson, *Sacrifices and Offerings in Ancient Israel* (Atlanta, 1987). Jacques Berlinblau, *The Vow and the "Popular Religious Groups" of Ancient Israel* (Sheffield, 1996). Baruch A. Levine, *In the Presence of the Lord* (Leiden, 1974).   S.M.O.

Anatolia

Offering or sacrifice may be defined as the rule-governed, ceremonial transfer of a foodstuff or other physi-

cal object from an individual or community of humans into the possession of a deity, demon, ghost, or personified numinous entity. The purpose behind this activity is the continued sustenance of the parahuman being in question and/or the securing of his/her goodwill and thereby influence over his/her/its actions. Within the ancient Near East, evidence from the Hittite capital of Bogazköy/Hattusha and other Hittite sites constitutes the single largest body of material available for the study of sacrifice. In accordance with the multicultural nature of Hittite religion, sacrificial practice was not a homogeneous system, but a continuously changing congeries of conceptions and procedures drawn from the Indo-European, Mesopotamian, Hurrian, and indigenous Hattic strata.

The Hittite archives preserve innumerable cuneiform texts describing offering procedures in great detail. The rites considered are of two main types: the periodically celebrated "festivals" (EZEN) of the state cult and the "rituals" (SISKUR) presenting magical procedures to be performed only irregularly, in the event of an emergent problem. Further information may be drawn from administrative lists recording the quantities of livestock or other materials to be offered at particular festivals and the bureaucrat or community responsible for their supply. Scattered passages in texts of other genres, including instructions for temple personnel, prayers, vows, and divination reports, also contribute to our knowledge of Hittite sacrifice.

Those receiving offerings included innumerable gods and goddesses, many known only from their appearance in sacrificial lists. Anthropomorphic deities customarily participated in sacrifice in the form of statues or stelae that represented them. Offerings to divinized mountains and springs and gifts to sacred objects and places, such as the throne and locations in temples (including the four corners, pillars, wall[s], windows, and hearth), were usually delivered directly to the recipient. Kings, queens, and princes attained the status of minor deities upon their deaths, and their ghosts might be allotted modest offerings in the course of their funerary rites and periodically afterward. Demonic forces such as Wishuriant (the Strangler) could also be appeased with appropriate gifts.

In principle, the Hittite king was the chief priest of all of the gods, and accordingly he was the usual sacrificer in ceremonies of the state cult; however, cultic culinary specialists commonly handled the actual slaughter and butchery involved in animal sacrifice. The queen might assist the monarch with an offering or even preside in her own right. A prince could sometimes be delegated to represent the royal house. Religious professionals and palace personnel also performed offerings in the state cult. Responsibility for the poorly documented routine sacrifices in provincial temples and village shrines undoubtedly fell to local officials. In magical rites, various freelance practitioners (e.g., "the old woman" or "the seer") were in charge. The client or patient for whom a

Libation made by king and queen before a bull figure, 1300 BCE. Ankara, Museum of Archaeology. *Hirmer Fotoarchiv*

magical rite was carried out might also make simple offerings on his or her own behalf.

The more important gods and goddesses of Hatti received daily offerings of bread and beverages. Thus, temple employees were required to be at their posts "in the morning at the gods' breakfast." Depending on local tradition, various periodic (monthly, yearly) and seasonal festivals (spring, autumn, and others tied to particular agricultural activities), featuring lavish sacrifices, were also dedicated to these divinities. Certainly the cultic calendar of the capital was an elaborate one, including offerings for most, if not all, of the deities honored in Hittite territory. In addition, every spring and autumn the king and members of the royal family performed a procession through the realm, sacrificing to the pantheons of the numerous towns they visited.

Other ceremonies were executed along with their attendant offerings as need arose. These occasions included the (re)construction of sacred buildings, the purification of a defeated army, *rites de passage* such as birth, puberty, and death, personal crises such as impotence, insomnia, family strife, and so on.

Offerings were most often performed in a place set apart from the profane sphere. Monumental buildings or parts thereof—temple, chapel, enclosed courtyard, and palace—were frequent locations for sacrifice in the state cult. In such a setting, the divine image, the altar, and/or an offering table provided the focus of activity.

Offerings in magical rites might take place in a special small building reserved for purifications, in an uncultivated place, or at some other location far removed from habitations and agricultural plots—for instance, on a rock outcropping, on a riverbank, at a spring or well, or simply in the open air. Some offerings to chthonic deities required the digging of an artificial offering pit.

Often the texts specify the time of day at which an offering should be given. A rite might be scheduled for the early morning, at midday, or in the afternoon. Evening

is frequently specified, occasionally described as "when at night a star twinkles." Nighttime and predawn twilight also are mentioned.

As in Mesopotamia, the gods were believed to be literally dependent upon humans for their sustenance, and food, therefore, was the most common offering: honey, oil, and fruit; processed foods such as flour, ghee, and cheese; and a wide array of baked goods, some of special shape. Potable liquids (wine, beer, milk, etc.) were frequently employed as libations.

Hittite deities enjoyed a diet far richer than that of the ordinary Anatolian peasant, as evidenced most strikingly in their prodigious consumption of meat, sometimes in astounding quantities (in one festival, one thousand sheep and fifty oxen were offered). The usual sacrificial animals in Hatti were those domestic creatures whose meat humans also ate most frequently—sheep, goats, and cattle. Wild animals, such as gazelles, stags, bears, boars, and leopards, were only seldom offered. Dogs, swine, and horses were killed only for special purposes, primarily to appease chthonic forces and the dead.

Sacrificial victims had to be "pure," that is, healthy and unblemished. Temple workers were threatened with severe sanctions for substituting their own inferior animals for the prize specimens intended for a deity. On occasion, it was required that a female animal be virgin, and sometimes the victim had to be of the same gender as the offerant. As a general rule, black animals were offered to chthonic gods, and white or light-colored ones to all other divinities. Although eagles and falcons already appear, although infrequently, in early rites, the regular sacrifice of fowl, usually through incineration, was introduced rather late, as part of a Hurro-Luwian cult borrowed from southern Anatolia and Syria. Nonfood items, including silver, precious objects, land holdings, and persons, are mentioned in vows by which an individual promised a gift to the gods in return for divine favor, usually in the form of healing. These pledges

King Shulumeli pouring libation to the weather-god (in conical hat with raised arm). Relief from Malatya, late Hittite period. Ankara, Museum of Archaeology. *Hirmer Fotoarchiv*

were doubtlessly assigned to temples and their associated economic establishments.

This bewildering variety of Hittite sacrifices can be reduced to five basic types: (1) attraction offerings, in which paths of fruit, sweets, and colored cloth intended to draw in the honored deities were laid out converging on the ritual site; (2) bloodless offerings consisting primarily of baked goods and libations of beer, wine, and so on; (3) animal sacrifice followed by a communal meal; (4) burnt offerings (restricted to ceremonies adopted from Syrian or Cilician sources); and (5) "god drinking." It must be recognized, however, that these ideal types do not reflect any native Hittite terminological distinctions. Only in the 14th and 13th centuries was an elaborate vocabulary borrowed from the Hurrian and Luwian languages to designate types of offering. Some of these numerous terms designate the procedure to be followed (e.g., burnt offering), others the material employed (blood), the purpose of the rite (purification), or the problem to be addressed (sin).

The general principle underlying Hittite offerings was that the material given had to be destroyed, in whole or in part, in order for it to pass over to its recipient in the parahuman world. Thus liquids were poured out (on the ground, offering table, or altar), breads were broken or crumbled, vessels were smashed, and animals were killed. Bearing in mind that any particular rite might show considerable variation and that the scribes frequently omitted mention of one or more features, we may summarize Hittite sacrificial procedure as follows.

The priest or officiant, cultic implements, and the offering itself were ritually purified, after which the offerant washed his hands in water. In the state cult, either of these acts might involve the use of an aromatic substance. If the offering were small in size, it was handed to the offerant; if it were large, he set his hand upon it, thereby establishing his patronage of the ceremony. The offering was made (through breaking, scattering, libating, etc.) by either the officiant or the offerant himself or herself. The sacrifice concluded with the obeisance of the offerant before the deity.

Animal sacrifice was somewhat more complicated. After the initial ritual cleansing, the victim, which might have been decorated with ribbons or objects of precious metal, was driven into the temple or sacrificial location and dedicated to the recipient. A sample of the animal—probably a lock of hair—was conveyed to the deity, after which the beast was driven out once more. The victim was then killed and butchered or dismembered, usually at a location away from the immediate offering site. The animal's death might be accompanied by a joyous shout from the participants. There followed the consumption of the slaughtered beast by the god(s) and worshipers. Divine taste favored fat and those internal organs that were thought to be the seat of life and the emotions—liver and heart above all, but also the gall bladder and kidneys. These entrails were roasted over the flame, chopped, and served to the god on bread. The remainder of the carcass was dismembered, cooked as a stew, and shared by those humans who were present. The skin or hide of the victim became the property of the offerant, the officiant, or the butcher.

Certain rites attributed particular importance to the victim's blood. In these instances, the throat of the animal was slit in the presence of the deity and the stream of blood directed from the neck arteries upward toward the divine statue or symbol or downward into a bowl or a pit. If purification was the purpose of the ceremony, the person or object to be cleansed might be smeared with the blood.

Later Hurro-Luwian burnt offerings were holocausts, with little or nothing remaining for the human participants to enjoy. The victims—most often birds but sometimes also sheep or goats—were incinerated in a portable brazier, optionally accompanied by condiments such as bread crumbs, honey, fruit, flour, salt, and so on.

A practice peculiar to the Hittites was "god-drinking," which was performed only by the king or by the royal couple, often for a long series of divinities in succession. This act is expressed verbally by a grammatical construction in which the divinity is the direct object, and some scholars believe that we must understand this as denoting mystical participation by the royal person(s) in the essence of the god or goddess. Others interpret "god-drinking" as a shorthand expression for "drinking to the honor of" or "toasting" a deity. The matter remains uncertain.

Substitute or "scapegoat" rituals do not belong to the topic of offerings as discussed here, because their purpose was not the bestowal of a gift on a deity, but rather the disposal of impurity, sin, blood guilt, or some other unwanted quality. This goal was accomplished through the transferal of the moral or literal pollution from the patient onto a living carrier, who was then either driven off into the wilderness or killed. The few attestations of human sacrifice found in Hittite texts are to be interpreted in this manner.

BIBL.: B. J. Collins, "Ritual Meals in the Hittite Cult," in *Ancient Magic and Ritual Power* (ed. P. Mirecki and M. Meyer; Leiden, 1995), 77–92. O. R. Gurney, *Some Aspects of Hittite Religion* (Oxford, 1977), 28–34. V. Haas, *Geschichte der hethitischen Religion* (Leiden, 1994), 640–73. C. Kühne, "Hethitisch *auli-* und einige Aspekte altanatolischer Opferpraxis," *Zeitschrift für Assyriologie* 76 (1986): 85–117. G. McMahon, "Theology, Priests, and Worship in Hittite Anatolia," in *Civilizations of the Ancient Near East* (ed. J. Sasson et al.; New York, 1995), 3.1981–95.   G.M.B.

Iran

According to Zoroastrians, the best things in life are to be offered to Ahura Mazda and to the invisible spirit powers of his good creation. These offerings, such as consecrated bread and drink, fruits, sacrificial animals (in ancient times), cooked dishes, and—equally importantly—good thoughts, words, and deeds, express the gratitude felt for the bountiful gifts of life and are offered to the good spirit powers in order to both please and strengthen them.

The meaning and significance of these offerings are best understood within the context of the Zoroastrian worldview. Metaphysically, the temporal-spatial world in which we live includes not only the visible, tangible, empirical world, but also invisible realms of powers and principles that make existence intelligible and sustain us in all our needs. The latter constitute the universal archetypal principles of Life and Health, Dominion, Good Mind, Bountiful Devotion, and Righteousness. Zarathustra referred to these invisible powers as the Bountiful Immortals. The ultimate reality, the source of this goodness, is Ahura Mazda (Lord of Wisdom, or Wise Lord; Pahlavi Ohrmazd).

All the Bountiful Immortals are understood as being intimately associated with an aspect of the material creation. This physical world (Pahlavi *gētīg*) is an extension of, or more accurately, a completion of the spiritual realm *(mēnōg)*. The radiant light of fire, for example, whether the warm fire of the sun, the simple but indispensable fire of the hearth, or the consecrated fire of priestly rituals, is understood to be in essence the living, physical embodiment of the light of Wisdom itself, a spark of the infinite light. In other words, a purified fire is a visible, dynamic presence of the vital energy that animates life itself. As such it is an exemplification, not a mere representation, of the Bountiful Immortal Righteousness, the principle of cosmic order and vitality. Likewise, the archetypal powers of Life and Health are instantiated in plants and water; Bountiful Devotion and Good Mind are manifest in the earth and cattle; and Dominion is evident in the overarching sky, which Zarathustra conceived of as metallic.

Opposed to these creative and sustaining creations of Ahura Mazda are the forces of unrighteousness, falsehood, disorder, arrogance, ill health, and destruction. The source of these powers is the Hostile One (Avestan Angra Mainyu; Pahlavi Ahriman), whose nature is one of deceit and lies. All these powers of decay manifest themselves in the material creation in multiple forms: smoke that diminishes the light of fire, rust that destroys metals, wolves that kill cattle, drought and sterility that destroy the life-giving powers of water and vegetation, and bad thoughts, words, and deeds that plague all human endeavor.

The divine purpose of humanity, consequently, is to combat and defeat these powers of destruction that diminish the powers of life. This is accomplished by purifying the good creation, freeing it from all the negative powers and thereby strengthening and restoring it to its original sacred condition. Anything that is ritually purified and dedicated to the cause of eliminating evil, therefore, is an offering. The fire that has been ritually purified by priests, for example, is an offering of metaphysical import, for it is an actual physical instance of the cosmic order untainted by the counterforces of disorder. In this way a purified fire both strengthens and pleases the powers of Wisdom and helps bring about the time when the whole of creation is rehabilitated.

This is true of all the offerings consecrated in Zoroastrian rituals. The most important daily ritual of offering is the *yasna* liturgy. From beginning to end, this service reveals its creative and sustaining purpose, as each item used in it embodies the presence of its corresponding

Bountiful Immortal. In addition to the ritual fire, the sacramental bread (dron), the selected bundle of twigs or metal wires (barsom), and the crushed pomegranate and hom twigs (perhaps a species of ephedra) are exemplifications of the Bountiful Immortal Life. Likewise, the sacramental drink (zohr) from consecrated well water exemplifies all the waters of the world that promote Health. Hairs from a white, unblemished bull instantiate the whole good animal kingdom and the spiritual principle of Good Mind. The iron mortar and other metallic ritual implements participate in the overarching Dominion of Ahura Mazda's Wisdom, and the purified earth that defines the ritual area is itself the visible, physical presence of Bountiful Devotion.

The priests themselves, dedicated to good thoughts, words, and deeds and bearers of ritual power, become the embodiments of Wisdom in this visible arena of the cosmic battle against Druj (Lie). Their recitation of Avestan manthra (holy utterances) encircles the entire yasna liturgy from beginning to end. Such manthras both protect the offerings from any pollution and consecrate them in order to bring about the increase, prosperity, and salvation of the entire creation.

The twenty-one words of the Ahunawar manthra, which epitomizes the whole revelation of Zarathustra, is the holiest and most powerful invocation. According to Zoroastrian theology, the Ahunawar manthra was spoken by Ahura Mazda before the good creation was brought into being, and the manthra of prosperity (Yasna 58) will be uttered by Ahura Mazda at the time of the last judgment, just prior to the restoration of the cosmos. The manthra of prosperity declares that the righteous—through their piety, industry, charity, wisdom, and humility—protect and bring about the prosperity of the world. Thus manthras, invoked by righteous priests, not only encircle the yasna liturgy but also frame cosmic history. For these reasons, the holy word (manthra spenta) is considered the very soul of Wisdom itself—a voiced offering of protective and consecrating power.

In addition to the daily yasna service celebrated inside the temple areas, there are also ceremonies outside, which invoke the presence of the Bountiful Immortals through consecrated offerings. In the ceremony of blessings (Pahlavi afrinagan), for example, an abundance of fruits, flowers, and cooked foods are set in front of a purified fire and consecrated by manthric invocations and dedicated to the powers of the good creation. Likewise, lay Zoroastrians offer up their individual thoughts, words, and deeds to Ahura Mazda on a daily basis and, when they enter the sanctum sanctorum of the fire temple, offer sandalwood and manthric prayers to the fire, the "son of Ahura Mazda." In all such instances, these ceremonial offerings advance the whole of creation toward the goal of cosmic rehabilitation.

BIBL.: Mary Boyce, "Ātash-Zōhr and Āb-Zōhr," Journal of the Royal Asiatic Society (1966): 100ff. Firoze M. Kotwal and James W. Boyd (ed. and trans.), A Guide to the Zoroastrian Religion: A 19th Century Catechism with Modern Commentary (Chico, Calif.: Scholars Press, 1982). Idem, A Persian Offering: The Yasna, a Zoroastrian High Liturgy (Paris: Association pour l'avancement des études iraniennes, 1991).

J.W.B., F.M.K.

Greece

Sacrifice was the core ritual of Greek religious practice. Its most typical form was the offering of a farm animal—a bull or a cow, a sheep or a goat, a pig, sometimes combined into a "triad starting from the bovine" (trittys boarkhos, i.e., bovine, sheep, pig)—to an Olympian deity, during which some, mostly inedible, parts of the animal were burned for the gods, while most of the meat was consumed by the humans. Its form was relatively stable throughout antiquity; the description in Homer, Odyssey 3.417–72 would have been, in most of its details, still valid a millennium later, despite variations due to local traditions and developments. There were, however, other forms of sacrifice that, inside the culture, gave rise to distinctions and categorizations that have been developed and refined by modern scholarly theories: the interplay and the variations of the different elements of sacrifice formed a complex symbolical system that informed participants about the status of both the participants and the divine recipients and about the concerns of the sacrificing community.

The ordinary sacrifice. The ordinary sacrifice took place under the open sky, at the altar of a sanctuary; altars usually were stone constructions, often opposite the main faces of temples (when there was a temple), raised several feet aboveground, with fires burning on top. The animals had to be perfect and, in an ordinary sacrifice, fully grown—only extraordinary sacrifices asked for young or sometimes even pregnant animals. Once selected, sometimes in a complex and lengthy process, the animal was adorned (in the case of bovines, often by gilding its horns). The participants in the sacrifice led it to the altar in a procession, where larger animals were firmly tied: in some sanctuaries, the foundations for iron rings around the altar are still preserved—resistance or escape of an animal was a bad sign (Vergil, Aeneid 2.223). Preliminary rituals of washing and libating prepared the group and obtained the consent of the animal to its sacrifice (what Karl Meuli called Unschuldskomödie [comedy of innocence]). After the prayer that called upon the divinity to participate, the sacrificer cut a few hairs from the animal's head. Then, the animal was stunned and bled to death; the blood was collected in a container and sprinkled over the altar. The animal was opened, a seer examined the entrails (a ritual absent in the Homeric descriptions), the innards (splanchna) were taken out, cut up, roasted on spits, and eaten on the spot by the core group of the participants. The animal was cut apart; bones, especially the

The goddess Bendis (right, in Thracian costume) receives a team of victors in her torch races, the bearded leader carrying a torch. Attic marble votive relief from Piraeus, 450–428 BCE. British Museum. © *The British Museum*

thigh bones, and fat were burned on the altar, while the meat was cooked for the ensuing common meal. Sometimes, the hip bone of the sheep or the pig was placed in the fire with the tail still on; the way it curled indicated the gods' acceptance or rejection of the participants' wishes. Libations of wine accompanied the entire ritual and articulated its structure. The distribution of the meat followed strict rules of hierarchy, the person organizing the sacrifice being singled out as the host of the gods whose parts often were placed on a sacred table *(trapeza),* sometimes on the hands or knees of the image. These parts *(trapezōmata*—tongue, thighs, the hide) usually went to the officiating priest; in Athens, the hides of state sacrifices were sold on behalf of the city's treasury. Ordinarily, leftover meat from the banquet was taken home or sold; the Christian refusal to buy sacrificial meat for domestic consumption left pagan temples with piles of unsold meat (Pliny, *Letters* 10.96.10).

For most public and private sacrifices, the sheep was the regular sacrificial animal; it was the cheapest farm animal in Greece. In more lavish sacrifices, bovines, which were much more valuable, were sacrificed; some very important festivals required sacrificing one hundred of them (a "hecatomb"). The selection among the main species of sacrificial animals as well as among animals of different genders or colors followed a complex and not fully understood logic, in which the value of the animal, the occasion of the sacrifice, the nature of the sacrificial group, and the nature and gender of the divinity addressed all played a role. Some animals were connected with specific divinities, either because they were welcome (e.g., the ram was welcome to Persephone) or forbidden (e.g., it was forbidden to sacrifice billy goats to Asclepius). Other domestic animals, such as horses, dogs, or chickens, were sacrificed only to a few specific deities or on rare and specific occasions (roosters for

Asclepius, horses for Helios, dogs to birth-goddesses), while the sacrifice of wild animals was very rare; this reflects the absolute dominance of farming over hunting in Greek meat production.

Greeks conceptualized the sacrifice as a gift to the gods (Plato, *Euthyphro* 14d), who felt obliged to the humans who offered them rich sacrifices (Homer, *Iliad* 22.170). Already early, Greeks were puzzled by the paradox that the gods were given mainly the inedible parts of the animal, portions that in fact constituted the refuse from slaughtering. Hesiod explained it by the myth that Prometheus had introduced this form in order to deceive Zeus or rather to test his omniscience (*Theogony* 535–617). Modern research (e.g., Karl Meuli, Walter Burkert) has situated the origin of the ritual form in prehistoric hunting rituals, in which the bones and the hide were preserved in order to restore the killed animal; the paradox that the rite presented inside Greek culture, however, remains unexplained. The Paris School (e.g., Jean-Pierre Vernant, Marcel Detienne) stresses the communicative and culinary function of animal sacrifice: the rite defines the human situation between animals and gods, using the former both for eating and for establishing contact with the latter.

Other forms of animal sacrifice. Major variations are characterized mainly by the absence of elements that belong to the usual ritual (which scholars, following later Greek use, call the Olympian sacrifice). Only rarely was the sacrifice not accompanied by a flute player who, ordinarily, helped create a festive atmosphere; such an absence required explanation (Apollodorus, *Library* 3.15.5). Another, more common form of sacrifice used wineless offerings only *(nēphalia);* in yet another variation, the meat had to be consumed on the spot and could not be carried away *(ou phora)* or participation was restricted to citizens, to one gender, or to freemen only—most cases are mentioned as exceptions in sacred laws, and often myths explain them. But the major variation of the standard sacrifice is the total destruction of the animal on a low hearth or even in a pit. Such sacrifices often addressed divinities of the underworld, hence its modern designation as chthonic (from Greek *chthōn* [earth]): the opposition Olympian-chthonic was introduced in the early 19th century (Carl Otfried Müller), reflecting the more complex late Greek classifications of ritual. In this type of sacrifice, humans really give away something valuable, although the animal burnt often was small, either a sheep or a piglet. In very rare cases only, a large group of animals was entirely burnt—prominent is the burning alive of a large number of wild animals in the festival of Artemis Laphria in Patras (Pausanias 7.18.11–13).

Animal sacrifice is attested already in Bronze Age Greece, if only in archeological contexts, and the widespread symbol of the double ax, familiar from Crete and Mycenae, might derive from the sacrificial instrument. Some details seem to be different from the Iron Age practice, and it is unclear whether it continued Bronze Age traditions or was introduced from or at least influenced by Near Eastern practices, where animal sacrifice had a much longer history.

Bloodless sacrifice. There were also bloodless sacrifices, where fruit or more often cakes in different shapes were offered: their form corresponded to specific ritual circumstances. Regular food, such as the suppers for the dead or for Hecate at crossroads, and dishes especially prepared for a ritual, such as a bean dish for Apollo, were rare. Libations of wine, water, milk (sometimes honey-milk), or oil not only accompanied other rites, such as animal sacrifices or oath ceremonies, but were also performed as isolated rites both in Bronze Age and Iron Age Greece; wineless libations belonged also to the cult of the dead. Philosophical criticism of animal sacrifice constructed an evolutionary history that led from harmless and acceptable offerings of herbs and fruit to the killing of large numbers of animals (Theophrastus, *On Piety,* known mostly through Porphyry, *On Abstinence*). The first opponents of animal sacrifice, the vegetarian Pythagoreans, proposed to offer cakes made in the forms of animals instead or looked for other compromises, since the refusal to participate in public animal sacrifices excluded one from civic life in a Greek city altogether. Given this crucial role of animal sacrifice in ancient society, no philosophical criticism succeeded in abolishing it. It was only the Christian opposition that finally succeeded—and only after prolonged resistance and much more than a century of very restrictive legislation by the emperors, from Theodosius I in 392 CE (*Codex Theodosianus* 16.10.10–12) to Justinian in 528–29 CE (*Codex Iustinianus* 11.10).

Votive offerings. Besides gift giving in the form of sacrifices, votive gifts (*anathemata* [lit., what is put aside high up]) were offered; the archeological evidence is as rich for Bronze Age as it is for later sanctuaries, and the

Mycenaean texts show how the palaces sent rich gifts (oil, wine, honey, animals, slaves, gold vessels) to certain sanctuaries. In historical times, animal sacrifices could result in votive offerings: a sacrifice could be recorded in the sanctuary by mounting the bovine skulls on a temple wall, by leaving the plates or drinking vessels in the sanctuary, or by dedicating a stone relief or painted terra-cotta plaque depicting the ritual in a fairly standard form, with the sacrificing group leading the animal toward the altar on whose opposite side the divinity was represented.

Ordinarily, votive gifts signaled recognition of divine intervention; sometimes, we learn that the divinity had ordered the dedication by appearing in a dream. Such gifts abound in healing sanctuaries all over the ancient world. While relatively costly dedicatory reliefs depicted the healing intervention, much more often the healed person dedicated a replica of the healed limb in bronze or silver, stone, or terra-cotta. Similar gifts were dedicated after rescue from any other danger or crisis, especially from dangers at sea (although the atheist Diagoras of Melos or Diogenes the Cynic remarked that the sanctuaries would be much fuller if those not rescued could dedicate a gift as well; Cicero, *On the Nature of the Gods* 3.89; Diogenes Laertius 6.59). Other gifts recorded a life change that often took the form of a rite—hair or toys dedicated by young men and women when reaching adulthood or when marrying, small wine jugs dedicated in Athens by boys at the age of three or four, tools dedicated at the end of a professional career. The majority of dedications, however, were much humbler. Small and mostly mold-made statuettes of the divinities, votaries, or animals, miniature weapons, and vessels of terra-cotta, lead, or bronze are known from most sanctuaries all over the Greek world. Small objects in silver and gold are lost, but they must have been considerable as well, as the power of the silversmiths around the sanctuary of Artemis in Ephesus shows (Acts 19.28). Overall, it appears that virtually anything could be dedicated, and the modern observer is at pains to formulate rules that go beyond fashion and personal taste—but they already ancient observers had to use the dedicatory inscriptions as the only certain guide to the divine possessor of a sanctuary (Apuleius, *The Golden Ass* 6.3).

A votive gift was not only the very personal expression of individual or collective gratitude for help, it also announced publicly the piety and divine protection of the dedicant. This helps to explain the impressive dedications by cities and kings in Panhellenic sanctuaries—from Croesus's impressive gifts to Apollo in Delphi (Herodotus 1.50–51) to the dedications of booty and weapons by Greek states in Olympia and the magnificence of Hellenistic and Roman rulers (e.g., the Nike of Samothrace, dedicated in the sanctuary of the Great Gods of Samothrace).

Anything dedicated in a sanctuary belonged to the divinity. This made theft an act of impiety against the gods *(hierosylia)*, punished by both human law and divine interaction, and thus protected the dedications, but it also made it impossible to sell or remove a dedicated object, even if severely damaged, to a spot outside the sanctuary. From early times, the many small objects that were filling much of sanctuary space were regularly buried inside the sanctuary, while damaged or superfluous objects made from precious metals were recast into ritual vessels.

BIBL.: Harold W. Attridge, "The Philosophical Critique of Religion under the Early Empire," *Aufstieg und Niedergang der römischen Welt* 2.16/1.45–78. Walter Burkert, *Homo Necans: The Anthropology of Ancient Greek Sacrificial Ritual and Myth* (trans. Peter Bing; Berkeley: University of California Press, 1983). Marcel Detienne and Jean-Pierre Vernant, *La cuisine du sacrifice en pays grec* (Paris: Gallimard, 1979). Cristiano Grottanelli and N. F. Parise (eds.), *Sacrifico e società nel mondo antico* (Rome: Laterza, 1988). Valasia Isaakidou, Paul Halstead, Jack Davis, and Sharon Stocker, "Burnt Animal Sacrifice at the Mycenaean 'Palace of Nestor,' Pylos," *Antiquity* 76 (2002): 86–92. Olivier Reverdin and Bernard Grange (eds.), *Le sacrifice dans l'antiquité: Entretiens sur l'antiquité classique* (Geneva: Hardt, 1981). W. H. Rouse, *Greek Votive Offerings* (Cambridge: Cambridge University Press, 1902). Folkert T. Van Straten, *Hierà Kalá: Images of Animal Sacrifice in Archaic and Classical Greece* (Leiden: Brill, 1995). F.G.

Etruria

The evidence for Etruscan sacrifices is elusive, although not as elusive as for other parts of Etruscan religion; but here as elsewhere, when written texts are few and difficult to understand, iconography and other archeological evidence must, in the absence of texts, rely on inference from a general phenomenology, particularly because information from Greek and Roman sources might be biased or otherwise flawed. The main written evidence comes from two long texts, the Capua Tile and the Zagreb mummy wrappings. Although the debate as to single expressions is far from over, there is more-or-less agreement as to the overall meaning of these texts. Both contain parts of a religious calendar with names of deities, dates, and references to sacrifices; nouns referring to gifts and offerings, sacrificed animals and liquids (wine), and vessels containing offerings; and also the verb *to sacrifice (nunthen)* can be made out. As for the specific practices of approaching deities with offerings, the best evidence comes from tomb paintings, reliefs, bronze and clay statuettes, and miniature pottery.

Well documented, both from texts and especially from visual sources, are animal sacrifices (bull, goat) and offerings of grain or incense, as well as libations. These were presented by priests and worshipers, often accompanied by a flute player, in processions to altars found in sanctuaries. Sacrificial processions are shown on reliefs and in tomb paintings; offerings of grain and libations were presented in bowls or jugs held by the worshipers or in the thousands of miniature vessels found in votive pits in sanctuaries or other sacred places.

For a long time, earlier scholars accepted the existence of human sacrifices in Etruria. This was based solely on Livy's account (7.15) of how in 358 BCE the victorious Etruscans at Tarquinia killed 307 Roman prisoners—but this must be not more than an occasional execution of prisoners of war, such as Herodotus (1.166) attests also for Tarquinia after the defeat of the Phocaean Greeks at Alalia on Corsica in 540 BCE—an exceptional event that led the Tarquinians to institute, at the command of a Delphic oracle, games and horse races in honor of the dead.

Votive offerings are attested in large numbers from many sanctuaries; and they were deposited also at specific locations outside a sanctuary, such as city gates, sources of water, or other sacred places. Almost any object could serve as a votive offering, including miniature pottery, coins, weapons, bronze and clay statuettes of human figures and animals, and clay representations of body parts. These anatomical votives are common and widespread in many sanctuaries of central Italy; they begin to appear in southern Etruria in the 4th century BCE, while bronze statuettes of deities and worshipers date back as early as the 6th century BCE and are mostly found in northern Etruria. The wide distribution and large number of these votive objects make it impossible to assume that specific types were reserved for specific deities or purposes, although anatomical votives are commonly assumed to refer to divine healing.

BIBL.: G. Bartoloni, G. Colonna, and C. Grottanelli (eds.), *Atti del convegno internazionale Anathema in Scienze dell'Antichità* (Rome, 1989–90), 3–4.619–50, 695–704, 875–904. Helen Nagy, "Divinities in the Context of Sacrifice and Cult on Caeretan Votive Terracottas," in *Murlo and the Etruscans: Art and Society in Ancient Etruria* (ed. Richard D. De Puma and Jocelyn P. Small; Madison: University of Wisconsin Press, 1994), 211–23. I.E.-B.

Group at an altar preparing a sacrifice. Etruscan stele from Chiusi, 5th century BCE. Louvre. *Réunion des Musées Nationaux/Art Resource, New York*

Rome

A common criticism of Roman religion is that it was merely formulaic and that the relationship between an individual or community and the gods demeaned the power of the latter: the formula of offerings and sacrifices is portrayed as one of *do ut des* (I give that you should give)—in other words, it sought to bind the gods into a tightly contractual relationship with humans. In fact this view is false. It parallels and may originate in Protestant criticism of Catholic formalism, a criticism that is itself highly tendentious. Romans themselves would not have accepted the criticism, although they might have understood it.

To explore this further, the best place to start is with Roman public *vota* (vows and their fulfillment). The most important of these were the annual *vota* performed at the beginning of January each year (e.g., Ovid, *Fasti* 1.79–88; *Ex Ponto* 4.4.27–34; 4.9.47–52). A grand procession of all the people, dressed in festal clothes, wound its way up onto the Capitol, where *vota* were performed by the new consuls and by all the colleges of priests. In the republican period the *vota* were performed on January 1; under the empire the original rites of January 1 were maintained for a time, but then replaced by new ones on January 3 on behalf of the emperor. We know more about the *vota* described in the records of the Arval Brothers (a priestly college connected mainly with the goddess known as Dea Dia) than others, but they may be taken as representative.

The ritual had two distinct elements: the discharge of the previous *vota* and the pronouncing of new *vota*. Drawing particularly on the lengthy record for 87 CE (which details the words spoken by the acting president of the college on the porch of the temple of Jupiter Optimus Maximus), we may see clearly the logic of the Roman system of *vota*. First, prayers were made to a specific deity (or set of deities) for a specific objective, in this case the well-being of the emperor and the imperial house:

> Jupiter Optimus Maximus, if the emperor Caesar Domitian Augustus Germanicus, son of *divus* Vespasianus, *pontifex maximus,* possessing tribunician power, perpetual *censor,* father of the country, Domitia Augusta, his wife, and Julia Augusta, whom I intend to mention, are alive and their house is secure on January 3 next year, for the Roman people, the Quirites, for the state of the Roman people the Quirites, if on this day you have preserved them safe and sound from all dangers that occur or might occur before this day, and if you have brought about as good an outcome as I intend to specify, and if you have preserved them in the same or better condition in which they are now, if you have done this in this fashion . . .

If the gods heard the prayer and the objective was met, then a sacrifice would be made to the deity (or deities) as a token of gratitude: "Then I vow that there will be an offering, an ox with gilded horns will be sacrificed to you in the name of the Arval Brothers." And indeed this vow had been preceded by the paying of the similar vow from the previous year: "Since the immortal gods, whose power has been made favorable, have hearkened to the *vota* that the whole world had eagerly pronounced for the well-being of the emperor Caesar Domitian Augustus Germanicus, son of *divus* Vespasianus, *pontifex maximus,* of Domitia Augusta, his wife, of Julia Augusta and of their whole house, it is fitting that the college should discharge the previous *vota* and pronounce new ones" (*ILS* 5034; Scheid 1998: no. 55, column 1). Conversely, if the objective were not met, then the sacrifice would not necessarily be offered (there are some cases in the Arval records when the *vota* were not discharged, explicitly so for 101 and 105 CE, presumably because the gods had not met their side of the bargain).

Vota thus articulated a set of relationships between gods and humans. The Romans promised honor and worship in return for divine benevolence. The gods might not hear the prayers, and if so there was no obligation on humans to grant continuing honors to the gods. This system, often characterized pejoratively as merely "contractual," in fact established a set of reciprocal relationships, which required skill on the part of humans to ensure that the gods remained on their side.

The expression of this system in the context of major public sacrifices in Rome is emblematic of the way that the system worked in other contexts, both public and private. For example, in 217 BCE, after consultation of the college of *pontifices,* the Roman people were consulted about the possibility of offering a "sacred spring": should a *votum* be made to Jupiter that if the Roman state were preserved for the next five years during the wars against the Carthaginians and Gauls, then all the animal produce of the appointed spring—swine, sheep, goats, and cattle—would be sacrificed to Jupiter? The assembly agreed to the proposal, and very precise conditions were laid down to ensure that proper discharge of the *votum* be possible. In fact, the sacrifice of the animals took place only in 195 BCE, twenty-one years after the *votum,* and then had to be repeated the following year because of a flaw in the performance of the ritual (Livy 22.10; 33.44.1–2; 34.44). The ritual was of course extraordinary, but it rests on the normal practices of regular public *vota.*

At a private level, individuals followed similar rules in their own dealings with the gods. For example, a monument, probably of early imperial date from just outside Rome, records the following: "Felix Asinianus, public slave of the *pontifices,* discharged his *votum* of a white heifer, gladly and sincerely to rustic Bona Dea

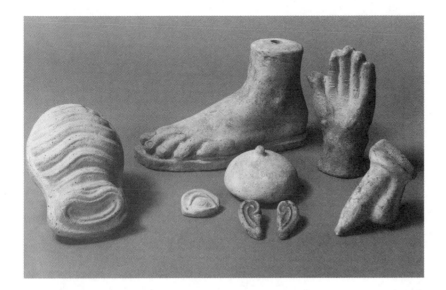

Roman votive objects. Terra-cotta representations of body parts were offered to healing deities in the hope of a divine cure or in thanks for one received. British Museum.
© *The British Museum*

Haruspex examining entrails of a sacrificed animal. Relief from Trajan's Forum, about 120 CE. *Réunion des Musées Nationaux/Art Resource, New York*

Felicula for the restoration of his eyesight. The doctors had abandoned him after ten months, but he was cured by favor of the Mistress and her remedies. All [the monument] restored under the care of Cannia Fortunata" (*CIL* 6.68 = *ILS* 3513). This text implies that Felix Asinianus had made a *votum* to the deity that if his eyesight were restored he would sacrifice to her an (expensive) animal. The procedure was so common that thousands of Latin inscriptions from the western empire use abbreviations to refer to the procedure: "v.s.," for *votum solvit* (he discharged the vow), "v.s.l.m.," for *votum solvit libens merito* (she discharged the vow freely and deservedly). The use of such shorthand on texts set up in public is strong testimony to the normality and pervasiveness of the system.

Detailed written descriptions of sacrifices performed as a result of *vota* or in other contexts are rarely preserved. The most that the documentary record preserves is the following type of information. At the initial sacrifice in 87 CE in the porch of the temple of Jupiter

Sacrifice of a bull to the Genius Augusti; the sacrifant at left is pouring a libation over a tripod. From the Altar of Vespasian, Pompeii. *German Archaeological Institute, Rome*

Optimus Maximus by the acting president of the Arval Brothers: "He sacrificed incense and wine on the flames of the altar and immolated with wine, grains, and knife an ox to Jupiter Optimus Maximus, a cow to Juno Regina, a cow to Minerva, a cow to Salus Publica of the Roman people the Quirites; he offered the entrails cooked in pots." It is nevertheless possible to reconstruct, from passing references in literature and from images in sculpture and other media, the main lines of a "standard" Roman animal sacrifice in civic cult. As in the Greek world, sacrifice took place in the open air. The animal was brought to the altar and the main officiant recited a prayer, offering incense and wine on the altar as a libation. Wine and specially prepared meal *(mola salsa)* was then poured over the animal's head, before it was killed by slaves and its entrails examined for omens. The final stage normally involved burning parts of the animal on the altar and a banquet (from the rest of the meat) for the participants.

Many of these stages are widely featured on public monuments depicting Roman sacrifice, both in Rome and in the Latin West. For example, a distance slab from the Antonine Wall in Scotland shows a legionary commander offering the preliminary libation of wine on an altar; a flute player plays music to drown out ill-omened sounds; the three sacrificial animals (boar [*sus*], ram [*ovis*], and bull [*taurus*]) to be offered in sacrifice (the combination is called a *suovetaurilia*) wait at one side, their apparent willingness an important element in the procedure. This somewhat crude carving parades at the farthest reaches of the Roman Empire a Roman sacrifice that would have been perfectly at home in the capital itself.

Dionysius of Halicarnassus, a Greek historian living in Rome and trying to explain Rome to the Greek world, offers the fullest description of a Roman sacrifice

(*Roman Antiquities* 7.72.14–18). Dionysius, however, had a particular agenda: to demonstrate that Roman practices had their parallels in Greece (in this case in Homer's descriptions of sacrifices). Later Christian writers, with a different agenda, also responded to the Roman system. Arnobius, writing in North Africa around 300 CE, dedicated a substantial section of his treatise against paganism to the perceived follies of animal sacrifice. For example, picking up points made by pagan philosophers, he argued that animal sacrifice was cruel, unfair, and illogical (*Against the Gentiles* 7.9).

The details of the traditional practice of Roman sacrifice were, of course, much more varied than any summary of its standard form suggests. Sacrifice could be performed without the shedding of blood (with wine, incense, or cakes offered to the gods). Subtly different procedures—such as whether the main officiant performed the ritual with his head covered or with his head bare (the so-called Greek rite)—might be applied in the context of different rituals or festivals. More generally the norms of sacrifice were a marker of traditional *Roman* cult. At the extreme, human sacrifice (although one or two exceptional cases are attested at Rome) was seen as utterly foreign. But alternative religions within Rome (such as that of Magna Mater or Mithras) defined their separation from traditional civic cult partly by a different sacrificial procedure. The *taurobolium* (bull killing) in the cult of Magna Mater, for example, seems to have involved the officiant being drenched with blood rather than staying unsullied, as in civic sacrifice.

The overall logic of the Roman system of vow plus sacrifice was very different from the systems around it. Despite Dionysius's claim, it differed from Greek sacrifices, which lacked an explicit conditional element, but it had similarities to Jewish vows, which, scholars argue, were also conditional. On the other hand, as Arnobius shows, the approach of Christians was different. Christians were expected to offer praise and thanks to God without obligation and without expecting anything in return. Such a view may lie at the root of subsequent scholarly misunderstandings of the Roman system.

BIBL.: G. Bartoloni, G. Colonna, and C. Grottanelli (eds.), *Atti del convegno internazionale Anathema in Scienze dell'Antichità* (Rome, 1989–90), 3–4. Mary Beard, John North, and Simon Price, *Religions of Rome* (2 vols.; Cambridge, 1998). R. L. Gordon, "The Veil of Power: Emperors, Sacrificers, and Benefactors," in *Pagan Priests* (ed. Mary Beard and John North; London, 1990), 199–231. I. S. Ryberg, *Rites of the State Religion in Roman Art* (Memoirs of the American Academy in Rome 23; New Haven, 1955). John Scheid, *Commentarii fratrum arvalium qui supersunt* (Rome, 1998). Idem, "Graeco ritu: A Typically Roman Way of Honoring the Gods," *Harvard Studies in Classical Philology* 97 (1995): 15–31. Idem, *Romulus et ses frères: Le collège des frères arvales, modèle du culte public romain dans la Rome des empereurs* (Bibliothèque des écoles françaises d'Athènes et de Rome 275; Rome, 1990), 285–676. S.R.F.P.

Christianity

Christianity emerged amid varied and competing systems of offering. Jewish and pagan traditions alike had distinctive forms of sacrificial practice and theory, including traditions of critique, and were already in some dialogue. Christian communities variously used, combined, developed, and countered these elements for their own theological and ritual purposes.

Jesus's own attitude to the Jerusalem temple and its system of offerings stood in the prophetic tradition of critique and expectation of renewal (Mark 11.15–19; cf. Hos. 6.6). The earliest Jewish Christian communities continued participation in the life of the temple (Acts 2.46), probably including sacrifices (Acts 21.26 [cf. Num. 6.1–21]; Matt. 5.23–24). Early Christian literature, however, also continued a Jewish tradition of "spiritualization" (Prayer of Azariah 15–17; Philo, On Dreams 1.215), applying sacrificial language and images to a variety of actions and ideas, sometimes implying the redundancy of cult. Jesus's life could be understood as priestly (Hebrews, passim), and his death in terms of the Day of Atonement ritual (Rom. 3.25) or of the Passover lamb (1 Cor. 5.7). Already somewhat abstracted from the specifics of Israelite religion, these sacrificial motifs were further developed in terms of a generalized sacrificial theory in the Christology of the following centuries (see Origen, Commentary on John 6). Prayer and worship (Heb. 13.15; 1 Pet. 2.5), as well as benevolence and offerings of money (Phil. 4.18; Heb. 13.16), also helped to expand sacrificial notions to the whole of life (Rom. 12.1) and to make images of temple and altar meaningful to Christians themselves (1 Cor. 3.16; Irenaeus, Against All Heresies 5.6.2).

Spiritualization and critique of Jewish sacrifice tend in a more clearly supersessionist direction after the destruction of the Jerusalem temple (see Epistle of Barnabas). While literal participation in these offerings necessarily ended, and some Christians saw all sacrifice as having been eliminated (Gospel of the Ebionites in Epiphanius, Panarion 30.16.4), interpretation of ritual law continued to be of interest to Christians, and appropriation of its sacrificial images was common.

Although some Christians from the earliest times (1 Cor. 8; Rev. 2.20) accommodated themselves to pagan sacrificial practice because of social and other benefits, the dominant attitude to this practice was negative, combining the Jewish tradition of opposition to idolatry with religious exclusivism. Although a degree of syncretism or fluidity of religious boundaries is attested in some cases (see Hippolytus, Refutation of All Heresies 5.1–6), formal rejection of pagan sacrifice became a touchstone of Christian identity. Persecution was often precipitated by refusal to sacrifice, and public executions attracted competing religious interpretations, pagan and Christian (Martyrdom of Polycarp 14.1; cf. Martyrdom of Perpetua 18.4). Reflection on martyrdom had employed sacrificial metaphors from the beginning (Rev. 6.9; Ignatius, Romans 2.2; 4.2), and such noble deaths could be understood as literally effective sacrifices, supplementing Jesus's own death (Origen, Commentary on John 6.54.36; cf. 2 Macc. 7.37–38; 4 Macc. 6.26–27).

Christian prayer and worship were understood in sacrificial terms from an early point, but some ambivalence remained. The absence of the obvious elements of cult meant pagans could infer that Christians actually had no concept of sacrifice (Minucius Felix, Octavius 10). The earliest depictions of the Eucharist as a sacrifice (Didache 14) should be understood as an instance of "spiritualization," rather than as essentially bound either to the death of Jesus (which the Didache does not mention) or to the foods of the sacred meal. The eucharistic meal is implicitly comparable to pagan sacrificial banquets (see 1 Cor. 10.21), especially when the "body" and "blood" of Jesus are spoken of, but the usual elements of the Eucharist (bread and wine or water) are to be contrasted with meat, the paradigmatic sacrificial food. Apologetic accounts of the Eucharist exemplify the tension, combining rejection of (pagan and Jewish) sacrifice with depictions of Christian practice as a superior equivalent (Justin, Apology 1.13; Dialogue with Trypho 29.1).

Other concrete offering practices accepted or continued by Christians included the bringing of additional foods as in harvest offerings (Apostolic Traditions 31–32) to eucharistic celebrations; surplus food offerings were used to provide charitable aid. Monetary contributions for social welfare were also made and regarded as means of expiating sin (2 Clement 16.4; Cyprian, On Works and Alms 5). Financial support of the clergy could also be seen as a votive or first fruits offering (Origen, Homilies on Numbers 11.2; Eusebius, Church History 5.18.2).

There was a gradual (if not consistent) movement through the 3rd century toward more directly sacrificial understandings of the Eucharist. In the Apostolic Tradition attributed to Hippolytus of Rome, the food and drink of the meal, brought to the celebration by participants, are called "offerings" (Apostolic Tradition 4). In the mid-3rd century, Cyprian of Carthage makes the explicit and literal identification of the Eucharist as sacrifice and of its ministers (bishops) as sacerdotes. Texts of the 4th and following centuries regard the Eucharist as sacrificial, a participation in the death of Jesus, yet still to be contrasted with animal sacrifice: the offering of bread and wine is "rational" and "bloodless" (this following on earlier philosophical critiques of sacrifice). This fuller cultic identification must be understood in the context not only of a more elaborate Christology and sacramental theology but also of the emergence of the church as rival to, and then replacement of, the state religion of the Roman Empire and its inheritance of Roman religion's roles in creating and maintaining civic order.

Changes in the relationship between Christianity and the wider culture and society allowed the emergence of a larger and more varied set of offerings in Christian settings, including some that were earlier rejected or contested, at least institutionally. Votive offering of objects seems to have proliferated; Roman imperial monuments were now routinely rededicated to the Christian deity, and church vessels and ornaments were offered to fulfill vows; even animal sacrifice could now be Christianized (Paulinus of Nola, *Carmen* 20; Bede, *Ecclesiastical History* 1.30), as a sort of strategic syncretism. These developments sometimes amounted to the emergence of practices from popular devotion into a clearer institutional light, rather than a radical compromise or collapse of principle. Nor did all controversy over or critique of sacrifices and votive practices disappear. Veneration of paintings of Christ and the saints, for instance, is attested even in the 2nd century (Irenaeus, *Against All Heresies* 1.25.6; *Acts of John* 26–29), and the votive inscriptions that characterized pagan icons are also found on the earliest surviving Christian examples; yet icons were to remain controversial long after Constantine.

BIBL.: Robert J. Daly, *Christian Sacrifice: The Judaeo-Christian Background before Origen* (Washington, D.C., 1978). Everett Ferguson, "Spiritual Sacrifice in Early Christianity and Its Environment," *Aufstieg und Niedergang der römischen Welt* 23.2.1151–89.   A.B.MCG.

Prayers, Hymns, Incantations, and Curses

Introduction

In the Hebrew Bible, Naaman, the celebrated general of the king of Aram, is afflicted with leprosy and consults with the Jewish prophet and healer Elisha, who tells him to bath seven times in the Jordan River as a cure. Naaman, however, gets angry and complains, "I thought that he would surely come out to me, and stand, and call on the name of the LORD his God, and wave his hand over the place" (2 Kings 5.11). His response underscores a deeply felt need in the ancient world to recite specially crafted words with the appropriate rhetorical gestures as one undertakes a ritual: in short, every *praxis* needs an attendant *logos*. It is important, moreover, that these words be marked linguistically as special and formal, either by archaic diction and syntax or by metrical and rhetorical form, and that they be performed in a special manner, for example, with musical accompaniment or dance, and in a special place.

The taxonomy of such formal speech acts is a modern problem—a difficulty that is evident in the very title of this chapter, which seeks to be inclusive rather than definitive. There are, in fact, many ways to divide up the territory. Prayers and hymns, for example, blend into one another imperceptibly along a spectrum of speech acts (all addressed to the gods), which runs from the simple, personal, practical, and prosaic requests of individuals to the more complex, public, generalized, and poetic requests of communities, and which regularly weave together the praise of a deity and present themselves as beautiful offerings similar to the glittering gold votives and other gifts used to attract divine attention—all a necessary prerequisite to a successful petition. A similar and similarly crude distinction is often made between curses and imprecations: the former are thought to be the selfish speech acts of individuals used with an eye to personal gain or revenge, while the latter designation usually refers to public curses invoked against the enemies of the state or against a class of universally recognized criminals, such as grave robbers. Curses and imprecations are also thought to differ along another popular modern division between magic and religion: if a speech asks the gods for the destruction of an enemy in a polite and deferential manner, it is deemed to be a prayer (i.e., "religious" speech), but if it addresses the gods brusquely or with threats—or if it fails to address them at all—then it is deemed an incantation or a curse (i.e., "magical" speech).

All of these modern taxonomical divisions are to different degrees helpful, but we must recognize that they are crude and simplistically dyadic and that they are often based on highly subjective criteria drawn from the religious experiences of the three major world religions—Judaism, Christianity, and Islam—that are influential in the places where the study of the ancient world has flourished most vigorously: the Mediterranean, Europe, and the Americas. In fact, there is a curious lack of such divisions in the vocabulary of some of the ancient peoples under discussion, especially the polytheists. The Greeks can, for example, use the word *hymnos*—the very source of the English word *hymn*—to refer to both Sappho's delightful lyric poems to Aphrodite and the *hymnos desmios* (the binding song) of the Furies in Aeschylus's *Oresteia,* and likewise the Romans use the word *carmen* (song) to refer to all of the speech acts discussed in this chapter.

Finally, how does one go about explaining the appearance of similar forms of prayers and hymns, incantations and curses, throughout the ancient Near East and Mediterranean? As always with cultural parallels there are (broadly speaking) two possible explanations: either the similar forms were generated separately from a shared human experience; or they arose in one spot in history and gradually spread by diffusion to their neighbors and beyond. The first, somewhat essentialist, approach must at some level be in operation. When we see the widespread use of images in cursing, for example, it makes sense to see some very old, shared human idea in play: if you can harm an image of your enemy, then you can harm your enemy. On the other hand, the diffusionist

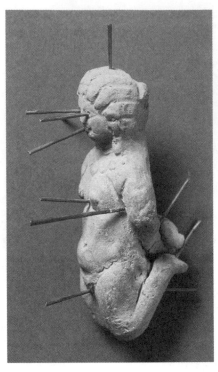

Doll pierced with pins, used in a love incantation (see p. 147). From Roman Egypt. Louvre. *Réunion des Musées Nationaux/Art Resource, New York*

approach has been very helpful in explaining the movement of technology in the Mediterranean, a persistent east-to-west drift of various kinds of technologies, such as the manufacture of the composite bow or bronze-working. Burkert notes a similar drift of what he calls "religious technology" in the Greek archaic periods, for example, incense burning or divination by the liver (1992: 14–25). In these cases, we can follow the progress of technology both in a series of archeological artifacts (e.g., distinctive types of incense burners and models of livers used to teach and explain hepatoscopy) and in the use of loanwords in Greek and then Latin for types of incense and for the terms used to describe the surface of a liver ("gate," etc.). We can see this same east-to-west drift in the diffusion of cursing techniques as well: the use of melting wax, spilt wine, or dismembered animals in oath-curses seems to have originated in the Levant and moved steadily to Greece and Macedonia; likewise the so-called judicial prayers and especially "curses against thieves" (see Sherwood Fox 1913–14) are first used in the west by Semites and then gradually appear in the central Mediterranean and then western Europe as far as Britain. But in the later periods, this east-to-west drift is not the only model, and we can trace, for example, how the originally Greek use of curses (*defixiones*) to bind but not destroy a rival in advance spreads gradually in every direction.

BIBL.: W. Burkert, *The Orientalizing Revolution: Near Eastern Influence on Greek Culture in the Early Archaic Age* (trans. M. E. Pinder and W. Burkert; Cambridge, Mass., 1992). W. Sherwood Fox, "Old Testament Parallels to *Tabellae Defixionum*," *American Journal of Semitic Languages* (1913–14): 111–24.

C.A.F.

Egypt

Hymns

Contexts and functions. The Egyptian term for "hymn" is the infinitive of a verb meaning "to adore, worship." Adoration is a rite within the morning ritual, and the words *morning* and *to adore* are etymologically related. Adoration is the "morning rite" *par excellence*. When, after the introductory purification rites, the doors of the shrine are opened, the statue is greeted with a morning hymn. In the sun cult, hymns are addressed, not to an uncovered statue, but to the rising sun. Also at sunset, the sun-god is addressed with a hymn. The original *Sitz im Leben* of the hymn, therefore, is the temple cult.

The earliest preserved hymns date from the Middle Kingdom, but the custom of singing hymns may be much older, for hymnic passages appear already in the Pyramid Texts (ca. 2500 BCE). In the course of time, hymnic poetry spread from its cultic origin to other contexts as well. With the New Kingdom, the monumental tomb becomes the most popular context for hymns. At the entrance, the thicknesses of the tomb walls were decorated with hymns: on the southern thickness a hymn to the rising sun (with the tomb owner leaving the tomb) and on the opposite thickness a hymn to the setting sun or to Osiris (where the tomb owner is entering the tomb). Representations of the funerary procession, usually located on the southern wall of the passage, frequently show the tomb owner addressing Osiris with a hymn. During the Ramesside age, hymns to Amun-Re, the sun-god, Osiris, and also other deities may appear on every possible place in the tomb. Hundreds of hymns, mostly to Re and Amun-Re, are preserved from this period, which in fact was the heyday of hymnic poetry in Egypt.

A third context for hymns was scribal education or literature. Hymns were to be composed, learned by heart and copied in school, and circulated among the literate elite. Many important anthologies of hymns are attested in literary manuscripts, among them Papyrus Cairo 58038, Papyrus Leiden I.350, Papyrus Leiden 344 verso, and Papyrus Chester Beatty 4.

A fourth context is "magic." The term *magic* has a double meaning in Egyptological parlance. On the one hand, it refers to the Egyptian concept of Heka as an all-pervading coercive power, by which the world was made and is daily maintained and by which humankind is ruled. On the other hand, it refers to the domestic application and personal use of Heka, denoting a specific family of texts and objects classified as "magical." In the temple, the performance of hymns is obviously not meant as a form of coercive power. There is no need to use Heka in order to invoke the divine; the deity

Hymn to the rising sun presented by Hunefer and his wife (at left). Their posture of adoration is reflected in the heavenly baboons greeting the falcon-shaped sun-god and (below) Isis and Nephthys calling Osiris back to life. From Book of the Dead. © *The British Museum*

is already there, the sacred place is already charged with divine presence, which wants to be properly addressed and served. In the domestic sphere, the situation is different. The divine is not there and needs to be invoked. The same hymns, when performed in the magical context, fulfill a different function. They no longer respond to the preceding apparition of the divine but serve as a means of its invocation. The text—without the alteration of a single word—loses its communicative meaning of service and assumes the coercive or theurgical power of an evocative incantation. Whereas in the temple cult, the hymn is used to greet a deity who is present and visible in his/her cult statue, in magical contexts similar hymns are used to make an absent deity appear and intervene on behalf of the speaker or the patient during a situation of crisis. Hymns are sung, for example, on the road or the river in order to avert the crocodile and other dangers (Papyrus Magica Harris).

Forms. Egyptian hymns are couched in either nominal or verbal style. Only literary hymns and later "theological hymns" (after ca. 1350 BCE) combine both forms. The nominal style consists of appending to the name of the deity a series of epithets, participles, and other nominal syntagmata; the verbal style uses phrases containing finite verb forms. Whereas the nominal style is used for hymns to virtually all deities, the verbal style is restricted to hymns to the sun. The basic function of the nominal style is appellative; it is an elaboration of the name of the deity who is to be called and praised "in all his/her names." The basic function of the verbal style, on the other hand, is descriptive; it refers not to a timeless essence as the nominal style does, but to a temporal state or process.

The most conspicuous specificity of Egyptian hymns

is the absence of the first-person singular; as a rule, the speaker never refers to himself or herself while praising the deity. This is also the distinctive feature that sets off hymns from prayers. The speaker appears only at the end, in a closing statement, in which the speaker presents himself or herself, explains his or her activity for the deity, and asks for favors in return.

Themes. In harmony with its verbal form, the theme of the sun hymn is not the timeless nature of the sun-god, but the temporal process of the solar circuit. In the imagination of the Egyptians, the solar course is divided into three phases, corresponding to three "transformations" *(cheperu)* of the sun-god and to three times of the day: morning (Chepre: scarab beetle), noon (Re: falcon-headed man), and evening/night (Atum: ram-headed old man). Sun hymns give a description of this tripartite structure. The main topic of nominal hymns is divine rulership. Most of the epithets consist of proclamations of dominion: "Lord of heaven, master of the netherworld, king of eternity, ruler of everlastingness, lord of Abydos, chieftain of Busiris," and so on.

In the course of the New Kingdom, especially after 1350 BCE, hymns become the most important vehicle of the theological discourse that arose in the New Kingdom (15th–12th centuries BCE) around one particular problem: the concept of the Highest God or Supreme Being and his/her relation to the other members of the pantheon. The emergence of theology as a form of discourse obviously has much to do with the professionalization of priesthood in Egypt and the increasing importance of literacy in Egyptian religion. Its development and rapid expansion, however, have to be seen in connection with the religious developments leading to the monotheistic revolution of Akhenaten and its subsequent refutation. Typical themes of theological discourse are cosmogony, divine immanence in the life-giving elements (air, water, light), and justice (god as judge, as ethical authority, and as savior). The relation between God and world (including the other gods) is conceived of in terms first of supremacy (God, lord of gods) and then, after the fall of the Amarna religion, of pantheism (the Hidden One, manifest in the world including the gods).

Prayers

Prayers as an independent genre occur in Egypt only outside the official cult (where they are annexed to hymns as "closing statements"). The most important context is personal piety, which developed during the New Kingdom in various forms, including votive stelae, ostraca, and graffiti, all of which might carry prayers. The earliest documents are ostraca presented to a deity on the occasion of a procession. After Amarna, the custom of erecting votive stelae arose; those from Deir el-Medina are usually inscribed with prayers, some of which are comparable to biblical psalms in poetic beauty and religious expressivity. In prayers, unlike hymns, the first-person singular of the speaker and his or her relation to the deity play a dominant role. Sometimes, these stelae were erected in times of distress and contain a confession of guilt and a promise to tell the power of the god or goddess to the whole world. These texts may be classified as penitential prayers *(Busslieder)*. In most cases, however, a stele was erected after an experience of healing and salvation. These texts are called prayers of thanksgiving *(Danklieder)*. There are many parallels for both forms in the biblical Book of Psalms. Most characteristic of these confessions is a certain pathos of public announcement, an intention of making known to the whole world a private experience of a rather shameful kind:

> I am a man who swore falsely by Ptah, Lord of
>   Truth,
> and he caused me to see darkness by day.
> I will declare his might to him that knows him not
>   and to him that knows him,
> to little and great.
> Be you wary of Ptah, Lord of Truth!

This prayer is entitled "Proclamation of the Might of Ptah." "Proclamation of divine power" seems to be a designation of this genre. The basic idea is that an act of divine intervention in the private affairs of an individual requires public proclamation. The manifestation of divine power is regarded as a miracle and has to be proclaimed. The Greek term for this literary form and function is aretalogy, the telling of the *aretē* of god: his power, righteousness, and efficacy. Very similar prayers occur also on ostraca and papyri belonging to the context of literature and scribal education. During the

Ramesside period (ca. 1300–1100 BCE) the personal prayer was a rather popular literary genre.

Curses

In Egypt, unlike Mesopotamia and many other Mediterranean cultures, curses occur only rarely, and they have nothing in common with hymns and prayers. The Egyptians resorted to cursing in cases where justice, that is, legal institutions, had failed. Curses appear mostly in tomb inscriptions and are directed against potential violators, because the violation of (private) tombs was normally beyond the reach of legal prosecution. The distinction between laws and curses, legislation and imprecation, is that the one refers to the agency of social institutions and the other to the intervention of supernatural powers. Legislation establishes a nexus between crime and penalty to be enforced by judicative and executive institutions. Where justice fails, as in the case of undetected crimes, imprecation is used in order to relegate the maintenance of this nexus to other agencies. A curse establishes a link between crime and penalty that is independent of sociopolitical institutions and therefore quasi-automatic. Legal sanctions differ from curses in that curses are complemented by blessings, whereas sanctions have no positive complement. The curses typically threaten trespassers with deprivation of burial, bodily destruction (e.g., by burning), exclusion from divine communication (offering) and social memory, a kind of excommunication, usually complemented by blessings for someone who will act piously: "As regards any nome governor, any son of a man, any nobleman, or any civilian who will fail to protect this tomb and its contents, his god will not accept his white bread, he will not be buried in the west, and their flesh will burn together with that of the criminals, they having been turned into ones who do not exist."

Starting in the New Kingdom, imprecation formulas almost disappear from tombs, but appear in other contexts, above all in inscriptions documenting royal and private donations. Very typical is a curse in which divine vengeance is apportioned to a triad of gods: "As to anyone who shall be deaf to this decree, Osiris shall be after him, Isis after his wife, and Horus after his children, and the great ones, the lords of the holy land, will make their reckoning with him."

The most elaborate example is an inscription pretending to be the copy of a foundation document of the funerary temple of the sage Amunhotep son of Hapu.

BIBL.: J. Assmann, *Ägyptische Hymnen und Gebete* (2nd ed.; Fribourg, 1999). A. Barucq, *L'expression de la louange divine et de la prière dans la Bible et en Égypte* (Bibliothèque d'étude 33; Cairo, 1962). G. Fecht, *Literarische Zeugnisse zur "Persönlichen Frömmigkeit" in Ägypten* (Abhandlungen der Heidelberger Akademie der Wissenschaften: Philosophisch-historische Klasse; Heidelberg, 1965). Scott Morschauser, *Threat-Formulae in Ancient Egypt: A Study of the History, Structure, and Use of Threats and Curses* in *Ancient Egypt* (Baltimore, 1991). Katarina Nordh, *Aspects of Ancient Egyptian Curses and Blessings: Conceptual Background and Transmission* (Uppsala Studies in Ancient Mediterranean and Near Eastern Civilizations; Uppsala, 1996).   J.A.

Mesopotamia

Akkadian prayers and incantations composed in Standard Babylonian during the post–Old Babylonian period are known from 1st-millennium copies found in libraries or collections in such Assyrian and Babylonian cities as Nineveh, Asshur, Nimrud, Sultantepe, Sippar, Babylon, Ur, and Uruk. In Mesopotamia, there was a range of sacred speech forms that included lengthy literary hymns and prayers, royal prayers (especially of the kings of the Neo-Assyrian and Neo-Babylonian periods), prayers of diviners, lamentations, penitential psalms, folkloristic and learned incantations, and so on. Here, however, we pay particular attention to some of the major types of prayers and incantations of the *āšipu* (exorcist), over against those of the diviner or temple lamentation priest. The oral rites of the exorcist are invocations to gods and addresses to evil forces.

Prayers. Of special interest are laments or prayers of the individual known as *šuilla*s, according to the native designations found especially in their rubrics. The *šuilla*s are directed to many of the gods of the Babylonian pantheon, but most often to Marduk, Shamash, and Ishtar. The *šuilla*s are often referred to as *Gebetsbeschwörungen* (incantation prayers) because they have the form and thematic makeup of prayers, but open with the designation ÉN (incantation), are identified by rubrics normally found with incantations, and are linked to ritual activities that are referred to within the prayer and/or in ritual instructions that accompany the prayer. This terminology reflects a modern Western and often artificial distinction between magic and religion. Assyriological scholarship distinguishes, furthermore, between general and special *Gebetsbeschwörung*. The former carries the designation *šuilla* in at least some of its manuscripts; the latter has the form of a *šuilla* but does not carry that designation. The special *šuilla*, moreover, is often directed against specific types of evil and is recited as part of a magical ritual.

The basic format of the Akkadian *šuilla* contains three elements:

1. An address to and praise of the god by means of epithets and whole sentences. This part of the *šuilla* prayer will often provide a laudatory description of the god, first in terms of his/her place within the divine community and then in terms of his/her relationship to earth and the human world. This descriptive praise, particularly the description of the god's relationship to humanity, provides the backdrop and jumping-off point for the request to the god to listen to and help the petitioner. It warrants the human address to the god and explains in very general terms why the supplicant turns to the god for help. Even more, praise here elicits the power that inheres in the addressee; it activates the god by reminding him/her of his/her powers and functions and perhaps by flattering him/her.

2. A supplication centering upon a petition to the god asking him/her to come to his aid. Usually this central part of the prayer also includes an introductory lament in which the supplicant describes his/her suffering and perhaps its cause. Personal suffering may include the individual's experience of physical and/or psychological illness or difficulties and/or socioeconomic crises such as the loss of wealth and status, breakup of family, and social isolation. This part of the prayer may also contain an explicit presentation of the supplicant and a mention of the ritual act(s) accompanying the recitation.

3. Finally, a promise of praise should the petition be granted and the deity allow the supplicant to regain a normal life. In the most common form of promise, this praise serves to express thanksgiving, to affirm the individual's loyalty to this god, to give honor to the god, and to publicize the god's saving deeds so as to attract other loyal followers to his/her service.

The following prayer to Nergal (King 1896: no. 27 and duplicates = Mayer 1976: 478–81, Nergal no. 2), a god of war and pestilence and ruler of the netherworld, is an excellent example of a general *šuilla*:

Mighty lord, exalted son of Nunammir,
foremost among the Anunnaki, lord of battle,
offspring of Kutushar, the great queen,
Nergal, all powerful among the gods, beloved of
    Ninmenna.

You are manifest in the bright heavens, your station
    is exalted,
you are great in the netherworld, you have no rival.
Together with Anu [variant: Ea], your counsel is pre-
    eminent in the assembly of the gods.
Together with Sin, you observe everything in the
    heavens [variant: and earth/netherworld].

Enlil, your father, gave to you the black-headed ones,
    all the living,
he entrusted into your hands the herds, the animals.

I am so-and-so, son of so-and-so, your servant.
The anger of god and goddess has beset me [so that]
expenses and losses befall my estate [and]
giving orders but not being obeyed keep me awake.

Because you save, my lord, I have turned toward
    your divinity,
because you are compassionate, I have sought you,
because you are merciful, I have stood before you,
because you are favorably inclined, I have looked
    upon your face.

Favorably look upon me and hear my supplication.
May your furious heart become calm toward me,
pardon my crime, my sin, and my misdeed,

may the indignation of your great divinity be appeased for me.

May the offended, angry, and irate god and goddess be reconciled with me.

Then will I declare your great deeds and sing your praise!

The *šuilla* type may be used to invoke not only anthropomorphic gods and stars, but also materials used in magical rituals such as amulets, salt, oil (the so-called *Kultmittelbeschwörung* or *Kultmittelgebet*). An excellent example of this type is the following *šuilla*:

O Salt, created in a clean place,
for food of gods did Enlil destine you.
Without you no meal is set out in Ekur,
without you god, king, nobleman, and prince do not smell incense.
I am so-and-so, the son of so-and-so, whom witchcraft holds captive,
whom bewitchment holds by means of [a skin] disease.
O Salt, break my witchcraft! Loosen my spell!
Receive from me the bewitchment so that, as my creator,
I may praise you.
(Maqlû 6.111–19)

There are variations on the basic pattern of the *šuilla*. Some deviate from the norm and represent creative innovations. An excellent example of this is a 27-line *šuilla* addressed to Marduk (King 1896: no. 9 obverse and duplicates). It exhibits a new design that is created by the inclusion of two related summary statements of invocation, prayer, and thanksgiving, with the first being placed between the hymnic introduction and the prayer, and the second between the prayer and the concluding benediction. Although deviating from the usual liturgical pattern, this *šuilla* does not lack a meaningful order and creates a new religious effect.

Other *šuilla*s are longer and less orderly than these three. An example drawn from among the most important *šuilla*s is the famous Great Prayer to Ishtar known from both 2nd- and 1st-millennium copies. The later version runs to about 110 lines and while thematically very rich and powerful and dynamic in its representation, its *šuilla* structure is less clear, as its sections of praise, complaint, and prayer are somewhat jumbled and repetitive.

Here we turn to some general problems relating to the makeup of the *šuilla* corpus. But first, we recall that the *šuilla* is not part of the temple liturgy; rather, it is to be compared to the biblical laments of the individual, the most prevalent type of prayer in the Hebrew Psalms. The *šuilla* was part of a ceremony meant to heal or protect an individual and was recited at the home of the

supplicant (or palace of the king) or in a secluded outdoor area. Originally, the magician viewed natural and material powers holistically. But although the *āšipu*'s activities on behalf of supplicants were not part of the temple cult and took place outside the temple, it seems that he increasingly thought in terms drawn from the urban temple as he became a servant and representative of the elite. He thus came to address both natural forces and material objects in forms drawn from the temple cult, that is, modeled on the image of the god in the temple, who himself/herself was conceived in accordance with the image of the human ruler. The evolution of the *šuilla* reflects this suggested development.

This perspective may help to explain the use of a temple-oriented text for home service, the place of the personal god in the *šuilla*, and the wide variety of texts that are designated as *šuilla*s. In addition, it may help to understand the formation and existence of the special *šuilla*.

Composers of *šuilla*s did not simply compose their works on the basis of one design. The development of this body of material is complicated. The sources upon which the composers drew were various, and some of the same tendencies apply to both general and special *šuilla*s.

The *šuilla* type as well as many of its actual examples seem to have their origin in prayers that were recited on behalf of individuals and did not contain developed hymnic introductions. These supplications for the individual derived from various sources; but prayers to the personal god or, more properly, the god of the family were a particularly important source. Prayers to the personal god were recited originally in a family context; they reflect the problems of the individual householder or family head and represent an attempt to rectify personal or family problems caused by a rupture of relations between this person and the god—a rupture that led to abandonment and suffering and a rectification that involved forgiveness and reconciliation. That originally these supplications did not contain extended praise is supported by biblical laments of the individual; many of these laments seem to have been recited to the family or clan-god in a nontemple context and call directly upon the god for help without first offering significant praise (cf., e.g., Ps. 6, 13, 35, 38). Not infrequently, the divine recipient was identified with a cosmic or urban deity normally worshiped in a temple, and the address was modeled on temple liturgies by *āšipu*s with temple orientation. An hymnic introduction of praise would then have been added to the supplication; for the new praise section, the composer drew upon temple imagery and experiences associated with gods of the temple. (This suggestion regarding the development of the *šuilla* explains, by the way, why the biblical and Mesopotamian laments of the individual, two obviously related literary corpora, are both similar and different.)

The family background of the original prayers explains the frequent mention of the personal god in many *šuilla*s. Of course, the social location of many of the *šuilla*s was now changed; concerns internal to the family are sometimes found alongside or even replaced by the court concerns of the elite members of society for whom the developed *šuilla*s were composed or adapted. This development may also explain some of the different roles of the personal god in this body of literature. Sometimes the role of the personal god is taken over by the urban god to whom the *šuilla* is addressed; at other times, the family god is mentioned in the text, but has been transformed into a mere reflection or manifestation of the major god, on the model of the royal court with its king (temple god) and courtiers (personal gods), in which circles the elite moved. (The earlier role of the personal god as an intercessor may also have been colored by the image of the courtier; but this role seems to recede in the developed *šuilla* and is replaced by the model of the courtier who simply reflects the disposition and moods of the king.)

The special *šuilla* is often recited as part of a magical ceremony, and the ritual as well as the prayer, the *Gebetsbeschwörung*, focus on the specific evil to be combated by the ceremony, evils such as roaming ghosts, witchcraft, *māmīt* (oath), evil omens, demons. Shamash is the most common addressee of the special *šuilla*s (see *KAR* 80 obverse 12–reverse 14 and duplicates and Köcher 1963: 323 obverse 19–35 and duplicates).

The formation of the special *Gebetsbeschwörung* type is a result of the transformation of magical incantations to divine forces into prayers with hymnic introductions. As I have argued elsewhere, the different forms of a text may attest to this development. Thus, for example, manuscript variations of a Shamash incantation seem to reflect the exorcist's attempt to transform an incantation rooted in nature and ritual into a hymn and prayer to the god. The incantation is thus transformed into a *Gebetsbeschwörung*, taking on the form of the standard *šuilla* prayer type. This development reflects a similar process whereby popular material, in this case magical, is transformed into the literary form of a centrist institution, that is, a temple, by a literate clergy, knowledgeable in the forms of temple imagery and worship. A further example, perhaps, of the same general process is the use of forms derived from juridical practice in the prayers, thus turning the encounter with an evil force into a case at law and the prayer itself into an address to a judge.

Incantations. There are many different kinds of incantations; in the main, they address evil forces as well as beneficent forces that are meant to aid in the fight against evil forces. Such causes of suffering as demons, witchcraft, evil omens, roaming ghosts, and so on are confronted so as either to expel them or to keep them at a distance. Originally, incantations were recorded only in part as an *aide-mémoire*, but eventually the entire incantation was committed to writing, and instructions regarding the time, place, and manner of ritual performance as well as other types of information (particularly an objective description of the problem, a diagnosis, and a statement of purpose) were subsequently added. Incantations are found in various written contexts: (1) individual incantations as part of short rituals, (2) short collections of incantations (with some ritual instructions), and (3) standardized scribal series—some were collections, others represented complex lengthy ceremonies such as Shurpu and Maqlû. Among the themes in which incantations are particularly rich are the imagery used to depict evil beings; the nature and cause of the suffering; and, finally, the ritual acts that are performed alongside the recitation and are often reflected in one way or another in the incantation itself.

BIBL.: T. Abusch, "Blessing and Praise in Ancient Mesopotamian Incantations," in *Literatur, Politik und Recht in Mesopotamien* (ed. W. Sallaberger et al.; Wiesbaden, 2003). Idem, "The Demonic Image of the Witch in Standard Babylonian Literature: The Reworking of Popular Conceptions by Learned Exorcists," in *Religion, Science, and Magic in Concert and in Conflict* (ed. J. Neusner et al.; New York, 1989), 27–58. Idem, "The Form and Meaning of a Babylonian Prayer to Marduk," *Journal of the American Oriental Society* 103 (1983): 3–15. Idem, *Mesopotamian Witchcraft: Toward a History and Understanding of Babylonian Witchcraft Beliefs and Literature* (Ancient Magic and Divination 5; Leiden, 2002). L. W. King, *Babylonian Magic and Sorcery* (London: Luzac, 1896). Franz Köcher, *Die babylonisch-assyrische Medizin in Texten und Untersuchungen* (Keilschrifttexte aus Assur 1; Berlin: de Gruyter, 1963–). W. G. Kunstmann, *Die babylonische Gebetsbeschwörung* (Leipziger semitische Studien n.s. 2; Leipzig, 1932). W. Mayer, *Untersuchungen zur Formensprache der babylonischen "Gebetsbeschwörungen"* (Studia Pohl: Series maior 5; Rome, 1976). M.-J. Seux, *Hymnes et prières aux dieux de babylone et d'assyrie* (Paris, 1976). T.A.

Syria-Canaan

Syro-Canaanite literature contains a variety of divine invocations intended to honor, entreat, or influence the gods. Written in Ugaritic, Aramaic, and Canaanite dialects, these hymns, prayers, curses, and incantations are recorded in liturgical texts, royal stelae, funerary inscriptions, votive offerings, and amulets.

The most illuminating Syro-Canaanite hymns and prayers are from the archives of Ugarit. While invocations introduce or conclude various mythological texts, independent hymns and prayers are rare. One Ugaritic hymn (*KTU* 1.101) celebrates the victorious god Baal-Hadad as he sits enthroned upon his divine mountain, brandishing seven lightning bolts and eight peals of thunder. Another text (*KTU* 1.108) describes Rapau, the King of Eternity, "whom men hymn and honor with music, on the lyre and the flute, on drum and cymbals," and concludes with a benediction:

[May] your strength, your help, your power, your
   rule, your splendor,
[be] in the middle of Ugarit
throughout the days of the sun and moon and the
   gracious years of El.

The clearest Ugaritic example of a liturgical prayer (KTU 1.119) assures divine protection against military attack:

When a mighty one attacks your gates,
   a warrior your walls,
You will lift up your eyes to Baal [saying]:
"O Baal, drive the mighty one away from our gates,
   the warrior from our walls!
A bull, O Baal, we will consecrate [to you],
   a votive offering, Baal, we will fulfill!
A male, Baal, we will consecrate [to you],
   a sacrifice we will fulfill.
A libation, O Baal, we will pour out.
We will ascend to the sanctuary of Baal,
   we will process through the paths of Baal's
   temple."
Then Baal will listen to your prayer.
He will drive the mighty one from your gates,
   the warrior from your walls.

First-millennium prayers are attested in short Phoenician inscriptions on burial stelae and votive gifts deposited in shrines throughout the Mediterranean area. Many votive texts ask for a long life or thank a deity for an answered prayer; others are petitions for profit, good fortune, and an heir. A more-elaborate stele discovered in Karatepe commemorates the 8th-century BCE reign of Azitiwada (KAI 26; ANET 653–54), who asks Baal for "life and health . . . , length of days, many years, a pleasant old age, and mighty strength above every other king!" He continues, "And may this city be the owner of plenty [of grain] and new wine. And may this people who dwell in her be owners of oxen . . . and sheep . . . and may they bear many children. And as they grow may many become powerful . . . by the grace of Baal and the gods." The 8th-century Aramean King Zakkur claims (KAI 202; ANET 655–56) that he raised his hands in prayer to his god, Baal-Shamayn, who answered him through seers and diviners with an oracle of salvation.

In contrast to entreating the gods for blessings, curses often seek divine power to harm one's enemies. Whether based upon the inherent magical quality of spoken words or the agency of a complicit deity, imprecations are performative utterances, meant to bring about a desired result within a culturally appropriate context. In Ugaritic

poetry, Kirta reprimands a traitorous son with a traditional curse (KTU 1.16 6.54–58):

May Horon smash, O my son,
   may Horon smash your head;
   Athtart, the Name of Baal, your skull!
May you fall at the height of your years!

Danel also pronounces eternal curses, using agricultural metaphors, upon the towns near the location of his son's murder: "May your root not sprout upon the earth, / your head droop at the hands of your harvester!" (KTU 1.19 3.53–54). He curses another town for its possible witness to Aqhat's murder: "May Baal strike you blind!" (4.5). Kilamuwa of Zincirli also fashions a curse appropriate to the crime in his 9th-century commemorative stele (KAI 24; ANET 654–55): "And if anyone smashes this inscription, may Baal-Samad smash his head!"

The burial inscriptions of Phoenician kings contain numerous sanctions against those who would violate their graves. A particularly interesting example belongs to 5th-century BCE King Eshmunazar of Sidon, who bemoans that he has been struck down in his prime and denied a long life. He invokes an extravagant curse upon those who would disturb his sarcophagus (KAI 14; ANET 662): "May they have no resting place among the shades, may they not be buried in a grave. May they have no son or heir to succeed them, but may the holy gods deliver them up to a mighty ruler who will have dominion over them so that they perish. . . . May they have no root below nor sprout above nor renown among those living under the sun!" An Aramean priest of the moon-god in Nerab more tersely curses one who would disturb his tomb: "May Sahar and Nikkal and Nusk make his dying odious, and may his posterity perish!" (KAI 225; ANET 661).

The most extensive Syro-Canaanite curses are from 1st-millennium Aramaic royal monuments. The 9th-century King Hadyisi of Gozan curses any future king who would efface his statue: "May my lord Hadad not accept [sacrificial] bread or water from him. . . . May he sow but may [Hadad] not let him reap. . . . May his people scavenge barley from the garbage dumps to eat. May pestilence, the staff of Nergal, not cease from his land!" (Tell Fekheriye inscription). A lengthy vassal treaty from Sefire (KAI 222; ANET 659–61) invokes divine witnesses to inflict extensive sanctions against the king of Arpad should he become disloyal. All manner of sterility, starvation, and desolation are delineated, as the text asks that Hadad pour out "every sort of evil which exists on earth and in heaven" so that Arpad become a deserted mound visited only by desert animals.

Incantations provide another means of entreating the gods. An Ugarit exorcism directly addresses demons (KTU 1.169): "At the command of the exorcist, you will exit [the patient] like smoke through a chimney!"

Although their authenticity is contested, two inscribed plaques from Arslan Tash contain incantations against various flying demons (*KAI* 27; *ANET* 658). These rare texts are the forerunners of numerous Aramaic magical bowls and amulets from late antiquity.

BIBL.: Ali Abou-Assaf, Pierre Bordreuil, and Alan Millard, *La statue de Tell Fekherye et son inscription bilingue assyro-araméene* (Étude assyriologiques 7; Paris: Éditions recherche sur les civilizations, 1982). John C. L. Gibson, *Textbook of Syrian Semitic Inscriptions* (3 vols.; Oxford: Clarendon, 1971–82); Gregorio del Olmo Lete, *Canaanite Religion according to the Liturgical Texts of Ugarit* (trans. W. G. E. Watson; Bethesda, Md.: CDL, 1999).   N.W.

Israel

In Judaism there is a fundamental conviction that it is both possible and desirable for humans to address God and that God can and will respond. The God of the Hebrew Bible is characterized as "you who listen to prayer" (Ps. 65.2 [= 65.3 Hebrew]). Words of prayer can be articulated by an individual or by a community; spontaneously or according to a set formula; in the elevated language of poetry or in ordinary prose style; set to music and sung or simply spoken; formulated in the second person to address God directly or in the third person to speak about God. Although there are many different ways to categorize prayers, the most fundamental division is between the "glad prayers" of praise, thanksgiving, and blessing and the "sad prayers" of lament, petition, and curse.

In the Hebrew Bible, there are numerous places where it is said that individuals or communities "cried out to the Lord" but the actual words of their prayer are not given (e.g., Gen. 25.21; Num. 11.2). There are, however, close to one hundred passages in the narrative and prophetic sections of the Bible where the specific words of prayer spoken on a specific occasion are given in the text. These range from very short, direct petitions (e.g., the prayer of Moses when his sister Miriam is afflicted with leprosy: "Heal her, O God"; Num. 12.13) to longer, more formal prayers that combine elements of praise and petition (e.g., Solomon's prayer at the dedication of the temple; 1 Kings 8.22–53). Most scholars have paid little attention to these prayers that are embedded in narrative because of their seemingly spontaneous, onetime nature; yet although such prayers are clearly literary compositions, they can provide an important glimpse into popular forms of piety and religious expression. From the postexilic period, there are examples of lengthier, formalized prose prayers that combine confession of sin with historical remembrance (Ezra 9.6–15; Neh. 9.5–37; and Dan. 9.3–19), and these may have originated in liturgical rituals of lament and penitence.

An important body of prayers, often much neglected, are those in the Apocrypha and Pseudepigrapha. The

Incantation bowl. The humanlike face on an insectlike figure is encircled by reptiles. The Aramaic text includes the words "that you may turn away spells and curses and afflictions from Mahdad." Hebrew University Institute of Archaeology. *Photo by Z. Radovan, Jerusalem*

Greek versions of Esther and Daniel contain prayers that were not part of the Hebrew versions (the prayers of Mordecai [Esth. 13.8–18] and Esther [14.1–19]; the Prayer of Azariah and the Song of the Three Young Men inserted after Dan. 3.23). The Greek apocryphal book *The Prayer of Manasseh* supplies the missing prayer of penitence that is only referred to in 2 Chron. 33.10–13, 18. In independent works that retell and rework the biblical narratives with explanations and elaborations, it is often prayers that are added (e.g., in *Genesis Apocryphon* the prayer of Abraham when Sarah is taken from him [20.12–16]; in *Jubilees*, the prayers of Moses [1.19–21], Noah [10.3–6], and Abraham [12.19–21; 22.6–7]).

The sentiments of praise and thanksgiving, lament and petition, are also expressed in poetic compositions. One hundred fifty poems (one hundred fifty-one in Greek manuscripts) collected into a single book are called by the Greek term *psalmoi* (psalms). Although originally designating a text that is sung to a musical accompaniment, the term *psalm* is sometimes applied by extension to other compositions and collections that are similar in style and content (e.g., *Psalms of Solomon, Thanksgiving Psalms* from Qumran). The biblical book as a whole came to be known as "the Psalter" or by its Hebrew title "The Book of Praises."

Modern scholarship categorizes the psalms on the basis of repeated forms and patterns that are linked in some way to usage. On the basis of such formal criteria, there are seven or eight distinctive types of psalms, although these are not rigidly fixed, and many psalms do not fit neatly into a single category. The largest single group, numerically, is the lament, whether of the individual or the community (e.g., Ps. 3–7, 22, 51, 74, 79, 137); psalms of this type follow a regular pattern of address to God, a description (often at length) of the situation of distress, a petition for divine help, an articulation of the motivation for God to act, and a concluding statement of trust and confidence. Thanksgiving psalms (e.g., Ps. 116, 75) praise God for deliverance that has already been granted, although they often include a lengthy recounting of the past condition of distress. Hymns (e.g., Ps. 8, 100, 135, 136, 150) call the community to praise or express praise directly for what God is and what God has done, especially in creation and in past acts of deliverance. Other types of psalms take as their specific focus the praise of Zion (Ps. 46, 48), the king and the promises made to the line of David (Ps. 2, 45, 89, 110), or God as eternal king (Ps. 47, 93, 96–99). The so-called wisdom psalms (Ps. 1, 19, 73, 119) offer extended meditations on the Torah, the righteous and the wicked, and the problem of the suffering of the just.

The individual psalms were written over many centuries, and the collection as we have it now is the result of a complex, and not totally recoverable, process of development. More than two-thirds of the psalms have some sort of superscription, but many of these are rubrical or musical notations whose original meanings are virtually unintelligible. Seventy-three psalms are attributed to David and thirteen of these are linked to specific events in his life (e.g., Ps. 3, 18, 51); Ps. 72 is attributed to Solomon and Ps. 90 to Moses. These titles are late, secondary attributions, and over time the tradition of David as psalm-writer *par excellence* (1 Sam. 16.4–23; Amos 6.5; 2 Chron. 23.18) led to the attribution of the whole Psalter to David. There are traces of other subgroupings (the psalms of Asaph [73–83], the psalms of the Korahites [42–49, 84–88], and the Elohistic psalter, distinguished by the use of *'ĕlōhîm* rather than the tetragrammaton *yhwh* as the designation for God), although little is known with certainty of their origins and purpose. Numerous references to the temple, sacrifices, and processions suggest that many of the psalms were composed for use in worship at the temple. According to descriptions in the Bible (1 Chron. 6.31–32 [= 6.16–17 Hebrew]; 16.4–7) and later sources (Sir. 50.18–19; Mishnah, tractate *Tamid* 7), specific psalms were sung by the Levites and temple singers after the daily sacrifice and at the major festivals. The inclusion of psalms in biblical narratives, however, indicates that they could also be used by an individual in times of crisis, apart from the temple cult (e.g., when Jonah is in the belly of the whale he is portrayed as praying a psalm; Jon. 2.1–9 [= 2.2–10 Hebrew]). The psalms were collected and organized during the Second Temple period, although the multiple copies found among the manuscripts in the caves of Qumran may give evidence of divergent collections and

orders, especially for the final third of the book, as late as the 1st century CE. In its final form, the Psalter was divided into five books (perhaps on analogy with the five books of Moses), each concluding with a doxology of praise (Ps. 41.13 [= 41.14 Hebrew]; 72.18–19; 89.53; 106.47–48; 150.6). Indeed the macrostructure of the Psalter as a whole in its final form moves from lament (in the majority of the psalms in the first half) to praise (especially in the final grouping of Ps. 145–50).

The composition of religious poetry continued throughout the Second Temple period, with new compositions usually modeled on the biblical psalms in style, language, and content. Much material is preserved only in the manuscripts from the caves at Qumran, for example, a pseudepigraphic collection of psalms attributed to the kings and prophets of Israel (4Q380–81) and another collection of psalms that each begin with the words from Ps. 103.1 and 104.1: "Bless the LORD, O my soul" (4Q434–38). More than thirty poems of thanksgiving, arranged in somewhat different collections (cf. 1QH and 4QHa), are designated as *Hodayot* or *Thanksgiving Psalms*. Opening with a standard introduction, "I thank you, Lord," or "Blessed are you, Lord," they share distinctive vocabulary and themes, with a strong emphasis on salvation, knowledge, predeterminism, and union with the angels. These psalms seem to be compositions of the Essenes, and at least some may have been composed by the Teacher of Righteousness (the original leader of that sect). Another collection of eighteen *Psalms of Solomon*, preserved in Greek and Syriac, reflect on the political situation in the 1st century BCE (Ps. 2) and the expectations for a Davidic messiah (Ps. 17).

The practice of the community reciting fixed prayers at specific times developed relatively late, probably in the latter part of the Second Temple period. While the temple existed, the central act of cultic worship was sacrifice, and the sacrificial cult per se seems to have been conducted in silence without accompanying words of prayer. There are hints of a shift in emphasis toward linking prayer and sacrifice in the postexilic period, and the temple itself came to be designated as the "house of prayer" (Isa. 56.7). Our earliest evidence for the composition of fixed communal prayers is a manuscript dated to the first half of the 2nd century BCE (4Q504); although preserved at Qumran, these *Words of the Luminaries*, as they are entitled, originated in some pre-Essene pious community, but it is uncertain how widely they were used. The Dead Sea Scrolls contain collections of prayers for the morning and evening of each day of the month (4Q503), a unified literary composition of prayers for each day of the week (4Q504, 4Q506), prayers for the cycle of feasts (1Q34, 4Q507–9), and a collection of prayers for thirteen sabbaths (*Songs of the Sabbath Sacrifice*) (4Q400–407). Certain features that came to be distinctive of Jewish prayer are already attested here, in particular the use of a blessing formulary at the beginning and/or end of each prayer (although the exact wording is not yet standardized) and the practice of petitionary prayer on weekdays and prayer of praise on the sabbath.

After the destruction of the temple in 70 CE, communal statutory prayer three times a day (morning, late afternoon, and evening) became the norm. A rabbi named Simeon Hapaquli is credited with "arranging" the Eighteen Benedictions "according to [their] order at Yavneh" (Babylonian Talmud, tractates *Berakhot* 28b and *Megillah* 17b). It is much debated by scholars whether this statement means that the benedictions were composed at this time or whether they existed to some extent much earlier and were now standardized, at least in terms of number, topics, and overall framework, although not precise wording. The core of the prayer service came to be the Eighteen Benedictions (Amidah), the recitation of the Shema (the fundamental, monotheistic statement of Judaism; see Deut. 6.4), and a series of blessings surrounding the Shema focusing on the themes of creation, Torah, and redemption. Gradually, poetry in the form of biblical psalms and of new compositions, *piyyutim,* were added to supplement the statutory prayers. The service of prayer was not canonized until the Gaonic period (6th–7th centuries CE), and the earliest copies of the prayer book (the Siddur of Rav Amran) that have survived are from the 9th and 10th centuries.

BIBL.: Samuel E. Balentine, *Prayer in the Hebrew Bible: The Drama of Divine-Human Dialogue* (Overtures to Biblical Theology; Minneapolis: Fortress, 1993). Esther Chazon, "Prayers and Hymns in the Dead Sea Scrolls," in *The Dead Sea Scrolls after Fifty Years: A Comprehensive Assessment* (ed. J. C. VanderKam and P. W. Flint; Leiden: Brill, 1998), 244–70. Hans-Joachim Kraus, *Psalms: A Commentary* (2 vols.; Minneapolis: Augsburg, 1988–93). Stefan Reif, *Judaism and Hebrew Prayer: New Perspectives on Jewish Liturgical History* (Cambridge: Cambridge University Press, 1993), 1–152.   E.S.

Anatolia

The only knowledge we have of Hittite prayers comes from the cuneiform archives of Hattusha, which recorded the official prayers, generally pronounced by a high priest in the name of the king, the queen, or a princess. The majority of them go back to the Hittite Empire and chiefly concern kings Murshili II, Muwattalli II, and Hattushili III and his wife, Pudukhepa. The gods invoked are the great gods, who were venerated as early as the Hatti period, although sometimes one of them is combined with a Hurrian god: the great Weather-god of Hatti (identified with the Hurrian god Teshub), the Sun-goddess of Arinna (identified with the Syro-Hurrian goddess Hepat) and her circle, Telipinu, or the Weather-god of Nerik. There is no trace of any spontaneous prayer or of any prayer that was purely adorative. The

pragmatic Hittites turned to the gods, whom they invoked as if they were sublimated kings, when they were in trouble. For instance, the many prayers of Murshili II were motivated by an ongoing plague that was decimating Hatti.

The genuine Hittite prayer is called *arkuwar* (argumentation, plea), a verbal noun that is in origin a legal term and that is loaded with specific religious value; in the end, the nature of all extant Hittite prayers comes down to this concept. The individual who prays presents his or her case to the god (or, often, has scribes present it for him or her); the outcome, happy or not, depends on the quality of the arguments put forward. As such, prayer is properly the work of a specialist. It tends to emphasize the relative freedom of humans, who are not to be crushed by the arbitrary will of the gods. There is, then, a place for the human even in the face of the divine world.

In order to ensure its maximum efficacy, the Hittites inserted the *arkuwar* prayer into a frame consisting of other kinds of prayers. The *mugawar* (a noun derived from the verb *mugai* [to set in motion]) involves magical words and actions that are likely to bring an angry god out of his hostile, sulky state. Prayers were often preceded by a hymn that was intended to win the god's benevolence, that is, a *walliyatar* (a word derived from *walliya* [to strengthen], cf. Latin *valere, validus*), in which the god was praised; these prayers generally were translations or adaptations of Babylonian models. The prayer concluded with a *malduwar* (a noun derived from *mald* [to promise]), a short votive prayer in which an individual promised to present the god with rich offerings if his or her plea was answered favorably. One more type of prayer, the *wekuwar* (a noun derived from *wek* [to ask for insistently], cf. Latin *vocare, vox*), could be short and sometimes attached to the *arkuwar* prayer; in it, one insistently asked the divinity to protect the king and royal family as well as the whole land of the Hittites.

One classical and typical prayer, the second prayer of Murshili II (1321–1295 BCE), asks for help against the plague. Here, he addresses the Weather-god of Hatti, because he thinks that his father, Shuppiluliuma I, has committed a serious crime (lines 20–29):

Now I present my prayer [*arkuwar*] to the weather-god, my lord, on account of the plague. O weather-god, my lord, listen to me, save me! I remind you: "The bird gets back to his cage so that the cage saves him [a proverb]." Or let us assume that a situation overwhelms a servant. He will then present his defense [*arkuwar*] to his lord. In this case his lord will listen to him and will sort out what makes him anxious. Let us also assume that a servant makes a mistake, but that he confesses his mistake to his lord. In this case, although his lord is entitled to do whatever pleases him, because he [the servant] confesses his mistake to his lord, the mind of his lord is calmed down and his lord will forgive this servant. Now there! I have confessed the mistake of my father; sincerely, I have done it.

Murshili II then indicates that the gods nevertheless are not satisfied, since the plague still rages. Perhaps the gods are waiting for a new, more specific form of compensation, or perhaps the most serious crime has not yet been discovered. If that is the case, then the gods should let this be known through a dream to the king or by way of an oracle. In line 37, the king becomes insistent: "Now, I present you plea after plea, Weather-god of Hatti, my lord; save me!"

BIBL.: H. G. Güterbock, "Some Aspects of Hittite Prayers," in *The Frontiers of Human Knowledge* (ed. T. T. Segerstedt; Uppsala, 1978), 125–39. R. Lebrun, *Hymnes et prières hittites* (Louvain-la-Neuve, 1980). I. Singer, *Muwatalli's Prayer to the Assembly of Gods through the Storm-God of Lightning (CTH 381)* (Atlanta, 1996).   R.L.

Iran

Prayers and devotional recitation in Zoroastrianism constitute an integral and continuous act of worship. They connect the believer with the physical and spiritual world in time and space and in the fundamentally cosmological and eschatological outlook of the religion contribute to the fight against evil and thus to the "healing the world" and its ultimate transfiguration at the end of a cycle of twelve millennia. The form, function, and attitude toward prayer reflect the central role and mediating power of the word in this religion. It is encoded in the Zoroastrian rule of conduct, "Good Thoughts, Good Words, Good Deeds," which in pragmatic terms is a rule of proper thought-speech-act. All prayers, whether private or sacerdotal, are recited in standing position, facing the sacred fire, the sun, or any other source of light; sacerdotal prayers require at least two priests.

For the devotional life the most important reference is the *Khorde Avesta* (Little Avesta), which is the Zoroastrian book of common prayer. It is a varying collection, for both priests and laypersons, of frequently used prayers, hymns, and other devotional texts. The major sets of prayers and devotional recitations may be grouped as follows: (1) the confession of faith *Fravarane*, which significantly includes the renunciation of the Daewas (false gods and demons) and the first phrases of which begin all major recitals and actions: "I profess to be an adherent of Mazda, a Zoroastrian, an opponent of the Daewa, accepting the law of Ahura, praising the Beneficent Immortals, worshiping the Beneficent Immortals"; the sacred-cord prayers, which include a special protective formula against the powers of evil; the confessional formularies *Patet*, both personal and on behalf of others, living or dead; (2) prayers related to life cycles of which cyclical memorial prayers

and blessings for the deceased and for the ancient forebears of the religion are an integral part; (3) prayers relating to temporal cycles and dedicated to their tutelary deities, specifically, the prayers during the five daily periods *(Gah)*; the five *Niyayeshn* (praises) addressed to the sun, the deity Mithra, the moon, the waters, and the fire, likewise to be recited daily; prayers on the thirty days of the month *(Si-roza)*; prayers on the six seasonal festivals *(Gahanbar)* and on the holy days of Nowruz at spring equinox; (4) the *Afrinagan* (blessings), to be recited during the five last holy days of the year at spring equinox, at the six seasonal feasts, and at the beginning and end of summer and in honor of the dead; grace at meals, both in secular and ritual settings; (5) most powerful, the so-called great prayers, in particular the four formulas that frame the Gathas of Zarathustra and thus also frame all secular and ritual acts, characteristic in specific numbers of repetitions and combinations, as is also the case with other formulaic sets and even longer texts.

The basic text of the religion is the Yasna, a liturgy accompanying the Zoroastrian *yasna* ritual, which consists of seventy-two chapters and is performed every morning by two priests in the fire temple. It is a composite text where sections in the Old Iranian language known as Young Avestan symmetrically frame two ancient hymn cycles composed in the language known as Old, or Gathic, Avestan (with a total of twenty-five chapters, Yasna 28–53, with some later additions): (1) the fundamental text of the religion, the Gathas (Songs), attributed to Zarathustra, which constitute a cycle of five sets of speculative hymns of wisdom, formally arranged according to their stanzaic syllabic meter, with a total of seventeen chapters; and (2) the liturgically central text, the *Hapta-hati* (Seven chapters), which itself is framed by the Gathas (inserted after the first Gatha) and is a hymn in stanzaic prose, perhaps composed shortly after the Gathas, in praise of the sacred fire and water and dedicated to Ahura Mazda and the six fundamental principles and divine entities, the Amesha Spentas (Beneficent Immortals). These two texts represent unique developments of specific types of the Indo-Iranian sacrificial hymns and share many basic features with those of the Rig Veda, including the basic dialectic of invocation of the divine beings with an offer of service, presentations of novel praise of their prominent features and deeds, requests of due reward, and much of their rhetoric and phraseology.

In terms of compositional techniques, the Gathas are extremely complex in structure, often enigmatic in diction, and marked by symmetry and chiastic structures on all levels. Most of the seventeen chapters have the form of a "ring composition," and the five Gathas as a whole form a single cycle, in a hierarchic verbal architecture of the "true spoken word," which, marked by significant numerical patterns, functions as the most effective defense and offense. Such structures appear to reflect both the comprehensive perception of the cosmos and the ideological tenor of the religion which opposes the fundamental principle of the divine Asha (order, truth) to the primary destructive principle Druj (lie). These two terms thus reflect the recognition of the central role of the word, which is also captured in Zarathustra's terms *House of Songs* and *House of Lies* for the final abodes. While the Gathas are ritual, not didactic texts, where the paradigmatic Zarathustra appears standing in front of the congregation in elated dialog with Mazda, which is expressed in various terms of mental perception and immediacy, they are on the whole predicted by the divine principle entity Vohu Manah (good mind), paired with the female Armaiti (proper thinking, devotion), which are the two determining benevolent principles of Ahura Mazda.

An essential constituent of the Gathas are *manthra*s (lit., instruments of thought). These are complex and enigmatic magic spells, the most important of which is believed to have been first spoken by Ahura Mazda against the Evil Spirit at initial creation. Such *manthra*s serve as both weapon and curse, such as, "Tell me how to destroy the Lie with the manthras of thy instruction; let one put the powerful sword on the adherent of the Lie to bring ill and harm over them" (Yasna 44.14; Humbach et al. 1991).

The four most sacred formulas capture the essential tenets of the religion and protectively enclose the Gathas in the liturgy, three at the beginning and one at the end, traditionally referred to by their initial phrases: Ahuna Vairya, Ashem Vohu, Yenhe Hatam, Airyema Ishyo. The first two are considered the most powerful and accordingly open and conclude all texts and actions in various combinations and repetitions. They may substitute for all other prayers and religious acts and are the first texts memorized by children. The very nature of these two allows for multiple grammatical and conceptual interpretations, which makes them virtually impossible to translate, so that the renderings suggested here can be only tentative at best:

Ahuna Vairya: "Whereas he shall be chosen by the world, so, according to Asha, the judgment of the deeds done by the world in Vohu Manah is yielded to Mazda, and the Khshathra to the Ahura whom they shall assign as pastor to the poor." (Yasna 27.13)

Ashem Vohu: "Asha is the best Good [blessed, rich life]. [All] wishes are [granted] to him who wishes [to strengthen] Asha for the sake of best Asha." (Yasna 27.14)

Yenhe Hatam: "Ahura Mazda knows whose [power] is stronger [lit., better] among the Beings in our Yasna, according to Asha. Those we worship, male and female." (Yasna 27.15)

Airyema Ishyo: "May the vigorous Aryaman come to the support of the men and women of Zarathustra, to the support of Vohu Manah. I seek [the paths] of

Daena, who will gain the desirable prize and the invigorating Ashi [reward] of Asha, which Ahura Mazda has designed." (Yasna 54.1)

The first of these four once was probably the first stanza of the Gathas, later separated for the manthric power attributed to it. It has been compared to the Christian *paternoster* and indeed is a nuclear profession of faith, apparently in the form of the legal judgment by a celestial council (reminiscent of Yasna 29.6). It cites, in addition to Asha and Vohu Manah, the third in the ranking of the Amesha Spentas, Khshathra (rule, sovereignty, power), and as a whole is paradigmatic for the Right Choice by humans. The second formula (probably derived from the first stanza of the second Gatha; Yasna 43.1) appears to be a cosmic spell about Asha, who is the guardian of fire and functions as the closure to most devotions. Its twelve words are perhaps reminiscent of the twelve constellations and the twelve millennia of Zoroastrian eschatology. The third formula acknowledges all spiritual beings and powers, significantly including female ones (unlike its model, Yasna 51.22), and is essentially confined to liturgical citations being regularly recited at the end of litanies. The fourth formula closing the Gathas appears to have been originally the last stanza of the last Gatha, Yasna 53, calling the Aryaman, probably the allied families of both believers and the divine, toward the path of the religious vision, Daena, and the achievement of universal fortune, Ashi, following the divine plan. This formula once functioned as the most powerful spell of physical and spiritual healing and had exorcising power, but today is reduced to recitation as part of the matrimonial blessings.

Two further Young Avestan collections, interspersed with the *yasna* liturgy on special occasions, are essential for the ritual and provide Avestan formulas for prayers: (a) the Visprad (all the lords), litanies to the different classes of divine beings, included especially at the six seasonal festivals and Nowruz at spring equinox; and (b) the Vendidad (law against the Daewa, the false and destructive gods and powers), which is not a liturgical text in origin, but mainly a vast collection of rules against physical and spiritual pollution.

A separate set and type of hymns are the Yashts (venerations; variant of Yasna), traditionally twenty-one in number and of various length in their present form. They are organized by extended cola in simple rhythmic prose, some suggesting octosyllabic meter, of which the so-called great Yashts still reflect their ancient origin. They are dedicated to Iranian deities, most of whom are not mentioned in the Gathas, but function as tutelary deities of specific days or months or both; that is, they are the guardians of the proper progression of the skies and of temporal cycles. Their hymns are to be recited according to their calendar days and months, particularly when both coincide. Among others, the Yashts include hymns to the following: the Fravashis, the protective and ancestor spirits (Yasht 13), a hymn ritually most important as part of the funerary rituals; the genius of the brightest star of the sky, Tishtrya (Sirius) (Yasht 8); and Mithra, the god of contract and social and solar cycles (Yasht 10). These three significantly guard three of the four cardinal points of the year in the Zoroastrian calendar, namely, spring equinox, summer solstice, and fall equinox, while the winter solstice at the darkest point of the year is guarded by Dadwah (the creator, establisher). Structurally, the longer Yashts are of two types, defined by formulaic pattern and deity, one set addressing the present continuous workings of the deity and the believer's appropriate ritual performance, the other celebrating mythical or "epic" heroes and their successful prayers to the deity, models for the present believer. Among those are the hymn to Anahita Aredvi Sura, the goddess of the cycles of natural flows and fluids (Yasht 5); to Good Vayu, the deity of the atmospheric cycles and space (Yasht 15); and to Khwarnah, the mysterious Iranian glory (Yasht 19), relatively more recent than the others and hailing the cosmic cycle of Iranian history from the beginning of the material world through Zarathustra's coming to the final transfiguration of the world. Not included in this collection, but in the *yasna* liturgy, are the hymn to Haoma (Yasna 9–11), the deity of the invigorating drink by the same name which is prepared and oblated in the act of the *yasna,* and two hymns to Srausha (listening, obedience), the god of prayer and protector of souls (Yasna 56–57). Also included in the Yasna is the Mazdean profession of faith (Yasna 12), immediately following the hymn to Haoma.

All Zoroastrian texts reflect the developments of a tradition that probably began in the 2nd millennium BCE, continued to be transmitted orally, and, exposed to the changing knowledge of the times, was finally codified in writing under the Sasanids (224–651 CE), for which a sophisticated phonetic alphabet was devised. It was organized in a canon of twenty-one thematic collections, Naska, a good many texts with Middle Persian translations and commentary. Thereafter much was lost so that the extant Avesta represents about two-fifths of that canon. New compilations and other works in Middle Persian were made mainly in the 9th and 10th centuries, later followed by works in New Persian and later also in Gujarati.

Throughout, the utterance of holy Avestan words, Middle Persian *wāj* (word) and Modern Persian *bāj,* remained the central feature and anchor. Prayer texts in particular typically combine a set of appropriate passages in Avestan with those in Middle Persian (some also in New Persian) and are audibly distinguished by being enunciated aloud while non-Avestan passages between such passages are recited inaudibly. A characteristic feature of Zoroastrian prayer and ritual is the function of two appropriate Avestan formulas to consecrate and protectively frame a prescribed act, in daily life as in ritual. These sequences thus constitute a performative

unit of variant internal complexity, technically referred to as a *wāj/bāj.* On a larger scale, the *yasna* liturgy itself includes numerous such *bāj*s, recited antiphonically by the two priests, typically opening major ritual sections. Certain of the shorter *bāj*s have become more widely used, such as the *bāj* of Srausha for its efficacy in protecting the souls.

Part of the modular structure of the texts are certain common components. Thus, typical in larger rituals is the *khshnuman* (for the pleasure of) (Avestan *khshnumaine*), a recitation in honor of the deity or spiritual being to whom the ritual is dedicated and a remembrance *(yād)* of the person, living or dead, for whose sake it is performed and the naming of the person who commissioned it. Similarly, each religious service has its dedicatory introduction in Middle Persian, known by the New Persian term *dibacha,* in anticipation of the Avestan dedication that follows during the ritual. A further distinctive feature is the dedication to the spirit of the specific period of the day.

The sacred-cord prayer, performed at the five periods of the day, may serve as an example of the composite nature of these texts: (after the initial ablution of hands and feet) beginning of *bāj,* with the *khshnuman* of Ahura Mazda; then recitation of the Ashem Vohu *manthra;* at untying, recitation of the exorcising Avestan Kem na Mazda, followed by one Ashem Vohu; other short Avestan prayers, including part of the confession of faith; at untying, the recitation of the Middle Persian Ohrmazd Khoday (Ohrmazd is the Lord, he keeps the Evil Spirit away). The Kem na Mazda itself is a composite of verses from the Yasna, embedding a crucial one from the Vendidad (Yasna 46.7 + 44.16 + Yasht 8.21 + Yasna 49.10.1.c).

BIBL.: Helmuth Humbach, Josef Elfenbein, and Prods O. Skjaeervø, *The Gāthās of Zarathushtra and the Other Old Iranian Texts* (2 vols.; Heidelberg, 1991). Jean Kellens, "La prière d'identification dans la tradition zoroastrienne," in *L'esperience de la prière dans les grandes religions* (ed. Henri Limet and Julien Ries; Louvain-la-Neuve, 1980), 119–28. Prods O. Skjaeervø, "The Literature of the Most Ancient Iranians," in *Proceedings of the Second North American Gatha Conference* (ed. Sarosh J. H. Manekshaw and Pallan R. Ichaporia; Womelsdorf, Pa., 1996), 221–35. Eva Tichy, "Indoiranische Hymnen," in *Hymnen der alten Welt im Kulturvergleich* (ed. Walter Burkert and Fritz Stolz; Göttingen, 1994), 79–95. Gernot Windfuhr, "The Word in Zoroastrianism," *Journal of Indo-European Studies* 12 (1984): 133–77.   G.L.W.

Greece

Greek hymns and prayers are generally part of the much larger practice of sacrifice: they explain or focus the ritual so the gods can understand precisely what is at stake and what is desired. They have a recognizable formal structure. The first part is the "invocation," in

who is the object of an assassination plot. Although this prayer, as many others, is focused on the request to the deity, there is also an element of self-assertion and confidence: the divinity will fulfill the request because the petitioner is worthy of it or it is somehow owed to him or her for past service (see Depew 1997: 232–36). The same self-confidence expresses itself both in gesture and terminology of prayer. Greeks stood with upraised hands during prayer; kneeling was understood as abasing oneself. The standard Greek verb for praying, *euchesthai,* means in Homeric Greek "to boast" or "to make a vaunt": a prayer is a speech act that makes a claim on the deity on the grounds that the person speaking is of some worth.

Another implication of this terminology is that Greek prayer usually was audible prayer. There might be special circumstances that recommended silent prayer—the wish not to be heard by the enemy, as at *Iliad* 7.195, the necessity not to betray one's real feelings, as with the disguised Orestes, who participates in Aegisthus's prayer, but whom he presently will kill (Euripides, *Electra* 809), or the character of a divinity, as in the case of the Erinyes (Sophocles, *Oedipus at Colonus* 489). But sometimes—and more often so in later periods—silent prayer was viewed with suspicion, as hiding dishonorable wishes (Clement of Alexandria, *Stromateis* 4.26).

Extant Greek prayers cover the full range of possibilities, from the highly formalized prayers in state festivals of the Greek cities to the very personal reaction of a human to an event that provokes a call for divine help, although, of course, filtered through the medium of a text. At the very end of this spectrum is the simple address to a god ("O god!"); at least in Athens, this interjection is gendered, with women invoking the "Two Goddesses" (i.e., Demeter and Persephone) and men invoking Heracles or Zeus. As literary prayers show, the sequence of argument and request can be reversed in order to express the urgency of the request; it is so much on the mind of the person making the prayer that the justification comes as an afterthought.

Hymns. Hymns can be distinguished from prayers in several useful ways. In general, Greek hymns are prayers that have become far more formalized: hymns are often sung in elaborate poetic meters and accompanied by dance and music. They are, moreover, often publicly sung by a chorus of young men or women, whose combined voices represent the voice of the community. When Apollo sends plague upon the Greeks (or, as Homer calls them, the Achaeans) at Troy, Chryses (Apollo's local priest), after having been mollified by the Greeks, first propitiates Apollo with a prayer and a sacrifice on behalf of the sufferers (*Iliad* 1.145–56), but then "all day long these young Achaeans propitiated the god with singing, chanting a splendid hymn to Apollo . . . who listened and was glad" (1.472–74). Apollo is said to hear the prayer, but he is gladdened by the singing of hymn, a detail that calls to mind yet another dis-

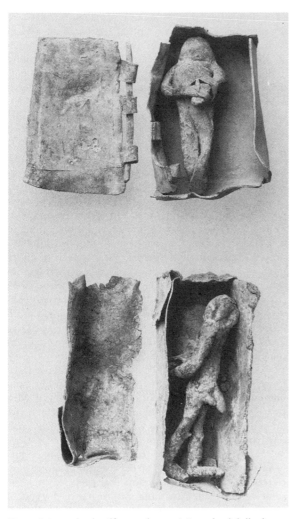

Two miniature lead coffins, each containing a lead doll whose hands are bound at its back. Athenian, late 5th–early 4th century BCE. Kerameikos Museum, Athens. *German Archaeological Institute, Rome*

which the worshiper "calls on" the deity and names her in a way that includes mention of her many epithets and the many places in which she is worshiped. The second part, the "argument," explains why the deity should be interested in helping the worshiper. And the third and final part, the "petition," makes a formal request to the god for some new or continued good or to ward off some evil. A brief prayer by Penelope is illustrative (*Odyssey* 4.759–66): "Tireless child of Zeus, graciously hear me! If ever Odysseus burned at our altar fire thigh bones of beef or mutton in sacrifice, recall it for my sake and save my son!" This prayer contains a brief invocation of Athena, the argument that she should respond because of gifts that Penelope's husband had made to her, and the imperative to save Telemachus,

tinction between the two forms: just like the unblemished sacrificial animals decked out in ribbons and gold leaf or the glittering silver and gold votives that line the temple of the god, hymns themselves are beautiful offerings, designed to catch the attention of the gods and give them great pleasure; this is why hymns, sometimes even with their notation, could be inscribed on marble and dedicated in sanctuaries in order to preserve the otherwise ephemeral pleasure derived from their performance (see Pulleyn 1997: 49–50).

A wide range of forms are preserved among the hymns found in inscriptions and ancient authors. A seemingly archaic hymn is sung by the women of Elis to call Dionysus: "Come, O Lord Dionysus, to the sacred temple of Elis's people . . . storming on your bovine foot, worthy bull, worthy bull" (Plutarch, *Moralia* 299B). Among the more elaborate hymns, two forms are singled out already in antiquity, the paean and the dithyramb. The paean is "nowadays composed to all the gods but originally belonging properly to Apollo and Artemis, being sung for the cessation of plagues and diseases" (Proclus in Photius, *Library* 320a21), an ancient definition that merits some credit, even after intensive modern discussions (Furley and Bremer 2001: 1.84–91). In *Iliad* 1, the young Greeks sing a paean to Apollo at the end of the plague; several later paeans are addressed to the healing son of Apollo, Asclepius, one of them composed by Sophocles. The dithyramb is Dionysus's song already in Archilochus (frag. 120 West; mid-7th century BCE) and remains the god's hymn, even as its form becomes increasingly elaborate throughout antiquity, not the least because a contest of dithyrambs remained an important event of the Athenian Greater Dionysia until the 2nd century CE.

Curses and imprecations. Curses and imprecations seek to harm individuals or whole cities by their use of words, either by making a request to a god (in the form of a prayer or hymn) or by using an incantation that alone (or accompanied by a significant and persuasive act) causes the harm to occur. There seems to be little benefit in separating Greek curses and imprecations along traditional lines, because they share very similar language, performative contexts, and purposes. It seems more profitable to divide them into categories that reflect Greek use and usage.

Revenge curses. Like all Greek curses, revenge curses clearly originate as a verbal art. They are the most popular kind of curse in literary texts, where they often take on a form that is indistinguishable from prayers. Chryses' first prayer to Apollo (*Iliad* 1.42) ends with a simple but deadly wish: "Let your arrows make the [Greeks] pay for the tears I have shed!" In Greek tragedy we find similar wishes motivated by the desire to pay back or punish an unjust act, such as Thyestes' curse against Atreus and his descendants (Aeschylus, *Agamemnon* 1601) or the curses of Theseus against his son (Euripides, *Hippolytus* 1167–68). There are, how-

ever, indications that in some cases such words were accompanied by special ritualized actions. When Althaea, to avenge her brother's death, curses her own son Meleager, she lies down full length upon the ground and "many times beating on the abundant earth" calls upon Hades, Persephone, and the Erinyes to give death to him (*Iliad* 9.566–72). The choral poet Bacchylides, on the other hand, tells us that she destroyed him by burning a special piece of wood (i.e., something like a "voodoo doll"), but he does not mention any verbal curse (5.136–42). Another type of ritual action, this time a public one, accompanied the cursing of Alcibiades at Athens: priestesses and priests stood up facing west and cursed him as they shook out their purple robes, "according to an old and traditional custom" (Lysias 6.51). Several Greek inscriptions belong to this class of revenge curse. Recently dubbed "judicial prayers," these texts are the legalistic appeals of an injured or abused person, who implores a deity to punish or destroy the person who has harmed them. Such curses seemed to be especially useful when the perpetrators were unknown, as in the theft that triggered this inscription from Hellenistic Cnidus (Audollent 1904, 2): "Artemeis consecrates to Demeter and Kore [and] all the gods with Demeter, whoever did not return . . . the cloak and stole, that I left behind, although I have asked for them back. Let he himself . . . burn and let him publicly confess his guilt. . . . For I have been wronged, Mistress Demeter." In all of these instances, the curses are uttered by an angry person who hopes to punish someone who has personally done them harm in the past.

Binding curses. Called *katadesmoi* in Greek and *defixiones* in late Latin, these curses aim, in contrast, at restraining rivals in any action that they may take in some future contest, without any reference to right or wrong. In literature they appear infrequently: Pelops, for example, asks Poseidon to "bind" the spear of Oenomaus so that he may safely win a deadly chariot race (Pindar, *Olympian* 1.75–78), and the Erinyes sing their "binding song" *(hymnos desmios)* in order to prevent Orestes from making a credible defense in his upcoming trial for matricide (Aeschylus, *Eumenides* 306). The enormous amount of epigraphic and archeological data suggests, however, that these types of curses were very popular. The most numerous are the so-called lead curse tablets. The earliest examples are found in Sicily, Olbia, and Attica and date to the late 6th/early 5th century BCE; by the 2nd century CE, they begin turning up in every corner of the Greco-Roman world. In the classical period, they are usually small, inscribed sheets of lead, which have been folded up, pierced with bronze or iron nails, and then either buried with a corpse, thrown into a well, or placed in the sanctuary of a deity associated with the underworld. The overwhelming majority of the pre-Roman examples aim at binding (but hardly ever destroying) a rival in athletics, law, commerce, or love. Occasionally these verbal or written curses are accompanied by the use of bound effigies. Four bound lead figurines each enclosed in a curse-inscribed coffin were apparently used to preempt the legal testimony and arguments of rivals in a series of Athenian lawsuits that took place about 400 BCE.

Conditional curses. Conditional curses are potential curses that are set like a trap to strike someone who might do wrong at some future time. Such curses appear fairly frequently in inscriptions designed to protect property, for example, a small 7th-century BCE flask from Cumae (*IG* 14.865: "whoever steals me shall be blinded") or a 6th-century BCE tomb inscription from Camirus (*IG* 12.1.737), which contains the simple wish that Zeus may destroy anyone who harms it. Such curses often imply a kind of helplessness on the part of the person who inscribes the curse, for he seems unable to protect family property on his own. At the end of Sophocles' *Ajax,* Teucer, helplessly surrounded by his brother's enemies, uses a similar curse to protect Ajax's wife and son from abuse by cutting some of their hairs and saying: "If anyone in the army tries to remove you with force from this corpse, may he . . . be cut off at the root with all his race, just as I cut this lock of hair" (*Ajax* 1175–79). Nor is the automatic curse limited to the private sphere. The 5th-century BCE public curses of the city of Teos claim that whoever among the citizens obstructs the grain supply or poisons the water supply will be utterly destroyed, along with their kith and kin (Meiggs and Lewis 1988: no. 30). But perhaps the most frequent use of these curses is in Greek oath ceremonies, where persons swearing oaths demand that destruction overtake them if they fail to uphold their oath. Conditional self-curses in oaths are often purely verbal, but they can also involve a concurrent ritualized action like Teucer's haircutting. These ceremonies could be very elaborate; the so-called Cyrenean Foundation Decree describes the oath of the 7th-century Theran colonists of Cyrene, who melted wax images and said: "May he who does not abide by this agreement but transgresses it melt away and dissolve like the images, himself, his seed and his property" (Meiggs and Lewis 1988: no. 5.46–49). Conditional curses are like revenge curses and unlike binding curses in that they aim at the total destruction of the victim and often involve some concept of cursing as a just action in recompense for a potential injury.

BIBL.: A. Audollent, *Defixionum Tabellae* (Paris, 1904). M. Depew, "Reading Greek Prayers," *Classical Antiquity* 16 (1997): 229–58. C. A. Faraone, "Molten Wax, Spilt Wine, and Mutilated Animals," *Journal of Hellenic Studies* 113 (1993): 60–80. C. A. Faraone and D. Obbink (eds.), *Magika Hiera: Ancient Greek Magic and Religion* (New York, 1991), esp. essays by C. A. Faraone (binding spells), J. Strubbe (grave curses), and H. S. Versnel (judicial prayers). W. D. Furley and J. M. Bremer (eds.), *Greek Hymns* (2 vols.; Tübingen, 2001). R. Meiggs and D. Lewis, *A Selection of Greek Historical Inscriptions to the End of the Fifth Century BC* (rev. ed.; Oxford, 1988). S. Pulleyn, *Prayer in Greek Religion* (Oxford, 1997). H. S. Versnel, "Religious Mentality in Ancient Prayer," in *Faith, Hope, and Worship* (ed. H. S. Versnel; Leiden, 1981), 1–64.   C.A.F.

Etruria

Prayers and hymns were almost certainly of great importance in the *disciplina Etrusca,* yet none survive. Most of our evidence comes from Roman sources, but even this allows us to make a general extrapolation of these Etruscan practices. Curses and charms were employed, as noted by Lucretius's allusion to *tyrrhena* [i.e., Etruscan] *carmina* (6.379), yet there remain only cryptic lead curse tablets and effigies of bound men and women, inscribed with names and deposited in tombs or wells (*defixiones* from Populonia and Volterra, and figurines from Sovana, cast into a centuries-old tomb around 300 BCE: *Corpus inscriptionum etruscarum* 5211, 52, 5234–35). Amulets such as *bullae* (lockets) worn by children and animals, apparently to avert all sorts of evil, including curses, may indicate that people were concerned about these matters.

The Prophecy of Vegoia, transcribed in the 1st century BCE, alludes to punishment (disease, storms, or famine) for people who transgress boundaries, suggesting one objective of imprecations. Etruscan *libri rituales* (books of rituals) contained formulas for the aversion of portents by prayers, vows, and sacrifices (Valerius Maximus 1.1), in phrases such as "may you [the god] be willing and favorable [*volens propitiusque sis*]" (Servius *ad Aeneid* 1.733).

The Capua Tile and the Zagreb mummy wrapping contain formulas for prayers and incantations to a variety of gods, not unlike the Umbrian *Iguvine Tables.* The Zagreb text lists public ceremonies and prayers to be performed on given dates. Their formal, repetitive phrasing leads scholars to assume that Etruscan rituals had to be performed perfectly and without interruption in order to be efficacious. Full interpretation of the Zagreb text remains controversial. Its lines instruct priests to "be benevolent and bow to the temples of the people, to the cities and the districts and the hearths" (1.7–8), illustrating the context of Etruscan prayers, in ceremonies involving designated groups of laity and professionals, with processions, sacrifices, incense, music, and dance.

Lucan's tale (*Civil War* 1.584–637) of the summoning of the Etruscan priest Arruns to avert portents from Rome describes a procession, "mystic hymns," incantations, sacrifice, and prayers. Etruscan hymns were probably metric, resembling those of other ancient cultures; a ritually destroyed *lituus* (horn), found in a 7th-century BCE deposit of the state sanctuary of Tarquinia, probably produced a sustained, low tone suited to accompany chanting.

Artistic representations show worshipers with hands

raised, palms facing an altar or statue; some gesture with their hands to their mouths or open their mouths as if speaking. In votive dedications, Etruscans addressed some gods as "father" or "mother" (as *ati Cel* [Mother Earth]). Some incantations were repeated many times, as in the charm of the Etruscan "Tarquenna" for healing feet, preserved by Varro (*Rerum rusticarum* 1.2.27).

BIBL.: Ambros J. Pfiffig, *Religio Etrusca* (Graz, 1979). Helmut Rix, "Les prières du liber linteus de Zagreb," in *Les Étrusques, les plus religieux des hommes* (ed. Françoise Gaultier and Dominique Briquel; Paris, 1998), 391–98.   J.M.T.

Rome

Prayers, hymns, curses, and imprecations: these terms may seem mutually exclusive, and there have been many attempts to separate their forms and function (e.g., prayer as a ritual act, hymns as a means of pleasing the deity). Yet for the Romans they all involved the human attempt to communicate with the divine or supernatural world, and all could be referred to as *carmen,* the common word in Augustan literature for poem. Isidore (*Origines* 1.39.4) defines *carmen* as a "rhythmical utterance." Prayers, hymns, and curses exhibit stylistic features common to poetic texts, as an early prayer for the purification of a field demonstrates (Cato, *Agriculture* 141.2–4). The prayer begins as follows: "Mars pater, te precor quaesoque, uti sies uolens propitius mihi domo familiaeque nostrae" (Father Mars, I beg and beseech you to be well disposed and propitious toward me, my household, and my family). Stylistic pairs ("well disposed and propitious"), rising tricola ("toward me, my household, and my family"), repetition, assonance, and parallelism, along with archaic specialized language, are the distinctive characteristics of the Roman religious *carmen,* as well as of early Latin poetry such as the *cantica* of Plautus.

Prayers and hymns, as well as curses and imprecations, cannot, then, be thought of as a category totally separate from poetry. However, the Roman religious *carmen* was highly formalized and conventional. Most of our evidence for the Roman prayer is late, preserved in Augustan writers, particularly Livy, and 4th-century critics, and it is difficult to tell to what extent authors normalized or rewrote ancient *carmina.* Quintilian (*Institutio Oratoria* 1.6.40) mentions that the ancient *carmina* of the Salii were unintelligible to his contemporaries, including the priests; Livy 1.24.6 pointedly claims that he cannot reproduce a long archaic *carmen.* Nonetheless, the arcane nature of ancient prayers appealed to Romans during a period of attempted moral revival and antiquarianism. Augustan writers recalled the pristine virtue of early Rome through the stable transmission of its sacred texts (cf. Ovid, *Fasti* 1.631–32: "If you love ancient rites, attend to someone who is praying: you will learn words you did not know before").

Prayers. Prayer was an essential feature of Roman re-

ligious life, both public and private, and set texts were used on specific occasions. Several types of officials, such as magistrates and generals as well as priests, offered public prayers before sacrifice, before war, and at important state occasions such as temple dedications. Private prayers were offered before the Lares (the household gods) and on important occasions such as birthdays and weddings.

In order to summon the correct deity and gain his or her good will, the use of precise language was of crucial importance (see Cicero, *On the Nature of the Gods* 2.4.10–11; Pliny, *Natural History* 28.3.11). To avoid mistakes, prayers were written in books and dictated to the chief magistrate beforehand; alternate names were often used for a deity. If the deity's identity was uncertain, as might be the case, given the specialized nature of many Roman deities, precautionary formulas such as *sive deus sive dea* (whether a god or a goddess) or *quocumque nomine* (by whatever name) provided a safeguard against offense. Outside noise was a distraction, hence prayers had to be uttered clearly against a silent background (Ovid, *Fasti* 1.71–74) or with, so Pliny suggests, a piper screening out inappropriate noise (*Natural History* 28.3.11). Indistinct prayers, muttered under the breath, on the other hand, were suspect and were associated with evil thoughts and intent (Martial 1.39.5–6).

The character of Roman prayer was generally pragmatic. Most extant prayers are petitionary; their language was aimed at achieving practical effects. Appel (1909) suggests that a Roman prayer resembled a commercial transaction between interested parties: both had a definite end in view, used precise wording, and generally provided a reminder of past services. Prayers of thanksgiving were rare. As Versnel comments, Roman gods had "to work" (1990: 16); "they did not have a moment's rest" (1990: 64).

Nonetheless, a prayer had also an important psychological component. Apuleius's hero Lucius prays to the moon-goddess when he is at his lowest moral and physical ebb, and he demonstrates both joy and grief (*The Golden Ass* 11.1–2). Fear was commonly felt when praying, an attitude parodied by Ovid in *Tristia* 3.1.53–54 when his poetry book, praying to the emperor, turns white and shivers.

Like a curse or imprecation, a prayer is a speech act. It is not uttered in a vacuum but in the context of other actions that precede, accompany, and follow it. Prayer not only imparts information but achieves results, performing the purification of a field (as in Cato's prayer), changing the mood of the speaker and the audience, or bringing about moral and physical change (as in the case of Apuleius's Lucius). Praying involved a variety of gestures and physical positions: heads might be veiled (Cicero, *On the Nature of the Gods* 2.3.10), hands outstretched (Vergil, *Aeneid* 1.93), or the right hand raised to the lips (Pliny, *Natural History* 28.5.25); the person might kneel or lie prostrate (Ovid, *Metamorphoses*

1.376); a statue or altar of the deity might be embraced (9.772).

The quasidivine status of the Roman emperor politicized Roman prayer, while correspondingly the traditional nature of prayer provided a relatively safe structure for writers presenting new and controversial views. Thus prayers to the emperor that begin a literary work and seek imperial endorsement can also be protreptic or even critical. The prayer at the start of Vergil's *Georgics*, while modeled on the conservative prayer of Varro's *Res rusticae*, addresses Augustus as a future god (24–42). The language of prayer softens Vergil's bold innovation; at the same time, in a period of political uncertainty, the poet skillfully fashions Augustus in his own self-interest, as a powerful being engaged with the arts rather than with war. Statius's prayers for Domitian's long life at the end of *Silvae* 1.1 and 4.3 may suggest anxiety about the emperor's lack of an heir and the consequent stability of the regime.

Hymns. A hymn is a sung prayer, designed for communal celebration. We have little evidence for early Latin hymns. The few extant texts of priestly hymns, the *Carmen Arvale* and the *Carmina Saliaria*, are heavily corrupt. Livy (27.37.7–15) alludes to a 3rd-century hymn composed by Livius Andronicus and performed by a choir of twenty-seven virgins as they processed through Rome, but little is known of how Roman hymns were performed or indeed of the important role that women may have played. Most extant Roman hymns come from Augustan literature and were heavily influenced by Greek models. ("Hymn" is etymologically a Greek word.) Horace in particular made the hymn a widespread literary form (see Williams 1968: 132–37).

In a hymn, the deity was solemnly invoked in circumlocutory style, with his or her titles and functions often varied in a *sive/sive* (either/or) sequence. Then followed the aretalogy of the god, that is, statements about his or her powers. Despite their stylization, hymns were a flexible form, open to parody (such as Horace's hymn to a wine jar; *Carmina* 3.21) and combination with other literary modes. Indeed, the very formality of hymns made them a safe venue for daring innovation. At the start of book 3 of *On the Nature of Things* (1–29), Lucretius boldly addresses the philosopher Epicurus in hymnic style, thereby suggesting a new concept of divinity.

As representations of a speech act, Roman literary hymns raise the vexed question of their artificiality. Horace's *Carmen Saeculare* was performed by twin choirs of twenty-seven boys and girls on an actual ritual occasion, Augustus's Secular Games. Yet the *Carmen Saeculare* has been criticized as a Hellenized literary exercise, an adornment rather than an integral part of the ritual. Feeney (1998: 32–38), however, argues that the *Carmen Saeculare* gives cogent expression to the new Apollonian ideology of Augustus. But how about the many hymns that have no clear relation to a historic cultic performance? Poetry, by reaching out to a wide readership, can activate a religious context in different ways. By evoking a performative context, hymns recall the poet's traditional role as the voice of the community; they can therefore suggest the need for greater poetic authority in the face of growing autocracy. The Roman hymn both comments upon and constructs political reality for a wide audience; it also provides a vehicle for poetic self-reflection.

Similar features can be found outside official civic cult. Highly formal and relatively standardized panegyrics (known as "hymns" or "aretalogies") were a distinctive feature of the cult of Isis. And prayers associated with the cult of Mithras still survive.

Curses. The line separating curses from prayers was a thin one. A curse is a deliberate speech act that attempts through utterance to do harm, particularly to the body through illness, mutilation, or painful death. Indeed, there was widespread belief that the very writing or speaking of a curse made it effective (Pliny, *Natural History* 28.4.19: "There is nobody who does not fear being the target of dire curses"). Curses had profound psychological effect in battle: according to Livy (10.41.3) the Samnites were terrified by the official curses pronounced against them by the Roman army. Yet since curses concern relations of power, they are often uttered by the powerless in an attempt to reassert dominance and social position.

Much of our evidence for curses comes from *defixiones*, curse tablets of lead, papyrus, or wax that, in order to communicate with the powers of the underworld, were commonly buried in graves, wells, or sacred waters such as at Aquae Sulis (Bath) in Roman Britain. Curses followed the *carmen* style; they were addressed, however, to underworld deities, most commonly Hermes, Prosperpina, Hecate, the Dirae, and unnamed spirits of the dead. *Defixiones* bound the underworld powers to perform the curser's will; a direct command replaced the respectful address of the petitionary prayer. Magical words were often used. The esoteric language of the curse conferred authority both on the curse and on the person uttering it, sometimes apparently a professional magician believed to have the specialized knowledge to communicate with the underworld. Common types of Roman *defixiones* involved frustrated love and, during the imperial period, were directed at influencing the outcome of competitions in the circus or amphitheater. Curses were also believed to bring about political change. According to Tacitus, the imperial heir Germanicus died mysteriously in a bedchamber that was afterward discovered to conceal curse tablets *(carmina devotionis)* inscribed with his name (*Annales* 2.69; see also Controlling Religion). In the imperial age, curses provided a means of empowerment for the politically disenfranchised.

Hellenistic and Roman curse poetry has been extensively studied by Watson (1991), who notes that there is some congruence between *defixiones* and literary curses. When they occur in literature, curses have no power as magic, for they are no longer secret, yet they can still express relationships of power and dominance. For instance, curses, which are prevalent in elegiac poetry, provide another strategy of domination: through condemning his girlfriend's procuress, the poet paradoxically achieves morally superior ground and reasserts his masculinity. One of the most famous curses in Roman poetry, Dido's fictional curse upon Aeneas and the Roman people (*Aeneid* 4.607–29), spoken by someone who was powerless, on the margins of the empire, and, moreover, a woman, acquired potency because of the historic enmity between Rome and Carthage.

Imprecations. The word *imprecation* (Latin *deprecatio*) is often used synonymously with curse, yet it can be regarded as a subcategory; Versnel (1999) defines imprecation as a conditional curse that refers to future events and is prevalent in the public domain. Magistrates and priests enforced communal laws, oaths, and treaties by cursing the person(s) who trespassed against them; such official imprecations were important in international relations. Indeed, they were foundational to the Roman world. The Twelve Tables record imprecations for protecting the crops and people from spells (Pliny, *Natural History* 28.4.18). Imprecations protected graves from violation (see *CIL* 6.13740: "Let the person who has urinated or defecated here feel the wrath of the gods above and below") and were written on walls to avert fires (Pliny, *Natural History* 28.4.19). Self-imprecations added authority to oaths; the inaugural consul swore before the emperor Trajan to consign himself and his family to the gods' wrath should he lie (Pliny, *Panegyricus* 64.3).

In general, the Roman preoccupation with prayers, hymns, curses, and imprecations demonstrates the faith that the Romans with their *carmina* put in the power of words.

BIBL.: G. Appel, *De romanorum precationibus* (Giessen, 1909). M. Clauss, *Roman Cult of Mithras: The God and His Mysteries* (trans. R. Gordon; Edinburgh, 2000), esp. 105–8. D. C. Feeney, *Literature and Religion at Rome: Cultures, Contexts, and Beliefs* (Cambridge, 1998), esp. 28–44. F. Graf, *Magic in the Ancient World* (trans. F. Philip; Cambridge, Mass., 1997), esp. 118–74. F. V. Hickson, *Roman Prayer Language: Livy and the Aeneid of Vergil* (Stuttgart, 1993). H. S. Versnel, "Curses," in *The Oxford Classical Dictionary* (ed. S. Hornblower and A. Spawforth; 3rd ed.; Oxford, 1999), 414–15. Idem (ed.), *Faith, Hope, and Worship: Aspects of Religious Mentality in the Ancient World* (Leiden, 1981). Idem, *Ter Unus: Isis, Dionysos, Hermes; Three Studies in Henotheism* (Studies in Greek and Roman Religion 6.1; Leiden, 1990), esp. 39–52. L. C. Watson, *Arae: The Curse Poetry of Antiquity* (Leeds, 1991). G. Williams, *Tradition and Originality in Roman Poetry* (Oxford, 1968), 132–57. C.E.N.

Christianity

From the beginning, Christian worship included prayer and song (Acts 16.25). While the form and substance of the earliest services derived from the sect's Jewish context, members of the post-Easter Christian movement quickly began to compose and disseminate hymns of their own. The texts were most likely set to simple monodies, although no melodies survive. New Testament epistles quote several Christological poems to remind listeners of ideas that were already familiar. Thus, singing was a common way of conveying basic Christian teachings. The hymns are remarkably consistent in depicting Christ as the heavenly redeemer who descended to earth and ascended again to heaven (Phil. 2.6–11; Col. 1.15–20; 1 Pet. 3.18–19, 22; Eph. 2.14–16; Heb. 1.3; 1 Tim. 3.16). Similarly, the prologue to the Gospel of John (1.1–5, 9–14, 16–18) conveys complex theological content to a late-1st-century community convinced of Christ's full divinity.

The precise performative contexts of these early Christian hymns is unclear. Like their Jewish precursors, Christians imagined heaven to be full of antiphonal singing (Rev. 4.11; 5.9–10; 7.15–17; 11.17–18; 15.3–4; 19.1–8). Thus the use of song imitated, or perhaps participated in, the celestial liturgy. Other New Testament songs that may have been used liturgically include the Magnificat (Luke 1.46–55) and the Benedictus (1.68–79), which together with some songs from the Hebrew Bible became canticles of the church. In time, Christians adopted the Jewish practices of reciting the Psalms either antiphonally or with a cantor and responsorial verse. Recitation of the gnostic Hymn of Christ from the *Acts of John* (94–96) may have been accompanied by dance, while the Hymn of the Soul preserved in the *Acts of Thomas* (108–13) is a complex allegory about the quest for knowledge and salvation and likely required explication. The Syriac *Odes of Solomon,* composed around 100 CE, is a hymnal containing some forty songs of thanksgiving for the coming of the Messiah.

In addition to rehearsing basic Christian theologies to bring about a unity of thought through a unity of practice, the Pauline correspondence expects that singing will instill order and convey moral instruction. Concerned with the chaos of ecstatic gatherings, where many speak in tongues, Paul calls on the Corinthians to pray and sing not only "with the spirit," but "with the mind also" (1 Cor. 14.13–15), and urges restraint. When he quotes a Christological hymn in Philippians, he emphasizes Christ's example of humility and service:

[He] emptied himself,
taking the form of a servant,
being born in the likeness of men.
And being found in human form
he humbled himself and became obedient unto death,
even death on a cross.
(Phil. 2.7–8)

Ephesians 5.18–20 recommends that congregants "address one another in psalms and hymns and spiritual songs, singing and making melody to the Lord with all your heart," as an alternative to drunkenness and in the larger context of ensuring hierarchical social structures: husbands over wives, masters over slaves, and parents over children. For the Pauline tradition, the discipline and obedience of collective singing could function to reinforce cohesion and conformity, achieving social harmony and balance.

Prayers both of petition and of thanksgiving feature prominently in early Christian traditions. The Gospel of Luke, in particular, emphasizes Jesus's piety by citing his frequent prayers. Three variants of the Lord's Prayer are preserved from the late 1st and early 2nd century (Matt. 6.9–13; Luke 11.2–4; *Didache* 8.2), suggesting that this form originated in the earliest Christian communities, perhaps even with Jesus himself. The early-2nd-century *Didache* (8.3) commands that the prayer be recited three times a day, on the model of the Eighteen Benedictions (or perhaps the Shema) in Judaism, and thus establishes a form for daily offices of prayer. The 3rd century saw the development of an evening service that included lighting the lamps, singing hymns, chanting psalms, and reciting prayers. The hymn *Phōs Hilaron* (O Joyous Light) may have been composed for this rite as early as the 3rd century.

Justin's description of Sunday eucharistic practice around 150 CE (*Apology* 1.65–67) shows the centrality of prayer in the sacrificial offering at the center of Christian cult. After scriptural readings and a homily, the assembly stood and offered petitions in common for the salvation of the congregation and of others before greeting each other with the kiss of peace (65). After the bread and wine were brought forward, the one presiding recited "prayers and thanksgivings" (i.e., the Eucharist) over these elements, to which the congregations assented "Amen." Church rubrics in the early-2nd-century *Didache* (9–10) and the early-3rd-century *Apostolic Tradition* of Hippolytus of Rome (4) sought to standardize the eucharistic prayers and establish a set liturgy. Prayers were also offered in preparation for baptism and at baptismal ceremonies (Justin, *Apology* 1.61, 65). Invocations connected with ritual practice or Syrian Christians are found in narrative sources such as the *Acts of Thomas* (27, 50).

Christians also used prayer and incantation to effect the miraculous. Jesus himself was known as an exorcist and miracle worker. Moreover, it was believed that he gave such powers to his disciples, explaining, "Whatever you bind on earth shall be bound in heaven, and whatever you loose on earth shall be loosed in heaven" (Matt. 18.18). The language of "binding" and "loosing" derives directly from Greco-Roman magical practices. Although Christians (and Jesus) were accused by detractors of practicing "magic" (Origen, *Against Celsus* 1.6, 38) and Christian leaders condemned the use of "magical arts" (Justin, *Apology* 1.14), Christians regularly invoked the name of Jesus to cast out demons and perform miracles (Matt. 7.22; Origen, *Against Celsus* 1.6; *Acts of Thomas* 47). Christians also employed liturgies of cursing and binding to harness and manipulate divine power, especially for healing (see Meyer et al. 1994). Christian incantations preserved on papyrus, ostraca, and lead are distinguished from more common Greco-Roman practice principally by the invocation of Christ and the use of Christian liturgical tags.

BIBL.: Mark Kiley (ed.), *Prayer from Alexander to Constantine: A Critical Anthology* (London, 1997), 205–318. John A. McGuckin, *At the Lighting of the Lamps: Hymns of the Ancient Church* (Harrisburg, Pa., 1995). Marvin Meyer et al., *Ancient Christian Magic: Coptic Texts of Ritual Power* (San Francisco, 1994). Jack T. Sanders, *New Testament Christological Hymns* (Cambridge, 1971). D.KR.

Divination and Prophecy

Introduction

Divination is one of the most revealing of all religious phenomena: embedded in the questions asked and the advice given are a society's fears and desires; implicit in the divinatory methods used are blueprints of how the society believes the world to work and how gods and humans interact.

"Divination" in this sense refers to all sorts of situations in which nonhuman entities communicate with humans. There are other, more specific ways in which scholars use "divination," however, particularly in distinction from "oracle" and "prophecy." These uses depend not only on which theoretical models one uses, but also on which culture one studies, as several of the essays make clear. It is worth noting that, *mutatis mutandis,* many ancient cultures attempted to distinguish between types of divination as well: one common division was between "natural" (e.g., visions, dreams) and "artificial," for the application of which skills were necessary (e.g., interpreting dice throws); another was between what the Romans called impetrative and oblative omens—those that were deliberately sought by humans and those that arrived unbidden; a third was between inspired divination (a god speaks through a human) and inductive divination (a human "reads" the signs that are available in the cosmos).

Such attempts to categorize methods of divination, and to articulate the ways in which the various methods worked, bespeak an ancient tendency to turn it into a "science." This is further manifested by the production of "dream books" that record each type of dream and what it means; the gathering of old oracles into collections for future reference and reinterpretation; and the creation of omen lists that work by a protasis/apodosis method: a given occurrence is stated ("it rained while the king was sacrificing"), what followed is stated ("a drought ensued the next summer"), and a causal re-lationship is assumed and recorded for later use. One more expression of the ancient desire to explain and validate divination is the theory of "sympathy" that developed in some cultures: what happened on the macrocosmic level—among the gods, planets, or whatever other entities were thought to affect mortals—was understood to be inscribed onto objects in the microcosm, the world in which mortals dwelled. Find the right object, read its "inscription," and you knew what the macrocosm had in store.

Because divination constituted communication between mortals and nonmortals, it often took place in a setting that had already been consecrated as a site for such interaction, such as a temple. Frequently, sacrifice accompanied divination, as a way of opening up the lines of communication; sometimes, indeed, the gods graciously wrote the divinatory information upon the sacrifice itself, within the entrails of animals that could be "read" for meaning. At other times divination occurred in a place that had been consecrated for the purpose only temporarily. Both the boundaries and the subdivisions of the place were ritually marked out; a bird that flew through the positively charged subdivision signified something different from one that flew through a negatively charged subdivision. This is one expression of a larger concern often found in connection with divination: everything had to be arranged very carefully before the procedure began, or else the results might not be trustworthy. In literature and folktale, this included the form of the question asked: if a loophole had been left by the phrases that the questioner used, the god exploited it, leading the questioner to misunderstand the answer, act incorrectly, and damage himself: "Should I go into battle against the Persians?" asked Croesus. "If you do," replied the Delphic Oracle, "a great empire will fall"—but the empire that fell was Croesus's own, not that of the Persians, as he had assumed the Oracle meant (Herodotus 1.53).

This sort of thing may not have happened very often in real life, but it was still important to ask the right question. This could be taken to extremes: in some cultures, divination acted mostly to rubber-stamp plans that humans had previously drafted: you submitted your carefully developed battle strategy or your shrewdest guess as to what had gone wrong in last week's ritual and brought on a plague of grasshoppers, and then you waited for confirmation. Human knowledge of what had been happening, and what was likely to be the right thing to do, was thus important in making divination work, even if all the sagacity was credited to the gods. Sometimes human acumen came into the process after divination had taken place, as well: an answer was given by the god, but then the worshipers argued about what it meant. In some societies, humans were bolder still: if they did not like the answer the god had given, they asked again and again—until they got an answer they liked. Fate was not always understood to be absolute; divination provided not an ironclad prognosis but a warning. Nor did divination always have to give an answer: some societies allowed for the possibility that the gods would not advise the questioner at all.

Most ancient Mediterranean divinatory systems did not seek to reveal the future but rather to clarify what had happened in the past, why it was affecting current events, and how the situation could be adjusted. Why were women suffering miscarriages? Because the goddess was angry. Why was she angry? Because temple attendants had broken her lamp and not replaced it. What could be done to atone for this and thus stop the miscarriages? Buy her *three* new lamps. Methods oriented toward the future developed predominantly in the eschatological contexts of Judaism, Christianity, and some late Egyptian venues; they emphasized moral admonishment and criticism of the current regime as much as they actually predicted the future. But all forms of divination had some capacity to criticize and thus threaten political power; for this reason, many ancient Mediterranean societies exercised control over diviners, attempting to limit the activity to priests associated with the ruling power or to banish diviners altogether.

Complete eradication of divination was never possible, however; the gods could inscribe their messages on such a huge variety of things—birds' flights, snakes' movements, animals' entrails, the patterns that flour makes when tossed on the ground or oil makes when dropped on water, the random comments of children at play, and so on—that everyone, whether specially trained as a diviner or not, was constantly tempted to read them. If the ancient Mediterranean world was full of gods, it was full of their messages as well.

BIBL.: G. Manetti, *Theories of the Sign in Classical Antiquity* (trans. Christine Richardson; Indiana University Press, 1993 [orig. 1987]).　　　　　　　　　S.I.J.

Egypt

"Divination" is often used broadly to include many phenomena, all of which aim at the acquisition of otherwise unavailable knowledge. Three rubrics reflect the ways in which Egypt divided such acquisition of knowledge: prophecy, oracles, and divination.

Prophecies. Defined generally as statements foretelling the future, prophecies appear frequently in our sources, although sometimes in literary texts that make us doubt their authenticity. According to a tale related by Herodotus (2.133), King Mycerinus (4th Dynasty) received a prophecy from Buto that only six more years were left of his life and that in the seventh he would die. The tale, which goes on to include the motif of fruitlessly attempting to evade the misfortune, must be taken, however, as a late folk-story without historical basis. Another famous early example of a (pseudo)prophecy written in a sophisticated literary style is the so-called Prophecy of Neferty (12th Dynasty; Middle Kingdom) in which the accession of Amunemhat I is foretold by a priest named Neferti, who lived during the reign of King Sneferu (4th Dynasty). From the 12th Dynasty, as well, is the tale of the Shipwrecked Sailor, in which the lord of a mythical island, a huge serpent of fantastic appearance, prophesies the safe return of the shipwrecked Egyptian to his homeland. There is also a prophecy in the Papyrus Westcar (Hyksos period; Old Kingdom). Here the magician Djedi foretells to King Cheops the founding of the 5th Dynasty, a prediction highly annoying to Cheops.

The reign of Thutmose IV (beginning of the New Kingdom) provides a remarkable prophecy concerning state affairs. The Sphinx Stele, dated to the first year of his reign, relates how the sun-god inhabiting the great Giza Sphinx revealed himself to the young prince and promised to raise him to the throne if he would clear away the sand that had started to inundate his image.

The most prolific period of prophetic literature was the Middle Kingdom, but much later phases saw a renewal of prophecy as well. The Demotic Chronicle, originating in the Ptolemaic period, is a collection of obscure prophecies and statements concerning the kings of the 28th to 30th Dynasties. The monarchs are judged by ethical standards, which probably indicates the influence of the Hebrew Bible. According to this chronicle, after Egypt had been occupied by the Medes (Persians) and the Ionians (Ptolemies), a savior king would appear in Herakleopolis.

Two further prophecies convey political messages. A demotic papyrus in Vienna relates that during the reign of King Bocchoris (24th Dynasty), a lamb predicted heavy trials for Egypt. The papyrus itself was written in the thirty-third year of Augustus's reign. A foreign conquest that it mentioned may well be that of the Assyrians or the Persians, but could be a reference to

Greek or Roman rule. The length of the period of misfortune would be nine hundred years. Later, the country would see better days again, and the generation living during this happy age would wish that their parents and grandparents could have lived to see its coming. After delivering its prophecy, the lamb died. It must have been a widely known story, since Manetho (3rd century BCE) mentions it as an important event during Bocchoris's reign.

Another political prophecy, the Potter's Prophecy, has survived in Greek, although its original language was Egyptian. Written in the second half of the 2nd century BCE, it displays considerable influence of the Prophecy of the Lamb. The "Potter" was actually the incarnation of the ram-god Khnum, who carried out the work of creation on his potter's wheel. Here the prophecy is told to King Amunhotep—this might mean Amunhotep III, during whose reign lived the wise Amunhotep son of Hapu who, according to Manetho, was versed in the art of prophesying. The text is clearly directed against the Greeks and Alexandria. The disturbances in the country and the struggles for the throne within the Ptolemaic royal family suggested to the prophet that the foreigners would perish by confronting each other. The tutelary gods of Alexandria, Agathos Daimon (Good Divinity) and Kneph, would leave for Memphis, the traditional royal residence of Egypt. There would follow a glorious fifty-five-year reign of a king descending from the sun-god and enthroned by Isis. People would wish that their ancestors could rise from the grave to enjoy the blessings of the age. At the end, as in the Prophecy of the Lamb, the prophet died and the king took care of his burial. All three prophecies—in addition to their political allusions—are dominated by an eschatological atmosphere.

Oracles. Between oracles and prophecies, although they are often merged in the literature, some distinction should be made, at least when we speak of Egypt. Oracles were not consulted primarily for the foretelling of future events but rather for obtaining knowledge of the divine will. They could refer to the near future, but mostly consulted the divine will about a specific issue. During the 18th Dynasty, oracles deal mainly with political questions and state affairs. For example, Queen Hatshepsut, who was made co-regent of Egypt by the statue of Amun on the occasion of a procession, went to Amun before her famous expedition to Punt in order to ask for his counsel. Similarly, Thutmose III was nominated king of Egypt by the statue of the same deity. We also hear about the oracle of Amun during the reign of Thutmose IV. In spite of these cases, however, it seems that the regular soliciting of the deity's opinion did not become a general practice during the 18th Dynasty. The commands of Amun were regarded at first as official oracles for the pharaoh, whereas the popular variety of the custom later flourished in the western side of Thebes, first of all in Deir el-Medina (settlement of the work-force of the necropolis) where, particularly in the later period of the New Kingdom, the deified King Amunhotep I and his mother, Queen Ahmose-Nefertari, became popular oracular gods, with whom people felt they had a particularly intimate relationship.

After consultation of oracles ceased to be a royal privilege, directions were given by the oracles in all sorts of cases, ranging from the highest affairs of state down to matters of stolen clothes. Sometimes grotesque situations occurred: if the suspect did not accept the decision of one oracle, a second or even third one could be consulted. Practically, the oracles attained judicial power and took over to a certain extent the functions of the courts of justice. Consultation persisted until the very end of Egyptian civilization and is attested even during the Coptic period.

We know the names of numerous oracle-gods. The most respected was Amun, also called Lord of the Gods. He also appears in the texts in various local forms. In addition to having an oracular site in Thebes, he was the lord of the world-famous oracle temple in the Siwa Oasis, which was visited by Alexander the Great. Amun also held an eminent position in the south of Egypt at Napata and Meroe. Amun's wife, Mut, also could give oracles and made a decision concerning the transportation of royal mummies; their son Khonsu could be consulted, too. This Theban triad played an important part in a group of amulet papyri, the so-called oracular amuletic decrees.

There were plenty of other oracular gods. The dwarf god Bes rose to the position of an eminent oracular god during the Roman period in Abydos, as did Ptah in Memphis and Seth in the Dakhla Oasis. Isis had the function of an oracular goddess in Coptos and Oxyrhynchus, and Herodotus (2.152; cf. 2.133) mentions the famous oracle of the goddess Uto (called Leto in his work) in the city of Buto. The ram-gods Khnum and Harsaphes also acquired the function of giving oracles. In addition, great importance was attributed to the behavior of the Apis bull; the bull Bukhis was probably also consulted; and sacred crocodiles were likewise supposed to give predictions. These practices, however, belong to the margins of oracles and divination.

There were several ways in which oracles might work, although we cannot always be sure of details. Given that Amun manifested his will during processions in which his statue was carried through the streets on his barque and exposed to the public gaze, it is unlikely that any clever mechanism was used to move the statue's head to give the semblance of nodding. In the case of Amun this would have been, in any case, pointless, since the statue was concealed within a shrine mounted on the barque. The statue of King Amunhotep I was, on the other hand, visible to the public. The oracle's approval was most likely manifested in the following way: if the priests carrying Amunhotep's barque approached the petitioner, this was the expression of approval. If they walked backward this meant disapproval. According to another interpretation the barque may have rocked in giving its answer.

Other oracular procedures are also known. At times, written demands or two contradictory documents were presented to the god. He could choose one of them or give his affirmative answer to one of them. Many very precisely worded oracular questions have survived on ostraca and potsherds, especially from Deir el-Medina.

At other times, the divine will was revealed through the priestly voice. Usually, the priest acted only as an interpreter of the god, but in the Greco-Roman period there may have been cases of priestly fraud by means of statues. A statue of Re-Harakhte and another of the Ptolemaic queen Arsinoe II (both made during the Roman period) had channels bored into them through which a pipe passed into the wall behind; a concealed priest could use the pipe to send forth a "divine" voice. Such manipulated talking statues were originally quite foreign to Egyptian practice.

Divination. Divinatory practices display considerable change over the course of time. In the Book of Genesis, Joseph appears in Egypt as a dream diviner, and during the pharaonic epochs as a whole, great importance was attributed to dreams. Just as everywhere else in the world, it was commonly believed that by correctly interpreting dreams it was possible to foretell the future. The oldest elaborate key to dream interpretation (Papyrus Chester Beatty III) probably originates in the Middle Kingdom. The compiler made a careful tabulation and divided all dreams into good and bad. The dreams of the "followers of Horus" and "followers of Seth," that is, the positive and negative character types, are treated separately, since the meaning of a dream was believed to depend on the "Horian" or "Sethian" nature of the dreamer. Numerous fragments of dream books are preserved from later epochs in Demotic script.

In addition to their importance in the private sphere, dreams appear in political contexts. In the Sphinx Stele of Thutmose IV, the sun-god foretells the accession of a prince to the throne in a dream. King Tanutamun of Napata had a dream; two serpents indicated to him that he would take possession of Upper Egypt and Lower Egypt. The dream of Nectanebo II, preserved on a Greek papyrus, includes a divine reproach for the king's neglect of the cult of the god Onuris. According to the Demotic ostraca from the middle of the 2nd century BCE (Saqqara), the withdrawal of Antiochus IV Epiphanes from Egypt was predicted in dreams of the scribe Hor.

Other divination methods existed. The intensity of the light of the star Sothis (our Sirius) at the New Year, for example, could be taken as an indication for the coming year. Necromancy (evoking the spirit of the dead or provisionally resuscitating the body for purposes of divination) was not unknown in pharaonic Egypt, although the bulk of the sources comes from the Roman period (*Papyri Graecae Magicae*). Among other

practices originally foreign to the pharaonic period are vessel inquiry (lecanomancy) and lamp divination (lychnomancy). The first instance of lecanomancy in Egypt is Joseph's silver cup, which he had used for divination (Gen. 44.5). Both lecanomancy and lychnomancy involve inducing a hypnotic trance in someone who gazes at the glittering surface of oil on water or at the light of a lamp. The gazer was supposed to acquire answers to questions from the gods; the gazer could be the questioner himself or a medium whom he employed for the purpose. Finally, we also hear about a so-called wise woman in Deir el-Medina, who provided explanations of problematic events such as the death of children. We cannot, however, be sure how widespread the presence of such women was.

BIBL.: J. Černý, "Egyptian Oracles," in *A Saite Oracle Papyrus from Thebes* by R. A. Parker (Providence, R.I., 1962), 35–48. I. E. S. Edwards, *Hieratic Papyri in the British Museum*, vol. 4: *Oracular and Amuletic Decrees of the Late New Kingdom* (London, 1960). L. Kákosy, "Prophecies of Ram Gods," *Studia Aegyptiaca* 7 (1981): 139–54. J.-M. Kruchten, "Oracles," in *The Oxford Encyclopedia of Ancient Egypt* (ed. D. B. Redford; Oxford, 2001), 2.609–12. S. Sauneron, "Les songes et leur interprétation dans l'Égypte ancienne," in *Les songes et leur interprétation* (Sources orientales 2; Paris, 1959), 18–61.   L.K.

Mesopotamia

Divination

The sources that attest to Mesopotamian divination span three millennia and cover all the common categories of practice. Mesopotamian divinatory knowledge was acquired through divine inspiration, through the observation of omens, or solicited from the gods by special techniques. However, inspired practices such as consulting professional ecstatics or dream incubation, valued by some cultures for their intimate and unmediated relationship with the divine, play a less significant role. Mesopotamia privileged divinatory knowledge when it was acquired through the trained application of the human intellect rather than through divine intervention in human cognition.

Mesopotamian divination is distinguished by the investigation of omens and by the literate scholarship that developed around it. An omen is a sign that stands as a warning of something that is latent and in the process of coming into being. Because the outcome predicted did not fully exist, it was not considered inevitable, and therefore steps could be taken to avoid it. Mesopotamia is generally known for two venerable and widely influential divinatory disciplines: extispicy (reading omens on the viscera of sacrificial animals) and celestial divination.

Typology of omens. The Romans made a distinction between omens that were deliberately solicited (*omina*

Model liver inscribed with omens, for use in divination. Babylonian, 1830–1530 BCE. British Museum. © *The British Museum*

impetrativa) and those that were simply observed *(omina oblativa)*. The contrast between these two forms of divination has been adapted by modern scholars and applied to Mesopotamian practice.

Impetrative divination consists of a question and an answer; it establishes a dialogue with a deity who is immanent and willing to answer. When properly queried, the sun-god Shamash or the West Semitic storm-god Adad answered by writing on the viscera of an animal about to be sacrificed. Extispicy (divination through examination of a sacrificed animal's organs), one of the earliest and most durable forms of Mesopotamian divination, enabled learned specialists to read these answers; they went on to produce a voluminous and varied textual record consisting of prayers, queries, and reports of actual extispicies, as well as omen compendia and related scholarly apparatus.

Other forms of impetrative divination, such as soliciting omens through oil dropped into water or from smoke rising from a censer, were also practiced in Mesopotamia but never commanded the same level of scholarly attention as extispicy. While extispicy texts are attested until the end of Mesopotamian civilization, texts that record oil and smoke omens are attested for only the Old Babylonian period.

Oblative divination consists of warnings that are simply offered, unbidden. Unsolicited omens are not based on a clearly defined system of occult communication and are typologically problematic. The observation of omens requires the observer to be alert to the possibility of a sign and to recognize and interpret it when it appears. While it is not difficult to construe the presence of a divine catalyst behind a phenomenon that is perceived to be an omen, it is a force that cannot be engaged through prayer or divinatory ritual and remains nameless.

Over time, the systematic investigation of unsolicited omens grew in variety and scope and came to dominate Mesopotamian practice. Celestial divination became significant for the life of the state, and terrestrial divination, although not exclusively domestic, had an impact on individual lives.

For the diviner-scholars, the world was inscribed with hidden meaning. Diviners were not interested in the regular or the routine, but were concerned with sudden ruptures, deviations in nature, and changeable patterns. In a world where many things were hidden and arbitrary, but nothing was meaningless, careful attention had to be paid not just to the singular, the anomalous, and the extraordinary, but to anything at all noteworthy or unusual. Celestial and meteorological events, behavior of animals, abnormal births, unusual patterns of vegetation, and features of human physiognomy and behavior were studied not as phenomena to be understood for their own sake, but as signs with extraordinary power to signify about matters of immediate human concern.

Development of the literature. In the middle of the 2nd millennium, an Akkadian literature began to develop around the observation of omens. Each omen was framed as a conditional sentence: the first clause, the protasis, recorded the ominous signifier, and the second clause, the apodosis, its signified. For example, "If a desert plant is growing in the city, the city will be desolate." Such omens have a casuistic structure, common to law and other forms of Mesopotamia discourse. This structure conveys information as a series of individual cases, presented as an itemized sequence. Omens of a similar type were recorded together to form collections. Once the systematic recording of omens began, divination became a complex, literate discipline. Omen texts were copied and recopied, passed from generation to generation and disseminated to different areas. Scribes at various sites not only recopied but also revised, edited, and systematically expanded the texts they inherited. They expended considerable effort on classifying signs and organizing them onto topically coherent individual tablets arranged in a logical sequence. As texts were combined into larger, more inclusive compositions, omens were added to fill in perceived classificatory gaps. Simple topical organization gave way to omens arranged in extended sequences, schemata, and permutations. In extending the classification patterns, the scribes not only formulated new omens but also determined their meaning.

Epistemological foundations. The epistemological foundations on which the omen compendia rest are unstated. However, they appear to be based on two underlying assumptions. First, omens seem to be recorded on the understanding that once a sequence (or conjunction) of two events was observed, it formed the basis for predicting a similar sequence in the future. Second, there are patterns in the universe, which may not be immediately apparent, but are nevertheless systematic and accessible to human scrutiny. The omen texts, therefore, appear to be created with the intent of delineating an autonomous signifying structure that operates independently of the will of a god. While most forms of divination produce meaning that is singular and applicable only to the problem at hand, the recording of omens suggests a process of abstraction: it transforms a singular perception into an intelligible object whose meaning is applicable in other contexts. The systematic study of omens, which preserves ominous observations and the events associated with them and organizes them into formal categories, stands apart from other forms of divination and appears to move into new epistemological territory. The scholarship that produced the omen compendia has been described in modern terms as Mesopotamian "science."

The problem with defining the study of omens as a Mesopotamian science is not that it is inaccurate, but rather that it obscures the features of the material that are essential elements of divination. Its very success depends on suppressing the fact that the receiver had a hand in the sending, the reader had a hand in the writing. A cat, a flash of light in the sky, a crow either standing on the side of the road or flying overhead becomes an omen only when the circumstances demand it. The underlying tension of a personal dilemma kindles the signifying power of an omen and triggers the expectation of meaning that will speak to the problem at hand. The system may be seen by the participants as universal. However, an omen cannot be separated from the individual observer nor can the omens of the compendia be separated from the subjective cultural dilemmas that govern the formulation of the signs and attribution of specific meaning.

An ominous sign, moreover, is composed of at least two components: the sign and the context. The context of the omen functions as a key contributor to the meaning. The structure may be rather simple, as when something appears anomalously in a context not its own. Omens are often based on the conjunction of nature and culture (a desert plant or a wild animal appears in a city, a house, or any urban context). In more elaborate systems, the omen complex can be described as a variable (a bird, a mark on a liver, or a celestial occurrence) imposed on a field of observation that is defined by cultural categories (on the door, the window, the roof, the wall) or by the observer's position (right/left, above/behind). Both the viscera and the sky are divided into zones whose names reflect aspects of or categories of human existence.

System of interpretation. The divinatory language of the compendia is inherently binary. Binary oppositions based on normal and reverse polarity are tools of divination. The benefic or malefic predictions in the apo-

doses define a basic binary structure. A favorable or unfavorable prediction is determined by the compound product of a positive or negative attribute of a sign (bright/dim) and of a positive or negative attribute of the field (right/left). The right (positive) side of the viscera refers to the ego and the left (negative) to the enemy. Binary logic based on the correlation of two pairs of symmetrically polar oppositions is a constant in many of the omen collections. Sets of polar pairs (right/left, high/low, front/back) are the most salient features of the protases.

Categories based on primary egocentric perceptions of the physical world also have an inherent polarity. What is above, on the right, or in front is positive, and what is below, on the left, or in back is negative. Negative and positive values vary little from culture to culture, but the uses to which they are put as conceptual tools are infinitely variable.

In the Mesopotamian omen compendia, sets exist in relation to each other; they adapt to different divinatory contexts and interact with other figurative patterns. Complex secondary patterns of polarity based on sets with more than two lexemes occur throughout the compendia. When applied to new contexts, basic values are inverted and refracted, producing new and unusual readings of omens.

Reading through the omen compendia, one gets the feeling that the scribes were using language as a tool of divinatory inquiry. The resulting linguistic structure is analogous to the configurations that occur in other forms of divination when actual objects are physically shaken and rearranged. It is important to note that the constant segmentation functions in opposition to the metaphoric enlargement that characterizes magic.

Misfortune revealed by an omen could be averted by apotropaic rituals. Referred to as "an undoing," the ritual is a magical act that annuls a misfortune and denies it existence.

Theological context. Shamash and Adad are the Mesopotamian gods of divination. Prayers and queries addressed to Shamash and Adad or later to Shamash alone show the gods as personally involved in the divinatory process. Shamash's divinatory function is a corollary to his role as god of justice: he decides cases and makes decisions.

According to one account, divination was a secret of the gods until Shamash and Adad disclosed the arts of oil and liver divination to a single individual, Enmeduranki, an antediluvian ruler of Sippar. As the techniques for accessing this exceptional source of wisdom passed from the gods to the human domain, they were still considered secrets that could be entrusted only to a select group of scholars.

Divinatory knowledge is obtained within a religious context, but the various forms do not present a consistent theological perspective. Gods could be directly addressed and they responded by sending messages into the sensory world embodied in natural phenomena. At the same time divinatory knowledge can also derive from a signifying system operating independently of a divine will.

BIBL.: Jean Bottéro, "Symptoms, signes, écritures en Mésopotamie ancienne," in *Divination et rationalité* by J. P. Vernant et al. (Paris, 1974), 70–196. S. M. Freedman, *If a City Is Set on a Height: The Akkadian Omen Series šumma alu ina mēlê šakin*, vol. 1: *Tablets 1–21* (Philadelphia, 1998). A. K. Guinan, "Left/Right Symbolism in Mesopotamian Divination," *State Archives of Assyria Bulletin* 10: 5–10. Ulla Koch-Westenholz, *Babylonian Liver Omens* (Copenhagen, 2000). Idem, *Mesopotamian Astrology: An Introduction to Babylonian and Assyrian Celestial Divination* (Copenhagen, 1995).   A.K.G.

Prophecy

The term *divination* covers the entire spectrum of techniques designed to capture a message from the powers above; strictly speaking, then, prophecy, the inspired utterances of someone acting as a god's mouthpiece, is a branch of divination. As their modes of communication with the gods differ quite fundamentally, however, divination and prophecy are treated here as distinct phenomena.

The biblical ring of the term *prophecy* is not entirely misleading. As a historical phenomenon, prophecy, both Israelite and Mesopotamian, is the inspired utterance of someone who, at least temporarily, acts as the mouthpiece of a god. Prophecy, by its very nature, is oral; written prophecy is a derivative. In some respects the prophetic utterance resembles the symbolically significant chance utterance (Akkadian *egirrû*). The inspired utterance, likewise, could be in need of interpretation, consisting as it sometimes did of a few disjointed words or a mysterious phrase. More often, however, the message of the prophet was quite intelligible. Claiming a divine revelation—and sometimes exhibiting the outward signs of possession (usually referred to as *immaḫi* [he/she went into a trance])—the prophet spoke promises of victory, admonished in the name of the god, or delivered oracles of encouragement. Unlike the professional diviner, the prophet received no special training—for which reason the prophet never enjoyed the prestige of the diviner, even if some prophets were held in high esteem by the general population. What is striking, too, is the number of women active as prophets in Mesopotamia, which confirms that the phenomenon is rooted in the popular religion—not the religion of scholars.

If the written evidence can be relied on, prophecy never gained a central place in Mesopotamian divination. It is possible that prophecy enjoyed a more-or-less constant popularity with the middle and lower classes of society. However, the records we possess document prophecy as a phenomenon of some importance only in the Old Babylonian period, especially in the kingdom of Mari, and in the Neo-Assyrian era, under such kings as Esarhaddon and Assurbanipal. The Assurbanipal library at Nineveh even contained collected oracles concerning the dynasty, similar to what must have formed the nucleus of some of the biblical prophetic books. These texts attest to the literary use of prophecy, an earlier prophecy being recycled for a new situation. Mesopotamian prophecy never served the role, however, that the prophetic books of the Bible came to play. Prophecy did not enter the stream of tradition and was not, in that sense, canonized.

BIBL.: Jean-Marie Durand, *Archives épistolaires de Mari*, vol. 1.1 (Paris: Éditions recherche sur les civilisations, 1988). Wilfred G. Lambert, "The Qualifications of Babylonian Diviners," in *Festschrift für Rykle Borger zu seinem 65. Geburtstag am 24. Mai 1994* (ed. Stefan M. Maul; Cuneiform Monographs 10; Groningen: Styx, 1998), 141–58. Martti Nissinen (ed.), *Prophecy in Its Ancient Near Eastern Context: Mesopotamian, Biblical, and Arabian Perspectives* (Society of Biblical Literature Symposium Series 13; Atlanta: Society of Biblical Literature, 2000). Idem, *References to Prophecy in Neo-Assyrian Sources* (State Archives of Assyria Studies 7; Helsinki: University of Helsinki Press, 1998). Simo Parpola, *Assyrian Prophecies* (State Archives of Assyria 9; Helsinki: University of Helsinki Press, 1997).   K.V.D.T.

Syria-Canaan

Extensive numbers of small figurines of deities, both Canaanite and Egyptian, found throughout Syria-Canaan from the Bronze and Iron Ages confirm a personal attachment by the population to the divine realm. It is likely that the owners of these images inquired for information directly from their gods by means of petition and prayer (see Ezek. 21.21 [= 21.26 Hebrew], where images are used for divination; see also Zech. 10.2); however, no evidence, save the figurines themselves, survives to confirm this. Amulets, some containing inscriptions, are found throughout the area, demonstrating the belief that deities and demons acted within the human world in such a manner that humans could know what to expect from the individual deities and thus petition for such action.

On the basis of the legal prohibition of divination by augury, magic, and necromancy in Deut. 18.10, it is generally assumed that these practices were common throughout Canaan; however, the evidence for such practices is slim. Augury, or perhaps more accurately ornithomantics, is attested at Alalakh in the 2nd millennium BCE on the Idrimi stele, where mention is also made of extispicy (reading the signs on entrails) of sacrificial sheep. Inscribed arrowheads have been interpreted as evidence for belomancy (divination by means of pulling an arrow out of a group in a quiver), while excavated models of livers from Megiddo, Hazor, and Ugarit clearly show that hepatoscopy was practiced where Mesopotamian influence was felt. A few textual remains at Ugarit suggest that an interest in the stars and planets existed, but whether this also reflected astrology in any form is unknown. Necromancy, calling up spirits of the dead in order to gain information from them, is unattested outside ambiguous cases. Emar, where West Semitic and Mesopotamian cultures met, incorporated an extensive tradition of Mesopotamian omen literature during the 2nd millennium BCE; this highly developed and professionally executed method of divination may have been dispersed westward since cultural contacts in that direction are extensive from Emar, but current evidence on the diffusion of divination practices is sparse.

Night appears to have been the propitious time to receive divine revelation. The practice of incubation rituals (sleeping in the presence of deities, e.g., in their temples, in order to receive communications from them) is attested by the Ugaritic Legend of Aqhat, where the gods themselves appear. In the Ugaritic Legend of Kirta, a divine message is delivered from the deity El to Kirta by means of a dream as he sleeps. Balaam's gods, according to the inscriptions at Deir Alla (cf. Levine 2000: 241–75), came to him by the order of El in a night vision, allowing him to attend their divine assembly. The biblical traditions about Balaam also place some of his revelations at night (Num. 22.8, 13, 19, 21).

Prophets are well represented in the surviving literatures of Mari to the east and Judah in the south of our area, making it clear that these intermediaries between the divine and human realms were common fixtures of the culture. The actual examples of prophets from Syria-Canaan, although few, do confirm a situation consistent with the wider ancient Near East. Prophets were both amateur and professional, serving as conduits for divine messages in either an ecstatic or a technical manner. A deity wishing to deliver a statement to a human could simply seize any convenient person and force him or her to speak in the name of the god. In this manner, the local deity at Byblos seized a page, as recorded in the report of Wen-Amun, a character in an Egyptian story, who traveled to Phoenicia (*ANET* 25–29), where the message was taken seriously enough to cut through bureaucratic red tape. More often, the deities made use of professionals known as "seers" or "prophets" to make their will known; this appears to be the position held by Balaam, whose presence in the divine assembly is preserved at Deir Alla.

For rulers, whose desire to know the will of the divine world on matters mundane (where to build a hallway according to the Milcom proclamation at the Ammonite citadel; Jackson 1983: 10; cf. *ANET* 655–56) and serious (who should be king, according to Zakkur's inscription at Hamath; cf. *Context of Scripture* 2:139) a ready entourage of prophets who could determine the will of the gods on demand was necessary at any court. Zakkur's inscription indeed states that the God of the Heaven was asked for the information and that the de-

ity responded through seers and prophets. The use of sacrificial livers reflects a highly technical manner of inquiring of the divine world, used by professional diviners (sometimes actually referred to by the Akkadian term *barû*). It is less clear whether governmental staff included professional ecstatic prophets, known for their capacity to receive and deliver divine messages, although Balaam may have held such a position. The proclamations of professional prophets were of more than passing interest, judging from the prophecy of the god Adad, delivered by the prophet Abiya in Aleppo concerning Zimri-Lim and speedily sent on to Mari by ambassador Nur-Sin along with a lock of Abiya's hair and a cutting from his robe to prove the reliability of the message.

The concerns expressed in divinatory records from Syria-Canaan are primarily political in nature. Abiya's Aleppo prophecy deals with the proper historical procession of kingship and the establishing (with the very weapon of Adad used to defeat Sea) of Zimri-Lim as king. The Zakkur inscription also deals with the divine assurance of a proper ruler while King Hamiyatas of Masuwari (Til Barsib) is divinely assured that the granaries of his father will be protected during his reign. The protection by deities of rulers is encountered in the Abiya, Hamiyatas, Zakkur, and Ammonite citadel prophecies. The Balaam inscriptions contain warnings about abnormal natural phenomena and social abominations that cause the deities to debate cutting off sunlight to the world. The Legend of Kirta includes a section reflecting an interest in ascertaining from the divine world information relating to diseases. Bes figurines possibly indicate petitions and inquiries regarding childbirth, which was among the concerns addressed by this Egyptian god.

With the increased political and cultural control of Syria-Canaan, first by Greece and then by Rome, the area took up Greek and Roman divination late in the 1st millennium BCE. Extispicy of a Greek and Roman type was incorporated into the religions of the area, replacing older local and Mesopotamian divinatory rituals. The zodiac, unattested in Syria until the Hellenistic era, then became a common feature of the artistic culture and, one assumes, of common life. References to oracles among the Syrians also are found in Greek authors; especially noteworthy is Lucian's (or pseudo-Lucian's) reference to the statue of "Apollo" in *On the Syrian Goddess,* which delivers messages to the priests on its own volition. In addition, Herodotus credits "Eastern" rulers of all nationalities with a great respect for Delphic oracles.

BIBL.: *The Context of Scripture*, ed. W. Hallo (Leiden: Brill, 2003). Kent Jackson, *The Ammonite Language of the Iron Age* (Harvard Semitic Monographs 27; Chico, Calif.: Scholars Press, 1983). Baruch Levine, *Numbers 21–36* (Anchor Bible 4A; New York: Doubleday, 2000).   L.K.H.

Israel

Like all of the civilizations of the ancient Near East, early Israel recognized the existence of divine or supernatural powers and believed that the human and divine worlds could communicate with each other in various ways. The earliest evidence for Israel's beliefs on this subject is found in the Hebrew Bible, which contains numerous narratives of divine-human interaction and relatively large collections of divine oracles. These texts provide reference points for all later Jewish thinking about prophecy and divination, and they also provide a paradigm for the figure of the prophet, a paradigm that later had a profound influence on religious thought in the West.

Terminology. Some modern anthropologists distinguish the diviner from the prophet by suggesting that the diviner possesses specialized training that allows the individual to contact the divine by manipulating physical objects or by interpreting natural phenomena, while the prophet simply speaks to the people a divine word concerning the present and future. This clear-cut distinction does not seem to have existed in ancient Israel, which knew several different types of individuals capable of facilitating communication between the human and divine worlds.

In the Hebrew Bible, the most visible of these intermediaries are the prophets, but even here, the Hebrew text distinguishes several different types of figures who originally may have had different characteristics and functions. The most commonly used title applied to prophetic figures is *nābî'*, a word that occurs more than 250 times in the Hebrew Bible to designate individuals associated with Israel's God, YHWH. However, the Hebrew Bible also applies the title to representatives of other gods as well (1 Kings 18), and it is attested in much earlier texts discovered at Mari and Emar. Scholars still do not agree on the meaning of the title, which is related to a verb meaning "to call." Some interpreters take the word as a passive participle, in which case the title would designate "one who is called" (by a deity). On the other hand, a growing number of scholars see the word as an active participle and understand it to mean "one who calls out" (the word of a deity) or even "one who invokes" (the name of a deity). In either case, the etymology of the title sheds little light on the behavior and functions of the figures that bear it.

Much less common is the title *ḥōzeh* (visionary), a designation that presumably refers to the means by which the figure received divine revelation. In the Old Testament it is applied particularly to figures associated with the kingdom of Judah, its government, and its cult. As is also true in the case of the *nābî'*, the visionary is attested in other Near Eastern texts.

The remaining prophetic titles are not well attested and are usually associated with particular individuals and biblical stories. Samuel is called a *rō'eh* (seer) (1

Sam. 9.11, 18–19) in a story that portrays him as an individual to whom people could come to seek information from the deity. The story also explains that *rō'eh* is archaic and has been replaced by the more common *nābî'*. Samuel and others are sometimes called "man of God" (or perhaps "servant of God"), an honorific title often appearing alongside *nābî'* and referring to the same individual (3.20; 9.6–8). Finally, the title "sons of the prophets" appears often in the stories about Elijah and Elisha (1 Kings 20; 2 Kings 2–9). This title is clearly a designation for a prophetic guild made up of the disciples of a single prophetic master.

No matter what distinctions may have originally been implied by the Old Testament's use of these various titles, it is clear that those distinctions had begun to blur within the biblical period itself. The Hebrew text sometimes uses the titles interchangeably, a trend that continues in the Greek translation of the Old Testament, the Septuagint. The Greek translators always render the Hebrew title *nābî'* with the word *prophētēs* (prophet), a word appearing in classical Greek texts as early as the 5th century BCE. The Greek term means "one who speaks forth or proclaims" the message of a deity, concerning either past, present, or future events. Since the words of the *nābî'* always addressed contemporary conditions and often predicted future events as well, this is an apt translation on the part of the Greek writers. However, it is clear that they did not recognize any distinctions among prophetic figures that might have originally been present in ancient Israel, for the Septuagint also applies the term *prophētēs* to visionaries and seers as well as, occasionally, to other religious figures (in accordance with Greek usage).

Prophets. Beyond the titles applied to various prophetic figures, biblical stories about them, as well as the words attributed to them, reveal a great deal of information about how ancient Israelites thought about prophecy and the roles of prophets in their society. Although the biblical sources do not contain much information about the process by which individuals became prophets, there is no indication that the prophet occupied a hereditary position or one that was achieved through a process of apprenticeship. Rather the prophets speak of being "taken" or called by YHWH (Amos 7.14–15; 1 Sam. 3). Sometimes the call took the form of a conversation (Jer. 1.4–10), while in other cases the prophet saw a divine vision that included the call (Isa. 6; Ezek. 1–3).

After the initial call, most prophets seem to have continued their normal occupations, which were occasionally interrupted by new messages from YHWH. Even well-known prophets such as Isaiah and Jeremiah seem to have gone through long periods of time when they did not prophesy, so it is clear that being a prophet did not always exclude living a normal life. Amos, for example, kept sheep and tended fig trees (Amos 1.1, 7.14), while Ezekiel and Jeremiah are both said to have been priests (Jer. 1.1; Ezek. 1.3). On the other hand, there is some evidence that prophets were attached occasionally to the central sanctuary or to the royal court (Joel; Ps. 2, 12, 46, 50, 60, 62, 68, 75, 81, 82, 87, 89, 91, 95, 108, 110, 132), and in the postexilic period the temple service of the Levites seems to have been considered a form of prophecy (1 Chron. 25.1–8; 2 Chron. 34.30). Such individuals presumably prophesied as a full-time occupation.

With respect to the process of prophetic revelation, there were differences of opinion among the major religious groups in Israel, although these differences ought not be too sharply drawn. Among those prophets associated with Jerusalem and its distinctive religious traditions, there seems to have been a tendency to talk about divine revelation as coming through visions. Prophetic books coming out of these circles tend to contain detailed reports of visions (Amos, Isaiah, Ezekiel), although the prophets involved also speak of receiving words directly from YHWH. On the other hand, the prophets influenced by the Book of Deuteronomy and the prophets portrayed in the Deuteronomistic History (Joshua, Judges, Samuel, Kings) tend to talk about receiving oracles directly from YHWH. They prefer to describe the experience of revelation as a form of spirit possession leading to a direct verbal communication from the deity (1 Kings 18.46; 2 Kings 3.15; Jer. 15.17; Num. 11.25–26). In the writings of some of these prophets, visions (and also dreams) may have been considered a secondary form of revelation (Jer. 23.23–32), although some of these same prophets occasionally give reports of their own visions (4.23–26).

Prophets who were possessed by YHWH's spirit may have exhibited stereotypical behavior that encouraged their audience to recognize them as prophets. Particularly noticeable in this respect are the regular speech patterns found in many prophetic oracles, particularly those from the preexilic period. Typically the oracle begins with an accusation against an individual or group. This is followed by the phrase "thus says YHWH," which in turn introduces an announcement of judgment. Along with the oracles themselves may have gone certain types of behavior peculiar to the prophets. In some cases, possession by YHWH's spirit may have led to ecstasy, a measurable physiological condition involving changes in concentration, loss of control over physical and mental processes, and hallucinations. However, this was by no means always the case. Particularly in the prophetic stories in the Books of Kings, prophets are also said to have performed miracles and other acts of power as part of their stereotypical behavior. Many of the later prophets used physical signs or symbolic actions that became the occasion for the delivery of an oracle. In the case of Ezekiel, the signs are so elaborate that they begin to take on a magical quality (Ezek. 4–5).

The prophets seem to have been able to exercise varying degrees of control over their receipt of divine messages. On the one hand, prophets speak of messages arriving unbidden and burning within them like a fire until they are delivered (Jer. 20.7–12; Amos 3.8). On the other hand, those prophets influenced by the picture of Moses as prophet in Deut. 18 saw their prophetic task to include intercession with YHWH on behalf of the people. Such prophets were thus specialists to whom individuals could go when they wanted to present a request to God or seek information from God (1 Sam. 12; 1 Kings 14.1–18; 2 Kings 3.4–27; Jer. 7.16–17; 11.14–17; 14.1–15.4). For the most part, the biblical texts provide no information about how prophets went about soliciting divine oracles, although on two occasions they are said to have used music to facilitate spirit possession (1 Sam. 10.5; 2 Kings 3.15).

As in any society where prophets are active, ancient Israel often faced the dilemma of prophetic conflict, occasions on which prophets delivered contradictory messages. This problem seems to have been particularly acute during the period before the fall of Jerusalem, when various prophets delivered conflicting oracles on how to deal with the political crisis (Jer. 23; 27–29), and it arose again during the Persian period, when prophets proposed conflicting plans for restoring the Israelite state (Haggai, Zechariah, Malachi). The biblical writers were clearly aware of the problem and suggested several solutions to it, although to the modern reader these solutions are less than satisfactory. In Deut. 18.21–22, the writer suggests that the true prophet is the one whose predictions come to pass, a criterion that unfortunately cannot be applied until after the fact. Jeremiah makes two suggestions: (1) the true word of God is self-authenticating because it achieves results in the world (Jer. 23) and (2) the prophetic oracle that most closely resembles true prophetic words from the past is the oracle most likely to be true (Jer. 28). After the biblical period, Jewish communities tended to adopt the second of Jeremiah's criteria and to present new revelation as the work of ancient prophets, whose status as true prophets had long been established. Tendencies in this direction are already at work in late biblical texts such as Isa. 40–66 and Daniel, where contemporary revelation is promulgated in the name of earlier prophetic authorities.

Other religious specialists. In addition to prophets, the Old Testament also mentions several other religious specialists who were thought to be able to communicate with the supernatural world and who operated in Israel at various times. The most comprehensive reference to these figures appears in a list in Deut. 18.10–11, although other texts refer to them as well (Exod. 22.18 [= 22.17 Hebrew]; Lev. 19.26, 31; 20.1–6, 27; Num. 23.23; 1 Sam. 15.23; 28.3–25; 2 Kings 17.17; 21.6; Isa. 3.2–3; Mic. 3.6–7). All of these intermediaries were individuals to whom an Israelite could go to obtain supernatural information and aid, although their titles are mostly obscure and say nothing about the ritual techniques that they employed. The witch of Endor in 1 Sam. 28 is an example. The list may include diviners of various sorts, and one specialist may have supplied charms or binding spells. Several of the titles have to do with seeking information from the spirits of the dead. From the standpoint of the biblical writers, all such figures are illegitimate and are to be banned from Israel, probably because they deal with supernatural powers other than YHWH.

Techniques of divination. The biblical writers also know various techniques of divination, although they usually associate such practices with foreigners, particularly the Assyrians and Babylonians. Thus, for example, Isaiah mentions Babylonian astrologers (Isa. 47.13), and Ezekiel gives a graphic picture of the Babylonian king determining the direction his army will march by shaking arrows (belomancy), consulting household gods, and examining the livers of sheep (Ezek. 21.21 [= 21.26 Hebrew]). Magicians and astrologers also appear frequently in stories set in the Babylonian royal court (Dan. 1.20; 2.2, 10, 27; 4.7 [= 4.4 Hebrew]; 5.7, 11, 15).

A few biblical narratives suggest the existence of divination in Israel, although the evidence is by no means straightforward. Joseph is said to have performed divination by using his cup, perhaps interpreting a mixture of oil and water (Gen. 44.5), and he was a skilled interpreter of dreams (37.5–11; 40.5–23; 41.1–36). Daniel also rose to power in the Babylonian royal court through his ability to interpret the king's dreams (Dan. 2, 4). It may be significant that the stories of Joseph and Daniel are both set in foreign contexts, although in Israel individuals also occasionally had ominous dreams (1 Kings 3.1–15 and perhaps 9.1–9 and 1 Sam. 3).

The most prominent type of divination in biblical Israel involved the priestly lots, the Urim and Thummim. There is no consensus on the nature of these objects, but the following is a plausible reconstruction. They were carried in an ephod, which was part of the vestments of the high priest (Exod. 28.30; Lev. 8.8), although Deuteronomistic traditions suggest that the Urim and Thummim could be operated by any levitical priest (Deut. 33.8; Judg. 18.5–6). The technique for the use of the lots involved a formal inquiry. An individual would come to the priest and ask a question that could be answered "yes" or "no." The priest would then instruct the lots to "give Urim" for one answer and to "give Thummim" for the other. The lots would probably then be shaken and thrown, a process that would either yield an answer or no answer at all (Num. 27.21; 1 Sam. 14.36–42; 23.9–12; 28.6; 30.7–8). In order to account for both possibilities, it is necessary to suppose that the Urim and Thummim did not resemble modern dice but were a pair of flat boards, each of which had "Urim" written on one side and "Thummim" written on the other. When the boards were thrown, a decisive answer resulted when the two upward-facing sides agreed with each other. If one upper side read "Urim" and the other

upper side read "Thummim," the procedure was inconclusive.

In addition to the sacred lots, there are also narrative references to ordinary lots, examples of which have been found in archeological excavations. They seem to have resembled modern dice and were possibly used in games as well as to obtain divine guidance to determine a course of future action (Num. 26.55–56; 1 Sam. 10.20–24; Jon. 1.7; Esth. 3.7; 9.24–26).

Decline of prophecy. While Israelites of the biblical period accorded great status to prophets whom they considered to be legitimate, the status of prophecy in Jewish communities of the later Second Temple period is more ambiguous. The apocalyptic writings present predictions of the future and disclosure of heavenly mysteries in the names of ancient figures such as Enoch. These writings typically contain vision reports that show clear continuity with prophetic visions and sometimes describe the ascent of the visionaries to the heavens. They also sometimes describe techniques for obtaining visions. Daniel fasts; Ezra eats a flower that is in the field and drinks a fiery liquid. Jews in the Diaspora also produced oracles in the name of the Sibyl, in imitation of the popular Hellenistic genre of Sibylline Oracles.

Rabbinic sources are normally thought to express the belief that prophecy in Israel came to an end after the last of the biblical prophets: "From the death of Haggai, Zechariah, and Malachi, the latter prophets, the Holy Spirit ceased from Israel. But in spite of that it was allowed them to hear messages from God by a Bath Qol [lit., daughter of a voice]" (Tosefta, tractate *Sotah* 13.2). It is not difficult to speculate about the rabbis' reasons for advocating this position. The biblical prophets of the postexilic period had become increasingly involved in political and religious advocacy, and the result was a good bit of social unrest. The rabbis generally wanted to avoid this sort of upheaval, and furthermore they very likely interpreted contemporary prophetic claims as a direct challenge to their own authority. By ruling out the possibility of contemporary prophecy, the rabbis were free to deal with the issue of revelation in their own distinctive way.

The rabbinic view of prophecy seems also to have been shared by the Jewish historian Josephus, who at points in his writings implies that prophetic inspiration diminished after the biblical period (*Against Apion* 1.41). However, in spite of these claims, the reality of the situation seems to have been somewhat different. Josephus himself describes several contemporary individuals whose activities resemble those of the biblical prophets, although he does not apply the prophetic label to them. He also mentions several "sign prophets," who all seem to have been leaders of movements and were involved in predicting future events. Finally, Josephus himself made predictions on the basis of dreams (*Life* 208–10).

Evidence on the beliefs of other Jewish groups in this period is difficult to obtain, but in at least two cases there is evidence of a continuing belief in prophecy. Some early Christian communities seem to have contained prophetic figures and very likely considered both Jesus and John the Baptist to have had prophetic characteristics. These groups also seem to have shared a growing Jewish belief of the period that prophetic inspiration in scripture was not restricted to only the prophetic writings. This belief is seen particularly in Christian interpretations of Psalms as prophecy.

Similarly the Jewish sectarian community at Qumran engaged in the interpretation of scripture as a collection of prophecies concerning its own times. This practice is visible in many of the interpretive works found at Qumran. It is even possible that the sectarians viewed the interpretations themselves as having prophetic authority if in fact they came from the Teacher of Righteousness (the original leader of the sect), who was accorded prophetic status.

While prophecy in various forms seems to have continued after the biblical period, the continued existence of divination is less certain. The rabbis claimed that the Urim and Thummim did not survive the exile, although they disagreed on exactly when the oracles disappeared (Babylonian Talmud, tractate *Sotah* 48b). Yet in spite of this claim, rabbinic references to divination suggest that the practice survived in later Jewish communities.

BIBL.: John Barton, *Oracles of God* (Oxford: Oxford University Press, 1986). Joseph Blenkinsopp, *A History of Prophecy in Israel* (rev. ed.; Louisville: Westminster/John Knox, 1996). Frederick H. Cryer, *Divination in Ancient Israel and Its Near Eastern Environment* (Sheffield: Sheffield Academic Press, 1994). Rebecca Gray, *Prophetic Figures in Late Second Temple Jewish Palestine* (Oxford: Oxford University Press, 1993). Robert R. Wilson, *Prophecy and Society in Ancient Israel* (Philadelphia: Fortress, 1980). R.R.W.

Anatolia

The Hittites considered their "thousand gods" to be concerned with the affairs of their servants, humans. The gods could see into the hearts of other beings and into the future. As future events were not fixed and immutable, but could be avoided or averted, both gods and humans had many reasons to keep as many lines of communication open as possible.

Humans could speak to gods and lesser spirits directly via prayers or in that mixture of oral and sign language that we often call magical rituals. Many examples of both of these survive. The gods could communicate with humans through a "man of god," presumably an ecstatic prophet, or through a female "seer." Unfortunately no examples of their utterances survive. Gods could also speak to humans through the language of omens. There were many such languages: marks on the liver and other internal organs of sheep, malformed

infants, events in the sky, earthquakes, patterns in oil, animal behavior. Gods could also come to people in dreams—either unsolicited dreams or those that occurred while the person incubated under a priest's supervision. Several texts recording requests made by gods or vows made to gods in dreams are preserved. Long before the Hittites were literate, ancient Mesopotamian scholars studied these languages and created vast dictionaries. Many of these were later passed on to the Hittites, often as modified by the Hurrians.

When the Hittites wanted to question their gods by oracle, they typically asked a long series of questions designed to solve a particular problem. Many questions involved an illness suffered by the king. Was a god responsible? If yes, was such and such a god angry? If yes, was this the only god? If no, then a second, third, fourth god, and so on was asked about until the question "Is this all?" got an affirmative answer. In this way in one text a new god was discovered and the questioning then turned to learning what this new god was god of, where he lived, and other relevant details. Having established that a particular god was angry, the questioning proceeded to discover why. Was the god angry at something in his temple? If yes, often members of that temple's staff would be questioned and all sorts of derelictions—festivals unperformed, cult objects broken and left unrepaired, cultic impurity ignored—would be laid before the god who would be asked, "Is this why you are angry?" Again, this type of questioning would go on until a positive answer to the question "Is this all?" was received. Then for each dereliction about which the god was found to be angry, he was asked whether he was angry at the king, at the priest, and so on. Once this was established, it was time for each person to settle accounts with the god or gods. Would fixing the dereliction suffice? If no, would an additional one-shekel penalty suffice? Two? A certain garment? and so on until all problems and payments had been resolved.

Some questions involved getting permission from the deity for cultic changes, others checking the validity and meaning of dreams and unsolicited omens. A series of questions asked where the king should spend the cold Anatolian winter and whether anything terrible would happen to him or his entourage while there (death, sickness, revolt, fire, storm, accidents), and if so, what could be done to avert it ("shall we give sworn instructions to the chariot drivers concerning road accidents?"). Questions asked whether a particular country, person, or ghost would cause trouble. The reliability of tributary kings and of potential officeholders was checked. Sometimes whole army campaigns would be laid out for divine approval. It is interesting to note that these series of questions were meant to find out of which cities, campaigns, or leaders the gods approved and disapproved, thus still leaving it to the king to choose from the approved ones. A single text asks, "Will the grains mature this year?"—which shows that the Hittites were not as obsessed with fertility as modern scholars of the an- cients are.

All of these questions were phrased in a yes-or-no format, and the gods were asked to reply in one of six specific languages. One particularly common language was written by the gods onto the entrails of specially slaughtered sheep. Various lumps and crevasses on the liver and gallbladder and different numbers of turns of the intestine were either favorable or unfavorable. If one of the signs was unfavorable, the answer was unfavor- able. A second, rather rare language was read in the behavior of a sheep on the way to slaughter. Both of these languages were learned from the Mesopotamians via the Hurrians and were read by a male diviner-exor- cist whose specialty also included the performance of magical rituals. A third language involved reading the movements of a symbolically named water snake across various symbolically named locations in a basin. A fourth was a particularly popular variant of this snake oracle in which a symbolically named token was said to take one or more other symbolically named tokens and deposit them with another symbolically named token. The mechanism of movement is unknown, but a mouse in a box has been suggested. The languages of the snake and the token oracles, both purely Anatolian, were read by a female practitioner, whose job also involved per- forming magical rituals. A fifth, also Anatolian, divine language was written in the actions (in flight or on the ground) of birds above or on a marked field of viewing. These movements were translated by a male augur.

In oracles involving these five languages, our texts normally describe what has been observed and then give the diviner's interpretation, that is, whether it was posi- tive or negative. A sixth language, which somehow in- volves shelducks (HURRI birds), was interpreted not by the augur but by the male diviner-exorcist, and in virtu- ally all occasions the texts simply record the positive or negative outcome. One presumes that this last was considered cheaper and slightly less reliable than the other methods of divination. Frequently, important an- swers would be checked, generally by asking for the same question to be answered in a different divine lan- guage.

BIBL.: A. Archi, "L'ornitomanzia ittita," *Studi Micenei ed Egeo-anatolici* 16 (1976): 119–80. R. Beal, "Gleanings from Hittite Oracle Questions on Religion, Society, Psychology, and Decision Making," in *Festschrift Maciej Popko* (ed. P. Taracha; forthcoming). Idem, "Seeking Divine Approval for Campaign Strategy," *Ktèma* 24 (1999): 41–54. O. R. Gurney, "Babylonians and Hittites," in *Oracles and Divination* (ed. M. Loewe and C. Blacker; Boulder, Colo.: Shambhala, 1981), 142–73. A. Ünal, *Ein Orakeltext über die Intrigen am hethitischen Hof* (Heidelberg: Winter, 1978). R.H.B.

Iran

In ancient Iranian divination, prophecy and ecstatic vi- sion were closely related, but few sources describe the actual performances and procedures of divination or prophecy. Zoroastrian texts that bear the mark of myth and legend, together with some short passages from Greco-Roman literature, provide our basic material for information.

Reports by Greek and Roman authors show the magi *(magoi)* in the role of interpreting cosmic signs or dream-visions. Herodotus refers to "interpreters of dreams" *(oneiropoloi)* among the magi as interpret- ing the dream-visions of Astyages (Herodotus 1.107–8) and also mentions *oneiropoloi* in the service of Cyrus (1.128). Similarly, a dream-vision of Xerxes is explained by the magi (7.19), and they interpret for Xerxes a cos- mic portent (7.37). Cicero states explicitly that in Persia it is the magi who perform divinations *(augurantur et divinant; On Divination* 1.41). Referring to Dinon's lost *Persica*, he mentions the magi interpreting a dream- vision of Cyrus *(On Divination* 1.23). Although cast in Greek and Roman terminology, the repeated references to the magi interpreting dreams and making predictions suggest that this priestly group assumed divinatory and prophetic functions in addition to their main roles as sacrificers and transmitters of religious traditions.

Our Zoroastrian sources (mainly the Pahlavi texts) confirm this and convey further aspects of prophecy and divination. Sacrificial rituals seem to have provided the most important context for these phenomena. The Gathas were, from the very beginning, recited within the framework of a sacrifice, which also had an eschatologi- cal purpose in preparing the road for the sacrificer's soul (Avestan *uruuan*) to paradise. The sacrificial site was the meeting place between gods and human beings and con- sequently the appropriate scene for divinatory rituals. Some stanzas suggest that the sacrificer had ecstatic ex- periences; in the Gathas, the sacrificer is condensed into the figure of Zarathustra. He is qualified as "the know- ing one" *(viduuah-;* e.g., Yasna 31.19) and as "possess- ing the divine word" *(mathran-;* e.g., Yasna 50.6).

From late Achaemenian times onward, the fire tem- ples emerge as the foremost places where both cult and divination were practiced. According to Cicero, the magi gathered in a sanctuary *(fanum)* when seeking the will of the deity *(On Divination* 1.23). In Sasanian tra- dition, represented by the story of Arda Viraz, the per- son who is to undergo an ecstatic, divinatory procedure is taken to a fire temple and, once the séance is finished, takes food and drink and performs a religious ceremo- nial (Arda Wiraz Namag 3.3, 24).

This represents a particular type of divination in which a chosen person is sent on an otherworldly jour- ney that ultimately ends in paradise, where guidance is given by the supreme deity. On returning, the visionary conveys the divine message to the community, which is reassured of the effectiveness of their rituals and of the truth of their beliefs. To prepare for the journey a state of trance is induced by means of a specific technique performed in a ritual context. The essential moment is the drinking of a cup with sacred juice *(hom)* and henbane *(mang)*, after which the visionary falls into a deep sleep. The part of the human personality called *ruwan* (Middle Iranian meaning "soul") leaves the body and sets out on its way to paradise. This kind of mantic practice is associated with important figures of the religious tradition: in the first place Zarathustra and Vistaspa, but also with historical persons in the Sasanian period, such as high priest Kirdir (end of the 3rd century CE) who in his inscriptions records an ecstatic otherworldly journey that had the purpose of obtaining divine confirmation of his religiopolitical mission. The perhaps legendary Arda Viraz is the best-known example of a visionary who, just like Kirdir, was granted a vision of paradise and hell during his ecstatic journey.

Some sources deal with the mode of conveying the capacity of ecstatic vision in more detail (Bahman Yasht 3.6–13; Pahlavi Rivayat 36.5–13; Selections of Zatspram 22.7–9; Denkard 8.14.7–8). The visionary receives the divine quality of omniscience (Middle Iranian *xrad i harwisp agaghih*), which is thought to be transmitted in liquid form, as told in Bahman Yasht: "[Ohrmazd] put the wisdom of omniscience in the form of water into the hands of Zarathustra and said: 'drink.' Zarathustra drank from it, and [Ohrmazd] mingled his wisdom of omniscience with Zardust. For seven days and nights Zarathustra remained in the wisdom of Ohrmazd" (Bahman Yasht 3.6–8).

According to the Avesta, the quality of omniscience belongs to the gods, in particular Ahura Mazda and Mithra, but can be transferred to human beings, in the first place to Zarathustra (Yasht 14.29–33; 16.7–13) and in later tradition also to Jamaspa (e.g., Ayadkar i Zareran 35–37).

The Pahlavi books, compiled in the early post-Islamic period but based on earlier traditions, have recorded many predictions that they put in the mouth of Zarathustra and Jamaspa. Extensive prophecies make up the content of the Bahman Yasht, a compilation which in its core goes back to the early Hellenistic period and which is set in the framework of divine teachings conveyed to Zarathustra during particular encounters with Ahura Mazda, called in Middle Iranian *hampursagih* (consultation). These encounters, mentioned in the Avesta (Yasna 12.6; Vendidad 2.1–2), are frequently alluded to in the Pahlavi books, but the underlying myth has been preserved only in Denkard 8.3.60–62 and Selections of Zatspram 21.7–11, and only incompletely. Zarathustra was fetching water for the *haoma* sacrifice at the river Daitya when Vohu Manah appeared and took him to the encounter with Ahura Mazda. Upon arriving, Zarathustra greeted the deity with the formula *namaz o Ohrmazd* (homage to Ohrmazd), and then "he sat down in the place of the inquirers." This piece of myth probably reflects actual oracular rituals performed by Iranian priests taking Zarathustra as their mythic model. The Oracles of Hystaspes, known through citations and secondary summaries in Clement of Alexandria and Lactantius, are ultimately derived from Iranian prophecies that were revealed in a dream-vision to Hystaspes (= Vistaspa) and interpreted by a prophesying youth (*sub interpretatione vaticinantis pueri*; Lactantius, *Divine Institutes* 7.15.19).

The prophecies that have come down to us concern mainly the future destinies of the Iranian nation, but in that connection also the history of the world. The Zoroastrian doctrine of the coming saviors (Avestan *saosyant-*), the ultimate battle between the good and evil powers, and the renewal of the world is often transmitted in the form of prophecies.

BIBL.: Mary Boyce and Frantz Grenet, *A History of Zoroastrianism*, vol. 3 (Leiden, 1991). Anders Hultgård, "Persian Apocalypticism," in *The Encyclopedia of Apocalypticism* (ed. John Collins; New York, 1998), 1.39–83. H. G. Kippenberg, "Die Geschichte der mittelpersischen apokalyptischen Traditionen," *Studia iranica* 7 (1978): 49–80. A.H.

Greece

Divination—the receipt and analysis of information from gods, ghosts, and other nonhuman entities—was everywhere in ancient Greece. Almost any object, person, statement, or event could carry information; the trick was to interpret and act upon that information correctly. Indeed, the receipt of divinatory information often led to spirited debate among those who had to interpret it. A classic case involved receipt of an oracle by Athens during the Persian Wars in the early 5th century BCE, which advised the citizens to protect themselves "by wooden walls." One Athenian, Themistocles, convinced his fellows that this meant they should increase the size of their navy (ships being built of wood), rather than adopt an alternative interpretation and seek refuge on the Acropolis, which had in former times been protected by a "wall" of thorn bushes. The fortified navy subsequently saved not only Athens but all of Greece, proving Themistocles' interpretation correct (Herodotus 7.140–43; cf. Religious Personnel and Religion and Politics).

The anecdote demonstrates not only that interpretation of divinatory information was just as important as receiving it in the first place, but also that anyone, not only specialists, might succeed at interpretation; in fact, professional interpreters of oracles (*chrēsmologoi*) had urged the Athenians to abandon their city altogether and establish a new home elsewhere after they heard the oracle, but had been ignored. In this characteristic, divination followed the general trend of Greek religion, which assumed that most functions could be carried out by most people. Professional seers (*manteis*) traveled with armies to provide advice based on their interpretations of omens, but a remark by the general Xenophon reminds us that theirs was not always the final word: Xenophon says that he himself was knowledgeable enough in the arts of divination that his seer

King Aegeus of Athens receives a prophecy from Themis, the mythical predecessor of the Pythia at Delphi, who sits, like the Pythia, on Apollo's tripod. Attic red-figure cup by the Kodros Painter 440–430 BCE. Staatliche Museen, Berlin. *Foto Marburg/ Art Resource, New York*

could not deceive him with false information (*Anabasis* 5.6.29). This statement, which finds echoes in other ancient sources, also reflects the presumption that, far from being unimpeachable due to some special relationship with the gods, professional diviners were motivated by the same things as other people and sometimes put their own interests before those of the people they advised. Even when the source and interpretation were considered accurate and trustworthy, divinatory information might be rejected or challenged. The "wooden walls" oracle that Themistocles successfully interpreted was the second oracle the Athenians envoys had received; they had rejected an earlier one because it offered the city no hope at all, and after begging the god for mercy tried a second time with better luck. In sum, information obtained through divination was open to multiple interpretations, which had to be winnowed by human intelligence.

Institutional oracles. Both of the oracles that Athens received came from the Delphic Oracle, one of the oldest (perhaps dating to the late 9th century BCE) and most prestigious of Greek institutional oracles—that is, oracles situated in a fixed spot and administered by a priesthood. At Delphi, in an inner chamber of Apollo's temple, a woman who had pledged to remain celibate, called the Pythia, sat on a sacred tripod, wore a crown of sacred laurel, and was inspired by the god himself. Through her mouth, Apollo spoke words that were transmitted to inquirers by priests who were called

prophētai (lit., those who speak for someone else). Whether the responses were already coherent and in good poetic verse when the Pythia spoke them or whether the *prophētai* made them so continues to be debated among scholars. Whatever the answer to that question, the responses sometimes were worded in such a way as to require interpretation on the part of the recipient, as we have seen. In other cases, however, the Delphic Oracle acted simply to rubber-stamp decisions that had been reached previously through completely human means; a city might formulate new regulations for a local cult and then submit them to Apollo at Delphi for approval, for instance. The truly enigmatic Delphic response, whose meaning proves to be quite different from what it seems, is primarily a literary *topos:* we encounter it in stories such as that of Oedipus but seldom in our records of historical responses.

Although Delphi was the preeminent oracular institution in the Greek world, others existed as well. Most were sponsored by Apollo (notably the oracles at Didyma and Claros in addition to that at Delphi), but Dodona was under the aegis of Zeus, and other gods had oracles, too. Some oracles conveyed information given by dead heroes, such as that of Amphiaraus in Oropus and of Trophonius in Lebadeia. Didyma, like Delphi, used inspired females; Claros used an inspired man. At Dodona priests may have interpreted the sound of wind blowing through sacred oak trees; at the Amphiaraon inquirers received information in a dream, while sleeping in the sanctuary; and at the shrine of Trophonius, inquirers apparently descended into an underground shrine and perhaps experienced an encounter with the hero himself. Herodotus lists a few more institutional oracles (1.46), and from other sources we can bring the number to about twenty that existed during the classical and Hellenistic periods; in later antiquity, we hear about yet others.

Independent practitioners. Divination was also provided by independent experts called by a variety of titles, a few of which were *ornithomantis* (interpreter of birds' behavior), *oneiromantis* (dream interpreter), and *teratoskopos* (interpreter of portents). *Mantis,* which might be translated simply as "diviner," was the most general term of all. The titles and the methods they represent were by no means mutually exclusive, and many practitioners probably were skilled in more than one technique, including some for which there were no special titles, such as reading the entrails of sacrificed animals; this was regularly done after any sacrifice, even if the primary purpose of the sacrifice was not divinatory. *Manteis* might offer other religious services as well, such as purification and initiation into private mystery cults.

Some independent diviners tried to borrow the prestige of institutional oracles. "Belly-talkers" (*engastrimuthoi*) prophesied via voices coming from their stomachs and were called "pythons," as if to imply kinship to the Delphic Pythia through whom Apollo spoke (Plato, *Sophist* 252c; Plutarch, *On the Obsolescence of Oracles* 9.414e). In later antiquity we encounter an even broader spectrum of divinatory techniques that private practitioners might employ either for themselves or on behalf of a client: scrying (gazing at water or some other reflective surface), lychnomancy (gazing at a flame), and the invocation of a "direct vision"— that is, a face-to-face encounter with a god such as Apollo—are among them. (It is not unlikely that some of these techniques were employed in earlier periods, too; we know a lot about the late antique phenomena due to the happy survival of numerous "recipe books" from that period that were written and used by the practitioners [see the Greek and Demotic Magical Papyri], but we lack any comparable sources for earlier centuries.) Two further interesting points emerge from these late antique sources that may be valid for earlier periods as well: independent practitioners made use of young children both as mediums and in other sorts of divinatory procedures, where their assumed honesty would be valuable; and independent practitioners did not hesitate to combine and adapt divinatory procedures that we would otherwise view as separate from one another. Thus, a practitioner might call a spirit into a child to prophesy and yet simultaneously ask the child to gaze into a bowl of water and scry.

Chrēsmologoi (interpreters of oracles) not only interpreted oracles delivered by the Delphic Oracle and other institutional oracles, as mentioned in the story of Themistocles, but also oracles that had been collected in books and that were believed to be very old, such as those of Bacis and the Sibyls. During the late 6th century, one famous *chrēsmologos*, Onomacritus, enjoyed the patronage of the Pisistratids, a prominent Athenian family, but was caught forging oracles that he attributed to the legendary seer Musaeus (Herodotus 7.6). The story, like the anecdote about Xenophon, represents the general attitude about independent diviners: potentially useful but never to be trusted completely. Although myths that made *manteis* such as Melampus and Amphiaraus members of prominent royal families may reflect the real status of *manteis* during some early period of Greek history, by the classical age, *manteis* were marginalized members of society. For really important matters, states and individuals alike preferred, when possible, to consult one of the institutional oracles.

Divination by the average person. Not that ordinary people were without resources; there were methods of divination available to them as well. Many of these were circumstantial—that is, an individual interpreted some spontaneous occurrence that he or she took to be significant. Thunder, especially when it came from an otherwise clear sky, was taken as a sign from Zeus. In *Odyssey* 17.541, Telemachus sneezes unexpectedly and his mother, Penelope, interprets this to mean that she will soon be rid of her troublesome suitors.

Just as now, some dreams (but not all of them; see,

e.g., *Odyssey* 19.562–67) were viewed as having hidden meanings. Although one might call in an *oneiromantis* to interpret particularly tricky ones, the average person usually could do it for himself or herself. Dream divination particularly caught the attention of intellectuals. In the 4th century BCE, Aristotle wrote a short treatise entitled *On Divination in Sleep* in which he denied that dreams could really be predicative, but this was far from the end of the discussion. The Stoics subsequently discussed the "scientific" reasons that dreams might be predicative at some length. A famous "dream diary" kept by Aelius Aristides in the 2nd century CE details his nightly visions and his proposed interpretations of them. Artemidorus's dream book, also composed in the 2nd century, is a formal collection of dreams drawn from people whom he interviewed, with notations as to what subsequently befell the dreamers—an attempt to systematize and test dream interpretation. At the shrine of Amphiaraus inquirers slept in a special building and waited for the hero to advise them in their dreams. This practice, called "incubation," was also employed at healing shrines such as that of Asclepius at Epidaurus. Priests of these shrines might help the dreamers interpret the dreams and put their advice into effect.

Finally, there are several divinatory methods about which we hear only a little, which makes it hard to judge how widely used or respected they were. Aristophanes describes a woman asking the statue of Hecate that stood before her door whether she should go out that day (*Lysistrata* 63). Dice oracles, established in some marketplaces of Greek Asia Minor during the imperial period, apparently left it up to the merchants who wished to consult them to roll the dice and then look up the meaning of the roll on a nearby chart. In Roman imperial sources we hear about a few legendary people who were what we would call "clairvoyant"—that is, they could "see" what was happening simultaneously in distant places (Philostratus, *Life of Apollonius* 8.26; Eunapius, *Lives of the Sophists* 468). The silence of our earlier sources concerning this phenomenon is hard to gauge.

In certain circumstances, the conversation of other people (especially children), overheard by someone who needed advice, could be interpreted as a divine message. Pittacus, one of the Seven Wise Men of Greece, advised a friend who could not decide between two brides to listen to boys spinning tops in the street. The boys cried out to each other "keep to your own traces!" which in their context meant that each should keep his top out of the others' way, but which Pittacus's friend interpreted to mean that he should keep to his own social rank and marry the humbler woman (Callimachus, *Epigrams* 1). Augustine's story of his conversion to Christianity is built on this practice: while sitting in his garden he heard a child sing out "pick it up and read it," which Augustine interpreted as referring to the Bible that lay by his side; later, after he had become a Christian, Augustine decided that it must have been the voice of God's angel instead (*Confessions* 8.12.29).

BIBL.: A. Bouché-Leclercq, *Histoire de la divination dans l'antiquité* (4 vols.; Paris: Leroux, 1879–82). E. R. Dodds, *The Ancient Concept of Progress* (Oxford: Oxford University Press, 1973), 156–210. F. Graf, "Rolling the Dice for an Answer," in *Mantikē: Studies in Greek and Roman Divination* (ed. S. I. Johnston and P. T. Struck; Leiden: Brill, forthcoming). S. I. Johnston, "Charming Children: The Use of the Child in Ancient Divination," *Arethusa* 34.1 (2001): 97–117. R. Parker, "Greek States and Greek Oracles," in *Crux: Essays Presented to G. E. M. de Ste. Croix on His 75th Birthday* (ed. P. A. Cartledge and F. D. Harvey; History of Political Thought 6.1/2; Sidmouth, Devon, U.K.: Imprint Academic, 1985), 298–326.   S.I.J.

Etruria

Most of our written evidence for Etruscan divination comes from Roman literature, and its technical vocabulary is now usually rendered in Latin, for the Romans drew heavily on what they saw as the Etruscans' special skills in divination, and they regularly consulted Etruscan diviners (Latin *haruspices* [pl.], *haruspex* [sing.]). We cannot be certain how far this Roman perspective has distorted our picture of "native" Etruscan practices. Outside specifically Roman contexts, we rely heavily on evidence of visual images and material objects.

Divination belonged to the "science of the Etruscans" (*disciplina Etrusca*) and involved two principal divinatory techniques: the examination of the liver of sacrificial animals and the observation of lightning bolts. Our earliest clear evidence for Etruscan divination comes from a bronze mirror from Vulci (ca. 400 BCE) engraved with a winged Chalchas, the Etruscan version of the famous Greek seer Calchas, who is attentively studying a sheep's liver, held in his left hand. Another crucial archeological document is the famous bronze liver from Piacenza (dated ca. 100 BCE, when the Etruscan cities had been absorbed into the Roman world); it is a model of a liver, probably used as a template in the examination of the entrails of sacrificial animals. One side is inscribed in considerable detail: around the margin sixteen regions are marked out, each bearing the name of one or two gods; in the interior twenty-four further regions are designated with divine names; there is also a sharp extrusion—a *processus pyramidalis* or the "head" (*caput*) of the liver. The other side is convex and mentions only Usil (Sun) on the right and Tiv (Moon) on the left.

Liver consultation was important in critical situations for determining whether a planned action could be undertaken successfully. In divination that used the liver, it seems that the organ acted as a microcosm reflecting the wider divine macrocosm. It is no doubt significant that the sixteen regions on the margin of the bronze liver correspond to some degree with the regions of heaven described by Martianus Capella in his *On the Nuptials of Philosophy and Mercury* (5th century CE), which presumably reflects Etruscan cosmological traditions. For example, Jupiter (Etruscan Tin) "lived" in three regions of the north and Vedius (Etruscan Vetis), an underworld-god, "lived" in the northwest. We do not know exactly what methods were used to decode the liver. But according to Roman literary sources, the presence of the head was a good omen and its absence was negative. The ritual importance of the head may originate in Greece. About twenty Attic vases, dating from 530 to 490 BCE, show a nude boy holding a bull's liver while a soldier checks for the presence of the head. It is probable also that anatomical and pathological anomalies were taken to indicate a positive or negative sign given by a god. In his *On Divination* (esp. 1.118–19; 2.36–37), Cicero offers a variety of rationalizing speculation on how divination from entrails (including the liver) could work.

The interpretation of lightning included observation of its type, intensity, color, sound, and effect—or so the Roman author Seneca implies (*Natural Questions* 2.40–41). Seneca also refers (2.32) to the accounts given by Etruscans (presumably in the 1st century CE) to explain the principles of divination by lightning. They apparently accepted the explanation of lightning advanced by contemporary science, which saw it as a collision between clouds. But the Etruscan approach added a religious dimension: collisions of clouds were provoked by the gods in order to send mortals a sign.

Divination by lightning depended on correctly dividing the heavens into sections. The eastern part of the heavens was the *pars familiaris* (the part belonging to one's own people), and the western part was the *pars hostilis* (the part belonging to the enemy). When preparing to read the signs that were to appear in the heavens, the diviner turned toward the south. Signs that appeared in the northeast were considered very lucky; those in the southeast, lucky; those in the southwest, ominous; and those in the northwest, very ominous. This system was almost certainly linked to the orientation of Etruscan cities. Etruscan settlements that were founded at the end of the 6th century BCE show an orthogonal pattern of streets that are oriented exactly north-south and west-east. The principal street in Marzabotto, near Bologna, has the same southward orientation as the temples on the nearby hill and the recently discovered temple to Tin in the city itself. Observers standing in the temples faced south and could easily watch for lightning in the east and west. The religious character of the city layout is confirmed by stones with a cross-shaped incision located in subterranean holes at crossroads; it was into these holes that *haruspices* placed their surveying poles, which enabled them to divide the heavens into favorable and unfavorable realms. According to the *Corpus*

Etruscan model of sheep's liver for divination. Bronze, 2nd–1st century BCE. Museo Civico, Piacenza. *Scala/Art Resource, New York*

Agrimensorum Romanorum, surveying in general had its origin in the *ars haruspicina.*

Etruscans also practiced divination by lots *(sortes)* and observed portents; there also are some indications that they consulted the flight of birds, as well as had a tradition of inspired prophecy. The earliest chest of lots has been found in the sanctuary of Menerva of Veii, near Rome, and dates to the 6th century BCE. Other lots mention Suri, a divinity similar to the Greek god Apollo. A story in Livy (1.34.8–9) tells of an eagle picking up the hat from the head of a man named Lucumo and putting it back upon his head. His wife, Tanaquil, interpreted this as a sign that her husband would be Rome's first Etruscan king, Tarquinius Priscus—but this may reflect Roman, rather than Etruscan, traditions of the interpretation of signs. The Latin *gromatici veteres* (texts of the land surveyors) include fragments of the prophecy of a nymph, Vegoia.

Tomb paintings and lid figures of sarcophagi and urns suggest that (whatever we are to make of Tanaquil's interpretative skill) only male members of aristocratic families could be official diviners. It is also clear that the same individuals could practice both of the major types of divination. A bilingual inscription in Etruscan and Latin from Pesaro (Pallottino 1968: 697) commemorates a man named Cafates (Cafatius) who was a *netśvis* (a *haruspex*—in the sense of an interpreter of livers), a *trutnvt* (interpreter of portents), and a *frontac* (*fulgurator,* interpreter of lightning). There are reports of *haruspices* being summoned from Etruria to Rome from early in the Roman republic to advise the senate on prodigies, and, probably in the 2nd century BCE, the senate intervened to encourage recruitment and training of *haruspices.* A college *(ordo)* of sixty *haruspices* is first attested at the end of the republic or beginning of the empire (CIL 6.32439); the *ordo* was reorganized under the emperor Claudius (Tacitus, *Annals* 11.15), and *haruspices* were still active in the 5th century CE (Zosimus 5.41.1).

BIBL.: D. Briquel, *Chrétiens et haruspices: La religion étrusque, dernier rempart du paganisme romain* (Paris, 1997). B. MacBain, *Prodigy and Expiation: A Study in Religion and Politics in Republican Rome* (Brussels, 1982). A. Maggiani, "Qualche osservazione sul Fegato di Piacenza," *Studi etruschi* 50 (1982): 53–88. L. B. van der Meer, *The Bronze Liver of Piacenza* (Amsterdam, 1987). M. Pallottino, *Testimonia linguae etruscae* (2nd ed.; Florence, 1968). C. O. Thulin, *Die etruskische Disziplin* (3 vols.; Göteborg, 1905–9; repr. Darmstadt, 1968).   D.BR., L.B.V.D.M.

Rome

Divination systems purport to reveal what an inquirer cannot learn by more normal cognitive means. But they may themselves be diagnostic of the society that employs them: the anthropologist Victor Turner liked to say that after studying a people's social structure he could predict the key themes of their divination system; and conversely Jon P. Kirby, who was himself initiated into a method of cowrie divination in northern Ghana, thought he could read off from his signs the ideal social order of the Anufo. But the divination system of the two last centuries of the Roman republic (virtually nothing is known of the archaic period) offers few insights into the Roman social order: the private system is all but unknown to us, and the public system was essentially political. The plain message of the latter system, however, is that the otherworld was preoccupied with the legitimate ambitions of Roman magistrates and of the Roman people.

We tend to think of divination—reading tea leaves and tarot cards, palmistry, newspaper astrology columns—as directed toward the future. Traditional divination systems, however, are largely directed toward establishing past facts, often relating to the otherworld, in order to resolve present problems. That is certainly the case with republican Rome: prodigies relating to individual destinies are reported only in the regal period (traditionally 753–509 BCE) and then again of the generals in the crisis of the late republic (2nd and 1st centuries BCE), but mainly of emperors and would-be emperors during the principate. Why should lightning strike the tomb of Caesar's daughter if not to indicate Octavian's destiny (Suetonius, *Augustus* 95)? Why should a fallen cypress tree on Vespasian's estate sprout again (Tacitus, *Histories* 2.78.2)? Emperors and their subjects liked to squint at the imperial purple through a haze of predestination. But even these signs are never recognized in advance for what they are; only in retrospect do they foretell the future.

Divination systems are conventionally divided into intuitive and inductive forms, otherwise known as inspirational versus technical or natural versus artificial. In antiquity both Platonists and Stoics—and their opponents, the Cynics—were primarily interested in the first type. But the Roman public system relegated inspiration, even in the mild form of dreams, as far as it could to myth and the social margins. Although it later possessed a shrine in the grove of Vesta at the corner of the Palatine, for example, the prophetic voice named Aius Locutius is mentioned in history but once, when it warned of the Gallic invasion of 391 BCE. The only person to hear it was a plebeian named Marcus Caedicius, whom the magistrates duly ignored (Plutarch, *Life of Camillus* 14.2–4). Alternatively, inspiration could be routinized: though the Sibyls were reputed to be divinely inspired and the value of their oracles was confirmed by the famous story of their purchase by King Tarquin (Aulus Gellius 1.19.2), the few whose gist we know, tamed in the transition from inspired utterance to written document, concern merely the ritual expiation of prodigies.

The Roman inductive system had three main aspects: (1) the taking of the *auspicia impetrativa* (signs "requested from" the gods), which in the high republic meant observing whether, and how, the divinatory chickens pecked at their food *(ex tripudiis)*; (2) extispicy, a considered judgment by a *haruspex* (seer) of the state of the inner organs of a sacrificial animal; and (3) the observation and interpretation of *prodigia*, events classified as unusual or extraordinary. Negative signs warned of calamity in the event of their being ignored; the primary effect of divinatory practice was to free magistrates in a specific context, the conduct of an election, say, or setting out with the army, from the consequences of committing a ritual fault. Although our sources, most obviously the records of prodigies, concentrate on cases of divine displeasure, on the rupturing of the *pax deorum* (the proper relations between gods and mortals), the

system was in fact very effective, achieving the highest level of routinization compatible with the premise of extreme divine irritability. And, by limiting responses strictly to the level of ritual action, the system both imputed to the otherworld a thoroughgoing rationality and sustained an implicitly optimistic worldview, which confirmed the settled opinion of the Roman elite, that they deserved every success they enjoyed.

Unless a divinatory system is managed by a full-time priestly caste, it needs to compromise between the competing ideals of amplitude and ease of use. Too much routine induces skepticism; complexity causes confusion. The Roman system answered this problem by employing several methods (subsystems) but strictly limiting interpretation of the information they provided. But it also acknowledged the value of writing in accumulating and fixing standardized meanings. At some point in the late archaic period, one aspect of the elaborate Etruscan system was introduced to Rome, a simplified procedure of extispicy applied in all contexts involving public sacrifice. The significances of the signs occurring in the internal organs were written down. This subsystem, which must have been accepted by the senate on the promise of its exoticism (Etruscan divination was highly regarded), probably encouraged the corresponding reduction of the system of auspices, which nominally contained five branches, to the observation of the behavior of the sacred chickens. Both subsystems thus limited themselves to an extremely narrow observational frame. And in both cases the answer, permissive or the reverse, was valid for just one day—indeed sacrifices might be repeated indefinitely on a single occasion until a permissive answer was obtained.

The third subsystem, however, divination by prodigies, acknowledged a much wider range of signs, many of which could be sighted by anyone, even outside Rome—lightning, eclipses, comets and meteors, monstrous births human and animal, wild animals entering Rome, unchaste Vestals, all of them infringements of categorial or sacred boundaries—and applied to the state as a whole. Constraints upon the recognition of such signs were correspondingly sharp: if they occurred, say, on private land or on nonmunicipal Italic soil, they might be refused; witnesses from the lower orders were not entitled to utter a word when their prodigy was reported to the senate; although that body often referred the signs to one of the priestly colleges, the *decemviri/ quindecim*, who might in serious cases consult the Sibylline Books (see Sacred Texts and Canonicity) or, from the 2nd century BCE, the major Etruscan *haruspices*, the senate always took the final decision concerning the response. (These *haruspices*, who eventually formed a quasicollege of sixty enrolled in the Equestrian Order, are to be distinguished from other Roman diviners who went under the same Latin name, the magistrates' entrails-gazers or even unofficial "street-corner" fortune tellers.) Except in times of emergency, however, prodigies, too, were a mainly routine matter: they were totted up over the year and then expiated *en bloc,* generally by removing the animal/object, closing it off, or reconfirming the ruptured boundaries.

Yet a fourth public system, the augural law, was believed to have been instituted by Romulus. The priests known as augurs were considered Jupiter's interpreters (Cicero, *On the Laws* 2.20–21). Their discipline covered the procedures of inauguration and the delimitation of a field of vision, or *templum,* for observing signs as well as the system of rules under which individual *augures*—almost all of them prominent members of the aristocracy—were entitled to observe signs (*auspicia oblativa,* signs offered by—rather than requested from—the god); these included, especially, lightning, thunder, and the flight of ominous birds, all of which might indicate divine displeasure. It was the augurs' right of intervention *(obnuntiatio)* in the conduct of magisterial business that made the augurate a key priesthood in the political conflicts of the late republic. The augural college, on the other hand, also replied to inquiries by the senate concerning possible cases of *vitium* (ritual fault) arising within the subsystems of divination. A considerable body of casuistry was thus created, which was the topic of books by several prominent *augures* in the later republic.

The most interesting ancient text concerning divination, both Greek and Roman, is Cicero's *On Divination,* written in 44 BCE. It presents an articulate, well-informed debate between Cicero and his brother Quintus on the merits of belief in divination. In the first book Quintus resumes the Stoic arguments, mostly formulated by Chrysippus in the second half of the 3rd century BCE, in favor of belief in the system; in the second, Cicero mainly picks up the Cynic and Academic arguments against. There is no resolution: the book belongs to the Academic genre *ex utraque parte,* giving both sides of an issue. That said, the equivocation of Cicero's text reflects a quite general ambivalence, though hardly ever amounting to thoroughgoing disbelief, about divination. An apocryphal story has Gaius Flaminius, disastrously defeated by Hannibal at Lake Trasimene in 217 BCE, discuss the *ex tripudiis* procedure with the chicken keeper *(pullarius),* who has just advised him not to join battle: "And if the chickens do not even eat later on, what do you advise?" The *pullarius* says that in that case Flaminius should stay put. "A wonderful sort of divination," replies the consul, "that allows one to act if chickens eat, but not if they do not" (Cicero, *On Divination* 1.77; see also 2.71–74). The story has it both ways: it links Flaminius's defeat to his disrespect of divination but registers a disquiet about the method. Even in the elder Cato's day (late 3rd/early 2nd century BCE), purists complained that the system was often flouted or ignored (Cicero, *On Divination* 1.28; *On the Nature of*

the Gods 2.9); but who could say whether such laxity truly affected the *pax deorum?* At any rate, since public divination was central to the senate's control of the religious system, it was convenient for members of the elite to confine themselves to mocking the inadequacies of popular divination (Cicero, *On Divination* 1.132).

Although auspices were at one time also taken in family contexts, for example, at marriage (Valerius Maximus 2.1.1), our sources ignore private divination almost completely. In turn, the great majority of the population ignored the public system. We hear of the deities Silvanus, Faunus/Fatuus, and perhaps Carmentis offering predictions, to say nothing of the lot oracle of Fortuna at Praeneste or of that other kind of *haruspices, (h)arioli,* and various types of wise men and women, who provided answers to everyday anxieties, about marriage and children, harvests and journeys, health and sickness, dangers from malign spirits and were-owls *(striges).* Their methods often imitated those of public systems; many were probably adapted from those practiced in the areas of Greek colonization: for example, we hear of women consulting the livers of geese and "reading" the fall of knucklebones or the bobbing of hazelnuts in a beaker of water. From the 2nd century BCE, catarchic astrology, introduced by Manilius of Antioch (Pliny, *Natural History* 35.199), provided a powerful new book-based method of divination, whose disadvantages were rapidly realized by the senate—astrologers were expelled from Rome for the first time already in 139 BCE (Valerius Maximus 1.3.3).

With the passing of the republic, its system of public divination gradually reinvented itself as "tradition." Augustus may have transferred the Sibylline Books to the temple of Apollo near his Palatine house and insisted that the auspices were his alone; but once emperors began to be singled out by providential signs and to keep their own staff astrologers, the neuralgic points were the prophecies and portents bombinating around candidates for the purple and the forebodings of the stars. Emperors became simultaneously the beneficiaries and the victims of these types of knowledge practices: seeking astrological information about them became a capital offense early in the reign of Tiberius. The otherworld became, as it were, preoccupied with emperors (see Controlling Religion). Over the long haul, then, Roman divination is perhaps in a sense diagnostic of Roman politics and culture after all.

BIBL.: Mary Beard, "Cicero and Divination," *Journal of Roman Studies* 76 (1986): 33–46. Marie-Theres Fögen, *Die Enteignung der Wahrsager: Studien zum kaiserlichen Wissensmonopol in der Spätantike* (Frankfurt am Main, 1993). Bruce MacBain, *Prodigy and Expiation: A Study of Religion and Politics in Republican Rome* (Collection Latomus 177; Brussels, 1982). John North, "Diviners and Divination at Rome," in *Pagan Priests: Religion and Power in the Ancient World* (ed. Mary Beard and John North; London,

1990), 49–71. D. S. Potter, *Prophets and Emperors* (Cambridge, Mass., 1994). Veit Rosenberger, *Gezähmte Götter: Das Prodigienwesen der römischen Republik* (Stuttgart, 1998). John Scheid, *An Introduction to Roman Religion* (trans. Janet Lloyd; Edinburgh, 2003 [orig. 1998]).   R.L.G.

Christianity

"Divination" is a general term for a broad spectrum of revelatory phenomena practiced throughout the ancient Mediterranean world. The term is also used more restrictively for the art or science of interpreting symbols understood as messages from the gods, while "prophecy" (from the Greek word *propheteia*) can be used, as it will be here, to refer to the reception of communications in human language from the gods mediated by divinely inspired individuals.

Although rabbinic sources no earlier than the end of the 2nd century CE insist that the spirit of prophecy was absent from Israel following Haggai, Zechariah, and Malachi, the last of the canonical Old Testament prophets, this is primarily a theological justification for the authority of rabbinic Judaism. There is in fact evidence that various forms of prophecy were still practiced throughout the Second Temple period, although often in socially deviant contexts. The movements surrounding John the Baptist and Jesus of Nazareth are part of the emphases on reform and revitalization characteristic of the late Second Temple period. John the Baptist, popularly honored as a prophet (Mark 11.32; Matt. 14.5; Luke 20.6), reportedly rebuked Herod Antipas for immorality (Mark 6.17–18) in a manner reminiscent of Old Testament prophets. The gospel tradition also preserves short prophecy-like denunciations attributed to John, one in the Q tradition (Luke 3.7–8; Matt. 3.7–10) and the other in both Mark and Q (Mark 1.7–8; Matt. 3.11–12; Luke 3.16–17). Jesus of Nazareth, who began as a disciple of John, claimed prophetic status only indirectly (Mark 6.4–5; Luke 13.28) and like John was considered a prophet by his contemporaries (Mark 6.15; Matt. 21.11; Luke 7.16; 24.19; John 4.19; 9.17). Unlike Jesus, John was not remembered as a miracle worker, but the miraculous signs performed by Jesus coupled with his powerful, authoritative, and memorable words gave him the reputation of "a prophet mighty in deed and word" (Luke 24.19), modeled on the miracle-working prophets of the Old Testament, Elijah and Elisha (1 Kings 17; 2 Kings 4).

The author of Luke-Acts (written ca. 90 CE), a quasi-historical narrative covering the period from the ascension of Jesus to the imprisonment of Paul in Rome (ca. 30–54 CE), provided an idealistic portrayal of early Christianity as a movement characterized by various forms of prophetic and divinatory phenomena. To determine the will of God in the choice of a successor for the reprobate Judas Iscariot, for example, lots were cast selecting Matthias over Joseph Barsabbas (Acts 1.26).

Shortly thereafter, more than one hundred assembled followers of Jesus are described as being "filled with the Holy Spirit" and as speaking in other languages on the day of Pentecost (2.1–13). The phenomenon of glossolalia ("speaking in tongues") is a type of revelatory speech in which inspired individuals often believe that they possess the ability to speak foreign languages that they have never learned (the view of 2.1–13). In fact, glossolalia is not a comprehensible language, but is the product of an altered state of consciousness. Mention of the presence and activity of Christian prophets punctuates the narrative of Acts (11.27; 13.1–3; 15.32; 21.10), where the source of divine inspiration is identified as the Holy Spirit, a designation for the active presence in the world of the God of Israel. The author also includes numerous dreams and visions in the narrative, which underscore that virtually all developments in early Christianity are in accord with the will of God (16.9–10; 18.9–11; 20.22–23; 21.4, 10–11; 22.17–22; 23.1; 27.23).

Of the divinatory and prophetic phenomena described idealistically in Acts, prophecy and glossolalia are given historical attestation as typical phenomena during the mid-1st century CE in early Christianity in the letters of Paul, written in about 49–57 CE. In 1 Thessalonians, Paul's earliest letter (ca. 49 CE), he admonishes the local Christians not to despise prophesying but to test everything (5.20), suggesting that prophetic utterances were the subject of some controversy and were thought to require regulation. Prophecy and glossolalia are thematized in 1 Cor. 12–14 (written ca. 56 CE), a passage that provides much of our knowledge of the practice of revelatory phenomena in early Christianity during the 1st century. Here, Paul is particularly concerned with regulating the behavior of prophets and speakers-in-tongues. The Corinthian prophets constituted a group whose contribution to communal worship consisted of making and critiquing prophetic pronouncements (14.29–33), although professional prophets did not exclusively monopolize prophesying (14.31). Paul was also concerned with regulating the practice of glossolalia among the Corinthian Christians by insisting that those speaking in tongues take turns and by demanding that what they said be interpreted, since it was otherwise incomprehensible (14.13–28).

The Apocalypse of John, the only extant 1st-century Christian prophetic work, combined prophetic with apocalyptic traditions. The author does not explicitly designate himself a prophet, but does relate two experiences that closely resemble Old Testament prophetic call narratives (Rev. 1.9–20; 10.8–11), and he describes what he was commanded to write as "prophecy" (1.3) and as a "prophetic book" (22.7, 10, 18–19). The author appears to have been the leader of a circle of itinerant Christian prophets active in Roman Asia (22.6–9). He roundly condemns "Jezebel," a female prophetess and her followers active in Thyatira, for justifying idolatrous and immoral practices (2.19–29). The Apocalypse itself is an extensive vision narrative with a heavenly ascent, which combines prophetic exhortations, admonitions, and threats directed to Christians (Rev. 2–3, 22) with apocalyptic visions of the divinely inflicted punishments that all unbelievers will experience.

During the 2nd century, only scattered evidence for Christian prophecy survives. The *Didache,* a pseudepigraphic church order compiled in rural Syria (late 1st or early 2nd century CE) reports the existence of itinerant prophets and ways for determining whether they are true or false (Did. 11–13). The *Shepherd of Hermas* (compiled in Rome, ca. 90–150) condemns prophets who practice privately and accept money, comparing them unfavorably with their pagan counterparts (Shepherd, *Mandate* 11). During the second half of the 2nd century, a prophetic revitalization movement called Montanism arose, inspired by the Apocalypse of John. Led by the prophet Montanus and two female prophetesses, Montanism was a rigorist and ascetic response to the perception of moral laxity in Christianity of the period. Thereafter, prophecy was generally repressed throughout the Christian world, appearing only sporadically in socially and theologically deviant contexts.

The apologetic argument from prophecy continued throughout the patristic period. In the 2nd century, Justin Martyr's *Dialogue with Trypho* creates a fictive argument with a Jewish interlocutor defending the Christian interpretation of biblical prophecy as a prediction of Christ. The tradition continues through Augustine in the 5th century, whose *City of God* 17 offers an elaborate catalogue of biblical prophecy fulfilled in Christ. Augustine at the same time refutes notions of fate (5) and criticizes reliance on "demons" as a source of divination (8.16–17).

BIBL.: David E. Aune, *Prophecy in Early Christianity and the Ancient Mediterranean World* (Grand Rapids, 1983). Ronald E. Heine, *The Montanist Oracles and Testimonia* (Macon, Ga., 1989). Jannes Reiling, *Hermas and Christian Prophecy: A Study of the Eleventh Mandate* (Leiden, 1973).   D.E.A.

Deities and Demons

Introduction

The ancient world was full of gods. Wherever lists were made—which was regularly done by the priests of Egypt, Rome, and Anatolia—this becomes evident: they count by the hundreds, if not by the thousands. To the Greeks, however, who are no less polytheistic than their neighbors, the number twelve seemed sufficient to designate the shifting group of principal gods, whereas Zoroastrian Persia (another peculiar case, in this respect) succeeded in subjecting their multitude to the rigorous principle of an ethical and cosmic dualism. In Mesopotamia, and presumably elsewhere as well, religion evolved in step with forms of authority. The more complex and hierarchical that society became, the more the ME (rules of tradition) yielded to the decisions of the sovereign. In the course of this movement, the concept of a divine creator at the top of the pantheon emerged, without ever leading, however, to the question of a *creatio ex nihilo*. The ancient Hebrews sometimes entertained the notion of a supreme god who divided the descendants of Adam into as many nations as Adam had sons and reserved Israel for himself. This is a sort of "mono-polytheism": each nation has its own gods, and the entire world is structured in a patriarchal way, like one large family with the god of Israel as its patriarch. In other passages of the Hebrew Bible, angels and demons work for YHWH; even Satan is a member of the heavenly court. One has to wait much longer for an explicit monotheism to emerge in Judea, in the 6th century BCE. And even after that, relapses into a form of polytheism (especially with regard to angels and demons) surface from time to time in Jewish and even more in Christian traditions.

How does one handle a plurality of gods? How does one classify and organize them into pantheons? Each culture invented its own method. Scribal classifications range from a list of functions (Rome) or one following geographical distribution (Egypt) to the thematic classification of ancient Anatolia. One of the easiest methods is the arrangement in divine families, along a genealogical tree forming the topic of major narrations that earned fame as literary creations—the theogonies of Egypt, Mesopotamia, the Hittite-Hurrites, and the Greeks. But often enough, these literary creations kept their distance from local cultic realities. Etruscans, and after them Romans, had no divine families until after they had come under Greek influence.

The function of traditional narrations about the gods, whatever their principle of organization—etiological, genealogical, historical—cannot be separated from the function of rituals. Whatever persuasive force mythological narratives exerted, it only paralleled and supplemented the steady and efficacious pressure of the rituals that were the foundations of human social life.

This leads to the question of what ancient civilizations thought their gods were and how they represented them. Here again, the possibilities are numerous. Cosmic elements (sun, moon, sky, sea, rivers), luminous or radiant entities, visible or invisible ones, humans made into gods, personifications of abstract concepts and values—there are many forms to choose from, from pure and simple aniconic representations to fully anthropomorphic shapes, with many combinations in between, including animal forms or symbols. A god can be several of these things at once: Greek Zeus is a bearded king whose palace is on Mount Olympus, but he is also the rain that fertilizes earth, the bull that abducts Europa, or the lightning that kills Semele. Persian Mithra is at the same time a warrior on his chariot and the personification of the contract between humans.

One of the fundamentals of the history of ancient religions is what we could define as "the gradual increase of the field of alterity." We can discern some major steps in this development, not the least the Greek discovery of Near Eastern polytheism, which initiated a comparativist interpretation. The Greeks decided to translate the names of foreign gods into Greek, using the names of their own gods. But although they noticed resemblances between the cults of the others and those they practiced themselves, they clearly distinguished between foreign and Greek cults. We call this mechanism of translation *interpretatio*, a word introduced by Tacitus (*Germania* 43.4); we thus speak of *interpretatio Graeca* or *interpretatio Romana* when we mean the way that the Greeks or Romans used their own divine names to designate the gods of the Persians, Egyptians, or Celts.

The most famous example on the Roman side is Caesar's chapter in his *Gallic Wars* (6.17) about the gods of the Celts, whom he designates simply by Latin names: "At the head of the gods, they put Mercury. His images are the most numerous, they consider him inventor of all the crafts, the protector of roads and of travels, the master of gain and commerce. Then Apollo, Mars, Jupiter, and Minerva. They attribute the same fields of action to them as do other peoples: Apollo drives out disease, Minerva teaches the crafts and arts, Jupiter reigns in the sky, Mars presides over wars."

This capacity to appropriate alterity is fundamental for Greek and Roman culture. It assumes the existence of one universal religious language. This assumption is not shared by all the cultures presented in this volume—one might think of the Hittites, who opposed altogether any form of syncretism or assimilation and simply accepted foreign gods as they were.

In a monotheistic framework, acceptance of one religion equals rejection of all the others. Christianity in particular, as taught by the early church fathers, is a doctrine that fights all others, that opposes its truth to that of the Hellenes (Greek and Roman paganism), the Jews, the gnostics, the Manicheans, or, of course, the heretics.

In this view, it is interesting to see how the imageless monotheism of the Jews was able to appear to pagan polytheists either as an admirable way to respect the divine's otherness—as shown by religious thinkers of the epochs of Caesar and Augustus, especially Varro and the geographer Strabo—or as the ultimate rejection of all the gods and thus as a form of atheism and isolationism. This explains why the Greek discourse on monotheism so often appears as a "Judeophobic" retelling of the story of the Mosaic exodus, most notably shortly after the destruction of the temple by Titus, in the extreme version of Tacitus's *Histories* (5.2–5).   PH.B.

Egypt

If one wants to provide a brief overview of Egyptian divinities, including demons and the multitude of personifications, it is a good idea not to get bogged down in details. The sheer number of such beings can make it difficult even for specialists to see the big picture. Besides the fifty to one hundred known divinities that would occur to every Egyptologist after a moment's

Isis kneeling, from the sarcophagus of Amenophis II in the Valley of the Kings near Thebes. *Hirmer Fotoarchiv*

thought, there are thousands upon thousands of further entities one could call minor gods to avoid placing them in the same category as "demons." A precedent for using the terms *major gods* and *minor gods* is provided by a stele of Rameses IV (ca. 1152–1145 BCE) from Abydos. Furthermore, no opposition between gods as greater and demons as lesser divine beings existed in ancient Egyptian terminology. And finally, the creatures that today one might readily characterize as demons, such as many inhabitants of the Egyptian underworld—as depicted in the Book of Caverns, for instance—are rarely referred to as gods in Egyptian texts.

Despite these difficulties, scholars have of course tried to determine what conditions must be fulfilled in order to speak of an ancient Egyptian supernatural being as a god. One definition that has found wide acceptance was proposed by Jan Assmann, who suggested that for the term to be properly applied three conditions must be fulfilled: the divinity must be associated with a cult or topographical site and must possess both a cosmic and a mythic dimension. In the case of Osiris, for example, who clearly qualifies, long litanies (e.g., Book of the Dead, utterances 141–42) list the places where he was worshiped; a large temple to him remains preserved in Abydos, and countless inscriptions have survived in which individuals directed prayers to Osiris. The cosmic dimension is addressed when Osiris is conceived as

Isis suckling her son Horus, 1st millennium BCE. Louvre. *Foto Marburg/Art Resource, New York*

by his younger brother Seth, who dismembered the body and distributed the parts throughout the country. However, Seth was unable to prevent their collection, reassembly, and embalming, which made it possible for the dead Osiris to sire a legitimate heir, Horus, with Isis. Horus grew up amid all kinds of perils, but finally defeated Seth and ascended the throne.

The Egyptians developed several ordering principles for the world of their divinities. The simplest principle involved linking three gods together as a triad. As a rule, the triad consisted of father, mother, and son, so that Amun, the god of Karnak, was venerated with his wife Mut and her son, the moon-god Khonsu. This becomes particularly clear at the Theban temples of the New Kingdom, which contained three shrines: one at the center for the barque of Amun, one to the right for the barque of Mut, and one to the left for the barque of Khonsu. The next, more complex principle consisted of associating many gods in enneads, or groups of nine (in which the number nine stood for the idea of "many" rather than the actual number of divinities in each group). The best-known and most important such group is the ennead of Heliopolis, which has a clear genealogical structure spanning four generations. At the top is Atum, the sun-god of Heliopolis, who created his progeny Shu, god of the air, and Shu's wife Tefnut out of himself. The third generation consists of Geb, god of the earth, and Nut, goddess of the sky. Together with the fourth generation—Osiris, Seth, Isis, and Nephthys—they make up a group that does in fact consist of nine members. Most of the known enneads comprise divinities venerated at a particular site; in many cases it is not possible to determine exactly how many members each group had or to identify them by name.

The recent publication of a papyrus from Tebtunis, dating from the Roman era, has revealed a quite different system, in which each of the great gods has a title corresponding to an official in the Egyptian palace administration. At the apex is Re-Harakhte as king, followed by Shu as crown prince and Thoth as vizier. Anubis, represented in the form of a jackal, is in charge of cattle—a role known from other texts. The role of Seth as head of the physicians of upper Egypt, on the other hand, is entirely unexpected. This identification of gods with government officials is only part of a larger system. In principle, Egyptian divinities could be associated with any class of animate or (from today's perspective) inanimate entities; there are documented cases of identification with snakes and other animals, stars, and minerals.

The lesser gods number literally in the thousands. A good example is Coffin Text 627 from the Middle Kingdom, inscribed on two coffins from Siut and el-Bersheh, which mention the companions of the lord of all things, to be understood as a group of eighty-one gods. Only the coffin from el-Bersheh lists the names of all eighty-one, and while almost none of these beings appear any-

floodwaters or as the corpse of the sun-god. The best-known example of the last dimension is the Osiris myth that has come down to us in complete form only in Plutarch, although single references or episodes play a central role in a large number of Egyptian texts. Briefly, the story involves the murder of the legitimate ruler Osiris

where else in surviving Egyptian texts, both their determinatives and phonetic representations indicate that they must unquestionably be identified as gods. There is little evidence of any topographical association or cosmic and mythical dimension—the three marks of divine status—and yet they are gods all the same, who must have had a certain importance four thousand years ago, although perhaps only locally and for a brief period. The reasons behind the order in which they are listed are completely unknown, as is the case for many other lists; scholars are at a loss to interpret them—understandably, given the sparseness of surviving artifacts. Nevertheless these little-known deities seem to have been important to Egyptians, for otherwise they would not have recorded their names (and often their appearance) in so many texts.

The lesser gods appear in the greatest numbers in the Books of the Underworld that decorated the royal tombs of the New Kingdom. These great compositions—such as the Amduat, the Book of Gates, and the Book of Caverns—describe the night journey of the sun-god through the underworld and provide a detailed description in words and pictures of all the creatures whom he encounters during the twelve hours of darkness. The Amduat alone, the oldest work (first documented under Thutmose I, ca. 1504–1492 BCE, but presumably created during the Middle Kingdom), lists 908 divinities; in all the Books of the Underworld combined, some 2,500 deities occur. A further group of sources, still largely unresearched, consists of funerary artifacts, both the wooden coffins of the Third Intermediate Period and, perhaps even more important, the later stone sarcophagi. The latter display long rows of gods with animal heads, most of them holding a long knife in each hand, on their outer sides, where they function as guardians. Each of these gods has a name, and the extensive accompanying texts assign each one a precise function in protecting the sarcophagus.

The power of these beings was summoned solely as a defense against robbers, who might later come to desecrate the tomb and rob the deceased. The same function was served by whole armies of protective deities who watch over the outer walls and entrances of the great temples of the late period. At the temple of Horus in Edfu, for instance, four companies of guardian deities (falcons, lions, snakes, and bulls), each with its own commander, are positioned to defend the temple against potential attackers from any direction. At Dendara another such group, consisting of seventy-seven members, guards both the entrance to a chamber of Sokar inside the temple and a shrine of Osiris on the roof. The gods in this last group are also depicted on several coffins. A final example for this class of divinities is the waterspouts in the form of lions on the outer walls of the great temples of the late period, whose power was meant to ward off all attacks from the air.

The Egyptians' preference for representing the order of their world in lists indicates a connection between certain divinities and specific divisions of time. This system extends from gods associated with individual hours of the day or night to monumental lists showing that each day of the year possessed its own god. Most of these catalogues of "chronocrats," or gods of a single day, come from the temples of the Greco-Roman period, but the tradition extends back at least to the New Kingdom. Amunhotep III (1388–1351/1350 BCE) had 365 large granite statues of Sachmet erected in the temple of Mut in Karnak: a comparison with the late lists shows that each was associated with a calendar day. The Egyptians of the late period also filled the remaining gaps by naming protective divinities for the twelve months and the thirty days of the lunar month. While these gods were considered to be helpers or benefactors as a rule, there were many others whose activities were viewed as menacing. Some of them were demons of disease, to whom Egyptians attributed a considerable number of illnesses. The most notable example is the annual pestilence that occurred when the Nile floods subsided, which may have been bubonic plague. It was thought to be spread by the so-called knife demons and wandering demons sent out by Sachmet, the goddess of disease.

Other beings universally feared were the dead—not the blessed dead who had received proper burial, but the unburied, who could haunt the living and inflict many kinds of harm. According to a mythological calendar dating from the New Kingdom, great heat would cause the ground to crack on a day with particularly negative associations, allowing the evil spirits to rise through the fissures. But they could also enter a person in dreams or through bodily orifices and release their poison; amulets, spells, and other magical practices were among the means used to protect against such spirits.

An entirely different group of gods widely venerated at certain times consisted of deified human beings. Both the living and the deceased could be deified, although the former practice was restricted to kings. The best-known examples are the deification of Sesostris III (1836–1818 BCE) in Nubia and of Rameses II (1279–1213 BCE), whose veneration was clearly more prevalent in Nubia than in Egypt. Nonroyal persons were always deified only after their death. The most important among them was Imhotep, who built the Step Pyramid for King Djoser in the 3rd Dynasty (27th century BCE). In the late period Imhotep was considered a god of healing, and shrines were built for him in various places around Egypt, such as Memphis, Philae, and Deir el-Bahri.

Personifications were another widespread phenomenon in ancient Egypt. These were objects or areas that were represented and addressed as persons, and it was also thought that they could initiate action. Egyptian personifications can be categorized according to their significance in cult rites and the magnitude of personality attributed to them or sorted thematically according to the objects and areas for which they stand. One instance of an important personification for the entire period of ancient Egyptian history is Maat, the goddess of order in the world and in life; Hapi, god of floodwaters, is another.

The variety of themes is striking. Numerous objects and abstractions connected in the broadest sense to human nourishment could be personified, and so two beer jugs became Menquet and Tenemit, goddesses of beer who were responsible for brewing. They were often depicted in processions of people bearing offerings in the Greco-Roman period. They were accompanied in these processions by other personifications such as Neper, the god of grain, Aqyt (bread), and Hab (fishing and bird catching), to name a few. From this type of personification, it was only a small step to personifying the geographical areas that supplied different kinds of food; thus we find various denominations for fields, canals, and rivers personified in the same processions.

There are also depictions of geographical processions, which in terms of iconography and location (in the lowest register in the temples) are hardly distinguishable from the processions of gift bearers. They include long rows of personifications of the regions of Egypt, frequently divided into four main groups; they are shown in geographical order from south to north, offering products typical of their region to the temple or the main god of the temple. Furthermore, individual toponyms could themselves become objects of veneration; examples include the two personifications of the region on the western bank of the Nile at Thebes: Meresger (She Who Loves Silence) and Cheftethernebes (She Who Faces Her Lord) (a reference to Karnak). An example from a later date is the personification of the Temple of Isis in Dendara, who is shown being honored by the king, just like Hathor or Isis, in a ritual scene on the outer wall of both the *pronaos* and *naos* of the temple of Hathor there.

Still other personifications are derived from the area of religion or the royal palace, as when two whips or the king's beard are portrayed as divine beings. A last important group consists of personifications of abstract concepts, such as the goddess Maat. Other important divinities in this category are Hu, the god of divine utterance, Sia, god of knowledge, and Heka, god of magic, who was venerated as a child-god in the Greco-Roman era at the temple in Esna.   CHR.L.

Mesopotamia

Deities, demons, and personified concepts cannot be assessed without reference to the symbolic and social wholes in which they function. The theoretical perspective can be outlined as follows: religion projects an image of purpose on whatever is beyond human control; the cosmos is the imaginary complement of boundless reality, which it models and explains; gods identify is-

lands of intent, permanent cosmic consciences shaped after their mortal designers and therefore reassuringly communicative; ritual gives form to shared beliefs and commits the individual to the group; myth specifies the essentially ambiguous ritual order and thus may adapt traditional forms to a changing environment. Mesopotamian religion, deities and demons included, is not a monolithic whole, but a social tool changing in step with an increasingly more complex and hierarchical society. From prehistory to the end of the cuneiform tradition, six stages of development can be discerned, defined basically according to the religious justification of power relations and rulership, the variable factor:

1. Prehistoric stage (ca. 4500–3500 BCE). Society is organized into small agricultural villages with little internal or regional stratification; day-to-day behavior is regulated by "rules of tradition" (ME); decision making is structured by the family, focused on an ancestor cult. The myth of the marriage of (father) Heaven (An) and (mother) Earth (Ki) may belong to this early period and affords a mechanism for human and nonhuman fertility; a pantheon of deified cosmic elements (Moon, Sun, Venus) can be assumed, while certain animals were viewed as manifestations of the divine. The cosmos was thought to be regulated by the same type of traditional rules (ME) as society; occasional mishap was imputed to the *azag* demon (infringement of a taboo); and compromised purity was restored by magical means (ablution with holy water).

2. Eridu stage (ca. 3500–2500 BCE). The villages grow into cities, and leadership is no longer based solely on family relations. The gods of nature expand their power to become city gods, anthropomorphic heads of state holding court with spouses and servants in the city's main temple: Inanna (Lady of Heaven) (Venus) in Uruk, UTU (Sun) in Larsa, Nanna (Heavenly Lord) (Moon) in Ur, Enlil (Lord Ether) in Nippur, Ninhursag (Lady of the Wooded Hills) (Mother-goddess) in Kish, to mention the most important. Enki (Lord of the Earth), the god of water and white magic, is seated in Eridu, which has become a "national" religious center, the touchstone of correct behavior (ME), and probably the authority behind the complementary assignment of gods to cities. The actual human ruler derives his right to rule from his relation to the city god: in Uruk he is "married" to Inanna, and as her husband he supervises her dominions, the city, and its inhabitants; elsewhere the ruler is the deity's son or chief tenant *(ensig)*.

3. Nippur stage (ca. 2500–1500 BCE). The religious and political regimen developed in the south (Sumer) allows only city-states, while in the tribal north (Akkad) an inheritable regional kingship prevails with wider aspirations. Halfway through the 3rd millennium a northern king, Emenbaragesi of Kish, gives Nippur a privileged national position by calling his new Enlil temple there Urunanam (It Is Indeed the City), and by the Akkad period (2334–2154 BCE) Nippur is correspond-

Cylinder seal of the Akkadian period portraying gods fighting among themselves. *Metropolitan Museum of Art, Anonymous Loan, 1992. (L.1992.23.4)*

ingly the seat of the divine council, a cosmic capital from where Enlil appoints one of the city gods, who in his turn appoints a king to rule the nation (dynasties of Akkad, Ur, Isin, Larsa, and Babylon). Concomitantly a new concept of cosmic order takes shape, in which the unchangeable "rules of tradition" can be overruled by the "decisions" (NAMTAR) of Enlil, a reconfiguration of cosmic power that reflects the growing ambitions of the national king. During this period the original Sumerian names of the gods are replaced by their Akkadian counterparts: Inanna by Ishtar, UTU by Shamash, Nanna by Suen (later Sin), Ninhursag by Mami, Enki by Ea. Gods (such as Enlil) without counterparts in the Akkadian pantheon retain their ancient names.

4. Babylonian stage (ca. 1500–1000 BCE). During its First Dynasty, Babylon becomes the uncontested capital of the nation. The prevailing political situation has its theological foundation in a reworked creation myth, the *Enuma Elish,* which makes Babylon's city god Marduk independent of the decisions of Enlil and uncontested ruler of the universe. The remoteness and inscrutability of divine rule leave a spiritual vacuum in which alternative forms of religion give humanity guidance; magic and divination are on the rise, and their practitioners are the sages who compose the wisdom literature.

5. Asshur stage and second Babylonian stage (ca. 1000 BCE). Like the Assyrian and Babylonian kings, the head of the pantheon (Marduk = Assyrian Assur) claims universal power over humankind and nature, a virtual monotheism that is limited only by the pressure of tradition and the local cults of the ancient city gods. The official pantheon consists of a handful of deities, who in learned texts may be represented as aspects of the supreme deity.

The main trend in the development of the pantheon is a shift from many deified phenomena to a few divine rulers over the same phenomena and a concomitant shift in the way that divine power is manifested. The most primitive (and longest lasting) notion is that of an awe-inspiring sheen that radiates from a phenomenon

and reveals it as divine. Related concepts are those of the day on which the god reveals himself and, more anthropomorphically based, of his throne, his weapon, or his word; most of these can be personified and function as minor gods in the deity's court: viziers, messengers, executioners. Wise gods such as Ea and Marduk may use their knowledge of spells to operate the universe.

Our major sources of information about the pantheon are lists of gods, the earliest of which date to the second half of the 3rd millennium. Some of these are scholarly products, others are related to the cult (litanies or records of offerings). Most of the myths, hymns, and prayers are related to cult as well, but are hard to date or situate because of their literary transmission, which divorces them from any certain context. Royal inscriptions may cite any number of gods and have the advantage of being firmly dated, but have the disadvantage of being biased in favor of centralistic views. The impression of confusion that prevails in the sources is due mainly to their covering a long time scale, their haphazard updating, and an unknown degree of inexplicit reinterpretation.

Cosmic order. Explanation in Mesopotamia is not logical deduction from principles, but historical derivation from origins; cosmogony accordingly is the proper method to set out the divine order imposed on the universe. Besides the myth of the marriage of heaven and earth, Mesopotamia produced two subsequent cosmogonies, the second a thoroughly reworked version of the first.

In the earlier cosmogony the first principle is a primeval ocean, Namnam (Creatrix), the "mother who gave birth to [unseparated] Heaven-Earth." Inside Heaven-Earth a latent cosmos comes into being, the Enki and Ninki (Lords and Ladies Earth), who produce the (lord and lady) Dukug (Holy Mound), from which, subsequently, Enlil is born. By his very nature Enlil (Lord Ether) separates Heaven and Earth and establishes the known cosmos; at the same time, the frayed edge around the lowlands comes into being in the form of

Winged female with bird talons, perhaps the goddess Inanna, the underworld aspect of Ishtar, or perhaps the demoness Lilitu (Lilith). Babylonian, 1800–1750 BCE. British Museum.
The Art Archive/Eileen Tweedy

Enlil's sister and wife, the Lady of the Wooded Hills (Ninhursag). The only struggle that takes place is the one that establishes Enlil's rule *(namtar)* over the mechanical cosmos of the ME, represented by Enlil's ancestor Enmeshara (Lord of all ME).

The basic source for this mythological scheme is a (variable) list of "fathers and mothers of Enlil" that functioned in an ancestor rite for the gods in the month Dukug (Akkadian Tashritu [beginning]). A close variant is the Egyptian cosmogony with a primeval ocean (Nawnaw, Nun), a primeval mound *(beriben),* and a separation of Heaven and Earth by Air (Shu).

The later cosmogony is given form in a highly regarded mythological poem, *Enuma Elish.* The first element is a cosmic ocean containing female saltwater (Tiamat [Sea]), male sweetwater (Apsu), and a creative principle Kummu. After a series of generations the cosmic gods are born: Anu (Heaven), his son Ea, and his son Marduk. The older gods (i.e., the latent, sleeping universe) object to the noise (liveliness) of the younger gods and try to destroy them. Marduk, the champion of the younger gods, defeats Tiamat in a cosmic battle and is rewarded by his peers with everlasting cosmic rulership. He separates Heaven and Earth by splitting Tiamat's body, then installs the heavenly bodies and

fixes their functions. In accordance with the general trend, the cosmos in this view does not *come* into being by the birth of the gods that represent the phenomena, but is *brought* into being by the conscious act of a creator whose power extends over the phenomena.

After the cosmos is finished, the "dead" or "bound" gods of the latent protocosmos remain as divine but inactive elements of the contemporary world (Tiamat, saltwater; Apsu, sweetwater; and Enmeshara, Lord of all ME); this scheme is current also in Egypt and Anatolia. Remarkably, Mesopotamian cosmogony lacks an underworld of the dead. Ereshkigal (Queen of the Big Earth) and her son Ninazu (Lord Healer) belong to a group of chthonic gods concerned with growth and decay; the "big earth" that they rule is the ground underfoot, where dead bodies decompose. At least in one view, the souls of the dead travel through the desert to a cosmic river in the west, opposite of which lies their final destination, the Big City, ruled by Nergal (Lord of the Big City). In the 2nd millennium, Ereshkigal becomes Nergal's wife, while their domain was an underworld of the dead (this reformulation may be due to western influence).

Since the cosmogonies depend on sexual reproduction, the resulting cosmos is one big family, the relative importance of its parts being determined by family relationships. In practice, the political importance of a deity may interfere with his or her cosmological relevance, so that the actual genealogies are highly variable.

A human's spiritual being is a composite whole. Aspects of personality are represented by deified external souls, someone's aggressiveness by the male *udug,* his receptivity by the female *lamař; teš* (Akkadian *baštu* [shame]) denotes one's social presence. The same supernatural qualities are ascribed to buildings (temples) and even to the nation. The contribution of someone's DINGIR (Akkadian *ilu*) is essential, a divine life force that emanates as health, prosperity, and offspring and as such guarantees the continuity of the family. After death a part of the soul turns into a zombielike ghost. A family cult takes care of its demand for food, water, and being remembered.

In accordance with the general trend, the external souls, especially the *ilu,* develop into personal gods who monitor the moral conduct of their private subject and if necessary abandon him or her. Since without personal gods life is virtually impossible, the threat of abandonment keeps the individual on the track of righteous behavior and integrates him or her with the religious and political regimen. The central divine government operates in a similar way: it may emanate minor gods (angels) to implement its decisions and punish misconduct, or it may simply leave the nation to its fate. Humans have a choice, but they must suffer the consequences.

Not all suffering is the consequence of human misconduct and lawful divine retaliation. The protocosmos and the mountains, the periphery where divine rule is in doubt, produce the nameless evil *udug,* lawless bastard gods without cults, who may overrun the nation, in which they have no stake. The baby-killing demoness Lamashtu can be called their sister; she is thrown out of heaven because of her evil intentions. In the Iron Age (and in Jewish magic) the baby-killing demoness is confounded with Ardat Lili (or Lilitu), the Maiden of the Wind (later understood as She of the Night), a succubus who seduces mortal men; to become such a ghost is the fate of women who die before fulfilling their destiny of love and childbirth. The presumed wicked intentions of unidentified others are personified in the quasidemonic Evil Eye, Enemy, and Witch.

BIBL.: J. Bottéro, *Mesopotamia: Writing, Reasoning, and the Gods* (University of Chicago Press, 1992 [orig. 1987]). T. Jacobsen, *The Treasures of Darkness: A History of Mesopotamian Religion* (Yale University Press, 1976).   F.A.M.W.

Syria-Canaan

The deities of Syria-Canaan appear to have originated as manifestations of nature; however, Bronze and Iron Age texts and inscriptions in the region present urbanized adaptations of the divine realm. Although the only

extensive narrative mythology comes from Ugarit, the Greek essay *On the Syrian Goddess* (ascribed to Lucian), fragments of Philo of Byblos incorporated into the *Preparation for the Gospel* by Eusebius, and the Hebrew Bible provide secondary material. Mesopotamian influence on the pantheon is clear throughout the region; Egyptian influence is most marked along the Mediterranean. The rural and agricultural origins of most deities reflect communities dependent on the fertility of plants and animals; urban populaces conceive of these deities on a royal model with a familial-bureaucratic notion of the governance of the cosmos. In representations, these deities were portrayed as human, sometimes with such symbols of divinity as bovine horns or astral images.

In mythology, a divine pair reigned in heaven over both divine and human realms. For some Syro-Canaanites this couple was El and Asherah, responsible for establishing and maintaining order through a hierarchy understood to extend through all levels of divine and human social structures. Immediately under them, a very active level of deities vied for power among themselves and for the favor of their parents. Beneath these squabbling gods and goddesses were deities who were very gifted in highly specialized areas, but who lacked the leeway allowed their superiors. At the bottom of the divine realm were the messenger-gods, essentially slaves on the divine level.

Demons and deities appear often to have been one and the same, dependent upon whether one was on their good or bad side. Chthonic deities such as Mot, Molech, and Resheph were considered demonic forces of death and disease, but also could be worshiped as useful deities: for example, Resheph as warrior and metallurgist. Amulets and incantations reflect fear of demons' activities in human and animal illnesses, childbirth, warfare, and general bad luck or evil.

The pantheons of the various peoples living in Syria-Canaan shared many deities, but maintained local identities as well. Gods of minor importance in most pantheons could be major, or even patron, deities in others; Chemosh was patron of Moab, but was peripheral elsewhere. Fights among peoples, seasons, weather, and abnormal occurrences of all kinds were described as conflicts among the various deities.

El and Asherah, who had their separate residences, provided the final venue of appeal for deities and humans. El did not actively participate in the direct governance of the world, but would intervene if the second tier of gods let order collapse. Asherah selected her children for

Ivory carving of a goddess, perhaps an Aegean goddess of wild beasts, 14th–13th century BCE. Found near Ras Shamra (Ugarit), Syria. Louvre. *Réunion des Musées Nationaux/Art Resource, New York*

Canaanite god, possibly El; bronze statue found at Megiddo. *Courtesy of the Oriental Institute of the University of Chicago*

Weather-god Baal with weapon raised in threatening stance, 1700–1400 BCE. From Ras Shamra (Ugarit). Louvre. *Réunion des Musées Nationaux/Art Resource, New York*

their positions and nurtured human rulers. Both were depicted as all too capable of playing favorites, which brought about sibling rivalry with cosmic repercussions. El was presented as having an eye for young goddesses and for indulging his violent, spoiled daughter Anat, while Asherah favored her son Athtar, an incompetent would-be replacement for Baal. Nonetheless, both parents would remove divine or human rulers from their positions if they were incompetent.

The extant Ugaritic myths primarily relate stories about Hadad, designated usually by his title Baal (Lord). Baal fights Yamm (Sea) and Mot (Death), attempting to gain kingship from them. This reflects the desire for order, prosperity, and fertility in a city depen-

Perhaps an Astarte figure. A 6-inch ivory image of Phoenician or Syrian workmanship, found at the Assyrian city of Kalhu (modern Nimrud). *All rights reserved. The Metropolitan Museum of Art*

dent on both shipping and agriculture. Hadad was the popular storm deity throughout Syria-Palestine, with both Aram and Ugarit acknowledging him as their patron. The myths depict a strong, virile, action-oriented deity who happens to be rash and sometimes simply stupid. His sister and consort, Anat, goddess of war,

needed to intervene on Baal's behalf with their parents and to physically extract her brother from Mot's grasp. Mot, a favorite of El, ruled the netherworld and desired to rule the rest of the cosmos. Baal and Anat protected life and held death at bay, with intervention by El through the sun-goddess Shapshu (in other Semitic pantheons the sun is a male, Shemesh), who serves El in maintaining divine order and justice.

Many other active deities, recognized throughout the region, appear in the myths and ritual texts of Ugarit and in regional inscriptions. Highly important was Dagan, god of grain. Iconography of the moon deity (having several names) appeared throughout the ancient period in all of Syria-Canaan. The goddess Astarte's name was common, but her function remains unknown from Syro-Canaanite sources; Greco-Roman texts suggest fertility, Egyptian texts war. Horon appeared in numerous inscriptions and incantations as a demon/deity capable of curing diseases and controlling demons.

The artisan deity Kothar-wa-Khasis was Baal's useful subordinate in Ugarit's myths. Manufacturer of weapons for Baal as well as architect of Baal's house, this tertiary-level deity knew his own work better than his superiors did and made no apologies for being right, over Baal's objections. *On the Syrian Goddess* suggests that there were several deities on this level of the pantheon, some of whom appear in the ritual texts from Ugarit, if only marginally or not at all in the myths (Fire [*išt*] and Righteousness [*ṣdk*] are examples). Divinized deceased rulers, the Rephaim, bridged the mortal and immortal realms; these dead were both revered and feared among humans.

Messenger deities (similar to angels) carried communications from one deity to another. These deities had names (Asherah's messengers were Qudshu and Amruru), but no individual volition or characteristics aside from those of obedient court servants. In the Ugaritic narratives, the gods themselves appear before humans, not their intermediaries.

Regular ritual cycles as well as names of months, in towns where evidence has been found, show a continuous devotion to the deities. Usually, the number of divinities who received offerings far exceeded the characters appearing in the extant myths. The theological world behind these lists of deities is elusive. In political treaties the deities of the constituent parties were asked to witness the agreements and to punish a partner who broke the treaty. Shemesh, as the god who transverses the world and who represents justice, was a common witness to such political negotiations.

BIBL.: Lowell K. Handy, *Among the Host of Heaven: The Syro-Palestinian Pantheon as Bureaucracy* (Winona Lake, Ind., 1994). Gregorio del Olmo Lete, *Canaanite Religion according to the Liturgical Texts of Ugarit* (trans. Wilfred G. E. Watson; Bethesda, Md., 1999). L.K.H.

Israel

Ancient Israelite religion has been understood as essentially monotheistic on the basis of the biblical evidence, but critical discussions of the relevant biblical texts as well as extrabiblical evidence call this into question.

Biblical presentation. Traditional assessments of deities and demons in the Hebrew Bible customarily focus on the belief in YHWH as the only god of Israel. Biblical texts that explicitly express monotheistic belief include Deut. 4.35, 39; 1 Sam. 2.2; 2 Sam. 7.22; 2 Kings 19.15, 19; Neh. 9.6; Isa. 43.10–11; 44.6, 8; 45.5–7, 14, 18, 21; 46.9; Jer. 16.19–20; Ps. 82.7; 86.10; 96.5 = 1 Chron. 16.26. Isaiah 43.10–11 offers a classic example: "Before me no god was formed, / nor shall there be any after me. / I, I am the LORD, / and besides me there is no savior." These texts are dated by scholars to the 7th and 6th centuries or later (1 Sam. 2.2 may be older). Texts often thought to be earlier, such as the Ten Commandments ("you shall have no other gods before me"; Exod. 20.3 = Deut. 5.7) or the Shema ("hear, O Israel: The LORD our God is one LORD"; Deut. 6.4), are considered also to be indicative of early Israelite monotheism. Indeed, many traditionally minded scholars would reaffirm that monotheism was an original feature of the covenant made by God with Moses and the Israelites on Mount Sinai and argue that biblical recognitions of other deities are deviations from the original monotheistic norm. Prophetic condemnations of the worship of other deities are likewise understood as affirmations of monotheism.

The discussion of demons presents similar issues of interpretation. It is clear that demons were recognized not only in ancient Israel, but also in later Judaism. Biblical demons include Lilith (Isa. 34.14); Rabisu who lies in wait (Gen. 4.7); Azazel, a desert demon known from the ritual of the Day of Atonement (Lev. 16); and Mot (Death), evidently presented as a demon who enters houses and threatens their inhabitants, perhaps in the form of pestilence (Jer. 9.21 [= 9.20 Hebrew]). Of these biblical demons, the most famous in later Jewish literature is Lilith, who is understood as Adam's first wife and characterized as a seductress of men and destroyer of young children (Babylonian Talmud, tractates *Shabbat* 15b; *Eruvin* 100b; *Niddah* 24b). Demons are commonly recognized in New Testament literature, and casting out demons is a hallmark of the ministry of Jesus and his disciples. In traditional assessments of the evidence in the Hebrew Bible, demons are disassociated from the understanding of YHWH as the one and only god of Israel. Many passages seem to present demons as working for YHWH (such as the destroying angel in Exod. 12.23, the deadly angels in Ps. 78.49, the apparently demonic figure in Exod. 4.24, and the lying spirit in 1 Kings 22.22); these are often disregarded in assessments of monotheism, as they are viewed as servants of the devil or Satan. This latter figure appears in the Hebrew Bible, but as a member of YHWH's heavenly court (Job 1–2) and not as the leader of hell or fallen angels, which are concepts attested in later Jewish and Christian literature.

Problematic evidence. In recent decades, this view of biblical monotheism has been questioned. Some biblical evidence militates against viewing ancient Israel as originally monotheistic. For example, the first of the Ten Commandments, with its prohibition against having "other gods before me," presupposes that other deities were acknowledged in ancient Israel, even if they were to be shunned. While this passage and similar ones could be viewed as expressive of a functional monotheism, other biblical passages are more problematic. Biblical expressions in praise of YHWH include uncritical recognition of other deities: "Who is like you, O LORD, among the gods?" (Exod. 15.11). The divine council, understood as consisting of children of the chief god, is also preserved in biblical passages dating to various periods (e.g., Ps. 29; 82; Job 1–2). YHWH is said to lead a military retinue that includes the divine figures Resheph and Deber (Hab. 3.5); in texts outside the Bible, these figures are attested as gods. The Bible even preserves the notion of a divine family, headed by a god El, with YHWH as one of his seventy sons, having Israel as his earthly patrimony (Deut. 32.8–9 in the Septuagint and the Dead Sea Scrolls, but not in the traditional Masoretic text). Elsewhere in biblical literature YHWH and El are understood as a single figure (Exod. 6.2). In addition to biblical evidence for various sorts of Israelite polytheism, there is also inscriptional and archeological evidence. The most dramatic instance involves inscriptions from the site of Kuntillet Ajrud (ca. 780 BCE). These inscriptions refer to "YHWH and his Asherah." The latter word is interpreted as the name of the goddess Asherah, or at least her symbol. Both the goddess and her symbol are known from the Bible.

Critical reconstruction of deities and demons. A new picture of Israelite polytheism and monotheism is emerging, based not only on biblical passages and contemporary extrabiblical evidence, but also on earlier texts discovered at modern Ras Shamra (ancient Ugarit).

In the Ugaritic texts, deities are conceived anthropomorphically both in familial and political terms. They constitute a family, headed by the patriarch El and his spouse, the matriarch Asherah, followed in status by a host of powerful children (sometimes called the "seventy children"), including the warrior storm-god Baal. Below these two ranks in the divine household are two levels of divine workers, which include the messenger-gods, better known in later biblical texts as angels. This divine family is often presented as a deliberative political body, known as the divine council. The hierarchical structure corresponds to the dominant social structure of the Late Bronze Age (ca. 1600–1200 BCE) and the earlier part of the Iron Age (ca. 1200–800 BCE), namely the patriarchal household. This structure was realized at various levels of society, including the monarchy or royal household. The deities are understood as a divine version of the royal household; as a result, the chief god is regarded as both a father and a king over the deities. The divine and human social structures correspond in even more fundamental ways. Ugaritic administrative texts often list persons according to their families ("sons of X"), suggesting that the highest form of social identification is not the individual, but the family. In this sort of society, the polytheism of a divine family would have been more intelligible than a notion of monotheism. Indeed, the divine family was for polytheism a sort of "monotheism." The monotheism of the sort presented later in the Bible may have resulted partially from the deterioration of the family structure in Judah.

Biblical texts surviving from early Israel are not nearly as abundant as texts dating from later periods. Despite this problem, some evidence of early Israelite polytheism has survived in the Bible. The divine family is headed by the god El, with YHWH as one of his seventy sons who has Israel as his earthly patrimony (Deut. 32.8–9 Septuagint). This divine family also constitutes the divine council, which consists primarily of the chief god and his sons. Some texts seem to reflect the older idea of El as the chief god, with YHWH as one of the second-tier deities (Ps. 82), but other passages clearly regard YHWH as the chief god over the "divine children" (Job 1–2). As the divine king and warrior, YHWH—like second-tier deities in the Ugaritic texts, such as the god Baal—leads a military retinue of divinities (Hab. 3.5) and rules over the gods more generally (Ps. 29). Older references to Asherah ("breast and womb" in Gen. 49.25?) and astral deities ("the sun, moon, and stars" or "hosts of heaven"; 1 Kings 22.19) suggest that they, too, constituted members of the divine family and council. Later biblical criticism against Asherah (1 Kings 18.19; 2 Kings 21.7; 23.6) and astral deities (21.5; 23.5) may represent an inner-Israelite critique against these divinities, not merely denunciation of foreign gods. With the identification of YHWH and El (accomplished around the 8th century in Judah), Asherah, who is known from the Ugaritic texts as the wife of El, seems to become YHWH's consort in some circles (reflected evidently in the Kuntillet Ajrud inscriptions). Demons and cosmic enemies continue to exist as divine powers, manifest in the human sphere as illness and destruction.

In the second half of the monarchy, ancient Israel witnessed a development toward a monotheistic construction of divinity in competition with the view that YHWH was sovereign in a polytheistic context. While the latter view may have been the dominant form of Judean worship (Jer. 44), other quarters of Judean society offer an alternative view of divine reality: Asherah is denounced, as are other deities such as the sun, moon, and stars. The divine world appears almost entirely to have been shorn of the familial concept. The notion of a council remains, but it is no longer invested with a multi-tier structure of deities. Instead, power is polarized between YHWH and servile figures such as angels. Demons also continue as threats to humans (Jer. 9.21 [= 9.20 Hebrew]), but they are portrayed in postexilic literature as denizens of the underworld and in later Jewish and Christian literature as minions of the devil or Satan.

Emergence of monotheism in Judah. The critical question is why the great bulk of monotheistic expressions in the Bible date from the 7th or 6th century onward. This shift may be correlated with two developments. The first involved the loss of traditional family patrimonies ravaged by warfare and economic pressures, from the 8th century onward. This shift is reflected in 6th-century biblical texts, including Jer. 31.29–30, Ezek. 16, and Deut. 24.16, which preach individual accountability instead of family accountability. Such a shift corresponds to the attribution of divine accountability to a single deity. The second development is the rise of empires. As long as Israel and Judah were independent, the notion of various gods ruling over their own nations posed little conceptual challenge to YHWH's status as their national god. The various other national gods could be understood as powerful in their own realms. The rise of the Assyrian Empire followed by its successor, the Babylonian Empire, destroyed any conceptual framework that correlated human and divine power. Israel and then Judah suffered political and social reduction in the world, but Israel then elevated its understanding of its deity's mastery of the world. Put summarily: Israel and Judah were no longer nations, but the gods of other nations, including the greatest powers, were not truly gods but illusions; YHWH was the sole force over all.

From the 6th century onward, the monotheistic presentation of Israel's deity appears in the Bible, often in monotheistic statements (Neh. 9.6; Zech. 14.9) or representations (Gen. 1). These passages do not preclude hosts of heavenly servants, whether angels or other heavenly beings. Later presentations of divinity would essentially eliminate divine forces comparable to YHWH in the cosmic realm. For example, the old notion of the divine family's seventy sons, vestigially assumed in Deut. 32.8–9, later reappears as the seventy angels who guard the seventy nations of the world. Other texts would preserve, albeit in modified form, vestiges of the older El-Baal mythology. For example, the vision of "the Ancient of Days" and "one like a Son of Man" in Dan. 7 reflects the older presentations of El and Baal, but in a monotheistic framework. Finally, Isa. 57 shows that not all Judeans of the later periods conformed to the monotheistic ideal as presented in the Bible. Later Jewish and Christian texts reflect continued traditions that reorganize older polytheistic themes in various monotheistic forms.

BIBL.: E. T. Mullen, *The Divine Council in Canaanite and Early Hebrew Literature* (Harvard Semitic Monographs 2;

Chico, Calif., 1980). M. S. Smith, *The Origins of Biblical Monotheism: Israel's Polytheistic Background and the Ugaritic Texts* (New York, 2001). K. van der Toorn, B. Becking, and P. W. van der Horst (eds.), *Dictionary of Deities and Demons in the Bible* (Leiden, 1999).   M.S.S.

Anatolia

Assimilation and syncretism. The Hittite pantheon formed through a process of territorial expansion and assimilation. On their arrival in Anatolia, the Hittites encountered the indigenous Hattian-speaking peoples, and, as they infiltrated the region, they adopted the gods of their new homeland. In time, the gods of the Indo-European Palaians and Luwians were assimilated as well. The pantheon expanded with the size of the kingdom. All of the deities encountered in the towns and villages who were absorbed into the kingdom were recognized by the Hittite state, and great care was taken to ensure that each deity was worshiped according to proper local tradition. Eventually, the expansion of the Hittite state resulted in the introduction of gods not only from other parts of Anatolia, but also from Syria and Mesopotamia. Because of this ongoing process of assimilation, by the end of the imperial period the Hittite pantheon had developed into a highly complex polytheistic system.

The Hittites worshiped so many deities that they sometimes abbreviated the list to "the thousand gods of Hatti." The actual total known to modern scholars has not yet reached this number but it is still growing, even if many of its deities are completely unknown to us except for their names. The complexity of the Hittite pantheon may be attributed to the Hittite resistance to syncretism; that is, in general, the Hittites tended not to identify their own gods with either foreign or native deities of a similar type. An attempt was made to bring order to this system insofar as the scribes grouped together local deities who showed a common character. For example, all bringers of rain and thunder were designated by the scribes with the same cuneiform sign indicating a storm-god. To this would be appended the city of origin, to distinguish them; thus, the storm-gods of Nerik, Zippalanda, Halpa, and Arinna are attested. We know, however, that the gods were worshiped individually because they appear side by side in the texts as separate entities.

This systematization of the pantheon sometimes renders it difficult to tell which deity is meant by a generic designation—the sign for Tutelary Deity LAMMA could refer to any number of deities, including Zithariya, Hapantaliya, and Inara—and often the original names of the deities are entirely lost. We owe the many cases where the original names of the gods do survive to the Hittites, who, in an attempt to please the gods, sometimes addressed them in their native tongues, thus allowing us better to trace their cultural point of origin. For example, the Sun-god of Heaven in Hittite is called

Isanu, but in Hurrian is worshiped as Simegi, in Luwian as Tiwat, in Palaic as Tiwaz, in Hattian as Estan, and in Akkadian as Shamash.

Ultimately, a sort of syncretism was achieved within the official pantheon by creating a divine family, at the head of which were the Sun-goddess of Arinna (Hurrian Hepat) and the Storm-god of Hatti (Hurrian Teshub), with their son, the Storm-god of Nerik (Hurrian Sarruma). The reliefs carved into the rock sanctuary at Yazılıkaya (end of the 13th century BCE), where a total of seventy-one divine figures are represented, reveal the syncretism of the Hittite and Hurrian gods in their official and final form. But this syncretism was artificial, manufactured at the state level as a means of promoting the Hurrian element within the empire. In spite of these efforts, however, at no point was an established divine hierarchy ever attempted on a wide scale. The local cults were left to worship and develop as they pleased.

Nature and function. The myths reveal that the gods of the Hittites were conceived of in human terms. They required sustenance, exhibited a range of emotions, and were negatively affected by the acts of other gods—if one god failed to perform his or her divine duties, all suffered. In the cult they were subject to a schedule probably not unlike that of a royal personage: they slept, arose, dressed, dined, enjoyed entertainments, and held court. The gods were neither omniscient nor omnipotent but made mistakes and were capable of being deceived. Still, they possessed wisdom and power that were far above that of humans. The level of wisdom and power varied widely, depending on each deity's status within the pantheon, which itself often depended on the importance of the natural phenomenon that that deity represented.

Each deity had his or her own role and function in the cosmos, which was usually tied directly to natural phenomena and reflected the agrarian interests of the population. Most important were the storm-gods, who brought the rain and winds that fertilized the crops. Heavenly deities of both genders (sun, moon) were also prominent. Deities of grain (Hattic Kait, Hittite Halki), vineyards, and orchards were directly responsible for the prosperity of the crops (Palaic Zaparwa). There were also gods of wildlife, gods of war and pestilence, and personal protective deities, who often served as intermediaries to the other gods on behalf of their mortal charges. A king could claim a major deity as his personal god. Thus King Hattushili attributes his good fortune to the intervention of Ishtar, Tudkhaliya represents himself in the arms of his personal god, Sarruma, on his seals and at the rock sanctuary Yazılıkaya, and Muwattalli composes an elaborate prayer to his god, the *pihassassi* storm-god. The mother-goddesses were responsible for the creation of humanity and for birth in general, while the goddesses of fate determined human destiny. Other groups of gods, some of inchoate character, are attested, including the Heptad (the "Seven") and the primordial (underworld) deities. Finally, god lists in

King Warpalawa standing before a fertility-god carrying grapes in one hand and grain stalks in the other; stele from Ivriz (near Tarsus), 8th century BCE. Archaeological Museum, Istanbul. *Hirmer Fotoarchiv*

the treaties often end by listing in generic fashion the mountains, rivers, streams, heaven and earth, winds, and clouds, and in most cases we never learn their individual names.

The pantheon. The evidence does not suggest a well-defined divine hierarchy, although in the treaties of the imperial period there is a fixed sequence in the lists of divine witnesses, with primacy of place given to the more important gods. Similarly, the processions of gods at Yazılıkaya impose an order on the pantheon. The myths, in which otherwise minor deities (Telipinu, Inara, and Kumarbi) play more important roles than the cultic documents would lead us to expect, do not support these hierarchies and thus reflect separate local or ethnic traditions.

The supreme male deity of the Hittite pantheon, the Storm-god of Hatti (Hittite Tarhunt) was an Indo-European import, later identified with the Hurrian Teshub. In Hurrian tradition the divine bulls Serri and Hurri drew his wagon. The Storm-god of Hatti shared the Great Temple at Hattusha with the supreme goddess of the land, the Sun-goddess of Arinna. Assimilated into

the pantheon from the native Hattian tradition, the Sun-goddess was the special protector of the kingship. Her Hattic name is Wurusemu, later identified with the Hurrian Hepat. Their sons, the Storm-gods of Nerik and Zippalanda, their daughter Mezzulla, and their granddaughter Zintuhi completed the divine first family in the Old Kingdom. During the imperial period, the Storm-god of Nerik came to be identified with Hurrian Sarruma, a minor mountain deity, as the only son of Hepat and Teshub, and his importance tied in part to his personal relationship to King Tudkhaliya IV.

According to the mythological texts, Telipinu and Inara are also important in the Old Kingdom pantheon. Inara is the daughter of the storm-god and the protective deity of Hattusha. She is a goddess of the hunt and wild animals. Some scholars identify her with Hattian Teteshapi, whose name means "Great Goddess." Telipinu, a lesser storm-god and god of cultivation, is also the son of the storm-god and the main protagonist in the so-called Telipinu myth, which is the best preserved of the numerous "missing deity" myths. Kamrusepa also figures prominently in Anatolian mythology, as a figure associated with magic, while Hannahanna, the "grandmother," is consulted by the other gods for her wisdom. Her special animal is the bee, symbol of hearth and home.

Istanu, the Sun-god of heaven, held a high status in the pantheon from the Old Kingdom on and was the all-seeing dispenser of justice to humans and animals. In this respect, the Hittite king was his earthly counterpart and was often identified with him both in costume and in his title, "My Sun." Because of his judicial powers, Istanu is most frequently invoked in prayers and hymns of praise that seek some kind of legal recognition or justification. Although not the supreme deity of the land, as the dispenser of justice he is given priority in the canonical treaty god lists.

Mesopotamian imports of the imperial period include Ishtar (Hurrian Sausga), who gained much popularity in Anatolia at the end of the Bronze Age (due perhaps to her patronage of Queen Pudukhepa and King Hattushili), when many local deities began to appear with her name. Her role in Anatolia as the goddess of both love and war mirrors her role in Mesopotamia. In god lists, she is accompanied by her handmaids, Ninatta and Kulitta. From Syria comes Ishhara, whose epithet, "Queen of the Oath," identifies her primary role as divine witness to treaties and vows. She might have been

King Tudkhaliya IV under the protection of the god Sarruma; rock carving from Yazılıkaya, 1220 BCE. *Hirmer Fotoarchiv*

considered an effective enforcer of these, since she seems to have been associated with both sickness and healing; in one text, diseases are called the "children of Ishhara."

The Hittites seem to have picked up the concept of the tutelary, or protective, deity from both the Hattian and Mesopotamian traditions. The Tutelary Deity (written with the Sumerogram LAMMA) has numerous manifestations identified by geographic and other epithets. This deity is particularly popular in Hittite reliefs, where he is shown standing on a hart and holding a weapon in one hand and a bird of prey and a hare in the other.

The underworld was also populated with deities. In early tradition, these included Hittite Lelwani (king [later lady] of the underworld) and Hattian Isdustaya and Papaya, the Fates who spin the years. The Sun-goddess of the Earth headed the pantheon that dwelled within the earth in later Hittite tradition. An avatar of the Sun-goddess of Arinna, she represented the sun's course during the hours of the night. Her underworld nature, perhaps a result of her syncretism with Hurrian Allani, who guarded the gate that separates the underworld from the upper earth, is attested by invocations directed to her in rituals performed for the dead. She conveyed the spirits of the dead to the underworld, and her worship involved placing offerings and sacrifices in the ground. With her, in the regions beneath the earth, lived the primordial ("inferior") gods, who were twelve in number according to the canonical lists of divine wit-

nesses in the treaties (in rituals their numbers vary from five to fifteen). Their role was to judge the cause of an evil and remove it to the underworld.

Demons and lesser deities. The Hittites did not have a separate word to identify lesser deities or demons, although divine status was bestowed on many supernatural entities who clearly were not counted among the great gods. In addition to the divine mountains, springs, rivers, and the sea (Aruna), whose lack of individuality in the texts suggest their lesser status, imaginary creatures are attested in both art (sphinxes, bovine-headed demons, and winged bird-headed genii) and texts, and in rare instances sacred animals of a more familiar earthly type also held supernatural status. Among the imaginary creatures, the *awiti* animal is listed in cultic inventory texts, particularly in association with Ishtar, and this creature has tentatively been identified with the winged feline that appears with the same goddess in the iconography. The *damnašara* creatures appear, among other places, in the mythological story of Kessi. In a dream, the hero encounters snakes *(elliyanka-)* and *damnašara-* at a gate. They are thought to be either sphinxes or bovine-headed monsters, in either case probably corresponding to creatures known from the iconography.

Both examples of sacred animals with divine status stem from Hurrian tradition. The bulls of the storm-god, Serri and Hurri, not only were considered divine, but received offerings. Eagles were the messengers of the gods who dwelled in the heavens and a main communicative link between king and god. But only in the cult of the Hurrian deity Manuziya, within the context of the *hisuwas* festival, are cult images of the divinized eagles, Esuen and Eribuski, manipulated.

Abstract concepts. In a few cases, abstractions might be divinized. Halmasuitta was a female personification of the throne, and her cult is attested at Hattusha. She appears in the Anitta Text as a symbol of the crown (in this case, Anitta), into whose hands Hattusha is delivered. In a ritual for the foundation of a new palace, she delivers to the king the insignias of power (KUB 29.1 1.23–24). Siwatt, a deity whose name means "propitious day," is a euphemism for the day of death. This deity comes from Hattic tradition and appears mainly in the funerary rituals. So important was the pit as a channel of communication between the upper and lower worlds that it was itself considered divine and was counted among the primordial underworld-gods.

BIBL.: Alfonso Archi, "The Names of the Primeval Gods," *Orientalia* 59.2 (1990): 114–29. Gary M. Beckman, "The Religion of the Hittites," *Biblical Archaeologist* 52.2–3 (1989): 98–108. Ben H. L. van Gessel, *Onomasticon of the Hittite Pantheon* (2 vols.; Leiden, 1998); Volkert Haas, *Geschichte der hethitischen Religion* (Leiden, 1994); Gregory McMahon, "Theology, Priests, and Worship in Hittite Anatolia," in *Civilizations of the Ancient Near East* (ed. Jack M. Sasson et al.; New York, 1995), 3.1981–95. Itamar

Singer, "'The Thousand Gods of Hatti': The Limits of an Expanding Pantheon," *Israel Oriental Studies* 14 (1994): 81–102.

B.J.C.

Iran

Although a few deities are revealed exclusively outside the Zoroastrian tradition, a great deal of what we know about the divine and demonic entities who populated the Iranian cosmos is mediated through Zoroastrian sources. Nevertheless, it is possible, in many cases, to distinguish pre-Zoroastrian or non-Zoroastrian concepts of deity from strictly Zoroastrian innovations. As in most cultures of the world, deities themselves are sometimes inseparable from abstract concepts that they personify, sometimes not obviously associated with a concept, and sometimes simply the bare concept without flesh and blood. For example, Mithra is a real flesh-and-blood god who travels about in a chariot, his great bronze mace in hand, as he seeks out violators of covenants. At the same time his name means "covenant," that is, he is in some way the personification of the concept of an important social institution. One can contrast Tishtrya, the star Sirius, who has a rich mythology, with Mah, the moon, who is hardly distinguishable from the heavenly body itself. Further, we encounter, especially in liturgies, deities such as Saoka (Profit) who is identified by only a few colorless epithets. As in Vedic tradition, the two deities essential to the cult, Atar and Haoma, are personifications of the element fire and the divine drink respectively.

A striking aspect of the Iranian pantheon is its radical partition into two general categories of deity, a partition based on the fundamental ethical and cosmic dualism of the Truth (*asa;* Old Persian *arta*) and the Lie (*druj;* Old Persian *drauga*). In terms of gods, demons, and personified powers, the dualism is expressed through the terms *ahura* and *daēwa* (Old Persian *daiwa*); the former belong to the Truth, the latter to the Lie. This dichotomy ran so deep that even the lexicon embeds a dualistic doubling of ahuric and daiwic words, nominal and verbal. The reasons for such a division of the pantheon are not altogether clear, although ritual, particularly sacrificial practices, may be at the root. In ancient India we find an inversion, namely, that after the early period of the Rig Veda, the *asura*s became demonized while the *deva*s retained their status as "good" deities; and in the ritual literature the two groups are frequently found in contention over control of the sacrifice. In the Avesta the common word for deity is, however, *yazata* (worthy of worship), in the Achaemenid inscriptions *baga*.

At the head of the ahuric pantheon stood Ahura Mazda, whose name can be taken to mean either "Wise Lord" or "Lord Wisdom." He was a creator-god in the sense that he established the world order in accord with the principle of Cosmic Order/Truth (*arta, asa*). There was also a demiurge, Warstar (Craftsman; Avestan

Relief showing the creator-deity Ahura Mazda granting a king a diadem of sovereignty while Mithra protects the king's back; 4th century CE, from Taq-i-Bostan, Iran. *Archive J. K. Choksy*

Thsorestar), whose creative function Zarathustra assigned to Spenta Mainyu (Beneficent Spirit). Because of his intimate connection with Truth, Ahura Mazda was the source of Zarathustra's revelations. In this respect he is comparable to the Vedic god Varuna; but unlike Varuna, the judicial role was assumed by Rasnu (Judge), along with the bellicose Mithra. One may speculate on the basis of a few references that Ahura Mazda was paired with the earth-goddess, Spenta Armaiti. In the religiopolitical ideology of the Achaemenids, Ahura Mazda is magnified as the great god, the creator, who not only established heaven and earth, but also established the legitimate rule of the king, who in turn established order on the earth by overcoming the rebellious forces of the Lie.

Iranian traditions show a tendency to transform older mythological motifs in a program of dynastic history which merges the legendary with the historical. The primordial twin, Yemo, reflected in various Indo-European traditions, becomes Yima, the first king who ruled during a golden age. He was overthrown by the serpent (in later traditions a dragon) demon Azi Dahaka. In the Vedic hymns the Indo-Iranian serpent appears as the anticosmic monster Ahi Vrtra, whom Indra slew in order to complete the creation of the world. After a period of misrule, Azi Dahaka was in turn overthrown by the hero Raetaona, who has his origins in a shadowy Indo-Iranian deity Trita (the Third). These and the Kayanid Dynasty that follows receive their power from the goddess Aredwi Sura Anahita. She was a favorite of Artaxerxes and so strong was her association with royal power that she appears on Sasanid investiture rock reliefs and even survives into the Islamic period as the Sahrbanu of Persian romances. Legitimacy and power were also vouchsafed through the possession of the royal Splendor called X^warnah (also Farnah), a shining appearance of fortune that attached itself to the legitimate ruler, yet remained unobtainable by usurpers. Connected to the martial aspect of royal power was the warrior-deity Werethrana, whose name originally meant "the smashing of obstruction" and then "victory."

The archdemon was the Druj (Lie)—like her opposite, Truth, a somewhat colorless abstraction of one pole of the ethical/cosmic duality. The instrument of her power, however, was Angra Mainyu (Evil Spirit). In Zarathustra's theology he was the primordial twin spirit who chose what was bad. In later Zoroastrianism he became the author of the evil, daiwic creation and was the adversary of Ahura Mazda's creative agency, Spenta Mainyu. Another archdemon was Aeshma (Wrath), who carried a bloody club and was opposed by Sraosha (Obedience). Much feared and loathed was the Nasu Druj, the Corpse Demon, the agent of putrefaction manifest in the form of a disgusting fly. Three *daēwa*s mentioned in the Vendidad appear in the Vedic pantheon: Indra, Saurwa (Sarva), and Nasatyau.

Although both the pantheon and pandemonium are richly populated with personified concepts, the most theologically significant are the group of abstract entities, in Avestan the Amesha Spentas (Beneficent Immortals), who seem to be the product of Zarathustra's innovative theology. These are Asa Wahista (Best Truth), Wohu Manah (Good Mind), Xsathura Wairya (Desirable Dominion), Spenta Armaiti (Beneficent Devotion), and the pair Haurwatat (Wholeness) and Ameretatat (Immortality). As, perhaps, hypostases of Ahura Mazda, they appear to assume functions performed, in part, by deities and powers in the ancient Iranian religion, though they are not simply sublimations of well-known deities whom Zarathustra ignored.

BIBL.: Mary Boyce, *A History of Zoroastrianism* (2 vols.; Leiden, 1975–82). L. H. Gray, *The Foundations of the Iranian Religions* (Bombay, 1929). W.W.M.

Greece and Rome

For most parts of the ancient world, it is literature that offers the most outspoken evidence about the gods. Greek and Roman religions are not different in this respect, and it is not always easy to discern what, within this evidence, is literary and theoretical and what is part of the living texture of religious practice.

The gods in myth. To begin with the theoretical side: what the Greeks, and after them the Romans, called "theology"—that is, in their meaning of the word, "narrations about the gods"—is part of their mythology, a body of traditional and meaningful stories. But it is only a part, albeit an important one. The great poems of the archaic age, especially Homer's and Hesiod's, display the essential elements of this theology in a systematic way. The ancients were aware of this, as Herodotus shows (2.53): "It was only the day before yesterday, so

Claudia Quinta, a Vestal, pulling in the ship of the goddess Cybele or Magna Mater. The goddess (represented as a black stone in her temple at Rome) was brought to Rome from Phrygia in 204 BCE, accompanied by her eunuch priests, the *galli. German Archaeological Institute, Rome*

to speak, that the Greeks came to know whence each of the gods originated, whether all of them existed always, and what they were like in their visible forms. For I reckon that Homer and Hesiod lived no more than four hundred years before my time. They are the poets who composed a theogony for the Greeks and gave the gods their epithets [*epōnymiai*], assigned them their honors [*timai*] and special skills [*technai*], and described their visible forms [*ideai*]. The other poets who are said to have been living before them, actually lived, at least in my opinion, only after them." Homer and Hesiod, then, according to Herodotus, built the framework of a Panhellenic representation of the gods, ordering and parsing out a pantheon that everybody could recognize. Thus, literature put into place a system that transcended diverse local ritual traditions and theologies. Being the outcome of reflection that was more or less explicit, the poetical texts transmitted what one could call an indigenous and abstract discourse on the gods, even what we, in our modern languages, would call a theology.

The fundamental object of this theology is a polytheistic system. The plurality of gods necessitates the organization of a pantheon. And the organization of a pantheon provides a starting point from which we can understand the difference between literature and cult. In

Procession of the twelve major Greek gods, led by Apollo, playing the cithara; followed by Artemis; Zeus, with thunderbolt; Athena; Poseidon and a goddess (his consort?); Hephaestus; Demeter; Ares and Aphrodite; Hermes; and, probably, Hestia. Marble relief said to be from Tarentum, late archaic (about 460 BCE) or archaizing (late 1st century BCE). *Walters Art Gallery, Baltimore*

literature, the gods are organized in a way that is acceptable to the largest possible number of Greeks. That is why one talks about Olympian gods, choosing the wild and remote top of Greece's highest mountain, Olympus, rather than any individual city, as their dwelling place. Hesiod's *Theogony* functions on this same Panhellenic level. On this level of a shared civilization, Zeus is Zeus, without the necessity of clarifying which Zeus is meant. This "father of gods and men" gained sovereignty after a series of crises that ended in his fair division of prerogatives and fields of action among the gods. A famous text of the *Iliad* tells how Zeus was allotted the sky, while his brother Poseidon received the sea, and a third brother, Hades, the subterranean world of the dead (*Iliad* 15.187–93). All the gods share the earth, which is another way of saying that on earth the gods contend with each other, and the humans have to intervene in order to keep them apart: in their cities, which are separate and different from each other, humans make choices that sometimes have dramatic consequences and give rise to specific myths of origins.

Greek gods, unlike humans, do not die, at least in principle, nor do they age. A god is at the same time *athanatos* (a being that has no share in *thanatos* [death]) and *agēraos* (a being that is not subject to *gēras* [old age]). The unhappy fate of Tithonus easily demonstrates what this means. Tithonus, a Trojan prince and mortal lover of Eos, goddess of the dawn, received immortality after Eos asked Zeus to bestow it upon him, but she forgot to ask also for the gift of eternal youth. Dried out by old age like a cicada, Tithonus lived on forever in a state of never-ending bodily decline. This calamity contrasts with the ordinary fate of the gods. They enjoy eternal life and eternal youth and feed on ambrosia and nectar; well sheltered from the necessities of daily sustenance that plague humans, the gods receive from humans only the smoke and the smell of sacrifices and bloodless offerings. Nor do they have blood in their veins, but a dif-

ferent liquid, *ichōr*. This does not prevent them from suffering or being subjected to desire and pain or from adopting bodies and making love. One sees them quarreling with each other and sometimes even picking fights with mortals. One finds them participating in all sorts of deception and shape-changing in order to copulate with mortal women and men, in homosexual and heterosexual relations. The gods, that is, although immortal and eternally young, do not essentially differ from humans. They share their origin with humans, moreover: both have Earth (Gaea) as an ancestor, the mother of gods and mortals.

From the primordial beings Void (Chaos), Earth (Gaea), Starry Sky (Uranus), Desire (Eros), and Water (Oceanus) to the Titans and then to the Olympian gods and the mortals, the evolution of the cosmos is seen as the slow splitting up of an initial power into a growing number of entities and finally, step by step and without rupture or break of continuity, the appearance of humanity. Although humans are closely related to the gods, they are mortal. There exist intermediaries between their mortality and the immortality of the gods who never age, notably the nymphs, who have a very long life but are not immortal. The hamadryads—whose name indicates that their life is tied to an oak *(drys)*—do not survive the murderous actions of lumberjacks.

For a long time, the protohumans, creatures born before the great flood, lived together with the gods, ignorant of death, work, and marriage and sharing their table with the gods, as a fragment of the Hesiodic *Catalog of Women* has it (frag. 1 Merkelbach-West). This common life ended, however, when the humans were encouraged by Prometheus, a divine "culture-hero," to test the gods. The flood that followed, from which only Deucalion, Prometheus's son, escaped with his wife, Pyrrha, marks the separation between gods and humans and, at the same time, the emergence of a specifically human way of life. This life is characterized by a loss of im-

409

mediacy between humans and the world in which they dwell and thereby necessitates a series of mediations between humans and nature and between humans and gods. In order to eat and survive, work becomes necessary, which presupposes arts and crafts and rules for life in society. The relationship with the invisible world becomes ritualized: Deucalion, the Greek Noah, performs the first sacrifice, and all sacrificial meals thereafter are both reminders of the original lapse that separated humans from gods and temporary resumptions of the interrupted communication, accomplished by the smoke and smell of incense that rises from the altars.

The gods in cult. On the level of ritual practice, things are much more complex than in literature. Everybody agrees by now that a divinity cannot be reduced to the picture given by the great Panhellenic poets. Every Greek community had to create a pantheon of its own, which was different from the pantheon of every other city, although the same gods, whom everybody could recognize, were part of it. In Greece's numerous sanctuaries, one never met simply Zeus or Aphrodite, but rather a specific form of Zeus or Aphrodite, distinguished by an "epiclesis," a local and cultic epithet different from the poetical epithets, which described one of his or her particular functions or connections—Zeus Agoraios (of the marketplace) or Zeus Polieus (of the city), Aphrodite Ourania (of the sky, celestial) or Aphrodite Pandemos (of the entire people). And in every place, on every liturgical occasion, each divinity was associated with other divinities in a network that changed from context to context and constituted, each time, a pantheon of its own.

Groups of various sizes and functions—cities, phratries (brotherhoods), villages, or clans and families—had to organize a specific pantheon and realize a specific relationship with the divine—each group in concert with others but also in its own specific way. Thus, religious activity offered many possible roles and an almost endless spectrum of nuances, which might concern the entire city, groups inside the city, or even each individual worshiper. To choose the wrong epiclesis and, in doing so, to assign the wrong ritual roles to the gods meant that the efficacy of the ritual would be annihilated. While Xenophon often enough offered a sacrifice to Zeus Basileus during the course of his expedition into Asia, at the end of that expedition he was reproached by a seer for having neglected Zeus Meilichios (*Anabasis* 7.8). This neglect—not of Zeus himself, but of a specific Zeus who paid more attention than others to household matters—was responsible for Xenophon's financial predicaments, which could have thwarted his return to Greece. Once this mistake was rectified with the seer's help, Xenophon's affairs went smoothly again. The positioning of this specific god in a precise ritual context also implied differentiated relationships within a group of other divinities. Religious activity thus demanded, in all circumstances, a specific definition not only of the particular being to whom a rite would be addressed, but also of the entire pantheon, of which the particular being was but a member and part.

A divine presence could be felt and recognized in any part of nature, even if one could not assign it a specific name. Evander expressed this idea when, showing Aeneas and his Trojans around the future site of what later would become Rome, he pointed to the specific hill that would become the Capitoline, which in Vergil's time would include a temple of Jupiter, shining with gold. For Evander, the place was simply a wilderness of brush and thorns. Yet already then, the timorous shepherds felt a superstitious dread of it; its woods and rocks made them uneasy: "This forest, this hill with its green crest, are inhabited by a god. Which god? One does not know" (*Aeneid* 8.352). Seneca cites this passage to explain how a forest, a grove, a cave, or a river's source can evoke in a human's mind and feelings the idea of divine, supernatural presence (*Letters to Lucilius* 4.41). For a Greek, a heroic cult sometimes preserved the memory of the person who first recognized a divine presence and shaped the cultic space, cutting some trees, carving some steps into the native rock, and sculpting images of the local divinities. In contrast, sometimes a divine presence imposed itself upon a product of human activity. In the plain outside Egyptian Thebes, a colossal image of Amunhotep III, whom the Greeks identified with Memnon, the son of Eos and Tithonus, whom Achilles had killed under the walls of Troy, resounded at sunrise: this sound (which we presume resulted from the change of temperature in a crack of the stone) was understood by Greeks and Romans as Memnon greeting his mother. A visit by the emperor Hadrian even started a cult of this image: its sound was understood to be oracular, and libations and sacrifices began to be offered.

The experience of theophany, thus, often precedes identification and name-giving. There may be hesitation, and it may be necessary later to become more precise about what one experienced, but such matters concern the identity of the god, not the reality of the theophany itself. Once the divine object has been identified, prayer and sacrifice can be addressed to it, at least in a tentative way, by constructing a polar opposition between mortal and immortal and a hierarchy that depends on personal inclinations of the individual or the community that performs the rite. The prayer, although primarily addressing the single most relevant divinity, is scrupulous not to omit other gods. Thus Socrates, while walking along the Ilissus River, addressed not only Pan but also "all the other divinities of this spot" (Plato, *Phaedrus* 279b).

For the Greeks and Romans, to scan the pantheon in order to individualize one god among the many meant to undertake an experiment. In fact, choosing one god always meant choosing a multitude of aspects and functions that were shared by and contrasted with those of other gods. In a ritual context, a god always appeared as a nodal point, as the provisional result of conjecture. This concrete and shifting rapport between the human interlocutor and the superhuman power was the locale in which gods were identified and the pantheon was defined. Such definitions, however absolute they may seem, were not fixed in advance. In the Athenian agora, there was an altar of the "Twelve Gods," and an ancient tradition, valued in Rome as well as in Greece, often assumed that there were twelve principal gods. Recent studies, however, have shown the difficulty of drawing up a list of these twelve gods that would have met with consensus everywhere in ancient Greece or Rome.

Gods in Rome. It helps to compare Rome with Greece. In Rome, the gods were not organized in a pantheon. In this city where every god had his *flamen* (priest) and thus depended on a sacerdotal structure that was heavily hierarchized, the classification of gods took place along two axes that were both controlled by the state: the calendar and sacred topography. It is well known that, according to that very learned contemporary of Caesar, Marcus Terentius Varro, there were three *theologiae* (discourses on the gods); in this, Varro followed the analysis of the *pontifex maximus* Quintus Mucius Scaevola. First, there was the discourse of the poets, that is, Greek mythology, which had no intrinsic value of its own. Then, there was the discourse of the philosophers, who adhered to the physical allegorization that Varro, being the good Stoic he was, valued very highly, although he cautioned readers not to disseminate this knowledge too widely among the uneducated. And finally there was the discourse of politics—what was called civic theology; one could read it simply as an exhortation to scrupulous respect for ritual orthopraxy, teaching and reminding one what gods had to be approached by what priests in what cults, under what circumstances, and in what places (*Divine Antiquities*, frags. 6–10). Concerning physical allegorization, Varro remarks that many truths would be useless to teach to the uneducated masses; he also tells us, when considering the civic use of poetical theology, which attributes human shapes and feelings to the gods, that although it includes many errors, the masses are better off accepting them as truths (in Augustine, *City of God* 4.31). And, as a scholar who had a deep respect for traditional practice, Varro confessed that, if he had to reconstitute the city, he would prefer to consecrate the gods and their names according to rules taken from nature. Nevertheless, Varro believed that, since he belonged to a very ancient people, he had to preserve divine names and epithets exactly as traditions had handed them down to him.

In the same spirit, Varro asserted that the ancient Romans had adored their gods for 160 years without using images. "If this usage had been kept until this day," he added, "the cults of the gods would be much purer." He even referred to the Jewish people as living

proof of the correctness of his religious ideas and did not hesitate to conclude that whoever had introduced the cult of images may have removed fear of the gods from among the people but had also introduced more errors. Varro dates the appearance of the first divine images in Rome to the reign of Tarquinius Priscus, who in fact is said to have commissioned the monumental image of Jupiter for the new Capitoline temple from an Etruscan artist (Pliny, *Natural History* 35.157). It is obvious that we deal with an idealized version of Rome's past: the most ancient Roman cult, as established under King Numa, was not only closely akin to Jewish practices but also to those of the Pythagoreans and the Persians, and as such it had neither statues nor temples: "The religion was without ornaments, the rites were poor, and there were no Capitols but rather altars made of turf—made to be used only once—and simple vessels" (Varro, *Divine Antiquities,* frag. 38, in Tertullian, *Apology* 25.12). In his *Life of Numa* (8.12), Plutarch attributes ideas to Numa that were close to those of the Pythagoreans:

His opinion of images is also very close to the doctrines of the Pythagoreans, who conceived of the first principle of being as transcending sense and passion, invisible and incorrupt, and to be apprehended only by abstract intelligence. So Numa forbade the Romans to represent divinity in the form of a human or beast, nor were there any painted or graven images of divinity admitted among them for the space of the first 170 years, during all of which time their temples and chapels were kept free and pure from images. To such baser objects they deemed it impious to liken the highest [lit., the best], and they thought all access to divinity to be impossible, except by the pure act of the intellect.

This tradition concerning the prohibition of images in early Rome aligns with Dionysius of Halicarnassus's account of Romulus's institutions (*Roman Antiquities* 2.18; late 1st century BCE): "As to the traditional myths about the gods that are full of blasphemy and slander about them, [Romulus] regarded them as harmful, useless, and unbecoming, unworthy not only of the gods, but even of decent humans. Thus, he rejected them all and trained the Romans to speak about the gods and to imagine them in the most dignified way and never to ascribe to them behavior unworthy of immortal beings." When he wrote these lines, Dionysius must have had Varro's *Divine Antiquities* in mind. He does not say that the Romans do not have myths; he simply says that this colony, founded (as his theory on Rome's origins has it) in the likeness of a Greek city by the reformer Romulus (who easily could have read Plato's *Republic*), had rejected the hoary, traditional, but scandalous stories about the Greek gods—which is another way of saying that the Romans did not possess any of the traditional opportunities to be exposed to divine mythology, at least not in their most ancient and most prestigious institutions, which were supposed to go as far back as Romulus. Thus, they were not guilty of projecting human forms and qualities onto the gods, and they practiced a religion that was close to what the religion of Greece was imagined to have been before Homer and Hesiod: no images, no anthropomorphism, and thus neither genealogies nor family histories—in short, no stories about the gods except about their interventions in Rome's history.

Demons and heroes. For their Christian opponents, the pagans' gods were dead mortals who had been divinized, according to the Greek theory of Euhemerus of Messene (late 4th/early 3rd century BCE). Alternatively, and in contrast, the Christians acknowledged the gods' superhuman reality but turned them into demons, downgrading this class of beings into devilish creatures. "The demons whom they accept as their gods" calls out the voice of Eusebius in the early 4th century CE (*Preparation for the Gospel* 5.51.1), following an identification made famous by Paul (1 Cor. 10.20). But traditional Greek religious thinking had never established such a separation between gods and demons. For a very long time, the two terms were synonymous. Under Platonic influence, the demons had developed into largely beneficent intermediary beings, similar to angels. Much more important, however, in traditional Greek polytheism, was another distinction, between gods and heroes who, as ancestors and founders, were rooted in funerary cult.

Yet there were, nevertheless, some sorts of immortal beings who carried negative connotations. The universal fear of the dead and the desire to influence destiny can lead people to look for ritual forms that are specifically magical and associated with more disturbing divine beings, such as Hecate. This goddess, like the Great Mother and Pan, was thought to be responsible for epileptic fits, which were diagnosed as acts of possession by a god; in order for a sufferer to be cured, the responsible god had to be appeased and made beneficent by rituals (Hippocrates, *On the Sacred Disease*). Enthusiasm—that is, to be a puppet in a god's hands, a toy with which he or she was playing, as Dionysus played with Pentheus in Euripides' *Bacchae*—was a privileged but nevertheless fearsome form of ecstasy. As we know, there are good and bad ways of losing self-control. Myths make it clear that the bad form, alienation, is caused by refusal of the good form: Pentheus was made into Dionysus's toy and finally destroyed because he had rejected the god and the maenads, women who worshiped him. Ecstasy, in Greek, did not mean that something, such as the soul, escaped from the body and joined the god; it was not a departure of the self, but rather the sudden movement of an entire individual out of an ordinary state in which he or she felt what everybody else felt. Ecstasy was perceived as a change, an alienation of both the body and the soul, and its language consisted of terms that marked the junction of transformation, metamorphosis, madness, and erotic passion. When ecstasy came from the gods, it was often triggered by contact and touching. In Euripides' *Bacchae* (v. 932), Dionysus himself arranged, with his own hands, Pentheus's robes, encouraging him to dress as a woman. It was the god's touch that drove the human off course and made him crazy. In another story, the boy Hylas bent over a spring in order to refill his water jug; his arm penetrated the surface of the water that reflected his image. The nymphs who were living in the spring, on the other side of the water's mirror, were seduced by his beauty; they touched, grasped, pulled down, and finally took possession of his young body, which disappeared forever, although his voice survived through the action of an echo. The ecstasy of Hylas, carried away by the nymphs (and who therefore, in Greek, would be called a *nympholēptos* [one taken by the nymphs], another term for a person experiencing ecstasy), was understood to have metamorphosed into sound, a bizarre materialization of desire and grief in music and ritual.

Personifications and divine rulers. Over time, this ever-changing world of gods in Greece and Rome came to contain yet other divine beings, both as subjects of stories and objects of cult: personifications of concrete and abstract entities and divinized rulers. Former generations of scholars, caught up in a Judeo-Christian perception of the divine, were apt to regard their rise as a sign of the decline of "true" religion; more recently, we have learned to distrust such easy evaluations.

Some personifications are old. The hearth as an object of cult is called Hestia in Greek, Vesta in Rome. Earth (Gaea) is a primordial power in Hesiod and received cult in many cities. Abstract powers are just as old, at least in narration: in Homer, Fright (Deimos) and Panic (Phobos) accompany Ares as his helpmates (*Iliad* 4.440); Sleep (Hypnos) and Death (Thanatos) do the gods' bidding (16.454); and Youth (Hebe) acts as their radiant steward (4.2). Hesiod's theology firmly embedded these characters into the fabric of the cosmos, from the primordial Eros, who is as old as Earth (*Theogony* 120), to the terrible offspring of Night (211–31). During the classical and Hellenistic ages, many such entities acquired cults: in their religious analysis of events, the Greeks never hesitated to conclude that divine powers were at work who previously had been without cult, who had not even been thought of as divine. Democracy (Demokratia) received altars in 4th-century Athens; Victory (Nikē) and Concord (Homonoia) were revered in many cities. Already in early times, the Romans turned *venus* (beauty) into a major goddess; the social unrest of the middle republic brought Greek Homonoia as Concordia to the Forum Romanum—her temple was allegedly dedicated by that second Romulus, Camillus, in 367/366 BCE (Plutarch, *Life of Camillus* 42.4). Rome's expanding power provoked many Greek cities into founding a cult of the Roman People and the Goddess Rome, Thea Rhome—yet another overwhelming but capricious power whom prayer and sacrifice could appease.

With the ascent of Augustus, Thea Rhome was easily supplemented or supplanted by Theos Sebastos (the August God). In fact, the cult of Augustus simply continued the worship of Hellenistic kings and Roman generals that was familiar all over the Greek world. The cult of the dead transformed itself into heroic cults, which portrayed the power of deceased humans as effective beyond the grave. Cultic honors paid to a living person recognized his or her power to interact with the living in the present and the future, as a "hearing and helpful god" *(theos epēkoos, deus praesens),* closer and more immediate than the Olympians. Such cults also honored past deeds of great humans—we seem to draw closer to Euhemerus's theories. In 422 BCE, the city of Amphipolis decreed a heroic cult for the Spartan general Brasidas, who had delivered it from Athenian control but died during the effort (Thucydides 5.11); not much later the city of Samos decreed an altar and a festival for the still-living Spartan general Lysander, who liberated them from the Athenians in 404 BCE (Duris of Samos, *FGrH* 76 F71). In both cases, native analysis of the event agreed that more than ordinary forces had been at work, and the cities responded with a cult; since Lysander was still alive, he was treated as a god, not as a powerful dead person. This foreshadowed the future: Alexander, many of his successors, and then Roman generals and emperors were honored by Greek cities with altars, temples, and festivals.

Augustus disapproved of such honors during his lifetime, at least in the West, but nothing prevented him from becoming a god, or rather a "divine personality" *(divus),* after death (see color plate)—as had Caesar and as had, long before him, Romulus, who became the god Quirinus. Romulus's apotheosis, in fact, was the model after which Rome fashioned the divinization of its dead emperors. In the Hellenistic cities, it was the assemblies that decreed the introduction of a new god; similarly, in Rome it was the senate that approved of these new cults—or it was even, in the parody that shows so much of the underlying ideology, the assembly of the gods that voted on the adoption of a future god (Seneca, *Apocolocyntosis).*

Ruler cult, in Hellenistic and Roman times, is not so much the breakdown of a firm boundary between mortals and immortals, humans and gods, as it is an insight into the permeable character of such a borderline. Just as in theogonical thought, immortality changed imperceptibly into mortality, so in the cities' cults, mortals could rise into a realm where they shared not only the form but also the prerogatives and even the names of the gods.

BIBL.: Marcel Detienne, *Apollon le couteau à la main* (Paris: Gallimard, 1998). Georges Dumézil, *Archaic Roman Religion* (Chicago: University of Chicago Press, 1975). Stella Georgoudi, "Les douze dieux des grecs: Variations sur un thème," in *Mythes grecs au figuré de l'antiquité au baroque* (ed. Stella Georgoudi et Jean-Pierre Vernant; Paris: Gallimard, 1996), 43–80. Vinciane Pirenne-Delforge, *L'Aphrodite grecque* (Liège: Centre international d'étude de la religion grecque antique, 1994). Jean Rudhardt, *Du mythe, de la religion grecque et de la compréhension d'autrui* (Revue européenne des sciences sociales 19; Geneva: Droz, 1981). John Scheid, "Numa et Jupiter ou les dieux citoyens de Rome," *Archives de science sociale des religions* 59 (1985): 41–53.   PH.B.

Etruria

Etruscan deities are often treated as closely equivalent to Greek and Roman gods and goddesses: Etruscan Tinia is thus the equivalent of Greek Zeus or Roman Jupiter, Menerva of Greek Athena or Roman Minerva. This is partly encouraged by the ancient evidence itself (there were close contacts between Etruria and other parts of the ancient Mediterranean, and, at least by the 5th century BCE, Etruscan gods were regularly visualized in Greek form, as is clear from the engraved scenes on Etruscan mirrors). It is also encouraged by the similarity of names, which suggests a common character, if not origins or borrowing (Etruscan Aritmi :: Greek Artemis; Etruscan Apulu :: Greek and Roman Apollo). But this is

Head of the Etruscan god Turms (= Hermes/Mercury), about 500 BCE. Villa Giulia, Rome. *Scala/Art Resource, New York*

Wall painting showing the Etruscan gods Charun and Vanth, from tomb at Tarquinia, end of 4th century BCE. *German Archaeological Institute, Rome*

Image of the Etruscan god Tinia (= Zeus/Jupiter). Museo Etrusco Faina, Orvieto. *Alinari/Art Resource, New York*

almost certainly to oversimplify the Etruscan pantheon. We need constantly to bear in mind the many local variants throughout the Etruscan cities, the fact that significant differences in function and interpretation can coexist with a similarity of name or representation, and that there are likely to be major differences over time. The picture is further complicated by the large proportion of surviving evidence that comes from funerary contexts.

In prehistoric Villanovan culture (ca. 1000–700 BCE) and during the 7th century, deities were often represented as monsters (although the distinction between monster and deity is obviously difficult to draw). A bronze urn from Bisenzio (ca. 700 BCE) shows a magical procession of warriors and farmers going around a chained, monstrous death demon. An apelike demon is visible on the famous Etrusco-Corinthian oinochoe from Tragliatella that shows several rites of passage (ca. 630 BCE). The earliest names of gods are found on a kylix from Narce: Turan, Achaviur, and Ithavusva, goddesses of love, birth, and the toilette.

In the 6th century BCE, gods start to be represented anthropomorphically. The Etruscan underworld-god Suri, for example, became associated with Apollo. He was first depicted as a wolf, only later like the Greek god. Important to this process of assimilation were the cultural contacts that took place along the Italian coast, in harbor sites where Etruscans and others shared religious sites (such as Gravisca near Tarquinia).

The equation of Greek with Etruscan deities does not mean that Etruscan gods functioned like Greek gods; we need, rather, to look at it within the context of native Italic religion. Epithets and votive material indicate that, for example, Tinia Calusna was considered not simply as the equivalent of the Greek Zeus, but as a god of the underworld; and, although Menerva is represented like Greek Athena, she had many roles in Etruscan religion including oracular abilities, the protection of warriors, growth, and birth, not all of which Athena shared. The familial structure of the Etruscan pantheon differs from that of the Olympian family of gods. Epithets such as *ati* (mother), *apa* or *sans* (father), *clan* (son), and *sech* (daughter) are known, but there are few significant familial relationships. The representation of Tinia (Zeus) and Uni (Hera) as a couple, for example, may itself be a reflection of Greek influence. The famous Bronze Liver of Piacenza (ca. 100 BCE) mentions about forty gods. At the top of the hierarchy is Tin(ia) (Zeus). Apart from Hercle (Greek Heracles), all gods are Etruscan or Etruscanized Italic gods.

To judge from funerary representations, at the end of

the 5th century BCE the number of divinities connected with death, such as Charun (Greek Charon) and Vanth, Aita and Phersipnai (Greek Hades and Persephone), increased. However, Charun was not usually depicted as the old Greek ferryman on the Styx, but with a hammer as his attribute, indicating the end of life. Another example of this *interpretatio etrusca* is Athrpa, who did not handle scissors like the Greek fate Atropos, but instead held on to a hammer and a nail, symbolizing death.

BIBL.: G. Colonna (ed.), *Santuari d'Etruria* (Milan, 1985). I. E. Edlund, *The Gods and the Place* (Stockholm, 1987). F. Gaultier and D. Briquel (eds.), *Les étrusques: Les plus religieux des hommes: État de la recherche sur la religion étrusque* (Paris, 1997). R. Herbig, *Götter und Dämonen der Etrusker* (ed. E. Simon; 2nd ed., Mainz, 1965). A. J. Pfiffig, *Religio etrusca* (Graz, 1975). L.B.V.D.M.

Christianity

The transformation of the Galilean peasant movement begun by Jesus into a missionary religion of salvation, spreading across the Roman world, followed no single geographical or ideational path. As the emerging Christianities formulated their beliefs, they refashioned the prevalent spiritual hierarchies to account for the human predicament and the origins of the salvation they taught. They participated in the general move toward monotheism, worshiping one god who was, in most cases, understood as the source of all things. All other divine beings were generally denied the rank of god and arranged beneath the one god in the form of good and evil spirits. The Christian tradition emphasized, more than its predecessors had, the radically antithetical natures of these beings, and it employed the division against its opponents. Rather than deny the existence of pagan gods, Christian apologists, such as Justin Martyr (*Apology* 1.56) relocated them within the spiritual hierarchy as demons.

The general pattern, however, conceals a remarkable diversity and development in the Christian treatment of deities and demons. While the proto-orthodox communities followed the earliest Jesus movement and Paul in embracing a monotheism that equated the Hebrew God with the God they worshiped, for example, various other teachers distinguished between the two. The Hebrew God can appear in such systems as one of three primordial principles, the highest of which is the Platonic Good (Justin the Gnostic); as a late and errant product of the true God's expansion, who functions as an ignorant or evil demiurge and rules over wicked archons (heavenly rulers of this world inimical to human beings) and demons (Basilides, the Valentinian Ptolemy, the *Apocryphon of John*); or as a completely independent god whose legalistic and vengeful treatment of his human creations led the alien Christian God to graciously intervene and rescue humankind from the control of the Hebrew God (Marcion of Sinope).

Christian teachers of the 2nd century, particularly those who came to be regarded as heterodox gnostics, while denying the divine status of Greek and Roman gods, also explored more fully the unity and complexity of the deity revealed by Christ. Followers of Valentinus, an Alexandrian Christian active in Rome in the mid-2nd century, postulated a primordial divine source sometimes described as a dyad, sometimes as a monad, from which a whole "pleroma" or fullness of deity emerged. From the original Silent Depth there initially emanated an Ogdoad, or group of eight syzygies or paired entities, personified principles or aeons such as Humanity and Church, Life and Truth. The Ogdoad in turn produced further principles, thirty in number, ending in Sophia or Wisdom, whose quest for knowledge of the unknowable God produced the realms of soul and matter. Such emanations, inspired in part by the Platonic notion popular in the early imperial period of ideal forms as concepts in the mind of God, enabled these theologians to understand the emergence of the universe, the human predicament, and the divine origins of salvation. In many gnostic systems, Jesus or Christ appears as an emanation of God that descends to the material realm to save humankind from the control of the demiurge, the creator of the material world who is an amalgam of the God of the Old Testament and the Craftsman (Demiurge) from Plato's *Timaeus*.

Most Christian thinkers of the 2nd century united in rejecting the sharp division between the God of Jesus Christ and the creator found in Marcion and some gnostic systems (Tertullian, *Against Marcion*). Heresiologists also rejected the divine complexity about which particularly gnostic teachers speculated (Irenaeus, *Against the Heresies*; Hippolytus, *Refutation of All Heresies*). Nonetheless, the understanding of the godhead in emerging orthodox Christianity also involved complexity. Christian worship of the divine triad of Father, Son, and Holy Spirit, already attested in the 1st century (Matt. 28.19; 2 Cor. 13.14 [= 13.13 Greek]), also generated speculation and debate about the nature of Christian monotheism. The earliest Christians, including Paul, did not explicitly identify the Son and Spirit as God. Over time, however, their status within the divine hierarchy advanced. While they were most often ranked above the angels (Heb. 1.5–13 for the Son) and their nearness to God was emphasized, Christian authors still frequently situated them beneath God as part of the created order. Second-century sources explored the implications of considering the Son as the Word (Logos) of God (John 1.1–14). They took inspiration from Stoic linguistic theory, which related thought and speech as two aspects of the same reality, and from Alexandrian Jewish attempts to reconcile Plato and the Bible, particularly those of the 1st-century philosophical exegete Philo. Christian theologians such as Justin Martyr and Irenaeus suggested that the Son was a part of God as his "thought" *(logos endiathetos),* which came to expression in "speech" *(logos prophorikos)* as the incarnate

Jesus. Other attempts to express unity and distinction between God and the Son used imagery such as "beam of light and source" or "stream of water and font." The 3rd-century theologian Origen of Alexandria argued for the intimate association of Father and Son, but explicitly considered the Spirit to be created (*On First Principles* 1.3.3 [Greek]; *Commentary on John* 2.75).

The unqualified assertion of the full divinity of Christ and the Holy Spirit in hypostatic union with the Father, which defines the orthodox doctrine of the Trinity, occurred in the 4th century. The Council of Nicea, called by the emperor Constantine in 325 CE, marked the first stage of the revolutionary process. At issue was the status of the Logos, or Son. Was he fully divine or merely similar to God? The council's decision that he was of the "very nature" *(homoousios)* of the Father, although formulated in a creedal statement, did not win the day against those who argued for his "similar nature" *(homoiousios)*, two terms with literally an *iota* of difference. After decades of controversy, in which stalwart supporters of Nicea, such as Athanasius of Alexandria, played a major political role, and in which the Cappadocian Fathers, Basil of Caesarea, Gregory of Nyssa, and Gregory Nazianzus, played a major conceptual role, the Nicean formula was accepted as orthodoxy. The status of the Spirit remained vague until the second ecumenical council, at Constantinople in 381 CE, which reaffirmed the Nicean position and affirmed as well the full deity of the Spirit.

Final acceptance of the doctrine of the Trinity depended in part on the conceptual clarification of key terms such as *hypostasis* (entity, person, substance) and *ousia* (nature, being, substance), which had a variety of uses, sometimes contradictory, sometimes overlapping, in philosophical language. The doctrine of the Trinity wanted to affirm the fully divine status of the second person in order to insure an effective cause for salvation (what is not divine cannot save) and to preserve the distinction between Father and Son, in order to be true to biblical data distinguishing Father and Son. Theologians wanted to avoid collapsing Father and Son into one entity with different modes of relationship to the world (the Sabellian position, named for a teacher in early-3rd-century Rome), and they equally wanted to avoid polytheism. The elucidation of the language of Nicea affirming three "persons" *(hypostaseis)*, in loving relationship to one another, sharing one divine "nature" *(ousia)*, presented the most satisfactory solution to 4th-century Christians. Theologians who accepted the creeds of Nicea and Constantinople continued to explore the doctrine of the Trinity. Augustine of Hippo *(On the Trinity)*, for instance, developed an elaborate psychological model for understanding the godhead.

While Christians debated the character of divine complexity, another important strand of thinking about God insisted on the divine transcendence. Origen *(On First Principles* 1.1) insists that God is Spirit, against those who assume that God has a body. Gnostic teachers of the 2nd and 3rd centuries, perhaps inspired by the increasing insistence in Platonic circles of the 2nd and 3rd centuries on the transcendence of first principle or "the One," evidence a tendency to speak of God in apophaticly or in negative terms: one cannot say what God is, only what God is not *(Apocryphon of John, Tripartite Tractate)*. This insistence on the divine transcendence of the created order would dominate later patristic theology.

Beneath God, early Christians imagined a universe filled with good and evil spirits. The Pauline corpus labels such entities more generally as powers, principalities (archons), authorities, dominions, and thrones (a peculiar term for heavenly beings perhaps derived from the vision in Ezek. 1 of the divine "throne" composed of living beings), often identifying them with the "spiritual hosts of wickedness" (Eph. 6.12). Later Christians, following Jewish precedent, distinguished good and evil spirits linguistically as angels and demons. Others preferred the language of "aeons" and "archons." While most forms of Christianity predicated the ultimate origin of both good and evil spirits with God, various systems arose to account for the radical division. The sons of God who descended to earth in the myth narrated in Gen. 6, interpreted as fallen angels, supplied biblical evidence for the emergence of the wicked angels or demons. In many so-called gnostic cosmogonies, the divide occurred as a result of a wayward act attributed to the lower aeon, often identified as Sophia, or Wisdom. This event led to the emergence of the demiurge who, in turn, created a counterspiritual world replete with archons and demons.

In early Christian sources, angels, who serve God, correspond with or oversee elements of the universe, serve as intermediaries, minister to the church, function as guardians, and model the awaited existence in the life to come. They are eventually given names and organized into ranks. Gabriel, Michael, Raphael, and Uriel, for example, are identified as the four archangels. Over against the angels, Satan and his demonic forces serve to explain earthly evils and woes. In many so-called gnostic systems, the demiurge and his archons assumed this role. While the early gospel traditions focus on demonic possession, later Christian sources expanded the demons' responsibility for evil. Nourished by animal sacrifice, their efforts explain the miracles, oracles, and other successes of non-Christian religions. They cause natural calamities, incite persecutions and heresy, and encourage sin by tempting humans through the passions. Christian teachers, such as Valentinus, Origen, and Evagrius Ponticus, developed extensive theories on the demonic challenges faced by believers and devised techniques to aid in the struggle against them. Christian ascetics of the 4th century embodied the struggle between the angelic and demonic hosts as they sought through their rigorous practices to control the passions and approach the angelic life.

While the intellectual purveyors of Christian belief fashioned their various theories about deities and demons, their converts more often simply found in the religion a new language through which to communicate with and influence the supernatural powers that infused their world and governed their lives. The emerging cult of the saints provided a new system of spiritual patronage through which humans could approach the divine. Christians found in the sign of the cross a powerful tool against the demons, and numerous amulets and texts of ritual power (magic) supply plentiful evidence of Christianity's continuity with the past. Jesus Christ, Sabaoth, the various archangels, Mary, and other biblical figures appear not only in the writings of the theological elite, but are invoked as well in oracular texts, curses, exorcisms, and healing and protective spells.

BIBL.: Aloys Grillmeier, *Christ in Christian Tradition*, vol. 1 (2nd ed.; London, 1975). R. P. C. Hanson, *Search for the Christian Doctrine of God: The Arian Controversy, 318–381* (Edinburgh, 1988). George L. Prestige, *God in Patristic Thought* (London, 1969). J.E.G.

Dictionary of Deities and Demons

EGYPT

Amun. Appears first in the Middle Kingdom in Thebes and acquires a preeminent position throughout Egypt from the New Kingdom on, usually in the form of Amun-Re. Amun's temple in Karnak was the largest in terms of square feet, and he was the most important landowner in Egypt. His sacred animals were the ram and less often the Nile goose.

Aton. Strictly speaking, a designation for the solar disk. Aton acquired great significance under Akhenaten, who venerated him as sole god and had him portrayed as a sun with rays that end in human hands.

Atum. Sun-god of Heliopolis, who stands at the top of the ennead there. Atum is one of the original *Ur*-gods, who created his children Shu and Tefnut by masturbating or coughing them up and spitting them out. He appears in numerous animal shapes, as snake, eel, or mongoose (in his role as adversary of the serpent Apopis).

Geb. God of the earth, a member of the ennead of Heliopolis, and son of Shu and Tefnut. Geb is often depicted lying under his wife Nut, with his body covered in reeds. In addition to his primary role as lord of the earth and plants, he also functions as a judge, particularly in the Coffin Texts of the Middle Kingdom.

Hathor. Goddess known already in the early period of Egyptian history. Hathor's temple in Dendara is the largest of the temples from the late period still standing. It contains more inscriptions than any other surviving temple in Egypt. Among her other functions, she was the goddess of love, for which reason the Greeks identified her with Aphrodite. She was depicted in human form, but also frequently as a cow or with the head of a cow.

Horus. Son of Osiris and Isis, who defeats the illegitimate ruler Seth and ascends to the throne. An Egyptian king was considered an earthly Horus, and two of his five official titles are names of Horus. Horus is usually represented as a falcon or with a falcon's head.

Isis. Wife of Osiris, daughter of Geb and Nut, and a member of the ennead of Heliopolis. Isis is the grieving widow of Osiris, who rears his son Horus and saves him from persecution by Seth. Independently from Osiris, she plays the role as a mistress of spells, which can cause difficulties even for Re, the king of the gods. One important temple of Isis was in Philae, which was the last Egyptian temple to be closed in 537 CE. She was the Egyptian divinity with the largest cult outside Egypt during the Roman period.

Nut. Goddess of the sky belonging to the ennead of Heliopolis, like her husband, Geb. Nut's parents are Shu and Tefnut. She wears the stars on her body and is the mother of the sun-god, whom she swallows in the evening and gives birth to again in the morning. (These acts are often represented pictorially, in the Books of the Underworld or on the ceilings of temples from the late period.)

Osiris. Son of Geb and Nut and a member of the ennead of Heliopolis. Osiris is killed by his brother, Seth, and dismembered. The corpse is reassembled by Anubis, the god of embalming, and so Osiris is able to sire his successor, Horus, and becomes ruler of the underworld. This ensures him a prominent position as judge of the dead. In addition, he was considered the god of floods and vegetation, the last suggested by depictions of him with green skin.

Ptah. Chief god of the old royal capital Memphis. Ptah's wife is Sachmet, the lion-goddess. He is always depicted in human form, with a distinctive straight beard and blue cap. He was held to be the primal creator, who created the world with his intelligence and craftsman's skills.

Re. Sun-god held to be the king of the gods. Re's center of worship was Heliopolis from the time of the Old Kingdom. From the 4th Dynasty on, many royal names contained the element *Re,* and the king's official titles included the designation *son of Re.* Re was worshiped as the lord of all creation, the first of all the gods, and creator of the world. He is usually shown in the shape of a falcon or with a falcon's head, but in representations of his nightly journey through the underworld he is shown in the shape of a ram, traveling in his boat, in a shrine encircled by a snake.

Sachmet. Wife of Ptah. The center of Sachmet's worship

was Memphis. She is usually shown with the head of a lion and is the goddess of disease, which she can both spread through her messengers and cure.

Seth. Son of Geb and Nut and a member of the ennead of Heliopolis. Seth murders his brother, Osiris, but is later defeated by Horus, the son and legitimate successor of Osiris. In addition Seth plays a positive role as the god of war in the New Kingdom. In the underworld he defeats Apopis, the serpent-shaped opponent of the sun-god.

Thoth. Moon-god. Thoth's two sacred animals are the ibis and the baboon. He was the god of wisdom and writing, who also functioned as the messenger of the gods. The Greeks therefore identified him with Hermes. His chief center of worship was Hermopolis in Middle Egypt.

MESOPOTAMIA

An (Akkadian Anum). Heaven, the god who presides, in name, over the divine assembly. An was at home in Uruk, but was not its city god.

Assur. City god of Asshur, in origin nothing more than the deified rock on which his city was built. To give Assur the status he deserved as god of a mighty city, the Assyrians identified him at first with Enlil and later with Marduk.

Enki (Akkadian Ea). Lord of the Earth (Akkadian "the Living One"). Enki presided over an underground domain called *abzu* (Akkadian *apsûm*), the source of sweet waters and the home of supernatural beings such as *laḫamu* ("the Hairy One"). In the earliest cosmogony his mother Namma represents the primeval cosmic waters from which everything came forth; in 1st-millennium cosmogony she is replaced by Tiamat (Sea).

Enlil. Lord Ether, the god who organized the world after creation and in fact dominated the divine assembly that met in his city, Nippur. Enlil's son Ninurta (Lord of the Arable Earth) colonized the land and freed it from the forces of evil. In Girsu, Ninurta's name is Ningirsu (Lord of Girsu).

Ereshkigal. Lady of the Big Earth and mistress of the city of the dead in the netherworld. Ereshkigal's husband is the death- and war-god Nergal.

Inanna (Akkadian Ishtar). Venus, the morning and evening star. Daughter of the moon-god and sister of the sun-god, Inanna was responsible for love and war.

Ishkur (Akkadian Adad). Storm-god. Ishkur's wife is the naked goddess Shala.

Marduk. City god of Babylon, important only after the rise of his city to political power. As creator and cosmic ruler, Marduk replaced Enlil and Ninurta in the mythology of the 1st millennium.

Nanna (Akkadian Sin). Moon-god, son of Enlil, and responsible for the division of time. Nanna was at home in Ur.

Ninazu. Lord Healer, a chthonic snake-god responsible for the death and regeneration of plant life. Ninazu is at home in Eshnunna.

Ninhursag. Lady of the Hills, sister of Enlil, and, in early sources, also his wife. Ninhursag is the mother-goddess, who, together with Enki, created humankind. In Akkadian she is known as Belet-ili (Mistress of the Gods) and as Mami (Mama).

Ninisina. Lady of Isin, goddess of healing, and at home at Isin.

UTU (Akkadian Shamsh). Sun-god and son of Nanna (the moon-god). UTU was the god of justice and at home in two cities, Larsa and Sippar.

SYRIA-CANAAN

Anat. Goddess of war in Ugarit and Egypt. Anat is daughter of El and Asherah, as well as sister/consort of Baal (Hadad) in the Ugaritic myths.

Asherah. Ruling goddess found throughout Syria-Canaan. Asherah is the mother of the deities and consort of El in the Ugaritic myths, where she plays an active role in sustaining order in the world.

Baal. See Hadad.

Chemosh. Patron deity of Moab. Although a deity from early times in the pantheons in Syria, Chemosh's function is debated, usually between a god of military victory and one of the underworld.

Dagan. Widely worshiped god of grain. Dagan was the patron deity of humans, but appears throughout the Syrian and Canaanite cults.

El. West Semitic word for "god" and the ultimate object of appeal. Consort of Asherah in the Ugaritic myths, El is presented as a willful and manipulable father of the deities.

Hadad. Storm-god and patron deity of Aram and Ugarit. Known in many West Semitic pantheons simply as Baal (Lord), Hadad was a central and popular character in the Ugaritic myths, where he appears as a boastful, virile, and somewhat thickheaded deity.

Horon. Demon or deity associated with curses and serpent cures. Horon appears to have had authority over lesser demons, as petitions to him seek aid in fending off misfortune.

Mot. God of death. The personification of death is presented in the Ugaritic narratives as ruler of the netherworld, insatiably consuming the living, and as a favorite of his father El.

Resheph. Highly popular god of the netherworld. Throughout Syria, Canaan, and Egypt, Resheph was honored and feared as guardian of the underworld, warrior in battle, and bringer of disease.

Shemesh. Sun-god, in Ugarit appearing as the goddess Shapshu. The sun serves in Ugaritic myths as both messenger for the deity El and as deliverer of divine judgment.

Yamm. God (or demon) of the sea. In Ugaritic mythology, Yamm is an enemy of Baal and appears as the sea serpent Lothan.

Yarikh. Moon deity, also referred to as Yareah and by the Mesopotamian name Sin. The lunar calendars of the Syro-Canaanite world depended on the regular stages of Yarikh. Iconography of lunar deities is omnipresent throughout the Levant in the Bronze and Iron Ages.

ISRAEL

Anat. Canaanite goddess. Anat appears as Anat-Yahu (Anat, the consort of YHWH?) in the Jewish documents from Elephantine in southern Egypt (5th century BCE).

Asherah. Canaanite mother-goddess. Asherah was widely worshiped in Israel before the reform of King Josiah in 722 BCE and attested in inscriptions that refer to "YHWH and his Asherah."

Astarte. Canaanite goddess. Astarte was worshiped in Israel as the queen of heaven.

Baal. Canaanite storm-god. Baal was the great rival of YHWH in ancient Israel.

El. Canaanite high god. El was identified with YHWH in the Hebrew Bible.

Elohim. Plural form of El, used as a generic word for god or gods, singular or plural, in the Hebrew Bible.

YHWH. God of Israel. According to one tradition, the name YHWH was first revealed at Mount Sinai.

HITTITE

Hepat. See Sun-Goddess of Arinna.

Inara. Daughter of the storm-god, goddess of the hunt, perhaps identifiable with Hattian Teteshapi.

Istanu. Sun-God of heaven.

Kamrusepa. In mythology, associated with magic.

Kumarbi. Grain and fertility deity, associated with the underworld, from Hurrian influence.

Storm-God of Hatti. Hittite Tarhunt, a chief deity. Originally an Indo-European deity and later identified with Hurrian Teshub, the Sun-God of Hatti shared a grand temple at Hattusha with the Sun-Goddess of Arinna.

Sun-Goddess of Arinna. Hattic Wurusemu, a chief deity. The Sun-Goddess of Arinna was later identified with Hurrian Hepat.

Telipinu. A lesser storm-god and a god of agriculture. Considered the son of the storm-god, Telipinu is the main figure in the Telipinu myth.

Teshub. See Storm-God of Hatti.

IRAN

Aeshma (Xeshm). Zoroastrian "Wrath with the bloody cudgel." Aeshma is one of the archdemons of the Lie (Druj) who disrupts the world of Truth (Asha). His primary opponent is Sraosha.

Ahura Mazda (Ohrmazd). "Wise Lord" of the Iranians and the supreme deity. Ahura Mazda created the material and spiritual worlds and is the source of Truth. He was worshiped by the Achaemenid kings and revealed the Good Religion to Zarathustra.

Anahita (Anahid). "The Immaculate" goddess of the Iranians. Anahita was worshiped with Mithra and Ahura Mazda by the Achaemenid kings, she was closely connected with royal power, and her cult was widespread in the western parts of the Persian Empire. In the Avesta she has joined a river-goddess Aredwi Sura (Ardwisur) (the Moist, Strong).

Angra Mainyu (Ahriman). Zoroastrian "Evil Spirit." Angra Mainyu is the archdemon, the very Lie (Druj). In Zarathustra's theology he is one of twin spirits whom, presumably, Ahura Mazda created, but in later dualistic theology he is the primordial embodiment of the lie and author of all evil. He is opposed by either Ahura Mazda's creative aspect, Spenta Mainyu, or by Ahura Mazda/Ohrmazd himself.

Azi Dahaka (Azdahag). "Snake Barbarian." Azi Dahaka derives from the Indo-Iranian myth of the cosmic snake who prevents the full unfolding of the cosmos by withholding water. In the Iranian national myth of kingship, he overthrows the first man and king (Yima, Jamshed) and subjects Iran to evil rule until he is slain by the hero Thraetaona (Fredon).

Frawashis (Frawahran). Guardian spirit. In Zoroastrianism each (righteous) individual has a guardian spirit, a spiritual double, a Frawashis. Together all such spirits join to form a large army that fights in the service of Ahura Mazda against the forces of Angra Mainyu. Further, they function as the ancestor spirits who must be propitiated in rituals just prior to the New Year.

Jeh. The "Whore." Jeh is absent from the Avesta but prominent in later Zoroastrian theology as one of Ahriman's most evil creations. Opposed to the beneficent female, Spandarmad, created by Ohrmazd, the Whore brings pollution upon humans through the filth of menstruation.

Mithra (Mihr). Iranian god "Covenant." Through strong martial attributes, Mithra enforces the sanctity of all contracts, treaties, and covenants among people. He acquired solar associations, and his name, through the cult of Mithras, was spread widely by the Roman legions throughout Europe and the Near East. In Zoroastrianism he played a role as a judge of the dead.

Sraosha (Srosh). Personification of "Obedience." Sraosha was a popular Zoroastrian god because of his effectiveness in combating the demons, especially the archdemon Aeshma. He acted as a judge of the dead, and his role of intermediary carried him over into Iranian Islam as the angel Surosh.

Tishtrya (Tishtar). Iranian astral god, the star Sirius. In the Avesta, Tishtrya overcomes the demon of drought, Apaosha, and the demoness of famine, Duzyairya. In the Pahlavi books he appears as the general of the east, pitted against the planetary god Tir (Mercury).

Werethrayna (Wahram). Iranian god of war or "Victory" (lit. "the Smashing of Resistance"). Werethrayna appears in ten avatars, the most important being the wild boar and the falcon. In the Avesta he shares martial traits with Mithra. A favorite of Parthian and Sasanid kings, he came to be identified with Heracles under the Arsacids.

Zurwan. Iranian god "time." Zurwan emerges during the Arsacid period as the ultimate creator of the dualistically opposed deities Ohrmazd and Ahriman, who themselves create the worlds of good and evil.

GREECE AND ROME

Aphrodite. Although presiding over erotic seduction and sweet whispers, Aphrodite is dangerous when her power is challenged or she is snubbed. Like her Mesopotamian homologue Ishtar, Greek Aphrodite also has a warlike character at times. Passing through Etruria, she brought the month April to the Romans and to us.

Apollo. Associated by both the Greeks and the Romans with prophecy, music, healing, and the foundation of colonies and sanctuaries. Apollo also has a dark side, whatever Nietzsche may have thought; he brings plague as well as cures it. He entered Rome as a healer and in Roman imperial ideology, he was the protector of Augustus.

Ares. Greek god of the madness and fury of war, seldom worshiped in cult. In myth, the paramour of Aphrodite.

Artemis. A virgin. Savage and connected with the moon, beautiful and capricious, Greek Artemis loves green valleys and forest clearings and protects the young of humans and animals.

Athena. Another virgin. Pursued by Hephaestus, Athena escaped his embrace, while his sperm impregnated Earth, who gave birth to Erichthonius, the ancestor of the Athenians. Athena adopted Erichthonius as her foster son. She is the goddess of skilled performance in many fields—sailing, cattle and horse breeding, war and handicraft.

Ceres. Personified Growth. Roman Ceres is the goddess of the plebeians. Very early, she was assimilated to Greek Demeter and connected with Liber (Dionysus) and Libera (Persephone).

Demeter. Mother of Persephone and nurse of the Eleusinian baby prince Demophon. Demeter brought laws and civilization, taught the cultivation and use of grain, and founded the Eleusinian Mysteries.

Diana. Goddess of the Latin League. Diana protects women in birth and their children. The ritual connected with the golden bough, made famous by Sir James Frazer, starts and ends at her sanctuary of Aricia, at Lake Nemi near Rome.

Dionysus. Greek Dionysus is an intimate stranger, a virtuoso of illusions and raptures, voluptuous and cruel. Ariadne's spouse, he protects the theater and wine. He was a great god in the ideology of a mystery religion whose sacred texts were attributed to Orpheus, which claimed that Dionysus's death led to the creation of humanity. Dionysus is also called Bacchus and, in Rome, Liber.

Eros. Greek cosmic power older than Aphrodite—or, more often, a boy and archer, Aphrodite's winged son and servant.

Fortuna. Associate of Mater Matuta with whom she shares her Roman sanctuary. Fortuna is a goddess of destiny, who likes to deceive her favorites (such as King Servius Tullius).

Hades. Greek god of the underworld, which is also called Hades. He is seldom honored in cult but in myth plays the important role of Persephone's abductor and husband.

Hephaestus. Greek god of potters and blacksmiths and a blacksmith himself. Hephaestus was lame since birth or early childhood. He is the husband of Aphrodite.

Hera. Greek goddess of marriage and many women's concerns. Hera is also a protector of cities. In myth, she attacks the many lovers and illegitimate children of her husband, Zeus.

Hermes. Present on herdsmen's trails and public places, in commerce, sport, and gambling, at the heart of language and the doors of dreams and of the underworld, Greek Hermes has a somewhat slick character. He is not necessarily a serious god, as his elder sibling Apollo good-humoredly points out in the Homeric *Hymn to Hermes*.

Hestia. Greek goddess of the hearth, worshiped in domestic cult primarily. Hestia is a virgin and seldom appears in myth.

Janus. Roman god of all beginnings. In time, space, and actions, Janus is always invoked first. As god of passages, he has a double face that looks both forward and backward.

Juno. Roman goddess of women. Juno also protects young citizens, and she is, with Jupiter and Minerva, one of the three divinities that preside over Rome (the Capitoline triad).

Jupiter. Somewhat different from Zeus, Jupiter embodies Roman sovereignty, protects vineyards, and presides over the middle of every month, when he accepts a sheep on the Ides *(ovis Idulis)*.

Magna Mater (Mother of the Gods). The name Magna Mater makes her the female counterpart of Zeus, "father of gods and mortals" in epic poetry. An aristocratic and violent mountain-goddess, she is said to originate from Phrygia or the Troad and plays the role of an ancestor both on the Palatine in Rome and on the Athenian Agora. Her weak point is Attis the royal shepherd, with whom she falls in love.

Mars. Much more complex than Ares. Rome's imperial destiny is proof that this warlike god, who also has an agricultural side, is really Romulus's father.

Mater Matuta. Goddess of dawn, of maternal aunts, and of the young children of Rome. Mater Matuta watches over legitimate citizenship. In her festival, the matrons chase a slave girl out of her sanctuary.

Minerva. Goddess of crafts and skills. Minerva's name denotes mental power *(mens)*. A *minerval* is the gift or honorarium given to a teacher.

Neptune. Roman god of springs and deep green shadows. When assimilated with Greek Poseidon he also became god of the sea.

Pan. Arcadia's goat-legged god, son of Hermes. Pan is a syrinx player, dancer, and hapless seducer of nymphs. He brings fertility to goats and sheep and sends panic into military camps in the silence of the night. The death of the Great Pan is a famous story in later antiquity and beyond.

Persephone. Greek queen of the underworld and unwilling wife of its king, Hades. Persephone and her mother, Demeter, are the central deities worshiped at the Eleusinian Mysteries, which promised a better existence both in life and after death. In sacred texts attributed to Orpheus, she is Dionysus's mother and associated with his mysteries.

Poseidon. Lord of the swirling waves of the sea, but also of earthquakes, springs, and the fury of horses. Poseidon is also sometimes a physician.

Saturnus. Reigned over Italy during the Golden Age. He had a temple on the Roman Forum. Sometimes he was assimilated with the Jewish god.

Venus. Adored and venerable Roman goddess. Her name indicates "beauty, attraction." Venus is the mother of Aeneas and, through his son Ascanius, who was also called Iulus, ancestor of Julius Caesar, or simply of all Romans.

Vesta. Roman goddess of the hearth. Vesta was worshiped as a guarantor of the state and sometimes domestically. A virgin, she was attended at her temple in Rome by six Vestal Virgins, sworn to celibacy.

Vulcan. The devouring fire, with an old cult on the Roman Forum (the Volcanal).

Zeus. Victor over the Titans and the Giants, king of the Olympian gods and supreme divinity of the age. A great politician, armed with lightning and deception, Zeus often changed shape to make love to mortal women.

ETRURIA

Cel. Goddess of earth; Celsclan: son *(clan)* of Cel, a giant.

Charun. God of death (from Greek Charon), holding a hammer to indicate the end of life.

Culsans. Male god protecting gateways (from Etruscan *cul* [gateway]), depicted with a double head.

Culsu. Female god of the gateway to the underworld.

Fufluns. God of vegetation, wine, and fertility. Fufluns looks like Greek Dionysus; he is a soteriological god, also appearing in underworld scenes.

Laran. Martial god, comparable to Greek Ares.

Lasa. Minor love-goddess, very popular in the last centuries BCE.

Menerva. Divine name of Italic origin (cf. Latin Minerva). Menerva's appearance is like that of Greek Athena.

Sethlans. Comparable to the Greek Hephaestus.

Thalana and Thanr. Goddesses of birth.

Thesan. Goddess of dawn, looks like the Greek Eos.

Tinia. Chief god, looks like the Greek Zeus, depicted with one or two lightning bolts in his hands.

Tiv. Goddess of the moon.

Turan. Goddess of love (cf. Etruscan *tur-* [to give]; *turan* [giving]), looks like the Greek Aphrodite.

Turms. The Etruscan Hermes.

Uni. Spouse of Tinia (cf. Latin Juno), looks like the Greek Hera.

Usil. God of the sun, often depicted with the attributes of the Greek Apollo.

Vanth. Goddess of death, looks like a Greek Fury, often represented together with Charun.

EARLY CHRISTIANITY

Aeon. A Greek word meaning "age," "eternity," or "realm." Aeon serves in so-called gnostic thought as a generic label for the positive emanations of the true God. The aeons often appear as personified concepts, such as Forethought and Eternal Life, and represent the unfolding outreach of the unknowable God. As the Trinity and the angels in proto-orthodox Christianity, they serve to connect God and humanity.

Archon. The Greek word for "ruler" or "governor." Archon is employed in early Christian thought to refer to spiritual authorities or beings that affect human life, especially in a negative or evil way. In so-called gnostic thought, the archons are produced by the lower and often evil demiurge as he seeks to emulate the spiritual realm of the true God and his aeons. The archons serve a demonic role, working to thwart human salvation.

Beelzebub. Meaning literally "Lord [Baal] of the Flies," the name Beelzebub is used in early Christian sources for the prince of the demons. It equates him with the devil and Satan.

Gabriel. An angel of God in Jewish and early Christian sources. Gabriel serves as an intermediary between the divine and human realms and eventually emerges as one of the four archangels in Christian tradition.

Ialdabaoth. The demiurge in various so-called gnostic systems. Ialdabaoth is responsible for material creation and strives with his archons to thwart the salvation efforts of God and retain control of humankind.

Logos. A term with a complex linguistic history, Logos appears in early Christian thought as a synonym for Christ. Often translated simply as "word," the usage reflects the common practice of using personified concepts as names for spiritual beings or aspects of God.

Michael. An angel of God in Jewish and early Christian sources. Michael serves as an intermediary between the divine and human realms, often appearing as a mediator of righteousness. He eventually emerges as one of the four archangels in Christian tradition.

Raphael. An angel of God in Jewish and early Christian sources. Raphael serves as an intermediary between the divine and human realms, often appearing as a healer of the faithful. He eventually emerges as one of the four archangels in Christian tradition.

Sophia. Sophia, or Wisdom, appears in Jewish and early Christian thought as a personified divine being. Proto-orthodox Christians equated the Jewish notion of Sophia as an entity who aided God in creation with the preexisting Christ, or Logos. Gnostic Christians identified Sophia as an emanation of the true God. Her actions led directly to the emergence of the demiurge and the creation of the material world.

Uriel. An angel of God in Jewish and early Christian sources. Uriel serves as an intermediary between the divine and human realms and eventually emerges as one of the four archangels in Christian tradition.

Religious Practices of the Individual and Family

Introduction

Western views on religion have been determined, for a very long time, by the concept of Christianity as a universal religion informed by a unified doctrinal system. This idealized notion of Christianity served as a model and a yardstick for the description and analysis of other religions, whether ancient or modern. Hence the emphasis, in textbooks on religion, on the ideas and written documents of the various religions. The principal ingredients of an introduction to Mesopotamian religion, for instance, consisted of a survey of the main deities—the top ten of the pantheon—and a summary of the myths transmitted in writing. Scholars did realize that there was also the realm of popular religion (referred to, rather pejoratively, as *Volksreligion*), but they considered the latter as a degraded expression of religion not belonging to its pure and true essence.

Despite its longtime dominance, the approach to religion as a single entity characterized by its doctrinal system no longer rules supreme. The early 20th century saw a growing sensibility to religious practices, as distinguished from doctrines. From that time onward, religious ritual came to be an object of study alongside the study of mythology. Owing to the impact of contemporary visual culture, the later 20th century became increasingly aware of the role of images in religion, not merely as an illustration of texts, but as a level of content in its own right. The revaluation of ritual is reflected in the—mainly Scandinavian—"Myth-and-Ritual School" and the new appreciation of religious iconography in such journals as *Visible Religion*.

Another development in 20th-century scholarship is the acknowledgment of the inner multiplicity of religion. No religion is monolithic; each is a compound consisting of historical sediments as well as regionally diversified and sociologically stratified layers. That the role of religion in the life of the state differs from its role in the private lives of citizens has led scholars to distinguish between official and popular religion. Many feel that the latter distinction is in need of refinement; in addition to the religion of the state and the religion of the individual, there is also village religion and the religion of the region. Others advocate a distinction along the lines of profession; thus, there is peasant religion and the religion of scholars, the religion of soldiers and the religion of merchants. The stress on the internal pluralism of religion has triggered a tendency to speak of religion in the plural. "Mesopotamian religions," "Israelite religions," and "Greek religions" figure in the titles of books whose counterparts twenty-five years ago spoke of religion in the singular.

One need not abandon the singular in favor of the plural in order to recognize that religion of the individual and family represents a distinct facet of ancient Mediterranean religions. This level of religion is best seen in contradistinction from the religion of the state. State religion is the religion practiced in the state temples and, in some cultures, transmitted in the schools and academies. The religion of the individual and family is religion as it was practiced in private households and local shrines for the benefit of the individual and the family. Finer distinctions can be proposed, but they would disturb the balance between the common (e.g., "the Mesopotamian religion") and the particular ("official" versus "popular" religion). The religion of the individual and family functions within, and presupposes, the wider context of the official religion. Also, its practices are not mere gestures, but are informed by notions and ideas adopted from the doctrines of the reigning religion.

The relationship between the individual and the family requires some elaboration, as here the situation differs fundamentally from the one prevalent in most modern societies. In the ancient world, a person was not an individual in our sense of the word. Individuals were first and foremost members of groups, the principal one being the family. The nuclear family, consisting on average of four or five persons (parents plus two or three children), was part of a larger social body best referred to as the clan or the neighborhood. It is true that clan membership implies kinship, whereas neighborhood implies topographical ties. In many ancient cultures, however, the kinship supposed by the clan or the lineage group is putative rather than demonstrable; families living in the same town or neighborhood, moreover, were credited with a common ancestor and thus considered themselves as kin. For all practical purposes, clan and neighborhood are often coterminous. The religion of the individual was the religion of the family, the latter notion being embedded in, as well as being an expression of, the religion of the clan, town, or neighborhood. There is then very little difference, if any, between family religion and village religion.

The data needed for the reconstruction of the religion of the individual and the family must be gleaned from a quite different type of evidence from the kind used in the case of state religion. Texts from the "stream of tradition" are of little use. Formulary prayers (such as the "prayers of the lifting of the hand") do attest that individuals worshiped private gods, but leave us uninformed about the identity of the latter and the nature of their worship. In this respect, the study of private documents, such as letters, deeds of inheritance, adoption contracts, and the like, is far more rewarding. Private seals, too, are a source of information in the case of Near Eastern cultures, as their legends frequently refer to the personal god of the owner. Nonverbal evidence, as furnished by the archeological record of private houses and neighborhood shrines, is important as well, although its interpretation is often hazardous. To some degree, comparative evidence from neighboring cultures makes up for the gaps in the evidence in a particular case.

In anticipation of the contributions to our understanding of the religion of the individual and family in the various civilizations of the ancient Near East, it may be said that private religion addresses itself to family gods and family ancestors. The god of a family is not anonymous; ordinarily, the family honors a specific member of the pantheon to whom, for reasons of tradition and/or topography, it feels particularly close. The family dead are an object of care and veneration up to four or five generations back; those of earlier times are no longer mentioned by name, but have joined the ever-increasing community of the dead with neither face nor name. Given the tendency, common to the ancient Mediterranean in general, to credit the dead with special powers—such as foreknowledge and fertility—the cult of dead kin bears some similarities to the cult of the family gods in those cultures that practice it. The primary function of family religion in the eyes of its practitioners is utilitarian. The family worships its god and honors its dead in order to obtain their blessings and to avoid their displeasure. Health of the household, a good harvest, male offspring, and the esteem of the neighbors are often considered to be matters too trivial for the gods of the state to be bothered with; but the family god and the ancestors are close and they care. In the eyes of the modern scholar, the religion of the family served a role primarily as an identity marker. The cult of the ancestors provided a historical focus of identity and the cult of the family god provided a topographical focus of identity. For the individual members of the family, participation in the rituals of family religion was a reaffirmation and celebration of their rightful place within the family. They belonged to a body that was larger than the life of one human only, protected by the family god and linked to the past—and hence legitimated—by the ancestors.

K.V.D.T.

Mesopotamia

The basic nucleus to which the Mesopotamian individual belonged, whether living in the city or in the country, was the *bīt abim* (house of the father), that is, the family. To be a member of a family was to partake of the same flesh and blood by virtue of which all those belonging to the family could refer to each other in terms of consanguinity. The boundaries of the family depended on the perspective that the speaker adopted: the "house of the father" might refer either to what we call the nuclear family or to the extended family. The nuclear family was the household, consisting of a father and mother plus an average of two or three children, with a couple of otherwise unattached relatives (grandparents, uncle, or aunt) and possibly servants sharing the same domestic space. The extended family or clan comprised a significantly larger group defined by consanguinity, whether real or presumed, and topographical vicinity. In many instances, the clan was more or less coterminous with the village or the city neighborhood.

In Mesopotamia, family religion was an important means of expressing the identity of the family and fostering solidarity among its members. The latter observation is not meant to imply that religion might be reduced to such functions, let alone that such an objective was paramount in the minds of those participating in the rites. Yet, however one feels about the nature of religious experience, it can hardly be denied that the effects of Mesopotamian family religion symbolically consolidated the bonds that existed on nonreligious grounds.

Mesopotamian family religion was a marriage of the cult of the ancestors, on the one hand, and the veneration of "the god of the father," that is, the family deity, on the other. The two facets are best dealt with separately.

For the ancients, the ancestor cult consisted of the proper care and feeding of the dead under the invocation of their names. One of the duties of a pious son was to bring regular offerings to the ancestors of the family and in particular to his own father. Although the duty was incumbent upon all children, primary responsibility

Sumerian statues, worshipers with clasped hands, found at the square Abu Temple at Eshnunna. Oriental Institute, University of Chicago. *Courtesy of the Oriental Institute of the University of Chicago*

lay with the one who succeeded his father as *paterfamilias*. Normally, this was the eldest son. That is why he received, as part of his inheritance, such paraphernalia of the domestic cult as the "ceremonial table." Since the son received his authority not by delegation from the rules, but by transmission and assumed devolution from the ancestors, his leadership in the cult of the ancestors had the attendant effect of legitimizing his position. On exceptional occasions a daughter might attain to this position.

The common word for the offering to the dead is *kispu*, a noun derived from a verb meaning "to break into small pieces." The etymology suggests a reference to the presentation of crumbs of bread, but flour instead of bread was standard. A bowl of water accompanied the food. Offered on a daily basis, the *kispu* was a modest meal. On special occasions, more solemn rites were performed, including the presentation of a full meal. The privileged period for this ceremony was the end of the month, during the time when the moon was invisible and believed to be visiting the underworld. The absence of the moon was taken as a warning of looming danger; the day was unpropitious and holy. People used the holiday to come together as family for a festive meal. As the family joined in a meal of plenty, it did not forget its ancestors: the latter received their share of the dishes. There are indications that once a year, at the end of the month of Abu (August), there were nightly vigils across the land in honor of the dead. This Mesopotamian version of All Souls' Day fit the pattern of monthly family meetings, but turned the family dead into the main guests.

The central rite of the cult of the ancestors was the invocation of the dead by their names. That is why the eldest son, as the leader of the ceremony, was called the *zākir šumim* (the one who invokes the name [i.e., of

the ancestors]). From the perspective of the dead, so to speak, the purpose of the cult devoted to them was to ensure that their names did not perish. By the same token, piety toward the ancestors endowed the living with a family identity that was anchored in the past. Judging from the way that ancestor cult is reflected literarily in prayers, "past" went back five generations at most. As a rule, family members addressed gifts and invocations only to those forebears who were still remembered as having been present among them. Women were included in the list of invoked ancestors only as wives and mothers or as daughters who did not marry. The invocation of the family dead, in other words, tallied with the patrilinear nature of the Mesopotamian family.

From the existence of exorcistic rituals against dissatisfied ghosts, one might gain the impression that the ancestors were fundamentally malevolent and that the function of the offerings was to keep them at bay. Under ordinary circumstances, however, the purpose of the rites for the dead was communion between family members alive and dead and the maintenance of mutual goodwill. The ancestors were not powerless. Not only could they harm when they felt neglected, but they could also act as moral authorities in cases of family tension and, when they were so disposed, bless their offspring with offspring of their own.

The second facet of the religion of the individual and the family in Mesopotamia focused on the veneration of a family god, referred to most often as "your god" or "the god of your father." This is an area of Mesopotamian religion that, until recently, did not receive a great deal of attention. Traditionally, historians of Mesopotamian religion have given pride of place to the study of the official national religions, with their theology, myths, and temple worship. That is why it is necessary first to demonstrate the existence, identity, and

425

A votive statue of a worshiper from the temple of Ishtar at Mari. The inscription reads, "Statue of Ebih-il, the steward, to Ishtar . . . he devoted it." Louvre. *Réunion des Musées Nationaux/ Art Resource, New York*

Marduk, for instance, son of Sin-gamil, professed himself to be "*shangum* priest of Shamash, servant of Marduk." The last line of the seal legend, then, refers to the god to whom the individual is privately devoted.

Private letters are another source of information about personal gods. The rules of the epistolary genre required the writer to open the letter with the wish, "May god A and god B keep you in good health." Normally the reference was to two gods; sometimes one, and exceptionally three or more. A study of the several thousand Old Babylonian and Old Assyrian letters reveals a pattern in the choice and the sequence of the divine names. As a rule, the last (and thus ordinarily the second) god mentioned was the personal god of the addressee. Some examples illustrate the practice:

May Shamash and your god keep you in good health!

May Shamash, Marduk, and Amurru your creator keep you in good health forever for my sake!

May Shamash and the god of your husband keep you in good health!

May Shamash and Ninshubur your creator keep you in good health forever for my sake!

In all of these cases, the personal god of the addressee comes last and may be mentioned by name and the epithet "your creator" or simply as "your god" or—when the letter is to a woman—"the god of your husband." Shamash and Marduk, the gods mentioned first, represent universal (Shamash the sun-god) or national (Marduk) deities. They are gods that concern every citizen; the last deity mentioned, on the other hand, is the private god of the recipient of the letter.

To call the god mentioned on the seal or as the last one in the greeting formulas of letters a personal or private god may be misleading in an age such as ours, which puts so much weight on the person as an individual. In ancient Mesopotamia, the cult of the personal god was collective, as the evidence shows. A synoptic study of seals belonging to different members of the same family reveals that different generations mentioned the same deity as their personal god. It is in line with this observation that the deity referred to as "your god" might alternatively be referred to as "the god of your father." Veneration of the personal god was handed down from father to son; a woman, upon her marriage, adopted the same god who could, in her case, be referred to as "the god of your husband." The father was the *paterfamilias,* whose devotion to one god determined the object of devotion of his sons and grandsons. My "personal god" (*ili rēšiya* or *ili qaqqadiya* [lit., the god of my head]) was, in fact, "the god of [my] family" (*ili kimtini* [the god of our family/clan]).

Devotion to a specific deity as personal god, then, was not a matter of choice but of inheritance. Yet there must

nature of family gods before we can assess their role in the life of the Mesopotamian family and its individual members.

There is ample evidence that the Babylonians and Assyrians had "personal gods," according to the terminology of the scholarly literature on the subject. Two types of data are particularly striking in this respect: the legends of the personal cylinder seals and the greeting formulas in private letters. The cylinder seal, which left an imprint by rolling over a malleable surface such as clay, served as an identity marker. The usual legend of the Old Babylonian seal consists of three lines: the first stating the name of the owner of the seal, the second defining him as "son of so-and-so," and the third defining him as the "servant of god so-and-so." The religious affiliation that was added to the personal name and the patronym was not, as a rule, a professional one. Someone belonging to the temple bureaucracy, for instance, might refer to himself as "priest of god A" but would then add "servant of god B." One Shalim-palih-

be historical reasons that some families worshiped one deity as their god and other families another. Analysis of available data cannot elucidate all the particular motives of choice, but points to three considerations that played a role. It is quite striking that nearly all of the family gods we know belong to the second or third echelon of the pantheon. The most satisfactory explanation of this fact is that the ordinary Mesopotamian considered intimacy with the highest gods presumptuous and therefore directed devotion to gods who could act as intercessors with their superiors. Seals depict and prayers describe the personal god as an intermediary between the worshiper and the supreme deities. Profession could also be a motive of choice: scribes had a preference for Nabu and Nissaba, the gods of writing, as their personal gods. Topographical proximity between the family and the shrine of the god it worships was also a factor of importance. There are several cases where it is clear that families focus their devotion on a god who has a sanctuary in the neighborhood, city quarter, or village where they live. Finally, in the case of the Amorite part of the Mesopotamian population, the family gods (or the gods of the clan) belonged to the restricted circle of typically Amorite gods such as the moon-god (Sin or Erah), Amurru, Dagan, and the storm-god Addu (or Adad).

Allegiance to a family god was more than a formal marker of family identity. According to the popular theology of the time, the family god was the creator of its individual members: your god was "your creator" (bānīka). For health, social status, prosperity, and success in life generally, the individual depended on the benevolence of this god: your god was "your protector" (nāṣirka). When the god was at peace with the family living under his tutelage, he surrounded them with loving care: your god was "the one who loves you" (rāʿimka). From a sociological point of view, the doctrine of the family god as divine family patron worked in two ways: it provided the family with hope that a higher power might secure their fortune, and it legitimized their superior position against the envy of those less well off. If wealth, power, and fame are gifts of the god, who could contest them?

The mutual bond between a family and its god also entailed obligations for the former. Their devotion was supposed to materialize in various acts of worship. The family god was entitled to prayer and praise; both were ways of acknowledging the god's powers. Family members were expected to daily "bless" (karābu) their god. To bless one's divine benefactor was to speak highly of him in the presence of others. If daily acts of blessing could not be performed in person, one might dedicate a votive object representing the individual in a pose of obeisance; the image was appropriately called a kāribum. Regular sacrifices were another ingredient of the cult of the family god. The demands of the deity were not merely ritual, however. "Fear of one's god," as the Akkadian expression runs, included respect for the socially accepted code of conduct. Acts of human kindness were an essential part of that code, particularly for those enjoying a superior social position.

The cult of the ancestors and the veneration of the "god of the father" constituted the two facets of Mesopotamian family religion. The religion of the individual was embedded in and formed part of the religion of the family. Outside the family or clan the individual would be without an identity, both personal and religious. Personal religion was the symbolic yet effective means to partake of the family identity and thereby to affirm oneself as belonging to a collectivity with ties to the past and to the local community. Family religion was the channel through which the individual secured the claim to his or her legitimate place in the Mesopotamian society.

BIBL.: Karel van der Toorn, *Family Religion in Babylonia, Syria, and Israel: Continuity and Change in the Forms of Religious Life* (Leiden: Brill, 1996). K.V.D.T.

Syria-Canaan

Family religion and individual devotion in ancient Syria constitute an area where historians must be cautious not to extrapolate from Mesopotamian and biblical sources in order to remedy the lack of evidence from Syria proper. Although it is clear that Syrian family religion conforms to the general ancient Near Eastern pattern of a dual devotion, to the family ancestors on the one hand and to the family god on the other, the written sources on the subject are scant, and other testimonies to private religion (such as votive objects) allow for more than one interpretation. The relevant written data we do have at our disposal, primarily from Ugarit in the 13th century BCE and from Samal, almost half a millennium later, reflect the religion of the royal family. It is mainly by assuming that dynastic religion is a special form of family religion that we may draw the contours of Syrian family religion in general.

As in Mesopotamia and Israel, the Syrian family is both patrilineal and patrilocal. It is headed by the *paterfamilias*, normally the eldest son who has succeeded his father in this function, even though the latter may still be alive. The duties of the *paterfamilias* are listed, paradigmatically rather than exhaustively, in a passage from the Ugaritic Aqhat epic. One of the themes of the epic is the desire of King Danel for a son and an heir. Owing to a divine intervention his wish is to be fulfilled, and encapsulated in the oracle that announces the birth of a son is a list of the duties to be performed by the latter. He will grow up to be a man

who erects the stele of his divine ancestor,
in the sanctuary the symbol of his kinsman;
who, on earth, makes his smoke go out,
on the dust, tends his place;
who crushes the jaws of those who revile him

Individual making an offering to a bearded deity (perhaps El), with horned crown, seated on his throne; the god's hand is lifted, perhaps in blessing. Stele from Ugarit (Ras Shamra), 13th century BCE. Aleppo Museum. *Erich Lessing/Art Resource, New York*

and drives away those who act against him;
who takes him by the hand in his drunkenness
and supports him when he is sated with wine;
who eats his emmer in the temple of Baal
[and] his part in the temple of El;
who plasters his roof in the [fou]l season
and washes his garments when they are dirty.
(KTU 1.17, 1.26–33, and parallels)

The pronominal suffixes in this passage refer back to the father: the son he hopes for will help him in his drunkenness and will wash his clothes. By including such menial chores as plastering the roof and washing the father's clothes, the list enumerates traditional duties incumbent on every son who succeeds his father; a prince of royal blood would have servants to keep the roof in repair and to do the laundry. The activities listed, moreover, are typically those of a grown man: crushing the jaws of one's father's adversaries is beyond the strength of a child or an adolescent. What are customarily referred to as the duties of a (royal) son, then, are in fact the duties of any son in charge of the house whose father is incapacitated by age.

The religious obligations that the heir is to fulfill illus-

trate in a striking fashion the dual nature of Syrian family religion. The son was to take care of the ancestors and participate in the sacrificial meals in the temples of El and Baal. The ancestor cult is summed up in the action of erecting a stele for the "divine ancestor" of the father, echoed in the parallel line by what has been tentatively translated as the "symbol" of his kinsman. The word for "divine ancestor" is *ilib,* a combination of the words for "god" *(il)* and "father" *(ab,* vocalized *ib* under the influence of *il).* In view of the parallelism with "kinsman" *('m),* the term *ilib* is best taken as a designation of the "father" in the wider sense of the term, which leads to the translation "ancestor." This ancestor is qualified as a "god," which is consonant with the parallelism between "the shades of the dead" *(rpim)* and the "divine ones" *(ilnym)* and that between the "gods" *(ilm)* and the "dead" *(mtm)* in a Ugaritic hymn to the sun-goddess. *Ilib* does not refer to "the god of the father" (as some commentators have argued) but to the "divine ancestor" or to the deified ancestors in the plural—that is, if we follow the lead of the Hurrian translations *enni attanni* and *enni attanniwena.* According to the beliefs of the time, then, the ancestors joined the gods upon their death.

According to the Aqhat passage, the cult of the ancestors took place "in the sanctuary." This particularity seems characteristic of family devotion to ancestors in the Syrian civilization. In a dedicatory inscription on a large statue for the storm-god Hadad (ca. 750 BCE), King Panammu of Samal enjoins his successors to bring sacrifice to the statue under the invocation of his own name: "Let him [i.e., the future king] say: 'May the soul of Panammu [eat] with you, and may the soul of Panammu drink with you.' Let him always invoke the soul of Panammu alongside with Hadad."

An early-1st-millennium BCE inscription found at Tell Fekherye (ancient Sikan) confirms the impression that the god was believed to act as a mediator between the family and its ancestors. In a curse formula against anyone who would erase the inscription, the gods of the ruler are entreated not to accept the bread and the water that the perpetrator might offer. Bread and water were highly unusual as offerings to the gods, but common in ritual meals for the ancestors. The image that these texts convey, then, is that of descendants bringing gifts to the gods who shared them with, or passed them on to, the family ancestors. It is possible that the "stele" and the "symbol" mentioned in the Aqhat passage refer to artifacts commemorative of such offerings to the ancestors, in spite of the more customary interpretation of "funerary stele."

In Syrian family religion, the cult of the ancestors was coupled with the veneration of a god or gods who were presumed to extend protection over their family especially. The patron deity of the royal family of Ugarit is referred to in the ritual texts as "the god of the house"—"house" being a designation of the dynasty. A synoptic study of the relevant texts suggests that this god had Ushhara as his consort. This goddess, referred to in another text as "the Hurrian goddess," resembles Mesopotamian Ishtar and is represented by lizards, symbols of fertility. The most plausible identification of the anonymous dynastic god is Baal-Zaphon, an epithet of the storm-god Haddu. King Idrimi of Alalakh referred to the same couple (Ishhara and the storm-god) as his "lady" and his "lord." Other expressions for the family god (or gods) are "the god of my father," "the gods of the house of my father," or, in texts from Samal, "the lord of the house." The occurrence of such terms in graffiti and inscriptions from the Hellenistic and Roman periods shows that, at least in later times, nonroyal families had their family gods as well. The practice is likely to have been a continuation from earlier times.

The available evidence does not allow conclusions concerning the nature of the cult of family gods beyond the rather general observation that it included sacrifice and prayer. A particular form of prayer, reflected both in the Ugaritic epics and in inscriptional evidence, is the vow. The solemn promise to honor the god with a substantial gift, provided that the god grant the wish of his servant, stresses the urgency of the request and illustrates the mutual self-interest as an aspect of the relationship between the family and its god. Self-interest did not exclude fervor, however, and gifts were also a means of strengthening mutual ties.

The list of filial duties in the Aqhat epic shows that the head of the family was expected to participate in communal rituals in the local temples. In addition to involvement in the religion of the city-state, however, families in Syria also had their private religion. As in Mesopotamia, the latter expressed itself primarily through the cult of the ancestors and the attachment to family gods.

BIBL.: Karel van der Toorn, *Family Religion in Babylonia, Syria, and Israel: Continuity and Change in the Forms of Religious Life* (Leiden: Brill, 1996), 153–77.   K.V.D.T.

Israel

Up to the 7th century BCE, the individual Israelites lived in a religious sphere that was clearly separated from the official religion of the Israelite and Judean states. Managing their daily lives as members of their own families, they had their own religious experiences, practices, and symbolic systems, which differed plainly from those of the nation, its main sanctuaries, institutions, and religious elites. The differences could even go so far that different gods were worshiped here and there. While YHWH, as the national god, was asked for help in cases of national distress, individual families preferred to trust in local deities when it came to problems of everyday living (Jer. 2.27–28). That family religion constituted a different religious sphere from the spheres of local and official religions produced a phenomenon that scholars call "internal religious pluralism." It can be observed in other religions as well.

Most early Israelite families probably had domestic shrines. In Megiddo, a cultic installation was found *in situ* next to the entrance of a private house, consisting of two small limestone horned altars and many goblets, shells, and cans that were suitable for incense and vegetable offerings. A more luxurious house cult is attested by Judg. 17–18, which has a silver divine image (teraphim) and an instrument for oracles (ephod). It was here that most of the subsidiary family cult took place: in the case of illness or distress of a family member the ceremony of lament was performed by the father, a man of God, or a prophet (1 Kings 17.17–24; 2 Kings 4.32–37). It was accompanied by offerings, magical rites, and exorcism (Isa. 38.21) and found its climax in the recitation of a psalm of lament, probably spoken by the liturgist line by line, to be repeated by the sick person. Similar rituals took place in connection with pregnancy and birth. Perhaps some of the numerous figurines and plaques of a naked woman found in many Israelite sites were used in such rituals. The woman who gave birth often praised God by giving her baby a name indicating thanksgiving. Finally, ancestor worship, which was performed daily and monthly, might have taken place in the domestic shrine, since the teraphim, which seem to have been figurines of the deified ancestors (Gen. 31.19, 34–35), belonged to the house chapel, according to Judg. 17.5. The ancestors were fed with vegetable offerings (cf. Deut. 26.14) in order to insure their protection of the family.

Another sort of familial practice, in this case including relatives and neighbors, took place at the local sanctuary (*bāmâ* [hill shrine]), which was typically situated outside the settlement. All such rites involve ceremonial meals (*zĕbāḥîm*), for which cultic purity and a bigger altar than was available at home were needed. If a family member had been healed or rescued, the family performed a thanksgiving ceremony (*zebaḥ hattôdâ*). With the assistance of a priest or a seer, the father slaughtered a sheep or a goat; parts of it were dedicated to God, but most of it was consumed by the family and the invited friends and neighbors (1 Sam. 9–10). During the festive meal, the person who had been healed spoke of his distress, his lamentation, and his rescue by God (song of thanksgiving) before the assembly. Through the shared feast, he was fully accepted again into the village community. Such a ceremonial meal could also take place as a fulfillment of a vow that had been made to God in a situation of distress (1 Sam. 1.11; 2 Sam. 15.7–8). Ancestor worship that was carried out once a year, on the occasion of a new moon, and in which all clan members had to participate (1 Sam. 20.6, 29) probably took place in the local sanctuary.

Passover was also a family ritual until the 7th century BCE. Possibly, after it had been slaughtered and roasted in the local communal sanctuary, each family's sheep was eaten by that family at home, together with unleavened bread and bitter herbs (Exod. 12.1–13). Perhaps rooted in an old nomadic ritual, originally celebrated before the herd was transferred from the winter to the summer pasture (cf. the staff and sandals in 12.11), the Passover sacrifice retained a clearly apotropaic function: the sheep's blood smeared on the lintel and on the two doorposts of the entrance to each house was intended to protect the family against a child-killing demon.

In addition to the practices already described, families had to observe several taboos, such as the weekly day of rest for the domestic animals and slaves (Exod. 23.12) and allowing fields to lie fallow every seventh year (23.10–11). Behind this stands an age-old human awareness that complete exploitation of nature endangers the power of blessing and fertility.

Family cult and official cult came into contact during the offering of first fruits. On the one hand, these sacrifices of the year's first produce were firmly related to the family's agricultural prosperity and thus its economy; on the other hand, the first fruits of barley and wheat were offered during the main annual feasts, the period between the feast of Unleavened Bread and the feast of Weeks (see Sacred Times and Places). Before the 7th century, the former was probably the only occasion on which the families commemorated a date of Israel's official history, the exodus (Exod. 23.15; 34.18). Family piety was based on nature rather than on the "salvation history" of Israel.

Beginning with Josiah's reform in 622 BCE, several efforts were made to link family religion more closely to Israel's official religion. The Passover ritual was withdrawn from the family cult; it became a pilgrimage feast celebrated in the central sanctuary and focused on the historical event of exodus (Deut. 16.1–8). During every offering of the first fruits, the father had to recite Israel's official "salvation history" (Deut. 26). The worship of any other god than YHWH was strictly forbidden. Family members are even told to kill relatives who worship other gods (13.6–11 [= 13.7–12 Hebrew]).

When the official institutions collapsed in 587 BCE, the Judean families became the main tradents of Israelite religion during the Babylonian exile. New or reformed family rites and customs such as circumcision, observation of the sabbath, and dietary rules now became clearly defined signs of identity, which enabled Judaism to survive the crisis.

BIBL.: R. Albertz, *A History of Israelite Religion in the Old Testament Period* (2 vols.; Louisville: Westminster, 1994), esp. 25–39, 94–103. Karel van der Toorn, *Family Religion in Babylonia, Syria, and Israel: Continuity and Change in the Forms of Religious Life* (Leiden: Brill, 1996).　　R.A.

Anatolia

In Hittite society, religious practices of the common people, that is, "popular religion," were performed without any official intermediary, in contrast to state religion, whose deities were venerated in the capital and served by the official priesthood. In other words, private

Worshiper standing before a seated Anatolian deity, 1300 BCE. Ankara, Museum of Archaeology. *Hirmer Fotoarchiv*

rituals are to be distinguished from royal festivals in that they were not performed at regular intervals by official priests and temple attendants, but only in certain circumstances to deal with specific problems. Also, they were not intended for the good of the state, but rather for the good of individuals.

These rituals have come down to us thanks to Hittite King Tudkhaliya IV, who set out to collect them from all over the Hittite domain and to keep a record of them in the Hittite state archives. The greater part of these rituals dealt with individuals possessing enough wealth to afford all the expense that a ritual entailed. However, we may assume that the common people also performed such rituals, but in simpler and more modest ways.

Rituals were employed to address a variety of disturbances, encompassing all aspects of the life of an individual or family, such as building a new house, illness and death, impotence, birth, family quarrels, ceremonies against curses and witchcraft, summoning absent deities, and so on. These rituals were similar to medical prescriptions, and each was a specific formula credited to a particular person, often from some distant part of the Hittite Empire.

Naturally, rituals were used in rites of passage such as birth, puberty, and death. Various Hittite texts describe rituals for obtaining fertility or for curing a specific ailment such as impotency, barrenness, or repeated miscarriages. Other rites and incantations were performed during the course of a pregnancy to avert evil spells or to prepare a woman for childbirth or during the birth itself.

The Hittites also performed purification rituals for the mother and baby, as well as propitiatory rites to secure a favorable destiny for the newborn and instate its proper sexual identity. The texts mention a ceremony that occurred in the third or fourth month of the baby's life, celebrating the reentry of the mother and the first entry of the baby into the community.

Little is known otherwise about family and individual religion. We can imagine, however, that individuals employed prayers to some extent similar to royal prayers and that they believed in an afterlife (see also Illness and Other Crises).

BIBL.: Gabriella Frantz-Szabó, "Hittite Witchcraft, Magic, and Divination," in *Civilizations of the Ancient Near East* (ed. Jack M. Sasson et al.; New York: Scribner, 1995), 3.2007–19. O. R. Gurney, *The Hittites* (London: Penguin, 1990). Fiorella Imparati, "Private Life among the Hittites," in *Civilizations of the Ancient Near East* (ed. Jack M. Sasson et al.; New York: Scribner, 1995), 1.571–86.   H.H.

Iran

Centrality of the individual in Iranian religiosity has ancient roots. In the Gathas or songs of the devotional poet Zarathustra (2nd millennium BCE), each individual bears responsibility for choosing between order and chaos, good and evil: "Between these two, the wise choose rightly, not so the unwise" (Yasna 30.3). Those individuals who "chose rightly" were regarded as righteous persons who would "approach you, O Ahura Mazda, with good thought" (28.2). In time, the notion of choice as to how life was to be lived gained cosmogonical dimensions with people—both individually and collectively—finding representation as troops in a universal conflict between the forces of creation and destruction: "Ahura Mazda deliberated with the perceptions and immortal souls of humanity . . . [saying], 'Incarnate you can battle with evil and vanquish it.' . . . [Humans] agreed to enter the material world to become perfect and immortal in the final body at eternity" (*Bundahishn* 3.23–24). Similarly, the notion that each person needed to focus actively on religious issues was acknowledged by followers of the prophet Mani (216–ca. 276 CE): "If, in the material world, an individual does not perceive . . . good, evil, and the mixture of these . . . the thought to come to righteousness would not reach that individual" (M 91).

In early Iranian culture, each individual (Avestan *mareta* [mortal], Old Persian *martiya*, Middle Persian *mard*) could be affiliated through kinship and alliance within spatial settings to a household unit (Old Avestan *demāna/nmāna*, Old Persian *taumā*, Middle Persian *mān, tōm/tōmag*), a village or settlement (Avestan *vis/vīs*, Old Persian *vith*, Middle Persian *wis/wīs*), a territory or tribal region (Avestan *shaithra, zana/zantu*, Old Persian **zana/zantu*, Middle Persian *zanag/zand*), and a district, province, or country (Avestan *dahiiu*, Old Persian *dahyu*, Middle Persian *deh/dēh*). Each individual could be associated within social settings to an extended family (Avestan *x^vaētu*, Old Persian **uvāitu*, Middle Per-

sian *xwēshīh*), a community or neighborhood (Avestan *verezēna*, Old Persian *vardana*, Middle Persian *wālan*), and a cohort (Avestan *airiiaman*, Old Persian **ariyaman*, Middle Persian *ērman*). Each person also would belong to a variety of social classes—initially farmers and pastoralists (Avestan *vāstriia*, Middle Persian *wāstaryōsh*), priests (Avestan *zaotar, āthrauuan*, Old Persian *magu, magush*, Middle Persian *mog/mow, mogmard/mowbed*), and warriors (Avestan *rathaēshtar*, Middle Persian *artēshtār*); later slaves, pastoralists, farmers, artisans, mercantile families, scribes, free men and women, lower noble families, priestly families, feudal noble families, and ruling families.

The social hierarchy was ratified by religion through attribution to divine will as a central aspect of the corporeal manifestation of order or righteousness (Avestan *asha*, Old Persian *arta*, Middle Persian *ardā*) and recorded in religious texts. Thus transgression of class boundaries by individuals and families—through actions as diverse as marriage ties and occupation changes—technically was regarded as violation of doctrinal tenets and, correspondingly, religio-secular law (Shkand Gumānīg Wizār 1.11–30), although social mobility proved unavoidable in practice.

Those social structures' impact crossed sectarian boundaries. So each Zoroastrian, Jew, and Christian in Iran had affiliations of kinship, alliance, and class. Individuals and families following Manicheism and Buddhism, while having ties of kinship and alliance, were cut off from the class hierarchy by being labeled heretics (Middle Persian *zandīk*) and idolaters (Middle Persian *butparist, uzdēsparist*) respectively. Manicheans replaced the regular Iranian social order with a sectarian one comprising hearers (or auditors) and elect including elders, bishops, and teachers (M 36). Men and women could belong to all five classes. Elect individuals were expected to practice celibacy, monasticism, and proselytism because they had "abjured the whole world" including secular careers and pleasures (M 8251 I). Their home was the monastery, their family comprised other bearers of faith (Middle Persian *dēndārān*), and each individual elect depended on "a hearer who brings alms" (M 221). Laypersons or hearers could live within family units but were urged to disavow that social arrangement in favor of an austere life focusing on the spirit (M 49 I; M 5794 II).

At the levels of the individual and the family, all Mazda worshipers or Zoroastrians shared certain basic practices. The origin of initiation into the sectarian community is unclear but probably became standard by late Achaemenian and early Parthian times, around the 4th and 3rd centuries BCE. During the ceremony, which symbolizes advent to adulthood, acceptance of religio-legal responsibilities, and spiritual rebirth, each child would be vested with a cord (Avestan *aiwiiānghana*, Middle Persian *kustīg*) around the waist and an undershirt (Middle Persian *shabīg*). Failing to

Artaxerxes II (404–359 BCE) worshiping in front of a fire altar, with winged disk and moon above. Rock relief at Persepolis. *Archive J. K. Choksy*

wear these items was regarded as a sin and equated to "scrambling around naked" (Vendidad 18.54; Shāyest nē Shāyest 4.10). Five canonical prayer times were supposed to be observed: at sunrise, noon, afternoon, evening, and before sunrise. Worship involved praise of divine entities (Avestan **upa.stāuuaka*, Middle Persian *abestāg*), which when recited exactingly was believed to "bind" the devotee to the spiritual realm (Yasna 48.7); libations (Avestan *zaothrā*, Middle Persian *zōhr*) of *haoma* (perhaps the ephedra plant) pounded and mixed with milk (9.1–3; 10.6–14); and sacrificial offerings of fruit, wine, goats, sheep, less frequently cattle and horses (Yasht 9.8, 13; Herodotus 1.132; 7.113; Xenophon, *Cyropaedia* 8.3; Arrian, *The Anabasis of Alexander* 6.29).

Manichean community life centered on a regime of seven daily prayer sessions for elect individuals and four for hearers, recited facing the sun during the day and the moon at night and focusing on symbols of Pidar Roshn or the divine father of light. Confession of sins usually accompanied prayer sessions. A central function of prayer was to praise divine entities such as Pidar Roshn, Madar i Zindagan (the mother of life), the Amahraspandan (beneficent spirits or elements), Zarathustra, and Jesus and to glorify Mani "the apostle of light" and other teachers (M 5; M 7; M 311; M 801; M 817I). Another function of prayer was to thank those divine entities who assisted individuals in attaining gnosis (M 67 R ii). Conversely, the goal of weekly confession was to expiate individual weaknesses and transgressions believed to have caused gnosis-inhibiting sins (M 210; M 6221; Xwāstwānīft 13 a). No individual

elect was permitted to store food for more than one day nor clothing for more than one year, to prevent attachment to material objects and concomitant distraction from the spiritual quest.

Initially, worship by Zoroastrians occurred outdoors (Herodotus 1.131), as attested by stone altars at Pasargadae and by reliefs upon the rock-cliff tombs of Darius I (522–486 BCE) and other Achaemenian rulers at Naqsh-e Rostam, which depict kings publicly venerating fires burning in altars upon open-air platforms. Sasanian monarchs such as Ardashir I (224–40 CE) even founded regnal fires, by that time within temple complexes. In more private settings, the hearth fire was supposed to burn during each male householder's life, to be extinguished upon his demise. Offerings of animal fat, incense, and scented wood were made to such ritual fires.

Five fasts, each two days long, were held by Manicheans during their religious year (Xwāstwānīft 12 a). The final fast was intended to remind the congregation of Mani's demise in a Sasanian prison. At the Bema (or throne) feast that followed the final fast, Mani's portrait was placed on a seat facing his followers (Xwāstwānīft 14 a–b; M 801 a; Augustine, *Contra epistulam fundamenti* 8). In between fasts and the Bema feast, the elect were expected to consume only one meal of fruits and vegetables each evening—abjuring meat and wine, which were regarded as polluted by evil (M 177 R; M 6020 I). Each elect's body was envisioned both as a system for separating spirit or light from matter through digestion of the food and as a vessel for storing the separated spirit until death when it could return to paradise. Thus, the "seals" of the mouth, hands, and chest had to be observed strictly to prevent sin and pollution of the body (Augustine, *On the Customs of the Manicheans* 10–18).

The divine entity *par excellence* of the Zoroastrian home and family was Hadish, regarded as the "spirit of the house" who rewarded pious individuals and families with pasture, grain, and well-being (Visperad 1.9; 2.11; 9.5, with its Pahlavi exegesis). Often circumscribed by domesticity, women were expected to be maternal, chaste, and obedient—duplicating, within their homes, attributes ascribed to the Zoroastrian feminine divine entity Spenta Armaiti (Wizīdagīhā ī Zādspram 4.8; Dādēstān ī Dēnīg 8.4; Denkard 415). Ideally, women were expected to resemble physically the divinity Ashi, who was said to be "narrow waisted, fair bodied, long fingered, [so] beautiful in form as to delight beholders" (Yasht 17.11; compare Xusrō ud Rēdag 96). Just as men prayed to the divine entity Aredwi Sura Anahita (or Anahid) for power and protection (Artaxerxes II Susa inscription a.3–4, Susa inscription d.3–4, Hamadan inscription a.5–6), women were expected to pray to Ashi to grant "easy childbirth . . . [and] milk" (Yasht 5.2). Regarded as defiled by the demonesses Jahika (or Jeh) and Nasush (or Nasa) during menstruation and childbirth, women were required to seclude themselves from the rest of the family during those times so as not to spread ritual impurity. A similar attitude prevailed among Manicheans, focusing on the "insatiable and shameless" demoness Az as the source of lust and procreation that allegedly spread to humans resulting in entrapment and pollution of spirit within matter (Xwāstwānīft 12 b; M 7984; M 7983). Manichean women were expected to be particularly cautious not to spread ritual pollution to the community while menstruating and not to arouse men sexually by their appearances and actions. The best women were said to be "holy virgin sisters" or elect women (M 801). The worst women, like their male auditor counterparts, were those who could not obey the injunction to "keep away from lewdness and fornication" (M 491). Consequently, physical beauty was not accorded praise by Manicheans, but temperate behavior was.

All in all, the family unit—be it a biological one in the case of Zoroastrians or a communal one in the case of Manicheans—was central to Iranian religiosity and social structure. Within that unit, ethics and law were instilled, illness and other crises were resolved, and purity and absolution achieved by the individual. Parents were expected to teach their children about proper behavior, honor, virtue, and religiosity (Handarz ī Ādurbād ī Māraspandān 1–2, 10, 37, 82–89). Children, in turn, were advised to "listen to them and obey them—for as long as an individual's father and mother live he [or she] is like a lion in the jungle fearing no one at all" (Handarz ī Ādurbād ī Māraspandān 90).

BIBL.: Jason D. BeDuhn, *The Manichaean Body: In Discipline and Ritual* (Baltimore, 2000). Jamsheed K. Choksy, *Evil, Good, and Gender: Facets of the Feminine in Zoroastrian Religious History* (New York, 2002). Wilhelm Geiger, *Civilization of the Eastern Iranians in Ancient Times* (trans. P. Sanjana; 2 vols.; London: Frowde, 1885–86). Louis H. Gray, *The Foundations of the Iranian Religions* (Bombay, 1929). Gernot L. Windfuhr, "A Note on Aryaman's Social and Cosmic Setting," in *Aryan and Non-Aryan in South Asia: Evidence, Interpretation, and Ideology* (ed. Johannes Bronkhorst and Madhav M. Deshpande; Cambridge, Mass., 1999), 295–336.   J.K.C.

Greece

The Greek household, the *oikos*, constituted an economic, social, and religious unit placed under the authority of the head of the family: father, husband, master of slaves, and citizen. As such, the household was part of the city-state: "Every city-state is composed of households," Aristotle declared (*Politics* 1.2.1). A household was also an aggregate of individuals, whose status was defined by their relationship to the authority under which the familial community lived and perpetuated itself. Any discussion of domestic religion, then, must refer to individual and collective practices within the *oikos* and within the larger entities with which the family was identified.

The practices by which individuals were integrated into this community were all centered on the hearth *(hestia),* placed under the protection of a deity with the same name, Hestia, who presided over the connection of city-states and sanctuaries to the soil. Newborn infants were cradled near or walked around the hearth; a few days after the biological birth, the child's social birth was sanctioned in Athens by the festival of the Amphidromia, which centered on the hearth and included a sacrifice and a meal shared by the permanent members of the *oikos.*

The hearth was the place where young newlyweds, too, were welcomed and where the members of the household showered them with dried fruit *(katachysmata),* signs of prosperity and fertility. Leaving their *oikos* for a new hearth, new brides had to be integrated into their new households, as did anyone else coming in from the outside. The same ritual was applied to newly purchased slaves, who were thus introduced into the community to which they would henceforth belong and to whose prosperity they would contribute. In all these cases, the entire family group, as defined by its participation in the rituals of the *oikos,* welcomed the newcomer and ratified his or her integration into the domestic hearth.

Everyday practices in the *oikos* were organized around several key points in the family space. Hestia presided over meals cooked on the altar of the family hearth: before every meal, a libation of wine was dedicated to her (Homeric *Hymn to Hestia* 4). Apart from Hestia's hearth—which also could be protected by a rather elusive Zeus Ephestios (Overseer of the Hearth), whose image was hung close by—two altars to Zeus played a central role. The head of the household conducted a regular service at the courtyard altar of Zeus Herkeios (Zeus of the Courtyard). The Homeric bard Phemius mentions, for example, the sacrifices carried out on this altar by Laertes and his son Odysseus (*Odyssey* 22.334–36). In the *Heracles,* Euripides shows the hero's entire family group—father, wife, children, and slaves—gathered to celebrate the cult of Zeus Herkeios with a sacrifice that, given the tragic turn of the play, turns into a massacre (*Heracles* 925–28). Zeus Ktesios (Zeus Who Guards Possessions) was the protector of household goods; the orator Isaeus refers to him in connection with the sacrificial rites performed in common by Ciron and his grandsons to attest to their status as heirs (Isaeus, *Oration* 8.16). The sign of Zeus Ktesios, ritually set up and regularly renewed in the pantry, was a pot, wreathed with white wool and filled with foodstuffs (*Athenaeus* 11.46).

The rhythm of life of the permanent members of the *oikos* was marked by the celebration of these family rituals, with which the slaves of the household could be associated if the slave owner so wished. The slaves were excluded from the family table, however; shared meals were reserved for free members of the family, except at the festival called Kronia, if we are to believe Philochorus's account (*FGrH* 328 F97). The narrow circle of the nuclear family—the head of the family, his wife, his children, and his slaves, extending to the sons' wives and children—thus brought together various groups of individuals whose status was in part defined by their religious function within the *oikos.*

The religious and social unity of the *oikos* was not a closed structure, however. It could occasionally be opened to members outside this community and even to strangers. The welcoming of a stranger to the hearth and to the table of the master of the house gave rise to ritual practices attached to the *xenia,* or hospitable reception. These practices, which established a social bond calling for reciprocity, were placed under the sign of Zeus Xenios (Hospitable Zeus), guarantor of mutual commitments. Other festive occasions opened the family group to celebrations shared with other family groups within the city-state. For example, during the Diasia, an Athenian festival honoring Zeus Meilichios (Kindly Zeus), families gathered together around a sacrifice and a meal in a civic context (Aristophanes, *Clouds* 407–8). The relation between families and phratries (brotherhoods, a group based not on real but on virtual descent) constituted another dimension of the bonds between the *oikos* and the individuals of which it consisted, on the one hand, and broader groupings that operated between the *oikos* and the city-state, on the other. The same is true for the somewhat more clusive relationship between *oikoi* and *genē* (lineages). Lineages had their own sanctuaries, cults, and priests; as in the case of the phratries over which Zeus Patroios (Ancestral Zeus)

or, in Athens, Apollon Patroios presided, their divinities were often distinguished by the epithet Patroios, which might designate the divinity as ancestor of the lineage.

The women of the household played an essential role in the purification rites that followed birth, in the rites and baths that accompanied wedding preparations, in the preparation of the dead, and in mourning within the *oikos,* as well as in daily worship services, particularly those devoted to Hestia. But their participation was always subject to the authority of the head of the *oikos,* who was also their legal *kyrios* (guardian).

BIBL.: F. Bourriot, *Recherches sur la nature du genos* (Paris, 1976). S. C. Humphreys, *The Family, Women, and Death: Comparative Studies* (London, 1983). L.B.Z.

Etruria

In the archeological record (on which most of our direct evidence about Etruscan religion depends), it is very hard to separate the traces of individual and family cult from those of the community at large. The largest body of material comes from Etruscan tombs, which—beyond providing evidence for funerary practice, the cult of the dead, and views of the afterlife—suggest a strong sense of family tradition and continuity; they are often associated with a single family and are reused over generations. Some family names are derived from divinities, for example, Uselna, from Usil (sun).

The excavation of Etruscan houses provides little evidence for specific cult practices, although remains of aristocratic buildings at Murlo, Acquarossa, and Rome, dating to the 6th century BCE, may shed some light upon the religious practices of the house. At Murlo a small enclosure inside the inner court may have been associated with ancestral cult. The 6th-century BCE terra-cotta friezes from the same site, representing banqueting, games, and a procession, as well as two godlike families who probably watch these activities, at least appear to show religious imagery within a partly domestic context; one section of the frieze may depict a marriage ceremony. It has been suggested that the terra-cotta statues that stood on the roof of the palace represented divine or semidivine ancestors.

Further evidence for private religious ideology are 1,500 bronze mirrors, which were used in domestic contexts from approximately 500 to 200 BCE. These mirrors are engraved with mythological representations, often scenes derived from Greek mythology in Etruscan reinterpretations. The themes include immortality, healing, rescue, birth, rejuvenation, and divine couples. They may reflect something of the religious views of those who used them—men, no doubt, as well as women. Importantly, they demonstrate that Hellenizing mythology was mediated on highly personal objects and that Greek influence in Etruscan religion operated in the most private spheres.

Other evidence for private religion (although hard to

interpret in any detail) includes terra-cotta votives of anatomical parts, such as uteri, breasts, and phalli, and bronze votive figurines representing gods such as Hercle (Heracles) and Laran (Ares). Evidence for cults of initiation is found in a house at Bolsena, Roman Volsinii (3rd century BCE), where a subterranean room with a terra-cotta throne seems to have acted as a site for Dionysian worship (suppressed by the Roman senate in 186 BCE).

BIBL.: R. De Puma and J. P. Small (eds.), *Murlo and the Etruscans* (Madison, Wisc., 1994). L. B. van der Meer, *Interpretatio etrusca* (Amsterdam, 1995). A. J. Pfiffig, *Religio etrusca* (Graz, 1975). S. Stopponi (ed.), *Case e palazzi d'Etruria* (Milan, 1985).   L.B.V.D.M.

Rome

Home is at all times a powerful notion in the psychology and ritual of human beings, and household rituals, therefore, form part of any religion. The two principal classes of Roman household gods are Lares and Penates. Attempts to see the Latin word for "ghost" *(larva)* in Lares (ancient Latin Lases) are colorful but remain guesswork (the word and concept could even be Etruscan). There may be more substance in the view that Penates are the gods of the inner house (connected with the Latin *penus* [household provisions or store cupboard]). This is usually thought of in modern times as the larder, but may imply no more than something hidden deep in the fabric of the house, to judge by Old English *cofgodas* (room gods) or Prussian *coltky* (who live in the hidden parts of houses).

Penates, like goblins, are an indiscriminate class of being and lack a theology of their own. They do not have names, unless the goddess Vesta (Hearth) is to be counted as one. This same theological gap also makes it difficult to deal with Lares. There is, however, a crucial difference between the two: the Lares are part of the local geography and protect you by virtue of your living on that land; when you move, you acquire new Lares, but you take your Penates (and your Vesta) with you, as Aeneas did. Originally, there may have been only one Lar at a time, the Lar that protected your land and those who lived on it, your *familia;* he was therefore known as the *Lar familiaris.* As there are many families, there are obviously many Lares; but equally, the plurality of gods in the house—Lar, Penates, and Vesta—leads to a collective sense of Lares. Where properties meet, at a crossroads *(compitum),* there is a negotiation of spiritual property rights and a shrine is erected to the Lares of the various properties. It was at crossroads that the festival called Compitalia took place, an integrative ceremony held at the New Year, mainly for peasants and slaves, where each free person was represented by a doll hanging from a tree and each slave by a ball of wool. Transferred into the inner city, this rite formed the basis of district organizations, a threat to authority in the late republic, but transformed by the genius of Augustus into a religion of loyalty, praising the *Genius Augusti* amid the Lares.

Inevitably, day-to-day practice varied during different periods, in different parts of the Roman world, and from family to family. But we can detect some basic patterns in household cult. Beings such as Lares and Penates needed respect and food. The hearth fire was one place of communication. On all feast days, including the three named days of the month (Kalends, Nones, Ides), a wreath was placed there, and an offering of food was cast into the flames. At every mealtime, a token offering would be made, typically of grain, grapes, cakes, honey, or wine. These entities might, moreover, receive sacrifice of a smaller animal (a lamb or goat) on some special occasions. This presumably was related to the dietary habits of the household—an animal could scarcely be slaughtered without the propriety of sacrifice to some divine power.

There is a striking amount of archeological evidence for a second place of communication, house shrines, particularly in the best-preserved ancient towns such as Pompeii and Herculaneum. Here we find miniature temples marked by mini-pillars and mini-pediments, known originally as *sacella* (mini-shrines) but since later antiquity as *lararia.* They may be freestanding cupboards containing lucky statuettes, a Lar holding a *cornucopia* (horn of plenty) and a *patera* (saucer for making offerings), sometimes including other personal deities, such as Isis-Fortuna with a *cornucopia* and a rudder to steer one's life. A *lararium* might also be a niche containing depictions. Typically these were a pair of Lares dancing, Roman conceptions brought to life by Greek art (perhaps in the 3rd century BCE when Theodotus painted the *Lares ludentes* for the Compitalia—as mentioned in a surviving fragment of Naevius's comedy *Tunicularia,* written in the late 3rd century BCE; see Warmington 1936). And between the dancing *Lares* was regularly a figure wearing a toga, together with a prominent snake. This partnership of human and snake represents the *genius,* something between a guardian angel and an embodiment of procreative power (from *gigno* [to procreate]). This man projects the *paterfamilias* at worship, the person whom the *genius* specially invests with power and whose *genius* he appears actually to be. Beneath these figures, a snake with its coils embodies the protective and fertilizing qualities of the earth and the *genius* itself in a different way, as the *genius loci* (genius of the place).

Moments of transition, always felt to be perilous, were marked by prayers and offerings to the Lar. These transitions included return from a journey (*Lares viales* [Lares of the highways], *Lares permarini* [Lares of sea crossing], and *Lares militares* [Lares of being a soldier]—to protect one while outside the embrace of home) and marriage (the bride would offer three coins—one to the *paterfamilias,* one to the Lares at the hearth, and one to the *Lares compitales* at the crossroads). It was also to the Lares that boys, on reaching adulthood, dedicated the *bulla* (locket) that they had worn since childhood. Lares were part and parcel of the life of the home, and their little statues might be seen decorated with miniature garlands of flowers on special occasions.

The religion of the household is also the religion of the community, and at the highest level Roman culture operates with a model of the state as a household. It has a father, instantiated in historical times in the acclamation as *pater patriae* (father of the fatherland, like Cicero or the emperors; see, e.g., Augustus, *Res gestae* 35) and in mythic time as Aeneas carrying the *Penates publici* out of blazing Troy so that the Roman state might be established, with its own hearth and worship of Vesta. This public form of the Penates was, however, rather different from the household gods. In their temple in Rome, they were represented as two young men holding spears, and some ancient authors identified them with Castor and Pollux (Servius, on *Aeneid* 3.13; with Weinstock 1960).

BIBL.: Annie Dubourdieu, *Les origines et le développement du culte des Pénates à Rome* (Rome, 1989). D. G. Orr, "Roman Domestic Religion: The Evidence of the Household Shrines," *Aufstieg und Niedergang der römischen Welt* 2.16/2 (1978): 1557–91. Tran Tam Linh, "Lares," *Lexicon iconographicum mythologiae classicae* 6.1 (1992). E. H. Warmington (trans.), *Remains of Old Latin*, vol. 2 (Loeb Classical Library; Cambridge, Mass., 1936). S. Weinstock, "Two Archaic Inscriptions from Latium," *Journal of Roman Studies* 50 (1960): 112–18. Georg Wissowa, *Religion und Kultus der Römer* (2nd ed.; Munich, 1912).   K.D.

Christianity

While a good deal of information is available about ancient practices of religion specific to individuals and families in Greece and Rome (the cultures in which Christianity developed), very little is known about the actual practices of ancient Christians themselves, their family rituals, and the contents of their family prayer, other than the Lord's Prayer, which early on became the normative Christian personal prayer (Matt. 6.7–15; *Didache* 8.2–3, to be prayed three times a day). The extant evidence indicates a triple practice of fasting, prayer, and almsgiving, already taught during the New Testament period (Matt. 6.2–18); all three of these had Jewish precedents.

Fasting. The practice of fasting could include both partial and total abstinence from food; the distinction is not always clear. However, Hippolytus's *Apostolic Tradition* 23 seems to presuppose total abstinence from food, even the Eucharist: widows and virgins should fast and pray for the church often, presbyters and laity if they wished, but the bishop could fast only when everyone else did, since he might be asked to "make the offering," in which case he had to taste of it. *Didache* 8.1 notes that fasting should be done on Wednesdays and

Fridays, a choice of days that deliberately differed from the practice of "the hypocrites," presumably religious authorities among non-Christian Jews (see Matt. 6.2, 5, 16). The *Shepherd of Hermas* depicts the protagonist, Hermas, as praying and fasting at home alone, which is sometimes the locale for Hermas's dream-visions (*Visions* 2.2.1; 3.1.2; 3.10.7). Later, he fasts while sitting alone on a mountain and is rebuked by his heavenly revealer for not including the necessary component of doing justice (*Similitude* 5.1). Here he calls his fast a *statiōn*, a Latin loanword into Greek, arising either from a military context (suggested by Tertullian, *On Prayer* 19; *On Fasting* 10; *To His Wife* 2.4; i.e., being "on guard") or more likely from the posture of standing in prayer.

Tertullian devoted an entire treatise to the subject of fasting, both to demonstrate its legitimacy, based on scripture and the example of Jesus, and to refute the excessive fasting practices of Montanists and others. His attempt to argue against the mixed marriage of a Christian wife and a pagan husband includes the wife's obligation to fast on certain days—when the unbelieving husband will be sure to schedule a major dinner party, thus causing conflict for the wife between her religious practices and her family responsibilities (*To His Wife* 2.4).

Prayer. Recitation of the Lord's Prayer several times a day seems to have been widely practiced and considered normative in many places. Already the *Didache* at the turn of the 1st century prescribes it. Again, Tertullian devoted a whole treatise to commentary on this prayer (*On Prayer*). Hippolytus's *Apostolic Tradition* 41 instructs Christians to wash their hands and pray immediately upon rising, before going to work. When instruction is given in church, all should attend. On days when there is no such instruction, spiritual reading at home is encouraged. If at home, believers should pray at the third hour (midmorning), the sixth (noon), and the ninth (midafternoon). If not at home, they should pray in their hearts privately. There should also be prayers before going to bed. Christians should rise in the middle of the night to pray; in the case of a mixed marriage, the Christian spouse should go to another room to pray so as not to disturb the unbelieving spouse. Thus, by the early 3rd century and probably earlier (Tertullian, *On Fasting* 10), the rhythm of daily prayer that was later to become the monastic office was already established, probably with Jewish precedent (e.g., see Dan 6.10 [= 6.11 Hebrew]).

Intercessory prayer was an important part of the content of Christian prayer. First Tim. 2.1–2 encourages prayer for all, especially civil rulers, so that they will leave Christians in peace. *First Clement* 61 and Tertullian (*Apology* 30.1, 4; 39.2) reinforce that message, while *1 Clement* 60.4 prays that Christians will be obedient to civil authorities.

Almsgiving. The giving of alms individually to the

The figure of a person praying with arms outstretched (termed an "orant" figure), a common image in pre-Constantinian Christian art. Fresco from the Catacomb of Priscilla, Rome. *Scala/Art Resource, New York*

poor and needy was already a well-established Jewish practice, and synagogues were also centers of relief to those in need. Greco-Roman professional guilds and service organizations, too, had their systems of centralized funding of the needy. Among Christians, personal patronage as a way of giving alms continued, but there was also a strong tendency to centralize this function in the hands of church leaders, who were seen to have wider knowledge of neediness. Justin (*Apology* 1.67) and Tertullian (*Apology* 39) among other Christian writers speak of a weekly or monthly collection among those who wish to contribute. According to Tertullian, the causes for which the funds were disseminated included burial of the poor, relief to destitute children and the elderly, shipwrecked sailors, and prisoners and exiles for the sake of Christ. Visiting the sick and those in prison and feeding the needy were also works of charity expected from ordinary believers (Matt. 25.35–36; Tertullian, *To His Wife* 2.4; Hippolytus, *Apostolic Tradition* 30).

Celibacy and other practices. The personal choice of celibacy is a very old custom in Christianity. Already Paul in 1 Cor. 7 advocates it as part of eschatological preparedness. First Tim. 4.3 takes the opposite position and by so doing reveals the growing importance of the discipline. Justin speaks of both men and women living in perpetual celibacy (*Apology* 1.15), as do many other writers, such as Athenagoras and Methodius. All of the early apocryphal acts of the apostles assume celibacy as the norm for Christian life—which was certainly not the reality. Yet the numbers of consecrated celibates, both male and female, must have been significant by the end of the 2nd century.

Certain practices taken for granted in the broader culture were not observed by Christians. Christian writers declared that believers did not engage in the two most widely practiced methods of family planning: abortion (Tertullian, *Apology* 9.8) and abandonment of newborns (Justin, *Apology* 1.27.1) Participation in or attendance at theater, arena, and circus were suspect (Tertullian, *Apology* 38.4), yet other texts indicate that these bans were not universally observed.

BIBL.: Peter Brown, *The Body and Society: Men, Women, and Sexual Renunciation in Early Christianity* (New York, 1988). Carolyn Osiek and David L. Balch, *Families in the New Testament World: Households and House Churches* (Louisville, 1997). Rosemary Radford Reuther, *Christianity and the Making of the Modern Family* (Boston, 2000). C.O.

Rites of Passage

Introduction

Ritual became an object of study only toward the end of the 19th century, and rites of the life cycle were analyzed first by Arnold van Gennep in his classic study *The Rites of Passage* (1909). According to van Gennep, these rites were characterized by a separation from the old status, a liminal phase "betwixt and between," and the incorporation into the new condition. His insights have been very useful, but they did not exploit all the possibilities that his material provided. Following long neglect, these rites have attracted much attention since the 1960s when, significantly, van Gennep's study appeared in an English translation. A more detailed analysis of these rituals should also discuss which parts of these transitions are important, which symbols are used, and what the social significance of these symbols is.

However, let us start with the sources. It is clear that there are enormous differences among the various cultures of the ancient Mediterranean. Whereas in Greece we probably have the richest and most varied set of data, ranging from epic, lyric, tragedy, comedy, mythography, and lexicography to a wealth of archeological remains, Israelite rites can be studied from virtually only one book and Hittites and early Christians can be studied for only a few centuries. This means that we always have to be conscious of the limitations of our sources as well as of their often stylized and idealized characters. We rarely come eye to eye with life as it "really" was.

The main passages in the rites of the life cycle were birth, entry into adulthood, wedding, and death. The last category is studied elsewhere in this volume. The others are not in all places equally present or important. Early Christians seem to have given little thought to the elaboration of a new ritual idiom. Circumcision was clearly a local phenomenon, restricted to certain areas of the ancient Near East, and (the onset of) pregnancy seems to have been dramatized only in some cultures, such as the Hittite. Moreover, birth itself seems not to have been ritualized everywhere to the same degree. We hear little about it in Israelite or Zoroastrian rituals. It is, of course, a rather private affair, which seems often to have taken place among women only. Gender bias is a problem that bedevils all accounts of ancient ritual, where male rites are always better attested and, presumably, also were more important, given the male dominance in society.

Birth also illustrates the different stresses within ritual. In Greece and Rome, the handing over of the baby to the father was ritualized, unlike, for example, among Israelites or Zoroastrians. Varying ideas about legitimacy and the place of the father within a society seem to be contributing factors here. It is even more difficult to trace differences over time. Whereas on Attic black-figured vases of the late archaic age the public procession of a Greek couple to the bridegroom's home received all the attention, 5th-century red-figure vases focused on the relationship between the Greek bride and groom. (This is also a nice illustration of a shift in attention from the public to the private sphere during these periods.) Unfortunately, our information about rites is usually so fragmentary that developments within these (as in other) rites is hard to document.

Perhaps the greatest differences of these kinds are to be found in the area of initiation, an institution that to varying degrees existed in all ancient Mediterranean cultures. The attention that the Greeks gave to their youths is remarkable; we know of many myths and rituals involving male and female adolescents. But it seems that Greece was exceptional in this respect; in Rome, initiation (gradually?) disappeared at a relatively early period, and only traces of these institutions have survived, although the myth of Romulus and Remus demonstrates that Roman initiation was still alive around 500 BCE. It seems that urbanization and a more rationalized form of political organization were not favorable to the continuation of this institution. Rather striking, also, is the difference between boys and girls in this respect. There is hardly a trace of female initiation left among the Romans, the Hittites, or the Mesopotamians, whereas in Israel male initiation seems to have disappeared without a trace; the adventures of David, however, may be fruitfully exploited in this respect, as his wanderings, his membership in Saul's *Gefolgschaft,* and his defeat of a giant all fit an initiatory scenario.

Prominent symbols of transitions were bathing or washing, changes of clothes and hairstyle, and the use of crowns. It is important to look at the timing and the shape of the symbol: when does a haircut take place, do the initiates wear black or white clothes, and are they wreathed with fertile or infertile plants? It is only the combination of symbols that gives meaning, not the individual symbols themselves: in Greece, both the dead and bridegrooms wear white clothes, but they have different crowns. Here, one might also see some rationalization over the course of time. During what seems to have been the presentation of the new adults in Mesopotamia during the New Year festival, the boys wore both masculine and feminine clothing. In Greece, we have similar mythical and ritual indications that young males were dressed as females before they became "real" males, whereas the female warrior Amazons may have been reminiscent of a time when girls were dressed as males before becoming "real" women. In later times, such striking symbolism seems to have been abandoned.

Finally, ritual is also indicative of social relations. We nowhere hear of the father being polluted after birth, in contrast to the mother and those who assisted with the birth. Apparently, the father's private and public functions are too important to allow him to be impeded by pollution. In rites of initiation, there seems to have been a clear difference between aristocrats and lower strata of the population. Significantly, among Hittites it is a prince whose ritual transition into manhood is preserved; the presence of twelve prostitutes seems also to presuppose a more-than-normal virility on the prince's part. Initiation of the common people hardly seems to have been an important ritual moment. In short, rites of the life cycle can teach us much about ancient cultures.

BIBL.: C. Bell, *Ritual: Perspectives and Dimensions* (Oxford, 1997). J. N. Bremmer, "'Religion,' 'Ritual,' and the Opposition 'Sacred vs. Profane': Notes towards a Terminological 'Genealogy,'" in *Ansichten griechischer Rituale: Festschrift für Walter Burkert* (ed. F. Graf; Stuttgart: Teubner, 1998), 9–32. A. van Gennep, *The Rites of Passage* (trans. M. Vizedom and G. L. Caffe; Chicago, 1960 [orig. 1909]). J.N.B.

Egypt

Any discussion of rites of passage or life-crisis rituals in pharaonic Egypt is limited by the lack of pictorial and written evidence. Such rituals generated very little written documentation, and the taboo conventions of Egyptian visual art forbade them being depicted explicitly. Consequently the archeological evidence for rites of passage—such as that from the goddess Hathor's shrines at Deir el-Bahri—is now difficult to interpret. It is possible, however, to make two general statements about Egyptian life-crisis rituals. The first is that they were related conceptually to funerary rituals, all such ceremonies being part of the cyclical process of death and rebirth. The second is that they often involved some kind of cultural work upon the body, whether permanent (such as circumcision) or temporary (such as wearing a special hairstyle). The life stages we know to have been marked by rituals were birth and coming-of-age, but not marriage. The ancient Egyptians did not have any formal marriage ceremony, a marital union being determined by the partners agreeing to cohabit.

Pregnancy and parturition were dangerous liminal periods during which the mother-to-be needed supernatural help from deities such as Bes and Taweret, who combined diverse human and animal elements and thus defied normal body boundaries. Having such physically unclassifiable gods as patrons of this stage in the life cycle set it apart as special and liminal. Some kind of ritual was therefore needed to mark the end of this special time and the return to a normal state of being. After a birth, mothers and children seem to have been somehow secluded so that the pollution of the birth could be contained and dispelled. Fourteen-day purifications are known from the Old Kingdom; during later historical periods, we hear about rituals taking place after forty days. The ritual nature of these purifications is unclear. Archeological evidence suggests that they could involve visits to temples or local shrines to make offerings to the gods or the ritualized disposal of birth debris such as the placenta and umbilicus. Archeological analysis of New Kingdom houses at the village of Deir el-Medina also points to domestic space being altered temporarily to accommodate the requirements of postpartum ritual. From the same site, accounts mentioning "the festival of so-and-so's daughter" as a recurrent community or family event may refer to celebrations after births; but this is not at all clear from the context, and other interpretations are possible. This was probably the moment when babies were named to mark their new status as social beings with rights and privileges. Personal names tended to place the child under the protection of a divinity, frequently a local one. These rituals of inclusion therefore underscored broader local identities as well as membership in the immediate kin-group, something that is also true of maturation rituals. In order to demarcate children as a separate social category, they might wear special hairstyles such as the "Horus-lock," a sort of plait worn on an otherwise shaven head, sometimes decorated with appropriate amulets. (The name comes from Horus having sported it as a child.) Such age-specific hairstyles were modified to indicate the change of status on maturation, but there is no evidence earlier than the Roman period for how this event might have been ritualized.

The best-attested coming-of-age rituals in pharaonic Egypt are those of the male elite. Nothing specific is known about how the coming-of-age of royal males might have been marked. For nonroyals, most of the evidence (and it is pretty scanty) relates to circumcision and dates to the Old Kingdom or First Intermediate Period. Circumcision may not have been regarded as necessary for all males, only for some as representatives of the larger community. We do not know at exactly what age circumcisions took place or whether their timing was related to an individual's biological maturation. Some Egyptian coming-of-age rituals were apparently communal events for large groups, so it is unlikely that personal physical development was the sole factor. And in anthropological terms, coming-of-age is essentially a social notion of what it means to be adult, to which biological adulthood may be irrelevant.

Funerary inscriptions honoring the deceased as a man of praiseworthy social conduct sometimes refer to his circumcision ceremony. These inscriptions suggest that circumcision was seen as a social induction and a prelude to a man performing acts of general benefit to his community. Suitably manly conduct was important at this initiation to social manhood, as illustrated by the funerary inscription of a man named Wah, now in the Oriental Institute, Chicago. Wah says, "I am one beloved of his father and praised of his mother, whom his brothers and sisters love. When I was circumcised along with 120 men there was none whom I struck and none who struck me among them; there was none whom I scratched and none who scratched me." This stresses the primarily social nature of the festival, for which mythology does not seem to have provided a template. Carvings from the tomb of Ankhmahor give some sense of how the circumcision may have been medicalized with the use of high-value commodities, such as linen and unguents. Providing for the expense of these circumcisions was perhaps seen as an act of social utility. A fragmentary funerary inscription from Dendara mentions an individual who arranged for both burials and circumcisions in a particular town. The juxtaposition of funerals and circumcisions may hint at the Egyptians seeing these rites of passage as somehow connected.

Nothing concrete is known about rituals at maturation for females before the Roman period, when a festival for girls called the *therapeutēria* is attested. This lack of written documentation shows the male bias of the sources rather than implying that such events did not take place. A closer analysis of the archeological material might reveal more about these aspects of women's lives. Contrary to popular belief, there is nothing to prove that female circumcision was ever practiced in pharaonic Egypt, despite the assertions of several classical authors that it was.

BIBL.: Dominic Montserrat, *Sex and Society in Graeco-Roman Egypt* (London, 1996), 44–49. Geraldine Pinch, *Votive Offerings to Hathor in Her Temples at Deir el-Bahri* (Oxford, 1994). Ann M. Roth, *Egyptian Phyles in the Old Kingdom* (Chicago, 1993), 99–108.　　　D.A.S.M.

Mesopotamia

According to the Mesopotamians, the destiny of every human being was characterized by four major stages, each marked by rites of passage that no one could avoid without running counter to the laws of society: birth, entry into adulthood, marriage, and death. Another rite of passage involved the integration of strangers into society. All these rites, with the exception of those surrounding birth, were believed to have been created by the goddess Inanna/Ishtar or at least to take place under her authority.

Birth. For the child, birth meant entry into the world of the living; for the father, it meant the birth of an heir, while the mother's essential concern was to give her husband a child and reinforce her husband's status.

When the mother was ready to give birth, a ritual was performed to encourage and safeguard the delivery. It had three essential moments: the anointing of the woman; the delivery itself, with the assistance of midwives; the baby's arrival—if a boy, a weapon was placed in its hand, if a girl, a spindle. A good deal of evidence suggests that the woman in labor assumed a squatting position, her chest inclined forward, her body held above a brick, the "brick of childbirth" that is mentioned in a wide variety of myths.

The final operation, focusing on the child, consisted of cutting the umbilical cord. The act was performed with a blade made of reeds; one text describes a silver knife. The child's destiny was sealed at this moment, and thus it is significant that an incantation was recited precisely at this point to protect the child against all forms of aggression. Fear of the demon Lamashtu, devourer of children, accounted for the many precautions taken.

Immediately after cutting the cord, the midwife picked up the newborn infant and held it upside down to facilitate its crying. She then bathed it, and it was at this point that the father acknowledged it; this was probably the moment when the child was given a name. The Mesopotamians did not practice circumcision.

Initiation into adulthood. The transition into adulthood is still not very well understood. As far as we can tell, during the celebration of the New Year, in Isin at the beginning of the 2nd millennium, young men paraded to the sound of an orchestra, miming scenes of war in homage to the goddess Inanna and performing in front of the royal couple, who presided over the ceremony. They were dressed in women's clothing on the right side, men's clothing on the left; each brandished a combat weapon. Young women and also an older woman accompanied them, as did the *kurgara,* an enigmatic individual resembling a berdache, who held a knife; one final performer, unless it was the same berdache, made blood flow. All the details of this scene inevitably recall rites of initiation known to be practiced elsewhere.

Marriage. Marriage was a commitment underwritten by two social groups who used marriage to make manifest the mutual obligations that each group acknowledged toward the other. In Sumerian, as in Akkadian, there was no word for marriage. To designate marriage, it sufficed to associate two abstract terms: "the attribute of wife and the attribute of husband"; more simply, it was said of a man that he "took a wife"—or in other words, marriage consisted in a man's taking possession of a woman.

In practice, marriage could be arranged even in infancy. Thus the Mesopotamians were acquainted with inchoate marriage. The first step in this practice was the intervention of the future groom's father, who chose a wife for his son and gave the bride's family a gift in kind or in cash, NIMIÚSA or *terḫatum;* the gift functioned as a kind of promise of marriage.

Only one formality, the contract, was actually indispensable in the making of a true marriage. Once the contract was concluded, the woman belonged to the man. It was an oral contract consisting of a solemn statement. In the old Babylonian era, the groom-to-be declared to his future spouse: "You be my wife; I shall be your husband." In the same period, the husband-to-be made this declaration to his intended wife in his father-in-law's house. Later, the formula was modified: "Assuredly, she is my wife"; the words were no longer addressed to the betrothed but to her father. Written contracts existed, of course, but they were never more than reflections of specific concerns. The introduction of the bride into the groom's house was the final step in the process.

A succession of ceremonies contributed to the celebration of a marriage. Each stage was underscored by collective celebrations and banquets. Four moments in particular were singled out as significant, four steps through which the union came about gradually.

First, the young man paid court to his betrothed; for her part, directly or through the intermediary of her father, she gave him a present, the *quištum,* usually clothing and precious metals.

This courtship continued until the day the family of the aspiring groom brought the *biblum,* a contribution consisting of food and drink, sometimes supplemented by nonconsumable goods that were meant to be saved. Custom required the young woman's father to return the platter, similarly provisioned, to the parents of the future husband.

With the completion of the rites by means of which the young couple acquired a different status—that of married persons—and made their entry into a new life, the rhythm of the ceremonies accelerated and the marriage took a more concrete turn. The young man's mother made the first official gesture in letting the son

depart. Later, a similar, reciprocal gesture took place at the home of the young woman's parents, with ceremonies of bathing and anointing preparations focusing on the woman's body. She was washed with soap and rinsed with purified water to remove all traces of taint; the young man or his father came afterward to anoint her with oil of cedar and various other perfumes. Anointing the bride or providing *ḫuruppâte* (metal dishes) intended for a banquet sufficed, in Assyria at the end of the 2nd millennium, to establish an irrevocable marriage.

From that point on, there was no further obstacle to the admission of the future husband into his father-in-law's house, at the head of the cohort of *susapinnu* (best man) who escorted the bride and groom to their nuptial chamber. Eventually, the bride left her father's household and entered her husband's. From then on, she was required to wear the veil. At that point, when the woman left her own family, she received her dowry, *šeriktum* or *širku.*

Integration of the stranger. The stranger was perceived first and foremost as an enemy. Potentially hostile by definition, he could be eliminated; alternatively, he had to be domesticated according to conventional practices in order to be admitted into society. One could try to assimilate a stranger through rituals of hospitality. Various sources make it possible to reconstitute the ritual surrounding the reception of a stranger as follows: the stranger identified himself and brought gifts; dressed and perfumed by his host, he was invited to share a meal; during this meal, a toast was proposed and a sparring match was initiated, either a simple oratorical contest or real hand-to-hand combat, in which the stranger's status was at stake; there had to be a winner and a loser; if the stranger won, he was admitted into society; if he lost, however, his introduction into society depended on the victor, who might have him put to death or might make him his slave or his friend. Such was the scenario that governed Enkidu's acceptance into Urukean society in the Epic of Gilgamesh.　　J. J.G.

Syria-Canaan

Arnold van Gennep's influential *Rites of Passage,* introduced in 1909 and much elaborated and modified since that time, has had no small effect on how contemporary scholars understand the transitions of the life cycle in any given society and cross-culturally. Changes in social status are both realized and communicated by rites that separate persons in transition from others, assign them a liminal status, and reincorporate them into the quotidian life of their community as socially transformed individuals. Such rites of passage function primarily to create and recreate a bounded social order.

In the Syro-Canaanite cultural sphere, rites of passage are evidenced in various texts, including narratives, legal collections, contracts, and prescriptive rituals. These represent or prescribe rites for social transitions such as betrothal and marriage, pregnancy and childbirth, divorce, adoption, entry into slavery, manumission, entry into cultic service, and death. Various manipulations of the body, changes of physical locus, restrictions of movement or access, purification procedures, oaths, sacrifices, and gift exchanges, among other examples, characterize the ritual processes that accomplish and communicate changes in social status. Examples of rites of transition from Syro-Canaanite texts include circumcision to establish and signal community membership; the rites of betrothal, marriage and divorce; and the rites of initiation for cultic servants.

Male circumcision, a common rite of initiation cross-culturally and much discussed by social anthropologists, is attested among the peoples of the Syro-Canaanite cultural sphere in texts and in artifacts such as figurines. Although circumcision is best documented in biblical texts, evidence suggests that forms of circumcision were also practiced by some of Israel's neighbors, including the Phoenicians and, at times, at least some Egyptians (Herodotus 2.104; Jer. 9.25–26 [= 9.24–25 Hebrew]). Biblical evidence suggests that male circumcision did not become a distinguishing characteristic or marker of Israelite status until the Babylonian exile of the 6th century BCE, when Judeans lived for the first time among peoples who did not utilize the practice.

Betrothal, marriage, and divorce had their own distinct rites that functioned to transform the social status of participants. Texts of varying provenance suggest that the presentation of bride price *(mōhar)* by the potential groom or his father to the potential bride's male guardian(s) (usually, her father or brother[s]) secured the man's claim to the woman in advance of the wedding itself, transforming her status to that of one who is betrothed. Some texts mention gifts as well. Of the rites of the wedding itself little can be said, due to a dearth of surviving evidence and because customs very likely varied from place to place. However, Mesopotamian parallels and biblical allusions suggest that some combination of feasting, the ritualized movement of the bride to the groom's home, and sexual intercourse played a role in establishing the transformed social status of bride and groom. Surviving contracts from the Judean military colony at Elephantine in southern Egypt (5th century BCE) bear witness to the use of a marriage formula to be recited by the groom ("She is my wife, and I am her husband from this day and forever"). Divorce meant the formal dissolution of the marriage bond, accomplished through a series of rites alluded to in Isa. 50.1; Jer. 3.8; Hos. 2.2 [= 2.4 Hebrew], but most clearly described in Deut. 24.1–4. Initiated by a dissatisfied husband, the rites of divorce include the writing of a "divorce document" *(sēper kĕrîtût),* the placing of the document into the wife's hand, and her expulsion from the husband's house. Elephantine contracts describe a divorce process whereby husband or wife makes a solemn statement before an assembly: "I hated my wife/ husband." Hosea 2.2 [= 2.4 Hebrew] records a comparable formula: "She is not my wife, and I am not her husband," evidently a reversal of a marriage formula.

The rites that effect and communicate entry into priesthood or other cultic service are documented in several surviving texts. A 2nd-millennium text from Emar describes the extended ritual process of the installation of the NIN.DINGIR, the high priestess of the storm-god. The NIN.DINGIR's transition from common woman to high priestess is accomplished over a nine-day period by means of a series of rites. These include anointing, shaving the body, offerings, processions with song, donning special clothing and jewelry, enthronement, and, finally, change of residence. The dedication of the Levites as described in Num. 8 is similar, in that it involves a series of rites that eventually result in permanently changed status. These include purification by means of sprinkling water, shaving the body, and washing of garments. Offerings and other ritual actions follow, leading to the dedication of the Levites to YHWH's service in a position subservient to that of the priesthood. Their dedication takes place in a public setting, witnessed by the congregation of Israel. It concludes with the Levites assembling to begin their service in the sanctuary.

Several different rituals are associated with death. In the Bible, people who come into contact with the dead become impure, for seven days according to the Priestly legislation (Num. 19). Purification rites serve as a transition from that state and symbolically separated the mourners from the dead who are buried or entombed. While the Bible contains no explicit rituals connected with burial, several Ugaritic texts deal with dead kings. The king was deified upon death. The entry of the king into his divine state may have been celebrated for three days, according to one interpretation of *KTU* 1.111 (see Olmo Lete 1999: 198–207; see also *KTU* 1.113 and Olmo Lete 1999: 184–98). Sacrifices were given to provide maintenance to deceased kings (e.g., *KTU* 1.39). Phoenician royal tombs imply that their kings were laid to rest with proper ritual procedures.

BIBL.: Arnold van Gennep, *The Rites of Passage* (trans. M. Vizedom and G. L. Caffe; Chicago, 1960 [orig. 1909]). J. S. La Fontaine, *Initiation* (Manchester, 1985). G. del Olmo Lete, *Canaanite Religion according to the Liturgical Texts of Ugarit* (trans. Wilfred G. E. Watson; Bethesda, Md.: CDL, 1999). S. M. Olyan, "What Do Shaving Rites Accomplish and What Do They Signal in Biblical Ritual Contexts?" *Journal of Biblical Literature* 117 (1998): 611–22. S.M.O.

Israel

The rite of passage best known from early Israel and Judaism is circumcision. According to biblical law and later Jewish tradition, circumcisions were performed on males eight days old and symbolized entry into the Israelite covenant community (Gen. 17.9–14; Lev. 12.3; Jub. 15.25–26; Luke 2.21; Phil. 3.5). Other (and arguably older) biblical materials, however, associate circumcision with adolescence (Ishmael's circumcision at thirteen; Gen. 17.25) and the closely allied institution of marriage (Jacob's sons requiring the Shechemites to circumcise themselves in Gen. 34.13–17 before Dinah marries into their community; circumcision's association with the phrase *bloody bridegroom* in Exod. 4.24–26; and Saul's demand in 1 Sam. 18.25–27 that his prospective son-in-law, David, pay a bride-price of foreskins). Biblical texts also associate circumcision with Passover (Exod. 12.43–49; Josh. 5.2–9), which represents a powerful combination (according to Propp 1998: 382–461) of traditions involving an individual male's rite of passage and the communal rite of passage undertaken by God's firstborn son, Israel, in its movement from Egypt into Canaan. Furthermore, biblical circumcision seems to have had an apotropaic function, for example, the circumcision ritual in Exod. 4.24–26 that wards off YHWH's murderous attack. Flusser and Safrai (1980) show that this belief survives in early Judaism.

Flusser and Safrai have also described circumcision's association with child sacrifice in the ancient Near East (Eusebius, *Preparation for the Gospel* 1.10.33) and in the Abraham saga (Gen. 17; 22), which may suggest that, as circumcision was originally a coming-of-age ritual for young men, so too was a related sacrificial ordeal. While not explicit, the Gen. 22 story does intimate that Isaac is an adolescent or nearly so at the time of his near sacrifice: he is not yet married but is physically mature enough to carry the wood for the sacrificial fire and mentally mature enough to question deviations from normal sacrificial ritual. Also significant is that the Gen. 22 story takes place in the wilderness space typical of a rite of passage's liminal phase and that it incorporates the typically liminal theme of trial at the hands of the participant's elder.

An analogous coming-of-age ritual for young women may be alluded to in Judg. 11.37–40, which describes how the daughters of Israel annually engaged in a four-day wilderness retreat to commemorate the two-month ritual that Jephthah's daughter undertook before Jephthah sacrificed her to God in payment for a vow. According to most translators, the purpose of the daughter's rite was to "bewail her virginity," but, as Day has demonstrated (1989), the word translated "virginity" *(bĕtûlâ)* does not refer to the physical state "virgin" but to a young woman who has reached puberty. Day further suggests that Jephthah's daughter ritually marks this transition by bewailing the "death" of her prepubescent stage in life and that this story of the daughter's rite of passage served in Israelite religion as a foundation legend for an annual ritual engaged in by young women who were making the same journey from immaturity to adolescence.

We know less about other Israelite and early Jewish rites of passage. Biblical accounts suggest that the primary rite associated with birth in early Israel was the naming of the newborn child, which was typically done by one of the child's parents, somewhat more often by the mother. This may suggest an important role for women in ancient Israelite birth rites, consistent, perhaps, with the roles that women have been posited to assume elsewhere within the Israelite household cult but in striking contrast to the general dearth of ritual roles attested for women in the public religious sphere. In later Judaism, names were bestowed by both parents at circumcision (Luke 1.59–63; 2.21).

Concerning marriage rituals, we also know little. Ancient Near Eastern parallels and a few biblical passages suggest that Israelite marriage was formalized by the groom's uttering some form of the vow, "You will be my wife, and I will be your husband" (cf. Hos. 2.2 [= 2.4 Hebrew]); whether the bride uttered the reciprocal form of this pledge is not known. At the Jewish military colony of Elephantine (late 6th and 5th centuries BCE), the husband's vow was recorded in a written contract. The earliest reference to a *kĕtûbâ* (marriage contract) elsewhere in Jewish sources is Tob. 7.13. Tobit and other early Jewish sources also prescribe a formal period of betrothal preceding the marriage (Matt. 1.18–19; Luke 1.27). These betrothals and the subsequent matrimonials were contracted between the bride's father and some representative of the groom (*Joseph and Aseneth* 20.9; 21; Tob. 7.9).

The accounts of Jacob's marriage in Gen. 29.22 and Samson's marriage in Judg. 14.10–20 suggest that in early Israel, weddings were an occasion for feasting, and the word *mišteh,* used in both texts, related to the verb *šātâ* (to drink), suggests that the consuming of wine was central. The New Testament account of the wedding at Cana (John 2.1–11) indicates that this tradition persists in early Judaism. The Samson story may also imply that the wedding feast, which is said to last seven days, could be a full-fledged drinking bout, with riddling contests and the like. Many commentators have assumed that Samson was attended at his wedding by a "best man," the companion to whom Samson's wife is given after Samson abandons his father-in-law's house (Judg. 14.20; 15.2), but at no other point in the Bible does the word *rēʿâ* (friend, associate) have this specialized meaning. There is, moreover, no requirement prescribing such a specially designated companion in early Jewish tradition.

BIBL.: P. L. Day, "From the Child Is Born the Women: The Story of Jephthah's Daughter," in *Gender and Difference in Ancient Israel* (ed. P. L. Day; Minneapolis, 1989), 58–74. D. Flusser and S. Safrai, "Who Sanctified the Beloved in the

Womb?" *Immanuel* 11 (1980): 46–55. W. H. C. Propp, *Exodus 1–18* (New York, 1998). S.A.

Anatolia

Although ritual texts are relatively plentiful among Hittite documents, activities specifically designed to mark the passage from one stage of life to another are scarcely mentioned. We can assume that many elements that went into the enactment of such rites replicated activities known from surviving festival and ritual texts that have other purposes. However, the psychological and social impacts of such rituals are not preserved and cannot be reconstructed.

Among the few pieces of Hittite evidence is a single ritual that testifies, perhaps, to a rite of initiation into manhood. The EZEN *haššumaš* (festival of potency/procreation) describes a ceremony that takes place in a tavern or an inn (an *arzana* building). In this establishment, the Hittite prince sits and eats with twelve prostitutes. Later, the temple priests, who are overseeing the operation, consecrate him and make him lie down. They place loaves of bread around him and pour out beer in a circle around him. The priests then bring in the twelve prostitutes—at which point the tablet ends. We infer that the prince had sexual intercourse with the women, but the significance of these events and the age and identity of the prince are not revealed.

Pregnancy could be marked by a special festival celebrated in honor of the mother-goddesses, although the details of this festival and information as to whether it was celebrated for every woman who became pregnant or only for those whose social status warranted the expense is not preserved. After the birth of a child, apart from the requisite rituals to purify mother and child, there were rituals to secure the mother's continuing fertility and a happy fate for the child. A ceremony of reentry into the community was performed for mother and child after three months for a boy and four for a girl, although, again, details of the rite are lacking.

Marriage, too, was marked by ceremony, although no marriage ceremonies are preserved in the textual sources. The existing evidence of preparations for arranged political marriages does not tell us about the practices of the population at large. However, two Old Hittite relief vases found in the vicinities of Inandik and Bitik may depict such ceremonies. In one scene on the former vase, a bride(?) is led by her father(?) in a procession. Musicians, acrobats, and an animal sacrifice are all depicted as components of the festivities. The top tier of the vase also depicts two performers in an act perhaps meant to induce fertility in the newlyweds. In one preserved scene on the Bitik vase, the bride and groom are seated on a marriage bed as the husband raises his hand to remove the bride's veil.

BIBL.: Gary M. Beckman, *Hittite Birth Rituals* (Studien zu den Bogazköy-Texten 29; Wiesbaden: Harrassowitz, 1983).

Harry A. Hoffner Jr., "The Arzana House," in *Anatolian Studies Presented to Hans Gustav Güterbock on the Occasion of His 65th Birthday* (ed. Kurt Bittel, Philo H. J. Houwink ten Cate, and Erica Reiner; Istanbul, 1974), 113–21. Tahsin Özgüç, *İnandiktepe: An Important Cult Center in the Old Hittite Period* (Ankara, 1988), pls. 36–59 and fig. 64. B.J.C.

Iran

A recurrent problem in the study of ancient Iranian religion is that we are seriously limited in many areas by the paucity of the sources. This is especially true with respect to what we know about rites of passage. Although there is a wealth of information about death and funerary practices, surprisingly little is recorded concerning birth, initiation, marriage, and aging. There does exist fairly extensive documentation of an ethnographic nature for rites of passage performed within the last two hundred years by the surviving Zoroastrian communities of Iran and India. These accounts are highly interesting, and the practices described are, in some of their details, undoubtedly of great antiquity, for these details can be checked against scattered references in the Pahlavi books of late antiquity or in the surviving Avesta itself. As one might expect, during the millennium that effectively separates the two branches of Zoroastrianism (Iranian and Indian), many changes in the performance of ritual evidently took place. Parsi ritual differs from Iranians, but one must assume that neither tradition remained static. There is a universal human propensity to believe that in the good old days there was strict and authentic observance; only now have customs been changed or compromised. The truth is that, while rituals are conservative, they do change over time, whether that time is the present or any point one might choose in the past. Further, except in times of strict, centralized ecclesiastic control, there undoubtedly was always variation from place to place. This is to suggest that the witness of modern observers helps locate a type of ritual in a live context, yet it can serve as only a rough guide to what little remains to us from antiquity.

Although Iranian tradition does not present tight schema of life's stages and their transitional rituals such as we find in the ancient Indian *dharmaśāstra*s and *gṛhasūtra*s, we can identify rituals for birth, initiation, and marriage.

Birth. While childbirth is mentioned as the particular concern of the goddess Aredwi Sura Anahita (Yasht 5.2), there is no real information about rituals pertaining to birth as a rite of passage. The legend of Zarathustra's birth as narrated at Denkard 7.2 (an important Pahlavi text dating to the 9th century CE) recounts many miraculous events involving the creation of the fetus in his mother's womb, her pregnancy, and the delivery. Owing to Zarathustra's nature as the archetypal human, there may be material here that reflects ritual practice. Particularly suggestive is that Zarathustra's parents drink the sacred *hōm* and milk infused with his *frawaši* (preexistent guardian spirits) and bodily substance.

Initiation. In contrast to ancient Israelite and Hindu practice, Zoroastrians (if not Iranians generally) initiated both boys and girls. It was necessary to initiate girls owing to the purpose for which human beings were created, namely, as the pinnacle of the material creation in the struggle against the Evil Spirit and his creation. The child should be initiated at age seven, but must be by age fifteen. The Vendidad, an ancient text containing instructions for all sorts of rituals, implies that up to age seven, a child is closely guarded by the parents; then at seven begins a maturation process, marked by education, leading to adulthood at fifteen. In response to a question posed concerning when a puppy is able to protect and nourish itself, Ahura Mazda answers, "When these dogs are able to encircle seven houses twice. Afterward, according to one's desire, [the dog] may stay outside in winter, so [too] in summer. [The period for] the guarding of a dog is six months; of a boy seven years . . . so [too] of a girl" (Vendidad 15.44–45). The upper limit of fifteen years is explained as follows (18.30–57). To the question whether the demoness Druj (Lie) is the only one in the material world who bears offspring without sexual intercourse, she responds that there are four categories of men who belong to her and who "impregnate me in the way that also other males deposit their semen in their wives." Although there are expiations that three of these may make, the fourth has no recourse. Specifically, this is "when a man, a woman [apparently a later interpolation], after the fifteenth year, who is either ungirdled or has not put on [the shirt], goes forth." In the Pahlavi books this is the sin of *wisad-dwarisnih* (going about open), that is, without sacred girdle or shirt. The actual ceremony of initiation involved investiture with a belt or girdle and with a shirt, both worn under the outer garments. Worn for life, these two sacred garments both marked the individual as a ritually consecrated member of the Zoroastrian community and provided a physical defense against demonic attack.

Marriage. Marriage is already the subject of a Gatha (Yasna 53) ascribed by tradition to Zarathustra, who composed it on the occasion of the marriage of his daughter Pourucista to Jamaspa. Whether or not Zarathustra himself is the author, it appears to be a kind of general sermon to brides and grooms on the importance of righteousness. The Vendidad (15.14) enjoins the giving in marriage, at the age of fifteen, of one's sister or daughter, who is healthy and has had no sexual contact with men. This text specifically mentions earrings, suggesting that they have a strong symbolic function of one sort or another. According to another passage (4.44) one was obliged to give a wife to a coreligionist brother or friend who has come suing for a wife. That is, marriages seem to have been arranged by men. While the creation of legitimate children was a pri-

mary goal of marriage, wives were recognized as part of the general prosperity a man could hope for, as is poetically described in the hymn to the goddess Asi (Yasht 17).

BIBL.: Mary Boyce, *A Persian Stronghold of Zoroastrianism* (Oxford, 1977). J. J. Modi, *The Religious Ceremonies and Customs of the Parsees* (New York, 1979).　　　W.W.M.

Greece

From ancient Greece we have abundant details concerning the main rites of the life cycle, easily spanning a period of more than a thousand years. This does not mean, however, that we are equally well informed about the whole of Greece or that the rites were everywhere the same. Undoubtedly, we know the least about the areas of northern Greece and the most about Athens, with Crete and Sparta coming second due to the interest of ancient Greek historians in those cities' archaic customs. Athens was also the city where the state interfered relatively little in the rites of the life cycle, whereas Sparta and Crete exerted considerable control over the maturation of their members. Although this wealth of documentation means that we sometimes can follow the development of rites over long periods of time, the picture given below will concentrate on the archaic and classical periods (ca. 800–300 BCE), about which our sources are the most informative.

Birth. Birth often was a joyful event, attended by female neighbors and, usually, a midwife, although the father was absent. As the labor pains began, the mother untied her hair and loosened her dress; this change from everyday appearance signaled a vital moment and also was understood by the participants as a means of undoing all sorts of binding and thus helping to hasten the birth. When the child appeared, attending women shouted the *ololygē* (a strident noise), signifying relaxation after the tense atmosphere of travail. Immediately after the umbilical cord had been cut, mother and baby were bathed. Yet in spite of this bath, the mother remained impure for ten days, and her helpers lost their impurity only after five days: society needed some time to adjust to the new situation created by the birth of a child. In Athens, the child was officially accepted into the family a few days later through a ritual called the Amphidromia (Running Round): the father circled the hearth with the baby, integrating it into the household. Most people named their child on the tenth day, when the mother returned to her normal place in society; this was celebrated in a ritual called the Dekatē (Tenth Day), which included a common meal attended by blood relatives, kin, and friends. In thanksgiving, mothers dedicated objects connected with the birth to Eileithyia, the main birth-goddess, such as their girdles, dresses, or votive reliefs with a representation of birth. Midwives were often older, postmenopausal women, and Eileithyia's sanctuary was usually situated on the mar-

A bride leaves home to go to her husband's family; in front, attendants with implements prepare for the wedding ceremony. Attic red-figure *pyxis* (perfume container) by the Marley Painter, 432–420 BCE. British Museum. © *The British Museum*

gin of the city; males kept away from birth's messy and often dangerous business. That does not mean that they had no interest in children: one early-4th-century defendant declares that, after the birth of their first child, he completely trusted his wife (Lysias, *Oration* 1.6), and childless marriages ran a much-greater risk of divorce: the production of a child was a mother's only passport to recognition by the male world.

Initiation. Ancient Greek did not have a word corresponding to the term *initiation* in the anthropological sense of adolescents' rites of social integration, but the same initiatory pattern that can be often found among "primitive" peoples also existed in ancient Greece, although it sometimes was developed almost beyond recognition. The great events of Greek mythology—the Trojan War, the expedition of the Argonauts, and the Calydonian Boar Hunt—all bristle with initiatory motifs, but in historical times only Crete, somewhat isolated from the Greek mainland, may well have preserved best the older forms of male rites of initiation. Initially, young boys were harshly disciplined through deprivation of food, wine, and adequate clothing. At seventeen, they were organized into private *agelai* ("herds" [of "horses"]; Greek boys and girls were widely seen as unruly foals or calves who had to be "domesticated"). Aristocratic boys had to assemble a "herd" in competition with one another, and they were

supervised by the fathers of these boys, who had the authority "to punish anyone who was disobedient" (Ephorus, *FGrH* 70 F 149). Initiation thus helped to bolster the Cretan feudal system. In the "herds," the boys learned their communities' traditions through dancing and songs, but also learned to run, march, and use the bow, the Cretan weapon *par excellence,* as well as how to prepare ambushes—acquisition of cunning behavior being a standard part of Greek initiation.

In various Cretan cities, the term for entering the *agela* was "to undress," and the adolescents in the final stage of the *agela* were called the "very nude ones"; the city of Phaestus even had a festival called Undressing, Ekdysia, which was connected with myths and rituals of coming-of-age (Antoninus Liberalis 17). This "nudity" came to an end in different ways for aristocrats and nonaristocrats. Aristocratic boys were "kidnapped" by an aristocratic older lover, with whom they spent two months in the country; in a mythological reflection of such relations, Zeus carried off Ganymede. Pederasty was widely accepted in Greece as part of a male's coming-of-age, even if its function is still widely debated. At the end of the stay in the "bush," the boy received a warrior's robe and a cup, his "passports" into the symposium, where he would associate with the other adult males (Ephorus, *FGrH* 70 F 149). The other youths probably showed off their new robes during "graduation" festivals, one of which was significantly called Periblemaia (Feast of the Dressing); moreover the boys married upon graduating from the *agela*—marriage being a very public rather than a private affair. As virtually everywhere in Greece, the definitive transition into adulthood took place at the age of twenty. In Crete, however, this event probably took the form of a footrace, since Cretan adults were called *dromeis* (runners), and the name of one of the Cretan months, Dromēios, suggests that the graduation, at least in one city, happened during a festival called Dromaia (the Running).

In Sparta, the whole initiatory system, the *agōgē* (lit., the leading [of a horse by the hand]), was monopolized by the state at an early stage. Moreover, initiation was intensified by introducing age classes, when the number of citizens became smaller during the 4th(?) century BCE. Boys had to go through many years of bad food, harsh discipline, humiliation, and strenuous exercises, although Spartan society also reveled in the dances of its youths. The frugal diet was meant to make the boys tall and beautiful. In the 3rd century BCE, the boys were even regularly paraded naked in front of the ephors, in order to show whether the exercises had had the right effect on their bodies; those who appeared well trained and powerful were praised; the weak were punished. A slim and well-trained appearance was one of the aims of Spartan education. Just as they had extended the training, so also the Spartans prolonged "graduation" by introducing several festivals, such as the

Hyakinthia and Karneia, to make the contrast between youths and adults as marked as possible. Xenophon (*Spartan Constitution* 3.3; 10.7) tells us that those who had backed out of the *agōgē* were excluded from "the nice things." He provides no further details, but the message is clear. There was only one way to become a fully qualified adult Spartan and that was the passage through the Spartan *agōgē*.

In contrast, Athens had more or less abandoned the "old-fashioned education" by the end of the 5th century BCE. Remnants might be seen in sacrifices to Apollo Patroios (Ancestral Apollo), which marked an individual's connection to the civic subgroup of the phratry (brotherhood, a virtual kin group); sons were formally introduced by their fathers at age three and then again as ephebes; new wives were introduced by their husbands (Plato, *Euthydemus* 302C). Around 336 BCE, Athens reorganized the so-called *ephēbeia,* a kind of military service at the age of eighteen. The date is significant. The defeat of Athens by the Macedonians at Chaeronea in 338 BCE had made the military situation critical, and the Athenians had to take urgent measures. The new service still displayed some typically initiatory features such as the wearing of a short black coat, a stress on discipline, sojourns in liminal places, and training in the use of light weapons. Apparently, Athens still preserved memories of earlier initiatory customs.

Traditionally, girls were less severely treated, and their rites receive less attention in our male-biased sources. In Sparta, girls particularly received their education in choruses led by girls from the highest aristocracy. This prominent position of the Spartan aristocratic girls was hardly unique in Greece: in Croton, the city in southern Italy where Pythagoras had settled, his daughter was also the leader of a maiden chorus. The girls called each other "cousin," but the term should not be taken to mean that all the girls were really related to each other: it rather denoted their close relationship within the chorus. There are a few indications that such girls also received a female lover, in analogy to the boys' education; the tradition is most visible in the poems of Sappho of Lesbos. In addition, they received athletic training. Running, in particular, was intended to make them strong; vases depicting small girls running have been found in the sanctuary of Artemis in Brauron in Attica, Artemis being the goddess of female initiation *par excellence*. The eventual aim of the ritual was to make the girls as attractive as possible to suitable young men. This aim is well illustrated by the exemplary maiden in Arcadian mythology being called Callisto (the Most Beautiful; she was seduced by none other than the most powerful god, Zeus); in Sparta, Helen (the most beautiful woman of Greek mythology) was connected with the completion of initiation. In fact, in several Greek cities the girls' graduation, at the age of twelve to fourteen years, included a beauty contest.

Wedding. The wedding was considered the high point of a girl's life, corresponding in importance to the boy's graduation into adulthood. Girls said farewell to their maiden years by dedicating a lock of hair and their toys to Artemis. However, they had no say in the arrangement of the wedding, which the father concluded with the groom, who must have often been twice the age of the bride, with the formula "I betroth my daughter for the siring [lit., plowing] of legitimate children." The formula sums it all up: the wedding was primarily an institution to ensure the birth of legitimate children. To that end the bride had to look as beautiful as possible. After a bath she was dressed in a red garment (the color of love), with elaborate jewelry, special shoes, and a wreath of myrtle, the plant dedicated to Aphrodite, whereas the groom was dressed in a plain white garment. His wreath consisted of plants, such as sesame and poppy, whose many seeds symbolized the couple's hoped-for fertility.

After a sacrifice to the wedding-gods, Zeus Teleios and Hera Teleia (the "Fulfillers"), and festivities in the bride's home, the wedding was "officiated" by a public procession to the house of the groom at the end of the day. Accompanied by their parents and by friends holding torches, the couple drove to the new house, where the groom's mother awaited them. The couple was also welcomed with the *katachysmata,* a shower of dates, figs, little coins, and nuts—symbolizing the good wishes of the wedding guests. During this shower, the bride stood near the hearth, the focal point of her new home.

The guests celebrated together the entry of the bride into the heavily decorated bridal chamber. When they had left the chamber to continue their festivities, the contemporaries of the bride sang songs in which they hailed the couple, but which also served the purpose of ensuring that "the voice of the virgin might not be heard as she is violated by her husband, but might go unnoticed, covered by the voice of the maidens," as the ancient commentator on Theocritus's *Epithalamium* (song sung at the doors of the wedding chamber) dryly notes. Amid this pandemonium the defloration of Greek girls took place.

From now on, the bride would have to live with a man she perhaps had seen for the first time in her life only recently. The wedding ceremony, however, had already clearly stressed her position and duties in life: she was to obey her husband, to look after the house, and, above all, to produce legitimate heirs. Living with a virtual stranger, the new environment, and the abrupt separation from her own family must have been a trying experience for many a young woman.

BIBL.: G. Binder, "Geburt II," in *Reallexikon für Antike und Christentum* 9 (1976): 43–117. A. Brelich, *Paides e parthenoi* (Rome, 1969). C. Calame, *Choruses of Young Women in Ancient Greece* (trans. Derek Collins and Jane Orion; Lanham, Md., 1997 [orig. 1977]). R. Parker, *Miasma* (Oxford, 1983), 48–66. A.-M. Vérilhac and C. Vial, *Le mariage grec* (Athens, 1998). Katharina Waldner, *Geburt und Hochzeit des Kriegers:*

Geschlechterdifferenz und Initiation in Mythos und Ritual der griechischen Polis (Berlin, 2000).   J.N.B.

Rome

In Rome, the life of the individual was intimately bound to the house and family, with the head of the household, the *paterfamilias,* as its main source of authority. Rites of passage—rituals that accompanied and socially enacted the major transitions from birth to adulthood—thus were *res privatae,* family affairs only.

· Roman antiquarians and Christian detractors describe many quaint rites and strange powers *(Sondergötter)* concerned with birth, adolescence, and weddings; often, the significance of these gods and rites was lost already to them. We should not assume that all these rites were scrupulously performed and all the powers fearfully invoked by Cicero's and Augustus's contemporaries; often, what mattered to them was more the social event than the traditional rite. Unlike with public rituals, there was no firm authority to safeguard tradition—especially in the case of marriage ceremonies, where a Roman seemed to have a much wider choice than antiquarian sources or modern handbooks would have us believe and where personal taste, political considerations, or simple expedience (Cicero did not even bother to travel from Cilicia to Rome to attend his beloved daughter's wedding) was important. The following account, like those of the learned antiquarians, thus is sometimes less a reflection of Roman realities than a folkloric idealization, nor will it deal with what the antiquarians were silent about, but what archeology in recent decades has taught us, namely, that there were sanctuaries in Latium where, as late as the end of the 3rd century, rites of passage for adolescent boys and girls that were much more reminiscent of Greek paradigms than of any later ritual were performed; suffice it to say that the social changes of the 2nd and early 1st centuries BCE must have drastically changed the form of the rituals.

Birth brings a new individual into the house. Its first stages took place exclusively among women—the mother, female relatives and servants, and the midwife. Besides performing more practical tasks, the midwife also laid the newborn on the floor, lifted it up again *(tollere infantem),* and put it on its feet *(statuere infantem),* perhaps symbolically anticipating the upright walk specific to a human (see Ovid, *Metamorphoses* 1.72). Only then, and after it had been bathed and swaddled, was the baby handed over to the father, who accepted it into the house. Several days later, the new family member was given a name—girls on the eighth, boys on the ninth day. Birth was accompanied by rituals and prayers to invoke divine helpers (such as Carmentis, Postvorta, and Praevorta) and to avert evil powers, such as the child-snatching striges (Ovid, *Fasti* 6.132–68) or the god Silvanus.

Woman in bridal dress clasping her husband's hand in the presence of Venus and Cupid (with torch); a Grace (with bared shoulder) touches the bride's hand. Relief on sarcophagus, 2nd century CE. Mantua, Ducal Palace. *Alinari/Art Resource, New York*

Between the ages of fourteen and seventeen, a Roman boy became an adult. The rituals that celebrated this transition, usually at the festival of the god Liber on March 17, describe his passage from the private world of the house and its gods, the Lares, to the public sphere. The boy deposited the signs of his boyhood—the toga with the broad purple border and the *bulla,* a hollow metal sphere filled with amulets and worn around the neck. The *bulla* was deposited in the shrine of the Lares, and the new adult put on a pure white toga, the formal dress of a free Roman adult male *(toga virilis).* Then, the father—at least when he was a knight or senator—brought his son to the Forum; a sacrifice to Jupiter Optimus Maximus on the Capitol, in which family members, friends, and clients participated, closed the day. Only ungainly Claudius, that unlikely future emperor, had to sacrifice on the Capitol at midnight of the previous day, in order to avoid the public gaze (Suetonius, *Claudius* 2.2). Presumably under Greek influence, the dedication of the boy's hair could also accompany this transition; ambitious parents sent the hair to Apollo in Delphi or Asclepius in Pergamum (Statius, *Silvae* 3.4). Sometimes, the shaving of the first beard was celebrated as well, and the shavings, in a precious box, were dedicated to the Lares—or more extravagantly, as in the case of young Nero, to Capitolian Jupiter (Suetonius, *Nero* 12.4).

The corresponding passage for a girl was the wedding. Romans of both genders married young, the law and the doctors stipulating that physical maturity was the minimum requirement; twelve was the minimum age for girls. The traditional wedding, the *confarreatio,* was an elaborate ritual that transferred the bride from her father's power into the power of her husband. From the late republic on, however, society began to prefer looser forms that granted more independence to the woman. Whatever its form, an upper-class wedding (the only type we are informed about) usually took place in the town house of the bride's family (although circumstances could make a couple prefer a quiet wedding out of town; Apuleius, *Apology* 87), and attendance was compulsory for all who were invited. Already on the evening before the wedding, the bride put on a long white tunic with a belt that her mother tied with a special knot, the *nodus Herculis,* which the groom would have to untie on the wedding night. Her hair was parted with the tip of a lance, then bound with wool; over this elaborate coiffure she wore a garland and a red veil called the *flammeum* (to marry meant, for a Roman girl, to be veiled [*nubere*]).

The next morning, omens were sought—the *auspex* who did this was more a best man than a professional; sacrifices and prayers were offered. Then, as the high point in the rite, bride and groom joined their hands. In the traditional rite, they divided and ate a spelt cake *(far),* and the priest of Jupiter sacrificed fruits and spelt bread. A day-long banquet ensued. At its end, a merry torchlight procession (torches were symbols of weddings) brought the bride to the groom's house (with someone carrying spindle and distaff, the most common symbols of female virtue), while the guests threw nuts and made sexual jokes. The groom had come earlier, by a separate route; he now received his wife, and after her attendants had lifted her over the threshold (presumably lest she stumble ominously), he offered her water and fire, while she offered him a small coin, put a second one into the hearth, and kept a third one to offer to the gods of the district. Although a lavishly decorated bridal bed waited in the atrium, consummation of the marriage took place more discreetly in the master bedroom. Whatever the exact meaning of some of these rites, the themes of agriculture, war, and female virtue—stock items of Roman ideology—are obvious.

BIBL.: Thomas Köves-Zulauf, *Römische Geburtsriten* (Munich, 1990). Mario Torelli, *Lavinio e Roma: Riti iniziatici e matrimonio tra archeologia e storia* (Rome, 1984). Susan Treggiari, *Roman Marriage: Iusti Coniuges from the Time of Cicero to the Time of Ulpian* (Oxford, 1991).   F.G.

Christianity

The principal Christian rites of passage were the rites of initiation, which developed slowly over the first four centuries. They sought to provide prospective converts safe passage from their former religious worlds into the Christian world through rites of separation, transition, and incorporation.

The first three centuries. By the end of the 1st century, the rites comprised an extended period of instruction in the fundamentals of the Christian message, climaxing in baptism and the Lord's Supper (*Didache* 1–10). Conditioned by the mounting jeopardy of Christians during the next two centuries—Christianity was an illegal religion—the rites crystallized, emphasizing careful screening and rigorous formation. In Rome, for instance, initiation could take as long as three years (Hippolytus, *Apostolic Tradition* 1–21). The rite of separation, eventually called enrollment, consisted primarily of a searching inquiry by the bishop into a candidate's personal and professional status. If one had an unacceptable personal status or was engaged in an unacceptable line of employment, the requirement was, "Desist or be rejected!"

Those who passed muster entered the long transitional phrase, consisting of frequent (daily?) instruction—a blend of biblical, doctrinal, moral, and liturgical instruction given orally and laced with prayer and other rituals, including exorcism and fasting. The candidates were called catechumens *(katēchoumenoi),* a term derived from their oral instructions. One of the Greek roots of this term, *ech* (to make a sound), is captured by the English word *echo* and discloses the purpose of this transitional phase. The lives of the candidates were to echo the teaching they heard, a purpose heralded by an injunction: "Let reformation of life be the test" (*Apostolic Tradition* 17). No longer what they had been, nor yet Christians, the catechumens or "hearers" stood on the boundaries of their former sacred world and their new one. Neither here nor there, they were betwixt and between—a "threshold people," as Turner (1969: 85) calls it. Under normal circumstances, they were catechumens for three years.

Toward the end of the period, catechumens were subjected to another inquiry, this time into their conduct of life. Had they lived honestly? honored widows? visited the sick? done every kind of good work? If they had, they heard the words, "Let them hear the gospel" (*Apostolic Tradition* 20). Set apart from the other catechumens and considered "the chosen," they received special instructions based on the Gospels and participated in special rites, including a solemn exorcism intended to sort out those truly ready for the next stage—incorporation. After some three weeks, the day of baptism approached.

The rites of incorporation began at cockcrow on Sunday. The baptismal waters and oils were blessed. Ritually stripped, the candidates individually renounced Satan and were anointed for the baptismal bath. Individually immersed in the water, each affirmed his or her faith and, on emerging, was anointed with oil, dried, and vested in a white garment. They entered the church, where the bishop, extending his hand over them and

Right to left: Baptism, man carrying a ram (a Christian Hermes figure), a praying (orant) figure, and the Jonah story depicted on a sarcophagus in S. Maria Antiqua al Foro Romano. The Jonah story was connected with baptism in Christian imagery. *Alinari/Art Resource, New York*

spelling out the meaning of baptism in a prayer, anointed each of the newly baptized on the head in the form of a cross. In the company of the faithful, who had greeted them as new brothers and sisters with a kiss, they then celebrated for the first time the Lord's Supper. They were now incorporated into the community, had acquired a new family and a religious home, and could loudly acclaim, "I am a Christian."

The 4th and 5th centuries. The 4th century changed everything. Legalized in 311 CE, Christianity became the established religion of the empire in 381 CE. Whereas the social and legal jeopardy of the early centuries had forced Christians to guard the gates and screen entrants rigorously, legalization and establishment threatened to open the gates to floods of people who, for many different reasons—some of them far from religious—sought

entrance. The problem was how to keep the floodgates in place, so that the flood would not wash away the faith of the first three centuries. The rites of initiation remained the buttress. Although from the outset Christianity envisioned the possibility of infant baptism, initiation remained primarily an adult experience until the early Middle Ages. Men, women, and children continued to be enrolled as catechumens in a distinctive rite of separation and, as in the past, to live on the threshold of the church, sometimes for half a lifetime—as in the case of Augustine of Hippo who, enrolled as an infant, was thirty-three when he finally made the decision to seek baptism.

The decisive change in the rites appeared first in Jerusalem about 330. The final stage of the catechumenate—preparation for incorporation—transformed

Fresco-decorated baptistry in the Christian housechurch at Dura Europos (Syria), 3rd century; model in Yale University Art Museum. The figures on the wall gesture toward the central sacred space. *Yale University Art Museum, Z65, Dura-Europos Baptistry, reconstruction of NW corner*

the annual preparation for Easter, called "the Forty Days" (modern Lent). They began with a new inquiry and enrollment and inaugurated a rigorous fast. With the bishop as catechist, those about to be baptized participated in daily oral instruction, based on the Bible and accompanied by prayer and exorcism. Three weeks before Easter, the text changed from the Bible to the creed. During the week before Easter ("Great Week"), the focus was on the final events of the life of Jesus, and the rites correspondingly increased in drama, culminating in a Saturday night vigil, which ended with baptism at cockcrow on Easter morning and the Lord's Supper. The baptismal rites, now hallowed by ancient tradition, remained much the same as in the 2nd century. Nonetheless, the week following became one of daily celebration over the incorporation of the newly baptized, ending the following Sunday, when the catechumens removed their white garments and took their normal places in their new family.

Although the rites of initiation had changed much in content and articulation over the first four centuries, their general structure and function still sought to separate candidates from an old way of life, form them in their new way by instruction in a ritual setting, and incorporate them into their new religious community as brothers and sisters in a family where God was father, Christ was elder brother, and the church was mother. The rites of passage remained extensive and demanding until changed by the dominance of infant baptism in the 6th century.

BIBL.: T. M. Finn, *From Death to Rebirth: Ritual and Conversion in Antiquity* (Mahwah, N.J., 1997). Arnold van Gennep, *The Rites of Passage* (trans. Monika Vizedom and G. L. Caffe; Chicago, 1960 [orig. 1909]). Clayton N. Jefford, *The Didache in Context* (Leiden, 1995). Victor Turner, *The Ritual Process: Structure and Antistructure* (Chicago: Aldine, 1969). T.M.F.

Illnesses and Other Crises

Introduction

Individuals and communities of the ancient Mediterranean were constantly beset by crises and often sought to face them with the gods' help. This was logical: crises were believed to be caused by individual gods or demonic forces, so impotent humans required divine aid against them. This reliance on the gods' support in fighting afflictions and warding off future suffering and misfortune was common to ancient cultures, and, while each culture might have distinct or even unique features, we should recognize that the similarities among them far outweigh the differences and that the same general theological principles underlay often wildly disparate rituals. The reason for many of the apparent differences is that the sources for these cultures are so varied; for example, cuneiform tablets provide the greatest illumination regarding religion in Mesopotamia and Anatolia, while the Israelites' beliefs are mostly preserved in the Hebrew Bible, and, in contrast, the Etruscans left us practically no written sources—instead their religious practices and beliefs must be determined from archeological sources. Understandably, the sources for the earlier cultures are much more limited than for the later cultures, and this impacts our ability to evaluate how they responded to crises, as well as the extent to which their responses evolved over time. After all, the volume and variety of written sources from Mesopotamia and Anatolia are dwarfed by those of the Greeks and Romans, and this is true of archeological remains as well. Furthermore, whereas the ability to write became widespread among Greeks and Romans from different classes and backgrounds, writing in the earlier cultures was mostly limited to the royal courts and bureaucracies, and this skews our knowledge of their religions.

Thus, for example, the earliest sources for incubation (the ritual practice of sleeping at a holy site in order to solicit dream-advice from a god) describe kings or priests engaging in this practice—for example, King Sol-

omon (2 Chron. 1.2–13) and priests answering to the Hittite King Murshili II (*ANET* 396)—while the more varied literary and epigraphical sources of the Greeks and Romans record both rulers and commoners alike doing so: surely ordinary Israelites and Hittites were also practicing incubation, long before incubation by common folk was first recorded by the Greeks; indeed, this may be indicated by a line in the Hebrew Bible (Jer. 29.8).

Despite such contrasts in the sources, it becomes evident that ancient cultures faced the same crises and generally used the same types of approaches to deal with them. Entire communities in times of crises such as invasions, plagues, and earthquakes appealed to the gods together, but the sources are much richer for personal attempts by afflicted individuals to seek relief. In times of communal crisis, presumably, efforts were frequently duplicated, since people living in a stricken city might appeal to certain gods for help even as their community was doing so: one can hardly imagine, for example, that individual Romans suffering from the plague of 293–292 BCE would have patiently waited and taken no actions while their government responded by sending an embassy to Greece in order to bring Asclepius to Rome (Ovid, *Metamorphoses* 15.622–744; Valerius Maximus 1.8.2; Livy 10.47.6–7 and *Periochae* 11).

The most common type of personal crisis, by far, involved health, including not only issues of personal well-being but fertility as well. In each of these societies illnesses and communal plagues were attributed to divine powers, even after the great medical researchers of Greece first began to argue that the causes of some human ailments might not lie in the stars but in ourselves. Failure to understand the causes of contagious disease made regular illness a fact of life for so many: ignorance of germs meant that sanitary conditions were often terrible, and there should be little doubt that much needless suffering was brought about by the lack of underground sewers in many cities or harmful individual practices, such as the Romans' inadvisable use of communal sponges for cleaning themselves at public restrooms. While some suffering was brought on through such ignorance, the insufficient knowledge of medical practitioners prevented many ailments that today would be treated easily from being corrected through prescriptive medicine or surgery. Overall, the medical conditions in the ancient world were much more dire than they are in the modern world, and when the cause of a problem could not be understood, it would be blamed on a divine power and thus the sufferer would turn to either that or another divine power for help. Above all else, ancient peoples relied on their gods for the restoration and maintenance of their health: certainly the preoccupation with healing miracles so richly illustrated in the Gospels and Acts of the Apostles demonstrates that Christianity spread at least in part because of the need and reverence for divine healers.

Although some of those afflicted by illnesses or physical ailments immediately turned to the gods for a cure and others sought their help only after human medicine had proved inadequate and their problems chronic, often human doctors and divine powers were enlisted concurrently—nor was this considered incongruous. In many cultures, there was no sharp delineation between "rational" medicine and divine medicine: thus in Egypt, medical knowledge was intricately linked to religious rituals and beliefs, while the patron-god of Greek physicians was Asclepius, whose healing sanctuaries were frequented by doctors who, like their patron, practiced medicine at these sites. Even "rational" Greek medicine, which was based on the belief that diseases and physical problems had natural causes and therefore could be cured if these causes were scientifically determined, was sometimes influenced by what we would call irrationality; for example, the great physician Galen once criticized a colleague for following the tenets of astrobotany, a system for determining the times at which certain plants with medicinal qualities were most potent and prime for picking (Galen, *De simplicium medicamentorum temperamentis et facultatibus* [ed. Kühn, 11.797]), but Galen himself wrote a work entitled *Crisis Days,* in which he explored the importance of stellar and lunar influences on both the causes of illnesses and the optimal times for treating them (Galen, *De diebus decretoriis* [ed. Kühn, 9.769–941]).

In addition to undergoing specific treatments, whether dictated by a god or human, the sick and injured frequently used amulets, as attested by both literary sources and archeological remains. Amulets appear to have been the most common method of enlisting divine forces to achieve a recovery—especially in the case of brief illnesses not meriting a visit to a healing sanctuary—but they were also commonly employed as a means of heading off a future health crisis: protective charms, some targeting specific ailments and others intended to ward off all forms of physical suffering, were worn by countless individuals, and, similarly, talismans adorned homes and other buildings. Similar to this form of "preventive medicine" were the apotropaic devices intended to protect property: while cities might employ talismans to repel potential invaders or plagues, individuals decorated their homes with magical designs and objects to defend against the Evil Eye or other baleful forces or placed in their fields objects inscribed with magical texts to protect against hail, locusts, and other agricultural crises (e.g., *L'année épigraphique* [1939]: 136; [1984]: 933; Kotansky 1994: 11A–B). Protective spells were even employed in anticipation of posthumous crises: numerous funerary inscriptions, particularly in Asia Minor, include imprecations intended to bring down divine vengeance on any who would violate the tomb.

BIBL.: Campbell Bonner, *Studies in Magical Amulets, Chiefly Graeco-Egyptian* (Ann Arbor, 1950). Sally A. L. Butler, *Mesopotamian Conceptions of Dreams and Dream Rituals* (Münster, 1998). Angelos Chaniotis, "Illness and Cures in the Greek Propitiatory Inscriptions and Dedications of Lydia and Phrygia," in *Ancient Medicine in Its Socio-Cultural Context: Papers Read at the Congress Held at Leiden University, 13–15 April 1992* (ed. P. J. van der Eijk, H. F. J. Horstmanshoff, and P. H. Schrijvers; Amsterdam, 1995), 2.323–44. Christopher A. Faraone, *Talismans and Trojan Horses: Guardian Statues in Ancient Greek Myth and Ritual* (Oxford, 1992). Roy Kotansky, *Greek Magical Amulets: The Inscribed Gold, Silver, Copper, and Bronze Lamellae,* vol. 1: *Published Texts of Known Provenance* (Opladen, 1994). Johan Strubbe, *Apai Epitumbioi: Imprecations against Desecrators of the Grave in the Greek Epitaphs of Asia Minor: A Catalogue* (Bonn, 1997). G.R.

Egypt

The Egyptians were famous in the ancient world for their knowledge of medicine and their trained physicians, as mentioned, for instance, in literary texts such as Homer's *Odyssey* (4.229–32) or later by Herodotus, who visited Egypt in the middle of the 5th century BCE: "The practice of medicine is so divided among [the Egyptians], that each physician is a healer of one disease and no more. All the country is full of physicians, some of the eye, some of the teeth, some of what pertains to the belly, and some of the hidden diseases" (2.84, trans. Godley). Herodotus's observations are impressively confirmed by about twenty surviving medical, surgical, and pharmacological treatises from all periods of pharaonic history, dealing with a wide range of common diseases, including diagnoses and prescriptions. Although these medical texts focused on the ill person and treatment of the disease, the patient remained surprisingly anonymous. For this reason, authentic documents concerning specific sufferers are very rare. Among the few exceptions is one that also displays genuine individ-

Egyptian amulet: a Horus cippus (Horus on crocodiles).
Rijksmuseum van Ouheden, Leiden

woven with treatment based on supernatural intervention. Accordingly, most of the medical papyri contain a mixture of what we would call medical and magical treatment, and, correspondingly, most of the magical papyri include spells designed for either prophylactic protection against all kinds of threats and dangers or for healing diseases and injuries—thus the Egyptological term *medico-magical texts*. Moreover, the texts include passages that are mythological and religious in the same sense as are many passages outside a "magical" context. In Egypt, in short, what we call religion, medicine, and magic coexisted without apparent conflict, and it was not unusual for magical and practical remedies to be used side by side: "Powerful are spells over remedies and vice versa" recommends the Ebers Papyrus, by far the longest surviving medical papyrus, dating to approximately 1500 BCE.

Yet, there was clearly some sort of personal choice made as to how medical, magical, and religious remedies were combined in any specific case, and the supposed cause of the illness would have been an important factor in choosing among remedies. Certain symptoms might have religious associations, that is, might be attributed to divine intervention; so a religious cure, for example, the reconciliation of the offended deity, may have been the first resort; other symptoms might lead the patient to opt for "magical" associations, that is, the influence of malign spirits that should be exorcised. And although conventional, "rational" medical treatment (without involving spirits and deities) was practiced during all phases of pharaonic history, including complicated operations such as trepanation, tooth reimplantation, and fracture reduction, magic figured prominently in the treatment of diseases.

Magical remedies can be classified in two main categories: those that used spells and those that used amulets—although the two often were employed together. "Do not slight a small amulet when it is time to seek it. An amulet that has no harm saves its owner from it," reads the Ptolemaic Instructions of Papyrus Insinger. Some amulets were worn temporarily in situations of crisis; others were worn on a regular basis for permanent protection or benefit. They served many purposes, prominently the preservation and protection of the body in life and death. There were amulets that a mother could use to safeguard her newborn child, amulets to protect their owners against any person or force who would harm them, amulets for protection against an illness or during a dangerous journey. The huge number of surviving amulets of all sizes and materials attests to their enormous popularity and suggests that most people were convinced of amulets' positive effects and curative power. Therefore it would be quite wrong to dismiss magic as irrelevant to the healing process.

A powerful curative amulet that is recommended in several texts is a necklace made of a piece of cloth knotted with magical knots, generally seven in number.

ual feeling. In a draftsman's letter to his son, the misery and despair of blindness are clearly expressed in simple but touching words: "Do not desert me, for I am not well . . . May you bring me honey for my eyes as well as fat and genuine galena . . . Am I not your father? Now I am incapacitated. I am searching for my eyesight, but it no longer exists!"

Contrary to the scientific principles of some ancient Greeks, such as Hippocrates, conventional or empirical medicine in pharaonic Egypt was unequivocally inter-

In one case, a certain Aninakhte, son of the Lady Oubekhet, seems to have been a child or a young man who lived in the community of Deir el-Medina at the time of Rameses III (ca. 1193–1162 BCE). During excavations at Deir el-Medina in 1951, a linen necklace covered with magical signs was found in the debris of a village house. Seven knots had been tied into the cord. Still in its original place was an attached small papyrus, folded eight times. The short magical text was designed to heal Aninakhte from a cold and heavy fever. The disease was supposed to have been caused by a series of ill-disposed demons from the netherworld. With the help of Osiris, god of the dead, these demons were to be removed. According to the text, the amulet was to be tied around the neck of the ill person. To protect the fragile papyrus, it was originally kept in a cylindrical container, which now is lost. Seven was a number of great significance in magic: just as the knot had been tied seven times, so should the illness be. Popular belief in such magical practices outlived both Egypt's conversion to Christianity as well as the spread of Islam, showing an amazing continuity of tradition. Even nowadays, the fellahin of Upper Egypt use necklaces with seven knots and small attached boxes containing verses from the Qur'an to protect freshly circumcised young boys against fever.

Another sort of magical device used against illness, the so-called divine or oracular decrees, flourished after the end of the New Kingdom (ca. 1000 BCE). These decrees were issued in the name of deities who gave oracles. Written on a narrow strip of papyrus, the gods mentioned in the text promised the owner immunity from all kinds of afflictions and protection against every type of illness, including blindness, headache, fever, and ailments of the lung, stomach, and rectum. In addition to demons or other supernatural powers, the dead are quite often mentioned as the cause of a disease, as a threat to its cure, or simply as a cause of an unexpected misfortune, family tragedy, or other personal crisis. The background for this is the deeply rooted belief of the Egyptians that the dead had the power to influence the destinies of the living and were also regarded as capable of defending the living against sickness caused by their deceased confreres. "Letters to the Dead" became a recognized literary genre with its own terminology. Sometimes written on a linen strip or a papyrus, or more frequently on ostraca or complete vessels of pottery, they were placed in tombs and played part in the funerary cult. They range in date between 2700 and 1200 BCE. In one of the earliest letters, probably dating to 2500 BCE, a woman named Irti turned to her dead husband, reminding him of the promise he had given while dying, to take special care of his son. Soon after his death, a foreign couple had come and taken possession of her house, destroying it completely, taking away all her property—even the slaves—and forcing her son to stay with them. Finally she beseeched her dead husband: "Raise yourself up, haste against him, raise yourself

up, haste against her, together with your fathers, your brothers, and your friends and overthrow them!" In another example a widower addresses his dead wife. Soon after she died, he and his children ran into difficulties. They suffered from some blow of fortune that the widower describes as "these wounds" but which may be simply an expression for poverty or hunger. He protests that his departed wife never had any cause for complaint, and he seems genuinely in doubt how far she can be cognizant of his wrongs. Now he is asking for her support and protection. If the mischief is being done against her will, perhaps her dead father is powerful enough to counter such machinations. If, however, she still bears a grudge against him, he is begging her: "Please, forget it for the sake of your children. Be gracious, be gracious, and may the gods be gracious to you!"

During the 1st millennium BCE, it became more common to attribute problems to the envy or spite of people who possessed the Evil Eye. Spells written on wooden boards threaten anyone who might cast the Evil Eye on a person with the most terrifying divine punishments. There are certain specific types of medical problems where this and other kinds of magic seem to be particularly prominent. It is remarkable that while Egyptian medical literature of the New Kingdom (ca. 1550–1080 BCE) presents a great variety of prescriptions and remedies for a wide range of diseases, wounds, and injuries, we find that snake bites, scorpion stings, and wounds from other biting animals are mostly ignored and their cures seem to belong, instead, completely to the realm of magic. And it is not until the early Ptolemaic period that we find a remarkable papyrus, now kept in the Brooklyn Museum, that lists the types of snakes found in Egypt, the symptoms of snake bites, and the treatments of their poisons. Snakes, scorpions, and crocodiles must have caused the deaths of numerous Egyptians, as we learn from various texts. A stele from Hellenistic times speaks about the death of a certain Cleopatra, daughter of Memnon, who was stung by a scorpion in the sanctuary of a temple.

The assumption that the Egyptians resorted commonly to what might be called religious means of treatment in cases of such injuries is supported by the prevalence from the New Kingdom until the end of Roman times of a healing statue known as a Horus *cippus*. The main function of these *cippi* was therapeutic, although their presence in temples was supposed also to have prophylactic effects. The *cippi* are dominated by the figure of the divine child Horus, standing on top of two or more crocodiles and triumphing over dangerous animals. With his hands he grasps scorpions and snakes, as well as wild animals such as lions and gazelles. Smaller deities, religious scenes, and a canonical set of magical texts consisting of several antivenom spells are distributed on the fronts and the backs of the *cippi*. The healing strategy was to identify the ill person with a particular deity, namely the injured youthful god Horus, so that he might be cured as Horus had been. Large examples of such *cippi* were set up in special public areas of temples. In 1983, a chapel covered with magical texts was excavated at the temple of the goddess Mut in Thebes, originally erected in a public place accessible to the devotees. This chapel was probably built specifically to house a Horus *cippus* and thereby to serve the general community as a healing shrine. Smaller, medium-sized *cippi* were kept in houses to repel dangerous animals, and still smaller and lighter ones, many of them with holes for suspensions, were worn as amulets. The obviously worn surface on many *cippi* attests to the frequency with which devotees kissed or rubbed them—especially the face of the young Horus. Such acts may have been considered a perfect means of receiving a share of their curative power. The primary way in which the power of the *cippi* was transferred to patients was as follows: water was poured over them and, having absorbed the power of the spells and images, was drunk by the patient who hoped for a cure. For this reason, the *cippi* sometimes were provided with small basins to collect the curative water. Astonishingly enough, centuries later, when the Scottish traveler James Bruce stayed in Abyssinia (1768–72) and was shown a Horus *cippus,* he was told that it had the power to cure every disease.

BIBL.: Carol Andrews, *Amulets of Ancient Egypt* (London, 1994). John F. Nunn, *Ancient Egyptian Medicine* (London: British Museum Press, 1997). Robert K. Ritner, *The Mechanics of Ancient Magical Practice* (Studies in Ancient Oriental Civilization 54; Chicago, 1993). Heike Sternberg-el Hotabi, *Untersuchungen zur Überlieferungsgeschichte der Horusstelen: Ein Beitrag zur Religionsgeschichte Ägyptens im 1. Jahrtausend v. Chr.* (Ägyptologische Abhandlungen 62; Wiesbaden, 1999). Wolfhart Westendorf, *Handbuch der altägyptischen Medizin* (2 vols.; Handbuch der Orientalistik 36; Leiden: Brill, 1999).　　　　　H.ST.

Mesopotamia

Over the course of some 2,500 years (ca. 2600–100 BCE), cuneiform sources, written in both the Sumerian and Akkadian languages, refer to illnesses as well as to other personal crises and prescribe various modes of coping with illness and with personal difficulties. The most important sources are various types of therapeutic texts that describe symptoms, provide etiological or descriptive diagnoses, and prescribe treatments. Other texts, such as the forty-tablet manual SA.GIG, are diagnostic in intent and provide descriptions of illnesses in their protases and diagnoses and prognoses in their apodoses. In addition, many nontherapeutic texts are concerned with illness; these include, for example, literary compositions that deal with the problem of theodicy, treaties and dedicatory texts that call down curses upon any who disrespect their provisions, miscellaneous texts that describe healers and patients, and letters to and from courts reporting on illness and advising appropriate treatments.

Distress. Personal distress includes the individual's experience of physical, psychological, and/or social difficulties. Texts may focus on specific symptoms, such as gastrointestinal, respiratory, sexual, or psychological difficulties; on life-threatening circumstances, such as childbirth and infancy; on more generalized illnesses involving systemic physical and/or psychological breakdown; or on situations involving socioeconomic loss of wealth and status as well as social isolation. Examples of physical difficulties mentioned in the texts are toothache, blindness, earaches, skin diseases, jaundice, epilepsy, kidney stones, infertility, miscarriage, and impotence.

An example of a description and diagnosis is provided by the following (all examples in this section are drawn from texts that treat problems caused by witchcraft; examples could equally have been drawn from texts that center on other evils): "If a man is bewitched, his flesh sags, he is stiff, his knees are locked, he desires a woman but upon looking at her, he loses his interest [erection?]; that man, his semen has been deposited with a corpse" (Köcher 1963: no. 205).

Cures. Procedural texts prescribe the treatment of illness either by means of various ritual therapies or by means of traditional herbal therapy. The traditional scribal literature contains and occasionally juxtaposes both forms of treatment. According to the 1965 analysis of Mesopotamian medical texts by Ritter, the ritual and herbal therapies represent the practices of two different healing professions, the *āšipu* and *asû,* respectively. The argument has recently been advanced that one should distinguish not between ritual and herbal practitioners, but between the healer *(āšipu)* and the pharmacist *(asû),* with the healer making use of all modes of treatment. The present exposition follows Ritter's approach, for even if the suggested modification of her conclusions turns out to be justified, I would maintain that such a situation indicates only that the upper-class *āšipu,* in his typical monopolizing fashion, has taken over the tasks and functions of the traditional herbalist *(asû),* who would now function as a pharmacist to the upper class while retaining his original role as a herbalist for the populace in general.

How is a cure achieved? Herbal medicine: the practice of the asû. In the texts that preserve the lore of the herbalist, descriptions of symptoms are followed by instructions for preparing and administering medications. The *materia medica* consisted of mineral, animal, but especially plant substances. The herbalist employed potions, lotions, ointments, bandages, suppositories, enemas, and so on. The *asû* (usually a man, but occasionally a woman) bandaged wounds, cared for breaks, and treated external and internal illnesses. His approach was pragmatic; he was concerned with what might work, and far less with etiology. His therapy was directed toward the relief of acute and pressing symptoms. Occasionally he also utilized incantations; these tended to be secondary and random, and they served mainly as a reinforcing therapeutic measure. The treatment provided by the *asû* is seen in this example: "If a man has repeated headaches, sleep . . . , his dreams are terrifying, he is repeatedly frightened in his sleep, his knees are bound, his chest . . . paralysis, he is constantly sweating; that man is bewitched. You crush tamarisk, soapwort, and leaves of the *ḫaluppu* tree together. You wash him with water, you rub him with cedar oil. Afterward you put tamarisk, soapwort, and potash in . . . , you heat it in the oven, you wash him with it; he will then recover" (Thompson 1923: no. 86/1).

Ritual medicine: the practice of the āšipu. The *āšipu* was an expert in dealing with supernatural forces such as demons and was concerned with etiology and theory in addition to practice. In contrast to the *asû*, the *āšipu* may be regarded as a member of the clergy or, at least, of the temple personnel. The activities of the more learned members of the *āšipu* group comprised both theological scholarship and practical ministry. Yet, although the *āšipu* did have temple affiliations and may have participated in cultic activities, he generally performed his craft on behalf of private clients who belonged to the upper classes, the central administration, and the royal family. The ritual usually involved only the *āšipu* and his client or patient, who might be treated not only for physical, but also for psychosomatic and mental distress.

Normally, the *āšipu* used both oral and manual rites. In the course of a ritual, the *āšipu* recited one or more oral addresses. These addresses might be either incantations or prayers and served to legitimate the speaker, call upon the divine powers, identify the purpose of the ritual, and specify the rites that were being performed. The addresses could be directed to beneficent natural forces (who often appeared as well-rounded divine figures) and ceremonial objects, or to the evil itself. The beneficent powers would be called upon to help the client or patient; the evil would be expelled, chased away, or even destroyed. Alongside the addresses, the *āšipu* performed accompanying rites. The ritual might range from a relatively simple one to an extensively elaborated performance and could last a few hours or continue for a day or more. The ceremony often involved purification, food and drink offerings to the gods, the burning of incense, a central operation directed toward significant objects or symbols (e.g., the destruction of figurines, the use of substitutes), the tying and untying of knots, washing, the setting up of protective devices, the application of amulets, and the like.

An example of a short ritual performed by the *āšipu* occurs in a witchcraft ritual text that may be summarized as follows:

> After a description of a patient's symptoms, a diagnosis of witchcraft, and a statement that the release of witchcraft is the purpose of the ritual, the ritual instructions prescribe the setting out of offerings to Shamash, the sun-god, the preparation of statues of a warlock and witch, the raising up of these statues, and the recitation of an incantation to Shamash. In this incantation, the statues are designated as representing the evildoers who have harmed the victim, and their destruction by fire is described. Subsequent to the threefold recitation of this incantation, the statues are placed in a container, sprinkled with fish oil, and set on fire. Then, a second incantation, "I lift up the torch, I burn your statues," invoking the aid of Ea, Asalluhi, and Girra [gods of magic and burning] and addressing the burning statues, is recited, and the burned statues are trampled in water and their remains buried. The ritual is performed either at sunrise or at sunset. In sum, statues of the witch are raised to Shamash and burned; the burned statues are then drowned and buried. (*KAR* no. 80 and duplicates)

An example of a complex ritual performed by the *āšipu* is the Maqlû ceremony against witchcraft. This ceremony, preserved on nine tablets, centered on the recitation of one hundred incantations and the performance of such rites as burning of figurines, fumigation, washing, disposal, and protection and was carried out throughout a night and into the following morning at the end of the month Abu (July/August).

Causes. Why are humans struck by illness? Mesopotamian medicine certainly recognized natural events such as cold, fire, falls, blows, breaks, and wounds as causes of suffering. More frequently, however, the texts took a religio-magical view and treated distress or illness as the result of the action or inaction of supernatural powers. In this view, the universe was understood to be hierarchically structured and to be centered on divine powers. This approach seems, however, to have emerged from, or at least to have drawn upon, an earlier approach that was primarily magical and viewed the world holistically. The principal agencies and causes of illness in the religio-magical worldview were gods, demons, personal gods, ghosts, witches, evil omens, curses, and sins. Among the demons are *lamaštu* and the *lîl, udug,* and *asag* demons.

Suffering is usually understood to be a consequence of the interaction of human and nonhuman forces. The interaction will take different forms—that is, there will be different causal agents and chains of causation. The changing configurations probably reflect different social situations and can be explained in historical terms. The earlier mechanistic magical universe reflects the social context of traditional society: the village and pre-urban settlement. Here, illness is due partly to irregularity, disorder, and chaos. This disorder is manifested in attacks by demons on individuals who are vulnerable; vulnerability is due to the lack of protection, only occasionally to culpability. The demons are modeled upon irresistible natural forces, upon enemies and bandits, and upon the minions of newly emerging warlords or leaders trying to extend their rule.

This traditional worldview probably remained operative for the mass of rural and urban dwellers. But alongside this worldview and based upon it, a new worldview that reflected the values and interests of the emerging urban elite arose in the late 4th or early 3rd millennium BCE; in this new view, the gods increasingly gained more control over the world. This new worldview underwent changes of its own; different, emerging sociopolitical contexts led to new ways through which to view and understand the travails of life. New successive contexts generated new causes of evil and placed the already existing ones into new settings and relationships. The sociopolitical contexts that underlay the new worldview were city, tribe, nation, and empire.

City-state. Given the personal relationship between city god and ruler, when the individual citizen is afflicted, it is generally because he or she is a member of a community that is to be punished or corrected because of failures of the ruler or the collective (in the form of the community or of its individual members) toward the god.

Clan. If a man does not provide necessary or proper service to the personal/family god, either by offerings and service or by proper social behavior, then the god may either become angry and strike the man or withdraw his protection and leave the man vulnerable to various forces. The alienation of the personal god need not result in an attack by demons, but may simply serve as a metaphor for the loss of vitality and energy. The centrality and power of the personal god, who punishes the individual because of infractions that he has committed, is a Semitic feature; it reflects the life of newly arrived Semitic tribal/rural clans and is a conceptual intrusion into the Mesopotamian urban landscape.

Empire. With the decrease in viewing society primarily in corporate terms, a relationship is developed between the citizen and the national god(s). Here, the human is punished by the god for some sin or other. The punishment will often take the form of the god ordering a demonic force or some other evil to afflict the person or ordering the family gods to withdraw their support. A development in this human-divine relationship takes place with the subsequent emergence of the imperial state, in which powers are centralized and integrated. Centralization and integration cause various changes in religious outlook. For example, the personal god now comes to be regarded as simply a manifestation of the imperial god; thus, human success or

failure, which depends on the beneficence or alienation of the personal god, is no more than a reflection or a manifestation of the will of the major god (especially Marduk). During these last stages, the witch became a major force and was able to control personal gods and demons. The witch even came to represent an enemy of the state, sometimes a foreign force that could threaten the late empire. Thus, in the later periods, humans suffer not only because of sin, but also because of outside forces like witchcraft.

Actually, the case of witchcraft may serve as a useful illustration of a form of evil that seems to have changed over time. One possible reconstruction suggests, first, the existence of a popular village and/or domestic witch, then the transformation of this form into the counterpart of the emerging exorcist, and finally a further transformation and use of the image of the witch as an instrument of state propaganda during the 1st millennium. Thus, several stages can be identified in the development of Mesopotamian witchcraft. Its origins begin with an early stage of "popular" witchcraft, which may have taken an archaic shamanistic form. In this early popular form, the witch probably belonged to a rural, nonurban world. She or he was not of necessity an evil being and took the form of both a "white" and a "black" witch. Not infrequently, she helped her fellows by means of magical abilities and medical knowledge; in this popular form, she occasionally exhibited behavior otherwise associated with ecstatic types of practitioners. Originally, then, the witch was not primarily a doer of evil. Perhaps, because the witch was often a woman who possessed knowledge and power, the female witch eventually became a focus of interest and even a threat to the prerogatives of the male exorcist. This village witch was transformed into an antisocial, malicious, evil force that was the polar opposite of the *āšipu;* first she became the evil counterpart of the exorcist, and then she was even transformed into an alien and/or demonic force that threatened society as a whole.

BIBL.: T. Abusch, "The Demonic Image of the Witch in Standard Babylonian Literature: The Reworking of Popular Conceptions by Learned Exorcists," in *Religion, Science, and Magic: In Concert and in Conflict* (ed. Jacob Neusner, Ernest S. Frerichs, and Paul V. M. Flesher; New York: Oxford University Press, 1989), 27–58. Idem, "Witchcraft and the Anger of the Personal God," in *Mesopotamian Magic: Textual, Historical, and Interpretative Perspectives* (ed. T. Abusch and K. van der Toorn; Groningen: Styx, 1999), 83–121. W. van Binsbergen and F. Wiggermann, "A Theoretical Perspective, and Its Application to Ancient Mesopotamia," in *Mesopotamian Magic: Textual, Historical, and Interpretative Perspectives* (ed. T. Abusch and K. van der Toorn; Groningen: Styx, 1999), 3–34. Franz Köcher, *Die babylonisch-assyrische Medizin in Texten und Untersuchungen* (Keilschrifttexte aus Assur 1; Berlin: de Gruyter, 1963–). E. Reiner, *Astral Magic in Babylonia* (Philadelphia: American Philosophical Society, 1995). E. K. Ritter, "Magical-Expert (= *Āšipu*) and Physician

(= *Asû*): Notes on Two Complementary Professions in Babylonian Medicine," in *Studies in Honor of Benno Landsberger* (ed. H. J. Güterbock and T. Jacobsen; Chicago: University of Chicago Press, 1965), 299–321. R. C. Thompson, *Assyrian Medical Texts from the Originals in the British Museum* (London: Oxford University Press, 1923). T.A.

Syria-Canaan

Although our data are somewhat limited, it seems clear that illness in the Syro-Canaanite world was understood primarily as the result of divine instrumentality. Healing was consequently in the hands of the gods as well. Typically, there is a direct and causal relationship presumed between contracting an illness and disobeying a god's will and, likewise, a direct and causal relationship between healing and divine favor. Thus, in the Late Bronze Age Epic of Kirta from the city-state of Ugarit, on the north Levantine coast, King Kirta is inflicted with some debilitating malady by the goddess Asherah, seemingly as punishment for Kirta's failure to fulfill a vow he had made to her. Yet El, the high god of the Canaanite pantheon and Kirta's divine patron, eventually heals his protégé by creating a being named Shataqat (lit., the female who causes [illness] to pass), who expels the disease.

El indeed may have a special connection with healing, as he bears the epithet Rapiu (*CAT* 1.108), a title derived from the root *rp'* (to heal). Alternatively, the epithet Rapiu could indicate that El himself is the "Healthy" or "Hearty" one. Another Syro-Canaanite deity who may be associated with healing is Baal-zebub of Ekron, whom King Ahaziah of Israel seeks to petition when injured (2 Kings 1.2). Almost all scholars agree that Baal-zebub (Lord of the Flies) is a deliberate parody of this god's true name, Baal-zebul. Since one meaning of the root *zbl* is "disease," the name Baal-zebul could mean "Lord of Illness." A third god who can be associated with healing is the Sidonian deity Eshmun, identified in multiple sources with the Greek healer-god Asclepius (e.g., *KAI* 66). Finally, we can note the Syro-Canaanite god Resheph, who is a healing deity according to 2nd-millennium BCE Egyptian texts. Interestingly, however, Resheph is also seen as one who inflicts pestilence.

While we have some evidence for the use of healing therapies in Syro-Canaanite tradition (e.g., the trephination of skulls in Middle Bronze Age Jericho), illness, because it lay in the hands of the gods, was most commonly addressed through religious ritual. Perhaps most common was the use of petitionary prayer, assuming, that is, that the well-attested use of such prayers in the Mesopotamian and Israelite spheres is paralleled in the less well-documented Syro-Canaanite world. Mesopotamian and Israelite parallels also suggest that the home was the primary locus for Syro-Canaanite health care, although visits to temples for healing are

Phoenician amulet with an incantation to assist women in childbirth, 7th–6th century BCE. Below a sphinx is a wolf devouring a child (legs can be seen hanging from the animal's mouth); on the reverse (not shown) is a god brandishing an ax. Aleppo Museum.

known. In the Ugaritic Epic of Aqhat, the infertile King Danel offers sacrifice and engages in other ritual acts in order to induce a deity to appear to him in a dream and grant that he be cured. While the king's location during this ritual is unspecified, it is surely not his own palace, as Danel returns there after the rite; since such incubation dreams are typically undertaken at sacred sites, it is most logical to conclude that Danel received his healing vision in a temple. Stager (1991) has argued, in addition, that the approximately fifteen hundred dogs buried in 5th-century BCE Ashkelon were, as in the cult of Asclepius, associated with healing sanctuaries. Given the association of dogs with healing also in the temples of Mesopotamian Gula and at the 5th-century BCE Phoenician temple at Kition, Cyprus, such an interpretation seems likely, although no temple at Ashkelon has yet been found.

Avalos (1995) has similarly proposed that the several metallic serpents found in Middle and Late Bronze Age Syro-Canaanite sacred precincts (e.g., Megiddo, Hazor, Gezer, Timna, Tel Mevorakh) had a therapeutic function within temple compounds, as did serpents in Asclepius shrines, where Asclepius himself could take the form of a snake in order to heal. Serpent figurines may have especially been used to heal snake bites, as they were in Mesopotamia. Two Late Bronze Age texts from Ugarit also speak to efforts to reverse the effects of venomous snake bites, which it seems is to be accomplished by a ritual specialist reciting an incantation (*CAT* 1.100; 1.107). Several other incantation texts at Ugarit deal with health-related issues, especially matters of birth and fertility. Of particular interest are several Akkadian texts that seek to ward off the threat of Lamashtu, a female demon whose origins lie in the Mesopotamian realm and who preyed especially upon unborn and newborn babies; one incantation, for example, seems to encourage that offerings be made to Lamashtu so as to curb her appetite for fetal and infant flesh (Ras Shamra tablet 25.420). The relationship between these Akkadian incantations and the incantation texts written in Ugaritic is unclear, but it may be that older Mesopotamian incantation traditions played a role in the development of Ugaritic incantational practice.

Also unclear is the date of an amulet found at Ugarit that was apparently worn as a necklace by either a mother or an infant in an effort to ward off Lamashtu's attacks (Ras Shamra tablet 25.457). However, Lamashtu amulets from elsewhere in the Syro-Canaanite world tend to date from the 1st millennium BCE. These charms were perhaps carried west as personal talismans by merchants or soldiers from Mesopotamia. These Mesopotamian prototypes may yet again have helped to shape the development of a Levantine tradition involving the use of amulets and plaques, such as the two Phoenician-language plaques from 7th-century BCE Arslan Tash that seek to ward off malevolent demons, including, perhaps, a demon who spirits away infants and demons who endanger eyesight. Alternatively, the latter plaque may seek protection against the Evil Eye. These plaques were probably hung at the entrance to a home and were meant to keep hostile forces from crossing the threshold. Amulets inscribed with Aramaic texts that likewise seek to ward off spirits who bring illness and other evils are widely attested in the Syro-Palestinian world of the 4th to 7th centuries CE.

BIBL.: Hector Avalos, *Illness and Health Care in the Ancient Near East: The Role of the Temple in Greece, Mesopotamia, and Israel* (Atlanta, 1995). Mordechai Cogan, "A Lamashtu Plaque from the Judaean Shephelah," *Israel Exploration Journal* 45 (1995): 155–61. L. E. Stager, "Why Were Hundreds of Dogs Buried at Ashkelon?" *Biblical Archaeology Review* 17.3 (1991): 26–42.   S.A.

Israel

Illness and health care had a complicated evolution in ancient Israel. Although we have archeological evidence for healing practices from at least the Neolithic period (trephinated skulls at Jericho), the Hebrew Bible remains the most important source for the study of illness and health care in the biblical period.

The identification of most diseases in the Hebrew Bible is notoriously difficult, especially in cases of epidemics (Num. 25; 1 Sam. 5.6–12). The condition usually

translated "leprosy" (Hebrew *ṣāraʿat*) probably encompassed a large variety of diseases that produced a chronic discoloration of the skin (Lev. 13–14). There are also various references to blindness (2 Sam. 5.8) and musculoskeletal disabilities (9.3). Infertility, an illness often mentioned in the Bible, diminished the social status of the afflicted woman (Gen. 30.1–20; 1 Sam. 1.5–6). The stories of the plagues on Egypt in Exod. 7–10 recognize that epidemics can alter the course of history.

The Hebrew Bible has at least two principal explanations for illness. One, represented by Deut. 28, affirms that health encompasses a physical state associated with the fulfillment of covenant stipulations that are fully disclosed to the members of the society and that illness stems from the violation of those stipulations. Therapy includes reviewing one's actions in light of the covenant. The Book of Job offers a contrasting view, insofar as illness may be rooted in undisclosed divine plans. The patient must trust that God's undisclosed reasons are just.

As modern medical anthropology shows, health care should be considered a system of interacting ideologies, resources, personnel, and strategies meant to maintain and/or restore health in any ancient or modern community. Perhaps the most distinctive feature of the Israelite health-care system depicted in the canonical texts is the division into legitimate and illegitimate options. This division is partly related to monolatry, insofar as illness and healing rest ultimately upon YHWH's control (Exod. 15.26) and insofar as non-Yahwistic options are prohibited. There is no clear evidence for purely secular approaches to health care, and the terms *magical* and *nonmagical* are not useful when speaking of biblical health care.

Since it was accessible and inexpensive, prayer to YHWH was probably the most common legitimate option. Petitions and thanksgiving prayers, perhaps intended specifically for use by patients, are attested in the Bible (Ps. 38; 39; 88; Isa. 38.10–20). Tangible treatments in the Bible include bandages (Ezek. 30.21), mandrakes for infertility (Gen. 30.14), figs for boils (2 Kings 20.7), and balsam from Gilead (Jer. 46.11).

Illegitimate options, which were probably widely used by Israelites, included consultants designated in Hebrew as *rōpēʾîm* (2 Chron. 16.12; NRSV: "physicians"), non-Yahwistic shrines (2 Kings 1.2–4), and probably a large variety of sorcerers (Deut. 18.10–12). Female figurines found in most periods in Israel, especially in domestic contexts, may be fertility amulets. The largest-known dog cemetery in the ancient world was recently uncovered at Ashkelon and may be associated with a healing cult of the Persian period.

Prophets, who were often in fierce competition with "illegitimate" consultants, are the foremost legitimate consultants in the canonical texts. Deuteronomy 18.10–17 seems to advocate the monopoly, by the Yahwistic prophet, of all the consultation functions, including probable ones for illness, that had been previously distributed in a wide variety of Canaanite consultants. Yahwistic prophets provide prognoses (2 Kings 8.8) and intercede on behalf of the patient (5.11).

Shrines of YHWH were probably another significant legitimate option in the preexilic period. In 1 Sam. 1 Hannah visited the temple at Shiloh to help reverse her infertility. Second Kings 18.4 indicates that, prior to Hezekiah, the bronze serpent made by Moses as a therapeutic device (Num. 21.6–9) was involved in acceptable therapeutic rituals in the temple of Jerusalem. Metal serpents, such as those found in or near shrines at Timna, Tell Mevorakh, and Hazor in the Late Bronze Age, may have been involved in therapeutic rituals and/or used as amulets.

The centralization of the cult in Jerusalem and the reforms attributed to Hezekiah (715–687 BCE) and Josiah (640–609 BCE) wrought significant changes, even if only in theory, in the health-care system. Shrines that may have formerly functioned as therapeutic centers were destroyed. By the postexilic period the Priestly Code, which may be viewed as a manual on public health that centralizes in the priesthood the power to define illness and health for an entire community, severely restricted access to the temple for the chronically ill (e.g., lepers in Lev. 13–14; cf. 2 Sam. 5.8 on the blind and the lame). Such restrictions are intimately related to a system of purity laws that encompasses, but is not limited to, issues of illness and health. Nonetheless, such laws could serve to remove socioeconomically burdensome populations from society. In effect, the Priestly Code minimizes state responsibility for the chronically ill, leaving the eradication of illness for a future utopia (Ezek. 47.12; Isa. 35.5–6). However, thanksgiving or "well-being" offerings (Lev. 7.11–36) after an illness were probably always acceptable and economically advantageous for the temple.

Relative to the Priestly Code, the community responsible for *Miqṣat Maʿaśê ha-Tôrâ* (Some Precepts of the Torah), the Temple Scroll, and other Qumran texts expanded the restrictions for lepers, the blind, and the lame. The Dead Sea Scrolls (2nd–1st centuries BCE) also provide evidence for the laying on of hands (*Genesis Apocryphon* 20.28–29) and the forgiveness of sins in healing (*Prayer of Nabonidus*).

By the late Second Temple period there occurred a wide legitimation of the *rōpěʾîm* (cf. Sir. 38; 2nd century BCE), but various types of folk healers and midwives (see Exod. 1.15–21) may actually have been the most common health-care consultants through the end of the Second Temple period.

By the 1st century, various Jewish sects, including the one that became known as Christianity, attempted to reform traditional Jewish health-care practices and addressed problems of health care (e.g., fees and geographical accessibility) found in the Greco-Roman world. Greco-Roman health-care practices also became increasingly acceptable in rabbinic tradition.

BIBL.: Hector Avalos, *Illness and Health Care in the Ancient Near East: The Role of the Temple in Greece, Mesopotamia, and Israel* (Atlanta, 1995). John Wilkinson, *The Bible and Healing: A Medical and Theological Commentary* (Grand Rapids, 1998).   H.A.

Anatolia

The principal concerns of the people who lived on the Anatolian plateau in the Late Bronze Age were those that accompanied an agrarian lifestyle, namely, maintaining the health and fertility of their herds, crops, and themselves. The individual problems and challenges best attested in the Hittite corpus tend also to reflect this focus. The full range of concerns for which we have evidence includes illness, impurity, family discord, bad years (agriculturally?) and infertility of the fields, sorcery and other criminal offenses (perjury, physical injury), birth, human fertility, and impotence. Rituals also addressed crises that affected the community as a whole, such as plague, military defeat, bad omens, building rites, and cultic events, which included attracting absent deities, erecting divine images, and correcting offenses against the gods.

When misfortune befell an individual, at least within the royal family, he or she had recourse to prayer. One royal relation, Kantuzili, prays for relief from his suffering: "Because of sickness, my house has now become a house of anguish, and because of anguish, my soul is flowing to another place. . . . Now my sickness and anguish have become too much for me. I must declare it to you, my god" (KUB 30.10 2.14–17). Pudukhepa vowed to bestow gifts on the goddess Lelwani if she would give health and long life to her husband, King Hattushili. Other such vows are made to excuse a variety of cultic infringements.

Most frequently, however, problems were solved by means of rituals tailored to address specific situations. The documents that record these rituals were more-or-less standardized in their format, beginning with an introduction identifying the professional practitioner and his or her place of origin. This was followed by a statement of the problem and a list of ingredients (*materia magica*) that would be used to address the problem. Finally, the ritual recipe itself was written out in detail. These ritual prescriptions must have been used over and over again, judging by their existence in several copies (although always retaining the identity of the original author).

They reveal that the primary means of treating problems included analogic magic, transference (contagion), and substitution. In the course of a given ritual, any combination of these elements might be employed, repeated, or embellished to achieve the desired end.

Analogic (sympathetic) magic combines ritual action with an incantation that links that action to the desired outcome. For example, male impotence could be cured by restoring a man's masculinity by taking from him the attributes of a woman (spindle, distaff) that he has been given and then restoring to him the attributes of a man (bow, arrows). Indeed, the threat of femininity in curse formulas was considered to be an effective preventative against disloyalty among the troops and was incorporated into the Hittite soldier's oath: "He who transgresses these oaths and takes part in evil against the king, queen, and princes, may these oath deities make [that] man [into] a woman. May they make his troops women. Let them put a scarf on them. Let them break the bows, arrows, and weapons in their hands, and let them place the distaff and spindle in their hands [instead]" (KBo 6.34 2.46–3.1). The actions embedded in the incantation are carried out in reality as the words are recited. Such incantations are one of the simplest and most common components of Hittite ritual and, some have argued, its key concept. The vehicle of the analogy might be an animal, human, god, plant, foodstuff or other substance, or natural process. The images used were ones that would have been familiar to the participants. Thus the anger of the deity Telipinu is dissipated with the following words and accompanying actions: "Telipinu is wrathful. His soul and [his] figure were stifled [like] kindling. As they have burned this kindling, let the displeasure, wrath, [perceived] offense, and anger of Telipinu likewise burn. As [malt] is meager [in fertility], and one does not take it to the field to use as seed, nor does one make it into bread, [nor] does one place [it] in the storehouse, so let the displeasure, [wrath], [perceived] offense, and anger of Telipinu likewise become meager [in effect]" (KUB 17.10 3.13–20; trans. Beckman 1999: 524).

Analogic magic could employ the same object in different ways. Thus, as symbols of fecundity, pigs were manipulated to ensure the productivity both of the fields (KUB 43.23 rev. 19'–22', 57'–58; KUB 12.44 3.16–19) and of women (Bogazköy tablet 3617 1.4'–17' with duplicates; KUB 36.83 1.3–7; 4.5–9). In the former instance, the female sexual parts of the sacrificed animal might be buried in the field whose productivity was sought while the requisite incantation was recited. In the latter, a woman seeking to become pregnant would be made to stand over a live pig (sow?) in order to absorb its powers of procreation.

Many techniques were used to transfer an affliction from the patient to another object. These included waving an object or animal over the patient, touching or rubbing the patient with an animal or power-laden substance such as bread, meal, honey, or mud, or causing the patient to pass through the severed parts of animals or through a gate made of hawthorne (which had the ability to scrape off and retain the malignancy). To extract illness from an individual, the old woman Tunnawiya arranges the twelve body parts of a ram against the patient's twelve body parts, top to bottom: "Head is arranged against head. Throat is arranged against throat. Ear is arrang[ed] against ear. . . . Fi[nger] against finger likewise. . . . [Foot] against foot likewise" and so on. Tunnawiya reveals the purpose of this rite: "I have arranged for his twelve body parts. Right now the body parts of the ram are claiming the sickness of the body parts of this mortal" (KUB 55.20 + KUB 9.4 + Bogazköy tablet 7125 + Bogazköy tablet 8057 2.1–22). Or if the situation calls for purifying a sacred space: "They 'wave' the temple of the storm-god, the temple of Hepat, and all the temples of the gods with an eagle, a falcon, a *hapupi* bird, a shelduck, and a *hušti* stone. They [then] purify [them] with consecrated water" (KUB 30.31 4.36–40 + KUB 32.114 rev 4'–8').

The concept of substitution was also important. In such a rite, a human or animal (both live animals or models fashioned from clay or dough were acceptable), took the place of the patient so that the evil or impurity accrued to it, freeing the patient from its damaging effects. For the substitution to be effective, the material first had to be identified with the person to be purified. The old woman Mashtigga does this orally while presenting the sheep to the offerants: "Here is a substitute for you; let it be a substitute for your bodies" (Mashtigga Ritual, CTH 404; ANET 350–351). Alternatively, when Murshili II undergoes a ritual treatment for his aphasia, he places his hand on the ox that would serve as the carrier. Once the identification was complete, the impurity was "downloaded" to the carrier (Hittite *nakkušši-*) or substitute (Hittite *tarpalli-*). For example, in Pulisa's ritual to end a plague within the army, a ram and ewe are adorned with wreaths made from colored strands of wool that have been pulled from the mouth of the king—the wreaths being symbolic of the illness afflicting the troops. On the other hand, in Mashtigga's ritual, the patients simply spit into the mouth of the substitute sheep. Once the evil is fully transferred, the carrier *(nakkušši-)* is sent away, while the substitute *(tarpalli-)* is destroyed (usually through burning or burial or both). The purification is thus complete.

To ensure that the gods continued to attend to their human charges, it was sometimes necessary to perform elaborate rituals of attraction to draw them to the festivities being held in their honor. In addition to laying out honey, wine, milk, butter, and other irresistible offerings, paths would be drawn with colorful textiles and branches to attract the gods and assist them in finding their way. These efforts were supplemented by incantations summoning the gods: "[If you are in Nineveh] then come from Nineveh. If you are [in] R[imussi, then come from Rimussi]. . . . If [you are] in the rivers and streams [then come from there]. . . . If you are with the Sun-goddess of the Earth and the Primor[dial Gods] then come from those. Come away from these countries" (KUB 15.35 + KBo 2.9 1.23–24, 40, 43–45).

The use of amulets to prevent illness or misfortune must have been widespread, but such objects are difficult to identify among the finds recovered from ancient Hattusha and other Hittite-period sites in Anatolia. Common amulets probably consisted of unworked natural materials, such as agate, used to ward off the Evil Eye. In addition, small figurines of deities and demons made from gold, silver, bronze, ivory, rock crystal, and other precious materials have been found in quantity and may have been used to protect spaces from malign influences. Further, rituals describe the use of animal-shaped models of clay, wax, or dough used as apotropaic devices. In Huwarlu's ritual, for example, a tallow figure of a puppy is placed on a door latch to ward off evil from approaching the king and queen.

Magic and medicine were not separate categories in Hittite thought or practice, and purely medical approaches to physical ailments are rare. Hittite medical texts attest to treatments for disorders of the eyes, intestine, throat, and mouth, among other things, and medical cures included the use of honey, wine or beer, plants, animal substances, and minerals. But more often we see treatments that combine magical and medical means or that are purely magical. For example, Hebatarakki uses dung therapy to nullify the effects of sorcery. She mixes dog excrement with barley flour to make a dough. She then places two figurines of a duck made from this dough on the patient's shoulders and, as she knocks the figures off the patient's shoulders, recites the incantation, "I have removed [the demon] Agalmati from you. I have pushed [the demon] Annamiluli from your head. I have extinguished fire from your head and ignited it in the sorcerer's head. I have driven away the stench of the dog from you, but the dog's excrement, the dog's flesh, and the dog's bones, I. . . ." (KUB 24.14 1.18–24).

It is difficult to trace precisely the origins of the elements of Hittite magic ritual. Many of the practices attested in the Hittite texts originated not with the Hittites themselves but with the Hattians (who preceded them in Anatolia), the Luwians, the Hurrians (whose influence was felt most strongly in southeastern Anatolia), and with Mesopotamia. But the Hittite ritual practitioner, whether an old woman, physician, bird observer, or exorcist, was skilled at weaving these disparate elements into a variety of ritual tapestries designed to address any situation and to provide the individual with a level of protection against an uncertain world.

BIBL.: Gary M. Beckman, "From Cradle to Grave: Women's Role in Hittite Medicine and Magic," *Journal of Ancient Civilizations* 8 (1993): 25–39. Idem, "The Tongue Is a Bridge: Communication between Humans and Gods in Hittite Anatolia," *Archiv Orientální* 67 (1999): 519–34. Volkert Haas, *Geschichte der hethitischen Religion* (Leiden: Brill, 1994). Ahmet Ünal, "The Role of Magic in the Ancient Anatolian Religions according to the Cuneiform Texts from Bogazköy-Hattusa," *Bulletin of the Middle Eastern Culture Center in Japan* 3 (1988): 52–85.   B.J.C.

Iran

Iranian society during antiquity regarded illness and other crises as having demonic origins. The notion went back to Zoroastrian or Mazdean cosmogonical beliefs that Angra Mainyu or Ahriman, the evil spirit *par excellence*, had introduced all calamities including death into

the material world as a means of afflicting pain, suffering, and nonexistence upon Ahura Mazda's foremost creation—humans (Vendidad 21.2; *Bundahishn* 1a.1–21). A female ghoul named Jahika or Jeh was thought to assist in spreading such chaos, as she allegedly had done during the murder of the mythic first androgyne Gayo Maretan or Gayomard (*Bundahishn* 4.1–28). Zoroastrian clerics concluded that "all creations are mirrored in humans who are [in] Ahura Mazda's likeness" (Denkard 321). So, the existential problem was compounded by a theological one. If illness and death, as manifestations of Angra Mainyu's chaos, could eliminate humans, who were the reflection of the high god's order, then could not Ahura Mazda also be dissipated? Death thus represented the location of gravest danger, potentially the moment of absolute disorder. Not surprisingly, epidemics such as bubonic plague, which entered Iran and took a heavy toll in lives, were demonized as harbingers of apocalyptic events.

The advent of empires ruled by Iranian dynasties brought both doctors and medical knowledge from many countries into Iran. Democedes, a physician of the Pythagorean school of Croton, served King Darius I and Queen Atossa (whom he cured of a breast ulcer) around 522–513 BCE, according to Herodotus (3.125–37). Udjahorresne, a priest of Neith at Sais, was another court physician for the Achaemenians under Cambyses II (530–522 BCE) and Darius I. He also served as an advisor, as did Democedes subsequently. Combining medicine (Middle Persian *bizeshkih*) with other forms of learning continued—for example, Borzuya or Burzoy, who hailed from Nishapur, rose to legendary status as a physician and translator. Medical training and research, supposedly based upon Hippocratic traditions, especially by Christian physicians bearing names such as John and Gabriel, took place at Gondeshapur under the Sasanian regime—as recorded by later Muslim writers, drawing upon earlier records. Symposiums on medical issues occurred under royal patronage. Iranians practiced medicine of the knife (Avestan *karetō.baēshaza*), or surgery, and of plants (Avestan *uruuarō.baēshaza*), or pharmacology. Medicines (Middle Persian *darmān*) were used by persons who had access to trained physicians. For example, a short Sogdian-language fragment preserves prescriptions for aphrodisiacs and purgatives. Herbal remedies (Pahlavi *dārūg*) also were widespread.

In Iranian myth, however, the first healer was said to be the legendary Thrita, to whom healing plants supposedly had been presented by Ahura Mazda. Using those items, Thrita cast off fever, pain, and death (Vendidad 20.1–10). Thrita often was amalgamated with another legendary figure, Thraetaona or Fredon (Faridun), who likewise was praised as a healer of the body and the soul (Yasht 13.131). Thus despite advances in medical knowledge under the Achaemenians, Parthians, and Sasanians, popular belief held that illness and other crises should be vigorously countered using both medicinal and religious means because healing (Avestan *baēshaza*,

Middle Persian *bēshāz, bēshāzēh*) ultimately occurred by ministering to alleged spiritual causes of suffering. Medical theories were collated with Zoroastrian scripture and exegeses, according to the Denkard (412), making that field a part of the religious sciences—in conjunction with physics—and influencing writings on human physiology. Medical texts were illustrated with pictures of demonic figures believed to be the sources of human illnesses. Species of plants believed to have originated from a primordial bovine were held to possess curative properties when imbibed or applied (*Bundahishn* 13.1–9; *Wizīdagīhā ī Zādspram* 3.42–51). So whether it was to counter sickness (Middle Persian *washtagīh, wēmārīh, xīdagīh*) while alive or to ensure that the soul entered paradise after the body's demise, Zoroastrians were enjoined by the magi not to "forsake the soul and neglect it for the sake of the body" (Chīdag Handarz ī Pōryōtkēshān 56). The underlying assumption was that "in ministering to corporeal matters, a thousand rituals are nothing; in ministering to spiritual matters, a single ritual is paramount" (Denkard 576–77).

As a result, in addition to medicines, charms (Avestan *nīrāngāni*, Middle Persian *nērang*) that embodied the holy word became popular because it was thought that "he who cures with the holy word is the most curing of curers" (Vendidad 7.44; see also 21.6). This was the medicine of words. The Young Avestan Vendidad (or Code to Ward off Evil Spirits) contains a series of incantations to exorcise sickness (21.18–23). The most-powerful incantation was thought to be the Old Avestan prayer Ā Airiiēmā Ishiiō (Yasna 54.1, invoked in Yasht 3; see also Vendidad 20.11–12). Archeological evidence suggests that incantation bowls (bowls inscribed with incantations against demons and sometimes with pictures of demons) also were used. Members of both the Jewish and Zoroastrian communities in Iran seem to have produced, sold, and utilized such bowls—fusing magic and religion in daily praxis. It was believed, as well, that spiritual ailments that led to physical manifestations of illness could be expunged through regular confessionals, resulting in the advice, "Do not underestimate the power of confession" (Handarz ī Ādurbād ī Māraspandān 40).

Despite the inversion of Iranian dualism in Manicheism, with the body regarded as a creation of demonic forces to entrap, pollute, and corrupt spirit, Manicheans, too, regarded coping with illness and other crises of the body including death as necessary for spiritual progress. The human body, although despised as "a prison" (S 9 R 2.30), was the means of processing and purifying the trapped spirit or light—in foods consumed and in the hearer's or the elect's physique—and releasing it upon death for reunion with the high god Zurwan or Pidar Roshn. The human body was also the means of reproducing future generations of Manicheans to continue that purificatory process—notwithstanding that birth perpetuated the cycle of entrapment. Ideally,

unlike Zoroastrians, Manicheans were expected to abjure medicine—confessing and seeking forgiveness for "having taken a remedy or medicine into my mouth" (M 801) or gathering herbal remedies (M 112; M 146 a; M 336 c). Yet, it seems that some monasteries did have rooms set aside for ill persons with physicians in attendance (Compendium 121–22). Given that medicine was regarded as best avoided, Manicheans, like Zoroastrians, sought cure through supplication (Middle Persian *paywahishn*) and spells (Middle Persian *afsōn*) "against fever and the spirit [of fever]" (M 781). They used amulets (Middle Persian *zāwar*) to ensure good health by invoking Jesus to exorcise evil spirits (M 1202). Mani described himself as "a physician [*bizeshk*] from the region of Babylon" (M 566). He claimed to the Sasanian ruler Wahram I (273–76 CE): "Many and numerous were your servants from whom demons and demonesses were cast out by me. Many were those whom I made rise from their illnesses. Many were those from whom I averted numerous types of fever. Many were those near death whom I [revived]" (M 3). So the classification as a physician appears to have been used in both medicinal and spiritual contexts—drawing upon the Manichean image of Jesus (e.g., Coptic Ps. 248) which in turn was derived from the Synoptic Gospels. Indeed, it was when Mani allegedly failed to cure the king's sister that magi, nobles, and other courtiers were able to convince Wahram I to imprison the founder of Manicheism—a sentence that led to Mani's demise (M 3).

Essentially, therefore, in Iranian society of antiquity, whether among Zoroastrians or Manicheans, the art of healing was directed at both the physical and the spiritual aspects of people. Curing illness and mitigating other crises were in the broadest sense just particular means by which a religious personage, such as a priest (Old Persian *magush*, Middle Persian *mowbed*), or a physician (Avestan *vī-mad*)—often those two occupations overlapped—reestablished order, as reflected in Indo-European **med-* (to heal), from which the notion of medicine derives.

BIBL.: Harold W. Bailey, *Zoroastrian Problems in the 9th Century Books* (2nd ed.; Oxford, 1971). J. Kevin Coyle, "Healing and the 'Physician' in Manichaeism," in *Healing in Religion and Society from Hippocrates to the Puritans: Selected Studies* (ed. J. Kevin Coyle and Steven C. Muir; Lewiston, N.Y., 1999), 135–58. Bruce Lincoln, *Myth, Cosmos, and Society: Indo-European Themes of Creation and Destruction* (Cambridge, Mass., 1986). Joseph Naveh and Shaul Shaked, *Amulets and Magic Bowls: Aramaic Incantations of Late Antiquity* (Jerusalem, 1985). J.K.C.

Greece and Rome

As the anthropologist Clifford Geertz pointed out in his essay "Religion as a Culture System," one role of religion is to provide meanings for what does not make sense. As human beings, we live on the edge of chaos, as disease strikes apparently healthy people, babies die, personal relationships break down, wars flare up, and crops fail. In any system of knowledge there will always be experiences and situations that do not fit—what Gould (1985) called "the event which is uncanny"—and that require further explanations.

Although there were many other individual crises in the life of ancient humans, some of which had become standard topics of consolation texts (such as Plutarch's *Consolation to His Wife,* on the death of a child, or his *On Exile* and Seneca's *Consolation to His Mother Helvia,* consoling his mother on his own exile), the main focus of this section is how the Greeks and Romans used religion in addressing illness. Illness can be explained at a general level—what causes these symptoms?—or at an individual level—why has this happened now, to me? An example is Galen's patient, Eudemus, typical of elite patients during the period known as the Second Sophistic (2nd century CE) who required their doctors to explain precisely what was happening in their bodies: "He demanded a reason for my statement" (Galen, *On Prognosis* in *Corpus Medicorum Graecorum* 5.8.1.78). Personal crises make people search their own past to account for their present: in this process, religion plays many roles.

Disease: its origin and cure. Was the individual's disease regarded as coming from within his or her body or from outside? In Greek myth, *nosoi* (diseases) are presented as coming from outside. In the *Iliad,* Zeus is described as sending diseases not only as punishment for injustice or for failure to respect his priests (1.9–10), but also in an entirely arbitrary fashion (24.527–33). In Hesiod, *nosoi,* released from Pandora's jar, wander the world outside Zeus's express command; neither gods nor mortals can control them (*Works and Days* 102–4). Hesiod links diseases to aging and death, aspects of the present world, not of an earlier Golden Age. For ancient medicine, illness can be a more personal matter, arising from the individual losing his or her humoral balance, but is also a wider process influenced by season, climate, and environment, as in the title of one Hippocratic treatise, *Airs, Waters, Places.* Diet and drugs would restore the individual's balance. But it continued to be thought that, although "diseases" in general lay outside the gods' control, specific diseases affecting specific individuals (or groups) could be both caused and healed by gods.

The most obvious way in which religion responded to "the event which is uncanny" was through the sanctuaries of various healing gods. The most famous was Asclepius, whose most important sanctuary at Epidaurus was visited by people from all over the Greek world. His cult was officially welcomed to Rome in the early 3rd century BCE, but similar cults already existed in Italy at least a century before this. Many other gods and heroes, both inside and outside the Olympic pantheon, were claimed as healers at a more local level. Like Asclepius, they sometimes offered healing through incubation, in

which the sleeping patient received a dream in which healing occurred or a remedy was recommended. When one of the workers on the Athenian Acropolis building project fell and the physicians were unable to help, Athena appeared to the statesman Pericles in a dream and told him how to treat the patient (Plutarch, *Pericles* 13).

The main value of the sanctuary at Epidaurus to the subject of illness is the survival of the *iamata* (healings), which are publicly displayed inscriptions on stone recounting cures experienced by previous visitors to the site; reordered, possibly developed, and reinscribed during the development of the sanctuary as a Panhellenic center in the 4th century BCE, the *iamata* may have helped create a mood of hope and expectation, possibly as part of a tour of the site given to pilgrims. Pausanias, who visited the shrine in the 2nd century CE, still saw six stelae with healing stories, while "in former times, there were more" (2.27.3); two of them are still preserved today (stelae A and B), with fragments of two more (C and D). The *iamata* reuse the experience of individual bodies to create public documents that link that body to the divine and also to the promotion of Epidaurus as a sanctuary. Similar, although much shorter lists of healings come from several other sanctuaries of Asclepius, including the one on Rome's Tiber Island. The historicity of some stories appears doubtful, since they seem to manipulate traditional motifs of miracle cures—but even when partly fictitious, these inscriptions remain valuable documents for ancient attitudes to divine intervention in illness and other problems.

Options and alternatives. The temples of Asclepius (Asklepeia) flourished alongside the rise of Hippocratic medicine; so, would the temple or the Hippocratic physician be the first port of call? One answer is neither: in the ancient world, the family and community would be the first to offer their help in personal crises. For early Roman medicine, we have the highly polemical insistence of writers such as Cato the Elder (Plutarch, *Cato* 23–24) and Pliny (*Natural History* 29.5.11; 29.8.15–16) that physicians are unnecessary and that the *paterfamilias* should treat disease in his family, slaves, and livestock. In rural parts of the ancient world, this may long have been the norm.

Religious options also existed at this level, among them divination and prayer. Divination was often the first response to a disease of sudden and severe onset. In Euripides' *Hippolytus,* the chorus wonders what is wrong with Phaedra, speculating about which god lies behind her symptoms (141–50); Phaedra's nurse suggests they will need an oracle in order to determine which god it is (236–38; cf. Sophocles, *Ajax* 172–81). More prosaically, there is also speculation as to whether her husband has found another woman, she has heard bad news from home (151–60), or she has been harmed by a hostile spell (319). One response, if the disorder has a physical cause, is to call on Artemis: "Once this breeze rushed through my womb; and I called to the heavenly helper of labor, ruler of arrows, Artemis, and causing me to be envied, with the gods' blessing, she always comes" (161–69). This suggests that one could call on the gods for physical problems, but that they would not "always come" (cf. *Iliad* 16.249–52, 523).

Some of the *iamata* from Epidaurus promote the temple by noting physicians' failures. Similarly, Aeschines (*Palatine Anthology* 6.330) tells how, despairing of mortal *technai* (skills), he left Athens and was cured of the ulcer on his head by Asclepius. Bona Dea healed the Roman public slave Felix after ten months of blindness; the physicians had given up on him (*derelictus a medicis*; CIL 6.68 = ILS 3513). Despite such evidence, the model of opposition and rivalry is not appropriate; the story that Hippocrates copied out the *iamata* at the Asklepeion on Cos (Strabo, *Geography* 14.19; Pliny, *Natural History* 29.2.2), the presence of the gods as witnesses to the Hippocratic oath, and the attendance of physicians at the temples all point to a symbiotic relationship. The Hippocratic text *On the Sacred Disease*, which argues that epilepsy is no more sacred than any other disease, does not attack temple medicine; the writer condemns only individual healers who claim that they can somehow make the gods serve their will through purifications and incantations. Like Artemidorus, whose manual of dream interpretation was written in the 2nd century CE, he opposes those who make the gods "appear tasteless, malicious, and stupid" (Artemidorus, *Dreambook* 4.22).

The decision to go to a physician or a temple could depend on geographical availability—how near was a shrine with a healing reputation?—or economic availability: which cost more, not just in terms of the healing itself, but also in terms of the family's support while a person was absent at a temple? But another possibility is that people approached the gods when other approaches to the body had nothing to offer, for example, in highly unusual circumstances or when a condition had become chronic.

Many female patients coming to Asclepius for help at Epidaurus had problems connected with childbirth or conception. The end of stele B includes the story of Andromache of Ephesos, "uncovered" (*agkalypsai*) by a handsome young man, then touched by the hand of the god. As a result, a son was born to her by Arybbas (B31). Asclepius can grant a child of the preferred sex (B34), and further pregnancies later on (B39). Ancient medicine dealt with similar problems, but in a less dramatic and immediate way; an entire book of the Hippocratic corpus is known as *On Barren Women* and opens, "Now I will reveal by what causes women are completely sterile, and why they do not give birth until they are cured. I say the cause is this: if the mouth of the womb is tilted completely away from the external sexual parts, the woman does not conceive" (*Diseases of Women* 3.213, L 8.408).

The second most common female problem was worms, something for which answers existed outside temple medicine. For both men and women, a significant number of cases taken to Asclepius were of chronic diseases. In *The Sons of Asclepius* 10 (Behr p. 231), Aelius Aristides, who spent 145–47 CE at Asklepeion in Pergamum, condemns the mythic figure Odysseus for unjustly abandoning his companion Philoctetes on Lemnos, after having decided that Philoctetes' disease was incurable; although the disease had "grown for ten years," the sons of Asclepius were able to heal it (cf. Sophocles, *Philoctetes* 1333; Marcus Julius Apellas in *IG* IV² 1, no. 126). At Epidaurus, Gorgias of Herakleion had a suppurating arrow wound for a year and a half (B30), and other conditions are also clearly chronic rather than spectacular. These include bladder stones (A8; A14), blindness (A4; A9; A18; A20; B22; B32; C65; possibly D69), paralysis (A3; A15; B37; B38; C57; C64), muteness (A5; C44), and lameness (A16; B35).

Blindness, the problem that sent Felix to Bona Dea, is the most common condition brought to Epidaurus. At another Asklepeion, Phalysios of Naupaktos gave the temple two thousand gold staters in thanksgiving for the restoration of his sight (Pausanias 10.38), and in Aristophanes (*Plutus* 634–749) the god Plutus visits the Asklepeion for loss of sight and incubates there with Neocleides, a blind thief. In Greek myth, blindness often is associated with poetry and prophecy; absence of outer sight gives inner sight, bringing the individual closer to the realm of the gods. But it may instead be a punishment for overstepping the limits of mortal activity, for example, seeing a goddess bathing or telling a god what he does not want to hear. Much later, in the so-called Phrygian confession stelae (2nd/3rd century CE), blindness is a common form of divine punishment, healed by a sacrifice and a public confession to a major local divinity. Blindness could be taken to physicians or treated with amulets (Libanius, *Oration* 1), but these ideas about the eyes and the role of sight may have led people in the ancient world to think that the gods were a particularly appropriate source of help for blindness. Herodotus describes how, fighting on the side of the heavily outnumbered Athenians at the battle of Marathon (490 BCE), Epizelos lost his sight after having a vision of a giant warrior, "although nothing had touched him anywhere—neither sword, spear, nor missile." He remained blind for the rest of his life (6.117). But he is unlikely to have visited a sanctuary of Asclepius; instead he became a symbol in his own lifetime of the heroic nature of the Athenian achievement, even being included in the paintings of the battle in the Stoa Poikile (Aelian, *On Animals* 7.38). His blinding had no physical cause, as Herodotus stresses, but religion gave this uncanny event a meaning, putting a positive spin on the individual's suffering, but without offering a cure.

Inability to do one's job due to illness was one of the personal crises handled by Asclepius. Aelius Aristides was troubled by breathing difficulties that prevented him from delivering his orations; the god gave him prescriptions, but also advice, including the need to have a chorus standing by to sing if his voice failed (*Sacred Tales* 50.14, 26, 38). Stele B29 provides an earlier example of Asclepius's occupational therapy; Hagestratus was not only cured of his headaches and insomnia by the god, but also learned from him how to wrestle, and went on to win the pankration at the Nemean Games (cf. Aelius Aristides, *Oration* 42.11). In late antiquity, pagan intellectuals such as Libanius continued to turn to Asclepius; Libanius was healed by him in 367 BC (*Oration* 1.143) when vocal and breathing difficulties left him unable to declaim. Later, severe headaches prevented him from teaching; he saw a soothsayer and physicians (1.243–46) but was cured only when he discovered a mutilated chameleon in his lecture theater—evidence that a binding spell had been cast against him.

Illness and magic. Illness can be both caused and cured by magic. The personal crises listed on the Epidaurean *iamata* are restricted to those that replicate and maintain social values; no countercultural desires, such as the wish to harm an enemy, are brought to Asclepius, only acceptable goals such as wanting to get pregnant, hunting for a child lost swimming in the sea (B24), and searching for treasure buried by a dead husband (C46). In this last case, a soothsayer helps the widow to interpret the god's instructions to look "within the lion, at noon in the month Thargelion." In contrast, magic and incantations could be used in both socially acceptable and countercultural crises: winning back a husband from a rival, trying to stop him from marrying someone else, but also trying to hurt an enemy or gain revenge. But an incantation also was used to stanch the blood in Odysseus's thigh wound (*Odyssey* 19.457) and, together with a "sympathetic" ritual, to cure a dislocation (Cato, *On Agriculture* 160); Plato mentions in the same breath "drugs, burning, cutting, incantations" (*Republic* 426B); recipes for healing minor ailments (headache, toothache, cough) are recorded in the collection that we call the Greek Magical Papyri from late antique Egypt, together with considerably more harmful recipes.

Individual crisis? We could end by challenging the concept of "personal crisis" in antiquity. At Epidaurus we read that Arata was ill with dropsy, but it was her mother who went to the temple to sleep and saw a vision in which the fluid was drained from Arata's body. Arata had the same vision and was cured (B21). What we see as a personal crisis was understood as a family crisis. Explaining the uncanny is, in any case, a matter of showing that the event is not individual and unique, but something that has happened to other people before, for which there are established ways of behaving. The cult of Asclepius, with its focus on direct contact between god and believer in a dream, may seem to offer a personal contact absent from much of ancient religion. In his oration *The Sons of Asclepius* (8; Behr p. 231), Aelius Aristides claims that "they aided the Greeks thereby . . . setting to rights the personal misfortunes of each of them"; so, this worshiper of Asclepius sees the god's action in very personal terms. But later in the same oration he talks about the "civic ability" of the sons, who "removed not only the diseases of the body, but also cured the sicknesses of the cities" (19; Behr p. 233): Asclepius does not confine his help to the individual. Indeed, for a long-term resident of an Asklepeion such as Aelius Aristides, the fellow worshipers and cult personnel could act as a healing community in themselves, offering moral support. Some Asklepeia, such as the one in Cilician Aegae, went even further and turned into centers of religious philosophy where philosophers and holy men like Apollonius of Tyana took up temporary residence, in order to cure not the body but the soul.

BIBL.: E. J. Edelstein and L. Edelstein, *Asclepius: A Collection and Interpretation of the Testimonies* (2 vols.; Baltimore, 1945). John Gould, "On Making Sense of Greek Religion," in *Greek Religion and Society* (ed. P. E. Easterling and John V. Muir; Cambridge, 1985). Helen King, *Hippocrates' Woman: Reading the Female Body in Ancient Greece* (London, 1998). Lynn LiDonnici, *The Epidaurian Miracle Inscriptions: Text, Translation, and Commentary* (Atlanta, 1995). Georg Petzl, *Die Beichtinschriften Westkleinasiens* (Bonn, 1994). Louise Wells, *The Greek Language of Healing from Homer to New Testament Times* (Berlin, 1998).   H.K.

Etruria

The most common archeological expressions of Etruscan reactions to illness are anatomical votives. In the south of Etruria (e.g., Tarquinia) these were made of terra-cotta and were usually life-sized representations of different parts of the body, including feet, hands, heads, eyes, breasts, penises, and internal organs such as intestines or uteruses. In the north (e.g., Fonte Veneziana, Arezzo), although the range remains the same, bronze is the preferred material, and there is a tendency toward miniaturization. We normally assume that the votives were offerings made by individuals with afflictions in the specific part of the body that they represented; this may often have been the case, but they may also have indicated other functions of the body parts concerned (e.g., feet indicating speedy escape for attack).

Illness is not the only crisis expressed by Etruscan votive deposits, although it is almost impossible now to reconstruct the circumstances of the dedication. The presence of actual arms and armor and statuettes of armed and helmeted warriors may represent expressions of concern over the uncertainty of the outcome of warfare, either by the warrior himself or by his family. Perhaps the hope for happiness in a forthcoming marriage could be signaled by the presence of coupled male and female figurines. Such votives were deposited in pits or trenches within sanctuaries or in sacred lakes or springs. Occasionally, the name of the god to whom the dedication was made was inscribed on the votive, and a large range of divinities are named as recipients of such gifts. Sometimes the name of the dedicant or of the object itself is given as well.

There is also evidence for the use of protective charms in the form of *bullae*. Statuettes and engraved mirrors show these small, gold, lentil-shaped lockets being worn, sometimes several together, around the necks of children and certain divinities. Surviving examples consist of two lenses of beaten gold, soldered together or delicately hinged; occasionally they are embossed with mythological scenes. They may have contained a charm as protection against bad luck or evil. Similar apotropaic functions were served by scarabs and mask-shaped Phoenician glass amulets, both of which are common early grave goods.

In addition to calling on their gods for help and protection, Etruscans called on their gods to cause harm to others. Several lead curse tablets have been recovered from lakes and wells. Uniquely, a pair of lead figurines, one male and one female, have been found at Sovana, and each has a name engraved on its leg; these objects have been interpreted as death wishes for those named.

The votives, amulets, and curses must be seen as attempts to influence areas or events beyond the control of the individual dedicator. In each instance, the sphere of the divine is marshaled in order to restore health, maintain prosperity, or cause harm.

BIBL.: T. Linders and G. Nordquist (eds.), *Gifts to the Gods* (Proceedings of the Uppsala Symposium, 1985; Uppsala, 1987). J. M. Turfa, "Anatomical Votives and Italian Medical Traditions," in *Murlo and the Etruscans: Art and Society in Ancient Etruria* (ed. R. D. De Puma and J. P. Small; Madison, Wisc., 1994), 224–40.   V.E.I.

Christianity

In the Galilean village culture that was the original environment of the Jesus movement, people suffering from various ailments sought aid from folk healers. As modern medical anthropologists suggest, the healers might not be able to offer a biomedical cure for the villagers' physical diseases, but they might be able to offer healing. Jesus, perceived to be such a healer, was reported to have provided relief from various ailments, including leprosy (Matt. 8.1–4; Mark 1.39–45; Luke 5.12–16), paralysis (Matt. 9.1–8; Mark 2.3–12; Luke 5.18–26; John 5.1–9), palsy (Matt. 12.9–14; Mark 3.1–6; Luke 6.6–11), blindness (Matt. 9.27–31; 15.30–31; Mark 8.22–26; 10.46–52; Luke 18.35–43; John 9.1–7, a man blind from birth!), and even death (Mark 5.35–43; Luke 7.11–17; John 11). The mere touch of the hem of Jesus's garment was thought to be efficacious in healing a gynecological problem (Matt. 9.20–22; Mark 5.25–34; Luke 8.43–48). Such reports of Jesus's power locate him alongside prophets of old, Elijah and Elisha,

An amulet, of a type popular possibly among Jews and certainly among Christians, showing a warrior clearly labeled "Solomon" subduing a female demon, 1st–5th century CE. The image, common in ancient royal iconography, celebrates Solomon's mastery over demons, widely acknowledged in Jewish and Christian literature since the Hellenistic period. *Kelsey Museum, University of Michigan*

who healed lepers and even raised the dead (1 Kings 17.17–24; 2 Kings 4.8–37; 5.1–19).

A major cause of sickness in this cultural environment was thought to be inimical personal forces, other human beings with an Evil Eye, or demons, who might be kept at bay with apotropaic devices. When preventive measures failed, the healer could be called upon to expel the offending power. Stories of Jesus's exorcistic actions (Matt. 8.28–34; Mark 5.1–13; Luke 8.26–39; Mark 1.23–28) illustrate such a belief, but they also add touches of eschatological conflict with cosmic forces. In at least one case, the name of the possessing demons, Legion, has obvious political overtones (Mark 5.9; Luke 8.30). All of Jesus's healing actions could also be interpreted as the fulfillment of prophecy, appropriate for the "last days" (Matt. 8.17; 11.4–6; Luke 4.18; 7.22).

The evidence of the Gospels suggests that Jesus's early followers adopted a program of healing of various illnesses (Matt. 10.8; Luke 9.1–2; 10.9). The stories of the early apostles recorded in the Book of Acts suggest that charismatic healing phenomena continued (Acts 3.1–10, a lame man; 9.32–43, a paralytic man and a deathly ill woman; 14.8–10, a lame man; 20.7–12, a resurrection).

Although literary imagination is at work in those accounts, Paul's reference to "spirit and power" (1 Cor. 2.4) suggests that charismatic healing was part of his missionary activity. Paul's account of the spiritual gifts present in the Corinthian community also includes healing (12.28–30).

The community's concern with healing soon became ritualized as an anointing for the sick (Mark 6.13; James 5.14). Later liturgical texts provide prayers to be used to bless the healing oil (e.g., from the 3rd century: Hippolytus, *Apostolic Tradition* 5).

Second-century Christian tradition insisted on the importance of healing various illnesses, caused by the divine power present in the apostles of Jesus. The apocryphal acts dating from the 2nd and 3rd centuries are replete with tales of healing that replicate the miracles recorded in the Gospels, including exorcism (*Acts of Thomas* 30–33; 42–48), general healings (*Acts of John* 30–36), restoration of sight (*Acts of Peter* [*Actus Vercellenses*] 20–21), and resurrection (*Acts of John* 19–25; *Acts of Thomas* 51–54). Whether a healing practice lay behind such accounts is unclear, but the apologetic importance of healing power is transparent. At the same time, more philosophically inclined Christians pointed to the "spiritual" healing that Christ, the physician of souls, provided (Clement of Alexandria, *Pedagogue* 1.2; *What Rich Man May Be Saved?* 1.29; Eusebius, *Church History* 10.4.12) by offering forgiveness of sin. Other patristic interpreters of the healing accounts of the Gospels also interpreted the stories symbolically. Thus, Tertullian (*On Baptism* 5.5) and Augustine (*Commentary on John* 44.2) understand the healing of a man born blind (John 9.1–7) in terms of the baptismal symbolism of illumination.

Apologetic concerns also run through the discourse about healing in the 2nd century. Some of what Jesus is reported to have done during his healing activity may have raised suspicions. The use of Aramaic words to raise a dead girl, *talitha koum* (Mark 5.41), or to open stopped ears, *ephphatha* (7.34), shared generic similar-ity with what magicians did. Non-Christian critics, capitalizing on the similarity, could dismiss Jesus as another charlatan. Apologists, such as Origen, responded with a vigorous defense of Jesus's activity (*Against Celsus* 1.6; 3.24–29).

While theologians apologized for the miraculous or exploited the metaphor of spiritual healing, various Christian groups engaged in the practical treatment of physical ailments. The veneration of holy men and women, particularly martyrs, produced, from the 4th century onward, a development of new sacred spaces where the power of the divine, mediated through the saints' relics, might be made available for healing. Along with systems designed to invoke divine power to effect healing, Christians also developed more practical institutional mechanisms for dealing with sickness.

The 3rd and 4th centuries saw the development of a rudimentary Christian welfare system, under episcopal authority. One of the tasks of the deacons serving a bishop was to report on the sick in their jurisdiction, so that the bishop might visit (Hippolytus, *Apostolic Tradition* 34). Most influential for later history was the establishment of clinics in the new cenobitic (common life) monasteries of the 4th century. Although primarily directed toward dealing with the health needs of the religious community, they offered a model for more-pervasive communal health care. The leading figures of orthodox Christianity in the late 4th century, the Cappadocian fathers, particularly Basil of Caesarea, apparently drew on the experience of monastic health care to establish the first hospital for the in-patient care of the general Christian populace.

BIBL.: Andrew Crislip, *The Monastic Health Care System and the Development of the Hospital in Late Antiquity* (diss., Yale University, 2002). Howard C. Kee, *Miracle in the Early Christian World: A Study in Sociohistorical Method* (New Haven, 1983). J. J. Pilch, *Healing in the New Testament: Insights from Medical and Mediterranean Anthropology* (Minneapolis, 2000).   J.J.P.

Death, the Afterlife, and Other Last Things

Introduction

Throughout the ancient world, it was commonly believed that individuals survived in some form after death. From earliest times, people laid out food and drink for dead relatives and performed rituals on their behalf. In many places, people shared communal meals with the dead. These practices were meant to ensure the well-being of the deceased and also to appease the spirits of the dead and to protect the living from their displeasure.

In most of the ancient world, however, the lot of the dead was rather dismal. The inevitability of death for human beings was affirmed alike by the Epic of Gilgamesh, Homer, and the Hebrew Bible. Normally, the dead went to the netherworld, where they could not see the light of day. Mesopotamian tradition speaks about the house that those who enter cannot leave, where they dwell in darkness and have dust for food. According to Homer, souls in Hades lack the strength to speak until they are given blood to drink. The Hebrew psalmist complains that the dead cannot even praise God. Only rarely are exceptional individuals exempted from this common fate. The Babylonian flood-hero Utnapishtim was taken off to live with the gods. Homer's Menelaus was admitted to the Elysian Fields. Elijah was taken up to heaven on a chariot. Conversely, only exceptional individuals suffered torment in the afterlife. Greek tradition tells of Sisyphus and Tantalus. In the Semitic world, and in most cases also in the West, the dreariness of the netherworld was punishment enough, regardless of one's behavior in life.

The great exception to common ancient beliefs about the afterlife was provided by ancient Egypt. Here life was imagined to follow the cyclic pattern of nature. The sun-god Re and the god Osiris exhibited a pattern of death and resurrection. The transition to the afterlife required certain rituals. The body had to be preserved through mummification, to serve as the basis for the life of the spirit. To reach the realm of the dead, the deceased required special knowledge. From a relatively early period, there was also a judgment, symbolized by the weighing of the heart in a balance. In Egypt we find what are probably the earliest foreshadowings of hell: a place where unrighteous people are subjected to torments and "the second death," a notion that is taken up later in the Christian Book of Revelation. Righteous Egyptians could look forward to their counterpart to the Elysian Fields, the Field of Reeds.

Ideas of a blessed hereafter and of punishments for the damned also appear to be present in ancient Persia from a very early period, although it is notoriously difficult to establish the dates of Persian traditions, which are often attested only in late sources. On the one hand, there is a strong tradition, attested already in the Gathas, that after death the soul is escorted to a bridge that leads to paradise. There it is judged by a divine court. The righteous soul is able to cross the bridge; the unrighteous falls off to perdition. On the other hand, there is also a Persian tradition about the resurrection of the dead that is attested in Greek sources from the Hellenistic period and in later Persian traditions. The body would be restored to enduring youth as part of a new creation.

A revolution in attitudes to the afterlife began in the Greek-speaking world about the end of the 6th century BCE, in the teachings of Pythagoras and the Orphics and in the mystery cults, all of which involved ideas of reward and punishment after death. The philosopher Plato incorporated some of these myths about the afterlife into his dialogues and gave them currency in the philosophical world. Henceforth, the immortality of the soul would be regarded as a quintessentially Greek idea, but various mythic conceptions of the afterlife flourished in the Hellenistic age. These included belief in astral immortality, whereby a person might hope to be elevated to the heavens after death.

Only in the Hellenistic period did belief in reward and

punishment after death become accepted in Judaism. Usually, in Judaism, the afterlife required resurrection, in the sense that death was followed at first by an intermediate state. The earliest forms of resurrection involve a spiritual form of existence (although even spirits were commonly thought to have bodies of some kind, other than flesh and blood). Often the spirit is raised up to join the stars or the heavenly host. In some cases, however, most notably in the Dead Sea Scrolls, the spirit proceeds directly to the place of reward or punishment. Whether, or to what degree, Jewish concepts of the afterlife were indebted to Persian traditions remains controversial. The spread of these ideas in Judaism was hastened by persecution in the 2nd century BCE. Belief in the resurrection of the body of flesh and blood is first attested in the stories of the Maccabees from that time. The Greek-speaking Judaism of the Hellenistic Diaspora, in contrast, often conceived the afterlife in Platonic terms, emphasizing the immortality of the soul.

No religion of the ancient world attached greater importance to the afterlife than did Christianity. Christian beliefs were adapted from Judaism, but as Christianity spread in the Hellenistic world it was increasingly indebted to Greek thought. Occasional influence from Egyptian and Persian motifs can also be found in Christian writings on the afterlife. The distinctive character of Christian belief lies in the insistence on both the immortality of the soul, in Greek philosophical terms, and the resurrection of the body—on both immediate retribution for individuals and a public judgment and settling of accounts at the end of history. Both of these themes are prominent in Judaism before the rise of Christianity, although they are usually found in separate texts and separate cultural areas. Historically, however, these beliefs have occupied a place of much greater importance in Christianity than they ever did in the parent religion.

BIBL.: Jan N. Bremmer, *The Rise and Fall of the Afterlife* (London: Routledge, 2002). J.J.C.

Egypt

Earlier period

The ancient Egyptians considered human existence as cyclical, an experience that, like the rising and setting of the sun or the growth and death of vegetation, would be repeated eternally. The development of an individual from birth through maturity to old age and death was regarded as a series of changes; death was not an end, but rather a further change leading to another sphere of existence. Thus the natural fear of death and its consequences (deprivation of the senses, isolation from the society of the living, and a perceived inversion of the natural order of existence) was tempered by the assurance that death was a transitional state that led to a better world. Hence, although some texts attempt to control human destiny by denying the occurrence of

death, many accept it as a necessary evil and optimistically liken it to sleep, departure on a journey, or homecoming (even as a return to the womb of the mother-goddess).

Humans were perceived as composites of physical and nonphysical aspects or modes of existence. The most important of these were the physical body and the heart and the incorporeal entities called the *ka* and the *ba*. Each of these *kheperu* (manifestations) could act as the vehicle for survival after death, but only if the connection between them, which death temporarily severed, could be reestablished through correct observance of funerary practices. The decay of the corpse had to be frustrated, as it was required to act as a base for the *ka* and the *ba*. The first of these enshrined the notion of perpetuation of the life force through food and drink and the passage of seed from father to child, linking one generation to the next. The *ba*, originally the manifestation of an entity's distinctive powers, came to signify the capacity of the deceased to move freely between the earthly realm and that of the gods; as such it is represented as a bird with a human head.

Evidence for the existence of a developed concept of life after death can be found already in the late predynastic period (ca. 3500–3000 BCE), when corpses were provided with gifts of food, tools, and utensils and were buried in an embryonic posture suggestive of a symbolic return to the womb. However, it is only in the dynastic era (ca. 3000–305 BCE) that attitudes to the posthumous survival of humans were firmly enshrined in a framework of religious thought. The principal written sources for this are, in chronological order, the Pyramid Texts, the Coffin Texts, the Book of the Dead, and the Books of the Netherworld. These compositions reflect the evolution of a succession of different notions of survival beyond death. A multiplicity of approaches, typical of ancient Egyptian thought processes, meant that newer concepts did not displace older beliefs. Different ideas were maintained simultaneously, and, despite a degree of rationalization, the various systems of belief were never completely synthesized.

All of the principal notions link human existence to the great cycles of the cosmos. An early concept of the afterlife as an ascent to the starry night sky was steadily overshadowed from the late Old Kingdom by two more powerful systems of belief, one centered on the god Osiris, the other on the sun-god Re. Both myth cycles involve the central figure in a "death" and "resurrection." In the case of Osiris, he is murdered by his brother Seth and his body dismembered. After being mummified by Anubis (the god responsible for tombs and embalming), Osiris is restored to life to rule the subterranean netherworld. Re, the sun-god and creator of the universe, experiences a symbolic death each evening at sunset, but is rejuvenated during a nocturnal journey through the netherworld to emerge reborn at dawn, perpetuating life on earth. A close association of the dead with these gods

Scene of weighing of the deceased's heart in the Book of the Dead at Hunefer. British Museum. *The Art Archive/Jacqueline Hyde*

was perceived as the key to renewal of life, and hence funerary preparations made many allusions to the myths. The mummification of Osiris provided an ideological model for the prescribed treatment of the human corpse, and texts identified each dead person as an Osiris. To accompany the sun-god on his nightly journey or to be bathed in his life-giving rays equally made possible rejuvenation and new life. The two myths were eventually interlinked by the identification of Osiris and Re as the physical and incorporeal aspects of a single supreme divine being; their unification was the culmination of the sun's nocturnal journey and became the model for the merging of the *ba* with the corpse, an event that came to be seen as essential to human survival after death.

Successful attainment of existence after death transformed the deceased into an *akh*, one who had acquired certain qualities of the gods, particularly a creative energy that facilitated the transition from the inertness of death to eternal life. In order to reach this state, arrangements had to be made for the preservation of the corpse and the maintenance of the *ka* through the rituals of an offering cult. The passage to the next life was conceived of in funerary texts as a journey along prescribed paths. The actual location and topography of the realm of the dead vary in texts of different periods, but were usually either in the sky or beneath the earth. To reach this realm safely the deceased required special knowledge: the names of the inhabitants of the netherworld, the locations of paths, waterways, and gates, and the words and acts of power needed to pass these. A special genre of funerary texts, known as "guides to the hereafter," equipped the deceased with this information. From the Second Intermediate Period, the perils that the dead had to undergo were augmented by a judgment in the

presence of Osiris. This emphasized the notion of demonstrating one's personal integrity as a condition of admission to the next world. The judgment involved the denial of forty-two specific "sins" and the symbolic weighing of the heart in a balance to prove that one had lived a blameless life in accordance with *ma'at,* the principle of order, right, and truth.

The world of the dead, conventionally situated in the west, was a reflection of the earthly sphere and contained both positive and negative forces. Hence the sun-god's nocturnal passage to the eastern horizon involved conflict against hostile powers. The netherworld was also a place in which mortals of bad character (those who had denied *ma'at*) were separated from the righteous and condemned to horrifying punishments involving decapitation and burning. These and other forms of punishment constituted the "second death," the total extinction that was the fate most feared by the Egyptians. For the blessed, the afterlife contained an agricultural paradise known as the Field of Reeds. The effect of these beliefs was to shape a formal tradition of burial. In general the evidence points to the existence of a standard set of practices, but the textual and iconographic sources relate almost solely to the uppermost levels of society. For funerary customs among the peasants, graves provide the only evidence, and these by their very simplicity are difficult to date and have been often neglected by archeologists. What can be deduced—concern for the proper disposal of the corpse and provision of the basic necessities of life—is broadly comparable with the customs of the elite but required a much smaller economic commitment.

When a death occurred, a period of formal mourning began. The corpse was immediately taken to the place of

Egyptian coffin cover painting that shows things the deceased will need for the afterlife as well as prayers (Coffin Texts) to ensure safe passage. *Photograph © 2003 Museum of Fine Arts, Boston*

embalming, where it was treated to preserve it and to transform it into an eternal image, an appropriate repository for the *ka* and the *ba* in the netherworld. In early burials (predynastic period to early Old Kingdom) the treatment usually consisted of little more than wrapping the body in hides or linen, although attempts at artificial preservation involving evisceration and the use of resin were made as early as approximately 3400 BCE. The corpse was prepared in an embryonic position and laid on its left side in the grave. In the Old Kingdom, with the emergence of true mummification, the body was fashioned into a formal image closely resembling a statue, with the limbs fully extended, facial features, hands, and feet carefully delineated, and dressed in the garments of the living. This iconography was replaced around 2100 BCE by the classic mummy, in which the body and limbs were cocooned in linen swathings, with only the head emerging; the face was usually covered by a painted mask, the form and coloring (predominantly blue and gold) of which emphasized the divine qualities of the deceased. The time allotted to the treatments of

the corpse varied, but seventy days is most often mentioned as the ideal. The manipulations of the body during this period began with cleansings, extraction of the internal organs (except the heart), and desiccation of the corpse and the principal viscera using natron, a natural salt compound. These processes were aimed at purification of the corpse and the preservation of its physical integrity. Mummification concluded with anointing with resin, oils, and spices (to inhibit decay, provide a pleasant smell, and confer divine status), filling the body cavities with packing materials, and finally wrapping in layers of linen to create the appearance deemed appropriate for a transfigured being. The relative complexity of the mummification procedure was dependent on cost. It was usually performed by skilled workers, and contracts were entered into to ensure that the mummy was delivered to the mourners by a specified day, but embalming could also be carried out by relatives of the deceased. Some of the materials used were certainly provided by the family; worn-out household linen, such as clothes and bedsheets, was kept for the eventual wrapping of the owner's corpse. At its most elaborate the mummification process was performed in a heavily ritualized context, and papyri of the Roman period preserve instructions for the correct manipulations and ritual acts to be performed.

At the end of seventy days the mummy was placed in its coffin, ready for transportation to the tomb. This took place on the day of burial, an event that marked the end of the phase of body-treatment, and the deceased's entrance into the afterlife. The mummy formed the focus of a procession, beginning either from the home or from the embalming workshop and terminating at the tomb. The cortege was composed of family members, servants carrying goods for the tomb, priests to perform the funerary rituals, and mourners. Among the latter, the most prominent role was reserved for the women, who enacted vigorous gestures of lamentation, accompanied by cries of grief; the ideological model was the lamentation by the goddesses Isis and Nephthys for their brother Osiris.

At the entrance to the tomb, the Opening of the Mouth ritual was performed on the mummy. This act reanimated the corpse, restoring to the deceased the use of his or her bodily faculties. The corpse was thus able to house the nonphysical aspects of the individual, rendering him or her a member of the society of the hereafter and also effectively reestablishing contact with the community of the living.

Following this ritual, the mummy was sealed in the burial chamber. From this point onward, the tomb fulfilled its principal functions. As the earthly setting for the deceased's afterlife, the tomb comprised a protected resting place for the mummy (to which the *ba* could return periodically) and a cult place where ritual perpetuated the existence of the *ka*. The iconography and contents of the tomb provided a sacred environment, ensuring that the occupant was supplied with basic necessities and providing the magical aids required, through the media of image and text on the tomb walls, on the surface of the coffin, or on papyrus. The principal texts and images were placed in close proximity to the body. Other chambers in the tomb were filled with a range of objects. In the earlier periods (predynastic and early dynastic eras) these were predominantly food, drink, clothing, and utensils, but during the dynastic period the basic human needs were catered for increasingly by magic. Food, containers, tools, and so on were replicated in miniature; wall scenes and wooden models represented servants, livestock, and supplies; and funerary figurines known as *shabtis* (later *usliebtis* [answerers]) deputized for their owners when menial work was required in the netherworld.

The place of burial depended on one's abode and one's rank in society. The king's burials were in cemeteries linked either to the principal royal residence (as with the Old Kingdom pyramids) or associated with major religious centers. Important court members and officials were sometimes buried near the king, but many had tombs in the locality where they lived and worked, and this was the rule for the majority of the population. Cemeteries were usually situated on the west bank of the Nile along the desert fringes. They might develop organically but at important sites there was a high degree of organization, projecting social structures beyond the threshold of death into the next world. This is reflected in the spatial relationship of tombs. Those of persons of high status often occupied prominent sites and acted as focal points around which the tombs of their subordinates were grouped. Relatively few tombs were built to receive a single corpse. Most accommodated members of the deceased's family; husbands and wives in particular would usually expect to be buried together.

After the burial the well-being of the dead was maintained by the performance of funerary rituals—essentially the dedication of food offerings in the tomb chapel or (for kings) in a memorial temple. These rites were performed by members of the deceased's family or by funerary priests. Tomb inscriptions specify certain religious festivals throughout the year, at which the services were expected. Where family members were chiefly responsible, maintenance of the cult rarely continued for more than a few generations after the death of the tomb owner. In an effort to ensure the perpetuity of the rituals, persons of wealth and high status set aside an endowment (usually agricultural land), the profits of which paid priests to maintain the cult. Instances survive of formal contracts between provincial officials and the priests of the local temple to ensure long-term continuance of the funerary cult. On the occasion of the chief religious festivals, the relatives visited the tomb and shared a meal with the deceased ancestors; the best-documented event of this kind is the Festival of the Valley, which took place in the cemeteries of the Theban west bank in the New Kingdom. Activities such as this emphasize that contact between the living and dead members of a community was implicitly accepted. While physical manifestations of the dead on earth ("ghosts") are rarely mentioned, there was a strong belief in the capacity of the dead in their own realm to influence events among the living, either for good or ill. Letters written on offering bowls left at the tomb seek to persuade deceased relatives to alleviate illness or suffering or to intercede with some other entity in the netherworld to solve problems on earth. Contact of this kind was also channeled through domestic cults, of which small sculptured busts of ancestors (usually unnamed) are the principal surviving evidence.

Since ancient Egyptian burial practices required a substantial commitment of time, expertise, and material resources, there was a natural limit not only to the performance of cult activities but also to the inviolability of the tomb. Robbery was commonplace—often with the complicity of those responsible for the necropolis—and the official dismantling of older burials (the mummies being secreted in caches) released both tombs and funerary equipment for reuse and recycling. Pessimistic literature laments the ruin of ancient tombs and the consequent extinction of the memory of the dead and conveys a message of *carpe diem*. However, the momentum of centuries-old beliefs and customs ensured that standard practices continued to flourish up to and beyond the Roman domination of Egypt.   J.T.

Later period

Egypt under Ptolemaic and Roman rule was home to an influx of settlers from abroad who brought with them their own distinctive ideas and customs about death and the afterlife. These were often fundamentally different from the indigenous Egyptian ones, and so the range of funerary beliefs and practices expanded in response to foreign influence. In the Ptolemaic period, for instance, Greek-style cremations begin to appear in Egypt for the first time. Destruction of the body by fire is a very un-Egyptian idea, as it implies disbelief in the notion of the preserved corpse as eternal home for the incorporeal self. In due course, foreign settlers themselves adopted Egyptian customs, with Greek and Egyptian cultures becoming more interwoven and ethnic distinctions more fluid. Egyptians also adopted some aspects of foreign practices, while retaining their core funerary myths of the journey to the next world and enacting daily the cyclical process of death and rebirth. Examples of this integration are the realistic mummy portraits first produced during the early Roman period, from about 40 CE. The belief system that underpinned these images was a conventional Egyptian one, whereby the dead person was assimilated to the god Osiris and shared in his divinity. Yet the realistic portraits suggest a way of commemorating the social personality and life history of the deceased that one would associate more with Roman ideas. This dialogue of funerary cultures is also reflected in the appearance of new gods such as Hermanubis (a combination of Hermes and Anubis) and in Egyptian funerary-gods adopting classical attributes. The result of all this *synkrasis* was a complex set of attitudes to death and the afterlife, mediated not only by different spheres of cultural influence, but also by geographical region and social class. No standard set of practices emerges from the mass of detailed evidence: papyrus texts, funerary inscriptions, the material culture of death, and the archeology of Egyptian mortuary sites. However, the written documentation—wills, personal letters, accounts of funeral expenditure, and so on—conveys a vivid sense of the emotional experience of death and commemoration.

Immediately after a death, a mourning period occurred, during which dietary and grooming prohibitions were observed. The act of mourning per se was believed to contribute to the rebirth of the dead person. Mourning also seems to have been determined by gen-

der to some extent. It was apparently acceptable for women to mourn excessively, but not for men to do so (the same thing was also true of mourning in pharaonic Egypt). The time just after a death was when friends and relatives sent letters of condolence to the bereaved. These letters hint at the taboos surrounding those who were dead but still unburied—they never refer to the deceased by name, but instead use euphemisms such as "the fortunate one." On the third day after death, the body would be taken from the house to the embalmer's in a procession that Greek-language documents call the *ekphora* (carrying forth). Individuals would often leave precise instructions in their wills about where and how they wished to be buried, indicating the diversity of mortuary options open to people at this time. These instructions in wills usually refer to the rites surrounding death as occurring in two distinct stages, called in Greek the *peristolē* (wrapping up) and the *kēdeia* (grieving). The *peristolē* was the liminal time of body processing—embalming, wrapping, adorning, and so on—that went on before the preserved body was returned to the family. The *kēdeia* came after the body was embalmed and had been returned to the family. It encompassed the rituals that followed, including those performed at the interment. The *ekphora*, *peristolē*, and *kēdeia* may therefore conform to the classic tripartite structure of rites of passage, with a ceremony of separation *(ekphora)* demarcating a liminal period *(peristolē)*, whose closure is marked by a ceremony of inclusion or reintegration *(kēdeia)*. Egyptian-language sources also mention the processing of the body and burial as separate elements of the postmortem ritual.

Once at the embalmer's, the corpse was washed, eviscerated (usually), dried out with natron, lustrated, wrapped, and adorned. Prayers were repeated over the deceased to help bring about his or her gradual union with Osiris. For the same purpose, the body might be decorated, such as by applying gold leaf to the desiccated skin to transform it into the golden flesh of a god. Much care was expended on the decoration of the body's external wrappings, which also stressed the identification of the deceased with Osiris. Images commonly reproduced on mummy coverings include the celestial boat of Sokar-Osiris that carried the dead across the heavens or passages from the Book of the Dead. All these images helped the dead to complete the postmortem transitions successfully and therefore to be reborn in the most perfect and vital form. This emphasis on the external wrappings reflects a change in burial practices. By Ptolemaic and Roman times, people were rarely buried with elaborate collections of funeral equipment. The wrapped body itself had become a burial in microcosm, and everything required to undergo rebirth successfully had to be carried on it.

After these attentions, the mummy was returned home. When people died away from home, great importance was placed on taking them back to their place of origin, where they could receive cult from their family and perhaps be interred in a family tomb or chapel. Numerous letters and other texts mention mummies being transported for these reasons.

What happened to the mummy next is a matter of some controversy. It is certain that some mummies were kept unburied for a time while they received cult from their relatives. What is uncertain is where this cult took place. One theory argues that mummies were kept in the homes of the living and honored there; especially important was the practice of the living dining in the presence of the dead. This theory, largely based on references to such a custom by several classical authors, would be consistent with the increasingly home-based nature of cults in Egypt from the Persian period onward. There are two problems with the hypothesis, however. The first is that classical Greek and Roman writers use such vague language to describe the structures in which the Egyptians keep their dead alongside the living that it is impossible to be sure exactly what sort of buildings they mean. The second problem is that the theory ignores the domestic architecture of the time. Houses, even of the elite, would have been too small and overcrowded to accommodate large collections of family mummies. It is much more likely that the wrapped bodies were kept in special funerary chapels in the necropolis, like those discovered at the Hawara cemetery in the 1880s. Here the families of the dead could visit them on appropriate days of the year and eat a meal in their presence. Dining with the dead at a tomb was a time-honored part of the Egyptian funerary cult that certainly survived into Greco-Roman times. Several papyrus documents refer to this custom, apparently called "the banquet of Anubis," and excavations in the 1990s at Marina el-Alamein revealed mummies in funerary chapels with associated dining areas. Other cultic attentions were paid to the dead as well, including offerings of garlands and hair. Visits to the dead took place on the birthday of a particular individual or perhaps on a special day of the year (like los Días de Muertos in Latin America) when boundaries between the living and the dead were thought to be more permeable than usual. It is probable that these family cults did not last longer than a generation or two, by which time the social personality of an individual dead person had been forgotten. The bodies might finally be interred at this time, and there is archeological evidence for funerary chapels being cleared out. Such interments might take place in a multigenerational family tomb, frequently a reused pharaonic structure. These reused tombs were not randomly selected, as is often stated, but seem to have been chosen for their location near spiritually charged locales, such as an important monument or numinous natural feature. The Egyptians liked their burial sites to be sanctified by continuous usage. Throughout the Ptolemaic and Roman periods, many of the traditional religious sites remained in use, and people continued to choose to be buried there. Striking examples of these sites are Abydos (the supposed burial place of Osiris), various areas of the Theban necropolis, and Hawara in the Fayyum. People who lived in Fayyum towns near Hawara often left instructions in their wills that they wanted to be buried there.

Observing the funerary cult at the tomb was one way of keeping the dead satisfied and sustained in the otherworld. Inevitably this meant that sometimes the dead could not be propitiated and grew angry at the living. Several pharaonic-period texts discuss the relationship between humans and ghosts, but there is less evidence for this in Greco-Roman times. A powerful category of the dead seem to be those called in Greek-language sources the aōroi, young people who had died before their expected time and operated in a dangerous liminal zone that humans could not control by themselves (see Greece in this chapter). Magical papyri from Egypt regularly refer to the power of the aōroi in spells. The aōroi are also disproportionately represented in funerary portraits and epitaphs. Maybe these were a means of propitiating the aōroi and so forestalling their vengefulness. The drowned also seem to have been regarded as a special category of the dead.

Finally, it is important to stress the regional variability in both funerary customs and cultic practice at all social levels. These local differences might be dictated by the wealth of the community, its distance from major urban centers, or whether the place was near an important religious monument. Burials at Terenouthis in the Delta, a market town and center of the salt trade, are very different from burials at Deir el-Bahri in the Theban necropolis, a major religious site with many monuments. The dead of Terenouthis were buried without elaborate wrappings near mud-brick tombs that had a wide variety of shapes. The superstructures of these tombs usually incorporated a carved image of the deceased, who was often shown seated at an eternal funerary banquet or in a boat making the pilgrimage to Abydos. Sometimes a single image commemorates several individuals from one family, and the tombs were probably specific to particular families. They seem to be less elaborate versions of funerary chapels like those at Hawara. At Deir el-Bahri, however, bodies were covered with complex external wrappings, usually incorporating an image of the boat of Sokar-Osiris. Sometimes other objects were added to the body before burial, such as meshes of branches, to protect it and ensure its rebirth. The Deir el-Bahri mummies may have been interred in family groups but were not associated with tombs as such. Maybe the numinous monuments of the west bank of the Nile—the tombs in the Valley of the Kings, the temple of Hathor, and so on—were in themselves protective memorials for the dead. But the common denominator of all these local nuances remained the myth of Osiris and the belief that human access to the afterlife came through him.

BIBL.: E. Bernand, *Inscriptions metriques de l'Égypte greco-romaine* (Besancon, 1968). Morris Bierbrier (ed.), *Portraits and Masks: Burial Customs in Roman Egypt* (London, 1997). France Dunand et al., *La nécropole de Douch (Oasis de Kharga)* (Cairo, 1992). Dominic Montserrat and Lynn Meskell, "Mortuary Archaeology and Religious Landscape at Graeco-Roman Deir el-Medina," *Journal of Egyptian Archaeology* 83 (1997). Mark Smith, *Catalogue of Demotic Papyri in the British Museum*, vol. 3: *The Mortuary Texts of Papyrus BM 10507* (London, 1987).   D.A.S.M.

Mesopotamia

From time immemorial, the inhabitants of ancient Mesopotamia buried their dead in cemeteries and in private houses, together with meals and personal effects. The archeological finds point to a funerary cult, and the variations suggest differences in the social status of the deceased. The written sources are more explicit about the Mesopotamian conceptions of death and afterlife. Written in Sumerian and Akkadian between the late 3rd millennium and the middle of the 1st millennium BCE, these sources also incorporate much older traditions that were retained by the population. The combined material of text and archeology suggests a belief that, after death, the personality continued an animated existence in the form of a ghost, retaining the basic needs and emotions of any living being. The dead gathered in their own realm, which was segregated and distant from the world of the living, to prevent commingling. The netherworld was perceived in terms of terrestrial social reality, and its gods fulfilled official functions within it. However, due to the dramatic ethnic, social, and political changes in the national texture of ancient Mesopotamia, the image of the netherworld was subject to developments and adaptations.

Death had been established by the gods. Thus, an Akkadian fragment of the Epic of Gilgamesh from the 17th century BCE relates that

> when the gods created mankind,
> death they dispensed to mankind,
> life they kept for themselves.
> (George 1999: 124)

In the Sumerian narrative the Death of Gilgamesh, the legendary king of Uruk was thus informed of his death: "The bane of mankind is thus come" (George 1999: 203). And the late-2nd-millennium version of the folktale Enlil and Namzitarra reveals that the lifespan of humanity is 120 years.

According to the Epic of Atrahasis, a creation narrative from the 2nd millennium, humans were fashioned from clay mixed with the flesh and blood of a slain god. Therefore the human spirit was divine and immortal, endowing the body with life and lasting after its decay. This belief signifies an inherent duality in the composition of humanity—there is body and there is spirit, which coexist temporarily. Death is the point of time following the last breath, when human nature changes from a dual into a single entity and moves from one kind of reality into another.

The spirit was embodied in the breath, which is as tangible as the wind and therefore perceived as an actual being. Being the animated component of the human, it retained all the needs and emotions of its former earthly life, but being invisible it remained mysterious. In order to forestall danger, it was treated with reverence and venerated in a special cult. The contents of excavated graves and lists recording offerings for the cult of the dead make it clear that the ghost was universally held to be a real, animated being and that it was sustained by actual food and drink, provided by the living.

Properly cared for, spirits protected the interests of their family. Numerous incantations and rituals against evil spirits testify that neglected, hungry ghosts, in contrast, returned to the land of the living, haunted the people, and caused diseases and untimely deaths. These were chased back to the netherworld by means of special rituals and magic.

During the funerary ritual, the mourner proclaimed the release of the spirit from the body and then offered a meal to an icon of the deceased. Thereafter, the spirit departed to rest in the netherworld and returned regularly for its meals. Instruction for the funerary ritual are given in one Sumerian lament:

> After you have called my "his spirit [wind] is released,"
> set up a chair and seat the statue . . .
> place the bread offering and wipe it,
> pour out the water to the libation pipe.
> (Thureau-Dangin 1922: lines 55–59)

The same ritual was performed for a spirit that had returned from the netherworld and concludes with the statement: "The spirit [wind] has entered, the spirit has departed" (Kramer 1977: line 48; and van Dijk 1976: 15.1–6). Accordingly, the hero Gilgamesh fashioned a statue and performed the ritual for his friend Enkidu (George 1999: 65–69); the Death of Gilgamesh ends with a recital about statues of men to be fashioned and venerated in temples for future days (George 1999: 207).

The cult of the dead was conducted on specific days in the family circle at home, at graves, or in temples. Images of the dead ancestors moved with the family when the house was abandoned, in order that their cult might be maintained and the well-being of the family secured. Mostly broken, discarded figurines that were found in private houses, as well as the biblical story about Rachel stealing the teraphim when she left her ancestral home for Canaan (Gen. 31.19), illustrate this practice. The food offering made to the dead became taboo for a living person; its consumption was believed ominous.

Where was the realm of the dead? Sumerian cultic laments over the young, dead gods Dumuzi, Damu, and Ningishzida suggest that originally the Sumerians conceived of the netherworld in real geographical terms and thought that it was at the foot of a distant mountain in the highland beyond the northeastern borders of Sumer. This image differs from common burial practices, but complements a holistic geopolitical outlook on the world: the standard Sumerian word for the netherworld is Kur, which signifies both "mountain" and "foreign land." Thus Kur is a concept that diametrically opposes every sense of Sumer itself: geographically, it is the mountain range, as opposed to Sumer, the level land; politically, it is "foreign land" as opposed to "my land"; socially and culturally, it is the uncivilized barren land of the dead, as opposed to Sumer, the civilized world.

However, during the first half of the 3rd millennium BCE, the geographical and political horizons of Sumer extended, the mountain range became accessible, and the concept of Kur could no longer accommodate the mythological netherworld. Subsequently the concept of Kur disintegrated, and as the realm of the dead, Kur became no more than a place-name devoid of geographic and topographical significance. The Sumerians now adopted a vertical perception of the cosmos, in which the dead resided in a subterranean region, the netherworld, and thereby mythological reality was harmonized with actual burial practices. Additional neutral names—Ki (place), Urugal (big city), and Arali—then emerged.

The modifications in the image of the realm of the dead followed urban, social, and political developments in Mesopotamia. Descriptions of an uninhabited landscape in some Sumerian laments probably reflect an ancient tradition that dates to preurban times. The image of the netherworld as an urban society is dated to the middle of the 3rd millennium by the name Urugal (the big city). An inscription from about 2300 BCE, dedicated to Ereshkigal, the queen of the netherworld, is the earliest unequivocal evidence for the concept of the netherworld as a kingdom. The lament over King Ur-Namma of Ur (died about 2095 BCE) depicts the netherworld in terms of the terrestrial kingdom ruled by deities: Queen Ereshkigal, her vizier (Namtar [destiny]), a scribe, military officers, gatekeepers, judges, and bailiffs. Religious texts and god lists from the 2nd and the 1st millennia record developments in the rank and role of some deities and attest to the existence of additional offices in the administration of the netherworld taken over from the actual governmental system.

Moreover, the few architectural features of the netherworld bear similarity to the earthly urban centers. The entrance was through a gate guarded by a gatekeeper. The gatekeeper's name, Bitu, is derived from the Akkadian word *open!* and originated in the Semitic population of Sumer. This name suggests that the idea of a gate was adopted by the Sumerians later. A wall is not mentioned in the sources, but it may have been considered self-evident. The Sumerian myth of Inanna's journey to the netherworld and its late Akkadian version describe an entrance through seven gates. A complex of seven gates does not exist in Mesopotamian urban architecture, and the major literary function of the description suggests that it originated in the demands of the plot, but it is doubtful that this image became standard. In addition to gates, palaces are also mentioned. Each netherworld-god had his own palace and was seated on a throne. The inspiration for these images may have been the configuration of the city's temple precincts.

The face of the earth sealed the abode of the ghosts away from the world of the living, although whenever necessary, an opening was made especially for the passage, either by digging a grave or by magic. The road could be traveled by foot, in a chariot, or in a boat. The textual evidence is confirmed by models of boats and chariots. A couple of real chariots harnessed to oxen were found in the early dynastic cemetery of Ur. Typically, the road between the two domains was imagined as one way, although the dead might return for periodic rites, and a few deities were allowed to come out in exchange for a substitute (Inanna, Dumuzi, Enlil, and Ninlil). Otherwise, only evil spirits and restless ghosts could return; thus, an Old Babylonian incantation against the seven evil spirits describes their way out from the netherworld:

In the Arali the path is laid out for them,
In the grave the gate is open for them,
They leave towards the gate of sunset.
(Geller 1985: lines 250–52)

The essence of the netherworld is the topic of the Akkadian myth about Ishtar's descent: "To the dark house . . . to the house which those who enter cannot leave . . . where dust is their food, clay their bread. . . . They see no light they dwell in darkness. Over the door and the bolt dust has settled" (Dalley 1989: 154).

Darkness, mud, clay, and dust are the fundamental elements of subterranean reality, and the food is not victuals but grave materials. The earlier Sumerian sources deal mainly with the bad quality of the nourishment, but none allude to clay, and only a few sources mention the darkness. The most uncompromising Sumerian perception is found in the myth about the journey of the god Ningishzida to the netherworld:

The river of the Netherworld flows no water, its water you would not drink. . . .
The field of the netherworld grows no grain, flour is not milled from it. . . .
The sheep of the netherworld carries no wool, cloth is not woven from it.
(Jacobsen and Alster 2000: 321)

This passage signifies that the netherworld lacks the basic necessities for existence and, moreover, that it is the opposite of civilization, a primordial realm, null and void. Yet, it does not allude to subterranean reality. The focus on the availability and quality of the nourishment demonstrates an assumption that the dead received regular provisions but that the food was spoiled. It seems, therefore, that the oldest Sumerian tradition separated the netherworld from the grave, in parallel to the release of the spirit from the body during the funerary ritual. The speculation that it was situated beyond the confines of the grave allowed for development of the image of a vast community, suited to house its ever-increasing population.

The belief in afterlife is rooted in the human experience that the body is doomed to perish, but that the spirit that enlivens it is everlasting. While changing historical reality yielded various images of the netherworld, one fundamental concept was held universally: the realm of the dead was an unproductive, barren region. This view accounts for the common belief that the ghosts depend on support from living relatives and respond accordingly, for better or worse. This belief helped to explain sudden diseases and suffering as the work of neglected, hungry spirits. The image of the netherworld as a subterranean, inverted replica of the actual world signifies a mythological reality in harmony with the conventional burial practices.

BIBL.: Tzvi Abusch, "Ghost and God: Some Observations on a Babylonian Understanding of Human Nature," in *Self, Soul, and Body in Religious Experience* (ed. A. I. Baumgarten, J. Assmann, and G. G. Stroumsa; Studies in the History of Religions 78; Leiden: Brill, 1998), 363–83. Bendt Alster (ed.), *Death in Mesopotamia: Papers Read at the XXVIe Rencontre assyriologique internationale* (Copenhagen, 1980). Stephanie Dalley, *Myth from Mesopotamia* (Oxford, 1989). J. van Dijk, *Cuneiform Texts: Texts of Varying Content* (Texts in the Iraq Museum 9; Leiden: Brill, 1976). M. J. Geller, *Forerunners to Udug-Hul: Sumerian Exorcistic Incantations* (Stuttgart, 1985). Andrew George, *The Epic of Gilgamesh: A New Translation* (London: Penguin, 1999). T. Jacobsen and B. Alster, "Ningišzida's Boat-Ride to Hades," in *Wisdom, Gods, and Literature: Studies in Honour of W. G. Lambert* (ed. A. G. George and I. L. Finkel; Winona Lake, Ind., 2000), 315–44. Jacob Klein, "The 'Bane' of Humanity: A Lifespan of One Hundred Twenty Years," *Acta Sumerologica* 12 (1990): 58–59. S. N. Kramer, "The GIR₅ and the ki-sikil: A New Sumerian Elegy," in *Essays on the Ancient Neat East in Memory of J. J. Finkelstein* (ed. M. de Jong Ellis; Hamden, Conn., 1977), 139–42. F. Thureau-Dangin, "La passion du dieu Lillu," *Revue d'assyriologie* 19 (1922): 175–84. D.K.

Syria-Canaan

The various cultures of the Syro-Canaanite sphere, especially as evidenced by the literary and ritual texts of Ugarit, Ebla, and Emar, as well as Phoenician, Hebrew, and Aramaic inscriptions, seemed to believe that death was inevitable for all human beings and any continued existence of the spirit after death was more dismal than pleasant. There was no concept of an ultimate judgment with rewards and punishments after death, and immortality was generally reserved for the gods, although sometimes dead kings and heroes were thought to be deified at some level.

According to the Aqhat epic from Late Bronze Age Ugarit, upon death the spirit exited the nose like wind or smoke. Elsewhere in Ugaritic literary texts, the netherworld to which the spirit descended is often called simply 'arṣ (lit., earth) and is depicted as a muddy, putrid abode. It is ruled by the god Mot (or Motu), who is the deified personification of death and sterility, and its entrance is beneath two mountains at the edge of the earth. Mot is said to have a voracious appetite and an enormous gullet: he has "[one lip to e]arth, one lip to heaven . . . a tongue to the stars!" (*KTU* 1.5 2.2–3). This same deity appears in later Phoenician mythology, where he is Muth (also called Thanatos or Pluto), a son of Cronus (Philo of Byblos, *apud* Eusebius, *Preparation for the Gospel* 1.10.34). In the Ugaritic Baal Epic, the fertility-god Baal (or Balu) is swallowed by Mot and later rescued by the goddess Anat (or Anatu), who kills Mot. Fertility returns to the land when Baal is revived, and seven years later, when Mot himself comes back to life, Baal defeats him again. Thus death, however terrible, was probably seen as a necessary element in an ongoing cycle.

Mourning and burial rituals. The mourning activities of the gods and humans in Ugaritic myths may reflect actual practices. In the Baal epic, the gods mourn the death of Baal by weeping, sitting on the ground, throwing dust on their heads, donning mourning clothes, lacerating their bodies, and sacrificing animals. Elsewhere there are professional mourners who gash their flesh and wail. In the list of the important "duties of a son" in the Aqhat epic, at least some of the duties described are funerary or mortuary. The importance of these filial funerary duties is seen also on the Phoenician sarcophagus of Ahiram of Byblos from the 12th or 11th century BCE, in which the dead king is portrayed seated on a throne receiving the offerings of mourners in procession, with his son by his side in charge of the proceedings.

As for the archeological remains of tombs, we find in Late Bronze Age Ugarit the practice of intramural burials under residential houses and the royal palace. Staircases under the floors led to these vaulted tombs with multiple burials. At Phoenician sites of the Iron Age, cremation and inhumation were both practiced, but in contrast to Ugarit, cemeteries were set far from the living, outside settlements. The Phoenician dead were not to be disturbed, and tomb inscriptions contain dire maledictions against anyone who dared to do so.

Cults of the dead and the deification of kings. There

were probably regular offerings for the dead at Ugarit, Ebla, and Emar, with the understanding that their spirits maintained a connection to and could benefit the living. These offerings may have been quite similar to the Mesopotamian *kispu* rituals, which required an invocation of the dead and a presentation of food and water. However, at Ugarit the archeological evidence for a mortuary cult is meager—gutters and pipes in the houses, which used to be interpreted as means for libations to the tombs underneath, are probably ordinary drainage installations—and the relevant texts are not explicit in detail. For example, the funerary ritual *KTU* 1.161 summons dead kings to join a group called the *rapi'uma*, probably the shades of ancestral heroes and kings, at the funeral of King Niqmaddu III (cf. biblical *rĕpā'îm* and Phoenician *rp'm*). The ritual includes sacrifices and the blessing of the new king, but may only have been part of the initial funeral and not part of repeated cultic practice. On the other hand, the *rapi'uma* are invited to feast in some Ugaritic texts, and it is possible that the social drinking and banqueting institution known as the *marzēaḥ* in diverse Syro-Canaanite texts across two millennia (cf. biblical *marzēaḥ*, Ugaritic *marziḥu*) occasionally involved mortuary meals. The idea of the royal dead dining with the gods is found in the Aramaic inscription of King Panammu of Samal (8th century BCE). His son is to offer sacrifices to the god Hadad and say, "May the soul of Panammu eat with you [Hadad], and may the soul of Panammu drink with you!" (*KAI* 214).

Finally, in king lists at both Ebla and Ugarit the names of dead kings are preceded by a divine determinative, indicating that they were thought to be minor deities or preternatural beings; at Ebla these clearly receive sacrifices. However, the ritual texts are in tension with the pessimistic sense of human mortality in the literary texts. When the hero Aqhat is tempted by the goddess Anat's offer to give him eternal life in return for his bow, he responds: "Do not lie, Maiden, for to a hero your lies are rubbish! What does a mortal get as his fate? What does a mortal get as his end? Glaze will be poured on my head, lime on top of my skull . . . the death of all I will die. I too will certainly die!" (*KTU* 1.17 6.34–38).

BIBL.: Michel Gras, Pierre Rouillard, and Javier Teixidor, "The Phoenicians and Death," *Berytus* 39 (1991): 127–76. T. J. Lewis, *Cults of the Dead in Ancient Israel and Ugarit* (Atlanta, 1989). Dennis Pardee, "Marzihu, kispu, and the Ugaritic Funerary Cult: A Minimalist View," in *Ugarit: Religion and Culture* (ed. N. Wyatt et al.; Münster, 1996), 273–87.   T.L.H.

Israel

Ancient Israel. As in ancient Canaan and Mesopotamia, in ancient Israel the dead were normally thought to go to "the land of no return," which was known in Hebrew as Sheol. This was a place of darkness, dust, and silence.

Those who go down to Sheol cannot praise God. It has an insatiable appetite and is said to swallow its victims, like Mot in the Ugaritic myth. The biblical Sheol is not yet a hell, but merely a gloomy limbo. This was the normal fate of human beings throughout the biblical period. In the early 2nd century BCE, Ben Sira insists that "whether life is for ten or a hundred or a thousand years, there is no inquiry about it in Hades" (Sir. 41.4) (Hades is the Greek counterpart of Sheol).

The mythology of Sheol reflects one aspect of the Israelite view of death. Another aspect is reflected in burial customs. Those who die a peaceful death are typically said to be gathered to their ancestors. The idiom here reflects the burial customs of ancient Israel. Family members were buried together in underground caves; in the Iron Age, the use of caves declined as bench-tombs grew in popularity. Bodies were laid on the benches until they had decomposed, and then the bones were gathered into a repository under one of the benches in a secondary burial. Bench-tombs were the predominant form of burial in Judah during the late 8th through early 6th centuries BCE.

The degree to which a cult of the dead was practiced in ancient Israel is controversial. Throughout the period of the monarchy, bowls for food, jars for liquid, and sometimes a lamp for light were placed in tombs, as were jewelry and amulets. Various figurines and statuettes are also found. The precise function of such figurines is unclear, but they probably represent some kind of sympathetic magic or possibly reflect the hope that the dead can intercede on behalf of the living.

Deuteronomy forbids offering tithed food to the dead (26.14), but does not prohibit other offerings. It also forbids the consulting of ghosts or spirits or seeking of oracles from the dead (18.11) and self-laceration in mourning (14.1). Consultation of the dead is also noted in Isa. 8.19–9.1a [= 8.19–23a Hebrew]; 19.3; and possibly 29.4. Second Kings notes that King Manasseh of Judah consulted mediums and wizards (21.6) and that Josiah put them away (23.24). The most famous story about the consultation of the dead concerns King Saul and the witch of Endor in 1 Sam. 28. It is disputed whether such consultation was an ancient custom in Israel or was introduced only under Assyrian influence. (The story of the witch of Endor may be a Deuteronomic composition, from the late 7th century BCE.)

Beatific afterlife in the Hebrew Bible? A few biblical texts are adduced as evidence for belief in a beatific afterlife, primarily in the Psalms. The key passages are Ps. 16.9–10; 49.15 [= 49.16 Hebrew]; and 73.23–26. Psalm 16.9–10 can be interpreted in terms of protection from premature death. A stronger case can be made for 49.15 ("but God will ransom my soul from the power of Sheol, for he will receive me"). The use of the verb *lqḥ* (to take, receive) here recalls the fate of Enoch, who "walked with God; and he was not, for God took him" (Gen. 5.24). The verb is used in a similar way in Ps.

Entrance to a burial cave at Beth Shearim. *Photo by Z. Radovan, Jerusalem*

73.24. But the psalmist also affirms that the wise die together with the fool and the dolt (49.10 [= 49.11 Hebrew]) and twice declares that "humankind shall not live in glory; they perish like the beasts" (49.12, 20 [= 49.13, 21 Hebrew], my translation). It may be that the psalmist hoped that God would grant him an exception to the common fate. Such exceptions are granted in the Hebrew Bible to Enoch and Elijah. A case can also be made that the king was sometimes thought to be immortal. Psalm 21.4 [= 21.5 Hebrew] says: "He asked you for life; you gave it to him—length of days forever and ever" (NRSV). But this is an exceptional passage, and there is little evidence to suggest that the immortality of the king was commonly accepted in Israel.

Resurrection as metaphor. Language of resurrection is sometimes used as a metaphor for the restoration of Israel in the period after the Babylonian exile. The most vivid example is found in Ezekiel's vision of a valley full of dry bones (Ezek. 37). The vision implies familiarity with the concept of resurrection. In Zoroastrianism the bodies of the dead are exposed to be picked clean by the vultures, and this custom may have suggested the vision of dry bones. Ezekiel, however, is explicit in his interpretation: "These bones are the whole house of Israel" (37.11). There is no question here of the resurrection of individuals. A more difficult case is provided by Isa. 26.19: "Thy dead shall live, their bodies shall rise. O dwellers in the dust, awake and sing for joy!" Many scholars understand this passage as an affirmation of the resurrection of individuals. The context, however, is entirely concerned with the restoration of the people. The passage should be interpreted as analogous to Ezek. 37. Its language, however, would have a profound influence on the subsequent development of belief in resurrection.

Isaiah 26 is part of the so-called Apocalypse of Isaiah (Isa. 24–27), written early in the Second Temple period. It contains one other passage that is relevant to the discussion of death and afterlife. In 25.6–10 we are told that God will make a great feast "on this mountain" (Zion) and that "he will swallow up death forever." The language evokes the old Canaanite myth in which Mot (Death) swallows Baal. The promise is that life will be transformed and death will be no more. The removal of the threat of death does not require that the dead be raised, but it does imply a hope for an immortal state in the future. This hope, however, should not be pressed in too literal a fashion. Another passage in the Book of Isaiah, from roughly the same period, envisions a new heaven and a new earth. In this new creation there will no longer be "an infant that lives but a few days, or an old man who does not fill out his days, for the child shall die a hundred years old, and the sinner a hundred years old shall be accursed" (65.20). In the new creation people will still be mortal, even if the length of life is greatly expanded.

Early apocalypses. The first clear evidence of belief in a differentiated life after death in Jewish sources appears in the apocalyptic literature of the Hellenistic period. In *1 Enoch* 22, Enoch is shown "a large and high mountain, and a hard rock and four beautiful places, and inside it was deep and wide and very smooth." Here the souls of the dead are gathered to await the judgment. The souls of the righteous are kept apart, with a spring of water and light. Another place is prepared for sinners "accomplished in wrongdoing." We are told that "their souls will not be killed on the day of judgment nor will they rise from there." This is the oldest passage in Jewish literature that attempts to distinguish the lot of righteous and wicked in the afterlife. Its views are never repeated in other Jewish literature. Other formulations of the belief in judgment of the dead appear in other sections of *1 Enoch*. In some cases, resurrection comes as a public event at the climax of history (*1 Enoch* 90–91). In other cases, the emphasis is on the transformation of the individual, and the place in the historical sequence is less important. *First Enoch* 104, also in the section of *1 Enoch* known as the Epistle of Enoch, tells the righteous to be hopeful, because "you will shine like the lights of heaven and will be seen, and the gate of heaven will be opened to you. . . . Be hopeful, and do not abandon your hope, for you will have great joy like the angels of heaven . . . for you shall be associates of the host of heaven." A very similar concept is found in Dan. 12.1–3, as the climax of a historical sequence: "At that time your people shall be delivered, every one whose name shall be found written in the book. And many of those who sleep in the dust of the earth shall awake, some to everlasting life, and some to shame and everlasting contempt. And those who are wise shall shine like the brightness of the firmament; and those who turn many to righteousness, like the stars for ever and ever." As is clear from the parallel in *1 Enoch*, to shine like the stars is to become a companion of the host of heaven. The language, however, carries overtones of the idea of astral immortality that was widespread in the Greco-Roman world.

Prior to the Hellenistic age, only exceptional individuals were believed to be elevated to the angelic realm. The notion that such a destiny could be attained by the righteous as a group was novel in this period. In the Book of Daniel, this belief is brought to bear directly on the problem of theodicy. Those who are raised are the leaders of the spiritual resistance to the persecution of Antiochus Epiphanes. Some of them, we are told, fall (die), "to refine and to cleanse them and to make them white, until the time of the end" (Dan. 11.35). But in the resurrection, they are vindicated, when they are elevated to shine like the stars. The faithful could afford to lose their lives in this world if they believed that they would be elevated to join the angels in heaven. In the Epistle of Enoch (*1 Enoch* 91–107), the dynamic is similar, although the situation envisaged is not one of persecution, but simply of social injustice. The injustice of the present will be set right in the judgment. This is also the situation envisioned in Ps. 49 and 73.

It is often claimed that Jewish eschatology is distinguished from Greek by its emphasis on the resurrection of the body in contrast to the immortality of the soul. This distinction, however, is far too simple and fails to do justice to the kind of belief that emerges in the books of Daniel and *1 Enoch*. While this is not the Greek idea of immortality of the soul, neither is it resurrection of the physical body. It might better be described as resurrection of the spirit, the exaltation of *nepeš* from the netherworld to the heavenly regions. In the formulation of Jub. 23.31: "Their bodies shall rest in the earth, and their spirits shall have much joy." The spiritual nature of the afterlife is underlined in the Book of the Watchers (*1 Enoch* 1–36), in contrast to the earthly life of corruptible flesh and sexuality.

The idea of bodily resurrection is also attested in Judaism, beginning in the 2nd century BCE. The brothers in 2 Macc. 7 taunt their torturers, in full confidence that their limbs will be restored in the resurrection. (It should be noted that 2 Maccabees was written in Greek, adapted from the work of a Diaspora Jew, Jason of Cyrene.) The pseudo-Ezekiel text from Qumran (4Q385) interprets Ezekiel's vision of the dry bones in terms of actual resurrection, which is, accordingly, physical in nature. Ezekiel 37 also underlies a prophecy of bodily resurrection in Sibylline Oracles 4, another Greek text from the Diaspora. Bodily resurrection was one of several ways in which the afterlife might be imagined. It was in no sense normative or standard in ancient Judaism.

Dead Sea Scrolls. The people who wrote the Dead Sea Scrolls were certainly familiar with the idea of resurrection. They preserved multiple copies of the books of Daniel and *1 Enoch*. There are also clear references to resurrection in 4Q385 (pseudo-Ezekiel) and in 4Q521 (the so-called Messianic Apocalypse), which lists the raising of the dead among the wonderful works of the end-time and refers to God as "the one who gives life to the dead of his people." These texts, however, are not necessarily sectarian products; they may simply be part of the community library like the books of Daniel and *1 Enoch*. There is a long-standing controversy about the sect's own understanding of resurrection and life after death.

In part this controversy is fueled by conflicting accounts of the beliefs of the Essenes, who are widely thought to be identical with the Dead Sea sect. Josephus, who apparently relied on a Greek ethnographic source, wrote that they believed in the immortality of the soul (*Jewish War* 2.154–56). Hippolytus, who apparently drew on the same source, held that they believed in resurrection of the body (*Refutation of All Heresies* 27). There is no doubt that the sect firmly believed in reward and punishment after death. The debate about bodily resurrection centers on a couple of texts from the Hodayot, or Thanksgiving Hymns, which thank God for raising people up from the dust to the heavenly council (1QH 3.19–23; 19.10–14). The goal here is fellowship with the angels, as it also was in *1 Enoch* and Daniel. The difference is that the hymnist at Qumran claims to enjoy in the present the fellowship that was promised to the righteous after death in the apocalypses. The members of the community believed that they had already made the essential transition to the angelic life. Consequently, future resurrection was not so important. Josephus certainly distorted this belief when he assimilated it to the Greek idea of immortality of the soul, but he was correct in placing the emphasis on immortality rather than on resurrection.

The Qumran community buried its dead in individual graves, with the head to the south and the feet to the north. There were no family tombs, and this has been taken to lend support to the view that the lifestyle was celibate. But any attempt to deduce anything from the Qumran cemetery is put in question by the discovery of a huge Nabatean cemetery across the Dead Sea in Jordan, at Khirbet Qazone. This cemetery also has individual (shaft) graves, and the bodies are oriented north-south, like those at Qumran. The graves at Khirbet Qazone are clearly identified as Nabatean, not only by the location but also by the grave goods that were found, which include depictions of the Nabatean god Dushara. The discovery at Khirbet Qazone raises fresh questions about the cemetery at Qumran—specifically the possibility that it may have been a regional cemetery in the Nabatean style rather than a reflection of distinctively Essene beliefs about the afterlife.

Immortality of the soul. The apocalyptic idea of angelic afterlife was adapted in another way in the Hellenistic Diaspora. The Wisdom of Solomon, written in Alexandria early in the Roman era, is clearly acquainted with apocalyptic judgment scenes (see Wis. 5.4–5). But while the Wisdom of Solomon uses the apocalyptic judgment scene as a rhetorical device, it actually subscribes to a Greek idea of immortality, informed by the Platonic tradition: "God created us for incorruption, and made us in the image of his own eternity" (2.23 NRSV). The soul, then, is created immortal. In this life, "a perishable body weighs down the soul" (9.15) but the soul that is devoted to wisdom can gain immortality. There is no question here of resurrection of the body. This essentially Platonic idea of the immortal soul was shared by philosophically sophisticated Jews, such as Philo of Alexandria. Not all Diaspora Jews were as refined philosophically as Philo and the Wisdom of Solomon. The great majority of Jewish epitaphs from Greco-Roman Egypt simply express grief that a loved one has been snatched away to Hades. Some reject any hope for life after death. Only a few express any kind of belief in an afterlife.

Beliefs in later Judaism. It is difficult to say how widely accepted ideas of reward and punishment after death were in Judaism around the turn of the era. The Pharisees allegedly accepted belief in resurrection; the Sadducees did not. The evidence of Jewish epitaphs in this period is ambiguous. A few centuries later, belief in resurrection is well attested in the epitaphs from Beth Shearim, where a huge necropolis dates to the 2nd through 4th centuries CE. The majority of epitaphs from the turn of the era, however, simply wish the dead person peace.

By the end of the 1st century, there is evidence of more systematic reflection on the fate of the individual after death, in the apocalypses of *4 Ezra* and *2 Baruch.* These try to synthesize the various traditions about life after death, combining bodily resurrection and angelic transformation as two stages in a process. Other apocalypses from the same period *(3 Baruch, 2 Enoch)* ignore the general resurrection and take the form of ascents of the visionary through the heavens.

Resurrection of the dead is affirmed strongly in rabbinic Judaism. The central prayer of the daily Jewish liturgy, the Amidah, contains the benediction "Blessed art you, O Lord, who revives the dead." According to the Mishnah, tractate *Sanhedrin* 10.1–2, "All Israel has a share in the world to come." But it adds: "And these are the ones who have no portion in the world to come: he who says there is no resurrection of the dead . . ."

BIBL.: A. J. Avery-Peck and J. Neusner (eds.), *Judaism in Late Antiquity,* vol. 4: *Death, Life-after-Death, and the World-to-Come in the Judaisms of Late Antiquity* (Leiden: Brill, 2000). E. Bloch-Smith, *Judahite Burial Practices and Beliefs about the Dead* (Sheffield: JSOT Press, 1992). T. J. Lewis, *Cults of the Dead in Ancient Israel and Ugarit* (Atlanta: Scholars Press, 1989). G. W. Nickelsburg, *Resurrection, Immortality, and Eternal Life in Intertestamental Judaism* (Cambridge: Harvard University Press, 1972). E. Puech, *La croyance des esséniens en la vie future: Immortalité, résurrection, vie éternelle?* vol. 1: *La résurrection des morts et le contexte scripturaire* (Paris: Gabalda, 1993).   J.J.C.

Anatolia

Given the exclusively royal focus of the Hittite tablet collections of the 2nd millennium BCE (ca. 1650–1180), next to nothing is known about the average Hittite person's beliefs concerning death and the afterlife. What little we do know comes from archeology. The cemeteries excavated from the Hittite period convey a fairly uniform picture: inhumation and cremation were practiced simultaneously, and the funeral complexes contain no gifts of any great value. The most valuable depositions consist of bovines and equids—in their entirety or heads only—that sometimes accompany the dead. They were animals in the prime of their lives, constituting considerable movable wealth.

The situation concerning our knowledge of royal funerary practices is completely the opposite. One of the most extensive Hittite text compositions concerns a funerary ritual for the Hittite king and queen. It was known by its incipit: "When in Hattusha a royal loss occurs, that is, either a king or queen becomes a god" (a fate shared by kings and queens exclusively). The ritual lasted for fourteen days and was a rite of passage in the sense that its goal was to ensure that the inevitable transition would not endanger the country's stability and prosperity, which were embodied by the king. The composition consists of four separate series: a scenario giving a detailed prescription of who should do what where and when; a script with the text of prayers to be spoken with brief directions; a ration list with the materials needed each day; and a summary characterizing each day in a single line. The scenario originally comprised between 3,000 and 3,500 lines of text, half of which can be reconstructed with some confidence. The composition can be dated around 1400 BCE with certainty, but may well be older.

The body of the deceased was cremated on the night of the first day of the ritual. Then, at dawn, the pyre was quenched with several liquids. Women collected the remains of the bones, which were then dipped in oil, wrapped in cloth, and brought to the actual tomb or "Stone House." There they would be laid out on a bed. That same day, a wooden effigy was made of the deceased: a seated male with weapons in his hands for a king, a seated female with spinning gear for a queen. Eyes and mouth were indicated with gold plaques or inlays. The rest of the second day through the sixth day was filled with offerings that aimed at reconciliation. The latter were probably directed at the powers of the netherworld, the most important of whom was the Sun-goddess of the Earth. The royal body seems to have gone initially to the Stone House, and texts suggest that the king was escorted out from there by his mother.

The seventh through thirteenth days after death were devoted to rituals concerning particular spheres of life, such as agriculture, viticulture, and animal husbandry, including hunting. For example, among the numerous acts performed, a chunk of sod was cut off and presented to the sun-god for the benefit of the deceased, a plow was used and then burned, a grapevine was brought to the table of the deceased, and some ducks were caught and burned. The seventh day itself probably centered on the theme of kingship, considering the use of "fine oil" and "[royal] robes," which recall the ceremony in which a Hittite king was anointed. The thirteenth day was called the day "of the *lahhanzana* birds," probably some kind of ducks, but the purpose of this day's ritual remains obscure. No text of the fourteenth day has been preserved.

The pattern of days seven through thirteen is generally the same. In the morning the effigy was brought out of the Stone House, given food and drink, put on a cart, and brought to a place where the day's ritual was carried out. All the while, the effigy sat on the cart, perhaps reflecting the king's custom of going out on a chariot or cart and, for instance, pronouncing judgments or holding audiences from there. The effigy was then taken down from the cart for inclusion in a meal of all participants and finally transported back to the Stone House, accompanied by wailing women. The focus of each day—the sphere on which it centered—was symbolized by various objects that were subsequently burned. These objects were often inlaid with precious stones and metals that were removed before being thrown into the fire. The valuables were finally brought to the Stone House, while the remaining objects' ashes went to "the place where the heads of horses and oxen have been burned." Although the background of this ritual remains unclear, it does recall the heads of equids and bovines deposited along with inhumations and cremations found at Hittite cemeteries. Fire being an appropriate means of transporting things to another existence, the deceased would be able to enjoy the fruits of agriculture and other things that had been burned in his or her afterlife. More important, however, by securing these objects for the deceased, the survivors invoked his or her benevolence and, as a consequence, guaranteed the continued prosperity of the land and its people.

The logistics of the ritual were complex: scores of participants are mentioned, all of whom needed to be directed and fed. Hundreds of oxen and sheep were slaughtered, and enormous amounts of produce, beverages, and baked goods were prepared. The rituals had been committed to writing, which ensured that, whenever a royal death occurred, the relevant texts could immediately be retrieved from the tablet, and the memory of those who had participated in the last funeral rites would not have to be relied upon. The texts enabled participants to carry out the ritual correctly down to the smallest detail. This is not to say, however, that over the centuries, the texts and therefore the ritual did not undergo modifications, reflecting past experiences or changes in beliefs.

From archeology, in contrast, we learn very little. No obviously royal tombs have ever been identified, and perhaps they are not likely to be. What we would expect to find, left over from the fourteen-day ritual, are the ashes, bones, and valuables that had collected during the second part of the rites, but so far such a complex has not survived the ages. From texts we know that Hittite kings and queens were not necessarily buried in the capital Hattusha and that, like Egyptian royalty, they sometimes started planning and building their tombs already during their lives, at great expense. Rocky outcrops (called *ḫegur* houses) seem to have been the preferred spots to build a Stone House. Two such places are identified in Hattusha: in the very center of the Upper City was the *ḫegur* of King Tudkhaliya IV (ca. 1240–1210 BCE), while Room B at the rock sanctuary Yazılıkaya just outside the city walls likely served a funerary purpose, judging from the reliefs that decorate it. That the latter is clearly associated with King Tudkhaliya IV as well, however, presents a problem, as individuals did not have double tombs.

In the end, the deceased became part of the ancestor cult. Images were set up in the temples and became the object of regular offerings and devotion. The souls of the dead lived on and could be contacted. However, those same souls, if not properly treated, could also exert a negative influence from beyond their world, into that of the living.

BIBL.: Alexei Kassian, Andrej Korolëv, and Andrej Sidel'tsev, *Hittite Funerary Ritual: Sallis Wastais* (Alter Orient und Altes Testament 288; Münster, Ugarit-Verlag, 2002). Heinrich Otten, *Hethitische Totenrituale* (Berlin, 1958). T. P. J. van den Hout, "Death as a Privilege: The Hittite Royal Funerary Ritual," in *Hidden Futures* (ed. J. M. Bremer, T. P. J. van den Hout, and R. Peters; Amsterdam, 1994), 37–75. Idem, "Tombs and Memorials: The (Divine) Stone-House and Hegur Reconsidered," in *Recent Developments in Hittite Archaeology and History: Papers in Memory of Hans G. Güterbock* (ed. K. Aslihan Yener and H. A. Hoffner Jr.; Winona Lake, Ind., 2002), 73–91.   T.V.D.H.

Iran

For the ancient Iranians, humans were etymologically mortal (Old Persian *martiya*), and humanity also was called "mortal seed" (Middle Persian *mardōm*). The name of the first man, Gayomard, was explained as "the mortal life." These various words denote the importance granted in Iran to the mortal aspect of the human being. But the first human also was named Yima; that is, he was the first sovereign and the "king of the dead," for he built a *vara* (dwelling place) for the dead. Thus, death is the state at which all humans arrive, in contrast to the gods, who never die. According to Kellens (2000), the kingdom in which Yima received the souls of the departed and where he built a *var*, that is, the underground shelter in which he protected the living from a very murderous winter, hearken back to the same motif: a universe enclosed by clay walls, like the closed space of the tomb.

Those ancient Iranians who practiced burial thought that the dead lived miserably under the earth and, according to Herodotus, that each person had to pay for a better life underground by the sacrifice of living creatures; thus, Xerxes' wife would have buried alive fourteen noble Persian children in order to propitiate the underground god Yima on Xerxes' behalf. The relationship of Yima, who is described as "bright," with the sun may reflect another funerary ritual, in which corpses were exposed to sunlight and allowed to be consumed by dogs and the birds; this ritual was popularized during the Sasanian period (224–632 CE). By the Achaemenian period, one's experiences after death are correlated with one's life: the one who has been just will enjoy bliss in the next world as well as in this world. Xerxes proclaims:

If you think: "May I be happy while alive and may I become blessed when dead!" then behave according to the law which Ahura Mazda established and worship Ahura Mazda according to truth, with barsom in the hands, he will both be happy while alive and blessed when dead.

More than six centuries later, the great magus Kirdir affirms exactly the same doctrine:

He who sees this inscription [= Naqsh-e Rajab 13–22] and reads it, may he be generous and truthful toward the gods and the lords and his own soul, as I have been, so that this osseous body of his may have fame and prosperity, and that osseous soul of his may have blessedness. . . . He who does well and practices good deeds, may his osseous soul . . . have blessedness like I, Kirdir had.

Moreover we find in the Avesta, in the Vendidad 5.61–62, a very similar thought:

If these Mazdayasnians . . . over this departed one, then neither will be a follower of order [while] alive, nor will he partake of the Best Being [when] dead.

This doctrine is optimistic inasmuch as belief in another life is clearly affirmed, but one can obtain it only if one respects Asha (order) established by gods and the power of kings; moreover, one must respect Truth, as well, by rejecting Lie.

Journey of the soul after death. After death, the undying soul *(ruwān)* lies close to the body for three days and nights, during which a ritual must be accomplished and all that is terribly polluting must be kept away from the corpse. Then the soul undertakes its journey to the world beyond and follows the right path that leads to paradise. It is helped by its *daēnā*, the immortal soul that comes to meet it in the shape of a seductive maiden if the man was just, but in the shape of a hideous old woman, if the man was destined to damnation *(druwand)*. The right way, mentioned by Darius the Great (died 486 BCE) as well as in the Gathas of Zarathustra (Yasna 33), leads to the Bridge of the Piler, which is guarded by two dogs accompanying the *daēnā*. The bridge is, in all Mazdean traditions, the critical point of access to paradise. Before the bridge is assembled the court of the gods, composed of Ahura Mazda, Vohu Manah, Vaiiu, Mithra, Sraosha, and Rasnu, weigh the merits of the departed soul on golden scales and decide whether to grant it the right to cross the bridge. The bridge becomes larger for the just, but as narrow and as sharp as a sword blade for the damned, who cannot cross it and fall irretrievably into hell.

Extraterrestrial journeys. Iranians sought to know what was after death. They could undertake "shamanistic" practices, as attested in the Book of Arda Viraz (9th century CE) and in the description of a vision of the world beyond narrated by the magus Kirdir (perhaps end of the 3rd century CE), who relates in his rock inscriptions how he asked the gods whom he worshiped and honored for a vision of paradise. Viraz was a man chosen for his great piety and justice, and he was given a narcotic drink in order to induce in him a state of apparent death. During the time he was "dead," he made an extraterrestrial journey (all of this reminds us of rituals and journeys associated with shamans in Tibet and Bhutan). When he was once again conscious, Arda Viraz dictated all that he had seen to a scribe, namely, all the different punishments that the damned had to suffer. Most of these suited the crime. Thus, sexual sins were punished by tortures applied to the genitals. The writer's imagination abounds with respect to such scabrous tortures. By contrast, paradise is little described in the Pahlavi sources. It is a place where one meets with Ohrmazd and the other gods, full of perfumes and of material delights. There is also a kind of purgatory, an intermediate place *(hammistagān)* for humans whose sins weigh as much as good deeds.

Last things. The Iranians believed in the resurrection of the dead. Therefore, in eastern Iran (Bactria, Sogdiana) it was recommended that bones be kept carefully after the flesh was gone and collected in bone containers that often were decorated with religious scenes. According to the teaching of Zadspram, it would be no more difficult for Ohrmazd to revive the bodies of the deceased than it had been for him to create them in the beginning. The events at the end of time will be closely parallel to those of the original creation: the end will be a time of renovation *(frašgird),* with the arrival of the savior; the destruction of the small and great demons, including Ahriman, the adversary of Ohrmazd (Ahura Mazda) and his creation; celestial cataclysms; the final struggle against the Lie; and the reconstitution of the body to an enduring youth.

BIBL.: Philippe Gignoux, "'Corps osseux et âme osseuse': Essai sur le chamanisme dans l'Iran ancien," *Journal asiatique* 267 (1979): 41–79. Idem, *Le livre d'Ardā Virāz* (Paris, 1984). J. Kellens, "Yima and Death," in *Essays on Zarathustra and Zoroastrianism* (trans. and ed. P. O. Skjaervø; Costa Mesa, Calif.: Mazda, 2000), 95–98. P. O. Skjaervø, "Thematic and Linguistic Parallels in the Achemenian and Sassanian Inscriptions," in *Papers in Honour of Professor Mary Boyce* (ed. Jacques Duchesne-Guillemin and Pierre Lecoq; Leiden, 1985), 593–603.   P.G.

Greece

Few topics are as difficult to summarize as a culture's attitudes toward death and the afterlife. For even within a single individual, much less an entire culture, outlooks on these topics tend to vacillate. As grief over a friend's death shifts to resignation, as fear concerning one's own end shifts to hopes for postmortem bliss and back again, so shift the ways that death and the afterlife are pictured. This problem is compounded in the case of ancient Greece because, to build any picture at all, we

Odysseus (center) meets the ghost of Elpenor in the underworld; to the right is Hermes. At Odysseus's feet are slain rams. Attic red-figure *pelike* (pitcher) by the Lykaon Painter, 450–440 BCE. Museum of Fine Arts, Boston. *Reproduced with permission.* © 2002 *Museum of Fine Arts, Boston. All rights reserved*

must supplement the rather meager evidence we derive from archeological excavations, grave inscriptions, and textual descriptions of rituals with the richer—but more freely imaginative—descriptions found in literary texts. Of necessity, the survey that follows imposes an artificial tidiness on data that vary a great deal.

"Life" in the land of the dead. In earliest times, the Greeks apparently believed that everyone got the same deal after death. The disembodied soul descended into the underworld, the land of the dead that was ruled by Hades and his queen, Persephone (the underworld itself is sometimes called the "house of Hades" or simply "Hades" as well). There, the souls existed in a state that was not unpleasant but not particularly enjoyable; literary portrayals, such as that in *Odyssey* 11, suggest that the underworld was dank and dark and that there was little to do to pass the time. The souls were imagined to look like their former bodies; thus Odysseus recognizes his former comrades when he sees them in Hades. They also retain the desires and grudges they held while alive.

GREECE

Despite these resemblances, the souls lack the ability to communicate with the living; until they drink ram's blood that Odysseus pours out for them, they can only squeak like bats. Physical contact is impossible because they have no substance, as Odysseus learns when he tries to hug his mother.

A few individuals do suffer terrible punishments in Hades, although it is not clear from our texts whether they are truly dead or have been transported there while still alive: Tantalus endures eternal thirst and hunger, for example, and Sisyphus repeatedly pushes a boulder uphill. But these mythological sufferers are punished for heinous trespasses against the gods; there is no trace of the idea that the average person would be either punished or rewarded for deeds committed while alive. Similarly, we hear about a few mythic figures who escape death altogether due to their special relationships with the gods. Menelaus, Helen's husband and therefore Zeus's son-in-law, will be carried off to the paradisiacal Elysian Fields at the end of his life, for example (*Odyssey* 4.561–69).

In the late archaic period, however, the expectation of postmortem punishments and rewards for everyone begins to be expressed; it becomes commonplace by the classical period. In most cases, one's lot is said to depend on how one behaved while alive. Cephalus, an old man participating in the dialogue recorded in Plato's *Republic,* says, "When a man realizes that he is going to die . . . his soul begins to be tortured by the tales that are told of the world below, and how the people who have done wrong here must pay the penalty there" (*Republic* 1.330d–e). The *Republic* ends with a myth that makes this point at length: the souls of the wicked are punished for one thousand years, and the souls of the just dwell in bliss for the same length of time. Although the myth, which was invented by Plato, cannot be taken to represent common belief in all of its details, its broader message represents the contemporary opinion that things will be evened up for good and bad alike after death.

Preparing for the afterlife. Once postmortem fate is understood to be determined by one's actions while alive, preparation for death should require nothing more than good behavior. This is actually a tall order, however: few people lead lives of perfect virtue, and most are therefore left, like Cephalus, worrying about what awaits them. Perhaps because of this, we also find, beginning in the late archaic period, the idea that one can erase the effects of bad behavior and guarantee postmortem bliss by being initiated into one or more of the mysteries cults while still alive (see Mysteries). Initiates could expect to spend eternity in a sunlit meadow or other pleasant place, eating, drinking, and dancing. Those who were not initiated into the mysteries, however stellar their conduct had been, were believed to wallow in mire forever.

The flaw in this system, as its critics pointed out, was that once initiated, individuals could behave however they liked without fear of repercussion. "It would be absurd," said Diogenes the Cynic, "if Agesilaus and Epaminondas [two Spartan generals known for nobility of character] end up in the mire after death, while worthless people, simply because they have been initiated into the mysteries, dwell on the Islands of the Blest" (Diogenes Laertius 6.39). Although a few unusual mystery cults may have required initiates to follow certain rules of ritualized purity for the rest of their lives (e.g., vegetarianism), there seems to have been no expectation that initiates would adhere to a moral or ethical code.

A variation on these themes focused on the idea that all humanity was doomed to postmortem punishment because of its connection to the death of Persephone's son, the god Dionysus. Myth said that Dionysus had been murdered and consumed by violent gods called Titans; after Zeus destroyed the Titans, humanity grew out of their remains. Persephone thereafter held each human liable for the loss of her son. Unless one had been initiated into mysteries sponsored by the (subsequently resurrected) Dionysus, one would suffer at her hands in the underworld. These Dionysiac mysteries are particularly interesting because, among other things, they bestowed knowledge of underworld geography: initiates were taught which path to follow and which to avoid once they went below, which infernal bodies of water were safe to drink from and which would inflict forgetfulness. Forgetfulness was dangerous because the initiates had to remember to declare that "Dionysus had released them" through initiation when they appeared before Persephone. Reminders of exactly what one should say to Persephone and other underworld gods, as well as of which paths and waters to take and which to avoid, were engraved on tiny gold tablets that were buried with initiates.

Reincarnation also shows up in a few documents connected with Dionysiac mysteries and in some philosophical systems influenced by Pythagoras. The soul still was expected to win rewards or suffer punishments in the afterlife, but then would be sent into a new bodily life. Souls that managed to conduct themselves without blemish for several cycles might win release from incarnation altogether and enter into a permanent state of happiness in the underworld.

I have described the eschatological aspects of mystery cults in some detail for two reasons: they caught the imagination of ancient authors and thus are alluded to frequently in some of our best-known Greek and Roman literary sources; and they represent a novel way of thinking about the afterlife that subsequently influenced many religious and philosophical systems in later antiquity, including Christianity. But it must be stressed that, for whatever reason (lack of money? lack of opportunity? lack of faith in their benefits?), most ancient Greeks were not initiated into mysteries. The standard expectation for the afterlife was probably, at best, a

487

static and rather dull existence and, at worst, one of retribution for earthly deeds.

Funerary rituals. It was the obligation of surviving kin, especially children, to ensure that the dead received proper funerary rites; if they did not, they were not considered "fully dead" and their souls would be condemned to wander restlessly between worlds. What constituted proper rites varied from place to place and time to time, but at a minimum, honorable disposal of the corpse by burial or cremation was required, lest it become the food of birds, dogs, and insects. If a body were lost at sea or was otherwise irretrievable, rites might be performed for it *in absentia* and a cenotaph erected.

Ideally, women from the family of the deceased would wash and dress the body as soon as possible after death. A day of mourning would follow; the informal mourning of family members might be supplemented with that of hired mourners. Gifts would be given to the deceased; these included small objects such as he or she would have used in life (mirrors and cosmetic cases for women, weapons and athletic equipment for men, toys for children). The body was buried or cremated on the third day (counting inclusively). Libations of honey, milk, wine, water, and/or oil were then poured into the grave where the body or ashes had been buried. Libations were repeated periodically, usually for at least a year. Survivors might also cut their hair and lay it on the grave as a sign of their grief; a survivor who was absent at the time of the funeral could dedicate his or her hair at a later date. A grave marker was set up and could be decorated with ribbons and myrtle branches. Other rituals might also be performed, depending on the desires of the deceased and his or her family. We assume, for example, that the small gold tablets reminding the deceased what to say to Persephone were placed on corpses by surviving family members.

Ghosts. Although any soul could become a ghost—that is, revisit the land of the living—those souls who did not receive proper funerary rites or those who had died too early or under unhappy circumstances were particularly liable to return, wreaking vengeance on those whom they blamed for their misfortunes or causing problems for those whom they envied. Even whole groups of people might suffer because a soul was unhappy; the Delphic Oracle sometimes told residents of plague-ridden cities that they would find relief in locating and properly burying the remains of a local individual. Some cities sponsored rituals in honor of girls who had died before marriage in order to assuage the anger and envy of their ghosts; had they not, the girls' ghosts might return and drive living maidens to commit suicide. There were means of averting ghosts as well; wreaths of a thorny plant called *rhamnos* (probably our buckthorn) could be hung on doors and windows, for example, in order to prevent their entering a house. In some parts of Greece, during annual festivals, such as the Anthesteria, ghosts were invited back into the world

of the living and treated well; the hope seems to have been that, once contented, they would stay peacefully within Hades the rest of the year. Even then, precautions such as buckthorn wreaths were employed to ensure that the ghosts did not take too many liberties. A special libation and ritual pronouncement at the end of the festival sent them back into Hades.

Ghosts could be useful. Ritual specialists knew how to create "curse tablets" (small lead tablets engraved with words) that compelled ghosts to rise from the underworld and do their bidding (see Prayers, Hymns, Curses, and Incantations). Typically, the specialist commanded the ghost to attack or hinder someone on behalf of a client who had paid him to create the tablet; thus, a tablet might tell the ghost to impose insomnia on the woman whom the client loved until she capitulated to his demands. This was viewed as distressing not only for the ghost's victim but for the ghost itself, which preferred to rest peacefully in the underworld. One special type of ghost—the soul of a dead hero—falls somewhere between the categories of ordinary dead souls and the gods. Heroic souls were expected to help with all sorts of problems, from enabling women to conceive, to helping their native cities win battles, to giving prophetic advice.

BIBL.: R. Garland, *The Greek Way of Death* (Ithaca: Cornell University Press, 1985). S. I. Johnston, *Restless Dead: Encounters between the Living and the Dead in Ancient Greece* (Berkeley: University of California Press, 1999). D. C. Kurtz and J. Boardman, *Greek Burial Customs* (Ithaca: Cornell University Press, 1968).   S.I.J.

Etruria

The innumerable tombs that riddle the landscape of Etruria are our greatest source of knowledge concerning Etruscan culture as a whole; more specifically, they furnish us with evidence of Etruscan reactions to, and conceptions of, death. However, it must be stressed that only the elite in Etruscan society had access to formal, and thus archeologically visible, burial, so only an elite world is available for reconstruction. The death of an individual had implications not only for the deceased and his or her relatives, but for the whole community, and these two strands are equally prominent in Etruscan funerary remains.

Information on the funerary rites of Etruria is archeological rather than textual. The elaborate "houses of the dead" that the Etruscans of the 7th century BCE built in monumental mounds, or in the cliff faces of Etruria, testify to the care and wealth that was invested in the treatment of the dead. The discovery of chariots and remains of food in the tombs suggests that elaborate rites (including racing and feasting) accompanied the act of mourning and that the deposition of the corpse was supplemented by complex sets of grave goods. This scenario is corroborated by the recent discovery in the Tolfa region of evidence for a temporary, tentlike structure outside the mound, where various activities associated with the funerals may have taken place.

The importance of the relationship between the living and the dead is emphasized by the visibility of the monumental cemeteries that formed sacred halos around settlements, like those of Cerveteri or Veii. Roads leading into and out of Etruscan cities of the living passed through the impressive cities of the dead. The proximity of the dead was thus visibly emphasized in Etruscan culture, while at the same time, the dead were isolated by the physical separation of gorges and valleys.

The importance of ancestor cults and worship of the dead is suggested by the wealth and prestige of family tombs, often used over several generations. In addition, platforms on or at the side of the tombs were constructed for commemorative rites. Altars for such sacrifices survive inside several tombs at Cerveteri and on the façades of numerous tombs at Castel d'Asso and Norchia. The regular commemoration of the dead by the living underlines the significance of maintaining material and ideological links with the dead.

The rites outlined in a list of festivals and sacrifices on the Capua Tile show that underworld deities, such as Calu and Lethams, were worshiped in the cemeteries alongside ancestors. Wall paintings and carved reliefs on cinerary urns provide evidence for other deities associated with death. Turms, the messenger-god of the Etruscans, is often shown carrying or leading the deceased to the next world. Charu (possibly an adaptation of the Greek Charon) was the guardian of the world of the dead. He first appears in the late 6th century and has a terrifying aspect: he is a hybrid figure with animal ears and pointed teeth. He wears boots and a short tunic; he carries a hammer, a key, or a sword, all devices for guarding and allowing access to the underworld. Similar to Charu is the bearded demon Tuchulcha, whose name appears only once, beside a painted evocation. Like Charu, he has ass's ears, but his skin is blue-green, his nose is beaklike, he has wings, and he grasps a pair of serpents. Charu is sometimes accompanied by Vanth, a winged female figure who wears clothes similar to his, although she carries a burning torch. As another messenger of the dead, she is also shown escorting or carrying souls to the next life. Modern studies have suggested the importance of seeing these deities in terms of boundaries and liminality: both in their hybrid forms and in their functions as gatekeeper or messenger, these deities control passage between the worlds of the living and the dead.

Representations of the world of the dead change dramatically over time, and the interpretation of the colorful figured frescoes that Etruscans painted in their tombs has been controversial. It has been suggested that they represent scenes from the life of the deceased, the funeral itself, or the life beyond. Some, or even all, of these interpretations were no doubt correct at different times and in different places in Etruria. At the very least, that the frescoes are in graves gives them an important bearing on Etruscan eschatology.

Tarquinia was the main center of tomb painting (although the earliest examples are from Veii and Cerveteri), and the art flourished from the late 7th to the 5th centuries BCE. The paintings from the late 6th to the mid-5th centuries contain a range of scenes, including racing, hunting, fishing, and swimming. A common motif in the paintings is the representation of a door on the far wall of the tomb, suggesting the world in which the dead reside. However, most common are scenes of elaborate banquets, where couples feast reclining on benches, to the accompaniment of music, dancers, and jugglers. Alternatively, figures dance to double flutes, in a natural landscape, holding cups, wreaths, and shawls. Similar themes are represented on the archaic reliefs on the sandstone cinerary urns of Chiusi and on tomb markers from the Arno Valley, such as the stelae of Londa.

From the end of the 5th century, the character of the paintings changes. Although banqueting scenes continue, they are much less frequent. Gruesome events and monsters are represented, or somber painted ceremonial wreaths decorate the walls. Vanth and Charu stand on either side of the painted doors, ominously guarding the underworld. Sarcophagi from this period show scenes of the deceased parting from the living members of the community, accompanied by Vanth. It has been suggested—though this is very much speculation—that the sadness and solemnity of the later paintings were due to the influence of Orphic and Pythagorean ideas. Even more speculatively, this atmosphere of gloom, some have argued, may reflect uncertainty for the future of Etruria in the face of Roman expansion.

BIBL.: D. Briquel, "Regards étrusques sur l'au-delà," in *La mort, les morts, l'au-delà dans le monde romain* (ed. F. Hinard; Caen, 1987), 263–77. V. Izzet, "Engraving the Boundaries: Exploring Space and Surface in Etruscan Funerary Architecture," in *Approaches to the Study of Ritual: Italy and the Ancient Mediterranean* (ed. J. B. Wilkins; London: Accordia Research Centre Specialist Studies, 1996), 55–72. M. Torelli, "Pittura funeraria e celebrazione della morte: Il caso della Tomba dell' Orco," in *Tarquinia* (ed. M. Bonghi Jovino and C. C. Trere; [Milan]: Edizioni ET, 1987). C. C. Van Essen, *Did Orphic Influence on Etruscan Painting Exist?* (Studies in Etruscan Painting 1; Amsterdam, 1927). V.E.I.

Rome

We all die alone, but death, for the Romans, was a communal event. Roman society was built around the family, and Roman death ritual, activated and mediated by the family, perpetuated the foundations of the *res publica* by integrating the newly dead individual into the collectivity of ancestors, the *maiores* (greaters), whose ways *(mos maiorum)* provided the paradigm for

489

On a marble relief (1st century CE) from the tomb of the Haterii, the deceased lies on a funerary couch in a house, attended by mourners. *Alinari/Art Resource, New York*

Roman life. The proper observance of religion was fundamental to this process, but the precise religious function of many rites remains uncertain. We do not generally have the tools to bridge the gap between behavior and belief, and in the matter of Roman funerary customs, our knowledge of the basic architecture is rudimentary. At the most basic level, death brought pollution into the community. It was therefore in the public interest that religion be served and that corpses be duly buried (*Digest* 11.7.43).

Any reconstruction of Roman funerary practices must draw upon disparate sources and will therefore represent a synthetic ideal rather than any precise historical reality. At all periods there were Romans who did not conform: the patrician Cornelii, for example, inhumed their dead when most others preferred cremation (Cicero, *De legibus* 2.56–57). As the empire expanded and the ethnic identification "Roman" came to embrace increasingly diverse populations, the variety of death customs grew, but Roman mortuary practices, like those of the central Italian culture from which they developed, were characterized from the outset by diversity.

Burial and funeral rites. When a person died, his or her family and household became *funestus* or *funestatus* (polluted by death) and remained so until the completion of the funerary rites. Just before or immediately after death, the body was placed on the ground outside the house *(depositio).* Ideally a family member caught the last breath. The eyes were closed, and the deceased was called upon by name *(conclamatio),* a procedure that was continued periodically up to the cremation. The corpse was washed in warm water, perfumed (sometimes by a professional *pollinctor*), clothed in

finery, and then laid out for viewing in a public area of the house *(collocatio),* with feet pointing toward the door, on a high funerary bed with two mattresses surrounded by incense burners *(acerrae)* and torches. Hired mourning women *(praeficae)* chanted a distinctive lament *(nenia)* to the accompaniment of flutes and horns; family members covered their hair with ashes and donned a dark mourning gown *(toga pulla* or *atra);* a cypress branch outside the house door signaled the presence of a corpse inside. The body lay in state for up to seven days, during which time family members fasted or ate only meagerly.

On the eighth day following death, if not sooner (burial was not permitted on public holidays; Columella, *On Agriculture* 2.21.4), the body was carried out *(exferre)* by four to eight pallbearers, and the heir, as *everriator* (sweeper out), cleaned the house with a special kind of broom (Festus 68 L). Mourners followed the cortege (hence the proper term for this phase is *exsequiae* [following]) to the city gates or the pyre. Before the body was laid on the pyre—a rectangular pile of wood surrounded by cypress branches to mask the smell—a fingertip was cut off *(os resectum)* for subsequent interment (Cicero, *On Laws* 2.55, 57); a coin was sometimes placed in the mouth to pay the ferryman Charon (Juvenal 3.267); and the eyes were opened. Those in attendance ate a meal known as *silicernium* (also a type of sausage; Festus 377 L) at the gravesite and refrained from bathing on that day (Petronius 42.1). Upon returning to the community, mourners underwent a cleansing rite known as *suffitio* (fumigation), whereby they were sprinkled with water by a laurel and walked over fire (Paulus excerptor Festi

A Roman funeral procession depicted on a sarcophagus from Amiternum, 1st century BCE. National Museum of the Abruzzo at Aquilieia. *Alinari/Art Resource, New York*

3 L). On the following day, with the pyre extinguished, family members gathered the ashes and bones *(cineres),* wet them with wine and milk (to nourish the dead; Pseudo-Tibullus 3.2.16–20), deposited them in a tomb or grave, and sacrificed a sow *(porca praesentanea)* to consecrate the site (Veranius Flaccus, *Iura* 7).

Then followed holidays of rest and mourning known as *feriae denicales* (from *de nece* [from the death], according to Cicero, *On Laws* 2.55), which came to an end on the ninth day with a sacrifice of wethers to the Lar (in origin probably the spirit of a deified ancestor) and a final funerary banquet *(cena novendialis).* Unlike the somber *silicernium,* the *cena novendialis* was a convivial affair (Petronius 65–66), at which the diners, now dressed in white, ate traditional foods (eggs, vegetables, beans, lentils, and salt) and drank wine, sometimes to excess.

Roman funerary ritual was thus divided into two balanced nine-day units *(nundinae),* with the central events—the deposition of the body and the consecration of the grave—forming the fulcrum between them. The period was characterized by reciprocal inversions, which both grouped the grieving family and the newly dead together, apart from normal life, and distinguished them from each other.

The first stage of the burial began with the laying of the deceased on the ground and the washing of the corpse and ended with family members washing their hands and consigning the remains to the soil—a return to life-giving mother earth (e.g., Cicero, *On Laws* 2.56). For those returning from a funeral, the employment of the evergreen laurel in the ritual sprinkling of the *suffitio* signified a return to the vitality of the *res publica* (cf. Paulus excerptor Festi 104 L), just as the cypress, the plant that, once severed, never grew again, signaled the irrevocable separation of the deceased from life. A puri-

fying passage over fire effected the integration of the participants into the communities in which they belonged.

The second *nundinae* was framed by sacrifice and communal meals. The passages they marked—the reintegration of the family into public life and the translation of the dead to the community of deified ancestors—were signaled by symbolic exchanges: for the living, of corruption for purity at the meals (dark clothing for white; sausage, a mixed confection, for unadulterated foodstuffs); for the dead, of vitality for sterility in the sacrifices (a sow to Ceres, a fertile creature offered to a natural agent of generation, for a gelded ram to the Lar, a sterile and altered offering to a transformed ancestor).

Until 353 CE, when the emperor Julian issued an edict forbidding funeral processions by day (because dead bodies passing the open doors of temples polluted them; *Epistle* 77), funerals were normally conducted by daylight, except those of the poor and those who died young ("unripe" [*funera acerba*]), which were traditionally carried out at night. In both cases, the cortege was preceded by torches, which set the procession apart from daily life.

Graves, mourning, and disposal of the dead. A Roman grave was not a grave until earth had covered the corpse and the heir had sacrificed the sow to Ceres (Cicero, *On Laws* 2.57). Once consecrated, a grave became a *locus religiosus* protected by the pontiffs, who maintained its sanctity by ensuring regular observances at the site. Cultivating the dead required ownership of the land, since the pontiffs had ruled that "a public place could not be bound by private religious rites" (Cicero, *On Laws* 2.58). Roman graves in the provinces, although respected as such, were not legally *loca religiosa,* because the soil in which they lay belonged to the emperor or to the Roman people (Gaius, *Institutes* 2.7).

During the empire those without the means to institute an heir joined funerary societies *(collegia funeraticia)* in order to secure proper burial and commemoration.

A law of the Twelve Tables (ca. 450 BCE) prohibiting burial within city walls (Cicero, *On Laws* 2.58) remained in effect, with rare exceptions, throughout antiquity. Since Roman funerary ritual required attendance at the gravesite, suburban cemeteries and tomb-lined streets naturally grew up outside city gates. In rural areas the sanctity of tombs led to their use as boundary markers to protect the borders of private properties *(Corpus Agrimensorum Romanorum* 220–22, 252.31–32 Campbell).

Of the three principal ways that Romans disposed of corpses—inhumation, cremation, and (occasionally) embalming (Lucretius 3.890–93)—the first was believed to be the oldest (Cicero, *On Laws* 2.56; Pliny, *Natural History* 7.187), but the second was distinctly "the Roman custom" (Tacitus, *Annal* 6.16.2) until around 150 CE, when inhumation began to predominate. Religious explanations for this momentous change, "the biggest single event in ancient burial" (Morris 1992: 31), have often been sought and have never been found.

The formal period of mourning *(luctus)* for a dead family member ended for men with the *cena novendialis.* For women the period was extended variously according to the age or relationship of the mourner to the deceased, but it could be curtailed for a variety of personal, familial, and civic reasons (Festus 144 L). When in mourning men and women abstained from dinner parties, jewelry and other adornments, and purple and white clothing (*Pauli Sententiae* 1.21.2–14).

Cult of the dead. The spirits of deceased ancestors were considered divine (Cicero, *On Laws* 2.22, 55). Originally these *di manes* were perceived as an undifferentiated collective entity, but by the middle of the 1st century BCE the concept of personal *manes* had begun to emerge in Roman literature (Cicero, Livy, Vergil) and, increasingly, in epitaphs dedicated "to the divine spirits [*D.M. = Dis Manibus*]" of individuals.

The dead were cultivated with banquets and other offerings at gravesites, notably red flowers (symbolic of lifeblood) on the festival days of roses (Rosalia, *dies rosationis*) and violets (Violatio, *dies violares*) in May and June and during the official festival for deceased family members *(parentes),* the nine-day Parentalia on February 13–21, the last day of which, Feralia (Varro, *On the Latin Language* 6.13), was celebrated with public ceremonies (Ovid, *Fasti* 2.533–70). Whereas these *dies parentales* were occasions for communal daytime remembrance of kindly ancestors at the tomb, the other public festival of the dead, the Lemuria on May 9, 11, and 13 (all ill-omened days [*dies nefasti*]), called for the *paterfamilias* alone at night to rid the household of ghosts *(lemures)* and malevolent spirits of the dead *(larvae)* with a series of apotropaic rituals involving ninefold repetition of ritual formulas, casting of beans (imbued with life, according to Orphic/Pythagorean belief), washing with spring water, and clashing of bronze (Ovid, *Fasti* 5.419–93).

The days of both festivals were *dies religiosi,* during which magistrates doffed their insignia, temples were closed, and no weddings took place. In this respect and others (banquet/sacrifice for the dead, rites of purification, communal meals at tombs, sequences of nine), the community festivals of the dead reflected private funerary rites for individuals, of which they formed recurring annual counterparts.

Belief in an afterlife. Belief in an afterlife of some sort is implicit in the Roman cult of the dead, which presumed that the souls of the deceased wanted offerings of food and other amenities (wine, oil, perfume, flowers), and in the concept of the *di manes.* The festivals of the Parentalia and Lemuria suggest that the duly buried were imagined as residing underground, at the sites of their tombs, whereas restless ghosts might roam abroad, haunting homes. That the former were thought to be sentient may be inferred from such common epitaphic prayers as the formulaic *s.t.t.l. = sit tibi terra levis* (may the earth be light for you) and from the custom of inserting pipes into graves to receive libations.

Most of our literary evidence, however, dates from no earlier than the 1st century BCE, by which time Epicurean and Stoic teaching had infused a strain of skepticism about immortality into Roman thought. Fully developed conceptions of a topographically defined underworld, such as we find overlaid on a Pythagorean view of the transmigration of souls in Vergil's *Aeneid* 6, are alien to native Roman belief and illustrate the heady blend of Greek mythological literary convention and philosophical doctrine that infiltrated Roman culture during the 1st century BCE. By the 1st century CE, the influence of Eastern mystery religions offering personal salvation had begun to assert itself more forcefully. Long before the ultimate triumph of the most subversive of these, the range of conceptions of the afterlife attested by so-called Roman sources had grown so diverse that one cannot identify any single idea as predominant. In general, the increasingly turbulent ideological winds swirling around the core Roman beliefs about death carried the gratifying prospect that the soul of the individual survived and that, for the good or the saved, the world beyond was a happier, more godlike place than that on earth.

BIBL.: "Aspetti dell'ideologia funeraria nel mondo romano," *Annali del'Istituto Universitario Orientale di Napoli, sezione di archeologia e storia antica* 6 (1984). Franz Cumont, *Lux Perpetua* (Paris, 1949). Ian Morris, *Death-Ritual and Social Structure in Classical Antiquity* (Cambridge, 1992). J. M. C. Toynbee, *Death and Burial in the Roman World* (London, 1971). Fernand de Visscher, *Le droit des tombeaux romains* (Milan, 1963). J.B.

Christianity

Christian faith began with the conviction that Jesus of Nazareth, the crucified Galilean prophet, had been raised from the dead and reigned invisibly as Lord among his disciples. But for early Christians, the resurrection of Jesus was not an isolated wonder so much as the beginning of a victory over death that would eventually engulf all believers; in Paul's words, the risen Jesus was "the first fruits of those who have fallen asleep" (1 Cor. 15.20), and at his glorious second coming all the faithful, living and dead, would be "caught up" to meet him and live with him forever (1 Thess. 4.17).

This hope for resurrection and eternal life remained a defining feature of early Christian faith. The 2nd-century apologist Athenagoras pointed to this hope in arguing that those who expected that their bodies would rise for judgment and retribution could hardly be guilty of the moral outrages with which popular prejudice taxed them (*Embassy* 36), and Tertullian, in the first decades of the 3rd century CE, observed simply, "The Christian's confidence is bound up with the resurrection of the dead. That makes us believers" (*On the Resurrection of the Dead* 1). In the *Odes of Solomon*, ecstatic Syriac hymns from the early 2nd century, eternal life and incorruption are spoken of as gifts already bestowed on the singer and his hearers (11.11–12; 15.8–10). Ignatius of Antioch, coming probably from the same religious context, sees in the gospel of Jesus's death and resurrection "the realization of incorruptibility" (*Philadelphians* 9.2) and speaks of the community's eucharistic bread and wine as "the medicine of immortality" (*Ephesians* 20.2).

Early critics fastened onto this hope for resurrection as one of the most puzzling and repellent of all Christian beliefs. It raised a host of questions that Christian apologists needed to answer: how was resurrection possible, given our understanding of the natural laws of birth and decay? what would a risen body look like? what would become of the particles of matter shared by more than one human body—in the case, for instance, of a person who has eaten an animal which has itself eaten part of another human? More significant, perhaps, was the question of the appropriateness of resurrection. Origen quotes the critique of the 2nd-century Platonist Celsus: "God cannot do what is shameful, nor does he desire what is contrary to nature. . . . For the soul he might be able to provide an everlasting life. . . . As for the flesh, which is full of things which it is not even nice to mention, God would neither desire nor be able to make it everlasting contrary to reason" (*Against Celsus* 5.14).

The early Christian apologetic tradition developed a variety of arguments for the possibility of bodily resurrection, mainly appealing to the creative power of God, already manifest in our bodily existence, and pointing to the importance of this hope in motivating upright moral behavior. Second-century gnostic Christian writers, on the other hand, took a different position, interpreting resurrection in interior, spiritual terms as a transformation that begins in this life in an enlightened, nonmaterial understanding of revelation and that will be fulfilled in our release from the material body and the "divisions and fetters" of our present, sense-bound mode of knowing (*Epistle to Rheginos* 47.6–49.16). Origen, writing in the 230s and 240s, attempted to bridge the gulf between these two approaches by developing a conception of a future "spiritual body" (cf. 1 Cor. 15.44) identical with the present material one in its shape and intelligible form, but free from all the corruptibility and limitations of matter (*On First Principles* 2.10.1–3; 3.6). Since only God is completely incorporeal, in Origen's view, every created intellect must have a finite, spatial body of some kind to serve as its "vehicle" of activity, even if that body is not material in our ordinary sense (quoted by Methodius, *On the Resurrection* 3.17). The goal of the human transformation begun by God in Christ, for Origen and his later admirers, such as the 4th-century Gregory of Nyssa, is the purging of all the body's corruptible qualities linked with the present conditions of matter and its reemergence in the physical splendor and moral beauty of the risen Christ (*On First Principles* 2.10.8; see Gregory of Nyssa, *On the Soul and Resurrection* in *Patrologia graeca* 46.108A2–8, 156A6–10; *On the Dead* in *Gregorii Nysseni Opera* [ed. Jaeger] 9.62.18–63.3).

Early Christian writers were less clear about the condition and place of the dead in the interim between the death of individuals and the final, cosmic catastrophe that was expected to usher in the resurrection and judgment of all humanity. Although some were clearly hesitant to adopt the widespread Greek philosophical notion of an immortal soul, set free from its bodily fetters at death (see discussion in Origen, *Dialogue with Heracleides* 24–28), Christian writers from the 2nd century on tended to accept the idea as a way of assuring the identity of the present human person with his or her future, risen state. Second-century writers often stressed that the human soul is not naturally immortal, but will receive continuing life as a participant in God's immortality, through the gift of the Holy Spirit (so Tatian, *Oration to the Greeks* 7, 13; Athenagoras, *Embassy* 4, 31; Irenaeus, *Against the Heresies* 2.34.2–3; 5.6.1; 5.7.2). Virtually all early Christian writers agreed in rejecting the transmigration of souls into other forms of life, mainly because it seemed to rule out lasting personal responsibility for one's moral actions (so Tertullian, *Apology* 48; Gregory of Nyssa, *On the Soul and Resurrection* in *Patrologia graeca* 46.103B–121A), although Origen and some of his later followers considered it at least possible that souls might undergo a new bodily birth in later worlds, on their way toward permanent stability in the knowledge and love of God (Origen,

Jesus raising Lazarus from the dead. Fresco in the Catacomb of the Giordani, Rome, late 3rd century. *Scala/Art Resource, New York*

Commentariorum series in Matthaeum 96; *On First Principles* 2.3.1–2; Evagrius, *Kephalaia gnostica* 2.85).

There was less agreement about how to imagine the present existence of disembodied souls after death. Many authors continued to conceive of the soul's afterlife in the muted tones of the biblical Sheol or the Greek Hades, rather than as the vibrantly active life of an unfettered mind: a shadowy existence in the "lower parts of the earth" (Tertullian, *On the Soul* 55–58), in subterranean "storehouses of souls" (Ambrose, *De bono mortis* 10.45–48), or even a "sleep" that would last until the resurrection of the whole person at the end of history (Aphrahat, *Demonstrationes* 8.19–22; Ephrem, *Hymns on Paradise* 8.4–6; *Carmina Nisibena* 47.6; Hilary of Poitiers, *In Matthaeum* 27.4). Yet most Christian writers, inspired particularly by Jesus's story of the rich man and Lazarus, took it as biblical teaching that, even before the resurrection, the dead would experience different kinds of treatment in the underworld, corresponding to their behavior in life (e.g., Tertullian, *On the Soul* 7, 56). So Justin asserts that "the souls of the pious remain in a better place, while those of the unjust and wicked are in a worse, waiting for the time of judgment" (*Dialogue with Trypho* 5). Clement of Alexandria, at the end of the 2nd century, believed that those who have become "true gnostics," learning the inner meaning of their faith and freeing themselves from passion during this life, would be admitted directly after death, as souls, into the kingdom of God (*Stromateis* 6.13–14). And Cyprian of Carthage, in the middle of the 3rd century, echoed the widespread conviction that Christians who had lived heroically in the face of persecution, especially those who died as martyrs, could look forward to immediate blessedness (*Ad Fortunatum* 12–13; *Epistle* 31.3; 58.3).

In light of their hope in resurrection and in the reward of a virtuous life, many early Christian writers—especially those with a classical literary training—insisted that death was not something to be dreaded: it was a "liberation for the Lord" (Clement of Alexandria, *Stromateis* 4.11.80.1), a release from a life burdened with care and an entry into "the life that is above" (Gregory of Nazianzus, *Oration* 18.42; Ambrose, *De bono mortis* 4.15). The only death really worth fearing is the "death of sin," leading to the eternal death of punishment (Ambrose, *De excessu fratris* 2.35–38). So Christian "philosophers," who shaped their lives as "preparation for death," in Socratic fashion, by meditation and ascetical practice, would not be surprised by death, but would welcome it joyously as the gateway to union with Christ (Clement of Alexandria, *Stromateis* 2.20.109.1; Athanasius, *Life of Antony* 92; Gregory of Nyssa, *Life of Macrina* 23–25; Gregory of Nazianzus, *Oration* 8.21–22).

In the last decades of the 4th century, however, the Christian world seems to have developed a new sense of insecurity and crisis, a dramatic foreboding of the end of history. Along with this apocalyptic mood, many writers showed a new sense of the terrors of dying and a new interest in speculating about the details of what awaited the soul between death and resurrection. Peter Chrysologus, archbishop of Ravenna in the early 5th century, insisted in a sermon that talk about "death as a good" was simply a learned imposture; death is always an evil, "the mistress of despair, the mother of disbelief, the sister of decay, the parent of hell, the spouse of the devil, the queen of all evils" (*Sermon* 118.3). Writings from the Egyptian monastic milieu revived the older notion that powerful angels and repulsive demons fought over the souls of the dying, surrounding them as they passed through a searching examination by assessor spirits who held each soul minutely accountable for its past sins (Athanasius, *Life of Antony* 65; Cyril of Alexandria[?], *Homily* 14 in *Patrologia Graeca* 77.1072–90; cf. *First Apocalypse of James* [= Nag Hammadi V.3] 33.2–36.1; Origen, *Homily on Luke* 23.5–6).

The so-called *Apocalypse of Paul*, a narrative probably composed by Greek monks in Constantinople during the first two decades of the 5th century, combines this sense of death as challenge and struggle with a richly picturesque vision of the rewards and punishments awaiting each individual, even before the resurrection and universal judgment. Written as a tour of the regions of the afterlife, this work reflects the new conviction of many late-4th-century theologians and preachers that the human soul's existence after death cannot be thought of simply as a long wait for resurrection and judgment, in vaguely differentiated regions of the underworld, but that the final fate of each human being, everlasting blessedness or everlasting suffering, begins for the soul immediately after death (see, e.g., Jerome, *On Ecclesiastes* 9.10; *Epistle* 23.3; John

Chrysostom, *In Epistulam ad Galatas* 6.3; *On Lazarus* 7.3; *In Acta Apostolorum* 21.4).

In the writings of Augustine of Hippo, who spans the 4th and 5th centuries, many of these earlier traditions are worked together into a richly detailed tapestry of the church's future hope. Life and death, he often emphasizes, must be understood in both a moral and a physical sense: "There are two kinds of life, one of the body, the other of the soul. As the soul is the life of the body, so God is the life of the soul. So just as the body would die if the soul should depart from it, the soul dies if it departs from God" (*Enarratio in Psalmum* 70 2.3; cf. *On the Trinity* 4.3.5; *City of God* 13.2). So death in its most destructive sense is the "second death" of eternal damnation, which will occur only after the resurrection and final judgment (*City of God* 13.2). Augustine believed, for reasons drawn from the Platonic tradition, that the soul is itself naturally immortal *(On the Immortality of the Soul),* but considered such survival of little benefit if the person were permanently separated from God by sin. Human souls, he argued, are personally judged at the moment of their separation from the body (*On the Nature and Origin of the Soul* 2.4.8), and "the separated souls of the saints are now in peace, while those of the wicked are in pain until their bodies rise again" (*City of God* 13.8). Yet the souls of the dead, in this present age, still belong to time; so "the souls of the holy dead are not separated from the church" and remain "members of Christ" (*City of God* 20.9; *On the Nature and Origin of the Soul* 1.9.10), while the souls of sinners who are not hardened against God undergo only temporary punishments that will end in forgiveness before the final judgment (*City of God* 21.13). After that, the saints in their risen, transfigured bodies will enjoy the engaged leisure of simply contemplating and praising God (*Sermon* 362.30.31; *City of God* 22.30), while the damned—whose state can only be described in biblical images—will survive in the endless torture of knowing that they are deprived of the presence of God, the source of all happiness and genuine life (*On True Religion* 52.101; *City of God* 19.28). In Augustine's vision of the afterlife, one already finds all the seeds of the classic eschatology of western Christianity.

BIBL.: Henri Crouzel, *Les fins dernières selon Origène* (Brookfield, Vt., 1990). Brian E. Daley, *The Hope of the Early Church* (Cambridge, 1991). Joseph A. Fischer, *Studien zum Todesgedanke in der alten Kirche* (Munich, 1954). Éric Rebillard, *In hora mortis: Évolution de la pastorale chrétienne de la mort aux IVe et Ve siècles* (Rome, 1994). Alfred C. Rush, *Death and Burial in Christian Antiquity* (Washington, D.C., 1941). B.E.D.

Sin, Pollution, and Purity

Introduction

A general abstract definition and illustration of the concepts of sin and pollution are helpful here, in order to compare and contrast the discussions of these ideas in this chapter. The two phenomena or concepts overlap to some degree, but are not synonymous. Sin relates to behavior, while pollution relates generally to a result of behavior (e.g., a social transgression such as murder or a cultic offense such as not performing prescribed rites) or some physical state (e.g., suffering or contact with sexual emissions, disease, or death). While in many traditions, sinful behavior can cause pollution, it does not always create pollution, and an impure state is not always sinful. The concepts of sin and pollution gain their definition further in their dynamic relationship to what is holy, including the gods. Sin is an action that offends the gods and angers them. Pollution generally threatens what is sacred—what is defined as belonging to the gods—be it a sanctuary, sacrifices, or the holiness of persons. Although the relation to the gods is indirect, pollution can also anger the deity, with consequences as serious as in the case of sin.

In antiquity, the corners of this triangle—sin, pollution, and the holy (or the gods)—stood in tension with each other, a tension that is not merely ideational but based on human experience and perceptions of reality. It was important for people to make sense of these ideas, not just for intellectual satisfaction, but for enduring well-being in this world and, for some, in the world to come. Thus the texts, to the extent that their genres and preservation allow, reveal a tendency toward resolving questions and systematizing their understandings of these matters. For example, the Priestly source of the Pentateuch contains a complex system of gradations of impurity. It anchored its perception of sin and pollution in the sanctuary institution. Both severe personal impurities and sin pollute the sanctuary. This requires purification by the appropriate sacrifices. The Hittite laws show a gradation in incest and bestiality offenses and accompanying impurity. Certain more serious offenses are labeled *ḫurkel* (abomination) and may require capital punishment. Other offenses are allowed but may require avoiding the presence of the king. The early Christian fathers sought to define a hierarchy of sin and to explain the seeming genetic inclination of humans toward sin and the accompanying need for God's salvation. Egypt developed a more cosmic, even mythical, sense of evil. Apart from human and divine sources, evil could irrupt into creation from chaos. Its systematic thought can also be seen in its listing of ethical/moral and cultic offenses in the Negative Confessions.

The anger that pollution and especially sin generated was thought to be manifested in various human and natural misfortunes: sickness, death, agricultural failure and accompanying famine, defeat in war, storm, earthquake, and so forth. Various means, including divination and prophecy, were used to discover which god was offended and what specifically was the cause of offense. Examples include the Greek oracle tablets from Dodona or omen tablets and collections from Mesopotamia. Means were also developed to appease the gods' wrath. These include sacrifices, which often were foods or gifts of precious materials, given to calm the heart of the gods, in analogy to giving gifts to and pacifying or glorifying human masters. To take care of wrath caused by pollution, the pollution first needed to be removed. In addition to ablutions by humans, various cultic detergents, including blood and water, were used to purify the sanctuary or its parts. More complex magico-ritual practices were performed to remove pollution. Polluted items and polluted or sinful persons could be secluded in or exiled from the community. The impurity may be buried or may be sent away on animals or persons, as with the Greek *pharmakoi,* Hittite prisoners of war who bear plague to the enemy land, or the biblical scapegoat. An area affected by pollution may need purification by elaborate rites, such as the Roman *lustratio,* which purifies a region with animal sacrifices. Any irreclaimable sanctum that was destroyed through the pollution needed to be restored, sometimes with an additional penalty. Moreover, since the gods became angry because of the pollution, they also needed to be pacified through sacrificial means or gifts.

Those in Western culture tend to be more familiar with "sin-based" rather than "pollution-based" religions, due to the now-noncultic traditions of Christianity and Judaism. Thus they tend to see pollution-based systems as foreign and may judge them to be less interested in morality. It is therefore helpful to be aware of how the pollution-based systems blended morality and sin in their pollution schemes. The Priestly tradition, for example, has to a large extent integrated its moral code into its pollution system. Indeed, the cultic purity system could almost be seen as a symbolic or structural echo of the moral system. Greek religion ascribes severe pollution to homicide. This acts as a mechanism of social control. The conceptual tying of morality and impurity can otherwise be found in various traditions where individuals are said to become impure because of their sin. This sometimes appears more rhetorical than real because purification rites are not necessarily required to cleanse the individual. Rather, a different regimen—repentance, reparation, and perhaps individual suffering—may be required to "purge" the soul. The language of pollution in the context of morality is thus more of a metaphor—a way of understanding by analogy—than an inherent part of the moral system. This use of metaphor to explain an idea is found elsewhere in religious thought, especially where human features and institutions are used to formulate an understanding of the gods. The metaphor also has the effect of reinforcing moral concepts and defining immoral behavior as negative and offensive to the deity.   D.P.W.

Egypt

Sin, crime, pollution, and impurity are terms used to classify contact with various manifestations of evil. Absence of this contact, whether intentional (e.g., through abstinence) or unintentional, implies purity—be it moral, ethical, or cultic. Two conceptual realms intersect in defining sin in ancient Egypt: the varied nature of the manifestations of evil and the concept of being, which bring together cosmological and social perspectives.

Evil. Evil takes various forms, each with its *Sitz im Leben* in Egyptian ontology. First, evil, defined as "that which is not" *(iwtt)* or disorder, is the regenerative and productive component of nonexistence. It is capable of being transformed into the ordered world of existence, given that the ordered world encompassed conflicts between good and evil, life and death (which does not mean the end of life). The concept of being thus required continuous, cyclical contact with nonexistence in the form of "that which is not."

Second, evil, defined as *isfet* and subsequently *bwt,* is the nonproductive, immutable part of nonexistence, a realm beyond boundaries, deep, dark, and endless, encompassing all the forces antagonistic to creation. This was a realm of reversals and the habitat of those who died the second death. Evil from this realm of uncreation was constantly penetrating creation and had to be combated. In Egypt, the world was created according to and by means of *ma'at,* a word often rendered as "world order" or "truth." These first two forms of evil were indispensable constituents of that universe. In some sources they are even seen as embedded in the design of the creator. The clear distinction between the two as belonging to "being" versus "nonbeing" is illustrated by the existence of two separate concepts of killing (i.e., negating creation). One term indicates that the executed is capable of participating in the eternal cycle of life and death, while the other indicates that complete annihilation, the second death that makes its victim a member of the class of eternal enemies, is the goal.

Third, over time these two forms of evil, "that which is not" and *isfet/bwt,* became conflated with their derivatives. In later sources the blame for the existence of evil was attributed to human desire to do evil.

Bwt. Egyptian has no word for sin in the Christian sense of the term. The Egyptian (Coptic) gospel translations use the term *nobe* for sin. This term, it has been suggested, derives from Egyptian *bwt. Bwt* is a complex category. It denotes both the evil itself and the "sin" committed when doing—or merely having contact with—something classified as *bwt.* During the almost three millennia of pharaonic history a steadily increasing number of phenomena were included in the category of things *bwt.* The entire catalogue of phenomena classified as *bwt* shows a wide selection of sins, ranging from "social evils" (or ordinary crimes), such as killing and theft, to violation of ethical norms (partiality) and to numerous cultic offenses, such as breaking rules of purity related to contact with the holy. The treatises known as Cult Monographs, from the Greco-Roman period, list the constituent elements of each nome (province) and temple. These lists always included one or several *bwts,* such as certain species of animals (mammals, reptiles, fish) or parts thereof, members of the body, diseases, miscellaneous substances, people who momentarily or permanently were at the border of the social values of *ma'at* (menstruating women, homosexuals), and proscribed forms of sexual behavior or contact with forbidden food.

Closer examination of the material, however, reveals a hierarchy of evils in which the world of reversal epitomizes evil as well as provides the earliest examples of *bwt.* Evil defined as reversal implies eating excrement instead of food, drinking urine in place of water, walking upside down, having an anus as a mouth and a mouth as an anus, and so forth. The reversed world was the truly evil world. The concept of evil was rooted in the fear of hunger. This fear, presumably emanating from the first negative experience of the child, was developed by the Egyptians into an ontological category whose content of evil and the negative transcends the polarity of matter and inert matter as well as cuts across the social and cosmological spheres. Food is placed at the center of ontological concerns: nourishment was the precondition for life, and food was equated with *ma'at*. Consequently, it is logical to find hunger, thirst, and feces as prototypes of that which is not *ma'at*. As *ma'at* is food and thus life, then *bwt* is excrement and death, the true death of nonexistence, known as the second death.

In the historical material, *bwt* takes a place somewhere between what Assmann has called social *ma'at* and cosmic *ma'at*. It obviously had a social nucleus, but by the middle of the 3rd millennium BCE it had also found a place in the cosmology of the Egyptians. In the earliest evidence available, the prototypical experience of hunger was reduced to certain formulas. For the living, access to tombs and temples required abstinence from contact with certain unspecified forms of food. For the dead, the claim of lack of contact with feces—the embodiment of *bwt* against *ma'at*—was a prerequisite for gaining access to the afterlife.

At the this-worldly level, the prototypical fear of hunger also entailed a moral that proscribed individual appropriation of food at the expense of the social group as a whole. In the normative discourses on ethics, called wisdom texts, avarice is the *ma'at*-antagonistic offense *par excellence*. Originally, this sin was most likely that of the hoarder in a society where the abundance of food was the most basic form of wealth.

With the advent of the Middle Kingdom, historical experience had made the old formulas ("feces is *bwt* for me") in which the Egyptians had articulated the concept of "sin" insufficient. Alternative concepts evolved, coexisting—true to the principle of a multiplicity of approaches—with the ancient notion of *bwt*. Henceforth, many acts were seen as manifestations of evil, which were, in turn, attributed to humans having turned away from god. In this perspective, sin is no longer evil directed toward others, but evil committed against god. The category *bwt* remained productive, but at the same time it gradually degenerated to become a kind of taboo.

Negative Confessions and rules of purity. The blend of evils and "sins," which from a modern point of view belong to separate categories, social, ethical, or religious, finds clear expression in the discourse often labeled the Negative Confessions. Its earliest example is the posthumous trial of the dead described in chapter 125 of the Book of the Dead. Here the deceased enumerates the many "sins" that he or she has not committed. The full-scale presentation of this judgment of the dead dates to the New Kingdom, while possibly having originated in the early Middle Kingdom.

An interesting array of sins is collected together in the denials of the deceased, which may be divided into three groups. In the first we have the ethical offenses, comprising ordinary crimes, which were otherwise prosecuted by the society, such as "I have not stolen," "I have not killed," "I have not committed adultery." This group also includes moral phenomena: "I have not made anyone weep," "I have not made anyone suffer," "I have not been deaf to *ma'at*." In the second group we find offenses associated with the public role of the official: "I have not increased or reduced the measure," "I have not added to the weight of the balance." The third group, finally, contains prohibitions related to cultic practice: "I have not done the *bwt* of god," "I have not defiled myself," "I have not stopped a god on his procession."

A set of rules is implied in the denials of the Negative Confessions. Similar rules are found in the injunctions or prohibitions that the priests were required to observe when officiating in the temples. These regulations are abundantly attested in the temples of the Greco-Roman period, where they are found on doorjambs and other architectural elements at the entrance to the temple proper. It is possible that similar rules applied to the priesthood as early as the end of the Old Kingdom.

Purity, as a precondition for contact with the sacred and the otherworld, is described in similar terms for the deceased pronouncing the Negative Confessions before Osiris, for the officiating priest, and for the ordinary mortals prior to entering a tomb or a temple.

Purity and pollution. The texts state explicitly that the absence of *bwt* is the equivalent of purity for the living and the dead. "The mouth of NN is pure, the two enneads cense him, and pure indeed is this tongue which is in his mouth. Excrement is what NN *bwts,* NN rejects urine. . . . This is what NN *bwts,* he does not eat [it], this is what NN *bwts*" (a formula first attested in the Pyramid Text 127/128 = spell 210 (see Deities and Demons). Purity is defined as "being free from" any of the manifestations of evil, whether this-worldly or otherworldly, social or cosmological. This may also be expressed as lack of contact with *isfet:* "I am one whose mouth is pure and whose teeth are healthy, and what is *bwt* for me is that which is *isfet* to Atum" (Coffin Text 7.226g–h = spell 1011).

The relationship between purity *(wab)* and impurity *(abw)* is illustrated by the evident word play found in the terms describing these states. The attitude toward pollution and evil became, over time, gradated into a hierarchy of evil. This is reflected in the spectrum of sanctions and of means of nullifying the consequences of breaking the rules of *ma'at*. At the one end of the scale, the violation of a *bwt* brought about the second death. At the other end, a ritual ablution, entailing purification, could be used to remove the evil attached to a person. This ritual, depending on the specific ends and circumstances, would initiate the individual into a new phase of life, including the immortality of the next life, the role of officiating temple priest, and the assumption of the kingship through coronation.

Although the use of purification media such as natron and incense was common, water was the principal agent for this aspect of the process of regeneration. It was the manifestation of Nun, the primeval ocean from which and in which creation came about. In pictorial representations of rites of purification, water is often rendered as a linked chain of life signs. In keeping with the pivotal role of food, the mouth became the principal focus of purity. The omnipresent Egyptian predilection for animal categories and images—for "thinking in animals"—is reflected in the use of the calf to describe the state of purity brought about by an ablution as "your mouth is the mouth of a sucking calf on the day it was born," a formula attested from the earliest to the latest sources.

BIBL.: Sidney H. Aufrère, "Les interdits religieux des nomes dans les monographies en Égypte: Un autre regard," in *L'interdit et le sacré dans les religions de la Bible et de l'Égypte: Actes du Colloque Montpellier, le 20 mars 1998* (ed. Jean-Marie Marconot and S. H. Aufrère; Groupe de recherche biblique interdisciplinaire avec la collaboration de l'UPRES-A 5052: Religions et sociétés dans l'Égypte de l'époque tardive; Montpellier: Presses de l'Université Paul Valéry Montpellier, 1998), 3.69–113. Paul John Frandsen, "On the Origin of the Notion of Evil in Ancient Egypt," *Göttinger Miszellen* 179 (2000): 9–34. Dimitri Meeks, "Pureté et purification en Égypte," in *Supplément au dictionnaire de la bible* (Paris, 1975), 9.430–52.   P.J.F.

Mesopotamia

Sin, pollution, and purity are not primarily religious notions; they qualify acts and conditions as they occur in the interaction between humans and between humans and their surroundings. The common term for sin, *arnu*, means "offense, wrongdoing." The words for pure *(ellu, ebbu, namru)* mean "clean" or "brilliant, shining"; their opposites *(la ellu, la ebbu, la namru)* refer to the absence of cleanliness and brilliance—an absence that may also be qualified on its own merits as *lu'û* (soiled), *dalḫu* (blurred, muddy), or *ešû* (gloomy, dull). Due to the Jewish or Christian context in which such terms as sin, pollution, and purity are often used, these Akkadian terms have, in our ears, a religious ring to them. But while it is true that in Mesopotamia, too, they belong to the vocabulary of religion, it is appropriate first to assess their primary, nonreligious significance.

Sin and the code of conduct. A sin is an offense against the moral code that regulates human interaction. That code, as such, is not laid down in writing. It is a cultural heritage transmitted orally by implication as much as by explicit teaching. The rules of conduct by which the Babylonians and Assyrians were supposed to live can be recovered on the basis of allusions in letters, exhortatory texts, prayers of confession, liturgical litanies of offenses possibly committed, and the like.

The core of the Mesopotamian code of conduct can be subsumed under several principles that are remarkably close to the second part of the Ten Commandments: filial obedience and respect are crucial virtues; bloodshed, adultery, theft, and unfounded allegations are strongly condemned. Like their Israelite counterparts, Mesopotamian morals are conservative and biased; formulated from the perspective of the wellborn adult male, they serve the interests of the status quo. The command to "honor your father and your mother" expresses the principle of respect for the social hierarchy that defines the relationships in the ancient Near Eastern society. All those who hold a superior position are entitled to the obedience and respect of those who fall under their authority, whether it be king and subjects, mayor and citizens, master and servant, husband and wife, parents and children, or seniors and juniors. Such respect for hierarchies keeps the communities of household, family, town, guild, and kingdom from falling apart. The prohibition of bloodshed, adultery, and theft is likewise designed to maintain the fabric of society. It should be noted that the application of these rules is restricted to the society one belongs to; for a soldier, it is no sin to kill an enemy, to abuse a woman belonging to the enemy, or to despoil an enemy of his possessions. The ban against unfounded accusations, as much as against libel and slander, is crucial not only to the proper functioning of the judicial system but to social interaction in general.

If there are shame cultures and guilt cultures, the Mesopotamian civilization belongs to the former. Honor and dignity are essential values. Adultery is prohibited first and foremost because it brings disgrace to the husband, not because lust is considered as somehow wrong. There is no offense in visiting a prostitute. Also, there is scant evidence at best for a Mesopotamian view that would define sin as an evil inclination or a wrong intention. A sin does not exist until committed—or even more strongly: until discovered. To harbor desires whose fulfillment would be sinful is not a sin by itself. A good reputation is more important than a clear conscience. In the same vein, acts of philanthropy are enjoined on humanitarian grounds, but often performed as a display of generosity and social sensibility—virtues that reflect and confirm social status.

The code of conduct and the notion of sin had religious significance inasmuch as the gods were believed to endorse moral standards and to punish any infringements. The doctrine of retribution that underlies this belief is based on the idea that the gods, while possessing superhuman powers of perception and intervention, share human values and emotions. Owing to this combination of characteristics, the Mesopotamian gods were the patrons and guardians of justice. This was especially true of those gods associated with the distribution of justice, such as the all-seeing sun-god Shamash. Sins committed by one human against the other were conceived of as sins against the gods as well. In addition to the religious interpretation of social offenses, there was also a code of conduct *vis-à-vis* the gods. Failure to provide the prescribed offerings, temple theft, intercourse with a priestess, and a false oath were sins against the gods on account of the same principles by virtue of which filial disrespect, theft, adultery, and false accusations were offenses.

Pollution and purity. The notions of pollution and purity are only partially concomitant with the notion of sin. Someone guilty of murder is polluted with blood, and a condition of guilt, more generally speaking, entails a state of impurity. Sins, although acts, are conceived of as stains that need to be purged. The principal idea that informs the notion of purity, however, does not come from the realm of ethics. Purity stands for perfection and integrity—moral, physical, spiritual, and social. The candidate for priesthood must be pure in the sense that he should be of noble descent and have no chipped teeth, bruised limbs, or other physical imperfections. It is clear that the family one is born into or one's physical defects have nothing to do with proper or reprehensible behavior. Yet the gods demand that their closest servants also be pure from imperfections for which they could never be blamed.

Like the notion of sin, the notions of purity and pollution as metaphors of a spiritual condition must be understood by analogy with their meaning in social interaction. The distinction between ethics and etiquette may be helpful. Our code of conduct is informed in part by the opposition between good and evil, in part by the opposition between proper and improper, tasteful and distasteful. The second province of our precepts of behavior consists of rules of etiquette. An unkempt appearance, foul breath, and improper language are not morally reprehensible but offenses against good manners. Just as people shun the company of those with such uncivilized manners, so do the gods. Gods, like humans, are moved by impulses of pleasure and repulsion. Correct behavior, in every sense of the term, causes them pleasure; evil behavior and bad manners fill them with repulsion. Emotions of pleasure and repulsion are not elicited only by certain kinds of behavior. A pleasant face with regular features arouses sympathy for no other reason than its own perfection; gods, just as kings, wish to be surrounded by beauty, which in Babylonian parlance is tantamount to brilliance and—by the same token—purity. Anything that soils that purity—dirt, whether the result of bodily secretions or contact with contaminated matter—counts as pollution.

In a study entitled *Purity and Danger,* anthropologist Mary Douglas defines dirt as "matter out of place." Shoes, she argues, do not by themselves offend our sense of propriety; they are acceptable on the doormat, but a source of displeasure when found on the dining table. Purity and impurity are indeed qualifications that are very sensitive to context. The consumption of garlic en-

tails no impurity in a domestic context, but a prayer uttered by someone who has recently had garlic is unacceptable because spoken with a mouth that is not pure. The requirement of purity becomes truly severe in the presence of the gods. The gods being the embodiment of beauty, power, and perfection, they want everything and everyone in their vicinity to partake of that purity. It is in the encounter with them, on holy ground so to speak, that human impurity becomes dangerous. In this respect, the standards of the gods are higher than those at court, as the gods are also aware of imperfections and impurities undetected by human means of perception. Outside the perimeter of the divine presence, a state of impurity is innocuous. In fact, participation in human society entails almost inevitably conditions of impurity. No human is fit to perpetually breathe the thin air of Olympus. That is why the ritual specialist enjoins his client, once the healing rituals are over and done with, to visit the cafe or the crossroads, where one is bound to run into a pollution of some sort.

Causes of impurity. In order to give more substance to the notions of pollution and purity, it may be useful to go over the various causes and forms of impurity. The predominant aspect of purity is physical: cleanliness is the first prerequisite of purity. Such purity is impaired by pollution in the literal sense of the term: dust, spoiled substances, sweat, and contact with various other bodily fluids. Indeed, every substance that issues from the human body or the animal body is potentially defiling—tears being the only exception. Corpses and carcasses are to be avoided, as they are bodies in the process of decomposition. Actions that are perfectly legitimate and harmless, such as sexual intercourse of husband and wife or the nursing of a newborn child by its mother, defile nevertheless because they involve exposure to bodily secretions. Such secretions do not need to leave a trace perceptible to the human eye in order to pollute. Conspicuousness does add to the impact of pollution, however. That is why blood, irrespective of its source, tends to become a symbol of impurity. The "blood-stained rag of the menstruating woman" is a proverbial expression in cuneiform texts (and found in the Bible as well) to denote something abhorred by the gods. Defilement by blood can also have moral overtones because of the association with bloodshed. To say that one's hands are clean and that there is no blood on them is tantamount to saying that one is innocent of murder. Purity and defilement are notions that lend themselves quite easily to metaphorical use: moral guilt can be compared to a stain; the comparison may become so commonplace that its metaphorical nature falls into oblivion.

The primarily physical aspect of purity is also in evidence when we are dealing with the impurity contracted by a foul breath. Visits to the temple are best made before the main meal, because "if someone goes to the chapel of his god he is not clean if he has eaten leeks, cress seed, garlic, onions, beef, or pork" (*Cuneiform Texts from Babylonian Tablets* 39 38 recto 11; 36.107). These are not food taboos comparable to the dietary laws of Leviticus. The Babylonians did not think anything was wrong with garlic or pork apart from their consumption leaving traces on the breath.

Generally speaking, impurity follows from a lessening of integrity or wholeness; such a lessening may occur on account of substances that render impure because they add a foreign element: to be pure is also to be unalloyed, without admixture. Purity, in this respect, can also have an ethnic significance: the candidate for the Babylonian priesthood had to be "of pure descent." Integrity can also be lost through attacks from within or without that cause physical harm. Illness, whether caused by deities, demons, or other agents, entails a state of impurity. Mental disturbances, too, are defiling; the diviner who has had a nightmare needs divine clemency if he is to perform extispicy successfully.

Means of purification. According to Babylonian beliefs, then, humans might become impure in many different ways. Some impurities are permanent, such as physical deformations; other impurities are transitory, provided the proper measures are taken. The recovery of purity, essential for safe commerce with the gods, involved the use of water (to wash away dirt and stains) and various perfumes (to take away unpleasant odors). Ablutions with water are a universal means of purification, used in Mesopotamia as both a physical and a spiritual cleansing. Such a cleansing might even be referred to as "sanctification" *(quddušu)*. Not just any water was suitable for this purpose. Still waters from pools, ponds, or ditches had no power of purification since people might have bathed in them before and defiled them. Impurity could be contracted even by stepping in used bathing water. Only running waters brought purification. Hence the custom of locating places of worship on riverbanks; hence, too, the taboo of urinating or vomiting into a river (Shurpu 3.63). Washing rites were often coupled with the use of purifying perfumes. Fumigation, that is, the manipulation of a censer so as to surround the person to be purified with a sweet fragrance, was common practice. According to Herodotus, the Babylonians did not need a ritual specialist for this rite; they performed it themselves in the privacy of their homes, after sexual intercourse, for instance (1.198). In order to obtain a sweet-scented breath, another prerequisite of purity, it was also customary to chew on herbs, leaves, or twigs with a refreshing smell, such as those of the tamarisk or cedar.

BIBL.: Karel van der Toorn, *Sin and Sanction in Israel and Mesopotamia: A Comparative Study* (Assen: Van Gorcum, 1985). E. Jan Wilson, *"Holiness" and "Purity" in Mesopotamia* (Alter Orient und Altes Testament 237; Kevelaer: Butzon & Bercker/Neukirchen-Vluyn: Neukirchener Verlag, 1994).   K.V.D.T.

Syria-Canaan

Transgression and its punishment are significant themes in surviving Syro-Canaanite texts, including the Hebrew Bible, a collection in which an extensive and complex vocabulary of sin survives. Transgressions of various types are mentioned in extant texts: oath and treaty violations, adultery and other sexual sins, murder, and ritual infringements. Punishments for sin include fines, extirpation of lineage, and execution. Among the various types of sin, crimes involving holy places, items, foods, or ritual actions—often referred to as sacrilege—are of particular concern in extant texts. Sacrilege might involve the violation of a priestly prerogative by a nonpriest (e.g., King Uzziah's incense offering in 2 Chron. 26.16–21) or the misappropriation of materials devoted to a deity (Josh. 7). It might be intentional or unintentional, known to the transgressor or not known. It is punishable by some form of calamity or even death. An example of unintentional sacrilege is found in the Ugaritic story about Kirta, who did not fulfill the vow that he made to the goddess Athirat (Asherah). For this mistake, the goddess made Kirta deathly ill. Only the intervention of the high god, El, could restore Kirta to health. The boy Aqhat in the Ugaritic story named for him suffers worse. He directly offends the goddess Anat by refusing to give her a bow made for him and by insulting her. She eventually kills him for his affront. Several Phoenician inscriptions call for the punishment of those who would destroy a king's grave or efface the inscription (*KAI* 1, 24, 26, 30). This is implicitly a sin against the gods, since they have installed and sustained the monarchs. Those who break a treaty, entered into in the presence of various gods, are to suffer various natural calamities according to the Aramaic Sefire inscription (*KAI* 222). The Bible allows the sinner who commits sacrilege by mistake to restore his position by means of a "guilt" or "reparation" offering *(ʾāšām)* according to Lev. 5.14–6.7 [= 5.14–26 Hebrew]. Other sins may threaten to pollute the sanctuary and require a purification offering *(ḥaṭṭāʾt)* and other ritual actions such as blood manipulation to prevent this from happening (see Lev. 4; 16).

Pollution is a concept common to religions of the ancient Mediterranean world and elsewhere, although the degree to which it appears in surviving literary corpora is not consistent. Whereas the text of the Hebrew Bible preserves extensive legal and narrative material pertinent to a discussion of pollution and purity, the Northwest Semitic epigraphic corpus is far less rich in comparison. The Ugaritic texts contain strong indications, however, that a purity system operated there. The chief evidence is found in texts for festivals in which the king participates. He washes, which leads to his being "pure" *(brr)* (*KTU* 1.41; 1.46; 1.87; 1.105; 1.106; 1.112). Some of these texts also speak of the king being in a "common" or desacralized state *(ḥl)*, often coming about at sunset (see also 1.132). The status of purity thus appears to stand in contrast to a common status. Other than the Ugaritic texts, scholars depend mainly on the witness of texts such as *On the Syrian Goddess* 52–54, attributed to the Greek-speaking satirist Lucian, which describes the cult at Hierapolis in the 2nd century CE and mentions the defilement caused by corpses and polluting foods, and also mentions purifications.

Binary contrasts, such as found in the Ugaritic texts, are more visible in the biblical text. One opposition is between "unclean" *(ṭāmēʾ)* and "clean" *(ṭāhôr)*. This opposition is related to a second binary contrast, that of "holy" *(qōdeš)* and "common" *(ḥōl)*. Other purity-related vocabulary in the Hebrew Bible includes "despicable thing" *(šeqeṣ)* and "abomination" *(tôʿēbâ)*, as well as other terms for defilement. The deity, his sanctuary, his cultic staff, the sanctuary's accoutrements, and the offerings brought to the sanctuary are described as "holy" in various texts; all things external to the sanctuary sphere are properly "common." The holiness of the sanctuary sphere requires constant, vigilant protection by the priesthood and other attendants of the sanctuary, for what is polluting can defile the sanctuary, and a polluted sanctuary is not fit for a deity's continuing residence and cult (Deut. 23.14 [= 23.15 Hebrew]; Ezek. 43.7–9). Thus, the primary objective of purity systems in the Syro-Canaanite cultural context is to protect the sanctity of a deity's space from any sort of defilement. Only clean (i.e., unpolluted) worshipers, sacrifices, and offerings gain entry into the sanctuary; that which is polluted is kept out by the sanctuary's attendants.

Biblical texts bear witness to a range of polluting substances, actions, characteristics, or states that disqualify persons or offerings from entering the sphere of the sanctuary. They also present ritual prescriptions intended to facilitate the restoration of polluted persons to a clean state so as to allow them to participate once again in the cult. Sources of defilement include the blood of menstruation and parturition, skin disease, seminal emissions, venereal discharges, bones, corpses, tombs, and animal carcasses. According to some texts, excrement defiles (Ezek. 4.9–15; Zech. 3), as do idols (Ezek. 36.18), alien lands (Amos 7.17), and transgressions such as consulting a medium or necromancer (Lev. 19.31). Some of these sources of defilement are avoidable (e.g., touching an animal carcass); some are not (e.g., menstruation). Some sources of impurity render an individual polluted for a day (e.g., seminal emission); others for a week (e.g., contact with a corpse); still others for longer than a week (e.g., parturition). Long-term or permanent pollution is possible, as in the case of an individual with persistent skin disease. Secondary pollution may arise from contact with a polluted individual or item. A single, convincing explanation of what the various impurities share with each other has yet to be proposed, though some scholars have suggested that all are related to death in some way.

Rituals of cleansing are preserved in the detailed purity legislation of the biblical Priestly and Holiness sources. These might include laundering clothes, washing the body, or cleansing inanimate objects that came into contact with polluting substances or defiled persons. In certain texts, other ritual actions such as the sprinkling of the blood of a sacrificial animal (Lev. 14) or the use of a purifying agent such as water mixed with the ashes of the red cow (Num. 19) are prescribed. Sometimes sacrifices and offerings are required of the individual making the transition from a polluted state to a clean state. Although these vary in value, it would seem that the more severe the pollution, the more valuable the sacrifice required (compare the sacrificial animals demanded of the man healed of a venereal discharge in Lev. 15.14 to those of one who has recovered from skin disease in 14.10, 21–22). That sacrifices and offerings are required of the person being cleansed suggests that such pollution is constructed not only as a threat to the deity and his sanctuary, but also as a sin. It therefore requires both purgation and reparation. The requirement of purity in connection with holiness is found in the Ugaritic story of Kirta. Fatherless Kirta purifies himself before making an offering enlisting the aid of the gods El and Baal: "He washed himself and rouged himself, he washed his hands to the elbow, his fingers to the shoulder" (KTU 1.14 3.52–54). The father Danel in the Aqhat story, after mourning for his dead son Aqhat for seven years, dismisses mourners and renews sacrificial worship. This return to normalcy is indicative of the transition from impurity to purity.

BIBL.: G. del Olmo Lete, *Canaanite Religion according to the Liturgical Texts of Ugarit* (trans. Wilfred G. E. Watson; Bethesda, Md.: CDL, 1999). Jean-Michel de Tarragon, *Le culte à Ugarit* (Cahiers de la revue biblique 19; Paris: Gabalda, 1980). Karel van der Toorn, *Sin and Sanction in Israel and Mesopotamia: A Comparative Study* (Assen, 1985). David P. Wright, "Unclean and Clean: Old Testament," in *The Anchor Bible Dictionary* (ed. David Noel Freedman et al.; New York, 1992), 6.729–41.   S.M.O.

Israel

Pollution and purity are central concepts in Israelite religion. The distinction between the pure/clean and the unclean is mentioned for the first time in the Hebrew Bible in regard to the flood story. According to Gen. 7.2, God commanded Noah: "Take with you seven pairs of all clean animals, the male and his mate; and a pair of the animals that are not clean, the male and his mate." This distinction is connected to Noah's sacrifice after the flood (8.20): only clean animals can be offered on the altar, hence Noah had to take with him to the ark a larger number of clean animals. We have here a clear notion about the cultic significance of purity and impurity. These verses belong to the J (Yahwistic) source of the Pentateuch. However, according to the Priestly source, P, Noah heard a different command: "And of every living thing of all flesh, you shall bring two of every sort into the ark, to keep them alive with you; they shall be male and female" (6.19). There is no mention here of the distinction between the clean and the unclean: Noah is to take with him two of all flesh. This disagreement is connected with and explained by another debate: according to the J source, sacrifices were brought to YHWH from the very beginning of human history. Cain and Abel were the first people who made offerings to the Lord (4.3–5). However, according to P, there was no offering to God in the time before Moses. Thus, according to P, the cultic system with the distinction between the pure and the impure did not yet exist in the time of Noah! In the broader sense, we see here a debate about the scope of the cultic system: according to J this is a universalistic system that existed from the dawn of humanity; according to P it was ordained only for Moses and Israel.

It is in the priestly tradition that we have the clearest connection between sin and pollution. The central rite of the Priestly Code is the rite of the Day of Atonement (Lev. 16). Aaron, the high priest, is instructed to "make atonement for the holy place, because of the uncleannesses of the people of Israel, and because of their transgressions, all their sins" (Lev. 16.16). After the cleansing of the tabernacle, a scapegoat is sent to Azazel: "Then he shall take the two goats, and set them before the LORD at the door of the tent of meeting; and Aaron shall cast lots upon the two goats, one lot for the LORD and the other lot for Azazel. And Aaron shall present the goat on which the lot fell for the LORD, and offer it as a sin offering; but the goat on which the lot fell for Azazel shall be presented alive before the LORD to make atonement over it, that it may be sent away into the wilderness to Azazel" (16.7–10).

Azazel is not mentioned elsewhere in the Bible. In rabbinic literature there was an effort to demythologize Azazel and to make him into a place-name. This effort affected also the spelling of the name. The ancient spelling 'zz'l (a mighty god) was transformed into 'z'zl, thus dimming his identity as a divine being. His image in Lev. 16 is astonishing: he is represented here as a counterpart to God. There is even a sense of equality: "One lot for the LORD and the other lot for Azazel."

This surprising status of Azazel is to be explained with regard to the essence of the ritual. The aim of the ritual is atonement, cleansing of the tabernacle, and cleansing of the people of Israel. In order to get rid of iniquities and sins, the Israelites have to find an evil entity who will be ready to accept their evils. The God of Israel, who is the source of all good in creation, cannot play this role. For this task one needs a true representative of primeval evil. Azazel, a preexisting demon, is thus lifted up from the dust of antiquity and charged with playing the counterpart of the Lord and accepting all evils and sins.

What are the sins that cause impurity? Is it only cultic sins, or are moral transgressions also a source of pollution? In the Priestly Code, holiness and impurity are connected with only cultic objects and conceptions. However, already in the Holiness Code (Lev. 19) we see that the conception of holiness is broader and encompasses cult and morality. Isaiah rebukes the people of Israel for their moral sins and calls them to clean and purify themselves from these moral iniquities: "Wash yourselves; make yourselves clean; remove the evil of your doings from before my eyes; cease to do evil, learn to do good; seek justice, correct oppression; defend the fatherless, plead for the widow" (Isa. 1.16–17). Ezekiel rebukes the king of Tyre: "In the unrighteousness of your trade you profaned your sanctuaries" (Ezek. 28.18). This line is continued by the Temple Scroll of Qumran: "In all your gates you shall appoint for yourself judges and magistrates, and they shall judge the people with just judgment, and not show partiality in judgment, and not accept bribes, and not pervert justice, because the bribe perverts justice . . . and causes great guilt and defiles the House with the wickedness of sin." Thus, according to this view, amoral trade and the taking of bribes are sources of impurity and defilement.

According to the Hebrew Bible, however, only cultic impurity is contagious. The sources of contagious pollution are various: a corpse, leprosy, genital discharges, and so on. These types of impurity have nothing to do with morality. The purification from these types of contagious pollution is accomplished by washing and also, in high degrees of pollution, by sacrifice. The highest stage of impurity is caused by touching a dead person. Purification from this is accomplished by sprinkling water mixed with the ashes of a red heifer: "And the heifer shall be burned . . . and the priest shall take cedarwood and hyssop and scarlet stuff, and cast them into the midst of the burning of the heifer. . . . For the unclean they shall take some ashes . . . and running water shall be added in a vessel; then a clean person shall take hyssop, and dip it in the water, and sprinkle it . . . upon the unclean on the third day and on the seventh day" (Num. 19.5–6, 17–19).

The prophet Ezekiel uses this rite as a metaphor for the purification from sins and the spiritual renewal of Israel in the time of redemption: "I will sprinkle clean water upon you, and you shall be clean from all your uncleannesses, and from all your idols I will cleanse you. A new heart I will give you, and a new spirit I will put within you" (Ezekiel 36.25–26). God is described here as a priest who purifies Israel from its sins. Indeed, God is the ultimate source of atonement and forgiveness throughout the Hebrew Bible, in the past, in the present, and at the end of days. Nowhere in the Hebrew Bible is there a reference to the eschatological Messiah as the forgiver or expiator of sins. The prophet Zechariah speaks about the coming of the Messiah and the removal of transgressions: "Behold, I will bring my servant the Branch. . . . And I will remove the guilt of this land in a single day" (Zech. 3.8–9). However, it is God, and not God's servant, the Branch, who removes the guilt.

Yet, there are two cases where a human can atone for others by his own death or suffering. The first case is the expiatory death of the high priest in Num. 35. According to this law, a person who killed someone unintentionally should flee to a city of refuge and "must remain in his city of refuge until the death of the high priest; but after the death of the high priest the manslayer may return to the land of his possession" (35.28). Thus the death of the high priest serves here as an expiatory act for this slayer. The high priest atones for the whole community in his life. His death (i.e., probably his natural death) also has expiatory significance.

The other example is the suffering servant in Second Isaiah. The servant is a humiliated figure: "He was despised and rejected by men, a man of sorrows, and acquainted with grief" (Isa. 53.3). It is said of the servant: "Surely he has borne our griefs and carried our sorrows. . . . But he was wounded for our transgressions, he was bruised for our iniquities. . . . We have turned every one to his own way; and the LORD has laid on him the iniquity of us all" (53.4–6). It is an old debate whether the servant is a unique person or a collective figure. In any case, it is clear that we have here the phenomenon of vicarious suffering that atones for sins. It is important to note that the servant does not appear here as a redeemer or savior of the Israelite nation in the political sense. He is not going to fight against the nations or to liberate Israel from captivity. He is passive: "Like a lamb that is led to the slaughter" (53.7).

The notion of a Messiah or a savior who atones for his people appears for the first time in the Dead Sea Scrolls. In the composition known as the Damascus Document we read: "And this is the explication of the rules by which they shall be governed until the rise of the anointed of Aaron and Israel, and he will atone for their iniquity better than through meal and sin offerings" (Damascus Document 14.18–19 and 4Q266 frag. 10 1.12–13). Thus, according to this text, the expiatory force of the Messiah is stronger than that of sacrifice. Yet, it is not said here by what means the Messiah will atone. In another scroll, the Hodayot or Thanksgiving Hymns, there is a unique psalm known as the Self-Glorification Hymn. The speaker of this hymn describes himself as the suffering servant: "[And who] has been despised like [me? And who] has been rejected of man like me? . . . [And who] compares with m[e in enduring evil]?" (4QHᵉ frags. 1–2). In the following hymn is a lively description of the time of salvation that includes the saying "iniquity ends" (4QHᵃ frag. 7 2.6). Is it possible that the end of iniquity is connected with the suffering servant figure, the speaker of the first hymn?

Finally, in the document known as Pesher Melchizedek, we meet the divine redeemer Melchizedek.

Like the high priest of Lev. 16, he expiates for his people at the eschatological Day of Atonement. The metaphor used for the eschatological atonement is taken from the laws of the seventh and the Jubilee years in the Pentateuch (Lev. 25.10; Deut. 15.1): "And liberty shall be proclaimed to them, to free them from [the debt of] all their iniquities" (11QMelchizedek 2.6).

BIBL.: M. Newton, *The Concept of Purity at Qumran and in the Letters of Paul* (Cambridge: Cambridge University Press, 1985). D. P. Wright, *The Disposal of Impurity: Elimination Rites in the Bible and in Hittite and Mesopotamian Literature* (Society of Biblical Literature Dissertation Series 101; Atlanta: Society of Biblical Literature, 1987). I.K.

Anatolia

"Sins," whether committed willfully or accidentally, aroused the displeasure of the divine and could manifest themselves in pollution or impurity adhering to an individual. Sources of accidental or unwillful impurity included sorcery, stumbling upon an unclean object or location, or unknowingly transgressing a taboo. The maintenance of ritual purity was particularly important for those working within and around the temple precincts, but even for the average individual, potential ritual defilement, stemming from several unavoidable sources, had to be reckoned with. Once pollution had accrued to the individual, from whatever direction it may have come, it had to be dealt with by magico-ritual means.

The incomplete nature of the texts makes a reconstruction of purity rules difficult. Where there is better evidence, as in the categories of birth and pregnancy, we see clear purity-related restrictions on behavior. Elsewhere we may assume that bodily emissions were probably defiling to some extent, and certainly to differing extents depending upon who one was (and how often one came into contact with the gods). But by taking the proper measures, matters of bodily defilement could be controlled with minimal fuss. Much information is undoubtedly lacking; it is clear, however, that failure to maintain these purity rules was one way of willfully bringing trouble upon oneself.

Some texts indicate that sexual intercourse was considered defiling, but also that ritual washing in the morning after intercourse occurred was sufficient to nullify its defiling effects (KUB 15.36 1.11–13 with duplicates; KUB 13.4 3.68–74 with duplicates). Death was the penalty for failing to cleanse oneself after sex and prior to entering the sanctuary of the god. The emission of semen itself is never singled out, however, as the defiling element, as in the Hebrew Bible.

Military rituals designed to purify the army do not indicate that the purification is for uncleanness acquired through contact with blood. Nor is the blood of sacrificial victims treated in any special way. The ritual for the relocation of the Goddess of the Night uses blood to purify the statue and cella of the deity (KUB 29.4 4.28–40). The same meaning applies to the blood used in a purificatory birth ritual to counter a bad omen (KBo 5.1 1.25–27). However, in ritual incantations, blood is listed among other evils to be eliminated. The blood in such cases should probably be taken as referring to murder or bloodshed, so that the blood itself is not the defiling element, but the evil act it represents. There is no indication that the Hittites feared menstruation or imbued it with any supernatural significance. Nor is there any evidence that they required a complex set of purificatory rituals to cleanse the woman or anyone with whom she had had contact. Such rituals may well have existed, but if they did, evidence of them is lacking.

A festival marking the onset of a pregnancy is known to have been conducted, as were monthly rites during the pregnancy in honor of the mother-goddesses. Purificatory rites and offerings for and by the woman were performed as well. Dietary and sexual restrictions were incumbent upon the expectant mother. The sexual restrictions, however, did not apply, it appears, until the seventh month of the pregnancy (KBo 17.65 obverse 5). One birth ritual indicates that while the husband may continue to live with his wife during her pregnancy, they must eat using separate utensils and at separate tables (KBo 17.65 obverse 20–23 with duplicates). The husband also had to undergo some purificatory measures according to this text.

Directly following the birth, an incantation was spoken to remove evil from the newborn and to draw blessings upon it. Purificatory rites for the mother and the child are attested, the latter sometimes involving washing the mouth of the child. Further purificatory rites were performed periodically during the days and months following the birth. The birth was followed by a period of ritual separation of the mother and child from the community. A ceremonial reentry took place three months after the birth for a boy child and four months for a girl. There is no evidence of a midwife's association with birth causing her to be defiled in any extranormal way. The scribes could have omitted mention of such defilement, and purification after performing a birth ritual could have been automatic and assumed.

The act of spitting in ritual contexts served to purify the body and to pollute that to which it became attached. Spittle (Hittite *iššalli*) was therefore frequently used in purificatory rituals. Spittle was also an effective counter to sorcery, nullifying its effects. It is difficult to say whether the spittle was unclean because the person it came from was unclean or because all bodily emissions were considered unclean.

Dung and urine were a common source of filth in towns, to the extent that the image is used in a magic incantation (KBo 10.45 4.37–41). But there is no indication of personal defilement through contact with or production of feces and urine. Urine is used in ritual magic, although toward what effect is not clear. A passage from the Instructions for the Temple Personnel tells us that eating excrement and drinking urine was an unpleasant prospect, but not that ritual defilement was in any way forthcoming (KUB 13.4 3.64–68).

BIBL.: Gary M. Beckman, *Hittite Birth Rituals* (Wiesbaden: Harrassowitz, 1983). Annelies Kammenhuber, "Ketten von Unheils- und Heilsbegriffen in den luwischen magischen Ritualen," *Orientalia* n.s. 54 (1985): 77–105. James C. Moyer, *The Concept of Ritual Purity among the Hittites* (Ph.D. diss., Brandeis University, 1969). Ahmet Ünal, "Ritual Purity versus Physical Impurity in Hittite Anatolia: Public Health and Structures for Sanitation according to Cuneiform Texts and Archaeological Remains," *Bulletin of the Middle Eastern Culture Center in Japan* 7 (1993): 119–39.   B.J.C.

Iran

Iranian religions in antiquity represented purity (Avestan *yaozhdāh*, Middle Persian *yōjdarīh*) as a notion fundamental to individual and collective existence—in corporeal and spiritual terms—because of its perceived centrality in averting chaos. For ancient Iranians, purity was connected to righteousness and consequently to holiness as a manifestation of order, distinguished from pollution, falsehood, and sin, which were thought to epitomize disorder.

Zarathustra, the devotional poet whose followers established Mazda worship or Zoroastrianism as the major faith of ancient Iran, personified this dichotomy in a pair of primal entities called Spenta Mainyu, the holy spirit or hypostasis of Ahura Mazda (or Ohrmazd the wise lord), and Angra Mainyu or Ahriman, the destructive or evil spirit. He labeled them the "better one and the worse one," "the holier one . . . and the evil one" (Yasna 30.3; 45.2). Zoroastrian or Mazdean doctrine in late antiquity separated order (Avestan *asha*, Old Persian *arta*, Middle Persian *ardā*), also comprehended as good or the truth, from chaos (Avestan *drug, druj*, Old Persian *drauga*, Middle Persian *druz*), also comprehended as evil or the lie. Eventually, Ahura Mazda came to be regarded as the absolutely righteous creator—a pure, rational, and omniscient deity—who did not, indeed could not, produce any form of disorder (Shkand Gumānīg Wizār 8.101–10). As a consequence, all events that disturbed order were seen as pollution (Avestan *irimant*, Middle Persian *rēmanīh*), hence sinful (Avestan *vīnas*, Middle Persian *wināh/wināh* [to be destroyed])—necessitating penance (Avestan *paitita*, Middle Persian *petīt*) and repentance (Middle Persian *pashēmānīh*) so that absolution occurred with the person's soul turning away from evil.

Bad thoughts (Avestan *dushmata*, Middle Persian *dushmat*), bad words (Avestan *duzhūxta*, Middle Persian *dushūxt*), and bad deeds (Avestan *duzhvarshta*, Middle Persian *dushxwarsht*)—including impious ideas, lies, and harmful actions—were seen as increasing chaos. The far-reaching negative consequences of negative thinking—impacting every aspect of existence from a religious viewpoint—was expounded by Zarathustra himself: "Some of the divine entities did not choose rightly between these two spirits. Ignorance beset them as they pondered, so they chose the worst thought. Consequently, they sided with wrath, thereby afflicting human life" (Yasna 30.6). Bad words and deeds, in this case disobeying Ahura Mazda by claiming that creation arose from Angra Mainyu and by worshiping evil, were said to have caused the fall of the first mortal couple—Mashya and Mashyana—paralleling in some ways the biblical story of Adam and Eve (*Bundahishn* 14.11–29). The Achaemenian ruler Darius I (522–486 BCE) explained political uprisings in his empire by claiming, "It was the lie that made them rebellious" (Behistun inscription 4.34). Even physiological processes such as bleeding, urinating, and exhaling were given negative connotations for crossing the sanctified boundary of the body. A myth in which Angra Mainyu demonstrated sexual attraction toward Jahika or Jeh the Whore demoness developed to marginalize menstruation as a polluting aberration: "Angra Mainyu . . . arose from a stupor, kissed the Whore's face, [and] the pollution called menstruation flowed from her" (*Bundahishn* 4.5). Sex and reproduction, however, would not be viewed as intrinsically unclean because such acts resulted in the continued birth of Zoroastrians to combat evil in the material world. Given that the high god Ahura Mazda was held to have created the world and all good creatures and that life was meant to combat chaos, death became the symbol of disorder *par excellence* which, consequently, was thought to spread pollution far and wide—affecting elements such as earth, water, and fire and creatures such as plants and animals. The Denkard or Acts of the Religion, juxtaposing life with purity and demise with pollution, provides a description of death as an attack "upon an individual's essence—the soul, and upon the soul's instrument and garment—the body; . . . evil strives to annihilate and defile an individual's essence, instrument, and garment" (383–84).

All such occurrences of sinful pollution had to be rectified ritually, through a combination of words and deeds. Uncorrected disorder, however indirectly associated with an individual, supposedly weighed against his or her soul at judgment after death and could result in torment by evil spiritual entities in hell, as forewarned by Zarathustra himself: "In the end, those who follow disorder will gain the worst existence" (Yasna 30.4). Once consigned to hell as the result of nonabsolved evil actions while alive, a soul remains there until the eschatological renovation (Avestan *frashō.kereti*, Middle Persian *frashagird*) of creation (*Bundahishn* 34.5–32). At a most basic level, sin could be expiated and absolution earned by reciting a confessional called the Petīt Pashēmānīh.

Pollution caused by contact with unclean objects, especially corpses, necessitated purification rituals involving the polluted individuals, one or more priests who functioned as purifiers (Avestan *yaozhdāthrya*, Middle Persian *yōjdāhrgar*), substances such as water and dust that cleansed the body physically or the soul symbolically, and rites such as the Pādyāb and the Barashnūm, which lasted from a few minutes to nine days respectively. Given the belief that pollutants—doctrinally embodied in a female ghoul named Nasush or Nasa who traveled in the form of a fly, an insect believed to have been malformed by Angra Mainyu—could spread, major rituals of purification from contact with carrion would not be performed within devotional settings to prevent pollution, however indirect, of holy fires, pure priests, and pious devotees. Rather, sites were set aside for purificatory rites. Items such as clothes and utensils that had come into contact with the religiously unclean person also had to be purified by washing. Locales rendered ritually unclean would be cleansed via washing and/or fumigation. Pollution symbolically inflicted by death will be exorcised by Ahura Mazda during the final resurrection and cleansing of the world, as was claimed later in Zoroastrian eschatological texts such as the Zand ī Wahman Yasht.

Manichean doctrines and rituals drew upon many aspects of Zoroastrian thought and religious terminology, combining and modifying them with Judeo-Christian, Hindu, and Buddhist ideas, to develop notions of pollution and purity, sin and absolution, for explaining life and death within an esoteric framework. Unlike Zoroastrianism, Manichean dualism followed Christian and gnostic thought in regarding matter as unclean and, therefore, life itself as undesirable. The high god, variously named Zurwan (Time), Pidar Roshn (Father of Light), and Pidar i Wuzurgih (Father of Greatness) by the Manicheans, was "righteous . . . the blissful one among the lights" (M 10 R 11). Life was supposed to center on the need to liberate, through *gnōsis*, portions of spirit or light trapped by the evil spirit Ahriman within the darkness of matter and passed through cycles of human reincarnation by Az the demoness of lust, who was scorned as "the mother of all maleficent spirits, the source of all sin" (M 183 I). Consequently sex and procreation, plus physiological processes such as menstruation that are associated with reproduction, came to be viewed negatively by male and female Manichean elect or monks as transferring pure spirit from one unclean corporeal generation to another. In other words, such acts and bodily functions were completely polluting from the religious standpoint. Hearers or laymen and laywomen could bear children only if absolutely necessary—they, too, were encouraged to practice abstinence and regulate their lives so as to minimize discharge of semen and menstrual blood—because the human body, allegedly crafted by Az from "the carrion of demons and the pollutant of demonesses" was thought to form "a prison [that] shackled the miserable soul" (S 9 R 2.30).

The purpose of existence for Manicheans became purity and, through it, release from "the five pits of destruction" or the material world so that the soul could return to the perfect realm of light or heaven where there is "not chaos . . . not sin . . . not death" (M 507; M 183 I). Purification and salvation from corporeal life could be achieved by Manicheans, it was held, only through strict adherence to precepts that included celibacy and vegetarianism, coupled with a strict regimen of prayer, fasting, and confession of sins (M 49 I; M 135 B; M 801; M 5794 II). As in Zoroastrianism, once salvation of individual souls had been achieved there was to be a universal renovation. In the Manichean eschatological stage, all spirit or light would be freed from matter, purified by divine beings such as Jesus, reenter the heavenly realm of light, and reunite with the high god (M 473; M 475; M 477; M 482; M 472; M 470).

Through contrasting categories such as pollution and purity, sin and absolution, Zoroastrian and Manichean doctrines and practices sought to reassure congregations that the problem of disorder or evil is restricted to a particular place—the earth—and to a finite period—the phase between creation and eschaton. Thereafter, there supposedly would be order or goodness in both purified space and infinite time.

BIBL.: Mary Boyce, *The Manichaean Hymn-Cycles in Parthian* (Oxford, 1954). Jamsheed K. Choksy, *Purity and Pollution in Zoroastrianism: Triumph over Evil* (Austin, 1989). A. V. Williams Jackson, "A Sketch of the Manichaean Doctrine concerning the Future Life," *Journal of the American Oriental Society* 50 (1930): 177–98. David N. McKenzie, "Mani's šābuhragān," *Bulletin of the School of Oriental and African Studies* 42 (1979): 500–534; 43 (1980): 288–310. Robert C. Zaehner, *The Dawn and Twilight of Zoroastrianism* (London, 1961). J.K.C.

Greece

From the oracle of Zeus at Dodona in northwestern Greece there survive numerous lead tablets from the classical period, inscribed with actual questions put to the oracle. One runs, "Is it because of the impurity [*akathartia*] of a mortal that the god is causing the storm?" (*SEG* 19 [1963]: 149 no. 427). Evils much worse than bad weather are caused by pollution at the start of Sophocles' *Oedipus Tyrannus*: the crops have failed, neither women nor animals can give birth, plague rages—and the cause turns out to be the presence in the city of Oedipus, who has unknowingly murdered his father and married his mother. Generalized pollution of this kind is, as it were, fertility turned upside down.

The myth of Oedipus is one of many myths and pseudohistorical narratives that tell of some or all of the same triad of evils afflicting a city in consequence of pollution, usually the pollution of bloodshed. A set of model speeches of the late 5th century BCE, designed to show how to argue both sides of a case in murder trials

Apollo purifies Orestes at Delphi with a piglet; to the right stands Artemis, to the left the Erinyes are sleeping. Redfigure bell krater from Apulia, 390–380 BCE. Louvre. *Réunion des Musées Nationaux/Art Resource, New York*

(the *Tetralogies* of Antiphon), deftly bats the argument for pollution back and forth across the net: to acquit a killer plunges jury and city into terrible danger, but so, too, does condemnation of an innocent person. Myths also portray the sufferings of the polluted person; the extreme case is Orestes, hounded from land to land in madness by the avenging furies (Erinyes)—a kind of animate pollution of the mother he had murdered. The Greek term for this, and for many other types of pollution, is *miasma*, although other words, such as *akatharsia* (lit., lack of purity), expressed the general idea as well.

Pollution, however, was not necessarily indelible. Even killers could be readmitted to society, whether abroad (the commonest case) or, after a period of exile, at home. The elaborate purification ritual that they had to undergo—"washing away blood with blood [of a piglet]"—is most fully described in the *Argonautica* of Apollonius Rhodius (4.685–717). Often, the polluting offense that endangered a community was itself a collective one, the killing of suppliants or heralds, for instance (bloodshed aggravated by sacrilege), perpetrated by a large section of the citizens or by their representatives, the magistrates. Exile of the guilty parties being in this case impossible, a symbolic restitution or reparation might be attempted instead, by setting up statues of the victims or by granting them cultic honors.

Beliefs of this kind are instruments of social control. They reinforce inhibitions against killing (or rather the wrong kind of killing: killing during open warfare creates no pollution). When killing occurs, by an individual or a community, they press for something to be done about it. They could also have a secondary function as explanations for misfortune, and Greeks often traced communal disasters back to past crimes; Herodotus, for instance, ascribes the expulsion of the Aeginetans from their island in 431 BCE to a pollution incurred half a century earlier, which they proved unable to "sacrifice out" (6.91). For the Attic tragedians, Aeschylus above all, pollution could be inherited within families.

Did pollution beliefs also serve as guides to action for states and individuals when they were actually in the grip of affliction? Would a plague-ridden state seek to identify and eliminate a responsible pollution? Several Greek states performed an annual ritual expulsion of human scapegoats (the Greek term is *pharmakoi*, a cognate of *pharmaka* [medicines]), who took away with them the ills of the community (see Ritual). Some ancient sources state that the ritual was also performed as needed, in time of crisis. No actual case is known, however; and the question put to the oracle at Dodona is one of the few firm historical items of evidence for "pollution hunts" as a reaction to disaster. The response to crisis was often to propitiate the gods—old gods, new gods—with renewed fervor, rather than to seek to identify guilty individuals. It was apparently in response to the great plague of 430–427 BCE that in 426 the Athenians "purified" the sacred island of Delos: all existing graves were removed, and henceforth neither death nor birth was to be permitted on the island (Thucydides 3.104). Here, pollution was indeed identified as a cause of ill, but the pollution was a matter of bad ritual practices, not of murderers wandering the streets undetected. Sick individuals, too, might be offered treatment by certain self-styled "purifiers" (see the attacks on them in the Hippocratic *On the Sacred Disease*). But neither purifiers nor other types of religious healers seem regularly to have blamed diseases on the past conduct of the patient or on pollutions that he or she had incurred.

The intensity of Greek anxiety about pollution should not be overestimated, therefore. For most Greeks, most of the time, concern for purity amounted to respect for certain, not very arduous, everyday rules. Birth and death counted as pollutions; after attending a funeral or entering a house where birth had occurred, one could not approach a temple for a few days (and persons such as priests, required to live in conditions of special purity, had to avoid polluting contacts altogether). Kin of a new mother or a dead person remained unclean for a little longer than mere acquaintances did. These rules have nothing to do with modern rules of hygiene; the separation that the rules insist on is that between natural processes and the sacred—in the case mentioned earlier, the Athenians believed that the presence of tombs on Delos had polluted the sacred island. After sex, one had to wash before entering a shrine. Restrictions on diet are rarely attested, and menstruation seems not to have been a pollution. But sanctuaries had rules of their own about objects that could be introduced into them, and a violation of such rules might require purification of the shrine even if the offending object—a piece of iron or an elaborate dress, say—was not intrinsically impure.

Rules of this kind were often written up at the entrance to temples. A famous inscription over the entrance to the temple of Asclepius at Epidaurus introduced a new note: "Within the fragrant temple one must be pure; and purity is to think holy thoughts" (Porphyry, *On Abstinence* 2.19). (This last phrase is not an exhortation to pious contemplation; what is meant is to have nothing in one's mind that will offend the gods.) That worthy sentiment was often echoed later. But there was some artificiality in this attempt to assimilate rules of purity to rules of morality; the two things overlapped one another without coinciding. Some pollutions might be incurred through socially recommended behavior such as attendance at a funeral. And the Epidaurian couplet did not, in fact, signal a suspension of all or indeed any taboos. To enter a temple, it was normally necessary to have had no recent contact with a woman in childbed, as well as to have a pious mind.

A poem or a part of a poem by the early-5th-century philosopher and scientist Empedocles was called "Purifications." Here we encounter an application of the idea of purification quite different from any we have considered thus far. Empedocles belonged to a minority tradition in Greek thought, one hostile to the body and concerned for the fate of the soul. Empedocles believed himself to be a fallen god who had passed, by metempsychosis, through a series of incarnations and was now apparently on the point of returning to his original state of beatitude. An ascetic hostility to the body is found also in Pythagoreanism (a movement that started with Pythagoras in the 6th century BCE), while similar ideas of guilt and expiation of guilt were taught in poems (probably also written in the 6th century) ascribed to the mythical singer Orpheus. In these Pythagorean-Orphic contexts, "purification" began to refer not just to specific rituals but to a way of life (the chief element of which was vegetarianism), which would liberate the soul from inherited guilt and give it access to a better lot in the afterlife. Plato (in the *Phaedo* above all) was much influenced by such ideas. But they remained outside the mainstream, and for most Greeks "purity" remained a matter of humdrum precautions and routines.

Most Greeks would not have had much sympathy with the insistence of these esoteric movements on the badness of mortals, either. The main Greek religious tradition encouraged mortals to see themselves as powerless, indeed, in contrast to the gods, but not as flawed in a diffuse and general way. Religious guilt could be incurred and religious anxiety could be felt, but usually only over specific offenses committed by oneself or one's forebears. An omitted sacrifice, a serious pollution, a violation of the rules of a sanctuary, a broken oath—any of these might be "on one's mind" *(enthymios),* and if one had many such things on one's mind one forfeited "good hopes" for the future (and might even become anxious about the afterlife). But that was because one feared punishment from figures in authority, namely, the gods. The Greek gods had not created either the universe or humankind, and they were viewed as social superiors to be propitiated rather than parent figures before whom one might feel guilt and shame.

BIBL.: Andreas Bendlin, "Reinheit/Unreinheit," in *Handbuch religionswissenschaftlicher Grundbegriffe* (ed. Hubert Cancik, Burkhard Gladigow, and K. H. Kohl; Stuttgart, 1998), 4.412–15. Angelos Chaniotis, "Reinheit des Körpers—Reinheit des Sinnes in den griechischen Kultgesetzen," in *Studien zum Verstehen fremder Religionen,* vol. 9: *Schuld, Gewissen und Person* (ed. J. Assmann and T. Sundermeier; Gütersloh, 1997), 142–78. S. G. Cole, "*Gynaiki ou Themis:* Gender Difference in the Greek *Leges Sacrae,*" *Helios* 19 (1992): 104–22. Robert Parker, *Miasma: Pollution and Purification in Early Greek Religion* (Oxford, 1996 [orig. 1983]). Heinrich von Staden, "Women and Dirt," *Helios* 19 (1992): 7–30.   R.C.T.P.

Rome

In the "Banquet of Trimalchio," the sole extended episode to survive from Petronius's novel, the *Satyrica,* the conversation of the guests turns (as it usually does late on in dinner parties) to the decline of social standards. The society we are supposed to imagine is that of Petronius's own day (mid-1st century CE) in a substantial city of Campania; the attitudes are those of Trimalchio's freedman peers: prosperous, opinionated, unintellectual. One of them, predictably, speaks of the decline of religion:

> Whatever is to happen if neither the gods nor man will take pity on this town? As I hope to have joy of my children, I believe all these things come from heaven. For no one now believes that the gods are gods. There is no fasting done, no one cares a button for religion: they all shut their eyes and count their own goods. In old days the mothers in their best robes used to climb the hill with bare feet and loose hair, pure in spirit, and pray Jupiter to send rain. Then it used promptly to rain by the bucket . . . and they all came home wet as drowned rats. As it is, the gods steal upon us with wooly feet because we are sceptics. So our fields lie baking. (44.16–18, trans. Heseltine)

This extract portrays an ordinary Roman's attitude to pollution/sin and its expiation, captured by a genius of ancient fiction. Notice the inferred causal chain: something has gone wrong *vis-à-vis* the gods (in this case, general neglect of their cult); the consequence is manifest public misfortune (drought followed by scarcity of grain and escalating prices); the remedy is appropriate ritual action and intercession with the gods (a procession of matrons to the municipal Capitol and prayers to Jupiter).

Perhaps the first point to make is that neither "pollution" nor "sin" quite covers what we want to express, which is simply that sense of something (a person, an object, an activity) being amiss, out of order, in relation to the gods. Latin *polluo* means simply "to make dirty" and is more common in the literal than in the figurative religious sense. Although the verb has a passive participial adjective (*pollutus* [polluted]), there is no corresponding noun. There is no Latin equivalent with quite the evocative physicality of Greek *miasma.* If the Romans wanted to characterize something as thoroughly amiss supernaturally, they might call it *sacrum* (sacred) in the negative sense of "accursed." In this negative sense, a thing or (more usually) a person could be made *sacer* by ritual or judicial action, literally "cursed," and thus be excluded from the community because the thing or person was deemed irremediably at fault in relation to the gods. Our word *sin,* of course, carries altogether too much spiritual and specifically Christian baggage, although, as we shall see, the concept was not entirely alien to the Romans. The Latin verb that was to provide the standard term for sinning, *peccare,* originally meant "to stumble," hence "to make a mistake." It was frequently used for moral errors, but not necessarily or even usually with supernatural implications. There were, of course, other Latin words for wrongdoing, notably *scelus* (wicked action, crime), which could (but did not have to) carry religious connotations. For a mistake made in ritual, which would inevitably have negative consequences tantamount to "pollution," a Roman might speak of *vitium,* but without any connotations of the English derivative *vice.* Finally, a person who subverted, knowingly and systematically, right relations with the gods (and fellow humans) would be deemed and termed *impius:* in Roman eyes, there was nothing worse.

Although an absence is difficult to demonstrate, Roman culture seems to have been relatively free of the sense that there exists a class of naturally occurring things that pollute in and of themselves, for example, certain types of food source, menstruation, childbirth, and consequently women menstruating or giving birth. Death might appear to be the exception. Nevertheless it was not the corpse itself that polluted, as in contemporaneous Zoroastrianism, for there were few Roman taboos on handling corpses or on corpse handlers. What polluted was the continued presence of the dead in the home and community of the living; and that was a potential for pollution, rather than an actual pollution, and it was obviated by the removal and interment of the mortal remains beyond the formal city limits (*pomerium*) with proper *exsequies* (Latin *ex[s]equiae* [followings out]).

"Things go wrong" in relation to the gods when a ritual is improperly performed or a taboo is broken. That, rather than a full-blown moral offense, was in most cases the cause of the fault. Because virtually all action in the public sphere was hedged around with religious ceremony and all high public officials had ceremonial responsibilities, occasions for error were numerous and their consequences grave. Furthermore, although the fault might be an individual's, its consequences were communal. The gods whose rites were compromised inflicted collective punishment. Besides, how else, other than by the evidence of public disaster, could one know for sure that "religion" had indeed been compromised?

The official reaction to one of Rome's great military disasters, the destruction of a consular army by Hannibal at Lake Trasimene (217 BCE), provides an example. The report is Livy's (22.9.7–10), and for our purposes it matters little that it is his (very Roman) voice that we are hearing overlaid on those of the players two hundred years earlier: "Quintus Fabius Maximus, now dictator once more, convened the Senate on the day he took office. Beginning with matters of religion [*ab dis orsus* (lit., beginning from the gods)], he convinced the Fathers that the consul Gaius Flaminius had erred more through his neglect of the ceremonies [*neglegentia caerimoniarum*] than through recklessness and ignorance, and that they ought to consult the gods themselves as to what way their anger might be appeased [*quaeque piacula irae essent* (lit., what expiations of their anger there might be)]" (trans. Foster).

On consulting the Sibylline Books (prophetic texts held by the state), it was determined "that the vow made to Mars on account of this war had not been properly performed [*non rite factum*]." The remedy was not only to perform again the flawed rite more lavishly but also to hold a *supplicatio* (formal prayers) and a *lectisternium* (a feast of the gods' images) and to vow a major festival of games, two temples, and, should the war be fought to a successful conclusion, a sacred spring *(ver sacrum)*—that is, the sacrifice of an entire season of livestock. An extraordinary crisis, thought to have been precipitated by what to us would seem a trivial and venial mistake, called for extraordinary countermeasures. The Romans also had a more-routine ritual of purification, the *lustratio,* a procession with animal victims around the boundaries of the affected area, followed by sacrifice.

A second example is provided by the ritual cursing of the consul Marcus Licinius Crassus by the tribune Gaius Ateius Capito, as the former was about to leave Rome late in 55 BCE to make war on the Parthians. The case is interesting because the religious fault was imposed on, rather than unwittingly incurred by, its carrier and also because the fault had a moral dimension: Crassus's war was widely (and properly) considered unjust, being more about Crassus's glory-hunting than Parthian wrongdoing. Here is Plutarch's description (*Life of Crassus* 16.5–6; note the somewhat melodramatic Greek overlay):

[After a thwarted attempt at physical arrest] Ateius then ran on ahead to the city gate where he set up a brazier with lighted fuel in it. When Crassus came to the gate, [Ateius] threw incense and libations on the brazier and called down on [Crassus] curses which were dreadful and frightening enough in themselves and made still more dreadful by the names of certain strange and terrible deities. . . . The Romans believe that these mysterious and ancient curses are so powerful that no one who has had them laid upon him can escape from their effect. . . . So on this occasion people blamed Ateius for what he had done; he had been angry with Crassus for the sake of Rome, yet he had involved Rome in these curses and in the terror which must be felt of supernatural intervention. (trans. Warner)

Rome had good reason for dread: two years later, Crassus and his legions were annihilated at Carrhae. One wonders how Ateius felt: vindicated—or aghast at the magnitude of the loss his curses had precipitated?

In this second story moral guilt plays as large a part as formal impurity. Whatever Ateius's partisan political motives, right was on his side: on Roman criteria of just and unjust wars, the war against Parthia was wrong. The dead at Carrhae paid the price of public guilt; Ateius's curses, in a sense, merely sealed a doom incurred by Roman state aggression.

The period that saw the fracturing of the republican system, the civil wars of the 40s and 30s BCE, and the establishment of the principate (marketed as the republic's restoration) saw also a pervasive sense of unease, verging on national guilt. Rome, it was felt, was justly punished by the gods for a collective impiety in which the neglect of religion was the principal cause of divine displeasure but which was manifested also in the dissolution of social ties and obligations, obscene wealth accruing to a few individuals and families from the profits of empire, and outbreaks of internecine violence all the more cruel because no longer inhibited by traditional ethical restraints. These are some of the themes that permeate the works of the two great Augustan poets Vergil and Horace and are most clearly articulated in the first stanza of one of the latter's "state odes" (note how impiety in one generation may be punished in the next): "You will pay for your fathers' crimes, Roman, though you do not deserve it, until you restore the gods' collapsing temples and their images polluted with black smoke" (*Odes* 3.6.1–4).

A skeptic might say that "neglect" of religion was a fiction of the new administration promoting the statesman Augustus, who "restored" religion by, among other things, physically restoring and building so many of its temples. But that is beside the point, which is rather that a narrative of collective sin, divine punishment, and expiation entered Roman discourse, however engineered. We hear its humbler echoes in the talk at the banquet of Trimalchio with which this exploration began. Note there the causality: the pursuit of private gain and the collapse of a communitarian ethic trigger the anger of the gods, which manifests itself in drought. Note too that a change of attitude, not just ritual action, is called for: the barefoot matrons must climb the local Capitol "with pure minds" (although one textual scholar, finding this un-Roman, emends *mentibus* [minds] to *vestibus* [clothes]!). Anxiety that slighted gods could and did visit disaster on the commonwealth was widespread and persistent. It was a major factor in the persecution of Christians both in the 250s and finally at the turn of the 3rd and 4th centuries CE. By opting out of—or worse, by surreptitiously polluting—the cult of the gods, the Christian "atheists" drew down divine anger, its symptoms all too manifest whenever natural or human-caused (as we would see it) disaster struck.

Certainly, then, the Romans had a lively sense of collective guilt, its modalities, and its expiations. Was there a corresponding sense of personal sin and its personal expiation or absolution? There was, although it was probably untypical and concentrated, where one would expect it, in the cults focused on savior-gods, the so-called mystery cults, which in that respect parallel early Christianity. In the cult of Mithras, for example, initiates of the "Lion" grade were warned against and ritually purified from "everything grievous, noxious, and foul . . . and from everything sinful" (Porphyry, *On the Care of the Nymphs* 15).

We began this exploration with a vignette from Petronius's *Satyrica*, whose comic plot, incidentally, parodies the classic tale of religious crime and punishment in that its louche hero-narrator Encolpius has sinned against the ithyphallic god Priapus and suffers priapic misadventures accordingly. Let us conclude with a glance at Rome's other great novel, the *Golden Ass* by Apuleius, a work of equal playfulness but containing an altogether graver narrative of guilt, punishment, and restoration. It tells the story of a young man, Lucius, whose pursuit of the sinister art of magic leads first to his transformation into an ass but eventually—and providentially—to his rescue by the goddess Isis, whose devotee he remains. One finds in this context a scenario of moral and spiritual transgression, of consequent suffering, and of absolution and salvation extended by divine grace, which for all its bizarre detail (not to mention the much debated complications of authorial intent) is every bit as full-blown as any narrative of contemporary Christianity.

BIBL.: R. M. Ogilvie, "Lustrum Condere," *Journal of Roman Studies* 51 (1961): 31–39. H. S. Versnel, "Sacrificium Lustrale: The Death of Mettius Fufetius (Livy I, 28); Studies in Roman Lustration-Ritual 1," *Mededelingen van het Nederlandsch historisch Institut te Rome* 37 (1975): 1–19. A. Wallace-Hadrill, "The Golden Age and Sin in Augustan Ideology," *Past and Present* 95 (1982): 19–36. R. E. Witt, *Isis in the Graeco-Roman World* (London, 1971).   R.L.B.

Christianity

The forceful displacement of "pollution" by "sin" may seem indelibly inscribed into the very origin of Christianity. Jesus himself is frequently depicted contesting the Pharisaic appropriation of biblical purity laws that had previously applied more narrowly to the Jerusalem temple cult and its priesthood. In Mark's Gospel, he di-

rectly challenges the practice of hand washing before meals when he proclaims that "there is nothing outside a man which by going into him can defile him" (Mark 7.15; cf. 7.3–4). Jesus incurs impurity when he touches a leper (1.41), a corpse (5.41), and a woman with a hemorrhage (5.25–34). Not long after Jesus's death, the controversial Christian missionary Paul (himself a Pharisaic Jew) went so far as to reject the necessity not merely of ritual purity but of legal observance more generally. In effect denying that Jewishness was a prerequisite for salvation "in Christ," Paul argued famously that it is not the law—circumcision, *kašrût* (observance of dietary laws), and the observance of the sabbath and holidays—but "faith of Christ" that renders one righteous in the eyes of God. At the same time, Paul's writings foreground the universal sinfulness of humanity. Reading Gen. 3, he proposes an innovative history of salvation: the first human, Adam, introduced sin (and thus death) to all humanity, a sin exposed but not eliminated by the Mosaic law; correspondingly, Jesus Christ, "the last Adam," through his death and resurrection, has freed all humanity from the power of sin, death, and law (Rom. 5; 1 Cor. 15.45–49).

With spiritual "absolution" superseding material "purity" as the central goal of religious practice, the rise of the church may also be represented as the incitement of the guilty conscience and the unfolding of the interiorized, transcendental self. What Paul initiates, Augustine, author of the doctrine of "original sin," eventually perfects—the confessional subject of flawed desire, absolved through the arbitrary gift of a merciful God, for whom the flesh and its disciplines (in themselves neither clean nor unclean) have become a matter of relative indifference (*Literal Interpretation of Genesis* 6.24.35; 11.1.3; *On the Forgiveness of Sins and Baptism of Infants* 1.9.10; 1.20.27).

Hinging on conversion and thereby highlighting contrast, such a narrative illumines certain aspects of ancient Christianity while casting others in shadow. The constructed opposition of impurity and sin, together with the tendency to conflate impurity with other forms of legal transgression recognized by Judaism, may impede a full understanding of both Paul and Christians of a later antiquity. The contrast of pollution-based and sin-based religious orientations further obscures the enduring similarities between nascent Christianity and protorabbinic Judaism (together with the varied "pagan" religions with which these overlapped and interacted), as well as the diversity and complexity of late ancient Christian definitions of sin. Even within non-Christian Judaism, the discourse of purity blurred with ethics and asceticism and intersected with cosmology and liturgy, so that it is often difficult to distinguish sharply between notions of impurity, sin, or other forms of social taboo and transgression, particularly after 70 CE, when the Jerusalem temple and its priestly cult were destroyed. For their part, Christians not only retained concepts of purity in the very act of spiritualizing and superseding them (cf. Letter to the Hebrews), but also continued to interweave spiritual understandings of sin with material concepts of purity, working out of a multifaceted cultural heritage.

In reconstructing ancient Christian discourses of sin and pollution, the challenge lies in isolating what appears both distinctive and relatively constant, so as to make Christianity itself visible as an object of historical inquiry, while at the same time not losing sight of internal complexity and contradiction and of all that is similar to or shared with other religious traditions of antiquity. Three figures and contexts illustrate this challenge.

Tertullian. Tertullian of Carthage (fl. 196–212) is one of the first Christians to provide a view of sin sufficiently elaborate as to approach the systematic. Notorious for his misogynistic framing of the Pauline narrative of humanity's fall (*On the Apparel of Women* 1.1), like Paul he is also, paradoxically, notable for his egalitarianism: for Tertullian, the Holy Spirit is no respecter of persons, and the purity of priesthood is available to all believers. Practice and theory coalesce in his discussions of sin, sanctification, penance, and absolution.

"The principal crime of the human race, the highest guilt charged upon the world, the whole procuring cause of judgment, is idolatry." For Tertullian, all human transgressions derive from the root sin of "refusing to God, and conferring upon others, God's honors" (*On Idolatry* 1). Vigilance is required to avoid not only easily recognizable instances of immorality but also social actions that implicate one even indirectly in the worship of false gods. An inherent professional liability for artists, teachers, government officials, soldiers, and merchants, idolatry is a threat as well for any who observe public holidays, attend parties and performances, enter into contractual agreements, or exchange common greetings and blessings (see also *On the Shows* and *On the Chaplet*). The lifestyle of discipline that avoids the taint permeating the dominant culture thus serves not only to keep the individual soul pure but also to demarcate the boundaries of the Christian community—already sharply drawn in a time of intermittent persecution. Shunning idolatry, an imperative derived from the Jewish scriptures, is now framed as a law "peculiar to Christians." Comparing the church to the ark of Noah, Tertullian remarks that "no animal has been fashioned to represent an idolater," concluding, "Let not that be in the church which was not in the ark" (*On Idolatry* 24).

The waters that overwhelm the sinners who remain outside the ark also wash away the sins of those who enter it. In his treatise *On Baptism,* Tertullian admits that it may seem astonishing that "death may be washed away by bathing"; nonetheless, the purifying properties of water should not be underestimated. "The Spirit of God, who hovered over the waters from the beginning, continues to linger over the waters of the baptized" (*On Baptism* 4). An "angel of baptism" furthermore resides in the waters themselves, cleansing sins and thereby preparing the initiate for the reception of the hovering Spirit through the anointing and laying on of hands (5–8).

The purification and sanctification effected in baptism is not repeatable, but it is reversible. Hence the importance of the lifestyle of discipline: holiness, once won, must be protected. In an early work, Tertullian stresses the importance of repentance for postbaptismal sin and refers to the rituals of public penance and communal supplication through which absolution is granted (*On Repentance* 9–12). In a later work, however, he takes a more rigorous stance, denouncing the bishop of Rome for presuming to forgive sexual sins. Continuing to affirm that minor sins are pardoned by Christ through the church, Tertullian distinguishes other "graver and deadly sins"—murder, idolatry, injustice, apostasy, blasphemy, adultery, fornication. "The one who has been born of God will not commit them at all" (*On Modesty* 19). Neither the church nor its bishops can mediate forgiveness of such sins, and the sinner must remain outside the communion of the church. There is one exception to this rule: martyrdom, understood as the absolute rejection of idolatry, constitutes a second baptism, not of water but of blood, which cleanses and sanctifies the Christian soiled by even "deadly" sin.

Origen. Origen of Alexandria (ca. 185–ca. 251) shares with Tertullian a high valuation of both martyrdom and asceticism. His concept of Christian "witness" and "discipline" is, however, more elitist than separatist, and for him baptism is of less interest as a physical rite than as an image of the fiery purification of the spirit that is the goal of divine pedagogy.

Confident that rational spirits were created to love and contemplate God eternally, Origen, in *On First Principles* (his most speculative work), seeks to discover the reasons for the fall. Like his gnostic contemporaries (and here differing from both Paul and Tertullian), he discerns in that first, mythic lapse not merely the origin of sin but also the cause of the material creation: in a process of devolution replayed scripturally in the slide from Gen. 1 to Gen. 2, ardent spirits "wax cold" and thereby take on the drag of mortal flesh (*On First Principles* 2.8.3–4). In contrast to the gnostics, however, Origen understands the cosmos to be the gift of a loving God for the reeducation of fallen souls (*Against Celsus* 6.44). He also stresses that the precosmic fall, although collective, is only incidentally so. Any and all might have persevered in love, and indeed at least one did: the soul of Jesus never wavered in its desire for God (*On First Principles* 2.6.3–5). Others withdrew willfully from contemplation, whether due to negligence or to satiety (1.3.8–1.4.1), each in turn finding his or her own level in the variegated cosmic classroom. Free will, leading to the possibility of sin and the certainty of God's carefully calibrated response, is thus the source of diversity in the world: "Each intellect, neglecting goodness either to a greater or more limited extent, was dragged into the opposite of good, which undoubtedly is evil—

from which it appears that the creator of all things admitted certain seeds and causes of variety and diversity" (2.9.2).

Asceticism for Origen is both a discipline of the flesh and a method of transcending the flesh in the reascent to divine contemplation. (A 4th-century student of Origen's work, Evagrius of Pontus, later identified eight basic "thoughts" that impede contemplation: gluttony, lust, avarice, sadness, anger, acedia, vainglory, pride.) Asceticism is also closely linked to the allegorical interpretation of scripture, through which the Word draws the soul ever higher, in the rise from the literal to the figurative sense. If sin, for Origen, is the universal state of a humanity presently mired in materiality, he remains strongly optimistic about the power of pedagogy to restore all spirits to their original, ethereal purity.

Augustine. It is Augustine of Hippo (354–430) who finally makes sin a matter of controversy and thus also of official doctrine. In so doing, he not only breaks with the ascetic traditions conveyed by Origen and later by both Origenists in the East and Pelagians in the West; he also breaks with the separatist stance taken by Tertullian and later by the African Donatists. Blurring the distinction between saints and sinners, church and world, Augustine thereby acknowledges the profound and disturbing ambiguity of a Christianized empire—even as Roman rule begins to erode in the West. Ironically perhaps, he becomes a major resource and authority for the forgers of a European Christendom inclined to minimize the ambiguity of earthly institutions confidently identified with divine will.

Augustine's highly original reconceptualizing of human sin turns on the originality of sin itself. Returning to the Pauline narrative of the fall, he places new emphasis on the collective character of Adam's initial sin. A prolific writer, he offers an ever more literal interpretation of that fall, in works that span the exegetical and homiletic, the doctrinal and polemical, and the historical and novelistic—most famously replaying the history of sin and salvation in the grand narratives of self *(Con-*

fessions) and cosmos *(City of God).* When Adam pridefully turns against God, sin infects his soul like a disease, according to Augustine, turning the human against himself, dividing his will, and subjecting him to the ultimate perversity of loving what is not God, but merely creaturely, as if it were an end in itself. No more than Adam can subsequent humanity remove the stubborn psychological flaw transmitted genetically in the reproduction of the race through repeatedly staged consummations of lust. All are born out of perverse passion, destined to sin, and none is healed of sin except through the unmerited grace of God, mediated through Christ in the sacraments. Those sacraments, above all baptism, are understood as performative signs, the power of which is not dependent on the purity—ritual, moral, or doctrinal—of the priest, though their efficacy is conditioned by the attitude of the recipient. The church is not pure, but like Noah's ark includes both the clean and the unclean creatures (here Augustine puts a new twist on Tertullian's metaphor), and no soul is without the taint of sin: nonetheless, God is active in the world. Indeed, Augustine comes close to suggesting that God is the only actor, solely responsible for all instances of virtue (or, correspondingly, of sin—which introduces the controversial notion of "double predestination").

Although here positioned at the end of the narrative, as so often in accounts of Western Christianity, Augustine's thought, however influential, should not be represented as the culmination of ancient Christian teachings about sin. The "purist" positions represented by Tertullian and Origen, respectively, were and have remained historically lively alternatives.

BIBL.: Ernst Dassmann, *Sündenvergebung durch Taufe, Busse und Martyrerfürbitte in den Zeugnissen frühchristlicher Frömmigkeit und Kunst* (Münster, 1973). G. M. Lukken, *Original Sin in the Roman Liturgy: Research into the Theology of Original Sin in the Roman Sacramentaria and the Early Baptismal Liturgy* (Leiden, 1973). Stanislas Lyonnet and Léopold Sabourin, *Sin, Redemption, and Sacrifice: A Biblical and Patristic Study* (Rome, 1970).   V.B.

Ethics and Law Codes

Egypt

For a culture to have a set of ethical standards is a widespread human phenomenon; indeed, it might even be a universal. And ancient Egypt was no exception in this regard.

We have textual sources regarding ethical conduct from nearly all periods of Egyptian history. These sources are both secular and religious in nature. Our secular sources consist chiefly of didactic texts, while the religious sources are related to the beliefs and practices surrounding the cult of the dead.

In Egypt, it was the norm for kingship to pass from father to son. This, however, was only a single, special instance of a widespread custom, for it was normal for sons to enter their fathers' trades or professions. Even officials of the royal administration tended to be succeeded by their sons, although kings always retained the right to intervene in such successions and appoint whom they wished. It is thus not surprising that didactic texts (part of a genre known as wisdom literature) typically purport to be written by fathers (including kings) for the benefit of their sons. While this accords with the expectation of filial succession, as well as the expectation that a father would be a guiding influence on his children, there is an exceptional instance in which one such text purports to have been written by the father, Ankhsheshonqy, while he was in prison!

It is uncertain whether any didactic texts have survived from the Old Kingdom, for there is a growing opinion that the texts attributed to figures of that period are actually Middle Kingdom compositions. Of these texts, only fragments survive from The Instruction of Prince Hardjedef and The Instruction for Kagemni. The Instruction of Ptahhotep, of which we have an intact version, is mostly concerned with practical matters, such as proper demeanor when addressing superiors, peers, and subordinates and correct manners when attending a dinner party given by a superior. But instances of ethical behavior also come into play, such as being faithful to the trust placed in one when serving as an emissary, gaining the trust of others by treating them kindly, not approaching the women of the household when visiting the home of a friend, cherishing one's own wife, and not repeating slander.

The Instruction for King Merikare, attributed to a monarch of the Herakleopolitan period but probably written in the Middle Kingdom, is a sort of manual outlining the behavior of a wise ruler. Like The Instruction of Ptahhotep, it contains practical advice, along with exhortations to ethical conduct, such as ruling by the power of persuasion rather than repression, earning the loyalty of one's followers by rewarding them well, appointing officials solely on the basis of merit, and respecting the monuments of one's predecessors rather than using them as quarries for the construction of new ones.

Later didactic texts list still more instances of proper conduct, both practical and ethical. For the ancient Egyptians, proper conduct entailed loyalty to the king (the topic of a Loyalist Instruction, a Middle Kingdom composition) and being a responsible member of society, which of course entailed ethical behavior.

In addition to these didactic texts, there is an important Middle Kingdom literary text called The Eloquent Peasant, whose concern is the need for honest administrators prepared to dispense justice fairly. Deprived unjustly of his donkey and his wares by a dishonest minor official, a would-be itinerant peddler complains to the robber's superior, who is so impressed by the man's eloquence that he obliges the latter to make no fewer than nine petitions, which are set down in writing and ultimately sent to the king. The theme of the text is the importance of justice in maintaining the order and cohesion of society.

A final important secular source is legal material, most of which has survived from the New Kingdom in the form of royal decrees and legal texts, the latter mostly from the village of Deir el-Medina during the Ramesside period. By providing us with a list of acts of wrongdoing—which range from failure to make payments on time to the plunder of royal and private tombs—this material allows us to infer that the opposite of these acts constituted proper conduct.

Ethical conduct was not, however, a purely secular concern. The Egyptians were far less inclined than we are today to view the religious and the secular as distinct conceptual entities. Even the most secular of the didactic texts, The Instruction of Ptahhotep, is not free of religious allusions, notably mentioning an anonymous god. The Instruction for King Merikare deals with religious matters, among them an important the Judgment of the Dead and a concluding passage devoted to praise of the beneficent world of nature that the creator-god established for the benefit of humankind. Later didactic texts are even more preoccupied with religious matters, along with secular concerns.

It is essential to note the emergence in Egypt of a concept of a Judgment of the Dead, which is first mentioned in the Middle Kingdom. There are numerous allusions to it in the Coffin Texts, a corpus of mortuary texts written mostly on the insides of wooden coffins. There is also an important mention of the concept in The Instruction for King Merikare, in a passage that reads in part, "The court that judges wretches, you know they are not merciful on that day of judging the base, the hour of enforcing the stipulations. . . . Let not your heart trust in length of years, for they view a lifetime as [but] an hour. . . . He who does what they reprove is a fool. He who reaches them without committing misdeeds, he will be there [i.e., in the afterlife] like a god." Later, in the New Kingdom, spell 125 of the Book of the Dead contains a litany of denials of misconduct, often called the Negative Confessions. Like the contents of the legal documents, they invite us to infer that the opposite of these acts constituted good behavior. Among the misdeeds that the deceased claims not to have committed are murder, telling lies, stealing food, appropriating land, adultery, and cursing a god.

With the concept of such a last judgment in mind, it is easy to understand why tomb biographies, although they tend to be concerned with the behavior of the deceased in what we might consider secular matters, in fact take on a religious cast because of the context created by the Egyptian belief system. The deeds and virtues they enumerate constitute the deceased's claim to an afterlife.

Although we have no evidence for a belief in the Judgment of the Dead in the Old Kingdom, the genre of tomb biographies in fact originated during that period. But at least in the case of the royal cemeteries that were constructed around the pyramids of kings, we might consider that the biographies do constitute a sort of ethically based claim to an afterlife, for it was conduct on earth that resulted in the royal permission that was presumably needed in order to be buried and receive a mortuary cult in these privileged locales.

The genre, which was actually presented as autobiographical (i.e., the contents were placed in the mouths of the deceased), grew out of statements that were originally few in number and brief in length. They report virtues such as, "I spoke ma'at, I did ma'at," "I judged between two persons so as to satisfy them," "I gave bread to the hungry," and "I buried the one who had no son." To statements of this type were added narratives, some of which came to comprise rather lengthy accounts of the deceased's noteworthy accomplishments. The brief statements grew into a large stock of standard phrases and epithets that could be drawn on in composing such texts, and taken in its entirety, it constitutes a veritable catalogue of what the ancient Egyptians considered to be ethical conduct. These sources, as well as the others listed so far, reveal that the Egyptian view of ethics was enough like our own that it constitutes one of the ways in which this ancient non-Western culture seems so familiar to us today (although, of course, there are other aspects of their culture of which the same is not true).

One group of these texts deserves to be singled out for special mention. These are the texts of local leaders of Upper Egypt during the First Intermediate Period, and especially the texts from the tomb of Ankhtyfy of Moalla. These autobiographies stand out for their evocations of effective leadership at the local level during a period when Egypt was politically fragmented and unstable and suffering from low Nile inundations and famine. These leaders seem to have been persons of extraordinary ability and outstanding civic virtue.

It would be impossible to close a discussion of the topic of ethics in ancient Egypt without taking further note of ma'at. Ma'at was a basic concept whose semantic range embraced notions ranging from "truth" and "justice" to "social cohesion" and the very order of the created cosmos. For a deceased person to say, "I spoke ma'at, I did ma'at" was enough to evoke in embryo all the virtues that we see otherwise mentioned in the texts. Further, the word ma'at is feminine in gender, and the concept it represents was personified as the goddess Maat (see color plate). In the forty-second episode of the Daily Cult Ritual performed in temples throughout the land, we see the king (theoretically, at least; in reality it was an officiating priest) making a presentation of a statuette of ma'at, presumably symbolizing here the ordered society over which he successfully presides.

Since ethics is a widespread human phenomenon, while ma'at was a concept peculiar to ancient Egypt, it was deemed best here to begin by discussing the surviving sources and what they have to tell us about ethical conduct, proceeding next to the religious framework within which ethical concerns were placed, and finally to the concept of ma'at. Doing so avoided creating at the outset a misimpression that the surviving materials from ancient Egypt are irrelevant to those with comparative interests. But this misimpression was avoided at the risk of creating another: downplaying the role of religious sentiment and the concept of *ma'at* in the issue of ethical conduct. In fact, from what has survived from ancient times, there is every chance that if we had some means of asking an educated Egyptian to tell us about ethical conduct, he would begin with *ma'at* and the necessity of serving its interests by saying and doing it, for reasons ranging from individual survival in the afterlife through maintaining social order and cohesion to preserving the very fabric of creation itself, which was, at least hypothetically, in ever-present danger of dissolving back into the watery chaos of precreation.

BIBL.: Jan Assmann, *Ma'at: Gerechtigkeit und Unsterblichkeit im alten Ägypten* (2nd ed.; Munich: Beck, 1995). Miriam Lichtheim, *Moral Values in Ancient Egypt* (Orbis biblicus et orientalis 155; Freiburg: University Press/Göttingen: Vandenhoeck & Ruprecht, 1997). Pascal Vernus, *Affaires et scandales sous les Ramsès: La crise de valeurs dans l'Égypte du nouvel empire* (Paris: Pygmalion/Gérard Watelet, 1993).   D.L.

Mesopotamia

Sources

Ethics, as a philosophical system of priorities and criteria that provides the framework for exercising moral judgments, is unknown in Mesopotamian thought. Nevertheless, Mesopotamian literature does reflect central moral concerns and ideal standards of proper human conduct. Most of the literary sources bearing on this issue belong to the Mesopotamian "stream of tradition" transmitted over the millennia by Sumerian and Akkadian scribes. The most important sources may be divided into the following categories: law corpora, wisdom literature, religious texts, and collections of omens.

Law corpora. The compilation of legal rules, best exemplified by the corpus issued by Hammurabi of Babylon, is a well-documented Mesopotamian literary tradition. The major corpora within this tradition are the Laws of Ur-Namma or Ur (circa 2100 BCE), the Laws of Lipit-Ishtar of Isin (circa 1950 BCE), the Laws of Eshnunna (circa 1800 BCE), the Laws of Hammurabi of Babylon (circa 1750 BCE), the Middle Assyrian Laws (circa 1100 BCE), and the Neo-Babylonian Laws (circa 700 BCE). Comparisons of these law corpora with contemporary documents from the actual practice of law indicate that the Mesopotamian law corpora are not royally prescribed legislation. They are more closely linked to royal inscriptions, attesting to the king's fulfillment of his divine charge to establish justice and equity in his realm and to protect the weak from the more powerful elements of society. Some cases in the corpora seem to represent summaries of specific royal economic reforms and legal judgments rendered by a king during his reign.

Stele of the Code of Hammurabi, 18th century BCE. At the top is the image of Hammurabi, king of Babylon, before the sun-god Shamash. Louvre. *Hirmer Fotoarchiv*

Other cases seem to be more scholastic in nature and seem to reflect nonbinding Mesopotamian socioeconomic principles of equity, which have been transmitted over the millennia by its scholarly tradition. Hence at least some of the cases are ideal statements and may not reflect the actual practice of law in ancient Mesopotamia. Furthermore, since the law cases deal with violations of existing obligations and rights and the equitable adjudication of conflict, the corpora do not represent an ethical code of positive conduct. Nevertheless, these corpora do reveal the king's keen moral sense of right and wrong and provide valuable insight into the Mesopotamian conception of justice and its social values.

Wisdom literature. Mesopotamian wisdom literature is replete with proverbial sayings and didactic instructions that encourage a code of correct behavior. For example, The Instructions of Shuruppak state: "Do not return evil to your adversary; requite with kindness the one who does evil to you." The motivation for such behavior is based upon pragmatic and utilitarian considerations. The religious factor is most prevalent in Mesopotamian contemplative works, such as the Babylonian Theodicy, which states: "Unless you seek the will of god, what success can you have?" These works of theodicy question the foundations of correct behavior and explore the reasons for human suffering.

Religious texts. The theme of human suffering is carried over into the religious texts. Although Mesopotamian literature recognizes natural causes of illness, it tends to view prolonged human suffering and social adversity as possible signs of divine disapproval. Mesopotamian penitential prayers and cultic rituals, designed to release the afflicted from his or her suffering, mention sinful acts that may be responsible for the suffering. Most noteworthy is the second tablet of the ritual Shurpu (a series for undoing spells), which contains an extensive confessional, listing both social and cultic misdeeds. The confessions include approaching a neighbor's wife, shedding a neighbor's blood, setting up a false property boundary, and eating what is taboo to one's god. These texts bring into focus what is deemed to be appropriate human behavior.

Omen literature. Within the Mesopotamian stream of tradition, omen literature represents the largest attested single genre. This literature organizes Mesopotamian divinatory practices into various collections based on ominous phenomena and divinatory technique. Most relevant to the study of ethics are the human behavioral omens and dream omens, in which certain human actions, committed while awake or in a dream, bear a divine message. Scholars have assumed that these omens reflect speculations on proper and improper human behavior. What is not clear, however, are the circumstances under which routine human actions become ominous and how widely relevant these omens are to daily human activity. Although much socially accepted behavior is interpreted as auspicious, the issue is further complicated by examples of behavior that are deemed clearly unacceptable in the law corpora but interpreted as auspicious within the corpus of behavioral omens. Closely related to the omen literature are the Mesopotamian calendrical texts, which specify whether individual days of the month are propitious or unpropitious for various actions. Most of the specified actions deal with proper cultic actions.

Central moral concerns

Since these four sources derive from the royal and scholarly elite in the employ of the palace and temple, the behavior that they uphold and foster is geared to the preservation of the existing social order. Hence one of the central moral concerns is that of social ethics, pertaining to the maintenance of the social hierarchy and the promotion of harmony within the family and the community. The sources stress filial obedience to parental authority. As is evident from Mesopotamian adoption tablets, filial love and respect entail an economic responsibility to care for elderly and indigent parents. Filial obligation continues after death, with responsibility for ensuring proper burial and mourning rites and for maintaining offerings so that the ghost of the deceased will be at peace and not endanger the realm of the living. The hierarchy among siblings is based on age and gender, with special respect due to one's elder brother and sister. The filial respect and loyalty due to parents was a value that also was extended to one's superiors, including master, officials, king, and personal god.

Included within social ethics are those moral concerns that are essential for the cohesion of the community. Human life is safeguarded by the prohibition of homicide, which under certain circumstances may be a capital crime. Often the decision is left to the victim's kin, who may demand blood vengeance or blood money. The notion that bloodshed pollutes is also evident in the sources. An individual's right to private property is another primary value of Mesopotamian society and a major concern of the law corpora. These texts deal not only with violations against one's right to property such as theft and burglary, but also with liability incurred for the destruction of property. The sources also demand honesty in commercial relations. The use of false weights and measures and the moving of a neighbor's boundary stone are considered to be serious misdeeds. Closely related to issues of honesty is the reliability of one's spoken word. This value is essential for the proper functioning of the judicial system, which depends upon the validity of accusations and the trustworthiness of testimony. The legal corpora deal with such moral infractions as false witnesses, false oaths, slander, and blasphemy, while the legal contracts specify heavy penalties for breach of contract.

Much of Mesopotamian sexual ethics dealing with the violation of women is closely related to the concept of property rights, since an unmarried daughter is considered to be the property of her father, and a married woman the property of her husband. Thus the rape of an unmarried woman of free birth, like the rape of a slave girl, is viewed as a property offense, requiring monetary compensation to her parents. Similarly, the adulterous relations of a man with a married woman is an invasion of the husband's domain and may at times be a capital crime. The decision rests with the aggrieved husband, who may demand the death of the adulterer if he is willing to acquiesce to the death of his wife as well. In the law corpora, abortion and male homosexuality are mentioned only in the Middle Assyrian Laws. The law case dealing with abortion states that a woman who aborts her fetus shall be impaled and remain unburied. The severity of the crime seems to be based upon her act of insurrection in destroying her husband's potential progeny, since one who strikes a man's pregnant wife causing her to abort her fetus usually pays monetary compensation to the husband. The assailant is held capitally liable only if the woman's husband had no son. With regard to homosexuality, one who fornicates with his comrade is to be sodomized and turned into a eunuch. It is unclear whether the criminality is due to the homosexual nature of the act or to its being committed against someone of the same social standing. However, in the sexual human behavioral omens, homosexuality and other sexual acts are deemed to be auspicious and hence seem to be viewed in a more positive light than that found in other sources.

Mesopotamian religious ethics reflect principles similar to those found in its social ethics. Although little is known about the role of the common people in the practice of religion, it is clear that personal gods served as their intercessors with the great gods. Wisdom literature and penitential prayers focus on duties toward one's personal gods, who are viewed as the divine parents of the worshiper. The gods are to be honored materially with sacrifices and verbally with prayers. Blasphemy by swearing false oaths is a serious act of disrespect. Other offenses include seizure of temple property and the wronging of temple personnel, who were thought to be divine property. More is known of the roles of the king and the cult functionaries in the state religion. The major royal cultic duties were the maintenance of the temples of the great gods, the support of their cults, and the observance of their festivals. The performance of these duties was vital for the prosperity and security of the land. The cultic functionaries had to follow a cultic etiquette, requiring them to be physically sound, unblemished, and ritually pure. Physical cleanliness was demanded together with the wearing of clean clothing. Washing of hands was required before prayer, sacrifice, and the sacred meal. The hemerologies (lists of auspicious days) state that certain food restrictions were in force during certain cultic times and rituals.

The Mesopotamian sources also extol virtuous behavior, praising the god-fearing person for his or her reverence, obedience, humility, and trust. But most information concerns the royal ethos. Royal ideology demands the moral perfection of the king, who is divinely mandated to uphold the moral order. His duties are not only to secure the borders of the land but to maintain the socioeconomic well-being of its citizenry. As the faithful shepherd of his people, the king must enforce justice, render true judgments, protect the powerless, care for the weak, and support the helpless. He must be meek and humble in his devotion to the gods, fastidious in the execution of his cultic duties, and always be careful not to abuse his power.

Conceptual framework

In order to comprehend and appreciate Mesopotamian ethics more fully, it is necessary to place it within the conceptual framework of the Mesopotamian *Weltanschauung*. According to the Mesopotamian polytheistic worldview, the gods emerged from a preexistent primordial realm that harbored within it all of the natural and supernatural forces of the cosmos. Since this primordial realm preceded the gods in time, the gods, like humankind, were subject to the natural forces of biological existence as well as to the supernatural forces of fate, destiny, magic, and cosmic truths. Just as law is understood to be the embodiment of cosmic truths, so too, Mesopotamian moral norms seem to reflect a cosmic standard of propriety governing human and divine behavior with the aim of achieving harmonious social intercourse. This moral cosmic standard is viewed, like all of the primordial forces of the universe, as an innate force, which is not endowed with the power of self-expression and cannot communicate its "will" to humankind. This conception differs radically from that of a monotheistic worldview in which ethics is a divinely communicated religious code of morality with the aim of achieving personal righteousness.

This is not to say that the gods were unconcerned with moral norms and their enforcement. In Mesopotamia, the gods served as custodians of the primordial forces of the cosmos and as the personal link between humankind and the impersonal cosmic forces. The gods, who created humankind to serve them, demanded that humans uphold the cosmic order by creating a harmonious social reality, consistent with the cosmic forces of the universe. Hence certain legal and moral infractions were termed acts of sacrilege and taboo, which jeopardized and undermined cosmic stability. These infractions were punishable not only by social but also by religious and magical retribution. In their role as the personal link between humankind and the impersonal cosmic forces, the Mesopotamian gods inspire humankind with knowledge of the essence of these forces. However, Mesopotamian sources are acutely aware of humankind's inability to comprehend fully the mind of the gods. The penitential psalms and wisdom literature stress the limited capacity of humankind to understand what is pleasing to the gods, to distinguish between good and evil, and hence to perceive clearly the cosmic moral standard. This lack of knowledge does not exonerate humankind from blame or punishment for its misdeeds, but is rather viewed as an insufficiency inherent within the imperfect human condition. By contrast, the monotheistic conception that divine commandments reveal the will of the deity and thus enlighten humankind in its moral predicament is foreign to the Mesopotamian worldview.

BIBL.: G. Buccellati, "Ethics and Piety in the Ancient Near East," in *Civilizations of the Ancient Near East* (ed. Jack M. Sasson et al.; New York: Scribner, 1995), 3.1685–96. K. van der Toorn, *Sin and Sanction in Israel and Mesopotamia: A Comparative Study* (Studia Semitica Neerlandica 22; Assen: Van Gorcum, 1985). B.L.E.

Syria-Canaan

How humans were to conduct themselves was not theirs to decide, for the gods made the world for themselves, and humans were only slaves tending it. This order is by definition just and right, and humans who discovered it and conformed to it were right with the gods. Ethics was, therefore, not to be divorced from philosophical and theological presuppositions. Mesopotamian and Egyptian literature (and the biblical Job) had a tradition of skeptical protest and satire, but no Syro-Canaanite examples have been discovered.

Ethical reflection was done through narratives concerning revered personages (what they did and how they fared) and through gnomic and exhortatory literature. In the sparse and randomly preserved material, three individuals are sketched in sufficient detail to serve as models of ethical behavior: in the Ugaritic texts (before 1200 BCE), King Kirta and the noble Danel, and in Aramaic the courtier Ahiqar, whose story was composed around 7th century BCE and also contains wisdom sayings. All three heroes accept what happens. No Syro-Canaanite law code comparable to the codes and collections of Mesopotamia and the Hittite kingdom has been preserved.

The Kirta epic opens with the king unexpectedly bereft of wife, siblings, and sons, initiating the drama of finding a son for the throne. In a dream, the high god El authorizes Kirta to go on a campaign to take the daughter of a neighboring king. Prior to finding an heir (his eighth daughter Thitmanatu = Octavia), Kirta has to overcome the goddess Asherah and a usurper son. Never in his Job-like sufferings is Kirta anything but pious. In the Danel legend (also referred to as the Legend of Aqhat), Danel's beloved son, Aqhat, scorns the goddess Anat and her offer of life in exchange for his wondrous bow. He is struck down by an assassin hired by Anat. His sister Paghat kills the thug, and the story breaks off. Danel, too, is a model of piety, accepting the volatility and unfairness of the divine world, never shedding the dignity of a great sheik and judge. In the Aramaic tale, the childless Ahiqar, wise counselor in the Neo-Assyrian court, promotes his nephew to take his place, only to fall victim to the ungrateful youth's betrayal. Sentenced to death, Ahiqar is eventually saved and freed and, in some versions of the story, addresses the appended wisdom sayings to his nephew in prison.

Differently from the stories of Kirta and Danel, this story does not mention the gods. Events simply happen, although it would have been recognized that a protecting hand was at work. Ahiqar's extraordinary wisdom is from the gods and is the reason that he succeeds.

The only substantial Syro-Canaanite "wisdom literature" is preserved with Ahiqar. It is "international" in that its themes and genres are those of Mesopotamia and Egypt and indeed of the Bible. Its exhortations urge conformity to the existing order; never once do they urge changing it. Its proverbs help one to know one's place in a world that was made by the gods exclusively for themselves.

BIBL.: Edward L. Greenstein, "Kirta," in *Ugaritic Narrative Poetry* (ed. Simon L. Parker; Atlanta, 1997). James L. Lindenberger, "Ahiqar," in *The Old Testament Pseudepigrapha* (ed. James H. Charlesworth; Garden City, N.Y., 1985), 2.479–507. Dennis Pardee, "The Kirta Epic" and "The 'Aqhatu Legend," in *The Context of Scripture* (ed. William W. Hallo et al.; Leiden, 1997), 1.333–56. Simon L. Parker, "Aqhat," in *Ugaritic Narrative Poetry* (ed. Simon L. Parker; Atlanta, 1997). R.J.C.

Israel

Already in late preexilic Israel (7th century BCE), a distinction is made between law and justice. Beginning with the book of the covenant (Exod. 20.24–23.13), ethical rules that rely on the force of argumentation rather than on legal sanctions were singled out within legal traditions. Thus, a portrayal of early Israelite ethics begins with its early legal history.

The laws of the Hebrew Bible have a dual origin. The casuistic or case laws in the book of the covenant, composed of the protasis of the legal case and the apodosis of the judgment (Exod. 21.18–19), originate in legal practice and serve to resolve conflicts between families of a community bound by the same law. Their goal was the suppression of violence and the furthering of community by substituting reparation and healing for retaliation. This is also true in the case of bodily harm, where immediate redress of the victim and his relations had been sanctioned originally through the *lex talionis*, "an eye for an eye, a tooth for a tooth" (21.22–24), and so did not require public trial. Through the casuistic law concerning bodily harm (21.18–19), this retaliation was disallowed, and reparation became a legal requirement, under the supervision of the courts. The later rabbinic interpretation of the *lex talionis*, by means of a list of legal substitutes in cases of bodily harm, did not meet the law's original intention, but it continues a process of reinterpretation begun in the casuistic laws of the book of the covenant. It is a serious misunderstanding if the *lex talionis* is taken to be representative of the law of the Hebrew Bible and if the Hebrew Bible's God is interpreted as a god of vengeance. The principle of retaliation as a legal means of redress was already rendered obsolete by casuistic law, as a matter of the control of rights by legal process, before casuistic law ever was given the theological status of divine (Yahwistic) revelation.

The second root of early Israelite law is the apodictic or unconditional law, including the prohibitions of the Decalogue, the laws on capital offenses (Exod. 21.12–17), and the prohibition of incest (Lev. 18). The absolute, unconditional character of these laws reflects the authority of the *paterfamilias,* who originally had the power to enforce them and implement sanctions. Already in preexilic times, the local courts took over the legal functions and power of sanction that had been vested in families. They regulated these functions by replacing the automatic punishment for a crime with a process that takes the reasons and the circumstances of the crime into consideration. An example of this is the legal differentiation between murder and bodily injury followed by the death of the injured.

These two types of laws did not need explicit religious authorization, since their natural functions of conflict resolution and enforcement of norms provided adequate warrants. Behavioral norms not regulated by laws are grounded in the solidarity of families and clans. As the obligation for vendetta shows, the degree of solidarity within a group depends on family ties, based on the veneration of the ancestors. Only with the increasing social differentiation of rich and poor in the 8th century BCE in Israel and Judah was it necessary for the socially horizontal law for conflict resolution to develop into a socially vertical ethic of solidarity with the weak in society (Exod. 21.2–11; 22.21–27 [= 22.20–26 Hebrew]; 23.10–12). This development, in turn, needed the weight of religious authority in order to criticize the political and economical elites of the land. Social conflict gave rise to the religious interpretation of the law, which was then developed into a social ethic and, already in Exodus 23.4–5, required love of the enemy.

The third root of early Israelite legal tradition is the cultic law, which gave cultic obligations the status of divine law (Exod. 34.18–26). Priestly intellectuals transferred the structure of this cultic law to the sphere of noncultic law and ethics. The theologizing of law in the book of the covenant allowed the Judean Priestly intellectuals of the 7th century to replace the veneration of the ancestors and the ancestral ethic (both of which were destroyed by urbanization from the 9th century on and by the Assyrian crisis, which entailed resettling and deportation) with a program of brotherly ethics that found its literary expression in the Book of Deuteronomy.

Deuteronomy, being a reformulation of the book of the covenant, based itself on the latter's commandments of social ethics and developed Exod. 23.4–5 into the main principle of all ethics, demanding brotherly conduct even toward the enemy (Deut. 22.1–4). This approach gives rise to a program of social solidarity with the weak in society, debt release in each sabbatical year (15.1–11), the prohibition of interest (23.19–20 [= 23.20–21 Hebrew]), and the limitation of pledges (24.6, 10–13, 17b). The Judean intellectuals from Priestly Zadokite circles tried to use this program to prove the superiority of YHWH (in whose name Deuteronomy announces this program) over the Assyrian king as representative of the god Assur, whose decrees of debt release remain ineffective since they can be nullified through special contractual stipulations. In Deuteronomy, as in the book of the covenant, law and ethic are based neither on the state nor on the king, but directly upon the will of God, so that their validation does not depend on the state. Deuteronomy grounds the ethic of solidarity in daily life within the cultic community, in which there are no distinctions between persons because of gender or social status. In the central sanctuary, the integrated cultic community celebrates its origin in the liberation of Israel from slavery in Egypt. The ethic of Deuteronomy is summarized in the Decalogue (Deut. 5) and given religious legitimation through the motif of the divine revelation mediated by Moses.

The prophets measure the people by the standards that are attributed to God in the legal collections and hold them responsible for the consequences of their actions, which must necessarily lead to catastrophe unless they reverse their ways. Thus, the prophets do not develop a new ethic but draw out the implications of the religious interpretations of law and ethic in the preexilic law collections. In the period of the exile, Deuteronomy seemed to provide, with its blessings and curses (Deut. 28), the guiding principle for the success or failure of the entire people. After the exile, however, the failure to implement this legal program became a theological challenge.

The redactors of the Pentateuch placed the Decalogue, the book of the covenant, and Deuteronomy in the context of the Priestly theology of transgression and atonement. They then answer the question whether successful human life is feasible, in light of the experience of human failure to meet divine demands, by instituting cultic atonement. In the Holiness Code (Lev. 17–26), the scribes who redacted the Pentateuch interpreted Deuteronomy and the Priestly document by using the book of the covenant as their hermeneutical key. In Lev. 19.18, Deut. 22.1–4 is developed into a commandment to love one's enemy as one's neighbor. In Lev. 19.34, it is further developed into a commandment to love the stranger. The social program is further developed in Lev. 25 through the limitation of human rights over labor and land, leading to a prohibition of taking Israelite (but not Gentile) slaves. Rights with regard to land are limited to usufruct and are further limited temporally. Land could not be sold in perpetuity but should revert to its original owners in the Jubilee Year, which was to be celebrated every fiftieth year. These programs of social solidarity, which are based on parenetic persuasion as opposed to threat of sanctions, were scarcely implemented in Persian and Hellenistic times. The first attested Jubilee was in 164/163 BCE, while Jewish documents of the 3rd and 2nd centuries BCE as well as the New Testament consider the taking of interest to be a normal procedure.

Parallel to and partially in dialogue with Hellenistic philosophy, postexilic wisdom literature deals with the problems of happiness and innocence. The divine speeches in Job emphasize the role of God as creator and the superiority of God over the powers of chaos that find their expression in innocent suffering. The attempt to mediate between the absolute superiority of God, expressed in mythical terms, and the individual experience of suffering in the fairy-tale-like epilogue to Job is not convincing, since this solution can be made null and void by the opposite experience.

The Book of Qoheleth (3rd century BCE) undermines the association between conduct and happiness that is typical of a synthetic view of life. In dialogue with contemporary Hellenistic philosophy, it teaches that happiness cannot be understood as independence with respect to all external goods (the Epicurean ideal of *ataraxia* [imperturbability]), but rather that these should be understood as gracious gifts of the creator, God, and therefore not bound to the moral behavior of the human recipient.

Ben Sira introduces the thought that the doing of the good deed itself constitutes happiness (Sir. 10.22, 24) and thus approaches Stoic thinking. Only apocalyptic literature and its understanding of the resurrection of the dead (Dan. 12.1–3) can answer the question about the successful life of those who did not receive just treatment in their existence on earth.

Hellenistic, Greek-speaking Judaism walked the narrow path between the preservation of the Jewish identity and assimilation to an alien environment. For this purpose, the Torah was reinterpreted, and, at the same time, its ethical superiority over Hellenistic philosophy was asserted by Aristobulus, a philosopher who wrote in Alexandria in the 2nd century BCE. The roughly contemporary Letter of Aristeas takes the Torah as a *nomos,* whose goal is the happy life, thereby assimilating the Torah to Hellenistic categories of thought. This development becomes clear when one considers the reinterpretation of the Hebrew term *ṣĕdāqâ* (loyalty to the community) by the Greek word *dikaiosynē* (in the sense of just distribution) and of the Hebrew word *bĕrît* (covenant) by the Greek word *diathēkē* (testament), taken from the Egyptian-Hellenistic laws of inheritance. In the final speeches of the Testaments of the Twelve Patriarchs, the Torah is interpreted as moral code, and the Stoic ethos and the biblical *tôrôt* are identified in an ascetic lifestyle. The Wisdom of Solomon follows the Stoa in interpreting the Torah as a manifestation of the order of creation that can be grasped by human reason.

In contrast to Hellenistic Judaism, rabbinic Judaism struggles only indirectly with contemporary philosophical ethics. In light of the Mosaic Torah and its status as a criterion for all ethics, natural law is only of very limited importance. Rational explanation of the commandments is not considered normative in light of the revealed character of the Torah (Babylonian Talmud, tractate *Sanhedrin* 21b). Also, the hierarchical ordering and systematizing of ethics, on the basis of a principle such as love of the neighbor, is alien to rabbinic Judaism (*Sifra* 2.4 on Lev. 19.18). Sanctity of life, charitable deeds, and the protection of human life are the basic rabbinic values in individual ethics.

BIBL.: J. J. Collins, *Jewish Wisdom in the Hellenistic Age* (Louisville, 1997). Z. Falk, *Introduction to Jewish Law of the Second Commonwealth* (Leiden, 1972). E. Otto, *Gottes Recht als Menschenrecht: Rechts- und literaturhistorische Studien zum Deuteronomium* (Wiesbaden, 2002). Idem, *Theologische Ethik des Alten Testaments* (Stuttgart, 1994). R. Weber, *Das Gesetz im hellenistischen Judentum* (Frankfurt am Main, 2000). E.O.

Anatolia

The land of Hatti belonged to the gods; the king was merely their steward. The sun-god was god of justice and of kingship, and the king, who dressed in the sun-god's regalia, was the head of the system of justice on earth and was directly responsible to the sun-god for the quality of justice he dispensed as ruler and judge. King Khattushili I deposed a crown prince because "he was cold. He was heartless. He did not shed tears. . . . If he shows no sympathy when commanded by the king, how then can he show sympathy on his own toward Hattusha?" Anecdotes from the reign of Khattushili I bearing moral lessons were collected during the reign of his successor, perhaps for this young king's instruction. Khattushili himself, as well as his successors, often used history to illustrate the consequences of morality or immorality.

There are also many texts instructing officials in correct behavior, sometimes moral and sometimes strictly bureaucratic. The king's provincial governors and officers doubled as circuit court judges. In the king's instructions to them they are told to investigate cases thoroughly, not to take bribes, not to make the case of a superior win or one of an inferior lose, to pay particular attention to widows and the powerless, and to satisfy the litigants. It was also up to the governor to keep his eyes on war captives resettled in localities and to provide them with temporary tax breaks and the wherewithal to start a new life. Locally, justice was in the hands of the town or village elders, whose decisions could be appealed upward.

As part of his duty to justice, the king compiled tablets collecting some two hundred laws, which were modified by successive rulers. These discuss homicide, assault, abduction, theft, arson, contracts, land tenure, abuses of hired animals and property, sorcery and damage due to magical pollution, rejection of a royal verdict, marriage, inheritance, sexual offenses, commodity prices, wages, and rents.

The most serious offenses seen in the Hittite laws are offenses against the gods. These would be tried before the king or the governor, and, depending on the custom of the locality, the guilty would be executed or banished. One of these is the crime of *ḫurkel,* illicit sexual relations with one's mother, daughter, son, sister-in-law, mother-in-law, female cousin, brother's wife while one's brother is living, stepmother while one's father is living, knowingly with free sisters and their mother, and with a cow or sheep. These rules are clearly a reflection of the society's aversion to such practices. Interestingly, sex with a horse or mule was not *ḫurkel,* but made one permanently impure. Although apparently not *ḫurkel,* the rape of a woman, in such a circumstance that her struggle could not be heard, was a capital offense for the man, while anything that happened in her house was assumed to be consensual and a capital offense for her. A husband could, of course, kill his wife and her lover caught *in flagrante delicto,* but he could not ask the king to kill one and not the other.

Someone who caused an innocent person to be executed would in turn be executed. In earliest times, if anyone sowed seed on a field that had already been sown, the sower was torn apart by two teams of oxen, which were then themselves killed. Already early on, however, this baroque penalty was reduced to a sacrifice of three sheep and a reconsecration of the field, in line with other reductions in legal penalties. Such reforms also eliminated fines, so that penalties paid by criminals all compensated the victim or his or her heirs. Members of a temple staff (Instructions for Temple Officials; cf. *ANET* 207–10) were warned that "he who embezzles from a god, dies" and "whoever commits or allows a misdeed during his watch dies and cannot be pardoned." But since texts that describe such things actually happening do not mention an execution, the gods presumably were expected to exact the penalty themselves (as other sections of the same text make clear).

In early days, at least, malfeasance in office could result in execution. Losers in dynastic struggles sometimes wound up assassinated or executed, but some kings emphasized that this was wrong and they instead internally exiled their defeated opponents and gave them a house and ample food and drink to live on. Extradited political refugees were also not to be executed.

The laws stipulated that a monetary payment be given to the heirs of murder victims, as was the case with many other crimes, but the heirs also had the right to demand the culprit's death. The most serious form of homicide was killing a merchant for the merchant's goods, followed by killing someone during a quarrel and accidental killing. Shedding blood was an offense

against the gods, as well as against humanity, and the gods could be expected to exact their own revenge, particularly if a ritual of expiation of bloodshed was not performed. Causing a woman to miscarry required a ten-shekel payment (equivalent to ten sheep) if she was near term, but five shekels if it was her fifth month. If someone injured and temporarily incapacitated a person, the guilty person had to pay the victim for the assault, provide a substitute to work the land until the victim recovered, and also pay the medical bills. If someone kept another alive during a famine, the individual who had been sustained, if a free person, had to give his or her savior a person by way of compensation; if the sustained individual were a slave, he or she had to pay his or her savior ten shekels.

BIBL.: A. Archi, "L'humanité des Hittites," in *Florilegium anatolicum: Mélanges offerts à Emmanuel Laroche* (Paris: De Boccard, 1979), 37–48. P. Dardano, *L'aneddoto e il Racconto in Età Antico-Hittita* (Rome: Il Calamo, 1997). S. de Martino, "Nudità rituale e senso del pudore nella letteratura ittita," *Oriens Antiquus* 24 (1984): 253–62. W. W. Hallo et al. (eds.), *The Context of Scripture* (Leiden: Brill, 1997–2000), 1.150–51, 181–82, 194–204, 217–25; 2.79–81, 93–119. H. A. Hoffner Jr., *The Laws of the Hittites* (Leiden: Brill, 1997). R.H.B.

Iran

Ethics or moral values (Avestan *pantay;* compare Old Persian *pathi,* Middle Persian *pand*) and law (Avestan and Old Persian *dāta,* Middle Persian *dād*) were entwined with religious and secular notions of how people should live their lives—individually and communally—in the empires of ancient Iran. Ethical codes and legal stipulations would be viewed as means of ensuring that individuals "do not stray from the correct path" and that "the mightier not strike, not destroy, the weak" causing social chaos, as noted by the Achaemenian King of Kings Darius I (522–486 BCE) in royal inscriptions (Naqsh-e Rostam a.58–60 and Susa e.39–41, respectively). The influence of Mazdaism or Zoroastrianism on the development of ethics and law in Iran during antiquity is not surprising. Words attributed to the devotional poet Zarathustra refer to "truth and good thought" (Yasna 28.10–11). Ethics and law fell under "the rules that Mazda has laid down for good behavior" (30.11) for facilitating discrimination between order and chaos, good and evil, during daily life—thereby ensuring that faithful observers attained the best existence after death. But Zoroastrianism was not the only influence on the development of ethics and law among the early Iranians. Morals and legal injunctions also were assimilated from the Elamites, with whom the Iranians coexisted, and eventually absorbed, in the 1st millennium BCE, and from the Jewish community in the postexilic period.

Greek notions of reason as a precondition for a moral

Trilingual cuneiform inscription at Persepolis praising "order," denouncing "heretical deities," and urging people to follow "law," 5th century BCE. Shown: Old Persian version, lines 1–27, and Elamite version, lines 28–50. *Archive J. K. Choksy*

life complemented Iranian, Zoroastrian-based ideals after the advent of Hellenism in the region. The concept of moderation or the mean (Middle Persian *paymān*) became especially central to Iranian ethics, as it accorded well with the notion of "harmony with truth" that Zarathustra had extolled (Yasna 29.7). Later on, Sasanian-era literature became replete with Zoroastrian maxims (Middle Persian *handarz*) attributed to monarchs such as Ardashir I (224–40 CE) and Khusrau I (531–79 CE) and high magi such as Adurbad the son of Maraspand (lived 4th century CE). Such advice literature was intended to encompass all aspects of life for both men and women. So the Chīdag Handarz ī Pōryōtkēshān (Select Counsels of the Ancient Sages) recommends, "Be diligent in acquiring education, for it is the basis of knowledge, its product is wisdom, and wisdom is the order of both [the corporeal and spiritual] existences." More generally, ethical sayings in the Handarz Nāmag (Book of Advice) by Adurbad, for instance, range from "tell no lies to anyone," "listen to a wise man," and "respect your father and mother," to "drink wine in moderation, for whoever drinks excessively commits many sins." Sayings warn against "the luxury of pride," encourage "more attention be paid to the soul than the belly," and rationalize social inequalities: "Although a person may be very poor in material possessions, he could be rich in character." Ethics could even be used to structure life according to duties that should be performed on particular days of the month. Yet, the extant works seem to have been compiled by men for male audiences. The Handarz of Adurbad advised, "Cherish the woman who is modest and marry her" and thereby "not forsake the righteous law for lust."

Manicheans were similar to Zoroastrians in many aspects of their ethics. Hearers (or laypersons) and elect (or monks) were urged "to teach knowledge and wisdom to people and thus save them from lust and evil" as the prophet Mani had done (M 49 II). Like other Iranians, they were expected to follow an ethical code of "do not be false . . . do not be unjust . . . walk along the path of truth" (M 5794 II). Ethics informed daily life through a series of commandments concerning right and wrong actions. Moreover, all members of the community were enjoined "to fight lust and evil" (M 49 II) by focusing on the spiritual realm rather than the corporeal one.

At the inception of Iranian political control over the Near East, under the Achaemenians, a system of local government had been introduced under which the laws and customs unique to each ethnic, regional, and confessional group were honored. As an extension, religious minorities, such as the Jewish community in Babylonia and the Levant, eventually became protected communities. Yet problems arose in reconciling local customs and regional practices with one another, particularly in matters involving more than one area or community. According to biblical and Greek sources, Darius I promulgated "laws of the king," sometimes called the "law of the Medes and Persians." That imperial legal system provided a bridge across confessional and ethnic groups. Disputes involving members of the same community were judged within that community by its own laws, ethics, and customs. Intercommunal litigation was referred to regional administrators for settlement. Certainly, expediency and propaganda played a part in the formulation of such policies, yet their presence suggests a degree of tolerance unprecedented until that time. Communities were required—with some exceptions—to pay a poll tax (Middle Persian *gazīdag*) in exchange for freedom of religious practice, a levy that became widespread under Parthian and, later, Sasanian rule, as best evidenced by the Babylonian Talmud. In addition to Jews, Christians were accorded protected minority status by the Sasanians, especially once the Nestorian church became completely independent of the Western churches in 496 CE. Despite legal codes stipulating freedom of devotional praxis, however, intersectarian violence did occur, especially during the 6th and 7th centuries CE, when messianic ideas become popular among Zoroastrians, Jews, and Christians alike. Manicheans, on the other hand, were not accorded legal protection as a religious minority because they were regarded as heretics (Middle Persian *zandīkān*) who misinterpreted Mazdaism.

Iranian secular law followed Zoroastrian practice in many cases, as evidenced by a collection of judicial guidelines known as the Mādayān ī hazār Dādestān (Book of a Thousand Judgments). For example, a woman was not permitted more than one husband at a time, although men could take as many wives as they could support financially and treat considerately. Wives were accorded differential legal status within a family based on their social rank prior to marriage, clauses of the marriage contract, and motherhood. Divorce could be initiated by either the husband or the wife, but usually both parties' consent was necessary in a clerical court. The legal system of Iranian Christians is known as well, through a later Syriac version of a Middle Persian compilation attributed to Ishoboxt.

Essentially, ethics and law came to be regarded as having divine origins and, therefore, were held intrinsic to order or righteousness (Avestan *asha*, Old Persian *arta*, Middle Persian *ardā*). The Achaemenian King of Kings Xerxes I (486–465 BCE) even claimed in an official inscription that anyone who observed such aspects of society "becomes happy while alive and righteous when dead" (Persepolis h.54–56).

BIBL.: David M. Goodblatt, "The Poll Tax in Sasanian Babylonia: The Talmudic Evidence," *Journal of the Economic and Social History of the Orient* 22.3 (1979): 233–95. Anahit G. Perikhanian (ed.), *The Book of a Thousand Judgments (A Sasanian Law-Book)* (trans. N. Garsoïan; Costa Mesa, Calif., 1997). E. Sachau, *Syrische Rechtsbücher*, vol. 3 (Berlin, 1914). Shaul Shaked (ed. and trans.), *The Wisdom of the Sasanian Sages (Denkard VI)* (Boulder, Colo., 1979). Robert C. Zaehner, *The Teachings of the Magi: A Compendium of Zoroastrian Beliefs* (repr. New York, 1976 [orig. 1956]).   J.K.C.

Greece

Religion shaped Greek moral and ethical norms throughout antiquity. It also provided a starting point for critical reflection on human life and society and on ethical principles. This reflective movement gave rise to a branch of philosophy that since Aristotle has been called "ethics" and to reconstructions of the Greek worldview and the place of the divine in it. As a result the relation of religion and ethics was given a new foundation with a variety of ethical implications.

Ethical norms of traditional religion. Greek gods did not give moral commands, nor did traditional Greek religious practices incorporate formal codes of ethics. Greek deities were associated with forces of nature that are beyond human control. The Greeks regarded themselves as dependent on these divine powers for their survival and well-being. Most critical to their existence in the fragile natural and human ecology of the Aegean were the weather, the annual harvest, physical health,

social stability, and protection against aggressive neighbors, all shown by centuries of painful experience to be radically insecure and beyond human capacity to ensure. As long as the Greeks regarded the forces controlling their existence anthropomorphically, managing a relationship with the deities that determined these forces became the highest priority in their lives, while the personal quality of proper tendence of these deities (*eusebeia*) became one of the highest moral obligations. Failure to attend to the cult of the gods was not only an offense against the slighted deity, but also threatened the existence and well-being of the entire community and thus carried with it serious social and moral implications.

Moreover, divine tendence, with its rigid schedule of rituals, incorporated in its associated conceptions and narratives an array of particular ethical norms and assumptions and thus became the principal way in which the identity and worldview of Greek citizens were shaped. For example, the citywide festivals, which involved everyone in the community, established and maintained the bonds of civic society along with civic pride and attendant moral obligations to other members and to the city as a whole. The festivals also maintained the established social stratification; hereditary religious duties, distributed on the basis of social and economic status, publicly enacted the social position of members of the community.

Underlying most cultic practice, communal and domestic, was the fundamental moral principle of reciprocity, manifested in an exchange of favor (*charis*) between the deity and the people. Gratitude for the divinely generated gifts of nature, such as grain, wine, and oil, was expressed in first-fruits offerings. Sacrifices were routinely cited as the basis for requesting a favor of the god. Natural catastrophes due to weather or illness called for extraordinary sacrifices to avert the assumed divine displeasure.

The cult of Zeus was exceptionally rich in support of ethical norms. Zeus was the source of order in society and sanctioned respect for its institutions and their ethical values. He protected the household and established governments. He ensured the sanctity of guests and suppliants and enforced oaths. In democracies, such as Athens, he oversaw the council, the assembly, and the marketplace. In most cities the chief deity, if it was not Zeus, came to share with him the function of underwriting the social order with all its attendant ethical expectations, as did Athena in classical Athens.

By incorporating the moral norms of Greek society, the symbolic praxis of religious ritual both gave these norms divine sanction and ensured their dissemination from generation to generation. In this function it was assisted by the stories that clustered around the deities and their cults. Stories articulate connections between things and thereby construct a framework within which to interpret meaning and value. Divine sponsorship of the human civil order, implicit in the cult of Zeus, is set into an evolutionary historical context in Hesiod's *Theogony*, in which Zeus, after defeating Cronus, who reigned by force and violence, initiated a rule of justice in the universe. Zeus's justice underlies the story of the *Odyssey*, in which Zeus brings about justice by restoring Odysseus to his rightful throne in Ithaca and by punishing the suitors who had violated the divinely sanctioned social order. From Homer on, justice was venerated as a universal Greek moral norm, divinely sanctioned by the supreme deity and implicated in the reciprocity principle of cultic interaction with all deities.

The stories of Greek mythology not only undergirded established social and moral norms; they also supplied the vehicle for ethical reflection and discourse on moral questions. In Aeschylus's *Oresteia*, Zeus as an agent of justice was complemented by Apollo and Athena, who were portrayed as refining the administration of justice to secure civil unity and harmony in a democratic polis in the wake of ambiguous violence. Sophocles' *Antigone* explored the clash of divinely sanctioned obligations to the family with politically expedient measures to ensure the survival of the city. Virtually every Greek tragedy presented moral issues in the context of or in opposition to traditional religious notions.

The critical movement. Once the Greek deities had entered the arena of public discourse on the moral structure of the universe, they were destined to come in for critical appraisal and revision. From earliest times the Greeks were inclined to critique their own beliefs, and it was not long before some began to question the divine warrant for morality implicit in traditional religion. Already in the 6th century BCE, Theognis questioned the efficacy of divine justice; he took Zeus to task for giving the same portion to the evil as to the good (vv. 373–400). Xenophanes faulted Homer and Hesiod for undermining morality by attributing to the gods immoral actions, and he ridiculed the whole notion of talking about deity in human form (Diels and Kranz 1952: 21 B 11–16). It was not only the stories of the poets, but even the basic cult practices that came under suspicion. Heraclitus questioned the efficacy of prayer to cult images and purification rituals (Diels and Kranz 1952: 22 B 5).

In the 4th century, Plato consolidated these criticisms into a devastating attack on traditional religion as a basis for moral living. In the *Republic* he produced a scathing criticism of the poets' unworthy portrayal of the gods and their behavior. In the *Euthyphro* he called into question the divine sanction for moral norms on the grounds that one cannot have certain knowledge of which norms or practices the gods approved. He also attacked the religious practices of prayer and sacrifice in that they entailed an unworthy conception of god as weak, in need of gifts and services, and subject to human manipulation.

These attacks brought some to the point of virtual atheism during the last third of the 5th century. Intellectuals, such as the Sophists and Atomists, dismissed the gods as exalted linguistic symbols for natural objects or phenomena or as political inventions to ensure conformity to conventional social norms. Ethical debates were now often carried on without any religious considerations, solely in terms of the relative importance of nature and social convention in determining moral norms.

New cosmologies and philosophical ethics. For most Greeks, however, the criticism of traditional religion went hand in hand with a radical rethinking of the role of the divine in the universe and of the relation between religion and morality. Instead of conceiving of the divine on the analogy of an aristocratic family, with superhuman cosmic forces governed by human motivations such as pleasure and displeasure, Greek poets and philosophers began to tell the story of the origin of the cosmos and to describe the way the world works on the analogy of the social order of the city-state. The divine forces now came to be viewed as operating in the lawlike way of the city-state and through physical processes resembling those observed in contemporary crafts and technology. From the 6th through the 3rd centuries BCE, the Greek philosophers developed a new cosmology with numerous variants, in which deity was assigned variously to the ultimate source, elemental building blocks, primal forces, or underlying structure of the cosmos and often to its most enduring and regularly moving components, the heavenly bodies.

These new conceptions of deity became the basis for a new justification for ethics: moral norms were construed as built deeply into the structure of the universe. Underlying this new justification was the presupposition of regular, natural patterns of human behavior that not only can, but, in fact, must, be taken into consideration in establishing norms of behavior and social institutions.

Most Greek intellectuals divided human behavior into two types: actions arising from rational decision either in an individual life or in a sociopolitical context, such as the city-state, and actions beyond voluntary control and even opposed to rational choice. The role of the divine in determining each became the subject of bitter debate beginning in the 5th century BCE. On the one hand, the awesome power of irrational, psychic forces and the difficulty of rational control pointed to the irrational as a divine force in human life. This did not necessarily imply that the irrational was to be normative, but rather entailed the need to curtail the role of religion and society in cultivating it. On the other hand, the aesthetically satisfying order seen in the natural world and the practical and social benefits of a rationally planned course of action suggested that rationality was the central function of the divine and the divinely authorized norm for life. Plato gave the latter point of view a decisive advantage.

Although Plato never systematically delineated his

theology, he clearly associated the divine with order and rationality. He identified as god (1) the ordered cosmos as a whole, as well as the celestial bodies, which are its eternal, regularly moving parts; (2) the source of its ordered motion, that is, its intelligent soul; and (3) the cosmic creator (demiurge), who contemplated the eternal Form of the cosmos and imposed it as far as he could upon the material body. Human souls he derived from the divine souls that animate the heavenly bodies. Hence they were in principle capable of contemplating the eternal Forms and rationally ordering their possessors in accord with the Form of the Good. To do so, reason has to control the irrational movements of soul, which are initiated by the desires and create harmony within the soul. The virtues, as redefined by Plato, consist in the right relationship among these parts of the soul. To the degree that reason succeeds in directing the two nonrational parts and bringing about harmonious motion like that of the heavens, the human soul becomes like the divine world soul. This is tantamount to assimilating oneself to god (*homoiōsis theōi; Theaetetus* 176b). That is the essence of the philosophical life and preparation for the soul's escape from the material world at death.

Thus Plato claimed divine sanction for rationality as the norm for human behavior and the basis for ethics. In a morally ordered universe governed by divine benevolence, humans have an obligation to promote that order in society through good laws and government. A transformed version of traditional religion is central to this endeavor. Purified civic cult practices bond the community and instill the virtues that restrain passions, enable social life, and free people for the pursuit of rationality. Ecstatic and mystic rituals are reconstructed as avenues of access to the Forms that constitute the divine, rational, moral structure of the universe.

Plato represented a seismic shift in attitudes toward the divine. Whereas Greek gods were traditionally perceived as tyrannical, grudging in their benevolence, defensive of their superiority, and envious of human success, Plato's creator-god was good, without jealousy, and desirous that everything in the universe should be as good as possible, like himself. With that theological revision, the ancient aversion to any aspiration to divine status began to give way among the philosophically inclined to a desire for becoming like god. Aristotle conjectured that the divine prime mover moved the cosmos as an object of desire, and the Stoics strove to conform their minds to the mind of Zeus, by which they meant the divine intellect that moves the cosmos.

Plato's own followers, except for a lengthy diversion into skepticism, laid increasing stress on the importance of making contact with the divine or of ascending from the material world to the divine realms above. The Middle Platonists (1st century BCE to 3rd century CE) and Neoplatonists (3rd to 5th centuries CE) stepped beyond Plato in locating the Forms in the mind of god, with the result that philosophy and the pursuit of knowledge of

the Forms entailed entry into the mind of god and union with the divine (see Esotericism and Mysticism). This line of thinking became increasingly widespread and diverse during Roman imperial times, with a broad spectrum of potential ethical imperatives, including self-discovery, self-denial, the traditional virtues, mystic contemplation, and sometimes even vegetarianism.

Thus Plato's followers and most rival philosophers pursued Plato's agenda of grounding ethics in the divine source of order and motion in the cosmos. There was vigorous debate over the precise connection between the divine and morality and over the appropriate norms and aspirations to be derived from it. Equally contested was the treatment of traditional religious beliefs and practices. Allegorization was commonly used by the Stoics to reconcile the old with the new; Platonists were inclined to accept the traditional gods and *daemones* as subordinate to the supreme god and as a means of access to the divine mind. Epicureanism gave new life to atomism and the virtual atheism of the classical era, denying divine providence and divine interaction with the world. All approaches, however, created philosophical religions or substitutes that promoted the study of philosophy as the essence of piety and right thinking as the basis of the moral life. From the 4th century BCE on, these philosophical religions flourished alongside and in creative tension with traditional religions, creating a continually evolving array of configurations of the relation between religion and ethics.

BIBL.: A. H. Armstrong (ed.), *The Cambridge History of Later Greek and Early Medieval Philosophy,* vols. 1, 3, 4 (Cambridge, 1967). W. Burkert, *Greek Religion* (Cambridge, Mass., 1985). M. Despland, *The Education of Desire: Plato and the Philosophy of Religion* (Toronto, 1985). H. Diels and W. Kranz, *Die Fragmente der Vorsokratiker* (6th ed.; Berlin, 1952). L. P. Gerson, *God and Greek Philosophy: Studies in the Early History of Natural Theology* (London, 1990). M. L. Morgan, "Plato and Greek Religion," in *The Cambridge Companion to Plato* (ed. R. Kraut; Cambridge, 1992), 227–47. Idem, *Platonic Piety: Philosophy and Ritual in 4th-Century Athens* (New Haven, Conn., 1990). D.E.H.

Rome

In broad terms, the nature of ethics in Rome was similar to that in Greece. There was no single source of moral authority, no religion whose prime function was that of setting moral norms, no determinate set of moral laws. "Ethics" or "morality" was the product of a nexus of interrelated influences, including religion, social practices or ideals, and philosophy. If one asks "In what ways (within this broad resemblance) does Roman ethics differ from Greek?" the answer is bound to be complex; but some distinctive features can be singled out.

During the period from the 6th century BCE to the 4th century CE, Rome developed from a small Italian city-state to (for several centuries) the dominant power in the Mediterranean world, including the Greek-speaking eastern Mediterranean. One of the factors that promoted this development was a high degree of social and political cohesion, supplemented by an effective legal system. In analyzing their own success, the Romans highlighted the maintenance of traditional practices *(mores)* and the promotion of very high standards of commitment to the public good, especially through the idealization of exemplary figures of the past *(exempla)*. A second recurrent theme of Roman social ethics was concern about the way in which, during various phases of its history, social ethics declined from its own best standards of public commitment and order. These ethical ideals were characterized in terms of certain core virtues, such as justice and courage, seriousness and industry, and also in the notion of "duty" *(officium)*.

The Romans also often attributed their success to the maintenance of religion, which was strongly embedded in political and social life. Roman religion did not give a prominent role to ethical teaching; and the gods were not seen as, necessarily, morally good. However, this is not to say that religion had no stake in ethics in our terms. So, for example, some abstractions such as "concord," "good faith," and "honor" acquired cult status and indeed had temples in the city of Rome. Some crimes were seen as the concerns of the gods: Jupiter, in particular, could be seen as a guarantor of oaths; while some misconduct (such as incest or the killing of kin) could be seen as religious offenses. The Latin term *pius* (which is wider than the English "pious") covered proper behavior toward the gods, but also other forms of correct conduct (relations between parents and children, appropriate sexual relations). In his treatise *On Laws* (2.7), Cicero could claim that fear of punishment by the gods discouraged people from crime. In general, the regular performance of religious practices was seen as being, in itself, a vital part of Roman *mores;* and Romans were sometimes identified as exceptionally scrupulous in religious practice. Traditional norms and religion were important components of Roman ethics.

Nevertheless the formal articulation of ethics took place mainly through philosophy. Philosophy figured as a means of advanced education, intellectual interest, and a source of advice, for at least some members of the Roman elite. They thus gained access to the systems of ethical thought that had developed in Greek-speaking culture in the 4th and 3rd centuries BCE.

The main philosophical systems known to the Romans were Stoicism, Epicureanism, and versions of Platonism and Aristotelianism. There are certain general differences between these ethical theories and modern moral theory. Much modern moral thinking (and also religious systems such as Judaism or Islam) is centered on the idea of moral rules or laws and the obligations thus imposed. Modern Western thinking also tends to assimilate "moral" or "ethical" principles with benefiting others rather than oneself. The Greco-Roman theories are based, rather, on the idea that the supreme value is happiness, which is the natural objective of human action and desire. For most of these theories, happiness is realized, above all, by virtuous actions or by developing a virtuous character. Some at least of the virtues (notably courage and justice) are seen as benefiting others, although virtues in general, including wisdom and self-control, are also regarded as valuable because they benefit the person concerned. Thus, Greco-Roman ethics, taken as a whole, exhibits marked differences in conceptual framework from much modern ethics and also from theocratic moral systems; but it also recognizes in its own way some of the concerns (such as right actions and benefiting others) that are central to those other approaches.

Roman thinkers did not evolve any fundamentally new ethical theories. They assimilated existing Greek theories and debated their respective merits. This process can be seen clearly at work in the late republic (1st century BCE) in thinkers such as Lucretius and Cicero. Another marked feature of Roman thought, one shared with Greek thinkers in the late republic and early empire, is the emergence of practical ethics: the application of philosophical principles to the management of one's life. Both in ethical theory and in practical ethics, we can see Romans reflecting on the relationship between philosophical principles and the values of Roman social and political life (sometimes also those of religion). In some cases, the aim is to reconcile philosophy with the highest ideals of Roman social and political practice; this is clear in Stoic-influenced works such as Cicero's *On Duties* and Marcus Aurelius's *Meditations.* However, philosophy could also serve as a basis for challenging Roman values as a whole (as the Epicurean poet Lucretius did) or for condemning what was seen as corrupt moral or political practice. As a result, philosophical teachers or philosophically inspired politicians were sometimes seen as subversive, especially under the Roman Empire, and were exiled, executed, or forced into suicide (e.g., Seneca, the former adviser of Nero). From the 2nd century CE onward, arguments for or against Christianity were also framed in partly philosophical form. So, although the Romans were not major innovative philosophers, philosophy provides an important point of access to the larger discourse in which ethics was expressed and debated in Roman culture.

BIBL.: J. Annas, *The Morality of Happiness* (Oxford, 1993). C. Edwards, *The Politics of Immorality* (Cambridge, 1993). M. T. Griffin and J. Barnes, *Philosophia Togata*, vol. 1 (Oxford, 1989). J. H. W. G. Liebeschuetz, *Continuity and Change in Roman Religion* (Oxford, 1979).   C.J.G.

Christianity

Of the law codes that early Christianity inherited from Judaism as part of its scripture, the most important were the Decalogue (Exod. 20.1–17; Deut. 5.6–21) and parts of both the Holiness Code (Lev. 17–26) and the Deuteronomic Code (Book of Deuteronomy). The Decalogue (also known as the Ten Commandments or Ten Words), which was given in the form of apodictic ("absolute" or "ordained by God") rather than casuistic ("case") law, was ancient Israel's fundamental law code and intimately linked in biblical tradition to YHWH's covenant with the Hebrews at Mount Sinai. The binding character of its commands to honor one's parents, not to commit murder or adultery, and not to steal, bear false witness, or covet is assumed by Jesus in his response to the rich man in all three of the Synoptic Gospels (Matt. 19.18–19; Mark 10.19; Luke 18.20). Several of the Decalogue's commands also play an important role in the Synoptic Gospels' depiction of Jesus's teaching. For example, he accuses the scribes of violating the command to honor one's father and mother (Exod. 20.12; Deut. 5.16; see also Exod. 21.17; Lev. 20.9) by their practice of offering as gifts to God what should have been given to their parents (Matt. 15.1–9; Mark 7.1–13). In the Sermon on the Mount, Jesus quotes the commands against murder (Exod. 20.13; Deut. 5.17) and adultery (Exod. 20.14; Deut. 5.18) as a prelude to the condemnation of anger (Matt. 5.21–22) and of lust (5.27–28).

The Matthean Jesus's prohibition of oaths (Matt. 5.34–37) is also prefaced by a reference to another of the Decalogue's stipulations, although here he does not quote the biblical command but gives instead a common interpretation of the law. "You shall not commit perjury" (5.33) is not, as is often thought, a reference to the prohibition against false testimony (Exod. 20.16; Deut. 5.20), but an interpretive summary of the injunction against taking the name of YHWH in vain (Exod. 20.7; Deut. 5.11). In the ancient Mediterranean world, bearing false witness was a legal offense committed in a legal or quasilegal setting (see, e.g., Matt. 26.59–60; Mark 14.55–59; Acts 6.13) and did not presuppose that the person guilty of the crime was even under oath. Perjury, by contrast, was a religious offense committed against God, owing to the abuse of the divine name. It involved not only false statements made under oath but also failures to keep sworn promises. Not restricted to a legal setting, perjury occurred wherever and whenever an individual either took a false assertory oath or failed to keep a promissory one. The Matthean Jesus's condemnation of perjury (Matt. 5.33), his criticism of the Pharisees' casuistry in regard to oaths (23.16–22), and his aversion to oaths align him with other ancient moralists, who similarly rejected perjury and restricted or rejected the use of oaths.

Jesus's interpretation of the Decalogue was certainly not without controversy. For instance, his willingness to heal on the sabbath (Matt. 12.9–14; Mark 3.1–6; Luke 6.6–11; 13.10–17; 14.1–6; John 5.1–18; 7.21–24; 9.13–17) and to allow his hungry disciples to pluck heads of grain and feed themselves on that day (Matt. 12.1–8;

Mark 2.23–28; Luke 6.1–5) embroiled him in a hermeneutical debate about the proper interpretation of the Torah's command to keep the sabbath holy (Exod. 20.8–11; Deut. 5.12–15). The canonical Gospels offer a defense of Jesus's practice of engaging in controversial conduct on the sabbath, whereas one of the apocryphal gospels, the *Infancy Gospel of Thomas* 2, suggests that this practice began already when Jesus was a five-year-old child. At the other end of the spectrum of traditions about Jesus and the sabbath stands the (almost certainly inauthentic) saying found in the Coptic *Gospel of Thomas,* "If you do not keep the sabbath as a sabbath, you will not see the Father" (27.2).

The Holiness Code grounds the demand for moral and ritual holiness in God's very character (Lev. 20.26) and contains the divine command "you shall love your neighbor as yourself" (19.18). The latter is quoted in the New Testament, in whole or in part, no less than nine times (Matt. 5.43; 19.19; 22.39; Mark 12.31, 33; Luke 10.27; Rom. 13.9; Gal. 5.14; James 2.8), which underscores its fundamental importance. Whereas the Matthean Jesus includes it along with five of the Decalogue's stipulations as necessary for entrance into life in the kingdom (Matt. 19.18–19) and identifies it as one of the two commandments undergirding all the law and the prophets (22.34–40; see also Mark 12.28–34), Paul views this command as a summary of the demands made by the whole law, including the Decalogue (Rom. 13.8–10; Gal. 5.14). James also links Lev. 19.18, which he regards as the quintessential expression of "the royal law" (James 2.8), with the Decalogue, which he cites immediately thereafter (2.11).

The Deuteronomic Code contains the commandment that Jesus identified as "the great and first commandment" (Matt. 22.38; see also Mark 12.28–29), namely, Deut. 6.5, "You shall love the LORD your God with all your heart, and with all your soul, and with all your might." Jesus was not alone in giving this commandment priority (Luke 10.27); it formed part of the Shema (the ancient confession of faith used in the synagogue liturgy) and was given pride of place because it made clear that love of God was demonstrated above all by the keeping of the Torah (Deut. 6.4–9).

The Synoptic tradition thus presents Jesus in part as the messianic interpreter of Israel's ancient law codes, sometimes sharpening or intensifying the biblical laws, sometimes criticizing certain laws (such as the law about divorce in Deut. 24.1–4) as concessions to human sinfulness (Matt. 19.7–8; Mark 10.4–6), and at other times criticizing others' interpretations of the law. Whether he saw himself as abolishing any of the laws was debated by his followers. Mark, for example, thought that he had abolished dietary laws (7.19) when declaring that "there is nothing outside a person that by going in can defile" (7.15 NRSV). Matthew 15.11 quotes the same saying but does not draw the same conclusion; on the contrary, he insists that Jesus's teaching upheld the validity of the whole law until the end of the age (5.17–20).

Of the early Christians, Paul's attitude toward the law is the most intriguing. Although he regards the law as good and uses it in dealing with ethical issues (see, e.g., the quotation of Deut. 17.7 in 1 Cor. 5.13), his attitude represents a significant break from the traditional conception. For Jewish tradition, the only enduring freedom is one that is informed and structured by law; for Paul, on the other hand, the law is a barrier to human freedom and a catalyst to sin. Instead of linking liberty with the law, he links it with the Holy Spirit and views the moral life as the consequence of being led by the Spirit. Whereas the presence of the Spirit was traditionally tied to ecstatic behavior, Paul is the first to link it to ethics within a communal context.

In addition to using the law codes inherited from Judaism, early Christians generated numerous guidelines for the moral life, with some of these having the status of law. Jesus's own teaching was viewed as uniquely authoritative by his followers, with some of his individual sayings termed "commandments" (1 Cor. 7.10; 9.14). Non-Christians recognized the authoritative status that his words had for believers and occasionally referred to Jesus as the Christians' "first lawgiver" (Lucian, *The Passing of Peregrinus* 13). Because early Christian apostles were regarded as the personal envoys of Christ, their own ethical exhortations and mandates were also widely viewed as authoritative. The sayings of other Christian leaders, such as prophets, also carried authority; some of these were cast in the form of sentences of holy law. The latter had the status of eschatological divine law and often invoked the ancient principle of retaliation (see, e.g., 1 Cor. 3.17).

Evolving Christianity also produced many laws contained in various books of church order, many of which claimed to transmit authoritative apostolic teachings about ecclesiastical faith and practice. The earliest example is the *Didache,* a 1st- or 2nd-century handbook containing instructions about ethics (1–6), the liturgy (7–10), church order and discipline (11–15), and eschatology (16). Later manuals enumerating various church laws and regulations include the *Apostolic Tradition* attributed to Hippolytus, a compilation containing material from the 2nd to 4th centuries, and the massive eight-volume work known as the *Apostolic Constitutions,* dating from the 4th century, the early church's largest collection of liturgical and legislative material.

In emphasizing the importance of correctly understanding the nature of God and of leading a life that corresponds to the divine will, early Christianity continued Judaism's strong link between religion and ethics. Yet in the Greco-Roman world in which early Christianity developed, religion was not inherently concerned with either moral formation or theological exposition. These were primarily the tasks of philosophy. The nature of the gods, for example, was a topic discussed by philoso-

phers such as Cicero *(On the Nature of the Gods)* and Philodemus *(On Piety, On the Gods),* and ethics was one of the three parts into which philosophical studies were commonly divided. Many of the Greco-Roman philosophical schools (especially Stoicism and Middle Platonism) had a strongly religious character, engaged in various theological debates, criticized aspects of popular religion, and rejected the immorality of traditional mythology. Philosophers accordingly placed emphasis on humans having a correct and worthy conception of the divine and on upright ethical conduct. Although the ethical systems of the philosophers had a theoretical foundation, the concern during this period was eminently practical, and the instruction was designed to help humans achieve moral maturity.

Formal Christian attitudes toward philosophy ran the spectrum from warm embrace to critical distance. Christians tended to favor Platonism as an approximation to Christian belief (Justin Martyr, *Dialogue with Trypho* 1–15; *Apology* 1.59–60; Augustine, *City of God* 8.4). Others, such as Hippolytus of Rome in the early 3rd century, argued that philosophy was the source of all the heretical evils in the life of the church *(Refutation of All Heresies).* Most Christian thinkers were in constructive dialogue with philosophical traditions, nowhere more than in the realm of ethics.

Although there was no inherent link between cult and morality in the world of the first Christians, their ethical concerns were thus shared by an important and influential segment of society. And there was genuine cause for concern. Although the ugly picture of moral bankruptcy painted by satirists is often a caricature rather than a realistic depiction, it had a sufficient societal basis to indicate that many of the problems plaguing Greco-Roman society were real. The ethical emphasis in early Christianity not only attracted some and repelled others, but also set it apart from most religions of the Greco-Roman world, aligning it with both Judaism and popular moral philosophy. For that reason and others, the early Christians appeared to many of their peers as members of a new popular philosophical school, offering instruction about the nature of the divine and guidance in morality. Not surprisingly, early Christians drew not only upon the words of Jesus and various Jewish traditions (such as the "two ways" [i.e., the way of life and the way of death; see especially *Didache* 1–6 and *Barnabas* 18–20]) but also on the materials and methods of the philosophers and other moralists, and they used them in their own ethical teaching and exhortation. These materials included proverbs, apophthegms (sayings of notable people, such as Epimenides of Crete: "Cretans are always liars, vicious brutes, lazy gluttons"; Titus 1.12 NRSV), precepts (instructions on living addressed to particular situations), gnomes and ethical maxims (e.g., "the love of money is a root of all kinds of evil"; 1 Tim. 6.10 NRSV), *chreiai* (instructive anecdotes and sayings by particular people), quotations of poets, tragedians, and comic playwrights (e.g., Menander: "Bad company ruins good morals"; 1 Cor. 15.33 NRSV), pieces of advice on particular subjects (1 Cor. 7.25; 2 Cor. 8.10), lists of virtues and vices, the household code (which was derived from philosophical discussions of household management and gave instructions on proper conduct to various members of the household), the use of personal example and the citation of other individuals as role models, and conventional subjects (such as anger, neighborly love, civic responsibility, concord, envy, friendship, and greed), the unwritten laws, and codes of conduct derived from the national customs of various ancient groups.

Whatever the proximate and ultimate source of the materials used by the early Christians, they initially concentrated their attention on the conduct of those who claimed to be Christians, not on society at large. They appear largely to have agreed with one another on certain ethical issues (e.g., on prohibiting infanticide), but to have disagreed on others (such as the propriety of attending gladiatorial contests and other games; see Tertullian, *On Spectacles* 3). Like members of any other religious or philosophical group, some Christians saw themselves as a positive moral force who helped to better their society, whereas others contributed to its problems.

BIBL.: Richard B. Hays, *The Moral Vision of the New Testament* (San Francisco, 1996). Abraham J. Malherbe, *Moral Exhortation: A Greco-Roman Sourcebook* (Philadelphia, 1986). Wayne A. Meeks, *The Moral World of the First Christians* (Philadelphia, 1986). Idem, *The Origins of Christian Morality: The First Two Centuries* (New Haven, Conn., 1993).   J.T.F.

Theology, Theodicy, Philosophy

Introduction

The three notions forming the title of this chapter summarize the cultural traditions raising the ultimate questions of life: the structure of reality and the fundamentals of human existence. Since the cultures of antiquity have disappeared as living traditions, we are largely dependent on the remaining texts. The earliest and most generally attested answers take the form of religion. They envisage a plurality of divine powers behind the phenomenal world and develop various forms of cult and worship in order to enter into communication with the divine world. Normally, the concepts about the divine (i.e., its unity and diversity and the modes of divine impact upon the phenomenal world) remain implicit in the various practices of communication, among which the sacrificial cult takes the most prominent place. We have to wait for specific "discourse generators" converting implicit knowledge into explicit statements in order to find these themes treated in the textual tradition. Typically, such generators arise in situations of crisis when the implicit answers seem no longer valid. In Egypt, literary texts addressing fundamental questions occur after the breakdown of the Old Kingdom (2150 BCE). Mesopotamia saw many cultural catastrophes and periods of crisis and suffering: the end of the Sumerian city-states (2350 BCE), the end of the Sargonid Empire (2150 BCE), the breakdown of the Neo-Sumerian Empire (1900 BCE), and the struggles between the Assyrians and the Babylonians, each of which found rich expression in the literary tradition, leading to the evolution of new genres, forms, and motifs. In the Hittite world, the most conspicuous crisis is the plague that struck the country for twenty years (1340–1320 BCE). The texts dealing with this disaster, the annals of Shuppiluliuma and the plague prayers of Murshili, rank among the most important achievements of Hittite historiography. In Israel, the connection between crisis and theological literature is most obvious. The prophetical movement from Amos to Ezra is most closely linked to political breakdowns: the fall of the northern kingdom (722 BCE), the catastrophe of Jerusalem (587 BCE), the Babylonian exile, and the political reorganization under Ezra and Nehemiah. The genesis of the Hebrew canon falls in a period of no lesser conflicts: the Maccabean wars (167–160 BCE), the destruction of the Second Temple (70 CE), expulsion, and the Diaspora (135 CE). Even in Greece, where the political situation seems less dramatic, Ionian philosophy starts with the Persian conquest of Ionia (end of 6th century BCE).

The most important factor for converting implicit knowledge into explicit discourse is the experience of drastic change, for which catastrophe is the most typical, but by no means the only, cause. Drastic changes may be caused not only by trauma, but also by triumph. The Sargonid unification of Mesopotamia and its far-reaching conquests (2350–2200 BCE) affected the Babylonian worldview; the expulsion of the Hyksos and the ensuing conquest of Nubia and large parts of Palestine (1580–1450 BCE) changed fundamentally the Egyptian view of the world; and the same holds true, of course, for the Greek (especially Athenian) triumph over Persia and the ensuing flourishing of arts and sciences, philosophy and literature in the 5th century BCE. For the Jews, the advent of Cyrus II (537 BCE), the return of the refugees, the commission of Ezra, and the reforms of Nehemiah were doubtlessly more of a triumph than a trauma, in spite of all the accompanying conflicts.

Triumphant change typically leads to a breakdown of conceptual boundaries. God, or the divine world, is now seen to be responsible for the creation and the maintenance not only of one's own group but also of a great variety of different nations. Imperialism entails universalism. In Egypt, the conquests of the 18th Dynasty severely shattered the polytheistic worldview, triggering a theological evolution that eventually culminated in a monotheistic revolution (Akhenaten, 1360 BCE). Under the Ramesside kings (1200–1050 BCE), Akhenaten's exclusive monotheism was replaced by an inclusive monotheism. The gods were readmitted but subordinated to Amun (the Hidden One). These changes in cosmology and theology found their explicit expression in hundreds of hymns, dealing with purely theological questions such as the relation between the One and the many, cosmogony as creation and emanation, the divine impact on human history, the welfare of the state and of the individual, and so on. In Mesopotamia, Assyrian and Babylonian imperialism inspired a likewise universalistic theology, subordinating the pantheon either to Assur or to Marduk and arriving at similar forms of inclusive monotheism. The Hellenistic and Roman empires that fell heir to the oriental kingdoms found their intellectual and spiritual expression in the universalistic theologies of Stoic and (Neo)platonic philosophy. We must not forget, however, that the triumph of the one is the trauma of the other.

Traumatic change means an experience of absence. Where was or were God or the gods when those things happened? Theodicy is the most original and general answer to this experience. The idea of a punishing god is easier to bear than the idea of divine absence. In Israel, the trauma of the fall of Jerusalem and the Babylonian exile led to a theology of history that explains the catastrophe as divine punishment for the "sins of the fathers." Historiography, especially of the Deuteronomic school, arose as a form of collective confession. In Egypt, the discourse of theodicy is clearly linked to the First Intermediate Period, which is depicted in the texts as a period of suffering when many died of violence and famine. In one text, god is accused of being indifferent to human suffering. The creator is supposed to act as a good shepherd: does he sleep? Is he incapable of getting inflamed against evil and injustice (Ipuwer)? Another text that reads like an answer to these questions confirms god's pastoral care for his creatures. If god actually slew many of them, this was only because of their "crookedness," "like a father hits a son for the sake of his brother" (Merikare). In a third text, god asserts that he did not order evil to be done but that the human heart transgressed his orders (Coffin Text, spell 1130). Theodicy deals with the absence or hiddenness of justice, be it on the level of society as in Egypt or on the level of personal biography as in Mesopotamia and the Bible. Justice is conceived of as the nexus between doing and faring, which means that suffering is always caused by evil deeds. The only way of healing is by reconciling the offended deity through worship, confession, sacrifice, and repentance. The Mesopotamian and biblical theodicy texts destroy the nexus between doing and faring, guilt and suffering, by giving voice to suffering without leading into confession and repentance, amounting to a kind of "negative theology of justice."

The most prolific generator of theological discourse is the distinction between true and false, or the rise of orthodoxy. Questions of orthodoxy, about the true concepts of the divine, are never a matter of oral tradition and implicit knowledge; they always call for codification and even canonization. Since this distinction was unknown to those ancient religions that later came to be subsumed under "paganism" by the so-called true religions based on revelation and monotheism (Judaism, Christianity, and Islam), we must distinguish between theology in a more general sense, as defined above, and theology in the narrow sense, concerned with questions of truth and untruth, orthodoxy and heresy, which is the exclusive property of monotheism.

Philosophy may be defined as a form of dealing with the ultimate questions without religious consequences. In this respect, Akhenaten's reform, which has often been interpreted as a philosophy rather than a theology, must rank as theology because its religious consequences were fundamental and far-reaching. Philosophy is also based on the distinction between true and false, but the truth is seen as a matter of reasoning, not of revelation. This does not mean that philosophical answers to ultimate questions exclude the divine. On the contrary, most philosophical traditions include a full-fledged theology, but this theology is not linked to any religion implying cult and ritual. A cult of Aristotle's "unmoved mover" would be unthinkable. If a philosophical school forms those links, as in some Neoplatonic and Pythagorean groups, it turns into religion.

BIBL.: David Birnbaum, *God and Evil: A Unified Theodicy, Theology, Philosophy* (Hoboken, N.J., 1989). Robert MacKim, *Religion, Ambiguity, and Religious Diversity* (New York, 2001). E. P. Sanders et al. (eds.), *Jewish and Christian Self-Definition* (3 vols.; Philadelphia, 1980–82). J.A.

Egypt

Like any society, ancient Egypt developed theodicy, theology, and philosophy in an attempt to answer questions about the nature of good and evil, the universe, and the human condition. The insights preserved in these constructs are often as subtle and profound as those produced by other cultures, yet their contribution to intellectual history has generally been overlooked or undervalued. This is due in large part to the nature of Egyptian thought itself, which was typically informed by subjectivity and a multivalent logic—features antithetical to those of more familiar theologies and philosophical systems.

Subjective thought imparts the qualities of the observer to the observed. To the ancient Egyptians, objects and phenomena were felt to be capable of the same sentience and willful behavior as human beings themselves. Egyptian explanations of the universe and human society were therefore codified not as treatises about the nature and behavior of impersonal forces but as myths of gods and their actions, with causality and evolution couched in the human terms of birth and generations. Egyptian thought thus produced what we would call "religion" rather than "science."

Egyptian logic accepted differing explanations of a single phenomenon as equally valid. These were typically viewed as complementary rather than competitive, each providing a unique insight into the underlying reality without completely encompassing that reality as a whole. This view produced the multiple names and forms of the Egyptian pantheon, reflecting different facets of the natural or human phenomena that the gods represented. It also gave rise to the quintessential Egyptian practice of syncretism, whereby the names of several gods were combined into one, in this case reflecting the unity of the underlying phenomenon.

In its subjectivity, Egyptian thought made no distinction between theology and philosophy. The results of philosophical inquiry were understood and presented as theology. Egyptian epistemology, for example, recognized three fundamental characteristics of thought, each of which was incorporated in a deity. The god Sia (Perception) represented the initial phenomenon of thought itself, understood as the perception of things both as they are and as they ought to be. The god Hu (Annunciation) personified the expression of that thought; coupled with the principle of Magic (the god Heka), this explained the phenomenon of authoritative utterance, speech that produces tangible results by the mere fact of its utterance. Finally, the god Ptah embodied the process whereby thought informs concrete reality itself. These principles were seen to be at work in all intellectual activity, from the Creator's initial conception and formation of the universe to the sculptor's inspiration that takes shape in the form of a statue.

Viewed in this light, theology in ancient Egypt was not so much an end in itself as an expression of inquiry into the nature of reality. Because of the practical nature of Egyptian religion, this thought was recorded in liturgical and other sacred texts rather than in discrete philosophical treatises. Three basic themes emerge from such texts: the creation and structure of the universe, the cycle of time and life, and the problem of good and evil.

The Egyptian concept of the universe was similar to that of other ancient Near Eastern cultures. The known world was viewed as a void within an infinite ocean and the sky as the surface of that ocean, held above the earth by the atmosphere; beneath the earth lay a similar void, known as the Duat, through which the sun traveled at night. Egyptian accounts of creation deal with the process and causality through which this structure was thought to have come into being.

The process of creation is incorporated in the Heliopolitan Ennead, a group of nine gods representing both the fundamental structures and principles of the world and their evolutionary interrelationship. In the Heliopolitan myth, the god Atum (Finished, Completed)

existed from all eternity within the universal ocean. At the moment of creation, he produced (through ejaculation or expectoration) a pair of gods, Shu (Void) and Tefnut. These in turn gave birth to the earth (Geb) and sky (Nut), who then produced two further pairs of deities: Osiris and Isis (the principles of procreation and motherhood), Seth (the principle of disorder) and Nephthys.

The elements of this myth appear in the earliest extensive texts, about 2400 BCE. Although crude by the standards of later cosmogonies, its structure and metaphors conceal a fairly sophisticated concept of the causality of the creation. The Ennead's generational structure embodies a system of evolutionary dependence reflecting the Egyptian concept of the world. Atum's initial creation of a void within the universal ocean (Shu) produced in turn a top (the sky) and bottom (the earth) to the void, and the creation of this space allowed the process of life (represented by the four children of Geb and Nut) to begin. Atum himself represents the primordial source of all the matter and forces of nature, and the metaphors of ejaculation/expectoration and birth are nothing more than a means of explaining their physical evolution. In a 4th-century BCE text, Atum describes the same process in more abstract terms: "When I evolved, evolution evolved . . . and the evolutions of evolutions became many, in the evolutions of children and in the evolutions of their children" (Papyrus Bremner-Rhind). With its concept of the world's evolution from a primordial singularity, the Heliopolitan Ennead embodies a cosmogony not all that different from the modern notion of the Big Bang.

In Aristotelian terms, the Heliopolitan system dealt with the material and formal causes of the creation. The creation's efficient cause was the concern of two systems centered on the gods Amun and Ptah. Where other Egyptian gods were immanent in the forces and elements of nature, Amun was viewed as transcendent and thus ultimately unknowable (his name means "hidden"). Amun is attested as early as the Heliopolitan myth, but his theology does not seem to have reached full form until the New Kingdom, about 1500 BCE. By that time his transcendence had made him both the greatest of the gods and the logical personification of the creation's efficient causality. In the latter role, his contribution was based on Egyptian epistemology: by giving expression to his perception of the world's ultimate character, Amun initiated the process of Atum's evolution. The link between Amun's perception and the ultimate material form of the world was embodied in the god Ptah, similar to Plato's demiurge or the Word in the Gospel of John.

The creation of the world also began the cycle of life, whose paradigm was the daily cycle of the sun, proceeding from birth to death and, through the force of procreation, to new life. In the Egyptian mind, this was viewed as the continual repetition of an eternal pattern, much like recurrent performances of a single play. These two components are embodied in complementary terms reflecting the Egyptian concept of time: "eternal recurrence" and "eternal sameness." Each beginning was seen not only as unique but also as a recurrence of the initial instance: each sunrise equivalent to the original dawn, each king's accession reprising that of the first, each child's birth continuing the life of its parents.

The pattern of eternal sameness reflected the Creator's initial concept of the world, and this feature of existence was embodied in the Egyptian concept of *ma'at.* Personified as the goddess Maat, *ma'at* was an abstract term meaning essentially "things as they ought to be." Preservation of *ma'at* was the pharaoh's prime duty, and his fulfillment of it was recorded in scenes on temple walls showing the king presenting the image of *ma'at* to various gods. In concrete applications, the meaning of *ma'at* ranges from "truth" to "rightness" and "justice," and the concept therefore incorporates both ethics and theodicy.

Egyptian notions of good and evil were essentially practical rather than absolute. Good was that which contributed to peace, stability, and order. The preservation of *ma'at* required the establishment of harmony between opposing forces rather than the annihilation of opposition. In theological terms, the god Seth generally represents the opposite of *ma'at,* yet the god himself was not seen as inherently evil; in fact, one of his chief roles was to repel opposition to the sun's nightly journey through the Duat.

Although personified in Seth, the phenomenon of disorder was also understood as a uniquely human failing, a flaw introduced into the perfect pattern of existence by people themselves. In a text from around 2000 BCE, the Creator says, "I have made each person like the other and have not commanded that they make disorder: it is their hearts that damage what I have said" (Coffin Text, spell 1130). The reference here is not to divine commandments but to the principle of *ma'at,* which was brought into existence with the rest of creation through the Creator's authoritative utterance ("what I have said").

Human beings, however, also represent the final cause of creation in Egyptian thought, as a text from the Middle Kingdom (ca. 1800 BCE) makes clear: "Well provided for are people, the flock of the god. For their sake he has made the sky and the earth, for them has he driven off the ravening of the water. He has made the heart's air so that they may live when they breathe. They are his likenesses, who have come from his body. For their sake he rises in the sky. For them has he made the plants, flocks, and fish that feed them. . . . When they weep he is hearing . . . for the god knows every name" (Instruction for King Merikare). The sense of personal relationship between people and the god implicit in this text is fairly unusual for the period in which it was written. By the Ramesside period (ca. 1200 BCE), however, it

had become well established, in some ways similar to that reflected in the Bible. For all of Egyptian history, however, the temples remained the exclusive domain of the gods and their human attendants, rather than public places of worship.

The text's use of the singular, anonymous term *the god* (or perhaps *God*) also reflects a pervasive theme of Egyptian theology from the Middle Kingdom onward: the ultimate unity of the divine beneath the multiplicity of names and forms in the Egyptian pantheon. The beginnings of this notion appear in the phenomenon of syncretism, already attested in the Old Kingdom (ca. 2600 BCE), which combines the names of two or more gods into a single entity, such as Amun-Re (Amun manifest in the sun). Its ultimate expression appears in a text from about 1228 BCE: "All the gods are three: Amun, Re, and Ptah, without others. His identity is hidden as Amun, his is Re as face, his body is Ptah" (Papyrus Leiden I 350). Despite the triune expression with which this passage opens, its continuation in the singular ("his") makes it clear that a single deity is meant, manifest in the sun (Re) and physical matter (Ptah), yet ultimately transcendent (Amun).

Although Egyptian theologians apparently came to understand divinity as ultimately one, their multivalent logic accepted this notion as equally valid with the more common view expressed in the Egyptian pantheon. Only the aberrant theology promoted by Pharaoh Akhenaten (ca. 1352–1336 BCE) dispensed with the other gods in favor of a single divine force—in this case, the power of light. Akhenaten began his reign by emphasizing the predominance of his deity, but he eventually initiated an active attempt to suppress polytheism by having the plural "gods" corrected to the singular "god" in inscriptions throughout Egypt. In doing so, he instituted not only monotheism but also univalent logic, which insisted on a single explanation of reality as valid. Akhenaten's religion did not survive the death of its founder, and later pharaohs destroyed his monuments and forbade mention of his name. Given the continued acceptance of monotheism as an option in Egyptian thought, this rejection of Akhenaten's ideas probably reflects an aversion to the intolerance of univalent logic rather than to his unique theology.

BIBL.: J. P. Allen, *Genesis in Egypt: The Philosophy of Ancient Egyptian Creation Accounts* (New Haven, Conn., 1988). J. Assmann, *The Search for God in Ancient Egypt* (trans. D. Lorton; Ithaca, N.Y., 2001). H. Frankfort et al., *The Intellectual Adventure of Ancient Man: An Essay on Speculative Thought in the Ancient Near East* (Chicago, 1946). E. Hornung, *Conceptions of God in Ancient Egypt: The One and the Many* (trans. J. Baines; Ithaca, N.Y., 1996).   J.P.A.

Mesopotamia

In the Mesopotamian view, humankind was created for the sole purpose of serving the gods, maintaining their temples and estates, and worshiping them. The gods controlled the destiny of every single individual, decreed the course of one's life and the time of one's death. They made whom they willed to prosper, and, although there existed some belief in the equation between sin and suffering, they seemingly inflicted punishment at random. The purpose of the gods' actions was indeed almost entirely concealed from human beings, for in the absence of a clearly defined code of conduct enacted by them—as was the case in Israel, where the duties of humankind were decreed by God and sanctioned by a solemn alliance between him and his people—how could worshipers gain any sense of security in their relationship with the divine world, how could they know their duties and obligations and thus avert divine anger? Religious texts from the 2nd and 1st millennia BCE insist on the sufferer's unawareness of his or her sin, which could be the result of an ethical, behavioral, cultic, or ritualistic misconduct, all of which were put on an equal footing.

This led to the question as to why the gods, so all-powerful and solicitous, would sometimes let their most devout worshipers suffer from disease and depression. Such a drama is portrayed in five literary compositions of the 2nd millennium BCE. The earliest is the Sumerian monologue of the pious sufferer, composed during the Isin-Larsa period (about 2000–1800). An Akkadian Dialogue between a Man and His God, on the same theme, was composed later during the Old Babylonian period (ca. 1800–1600). The other three compositions are from the Middle Babylonian period. In the Sufferer's Salvation, found at Ugarit, the entreaties of the sufferer are directed to the god Marduk. Marduk also appears in the lengthy poem *Ludlul Bēl Nēmeqi* (Let me praise the Lord of Wisdom), where he is portrayed as a unity of opposites, as the god who punishes and saves. Finally, the Babylonian Theodicy is cast in the form of a dialogue between the sufferer and a friend. All these texts portray a pious person afflicted with disease, alienation from society, even paranoia. Not knowing his sin, he nevertheless turns to his god with an overwhelming sense of guilt. In the end, the deity, moved by the entreaty, restores favor and health to the sufferer. The Babylonian Theodicy describes how the rogue and the impious prosper while the gods let their most faithful worshipers suffer punishment. This seems to be a more ethical and ecumenical treatment of the question of divine retribution. Yet, as the purpose of the gods remains unfathomable, the sufferer must still passively await restoration of divine favor: "The mind of the gods is as remote as innermost heaven; it is most difficult to understand, and people do not know it."

Although the feelings expressed in these compositions are, in a sense, only more ambitious elaborations of the theology underlying the numerous hymns and prayers of the late periods, the answers they propose still seem intellectually unsatisfactory. Divine purpose remains mysterious, and the sole escape for humans lies in blind faith. Therefore, in this early, perhaps first, recorded instance of a debate between faith and reason, the Babylonians opted for a religion of the heart, for unflinching faith in the ultimate purpose of the gods. They reflect a general agreement that steadfast piety will eventually be rewarded, however long it takes for the gods to respond. These feelings eventually evolved into a vision of history and human destiny that favored fatalism and the *vita contemplativa*. In the wake of the collapse of the Assyrian Empire at the end of the 7th century, King Nabopolassar of Babylonia reasserted this theology of history in his building inscriptions. Passive faith in the god Marduk ensured Babylonian triumph over Assyrian brutality, the victory of steadfast piety over hubris, of good over evil. Future kings are enjoined to follow these precepts: "Any king whose name Marduk will call to exert rulership of the country, do not be concerned with feats of might and power. Seek the sanctuaries of Nabu and Marduk, and let them slay your enemies." This advice led to the almost eschatological climax: "He who is loyal to Bel [Marduk] his foundations will endure, he who is loyal to the son of Bel [Nabu] will last for eternity."

The Mesopotamian sense of theodicy could easily have led to the elaboration of a complex theology and philosophy speculating on the nature of the gods, good and evil, and the place of humans in the cosmos. The existence of such speculations can be inferred from the extensive mythological and religious literature in Sumerian and Akkadian. The creation of humankind from the blood of the slain rebellious god Qingu in the Babylonian epic of creation *(Enuma Elish)*, for instance, can be interpreted both as an etiology of humanity's kinship with the gods and as a recognition of its fundamentally corrupt nature, and indeed the latter notion is explicitly defined in the Babylonian Theodicy in relation to humankind's creation by the god Ea and the goddess Mami: "[They] gave twisted words to the human race, they endowed them in perpetuity with lies and falsehood." Thus, evil is not only an external force personified by demonic creatures, it is also embedded in the human heart. Brief theological statements of this sort can be gleaned from various sources, but texts that can be narrowly defined as essentially theological in content are of a quite different nature and aimed mostly at explaining the position of the gods in relation to the world and, more important, in relation to one another.

Lists of gods are the earliest attested and most widespread theological texts. Copies of such lists have been found as early as the early dynastic period and as late as the Hellenistic period. Most of them list gods in hierarchical or genealogical order, sometimes adding brief explanatory comments. The tradition of lists of gods culminated in the latter part of the 2nd millennium with the compilation of the great list An = Anum, whose seven tablets form an exhaustive divine encyclopedia listing some two thousand gods organized in a vast pyramidal hierarchy crowned by the great cosmic deities Anu, Enlil, and Ea. Each major god leads a divine court comprising family members and a retinue of servants and attendants. One of the primordial notions expounded in the list An = Anum is the belief that goddesses and gods are queens and kings in their own cities and that the heavenly hierarchy is organized as an imperial council crowning these local divine fiefs.

In the course of the late 2nd and 1st millennia, new theological texts were composed. Syncretistic, as well as henotheistic, hymns and lists of gods express a further development of the notion of the divine reflecting the increased centralization of Mesopotamian national and imperial states, as well as the extension of their system of control over the greater portion of the Near East. A hymn to the healing goddess Gula, composed by one Bullussa-rabi (whose name means "great is her healing") extols Gula as a universal and all-powerful goddess; a hymn to the goddess Nanaya explains how she assumes the personas of the protecting goddesses of major Babylonian cities; a text from Babylon lists all major gods as aspects of Marduk; and a hymn to Ninurta views gods and goddesses as parts of his body, which thus mystically sums up the entire universe. Theological reforms such as those of King Sennacherib (705–681) of Assyria, promoting the equation between Assur, Ansar, and Marduk in order to fuse Assyrian and Babylonian theologies and stress the primeval and universal character of the god of Assyria; of King Nabonidus (556–539), the last Babylonian monarch, assimilating Marduk to the moon-god Sin and extolling the latter's status as imperial god; and of late Achaemenid and Hellenistic Uruk, promoting the divine pair Anu/Antu to the status of highest gods—all testify to the intensity and complexity of theological thinking. Neither the Babylonians nor the Assyrians produced texts detailing the reasoning and motives underlying these theological constructions, that is to say, they did not produce a discursive written rationalization of their constructs.

It is often said in this connection that Mesopotamia did not produce a philosophy. This is true insofar as philosophy is defined according to the ancient Greek model as an autonomous activity, conducted outside established institutions by individuals in competition with one another, who propose various systems addressing the perennial questions that beset humankind, and especially insofar as it includes the invention of a metalanguage that defines, and eventually itself becomes, the subject of rational inquiry. However, if we define philosophy more generally as reflection on the human condition and as the investigation of the structure of the cosmos and the laws governing its workings, then it may be claimed that the entire corpus of Mesopotamian literary, religious, and scientific texts constitutes a philosophy. In Mesopotamia there was no countersystem of thought that aimed at overturning established notions, no avowed effort to reform the existing order. The activities

of scholars were incremental; they did aim at providing ever-better answers and solutions, but always within the frame of the tradition. In this sense the intellectual kin of Mesopotamian scholars were not the philosophers of Greece, but the talmudic sages.

Who were these scholars? Essentially they were expert scribes who had reached the pinnacle of their discipline and thus deserved the epithet of *apkallu* (wise man, sage) or *ummânu* (scholar, expert). Since the Middle Babylonian period, Mesopotamian scholarship was divided into three main branches: *āšipūtu* (lore of the exorcist), *kalûtu* (lore of the cultic singer), and *bārûtu* (lore of the diviner). But words such as "exorcist" and "diviner" are inappropriately restrictive for denoting disciplines that in fact covered substantial portions of the entire body of knowledge that was available in written form. An expert exorcist, for example, was expected to master a vast number of canonical series touching on magic, medicine, astronomy, divination, and mathematics. Writing served largely as an aid to memory, and the corpus of texts transmitted by the sages formed a backbone around which theories, comments, and explanations were elaborated and transmitted orally. As with the study of theology, that of Mesopotamian philosophy is therefore beset by a lack of written theoretical statements. One notable exception is the subscription to a compendium of extracanonical celestial and terrestrial omens from the 7th century: "Their good and evil portents are in harmony. The signs on earth, just as those in the sky, give us signals. Sky and earth both produce portents; although appearing separately, they are not separate [because] sky and earth are related." This is a general formulation of the theory of universal sympathy, which is indeed one of the cornerstones of Mesopotamian philosophy.

In a world in which the gods had to be appeased constantly, where diseases were often explained as divine punishment, where natural phenomena were read as omens—signs sent by the almighty gods to warn humankind and impart to it fragments of divine foreknowledge—and sciences such as astronomy very probably evolved from a desire to decipher the divine will as revealed in the cosmos, there is no need to stress that what we would call philosophy was integrated with science, magic, and divination or that philosophy was dependent on the religious system. In sum, if we want to contrast the philosophy of the Mesopotamians with another ancient system of thought, we are probably justified in asserting that their belief in an animated cosmos, as well as their overwhelming fear of the gods and feeling of absolute dependence on them, made their worldview the very antithesis of Epicurean freedom.

BIBL.: Jean Bottéro, *Mesopotamia: Writing, Reasoning, and the Gods* (Chicago, 1992 [orig. 1987]). J.-J. Glassner, "La philosophie mésopotamienne," in *Encyclopédie philosophique universelle* (ed. André Jacob; Paris, 1989), 1637–42. W. G. Lambert, *Babylonian Wisdom Literature* (Oxford, 1960).

G. L. Mattingly, "The Pious Sufferer: Mesopotamia's Traditional Theodicy and Job's Counselors," in *The Bible in the Light of Cuneiform Literature* (ed. W. W. Hallo, B. W. Jones, and G. L. Mattingly; Scripture in Context 3; Lewiston, N.Y., 1990), 305–48. Karel van der Toorn, *Sin and Sanction in Israel and Mesopotamia* (Assen, 1985).   P.-A.B.

Syria-Canaan

The theological and philosophical essay was unknown in Syro-Canaanite culture; instead, thinkers used narratives to explore the great questions that we usually call theological and philosophical. Their interpretation must be inferred from their retelling of the story, what they add, subtract, or change. Retelling stories was done not only to explore ideas, however; poets also wanted to delight and entertain their readers, which means that we must always be cautious about what we infer about theology and philosophy from any given narrative.

A good example of this is the major myth of Ugaritic literature, the Baal Cycle (13th century BCE), fragmentarily preserved on six tablets. It narrates the cosmic battle and victory of the storm-god Baal-Hadad over Sea (Yamm) and over Death (Mot); subplots tell how the enemy's threat and the storm-god's victory affected the rankings of the gods and reorganized and reinvigorated the universe. The genre of combat myth that includes this story is attested in three Mesopotamian compositions ranging in date from about 2100 to 1000 BCE, *Lugal-e, Anzu,* and *Enuma Elish,* each influencing its successor. The genre appears vestigially in the Bible, for example, Exod. 15 and Ps. 89. The plot involves a monster, typically in the form of Sea, who threatens cosmic order; the panicking gods commission an outsider deity who defeats the monster; the outsider god is acclaimed sovereign and restores or creates the world. Although the identity of the victorious deity may vary, he typically is the patron god of the dynasty that holds political control at the time.

The combat myth is a way of thinking about the world, differing from modern historical and political theory chiefly in that the ancients took for granted the existence and power of the gods and readily used analogies from human psychic and social life to understand them, whereas moderns take for granted a different (and less ultimate) range of forces, for example, the power of ideas, of free trade, of energy resources. The combat myth seeks to explain why life is precarious yet somehow goes on, why empires (and their patron-gods) rise and fall.

Philo of Byblos's *Phoenician History* is a much later example of theology (early 2nd century CE). It contains a cosmogony, which was used to explore contemporary values and institutions, for the essence of a phenomenon was regarded as most visible at its moment of origin. Philo's cosmogony describes the world as coming into being *without* a creator-god; the "history of culture"

that immediately follows tells how the human race discovered civilization without the help of the gods, and a "history of the god Cronus" teaches that the gods originally were only human beings. Although it is difficult to judge Philo's accuracy as a reporter of Phoenician religion, his strongly antitheological tendency closely resembles Greek (Ionian) science of the 6th century BCE, when a similar conflict between traditional beliefs and the new "science" took place.

No theodicy (which I define here as a "defense of divine justice") has been found in the extant literature, although scribes presumably were familiar with skeptical Mesopotamian works such as the Babylonian Theodicy (1400–800 BCE) and heartfelt prayers of sufferers like *Ludlul Bēl Nēmeqi* (Let me praise the Lord of Wisdom; as early as 1400 BCE).

BIBL.: Harold W. Attridge and Robert A. Oden, *Philo of Byblos: The Phoenician History: Introduction, Critical Text, Translation, Notes* (Catholic Biblical Quarterly Monograph Series 9; Washington, D.C., 1981). Richard J. Clifford, "The Roots of Apocalypticism in Near Eastern Myth," in *The Encyclopedia of Apocalypticism* (ed. John J. Collins; New York, 1998), 1.3–38.   R.J.C.

Israel

While the claim of monotheism needs considerable revision, Israelite religion was focused on a single deity to a degree that was exceptional in the ancient world (see Deities and Demons). Whereas belief in multiple deities enabled Israel's neighbors to attribute misfortune to malevolent forces, YHWH eventually absorbed the demonic into his own being, claiming responsibility for good and ill.

Within the Bible one finds a persistent attempt to define YHWH's essential nature. The classic text, Exod. 34.6–7, is actually quoted in part nearly twenty times, in addition to numerous allusions to it. The twin attributes of justice and mercy, extended to thirteen, and remembered even today in the Passover Seder, attest to the importance of merit but also the need for something more. The anomalies of existence frequently placed a huge question mark before life's cherished beliefs. Once corporate solidarity gave way to individualism, these jolts to reasonable expectation of reward for virtue and punishment for vice became unbearable. The collapse of the northern kingdom (Israel) in 722 BCE and of the southern kingdom (Judah) in 587 BCE, again in 70 CE and 132–35 CE, had to be explained in a way that exonerated YHWH. The Deuteronomistic history shifted the blame to Israel and Judah while understanding the punishment as instrumental and disciplinary. The people sinned; YHWH punished them through foreign powers; the victims cried out for help; YHWH sent deliverance. Other writings adopted similar tactics that invariably gave the impression of an incorrigible Israel.

The classic discussion of theodicy with reference to an

individual, the Book of Job, has precursors in a brief section within the Egyptian Admonition of Ipuwer, the Sumerian Man and His God, and two Babylonian texts, *Ludlul Bēl Nēmeqi* and the Theodicy. Remote texts, from the standpoint of genre, are Ecclesiastes and the Egyptian Dialogue between a Master and His Slave. A paradigmatic text, Gen. 18–19, has Abraham address the deity with the words, "Shall not the Judge of all the earth do what is just?" The sequel implies that YHWH was ready to act justly, indeed to go beyond mere justice to incorporate divine compassion by sparing the many for the sake of a few. In the story a sojourner, Lot, ventures to criticize the people of Sodom on the basis of his moral values, a strategy adopted by all practitioners of theodicy. Those practitioners in the Bible are numerous; the most notable of them include Job and Abraham but also the unknown author of Ps. 73 and the prophets Ezekiel, Jeremiah, Habakkuk, and Jonah. The psalmist struggles to retain traditional belief that God is good to the upright although experience seems to deny its truth. In the end this realist undergoes transformation in the sacred assembly and redefines divine goodness as presence.

Ezekiel insists on radical individualism, but views YHWH's departure from Zion as punishment, which, in his utopian vision, will give way to compassion in a restored Zion replete with eschatological fulfillment centered in a purified cult devoid of images. The laments attributed to Jeremiah accuse YHWH of egregious personal affront, a feeling shared by Jonah, who fumes over the deity's decision to pardon the guilty but repentant Nineveh. Habakkuk also ponders the fairness in YHWH's use of Babylon to punish Judah and sees no evidence of divine activity curtailing violence against the innocent. Joel credits YHWH with future retribution against foreign offenders, an exact measure-for-measure vengeance, while Zephaniah insists that YHWH is just and can do nothing wrong. The Book of Malachi records a lively debate between a defender of YHWH and others who question his justice.

Israel's sages continue the dispute. Qoheleth can detect no evidence of divine justice, or compassion either; the Book of Proverbs assumes both. Sirach (ca. 180 BCE) adopts traditional arguments and adds two more from Hellenistic sources, a philosophical one about opposite forces in nature and a psychological one that anxiety overwhelms sinners. Theodicy receives poignantly eloquent expression in an apocalyptic text, 2 *Esdras,* and even gives birth to the Prayer of Manasseh, an attempt to justify this king's long reign in light of his reputation for villainy. Rabbinic Judaism explains the prevalence of evil as a product of an evil inclination, which emerges twelve years sooner in individuals than does the disposition toward good. The destruction of the temple becomes a central issue demanding an explanation in postbiblical Judaism; 2 *Baruch* (Greek Apocalypse) has angels remove sacred vessels, knock a hole in the wall of the city, and invite the invaders into the city as punishing agents of the deity.

With Ecclesiastes and Wisdom of Solomon, theological concerns begin to take on philosophical dimensions. Indeed, wisdom literature generally resembles philosophy in both its manifestations, theoretical reflection about life's meaning, and moral observations about goodness, truth, and beauty. Its authors subscribed to an epistemology that gave precedence to religion; all knowledge consisted of faith seeking understanding, given classic formulation in the Book of Proverbs ("the fear of YHWH is the beginning/essential principle of understanding"). Wisdom, a divine principle of knowledge, exists alongside YHWH. This expression of divine thought, corresponding to the Logos in Stoic philosophy, delights in human beings and bestows understanding on those who cultivate self-discipline. The feminization of Wisdom in Israel has mythic precedent in the Egyptian goddess Maat, perhaps also in aretalogies to Isis. Mythic poems about Wisdom in Prov. 8, Sir. 24, and Wis. 7 culminate in full-blown hypostasis. The aim of knowledge is to build character; with moral rectitude comes life and its material benefits. Because knowledge derives from observation of natural phenomena, social interaction, and inspiration, it is both experimental and intuitive. Belief in the principle of act and consequence presumes a moral order governing the universe, one that enables humans to control their destiny.

Theoretical probings into this optimism issued in skepticism if not actual pessimism. Skeptics harbored a vision of a better world and lamented its disappearance. In Egypt various texts, most notably the Songs of Harpers, decry present existence and embrace the prospect of death. The Mesopotamian Dialogue between a Master and His Slave enjoins suicide as an appropriate response to life's ennui. The author of Ecclesiastes perceives the meaningless nature of reality and recognizes no escape from death's negating impact. For him, chance similar to fate in Greek thought has gained the upper hand, making life futile and rendering all the more urgent every quest for pleasure, a point also made to Gilgamesh by the barmaid Siduri. The operative phrase in Ecclesiastes' epistemology—"Who knows?"—functions as an emphatic negation.

Greek philosophical presuppositions permeate the Wisdom of Solomon; its language abounds in rhetorical tropes. A mixture of didactic exhortation and praise of wisdom, the 1st-century work also combines Platonism and Stoicism. The author believes in a transcendent deity and in an intermediate realm between the visible world and the hidden deity. The Logos, a rational principle governing the universe, corresponds to Wisdom, a hypostasis of the creator. By analogy, the human mind functions as the governing principle in daily life, as well as the point of contact with the divine. In short, one finds in this book teachings about the World Soul and its penetration of humans; the divine spark and its residence in human mental capacity; the significance of analogy; and the divine being made manifest in many attributes. Most surprisingly, one hears that God did not create death, which sprang from the devil's envy, and that the soul is immortal. Here, too, one discovers other peripheral teachings within Jewish literature of the Bible: a mystical inclination, natural theology, and ridicule of idolatry (explained as a way of venerating officials, expressing grief over a lost loved one, or a form of aesthetics).

The gnomic spectrum of wisdom, with precedents in Proverbs and Sirach, is taken up by Pseudo-Phocylides (early 1st century CE), who emphasizes Hellenistic virtues, the afterlife, and monotheism. Above all, he spiritualizes ritual, explaining the various actions mandated in the Torah as a means of purifying the soul. The best-known religious teacher of his day, the Alexandrian Philo, represents the other end of the spectrum: philosophical reflection. Probably a product of Greek-style education in the gymnasium, as well as a member of the upper class, Philo emphasized the Logos as an intermediate reality between the giver of Torah and the created universe. He understood the literal level of the biblical text in terms of allegorical prefiguration; the stories about Abraham, Jacob, Esau, Sarah, and others represent virtues rather than mere events on the historical level. Even the sabbath, in his view, is properly observed when devoted to the study of philosophy. With the aid of the divine Logos, the worshiper endeavored to ascend mystically, becoming like God.

To some extent, two figures of the 2nd century BCE, Ben Sira and Aristobulus, paved the way for such speculation by identifying the Torah with wisdom, denying any conflict between the truth revealed at Sinai and that discovered by use of reason. Nevertheless, not even Philo believed in autonomous reason; in some sense, all knowledge was understood as divine gift, a complement of the human capacity for reasoning.

Rabbinic Judaism, as well as other forms of Judaism such as that attested at Qumran, continued to reflect on divine justice in light of life's anomalies and on the afterlife (denied in Proverbs, Job, Qoheleth, and Sirach, but affirmed frequently in later texts, e.g., Dan. 12.2; 2 Macc. 7; 2 *Esdras*; 1 *Enoch* 37–71 [= Similitudes of Enoch]; and 4Q Instruction; see also Death, the Afterlife, and Other Last Things). The Pharisaic rabbis expended much energy on devising hermeneutical principles for interpreting classical but troublesome texts and carried on a tradition of natural theology (as did the convert to Christianity, Paul, in Romans). At the same time, an oral tradition in rabbinic literature offers a vital link to a revered past.

BIBL.: John J. Collins, *Jewish Wisdom in the Hellenistic Age* (Louisville, 1997). James L. Crenshaw, *Urgent Advice and Probing Questions: Collected Writings on Old Testament Wisdom* (Macon, 1995). Idem (ed.), *Theodicy in the Old Testament* (Philadelphia, 1983). Patrick D. Miller, *The Religion of Ancient Israel* (Louisville, 2000). David Penchansky and Paul L. Redditt (eds.), *Shall Not the Judge of All the Earth Do What Is Right? Studies on the Nature of God in Tribute to James L. Crenshaw* (Winona Lake, Ind., 2000).

J.L.C.

Anatolia

Among the Hittites, the human-divine relationship was one of servant and master. Human ambition could achieve no greater purpose than to serve the gods well, as a good servant served a master. Such a servant could hope to enjoy a life free of illness and hardship. Humans and deities also depended on one another for survival. The gods needed the sustenance provided by humans in daily cult. At the same time, humans were dependent on the beneficence of the deities, who controlled the forces of nature that ensured agricultural bounty and the growth of the herds. Thus King Murshili II (1321–1295 BCE) reminds the gods: "These few bakers of offering bread and libation bearers who [are still here]—if they perish [of the plague], no one will any longer give you offering bread or libation" (Beckman 1997: 157). The series of compositions known as the "missing deity" myths included ritual tools for coping with deities who failed to maintain their role in this symbiosis adequately (see also Myth and Sacred Narratives). If a deity left his or her post out of anger or confusion, the natural world could not function. But a ritual, performed by a human practitioner in the guise of the goddess of magic, Kamrushepa, was effective in restoring the deity to his or her place in the cosmos, and, with him or her, the cosmic balance, as in this instance from the Disappearance of Telipinu: "The mist released the windows. The smoke released the house. The altars were in harmony again with the gods. . . . Then the mother looked after her child. The sheep looked after her lamb. The cow looked after her calf. And Telipinu too [looked after] the king and queen and took account of them in respect to life, vigor, and longevity" (Hoffner 1998: 17–18).

Other than myth, humans had recourse to various forms of communication with the divine realm. Prayers form a distinct genre in Hittite literature and indicate a personal relationship with the gods, at least for the royal family. Communal meals with a deity in his or her temple also served to strengthen the bond between gods and humans. And when direct answers were needed to direct questions, oracles could be sought by various means. Thus Murshili writes in one of his prayers, asking for abeyance of a plague, "[Let the matter on account of which] people have been dying [in Khatti either be established through oracle], or [let me see] it [in a dream, or let a prophet] . . . speak [of it]" (Beckman 1997: 157).

Within official Hittite state theology, the king held a central place as intermediary between the mortal and the divine realms. While everyone had access to the gods through local places of worship, the king was the focal point of the state religion, serving to represent humankind before the gods and, as chief priest, being responsible on behalf of humankind for maintaining proper service to the gods. Thus, the worlds of gods and humans met in the person of the king. The king was identified to an extent with the sun-god, and both the king and queen had a special relationship with the Sun-goddess of Arinna, supreme goddess of the land.

Hittite priests received instruction in the proper maintenance of the cult and in proper conduct befitting their status within the temple hierarchy. But their education, so far as we know, did not include scribal training. The recording, preservation, and dissemination of sacred knowledge and tradition appears to have depended instead on the scribes attached to the palace and/or temples, many of whom were imported from Mesopotamia. Thus, sacred knowledge was in no way a monopoly of the temple priesthood, and the lack of scribal training within the priesthood may help to explain why theological discussions, in our sense of that term, are absent from the surviving religious documents.

No single divinity embodied goodness, and by the same token, neither was there a divinity who epitomized or explained the existence of evil. As one half of a cosmic duality, evil had no place in Hittite thought. The gods ruled by *para ḫandatar,* a concept that embodied divine justice as well as the power to impose it. By this attribute, the gods protected deserving humans—especially kings—from misfortune. Evil, or what might today be called "negative energy," had many sources in Hittite theology, including malicious gossip, murder, impurity, curse, threat, and sin. When bad things happened to good people, the cause was sought either in some accidental sin or transgression on the part of the afflicted individual or in the form of a sorcerer, demon, or angry deity.

BIBL.: Gary M. Beckman, "Plague Prayers of Muršili II," in *The Context of Scripture* (ed. W. W. Hallo et al.; Leiden, 1997), 1.156–60. Idem, "The Religion of the Hittites," *Biblical Archaeologist* 52.2–3 (1989): 98–108. Idem, "The Tongue Is a Bridge: Communication between Humans and Gods in Hittite Anatolia," *Archiv Orientální* 67 (1999): 519–34. Albrecht Goetze, *Kleinasien* (Munich, 1957). Harry A. Hoffner Jr., *Hittite Myths* (2nd ed.; Atlanta, 1998). Gregory McMahon, "Theology, Priests, and Worship in Hittite Anatolia," in *Civilizations of the Ancient Near East* (ed. Jack M. Sasson et al.; New York, 1995), 3.1981–95.   B.J.C.

Iran

It is well known that it was the German philosopher Gottfried Wilhelm Leibniz who coined the modern term *theodicy* (French *théodicée*) in order to refer to his theory of God's justification in view of (or in spite of) the physical and moral evil in this world. Leibniz's *Essais*

de théodicée were published in 1710. It may be less well known, however, that Leibniz's theory ultimately was a reaction to ancient Iranian religion and its fountainhead, Zarathustra. As a matter of fact, the *Essais* grew out of conversations that Leibniz held with the electress Sophie Charlotte in Berlin during the summer of 1702. These conversations were about the *Dictionnaire historique et critique* that the Calvinist Pierre Bayle, who was living as a refugee in Rotterdam, had first published in 1697. A revised and enlarged second edition was published in 1702.

Far from being a simple dictionary, however, Bayle's *Dictionnaire* contained many articles that were perceived as highly provocative and that stimulated some of the major philosophical debates of the 18th century. One of these articles was dedicated to the "disgraceful sect" of the Manicheans. Here, Bayle declared that the Manichean doctrine of two primeval beings, a good and a bad one, was almost impossible to refute by rational arguments alone. In order to illustrate this point, in a famous note to the article, Bayle set up an imaginary debate between the monist Melissus (a student of the Greek philosopher Parmenides) and Zarathustra, whom Bayle regarded as a pre-Manichean champion of the doctrine of two principles (which later, in the course of the debate around Bayle's article, came to be referred to as dualism). Bayle shows that neither Melissus nor Zarathustra would ultimately succeed in convincing his counterpart—that dualism, in other words, is irrefutable by rational means alone. Leibniz, in turn, tried to banish that dangerous thought by developing a metaphysical optimism that was able, he hoped, to vindicate the grace, wisdom, and justice of God.

In contrast to that, the Oxford orientalist Thomas Hyde, in what was the first-ever history of ancient Iranian religion, published in 1700 (i.e., shortly after the first edition of Bayle's *Dictionnaire*), tried to put Zarathustra and ancient Iranian religion in a different light altogether. Hyde argued that Zarathustra was a former student of a Hebrew prophet who sought to return ancient Iranian religion to its pristine "orthodoxy" (i.e., monotheism). Thus, in Hyde's scheme, ancient Iranian religion was some sort of a duplicate of the Jewish tradition. No wonder, then, that Hyde's Zarathustra was able to predict the birth of the Messiah.

Ever since these early stages, the question of dualism has been one of the hot issues of the modern scholarly debate about Zoroastrianism. While there certainly is a good dose of dualism already in the Gathas, the ancient hymns that many scholars attribute to Zarathustra, the idea that this dualism was the conscious answer of a philosopher-prophet (i.e., Zarathustra) who had pondered over the problem of evil seems somewhat far-fetched and out of focus from a historical point of view. However, available sources confirm that in a much later phase, when Zoroastrianism was facing the theologies of Judaism, Christianity, and—later even more importantly—Islam, the problem of theodicy actually came to be advanced by Zoroastrian theologians against their opponents. Among the Zoroastrian treatises in Middle Persian (Pahlavi), two stand out as attempts at an argumentative critique against what could be labeled a monistic variety of monotheism, distinct from its dualistic variety as advocated by the Zoroastrian thinkers. These works are the third book of a larger work called Denkard (Acts of the Religion) and a purely apologetic treatise called Skand gumānīg wizār (Doubt Dispelling Explanation), written by a certain Mardanfarrox, son of Ohrmazddad, who is generally held to have lived in the 9th century CE. While Islam is never explicitly referred to in these texts—although it is implicitly targeted—a later New Persian text entitled ʿOlamā-e Eslām (Muslim Scholars) presents a critique directed explicitly against Muslim theologians. Some of the arguments presented in this text—and similarly in the older ones—center on the notions of god and creation. According to the Zoroastrian thinkers, those systems that are based on just one "principle" are entirely mistaken because they necessarily have to attribute good and evil to this one principle, thus inevitably resulting in contradictions. For how can a good god create something evil? Either because he is no god, but a pretender (= contradiction 1), or because he is not good, but mischievous (= contradiction 2). Just as day and night, light and darkness, are distinct units, the Zoroastrian thinkers favor the distinction between two principles in order to preserve the uncontaminated purity of god, the creator. In their eyes, only by conceptually distinguishing evil as a separate, coeval principle can god be conceptualized as a pure being, acting in a responsible way, having nothing to do with lies, ignorance, and deceit. Only such a view of things allows a moral vision of the divinity and the cosmos, which is held to be essentially good because it is the creation of the pure god, whereas his adversary does not properly exist and is unable to create in the strict sense, but merely contaminates and manipulates the good creation.

Theodicy here implicitly corresponds to the moral and ritual dimensions of the religion: the refusal to conceptually contaminate the very idea of god by possibly attributing to him anything evil goes hand in hand with the moral and ritual duties to ward off evil and maintain the purity of the creation. In the course of history, however, theodicy has, by and large, ceased to be a dominant strategy of Zoroastrian apologetics. Many modern Zoroastrian thinkers instead emphasize the idea of freedom of choice that Zarathustra supposedly preached against the supposedly legalistic traditions of Judaism, Christianity, and Islam, which often strived to establish religions as matters of state and law.

BIBL.: Michael Stausberg, *Faszination Zarathushtra* (2 vols.; Berlin, 1998). Idem, *Die Religion Zarathushtras* (2 vols.; Stuttgart, 2002).   M.ST.

Greece and Rome

Archaic and classical Greek poetry. In the public and oral culture of archaic and classical Greece, theological questions are the domain of public communicators, the poets. They submit their thoughts, made more or less explicit in their texts, to the approval of their audience. In the absence of any institution that would shape and control dogmatic correctness, the poet's power of narration and the audience's willingness to approve his stories are the sole forces that shape early Greek theological thinking.

Already the four early Greek epic poems—Hesiod's *Theogony* and *Work and Days,* and the *Iliad* and *Odyssey* ascribed to Homer—give somewhat different answers to the problems of theodicy. There is no doubt that Zeus established the present order of the world and that he guarantees and defends it, and in both Homeric epics, the gods are depicted as beings whose personal interest and capriciousness override any ethical concerns that humans might have. But it is especially Zeus on whom theological thinking focuses. In the *Iliad,* he is the executor of a destiny over whose course he seems to have only limited influence once it is set in motion: despite his personal regrets and pains, he is unable to save the life of his son Sarpedon (16.431). In the *Odyssey* and in Hesiod's poems, Zeus is much more concerned with justice: early in the *Odyssey,* the murder of Agamemnon causes Zeus to emphasize human responsibility (1.32–43), and in the Prometheus episode of the *Theogony,* Hesiod is at pains to stress Prometheus's responsibility for the fate he decreed for humans. Evils existed as part of the overall structure of the cosmos well before Zeus came into being (*Theogony* 211–32) and were activated as the result of Prometheus's attempt to cheat on Zeus, which in turn made Zeus send Pandora and her jar to the slow-witted Epimetheus (*Works and Days* 47–105).

Justice is the major value that shapes early Greek theodicy. In the person of Themis (Divine Right), whom Hesiod assigns to the generation of Cronus, preceding the rule of Zeus (*Theogony* 135), justice is vital for the establishment of divine order; both Uranus and Cronus fail as rulers because their behavior flouts basic rules. As Dikē (Right), Themis's daughter with Zeus, and sister of Eunomie (Good Order), and Eirene (Peace) (*Theogony* 902), justice on earth helps to shape good societal order (*Works and Days* 220). Experience of social life, however, would also reveal that unjust behavior is not always punished. This observation led Hesiod, a social optimist, to construct an opposition between our present, imperfect society and a utopian, perfect one (*Works and Days* 213–48). The more pragmatic Solon, a social reformer, turned it into a problem of theodicy and developed an alternative model, according to which an evildoer could escape immediate divine punishment; but in the long run, the gods always punished transgressions, sometimes after several generations: "Zeus watches over the outcome of everything. . . . But unlike a mortal man, his anger flares not immediately up about each thing; however he never forgets the person who has an evil mind, and in the end he shows himself: one person is immediately punished, the other one later; others escape themselves and the gods' anger does not attack them; their innocent children pay the penalty, or their offspring" (Solon, *Elegy* 13 [ed. West]).

The debate becomes more intense in Athenian tragedy, which flourished in a period and in a society where traditional values were more radically debated and questioned than at any time before. This is especially true for the youngest among the three major tragedians, Euripides (480–406 BCE): his gods are often capricious and morally highly questionable, or at least so different from humans that they defy our empathy, but Euripides also exalted the irrational power of the divine, which could bring blessings as well as terrible distress (see his *Bacchae*). Closer to late archaic thinking, Aeschylus (525–456 BCE) continued its more optimistic theology, although with a new sound of awe. The world is well ordered, and Zeus stands for this and accounts even for suffering and evil: "It is Zeus who has put men on the way to wisdom by establishing as a valid law 'By suffering they shall win understanding'" (*Agamemnon* 176–78, trans. Fraenkel). At the same time, human perception of the divine world is not easy: "Zeus, whoever he be—if to be called and invoked by this name is pleasing to him, even thus I address him" (*Agamemnon* 160–61). Given the difficulties of perception, the traditions of myth and cult seem the better guide. Sophocles (496–406 BCE) is usually seen as the most pious of the three tragedians, and he had an active hand in introducing the cult of Asclepius to Athens. This did not prevent him from depicting a divine world that is far from being benign. In *Oedipus Tyrannus*, Apollo's oracle is fulfilled, whatever Oedipus has done to avoid it, and it is not easy to argue for any culpability on Oedipus's part that could justify his fate or, even more so, the fate of Jocasta, his mother and wife: at the play's opening, Oedipus is the good and caring king of Thebes, just as he was a caring and responsible young man who did not return to the couple who he thought were his parents after the oracle had announced that he would kill his father and marry his mother. One can sympathize with the French writer Jean Cocteau, who called his version of the Sophoclean play "La machine infernale"—although Sophocles did not intend to depict the actions of the gods as pure evil. It is rather that the world's working defies moral interpretation. At the end of the *Women of Trachis*—a play that shows Deianira accidentally causing the death of her husband Heracles out of sheer love and then killing herself, Sophocles' chorus states: "There is nothing here that is not Zeus."

Pre-Socratic philosophy. Greek philosophy developed as a literary discourse in prose books and, because it needed no public communication, could freely move away from tradition. The first philosophers, from Thales (early 6th century BCE) to Anaxagoras (500–428 BCE) and Democritus (ca. 460–380 BCE?)—called pre-Socratic philosophers on the assumption that Socrates introduced a radical new epoch in philosophy—were mostly interested in cosmology; although by no means simply materialist and areligious, pre-Socratic philosophers usually treated explicit theology as subsidiary to physics. Their outlook questioned the traditional role of gods who presided over the broad and basic laws of the cosmos and, at the same time, ruled the world in a sort of micromanagement that never hesitated to intervene in the daily affairs of humans. Cosmology was often mechanistic, even when the substance of the cosmos was assumed to be divine, and had no need for a detached divine creator. Theological discussions or a polemical stance toward traditional Greek religious thought and practice were absent, even when philosophers assumed a fundamental principle with a divine nature, be it the constant and eternal substance of the cosmos (such as the fire in Heraclitus) or a fundamental principle active in the cosmos (such as Nous [intellect] in Anaxagoras).

An exception was Xenophanes (ca. 570–460 BCE), the first pre-Socratic philosopher to use the medium of poetry in order to exert a public influence on the religious tradition. Xenophanes' criticism of traditional religion focused on its anthropomorphism, which had given rise to the morally unacceptable stories that Homer and Hesiod narrated. In place of the mythological gods, he posited a single, nonanthropomorphic divinity, "one deity, greatest among gods and humans, in no way similar to mortals either in body or in thought" (Diels and Kranz 1952: 21 B 23). But he did not confine himself to negative theology: "Always [god] remains in the same place, moving not at all. . . . Without toil he shakes all things by the thought of his mind. . . . All of him sees, all thinks, and all hears" (Diels and Kranz 1952: 21 B 26.25.24). This concept of the divine as a perfect intellectual being is rooted in traditional ideas about the nature of the gods, but Xenophanes drew all the inherent consequences. The divine is radically different from and absolutely better than humans, and Xenophanes expressed this difference and superiority in a physical and a moral key. It was especially the ethical radicalization of theology that was to become important in later philosophy and entered the theological mainstream during the Hellenistic age.

An entirely different approach was taken by Pythagoras (late 6th century BCE) and his followers, not the least Empedocles (first half of the 5th century BCE). In a movement that seems the opposite of Xenophanes', these thinkers made the borderline between the divine and the human world much more permeable than it had been traditionally, by introducing a split between body and soul. Soul was divine and eternal and only temporarily embodied in a body, because—as Empedocles has it—the divine being that was the soul had committed a crime, had been expelled from the society of the gods, and was forced to pass through a series of bodily incarnations (human, animal, or even plant), which purified it and made it fit to return permanently to the realm of the gods. For reasons different from those of Xenophanes and Heraclitus, Pythagoreans also were at odds with traditional cult: their theological approach to human psychology resulted in vegetarianism, since animals, which were receptacles for divine souls, should not be killed and eaten; this excluded Pythagoreans from the animal sacrifices and common meals of the polis.

Despite these differences, early Greek philosophy shared with religious tradition the belief that gods existed and that humans had the capacity to gain knowledge about them. The belief was based on the traditional way of interaction between the two spheres: humans performed cult in honor of the gods, and gods manifested their power by intervening in human affairs. Even Xenophanes' radical theology shared this common horizon. Shortly after Xenophanes, Parmenides broke with the prevailing cognitive model and introduced a radical split between a world of truth that was constant, certain, and "truly being," and a world of opinion that lacked the certainty of knowledge; he saw no possibility of communication between the two.

Although Parmenides seems not to have drawn any theological consequences from his ontology, other thinkers did, such as his contemporary Protagoras (ca. 490–420 BCE). He was the first of the so-called Sophists, philosophers who abandoned cosmology, concentrated on issues of society, and made their living as itinerant teachers of the polis's elite. They brought orality back into philosophy, and with it came the test of tradition; the Athenians promptly accused Protagoras of *asebeia* (contempt of the gods) because of his theological thinking. His otherwise lost book *On the Gods* opens with the memorable sentence: "As to the gods, I am unable to have knowledge, neither whether they exist or exist not, nor what their form would be; there are many things that impede knowledge, such as the difficulty of perception and the shortness of human life" (Diels and Kranz 1952: 80 B 4). One can see how this rather surprising opening of a book on the gods lent itself to the misunderstanding that Protagoras distanced himself from the gods: since cult relied on divine manifestation, and manifestation on the possibility of unambiguous perception, his position carried in itself the potential to abolish cult altogether. In reality, Protagoras must have simply drawn the consequences from Parmenides' ontology, and he must have found a way to preserve cults: he was the lawgiver of the Athenian colony Thurii (444 BCE), and part of a city's laws concerned its interaction with the divine. How he did this is unknown, and the underlying epistemology retained the potential of either removing the gods so far out of human perception that

they could not be reached at all or, on the contrary, claiming that they did not exist. The latter was rarely done (atheism was not popular in antiquity), the former signaled a peril inherent in the epistemology and theology of Plato, of the skeptical Academy, and of Neoplatonism.

Later philosophical schools: the Academy. Plato (428–348 BCE) crystallized the earlier debates into an entirely new and highly successful philosophical system. The fundamental split between the world of the senses, which lacks certainty, truth, and permanence, and the transcendental world of forms, which are eternal and true, locates the divine beyond our world; it is defined, in the last instance, as absolute good, its highest form being the form of the good that is identical with the supreme deity. Although Plato was highly critical of traditional mythology and, to a lesser degree, of traditional cult, he never rejected the polis cult: cult could provide ethical guidance to nonphilosophers, once the essential goodness of the gods was understood and translated into acceptable cultic action.

The divine interacts in several ways with our world. At the origin of the cosmos is a creator-god, the Craftsman (Demiurge), whose actions Plato describes in the *Timaeus*: he is the divine mind responsible for the regularity and rationality of the cosmos. Our own soul is divine, and when purified to pure rationality, it ascends to the gods and participates in their vision of the eternal forms, thus gaining knowledge and certainty (*Phaedrus* 247a–b). In the practice of philosophy, we remember this vision and enter again into contact with the divine world. This has consequences for the philosopher's life: his task is to assimilate himself as far as possible to the divine (*Theaetetus* 176b). It goes without saying how much this separates the religion of the philosopher from that of the other citizens of the polis, without, however, preventing him from participating in traditional cult; after all, the Academy was organized as a religious group, centered on a common cult of the Muses.

Evil enters Plato's theology only negatively: "It is impossible to abolish the evils . . . or to give them a place among the gods" (*Theaetetus* 176a). In his written work, Plato never talked at length about evil. The important point is that there is no dualism, even if evil is connected with matter, and the Craftsman's creation by necessity contains faults due to the imperfect realization of his perfect plan in space and time; space and time are his creations as well. Late in his life, however, Plato came close to dualism: in his last work, the *Laws*, he opposed to the beneficent World Soul, which is responsible for the perfect motion in the cosmos, "another capable of the contrary effect" (896e). This shifting of positions points to a more fundamental problem: any theology that makes the divine into absolute good, as did all Greek theology after Xenophanes, has difficulties explaining the existence of evil. Stoicism and later Platonism faced the same challenge, and Platonism offered a wide array of solutions, from an almost-dualistic position that is based on Plato's *Laws* (Plutarch [46–ca. 120 CE], *On Isis and Osiris* 48,370e) to the utter denial of evil as an empty concept (Proclus [410–85 CE], *Platonic Theology* 1.21.98). This wide spectrum has its roots in the way that Platonists situated the supreme god in the hierarchy of being: the closer he is to our world (as in Plato or Plutarch), the more the perception of evil threatens his supremacy.

Hellenistic schools. A new era opened with Alexander's conquests. Political and social conditions changed drastically during an epoch in which rival monarchs fought for power. Cities largely lost their political autonomy, individuals experienced political and economic insecurity and witnessed the seemingly arbitrary rise and fall of powerful rulers. Traditional religion was affected only slowly, philosophical theology reacted faster. The Academy retreated from Plato's metaphysical optimism into skepticism, and two new philosophical schools developed in reaction to Platonism: Epicureanism and Stoicism, which aspired to shelter the individual from the unsettling circumstances of life.

From early on, Epicurus (341–270 BCE) was accused of atheism; this was due to the paradoxical role that he assigned the gods. In his cosmology, the origin and function of the world need no divine intervention. In limitless space, eternal and indestructible atoms rain eternally downward; an unmotivated and unforeseeable swerve of an atom leads to a chain reaction of collisions; the colliding atoms congregate arbitrarily into objects that are never constant and that finally will dissolve again into their constituent atoms. In a mechanistic cosmology such as this, without creator or teleology, gods might seem superfluous, and if they are part of the system, theodicy becomes awkward. Epicurus imagined the gods as super-atoms in the interstices between the worlds; already ancient critics assumed that he did this in order to avoid the accusation of *asebeia*.

This cannot be correct. To Epicurus, both the general agreement that gods exist and the individual experience of divine appearances in dreams and visions proved the material existence of gods, since everything we perceive must have a material and therefore real origin (Diogenes Laertius 10.123). The gods, however, interact with humans by sheer chance: they are impervious to sacrifices and prayers, and their wills cannot be read by divination. They lead a life of absolute happiness, and since they are absolutely perfect, they have no need of human contact. Radically thinking through the earlier, especially Platonic, definition of the divine as absolute good, Epicurus arrived at an almost total dissociation between divine and human realms; what is left for the gods is to be examples of perfect existence. In his argument, Epicurus uses the Platonic definition of the ideal human life as an imitation of the divine: "When you will not suffer any irritation either when awake or when asleep, you will live as a god among mortals; a human who lives in immortal blessings no longer looks like a human being" (Diogenes Laertius 10.135). In the end, Epicurus, too, needed a theodicy, albeit an idiosyncratic one; it was given new prominence by the Roman Lucretius (94–55? BCE), in his poem *On the Nature of Things.*

Nothing could be more opposed to Epicurus's theology than the theology of Zeno (335–262 BCE) and Chrysippus (ca. 280–207 BCE), the founders of Stoicism. The world's active principle is something that is deity, intelligence *(logos),* and fire at the same time, fire understood not as material but as "a designing fire which methodically proceeds towards creation of the world" (Aëtius 1.7.33, trans. Long). The Stoic god acts not as a creator who is detached from his creation, as in the creation myths or in Plato, but as a constituent part of the world he is creating; once the world is created, this god persists in it as "breath [*pneuma*] pervading the whole world" (Chrysippus, in Aëtius 1.7.33). Thus, the cosmos is intelligent and rational, and there is no place in it for contingency. Stoicism is radically deterministic, and free will is, in the end, saved only through a complex and contrived psychology; in his mechanistic universe, Epicurus had to invent a similarly contrived physical construction to save free will.

But Stoicism is no more monotheistic than Platonism. The one god, whom the Stoics also called Zeus, created "the sun and the moon and each of the other stars" as divine beings who shared his intelligence and his fieriness (Stobaeus 1.213.15). Stoicism even came to terms with the gods of the religious tradition. Extensive physical allegorization saved the myths as accounts of how the world worked and interacted, and this opened the way to accepting the cultic traditions. In a formalization transmitted by Augustine (*City of God* 6.5) as the work of the Roman writer Marcus Terentius Varro (116–27 BCE), Stoic doctrine accepted three ways of "discourse on the gods" *(theologia):* the mythical, used by the poets and in need of allegorization; the philosophical, on "who the gods are, where they are and what they are"; and the political, used by the priests and cultic officials of the state (see also Deities and Demons).

The regularity and astonishing functionality of the cosmos and of all beings proved that there existed a planning rationality as the source of all creation (see Cicero, *On the Nature of the Gods* 2), and cosmology as observation of the world's perfect shape could turn into a meditation about the divine (Seneca, *Questions on Nature,* pref. 1). The intervention of gods in human affairs motivated and legitimated the cultic actions of the needy and grateful humans.

Academy. Early in the 3rd century BCE, the Academy lost Plato's confidence that the human intellect could reach out to the transcendental forms; knowledge became uncertain, of the gods as of everything else. Middle Platonism (1st and 2nd centuries CE) and especially Neoplatonism (starting with Plotinus, 205–70 CE) regained epistemological certainty, but at the price of rather complex theological constructions that vastly expanded upon Platonic antecedents. The world of humans who mixed material bodies and immortal souls was the lowest realm of sentient beings; above it was an entire chain of superhuman beings, from demons and the planetary gods to the supreme god who was pure Intellect *(Nous)*. Ordinary humans might be able to come into contact with the demons or the planetary gods; philosophers aimed at contacting the Supreme God—a highly difficult undertaking performed as an ecstatic ascent (see also Esotericism and Mysticism).

BIBL.: William Chase Greene, *Moira: Fate, Good, and Evil in Greek Thought* (New York: Harvard University Press, 1963). H. Diels and W. Kranz, *Die Fragmente der Vorsokratiker* (6th ed.; Berlin, 1952). Werner Jaeger, *The Theology of the Early Greek Philosophers* (repr. Berkeley: University of California Press, 1967 [orig. 1947]). Hugh Lloyd-Jones, *The Justice of Zeus* (Berkeley: University of California Press, 1971). Arnaldo Momigliano, "The Theological Efforts of the Roman Upper Classes in the 1st Century B.C.," in Momigliano's *Ottavo Contributo alla Storia degli Studi Classici e del Mondo Antico* (Rome, 1987), 261–77.   F.G.

Christianity

Theodicy, an amalgam of Greek terms for "god" and "justice," first appeared in its specialized sense in 1710 (G. W. Leibniz), but it was not a new star in the sky, for the issues that theodicy would address lie at the heart of every theistic system that views God or the gods as entirely good and of unlimited might. The motive for theodicy is the ubiquitous cry: "How can God allow this to happen?" Theodicy thus relates to the fundamental demand for fairness in the face of misfortune. Theodicy did not become a subdivision of theology until philosophy and science began to deconstruct the edifices of providence and teleology (ca. 1700). From an ethical perspective the challenge of theodicy is "why do the just suffer?" The theological problem concerns the evident failure of divine promises.

To address these dilemmas early Christians appropriated Jewish prophecy and wisdom. Those who shaped Israelite historical traditions applied a simple, potent formula: when the people were obedient, the nation thrived; disaster followed failure to comply. Ruin and misfortune were condign punishment. From a more individualistic and ecumenical perspective, oriental wisdom variously explained apparently undeserved misfortune. These included the notions that suffering is corrective, that God alone sets the time of retribution, that virtue is its own reward, that punishment may be purely internal, that vengeance may be displaced, and/or that puny humans cannot unravel the mysteries of divinity—in short, that things are not as they seem. Although each of these solutions had its applications and advocates, the final proposition energized two contrary approaches: apocalyptic and gnostic. Apocalyptic pits the eternal, celestial, and (largely) future world of divine justice against present, terrestrial, and transitory evil. In Gnosticism the phenomenal realm of matter is the world of sinful and deceiving appearance. Their respective responsive to the questions of theodicy greatly differ. The movements now called "gnostic" attributed evil to primordial disaster or conflict. The true god has no responsibility for material creation (i.e., evil). One challenge faced by proponents of the apocalyptic model is the difficulty of affirming a god whom many would find too dilatory. In this context the doctrine of resurrection first took visible shape (Daniel). Continuing delay helped generate one of the earliest Christian essays at theodicy: 2 Peter (ca. 130–50), which propounds time as part of the divine mystery, for time and the related cosmic structure belong to creation and do not control God. Matter posed similar problems, leading to the belief that God created the universe out of nothing, rather than shaping preexistent stuff.

The Jesus tradition includes nods to a popular view of providence (e.g., Luke 12.6–7, 22–31), as well as tart rejoinders to facile theodicies (e.g., Luke 13.1–9; John 9.1–3). In the background is the perennial understanding of misfortune as the result of divine displeasure and/ or due to intermediary beings ("angels" and "demons"). Most early Christians were blithely content to understand the recipe for misfortune as a blend of the devil and his minions, topped with a large portion of moralism. Were God not to reward the righteous and punish the wicked, all hell would break loose.

If Jesus of Nazareth is God's promised Messiah, why have so many Jews failed to acknowledge him? The apostle Paul wrestled with this issue, confident in the desired end, even if the plot did not match human expectations (Rom. 9–11). By the close of the 1st century CE, things had changed. The ruinous failure of the first Jewish revolt (66–74) invited Christians to usurp the prophetic model and hold that "the Jews" were punished for unbelief. Luke develops this judgment into a theology of Providence that accounts for Gentile salvation in a quasiphilosophical formulation.

By the middle of the 2nd century CE, the axis had shifted. While the issue of delay had received passable answers, there remained the problem of particularity: so unpromising a people and place for universal salvation! Paul (Rom. 1) and Luke (e.g., Acts 17) had once more shown the way. The true God has been made known to all people and is now willing to wipe every slate blank. Apologists such as Justin Martyr (mid-2nd century CE) mined the polytheistic religious and philosophical tradition to demonstrate a kind of "pagan Old Testament." This enterprise ultimately yielded a comprehensive *praeparatio evangelica* (groundwork for the gospel), fully elaborated by Eusebius (4th century CE).

By around 140 the Israelite heritage was a burden for many. A second revolt had further discredited the Jewish people, while much of the Hebrew Bible seemed barbaric. A Pauline theologian named Marcion found a way (with the evident help of gnostic theories) to loose the raft of Christianity from the endangered ark of Israel by positing the sharpest sort of discontinuity. The God of the Hebrew Bible is a potent, but inferior, being, who had far less to offer than humans could ask for or imagine. Justification of such a deity could be left to his followers.

One response to the challenges raised by Marcion and various gnostics came from Irenaeus (ca. 180), who fashioned an attractive synthesis that incorporated the Israelite heritage, diverse Christian traditions, and the life of the church, while also integrating the spheres of nature and grace. His evolutionary model built upon Paul and the apologists, viewing both creation and history as a theater for human growth in accordance with a divine plan disrupted by sin, but put back on track by Christ.

Irenaeus's theology did not comprehend the more adventurous Alexandrian tradition, which reached one climax in the work of Origen (died ca. 260), a Christian Platonist who apparently espoused a form of universalism. Misfortune and unbelief arise through the abuse of freedom, but all souls will be redeemed through purification. This view was condemned, one indicator that learned theology could not overcome the popular and pastorally expedient allure of moralism.

Fifth-century political crises raised one more great challenge for theodicy. How could God allow a *Christian* Rome to be plundered and the empire to be ravaged? These events stimulated Augustine of Hippo (died 430) to compose his *City of God,* a profound philosophy of history in the form of a theodicy. God tolerates evil, understood in Neoplatonic terms as the absence of good, because it can be used to good purpose. Augustine thereby rounded off the task first engaged by Luke: to ground theodicy in a doctrine of providence and a theology of history. From the antlike perspective of mere mortals, the divine writing seems jagged and purposeless. In the long view, God's intention produces a straight and significant line. Augustine's proposal was neither thorough nor perfect. The absence of free will is a problem for theodicy if the unfree are to be punished for their failures. Augustine was a Latin theologian. The "New Rome" (Constantinople) did not fall, nor were Eastern theologians often moved to construct theodicies.

BIBL.: Jaroslav Pelikan, *The Christian Tradition: A History of the Development of Doctrine,* vol. 1: *The Emergence of the Catholic Tradition (100–600)* (Chicago: University of Chicago Press, 1971).   R.I.P.

Religion and Politics

Introduction

Religion involves a particular style of ideology, where human institutions, patterns of social organization, and cultural preferences are represented as more than human and thereby invested with transcendent status, rather than more mundane types of legitimacy. This is the primary form of ideology employed by all societies prior to the Enlightenment, and it is virtually ubiquitous in antiquity. In practice, however, it can be used in many ways to serve a wide variety of purposes. These include both support and critique of institutions or social formations situated at different, even competing levels of integration, for example, family, tribe, age, gender, class, polis, nation, empire, and others. Thus, for instance, when Antigone wishes to defend the claims of loyalty to family against rival claims on behalf of the polis, she does so by styling her dispute with Creon as one pitting the "laws of the gods" against the lesser "laws of humans" (Sophocles, *Antigone* 450–61).

Given limitations of space, this chapter focuses most closely on the way that religious institutions, practices, and discourses articulated with ancient states. This choice subtly reflects, however, the state's point of view of how certain religious constructs served one state or another and how these states legitimated themselves, their officers, and their projects by making reference to religion. To be sure, this is an important part of the story and it makes appropriate use of available evidence, most of which—in one fashion or another—was produced by and for the state. We should not mistake it for the whole story, however, and must balance it with an awareness of other possibilities, since politics is hardly limited to the state's interests and perspective.

To take an obvious example, the common binary oppositions contrasting mortals and immortals, sacred and profane, heaven and earth, themselves have a political aspect, since they posit a cosmic order involving a foundational division between higher and lower levels of status and power. This provides a model and normalizes other divisions more social than cosmic: elder and younger, male and female, citizen and slave, native and foreigner, ruler and ruled. The homology between cosmic and social levels can cut in unexpected ways, however, as when Euthyphro cited the myth of Zeus and Cronus to justify the legal action that he initiated against his father for the crime of maltreating a slave (Plato, *Euthyphro* 6a).

Here, Euthyphro forged an unexpected connection, linking subordinate groups (sons and slaves) to the supreme deity, who is more usually associated with dominant power of every sort. And for all that the famed "justice of Zeus" usually served to protect the status quo, Euthyphro located a narrative where the same Zeus became the model for a different sort of justice, in which dominant strata (fathers and masters) were (re)defined as tyrants to be overthrown. In response, Socrates attempted to show that Euthyphro did not understand the stories he cited or the issues he raised and therefore should take no action without fuller reflection. Here, once again the religious and the political are so intertwined as to be virtually indistinguishable, for Socrates simultaneously defends the dignity of gods, myths, fathers, and masters from interventions—legal or hermeneutic—that he regards as intemperate and abusive.

Whenever a deity represents—or can be made to represent—some group or category of human subjects, discourse about that god and its relations to deities with similar associations to other groups has strong interest (and potentially serious consequences) for all the humans whose relations are implied in that discourse. Beyond this obvious point, two further interesting and subtle observations follow.

First, religious discourse does not mirror the social order in straightforward, undistorted fashion. Myth, epic, theology, cosmology, and the like offer experimental spaces of the imagination, in which one can entertain emergent or counterfactual possibilities. They are, moreover, instruments of persuasion, with which one can labor to change the perceptions, evaluations, assumptions, and ultimately the behavior of one's audience, thereby changing—or at least recalibrating—the social and political order, moving it toward that envisioned in the discourse. Thus, for all that Marduk and YHWH were gods associated with Babylon and Israel, propaganda developed for Cyrus the Great by his scribes, in conjunction with factions of the Babylonian and Israelite priesthood, had these gods hail the Persian as king and savior of their peoples, greatly facilitating his acceptance (Cyrus Cylinder, in *ANET* 315–16; Isa. 44.24–45.4).

Second, advancing political interests is never the sole project undertaken by religious discourse. Were it so, this motive would be so transparent as to render the attempt crude, offensive, and unconvincing. Rather, the political aspect must be integrated and reconciled with others of more disinterested nature—those whose concerns are more innocently speculative, descriptive, or aesthetic, for example—if the discourse is to command attention and credence. Darius's attempt to court priests of Apollo thus seems to have had some limited success (see his letter to Gadatas in Meiggs and Lewis 1969: 20–21), but even so, pro-Persian oracles gained little favor in most Greek cities.

Oracles and other mantic forms of discourse effectively claim divine status for the voice with which they seek to influence human relations, dispositions, perceptions, and practice. This is also frequently true of other genres, including codes of law; myth, epic, hymns, and inspired verse; blessings, curses, magical spells, and incantations; and royal proclamations and aristocratic genealogies.

One can also make similar observations regarding practices and institutions. With regard to the former, let me simply cite the example of sacrifice, a complex set of actions that (1) reasserts the categorical divide between divine, human, and animal actors; (2) charters human violence against animals when controlled by ritual prescriptions; (3) effects mutually supportive relations between people and gods as the former present offerings to the latter, calling forth reciprocity; and (4) reconstitutes the sociopolitical hierarchy by distributing differentially valorized portions of meat to those defined as their fitting recipients. Similar arguments could be made about the rituals of birth, marriage, death, and initiation, not to speak of civic festivals and royal or priestly consecration. In all of these, the precise locus of specific actors within a complex sociopolitical hierarchy is established and sacralized, while the order itself is naturalized and reasserted.

Many institutions stand out as deserving special attention. Not just the state, but temples, priesthoods, oracular complexes, centers of scribal activity and learning, places of initiation or pilgrimage, kingships, and palaces are all sites where human power was not only concentrated but also theorized—which is to say mystified and legitimated—in an idiom of the sacred, ineffable, pure, and divine. The same may be said of countless other sites, including theaters, athletic stadiums, royal gardens, family hearths, and others—each of which had its own particular agency and aura where the religious and political commingled.

BIBL.: R. Meiggs and D. Lewis, *A Selection of Greek Historical Inscriptions to the End of the Fifth Century* BC (Oxford, 1969).   B.L.

Egypt

In Egypt, religion was a complex phenomenon, and aspects of it affected, were related to, or were integrated with all other elements of the culture. Among other things, it directed one's behavior and thinking. It guided one in governing as well as being governed, and it showed one how to understand and perceive the universe as both a place in which one lived one's life as well as a place that one aspired to join in the afterlife. Its breadth was comprehensive, extending to both rich and poor, private and royal, male and female, child and adult.

It is possible, however, to identify and then describe separate areas of religion. For example, funerary beliefs are very visible and easy to isolate. But without integrating information about funerary cult into the larger subject of religion or taking into account other aspects of culture, such as politics, misunderstandings could occur. Politics and class structure played a significant role in the formation of texts and decorations, as well as in the very form that burial complexes might take. Middle Kingdom complexes belonging to private individuals from the Memphite area clearly appropriate royal models of the Old Kingdom in terms of texts, iconography, and building plan, perhaps illustrating the phenomenon of democratization. Pyramidal monuments, which had marked the burials of royalty for a large part of Egyptian history, begin to appear in the private domain, although on a smaller scale, as their use by royalty declined. The reverse, however, may also be indicated in the use of *shabtis,* funerary figurines that are employed first in the public sector, then later by royalty. In the New Kingdom, the artists who decorated the tombs in the Valley of the Kings apparently took some license and used textual and iconographic material from their royal models in their own tombs. Funerary texts inscribed in tombs are restricted to royalty at first, but appear by the following dynasty in private tombs. That certain standards were maintained, however, can be seen in the tomb of Rameses II's favorite wife, Nefertari. It was decorated with scenes and text from the Book of the Dead, not from the Amduat, as those were reserved at the time for pharaohs alone. Each of these cases illustrates the interplay between the funerary religion, politics, and social structure.

Theocracy. It is difficult to apply the term *theocracy* outright to ancient Egypt. In earlier periods the identification of the king with the godhead (Re, the solar deity) is more evident, while, from the Middle Kingdom on, there was a greater emphasis on the authority of the divine. Clearly, the Amarna revolution of the late 18th Dynasty, which attempted to equalize the status of the royal and the divine spheres, represented a brief reversion of this tendency. Tradition was, however, quickly restored, and by the 21st Dynasty, the god's oracles represented the ultimate authority in the land.

In general theory, the government was in the hands of the king, but the monarch functioned as the earthly vehicle for the actions of the sacred/divine realm. His conduct and deeds, when performed according to a complex doctrine before both the gods and the people, ensured that the world would function properly. The entire administration of the country was under his charge, and he structured a framework headed by officials (which evolved eventually into a bureaucracy). These roles were taken on not by clerics, but by administrators, whose titles would reflect their responsibilities, for example, *t3tj* (vizier) and *htmtj bjty* (seal bearer of the king of Lower Egypt [i.e., treasurer]). These individuals might also have designations that reflected their participation in religious activities, such as (high) priest of a particular god. Imhotep, an official of the 3rd Dynasty, was, among other things, a vizier, an architect, and high priest of Re. That said, the developing influence and power of the clergy is clearly evident in the New Kingdom, and its rise may have influenced Akhenaten in the formation of his untraditional doctrines. In any case, by the 21st Dynasty, those individuals who held the title "high priest of Amun" were essentially ruling the country from Upper Egypt. The most effective of them were powerful generals based in the south, whose control of the military was in large part responsible for their success. The last of the Ramesside kings, meanwhile, reigned from Tanis in the Delta with less authority.

Sacred kingship. That the king was a divine figure in Egyptian religion is a statement that needs some qualification. Did the populace always view their ruler in the same way that they perceived the gods? In order to answer this question, one must understand that there was a hierarchical organization in the ancient Egyptian belief system. It was in many ways similar to that in the mundane world. Deities did not exist as a monolithic structure; they were differentiated by types, including minor and major deities, local and national gods, deified mortals and kings, and native and foreign divinities. Moreover, they had a ruling class. The king fits into this structure in a distinct way, for his divinity had different levels or degrees, and, at different times during the long history of ancient Egypt, the nature of his kingship changed. It is clear that in the earlier periods (i.e., the Old Kingdom), the king's power and, hence, his divinity were based more on a direct identification with a god. In the Middle Kingdom and later, kingship appears to rely more on the divine realm, with the king deriving his power more from the gods, rather than coming into being with it intact. Akhenaten may have developed some of his doctrines in partial response to this trend. The New Kingdom also saw the visible manifestation of the concept of divine birth in royal temples, such as that found in reliefs in the mortuary complex of Hatshepsut and Amunhotep III's chapel in the Luxor temple. By the Ptolemaic period "birth houses" had become a staple in most temples in the south. Reference to this concept, however, is apparent from the Old Kingdom on in "the Son of Re," a title of the king. The Westcar Papyrus records a Middle Kingdom tale describing the divine birth of the rulers of the 5th Dynasty.

It is also possible to distinguish aspects of the king's divinity other than divine birth. One is related to his death, and from the earliest periods Egyptian rulers built extensive monuments to commemorate their ascension after death into the world of the divine and their unification with the beings there. They established elaborate mortuary cults around these structures in order to ensure the survival of religious rituals that would perpetuate their divinity. The continuation of these cults, in some cases for centuries, testifies to the extent of belief in this concept among the king and his subjects. By the end of the 5th Dynasty, royalty had aspects of this perceived existence inscribed on the walls of their tomb chambers: they continued to use them and other funerary texts and later augmented them with carved and painted scenes. Not limited to a single genre, reference to royalty's ascent to heaven is found elsewhere, for example, in Sinuhe, a popular story of the Middle Kingdom. Yet the continuous robbing of the royal burials and the equally blasphemous conduct recorded in late New Kingdom papyri testify to the equally obvious lack of belief in royal power beyond the grave among some members of the population. Deification of the living king is another dimension of sacred kingship. A phenomenon that may have been inherent in earlier periods, it becomes clearest in the New Kingdom. The religious changes that Akhenaten instituted were in part an attempt to elevate his own status to that of a deity, a god on earth. His predecessor, Amunhotep III, may have set the stage somewhat for his successor when he established his own cults as a deified living king. The 19th Dynasty ruler Rameses II developed this program further, instituting such cults throughout his kingdom.

Kingship in ancient Egypt had a dual nature, that is, there was an office as well as an individual who inhabited it. The office was both divine and constant. The individual, who by birth, position, or power, took it over, became divine through the ritual of coronation. Once in place, that ruler embodied the abstract and timeless concept of kingship and was identified with the deity Horus, who represented the heir to the throne. This duality is best visualized in the *serekh*, a frequently used image in which the name of the ruler is inscribed above the palace façade, above which perches Horus.

In the Old Kingdom, different designations are used when referring to the king either personally or officially. The later use of the term *pharaoh,* which means literally "great house," as a reference to the king, indicates the palace and his official position. In their understanding of kingship, the Egyptians were able to rationalize both the human and the divine nature of their rulers. Despite the use of a variety of means to elevate the status of the reigning kings, however, monarchs were apparently unable to erase completely their mortal origins from the minds of the people. For example, only the gods were able to perform miracles and were not susceptible to disease and death. Personal letters, graffiti, and episodes in stories contain passages, references to, and images of the monarch that are far from respectful, further testimony to the understanding among the populace that their rulers retained some of their humble origins.

Interplay between secular and religious power. Ancient Egypt was a society where the king was the supreme being on earth. Through ritual he was identified as a divinity. He was, at least in theory, the high priest of every god; he was the head of state; and he was also the chief of a large bureaucratic organization as well as the leader of extensive military forces. In such an environment, where the government operated for and by the king and the king functioned for and by the gods, a purely temporal world may not have existed as it does in modern Western society. In Egypt, the two blurred under the authority of a single individual (the king) and the comprehensive religious structure. Since the ruler's authority derived ultimately from a religious source and decorum evolved from the same principles, the basis of government in ancient Egypt can be seen as primarily religious.

On a practical level, however, many interactions must have occurred between the different departments of government. For example, the vast treasuries resulting from the collection of revenues for both royalty and the temples and how this income was divided, managed, and distributed must have presented a continual threat to the balance of power between the king and the priesthood. The priesthood's strong influence in other affairs is also evident in the introduction of oracles as a process to settle legal disputes as well as affairs on a much higher level of state. Prior to the middle of the 18th Dynasty, most courts were civil. Now, with oracular decisions, the high priest of the particular god and the officiating priests generally had authority over the procedure, even though officials of the state occasionally took some part, and the king ultimately could affect the decision.

By the New Kingdom, the high priests of Amun at Thebes had become a very influential group, and their increasing wealth and power may well have been an underlying motive for Akhenaten's proscribing the worship of Amun and eliminating the support of his cult

and priesthood. The king's changes were not accepted, however, and traditional religion and its organizational structure were reinstated. The office of high priest of Amun at Thebes was reestablished, and eventually it succeeded in eclipsing, to some extent, royal authority. By the 21st Dynasty, powerful generals based in the south appropriated this religious title and then effectively ruled part of the country, while the "legitimate" kings reigned simultaneously from a site in the Delta.

In the temporal world, the king was the head of his army, who waged war against those powers that threatened the borders of Egypt and its people, and he also led armies to conquer lands whose natural resources or strategic locations were valuable to his own kingdom. Hieroglyphs inscribed on the walls of temples record these victories and indicate that they were ultimately achieved through divine authority and were to be understood as gifts to the gods as well. The image of pharaoh triumphant had other religious significance, since the image of the victorious king represented the ruler in his role as the creator-god, symbolically bringing order out of chaos. Religious doctrine may not have been the prime motivator, but it played a significant role in all military activity.

Overall, one may see a shift to emphasize religion in more secular activities as time goes on. It does appear that earlier wisdom/instructional literature seems to emphasize proper behavior within accepted standards, while in later periods, texts in the same genre stress individual expressions of devotion. However, many of the changes may be more apparent than actual, indicating that the means of expression may have evolved, while the underlying beliefs remained constant.

BIBL.: Henri Frankfort, *Kingship and the Gods* (Chicago, 1949). David O'Connor and David Silverman (eds.), *Ancient Egyptian Kingship: New Investigations* (Probleme der Ägyptologie 9; Leiden, 1995). Georges Posener, *De la divinité du pharaon* (Paris, 1960). Dominique Valbelle, *Histoire de l'état pharaonique* (Paris, 1998).   D.P.S.

Syria-Canaan

Although leadership in the Syro-Canaanite world was occasionally exercised by a council of elders (e.g., El-Amarna tablet 100.4; Judg. 20.5), the predominant Syro-Canaanite political system was kingship. Syro-Canaanite kings exercised military, judicial, administrative, economic, and also religious authority.

Indeed, Syro-Canaanite kingship was religiously grounded. According to the Sumerian King List, Mesopotamian kingship was "lowered from heaven," and by all indications, the Syro-Canaanite world shared this view of kingship as divinely ordained. Certainly, individual kings describe their monarchies as sanctioned by divine decree; for example, the 8th-century BCE Aramean King Zakkur credits the god Baal-Shamem with making him king over his double kingdom of Hamath and Luash (*KAI* 202.3–4, 13), and the 5th-century BCE inscription of King Yehaumilk of the Phoenician city-state of Byblos identifies the monarch as having been made king by the city's patron-goddess, the "Lady of Byblos" (probably Asherah; *KAI* 10.2). In return for the gods' favor, kings built temples for their patron deities: the 10th-century BCE King Yehimilk (not to be confused with Yehaumilk, the similarly named 5th-century king) of Byblos built a temple and restored other temples for Baal-Shamem, the "Lady of Byblos," and "the assembly of the holy gods of Byblos" (*KAI* 4.1–4), and the 9th-century BCE King Mesha of Moab likewise built a "high place" or sacred precinct for Chemosh, the national god of the Moabites, after Chemosh enabled Mesha's military victories against the northern kingdom of Israel (*KAI* 181.3–4). In addition, Mesha dedicated spoils from his battle to Chemosh (*KAI* 181.12–13, 16–18), and King Yehaumilk of Byblos likewise dedicated a bronze altar, a gold gate, and a portico for the shrine of his patron, the "Lady of Byblos" (*KAI* 10.4–6).

King Yehaumilk further describes the Lady's gate as standing "opposite this gate of mine," an indication that the sacred precinct of the goddess stood next to the king's own palace. This conjunction of palace and temple is well attested elsewhere in the Syro-Canaanite world, most famously in Jerusalem, where the temple built by Solomon stood adjacent to the king's palace. It is also seen in Syria, at the Middle Bronze Age site of Alalakh and the Iron Age site of Zincirli, and in northern Mesopotamia, at the Iron Age site of Tell Halaf. What such proximity suggests is that the king is not only a ruler whose authority is sanctioned by divine decree, but that he actually represents the god or gods on earth, ruling on behalf of his divine patron over a region or nation of which the deity is ultimately sovereign. As part of his role as regent, the king serves the deity in the cult, offering sacrifice, presiding over religious ceremonies and festivals, and appointing priestly and related officials. Kings Eshmunazor I and Tabnit, of late-6th- and early-5th-century BCE Sidon, are even identified as priests of their patron-goddess Astarte (*KAI* 13.1–2).

So closely allied is the king with his divine patron that he can be said to be the "son" of the deity; this language is perhaps best attested in the Hebrew Bible (2 Sam. 7.14; Ps. 2.7–9; 89.26–27 [= 89:27–28 Hebrew]) but is also well known from the Late Bronze Age Epic of Kirta from the city-state of Ugarit, on the north Levantine coast. In this text, Kirta is called both the "lad" and the "son" of El, the high god of the Ugaritic pantheon. In one passage, moreover, Kirta himself is called a "god" (*CAT* 1.16.1.22–23), which may suggest that kings in the Syro-Canaanite world were, as in Egypt, actually considered divine. Most scholars prefer, however, to describe Syro-Canaanite kingship as "sacral," understanding the king to be not truly a god but one who metaphorically partakes of a familial relationship with a deity.

After the king, the most important political actor in the Syro-Canaanite world was the queen mother, who wielded considerable power. The queen mother of the Phoenician King Eshmunazor II (5th century BCE) seems to have served as regent for her minor son until he came of age (*KAI* 14.14–20). In fact, Heltzer (1982) has argued that at Ugarit the queen mother served as regent whenever a king was absent from court. At Ugarit also, the queen mother could own property (although this was generally not allowed for Ugaritic women), and, like Bathsheba in the Hebrew Bible, she played a crucial role in determining the royal succession upon her husband's death.

Arguably, the position of political power held by Syro-Canaanite queen mothers was, like the office held by their sons, grounded in religious ideology. As their sons served as earthly representatives of a region's or nation's patron-god or gods, so do queen mothers seem to have served as representatives of one of their region's or nation's deities, most often the Syro-Canaanite mother-goddess Asherah. The logic that underlies this association seems related to the tradition of a king's divine sonship: as a king (like Kirta) was considered the metaphorical son of a divine father (like El), so too would that king be considered to have a metaphorical divine mother, the mother-goddess Asherah. Yet a king also had a biological mother, his queen mother, and consequently these two maternal figures became identified, the queen mother serving as an earthly representative of her divine counterpart. Similarly, it may be that the king's biological father became identified with the king's metaphorical divine father; however, because a king's earthly father must necessarily have died before his son ascended to the throne, the identification between the divine and earthly father could happen only in the old king's afterlife. This might explain why dead kings are occasionally identified as gods in Syro-Canaanite texts, for example, in the Ugaritic King List (*CAT* 1.113) and in the 5th-century BCE Phoenician inscription from Pyrgi (*KAI* 277.9–11).

BIBL.: Susan Ackerman, "The Queen Mother and the Cult in the Ancient Near East," in *Women and Goddess Traditions: In Antiquity and Today* (ed. K. L. King; Minneapolis, 1997), 179–209. G. W. Ahlström, "Administration of the State in Canaan and Ancient Israel," in *Civilizations of the Ancient Near East* (ed. Jack M. Sasson et al.; New York, 1995), 1.587–603. Michael Heltzer, *The Internal Organization of the Kingdom of Ugarit* (Wiesbaden, 1982).   S.A.

Israel

Religion and politics were closely and contentiously intertwined in ancient Israel and nascent Judaism. Tribal Israel formed a decentralized association of agrarian and pastoral hill dwellers whose opposition to state power was reinforced by the cult of YHWH. Monarchic Israel, at first singular and then divided into northern (Israel) and southern (Judah) kingdoms, was a typical ancient Near Eastern tributary monarchy in which some strands of Yahwistic religion supported the state and other strands opposed the state. Colonial Israel, subject to foreign empires from Neo-Babylonian through Roman times, made uneasy accommodations with its overlords that involved religious controversy. The Hasmonean kingdom, in which for less than a century Israel once again achieved political independence, was likewise marked by religious dissension. With the emergence of rabbinic Judaism, Israelite Yahwists adjusted to their lack of secular power by forms of socioreligious self-rule that proved viable in retaining religious identity within hostile or neutral states and empires.

Biblical and postbiblical literary traditions. Broadly speaking, the biblical traditions locate Israelite history within three sociopolitical horizons: a stateless tribal period, a monarchic period with native Israelite states, and a colonial period dominated by foreign empires. Exodus through Joshua picture a united twelve-tribe system, joined by covenant and law, derived from YHWH, and mediated through Moses. Judges indicates a much looser association of autonomous tribes that is tenuously committed to the worship of YHWH and lacks the cohesive social and religious shape presupposed in the preceding books. Samuel and Kings, supplemented by Chronicles, describe the emergence of Israelite statehood, first under Saul, David, and Solomon, followed by a breakup of the united kingdom into the northern kingdom of Israel and the southern kingdom of Judah. The northern branch survives until its destruction by Assyria in 722 BCE, while the southern branch is brought to an end by Neo-Babylonia in 586 BCE.

The political rule of all these kings is reported and evaluated primarily by religious criteria that are set forth in the Book of Deuteronomy. These criteria stem from a reform movement in the 7th century, which mandated worship of YHWH exclusively at the Jerusalem temple and ruthless suppression of all forms of hitherto permitted religious beliefs and practices judged to be illicit by the reformers. As a result, all the kings of Israel and Judah are stigmatized as religiously apostate or deficient except for David and Josiah, the king who championed the Deuteronomic reforms. Mixed with this religious assessment is a fair amount of uncoordinated administrative, diplomatic, and military information. The prophets who were contemporaries of kings provide limited political information but generally focus on condemning the social, political, and religious conduct of Israel's leaders. In particular, prophets oppose foreign alliances and deplore the economic injustices inflicted on the general populace. Certain of the prophets anticipate the total destruction of the kingdoms, which, although unpopular at the time, ironically increased their stature in the eyes of Israelites who lived to experience the fulfillment of the dire prophetic predictions.

Israel's religious and political history in colonial times is far less extensively documented than its monarchic phase. The native religious and political institutions were destroyed and the key leadership was deported, both in Israel and Judah. The rebuilding of the temple and the reforms of Ezra and Nehemiah are recounted as steps in the eventual reconstruction of Judah as a province within the Persian Empire. The ongoing community of Judahites who were not deported is entirely ignored, so that the reconstruction of Judah is attributed solely to the return of descendants of the Babylonian exiles. There is no further historical record between Ezra-Nehemiah and the Maccabees, a gap of more than two centuries. The terms on which Judah was restored under Persian hegemony established it as an administrative unit in the larger empire, with a governor in charge of state affairs and a high priest supervising temple worship. Some version of the law of Moses found in Exodus through Deuteronomy was agreed upon as religious and civil law acceptable to Persia as long as taxes were paid and obedience to the crown was assured. Certain prophets during this period entertained aspirations for the revival of the Davidic Dynasty, but others envisioned reformed Israel as a self-sufficient religious community, subject to Persia and the later Hellenistic empires.

The accommodation between native religion and foreign political rule was shattered by the failed attempt to Hellenize Judahite religion in the early 2nd century BCE, which led to an independent kingdom of Judah ruled by Hasmoneans from 140 to 63 BCE, after which Rome imposed its rule on Judah. We learn of these developments from the books of Maccabees and the works of Josephus, the latter also providing considerable information about Judahite history under Rome down to the revolt of 66–70 CE. Rome retained the policy of previous empires in recognizing the authority of the high priest in religious matters, while alternating between administering Judah by Herodian kings and Roman governors. With the failure of the revolts against Rome, Judah ceased to be an administrative political entity in the Roman Empire, and a reordering and reformulation of Jewish communal life eventuated in rabbinic Judaism, as formalized in the Mishnah and Talmud.

Reconstructing and evaluating the religion-politics nexus. The basis of Israelite ambivalence toward the state was rooted in its decentralized tribal origins, which diffused group decision-making powers within the existing social networks. This stateless social formation was articulated by a religious cult that asserted YHWH to be the sole king of Israel. There was a significant overlap and concordance between "secular" and "religious" spheres. Covenantal linkages among the tribes provided both religious and socioeconomic measures aimed at leveling wealth and power. Decentralized religion and decentralized power arrangements cooperated to undergird a form of "regulated anarchy."

With the rise of the state in Israel, centralized power provoked conflicts and splits in Yahwistic ideology and practice. The resulting divisions in religious circles are sharply expressed in the so-called promonarchic and antimonarchic traditions in the Books of Samuel. On the one hand, a royal theology developed in support of the Davidic Dynasty as the means of mediation between YHWH and Israel. This ideology was concretized as a special covenant with David. The concomitant practice was obedience to the state and celebration of its religious efficacy. On the other hand, the tribal ideology and practice of covenants that resisted concentration and legitimation of power in state rule held sway among Israelites who resisted state power. This resistance to the state on religious grounds is evident in many prophets and in the final shape of the Deuteronomistic history in Deuteronomy through Kings.

The overriding perspective of the Hebrew Bible subordinates politics to religion, but the reasons for this subordination and the precise modes of subordination varied considerably over the centuries. The initiating impulse to privilege religion over politics seems to have risen from the clash between tribalism and state rule in which an established state religion stood in tension with local and regional forms of worship. These tensions were exacerbated by state policies that threatened the economic and social integrity and welfare of the very people who resisted the royal religious cult and ideology. When a realistic assessment is made of the conduct of the Israelite states, they appear to have been little different religiously or politically from other states in their environment. All of them buttressed state rule with religious cult and ideology, and all of them permitted diverse forms of religion as long as they did not entail political rebellion. Devotees of the cult of YHWH throughout the monarchic era employed many practices that the Deuteronomic reform attempted to prohibit in the late 7th century but that were not eliminated until the Judahite restoration from the late 6th century onward.

The decisive impulse in subordinating politics to religion was the colonial circumstances in which the Hebrew Bible was compiled and edited in its final form. In that context, Judahites had no sovereign political power, being subject to Persian and Hellenistic empires. Their colonial plight was a result of the failure of native Israelite political institutions to protect them from the great empires. Reluctantly accepting submission to foreign powers, the principal energy of Judahites was invested in culture and religion as the secure foundation for social cohesion and group identity. Their backward look over the long history of ancient Israel downplayed the role of the state, which, from their perspective, had been successful only when it followed the form of Yahwism that they themselves now practiced and that they understood to have been in force from ancient times—even though their preexilic forebears had repeatedly and wilfully violated the obligatory laws. This accounts for the treatment of the era of Moses as the golden age of Israelite life, from which stemmed the authentic regime of law and covenant and which alone could secure the commu-

nity's survival. The law of Moses, in its various literary embodiments, became the incontestable lifeline of Israel, which Israelite state rule had nearly severed. Nonetheless, how that body of diverse laws was to be applied to contemporary religious and sociopolitical practice remained a matter of continuing dispute.

Although political activism was sharply circumscribed, there were strong impulses in restored Judah to hope for, and perhaps eventually to attain, political sovereignty in which religion could be given the fullest possible expression. This impulse lay behind the Maccabean revolt against the Seleucids and the two uprisings against Rome. The success of the Maccabean revolt in preserving traditional religion did not issue in long-term political success. The ensuing Hasmonean Dynasty, while officially Yahwistic, was seen by many Judahites as religiously apostate and socially repressive, to such an extent that Rome was at first welcomed as a relief from their own rulers. All too soon, however, Roman rule stirred discontent, and two exhausting revolts against Rome proved to be failures. At that point, rabbinic Judaism was able to save the day, strengthening and regularizing community life by means of a mode of casuistic interpretation of the laws of Moses that updated their relevance to the new conditions. Rabbinic Judaism was highly successful in developing an apolitical, text-centered form of religion, with synagogue and rabbi-sage replacing temple and priest. In shaping the scriptural canon, apocalyptic writings that might legitimate further rebellions against Rome, Parthia, or the Sasanian Empire were discouraged. The Messiah became an otherworldy figure not to be identified with a human deliverer. Nevertheless, a restricted exercise of politics found necessary expression in the office of the patriarch (titular head of the Palestinian Jewish community) and the office of the exilarch (the comparable leader of the Babylonian Jewish community).

BIBL.: Norman K. Gottwald, *The Politics of Ancient Israel* (Louisville, 2001). Thomas E. Levy (ed.), *The Archaeology of Society in the Holy Land* (New York, 1995). Ira Sharkansky, *Israel and Its Bible: A Political Analysis* (New York, 1996). Mark S. Smith, *The Early History of God: Yahweh and the Other Deities in Ancient Israel* (San Francisco, 1990). Michael Walzer, Menachem Lorberbaum, and Noam Zohar (eds.), *The Jewish Political Tradition*, vol. 1: *Authority* (New Haven, Conn., 2000). N.K.G.

Anatolia

Although the Hittite king was the chief political officer of the kingdom, many of his duties were in the religious sphere. Of particular importance was his relationship to the gods. In a fashion that parallels later Old Testament practice, the Hittite king was anointed with oil, given royal robes, crowned, and addressed with royal titles. The king was invested by the gods with powers of almost mythical proportions: "His body they made of tin, his head of iron with eagle eyes and lion teeth." To his subjects who addressed him as "My Sun," he was the representative of the sun-god on earth. Great kingship in Hittite Anatolia was thus a derived theocracy. It was bestowed on the ruler by the "Gods of Kingship," that is, the two supreme gods of the pantheon, the storm-god and the sun-goddess.

The relation of the king to the gods could be expressed in different ways: he was either their governor, their priest, or their adopted child. The idea underlying the first image is that the gods entrusted "their" land to the king in much the same way as the Hittite king would hand part of his empire to a governor or vassal. Within the state religion, the ruler was also the highest priest of those same gods, and this priesthood was synonymous with kingship. Secular and religious power were in the same hands, therefore. In the third metaphor— that of the child—the king's originally human nature was not denied, but at an early stage in his life the gods "selected" the future ruler for kingship and "raised" him. The latter two metaphors are combined by King Muwattalli II (1295–1274 BCE) in his prayer to the assembly of gods: "I was a mortal while my father was priest to the Sun-goddess of Arinna and to all the gods. My father begat me but the Storm-god of Lightning took me from my mother, raised me, and made me priest to the Sun-goddess of Arinna and all the gods by putting me in kingship over Hatti-land." The human nature of the king is also implied in the expression used for a king's (or queen's) death: "becoming a god." Another image used for the king—this time expressing his relationship to his people—is that of shepherd (this image is well known from Mesopotamia as well). It is only occasionally found in Hittite texts but may be more prominent iconographically insofar as the image of the king as the sun-god often includes the so-called *lituus* (Hittite *kalmuš*), if the latter can be equated with a shepherd's crooked staff.

The special position of the king as both a political and a religious person is reflected by the emphasis that the texts place on his purity. His person was surrounded with the utmost care by personnel imbued with the importance of this. Defilement of the royal person could have implications for the entire country, as the land's fertility and prosperity were directly contingent on that of the ruler. The same concept underlies the extensive royal funerary ritual, which seems to be focused almost exclusively on agricultural aspects. References to the king as the supreme military commander, on the other hand, seem to be missing in funerary ritual. The manner in which pollution of the royal person could have repercussions for the country is exemplified by the link that Murshili II eventually made between his father's misdeeds and the epidemic that occurred during his (i.e., Murshili II's), reign.

Royal iconography emphasizes two main themes, each of which expresses the king's closeness to the divine world. The king and the sun-god are often portrayed identically, wearing a long robe and a tight-fitting cap and carrying the *lituus*. Alternatively, the king can be portrayed in more warriorlike attire: bare-breasted, wearing a pointed helmet and a short kilt and girdle from which a sword hangs down, and carrying other weapons. The helmet can even include "horns of divinity," as known from Mesopotamian iconography. When portrayed in this way, the king resembled all gods (except for the sun-god), but foremost the storm-god.

The ideology seems to have been fully developed already during the Old Hittite period (ca. 1650–1500). Most of the texts dealing with kingship date from that time and were regularly copied down to the very end of the empire in the early 12th century. A possible change in the royal ideology may have occurred during the second half of the 13th century during the reign of Tudkhaliya IV (ca. 1240–1210 BCE), but it may have been the result of developments introduced earlier. It may have been Muwattalli II who broke with a consistently aniconic tradition. This change could stand in relation to religious reforms during his reign. He is the first king of whom lifelike images are attested both on sealings and rock reliefs. Although there are in general no Hittite reliefs that can be dated prior to Muwattalli with certainty, there is a long tradition of royal seals from the Old Kingdom onward, up to and including Muwattalli II's father Murshili II (ca. 1318–1295 BCE), which lack iconic portrayals. The observed modeling of the king's image after divine examples may have led to a growing identification of the ruler with the gods, culminating in Tudkhaliya's demand for offerings to his person during his lifetime. The expansion of Hattusha attributable to him, the renaming of the city as "Hattusha-Tudkhaliya-city," and his use of the title "King of the Universe" are fully concomitant with such a development. Another phenomenon that existed before Muwattalli II but which became more prominent in his reign and gained in importance afterward is that of the patron deity. His father Murshili II had special reverence for the Sun-goddess of Arinna but the devotion shown by Muwattalli to the Storm-god of Lightning was unparalleled. It is likely to have been the reason for moving the residence from Hattusha to the as-yet-unknown site of Tarhuntasa in south-central Anatolia, where he established a new capital fully dedicated to this deity. This trend is sometimes considered a step toward henotheism.

BIBL.: Gary Beckman, "Royal Ideology and State Administration in Hittite Anatolia," in *Civilizations of the Ancient Near East* (ed. Jack M. Sasson et al.; New York, 1995), 1.529–43. O. R. Gurney, "Hittite Kingship," in *Myth, Ritual, and Kingship* (ed. S. H. Hooke; Oxford, 1958), 105–21. T. P. J. van den Hout, "Tuthalija IV. und die Ikonographie hethitischer Grosskönige des 13. Jhs.," *Bibliotheca Orientalis* 52 (1995): 545–73.   T.V.D.H.

Iran

"Thus says the LORD to his anointed, to Cyrus, whose right hand I have grasped, to subdue nations before him. . . . I call you by your name, I surname you, though you do not know me." This well-known passage from Deutero-Isaiah (45.1–4) is not only a bold theological statement about the role of Israel's god in history, but also an indirect comment on the religiopolitical policy of the Achaemenids toward conquered peoples within their vast empire. As architect of the new empire's administration, Cyrus II (549–530 BCE) adopted an overt policy of embracing the deities of these peoples. In a cylinder inscription in Akkadian, Cyrus, after mentioning the abominations practiced by Nabonidus in the worship of Marduk and sacrileges perpetrated against other gods, states that Marduk "scanned and looked through all the countries, searching for a righteous ruler willing to lead him [in the annual procession]. [Then] he pronounced the name of King Cyrus of Anshan, announced his name to be the ruler of the world. . . . When I entered Babylon as a friend and established the seat of government in the palace of the ruler . . . Marduk, the great lord, [induced] the magnanimous inhabitants of Babylon [to love me]." He goes on to say that, under instructions from Marduk, he restored various sanctuaries and returned images of numerous deities, which Nabonidus had brought to Babylon, to their proper cities (*ANET* 315–16). The return of the Israelite exiles under Cyrus and the rebuilding of Jerusalem's walls and of the temple under Darius, Xerxes, and Artaxerxes chronicled especially in the biblical books of Nehemiah and Ezra, show a continuation of Cyrus's policies. Although Herodotus entertained a particular view of the mental stability of Cambyses II (530–522), Cyrus's son, his account of the latter's involvement in the Egyptian cult of the bull Apis must reflect also the Achaemenid foreign policy with respect to religion.

Apart from the theologically colored testimony of the Bible and the propagandistic statements intended for a Mesopotamian audience, we know nothing about Cyrus's personal theology. In sharp contrast, Darius the Great (522–486) and his son Xerxes (486–465) published their personal theologies throughout the empire. Scholars continue to debate the question of whether the early Achaemenid kings were Zoroastrians and, if so, whether this begins with Cyrus or a later ruler. While the relationship of Zoroastrianism with the power of the state is crucial for the Sasanid Empire, it goes unnoticed in Achaemenid sources. What is important is that Darius and his successors were fervent Mazdeans, that is, worshipers of Ahura Mazda. After Darius had seized power, he needed an ideological framework in which to legitimize his rule. Through his long inscription at Behistun and in subsequent inscriptions, he promoted in nearly monotheistic language the supremacy of Ahura Mazda, "the great god who created this earth and yon-der heaven, who created man, who created the happiness of man" (Darius inscription at Naqsh-e Rostam a.1–5). Relying on ancient Indo-Iranian ideas of a social and natural dichotomy between order (*Arta/rta* [lit., Truth]) and chaos (*Drauga* [lit., Lie]), Darius expounded a religiopolitical theology that placed him as Ahura Mazda's appointee to overcome chaos (i.e., rebellion) and to establish order in the world: "By the will of Ahura Mazda I am king; Ahura Mazda delivered the royal power [*xšaça*] to me" (Darius inscription at Behistun 1.11–12). The inscriptions of Xerxes follow closely the formulas of his father. However, an element of intolerance toward the worship of the Daewas (evil deities) may signal a departure from the policies of his predecessors, as in his Daiwadana inscription (Xerxes inscription at Persepolis h.35–56) he proscribes the worship of the Daewas and describes the destruction of their sanctuary *(daiwadāna)*, while advocating the correct worship of Ahura Mazda. Unfortunately, we do not know where this *daiwadāna* was or whether the encouragement to worship Ahura Mazda was directed at Iranians only or at all peoples. Noteworthy is the promotion by Artaxerxes II (404–359) of the cult of Anahita, the goddess of royal power in the Avesta and in Sasanid ideology.

A matter of some uncertainty is the role played by the magi in the power structure of Achaemenid Iran. Herodotus, whose information can seldom be taken at face value, described the magi as a Median tribe who officiated at all religious ceremonies, where they recited theogonies. Although ignored by the eastern Iranian Avesta, they were certainly a powerful priestly caste in western Iran. In the initial struggle for power, Darius put to death a pretender, Gaumata the Magu. This is all he has to say about the magi. However, Herodotus (3.76–79) describes in detail a magian conspiracy that so outraged the Persians that its exposure led to a wholesale slaughter of magi. Thereafter there was an annual festival named the Magophonia (killing of magi), during which magi were obliged to remain in seclusion or risk death. Herodotus's story may reflect a festival of social inversion, but owing to the general awe that the magi inspired throughout the ancient world and in consideration of their prominence in the priestly nomenclature of Sasanid Iran, we can only assume that power had to be negotiated with this priesthood. A Manichean Sogdian ascription of *mywzt* (magophonia) to Alexander shows that subsequent to the downfall of the Achaemenid Dynasty, the magi were successful in rewriting the history of this embarrassment.

Very little is known about religion and politics in the Parthian Empire. Both their art and notices by Greek and Roman authors point to a high level of eclecticism. In the east, coinage of the Kushan Empire during the first two centuries of the common era preserves Hindu, Buddhist, and Iranian iconography, indicating a policy of religious accommodation consistent with

Achaemenid traditions. All that changes with the rise of the Sasanid state.

When Ardashir established the Sasanid Dynasty around 224 CE, he followed a deliberate ideological program which, emphasizing his revival of the Achaemenid heritage, promoted the distinctively Iranian nature of the state and the civilization that it embraced. Symbolic of the disavowal of non-Iranian influences was the demonization of Alexander "the Roman," who was blamed especially for the disorganization of the Zoroastrian religion. Concrete was the enfranchisement of the Zoroastrian (i.e., magian) priesthood and the establishment of the Zoroastrian church as the authority in all religious matters. Under his chief priest Tansar (or Tosar), a major attempt was made to compile an orthodox canon. But, it was not until the reign of his son Shapur (240–72) that the power of the Zoroastrian clergy truly asserted itself. The chief priest named Kirder, who had begun his career under Ardashir, became engaged in a power struggle for the loyalty of the king with the charismatic prophet Mani, the founder of Manicheanism. In the end, the priest was triumphant over prophet; and, even though Manicheanism exercised a wide influence in late antiquity from Rome to China, it was never allowed to prosper in the Iranian heartland. Kirder's unprecedented power is heralded in a series of his inscriptions, unprecedented since inscriptions were otherwise the prerogative of rulers. In the inscriptions Kirder established his authority in religious matters by recounting a marvelous journey to the otherworld in which reports are brought to him of paradise and hell. His ascendance and tenure as supreme ecclesiastical authority "at court . . . in all the land" is chronicled through the reigns of four emperors, culminating in the reign of Bahram II (276–93), under whom Jews, Buddhists, Hindus, Nazareans, Christians, Baptists, and Manicheans were being persecuted.

The Sasanids always insisted on the inseparability of religion and the state. Whereas the Achaemenids wished only to publicize their divine mandate to rule, the Sasanids claimed some sort of divine lineage by using the expression *from the seed of the gods (az cihr ī yazdān)*. Monumental sculptural scenes show the investiture of several emperors by the deities Ohrmazd and Anahita. In keeping with the general Zoroastrian theology of a cosmic dualistic struggle between Truth and the Lie, the king was held up as the one locus of the religiopolitical power necessary to accomplish the defeat of Ahriman. As the Denkard puts it: "The thing against which the Destructive Spirit struggles most violently is the coming together in full force of the glory [*xwarrah*] of kingship and the Good Religion in one person, because such a conjunction must destroy him" (M 129). While there are many reasons for the rapid eclipse of Zoroastrianism by Islam, this conception of power residing in the fusion of religion and kingship in the concrete person of the king resulted in a theological vacuum

that could not be filled after the death of Yazdagird III, the last king of kings.

BIBL.: Mary Boyce, *A History of Zoroastrianism* (3 vols.; Leiden: Brill, 1975–91). *The Cambridge History of Iran*, vols. 2 (ed. Ilya Gershevitch) and 3 (ed. Ehsan Yarshater) (Cambridge: Cambridge University Press, 1983–85). Arthur Christensen, *L'Iran sous les Sassanides* (repr. Copenhagen: Munksgaard, 1971 [orig. 1944]). Richard N. Frye, *The Heritage of Persia* (Cleveland: World, 1963). Idem, *The History of Ancient Iran* (Munich: Beck, 1984). W. B. Henning, "The Murder of the Magi," *Journal of the Royal Asiatic Society* (1944): 133–44. Roland G. Kent, *Old Persian* (New Haven: American Oriental Society, 1953). W.W.M.

Greece

Polis religion. The categories "religion" and "politics" are both inevitable and problematic. Any modern analysis must engage with modern categories, but it must at the same time recognize that they are rooted in contexts very different from those of ancient Greece. In particular, the assumption that religion is a differentiated institution that can have a process of interaction with political institutions—in the way the Christian church interacts with the secular state—is not valid for ancient Greece. The dominant current model for understanding Greek religion, the polis model, is an attempt to escape the misleading implications of the categories. It defines the principal context for Greek religious life as the polis (city-state), which had the authority to establish and run religious systems that organized the relationships between humans and gods (in some sense it could be said that the polis played the role played in Christianity by the church). The polis had the ultimate authority over all religious matters. Religious items were taken first at two of the four monthly meetings of the assembly. It followed that speakers in the assembly needed to be trained in religious matters: a 4th-century rhetorical handbook describes as the first of its seven types of public speeches those on sacred rites (pseudo-Aristotle, *Rhetoric to Alexander* 3.1423a20–1424a8).

At a more general level, the religious code of discourse was dominant in the Athenian assembly: speakers on a wide range of topics assumed that the gods were benevolent toward the city. Demosthenes, in urging Athenian action against Philip of Macedon, opens his *Second Olynthiac:* "There are many signs of the goodwill of the gods to our city, and not least the present situation." It was not the case that politics, even in democratic Athens, had become a wholly secular matter, a differentiated system with no relationship to religion. The state was the formal organizer of collective religious life and at the same time ultimately dependent on the good will of the gods.

A consequence of this relationship between politics and religion is that political change might entail religious change. The democratic reforms of Cleisthenes in

507 BCE are often seen as a radical move, which swept away the old and subordinated cult to politics. In fact, the reforms are marked by the creation of new group identities expressed through the medium of religion. Leaving the four old Ionic tribes untouched, Cleisthenes created ten new tribes, which were sanctioned by the Delphic Oracle. And again leaving the old brotherhoods (phratries) untouched, he reorganized villages (demes) as the basic unit of the state, and they celebrated their own cycles of festivals and sacrifices. Aristotle in his *Politics* derived from this case and the establishment of democracy at Cyrene a general proposition about the steps which can usefully be taken in establishing democracy: "New tribes and brotherhoods should be established, more numerous than the old, and ceremonies held at private shrines should be concentrated on a few public ones; and in general one must fix things so that there is as much social intercourse as possible and a breakup of former ties" (1319b23–28). Political and religious change might be expected to go hand in hand.

Equally, religious innovation was at least notionally the responsibility of the state. Foreigners living in Athens who wished to establish shrines to their ancestral gods needed to obtain permission from the assembly. Merchants from Kition on Cyprus were granted permission in 333 BCE to create a sanctuary to Aphrodite (born in Kition), on the analogy of permission granted previously to merchants from Egypt for a sanctuary of Isis. As foreigners, who normally could not own land in Attica, they needed a special right to own land on which they could then build the sanctuary. But only very exceptionally did the creation of such new sanctuaries affect the state cults. The one exception in Athens is the cult of Thracian Bendis. In the 5th century, the Athenians gave permission to Thracians for a sanctuary in the Piraeus for their ancestral deity and subsequently (perhaps following consultation of the oracle of Zeus at Dodona) transformed the cult into a state cult: it was paid for by the Treasurers of the Other Gods (i.e., treasurers of the gods other than Athena), and the nocturnal torch race in the festival became a notable event (immortalized in the opening of Plato's *Republic*). The public adoption of this cult, sometimes seen as a sign of religious decay, in fact remained almost unique at Athens. The ancestral religious system, under the authority of the state, remained very stable throughout antiquity.

Oracles. Outside the polis, the most obvious religious authorities were oracles, which at times played major political roles. The Delphic Oracle is the one that has attracted the most scholarly attention, in part because of its centrality to Herodotus's history of the Greek world down to the early 5th century BCE. Herodotus's narrative represents it as perfectly normal for states to consult Delphi on political issues. It was so usual to consult an oracle about founding a new city that Herodotus was not surprised that, when someone (a Spartan, Dorieus) omitted to consult Delphi the first time, the mission failed and that, when he went beyond what Delphi had told him the second time, he lost his life (5.42–45).

There is an evidential problem with the political enquiries of oracles in Herodotus: the enquiries by states securely attested in epigraphic documents are all on religious matters, and as some of the Herodotean political enquiries are certainly later fabrications, it could be argued that they all are. But such skepticism is excessive, and one key enquiry in Herodotus is surely to be accepted. When in 481 BCE the Athenians were undecided what to do about the threat of Persian attack they consulted the Delphic Oracle (7.140–44). The first oracle that the envoys received seemed too bleak (advising them, like other Greeks, to flee from the Persians and create a new city elsewhere). The envoys then managed to get a second consultation and received a second oracle that was seemingly less bleak, but also somewhat mysterious (a wooden wall would protect the Athenians, and divine Salamis would bring death to women's sons). The key point is that the envoys then presented this oracle to the Athenian assembly, where a major debate occurred as to the meaning of the wooden wall and divine Salamis. This public event has as much claim to historicity as any event in Herodotus's work, and it therefore authenticates the general category of archaic political enquiries of oracles (see further Divination and Prophecy).

After the Persian Wars, despite the Greek victory (at Salamis) being considered to have been dependent on the successful interpretation of this oracle, the Athenians did not again consult an oracle on a simply political matter. This was not because (as has been claimed) the Greeks lost faith in Delphi because of its alleged siding with Persia in the conflict or because of a general loss of faith in oracular authority. After all, the first item in a peace treaty between the Athenians and the Spartans in 421 BCE included the provision that people should be able to seek oracular advice from the Panhellenic shrines without let or hindrance and that Delphi should be autonomous (Thucydides 5.18.2). And other states did continue to consult oracles on political matters. Sparta consulted Delphi in 432 BCE as to whether it should go to war with Athens (Thucydides 1.118), and in the 4th century the Chalcidians made an enquiry as to whether they should make an alliance with their mighty neighbor Philip II of Macedon (Tod 1948: no. 158; Harding 1985: no. 67). What changed, at least for some states, was the nature of their political institutions. States such as democratic Athens, which had powerful political institutions that could reach decisions within the state even on very controversial matters, had no need to seek external advice from an oracle.

The role of the polis and its cults in the Hellenistic and Roman periods shows the continuing vitality of civic cults and the value of the polis model. The old scholarly view of civic cults, as of the polis itself, in these periods was of decline and loss of meaning. In the face of the great Hellenistic kingdoms and the Roman Empire, the polis was no longer an appropriate framework for human life. This view has now been largely abandoned in favor of one that stresses the ongoing significance of cities and their religious lives throughout this period. So, for example, the city of Ephesus in the 2nd century CE placed enormous emphasis on the cult of Artemis, born at Ephesus. A civic decree began as follows: "The goddess Artemis, presiding over our city, is honored not only in her native city, which she has made more famous than all other cities through her own divinity, but also by Greeks and barbarians, so that everywhere sanctuaries and precincts are consecrated for her, temples are dedicated and altars set up for her, on account of her manifest epiphanies" (*Inschriften von Ephesos* 24, lines 8–14; 162/163 or 163/164 CE). The city here defines its own identity in relation to a cult that has spread out from Ephesus all over the world. The Roman authorities were happy to accept this view and in this case to give official approval to a request from the Ephesians to extend the festival of Artemis to a month and to ban public business for this whole period. Civic organization of religion thus continued within a Roman political framework.

Marginal cults. A second area also points to the limits of the polis model: areas where religious life existed in a manner unregulated by and in some ways in opposition to civic religion. The most obvious example is provided by the so-called Orphic sect. This movement created a cosmology that was distinct from the dominant Hesiodic cosmology and that was meaningful only for members of the sect. The opening of the surviving text is: "I shall sing to those who understand. Bar your ears, you uninitiated." The Orphic cosmogony ascribes a key role to Persephone as guardian of the underworld and to Dionysus as protector of mortals in this world. The souls of the dead spend three hundred years in the underworld and are then reborn, but attempt to escape the cycle of death and rebirth through purification sacrifices and the assistance of Persephone and Dionysus. This view of the world is strikingly untraditional and is completely untrammeled by the institutions of the polis. Indeed the Orphic principle of abstinence from eating animal flesh set Orphics in opposition to the dietary code of the polis, which articulated the relationship between humans and gods through animal sacrifice and the eating of sacrificial meat (see further Mysteries).

Ruler cult. The civic cults also provided the framework within which cities and individuals perceived and expressed the relationship between cities and ruling power. When Greek cities came under the dominance of external rulers, whether Greek or Roman, they established cults of those rulers, using as a template the existing cult of the gods. That is, the idiom used to honor Hellenistic kings and Roman emperors was derived from the traditional civic cults: temples, altars, priests, sacrifices, and festivals. For example, after Athens had fallen to the Macedonian Demetrius Poliorcetes (Besieger of Cities), the Athenians welcomed him in 291/290 BCE with offerings of incense, crowns, and libations and sang a processional hymn comparing Demetrius, a name formed after the goddess's name, and Demeter, the goddess:

> For the greatest and dearest of the gods have come to our city: here indeed the time [of the Eleusinian Mysteries] has brought together Demeter and Demetrius. She comes to celebrate the solemn mysteries of the Daughter [Persephone] but he, as is fitting for a god, is here in gladness, fair and smiling. Something august he seems, all his friends around him and he himself among them, his friends the stars even as he is the sun. O son of the most mighty god Poseidon and of Aphrodite, Hail! For other gods are either far away or have not ears, or exist not, or heed us not at all, but you we can see in very presence, not in wood and not in stone, but for real. So we pray to you, first bring peace, you most dear. For you have the power. (Athenaeus 6.252f–54a)

Such language struck some later and perhaps some at the time as "flattery," but we cannot dismiss it so simply. It shows not the decay of the old cults, but their continuing ability to express the relationship of a Greek city to the ruling power.

Such patterns of behavior continued under Rome. For example, in one Macedonian town a local citizen volunteered to be priest of Zeus, Roma, and Augustus and displayed amazing munificence in the monthly sacrifices to Zeus and Augustus and in the feasts and games that he put on for the citizens (*SEG* 35 no. 744; 1 CE). Such divine honors, whether to the ruler alone or to him in association with the gods, formed a religious framework for the new political order, a framework that permitted subjects to represent external power in a manner familiar to and therefore acceptable to themselves.

BIBL.: Phillip Harding (ed./trans.), *From the End of the Peloponnesian War to the Battle of Ipsus* (Translated Documents of Greece and Rome 2; Cambridge, 1985). J. D. Mikalson, *Religion in Hellenistic Athens* (Berkeley, 1998). Robert Parker, *Athenian Religion: A History* (Oxford, 1996). S. R. F. Price, *Rituals and Power: The Roman Imperial Cult in Asia Minor* (Cambridge, 1984). C. J. Schwenk, *Athens in the Age of Alexander* (Chicago, 1985). Christiane Sourvinou-Inwood, "What Is Polis Religion?" in *Oxford Readings in Greek Religion* (ed. Richard Buxton; Oxford, 2000), 13–37 (repr. from *The Greek City from Homer to Alexander* [ed. Oswyn Murray and Simon Price; Oxford, 1990], 293–322). M. N. Tod, *A Selection of Greek Historical Inscriptions*, vol. 2 (Oxford, 1948). S.R.F.P.

Rome

Since Roman religion was neither a coherent nor a static system, the relationship between religion and politics was always fluid. According to tradition, Rome was originally ruled by kings, who must have played a leading role in public religion; many scholars have argued that a key element in the development of the republic was the transfer of religious authority from the king to public priests. But since the evidence for this process is both meager and late, any account of it must be highly speculative.

We are on firmer ground when we reach the Roman Republic of the late 3rd and 2nd centuries BCE. In this period, religious power meant essentially the ability to make authoritative decisions about relations between the community and the divine world and was rather widely diffused among the political elite. Although traditional religious knowledge was in the hands of public priests, they did not exercise their authority single-handedly or even, in many cases, directly. The annual magistrates were the ones who actually took the auspices, dedicated temples, and made and fulfilled public vows; the priests were generally responsible only for ensuring that they performed these rituals correctly. Likewise, it was the senate that normally made important decisions concerning relations with the gods, such as establishing a new cult or performing expiations. Moreover, the priests themselves were normally also senators and magistrates.

As a result, there was in Rome no significant distinction between religious and secular authority. Although it was not a theocracy, the ties between religion and politics were so close and complex that for all practical purposes the two formed an almost seamless whole. The same group of men from the social and economic elite had responsibility for all public affairs, whether these concerned the human sphere only or the divine sphere as well. Moreover, they conducted all their business, "secular" as well as "religious," within what we might describe as a sacred framework. For example, the senate could meet only in a *templum,* a space that had been marked out by augural ritual. Similarly, it was necessary to take the auspices and obtain signs of the gods' approval before all meetings of the public assemblies, including those for the election of magistrates and the passing of laws. On a fundamental level, then, all public affairs in republican Rome were bounded by religious rules.

The intersection of religion and politics was as close in the military sphere as in the civil. The declaration of war and the striking of treaties involved specific rituals, and there was an entire college of priests, the *fetiales,* whose role was to ensure their correct performance; these rituals were necessary for a war to be regarded as a *iustum bellum* (just war). Religious observances also had a role in the actual conduct of war: not only the usual rituals such as sacrifices and the taking of auspices, but also the distinctive ritual of the *evocatio,* in which the Roman general would summon the gods of the enemy to abandon their people in exchange for a cult in Rome. The vows of generals, to Roman as well as foreign deities, were responsible for many new cults

during the republican period. Lastly, a victorious general could be granted the honor of a triumph, in which the general (in a guise close to that of Jupiter), his army, and the captives and spoils of the war made an elaborate procession from the city walls to the Capitol.

In such a context it is not surprising that there were many situations in which religious considerations had a direct impact on political life. It was possible, for example, for a presiding magistrate to declare that the auspices were negative and so postpone an assembly; it was likewise possible for an augur to declare that the magistrate had not performed the ritual correctly and that any decisions made in the assembly were accordingly invalid. Religious personnel called *pontifices* and *quindecimviri* could also influence political affairs through their authority over public rituals. We know many specific cases of such actions, particularly in the 1st century BCE. For example, in 56 BCE, the consul Lentulus Marcellinus removed all the available *dies comitiales,* that is, days on which public assemblies could take place, by ordering the repetition of a major public festival, presumably because the *pontifices* had identified a flaw in its initial performance; Cicero commends him for thereby placing an obstacle in the way of those who were proposing some "highly pernicious" legislation (*Letters to His Brother Quintus* 2.4.4–5). In the same year, amid intense political debate over proposals to restore the exiled king of Egypt, the *quindecimviri* discovered an oracle in the Sibylline Books to the effect that "the king of Egypt should not be supported with a multitude" and so thwarted those who were scheming for this plum opportunity (Cassius Dio, *Roman History* 39.15–16). In 55 BCE, when Pompey was presiding over the elections, the initial vote went to one of his political enemies; Pompey thereupon announced that the auspices were unacceptable and dissolved the assembly (Plutarch, *Cato the Younger* 42).

Earlier scholarship tended to decry such stories as examples of an illegitimate manipulation of religion and as evidence that the Roman religious tradition had by the 1st century BCE lost all true religious significance and become a hollow political tool. But such objections presuppose a distinction between the religious and political spheres that does not seem ever to have existed in Rome. Although there was certainly debate over the legitimacy of particular maneuvers, and although some individuals were apparently quite cynical in their use of religious tactics, no one seems to have regarded the system as a whole as moribund or hopelessly corrupt.

More important in the long run was the gradual development of a different sort of religious authority, one based less on traditional public institutions than on individual claims to privileged relationships with the divine. We can see traces of this already in the late 3rd century BCE, when Scipio Africanus is said to have regularly visited the temple of Jupiter Optimus Maximus before dawn, as if consulting the god on the affairs of Rome (Livy, *History of Rome* 26.19). In the last century BCE, the same military leaders who amassed unprecedented political power also made unprecedented claims to unique religious status. The dictator Sulla apparently cultivated a special association with the goddess Venus, who as the mother of Aeneas could be considered the divine ancestor of the Roman people; Pompey topped him by building an elaborate temple to Venus Victrix (Venus of Victory); and Julius Caesar outstripped them both. Playing up traditions that presented Aeneas's son Iulus as the ancestor of the Julian family, he dedicated an even more elaborate temple to Venus Genetrix (Venus the Ancestress), thereby emphasizing his special descent from the common forebear of the Roman people. In the last years of his life, when he became the sole ruler of the Roman world, Caesar seems to have explored an almost bewildering variety of ways to associate himself with the divine. Although some of his experiments apparently offended the traditional elite of Rome, a large part of the population seems to have received them with enthusiasm.

Given the intimate association of religion and politics in the Roman tradition, it was inevitable that the creation of a new form of government, centered on the figure whom we call the emperor, would have religious as well as political aspects. Just as the old political forms of the republic were not abolished but rather transformed through the concentration of power in the hands of the emperor, so too the old religious institutions remained technically unaltered, although in practice the emperor now dominated all the major priestly colleges. But the practical significance of the old priesthoods rapidly dwindled, and the new emphasis on personal connections between the emperor and the divine soon came to dominate. The latter constitutes what is usually called imperial cult, although this term can be somewhat misleading. There was never a single organized cult of the emperor, or a single set of rituals to honor him, or even a single conception of his connection to the divine. Instead, the emperor's privileged relationship to the divine was represented in a wide variety of ways.

In one key respect the emperors built on the Roman tradition that political leaders were also responsible for maintaining the good will of the gods: the emperor became the intermediary *par excellence* between the inhabitants of the empire and the divine world. This conception spread chiefly through depictions on reliefs and coins of the emperor sacrificing to the gods. Although there is little to suggest that the emperor was in actual fact the "chief sacrificer" of the Roman Empire, the image effectively represented one aspect of his position. Conversely, because the emperor was so important for the prosperity of the empire, it became increasingly common for people to pray, sacrifice, and make vows on his behalf; in the Latin-speaking parts of the empire, the formula "for the well-being of the emperor" became a standard element in dedications to an extremely wide range of deities. In other ways the emperors were themselves treated like gods. Emperors could, for example, be depicted with the attributes of traditional deities such as Jupiter; such representations evoked an association between the emperor and the god without defining it too precisely. There were also priests of the emperors, temples of the emperors, and even sacrifices to the emperors. In all these respects, the emperor's unique connection to the divine was expressed through the deployment of traditional cult practices, although usually with certain subtle adjustments to maintain some distinction between emperors and the traditional gods.

This close connection between the emperor and the divine was crucial to the success of the Roman Empire. It served not only to characterize the emperor's unique status, but also to structure the hierarchical social relationships on which the effective functioning of the empire depended. Particularly in the provinces, where direct contact with the emperor was generally limited, symbolic proximity by means of cult was an important component of social and political status. The imperial priesthoods attested in many cities of the empire were prestigious local offices. Moreover, in many provinces an assembly of representatives met annually to celebrate a festival for the emperor and elect a provincial priest; this position was generally the capstone of a local political career. Even wealthy freedmen, who were otherwise normally excluded from public positions, could establish their standing through an association with imperial cult.

Yet the symbolic importance of the emperor should not be confused with his practical role in the religious organization of the empire. Emperors could certainly promote particular deities, as Julius Caesar had Venus, and several of them did so, such as Elagabalus (218–22), who declared his Syrian sun-god the supreme deity of the empire, and Diocletian (284–305), who adopted the titles Jovius and Herculius for himself and his colleagues. But the effects of such promotions were generally limited and temporary. Actual cults, including those of the emperor himself, continued to be locally established as well as locally organized. It was not until the promotion of Christianity by Constantine and his successors that emperors had a direct and drastic effect on the organization of religion. Indeed, the imperial promotion of Christianity brought about a fundamental restructuring of the relationship between religion and politics in the Roman world: because Christians had already developed their own hierarchy, there came to exist for the first time a powerful and officially recognized religious authority that was distinct from secular authority.

BIBL.: M. Beard, J. North, and S. Price, *Religions of Rome*, vol. 1 (Cambridge, 1998). Duncan Fishwick, *The Imperial Cult in the Latin West* (Leiden, 1987–2002). Richard Gordon, "The Veil of Power: Emperors, Sacrificers and Benefactors," in *Pagan Priests* (ed. Mary Beard and John North; Ithaca, N.Y., 1990), 201–31. S. R. F. Price, *Rituals and*

Power: The Roman Imperial Cult in Asia Minor (Cambridge, 1984). Stefan Weinstock, *Divus Julius* (Oxford, 1971). J.B.R.

Christianity

The earliest churches took root in polytheistic urban settings. Polytheism permeated every aspect of life in the cities of the Roman Empire, for religion was not simply one sector of society. Sacrifices and prayers were made at festivals, in gymnasia, at the baths, at concerts, during legislative meetings, in wartime, at peace treaties, at the sowing of crops, at harvest, with the slaughter of animals, at dinner parties, in homes, before childbirth, at funerals, and at other times. For mainstream society, polytheism defined the meaning of the world.

Early church members held views about deity that deviated from those of mainstream society, and such views had practical implications. Three particular factors are especially relevant. One was early Christian teaching on the use of power, for several early documents teach an ethic of love for one's enemies and the renunciation of force (e.g., Matt. 5.38–48; Mark 10.45–48; Rom. 12.14–21; 1 Pet. 3.8–13).

The second has to do with resources: most of the saints had neither the money nor the status to serve in public offices. Only members of the wealthiest elite families could afford the burden of political responsibility, for officials volunteered their time and normally supplemented meager civic budgets from their own personal wealth. Officials also benefited from their service, for they were able to influence a wide range of policies (regulating such things as prices, wages, labor, land use, banking, citizenship, and local criminal justice systems) in ways that enhanced their own fortunes and status. Most early church members, however, did not have the resources to break into this small group of elite leaders.

The third factor that separated the churches from political life was that government—like all aspects of mainstream society—was under the aegis of the Greco-Roman pantheon. In order to be involved in politics, a church member would need to sacrifice to various deities who nourished or threatened human communities. Even more reprehensible in the eyes of many church members was the worship of Roman emperors and members of their dynasties as deities. This phenomenon—known today as "imperial cult"—was a standard feature of polytheism in the empire that troubled early Christians. Most Christians (and Jews) considered it blasphemous to offer sacrifice to humans, yet mainstream society operated on the assumption that the emperors were related in some way to the Olympian deities by virtue of their accomplishments and authority. When Christians refused to worship the emperors, their refusal was taken as an act of sedition, a capital offense.

Because of these three factors—a nonviolent ethic, the lack of elite resources, and the polytheism of public life—the early churches tended to have a sectarian character. As nonconformists, church members usually remained on the margins of public life, and so they were often more vulnerable than most people to public harassment and political oppression.

Since the churches dissented from prevailing theories about government and the divine realm, they had to devise theories of their own. Most early churches agreed that the Roman Empire could not claim divine approval, but our earliest church documents display surprising variety in their assessments of Roman rule. The extreme positions are exemplified by Revelation and Luke-Acts. Revelation vilified the Roman Empire as the summation of history's oppressive regimes, empowered by Satan, bent on world domination, drunk on the blood of the saints (Rev. 12–13, 17–19). The author of Luke-Acts, on the other hand, sought a place for the churches within the imperial system. The author portrayed Roman officials in a positive light and downplayed the role of Roman authority in the executions of Jesus and Paul. The author also depicted the early churches as an innocuous movement, composed of law-abiding inhabitants who were falsely accused by Jews and by Gentiles of disturbing the *pax Romana*.

Paul's Letter to the Romans and 1 Peter are neither so pessimistic as Revelation nor as idealized as Luke-Acts and so provide examples of how some, and perhaps many, church members understood politics in the late 1st and early 2nd centuries. Both texts assert that government is ordained by God to reward the righteous and punish evildoers (Rom. 13.1–7; 1 Pet. 2.13–14). Since both of these authors knew that government did not normally live up to these standards, further explanation was in order. In both texts the problem is resolved eschatologically, but with different nuances. For Paul, the sufferings experienced by the churches—including governmental oppression—characterized this evil age, which would come to an end at the glorious revelation of the children of God (Rom. 8.18–39). The author of 1 Peter, on the other hand, emphasized judgment and purification: in the churches' sufferings God was disciplining God's own household as a prelude to judging the disobedient world (1 Pet. 4.12–19).

While the political views of Romans and 1 Peter probably represented a moderate position among the churches, these views were still deviant when compared with the official discourse on politics and religion. In public culture, the emperors and members of their families were gods, worshiped as latter-day Olympians. So a Roman governor such as Pliny the Younger (early 2nd century CE) had little sympathy for Christians. Pliny gathered information about the movement in Bithynia by torturing two female slaves who were deaconesses, but found no evidence of destructive practices. He allowed Christians to recant and win their freedom by sacrificing to the gods and to the emperors and by cursing Christ. Pliny decided, however, to execute Christians who would not recant. "If they persist, I order them to be led away for execution; for, whatever the nature of their admission, I am convinced that their stubbornness and unshakeable obstinacy ought not to go unpunished" (*Epistle* 10.96.3).

By the mid-2nd century CE, the churches were attracting more attention from elite writers and governmental officials as a movement clearly distinct from Judaism. Two complementary trends exerted a formative influence around this time. One was the emergence of Christian apologists. Using the tools of Hellenistic philosophy and rhetoric, the apologists attempted to give a reasoned defense of Christianity against accusations of deviance. They could deny the charges of criminal or ethical wrongdoing: Christians did not steal, practice cannibalism, or engage in sexual orgies. The apologists could redefine and rationalize other charges such as atheism by asserting that they worshiped the true God, not the false gods of polytheism. The charge of political sedition, however, was more difficult to deny. The apologists indicated that Christians prayed for the emperor and were valuable inhabitants of the empire. But the apologists stood firm on this point: ultimate authority belonged to God, not to the emperor. If the empire required them to do something contrary to God's will, Christians would rather suffer the consequences than comply.

The efforts of the apologists to defend Christianity accompanied a second trend: growing numbers of Christian martyrs during the mid- to late 2nd century. Only a small percentage of the church membership actually faced the beasts, the gladiators, the executioners, or the mobs. The majority of church members either lived without harassment, avoided confrontation, fled arrest, or renounced their faith. The martyrs, however, became the heroes of the churches. Written records of their ordeals were passed on, and commemorations of their deaths became part of Christian ritual calendars. Their uncompromising stance became the Christian ideal. Thus, by the end of the 2nd century CE a particular Christian political theory was becoming predominant. This theory asserted that government was subordinate to the God of the Christians, that government tended to disobey God, and that Christians should refuse unjust demands of government even if it meant loss of life.

This theory was severely tested in the 3rd century. Churches were widespread and fairly well organized, and popular resentment of Christians grew as the empire experienced serious upheaval in politics, economy, and defense. In 250, the emperor Decius inaugurated the first systematic effort to exterminate the churches and to restore polytheism throughout the realm. He ordered that all inhabitants of the empire should sacrifice to the gods, pour a libation, and eat meat from the sacrifice. Anyone who refused was to be executed. By the end of the persecution in 251, the Christian death toll was in the hundreds.

Other authorized persecutions punctuated the last half of the 3rd century but they were surpassed by one massive effort to eliminate Christianity. The so-called Great Persecution began in 303 under Diocletian and continued under Galerius. A series of decrees led to the demolition of church buildings, the destruction of sacred books, the imprisonment of clergy, and finally forced sacrifice upon pain of death. The persecution lasted until 311, when Galerius issued the Edict of Toleration from his deathbed. Local trials and riots against Christians persisted in some places for several months, but the churches had finally been granted the legal right to exist.

An event in 312, however, turned out to be more significant for the history of Christian politics. In that year, a vision convinced Constantine that the God of the Christians was on his side in his fight to rule the empire. He responded with edicts that required the return of Christian property and made Christianity preeminent among religions. Constantine built monumental churches, gave them huge benefactions, convened councils of bishops, and even contributed his opinions to theological debates. In the years before his death in 337, Constantine declared himself to be a Christian and established Christianity as the religion of the realm. Furthermore, he initiated the process of restricting acceptable forms of Christian monotheism to those who accepted the decisions of the Nicene Council (325 CE).

Some scholars have argued that this 4th-century shift toward a monotheistic political theology was part of a general cultural trend. It is true that certain earlier philosophical and religious groups described the divine world as having many beings under one high god or as having many emanations from one first principle. But these can seldom be described as monotheism or even as henotheism. The crucial factor in the 4th century was the intervention of emperors who sanctioned particular forms of Christian monotheism above all other perspectives.

This was an entirely new situation for the churches. Since the 1st century, Christians had been a peculiar movement within a polytheistic empire. Now they were the favored group in an empire moving toward monotheism. New theories of government were needed that would transcend the Christian sectarian ethos of earlier centuries without divinizing the ruler as in Greco-Roman imperial culture. One theory, associated especially with Eusebius of Caesarea (died ca. 340), exerted lasting influence in the Eastern churches of the Byzantine Empire. Eusebius Christianized ideas about divine rulers by comparing the emperor to Christ: both are empowered by God, both protect God's people, and both vanquish God's enemies. Eusebius also perceived a fundamental similarity between the kingdom of God and the empire: the empire was a reflection of God's kingdom, and both had the same mission. "Having been entrusted with an empire, the image of the heavenly kingdom, [the emperor] looks to that ideal form and directs his earthly rule to the divine model and thus provides an example of divine monarchic sovereignty" (*Praise of Constantine*

3). According to this theory, the emperor guides both empire and church toward God's kingdom.

A different theory of government developed in the West that drew more heavily on the churches' sectarian heritage by denying that the emperor had authority directly from God that gave him power over the church. This theory is associated especially with Ambrose of Milan (bishop 373–97) who asserted, "The church belongs to God; therefore, it ought not to be assigned to Caesar. For the temple of God cannot be Caesar's by right. . . . For what is more full of respect than that the emperor should be called the son of the church? . . . For the emperor is within the church, not above her" (*Sermon against Auxentius* 35–36). This theory grants the emperor responsibility to enforce Christian thought and behavior, but gives him no responsibility over the church. Ambrose successfully defended this position in several dramatic confrontations with the emperor Theodosius I in the late 4th century, and this approach came to characterize church-state relations in the Western church.

To summarize, over the course of four centuries, Christian political perspectives changed radically. All three early obstacles to political involvement were removed. The churches restricted teachings about love for enemies and renunciation of force to the point where they could encourage Theodosius I and other emperors to suppress polytheism, Judaism, and dissenting Christian groups by force. The second obstacle disappeared as the churches accumulated sufficient resources to participate actively in political life. The wealth and status came from many sources, including imperial benefactions, a history of courageous martyrdoms, and self-sacrifice on the part of many believers. The third obstacle was removed as mainstream culture gradually exchanged Greco-Roman polytheism for Nicene Christian monotheism. In less than four hundred years, the movement that began as an oppressed minority within the empire became an oppressive majority devoted to the maintenance of the empire, with two political theologies distinguishing the Eastern and Western churches.

BIBL.: Everett Ferguson (ed.), *Church and State in the Early Church* (Studies in Early Christianity 7; New York, 1993). Hugo Rahner, *Church and State in Early Christianity* (San Francisco, 1992).　　　　　　　　　　　S.F.

Controlling Religion

Introduction

Religion controls behavior: people should do what pleases the gods and avoid what displeases them. This applies inside religion, in everyday ritual behavior, and outside it, in society at large, both in public and in private. Certain acts or even attitudes are correct, legitimate, and desirable and therefore are approved of or actively encouraged, whereas others are wrong and therefore are frowned upon or outright forbidden. This does not necessarily mean that religion encourages the establishment of controlling authorities, although this can always happen; in a less strong and less intrusive way, it is tradition that often, through interiorization or group pressure, makes individuals behave in the way they should.

If religion controls society and its individual members, controlling religion can become vital. From an indigenous perspective, it is the supernatural that controls religion: the gods, or God, make manifest what is acceptable and desirable and what is rejected and forbidden; the controllers derive their legitimation and their guidelines from the divine realm. In theory, this control can be direct, from the supernatural directly to the worshiper. In practice, this is rarely the case. Religion is a social and communal phenomenon: the group controls what is desirable and correct and what is the contrary, and it does so mostly through its designated institutions. If individuals receive guidance and revelation from the gods as to what is correct, they receive it rarely for their own benefit alone but as guidelines to be communicated to and enforced within the group. The control exercised by the society's representatives might be weak, mainly providing for the correct execution of the rites, or it might be strong, sharply defining the boundaries of accepted religion and accepted behavior and punishing members of the group that act outside these boundaries.

In the religious cultures of the ancient Mediterranean, the entire spectrum of possibilities is present. In the city-states of the ancient Near East, control was either in the hands of the temple or of the palace or both, and it was relatively weak: it seems symptomatic that none of the Mesopotamian law codes deals with religious behavior. The same was true for ancient Egypt, despite its being ruled by a god-king and a priestly elite, and for most of preexilic Israel. Kings and a priestly elite were absent from the city-states of Greece and Italy, where the cities and its institutions—the assembly in Greece, the senate in Rome—were responsible for correct religious behavior; again, control ordinarily was rather weak, even if sacred laws in many Greek cities prescribed often small minutiae of cult. Ordinarily, tradition was enough to give guidelines, and tradition was stored in the living or written memory of the priesthoods and the performers.

Extraordinary circumstances, however, tightened control, especially religious reform or public crisis or both. When disaster was seen as the result of divine anger and divine anger as resulting from individual behavior, deviant rituals and beliefs could not be tolerated, and when religious reformers saw their reforms as the only way to vouchsafe divine goodwill, intellectual dissent became religious deviance and had to be suppressed. In Egypt, control became markedly stronger when Akhenaten pushed his quasi-monotheist innovation, even against the resistance of traditional priesthood, and when, after his death, the traditional temples reasserted themselves again. But even in this case, neither party seemed to have attacked religious behavior outside the narrow field of royal ritual: it was very much a dispute at the top. In Israel, the Yahwist reforms led to stricter control and to the exclusion of foreign gods and their rites already in preexilic times, while the prophets' claims provoked a battle for authority over religion which, in the end, the kings lost: the destruction of Samaria and Jerusalem and the catastrophic experience of the Babylonian exile could but strengthen the prophetic claims of divine anger and retribution. In postexilic times, Hellenization threatened an identity built exclusively in religious terms and provoked another tightening of control through the Jerusalem priesthood, as did the struggle with Rome and the destruction of the Second Temple. In Athens, in the later decades of the 5th century BCE, the nearly simultaneous outbreak of a war (431 BCE) and of a plague (430 BCE) and the city's final defeat and humiliation (404 BCE) led to trials and the capital punishment of several intellectuals; but only Socrates decided not to dodge the verdict by leaving the hostile city, and he was executed in 399 BCE. Even in imperial Rome, the persecution of the Christians became much more widespread during the dark times of the 3rd century with its economic and military decline.

Tight control sets in when a community defines itself exclusively through religion and feels the need to defend this self-definition against (true or imaginary) threats from the outside by weeding out any inside alternative. In the ancient Mediterranean, this was almost exclusively the case with monotheistic movements; polytheistic systems ordinarily were too open to serve as exclusive means of definition. While postexilic Israel set the tone in its resistance against outside influences, it was Christianity that more deeply changed the nature of religious control. A very exclusive self-definition soon was controlled by charismatic individuals such as Paul; and institutionally powerful leaders were instrumental in defining Christianity in opposition to polytheist paganism, Jewish monotheism, and the many alternative movements quickly defined as heresies and in setting up strict mechanisms of control. The necessity for definition and thus control survived the victory of Christianity: there were always pagans, Jews, and heretics who threatened the one church with its worldwide claim. The circularity of the process should not be overlooked: once strong instruments of control were in place, be it the bishops or, in Judaism, the rabbis, they created an institutional pressure for ongoing self-definition in the face of the many eroding influences—and thus for ongoing control.   F.G.

Egypt

"The Egyptians," writes Herodotus, "are the most god-fearing of all people" (2.37). He then goes on to describe a society subjected to considerable hierocratic control in day-to-day life, notably with respect to dietary taboos and generalized rules of purity. If any of this is true, it must represent a very late development, as the religious *nomoi* (laws) mentioned by Herodotus find no counterpart in older sources. In fact, the ideal conduct of life expounded by traditional Egyptian autobiographies and wisdom texts seems astonishingly worldly and secular in comparison. This is not to say that certain aspects of ancient Egyptian religion were not bound to prescribed patterns of behavior, but rather that the unbroken authority of fully developed tradition

required little scriptorial or institutional support to function properly. As always, there are some exceptions to the rule, most of which are found in the narrower context of liturgy. Thus, inscriptions on the doorjambs of late Old Kingdom tombs warn visitors not to enter the funerary chapel in a state of ritual impurity, making special reference to dietary taboos and physical cleanliness (Sethe 1933: 201.17–202.11). Other passages admonish the officiating priests to perform the ritual in a conscientious manner and in accordance to the rules of purity required in the Temple of the Great God (Edel 1953: 329), thus implying at least some degree of standardization in the performance of funerary and temple liturgies. Another contemporary tomb inscription even calls upon the lector-priest to perform the ritual "in accordance to this secret book on the art of the lector-priest" (Sainte Fare Garnot 1938: 22), thereby lending credibility to the assumption that the correct performance of the rituals had undergone at least partial codification.

This assumption receives further support from a short passage inserted in the Pyramid Texts, which alludes to correct ritual behavior in a context of priestly qualification or initiation: "NN [i.e., the deceased king] has kept away from the abomination of men, NN did not reach for the abomination of the gods, NN did not eat the *djais* plant, [NN did not omit to purify himself(?)] on the [feast of the] first of the month . . . , he did not sleep during the night[-service], he did not spend the day forgetting his duty at the appointed times of Khepri [i.e., the morning and evening liturgy]" (§2082c–83d). Notwithstanding the adaptation of this passage to a royal liturgy, it becomes evident that a strong interest in the correct performance of the rituals led to some sort of normative definition of ritual purity by the 5th Dynasty, ostensibly through the agency of the lector-priests who compiled a normative list of dietary taboos and ablution requirements, if not even more specific rules of conduct for the liturgical service.

In the standard Egyptological discourse, negative assertions of the type just encountered are regularly associated with so-called Negative Confession (spell 125 of the Book of the Dead) from the early New Kingdom. Consisting of a double list of social and cultic "sins" that the deceased person claims not to have committed, the Negative Confession is essentially a funerary "rite of passage" that was meant to be spoken at the Judgment of the Dead. Bearing formal similarities to the temple entrance liturgies of Ps. 15 and 24, the Negative Confession has attracted the attention of biblical scholars. Indeed, sentences of the type "I have not done such and such" seem to imply the existence of the corresponding prohibitives "do not" (that is, "thou shalt not") "do such and such." However, the use of prohibitives is extremely rare in Egyptian didactic literature, thereby suggesting that they were restricted to the sphere of cultic performance and binding only for the officiating priests.

How the Negative Confession came to include norms of social behavior, however, remains a much-disputed question. Conceivably, the Egyptian conception of the netherworld on the model of a temple precinct might have led to a broader priestly codification of the conditions necessary to enter this sacred realm, although the actual relevance of this funerary concept of holiness for the conduct of life appears rather doubtful. A compilation of prohibitives of the type "thou shalt not" in the Ramesside Ostracon Gardiner 2, apparently formulated with the intention of controlling the lifestyles of priests (and laypeople?), may, however, represent an early attempt at religious didacticism. A noticeable increase of references to the "counsels," that is, the "teaching of god," in the private inscriptions of the 19th Dynasty is no less symptomatic for the increasing relevance of religion in day-to-day life, although their interpretation must as yet remain conjectural.

It is not until the Ptolemaic period that one actually encounters religious teachings that come close to what one might have expected in conjunction with the Negative Confession. They are again found on doorjambs, although not of funerary chapels but rather of regular temples (cf. Grieshammer 1974 and Weinfeld 1982). The evident similarity to the inscriptions of the Old Kingdom is by no means fortuitous, since these texts frame the gates by which the officiating priests entered the temple, as did the lector-priests in the tomb-chapels. Accordingly, the inscriptions address the priests alone and exhort them to perform their cultic duties correctly and in the required state of purity, but also warn them to avoid theft, drunkenness, loud talking, singing, and so on. Somewhat surprising are the many prohibitives relating to the general conduct of life, notably with respect to causing harm to people, handling weights and measures, telling lies, gossiping, and so on. Conceivably, these reflect the central role of the priests in late Egyptian society, who had assumed the task of preserving the cultural identity of Egypt in the face of foreign conquerors, albeit through a profoundly priestly reinterpretation of tradition.

Although of varying length, all such inscriptions are obviously dependent upon a single textual source that might have been known as the "conduct" or "rule of the temple," as they exhorted the priests to educate their children in precisely this teaching. Furthermore, the "rule of the temple" was only a small portion of an extensive corpus of priestly writings pertaining to all aspects of the late Egyptian temple and providing a normative definition of sacral architecture, decoration, and symbolism, but also of festive and daily rituals, offerings, priestly rules of conduct, and administrative matters. The publication of the numerous papyrus fragments belonging to this corpus will undoubtedly elucidate many problems and questions pertaining to priestly literature in ancient Egypt. Whether it will also enable us to understand Herodotus's description of the late Egyptians' conduct of life, which seems somehow reminiscent of Jewish halakah, is by no means certain. In this context, it is worth noting that papyrus 215 of the Bibliothèque Nationale in Paris (cf. Spiegelberg 1914), dating from the late 3rd century BCE, preserves excerpts of several texts relating to a corpus of religious laws. In the light of the highly theological contextualization of these laws by the papyrus, one is of course tempted to equate at least some of them with the religious *nomoi* described by Herodotus. The arguments favoring such a position, however, tread on very thin ice. A priestly redefinition of late Egyptian society along the lines of a "kingdom of priests" would represent a plausible explanation for the tabooistic character of these *nomoi* and appears to find some confirmation in the cult-topographical texts of the Ptolemaic-Roman period, in which the whole of Egypt is interpreted as a virtual temple requiring the observation of priestly rules of purity from all Egyptians. Indeed, texts of this genre, such as Papyrus Jumilhac, the Geographical Papyrus Tanis, and the inscriptions accompanying the processions of the forty-two nomes of Egypt on the walls of temples, include extensive lists of generalized cultic taboos for day-to-day life. Should this be correct, late Egyptian religion might have come close to our understanding of a "book religion," although only the publication of relevant textual sources and new approaches to the religion of this period will provide a definitive answer to the questions raised by Herodotus's puzzling eyewitness testimony of Egyptian society.

BIBL.: J. Assmann, *Das kulturelle Gedächtnis: Schrift, Erinnerung und politische Identität in frühen Hochkulturen* (Munich, 1992). Idem, *Maat: Gerechtigkeit und Unsterblichkeit im Alten Ägypten* (Munich, 1990). E. Edel, "Die Stele des Mḥw-ḥtj (Reisner G 2375)" [= Inschriften des Alten Reiches 3], *Mitteilungen des Instituts für Orientforschung* 1 (1953): 327–33. R. Grieshammer, "Zum 'Sitz im Leben' des negativen Sündenbekenntnisses," *Zeitschrift der Deutschen Morgenländischen Gesellschaft*, supplement 2 (1974): 19. J. Sainte Fare Garnot, *L'appel aux vivants dans les textes funéraires égyptiens des origines à la fin de l'ancien empire* (Cairo: L'institut français d'archéologie orientale, 1938). K. Sethe, *Urkunden des Alten Reiches* (2nd ed.; Urkunden des ägyptischen Altertums 1; Leipzig, 1933). W. Spiegelberg, *Die sogenannte demotische Chronik des Papyrus 215 der Bibliothèque Nationale zu Paris* (Demotische Studien 7; Leipzig, 1914). M. Weinfeld, "Instructions for Temple Visitors in the Bible and in Ancient Egypt," in *Scripta Hierosolymitana*, vol. 28: *Egyptological Studies* (ed. Sarah Israelit-Groll; Jerusalem, 1982), 224–50. R.M.

Israel

Up to the 8th century BCE, the public sphere in the states of Israel and Judah was characterized by the rivalry of several important sanctuaries (Bethel, Gilgal, Jerusalem, Beersheba, and others). At the same time, the state sanctuaries (Bethel, Dan, Jerusalem) were under the control of the kings, but this control affected the financial, political, and cultic affairs more than religious questions (2 Kings 12.4–16 [= 12.5–17 Hebrew]; 16.10–20). The local sanctuaries (*bāmôt* [hill shrines]), were more or less uncontrolled. Up to the 7th century no priest or state official was interested in what individuals in their family cult practiced or believed.

Control of prophecy. Conditions changed from the 8th century BCE on. The prophet Amos (around 760 BCE) pointed out the contradiction between the injustices in everyday life in the kingdom of Israel and its thriving cult (Amos 4.4–5; 5.4–6, 21–27). The prophet Hosea attacked the cult of the local sanctuaries directly, criticizing ritual and sexual abuses that turned them into "Baal worship" (Hos. 4.4–14; 11.2). Likewise he rejected all idols used in the YHWH cult (4.17), especially the golden bulls of the state cult in Bethel (8.4–5; 13.2). Instead of unreflective cultic bustle, Hosea called for "knowledge of God" (6.6; cf. 4.1, 6; 6.3; *daʿat ʾĕlōhîm*), that is, that Israel should remember its unique history with YHWH since the days of the exodus (9.10–12; 10.1–2; 11.1–11; 13.4–8). Thus the discussion about the specific nature of Israel's religion was opened.

The radical criticism of the prophets provoked the first known exercise of religious control in Israel and Judah: Amaziah, the priest of Bethel, reported to King Jeroboam II of Israel: "Amos has conspired against you in the midst of the house of Israel; the land is not able to bear all his words" (Amos 7.10). Because of his prophecy, Amos was accused of high treason (7.11). Amos was not killed, but rather was expelled from Israel to his native Judah. He was banned forever from speaking in the king's sanctuary of Bethel (7.12).

During the 7th and 6th centuries BCE, the prophets of doom came to be more harshly controlled. When Jeremiah in 609 BCE announced the destruction of the Jerusalem temple (Jer. 7.1–15), the priests and the outraged crowd wanted to lynch him (26.7–9, 24). Only with the help of some officials could Jeremiah escape with his life (7.10–15). Jeremiah was forced to obtain a hearing in other ways. In 605 he wrote down all his previous prophecies and asked his friend Baruch to read them aloud in the temple (36.1–10). Again, this was possible only with the support of some officials. But the king burned the prophetic scroll and attempted, unsuccessfully, to persecute Jeremiah and Baruch, who were able to hide themselves for a long time (36.23, 26). Another prophet of doom, however, Uriah, was caught in Egypt and put to death (26.20–23). Later on, the chief officer of the temple police, Pashhur, put Jeremiah in the stocks for one night in order to stop him from prophesying the capture of Jerusalem (20.1–6)—again without success.

It can be seen that the religious control of the radical prophets carried out by the king and the temple priests did not succeed. The classical prophets of doom and their disciples resisted and found ways to undermine such control. They wrote down their radical messages (Jer. 36.1–8, 32; cf. Isa. 8.16–18; 30.8–11), which enabled the prophetic word to survive even if the prophet was forced to become silent or was expelled or killed. Therefore, most of the prophetic heritage was preserved after the fall of Samaria (capital of Israel, 722 BCE) and Jerusalem (587 BCE). Retrospectively, the tradents of the prophetic scriptures became convinced that this control of the prophets paved the way for the destruction by preventing the preaching of God's word (Amos 2.11–12; 7.10–8.3; Jer. 18.18–23). The reasons for these attempts to control the prophets of doom were mainly political rather than theological. Amos and Jeremiah could not be tolerated because they questioned the political and cultic institutions of Israel and Judah.

State-sponsored reforms. Beginning at the end of the 8th century BCE in Judah, another kind of religious control emerged. King Hezekiah tried to control the local hill shrines and removed an age-old idol from the central cult in Jerusalem, the bronze serpent Nehushtan made by Moses (2 Kings 18.4). We now have archeological evidence of this reform. The local sanctuary of Arad in the eastern Negev was closed and buried under a thick layer of earth during Hezekiah's reign. Likewise a huge limestone altar in Beersheba, on which a serpent was engraved, was dismantled during that time and its stones were reused profanely in a building for storing state taxes. Both findings point to a massive intervention by a supralocal authority. Insofar as we can connect the book of the covenant (Exod. 20.22–23.19) with Hezekiah's reform, we can make out how this control worked. The book of the covenant starts with a prohibition of all silver and gold idols (20.23). The local cult places were restricted to those that had an acknowledged Yahwistic tradition. Consequently, the veneration of deities other than YHWH, as had been allowed hitherto (cf. the formula "YHWH and his Asherah" testified by inscriptions of the 9th and 8th centuries in Kuntillet Ajrud and Khirbet el-Qom; see further Deities and Demons), was made a punishable offense (22.20 [= 22.19 Hebrew]). Even mentioning the name of those deities in the YHWH cult was forbidden (23.13). At the same time, the book of the covenant contains many commandments and laws in order to improve the situation of the poor (22.21–31 [= 22.20–30 Hebrew]), including a restriction of debt slavery (21.1–11).

The reformers used legislation to change the religious and social conditions in Judean society. All the commandments and parts of the law were stylized as the speech of YHWH. That means that YHWH himself was presented as the lawgiver, who would have control of enforcement (Exod. 22.23–24 [= 22.22–23 Hebrew]). Thus we recognize a new kind of religious control: the theologization of law. Probably the book of the covenant was read aloud during the main worship services.

The reform that was undertaken during the reign of Josiah (622 BCE) was even more ambitious. It can probably be connected with the core of the Book of Deuteronomy. By centralizing all sacrificial cult in the temple at Jerusalem, it effected the closure of the local sanctuaries (Deut. 12), which still existed after Hezekiah's reform and the Assyrian invasions. Their traditional cult installations, the sacred pillar and sacred pole, were officially forbidden (16.21–22). Because of this, most family cult, which traditionally was carried out at the hill shrines, became impossible. The families had to come to Jerusalem when they wanted to celebrate their ceremonial meals or to fulfill their vows. Deuteronomy allowed profane slaughtering of animals outside Jerusalem (12.15–16, 21–24). Thus the effect of controlling all cultic activities in the country was a far-reaching secularization of daily life.

In order to integrate family religion into the official religion of YHWH, the reformers created new rituals for it: dedicating his first fruits in Jerusalem, the father had to confess Israel's official salvation history (Deut. 26). The Passover feast, which had traditionally been celebrated by families at home, was redesigned as a pilgrimage feast, which the families should celebrate now in the central sanctuary, together with the Feast of Unleavened Bread, in order to commemorate the exodus (16.1–8).

The reformers tried hard to make sure that no god other than YHWH was venerated on all levels of society. Every prophet or dreamer who recommended the worship of another god to the people in order to ward off a certain danger had to be put to death, even if his prophecies proved to have been correct (Deut. 12.32–13.5 [= 13.1–6 Hebrew]). If a relative encouraged someone to venerate another god, one was obliged to institute legal proceedings against that relative (13.6–11 [= 13.7–12 Hebrew]). If a whole Judean settlement was led astray to worship other gods, it was to be banned and burned (13.12–19 [= 13.13–18 Hebrew]). Thus the Deuteronomic reformers wanted to establish an effective religious control over all the society. To avoid abuses, they required careful investigations and restricted sentences of death to cases proven by the testimony of two or three witnesses (17.2–7).

Even the king was subordinated to YHWH's Torah (Deut. 17.14–20). Practically speaking, control was to be the responsibility of local judges and elders; in difficult cases, a new supreme court, consisting of priests and officers, would declare the final verdict (17.8–13). Moreover, the reformers introduced a new idea of covenant, modeled on political vassal treaties and understood as mutual self-commitment of YHWH and his people. This was a quasi-juridical form of religious self-commitment, which again internalized religious control. Everybody who belonged to the covenant was obliged to live up to the Torah of Moses voluntarily.

Under the reign of Josiah, the covenant probably became the constitution of the Judean state (2 Kings 23.1–3) for a short time (622–609 BCE). But even when the re-

form failed after Josiah's death and the Judean state broke down, the covenant became the basis of the communal self-control that formed the characteristic shape of Judaism.

Postexilic Judaism. The situation during the postexilic period can be illustrated by the books of Ezra and Nehemiah. Both Ezra and Nehemiah carried out reforms in Jerusalem under the authorization of the Persian king. Nehemiah's reform is dated to the twentieth year of Artaxerxes I (445–444 BCE). Ezra's is dated to the seventh year of Artaxerxes, which could refer either to the reign of Artaxerxes I or II, and so either to 458 or 398 BCE. The later date is more plausible. In any case, both reformers seem to have encountered similar problems. Nehemiah obliged the people to make "a firm agreement in writing" (9.38 NRSV [= 10.1 Hebrew]), promising to refrain from intermarriage and to observe the law in all its details. When Ezra came to Jerusalem, he was shocked to find that Judean men had married women from "the peoples of the lands" (9.2). He assembled the people in heavy rain and demanded that they divorce their foreign wives and send them away. Only a few people opposed him. The rest sent the women away with their children and made sacrifices to atone for their guilt (Ezra 10). The high priests who ruled Jerusalem during the Hellenistic period, however, do not seem to have been so strict in their observance of the law. There was widespread acceptance of Hellenistic customs during the years preceding the Maccabean revolt (168–164 BCE).

During the Hellenistic period, Jews who wanted to ensure strict observance of the law formed their own sectarian communities. The community known to us from the Dead Sea Scrolls (probably the Essenes) had its own procedures for admission, discipline, and expulsion. We know that this community had some problems with the rulers of the day (the Hasmonean kings), but the sect was not suppressed. The Pharisees had their own separate rules and regulations. After the destruction of Jerusalem by the Romans, the Pharisaic view of Judaism prevailed. Yet it is apparent that the rabbinic authorities did not impose a uniform theology. One of the characteristics of the rabbinic writings is that they record debates among the rabbis and preserve dissenting opinions.

BIBL.: R. Albertz, *A History of Israelite Religion in the Old Testament Period* (2 vols. Louisville: Westminster John Knox, 1994), esp. 1.180–86, 195–242. R.A.

Anatolia

Given the exclusively royal focus of our corpus of Hittite texts and the predominantly official (i.e., royal, religious, or administrative) character of the archeological complexes found so far, one might easily arrive at the conclusion that religion in Anatolia was completely controlled by the state. The overwhelming majority of compositions belong to straightforward religious genres such as festivals, rituals, or oracles, while other, not primarily religious, texts nonetheless show a strong religious preoccupation. All sites excavated are dominated by temples accompanied by buildings of an administrative or palatial nature. Architectural structures, on the other hand, that qualify as houses are few and far between.

The Hittite state was controlled by the extended royal family, headed by the king and queen. Many, if not all, key positions—whether military, judicial, economic/administrative, or religious—were in the hands of family members, including in-laws. There is no evidence for an independent priestly class. The king and queen served as high priest and high priestess; kingship, indeed, was synonymous with priesthood. The extent to which religion was centralized is illustrated by religious compositions found in provincial centers having turned out to be largely the same as those from the capital. Hittite kings traveled the country performing religious duties in the towns they visited. Under King Tudkhaliya IV (ca. 1240–1210 BCE) a nationwide inventory of cults—sometimes described as a reorganization of cults—was undertaken. Officials were sent out to assess the temples and their cults throughout the empire. They reported back to the capital and appropriate measures then were taken, ranging from simple repairs of a leaking roof or a broken statue to changes in the cult itself. Moreover, this undertaking was not the first of its kind in Hittite history.

State taxes were likewise often levied for religious purposes. The logistics of state festivals were enormous, with large numbers of people gathering and huge quantities of foods required. The yearly cult provision of the important center of Tarhuntasa in the south, for instance, amounted to two hundred oxen and one thousand sheep. The city itself was exempted from providing this so that the burden of paying fell upon other communities.

In what might be called a very practical and politically motivated approach, state religion was very open in that it easily incorporated foreign deities of annexed territories into its pantheon. They were often assimilated to an already-known Anatolian god or added as a special hypostasis to a certain type of divinity. This combination of syncretism and incorporation led to the famous "thousand gods of Hatti" regularly invoked in the texts. As a consequence, the Hittite pantheon, with its mix of indigenous Hattic, Anatolian (Hittite-Luwian), Hurrian, and Mesopotamian (Sumerian and Assyrian-Babylonian) deities, faithfully reflects the empire's expansion and all the influences to which it had at some time been subjected. Similarly, the existence of deities worshiped by foreign powers was acknowledged, and in treaties the gods of both parties were called upon as witnesses. All of this is not to say that the Hittites had no sense of their own, Hittite gods, as opposed to foreign

gods. The earliest Hittite deity attested in the text of Anitta, an 18th- or 17th-century pre-Hittite ruler, and a text that is one of the oldest Hittite texts, was simply called "Our God" and contrasted with the Hattic Halmasuit as "their god." That same text, however, gives us the first example of the typical attitude of incorporating foreign deities when Anitta built Halmasuit her own temple in Nesha, the main Hittite city prior to Hattusha. What has been called a characteristic leaning toward a kind of cultural "cosmopolitanism" is thus attested from the very start of our documentation.

So far, the extent to which the Hittite state controlled religion may seem total. On the other hand, the anxieties that many texts convey also suggest that religion often controlled the state and its ruling class, dictating their conduct and perhaps their decisions considerably. Evidence for heresies and persecution seems to be lacking. This may be taken as an argument that popular beliefs and religious practices—assuming they existed—did not seriously run counter to the official creed or were simply condoned. Alternatively, it might point to the ruling class's very powerful grip over society as a whole. The lack of information concerning religion beyond the court circles does not allow a certain answer. In oracles we find occasional examples of manipulation. In such cases, the state did use religion as a pretext to get what it wanted all along. The only thing possibly hinting at popular practices and the state's reaction to them is the explicit prohibition in the Hittite laws of unauthorized use of magic.

Finally, one should be careful not to overinterpret the official character of the sources or the preponderance of religious texts among them. They might give an overly religious impression of life in the Hittite ruling circles. In the genre most closely reflecting the daily life of the empire's administration, that, is, the letters exchanged between the king and his officials and among the officials themselves, gods or religious topics do not seem to play a role of any great importance. The gods' role there is largely restricted to anonymous ("may the gods protect you") formulas of good wishes.

BIBL.: J. J. M. Hazenbos, *The Organization of the Anatolian Local Cults during the 13th Century: An Appraisal of the Hittite Cult Inventories* (diss., University of Amsterdam, 1998). Itamar Singer, "'The Thousand Gods of Hatti': The Limits of an Expanding Pantheon," *Israel Oriental Studies* 14 (1994): 81–102.   T.V.D.H.

Iran

Among the civilizations of the ancient world, religion played a central role in the internal control of their populations and external control against the incursion of foreign elements thought to challenge the internal structures of societies. Although scoffers and atheists could be found in ancient civilizations, the modern concept of secularism was never a factor in the exercise of religious control. That is, challenges to specific religious authority by rival social classes, oppressed segments of the population, or heterodox movements—all normally occurred in the context of religious ideologies.

In Iran, the starting point of the dominant ideology, throughout pre-Islamic history, was the fundamental view that the world is an arena in which the forces of the Truth (ṛta [Good]) contend with those of the Lie (druj, drauga [Evil]). In the archaic hymns of Zarathustra, the prophet, himself a priest and skilled hymnist, speaks in terms of both cultic and ideological conflict with rival groups of priests who venerate the Daewas (demonic deities) in contradistinction to his veneration of Ahura Mazda and the Ahuras (beneficent deities). The triumph of his religious vision (daēnā) over rivals was accomplished, however, through his alliance with the ruler (kawi) Vistaspa. The so-called Younger Avesta, presenting a basically pre-Zoroastrian ahuric religion with an overlay of Zarathustra's reform, constructs a legendary history as a succession of rulers (kawis) engaged with various demonic and threatening forces. Righteous rulers who prevail are accompanied by the royal Glory (xʷarenah; from evil rulers it flees).

Under the Achaemenid great kings, the dichotomy of ṛta and drauga was the ideological premise for the legitimization of imperial power. The Persian law (dāta) that held society together was the expression of arta. As shown there also, cultic control played a part, although this was probably confined to Iran proper. In contrast to the liberal policies of the Achaemenids toward the religious practices of other peoples, the Sasanids adopted one of intolerance that was soon to be adopted by Roman Christianity and later by Islam.

Iran seems to have had a basic tripartite division of society with two elite upper castes, the nobles and priests, and a broad class of agriculturalists, to which was added a caste of artisans. While not a great deal is made of the social structure in the Avesta, the maintenance of social boundaries and hierarchies was an important part of the Sasanid state religion. A challenge to the state-sanctioned oppression of the commoners by the nobility and the Zoroastrian clergy was mounted at the end of the 5th century by a charismatic figure, Mazdak. Drawing on Manichean ideas, he propounded a form of communism that was initially attractive to Emperor Kawad, who saw it as a means of stemming the power of the nobles. Suppressed by Khusrau I around 528, the movement persisted into Islamic times. One strong reason for the success of Islam in Iran was an egalitarian vision of society that appealed to those disenfranchised by Zoroastrian society.

Beyond the maintenance of orthodoxy, religion controlled most aspects of life. In the legal literature from the Sasanid period, one can read about the extent of control in matters such as lifecycle events (rites of passage), fixing of the calendar, oversight of women and children, economic practices, and so on—matters too detailed and obvious for mention here. One thing that is especially pervasive is the valorization of gender. In the dominant myth of creation, Ohrmazd and Ahriman fashion their respective creations in such a way that they are paired with opposites or opposing forces. Corresponding to the good creation of the female entity Spandarmad is the evil creation of Jeh the Whore, who pollutes the primal androgynous man Gayomard. From her fatal kiss comes not only the defilement of menstruation, but also the general corruption of human nature. Thus, by the very ontology of humanity, woman is ritually impure (excluded from cult), morally corrupt (necessary to control), yet indispensable for producing the males who will aid Ohrmazd in the struggle against Ahriman. There are also many other subtle strategies for encoding gender hierarchy. An example is an extensive treatise on embryology in the *Bundahishn*, in which a series of physiological factors in conception are consistently marked for male superiority.

BIBL.: Bruce Lincoln, *Death, War, and Sacrifice* (Chicago: University of Chicago Press, 1991), 209–27.   W.W.M.

Greece

Modern assumptions. If one starts to look for religious authority in Greece in the places familiar from most of the world religions, one will never find it. Sacred books there were none. The historian Herodotus, it is true, credits two early poets with huge influence upon subsequent religious tradition, and although he exaggerates he is not entirely wrong: "Not till the day before yesterday, so to speak, did the Greeks know the origin of each of the gods, or whether they had all existed always, and what they were like in appearance. . . . It was Homer and Hesiod who created a theogony for the Greeks, gave the gods their epithets, divided out offices and functions among them, and described their appearance" (2.53). One might suppose that the claim of such poets to be inspired by the Muses lent authority to their words, but as they said to Hesiod in his *Theogony,* "We speak the truth when we choose." A religion can scarcely be founded definitively on the words of Muses who may or may not be describing things as they are. Moreover, the accounts of Homer and Hesiod differed on many important matters—the identity of Aphrodite's father, for instance. There was a proverb that "many lies are told by poets." Poetic texts viewed in this way could have at best influence, not authority.

Priests and priestesses. Priests and priestesses, too, lacked the authority to control religion, although they possessed prestige. In one sense they were an indispensable part of Greek civic religion. Although there was virtually no ritual act that could not be performed by a nonpriest, in practice priests and priestesses had prominent roles in public rituals, and the many stories of, for instance, appearances of deities to priests and priestesses in dreams prove that they could be seen as privileged channels of communication between gods and mortals. So the points constantly stressed in modern accounts (priests' and priestesses' lack of training or qualifications, their part-time status, the complete absence of any ideal of a vocation for priesthood) did not rob priests and priestesses of dignity in Greek eyes: Chryses, the aged priest of Apollo depicted in book 1 of Homer's *Iliad* is a good counterexample. But there was no such thing as an organized priesthood in Greece (there were only individual priests and priestesses, each attached to a particular sanctuary) nor was there any organization whose authority priests supported and embodied. At Athens and in many other Greek states, front seats at the theater were reserved for the priests and priestesses of the various public cults. This is indeed a notable mark of respect. But it was only at the theater that they came together as a body, and, like any other citizen or official, they had to argue the case for their particular concerns in the assembly.

Several works of Greek literature portray what we might be tempted to identify as a clash between "church" and "state." In Sophocles' *Antigone,* for instance, Tiresias stands up for traditional burial practices against King Creon, who for reasons of state wishes to deny burial to a traitor. But the defender of religion here is not a priest but a quite different type of figure, a seer. And the seer speaks from a position of complete powerlessness. Seers may well represent the best example of full-time religious professionals that Greece has to offer. But there was no guild of seers. They were self-employed contractors, quite devoid of formal power. They could at best acquire prestige and influence, particularly if closely associated with a prominent politician. The seer Lampon, for instance, gained influence with and through Pericles, was engaged in drawing up an important law (*IG*³ no. 76), and participated in the Athenian founding of Thurii in southern Italy (Diodorus 12.10.3).

The role of the polis. Sacred books and a church, therefore, are not to be found. Instead, to find religious authority in Greece we must look for secular authority. The normal principle was that decisions about religious matters were taken by exactly the same bodies as took decisions about politics and war. In Athens, most meetings of the citizen assembly had a split agenda: first sacred matters were discussed, then nonsacred. Sacrifices, priesthoods, and the construction and siting of temples were routine business for council and assembly. Priests were required to make formal reports on the outcome of sacrifices to the council and were even subject to being audited, like state magistrates; priesthood was in fact a kind of magistracy. Most of the so-called sacred laws that are treated as a separate category by modern scholars are simply laws of the state concerned with religious actions, no different except in subject from its other laws. Magistrates had important sacral functions: Aristotle's *Constitution of the Athenians* has disappoint-

ingly little to say about priests, but lists which magistrate was in charge of which festival (56–58).

These are the reasons that in recent years scholars have come to speak of the dominant form of Greek religion as "polis religion." The claim is not that all religious activity in Greece was conducted by the city (polis) or by its subdivisions—that is manifestly not true, as sacrifices and dedications by individuals were commonplace. The claim is rather that, insofar as an organizing body, a "church," existed, that body was the polis. We see this principle in operation most clearly in the society that we know best, democratic Athens. But there is no reason to doubt that it applied, with the necessary adjustments, in every Greek city. At Sparta there were still kings in the 5th century BCE, and we duly find the kings prominent in religious as well as in secular affairs.

The role of oracles. To the proposition that religious and secular authority were largely identical, a crucial qualification must be added. When important decisions about questions of religion had to be made, Greek states consistently consulted an oracle, and, since the advice of the oracle on such an issue was never disobeyed, the decision was in effect delegated to the god. Plato in the *Republic* recommends (427b–c) that Apollo of Delphi be consulted about "the setting up of shrines, and sacrifices, and other forms of cult to gods and *daemones* and heroes, and the tombs of the dead and all the service one must perform to secure their favor. We understand none of these things . . . , [but Apollo,] the ancestral interpreter of such matters for all humankind, interprets them, seated on the navel of the earth." In so saying, Plato speaks not as a philosopher but as an ordinary Greek citizen. Examples are numerous; when, for instance, late in the 5th century the Athenians decided to appoint a priestess of Bendis, they asked the Oracle of Zeus at Dodona whether she should be an Athenian or a woman from Bendis's homeland, Thrace. Oracular consultation was a solution to the problem of securing an authoritative ruling on what was, and was not, acceptable in religious terms: the gods themselves could declare their wishes. This function of legitimating religious practice was one of the most important that the Greek oracles performed. In a sense, then, it was with the gods that authority rested. But the decision to consult a god lay with the secular decision-making body. Gods had no power to set their own agendas. Secular assemblies determined which religious issues needed to be so resolved.

According to Xenophon, if one asked the Oracle at Delphi how to act "concerning sacrifice or offerings to one's forebears or any such matter," Apollo's priestess normally responded "in accord with the tradition of your city" (*Memorabilia* 1.3.1). Tradition, too, had authority. Inherited practices had been validated by the test of time, which had proven them to be acceptable to the gods. In Athens and some other cities, a special body of experts known as exegetes provided advice on matters relating to ritual and purifications. What they preserved and expounded (or so they supposed) were the ancestral traditions of the city in these matters. But even the exegetes probably lacked power to enforce their rulings.

Religious tolerance? If religious authority lay with the state, did it exercise that authority in a tolerant or a repressive spirit? The question is very controversial. In book 11 of the *Laws,* Plato recommends that those who held certain impious opinions should be persecuted until they recant; if they will not, they should be executed. Plato is constructing an ideal society, not describing a real one, and some scholars contrast his bigotry in this matter with the easy-going tolerance that, they suppose, in fact characterized his native city of Athens. Others argue that he merely brought the unstated assumptions of most Greeks to the surface. Both positions are true in a way. Greek society was potentially intolerant in that it certainly had no principled objection to acting against an individual whose religious behavior it found unacceptable. Nobody speaks up for "freedom of conscience." There were political factors in the background of the trial of Socrates, but in the foreground and on the indictment stood a charge of "not believing in the same gods as the rest of the city, but other new gods." A seer, Diopeithes, is said to have proposed a decree in the 430s that "those who do not believe in the gods" and "those who teach about the things in the sky" (astronomers) should be prosecuted (Plutarch, *Life of Pericles* 32). It is doubtful that this led to the prosecution of the great scientist Anaxagoras, as Plutarch claims, but several women were prosecuted in Athens in the 4th century for organizing unofficial cult societies (Demosthenes 19.281; Pseudo-Demosthenes 25.79–80; Hyperides, frags. 171–80). Athens was not necessarily opposed to the introduction of new gods—in addition to the Thracian Bendis being received into the state religion in the 5th century, Egyptian Isis was similarly received in the 3rd century. But these were public decisions, and a private individual who established a new cult ran a certain risk.

On the other side, it is almost impossible to envisage any Greek state engaging in the kind of systematic persecution of freethinkers advocated by Plato. The objection to the cult societies whose leaders came under attack seems to have been that they were disorderly and socially disruptive; the issue was not one of belief and orthodoxy. A wide spectrum of religious attitudes was perfectly acceptable; even if an individual might be suspected of falling outside the spectrum, it was nobody's business to look into the matter; to motivate a prosecution, private malice would be required. Socrates, the one Greek we know of who died, in part at least, for his supposed religious beliefs, was as much an anomaly in his death as in his life.

BIBL.: Robert Garland, "Priests and Power in Classical Athens," in *Pagan Priests: Religion and Power in the Ancient World* (ed. Mary Beard and John North; London, 1990), 49–72. Emily Kearns, "Order, Interaction, Authority: Ways of Looking at Greek Religion," in *The Greek World* (ed. Anton Powell; London, 1995), 511–29. Robert Parker, *Athenian Religion: A History* (Oxford, 1996), chap. 10. Christiane Sourvinou-Inwood, "What Is Polis Religion?" in *The Greek City from Homer to Alexander* (ed. Oswyn Murray and Simon Price; Oxford, 1990), 293–322.   R.C.T.P.

Rome

Roman religion was practiced and controlled at every level of society: in the household collectively, by men and women privately and publicly, in public life by priests, by the senate, by popular assemblies, and eventually by emperors. It was also practiced by soothsayers, oracle mongers, astrologers, and magicians, with varying degrees of social prestige and legitimacy. Religion was pervasive in Roman society.

Precisely because religion was so pervasive, there were no specialized institutions or religious personnel, whose specific and primary responsibility was to control its content or police its boundaries. But controls existed and were repeatedly exercised. For example, when Cicero's house was razed to the ground and a shrine of Liberty erected on the site, the site became sacred. When Cicero contested this, it was restored to his private use in 57 BCE, on the decision of the senate following advice from the college of pontiffs (Cicero, *On His House* 104: "You are the guardians of sacred rites"). A few years earlier, when the women-only ceremonies of the Bona Dea (Good Goddess) were infiltrated by a man, the senate, after consulting the Vestal Virgins and *pontifices,* instructed the consuls to set up a formal public trial of the suspect (Cicero, *Letters to Atticus* 1.13.3).

In other spheres of religious activity, mechanisms of control were embedded in its very practice. In religious performance, a single mistake in a ritual or prayer reportedly and ideally necessitated its error-free repetition (Cicero, *On the Haruspices' Responses* 23; cf. Pliny, *Natural History* 13.10). But not only the act of repetition, but also each story told about infraction and its consequences, however ambiguous and mixed their interpretations, was itself an act of control. To a large extent, Roman religion policed itself.

But as the empire grew, Romans increasingly came into contact with new gods and new religious rites among enemies or conquered peoples. Gods, like slaves, intellectuals, priests, and traders, migrated to Rome. And it was then that the senate and high officers of state (consuls, praetors, and *quindecimviri*—one of whose responsibilities was the charge of foreign cults) had to maintain what we may now see as a delicate balance between conservative traditionalism and absorptive innovation. State control of, and political controversy about, religious innovation is visible in the dramatic stories that Romans told about the introduction of foreign cults. These stories are themselves important elements in Roman religious history and its system of control, whether legitimating or questioning cultic innovation.

One instance is both striking and well known. In 204 BCE, toward the end of Rome's war against Carthage, Magna Mater (the Great Mother or Cybele) was brought to Rome. The populace had been upset by frequent showers of stones. In response to this prodigy, the oracular Sibylline Books had been consulted. There the priests found an oracle, which they reported to the senate, stating that if a foreign enemy invaded Italy, it could be driven out only if the Idaean Mother (i.e., Cybele) was brought from her sanctuary at Pessinus in Asia Minor (modern Turkey). At the same time, Roman ambassadors came back from consulting the Oracle at Delphi with excellent news: Rome would soon win a glorious victory. Disaster, doubt, omens, the senate, sacred books, oracles, interpretations, hope, and above all awareness of the outcome—these are the mechanisms here of religious control.

So ambassadors were sent to Asia Minor, via the Oracle at Delphi. Once again she promised a favorable outcome, but also gave the mischievous instruction that when the goddess arrived at Rome, she must be welcomed by the "best Roman." After predictable competition, a young noble, not yet embarked on a political career, was selected. He went to Ostia, the port of Rome, to receive the image of the goddess, which was in the form of a black stone. The married women of the city then passed her from hand to hand, until she was safely installed in the temple of Victory on the Palatine, before her own temple was built. Her arrival came to be celebrated with a festival and games, the Megalensia.

This was the core of the story. It purports to explain how the cult of Magna Mater began in Rome. But the story did not stop here; religious stories thrive on complexity, variety, and ambiguities. In another version, the ship bearing the goddess gets stuck before it lands. No amount of tugging can release it, until a Vestal Virgin, wrongfully accused of having broken her vow of chastity, prays to the goddess and single-handedly pulls the ship ashore. Magna Mater, in other words, celebrated her own arrival with a miracle, which not only proved the Vestal's innocence but legitimated a problematic innovation: for the self-castrating, beggar priests of Cybele—who arrived as part and parcel of the new cult—were remarkably un-Roman. And although senior magistrates regularly performed sacrifice to the goddess and the Megalensia took its place in the Roman calendar, there were repeated attempts to draw a line between that and the goddess's more "foreign" rituals. Several sources record, for example, that by law no Roman citizen was allowed to walk in her procession (Dionysius Halicarnassus 2.19; Livy 29.10–11; 14; Ovid, *Fasti* 4.247ff.; Herodian 1.11; see illus. on p. 408).

The diversity of Roman religion and the welcome that the Roman state repeatedly gave to foreign cults some-times tempts us into thinking that Romans were religiously tolerant. But religious toleration as a concept warrants analysis. Tolerance presupposes disapproval—and forbearance in the face of such disapproval. It also implies a boundaried sense of what constitutes religion and elevates religious affiliation into a primary identifier. The concept sits easily with Judaism and Christianity, each of which is an exclusive religion; so Jews can properly be said to "tolerate" Christians and vice versa. Roman attitudes to alien cults varied enormously: there *was* tolerance (of Jews, for the most part); but many of Rome's reactions (from absorption through permissiveness or neglect to downright oppression) are not best understood in that way.

The vicious suppression of the rites of Bacchus in 186 BCE by the senate is a case in point (and the first time, so far as we know, that the Roman authorities took such concerted action against any religious practices). The story is told by Livy (39.8–19) with a rich embroidery of sex, violence, deceit, and murder. The unlikely heroine of the tale is a kindly prostitute; the hero is her lover, an innocent young man, whose mother—attempting to set him up for blackmail, so that he will not reveal the villainy of his wicked stepfather—persuades him to become initiated into Bacchic cult. Enter the courtesan, an ex-slave, who is horrified when the son explains what he is going to do. As a slave, she had attended the Bacchants' terrible rites, in which the noise from cymbals and drums was used to drown each young initiate's shrieks of pain as the priests took his virtue. Our hero is persuaded to change his mind and, driven from home, finds refuge with his aunt, who takes the story to the consuls. With great reluctance, the courtesan reveals to the authorities the horrid secrets. Originally, the cult had been for women only and practiced three days a year. But now it was for men and women, happened five times a month and at night, with wine, lust, ecstasy, violence, and sex. The numbers involved were large, including both men and women of high rank. The senate ordered investigation throughout Italy. According to Livy, the ringleaders were rounded up and executed; others committed suicide; women were handed over to their relatives for punishment. The cult of Bacchus was strictly regulated for the future, while the public was urged to return to the traditional gods of Rome, away from the debauchery of women and "men like women." The cult sapped the military strength on which the glory of Rome depended. "Nothing," said the consul, "is more deceptive than a wicked cult [*prava religio*]."

As with later anti-Christian stories, the highly rhetorical presentation makes the story more memorable and helps legitimate the persecution. But beneath the rhetoric is a description of cultic innovation, its rapidly growing popularity, and the state's repressive reaction, motivated apparently by fear of an alternative focus of religious loyalty. Alongside Livy's description, a copy of the decree of the senate regulating the cult survives (*ILS*

18): no citizen was to be a Bacchic priest, and no cult was to have communal funds, exact oaths of allegiance, or appoint its own officials. Significantly, the senate did not ban the cult as a whole; it proscribed those aspects that might allow it to grow large or to act as a rival community or power base within the state.

In preindustrial empires, without effective laws or police force, moral and religious control is operated on the frontiers of normality. Martyrs, monks, and nuns in early Christianity, film stars in Hollywood, and above all the stories told about them create desirable but for most of us inimitable ideals. So too in pagan antiquity with astrologers and magicians, owners and lenders of secret knowledge, stolen from the supernatural. They offered knowledge of the future and tools for its control. They were recurrently popular, of dubious reputation, admired, feared, and always at risk of control by the state. Gods were too powerful to be in anyone's private pocket. "Prophets who pretend to be inspired by god are to be expelled" (Paul, *Sententiae* 5.21).

The Roman historian Tacitus tells us that the exiled Tiberius was fond of consulting astrologers about his chances of becoming emperor. They were universally reassuring. He then asked them about their own futures; but if they did not know, he had them pushed to their deaths from a high cliff. But the great Thrasyllus, when asked the same question, shook with fear. He said he was in great danger. But Tiberius, convinced he had at last found the best astrologer, embraced him and kept him as his favorite. The future emperor now controlled the future—even though, paradoxically, Thrasyllus's answer had been wrong (Tacitus, *Annals* 6.21).

Tiberius's problem, shared with other emperors, was how to monopolize, or at least to control access to, supernatural knowledge. Augustus himself had more than two thousand oracular books collected and burnt. It did not solve the problem. Astrologers and magicians were recurrently popular, and they were repeatedly expelled from Rome; indeed, eleven expulsions are recorded in the 1st century CE. A classic case is the death of the young prince Germanicus Caesar in 19 CE. Remains of human corpses, spells, and curse tablets designed to subject human souls to deathly powers were found in his bedroom. According to Tacitus, Germanicus himself thought he was being attacked with magic (Tacitus, *Annals* 2.69–72). And that eventually was the official opinion of the senate. In the Roman world, there were dark forces that neither state nor nobles could control.

Roman behavior toward Jews ranged from support, through toleration, to mass murder. The principal cause of mass murder was the three Jewish rebellions in 66, 115, and 132, not the strangeness of their religious practices, separatism, or rejection of Roman gods. The Roman conquerors did not insist on participation in polytheism or even in the imperial cult. Indeed, the Roman government took considerable pains to accommodate, and sometimes even gave limited privileges to, local Jewish populations. But individual provincial governors sometimes allowed and perhaps provoked persecutions. A classic instance was the pogrom in Alexandria in 38 CE; the Jews there were beaten, tortured, even killed by pagans, with the apparent connivance of the governor (who was, however, recalled and punished). Soon afterward, the emperor Caligula, against huge Jewish opposition, went ahead with his plans to place a statue of himself in the Holy of Holies in Jerusalem. After Caligula's assassination, Claudius explicitly rejected his policy and attempted a fair settlement between the conflicting parties in Alexandria. They were instructed to live in mutual respect and peace (Hunt and Edgar 1934: no. 212). And it is striking that the Alexandrian Jews did not join the rebellion of 66.

In general, Roman policy and attitudes toward Jews were inconsistent and reactive. Hadrian built a temple to Jupiter in Jerusalem, renamed Aelia Capitolina. This act either provoked or followed the revolt of Bar Kochba. Afterward, central Judea was cleared of Jews. Some scholars think that Hadrian also prohibited male circumcision (but that depends on unreliable testimony and seems unlikely). On the other hand, some pagans clearly thought that emperors favored Jews, a recurrent theme in the political pamphlets known as the *Acts of the Pagan Martyrs*. No less recurrent is Jewish resentment against Roman injustice told in numerous stories in the Talmud and Midrash (where Esau is a figure for Rome). But there are also signs of other attitudes, as when the Jewish towns of Sepphoris and Lydda voluntarily, it seems, changed their names to Diocaesarea and Diospolis (celebrating the imperial name Caesar and the god Jupiter/Zeus—in the form Dio). Unsuccessful rebellion had taken its toll of Jewish identity. But the Romans did not, nor did they try to, crush nascent rabbinism or obstruct its codifications in the Mishnah (ca. 200 CE) and the talmuds. Quite the opposite, Christian emperors in the 4th century temporarily revived a specifically religious Jewish leadership in the patriarchate.

Roman policy toward Christians is difficult to reconstruct, partly because persecution and heroic martyrdom are central themes in Christian myth. From the earliest days, Christians portrayed themselves as victims of a combination of wicked Jews and cruel Romans. But as Christianity expanded, at least some of its leaders sought accommodation with Roman powers. They pleaded for religious toleration, and they pleaded not guilty to the crimes of which they were accused. The emperor was chosen, they might admit, by God (Tertullian, *Apology* 24, 32).

Why then did Romans attempt to control or suppress Christianity? It is always difficult to reconstruct motives. But it would be surprising if Roman irritation at Christian oddity in a polytheistic world and at their aggressive obduracy were not part of the answer. At the same time, it has to be acknowledged that the early persecutions were spasmodic, local, small-scale, and unsystematic. After all, by 100 CE there were very few Christians to attack (a few thousand perhaps in an empire of sixty million). And a letter from Trajan to a provincial governor makes it clear that persecution was not a primary government objective (Pliny, *Letters* 10.97). Early Roman emperors did not have an explicit or concerted policy on controlling religion. Nor did they have the resources or techniques to police beliefs. That said, the last three persecutions (249, 257, and 303–11) were on a much larger scale. They were specifically aimed at Christian leaders, church property, and the church as an institution. By then, Roman leaders perhaps again feared the creation of a state within a state. And by then, they were more conscious that polytheism needed to be defended. An imperial edict of 249 required the inhabitants of the empire to sacrifice to the gods. Several official certificates attesting the performance of sacrifice by individuals have survived from Egypt.

Persecutions effectively ended with the treaty of Milan (312), with Constantine's victory over his last rival Licinius (324), and with the foundation of a Christian capital at Constantinople. Paganism was outlawed in 391, and now pagans were spasmodically persecuted and their temples destroyed, or gradually converted into churches. Finally, the Roman Empire had an explicit policy of religious control, which involved the creation of a Catholic orthodoxy, the support of episcopal hierarchy, and the persecution of Christian heretics and Manichees. But whatever the intentions of its leaders, and they were both varied and changing, the central government's capacity to execute its will was capricious and often ineffectual. Religious control at a local level was more successful.

BIBL.: G. E. M. de Ste. Croix, "Why Were the Early Christians Persecuted?" *Past and Present* 26 (1963): 6–38 (repr. in *Studies in Ancient Society* [ed. M. I. Finley; London, 1974], 210–49). W. H. C. Frend, *Martyrdom and Persecution in the Early Church* (Oxford, 1965). P. Garnsey, "Religious Toleration in Classical Antiquity," in *Persecution and Toleration* (ed. W. J. Sheils; Studies in Church History 21; Oxford, 1984), 1–27. K. Hopkins, *A World Full of Gods: Pagans, Jews, and Christians in the Roman Empire* (London, 1999). A. S. Hunt and C. C. Edgar, *Select Papyri*, vol. 2: *Official Documents* (Loeb Classical Library; Cambridge, Mass., 1934). J. A. North, "Religious Toleration in Republican Rome," *Proceedings of the Cambridge Philological Society* 25 (1979): 85–103. J.-M. Pailler, *Bacchanalia: Le répression de 186 av. J.-C. à Rome et en Italie* (Bibliothèque des écoles françaises d'Athènes et de Rome 270; Rome, 1988). P. Schäfer, *Judeophobia: Attitudes towards the Jews in the Ancient World* (Cambridge, Mass., 1997).   K.H.

Christianity

During the 4th century CE, Christians, formerly the victims of state control of religion, became its perpetrators. The dramatic nature of this shift and its far-reaching consequences for the religious life of the ancient Mediterranean should not be minimized. Still, certain characteristics both of Christianity and of the Roman state remained constant in the centuries before and after the conversion of the emperor Constantine in 312, and these enabled and perhaps even made inevitable state control of religion in a Christian empire. On the one hand, emperors before and after Constantine believed that Rome's stability and prosperity depended upon a proper relationship with the divine, that the emperor was responsible for maintaining the health of that relationship, and that religious practices offensive to the gods (or God) (i.e., "magic," "superstition") should be suppressed. On the other hand, from the origins of their religion, most Christian leaders did not tolerate diversity within the movement: they rapidly developed a concept of heresy as demonically inspired deviation from original orthodoxy, and they formed a hierarchical system of governance to combat it, the episcopate. The combination of these religious attitudes in the era after Constantine fostered the intolerant Christian empire that emerged clearly during the reign of Theodosius I in the late 4th century.

The roots of Christian-sponsored state control of religion are to be found in the earliest surviving Christian literature, the New Testament. The early Christians inherited from their parent religion, Judaism, the belief that, however dispersed across the world they may have been, they formed a single people of God (see especially Ephesians). Shared beliefs, common rituals, and practices of hospitality gave substance to their unity as the body of Christ throughout the world. Although modern scholarship has revealed the extensive heterogeneity of early Christian groups, especially among different geographical centers, many Christians sought to contain this diversity within acceptable limits as soon as communication among churches made them aware of it. A very early meeting of the fledgling movement's leaders in Jerusalem (ca. 42), described in Acts 15 and Gal. 2, shows a willingness to tolerate some differences in Christian practice (in this case, between Jewish and Gentile converts), along with the concern that even such tolerance ought to arise from a universally shared policy.

Tolerance of diversity could go only so far, however, and conflict with internal opponents shaped many early Christian writings. The letters of Paul are filled with attacks on rival Christians, some of whom he accuses of teaching "a different gospel" (Gal. 1.6) and others whom he sarcastically ridicules as "super-apostles" (2 Cor. 12.11). The author of the Gospel of Matthew has Jesus criticize Christians whose views of the Jewish law were more relaxed than his (5.19). The letters of John label as "antichrist" fellow believers with a different understanding of the humanity of Christ (1 John 2.18; 2 John 7). In the early years, the practical methods of controlling diversity available to Christians were limited, for example, exclusion from or refusal to participate in shared meals and rituals (1 Cor. 5; Ignatius, *Smyrnaeans* 6–8) and withdrawal of hospitality from traveling missionaries (2 John 10–11; *Didache* 11–13). Thus, leaders relied on the coercive effects of rhetoric, itself an effective tool in a movement profoundly shaped by a powerful biblical narrative and its resonances.

During the 2nd and 3rd centuries, the monarchical episcopate arose in churches throughout the empire, in part to ensure unity and uniformity within and between Christian communities. Bishops portrayed themselves as guarantors of the sole tradition of proper belief and practice (the "rule of faith"), endangered by the speculations of independent philosophers or teachers (persons such as Clement of Alexandria or Origen), which could lead to such outright heresies as the gnostic sect and the Valentinian school. Bishops bolstered their authority (and mimicked philosophers) by producing lists of their predecessors that traced their succession back to one of the original apostles and ultimately to Christ himself (Irenaeus, *Against Heresies* 3.1–4). Often drawn from the elite strata of society, bishops began to function in ways similar to patrons in Roman society. They dispensed spiritual benefits to ordinary believers through the sacraments and material benefits through a welfare system. In turn, they represented their followers before God and at times before earthly governors. The withdrawal of such benefits, excommunication, was the ultimate punishment available to the bishop in his effort to control deviance within his community. Such deviance, the bishop knew, would offend the divine judge when he and his flock stood before him (see the works of Cyprian of Carthage, especially *The Unity of the Church* and *The Lapsed*).

Unity and uniformity were not only to characterize each individual congregation, but also to prevail between congregations, as befit a religion that claimed to be "universal" *(katholikos)*. Some individual bishops, especially of major Christian centers, claimed the authority to correct other bishops on their own. Drawing on the apostolic example of the Jerusalem meeting, bishops controlled diversity among themselves collectively through regional meetings (councils or synods). At these meetings a bishop of questionable orthodoxy might be publicly interrogated by a learned theologian, not always a bishop, and brought thereby to see the errors of his way of thinking. But a stubborn defendant could be excommunicated by the gathered bishops, who would name a replacement in his see. When a bishop of Antioch, Paul of Samosata, refused to give up possession of the church buildings after a synod deposed him, Christians petitioned the emperor Aurelian, who ordered that the civil authorities forcibly transfer control of the buildings to Christians who were in communion with the bishops in Rome and Italy (Eusebius, *Church History* 7.30.18–19). If the bishops who excommunicated Paul showed any hesitation about using state power to enforce their ecclesiastical decision, we do not

know it. When councils of bishops in different regions disagreed on a major issue, as did bishops in North Africa and Italy on rebaptism of schismatics in the 250s, it was not clear how such a difference ought to be resolved, although participants believed it should be.

Constantine, then, when he became an engaged supporter of Christianity in 312, inherited both an ancient Roman tradition of suppressing offensive religious practices to ensure a good relationship with the divine and a more recent Christian tradition of controlling diversity through the episcopate and its councils. Constantine himself appears to have been comfortable with a vague and inclusive monotheism to which Christians and "pagans" (and Jews?) could adhere, and he expressed exasperation over disputes (such as that over Arius) that to his mind concerned "small and utterly trivial" matters (Eusebius, *Life of Constantine* 2.68). Such was not the attitude of the newly empowered bishops, and the emperor soon found himself involved in state control of religion. For example, when he wished to bestow imperial patronage on the Christians of North Africa and to grant exemptions from costly civic offices to their clergy, he had to choose between two rival churches, the Donatists and the Caecilianists: he opted for the latter on the basis that they were in communion with the bishops in Rome and Italy (Eusebius, *Church History* 10.6–7). This direction of imperial patronage and clerical exemptions to one group or another fostered conformity across geographical regions.

Constantine sponsored and enforced the decisions of the Council of Nicea in 325. This meeting represented a significant advance in establishing and enforcing an international orthodoxy: as an explicitly (if not actually) ecumenical (worldwide) council, it claimed an authority superior to that of regional councils, which had differed on the orthodoxy of Arius and his supporters. The emperor paid for the meeting and presided at its opening (Eusebius, *Life of Constantine* 3.4–14). The full extent of his involvement in the bishops' deliberations is a matter of dispute, but he enforced the council's decisions by sending into exile those bishops who refused to comply. In accord with the long-standing Christian antipathy to internal diversity, the first objects of state religious control after Constantine were "heretics." Exile was the primary coercive measure available to emperors after Constantine, but by the turn of the 5th century heretics faced also imprisonment, heavy fines, and the confiscation of their places of worship (*Theodosian Code* 16.5.21).

Under Constantine and his successors before Theodosius, there was no concerted effort to eliminate traditional religions (i.e., "paganism"). After all, during its years of being persecuted, Christianity had developed a rhetoric of state tolerance of different religions (Tertullian, *To Scapula* 2, particularly eloquent). Eventually, however, it would be pagans who would need to voice such sentiments (Symmachus, *Memorandum*).

Public sacrifice fell into disfavor, and the emperors did not participate in it. In accord with Roman tradition, legislation sought to eliminate offensive religious practices such as harmful "magic" and private divination (*Theodosian Code* 9.16.1–3). While these laws may have fallen harder on pagans than on Christians, their actual effects are not clear since there is much evidence for the continued practice of such activities in pagan, Christian, Jewish, and multireligious forms. The emperors continued to hold the title *pontifex maximus,* and the civic cults in Rome (e.g., the Vestal Virgins and the priesthoods) continued to receive public funds. Most people lived in a hybrid culture composed of traditional and Christian elements. However, the generous imperial support for Christianity, including its building programs and welfare system, no doubt persuaded many to join the Christian fold.

A more aggressive stance toward paganism began to emerge in the 370s and gained momentum under Theodosius I (379–95), at which point one may speak of state persecution of pagans. In the later 370s, the Western emperor Gratian gave up the title of *pontifex maximus,* and in 382 he discontinued financial support of Rome's civic cults. In a move of great public symbolism, the altar to the goddess Victory in the senate house was definitively removed (having been removed and restored once before). In 391–92 Theodosius promulgated legislation that equated sacrifice and other forms of traditional religion with *superstitio* and thus with anti-Romanness: sacrifices were prohibited, temples were to be closed, severe penalties were attached to certain forms of divination (*Theodosian Code* 16.5.5–24; 10.7–12). A law of 408 called for the destruction of images that were the focus of worship (*Theodosian Code* 16.10.19). In the next decade, legislation concerning the Jews took a less protective, more punitive turn, even calling Judaism a *superstitio* (*Theodosian Code* 16.8.24). These laws were limited in their effectiveness because there was no standing police force and enforcement depended upon numerous bureaucrats at multiple levels, many of whom were not Christians or, if they were, sometimes did not share the imperial zeal for intolerance. Over the 5th and 6th centuries, state persecution intensified, as the number of Christian officials increased and emperors turned up the heat on those below them.

The government's official policy of suppressing paganism granted legitimacy to more ad hoc acts of persecution led by bishops or monks and/or carried out by Christian mobs. Two famous incidents in Alexandria—the destruction of the Sarapeum in 391 and the lynching of the philosopher Hypatia in 415—exemplify an escalating series of violent antipagan actions that Christians undertook with the tacit or explicit support of their religious leaders and without much, if any, restraint from secular authorities. A series of laws meant to protect Jews indicates repeated attacks on them. Although not sponsored by the state, such violence flourished in an empire in which non-Christian religion had been labeled "superstition."

As destructive as it was, state persecution of pagans and Christian heretics during the 4th and later centuries did not fully achieve its objectives. Despite the paucity of surviving literature from such groups (itself the result of organized suppression), the evidence amply attests to the lively persistence both of diversity within Christianity and of various traditional religions in the Mediterranean basin to the close of antiquity and beyond. Religious practices that bishops considered "pagan" found new places within a Christian culture. According to their frequent complaints on this score, Christian rulers learned, as did their pagan predecessors, that there were limits to the state's power to control religion.

BIBL.: Timothy D. Barnes, *Athanasius and Constantius: Theology and Politics in the Constantinian Empire* (Cambridge, Mass., 1993). Mary Beard, John North, and Simon Price, *Religions of Rome,* vol. 1: *A History* (Cambridge, 1998), esp. 364–88. H. A. Drake, *Constantine and the Bishops: The Politics of Intolerance* (Baltimore, 2000). Ramsay MacMullen, *Christianity and Paganism in the Fourth to Eighth Centuries* (New Haven, Conn., 1997).   D.B.

Myth and Sacred Narratives

Egypt

Wherever gods are viewed as living and acting beings, they are also believed to engage in various forms of interaction in much the same way as human beings do: positive and creative contacts, struggles, and fights. The gods' interactions, however, have profound implications for the universe and human society. Moreover, they are free from human constrictions as far as time and space are concerned. They are timeless, primordial, and ever present. What humans know and believe about interactions between deities may be called "myth."

In a broader sense, the word *myth* may also be used to refer to simple relations between gods. In ancient Egypt, many gods are associated through husband-wife, father-son, or mother-son relationships, which are posited without necessarily implying any particular action. (Scholars also call these groupings "constellations.") Myths define and characterize the individual gods and establish firm links between pairs or groups of gods who are involved together in a mythical event.

Transitivity is a basic characteristic of myth; the mythical event brings about some significant change in the world. The actual situation is explained as opposed to a former situation, as the result of some event in the sphere of the gods. Most myths are related either to the cosmic and natural environment or to social patterns. They offer explanations, prototypes, or parallels to these phenomena.

The principal myths. The most prominent belief complex with a mythical structure is the one involving Osiris, Isis, Seth, and Horus. Osiris was killed and dismembered by Seth, who wanted to usurp his kingship. After his death Isis recovered the pieces of Osiris's body and used them to conceive his son Horus, whom she brought up to avenge his father, to tend his funerary cult, and to succeed him on the throne. Horus contended physically with Seth and involved the whole pantheon in a long and complicated lawsuit in order to obtain their approval to take over his father's role as king.

This basic scheme can be enriched with countless details and individual episodes concerning the childhood of Horus, the fights between the two antagonists, or the different sessions of the court. It also accounts for most features of Egypt's social and political structure: it offers a model for father-son relations, for the son's inheritance of the father's function, and for the son's care for his father's afterlife through performance of funerary cult. Husband-wife relations, motherhood, childcare, and medicine are reflected in this myth as well. Human factors such as conflict and violence are addressed, and ways of dealing with antagonism are demonstrated. The myth also offers precedent for kingship as a divine function, Horus being the model and forerunner of every ruling king.

Another major mythical complex concerned the origin and functioning of the universe. It begins from the idea of an original, ever-present, fertile flood called Nun, in which potential existence was latent before the solar creator-god emerged, settled on a floating piece of land, and initiated life. Through the medium of his semen, spittle, tears, breath, word, and will, he created the gods, humanity, and the universe with all its components. This creator-god is called Atum; his name is based on a word simultaneously meaning "the nonexistent" and "the complete one." Very early on, he was assimilated to the sun-god, Re. From the middle of the 2nd millennium BCE onward, several other deities, such as Ptah and Amun, were viewed as creators, each of them closely associated with the sun.

This basic scheme of conceptions concerning the origin of the world can be drawn upon in many different ways. According to the context, various aspects can be stressed, different cult places identified as the creator's point of emergence, different means of creation associated with individual major or minor elements of the universe. These variants do not form local traditions and even less competing theologies; they are merely ways of highlighting certain features in accordance with a context outside the frame of the myth.

A third major mythical complex centers on a goddess who for some reason becomes furious and leaves Egypt, raging as a fierce lioness through the desert and through foreign countries, mainly Nubia. Her absence causes sadness and distress in Egypt. A god is dispatched to calm her, to make her change into a friendly cat and return home. Most goddesses of the Egyptian pantheon can be identified with this ambivalent lion-cat figure, and several gods can play the role of the appeaser who convinces her to come back. Many temples located close to the border of Egypt or on the edge of the desert, where caravan tracks met the Nile Valley, were considered to be the place where the furious goddess had reached Egypt once again and calmed down (see Junker 1911).

A variant of this myth tells of the creator sending forth his daughter to destroy disobedient humanity, which has disappointed him. She becomes a bloodthirsty lioness. Seeing that humans are about to be eradicated, the creator dispatches a god who pours out red-colored beer, which the goddess drinks like blood. It is only under the effect of this drink that she calms down and agrees to return. As a consequence of these events, the creator decides to withdraw from the earth and settle down, with the other gods, in the sky, apart from the humans (see Hornung 1982).

Not all gods act within the frame of myth. Some deities seem attached to a concept rather than to mythical interaction and groupings. This does not mean that they are completely abstract figures; if any mythical action involving them is known, it seems to be much less prominent or culturally central than for other gods. One such example is the god Anubis, with his typical black jackal's head; he acts on behalf of the deceased, caring for his mummy or introducing him to the netherworld. In spite of his being one of the most frequently depicted and mentioned gods of the pantheon, no relevant mythical event involves him. The same is true for the god Khnum, who fashions each human in his or her mother's womb like a potter who models an object on a wheel. These and many other gods carry out actions in this world that do not have any known mythical precedents.

The structure and use of myths. We know little about the Egyptian oral tradition, but it was probably quite well developed and important, considering that Egyptian society as a whole was largely illiterate. If so, it is possible that myths were narrated orally as stories. In the textual tradition, on the other hand, myths as narratives are largely absent, in contrast to ancient Greece, for example. No existing text refers to a myth for its own interest, for instruction, or purely for entertainment, and when a myth is mentioned, its details are assumed to be known by the audience already. This worked because in Egypt, myth was part of the society's cultural background and of each individual's religious knowledge. As such, it did not have to be explicitly narrated or taught. Nor were mythical conceptions linked to any specific, fixed wording; they could be expressed in many different ways. The same idea could be developed at length, summarized in a single epithet, or rendered iconographically. The few existing examples of longer texts seldom narrate an entire myth, but rather concentrate on certain episodes, sometimes developing many details in order to serve a specific purpose—to make an analogy or to serve as a parallel or comparison. Temple and cult were the principal domains where myth was deployed. Places, feasts, and ritual objects received mythical explanations and thus were rooted in the depth of mythical time, which conferred on everyday objects and actions a profound cultural significance. Egypt stressed these cultural roots increasingly as it came into closer contact with other cultures in the second half of the 1st millennium.

Funerary texts, hymns, ritual texts, and magical texts are particularly rich in myths. Historically, the funerary texts, written in pyramids and on coffins in the Old and Middle Kingdoms (2400–1700), are the oldest major documents that use myth. Many episodes of the Osiris myth are referred to as a sort of precedent, since the deceased wished to be treated well in the court of judgment, just as Osiris and Horus had been. The creation myth often is referred to as paradigm for regeneration and the emergence of the deceased into a new life. The New Kingdom (1500–1000) enumerates the achievements of the creator-god in long hymns in order to illustrate his overwhelming power. Every sunrise is compared to the first appearance of the sun-god and his rising from the primeval flood. A mystical union between the sun-god and Osiris was believed to take place each night, enabling the two principles of existence to regenerate themselves. Temple ritual often referred, too, to the figure of Horus, whose wounded and restored eye had become the symbol of every offering presented to the gods. Flowers and music were presented to the goddesses in order to cheer them and keep them peaceful. One sought to prevent them from getting in the state of a furious lioness again and leaving the country, as in the myth—a situation that would bring plague and disease upon the earth.

Magical procedures regularly consisted of formulating analogies between a given fact and a mythical event, so as to persuade the current circumstance to follow the mythic pattern—for example, a sick person is implicitly compared to Horus, who once was cured from a fever, in hopes that the sufferer will recover as well. The presence of mythical references and allusions in the sphere of magic, medicine, and motherhood and of objects such as amulets indicates that myth was, at least in part, popularly known, rather than restricted to the elite or the priests.

Myths were also mobilized in political contexts to serve as parallels for, and thus to help vindicate, certain decisions or situations. This politically oriented use of mythical conceptions generated several long and elaborate texts (see Verhoeven 1996). A New Kingdom text also offers an example of conscious borrowing of Near Eastern conceptions concerning a god's combat against the sea; this myth seemed especially pertinent to highlight King Amunhotep II's warriorship and to account for the institutionalization of foreign gods and cults in certain regions of Egypt (see Collombert and Coulon 2000). The 1st millennium BCE was particularly productive in creating new combinations of older conceptions with the addition of new details.

Throughout history, myth remained an open field through which many aspects of everyday life could be explained and made meaningful. Only very few new myths were developed during time. One new mythic conception, which appears only in later periods, is the idea of an original combat in which the creator-god fought against enemies before establishing the universe; it is prominent in texts from the 1st millennium, but is absent from older sources. Texts in the temple of Edfu, for example, present Apophis, the snake-shaped permanent threat to the created order, as primeval opponent to the creator-god (see Goyon 1985). For the most part, however, younger compositions and theological developments rely entirely on mythic conceptions that are known already from texts of the early 2nd millennium. The god Amun, for example, a relative newcomer in the Egyptian pantheon who gained national importance through political circumstances, was gradually embedded in a mythological setting that was entirely made up of older mythic conceptions originally developed for other deities. Theban temple texts of Greco-Roman times describe Amun as primeval creator-god who emerged from the Nun (primeval waters) as a child sitting in a lotus flower and who created the other gods, the cosmos, and humanity through his will and his spoken word. All elements of the Theban creation myth were long known, but their combination still allowed the theologians to express new speculative ways of approaching the unknowable.

Ancient Egyptian myth was a language in which theological and philosophical reflections could be uttered. Essential problems were discussed within the frame of mythical conceptions. Questions concerning matters such as the reasons for the imperfect character of humans, the origin of evil, the permanent threat to the universe, or the possible end of creation were outside the reach of human decision, and only myths were able to offer possible explanations.

BIBL.: Jan Assmann, *The Search for God in Ancient Egypt* (Ithaca, N.Y., 2001), chaps. 4–5. John Baines, "Egyptian Myth and Discourse: Myth, Gods, and the Early Written and Iconographic Record," *Journal of Near Eastern Studies* 50 (1991): 81–105. Idem, "Myth and Literature," in *Ancient Egyptian Literature* (ed. Antonio Loprieno; Leiden, 1996), 361–77. P. Collombert and L. Coulon, "Les dieux contre la mer," *Bulletin de l'institut français d'archéologie orientale* 100 (2000): 193–242. J.-C. Goyon, *Les dieux gardiens et la genèse des temples* (Cairo, 1985). E. Hornung, *Das Buch von der Himmelskuh* (Orbis Biblicus et Orientalis 46; Fribourg, 1982). H. Junker, *Der Auszug der Hathor-Tefnut aus Nubien* (Abhandlungen der Preussischen Akademie der Wissenschaften; Berlin, 1911). Heike Sternberg, *Mythische Motive und Mythenbildung in den ägyptischen Tempeln und Papyri der griechisch-römischen Zeit* (Göttinger Orientforschungen 4.14; Wiesbaden, 1985). U. Verhoeven, "The Contendings of Horus and Seth," in *Wege Öffnen: Festschrift für Rolf Gundlach zum 65. Geburtstag* (ed. Mechthild Schade-Busch; Ägypten und Altes Testament 35; Wiesbaden, 1996), 347–63.   S.B.

Mesopotamia

Myths are widely thought to constitute a separate literary category in ancient Mesopotamian literature. The fundamental reason is the assumption that myths are considered to be distinguishable from other narrative texts, perhaps more closely related to rituals, and thereby more "sacred" than other narrative literature. However, there is an increasing tendency to regard the well-known examples of myths from Babylonian and Assyrian literature, such as Ishtar's Descent to the Netherworld and the stories of Adapa and Etana, as literary creations rather than myths or religious literature in the strict sense, although there is no agreement as to what distinguishes the one group from the other.

Here I will support the premise that most myths are literary creations, but will also bear in mind that the cultural setting changed considerably over the three millennia covered by Mesopotamian civilization. Therefore, one cannot talk in the same vein of the key works of Akkadian (i.e., Babylonian and Assyrian) mythological literature, dating to the 2nd and 1st millennia BCE, as of the Sumerian mythological literature dating from perhaps a millennium earlier.

Inanna's Descent to the Netherworld. "Work of literary art" is a more fitting designation than "myth" for what is often regarded as an outstanding and representative example of early Mesopotamian mythology: the Sumerian text Inanna's Descent to the Netherworld.

Like most Sumerian literary texts, this one is known from numerous duplicating cuneiform tablets from the Isin-Larsa period (ca. 2000–1750 BCE). Whether the text existed earlier than the Isin-Larsa period cannot yet be decided, but it might go back to the Third Dynasty of Ur, one of whose rulers, King Shulgi (ca. 2095–2047 BCE) favored the Sumerian schools and so played an enormous role in the formation of Sumerian literature. Typically, there are some reminiscences of Inanna's Descent in the Akkadian Ishtar's Descent to the Netherworld, dating from the mid-2nd millennium BCE, although its scope is very different, more closely tied to rituals, and structured much more tightly from a narrative point of view.

Inanna, goddess of the upper regions (i.e., the sky), set her mind toward the lower regions, obviously in order to include them among the realms over which she ruled supreme. Her description is characteristically double-sided: what she left is not so much the sky as a series of earthly temples. Before she set out on her journey, she instructed her vizier, Ninshubur, to appeal to the major deities of Sumer, in case she should not return within three days.

On her arrival in the netherworld, Inanna was humiliated by being stripped of all her precious clothes. Nevertheless, she continued to behave most inappropriately with her noisy, aggressive, and pompous conduct. When she tried to drag Ereshkigal, her sister and queen of the netherworld, down from her throne, she was immediately sentenced to death by an assembly of the appalled gods. Ninshubur's appeal to the gods Enlil and Nanna to come to Inanna's rescue proved fruitless, but a third appeal, to Enki, god of wisdom and craft, led him to devise a plan to revive Inanna: Ereshkigal was tricked into handing over Inanna's corpse, which was hanging from a nail, as a gift of sympathy to two genderless beings, the *kurgarra* and the *galaturra*, who, finding Ereshkigal lying in great pain in childbirth, performed a mock ritual of sympathy. They revived Inanna, sprinkling her dead body with the food and waters of life. Yet, on her journey back to Uruk, she was accompanied by the gendarmes of the netherworld, who demanded that she send a substitute for herself to the realms of death. She spared her two loyal servants, who happened to be the first people she met on her way, but the third person she encountered, her own husband Dumuzi the shepherd, infuriated her by his failure to show any sign of mourning. So she handed him over to the gendarmes, who dragged him away to his fate.

Dumuzi appealed to the sun-god UTU, who helped him to escape in the shape of a snake, but he was finally found by the gendarmes and dragged away to the netherworld. The conclusion is full of surprises. Inanna, the goddess who had handed over her own husband to the realms of death, began to repent and bewail his disappearance. Finally comes the ultimate surprise: Geshtinanna, Dumuzi's faithful sister, is permitted to replace Dumuzi in the netherworld for half the year. An eternal cycle was thus established in which Dumuzi and Geshtinanna continually go down to the netherworld and then return to the realms of the living. The story ends with praise for Ereshkigal.

Related stories. It is not immediately evident to a reader unfamiliar with Sumerian literature that the final part of Inanna's Descent could have been told very differently. Nevertheless, many accounts of the same events were in circulation, and if we read the story with these in mind, our impression of the whole text is affected. Dumuzi's Dream is another so-called myth, which depicts Dumuzi as a guiltless victim of an unavoidable fate, not as the sufferer of a fate he had himself provoked by his thoughtless behavior. Dumuzi's Dream elaborates a theme virtually unknown in any other text:

there, an unnamed friend of Dumuzi betrays him. In a completely different and independent version of the concluding section of Inanna's Descent, the so-called Ur version, Dumuzi is seen as not responsible for his death, the blame being put exclusively on Inanna. That text elaborates a theme only hinted at in Inanna's Descent: Dumuzi's faithful sister, Geshtinanna, is tortured by the gendarmes, who try to force her to reveal Dumuzi's hiding place.

These differences are essential to the understanding of the text as a whole: Why were there different versions of the same myths? Do they reveal different trends in the cults of Dumuzi and Inanna? Is Dumuzi's unnamed friend who betrayed him a cover for a god who betrayed him on a mythological level? Or (more likely) do the different tellings simply reflect a desire for narrative variety?

How it has been understood. In modern times, a favorite way to understand such texts is to see them as reflections of particular historical events. Such interpretations appeal to the rationality of our time, but some caution is necessary. Inanna's Descent is not the reflection of any particular political situation—say, an old conflict between the Sumerians and the Akkadians. The suggestion has been made that the shepherd-god Dumuzi represents the Sumerians and Inanna-Ishtar the Akkadians, but such a concept is alien to the text itself.

Could the text, perhaps, rather be the outcome of a propagandistic attempt to expand the cult of Inanna to places where it did not originally exist? The cult of Inanna rivaled the cult of An in Uruk since the 4th millennium BCE. Thus, Inanna's attempt to rob An of his domain, the sky, in a newly published text may provide a parallel to Inanna's attempt to rob her sister Ereshkigal of her domain in Inanna's Descent. But this explanation, too, is unlikely.

Neither is it primarily an astral allegory relating to the goddess Inanna as Venus. It is true that Inanna says, "I am Inanna on my way to the place where the sun rises," that is, she is Venus on her way to her celestial appearance. Yet, this is merely a detail in the larger context.

Could Inanna's Descent primarily be a nature allegory intended to "explain" the annual death and revival of vegetation in a seasonal cycle? This was the opinion of Thorkild Jacobsen, the most influential writer in the field of Mesopotamian religion. In a more moderate form, such an interpretation may appeal to many readers, and one cannot miss the obvious similarity with the Greek myth of Persephone and her mother Demeter, a goddess of agriculture. It is tempting to suggest that this is primarily a cult legend belonging to the ritual of a dying and reviving god, a theme of great significance in the religions of the ancient Near East. Such rituals undoubtedly existed, and features from them may have been incorporated in the text.

That Dumuzi's and Geshtinanna's replacement of one another in the netherworld is an allegory of the changing seasons is an obvious suggestion. Yet, it makes little sense if pursued too carefully in detail. Dumuzi was a shepherd-god and Geshtinanna was a goddess of the wine grapes, so other more fitting candidates could have been found to represent the agricultural cycle, had this been the primary intent. The specific form in which the motif appears in Inanna's Descent seems to be an innovation in Sumerian literature. The motivation for including the motif in Inanna's Descent was hardly to introduce a new agricultural cult, but to retell old stories in a new and surprising manner.

The combined stories. Is Inanna's Descent, then, a "myth" of the dying-and-reviving god? The reason that such a perspective alone cannot "explain" Inanna's Descent is that it refers to only one of the two main themes of the text: First, there is the story of Inanna, the goddess who sought to conquer the netherworld, and second, there is the story of Dumuzi's death and disappearance. The latter is well known from Dumuzi's Dream, where it is elaborated with great narrative skill, but the return of Dumuzi to life is not even hinted at there. Many laments bewail Dumuzi's disappearance and death, but in none of them is Dumuzi's revival even hinted at. So, this leads to the conclusion that there was a strong element of storytelling in the so-called myths, and narrative elements seem to have been combined at times for the mere purpose of telling an entertaining story, rather than to teach a fully developed "sacred" or religious lesson or to conform to any particular ritual.

A multilevel answer. We might then look in a totally different direction and ask whether this is a satirical account of the goddess Inanna and her doings. Even if this is not the only or fullest explanation, it opens our ears to the story's humorous and entertaining features. These are not merely coincidental details, but force us to face the question: How sacred were such texts? The presence of wit and humor in sacred texts is a well-known phenomenon elsewhere, so this does not automatically imply that such a text could not be sacred. If our text is to be considered sacred literature in the sense that it had a religious function, say in a temple ritual, it seems impossible to find an occasion where it would fit. Yet, the text includes many features borrowed from cult songs that undoubtedly were used in existing rituals. There are reminiscences of processions and mourning rites in particular, the feeding and dressing of a divine cult statue, as well as a temple ritual suggesting that Inanna actually went down to the netherworld. So, rather, this was a text that sought to gather as many themes as possible with the purpose of making a good story out of them.

In sum I suggest that we view the myth, as we know it, as an innovative and original literary conglomerate of several features relating to hymnic and cultic phenomena, royal court literature, narrative art, including satirical and popular storytelling, as well as features of the Sumerian scribal school literature.

One might ask who would have had an interest in creating such a text and for what purpose. Certainly the Sumerian scribal schools played a primary role in the formation and transmission of most of the known Sumerian literary texts. Inanna's Descent shares some characteristics of the scribal training in literature, in that the form in which such texts are transmitted to us is not always stable, but is subject to the needs for variation prompted by the use of the texts for teaching purposes.

To be sure, the role of the royal courts and the Sumerian temples was also of primary importance, but we must remember that the text belongs to a setting where the retelling of old stories in new forms was appreciated by an audience, who could be listeners or readers of texts, especially those making use of irony. Irony was the most remarkable contribution of schoolmasters of the Sumerian scribal schools, and their pupils certainly formed an audience capable of appreciating their creativity. So it is highly likely that the Sumerian scribal schools were the place where such literary conglomerates were created.

There are many other myths from ancient Mesopotamia in addition to those about Inanna/Ishtar and Dumuzi/Tammuz. Some of the most important in Sumerian are Enki and Ninhursag, Enki and Ninmah, the Eridu Genesis, and *Lugal-e*. Some of the most important in Akkadian are Adapa, Anzu, Atrahasis, *Enuma Elish*, Etana, and Gilgamesh.

BIBL.: Bendt Alster: "Inanna Repenting: The Conclusion of Inanna's Descent," *Acta Sumerologica* 18 (1996): 1–18. Giorgio Buccellati: "The Descent of Inanna as a Ritual Journey to Kutha?" *Syro-Mesopotamian Studies* 4.3 (1982): 53–57. Stephanie Dalley, *Myths from Mesopotamia: Creation, the Flood, Gilgamesh, and Others* (Oxford: Oxford University Press, 1989). Thorkild Jacobsen, *The Harps That Once . . . : Sumerian Poetry in Translation* (New Haven: Yale University Press, 1987). Idem, *The Treasures of Darkness: A History of Mesopotamian Religion* (New Haven: Yale University Press, 1976). Dina Katz, "How Dumuzi Became Inanna's Victim: On the Formation of 'Inanna's Descent,'" *Acta Sumerologica* 18 (1996): 93–102. Idem, "Inanna's Descent and Undressing the Dead as a Divine Law," *Zeitschrift für Assyriologie* 85 (1995): 221–33. Pierre Marello, "Vie nomade," in *Florilegium marianum: Recueil d'études en l'honneur de Michel Fleury* (ed. J.-M. Durand; Mémoires de NABU 1; Paris, 1992), 115–25 (esp. 117 lines 42–44). B.A.

Syria-Canaan

The Ugaritic myths, most of which were written down by the same master scribe, were found in the house of the high priest, which was situated between the temples of Dagan and of Baal. None of them is completely preserved, and all include obscure passages, so their interpretation is often in doubt or at least in dispute. Comparison of three recent translations into English (Hallo 1997; Parker 1997; and Wyatt 1998) reveals those parts whose meaning is well established and those where different interpretations are still defended.

The Baal Cycle consists of six multicolumn tablets.

Basic scenes and episodes drawn from the life of the court—the sending to and fro of messengers, the paying of visits and providing of lavish hospitality, appeals and threats, alliances and conflicts, celebratory banquets—are transposed to the divine realm and used to express themes of cosmic significance. The plot falls into three parts, of which the first is the least well preserved. It concerned El's support of his current favorite Yamm/Nahar (Sea/River). Yamm demands the submission of Baal (Lord), who resists. In a fight, Baal prevails through the use of weapons made by the artisan/magician-god, Kothar-wa-Khasis (a single deity with a compound name: Kothar-and-Khasis). Later, Anat boasts of having killed Yamm/Naharu and other favorites of El.

The myth of Baal's defeat of Sea with specially effective weapons is alluded to some five centuries earlier in a prophecy reported to the king of Mari, in which an older manifestation of the storm-god, Adad of Aleppo, says: "I have given you the weapons with which I did battle with Sea." That this is not just a metaphor is made clear in another letter in which a servant of the king writes: "The weapons of Adad of Aleppo have arrived. I am keeping them in the temple of Dagan at Terqa." The king evidently claimed to be the possessor of relics of the mythological battle, bestowed by the victorious deity. Whether these were produced and the myth recited in some ritual involving the king we cannot say.

The second two tablets focus on Baal's need of a house appropriate to his new status. With gifts commissioned from Kothar, Asherah (El's consort) succeeds in gaining El's approval of the project. Kothar then undertakes the wonderful construction of the house. After a celebratory feast, Baal takes possession of numerous cities and asks for a window in the house, through which he thunders. We do not know whether this myth was ever related to the construction of an actual temple for Baal or an anniversary celebration of such construction. In its present form, the myth is more interested in the narrative development of the relations among the gods and the elaboration of various mythological details than in any traceable connection to a historical building.

Baal now presumes to take on the last enemy, Mot (Death). In the last two tablets, after lengthy exchanges of messages, Baal finally agrees to submit to the ravenous Mot. El mourns the loss of Baal, and Anat, with assistance from the sun-goddess Shapsh, recovers Baal's body and buries it on Baal's mountain, Mount Saphon. A proposed substitute for Baal, Athtar, is not big enough for Baal's throne. Longing for Baal, Anat takes hold of Mot and destroys him, scattering his remains over land and sea. Upon Baal's revival, the means of which are unclear to us due to breakage in the text but that are heralded in a mantic dream of El, Baal strikes down his enemies and resumes his rule. After seven years, Mot also reappears and the two fight to exhaustion. Shapsh then warns Mot that El will depose him if he continues to oppose Baal. The concluding lines, probably addressed to Baal, seem to assure him of the continued

support of Shapsh in her journey through the underworld and of Kothar in his magical power over the sea monsters. While different gods compete for spheres of dominion within the cosmos and Baal acquires the greatest power, El remains the old patriarch of the gods.

Several other fragments contain brief passages also found in the Baal Cycle, sometimes with previously unknown material. It is not clear whether they derive from different oral renderings of the same myth or from different myths using some similar material or whether they are the free compositions—or exercises—of scribes working within a broader tradition. Nor do these variant versions allow us to define any clear interpretative trends. It is necessary to look at the poets of Judah and even later Hellenistic writers to find significant reinterpretation of these myths (Yahwistic, henotheistic, euhemeristic).

The three recovered tablets of the Epic of Aqhat, although focusing on a human family, have in common with the Baal Cycle many poetic formulas and even groups of verses, as well as such thematic material as death and the response to it. Danel is depicted in a ritual that leads to El's blessing of him and the birth of a son, Aqhat. Kothar pays a visit and presents Danel with a bow, which he bestows on Aqhat. Anat offers Aqhat first riches and then immortality in exchange for the bow. Correspondingly, Aqhat refers her to Kothar, then accuses her of deceitfully promising the impossible. With a threat, Anat leaves for El's abode, where she extorts from him permission to have her way with Aqhat. She then contrives Aqhat's death by flying above him among birds of prey and launching against him a companion in arms whom she has tucked into her belt. Unaware of this, Danel and his daughter, Paghat, perform ritual words and acts to revive the now-dying vegetation. Messengers come and announce the news of Aqhat's death. With Baal's assistance, Danel recovers Aqhat's remains from the mother of the birds. After burying him, cursing the nearest settlements, and mourning for seven years, he responds to Paghat's request to bless her on a mission of vengeance. The third tablet concludes with Paghat's arrival at the camp of Anat's henchman, wearing male garb, including a weapon, under her woman's outfit, and drinking with him. The lack of an ending leaves the final resolution uncertain.

The gods reward dutiful piety or punish rash defiance, but the family largely fends for itself following Aqhat's death. The tale emphasizes family roles and especially rituals (particularly after Aqhat's death), and many of the critical events occur in conjunction with meals. Both Anat's relationship with Aqhat and Paghat's with Anat's henchman depict females assuming traditional male interests and roles.

Twice Danel is portrayed ensuring justice for widows and orphans, which leads some to conclude that he is a king (and to read the word for "king" in another difficult context). But good village elders also assure the weak of justice (see Job 29, especially vv. 12–17), and in general Danel is portrayed like a biblical patriarch, without any royal trappings or court.

The subject of the Epic of Kirta, however, is clearly a king, more specifically the relations between a king (the god's "son") and his god (the king's "father"). In the prologue we learn that Kirta has lost his entire family. El appears to him in a dream and directs him to mount a military expedition to a distant city to demand the king's daughter as his wife. Kirta goes and successfully negotiates for the woman, and El and the gods assemble to bless the marriage with multiple offspring. But Kirta forgets to fulfill a vow that he had made to Asherah, contingent on the success of his expedition. Consequently he becomes sick and the land suffers a drought. Neither the royal nor the divine court can do anything to help Kirta. Finally, El creates an ad hoc creature who flies to Kirta and removes the disease. No sooner is Kirta cured than his oldest son accuses him of neglecting his duties as the guarantor of justice and proposes to replace his father. Kirta curses him. This concludes the last of the three recovered tablets. Kirta suffers the three threats that all kings feared: lack of succession, sickness and death, and deposition (overzealous succession). El's extraordinary benevolence, wisdom, and effectiveness displace all other significant divine activity in providing the solutions to Kirta's problems and maintaining the unsteady institution of monarchy.

We have no external evidence about the contexts in which any of these works were performed. There are, however, some scenes in the major poems that suggest possible social settings. Baal 3.1.18–22 depicts a feast at which, while meat is served and the wine flows:

He rises, tunes his voice, and sings,
with cymbals in the musician's hands.
With lucid voice the young man sings
about [or for] the Lord on lofty Zaphon.

If the authors envisaged myths among such songs, we may speculate that as the musician sang them to the gods on Mount Zaphon, so minstrels sang them to the elite of Ugarit. Perhaps the Baal myths in particular were sung at religious feasts in the presence of the court. In Aqhat 1.6, Anat promises Aqhat life without death and depicts a scene that is a model for what she will do:

As Baal revives, then invites,
invites the revived to drink,
and they tune the voice, sing over him,
delightfully respond to him—
so I will revive Aqhat the Hero.

(Some scholars understand Anat's analogy as referring to Baal's own revival after his sojourn in the underworld.) This invites the speculation that some myths were sung in celebration of a recovery from serious illness (a confrontation with the realm of Mot).

There are a few shorter myths, all fragmentary. In one, a cow, pregnant by Baal, bears him a bull, which Anat tends. It ends with her ascending Baal's mountain and delighting him with news of the birth. This is reminiscent of a brief episode in the Baal Cycle (just before his submission to Mot), in which Baal copulates with a cow and produces offspring. Another fragmentary myth tells of two maids of the gods giving birth to tauromorphic creatures called Eaters and Tearers and of their relations with Baal. Three damaged and obscure tablets recount activities of the Rapiuma (shades of the [especially royal] dead). In different fragments, they are invited to a banquet, in one case at least in El's house; ride with horses and chariots to the threshing floors and plantings; and enjoy a rich feast for seven days, at the end of which Baal appears. Danel is also mentioned.

The main Ugaritic myths, especially Baal, but also Aqhat, have sometimes been interpreted as ritual texts, used especially in conjunction with the agricultural year. In the last three decades that approach has been severely criticized and largely abandoned, especially because of its failure to recognize the literary characteristics of the poems as we have them. Some of the shorter myths, however, have very clear indications of a ritual use or context.

One such text, almost complete, is unique in beginning with twenty-nine lines of liturgical material. Then, after a lengthy account of El's establishing the right relationship with two women, the myth tells of his impregnation of them and of the birth first of Shahar (Dawn) and Shalim (Dusk) and then of the "Gracious Gods" (although some think this is a repetition involving the same gods under a different name) who are characterized as all-consuming (like Mot). Insatiable, these gods are given over to the wilderness. After seven years of hunting there, they approach the guard of the arable land, seeking bread and wine. He apparently caters to their needs.

The opening liturgy calls on the Gracious Gods to eat bread and drink wine and speaks of the trimming of Mot as of a grapevine and of Shapsh's effect on the grapes. It has been suggested that the "gracious" gods represented a late threat to the grape harvest and that the myth and its accompanying ritual were designed to keep them away until the completion of the vintage, when they would be won over by a share in the harvest.

Although scribal errors indicate that the copies recovered, which date to the 13th century BCE, were not the first written versions of the myths, they are probably very close to their oral sources. They certainly depend heavily on traditional formulaic language (partially shared by later Hebrew poetry), epic repetition, and widely used motifs and tale types. It is difficult, however, to establish any direct borrowing from another culture.

BIBL.: W. W. Hallo et al. (ed.), *The Context of Scripture,* vol. 1: *Canonical Compositions from the Biblical World* (Leiden: Brill, 1997), esp. 239–356. S. B. Parker (ed.), *Ugaritic -*

Narrative Poetry (Writings from the Ancient World 9; Atlanta: Scholars Press, 1997). Nicholas Wyatt, *Religious Texts from Ugarit* (Sheffield: Sheffield Academic Press, 1998).   S.B.P.

Israel

The Hebrew Bible is part of ancient Near Eastern literature and religion. As such, it shares with the latter diverse genres, motifs, and terms—even as these elements have been molded (by many different circles and authors) to suit the reality of a new national religion centered on a supreme deity named YHWH, during a millennium of growth and creativity (between the 12th and 2nd centuries BCE). This deity is variously portrayed as a complex and powerful personality, evincing a forceful will (demanding allegiance) and mutable emotions (of wrath and mercy). Both of these characteristics are deemed actual traits manifested in the world in different ways. The divine will is communicated either directly or through interpreted signs to persons, whereas the emotions are expressed through the events of history and of nature, both of which serve as agents of divine purpose. Nowhere are these personality traits presumed to be mere tropes. Rather, all spheres of religious life (the cult, covenant, prophecy, and prayer) presuppose their ontological veracity, even if the "ways" of this deity surpass comprehension.

Typically, within this ancient Near Eastern horizon, mythic activity involves the divine world (the pantheon) at the time of world origins; at foundational events (such as temple building) or their destruction; and at the time of divine battles for their devotees. Among the vast anthology of traditions that comprise the Hebrew Bible, many of these mythic topics recur within the predominating historical genres; but also within the context of prophecy, prayer, and sapiential instruction. Over all, these diverse genres reflect numerous realizations of these mythic themes (i.e., of world origins, foundations of sacred sites, and divine advents to rescue the people), with different degrees of mythic poignancy and drama—all depending upon rhetorical purpose or narrative emphasis. But this does not mean that the more muted or allusive forms are only figures of speech or that the more magnified ones are mere hyperboles. Due caution is required for every term, in order to determine the valence of the mythic forms used. Such considerations have particular bearing on the evaluation or understanding of the austere account of creation in Gen. 1 or the evaluation of the more poetic depictions found in the Psalms. Moreover, the present arrangement of the texts of scripture should not be taken to indicate that certain accounts and their ideologies (like Gen. 1) were always the only or predominant version. Rather, ancient Israelite religious expressions are everywhere polymorphous and polyvalent; and this means that many mythic modes circulated for different purposes. Such caveats are crucial for understanding this complex subject.

Ancient Israel. The theme or account of world origins recurs throughout the Hebrew Bible in diverse renditions. In the opening narrative of Genesis (1.1–2.4) this event is depicted in schematic form, with little dramatic action and a greater emphasis upon verbal fiat. Traces of the widespread Near Eastern theme of strife with the ancient waters are muted here (a reference to the "deep," or Tehom, evokes the Babylonian sea dragon Tiamat, but without her malevolent antagonism); and an indication of the heavenly host is marked by God's proclamation, "Let us make humankind in our image, according to our likeness" (1.26 NRSV), although other details are wanting, and the subsequent statement reformulates the act only in terms of the creator-god's sole sovereignty and image (1.27). For all that, the account pulses with mythic realism. Elsewhere, more explicit references to a combat with the sea monster are given, even using divine names and verbs known from Canaanite myths. Particularly notable is a psalm reference to YHWH as the ancient who "crushed" the power of Yamm (Sea), "broke the heads of the sea dragons," and "smashed the heads of Leviathan" (Ps. 74.13–15), as well as a prophetic reference to the mighty "arm of YHWH," which in olden times "hewed Rahab and pieced the dragon" (Isa. 51.9).

These epitomes of ancient battles are recalled or evoked in order to induce the renewal of divine might in the present. Such living religious contexts attest to the dramatic reality of these mythic allusions and show how such events served as precedents for the present. Any simple distinction between myth and history is thus not tenable. Indeed these triumphs also served as models for depicting such historical victories as the quelling of the sea at the exodus, both in prayer (Ps. 77.16–19 [= 77.17–20 Hebrew]) and prophecy (Isa. 51.10), as well as in the narrative and epic versions of this event (in Exod. 14.16, Moses appears as the hero with his sea-cleaving staff of victory; in 15.7–8, God is portrayed as the sovereign victor who blasts the seas with winds and fury). Similarly, future victories over historical enemies draw on such scenes from mythic combats (note Hab. 3.5–13) and even use ancient epithets attributed to these monsters (Isa. 27.1). Comparison with Mesopotamian and Canaanite myths thus shows that the biblical language is part and parcel of a widespread mythic tradition, particularized in different forms in the cultures of each region. It even infiltrated wisdom circles for other rhetorical purposes (cf. Job 26.11–13). Hence the absence in the Hebrew Bible of mythic narratives in their own right does not diminish the palpable vitality of the imagery we do have or its effect.

The frequent portrayal of YHWH's advent with the imagery of a storm-god dominates the theophany of Sinai and shows how such mythic depictions could influence the presentation of a scene of covenant making and lawgiving (Exod. 19–20). And if the divine appearance here magnifies the meteorological effects and

The tabernacle shown on a wheeled vehicle in a relief at the synagogue of Capernaum, 3rd century CE. *Photo by Z. Radovan, Jerusalem*

mutes the presence of a heavenly retinue, this is reversed in epitomes of this event found in more poetic versions (cf. Deut. 33.2–3; Ps. 68.16–19 [= 68.17–20 Hebrew]). Such a topos also underlies other dramatic portrayals of the advent of God as a figure of justice and might, surrounded by enclosures of clouds and preceded by a vanguard of fiery flame (Ps. 97.2–6). This imagery (and its like) echoes similar ones in ancient Near Eastern texts, where such concrete depictions of the chariot and divine embodiments of doom (fire or plague) recur. By the same token, one should not assume that the depiction of God's chariot set on a foundation of "justice and right" (*ṣedeq ûmišpāṭ*) is mere piety or metaphor; for in old Canaanite god lists just this dyad (*ṣdq umšpṭ*) was the embodiment of these virtues, and this old tradition even survives into Roman-era sources under the name of Philo of Byblos). Hence the biblical formulation may also be a component of the chariot complex in the heavenly world, with the elements justice and right serving as divine realities of some sort—embodiments or agents of divine attributes and values.

The divine retinue appears in a host of biblical sources, in such a way that the realms of myth and history interpenetrate one another in diverse ways. The beings of this retinue are thus not only characters in some old mythic episodes, like the apocopated account of the miscegenation done by the "divine beings" (*běnê-hā'ĕlōhîm*) upon womankind in primordial times (Gen. 6.2–4); they also appear as agential "spirits" of the divine court in later historical narratives (cf. 1 Kings 22). In some cases, specific figures of this realm announce public or private benefits—as does the warrior-prince of YHWH's army (Josh. 5.13–15) or the mysterious "messenger" of good tidings to Manoah (Judg. 13.3). In other texts, such messengers bring divine dooms against humans (Ezek. 9). In still other mythic traditions, events pertaining to that realm are transmitted. According to

one instance, the eviction of some of these divine beings from this divine realm is linked to misdemeanors regarding their governance of the nations (Ps. 82); in other cases the precise reason for eviction is not specified, although the banishment serves as a literary trope for other rhetorical purposes (cf. the use of Helel ben Shahar's fall in Isa. 14.3–15). Similarly, the prologue to Job is evidently a fictive transfiguration of an established mythic topos, if not some mode of myth itself. A later and different version of this heavenly court scene informs the apocalyptic vision portrayed in Dan. 7. In it, myth transfigures the very facts of history.

The desert tabernacle and the temple in Jerusalem, as seats of God's indwelling on earth, are both rife with mythic notions and depictions. It will suffice here to note that the tabernacle and its appurtenances conform to a heavenly prototype (Exod. 25.40) and that the temple is the throne of the visible Glory of God, which is dramatically abandoned when the shrine is destroyed (cf. Ezek. 10.18–19; 11.22–23). Only in a later vision is there a depiction of the restoration of the Glory to its old seat on earth (43.2–4). Similar sequences of a god abandoning a cultic site (because of defilement) and a later resumption of presence are found in the lament genres of old Mesopotamia.

Altogether, the materials of the Hebrew Bible continue the rich mythic traditions of the ancient Near East, reformulated and reformed to fit the particular monotheistic modalities of ancient Israel. Although the dominant focus of this scriptural record is historical, these texts vibrate with distinct mythic valences—sometimes along the edges, but even at their theological core.

Early Judaism. A panoply of mythic elements and attitudes are found in the midrash collections (exegetical and homiletical) and two talmuds (Jerusalem and Babylonian) of ancient rabbinic culture. Two distinct trajectories are evident. On the one hand, older themes from ancient Israel and Mesopotamia are cited, revitalized, and even expanded with bold vigor; and on the other, newer themes are presented or invented, based on oral traditions otherwise unknown and on remarkable transformations of a host of biblical elements. Both tracks are aided by the phenomenon of a canonical corpus of sacred scripture. Its many topics and language were sifted and spliced to create new mythic forms and formulations, even as its words and images provide the authoritative anchor for independent developments or innovations. The linkage between the myths and the biblical text is a characteristic feature of rabbinic myths in their present form. Whether such links are matters of primary exegesis or secondary justification, their net effect is to give scripture new mythic dimensions.

The foundational events of the Pentateuch are of preeminent significance for rabbinic myth. The creation account in Gen. 1 is central and provides the setting for integrating pertinent mythic units from other parts of scripture, as well as traditions that survived orally (with many verbal and thematic continuities with ancient Near Eastern materials). Particularly notable are various accounts of a divine battle between the creator-god and a personified sea (cf. Babylonian Talmud, tractate *Baba Bathra* 74b–75a and Tanhuma [ed. Buber], tractate *Huggat* 1), although it is equally notable that such combats do not constitute a theomachy prior to the establishment of cosmic order but a rebellion of the waters in the course of the divine acts of creation—resisting the command to gather in certain areas, and the like. In some of these texts, the rebellious waters of Tehom were either suppressed or sealed over and lie below such sacred sites as the temple in Jerusalem. Among other mythic accounts of world origins found in rabbinic sources, one may mention the case of God throwing a stone into the watery deep (cf. Babylonian Talmud, tractate *Yoma* 54b).

The exodus from Egypt provides another foundational moment for rabbinic myth. Of particular dramatic moment are accounts of how God himself sympathetically participated in the servitude of the people (making brickwork in heaven) and was also liberated with the nation. These teachings provide poignant and powerful images of God's providential involvement with Israel's history and are linked to scriptural passages by bold exegetical elements (cf. *Mekilta de-Rabbi Ishmael, Bo* 14). Other myths portray the participation of God in several national exiles and promise his return with the people's redemption (ibid.). Different dramas even portray God as binding his own arm behind him for the duration of the exile, in sympathy with Israel's travail, and his liberation of his arm during the occasion of Israel's salvation. Such texts are bold and graphic and also linked to scriptural proofs (cf. *Pesiqta de-Rab Kahana* 17.5). In these instances, and many others, myth and history are complexly and boldly intertwined.

Temple traditions also have marked mythic reso-nances and include features of an erotic nature, echoing traditions about a sacred marriage in Mesopotamian myths—although these rabbinic cases are based on biblical proofs (Babylonian Talmud, tractate *Yoma* 54a). Other mythic traditions deal with the withdrawal of the Shekinah heavenward, after the destruction of the shrine, or its various travails and travels with Israel into the Babylonian exile. These myths were also recited in liturgical poetry, thus ensuring their occurrence within the ancient synagogue. In this way, as well, old rabbinic theology was suffused with the dramatic imagery of myth. There was therefore no gap between the features of biblical myth and their multiform elaborations in medieval sources, but rather an unbroken tradition of Jewish mythmaking and mythic theology.

BIBL.: Richard Clifford, *Creation Accounts in the Ancient Near East and the Bible* (Washington, D.C.: Catholic Biblical Association, 1994). Frank M. Cross, *Canaanite Myth and Hebrew Epic* (Cambridge: Harvard University Press, 1973). Michael Fishbane, *Biblical Myth and Rabbinic Mythmaking* (Oxford: Clarendon, 2003). John Rogerson, *Myth in Old Testament Interpretation* (New York: de Gruyter: 1974).M.F.

Anatolia

When discussing Hittite myth, rather than thinking in terms of "a tradition," we need to think about "traditions," for there were, as a matter of fact, two traditions that went into creating what we now call Hittite myth: an Anatolian (Hattic) tradition and another, foreign tradition—essentially Hurrian, but drawing on Babylonian myths as well. We also need to remember that Hittite myths were not merely narrated as stories; some myths were recited and enacted at important festivals in the hope that, by reminding the gods of how they had put an end to some disorder or calamity in mythic times, the myths would motivate the gods to act in similar ways again and benefit current worshipers. Cuneiform tablets relating Hittite myths were found in the library archives at Hattusha, the capital of the Hittite Empire: they generally date to the 13th century BCE but are copies made from more ancient documents, which were themselves translations or adaptations of Hattian, Hurrian, or Babylonian stories.

Anatolian myths. These very ancient stories were gradually adopted by the Indo-European migrants into central Anatolia. They are generally linked to the cycle of the seasons or to exceptional happenings in nature.

The myth of the dragon Illuyanka, associated with the spring festival, evokes the combat between a dragon and the weather-god, which probably symbolized the struggle between the forces of the reawakening nature and the sterile forces of winter. The goddess Inara, a Hattian divinity who protects the living forces of nature, invites the dragon to come up from his hole, gives him too much to drink and to eat, and binds him, once he is drunk, with a rope; she then hands him over to the weather-god, who kills him. Inara is helped in these tasks by a mortal, Hupasiya, whom she eventually locks up in a house and forbids to look out of the window, in order that he might not see his wife and children. Hupasiya disobeys Inara, and in her fury, Inara destroys the house. The myth thus emphasizes both that the gods need human help and that the gods are loath to allow humans freedom.

A second, but fragmentary, version of this myth says that the defeated weather-god recovered magically and slew the dragon as well as a son who had been born to the weather-god and a mortal woman because that son had married the dragon's daughter. In its general outline, if not in all its details, the story reminds one of the struggle between Zeus and the giant, dragonlike Typhon in Greek myth.

The theme of the missing god is typically Anatolian, although it is also found in other Mediterranean cultures: an irritated god has disappeared and has to be coaxed out of his bad mood and sulkiness, with the help of a *mugawar* prayer so that the disorder his disappearance has caused may end.

The most famous of these myths, as found in three parallel versions, is that of Telipinu, the great Hattian god of vegetation, son of the weather-god. Having departed in a fit of rage and hidden in a marsh, Telipinu sits, his whereabouts unknown to the other gods. They seek him unsuccessfully for a long time. When they do eventually find him, Telipinu refuses to move. Only the magician-goddess Kamrusepa can soothe Telipinu and placate his anger. The myth is, among other things, seasonal and etiological, linked to the return of spring. The same narrative scheme applies to stories that narrate the disappearance of a weather-god, of the sun (a solar eclipse), of the moon (a lunar eclipse), of Inara, of the goddesses Anzili and Zurki, or of another god particularly venerated by a Hittite queen.

We must also mention a myth that narrates the adventures of Telipinu and the ocean's daughter, which unfortunately exists only in a fragmentary state. We glimpse Telipinu trying to bring the sun-god of the sky back from the bottom of the ocean. The sun is accompanied, when he returns, by the daughter of the ocean, whom Telipinu marries. This myth probably emphasizes the connection between the fertilizing water born of the ocean and the fertility of nature.

Foreign myths. Hittite myths that are of an essentially Hurrian origin have reached us thanks to Hittite translations found on tablets in Hattusha. These texts evince what can genuinely be described as a theology, characterized by the combination of important Sumerian gods and beliefs with religious thought as it was developing among the Hurrians in northern Syria. Two great mythical stories, Kingdom in Heaven and the Song of Ullikummi, stand out, both of which concern Kumarbi and seek to establish the predominance of Teshub, the great Hurrian weather-god, who was victorious over Kumarbi and became king of the gods (as expressed by his Hurrian epithet, *šarri* [king]). This god served as the model of the ideal ruler—pugnacious and triumphant, surrounded by a court of gods.

The establishment of Teshub as the chief god occurs within the context of a theogony that tells of several successive divine reigns, each lasting nine years. In the penultimate reign, Kumarbi, the father of the gods, is dethroned by his son, Teshub. The part of the theogony that is called Kingdom in Heaven also includes allusions to the story of the origin of the world, which unquestionably display the marks of Sumero-Babylonian sources. We also discern within it the atmosphere of the royal courts; each rebellion that occurs in heaven makes one think of rebellion by a member of the (earthly) king's entourage and the king's subsequent dethronement. The following extract provides an example: "Long ago, in ancient times, Alalu was king in heaven. As long as Alalu sat on the divine throne, the mighty Anu, the first among the gods, stood before him, bowed down at his feet, and handed him the cup to drink. Alalu reigned in heaven for nine years. In the ninth year, Anu made war on Alalu and conquered him." Alalu fled, and for nine years Anu, too, held the throne from which Kumarbi, a sort of cupbearer, drove him. In the struggle, Kumarbi bit off Anu's genitals and swallowed them; from Kumarbi three gods subsequently were born: the Tigris river, Tashmishu (the vizier of the weather-god), and Teshub, the weather-god who was to eventually dethrone his father.

The Song of Ullikummi relates Kumarbi's attempt to recover his throne. With that aim in view, Kumarbi fathers a stone monster, Ullikummi, whom he places on the shoulder of Upelluri, the Atlas of Hurrian myth, who stands in the midst of the sea. Ullikummi grows so fast and huge that he reaches the vault of heaven and consequently the dwellings of the sun and of Teshub, which fills these two gods with dread and anger. When he sees the sun-god coming, Tashmishu says to Teshub: "Why does the sun come? . . . It must be a very grave matter, foreboding a hard battle, an uproar in the heavens as well as hunger and death on earth?" The weather-god then replied to Tashmishu: "Let them set up a chair for the sun! Let them lay out a table for his eating!" A long discussion (a part of which is unfortunately lost) takes place between the two great gods, both of whom are nervous and in despair; but, feeling somewhat reassured, the sun returns to his celestial dwelling. Moved by Teshub's dejection, the goddess Ishtar of Nineveh offers her help; she decides to seduce the stone monster, but being deaf and blind, the monster remains insensible to the goddess's maneuvers. Teshub eventually begins to fight against Ullikummi, but cannot defeat the stone monster, who continues to grow; the same thing happens to seventy other gods who are fighting under the command of Ashtabi the Hurrian war-god. Finally Ea, the god of wisdom, intervenes. After pointing out that the monster whom Kumarbi had fathered would cause the destruction of humanity and thus deprive the gods of efficient servants, Ea learns from ancient gods how he can disable Ullikummi, namely by cutting off his feet. And so, with this information, Teshub eventually can both eliminate Ullikummi and get the better of Kumarbi.

The Song of the Dragon Hedammu is another interesting Hurrian myth, but unfortunately we have only sixteen fragments of it. The dragon was born from Kumarbi and the sea. Several passages relate dialogues between Shaushka of Nineveh and Hedammu. Other fragments (both Hittite and Hurrian) concern Kessi the hunter and his beautiful wife. Kessi has several dreams, which his mother interprets for him.

The Myth of Appu deserves some attention. The archaisms of the Hittite text that we possess lead us to assume an archetype dating from the Old Kingdom, which was itself an adaptation of a Hurrian text or a Hurrian tradition. Judging from the fragments we have, the myth constituted a reflection upon the fate of humanity: Appu, although rich, is not happy, for he has no child. The sun-god advises him to have intercourse with his wife, who then bears him two sons: first a son named Wrong, and later a son named Right. The myth analyzes the sons' difficult coexistence, as well as the "justice" of the god who punishes Wrong for his bad behavior toward his brother (when the two brothers divided the estate after Appu's death, Wrong kept a very good cow for himself and left a barren one for Right).

I should also mention, although only briefly, some purely foreign myths, of which our Hittite texts are probably translations: the famous Mesopotamian myth of Gilgamesh, that of Atrahasis about the creation of humanity, and also the fragments of the Canaanite myth of Ashertu, with dialogues between Ashertu, her husband, and the god Baal. That the Hittites made translations of these stories shows how open they were to outside religious influences.

BIBL.: Pecchioli Daddi and A. M. Polvani, *La Mitologia Ittita* (Brescia, 1990). H. A. Hoffner Jr., *Hittite Myths* (Atlanta, 1990).   R.L.

Iran

Iran, as a region, is defined by borders that have fluctuated over time. For most of its history, it was more than a region: it was notionally an empire, meant to be ruled by a king of kings. Such a notion of a cohesive Iranian empire was predicated on a cohesive Iranian narrative tradition that is still evident in a monumental masterpiece of classical Persian poetry, the Book of Kings or *Shahnameh* of Ferdowsi, produced in the early 11th century CE. The roots of this narrative tradition go back to pre-Islamic times and far beyond, even into prehistoric times.

From the standpoint of prehistoric times, as reflected in the oldest narratives we may call Iranian, that is, in a

collection of sacred texts known as the Avesta, there already exists a notion of Iran as an empire. For example, the first book of a subset of the Avesta known as the Vendidad contains a catalogue of regions described as accepting, one after another, the teachings of Zarathustra, and the names of these regions correspond to the names of provinces in historical phases of imperial rule (Ariana, Sogdiana, Margiana, Bactriana, etc.).

The collective sense of identity that constitutes this so-called empire can be analyzed linguistically as well as narratologically. The notional Iran of all attested Iranian-speaking populations amounts to a linguistic as well as cultural—not to say national—grouping. The vast family of Iranian languages (Avestan, Old Persian, Parthian, Pahlavi, New Persian, Sogdian, Bactrian, and the list continues) is a subset of what linguists know as the Indo-Iranian family of languages, which in turn is a subset of an overall linguistic grouping known as Indo-European. The category of Indo-Iranian is especially important for understanding Iranian narrative traditions, since the earliest forms of Iranian narrative, as attested in the Avesta, are evidently cognate with the correspondingly earliest forms of Indic narrative, as attested in a body of sacred texts known as the Vedas (Rig Veda, Atharva Veda, and so on). Even the self-identification of the speakers of these earliest phases of Iranian and Indic languages is cognate: in their respective sacred texts, both linguistic groups refer to themselves as Aryans (not to be confused with the modern political usage). In fact, the name Iran is derived from the root form of Aryan.

On the basis of comparing Iranian narrative traditions as attested in the Avesta with the Indic narrative traditions of the Vedas, it is possible to reconstruct a shared Indo-Iranian heritage of narratives, especially sacred narratives, which in turn are linked to rituals. In other words, the myth-ritual complex of Avestan traditions is cognate with that of Vedic traditions. What is cognate in Iranian and Indic cultures doubtless extends to other forms of verbal art, but the fact remains that the most evident point of comparison is sacred narrative.

Granted, if one compares Iranian narrative traditions with those of other cultures beyond the Indo-Iranian linguistic grouping, it is easy to find alternative points of comparison. For example, one can find "epic" features in the *Shahnameh* of Ferdowsi if one compares it with the Greek epic the *Iliad*. A figure such as Rostam in the *Shahnameh* is readily comparable with Achilles in the *Iliad*: both characters are represented as superior to the kings who outrank them, and yet both ultimately uphold the kingship of men whom they would otherwise resist.

Still, the clearest evidence for distinctly Iranian elements in the *Shahnameh* is its heritage of sacred—even priestly—narrative, centering on the theme of a cohesive empire of moral righteousness founded on sacred principles that predate the time frame of Islam.

The *Shahnameh,* as a Book of Kings, dramatizes its own origin in these terms. It tells of a prototypical book of kings that disintegrated into fragments once upon a time when the empire was neglected. The fragments were scattered over all the regions of the empire. According to the story as told in the *Shahnameh,* this disintegrated prototypical book of kings was later reintegrated when a wise shah commissioned his vizier to assemble the most learned men of the empire, one from each region; each of these assembled men from each region held a fragment of the disintegrated book, and each recited his fragment in proper order, so that the prototypical book of kings was duly reconstituted. So too, by extension, the neglected empire can become reconstituted.

The central idea of an empire founded on righteousness reflects Iranian traditions that are traceable as far back as the Avesta, and the actual principles of righteousness are ultimately cognate with comparable principles found in the Indic Vedas. In the linguistically oldest texts of the Avesta, most prominently in the Gathas, the speaker who articulates these principles is Zarathustra. The wording that introduces his direct speech in the Avesta (Yasna 9) is "thus spoke Zarathustra" (well known from Nietzsche's appropriation, *Also sprach Zarathustra*). The same wording can be traced back to Indo-Iranian and, further, to Indo-European phases of ritual and mythological language.

As is evident from the very words of the Avesta, this text presents itself as the authoritative script, as it were, for sacrifice. As the prototypical speaker, Zarathustra is the prototypical poet-sacrificer, as Skjaervø has shown (1996). As the priestly master of ritual, the figure of Zarathustra in the Gathas complements—and is interdependent with—the figure of Vistaspa as the warrior-king. Moreover, as a prototypical sacrificer, Zarathustra prefigures an eschatological counterpart, the *saosiiant* (revitalizer) who will ultimately save the universe in the fullness of time.

No scholarly consensus has ever emerged about when and where Zarathustra actually lived. There have been crude attempts to euhemerize him as a religious reformer whose immediate historical circumstances can somehow be reconstructed from the words of the Avesta, but such reconstructions depend ultimately on unjustified assumptions about these sacred texts, as if they represented the products of contemporary reportage.

The cumulative evidence of Indo-Iranian traditions in myth and ritual points toward a different solution. The speaker Zarathustra can be understood only in terms of the Indo-Iranian religious heritage. In other words, Zarathustra as a religious persona speaks for the entire tradition of myths and rituals in the Avesta, and he can be understood only in terms of that tradition, which changes over time. As the tradition changes, so too does the speaker who is framed by it. Real empires rise and fall, but there remains the one who gives voice to the notional empire. The Zarathustra of the Avesta

and of later sacred texts reflects an entire system of rituals and sacred narratives that evolve through time. In other words, Zarathustra is a character in multiple interacting texts; the interpretation of what *he* says varies with changing audience evaluations of who and what that *he* is, but this character is continually read back into even the oldest texts, and he always speaks for the tradition as a whole.

When Zarathustra speaks, what he says is the essence of Iranian sacred narrative.

BIBL.: Olga M. Davidson, *Comparative Literature and Classical Persian Poetics* (Costa Mesa, Calif.: Mazda, 2000). Oktor Skjaervø, "Zarathustra in the Avesta and in Manicheism: Irano-Manichaica IV," in *La Persia e l'Asia Centrale da Alessandro al X Secolo* (Rome: Accademia dei Lincei, 1996), 597–628.   O.M.D.

Greece and Rome

Greek myth. Greek myths may be conveniently classified into three broad categories according to their content: origins, exploits of the gods, and deeds of the heroes.

First, cosmogonies and theogonies account for the formation of the world and the origin of the gods. Hesiod's *Theogony,* which posits two primordial entities, Chasm or Void (Chaos) and Earth (Gaea), and keeps their descendants carefully separated, has been preserved in its entirety, but we know of other cosmogonies attributed either to legendary characters such as Orpheus or Musaeus or to historical writers such as Pherecydes of Syros (around 550 BCE), which deviated from Hesiod's version. Creation myths narrated the first appearance of humans, either from the earth or from the soot of the Titans struck by Zeus's thunder, and linked the beginning of civilization to the gift of fire by Prometheus or the Argive Phoroneus. Mythical genealogies defined the relations between the various Greek ethnic groups, all born from Hellen or his sons, according to the Hesiodic *Catalogue of Women,* or singled out those who claimed to be "earthborn." Descent from or foundations by epic heroes also served to enhance the prestige of rulers, aristocratic families, and city-states. Etiological myths explained the origins of sanctuaries, rituals, or institutions. Second, tales about gods gave them a genealogy, defined their privileges, and narrated their interventions within the human world. Third, stories of heroes such as Heracles or Theseus listed their exploits and ordeals, whereas those about heroines provided positive or negative illustrations of the roles assigned to women in Greek society.

In a Greece divided into city-states, most myths clustered around a single city (Thebes, Argos, or Athens), but some (the Calydonian boar hunt, the Argonautic expedition, or the Trojan War) brought together heroes who originally belonged to various other cycles. As far back as we know them, Greek myths are characterized by their variety and plasticity. Each traditional story, while keeping a permanent core, could be retold with new meanings, incidents, and characters, for Greek religion had neither sacred books nor canonical authority.

These myths have various origins and status. Zeus's role as father can be traced back to an Indo-European protomythology in which sky-gods often are also father-gods. Hesiod's succession myth shows significant points of contact with the Hittite Song of Kumarbi and unmistakable similarities with the Babylonian poem *Enuma Elish*. But some tales, fabricated during the Hellenistic and imperial periods to provide recently Hellenized communities with heroic founders and good Greek pedigrees or account for names, customs, and institutions, were quite new. Some remained purely local and are known to us through Pausanias's *Description of Greece,* fragments of local historians, and use in local inscriptions, whereas others achieved Panhellenic recognition.

It is agreed that Greek myths were first transmitted orally. But we first encounter them only after they have begun to be fixed by images and enshrined in verse in the poems of Homer, which synthesize the diverse local traditions into a unified Panhellenic model, more or less at the same time, that is, at the end of the 8th century BCE. It is anybody's guess how far back the oral tradition reaches: there are vague indications of mythical structures in the divine names transmitted in Linear B texts—when, say, a god is defined as "son of Zeus," or when a goddess appears as Divine Mother, that is, presumably, Mother of the Gods, or even, more tantalizingly, when Dionysus, later Zeus's son, shares with him a sanctuary in Chania in Crete.

From Homer to Nonnus (around 450 CE), myths appear in nearly every genre of Greek literature. According to the *Odyssey,* the mythological epics of Phemius and Demodocus were performed in the limited circle of the aristocratic symposium (*Odyssey* 1.154; 8.62). This was also the case with elegy and lyric monody, whereas the performances of the rhapsodes and the songs of the choruses—which recast epic themes in lyric meters, sang the praises of the gods in their hymns, or celebrated the victorious athlete by setting his victory in relation to the paradigmatic world of gods and heroes—addressed larger audiences that gathered for local or Panhellenic festivals. During the classical period, tragedy, which drew its themes nearly exclusively from myth, and comedy, which often put mythical characters on stage, were also presented at festivals. Moreover, funeral orations gave pride of place to the mythical exploits of Athens, and Sophists included mythological topics in the lectures they gave either in private houses or at public meetings. The so-called *logographoi* (writers of stories) and local historians such as Hecataeus of Miletus or Hellanicus of Lesbos "translated into prose," sometimes with "corrections," mythical genealogies and "tales of heroes" (Clement of Alexandria, *Stromata* 6.2.26.7). Philosophers such as Plato were also busy creating "new myths" by combining motifs borrowed from traditional tales. With Hellenistic poets such as Callimachus,

Apollonius, and Theocritus, who delighted in recondite local versions, myth became the playground of the erudite elite. But agonistic festivals, private recitations, and symposia attest to the continued performance of mythological poems and declamations during the Hellenistic and imperial periods. Public speeches of any kind were also, as a rule, adorned with mythological allusions under the Roman Empire, and historians and geographers such as Diodorus of Sicily, Strabo, Dionysius of Halicarnassus, and Pausanias included "ancient mythic tales" (Diodorus 1.3.2) in their works, notwithstanding that Hellenistic rhetorical theory classified myth (Latin *fabula*) as "unlikely and impossible" and opposed it both to *historia,* which records true events, and to *plasma* (Latin *argumentum*), the fiction that bears likeness to truth (*Rhetorica ad Herennium* 1.12). Late antiquity saw a major revival of mythological poetry, culminating in the *Dionysiaca* of Nonnus.

Mythology permeated not only literature but also inscriptions and visual arts, whose importance for a better understanding of the functions of myths in Greek society can hardly be overstated. Depictions of myths were on view in temples, treasuries, and public buildings, as testified by the remains of architectural sculpture and the descriptions of paintings and other lost works of art by Pliny the Elder and Pausanias. Coin types often referred to local myths. Vases, wall paintings, mosaic floors, silver plates, engraved gems, and decorated sarcophagi also associated mythology with every aspect of the private life (and death) of the elite.

Several factors contributed to the omnipresence of myth. Artistic representation and poetic performance of mythical narrations were seen as pleasing not only to human spectators, but also to the gods, who were understood as the primary addressees: a sculpted or painted image made a powerful dedication, the performance of a hymn contributed to the splendor of the festival in honor of a divinity. Myths explained the world. Myths of origin made the world and the role of humans in it understandable. Every cult, every festival, had its explanatory (etiological) myth, as had rituals that provoked curiosity. Why do the Parians, in a sacrifice to the Graces, wear no wreaths? Because during his sacrifice, King Minos was told about the death of his son; thus he put down the wreath as a sign of his grief (Apollodorus, *Library* 3.15.7). Strange animals, surprising customs, but also curious rock formations had their explanatory myths—Ovid's *Metamorphoses* are full of them. Even after myth seemed to have lost credibility, it still retained this power of explanation and legitimation. Myth was also a powerful instrument of self-reflection: by staging its own versions of these traditional stories, Athenian tragedy, once a year, made the spectators step back and think about their city and about the fate and place of humans and gods in it.

Myths at Rome. From Dionysius of Halicarnassus to the first great scholars of Roman religion, G. Wissowa and K. Latte, it has long been taken for granted that

Romans lacked a fully developed mythology, perhaps because their founder Romulus had been wise enough to "reject all the traditional myths concerning the gods that contain blasphemies or calumnies against them" (Dionysius, *Roman Antiquities* 2.18.3). Others theories hold that the Romans were naturally deprived of any creative imagination, happened at some point to forget their native myths, or had consciously historicized them. So, instead of a genuine popular tradition, Romans supposedly were given only a pseudomythology, composed of late, artificial tales put together by Greeks or under Greek influence and addressed to an elite.

The most recent studies devoted to Roman religion strongly criticize this view as an unjustifiable denial. Indeed, the Romans did not have cosmogonies or stories about the adventures of their gods, but they did not lack etiological myths explaining the origins of festivals, rituals, social institutions, and public monuments. Rome had also one or even two foundation stories, and leading Roman families, like their Greek counterparts, were proud of their mythical genealogies. Moreover, it has long been acknowledged that the "history" of the first kings of Rome, full as it is of miraculous elements, is, in fact, myth in disguise.

As far back as we can go, Roman myth, like much of Roman culture, is an eclectic amalgam of both indigenous material and elements borrowed from neighboring peoples, most prominently from the Etruscans and the Greeks. Therefore it is overly schematic to set up a dichotomy between "genuine" Italian myths predating any regular contact with Greek culture and "secondary" myths produced under the influence of Hellenistic mythography by an antiquarian industry. It is far more fruitful to focus on the Romans' appropriation of Greek myths and their ability to adapt these foreign tales to their own vital concerns.

The account of the foundation of Rome is a case in point. The legends linking the origins of Rome to the aftermath of the Trojan War had gained circulation by the beginning of the 3rd century BCE, when the "Roman" story, that is, the foundation of the town by the twins Romulus and Remus, was already well established. But it was the tale associating Aeneas with Lavinium and not those ascribing Hellenic descent to the Romans that penetrated Roman literature toward the end of the 3rd century BCE by means of the epic poem of Naevius and the *Annals* of Fabius Pictor, becoming firmly entrenched with the *Annals* of Ennius and the *Origins* of Cato. This embrace of a Trojan origin, which enabled Rome to associate itself with the Hellenic tradition while emphasizing its distinctiveness, is typical of the Roman relation to Greek myth.

Like Greek myth, and for the same reasons, Roman myth is characterized by its plasticity. Even the foundation myths were somewhat flexible: there existed many versions of the killing of Remus or the death of Romulus. Multiple mythical interpretations were the rule rather than the exception for festivals and ritual practices, as demonstrated by the *Roman Questions* of Plutarch and the *Fasti* of Ovid.

Greek myths entered Roman literature right from the beginning with the tragedies of Livius Andronicus (around 240 BCE), which were derived from Greek models. Roman myths entered later, with Ennius and Accius. But the great literary monuments that encapsulate for us the essentials of Roman mythology all belong to the Augustan Age. Dionysius of Halicarnassus's *Roman Antiquities* have been said to be "a repository of Roman myths." Together with Horace, Ovid and Vergil redefined myth's value and meaning for Roman culture in poems that are the products of highly refined and self-conscious literary techniques, whereas Livy, in his *Books from the Foundation of the City [of Rome]*, gave what became the authorized version of the traditions associated with Romulus and the Roman kings. After them, poets, historians, and orators alike never stopped rewriting the myths and generating new meanings from them until late antiquity, as demonstrated, for instance, by the epic poems of Claudian (370–404 CE).

Images of naturalized Greek myths had already arrived in Rome at the end of the 6th century BCE. Under the late republic, myths were put on public monuments to serve the self-glorification of the aristocrats, and, in the form of paintings and mosaics, myths helped to transform their luxurious villas into dream worlds of beauty. Myths also permeated political life, with Antony entering cities dressed as Dionysus or Augustus styling himself as Romulus and decorating the temples he built with mythical analogues that celebrated his own victories. Under the empire, mythological stories, mimed by dancers or gruesomely reenacted in the arena by condemned criminals, were among the most popular entertainments.

From mythology to mythography. As opposed to writers and artists, who made use of myths for particular purposes, mythographers concerned themselves with myth in and for itself, simply collecting and writing down the old stories, either by following the most authoritative version or by juxtaposing various accounts in order to teach anyone with pretensions to culture how to make sense of a world where myth was omnipresent. The main collections known to us through manuscripts, summaries, and papyri date from the Hellenistic and early imperial periods. The *Mythographus Homericus*, the *Tragic Hypotheseis* (summaries of tragedies), or the *Catasterisms* (tales of humans transformed into starry constellations, and thus a mythological companion to Aratus's earlier *Phaenomena*), wrongly ascribed to the astronomer Eratosthenes, helped readers to elucidate mythological allusions in other texts, whereas Antoninus Liberalis's *Metamorphoses* and Parthenius of Nicea's *Love Stories* were organized around a single theme. The *Library*, mistakenly ascribed to the Athenian grammarian Apollodorus and written around 200 CE, presents the most complete narrative of myths, arranged according to a genealogical order, from the creation of the world to the return of the Heraclidae.

The Latin mythographical tradition begins with the *Fables* (mistakenly attributed to Hyginus) which combine genealogies, narratives, and catalogues. Together with the *Mythologies* of Fulgentius (late 5th century?), the so-called Vatican Mythographers (10th or 11th century?) attest to the survival of the *Fables* well into the Middle Ages. The collections of myths assembled in modern times by Natale Conti (Natales Comes, 1616), Thomas Bulfinch (1855), or Robert Graves (1955) attest the vitality of this ancillary genre.

Ancient and modern readings of classical mythology. Long before Plato's *Republic,* Greeks began to criticize their myths. At the end of the 6th century BCE, Xenophanes of Colophon attacked Homer and Hesiod for attributing to the gods "all that is shameful and disgraceful among humans" (Diels and Kranz 1952: 21 B 11), and Hecataeus of Miletus ridiculed the tales of the Greeks because of their absurdity. At the same time, a defensive interpretation of mythology was produced by Theagenes of Rhegium, who is said to have interpreted the Iliadic theomachy as a struggle among natural forces. After him, many authors attempted "to purify the mythical by submitting it to reason" (Plutarch, *Life of Theseus* 1.3), either by stripping a traditional story of its most marvelous elements, as Herodotus and Thucydides did occasionally and Palaephatus more systematically in his *Unbelievable Tales* (FGrH 44, late 4th century BCE), or by rejecting the morally shocking tales in favor of "sanitized" versions, as did Pindar when, in *Olympian* 1, he refused to believe that Demeter, absentminded because of grief for her lost daughter, had once eaten human flesh. During the early Hellenistic period, Euhemerus, in his influential *Sacred Scripture,* known to us from Diodorus and Eusebius, went a step further by transforming myth into history and proposing that the first gods were in fact deified human beings: Zeus, for example, was a powerful king who "gave laws and did many other good things and gained therefore eternal glory and memory" (Euhemerus, *Testimonia* 69 B Winiarczyk).

Together with historicization, allegorical interpretation that substituted a covert meaning *(hyponoia)* for the literal one contributed to rescuing myths from the charge of impiety and keeping them in step with contemporary philosophy. Physical and moral allegories such as Heraclitus's *Homeric Problems* elucidated the physical realities or moral truths hidden behind the names and stories of the gods—Hera (Greek *ēra*) thus was air (Greek *aēr*), in an easy transposition of the three letters of her name, which led to more sophisticated readings: "When Homer portrayed the wounding of Hera by Heracles [*Iliad* 5.392–94], he wished to show that Heracles . . . was the first to pierce the thick air that obscures our thought" (Heraclitus, *Allegories*

43.2). Myths were also interpreted "theologically" as expressions of the essence of the gods by Neoplatonist philosophers. As Sallustius, the friend of Julian the Apostate, wrote (mid-4th century CE): "Such is the tale that Cronus swallowed his children: since the god is intellectual, and all intellect is directed towards itself, the myth hints at the god's essential nature" (*Concerning the God and the Universe* 4, trans. Nock).

There is some continuity between these ancient interpretations and the scientific study of myths by 19th-century scholars. After all, the followers of K. O. Müller and his *Prolegomena to a Scientific Mythology* (1825) who attempted to extract the factual kernel from the legends of the Trojan War or discover the genuine population movements that may be preserved by the myth of the return of the Heraclidae are modern euhemerists. On the other hand, those scholars in the later 19th century who looked for a hidden meaning and interpreted myths as transcriptions of natural phenomena—such as thunderstorms (A. Kuhn), dawn (Max Müller), or growth and death of vegetation (James G. Frazer and followers)—are suspiciously close to natural allegoresis.

The search for origins is still alive and well in recent mythological studies. At the beginning of the 20th century, the myth-and-ritual theory of the so-called Cambridge School discovered the origin of the myths in rituals. Later, others tried to find the sources of some Greek myths in history, privileging the Mycenaean world (Nilsson 1932) or the ancient Near East (West 1997). Burkert (1983) went even further back and located the development of sociobiological patterns fundamental to human behavior, and the myths that expressed them, in the Paleolithic culture, while psychoanalysts S. Freud and C. G. Jung saw the origin of myth in hidden structures of the human soul.

Currently, the exclusive attention paid to a "primitive" core of the myth, to be isolated from all the "secondary" additions, is giving way, under the influence of structural narratology, to a new interest in all versions of a myth. In fact, because of anthropologists' emphasis on the social relevance of myth as pragmatic charter, many analysts of Greek and Roman myths tend now to focus on the reception and continuous reuse of myths rather than their origins. Viewed from this angle, invented traditions and creative adaptations deserve as much attention as stories passed on for generations and "original" tales. This change explains the growing interest in Roman mythology and the reevaluation of its innovative engagement with Greek myth.

BIBL.: J. Bremmer (ed.), *Interpretations of Greek Mythology* (Sydney: Croom Helm, 1987). W. Burkert, *Homo Necans* (trans. Peter Bing; Berkeley, 1983 [orig. 1972]). R. Buxton, *Imaginary Greece: The Contexts of Mythology* (Cambridge: Cambridge University Press, 1994). H. Diels and W. Kranz, *Die Fragmente der Vorsokratiker* (6th ed.; Berlin, 1952). R. Fowler, *Early Greek Mythography* (Oxford: Oxford University Press, 2000). T. Gantz, *Early Greek Myth: A Guide to*

Literary and Artistic Sources (Baltimore: John Hopkins University Press, 1993). F. Graf, *Greek Mythology* (Baltimore, 1993). Idem (ed.), *Mythos in mythenloser Gesellschaft: Das Paradigma Roms* (Colloquium Rauricum 3; Stuttgart: Teubner, 1995). *Lexicon iconographicum mythologiae classicae* (Zürich, 1981–97). M. P. Nilsson, *The Mycenaean Origin of Greek Mythology* (Berkeley, 1932). M. L. West, *The East Face of Helicon* (Oxford, 1997).   s.s.

Etruria

No mythological account in the Etruscan language has survived; but we know—thanks to Etruscan artistic representations and to references in Greek and Roman writers—that the Etruscans had sacred narratives about creation and the cosmos, the founding of their people and cities, the underworld, and the end of their civilization, as well as stories about individual deities and heroes. Because of the close relationship between Etruscan and Greek mythology, many scholars think quite wrongly that there is no Etruscan myth, only Greek myth in disguise. As a result, they have begun with the Greek material and tried to define Etruscan mythology from it. Yet, while it is true that the Etruscans had considerable knowledge of these alien gods and their myths, such an approach is mistaken.

A purely Etruscan myth, of primary importance for understanding Etruscan religion, is that of the child called Tages in Latin and Greek. Accounts relate the story to Tarquinia, a leading city of Etruria, where a farmer was plowing his field, when suddenly Tages popped out of a furrow and began to sing of the "Etruscan discipline" (*disciplina Etrusca;* see also Divination and Prophecy). The hero/founder Tarchon came to hear his songs and record them, and the revelations were then taught to people in the other cities of Etruria. This story appears on Etruscan carved gems, which show a head rising from the ground as one or more figures record its message, and on a famous Etruscan bronze engraved mirror found near Tarquinia, where a youth named Pava Tachies (perhaps "Child of Tages") reads a liver as Avl Tarchunus watches and meditates. Another prophet, Lasa Vecuvia (called "the nymph Vegoia" in Latin), who is also shown on gems and mirrors, is known to have revealed how the world was created and lands were measured and distributed. Finally, a uniquely Etruscan story known from mirrors and sculptured funerary urns pertains to Cacu, who, assisted by the youth Artile, sings prophetically, while soldiers, Avle and Caile Vipinas, come to seize him and learn his secrets.

When Greek myth is represented by the Etruscans, variations from the Greek versions are sometimes extreme. In Etruria, the Minotaur may be depicted as killed by Hercle (= Heracles) rather than Theseus, and Artumes (= Artemis) may be represented as male. The Trojan Horse is named Pecse (= Pegasus), and Uni, the Etruscan Hera, may be seen suckling not the infant Heracles but an adult, bearded Hercle. A hammer-wielding demon labeled Charu guards the door to the underworld rather than plying an infernal ferryboat, as Charon does. Examples could be multiplied, and one school of thought, increasingly discredited, sees these as "banalizations" of Greek mythology, in which "the artist made a mistake" or someone told the story "wrongly." Other scholars now allow for a genuine *interpretatio etrusca,* in which Greek myths were selected and molded in Etruria for themes or details that were especially Etruscan, such as the hurling of lightning by Tinia (= Zeus) in the story of Seven against Thebes or the delivery of the egg containing Elina (= Helen) by Turms (= Hermes).   N.T.DEG.

Christianity

The earliest Christian myths were constructive expressions of the significance of Jesus for his followers and for the cosmos and history as a whole. These myths were formulated orally and communicated by missionaries, such as Peter and Paul, to Jews, Gentiles affiliated with the synagogues, and polytheists. Paul wrote summaries of some of these early myths in his letters. They were based on the exclusive worship of the God of Israel and the myths associated with that figure, especially the apocalyptic myth of the kingdom of God. They interpreted Jesus as the anointed agent of this God, who proclaimed the nearness of the kingdom like a prophet and who would rule and sit in judgment like a king. The early Christians innovated with regard to the Jewish myth of the kingdom of God in two ways: by announcing that the awaited ideal king (Messiah of Israel) had come and by incorporating the death and resurrection of Jesus into the apocalyptic myth. The idea of resurrection was already a facet of Jewish apocalyptic myths (e.g., Dan. 12.1–3). The myth presupposed by the letters of Paul interprets the death and resurrection of Jesus as foundational events, both for the formation of a new king of community and for the ethical reformation and eventual glorification of individuals.

The earliest myths do not agree about the origin and ontological status of Jesus. The prose hymn in Paul's Letter to the Philippians implies that, before Jesus was born as a human being, he was "in the form of God" (2.6). This probably does not mean that he was already equal to God, but that he shared in the ontological status of divinity. The beings that came to be called angels also shared in this mode of being according to Jewish myths; they are called "gods," for example, in the Dead Sea Scrolls. Rather than language of resurrection, this hymn refers to the "exaltation" of Jesus. Because he was obedient, even to death on a cross, God highly exalted him and bestowed upon him the very status and name of God (2.7–11). In the context of the letter, this hymn has an ethical purpose: to encourage the Philippians to be reconciled to one another, instead of competing and disagreeing (1.27; 2.2–4).

In the opening of the Letter to the Romans, however,

Jonah emerging from the jaws of the sea monster that had swallowed him. Marble sculpture, 3rd century CE, believed to have come from a Christian family tomb in Asia Minor. The Jonah story had messianic significance for Christians. It was used as a type of the death and resurrection of Christ (Matthew 12.40; see p. 619). *Jonah Cast Up. Asia Minor, probably Phrygis (central Turkey), Early Christian, c. 270–80. Marble, 40.65 × 21.6 × 37.6 cm. © The Cleveland Museum of Art, 2003. Severance Fund, 1965.238*

Paul speaks as if Jesus had been, ontologically speaking, an ordinary human being until God raised him from the dead. He says that Jesus was descended from David "according to the flesh" and was appointed "Son of God" by the power of the Holy Spirit in the event of his resurrection (Rom. 1.3–4). In other words, Jesus was given divine status for the first time when he was raised from the dead. In this letter the preexistence of Jesus is

not an issue. Rather, the emphasis lies on the ethical and cosmic significance of the death and resurrection of Jesus (3.21–26; 8.1–11, 18–23). The formulation of the early Christian myth in Romans is connected with ritual. Baptism is interpreted as a "likeness" of the death of Jesus (6.5). Thus, in the rite of baptism, the believer shares in the death and burial of Jesus (6.3–4). The significance of the rite is ethical: the old sinful self dies so that the baptized person is no longer enslaved to sin (6.6). The resurrection of Jesus has a dual function: ethical and soteriological. As Jesus rose from the dead, the baptized person is expected to lead a new life by doing what is right (6.4, 12–14). This new life will then lead to the experience of a resurrection like that of Jesus (6.5). Myth and ritual are also linked in the reference to prayer in the Spirit, specifically the cry "Abba! Father!" (8.14–15). Paul interprets this prayer to mean that the believers are fellow heirs with Christ, who will be glorified with him, if they suffer with him (8.16–17).

The letters of Paul allude to and summarize early Christian myths in oral form. The four canonical Gospels are sacred narratives in the proper sense. They all emphasize the death and resurrection of Jesus, just as the oral myths do, although these events are variously interpreted. The Gospels do not agree about the preexistence of Jesus. The Gospel according to Mark was probably composed just before or just after the destruction of the temple in Jerusalem during the first Jewish war with Rome. According to Christian tradition from the early 2nd century onward, it was written by a companion of Peter. Mark portrays Jesus as "Son of God," but this epithet does not necessarily imply divinity. The phrase is applied to the king in the Hebrew Bible, and it can also apply to any righteous member of the people of Israel (Wis. 2.16). Mark does not portray Jesus as the incarnate Word of God, as the Gospel according to John does. It includes no narratives about Jesus's virginal conception, as Matthew and Luke do. The only passage that may imply divinity is the account of transfiguration, which has features in common with Greek accounts of the epiphanies of deities.

According to Justin Martyr's *First Apology,* written about 150 CE, the "reminiscences of the apostles" (i.e., the Gospels) were regularly read in Christian liturgical assemblies. It is often inferred that they were written for such a purpose. Many scholars believe that the author of Mark used a written account of the death of Jesus as a source. Some think that Luke and John had access to different versions of the same source. If the account of Jesus's last supper with the Twelve was part of this early source, it is likely that it had a ritual use. In the words over the bread and cup, the myth of the significance of Jesus's death is expressed. He died "for many" and his death is interpreted as a covenant-renewing sacrifice (Mark 14.24). Matthew's version implies that his death was a metaphorical sacrifice that effected the forgiveness of the sins of many (Matt. 26.28). The ritual may have been an annual commemoration of the death of Je-

Images of the suffering of Jesus leading to his crucifixion; in the center panel is an empty cross surmounted by a christogram (*chi-rho*, the first two letters of *Christ* in Greek). Late 4th-century CE sarcophagus. Vatican Museum. *Courtesy Robin Margaret Jensen*

sus, near the time of the Jewish Passover, or a weekly celebration of the Lord's Supper.

In the New Testament, the dominant framework for the mythic expression of the significance of Jesus was an adapted Jewish apocalyptic myth. In some Christian texts of the 2nd century, the significance of Jesus was expressed in the context of the gnostic myth of creation, which was dependent on Platonist interpretation of the myth of creation in Plato's *Timaeus*. The authors of these texts thus shifted the focus of early Christian myth-making from eschatology (teaching about the End) to protology (teaching about the Beginning).

This gnostic myth is the philosophical creation of literary theologians; it is not the spontaneous product of a tribe or culture, as early myths are believed to be. The *Apocryphon* or *Secret Book according to John* (Nag Hammadi II.1, III.1, IV.1) presents what has come to be considered the paradigmatic gnostic myth. It begins with the unfolding of a solitary first principle or god into a complex, elaborated spiritual universe or pleroma. The second stage involves the creation of the material world, which occurs by means of the theft of some of the spiritual, divine power and its falling into the hands of a nonspiritual being, a fatally imperfect version of Plato's cosmic craftsman. In the third stage, the craftsman creates Adam and Eve, and their children come into existence. In this stage, wisdom and the other spiritual powers trick the craftsman, with the result that some of the power is transferred to human beings, especially to the children of Seth, who are the archetypes or progenitors of gnostics. The final stage consists of human history in which the stolen power is gradually recovered by the spiritual world and gnostic souls return to god with the help of a savior. In some versions of the gnostic myth, Jesus of Nazareth is this savior. He can play this role because he is identified with a preexistent figure, such as the heavenly, eternal Christ or Word.

The gnostic texts speak about baptism, but it is not clear whether they refer to an actual ritual washing that gnostics practiced or whether they rejected the ritual as such, but used baptismal imagery as a metaphor for salvation by means of knowledge of one's true origin. In a work called *First Thought in Three Forms* (Nag Hammadi XIII.1), the gnostic baptismal ceremony is described as stripping off darkness, putting on a robe of light, washing in the waters of life, receiving a throne of glory, being glorified with the glory of kinship (a new state of life characterized by the reception of knowledge), and being raised to the luminous place of kinship. The *Gospel of Philip* (Nag Hammadi II.3) speaks about five mysteries: baptism, anointing, Eucharist, ransom, and the bridal chamber. Again, it is not clear whether these mysteries are actual rituals or metaphors for spiritual processes.

The complex and distinctive myth of origins created by such 2nd-century Christians expresses a strong sense of group identity in its genealogies and psychological analysis of humanity. This self-understanding is rooted in the idea that there are two types of human being. In some texts involved in such social mapping, the authors referred to themselves as the offspring of Seth, the offspring of the light, or the perfect race (*Hypostasis of the Archons*; Nag Hammadi II.4). They were hostile to outsiders and expected them to be damned and destroyed. The material universe of which they were a part was often referred to as "darkness." The school of Valentinus, a Christian theologian whose school appropriated many features typical of gnostics, divided the world into three camps. Members of the school called themselves "people endowed with spirit," "spirituals," or "the perfect." They expected to be reunited eschatologically with the heavenly father. They taught that ordinary Christians, "psychics" or "people of soul," would achieve at best a second-class paradise and rest forever with the creator of the world, not the heavenly father. Those totally outside the boundary of the church, the "hylics" or "material people," would be finally destroyed. These teachers and their followers were active from the mid-2nd century into the 4th century and even later.

While some Christians delighted in telling stories about Jesus or narrating the history of the transcendent godhead, others spent considerable energy denigrating the tales of Greece and Rome and "mere myths," replete with immorality and unworthy notions of the divine. The process begins in the latter stages of the New Testament (1 Tim. 4.7) and continues as a staple of the apologetic tradition, from 2nd-century authors such as Justin Martyr (*Apology* 1.25) and Theophilus (*To Autolycus* 1.9; 2.5) to Augustine (*City of God* 2.4–6, 12–17, 24–26).

BIBL.: A. Y. Collins, "Mark and His Readers: The Son of God among Greeks and Romans," *Harvard Theological Review* 93 (2000): 85–100. Idem, "Mark and His Readers: The Son of God among Jews," *Harvard Theological Review* 92 (1999): 393–408. Bentley Layton, *The Gnostic Scriptures* (Garden City, N.Y., 1987). Gerd Theissen, *A Theory of Primitive Christian Religion* (London, 1999).   A.Y.C.

Visual Representations

Introduction

The imaging of god, or the gods, is a crucial part of all religious systems—not least of those religions that tend to deny that divinity can be represented in iconic form. Such denial is, after all, one answer to the fundamental question of how the essence of divinity, or its form, is to be represented in this world. Whenever an ancient artist or craftsperson set out to make an image of a deity, he or (rarely) she inevitably negotiated a whole range of key religious issues: could a human being represent a god? if so, how? what is god "like"? what, indeed, would count as a "likeness" of the divine? The civilizations of the ancient Mediterranean produced a vast array of very different answers to those questions, from the anthropomorphizing forms of Greco-Roman statues to the attempts within ancient Israelite religion and Judaism to represent YHWH as "word." In between come the animal forms (theriomorphs) of various Egyptian deities, the natural stones, trees, and plants that were widely taken to stand for gods, as well as a range of divine symbols and emblems (such as the fish in early Christianity).

In religious terms, however, the community of viewers (and, notably in the case of Zoroastrianism, the ritual context) is as important a part of the whole process of imaging as is the artist himself. For it is just as much in the reception of the image as in its creation that its religious power or plausibility must lie. There is a complicated trade-off always at work, between the image and its makers (who may determine or, at least, influence human understanding of the divine) and the viewers (who may or may not accept the image as a likely or legitimate representation). At one extreme of this process is the practice of iconoclasm, or the deliberate destruction of religious images; far from ignorant vandalism (as opponents often paint it), this is the ultimate rejection of the legitimacy of a religious image or the legitimacy of the deity whom the image represents. But it is not only

in such extreme cases that we see the interpretative and critical involvement of the viewers at work. It is only with their collusion that a tree, for example, or a stone can be deemed a representation or a symbol of a god—rather than "just a tree." In fact, it is always up to the viewer to decide whether any particular image is to be seen as a representation or a symbol of the divine—and what difference (religious or otherwise) might be entailed by any such difference of terminology.

The importance of understanding the viewer's response has considerable consequences for our interpretation of the role of images within different religions in the ancient world or even within different communities of what we call the same religion. For it is only when we have some contemporary written tradition discussing, or responding to, divine images that we can offer any detailed analysis of how those images were perceived or functioned, let alone what impact they might have on wider questions of religious ideology. When we rely on archeological or visual evidence alone, we are almost always faced with extremely tricky interpretative difficulties. In many cases, without a written tradition, we even find it hard to determine which images are to be counted as "religious," still less what their religious significance might be. It is an old joke among archeologists that whenever they find an object that they do not understand, they call it religious. Like most old jokes, there is more than a grain of truth in this.

In prehistoric Crete, for example, the identity of the famous figurines commonly known as "snake-goddesses" is still keenly disputed, as is the idea that they attest to some form of worship of a "mother-goddess." Almost equally hard to interpret are the wall paintings from the Minoan palace at Knossos, the majority of which were ambitiously restored in the early 20th century: which of them are deemed to represent religious practices and which state-political ceremonial practices (and whether such a distinction should be made) tends to depend of the prejudices of the modern scholar (not to mention the modern restorer). In other cases covered in this volume, it is as much as we can do to attach some sort of name to the deity portrayed.

But even in religious systems where there is a comparative wealth of literary and other written sources, those texts usually give us access only to the discussions of a small elite and, by and large, to the practices of urban religion. As for the understanding of visual images among the illiterate peasantry (i.e., the vast majority of the inhabitants of the ancient world), we are left either to assume that it broadly matched that of the literate urban elite or to make risky extrapolations from the images themselves. One area where these difficulties are very clear is the range of "syncretistic" representations of deities in the western provinces of the Roman Empire—images that combine standard attributes of Greco-Roman gods and goddesses with the forms of their "native" provincial counterparts. How far these were understood as a "real" combination of the two traditions or essentially native deities with a classicizing veneer (or vice versa) is almost impossible to decide. Another side of this problem is revealed by the visual conventions of early Christianity, where many "pagan" forms were incorporated in the Christian repertoire: in other words, what is apparently the same iconographic image could have drastically different meanings within different religious contexts.

Whatever the difficulties of interpretation, it is absolutely clear that images played a leading role in the cult practice and religious ideology of virtually all the religions of the ancient Mediterranean. Although most of them are now seen as museum objects, precious maybe, but sanitized and essentially static, the challenge for the historian of religion is always to recreate their active role within the religious context. In very many ancient societies, ritual regularly involved an encounter with images, which were manipulated, paraded, anointed, and addressed. And those rituals themselves regularly became the subject of representation, painted or sculpted on the walls of temples, sanctuaries, and palaces, even in private houses. In a complex and intersecting profusion of representation, images gave permanent form not only to deities, but to many of the ritual practices that themselves focused on the images of the gods.   M.B.

Egypt

Earlier periods. Art was fundamental to Egyptian civilization, standing at the core of a pervasive high-cultural communicative system. Representation of crucial religious motifs, especially images of deities, was very restricted and for around half the dynastic period was used primarily for cult images and in the decoration of temple interiors, to which only the king and elite priests had access. The vast amount of surviving material must be set against a general paucity of images in human life and in all but leading religious institutions. It is much

easier to see a range of religious imagery now than it was in antiquity.

The restriction of images becomes apparent during the formative period of Egyptian civilization. In late predynastic times, pictorial imagery disappeared from all but prestigious contexts, the principal surviving examples being on symbolic weapons and on offerings dedicated in temples. These images depict the world of an elite whose values centered on conquest and on the domination of forces of nature. From the same period, colossal limestone statues of the ithyphallic and protective god Min, which must have been visible to many, have the only iconography of a deity that was later displayed publicly and so suggest that long-lasting conventions were already in place.

The context in which religious imagery is organized is the temple scene, which typically shows the king of Egypt offering to, and receiving benefits from, a deity or deities. Temple decoration uses the general representational principles of Egyptian art, but presents a still more idealized world. Scenes have an almost abstract setting that signifies the world, with the top line formed into the hieroglyph of the sky, while the sides are occasionally shown to be its support and the baseline the earth. Whole walls of scenes and complete temple structures represent the cosmos, so that there is a nesting of imagery. The separation of the divine and royal as against humanity and the secular world is crucial to the system of decorum that structured many domains of Egyptian life and art. In pictorial terms, figures in temple scenes focus on human form, which is used even for deities whose principal manifestation is not anthropomorphic. Deities strongly associated with animals are often shown with animal heads and human bodies, in a convention—misunderstood and the object of scorn in classical antiquity—that brings attributes together but does not signify that such mixed beings were believed to exist.

Qualities of deities and of the king were symbolized by a limited range of elements, such as crowns and clothing, flesh color, and the emblems held in the hands. Images are identified by captions that can also complement their meaning. Thus, a quality that a deity gives to the king may not be represented as such, while the king's reciprocal dedication of offerings to the deity may be depicted but not captioned. Over vast periods, scenes became a little more explicit. A relatively common feature is emblematic personification, in which hieroglyphs for such concepts as *life* and *power* are shown with human limbs, rendering them capable of action toward the king in particular.

As in numerous traditions, cult images often had forms not found in other domains. Hardly any such images survive, because they were made of coveted precious materials and were also destroyed by early Christian iconoclasts. Nevertheless, representations of the images convey a little of their character. Some images preserved ancient models, while others mimicked them; in the long term they tended to amass ever more symbolic attributes. Before any important representations, such as a cult statue or the decoration of a temple, could fulfill their roles, a ritual of "opening the mouth" (a procedure by which the statue was animated) had to be performed on them. This quasi-living character of images is also indicated by a term for a sculptor: "he who makes to live" or "he who sustains."

The scarcity of imagery is a mark of its importance. Depictions of deities had to be protected. In certain contexts living beings were shown mutilated, presumably so that they could do no harm. The best-known examples of this practice are hieroglyphs of human figures, animals, and birds in Old and Middle Kingdom inscriptions set up in mortuary contexts. Because these contexts are so specialized, it does not follow that other images were believed to be similarly hazardous. The power of images is, however, confirmed in magic, where they could be used for harmful purposes, for example, when figurines were destroyed while incantations were recited.

The frequent confinement of religious imagery to temple contexts makes it difficult to interpret significant categories, such as the decoration of Old and Middle Kingdom nonroyal tombs. Much of this material, which consists primarily of scenes of daily life, probably conveys religious symbolism, but it is so strongly encrypted that little of it can be recovered.

New Kingdom (ca. 1520–1075 BCE). From the New Kingdom on, restrictions on religious imagery lessened and its use proliferated. Although the most prestigious material was still the preserve of gods and the king, deities could now be represented in nonroyal monuments such as tomb chapels. Votive stelae showing gods were dedicated in temples, as was statuary from the colossal to small or miniature votive pieces and amulets; the smaller-scale categories proliferated still more in the 1st millennium BCE.

The largest numbers of surviving votive offerings date to the 18th Dynasty and come from temples of the goddess Hathor, of which the most important was Deir el-Bahri in western Thebes. The objects range widely in type and include clay figurines of women that are not within normal Egyptian conventions and that were dedicated in the quest for fertility. A group of votive cloths exemplifies how much of religious and pictorial practice must be lost. These very perishable objects bear scenes of worshipers, mainly women, adoring figures of Hathor, typically shown as a cow either emerging from the Theban mountain or surrounded by papyrus marsh. Such images are very rare on other categories of material.

The New Kingdom is the period that has produced the largest amounts of religious material from dwellings and palaces. Many houses in the 19th–20th Dynasty village of Deir el-Medina had paintings relating to women's fertility, notably figures of the protective minor deities Bes and Taweret. Stelae and busts of human figures acted as the focus for a cult of ancestors, an institution otherwise little known from Egypt, perhaps because of the dearth of material from settlement sites.

The next world was depicted on nonroyal mortuary equipment, from illustrated papyrus manuscripts of the Book of the Dead to coffins, and still more impressively on the walls of royal tombs in Books of the Underworld that mix picture and text to present the domain of the dead through which the sun-god was believed to pass in the night. The strict conventions governing images in temples and in the accessible areas of tombs did not apply in underworld contexts, although representational forms were comparable. Underworld depictions, too, were arranged in registers, with the sun-god on his barque traveling along the middle register of three. Hundreds of deities and demons with sometimes monstrous features are represented, named, and described. Some compositions, in particular those showing the end of the sun-god's journey through the night, are more grandly organized to fill the entire pictorial space.

Vignettes in the Book of the Dead have partly similar content to Books of the Underworld. A composite iconography of sunrise and sunset, which is a this-worldly counterpart to the images of the end of the night in the Books of the Underworld, shows the solar disk between mountains, helped on its way by various deities and adored by figures representing humanity, deities, and mythical beings in the form of baboons. The best-known vignette is the judgment, in which the deceased owner of a papyrus is shown before Osiris, the judge of the dead. The judgment process is a weighing of the heart against "right order" *(ma'at)*, performed by Anubis and registered by Thoth, with a monster called "Eater of the Dead," whose body is a composite of crocodile and hippopotamus, in attendance—should the verdict be adverse.

The reforms of Akhenaten (1375–1358 BCE) marked a sharp change in religious art. During his reign the representation of deities in bodily form was suppressed progressively. Only the image of the sun disk and its rays descending on the world was retained; where the rays touched the royal family and some elements of temples and palaces, they terminated in human hands that offered the hieroglyph for "life" (the *ankh* sign) to the protagonists' nostrils. This art, which was in a radically new style, emphasized nature and adapted a strand of solar belief in which the natural world celebrated the creator's beneficence.

Akhenaten's reforms were quickly rejected, and the violence of the reaction to their artistic side is another measure of art's importance in religion. The return to traditional forms brought profound change in decorum. Within a few decades the decoration of nonroyal tombs in particular included more religious material, while scenes of daily life largely disappeared. While mortuary religious display proliferated, few votive offerings are preserved from this period, although the role of deities in people's lives is well attested, notably by the use of oracles.

The 1st millennium and the Greco-Roman period. The 21st Dynasty saw a radical transformation in religious imagery, especially in burials of the Theban elite in nests of highly decorated wooden coffins. Decorated tombs ceased to be constructed in the region, and burials focused on the coffin and the treatment of the mummified body. Scenes on the coffins derived from material such as the Books of the Underworld, together with cosmological compositions that are not known from other sources. Some people were buried with pictorial "mythological papyri," a few of which contain otherwise unknown motifs. Imagery used in burials continued to develop into Roman times, when both Egyptian and Greek forms were available for use. Tombs, however, were less culturally salient than earlier, and the elite displayed their status more by setting up their statues in temples.

First-millennium temples are less well known than earlier ones because most were in the Delta, where they did not survive. The late period was marked by an archaizing artistic revival and an increase in the amount of material deposited in temples. Votive offerings again became widespread. The major surviving body of such offerings is small-scale bronze statuary of deities, dedicated principally by individuals, which has a somewhat different iconography from material of earlier periods; no doubt much else was offered in less durable media. Animal cults were a major focus of late period religious display, in forms ranging from the keeping of live exemplars, through statuary, to complex customs of sacrifice and burial, all attended by appropriate artistic forms. Visual representation associated with magical practices proliferated in media ranging from small amulets, through rare illustrated papyri, to statuary and stelae covered with images of often outlandish forms of a universal creator or of minor deities. The scarab beetle, a symbol of the solar cycle and regeneration that originated in the 3rd millennium, became perhaps the most characteristic single Egyptian motif and was adopted in many other cultures.

Ptolemaic and Roman temples in southern Upper Egypt and Lower Nubia are not very representative but are most impressive. Decoration was generally at a smaller scale than before and increased vastly in content, reaching a peak in early Roman times. The principles of decoration changed in detail rather than fundamentally, but the pictorial style and the hieroglyphic inscriptions were transformed, creating the richest body of material known from Egyptian temples of any period.

Temple forms and broader practices of Egyptian religious art were influential in Syria-Palestine from the Middle Kingdom on and increasingly in the Mediterranean world from the later New Kingdom until the end of Egyptian civilization. The diffusion of Egyptian cults throughout the Roman Empire was accompanied by Egyptian divine imagery, but also stimulated the creation of iconographies of deities such as Isis in Greek form.

BIBL.: John Baines, *Fecundity Figures: Egyptian Personification and the Iconology of a Genre* (Warminster, 1985). Erik Hornung, "Ancient Egyptian Religious Iconography," in *Civilizations of the Ancient Near East* (ed. Jack M. Sasson et al.; New York, 1995), 3.1711–30. Geraldine Pinch, *Votive Offerings to Hathor* (Oxford, 1993). Gay Robins, *The Art of Ancient Egypt* (Cambridge, Mass., 1997). John H. Taylor, *Death and the Afterlife in Ancient Egypt* (London, 2001). J.R.B.

Mesopotamia

Principles and social framework. Religious imagery, as any other imagery, is an instrument of communication, and as such dependent on a social and mythological framework that determines its form, meaning, and use. The readability of the imagery is limited by the measure in which this framework is known, and since archeology has little access to social and still less to mythological facts, it is only with the onset of writing that Mesopotamian religious iconography becomes readable. Through history it gains progressive definition, in step with the increasingly more refined notions of cosmic order and divine rule, which develop as the ideological counterpart of an increasingly more complex and hierarchical society.

Basic to Mesopotamian religion, and consequently to Mesopotamian iconography, is the idea that the great gods, in origin and through history embodying natural phenomena, need their creations, humans, just as much as humans need the gods. The gods own earthly domains and live as supernatural landowners in "houses" (temples from a human perspective); there they administer their possessions and expect to be fed and clothed by their human servants (the cult from a human perspective). The god has a divine spouse (sometimes a human

Tree of Life in a design on a stone bowl of about 2300 BCE found at Susa. Louvre. *Erich Lessing/Art Resource, New York*

Assyrian warrior-god surrounded by divine symbols. Relief in Vorderasiatisches Museum, Berlin. *Bildarchiv Preussischer Kulturbesitz/Art Resource, New York*

Griffin genie, bird *apkallu*, typically carrying bucket and cone. Relief from Assyrian royal palace, the palace of Assurnasirpal II at Kalhu, 9th century BCE. Bristol Museum.

one as well), children, a vizier, and a household staff consisting of minor deities. The divine landowner and his court are represented by statues of wood, stone, or metal; the great gods are fully anthropomorphic, while lesser ones may be represented by animals or mixed animal-human forms. Such statues are not just representations of deities, but the deities themselves; in order to shed their origin as objects made by humans and to take the food that is offered, they have to undergo the magical rites of the "washing of the mouth" and the "opening of the mouth." Most of the cultic statuary is lost, but depictions on cylinder seals provide a good impression of its temporal and spatial variety.

The king is the foremost servant of the gods and is responsible to them for the service of his people; he builds the temples and provides them with what is needed for the cult. Since most of the cult is concerned with the daily life of the temple's divine inhabitant, a cultic inventory consists of practical things such as beds, thrones, (offering) tables, household utensils, jewelry, weapons, a chariot to wage war on the infidels, and a boat for family visits—all of them made of precious materials and dedicated with the proper rituals. The king leaves a record of his pious deeds (providing for the cult, defeating the infidels) in the temple, in pictures carved on stone, or in writing, for instance, on a statue representing himself as the deity's humble servant. Through time the courts of especially the national temples fill up with the records of many generations, becoming the stone memory of the nation (fig. 1, p. 604).

Besides the king, wealthy citizens may contribute to the cult and honor themselves with a commemorative plaque or a statue in the temple. By receiving the contribution of his human servant and allowing his representation in his vicinity, the god implies approval of the servant's performance, prolongation of his service, and thus life, health, and protection against evil. On cylinder seals from the late 3rd millennium onward, reception by a seated deity becomes the standard expression of divine favor and implied prosperity; often a member of the deity's court guides the visitor (the owner of the seal) into the presence of his lord (fig. 2).

In the last quarter of the 3rd millennium, the palace replaces the temple as the center of administration. The images in the palace serve to impress visitors with the king's piety, his achievements, and the divine support of his rule: monstrous spirits of metal or stone guard the entrances, battle scenes adorn the walls, and mythological sages purify the king and his visitors with holy water. As in Egypt the royal hunt, in reality or in images, metaphorically expresses the king's superiority over the enemies of divine order (fig. 3).

Under the symbols of the sun disk (Shamash), crescent (Sin), and eight-pointed star (Ishtar), the goddess Nanaya receives the king and his daughter. The goddess is seated on a lion-footed platform. Kassite, 12th century BCE, found at Susa. Louvre. *Erich Lessing/Art Resource, New York*

cifically cylinder seals. The figurative scenes on the seals usually relate to the well-being of the bearer, although not everything is as yet understood: reception scenes denote good relations with the divine government; contest scenes express protection and the ascendancy of divine order; banquet scenes celebrate enduring achievement. The intimate life force of the individual is represented by a nude frontal female, who remains independent of the scene. Small additional faunal, floral, or geometric elements seem to serve as good-luck charms.

Mythological framework. An outline of the cosmic order is transmitted by the public cults, while the details are filled out by the specialists of applied religion, the conjurer and the diviner, who make house calls and instruct their clients concerning what must be said and done during the rituals.

A yearly festival celebrates the primeval passage from chaos to order; the gods (in fact, their statues) assemble, and Enlil (later Marduk), seated on a representation of the Dukug (holy mound), which brought him into being, decides the nation's fate for the coming year. The dependent position of humanity and the leadership of the king are thoroughly integrated not only in the cult, the care and feeding of the gods, but in the whole fabric of Mesopotamian society. The relations are aptly epitomized by the image of the king as good shepherd and of the people as the god's herd (fig. 4).

The insecurity of the cosmic order is revealed by the continuing threat of breaches. The steppes and hills beyond the rule of Mesopotamian kings breed enemies of all kinds, natural and supernatural, which may be visualized as nude gods being defeated on their mountains or as wild animals being overpowered and killed. Even the stones that support civilization in a land of clay can be imagined as "domesticated" foreign rebels who by implication praise their divine subduer. Representations of divine weapons symbolize permanent vigilance (fig. 5).

The mountains not only breed evil, but also harbor a pristine purity unstained by human hands. Since impurity, later reinterpreted as sin, is the ultimate cause of suffering, the restoration of purity plays a major part in the healing rituals of the conjurer, whose incantations transform water and vegetal elements (specifically parts of the date palm) into cosmic cleansing agents. A stylized version of the date palm symbolizing cosmic (royal and divine) order develops into an important emblem of Neo-Assyrian royal power (fig. 6).

The early cosmos is marked by the same ambiguity

Private lives are motivated in part by community religion and in part by religious themes proper to the continuity of the family and the prosperity of its members. A private house may be protected against the forces of evil by representations of apotropaic spirits, cheap downscaled versions of those that guard the palace. In case of illness or misfortune, a conjurer exorcizes the demons using an array of constructed and natural substances, transformed into *materia magica* by incantations; at the end of the proceedings the conjurer purifies the victim and ensures the permanence of the results by leaving a figurine of his role model, a mythological sage holding a bucket with cleansing water and a sprinkler. The family's dead, represented by objects or by an empty chair, are commemorated periodically during a communal meal.

The identity of the individual is publicized by details of dress, ornaments, and items of personal use, spe-

Fig. 1.

Fig. 2.

Fig. 4.

a   b

Fig. 5.

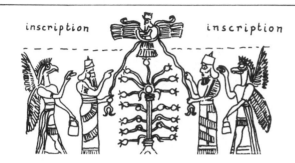

inscription   inscription

Fig. 6.

a   b   c   d   e   f

Fig. 7.

a   b   a

Fig. 8.

Fig. 9.

Fig. 10. *Courtesy Frans Wiggermann*

that makes the mountains the location of both the pure and the impure: it breeds demons as well as the primeval sages, the role models of the conjurer. They are fishmen, born in the stream, who share the wisdom of Enki, the god of white magic. In practice, images of these sages legitimize the tricks of the conjurer as the product of cosmic purity (fig. 7).

In between the otherworld of the periphery and the safety of home is a transit zone, which defines a set of beings of dubious allegiance. Their nature is mixed, neither human nor animal, neither domesticated nor wild, but they tend to follow orders of the gods and side with civilization in its struggle against disruption. The mythology of the Iron Age views them as the products of primeval chaos, which, once defeated by Marduk, support order in the service of the gods. In contest scenes, they overpower wild animals, and they guard houses and palaces against intruding evil (fig. 8).

Scenes from myth or epic are rarely depicted. One of the exceptions is Gilgamesh's defeat of the monster Humbaba, a pivotal episode of the Epic of Gilgamesh. As a variant of the contest scene, the image presumably has an apotropaic function, which explains its exceptional existence. By itself, the monstrous head of Humbaba is an apotropaion of the same type as the heads of the Egyptian Bes and the Greek Medusa: their terror scares off unwelcome visitors.

Individual figures. Mesopotamian mythology is concerned with the cosmic framework and the ensuing political order much more than with stories exploiting the character of individual figures. With the exceptions of Enki (Akkadian Ea) and the Mother-Goddess (who exhibit an abiding interest in humans, their creations), of Inanna (Akkadian Ishtar) and Dumuzi (the role models of courtship and love), and of the baby-snatching demoness Lamashtu, deities and demons remain just

faceless actors playing their narrow cosmic and political roles. Their iconographies reflect these limitations.

In the earliest historical periods, the anthropomorphic gods are not formally distinguished from human beings; only the position of a figure in the scene sometimes points it out as a deity (or a human being playing the part of a deity). From the first half of the 3rd millennium onward, deities may be distinguished by horns growing out of their heads (symbolic of light), by horned crowns, and later by feathered ones. From the second half of the 3rd millennium onward, deities may be distinguished from each other by added elements identifying their functions: gods of war and death carry weapons and are accompanied by fierce animals (lion, bull) or monsters; the water-god Enki (Akkadian Ea) has streams of water emanating from his shoulders, the sun-god UTU (Akkadian Shamash) rays of heat, the wargoddess Inanna (Akkadian Ishtar) maces and axes. Not all gods are clearly marked in this way, and especially the iconography of the main god Enlil remains uncertain; it seems, however, that his authority is represented by the lion-headed eagle Anzud (Akkadian Anzu), who also identifies Enlil's son and warrior Ninurta (fig. 9).

During the 2nd and 1st millennia, the Akkadian pantheon moves toward a kind of monotheism, in which the individual gods become aspects of one high god, Marduk. Concomitantly the added elements once identifying gods develop into a complete set of symbols identifying divine functions named after gods (fig. 10).

Besides wild animals that under certain circumstance may represent evil, the baby-snatching demoness Lamashtu is the only evil force with a definite iconography. The written sources reveal her as a countergoddess, the insurgent reverse of Ishtar, an unmotherly mother, who demands human babies for food. Her appearance matches her character: she is a mixed being composed out of the parts of various predators.

Textual passages show that Mesopotamian artists could recombine iconographic elements in order to create new beings expressing surprisingly abstract notions such as Zeal, Competition, or Strife. The metaphoric reading that this implies indicates that other images as well may have meaning beyond the literal.

BIBL.: J. Black and A. Green, *Gods, Demons, and Symbols of Ancient Mesopotamia* (London: British Museum Press, 1992). I. L. Finkel and M. J. Geller (eds.), *Sumerian Gods and Their Representations* (Groningen: Styx, 1997). N. P. Heessel, *Pazuzu: Archäologische und philologische Studien zu einem altorientalischen Dämon* (Leiden: Brill, 2002). U. Seidl, *Die babylonischen Kudurru-Reliefs: Symbole mesopotamischer Gottheiten* (Freiburg: Universitätsverlag, 1989). F. A. M. Wiggermann, *Mesopotamian Protective Spirits: The Ritual Texts* (Groningen: Styx, 1992). F.A.M.W.

Syria-Canaan

The visual arts (iconography) are an important source for studying Syro-Palestinian religion, complementing the texts and providing unique perspectives. The exact relationship between texts and images is still under discussion. Different types of representations are known: the enthroned god, menacing god and goddess, standing god and goddess, goddess on horseback, naked goddess (with an emphasis on prominent body parts). Ascertaining the function of an iconographic type (e.g., a warrior-goddess) is of greater importance than merely identifying it by a divine name (e.g., Anat). The function of many depictions still needs clarification. Very few items have inscriptions that identify the deities, and these are limited to Egyptian stelae that have representations of Syro-Canaanite deities.

Visual sources include media such as stone statues, relief, stelae, paintings, ivories, metal and clay figurines and plaques, metal pendants, painted pottery, seals, and amulets (available in abundance and especially of value when paintings and reliefs, such as those found in Egypt and Mesopotamia, are lacking); for the later period, coins are important as visual sources. The following discussion emphasizes the iconography of the gods, rather than the iconography of the cult.

From early Jericho come human skulls with modeled features—perhaps part of some ancestral cult. It is still debated whether the lime plaster figurines from Ain Ghazal in Jordan depict deities or deified ancestors (ca. 7000–5500 BCE).

The excavations at Ebla (2300 BCE) yielded a bull-man figurine—guardian of the heavenly gates who opened the gates at dawn so that the sun could come out, according to Mesopotamian mythology. Nineteenth-century BCE cultic basins with reliefs depict mythological scenes, and fragments of seal impressions on jars depict the weather-god (Hadad) with raised

Example of an Ashdoda figure: Philistine goddess enthroned—that is, in the shape of a chair. *Photo by Z. Radovan, Jerusalem*

mace, horned headdress, and bull figurine, accompanied by his female consort with bird on her head (Astarte).

Metal figurines from 2nd-millennium Byblos might represent deities. From the Syrian port of Ugarit (Ras Shamra) come various representations: seated chief god and creator Ilu (stele and bronze/gold figurine), his consort and mother of the gods Asherah (bronzes standing and seated with her hand in a gesture of blessing like Ilu), and weather- and warrior-god Baal (large stele and identified on the Baal-Zaphon stele). Sometimes he appears on seals (winged Baal-Seth on the back of a lion or serpent slayer). A winged figure (stele, ivory, and seal) might be his sister and consort Anat, closely connected with war.

At Megiddo in Palestine a seated bronze figure (Ilu-type) and Resheph-type warrior with shield were discovered, as well as ivories with Egyptian motifs (sphinx and household deity Bes).

Syro-Palestinian deities are known from New Kingdom Egyptian stelae (ca. 15th to 12th centuries BCE):

Head of a deity from an Edomite shrine, Horvat Qitmit, first half of 6th century BCE. *Courtesy Itzhaq Beit-Arieh*

Astarte (standing, warrior, equestrian), Anat (seated, standing, and warrior), Qedeshet (naked, holding flowers and serpents, sometimes on lions), and Resheph (menacing, with shield). Resheph also occurs on seal amulets on the back of horned animals as "lord of the animals." From Ugarit there are plaques of the Qedeshet-type in metal and in clay from Palestine. A goddess on horseback (Astarte as war-goddess) was found on a gold foil from Lachish, as well as graffiti of a god with spear (Baal as serpent slayer). Beisan stelae show Anat and the seated god Mekal. At Hazor a high place with stelae (one with hands worshiping the heavenly powers) and a stone statue of a god standing on a bull were found.

Several Phoenician deities have been identified on images. Baal-Melqart, chief god of Tyre, is shown with battle-ax over his shoulder on a stele (800 BCE) found near Aleppo. His consort Astarte is shown seated as a bronze figurine. Baal-Hammon of Carthage sits on a cherub throne, and stelae show the Tanit symbol. No clearly identified depictions of alleged child sacrifice have been found. The "lady of Byblos" is shown seated on a stele of Yehaumilk of Byblos (5th century BCE). At

Amrit a stele of the god Shadrapa on a lion in Egyptian style was found.

Aramean representations are known from several sites. Tell Halaf (Guzana): deities on animals, large bird, scorpion, and bull-men supporting winged sun; Ain Dara: mountain-gods; Arslan Tash (Khadatu): ivories (Egyptian motifs such as a god on a lotus); Zincirli: stele of god Hadad with horns, weather-god with ax and thunderbolt, and goddess Kubaba. A rare example of wall painting occurs at Deir Alla in Jordan depicting a winged sphinx. Later Aramean deities are known from Palmyra, including the gods Baal-Shamem (Lord of Heaven) and Yarhibol (a sun-god). At Hatra the god Maran appears with horns, a crescent, and sun.

Philistine religion is known from the early Ashdoda figurines (from Ashdod): a throne/seat in the form of a woman perhaps representing a mother-goddess and imported from Mycenae. Seals contain important scenes, and a bull figurine in a shrine comes from Ashkelon (1550 BCE). (Many other bull figurines are known from other sites.)

An Edomite shrine at Qitmit contained the head of a goddess (consort of Qaus) with three horns, and from En Hazeva come anthropomorphic cult stands of clay. Stone sculptures from Ammon might represent the god Milcom. A Late Bronze Age warrior-god comes from Sihan, and male and female deities are shown on a stele from Balua in Jordan.

Nabatean religious iconography is a mixture of the stelae cult *(betyl)*, sometimes aniconic and later anthropomorphic forms, as known from Petra. Dushara (Qaus) is shown flanked by bulls with thunderbolt. His consort Allat is shown as a *betyl* with a face.

BIBL.: Izak Cornelius, *The Iconography of the Canaanite Gods Reshef and Baal: The Late Bronze and Iron Age I Periods (c 1500–1000 BC)* (Göttingen, 1994). Othmar Keel and Christoph Uehlinger, *Gods, Goddesses, and Images of God in Ancient Israel* (Minneapolis, 1998), chaps. 2–3. Ora Negbi, *Canaanite Gods in Metal* (Tel Aviv, 1976).   I.C.

Israel

The ban on visual representations of YHWH or any other deity is one of the most distinctive features of biblical religion. Greek and Latin authors from the early Hellenistic period onward consider Jewish worship to be aniconic. Biblical tradition relates this image ban to divine revelation to Moses on Mount Sinai. Historians of religion have suggested various hypotheses to explain it, none of which is entirely convincing.

Biblical texts. The biblical prohibition does not concern visual art in general, but only the production and worship of cult-related images. Major references include Exod. 20.4 parallel Deut. 5.8 (the second commandment of the Decalogue); Exod. 20.23; 23.23–24; 34.13, 16–17; Lev. 19.4; 26.1; Num. 33.52–53; Deut. 16.21–22; and 27.15. The prohibition is primarily directed against anthropomorphic and theriomorphic cult statuary; more extensive catalogues also mention stelae, barely sculpted or nonfigurative standing stones, and sacred trees and may even include votive statuary (cf. Deut. 5.8; 4.16–17). Only Deut. 4.15–18 provides a reason: Israel only heard YHWH on Mount Sinai but did not see any definite shape *(tĕmûnâ)*. Other texts may conceive of a divine *Gestalt,* which might have been known to Moses (Num. 12.8; Exod. 33.11 vs. 33.20; Deut. 34.10) but was never revealed to all of Israel. A few texts require the destruction of non-Israelite sanctuaries together with their images, sacred stones and trees, and other ritual paraphernalia (Deut. 7.5; 12.2–3; cf. Mic. 5.12–14 [= 5.11–13 Hebrew]; 1 Macc. 13.47).

Iconoclasm is reported for the so-called cult reforms of the Judean kings Hezekiah (2 Kings 18.4) and Josiah (2 Kings 23). Yet, biblical texts offer numerous examples of iconolatry practiced by Israelites (e.g., Judg. 17–18; Exod. 32; Ezek. 16.17–19; 23.41). Best known among Israelite cultic images are the bull calves said to have been erected at Bethel and Dan by King Jeroboam I (1 Kings 12.26–32). These are regarded by Deuteronomist historiographers as an expression of the northern kingdom's basic sin against YHWH's covenant with Israel (2 Kings 10.29; Deut. 9.12; Ps. 106.19–20). The golden calf episode in Exod. 32 (cf. Deut. 9) is related to the Bethel tradition. In both instances the people who produced the bull-calf statues perceived them as visual representations of YHWH, the god of Israel. This interpretation concurs with a well-established Bronze and Iron Age tradition of storm-god iconography, which may have subsisted in Israel until at least the 8th century BCE but was rejected by the biblical writers. In Hos. 8.4–6; 10.5–6; and 13.2, YHWH disconnects himself from bull statuary at Bethel. Further iconolatrous features in both Israel and Judah include the Asherah (as a cult object: 1 Kings 15.13; 16.33; 2 Kings 21.7; 23.4, 6–7), the Nehushtan serpent said to have been made by Moses (2 Kings 18.5; cf. Num. 21.9), and the image of jealousy (Ezek 8.3). The tabernacle (Exod 25–26; 35–40) and Solomon's temple in Jerusalem (1 Kings 6–9), while lavishly decorated, are said not to have housed an image of the deity. According to 1 Kings 8.6–9, YHWH was represented in the holy of holies of the preexilic temple in Jerusalem by the ark, a mobile chest containing holy stones and protected by winged, human-headed sphinxes (the cherubim). However, Ezek. 8 hints again at the coexistence of several cults, some of them clearly iconolatrous, in the late preexilic temple precinct. Some exilic or postexilic prophetic texts mock artisans who produce idols, considering them to be actual gods (Isa. 40.18–20; 41.6–7; 44.9–20; 46.5–8; Jer. 10.1–8). Explicitly non-Israelite idolatry is a regular topic of biblical mockery (e.g., 1 Sam. 5), Babylon being considered the center of idolatry (Isa. 46.1; Jer. 50.38; 51.47, 52; Bar. 6 [The Letter of Jeremiah]; Dan. 5).

Extrabiblical evidence. A late-8th-century BCE Assyrian royal inscription from Nimrud mentions "the gods in whom they trusted" (i.e., divine images) among the spoil taken from Samaria in 720 BCE. Hebrew inscriptions from Kuntillet Ajrud in northern Sinai, dated around 800 BCE, feature blessing formulas: "by YHWH of Samaria [or of Teman] and his Asherah." According to some scholars, this should refer to the worship of a pair of divine statues; other scholars take "his Asherah" to refer to a nonanthropomorphic cultic symbol, possibly in the shape of a stylized tree (but note the reference to women weaving garments for "[the] Asherah" in 2 Kings 23.7). Asherah is generally thought to have provided the figurative model for the so-called *dea nutrix* pillar figurines of the 8th and 7th centuries that represent a well-dressed lady supporting or offering her breasts. Such small inexpensive statuary was mainly used in traditional Judahite family religion to provide blessing for the house and grave. It disappears from the Judahite and Samarian archeological record from the Persian period onward.

So far only one clearly Yahwistic sanctuary of preexilic times has been fully excavated: a small shrine that was part of the Judahite fortress of Arad, which controlled the southern Judahite hills during the 8th and 7th centuries BCE. A standing stone painted red (probably representing blood, i.e., life) seems to have been the only visual representation of the main deity worshiped there, most probably YHWH. A similar installation in Ahab's "temple of the Baal" at Samaria was considered abominable by Deuteronomistic writers and is said to have been purged by Jehu (2 Kings 10.26–27).

Origins, formation, and development of biblical aniconism. Some authors follow the main lines of the biblical texts, considering that Israelite religion was always aniconic in essence; they regard conflicting evidence as traces of non-Israelite, that is, "pagan," idolatry that persisted in Israel and Judah until at least the Persian period. Other scholars assume a dichotomy between an essentially aniconic state religion and iconolatrous popular religion. But terra-cotta figurines are attested even in royal palaces, and iconolatry was not restricted to cheap terra-cotta. A third group of scholars thinks that much of what the Bible depicts as heterodox deviations actually reflects practices that once were an integral part of Israelite religion. Some of these scholars favor a basically evolutionary view according to which sacred images became gradually suspect from the 8th century onward until the essentially aniconic worship of the postexilic period. However, biblical evidence such as Ezekiel's visionary description of idolatrous cults performed in late preexilic Jerusalem (Ezek. 8) or Jeremiah's debate with recently exiled Judeans over the legitimacy of worshiping the Queen of Heaven (Jer. 44), seems to exclude a simple linear development. A last group of scholars tends to ascribe late, postexilic dates to the biblical sources that require an exclusively aniconic worship of YHWH. They consider preexilic Israelite religion as essentially analogous to the neighboring cultures of Iron Age Palestine. The main difficulties in this debate are our inability to date precisely most of the biblical texts and to substantiate any of the four positions with unambiguous archeological evidence.

While possibly related to an old West Semitic tradition of stone worship, aniconism may have become more explicit following the loss of anthropomorphic statuary and other objects such as the ark in the wake of the Assyrian and Babylonian conquests. Exiled priests such as Ezekiel could no longer relate to the cult of their central sanctuary. As a consequence, new concepts of divine presence were developed, which concentrated on purely symbolical presence such as the "glory" or "name" of YHWH. The image-ban texts in the Torah apparently do not antedate the Babylonian exile; consequently, they should be explained against the peculiar background of the 6th and 5th centuries BCE. We know that after the exile, Deuteronomistic and Priestly theologians radically disconnected YHWH from all other deities of the region and even from traditional concepts of YHWH himself, which were now reviled as Baal worship. In this situation, the image ban effectively contributed to the strength of exclusive Yahwism.

Implementation of biblical and Jewish aniconism. The aniconic nature of the postexilic temple in Jerusalem is assured around 300 BCE by Hecataeus (reported by Diodorus 40.3). Late Hellenistic descriptions of Second Temple inventory mention the menorah, a table, and an incense altar as the most basic furniture of the holy of holies. After the loss of the Second Temple in 70 CE, Jewish synagogue worship focused increasingly on the Torah scroll in ways reminiscent of the treatment that other religions reserved for cultic images. Rabbinic tractates (especially *Avodah Zarah* [lit., idolatry]) discuss how aniconic worship of YHWH alone could be observed in a non-Jewish environment. Excavated synagogues of late antiquity show that the interpretation of the biblical image ban could vary according to sociocultural context. The 3rd-century CE mural paintings of the Diaspora synagogue of Dura Europos on the Euphrates or the 4th- to 6th-century CE mosaic floors of synagogues in Byzantine Palestine depict scenes from the Bible and even the "pagan" zodiac featuring anthropomorphic Helios (the sun) in its very center. These images may have been understood as merely symbolic pictures without any inherently sacred character.

BIBL.: Erwin R. Goodenough, *Jewish Symbols in the Greco-Roman Period* (abridged by Jacob Neusner; Bollingen Series 37; Princeton: Princeton University Press, 1988). Othmar Keel and Christoph Uehlinger, *Gods, Goddesses, and Images of God in Ancient Israel* (Minneapolis: Fortress, 1998). Silvia Schroer, *In Israel gab es Bilder: Nachrichten von darstellender Kunst im Alten Testament* (Orbis Biblicus et Orientalis 74; Göttingen: Vandenhoeck & Ruprecht, 1987). Karel van der Toorn (ed.), *The Image and the Book: Iconic Cults, Aniconism, and the Rise of Book Religion in Israel and the Ancient Near East* (Leuven: Peeters, 1997).   C.U.

Anatolia

Most of the information we possess concerning Hittite religion is drawn from textual sources, from the thousands of cuneiform tablets excavated at the capital city Hattusha. Among these texts we find hymns, prayers, detailed descriptions of ceremonies, and some cultic inventories containing descriptions of the divine images housed in temples and shrines. For example:

> The Storm-god of Likḫzina [as worshiped in the town of] Tiliura: The divine image is a wooden bull rhyton, standing on all fours, plated with silver; its head and breast are plated with gold. Its height is one span; beneath it is a socle. King Murshili donated a silver beaker, eight shekels in weight, to the Storm-god of Likḫzina. Ten bronze sun-disks have been nailed onto the offering table of the Storm-god [of Likḫzina]. We have built a new temple for him. (KUB 38.3 1.1–6.)

As indicated in this excerpt, the three-dimensional earthly representation of a god or goddess was often made in whole or in part of precious metals. Few objects of such valuable material have survived, but there are some exceptions to the general fate of plunder and melting down for reuse. Three silver rhyta—a bull protome (fig. 178—all figures come from Bittel 1976), a stag protome (fig. 169), and a "fist"—not only provide vivid confirmation of the occasional theriomorphic rendering of Hittite deities, but each of the latter two objects is also decorated with a frieze depicting a scene of worship. Ceramic libation vessels in animal shapes (figs. 156–66) should also be mentioned here. Small (10–20 cm) bronze anthropomorphic figurines (figs. 147, 149, 175, 262, 263) may be actual cult images from minor shrines, while tiny pendants of gold, silver, or electron (figs. 167, 168, 170, 171, 173, 179, 180) give us an idea of the likely appearance of the lost statues from great temples.

The most impressive artistic renderings of Hittite divinities, however, are those done in relief sculpture, both on the living rock as at İmamkulu (fig. 203), Fraktin (figs. 196, 198), and the rock sanctuary of Yazılıkaya (figs. 232–241, 249–254) and on stelae (figs. 207, 230, 247, 264) or orthostats, the last particularly numerous at Alaca Höyük (figs. 212–227). The cosmological scene at Eflatun Pınar, composed of blocks carved in low relief (fig. 257), is especially noteworthy. The use of orthostats would assume great importance in the Neo-Hittite culture of the 1st millennium (figs. 276–318), as exemplified most charmingly in a depiction of the battle of the storm-god with the serpent, an event well known from Hittite mythology (fig. 279).

Stone sculpture in the round—or nearly so—is known

Relief of a Hittite god in martial dress, with a pointed helmet, carrying an ax and sword. From the King's Gate, Hattusha, 13th century BCE. Ankara, Museum of Archaeology. *Hirmer Fotoarchiv*

chiefly for guardian figures in gate complexes (figs. 209–211, 258–261, 265–268). Theriomorphic column and statue bases are frequently found at Neo-Hittite sites (figs. 282, 303, 307).

Seals and seal impressions are another important source of Hittite religious imagery. The stamp seals characteristic of Hittite glyptic normally have space enough for the depiction of only a single god (figs. 185, 186, 193), but some large royal seals could accommodate a scene of a monarch in the embrace of his patron deity (figs. 191, 192). The long continuous design produced by the rolling of the much less common cylinder seal might picture two or more deities (figs. 182, 183) or even depict a religious ceremony (fig. 155) or mythological scene (fig. 152).

Presenting similar compositional possibilities is the relief vase, on which one—or more often several—bands of painted appliqué figures around the upper portion of the large vessel show scenes of worship. Well-preserved jars of this type are known from Bitik (figs.

140, 144), İnandik, and Hüseyindede Tepe, and fragments of such vessels have been excavated at Bogazköy and Alisar. The frieze is thus an important organizational element in surviving Hittite religious art, appearing on rhyta, cylinder seals, and relief ceramics and in the galleries of Yazılıkaya.

A comparison of these decorative bands with the motifs on cylinder seals in use in the Assyrian trading colonies in Anatolia from the period immediately preceding the establishment of the Hittite state leaves little doubt that the basic elements of Hittite religious iconography were borrowed from Syria and ultimately from Mesopotamia. This is seen particularly in the rendering of anthropomorphic figures in a combination of profile and frontal view, as well as the convention by which a personage's divinity is indicated by the presence of one or more pairs of horns. As for work in three dimensions, many of the small bronze statuettes of Hittite deities—particularly those of the "striding god" type—are practically indistinguishable from those found throughout the Levant in the Late Bronze Age.

A native Anatolian contribution, however, is the alternate representation of certain gods in theriomorphic and anthropomorphic form, a practice already attested in earlier local iconography (Alaca Höyük, Kanes). Thus the storm-god may appear as a bull, and the Tutelary Deity as a stag. It is also clear from both textual and artistic material that cultic implements in the shape of these animals, and the beasts themselves as sacrificial victims, were central to the worship of these particular gods.

Several deities enjoy an established standard iconography. For instance, the sun-god is inevitably dressed in a skullcap and long robe and bears a winged sun-disk upon his head. The storm-god wears a pointed hat and short kilt with a dagger tucked into his belt and often brandishes a mace and/or forked lightning bolt. The similarly clad Tutelary Deity shoulders a bow or less frequently a crook. Most divinities, however, are undifferentiated visually, although they may sometimes be distinguished, as in the procession at Yazılıkaya, by accompanying hieroglyphic writings of their names. In particular, each goddess (save the bigendered Sawusga) is depicted in the same voluminous mantle and long skirt, with a cowl, or later a high cylindrical *polos*, upon her head.

Finally, the friezes on ceramic and silver vessels complement textual descriptions of Hittite worship. Here we see the deities honored by libation or animal sacrifice, while being entertained with music, acrobatics, and other athletic activities, including bull jumping.

BIBL.: K. Bittel, *Die Hethiter* (Munich, 1976). H. G. Güterbock and T. Kendall, "A Hittite Silver Vessel in the Form of a Fist," in *The Ages of Homer: A Tribute to Emily Townsend Vermeule* (ed. J. B. Carter and S. P. Morris; Austin, 1995), 45–60. L. Rost, "Zu den hethitischen Bildbeschreibungen (I. Teil)," *Mitteilungen des Instituts für Orient-*

Sphinx with both a human head and a lion's head. Relief from Carchemish, late Hittite period. Ankara, Museum of Archaeology. *Hirmer Fotoarchiv*

forschung 8 (1961): 161–217. N. Willemaers, "Contribution iconographique à l'histoire du rituel hittite," *Revue d'archéologie et histoire d'art de Louvain* 6 (1973): 7–18. Idem, "Contribution iconographique à l'histoire du rituel hittite, II—Confrontation avec les textes," *Hethitica* 2 (1977): 53–78.   G.M.B.

Iran

The sacred fire is a major symbol of the religious insights of the Zoroastrian tradition. Another icon, the winged disk, also has come to be regarded by many as an important Zoroastrian emblem. All other major visual presentations, other than the image of Zarathustra himself, are significant liturgically and must be understood in their ritual contexts.

The visual image of a winged disk dates back to times and cultures prior to the Achaemenian Dynasty. In the palace complex begun by Darius at Persepolis in the 6th century BCE, on the edge of the Marv Dasht, are many carved images of a winged disk, often with a bird tail beneath it and two undulating appendages. Sometimes a male figure stands within the circle, with robe and kingly crown, his right hand raised in benediction and his left holding a ring. This image possibly represents the Avestan *khvarenah*, "the divine grace sought after by men to bring them long life, power and prosperity" (Boyce 1982: 103). A figure in the winged circle may symbolize the royal *khvarenah*, the divine power that attends each ruler and his dynasty. Contemporary Zoroastrians view this winged-disk figure as symbolic of the guardian spirits (Avestan *fravashi*) of the souls of the living and the dead. It is often displayed over entrances to fire temples, worn around the neck as a talisman, and more generally is used as a symbol of the Zoroastrian tradition.

Likewise, representations of the sacred fire and other liturgically significant items, including images of priests themselves, are important visual symbols of this tradition. A stone carving from Dascylion, the capital of the Achaemenian satrapy of Hellespontine Phrygia (late 6th or early 5th century BCE), depicts two Zoroastrian priests (magi) attentively standing side by side and each holding a long *barsom* (a bundle of twigs or metal wires) and performing what appears to be a ceremony for the spirits of the dead. Each is costumed in tunic and trousers with a sleeved mantle and a head covering. In the treasury at Persepolis pestles and mortars have been found, and at the tomb of Darius at Naqsh-e Rostam is a depiction in stone of a burning fire in a fire holder atop a raised base.

It is at this point, however, that a further distinction regarding the nature of visual representations in this tradition needs to be made. A stone image of a sacred fire may appear on the facade of a fire temple, but inside the fire temple resides a living fire, the focal point of ritual performance. The real art works of this tradition, it can be argued, are to be found in the celebration of the rituals themselves because the liturgies have an aesthetic dimension of their own. We can refer to them as major visual presentations of the tradition.

The great Fires of Victory (Pahlavi *ātash wahrām*) consecrated in temple sanctuaries, for example, are theologically understood as exemplifications of the infinite light of Ahura Mazda and physically visible instantiations of the animating principle of life itself (see color plate). Like the priests who constantly attend to them, these fires are thought of as warriors combating the dark forces of decay, deceit, ignorance, and death and thus serve as icons of the good creation's victory over the forces of evil.

Likewise, each individual fire ignited in a temple's rit-

or walking within the ritual area, a ritual priest always moves with disciplined, regulated gestures during a ceremony. The mask worn over his nose and mouth and his white costuming tend to erase his personal identity, and he visually takes on the role of purifier, one who is empowered to create a consecrated space in which to invoke the blessings of all that is good and beautiful in creation.

Within the context of such carefully orchestrated liturgies, the various implements and items used in the ritual ceremony also serve as living symbols of the Zoroastrian tradition. For example, the *barsom,* which was held by the priest in his left hand while performing high liturgies, or the mortar and pestle central to the performance of the daily *yasna* liturgy, are replete with symbolic meaning. A priest holds the *barsom* to exemplify the connection between the physical and spiritual worlds. The mortar and pestle are ritual implements used to extract liquid for a sacramental drink. The chief priest pounds *hom* twigs in the mortar, each blow of the pestle smiting the invoked presence of Angra Mainyu and all wicked demons. He also strikes the rim of the mortar with the pestle, rapidly and repeatedly, causing it to ring out with sounds of victory over the wicked Angra Mainyu.

In addition to these ritual items, water is equal to the fire in prominence in Zoroastrian liturgies. Visually, water provides a mirrorlike replication of light and is the source of health and an instrument of purification. For this reason, Zoroastrians in all walks of life often stand before open well water or face the ocean waters while performing their daily devotions. In the *yasna* high liturgy, the chief priest concludes the service by pouring a consecrated libation into well water, thereby infusing the whole of creation with its consecrated strength.

Rituals held outside fire temples, such as the ceremony of blessings (Pahlavi *āfrīnagan*), also provide images expressive of the tradition. This act of worship (Pahlavi *jashan*) is usually conducted on a patterned Persian rug on which are placed a wealth of offerings: fresh flowers, a silver tray laden with fruits and prepared foods, vessels of milk and wine, a living fire in a raised fire vase, and a metal tray containing fragrant sandalwood and frankincense. The scripted ritual gestures by the white-costumed priests visually culminate in a simple, thrice-repeated exchange of flowers between the two priests. This gestural act serves as a dramatic visual metaphor for the connection that such a ritual establishes between this physical world and the unseen realm, which bestows blessings on the whole creation. This celebration, in other words, comprises a visually rich and theologically meaningful expression of the Zoroastrian tradition.

BIBL.: Mary Boyce, *A History of Zoroastrianism,* vol. 2 (Leiden: Brill, 1982). Firoze M. Kotwal and James W. Boyd (eds. and trans.), *A Guide to the Zoroastrian Religion: A 19th Century Catechism with Modern Commentary* (Chico,

Mithra. Rock relief at Taq-i-Bostan, Iran, 4th century CE. *Archive J. K. Choksy*

ual area (Persian *dar-i mihr*) and exclusively dedicated to its role in a specific liturgical service is a major visual symbol of Zoroastrian ritual and theology. Elevated on a fire stand, such a ritual fire is approached with gestures of respect by qualified priests and is the object of manthric praise and devotion, all of which create the dramatic effect of the fire as a virtual "being." This response is reinforced by the theological definition of the fire as "he," the "son of god." The effect, in the words of one priest, is profound: "In the eyes of the faithful, this glow of fire and everything surrounding it would seem to be the presence of God" (Kotwal and Boyd 1982: 55).

Living, robed Zoroastrian priests are also significant expressions of this tradition. Whether standing, sitting,

Example of a winged-disk symbol (representing either Ahura Mazda or Farnah); rock relief at Persepolis, 5th century BCE. *Archive J. K. Choksy*

Calif.: Scholars Press, 1982). Ron G. Williams and James W. Boyd, *Ritual Art and Knowledge: Aesthetic Theory and Zoroastrian Ritual* (Columbia: University of South Carolina Press, 1993). J.W.B., F.M.

Greece, Rome, and Etruria

Images of deities filled the classical world. Archaic and classical Greek sanctuaries hosted a vast array of statues, from the divine figures crafted by leading artists that decorated temple pediments to the humble models of gods and goddesses offered as dedications. Etruscan tombs featured a now-baffling variety of deities and demons painted on their chamber walls. From the Hellenistic period at least, rich private houses might be adorned with choice sculptures drawn from the repertoire of divine images, gods and goddesses characterized by distinctive attributes and poses (Athena/Minerva clad in armor, the gorgon's head on her breastplate; Artemis/Diana at the hunt; Aphrodite/Venus with baby Eros/Cupid). Even humbler houses—from Roman Britain to Syria—boasted miniature bronzes, wall paintings, and mosaics that paraded local as well as distant foreign deities (strikingly, an ivory figurine of the Indian goddess Lakshmi was discovered in the excavations of Pompeii)—not to mention all those featured on coins, Greek ceramics, seal stones, pottery lamps, even cake molds. The classical world was a world full of (images of) gods.

We take all this for granted. These are the objects that fill museums and archeological sites. And through them classical antiquity has bequeathed to later ages how its deities are to be visualized (from Botticelli's *Birth of Venus* to Disney's *Hercules*). But they are also, in certain respects, a misleading guide to the form, role, and function of visual images within the religions of the Greco-Roman world. The term *Greco-Roman world* is, of course, itself something of a misleading shorthand. Over the thousand years or more of "classical antiquity," across the different parts of the classical world, there were all kinds of very different traditions of visual representation within religion. But, at the same time, cultural interchange across the classical Mediterranean, plus the interdependence of artistic forms and techniques, justifies thinking in such broad terms. Indeed, it would be very hard now to isolate from Greek traditions, a specifically Roman, let alone Etruscan, approach to religious image making.

There are three important preliminary considerations. First, it is only from the writing of the elite culture of Greece and Rome that we can gain any detailed insight into the key questions of how religious images were used, discussed, and understood. For this reason, what follows will focus very largely on Greco-Roman religion and on those subsections of Greek and Roman society whose writings are preserved. The fact is that for Etruria, as with most cultures without (surviving) literature, we can usually do nothing more than conjecture function and meaning from the images themselves or extrapolate from wider, Greco-Roman, traditions. The only case where major conclusions have been drawn directly from ancient images, independent of a written context, is the cult of Mithras, especially the standard icon of Mithraism (the image of Mithras slaying the bull) and the complicated layout of Mithraic temples,

Reconstruction of the colossal gold and ivory statue of Athena by Phidias that after 438 BCE stood in the Parthenon. The people in the lower right corner are a measure of the size of the statue. Royal Ontario Museum, Toronto. *Royal Ontario Museum*

often signaled by zodiacal signs and symbols of the cult's grades of initiation. Close comparison of apparently minor differences in these images in Mithraea across the Roman Empire has led to a variety of ambitious arguments about the symbolic universe of the cult and how it expressed its religious view of the world. But, even in this case, literary texts still offered a lead.

The second consideration stems from the obvious fact that the divine images that have come down to us from antiquity are (by definition) those that have survived the processes of damage and decay over two millennia—those made of virtually indestructible marble, limestone, ceramic, or terra-cotta or those that have been preserved through their sheer insignificance (such as hundreds of small bronze figurines) or lucky chance (the painted images from Pompeii or large bronze statues dragged from the sea bed). The great majority of the most prized divine images from antiquity are lost. Vast numbers of sizeable statues in bronze, silver, and gold were at some

point thought worth melting down or were accidentally destroyed in fire. The representations most renowned in the ancient world itself—the colossal constructions in gold and ivory that embodied Zeus in his temple at Olympia or Athena in the Parthenon—are entirely lost, apart from small-scale ancient copies. (The best glimpse we have of the appearance of these chryselephantine images is provided by the discovery at Delphi of a cache of badly burned gold and ivory images of the mid-6th century BCE, carefully buried after a fire in the late 5th century BCE.) But also lost are a range of no less prized, if intrinsically less valuable, images in other materials and often adopting a different mode of representation entirely: the "black stone" (probably a meteorite) that was brought to Rome from Asia Minor as the image of Magna Mater (Cybele; see illus. on p. 408) to be installed in the goddess's temple on the Palatine (204 BCE), the old image from Athena's temple on the Athenian Acropolis that seems to have been little more than a

Portrayal of Mithras killing the bull. The scorpion and snake in the foreground are images commonly associated with Mithras, and the rayed head at left represents Sol. In most depictions, Mithras looks away from the bull as he kills it; this is one of a few that show him looking at the bull. Relief from Rome. *Cincinnati Art Museum, Gift of Mr. and Mrs. Fletcher E. Nyce*

roughly shaped plank of wood, or even the myrtle plant that Pausanias saw as the image of Artemis "the savior" near Sparta (3.22). The immediate conclusion is that divine images were much more varied—in form, material, texture, and size—than first impressions would suggest. This variety turns out, as we shall see, to have crucial religious implications.

The third factor to bear in mind is the sheer fluidity of many of the "identifications" of divine images. In museums and picture captions, the images usually come labeled with a plausible name of god or goddess. But this often conceals something much less certain. Sometimes it is a question of a disputed identification: Pausanias, for example, describing the temple of Zeus at Olympia in the 2nd century CE, identified as the hero Pirithous the famous figure from the west pediment that we know as the god Apollo (5.10—we usually assume he made a "mistake"); we still cannot decide whether the famous 5th-century bronze statue pulled out of the sea at Artemision represents Zeus or Poseidon. Other times it is a question of misleading conventions. Most of the freestanding male statues of the Greek archaic period (now regularly known as *kouroi*) are entirely anony-

mous: they may have been intended to represent a god, to commemorate the dead, or to immortalize their commissioner; we do not know. Earlier generations of scholars, however, entitled them all Apollo, and in many cases that label has, erroneously, stuck.

Trivial as these puzzles of identification may seem, they hint at more important issues. First is the overlap between divine and human images, which inevitably comes with an anthropomorphic projection of the gods. Second is the emphasis that uncertainties of this kind must place on the processes of interpretation, now and in antiquity itself. Of course, in some particular cases, for us, it may simply be a matter of missing information (if the Artemision figure was still equipped with a trident, the debate would be closed). But in general they remind us how crucial the interpretative eyes of the ancient viewer must be to any understanding of the image and that ultimately the religious power of the image was a product of those who looked at it and colluded in treating it as such.

All divine images involve negotiations about divine form, essence, and character; but none more so than the so-called cult images in temples. Greco-Roman temples were not sites of congregational worship, but acted as homes for (an image of) their divinity; it was these images that made the deity present in the temple—in a variety of different forms, from what are essentially aniconic "symbols" (wooden "statues" of this type are often now referred to by the Greek word *xoana*) through more familiar marble to elaborate chryselephantine structures. Very few of these cult images survive (the most impressive remains are the colossal fragments from the temple of Despoina at Lykosura in the Peloponnese, ca. 200 BCE; also mentioned by Pausanias, 8.37). But, from literary descriptions, it is clear that they offered many different versions of divinity. The statue of Zeus at Olympia, for example, evoked the god's enormous bulk by having his seated figure fill the height of the temple (as Strabo remarked, *Geography* 8.353: "He gives the impression that if he stood up he would unroof the temple"—although Strabo himself thought that the sculptor misread the proportions). Even the gold of the chryselephantine images was not merely a sign of the conspicuous expense poured into the statue; it must also have evoked the "divine radiance" that was a common element of the epiphany of a god in classical poetry (see, e.g., *Homeric Hymn to Demeter* 188–89, also referring to the great height of the goddess "reaching the roof").

A particularly instructive comparison is found in the two "cult images" of Athena on the Acropolis. The more familiar is the great statue of the master-sculptor Phidias, almost twelve meters high, made of gold and ivory attached to a wooden frame. Produced about 440 BCE, it was the centerpiece of the new Parthenon and so valuable that all close contact must have been carefully controlled. The other is the image from the old temple of Athena that was destroyed in the Persian invasion of 480–479 BCE; the statue itself was eventually lodged in the small temple on the Acropolis that we know as the Erechtheum. This was a crude piece of wood, though dressed and decorated with jewelry (at the annual festival of the Plynteria, it was ceremonially undressed, carried to the sea for washing, then dressed again in the temple). Another story says that it was not made by humans at all, but had miraculously fallen to earth from heaven (Pausanias, *Description* 1.26). There are many ways of defining the differences between these two images. The old *xoanon* has been seen as "primitive" in contrast to the more "advanced" conception of the Parthenon image (it is true that ancient authors regularly explained aniconic images as early—but, for most of antiquity, these two statues were contemporaries, standing in adjacent temples). The "old image" has been taken to be a "cult image" in the strict sense (it was the object of—and indeed participant in—ritual), while the Phidian statue has been seen as, to all intents and purposes, a votive offering to Athena (it was involved, so far as we know, in no formal rituals). But the crucial contrast lies in the different versions of sacrality that

they represent: the one mysterious, miraculous, and delivered by divine hand itself, but at the same time familiar and touchable; the other an object of remote wonder and the most lavish conception of the sacred that human hand could model.

Other images negotiated other kinds of religious questions. In imperial Rome, for example, the awkward problems of imperial apotheosis—how exactly did the emperor become a god? what kind of process was involved?—found expression in visual as well as literary form. The Great Cameo of France (ca. 50 CE), a piece of precious craftsmanship often thought to have been a commission by the imperial family itself, attempted both to fix the layers of the imperial cosmos (from the subject barbarians beneath to the deified emperor above) and to show the routes of transition from earth to the realm of the gods: one imperial prince ascends to "heaven" on a winged horse, another (less convincingly) simply floats toward the sky (see color plate). A different solution was devised for the image of the apotheosis of Antoninus and Faustina from the pedestal of the column of Antoninus (161 CE). The enormous winged creature, which carries the emperor and his wife to the skies, fills most of the panel. Whoever exactly it was meant to be (and that has been the subject of innumerable studies, none of which has carried much conviction), it signals more than anything the sheer difficulty of envisaging the event represented.

Several ancient writers discussed the issues of religious representation (and of religion itself) that images raised. Already in the 6th century BCE, Greek philosophers confronted the question of the exact relationship between statues and the gods themselves. In a famous critique of a crude anthropomorphic vision of the divine (Diels and Kranz 1952: frag. B 15; Kirk, Raven, and Schofield 1983: 169), Xenophanes claimed that if animals made statues and paintings of gods, they would make them in the shapes of animals. And Heraclitus (Diels and Kranz 1952: frag. B 5; Kirk, Raven, and Schofield 1983: 241) attacked people who prayed "to statues, as if one were to carry on a conversation with houses, not recognizing the true nature of the gods or demi-gods [heroes]." His point was to contest the view (probably widespread) that the power of the god could be found in the statue, that images were not, as one writer has put it, just "empty shells" (Steiner 2001: 79). These themes inevitably played a part in the wider Platonic discussion of artistic representation and mimesis from the 4th century BCE on (see, e.g., *Laws* 931a). A particularly lively argument is scripted by Cicero in the first book of his *On the Nature of the Gods*, where Cotta (the spokesman for the Academic school of philosophy) shows how statues and paintings determine the human vision of the divine and how different versions of the gods are inferred from different statue types (1.81–88). Other ancient intellectual traditions looked at these problems from a different angle. In the 1st century BCE,

Varro considered the history of divine image making: his conclusion (obviously rooted in his own perception of a "primitive" religion) that the Romans had no divine images at all for the first 170 years of their history took on the status of fact (which it is not) for some later writers (Augustine, *City of God* 4.31; Plutarch, *Numa* 8).

Whatever the direction of the philosophical debate, images of gods were treated as more than precious artworks and were the focus of numerous rituals. In addition to a whole variety of ceremonies of anointing and dressing the divine image, many civic processions, particularly (but not solely) in the Greek world and the eastern Roman Empire, saw the gods' statues paraded through the streets. In the preliminary rituals before the City Dionysia in Athens, for example, the image of Dionysus was carried out to a temple on the outskirts of the city, then back in a torch-lit procession to the theater (perhaps a reenactment of the god's mythical entry into Athens); and the lavish bequest of a wealthy Roman citizen in 2nd-century CE Ephesus provided for statues in silver and gilt of Artemis, other deities, mythical founders, and the imperial family, which were to be paraded around the city in procession (*Inschriften von Ephesos* no. 27). Statues also participated in sacred banquets. At Rome the first of these so-called *lectisternia* (almost certainly introduced from the Greek world) took place in the early 4th century BCE (Livy 5.13). Predictably enough statues were commonly the recipients of private prayers and vows. But more strikingly they could themselves be treated as if they had the active power of protection: runaway slaves, for example, might cling to a god's image for asylum. In the Roman Empire this power was attributed not only to statues of deified emperors but also to those of living emperors—a significant indication of the blurring of the boundaries between human and divine.

In other senses, too, divine images played a major part in the negotiation of that boundary between human beings and the gods. When the general processed through the city of Rome in triumph, he was dressed not merely as Jupiter Optimus Maximus, but in the guise of the statue of Jupiter from his temple on the Capitol (the general's red-painted face mimicking the terra-cotta of the statue itself). Conversely there were a series of ancient stories of humans who took divine images "for real." The most famous example concerns a young man who fell in love with the statue of Aphrodite at Cnidus, hid in the temple overnight, and made love to her/it. Ancient images of this sort (and the stories told about them) always raised the question of exactly how far a representation was itself divine. But the moral of this particular tale—which ends with the suicide of the man—is an emphatic assertion of the illegitimacy of his actions (Pseudo-Lucian, *Erotes* 15–16; Pliny, *Natural History* 36.20–22).

Visual representation in the religions of ancient Greece and Italy was not restricted to images of divinities. Many aspects of classical religions were represented in visual form. Note, for example, the votive offerings made at sanctuary sites (often in the form of terra-cotta models of parts of the body), the bronze Piacenza Liver, which seems to have been a visual guide to the haruspical interpretation of that organ (see Divination and Prophecy); or the figurines used to image the victims of curses (a notable example from Roman Egypt, now in the Louvre, depicts a woman, in clay, pierced with needles according to the instructions of a spell; see illustration on p. 350).

A particularly important category of representation is images of ritual activity. These range from vignettes of ritual on Athenian painted pottery through scenes of Isis worship painted on the wall of a private house at Herculaneum (see color plate) to major works of public relief sculpture in Rome and its empire, often depicting sacrifice. Such images have often been used as evidence to reconstruct ritual procedures. But that is more difficult than it might seem, because of the inevitable gap between the representation and the ritual as it was carried out. The images are never documentary records, but selective interpretations of the ceremonies. In the case of Roman sacrifice, for reasons that are not entirely clear, the vast majority of the representations show the preliminary activity: the procession of animals to the altar, the libation poured by the main officiant at the altar. Few depict the crucial stage of the inspection of the entrails, and only one (possibly) shows the postsacrificial meal, which is often referred to in written sources. Even more problematic, in the absence of written accounts, are the paintings in Etruscan tombs, where it is almost impossible to decide whether the banquets commonly represented evoke the funeral ceremony itself, memories of the deceased in this life, or an imaginative projection of the activities of the next world.

The key to understanding such images is not to see them crudely as "evidence" for ritual. Many of these representations had a much more active function in the religious life of the classical world. By displaying in a permanent form various aspects of rituals that were themselves fleeting and transitory, they acted as a focus of memory of past ritual; they were also a powerful and often idealizing template against which the messy, improvised actions of day to day ritual could be set.

BIBL.: H. Diels and W. Kranz, *Die Fragmente der Vorsokratiker* (6th ed.; Berlin, 1952). R. L. Gordon, *Image and Value in the Graeco-Roman World: Studies in Mithraism and Religious Art* (Aldershot, 1996). Idem, "The Real and the Imaginary: Production and Religion in the Graeco-Roman World," *Art History* 2 (1979): 5–34. G. S. Kirk, J. E. Raven, and M. Schofield, *The Presocratic Philosophers: A Critical History* (2nd ed.; Cambridge, 1983). S. R. F. Price, *Rituals and Power: The Roman Imperial Cult in Asia Minor* (Cambridge, 1984), 170–206. J. Scheid, "Le flamine de Jupiter, les Vestales et le général triomphant," in *Corps des dieux* (ed. C. Malamud and J.-P. Vernant; Le temps de la réflexion 7; Paris,

1986), 213–30. D. Steiner, *Images in Mind: Statues in Archaic and Classical Greek Literature and Thought* (Princeton, 2001). J.-P. Vernant, *Mortals and Immortals: Collected Essays* (ed. F. I. Zeitlin; Princeton, 1991), 3.141–92.   M.B.

Christianity

Early Christianity developed in a world of abundant images of the divine and human, and Christian art was commissioned, produced, and received in competitive interaction with the late antique social and artistic world. Although fragmentary, early Christian art provides unique insights into the movement's beliefs and practices, cultural affiliations and aspirations. Christian art clearly was not restricted to heretics or an ill-educated laity, and claims of a constant theological tradition of official noniconic orthodoxy from earliest times to the iconoclastic controversies in the 8th century have proven wrong. Moreover, the second commandment never caused Christians to prohibit outright all iconographic art. The few texts referring to the second commandment warn only against idolatrous use of images (cf. canon 36 of the synod of Elvira, ca. 306). Thus, the early Christian approach to art resembled that of contemporaneous Judaism, which, despite its adherence to the second commandment, was also not totally aniconic.

The style of early Christian art remained rooted in ancient iconography, which sometimes renders difficult the identification of particular works as Christian or pagan.

Three early Christian symbols: the Christogram (*chi-rho,* the first two letters of *Christ* in Greek); fish (the Greek word for fish, *ichthys,* is an acrostic for the words "Jesus Christ, son of God, Savior" in Greek); and anchor (perhaps originally a crypto-cross symbol or a symbol of hope; cf. Hebrews 6:19). From Catacombs of St. Sebastian, Rome. *Courtesy Harold Attridge*

A distinctly Christian art style develops only around 500 when non-Christian artistic production declined. No identifiable Christian art is known from before approximately 200. Staurograms (representations of the cross) and particular forms to represent *nomina sacra* (sacred names) in manuscripts are the only clear traces of a nascent Christian material culture that date from the 2nd century (cf. Bodmer papyri P[66] and P[75]). However, early Christian art apparently evolved during the 3rd century from selectively adapted elements of traditional late antique art. Increasing wealth and practical needs fostered development of these elements into a repertoire increasingly suited to Christian beliefs and ritual (cf. Clement of Alexandria, *Paedagogus* 3.57.1–3.60.1).

Pre-Constantinian Christian art survives in the cities of Italy (Rome, possibly Naples) and southern France (Arles) and on the Euphrates (Dura Europos) and includes wall and ceiling paintings in communal (Dura) and funeral (Roman catacombs) contexts, sarcophagi (from ca. 240–60), magical symbols and gemstones, possibly a small corpus of statuettes (Cleveland Art Museum), and a certain lamp type (made by Annius, now in Berlin). Literary texts mention vessels decorated with Christian imagery shortly after 200. The iconographic repertoire from the catacombs and on sarcophagi is fairly constant, as is the imagery on sarcophagi from Rome, the western provinces, and Constantinople and on paintings from Rome and Dura. Distinct regional traditions are not recognizable before approximately 400 (especially Egypt).

Early Christian iconography uses traditions from the Bible (both Old and New Testaments), biblical Apocrypha and Pseudepigrapha, as well as nonbiblical traditions. Not surprisingly, many scenes from the Hebrew Bible have parallels in Jewish art. Famous are the Jonah cycles in catacomb paintings and sarcophagi, Abraham sacrificing Isaac, Moses, Daniel in the lions' den, the fiery furnace, and Noah surviving the flood. The earliest New Testament scenes show Jesus as miracle worker or as lawgiver/philosopher, the Samaritan woman at the well, the women at the tomb (Dura Europos), Peter and Paul, or Paul's companion Thecla. These depictions are not intentional "portraits" but stylized images with conventional gestures and apparel of elegant nobles or philosophers. Post-Constantinian depictions of Jesus attract attributes of Zeus (Christ as *pantokrator*) and elements of imperial imagery (cloak, *labarum* as sign of victory).

Pagan art supplies many iconographic motifs. Traditional representations of Hermes the ram bearer became depic-

Jesus teaching, a representation with clear parallels to the philosopher figure in Greco-Roman art. Late 4th-century CE sarcophagus. Arles Museum. *Courtesy Robin Margaret Jensen*

tions of Christ the Good Shepherd (cf. Tertullian, *On Modesty* 7.1–4; ca. 210). Christian funeral iconography continues pagan depictions of the afterlife, showing the deceased entering the heavenly banquet, but avoids pagan mythological imagery of death. Christian pictorial art invited viewers to identify with biblical characters and their experience of the divine as the power to overcome death. Many scenes, however, are too condensed to allow only one specific reading.

Apart from narratives, Christians adopted symbolic images such as the fish and dove and some noniconic symbols such as anchors, the *chi-rho,* or cruciform images (cf. Minucius Felix, *Octavius* 29.6–8; Tertullian, *Apology* 16.6–9). Constantine's use of the cross, starting in 315 with the silver medallion from Ticinum, encouraged widespread use of the empty cross in the 4th century. Depictions of Christ crucified do not appear before approximately 420. These include an ivory plaque in the British Museum and the wooden door of Sta Sabina in Rome, where both still remain part of narrative settings. The controversial Alexamenos-Graffito from the Palatine (ca. 200), with an ass on a cross, may be the work of an opponent. At least in its art, the early church located Christ's redemptive work not exclusively in the passion but in his whole miraculous ministry and teaching.

Portraits of individuals are rare before the 5th century (cf. late 4th-century gold glasses from Rome). The many depictions of persons standing erect with the arms extended *(orantes)* are generic representations of piety adapted from pagan art. Not strictly portraits, they inscribe the believing Christians in the narrated scene.

The Constantinian age effected profound architectural change. The house church originally provided the context of mission and worship. Considerable diversity in size and form reflected the communities' needs as well

as local building practices. With the common meal as the setting for worship, the dining room provided the context of instruction and liturgy. All this could take place within the normal context of a house, and even baptism was performed there, where water was available. Until the mid-3rd century, nothing indicates special rooms exclusively devoted to worship or that buildings were erected exclusively for rituals. By the 3rd century, after a period of numerical growth and liturgical formalization, Christian buildings became recognizable, although not architecturally defined. A Syrian chronicle describing a flood in Edessa in the year 201 first mentions an identifiable "holy place of the congregation of the Christians." Archeological evidence for a more formal type of building comes from Dura Europos. Here, in 232/233 and 240/241, two rooms in a private house were renovated for ecclesiastical use, one an assembly hall, the second a carefully designed baptismal pool. Domestic activities ceased, but the room's external look and internal arrangement remained virtually unaltered. Both rooms display elaborate wall paintings with suitable iconography. Dura is a fine, but certainly not the first or only, example of architectural adaptation for special religious and social purposes. Similar adaptation probably took place in the 3rd-century structures below the later Roman basilicas of S. Clemente *(titulus Clementis)* and SS. Giovanni e Paolo *(titulus Byzantis).* The origins of internal church architecture also clearly predate the 4th century. Literary evidence shows that during the 3rd century, the need for larger assembly halls, coupled with evolving liturgies, produced larger spaces with special areas for clergy and a raised platform *(pulpitum, tribunal)* (cf., e.g., *Didascalia apostolorum* 12.2.57–58).

The Constantinian era introduced the basilica as the model for church building (first S. Giovanni in Laterano in 314). Based on common public Roman architecture, the basilica proclaimed the new status of the church under imperial patronage. There is no apparent genetic connection between pre-Constantinian and Constantinian church architecture. Not all existing churches, however, were immediately adapted to the new style. In particular regions, basilicas were introduced very late (in North Africa rarely before the 5th century), and other house churches were never overbuilt at all (cf. rural Britannia in the 4th- and 5th-century villas of Hinton St. Mary or Lullingstone).

BIBL.: David R. Cartlidge and J. Keith Elliott, *Art and the Christian Apocrypha* (London, 2001). Paul C. Finney, *The Invisible God: The Earliest Christians on Art* (New York, 1994). Robin Margaret Jensen, *Understanding Early Christian Art* (London, 2000). Thomas F. Mathews, *The Clash of Gods: A Reinterpretation of Early Christian Art* (Princeton, 1999). L. Michael White, "Architecture: The First Five Centuries," in *The Early Christian World* (ed. Philip F. Esler; London, 2000), 2.693–746.   J.Z.

Sacred Texts and Canonicity

Introduction

Books and writing assume curious roles in nonliterate cultures, and those who study sacred texts from the perspective of modern, democratized, vernacular literacy do well to consider writing's fundamental anomaly in the ancient world before considering the range and types of sacred texts. For almost all ancient cultures, writing was the specialty of royal or priestly scribes who practiced their skills in a private domain that cultivated an aura of mystique and power, as scribes controlled history, cosmos, and fertility through their characters. And for those cultures such as Greece that were traditionally disinclined to place supreme authority in written text, writing was still a curiosity, but now a foreign one, bound to sap culture of its vital oral traditions and memory. Overall, we cannot think about ancient texts as either descriptive or prescriptive of their cultures but rather as existing in a tenuous, often politically charged relationship to the oral traditions and extratextual practices that dominated those cultures.

Sacred texts grew out of institutional functions. The rather mundane scribal enterprises of keeping lists of kings, shrines, deities, and omens develop in many ancient cultures into theologically constructed royal annals (1–2 Samuel, 1–2 Kings), mythographies (Hesiod's *Theogony*, Hittite materials), commentaries on oracles (Egyptian Demotic Chronicle), and collections of prophecies (Sibylline Oracles). Whereas these genres remained the purview of literate professionals and priesthoods, we find an analogous process in the case of early Christianity, where lists of sayings and miracles were pressed into narrative "gospels" for further interpretation in more popular (if still semiliterate) milieux.

Another scribal function, specifically associated with priestly duties, was the development and control of rituals—a paradox, given that ritual origins were supposed to lie always with the gods themselves. The paradox was resolved through the priestly scribes' role as maintainers of the words of gods; that is, whatever was written or performed stemmed ultimately and intrinsically from the gods or their authoritative human representatives (kings, heroes). Hence texts that establish festival rites, the dramatic recitation of myth or epic, hymns and prayers, proper methods or frameworks for sacrifice, and even procedures for healing or protection comprise another large portion of sacred texts in antiquity.

The sacredness of texts produced in these institutional contexts could take diverse forms. In Egypt, where hieroglyphic writing represented more or less the very writing of gods, everything written in this way was sacred to some extent; and the written description of ritual gesture or utterance could ultimately serve as a living, eternal substitution for the human performance—a dynamic we see, for example, in mortuary inscriptions. In Rome, by contrast, the texts of the *haruspices* and *augures* and the Sibylline Oracles served as repositories of precedent and authority for priestly guilds, but were not sacred in a concrete or ethical sense. In Israel, texts that originated in public oral performance, such as psalms, priestly curse (Num. 5), or proclamation (Deut. 6.4–9), became over time concretely efficacious—as amulets or, in the case of Num. 5, as ritual poison.

These "performative" uses of sacred texts such as amulets, mezuzahs (after Deut. 6.4–9), inscriptions, or papyri designed for otherworldly consumption (Egyptian funerary materials), divination (by Homer or by the Bible), liturgy (Iranian Yasna as context for ancient Gathas), or even theatrical presentation of books in procession are to be distinguished from what Gill (1985) has called the "informative" use of texts, which involves content-based interpretation. In the ancient world, as in many premodern and modern cultures where non-literacy predominates, the performative is the only way that nonreaders can interact with such vehicles of power. One can observe "magical" uses of writing and texts cross-culturally: touching, wearing, eating, drinking, and waving the sacred characters. Even for the scribes in cultures such as Egypt, Israel, and Mesopotamia, the acts of reading, writing, and interpretation carried a performative significance, insofar as the scribe was transmitting the sacred divine characters, discerning the intentions of a god in a heaven-borne text, or collating divine oracles. In Rome, however, the use of religious texts tended to be informative and instrumental, with the performative power lying not in the texts themselves but in the rituals and omen interpretations conducted by the priests (according to the texts' guidance). In a new religious movement such as early Christianity, oral prophecy might assume central authority apart from texts; yet the relative authority of oral and textual media could fluctuate radically: in the face of the widespread circulation of the seven Pauline letters in the later 1st century CE, the Book of Revelation tried to be both oral prophecy (1.3) and unchangeable heavenly book (22.18–19).

In its most basic sense of an authoritative body of texts, canon is but a literate version of any culture's tendency to embrace some common spectrum of tradition and lore as a frame of reference and often (even in some oral cultures) to maintain some concrete list or map of this tradition. In ancient scribal subcultures, one can see the force of such canons in the form of literary influences (the circumscribed nature, if diversified, of funerary manuals in Egypt); in the customary dependence on certain texts for managing ritual procedures (the divination manuals of Roman religion); and even in the consolidation, over early Jewish history (5th century BCE–1st century CE), of a common corpus of authoritative books. Yet in these cases of canon, the actual boundaries between texts of authority and texts regarded as irrelevant (or even reprehensible) are somewhat fluid. It is unique to post-70 CE rabbinic Judaism and to developing early Christian movements to attend to the boundaries, establishing the textual canon in detail and by official decree. The anxiety that led to such fixed canons was clearly social and political. For rabbinic Judaism, canon had the potential to replace the fallen Jerusalem temple, and its boundaries (against, e.g., apocalyptic works) circumvented forms of text-based dissent. For Christians such as Marcion and Irenaeus, canon defined a growing sect's history and identity (neo-Hebraic or post-Hebraic?), and its boundaries likewise served to exclude entire streams of interpretation and practice that were deemed "heretical" by canonizers. But in both cases, Jewish and Christian, the absolutely delimited canon of texts, once established as authoritative, became universal in its scope of application, capable of revealing the nature of reality, history, and divine will at any time or any place.

BIBL.: Alan K. Bowman and Greg Woolf (eds.), *Literacy and Power in the Ancient World* (Cambridge, 1994). David Frankfurter, "The Magic of Writing and the Writing of Magic: The Power of the Word in Egyptian and Greek Traditions," *Helios* 21 (1994): 189–221. Sam D. Gill, "Nonliterate Traditions and Holy Books," in *The Holy Book in Comparative Perspective* (ed. Frederick M. Denny and Rodney L. Taylor; Columbia, S.C., 1985), 224–39. Jack Goody, *The Logic of Writing and the Organization of Society* (Cambridge, 1986). Idem, *The Power of the Written Tradition* (Washington, D.C., 2000). Jonathan Z. Smith, "Sacred Persistence: Toward a Redescription of Canon," in Smith, *Imagining Religion: From Babylon to Jonestown* (Chicago, 1982), 36–51.   D.F.

Egypt

Early period. The religion of ancient Egypt was defined by practice rather than doctrine. Its sacred texts were therefore functional rather than dogmatic, lacking both the centrality and the immutability that characterizes canonical texts. Even those that survive in multiple copies usually exhibit significant variations in wording and content, unlike true canonical literature.

Such texts reflect rather than define the religion that produced them. Once created, however, they often came to be viewed as normative. To a certain extent, their sacred character was imparted by the very act of writing them down, since the Egyptians called their script "god's speech" (compare the Greek term *hieroglyph*, sacred inscription). Some texts were considered esoteric as well as sacred, an aspect occasionally emphasized in colophons such as "It is a very real secret: no one shall ever learn of it in any place, no people shall speak it, no eye shall see it, no ear shall hear it, except for the *ba* [spirit of the deceased] and the one who instructs him" (Book of the Dead spell 148, Papyrus of Nedjmet). A text's sacredness was also a factor of its age, and scrolls in temple libraries were often consulted so that important rituals could be conducted "in accordance with the writings of old" (tomb of Kheruef).

Because of their noncanonical nature, the identification of sacred texts reflects modern rather than ancient perceptions, and the genre as a whole is therefore not well defined. In any definition, however, it includes at least those texts that were used in conjunction with funerals, worship, and liturgy.

Funerary texts are the oldest and best attested of all ancient Egyptian sacred writings. They consist essentially of three different kinds of texts (usually called "spells"), which can be called ritual, personal, and apotropaic. Ritual spells, called "those that make [the spirit] effective," were used during the funeral itself. Some are addressed to the deceased, while others invoke the gods on his or her behalf. Personal spells were meant to be recited by the spirit each night during its journey through the netherworld toward rebirth at dawn. In these, the deceased speaks in the first person, although some copies were personalized by substituting the deceased's name in place of first-person pronouns. Apotropaic spells were intended to protect the tomb's contents from serpents and other inimical forces.

Funerary texts first appear in the late Old Kingdom (ca. 2325–2140 BCE), inscribed on the subterranean walls of royal pyramids. They are known as Pyramid Texts and consist of some eight hundred separate spells. During the First Intermediate Period and Middle Kingdom (ca. 2140–1750 BCE), these developed into the Coffin Texts, so called because they were inscribed primarily on nonroyal coffins. About twelve hundred Coffin Texts are known, including copies and altered versions of some Pyramid Texts together with a greatly expanded inventory of personal and apotropaic spells. They also introduced a new genre of funerary texts, known as netherworld guides, which were designed to aid the deceased's spirit in overcoming the obstacles of its nightly journey.

During the New Kingdom (ca. 1550–1050 BCE), the various genres of funerary texts were edited into discrete compositions. The ritual of the opening of the mouth, a funeral ceremony that symbolically restored the deceased's faculties, was based on the older corpus of ritual spells, while the personal spells of the Pyramid Texts and Coffin Texts were reworked into a collection of some two hundred spells known as the Book of the Dead. The genre of netherworld guides expanded to include some new compositions, including those known as the Amduat, the Book of Gates, and the Book of Caverns. Along with copies of the Pyramid Texts, many of these New Kingdom creations remained in use until the end of pharaonic civilization, occasionally enhanced by other new compositions, such as the Book of Breathing.

Sacred texts were also used in worship and rites other than funerary. Best attested of these is the genre known as hymns, which were texts of worship and praise addressed to individual gods. Some hymns were undoubtedly composed for temple ceremonies, but most occur in mortuary contexts such as stelae, tomb walls, and the Book of the Dead, although they do not belong to the genre of funerary texts as such. Since few exist in more than a single copy, hymns are the least canonical of all sacred texts. For that reason, however, they reflect contemporary developments in theology more closely than do other sacred writings.

Ritual texts of a nonfunerary character are represented by several liturgical compositions, such as the Daily Temple Ritual of the New Kingdom and Ramesside period (ca. 1525–1050 BCE), used by the acting high priest (theoretically, the pharaoh) in his daily attendance on the temple's cult image. Other examples of this genre are a liturgy of royal affirmation, preserved on a papyrus of the early Middle Kingdom (ca. 1950 BCE); the Shabaka Stone (ca. 700 BCE), containing the remnants of an older ritual enacted at the temple of Ptah in Memphis; a liturgy for reviving the god Osiris, preserved in several Ptolemaic papyri (4th–1st centuries BCE); and a ceremony inscribed in the temple of Horus at Edfu during

the 1st century BCE, which celebrated the god's triumph over the forces of chaos.

Although well represented by such compositions, the liturgical genre is actually the least well attested among ancient Egyptian sacred texts, probably because most such liturgies were entrusted to papyri in temple libraries, which have not survived. The ritual of royal renewal known as the *sed* festival, for example, was celebrated throughout the entire span of ancient Egyptian history, yet it is known from only a few representations of selected scenes in temples and tombs.

Funerary texts, hymns, and liturgies are the best-defined genres of Egyptian sacred texts. Other such texts are not as easily categorized, either as a corpus in themselves or as part of the broader genre of sacred writings. These include collections of magical spells, used for apotropaic purposes and in healing; a cycle of scenes and texts describing the divine birth of some New Kingdom pharaohs; and unique compositions such as Papyrus Bremner-Rhind, a compilation of funerary, ritual, apotropaic, and theological texts dating to the 4th century BCE. Egyptian oracular decrees are generally legal or historical rather than sacred in character, while the genre of moral teachings, or wisdom texts, was considered part of secular literature by the ancient Egyptians themselves.

BIBL.: Jan Assmann, *Ägyptische Hymnen und Gebete* (2nd ed.; Fribourg, 1999). Raymond O. Faulkner, *The Ancient Egyptian Book of the Dead* (London, 1985). Idem, *The Ancient Egyptian Coffin Texts* (3 vols.; Warminster, 1973–78). Idem, *The Ancient Egyptian Pyramid Texts* (Oxford, 1969). Erich Hornung, *Altägyptische Jenseitsführer: Ein einführender Überblick* (Darmstadt, 1997).   J.P.A.

Later period. Most of the Egyptian religious literature of the late, Ptolemaic, and Roman periods—temple inscriptions, texts of temple rituals, funerary papyri, and other religious texts from tombs—seems to reproduce traditions already known from pharaonic Egypt. Many rituals known to have existed or known only in fragments in earlier periods are extensively documented in Ptolemaic source material. The great temples of Edfu, Dendara, and Philae are treasuries of sacred texts, and they reflect an age with a marked interest in canonization. Sacred texts were considered *bȝw Rʿ* (manifestations of the sun-god), and, as an impact of the multicultural situation, the Egyptian priesthood made every effort to preserve the religious tradition of the country in a state of pure cultivation. Of central importance is the famous series of reliefs and texts in Edfu perpetuating the ritual drama performed every year to reenact the victory of Horus over Seth and to embody that victory in the reigning king. The dramatic form reflected in the reliefs and texts is that of a very redundant series of tableaux, in which Horus harpoons Seth as a hippopotamus and is crowned king of Upper and Lower Egypt. In the end, Ptolemy IX is declared victorious against the enemies of Egypt. The clear representation of the myth-ritual relation in this text from around 110 BCE is no doubt rooted in a ritual tradition at least as old as the late Old Kingdom, but it is also a typical feature of these late ritual texts. In the Greco-Roman period almost every sacrifice becomes a killing of Seth, and, on the whole, temple texts of this time reflect a still more emancipated priesthood's preoccupation with the meaning of the temple, its traditional rites, and its sacred texts. The temple itself was understood as an image of the process by which the world came into being—from the primeval darkness of the sanctuary at the rear of the temple, through the half-light and the papyrus wetlands of the pillared halls and colonnades, into the daylight of the open courts (Finnestad 1985). The border between the potential world-coming-into-being in the temple and the actual world outside was the huge pylon, an image of the horizontal mountains between which the sun appeared every day. Everything written or recited behind that pylon was situated behind the horizon, that is, on the threshold of coming into existence. And through that pylon, processions would march to impose afresh the order of creation on the world.

The mortuary literature of the late and Greco-Roman periods exhibits the same faithful adherence to tradition. The Book of the Dead is still the most common equipment for the hereafter, and it is invariably reproduced in the form it assumed shortly after the New Kingdom. Of approximately the same date is an ever-increasing tendency to supplement it with texts of temple rituals. Temple ritual was probably always an important source of funerary literature, but late funerary texts are more explicit on textual ancestry. For the authors as well as for the users of the texts, roots in ancient priestly traditions added to the sacredness and the efficacy of a text. In the 1st century BCE, novel funerary compositions such as the Books of Breathing established themselves as sacred texts by explicitly claiming an origin in the rituals performed for Osiris. A still more radical innovation was the Book of Traversing Eternity, which took the form of a long hymn to the deceased (Herbin 1994). Just as traditional hymns made the sun-god rise and accomplish his regular course or went through the ritual topography and the mythology of Osiris, the Book of Traversing Eternity made the deceased participate in the worship of Egypt's religious centers and the highlights of its festival calendar.

Such innovations demonstrate that the age-old traditions were both alive and under reconsideration. In phraseology and scope, however, the mortuary literature written in classical Egyptian language remains thoroughly traditional and shows no signs of foreign influence. This seems true also for the Demotic mortuary texts. Only in glimpses do these texts in the contemporary language betray that novel meanings may have been perceived in traditional religious phraseology. Thus in one papyrus (British Museum 10507 12.2), within traditional Osirian and solar mythical exemplars for the

regeneration of the deceased, we suddenly come across the invocation: "O heart, create; Mind, take thought!" Such isolated outbursts of a *religio mentis* do not permit a reinterpretation of late mortuary literature, but it is important to note that they do correspond to trends in other genres of religious literature.

The one literary genre of Hellenistic Egypt that exhibits change and foreign influence is the so-called magical literature in Demotic and Greek. In the Greek Magical Papyri, Egyptian, Greek, and Jewish elements are approximately equally numerous. Very much the same goes for the Demotic papyri, perhaps slightly in favor of the Egyptian element. The basis of both groups of texts is, however, the traditional genre of Egyptian magical literature, which can be followed from about 1500 BCE. In a wilderness of gods, demons, and magical names of varied extraction, the Egyptian magical formula survives with its mythological identifications, no longer limited to Egyptian mythology.

Of this literature, little is left that can be dated to the Ptolemaic period—in fact, just enough to show that the extreme syncretism we find in the many manuscrips of Roman date was begun at least a century before. In order to observe the changes that took place in the Ptolemaic period and are found accomplished in the papyri of Roman date, it is necessary to have an idea of the pharaonic magical literature. Pharaonic magical formulas had a very distinct *Sitz im Leben*; they were designed to ward off diseases, danger, enemies, evil dreams, and so on. In the ritual act of defeating these menaces, it is the task of the formula to subject the situation to the rule of cosmology, to reduce or transcribe it to cosmological categories. Cosmology is a means of exerting ritual control, and it is the formula that puts this means to work. This is done in a rich variety of ways; most often by citing a mythical antecedent of the situation to be ritually controlled. It is not uncommon to find a series of parallel statements, each representing its own mythological identification or its own transcription of the situation into cosmological categories. In this way several mythological identifications of different extraction may stand together, narratively unconnected, and with their reference to the situation as the only common denominator. Since they do not form a consistent narrative, they are interchangeable and may be replaced by other identifications. The genre of Egyptian magical formulas was thus extremely flexible and open to new motifs, including features of foreign mythology. It is no mere coincidence that their Demotic and Greek successors in Hellenistic Egypt exhibit an almost breathtaking syncretism. In a Demotic spell against a poisonous or bewitching potion the user identifies himself or herself both with Horus and with Yaho (i.e., YHWH). Another formula, against the bite of a dog, is introduced as "the fury of Amun and Triphis"; the bite of the dog is then mythologized as Seth against Osiris and Apophis against the sun, and eventually the patient is identified with Horus the son of Osiris and Isis. But Horus is also called the founder of the earth, and in the end Yaho, Sabaho (Sabaoth?), and Abiaho are addressed, probably as forms of Horus.

In a Greek spell, to be recited over an ointment with which a man smears his private parts before having intercourse, it is said: "Let her, NN, love me for all her time as Isis loved Osiris, and let her remain chaste for me as Penelope did of Odysseus."

The openness and the flexibility of the magical literature was, of course, also socially conditioned. It was not, like the temple literature, in the charge of institutions and hierarchies obliged to maintain traditional integrity. And in fact, the magical genre was not open only to motifs of foreign extraction, but also to new applications of magic—for example, erotic magic, which is extremely frequent in the Greek papyri—and to the apocalyptic tendencies of the time. The Demotic and Greek *grimoires* abound in the kind of "do-it-yourself apocalypticism" once called *Offenbarungsmagie*. It is a kind of divination procedure, in which a god is made to appear, sometimes in a dream, sometimes in a vision, in order that to answer questions. This divination procedure has, however, an elaborate and dramatic framework, in which a face-to-face encounter between the god and the user is arranged. The vision may be a dream, but there is nevertheless a ritual to bring it about; and the ritual and divinatory procedure is reinforced by the subjective religious experience. In short, the *religio mentis* with its desire for apocalypticism has entered the private sphere of magic and divination. One formula has no other explicit purpose than the one given in its headline: "To see the barque of Pre." There are spells that allegedly produce a "direct vision" or even a trance.

Side by side with the practical purpose of divination, there is in these instructions and spells an important element of self-initiation, of which the *Mithrasliturgie* is the most famous example. In these cases, the object of the prescribed ritual is the user himself. He is the person marked out for ritual, he is the one who beholds the god, and the one on whom the blessings of this spectacular revelation are bestowed.

In the Demotic and Greek "magical" literature, this subjective, revelatory experience is an outstanding novel feature, continuous with the Hermetic and gnostic currents of the 2nd to 4th centuries CE. There is also a new religious term to denote this novel focus on an epistemological or spiritual breakthrough: Demotic *swn*, Coptic *sown*, Greek *gnōsis*. Gnosis, the "knowledge" of god that makes the adept return to his or her own preexistence in god, is the core subject of the Hermetic literature, a group of devotional tractates surviving in Greek, Coptic, Latin, and Armenian, all claiming an origin in Egypt, in the circle around Hermes Trismegistus, the Greek translation of Thrice Great Thoth, the Egyptian god of writing and priestly wisdom (see further Hermeticism). For many years the claims to

an Egyptian origin were taken as a mere pseudepigraphic construction, but today, scholars tend to take them more seriously. In fact, a Demotic book of Thoth has now been restored (Zauzich and Jasnow, forthcoming).

It is, however, obvious how much these texts owe to Greek philosophy, notably Stoicism and Middle Platonism. But they cultivate an Egyptian heritage, not only as a framework, but closely tied to their very character as sacred texts. The 16th Hermetic tractate puts it in a rather programmatic way: The highly pretentious philosophy of the Greeks is nothing but a noise of arguments *(logos)*, whereas we (the Egyptians) have sounds full of efficacy. Hermetic texts are not without philosophical arguments, but like ancient Egyptian mortuary literature and self-initiatory "magic," they were designed as efficacious texts. Their ultimate aim, especially transparent in the 13th tractate and the Coptic text called On the 8th and the 9th, was to perform a spiritual breakthrough on their users.

BIBL.: Hans Dieter Betz (ed.), *The Greek Magical Papyri in Translation* (Chicago, 1996). B. P. Copenhaver, *Hermetica* (Cambridge, 1992). Ragnhild B. Finnestad, *Image of the World and Symbol of the Creator* (Wiesbaden, 1985). Garth Fowden, *The Egyptian Hermes* (Cambridge, 1986). J. C. Goyon, *Rituels funéraires de l'ancienne Égypte* (Paris, 1972). F. R. Herbin, *Le livre de parcourir l'éternité* (Leuven, 1994). Naomi Janowitz, *Icons of Power: Ritual Practices in Late Antiquity* (University Park, Pa., 2002). A. Piankoff, *Egyptian Religious Texts and Representations* (6 vols.; Princeton, 1954–72). K.-T. Zauzich and R. Jasnow, *The Book of Thoth* (forthcoming).
J.P.S.

Mesopotamia

The hallmark of Mesopotamian literary culture is the scholarly and scholastic tradition that accompanied, shaped, and defined nearly three millennia of textual production. The term *canon* can be applied to Mesopotamian texts and text corpora that reflect and preserve scribal editorial or bibliographical activities, whether or not their content appears to be primarily religious in nature. Scholarly activity on Mesopotamian texts is discernible not only from physical marks (such as indicators of line counts inscribed on tablet edges) that scribes made on the tablets they produced, but also in editorial changes made to texts over time. Because we lack native terms for "canon" or "sacred texts" as well as Mesopotamian handbooks of composition or literary theory, we must discern the native Mesopotamian criteria by which the texts may be designated as belonging to such categories.

In the Mesopotamian textual tradition, it was neither necessary nor sufficient for a text to be sacred to be considered canonical. If "sacred" is understood to refer to texts that invoke or praise deities or describe ritual or cultic practice, then the cuneiform corpus is replete with exemplars of texts that reflect sacred activity or thought but do not reveal the scribal conceptions or authority that would lead us to consider them canonical. Conversely, many genres of Mesopotamian texts (among them the scientific, lexical, and mantic corpora) appear, at first glance, to have little to do with sacred matters, yet are readily apprehended as canonical. Once parameters defining canon within the Mesopotamian cultural environment are recognized, the designation of these genres as canonical is readily understood.

Textual authority. Mesopotamian notions of sacred text and canon do not readily correspond to Western definitions of these terms. Above all, authority in the Mesopotamian literary tradition is characterized by the primacy and endurance of a scribal tradition that is as slavish in its attention to detail as it is comprehensive in its output. However, the existence of numerous exact (or nearly exact) copies of a text is hardly a sufficient criterion by which to designate it canonical. Therefore, the theoretical underpinnings for a native conception of canon must be sought beyond the fact of copious textual output.

Underlying the Western definition of canon is the existence of an authority (be it personnel or institution, most often of religious nature) that grants its imprimatur to a text or text corpus. One consequence of such approval may be the inclusion and use of the text in ritual activity or devotion. In Mesopotamia, however, the authority behind the production of texts originated and resided in the scribal academy. Thus, while the palace and temple were the dominant institutions in Mesopotamian life, royal endorsement of the creation of a text was not a factor that rendered a text canonical.

One example may be drawn from the history of the text of one of the most widely recognized documents from Mesopotamia, the Laws of Hammurabi. This collection of laws did not serve as the basis for the implementation or execution of justice but as a programmatic statement of Hammurabi's worthiness as a ruler. The text is considered canonical because of its transmission with remarkable consistency over a thousand-year period and not because of any practical function. Changes that appeared in the phrasing of the initial (conditional) statement of each paragraph reflect scribal preoccupation with the form of the text rather than an interest in the evolution of legal principles over time. The status of the text in the scribal curriculum, reflected in part by its repeated copying, imbued the Laws of Hammurabi with the authority of the academy (along with its scribes and scholars) responsible for the preservation of Mesopotamia's cultural and intellectual heritage. That this authority enjoyed a close (but not inherent) relationship to the sacred world is reflected in the nature of the prologue, in which Hammurabi's authority to rule is established through its origin in divine assignment of the task and not through a restatement of Hammurabi's political, military, or juridical achievements. Thus, there can

be no doubt that scribal authority is the foundation of this text's perception as canonical.

Berossus, a Babylonian scholar who wrote in Greek during the 3rd and 2nd centuries BCE, explicitly states that the source of textual authority originates in the intellectual community. He records that the entirety of revealed knowledge was given once for all by antediluvian *apkallus* (sages—in particular, seven mythological antediluvian sages, descendants of Adapa/Oannes), who were experts in diverse fields of learning. Therefore, any expert labeled *apkallu* carried, by association, a connection to Mesopotamia's mythological intellectual, but not necessarily historical, past. Scribes bearing other professional titles join the *apkallu* in professional competence and authority to produce or copy texts which moderns would designate as canon.

When the palace actively participated in the assembling of textual corpora, it did so for the king's personal political and propagandistic agendas, not with a view to creating an authoritative compendium. Most notable of Mesopotamia's collections of tablets was the great library that Assurbanipal amassed at Nineveh. A letter and several scribal exercises show that an individual charged with obtaining tablets for that collection may have determined which texts to include on the basis of whether tablets pleased the king or were good for the palace. Although the king may have taken an active and personal role in selecting the contents of his tablet collection, his ability and authority to do so derives from his claim to have mastered the scribal curriculum. That his was a personal, rather than institutional, library further evinces the subordinate role that political authority played in the establishment of a Mesopotamian canon.

Native terminology. Beyond determining the authority that lay behind canonical status of Mesopotamian texts, it is useful to consider the native designations of texts in order to determine how the scholar-scribes viewed the relationships among categories of texts *vis-à-vis* their textual validity. Some literary, scientific, and mantic texts bear the designations *iškaru* (series), *ahû* (external, explanatory, excursus), and *ša pî ummāni* (according to the word of the scholars [= oral tradition]). Although the term *iškaru* is frequently understood to be the Akkadian equivalent of "canon," such a translation is erroneous. *Iškaru* designates tablets that belong to ordered, numbered, authoritative series; a particular tablet's place in a series is typically indicated with the annotation "xth tablet of series [name]." Recent research demonstrates that traditions from different cities preserve alternate text sequences and contents for recognized series, thus indicating that a monolithic authority did not stand behind the creation, compilation, and transmission of textual series. The variability of the contents in a particular series is also evident from the existence of texts labeled *ahû* (extraneous, external), which are nevertheless equally valid with regard to their intellectual content and authority. That texts are labeled "extraneous" refers only to their lack of inclusion in a particular series and not to their textual validity.

The readiness of scribes to consult and cite *ahû* texts, particularly when attempting to provide the king with positive information upon which to base his activities, helps us determine the scope and meaning of canon in Mesopotamian textual tradition. Letters from Assyrian and Babylonian scholars to the king contain assurances that *iškaru* and *ahû* compendia, as well as the oral tradition, had been consulted in order to present the king with the most favorable interpretation of a mantic activity or astronomical sighting. These citations affirm the validity and continuity of the divergent traditions to which the term *ahû* alludes. Whereas in Western literature, the label *noncanonical* calls into question the validity and sanctity of the text, the relationship between texts designated *iškaru* and *ahû* reflects the survival and validity of divergent, rather than conflicting, traditions of scholarship. The authority of *ahû* texts may be equated with those labeled by the Aramaic term *brayta,* that is, Tanaaitic materials which, although not included in authoritative versions of Mishnah, are considered no less authentic.

Sacred text. Some texts designated *pirištu* and *nişirtu,* both meaning "secret," may also be considered canonical. These terms appear in colophons to literary and scientific texts, either in admonitions to "guard the secret" or in phrases describing the lore of professionals, such as *nişirti barûti* (the secrets of the extispicy priest), *nişirti apkalli* (the secrets of the sage), and *nişirti šamê u erşeti* (the secrets of heaven and earth). Rather than the specialized knowledge of a highly trained professional, *nişirti šamê u erşeti* articulates the relationship between world and word and may be the key term for understanding the Mesopotamian notion of textual sanctity.

The phrase *nişirti šame u erşeti uşur* (guard the secrets of heaven and earth) confirms the tradition already established by the Old Babylonian period that portentous signs were believed to be written on the livers of sacrificial animals by the hand of Shamash, god of justice, and "designer of the cosmic designs" *(muşşir uşurāti).* That is to say, physiological anomalies were considered to be equivalent to writing. The connection is strengthened with the recognition that the cuneiform signs used to write names of astronomical and astrological phenomena could serve as a secret form of writing (termed astroglyphs), as in the writing of some royal names and epithets. The Babylonian Diviner's Manual expresses the notion that astronomical phenomena are represented equally and have identical significance in the celestial and terrestrial realms:

The signs on earth just as those in the sky give us
    signals.
Sky and earth both produce portents
though appearing separately, they are not separate
    [because] sky and earth are related.

Thus, the lore of various personnel was seen as a written manifestation of the physical realm observed in the performance of their professional duties.

Writing as sacred activity. Mesopotamia was not the only literate community of the ancient Near East and Mediterranean to understand that sanctity inhered in the apparatus and process of writing. Smith suggests that the ritual activity associated with the production of the Greek Magical Papyri, texts that record the necessary tools and the correct order of ritual, replicated the function of temple sacrifice. The texts themselves demonstrate a shift in interest from purification, incubation, and sacrifice that accompanied ritual to a focus on *"the act of writing itself"* (Smith 1995: 26, emphasis original). The accurate transmission and process of writing achieves ritual status by the choice of ritually appropriate materials, and the process of writing "becomes a sort of *ritual of ritual,* existing, among other loci, in a space best described as discursive or intellectual" (Smith 1995: 27, emphasis original).

Similarly, the notion that execution of an orthographic task is imbued with sacred purpose is found in two contexts in the cuneiform corpus. The first is in those colophons to literary and scientific texts in which scribes indicated the purpose(s) (performance, study, or votive) for which a particular tablet was copied or written. Texts that bear purpose statements originating in the vocabulary of votive inscriptions (e.g., "for his long life, well-being, and the hearing of his prayers") make clear that their preservation and/or transmission was considered a sacred task, regardless of the contents of the text itself. However, these statements also appear along with purpose statements that indicate that the text was also written for scholarly reasons, for example, "for the reading," "for the learning."

The second context is in the superscription to secular texts from Seleucid Uruk and Babylon, which reads: "According to the command of Anu and Antu, may [this endeavor] be successful." The phrase is not a part of the body of the document on which it appears, but rather expresses the personal hope of the scribe that his work be pleasing to the gods. The phrase appears on legal documents that record the specifics of legal situations as well as on scientific texts belonging to various series, indicating that the term has no inherent connection to the content of a particular tablet. Thus, both contexts demonstrate that the act of writing is understood to contain sacred meaning in and of itself and that the integration of the mundane and the supernatural is manifest through the production of text.

This brief discussion of sacred text and canon in Mesopotamia can in no way address the multiplicity and complexity of issues attendant to these topics. However, several conclusions can be drawn. The first is that the concept of canon can be applied to Mesopotamian texts that endured through the imprimatur of the scribal academy. This authorization stemmed from the intellectual milieu of the scribal profession, a domain that operated in all areas of Mesopotamian life. Second is the recognition that canonical texts may demonstrate connections to the realm of the religious community, but were in no way dependent upon being a part or product thereof. Third, for Mesopotamian texts, the notion of sanctity is irrelevant to the rubric of canon, for the process of textual production could be easily considered as sacred as the text itself. And finally, the terminology employed by the Mesopotamian scribes reflects their understanding of the inherent connection of their textual output to the conception of their world as a place where the heavenly and earthly realms intermingled in every aspect of human endeavor.

BIBL.: W. G. Lambert, "Ancestors, Authors, and Canonicity," *Journal of Cuneiform Studies* 11 (1957): 1–14. S. J. Lieberman, "Canonical and Official Cuneiform Texts: Towards an Understanding of Assurbanipal's Personal Tablet Collection," in *Lingering over Words: Studies in Ancient Near Eastern Literature in Honor of William L. Moran* (ed. T. Abusch, J. Huehnergard, and P. Steinkeller; Atlanta: Scholars Press, 1990), 305–36. L. E. Pearce, "Statements of Purpose: Why the Scribes Wrote," in *The Tablet and the Scroll: Near Eastern Studies in Honor of William W. Hallo* (ed. M. E. Cohen, D. C. Snell, and D. B. Weisberg; Bethesda, Md.: CDL, 1993), 185–93. M. Roaf and A. Zgoll, "Assyrian Astroglyphs: Lord Aberdeen's Black Stone and the Prisms of Esarhaddon," *Zeitschrift für Assyriologie* 91 (2001): 264–95. F. Rochberg-Halton, "Canonicity in Cuneiform Texts," *Journal of Cuneiform Studies* 36 (1984): 127–44. J. Z. Smith, "Trading Places," in *Ancient Magic and Ritual Power* (ed. M. Meyer and P. Mirecki; Leiden: Brill, 1995), 13–27. L.E.P.

Israel

Judaism was born in the 6th century BCE out of the ruins of the old kingdoms of Israel and Judah and out of the ashes of Solomon's temple. Israel and Judah had been destroyed by the expansive Neo-Assyrian and Neo-Babylonian empires during the late 8th through early 6th centuries BCE. When the northern kingdom of Israel was overrun by the Assyrians in 722 BCE, many refugees fled to the southern kingdom of Judah, which the Assyrians failed finally to conquer. There the traditions of the two kingdoms (which we know as J, the Yahwist, and E, the Elohist) were interwoven into a unified story that formed the narrative base of what would become the Pentateuch or Torah of the later Jewish canon. During the last decades of the kingdom of Judah, in the course of the Deuteronomic reform, these traditions were woven into an even-tighter fabric and supplemented with the Deuteronomic law book.

The Deuteronomic writings, using ancient sources from both traditions, extended on into the history of the conquest, settlement, and final loss of the land to the Mesopotamian powers (Deuteronomy to 2 Kings). That history was woven out of old sources by (Deuteronomist) redactors, prisoners, and exiles in Babylonia, down to the story of defeat and deportation. It is a history that insists that God was after all the only true king that Israel and Judah had had and that the patriarchs, judges, prophets, and kings who had arisen to lead the people in stages in the preexilic period were but agents of God's rule, with the monarchies of both largely at fault for the disaster. Out of the ashes of the kingdom of Judah there arose a successor religion called Judaism, which would be dominated by priests. Efforts to reestablish a monarchy in the postexilic period failed early on and would not be resumed until after the successful Maccabean rebellion against Greek domination in the middle of the 2nd century BCE.

During the Second Temple period the Jewish canon, usually called the Torah and the Prophets, plus other writings, took its basic shape. Its tripartite form—Torah, Prophets, and a well-defined third section called the Writings (Tanak, a Hebrew acronym for Torah, Neviim, and Ketuvim)—would not emerge clearly until after the further disastrous defeat of Judea by Rome in the 2nd century CE. The priestly cast of the Second Temple period gave way between the two calamities to the lay leadership of rabbinic Judaism. The Jewish canon is thus in large part an attempt to salvage the religious literature of Judaism in the wake of national disasters.

Only thirty-five "books" stemming from this history made it into the Jewish canon (twenty-four in the Jewish mode of counting the Twelve Minor Prophets as one, or thirty-nine by a different mode of counting in the Christian First Testament, or what is usually called the Old Testament). Yet far more than thirty other unknown ancient literary works are referred to in the Tanak, and countless other later writings are attested in the so-called Apocrypha, Pseudepigrapha, and the writings found among the approximately eight hundred Judean Desert Scrolls discovered during the 20th century. Some of these writings that were not included in the Hebrew Bible are found in Catholic and Orthodox Christian canons, but most were not included in the canon of any ancient Jewish community so far as we know. We are not at all sure what a canon of scripture would have contained—beyond the Torah and Prophets—for the Jewish community at Qumran or for the Jews of the Hellenistic Diaspora. The Jewish scriptures were adopted by early Christianity as the Old Testament or First Testament, but the forms in which it is found in early Christian Bibles vary considerably in terms of content and even order of books. In addition, the Jewish Bible and the Christian First Testament differ in basic literary structure, the Jewish being tripartite and the Christian quadripartite, indicating quite different hermeneutics by which they were to be read by the faithful. For example, in the Christian First Testament, the Prophets are placed at the end, so that they lead directly to the New Testament, which was viewed as their fulfillment.

The Dead Sea Scrolls have shown that early Judaism

was considerably more diverse and pluriform than we had earlier thought and that the histories of the formation and the transmission of the biblical text and of the canonical process, leading up to differing Jewish and Christian canons, was more complex. Instead of there having been a normative Judaism and otherwise heterodox sects that produced the so-called Apocrypha and Pseudepigrapha, early Judaism was highly diverse ever since the postexilic period when Jewish communities scattered widely. But the one concept that unified all forms of Judaism was scripture and tradition, or Torah in its broader meaning.

The Pentateuch and the prophetic corpus were probably set, in the form we know them if not in their content, by the end of the 5th century BCE. In addition, collections of stories, psalms, and wisdom literature would have been read and reread, as well as a very Priestly review of the old history (in Chronicles). But the third part of the Tanak would not be stabilized in the form we have inherited until after the Bar Kochba disaster toward the middle of the 2nd century CE. The statement of the Jewish historian Josephus in the late 1st century CE that there were twenty-two books in the Jewish Bible may have been a first attempt to fix the number of books, which was still in flux.

What we once called canonization of the Hebrew Bible was actually a process of use and reuse of such literature in the widespread Jewish communities during the Persian and Greco-Roman periods. That which was picked up again and again and then shared with other communities, because of its relevance and helpfulness to the needs of those communities, would eventually have moved onto a sort of tenure-track toward inclusion in the canons of rabbinic and Christian Judaism.

The eventual stabilization of the prophetic corpus in the Persian period, and even of the writings that make up the third part of the canon in the Greco-Roman period, was probably a result of the survival (i.e., repeated use) of the most widely accepted literature, those stories that sustained a people living under foreign domination, in tenuous and threatening conditions.

But the canonical process of repetition and adaptation of early traditions actually started well back in preexilic experience. The biblical literature that is most clearly datable—the prophetic books—indicates that the prophet whose name the book bore often cited and alluded to earlier traditions in an authoritative way, with the aim of supporting his arguments concerning God's intentions in the public events of his time; and they did so in surprising and memorable ways. The students and editors of these prophets adapted what they had said so as to apply it to their later time, and some of it was incorporated into the newer text itself. In fact, there is hardly any biblical literature, no matter how early or late in date, that does not build on earlier tradition or literature.

Israel's early tradents seemed particularly adept at borrowing the wisdom of its neighbors and adapting it to address community needs. The story of the flood in Gen. 6–9 is similar to the earlier Mesopotamian flood stories. Many of Israel's laws were adapted from the laws of its neighbors in the ancient Near East, but Israel differed in how it presented God's relation to those laws. The gods of others might grant authority to the laws developed by a human such as Shamshi-Adad or Hammurabi, but in the Bible, in contrast, God is presented as a legislator himself, who gave the laws to Moses. The Temple Scroll from cave 11 at Qumran would press the hermeneutic case further, suggesting that God legislated directly without the mediation of Moses.

Many early traditions in preexilic biblical literature functioned authoritatively in the same manner that canonical written literature would function in later times. The canonical process had thus begun well before a canon in the full sense of the word was developed. Indeed, the Torah that Ezra brought back with him from exile in Babylonia (Neh. 8) undoubtedly functioned for communities in early Judaism much as it would later, when the Jewish canon was closed. And as is clear from Qumran literature, much of the prophetic corpus functioned in the same way. In fact, when the third section was added and the Jewish canon closed, the literature in the canon continued to function very much as early authoritative traditions, homegrown and borrowed, had functioned in preexilic times.

It is true, however, that the closing of the canon had the effect of attaching greater importance to the actual words in the written text. (Tradition could be formulated in various ways.) The focus thereby shifted somewhat from the ancient messages of biblical literature to the sanctity of the words themselves, which were being more accurately copied in the transmission of the text. Beginning in the 2nd century BCE, we begin to find biblical commentaries: the pesharim (which were primarily commentaries on prophetic texts) in the Dead Sea Scrolls and allegorical commentaries in Greek-speaking Judaism. These commentaries examine every word of the text and often play with different meanings. This process is carried much further in the midrashic commentaries of rabbinic Judaism, composed between the 4th and 12th centuries CE. But the canonical process of adaptation to ever-changing conditions, faced by the communities that found their identity and their *raison d'être* in scripture, hardly changed at all; and it continues to function in much the same way in the heirs of those communities today.

BIBL.: Lee Martin McDonald and James A. Sanders (eds.), *The Canon Debate* (Peabody, Mass.: Hendrickson, 2002). James A. Sanders, *From Sacred Story to Sacred Text: Canon as Paradigm* (Philadelphia: Fortress, 1987).   J.A.S.

Anatolia

Strictly speaking, there are no sacred texts in Hittite Anatolia, since Hittite religion was not a revealed one and because there was no "religion of the book" in the Hittite world. Reflecting upon the world in which he lived, *homo Hethaeus* built up his own conception of the heavenly realm mainly based on those of the Near Eastern, especially Syrian, culture. When we speak of "sacred texts" in the Hittite world, therefore, we ought to focus instead on three categories of texts that are related to religious practices: myths, texts connected with magical rituals, and texts connected with festivals. Myths are treated elsewhere in this volume and will therefore not be discussed here. The two other categories have much in common, but the festival texts assume an official character and are linked to the calendar: festivals occur at set dates, at which time a god comes to earth to visit the inhabitants of a town or a country. The activities at festivals are performed scrupulously according to certain rules, which are inspired by royal protocol, since the god is a sort of "super king." In contrast, the performance of magical rituals is dictated by circumstances (generally difficult situations that a community or an individual faces); the antiquity of their practices guarantees their efficacy. As luck would have it, excavations, chiefly at Hattusha, turned up libraries and "sacristies" of temples that are full of texts for both magical rituals and festivals, written on clay tablets that subsequently were burnt. These serve as venerable testimonies of Hittite religious practice.

Festival texts. The timing of great festivals is linked to seasons and agricultural work: it usually also presupposes the presence of the king or the royal couple. Two great festivals going back to early antiquity are especially important: the spring festival (AN.TAḪ.ŠUM [Crocus festival]) and the autumn festival (*nuntarriyashas* [festival of Haste]). The first festival lasted at least twenty-one days, and the second not fewer than thirty-eight. Both consisted of a kind of royal pilgrimage through the principal towns of Hatti. Texts from tablets specify the detail of the ceremonies to be performed in each town, providing a rich resource of information about ancient Anatolian liturgies. They describe the cult, the way of honoring the gods—they are a veritable handbook of "how to care for the gods." They also reflect on royal protocol, describing how to sacralize the "master of the ritual," the offerings, and the liturgical objects, how to make the gods come into their temple and then welcome and honor them, especially by means of a sacred feast at which the gods are offered food and libations and which the king and queen attend dressed in special ceremonial clothes. The presence of the king and queen, their activities, and their dress reflect the royal protocol. During the ceremonies, a group of dignitaries surrounded the king or the queen, all of whom had first undergone ritualized washing, since purity was a prerequisite of contact with the sacred. By way of illustration, we give here an excerpt from the ceremonies in the temple of the war-god, on the 16th day of the Crocus festival (*CTH* 612; cf. *ANET* 358–61):

Before the king and queen proceed to the temple of the war-god, the jongleurs, the narrator, and the crier proceed thereto and take their places. Then, the king and queen go to the temple of the war-god; the king reaches the portico, and at that time a dancer turns around once. The king and queen take their places in the court of the temple of the war-god. The chief of the guard holds the coat of the priest of the protector-god of nature, and, on the other hand, the priest of the protector-god of nature holds the perfumed lotion. Two palace sons bring the king and queen water for their hands. The king and queen wash their hands. The chief of the palace sons gives [them] a cloth so that they can dry their hands. The priest of the protector-god of nature presents to the king perfumed lotion; the king covers himself with it. The chief of the palace sons presents the cloth of the golden scepter to the king; the king washes his hands. A palace son takes the perfumed lotion back from the priest of the protector-god of nature. The priest of the protector-god of nature bows before the king. The palace son presents the perfumed lotion to the queen; the queen covers herself with it. The palace son gives back the perfumed lotion to the priest of the protector-god of nature. The chief of the palace sons gives the cloth of the golden scepter to the queen; the queen washes her hands.

Magical rituals. Most rituals pertain to magic and therefore aim at remedying some abnormality, including sickness. For the Hittites as for other peoples of the ancient Near East, all sicknesses and anomalies were the results of offenses, either one's own or inherited. In order to achieve healing, the magicians used healing rituals against fever, plague, women's sterility, or impotence. Many of these texts originate from Kizzuwatna (Cilicia). They are grouped under three types: (1) transfer rituals, where the evil is transferred into a substitute, which is then physically eliminated or sent into the steppe or a neighboring country (i.e., a scapegoat); (2) rituals of sympathetic magic based on analogy and meant to focus the attention of the concerned god on the positive response expected from him; and (3) rituals of purification of impure persons, buildings, and things, consisting in purificatory baths, temple aspersions, or distempering of the idol.

Appeasing rituals aimed at calming the irritation of a god as well as putting an end to the hostility between inhabitants of a country or between members of a family, especially father and son. The ritual of the Comanian priestess Mastigga against family quarrels is significant. Also very revealing are the rituals aiming at appeasing infernal forces, particularly the ritual concerning the Sun-goddess of the Earth in which the king and the queen evoke and pacify infernal forces by making offerings into a hole. We can put in the same category the *mugawar* rituals, which consisted of coaxing the god out of his bad mood and bringing him out of the place where he was in hiding.

Evocative rituals consisted of enticing the god from

one of the places where he was likely to reside (heaven, sea, depths of the earth) into a town, especially a temple. Several methods were used: a priest would call from the roof of the temple, or a red or bright thread would be strung along a way that the god would have to follow. The ritual of the "marking out of the ways" is very typical in this respect.

Execratory rituals aimed at calling down curses upon an enemy or a dishonest person. Meteorological rituals are typical of ancient Anatolia: they describe the ritual actions performed by the king when he heard the thunder considered to be a message of the weather-god: the offerings are black (bread, sheep, or oxen), and the libations are poured out of a black vase. Building and consecration rituals were performed at palaces and temples.

BIBL.: S. Alp, *Beiträge zur Erforschung des hethitischen Tempels* (Ankara, 1983). V. Haas and G. Wilhelm, *Hurritische und luwische Riten aus Kizzuwatna* (Neukirchen-Vluyn, 1974). L. Jakob-Rost, *Das Ritual der Malli aus Arzawa gegen Behexung* (Texte der Hethiter 2; Heidelberg, 1972). I. Wegner and M. Salvini, *Die hethitisch-hurritischen Ritualtafeln des Hiuwa-Festes* (Rome, 1991). R.L.

Iran

The religious history of Iran illustrates the necessity to distinguish between sacred texts, sacred writings (scripture), and canonicity. Unfortunately, in much historical writing, these categories have been mixed up and confused. Not all religious texts were written down, and while the medium of writing may in one instance be used to enhance the sacred character of a text, in another instance one observes a reluctance to commit sacred texts to writing.

For a very long period, the religious traditions of ancient Iran were transmitted orally. The text commonly thought to be the oldest document in an Iranian language, the so-called Gathas (hymns), is considered to be the core of ancient sacred traditions. Comprising five hymns of varying lengths, consisting of a total of seventeen chapters, the Gathas represent a very advanced form of priestly, ritual, or (some would claim) mystical poetry. This makes them extremely difficult to translate, let alone to interpret. Tradition claims that they were composed by or revealed to Spitama Zarathustra. While this is unlikely (the Gathas are normally dated by scholars to about 1000 BCE and Zarathustra to about 600), it remains safe to say that Zarathustra is the key figure among the people mentioned in the Gathas. Most scholars agree that the Gathas originated somewhere east of the country nowadays known as Iran.

At a certain period of time, about which it is impossible to be specific, the Gathas became part of a text known as Yasna (sacrificial liturgy). The Yasna also incorporates some other hymns and sacred literature, such as manthric utterances. (The name of a ritual still celebrated by current Zoroastrian priests in India is *yasna*.)

In the course of the *yasna* ritual, the text of the Yasna is recited.

The Yasna is part of what is known as the Avesta, a collection of texts composed in the Avestan language(s) and written in the Avestan script. All of these texts, including a treatise mostly pertaining to legal issues, are used either in priestly ceremonies or by laypeople in their prayers. It is unclear whether Avestan has ever been used as a "secular" language. The manuscript tradition is very late; the oldest Avestan manuscript is from the late 13th century CE. Not all Avestan texts have been preserved, and it is difficult to detect how much material has been lost. Later Islamic notions of a "sacred book" and modern printing techniques have contributed to changes in the perception and practical usage of the Avestan texts among Zoroastrians.

From the perspective of those performing a ritual, it may be less important to understand the texts recited in a ritual context than to perform them in an appropriate manner. In addition to the correct posture of the body, great care was taken to control intonation and pronunciation during recitation. Probably, the invention of the Avestan script, usually dated between the 4th and 6th centuries CE, was closely associated with this. The Avestan alphabet, which is based on Aramaic, is highly evolved from a phonetic standpoint. With its fifty-three letters (among them sixteen denoting vowels), it provides an excellent tool for transmitting specific requirements for pronunciation. Therefore, it provides a means of controlling a major feature of ritual practice. This trait distinguishes the Avestan script from other scripts that originated at roughly the same time and in the same cultural area, such as the Manichean, Georgian, and Armenian alphabets, all of which were aimed more at spreading religious ideas and texts among the people than at preserving priestly ritual instructions.

Probably, Avestan texts began to be translated into neighboring languages from an early period. However, only fragments of such early translations are preserved. At a later date, possibly already by the 3rd century CE, most, if not all, Avestan texts had been translated into Middle Persian. The texts and translations are provided with interspersed commentaries on the Avestan texts. Moreover, a new body of religious scripture developed, the so-called Pahlavi books (roughly 9th and 10th centuries CE). Some of these books claim to preserve ancient and authentic materials.

The commentaries on these texts, usually referred to as Zand, were a very sensitive issue. As commentaries could carry the seeds of religious dissidence and nonconformism—called heterodoxy by the establishment—religious and political authorities tried to keep the commentaries firmly under control; it is not by chance that the heretics were referred to as Zandik or Zandiq in Middle and New Persian respectively. The "heretics" *par excellence* were the Manicheans. This may have to do with their fondness for commenting on other religions' scriptures and thereby providing Manichean interpretations, which they claimed were authentic, rediscovered meanings. On the other hand, the Manicheans also had sacred texts of their own in different languages.

A final point often overlooked is that some Iranian kings, beginning with Darius the Great (reigned 522–486 BCE), made inscriptions at "sacred places," adding a religious dimension to their political decisions and positions.

BIBL.: Shaul Shaked, *Dualism in Transformation* (London, 1994). Michael Stausberg, "The Invention of a Canon," in *Canonization and Decanonization* (ed. Arie van der Kooij and Karel van der Toorn; Leiden, 1998), 257–77. Idem, *Die Religion Zarathushtras*, vol. 1 (Stuttgart, 2001).   M.ST.

Greece

Greek religion drew its strength from three inherent characteristics: its polytheism, a rich and complex pantheon with a large number of diverse gods; its ritualism, a culture of religious performance based on the scrupulous observance of a plethora of cults, festivals, and time-honored rites; and its regionalism, a broad and heterogeneous geographical base ranging from Sicily and Magna Graecia to the shores of the Black Sea. In stark contrast with the monotheistic "religions of the book," Greek religion survived for as long as it did without a canon of sacred scriptures, without a central religious authority, and without a belief system supported by authoritative texts and a cadre of professional exegetes to interpret them.

Egyptians were buried with the Book of the Dead and Romans consulted the Sibylline Books. Unlike its polytheistic neighbors, Greece did not produce a single sacred text of comparable rank. Yet religious texts of various kinds existed in abundance, from the representations of gods and rituals in high literature to cultic records on stone, even if none attained canonical status. The absence of such a canon suggests that writing was not essential to Greek religion and that written texts were extraneous to its core. Despite the widespread availability of writing, Greece remained largely an oral culture until the end of the classical age. In the early Hellenistic period, between 300 and 250 BCE, the classification of written texts and canonicity went hand in hand in the library of Alexandria. But the canon of "classical" Greek authors produced by Alexandrian scholars was based on the established genres of poetry and prose; it did not include sacred texts as a category.

That Greek religion lacked a canon, a clergy, and a spiritual center hardly comes as a surprise. Throughout its history, ancient Greece was a loose conglomerate of sovereign city-states, whose religious traditions and practices varied considerably from one place to another. Despite its Panhellenic tendencies, Greek religion retained a distinctly local and regional character. This is particularly true for the nexus between writing and religion. Texts used exclusively for religious purposes or in the context of religious institutions—such as cult regulations, sacrificial calendars, temple inventories, statutes of religious associations, oracles, and records of divine epiphanies and healing miracles—were recorded for local constituencies and did not circulate widely. More than four hundred of these texts survive; the vast majority existed in single copies on stone and never attained Panhellenic prominence. They document the practical side of Greek religion—the performance of ritual, the organization of festivals, the administration of public and private cults, and the behavior of religious groups.

One such text, a cult regulation from Selinus in Sicily, prescribes the following sacrificial ritual (*SEG* 43.630, B 12–13; ca. 450 BCE): "Whenever a sacrifice to the *elasteros* is required, perform the sacrifice as one sacrifices to the immortals. But [the sacrificer] must slaughter [the victim so that its blood flows] into the earth." As is often the case, the authority behind this regulation remains anonymous. The high level of ritual expertise points to a person or group—"those who make a craft out of rites" (Derveni Papyrus 20.3–4)—steeped in sacrificial lore that was ordinarily transmitted orally. Because texts of this type address matters of cult and ritual in a prescriptive manner, they have been collected twice in modern times under the generic title "sacred laws" (Latinized as *leges sacrae*). The underlying Greek term *hieros nomos* (sacred law or sacred custom) is attested in Plato, Demosthenes, and Hellenistic inscriptions, where it refers to a variety of cult-related texts and does not reflect a consistent category or concept. The modern classification implies, falsely, that a concept of "sacred laws" converging on "sacred texts" existed. In fact, for the Greeks, *hieros* (sacred) designated anything related to religion and the gods; it functioned as the antonym of "profane." Thus, the *hieroi nomoi* were considered sacred not in and of themselves, but because they dealt with sacred lore.

Another candidate for sacred-text status is Homer, whose poems have been called "the Bible of the Greeks." The Greeks had many books *(bibloi)* but no Bible. Yet Homer is indeed a special case. His role in the formation of Greek culture from around 700 BCE to late antiquity was pivotal. Does his preoccupation with gods and rituals make him an authority in matters of religion? The historian Herodotus certainly thought so. In his comparison of Greek and Egyptian gods he considers both Homer and Hesiod instrumental in the formation of the Greek pantheon: "It was only the day before yesterday, so to speak, that the Greeks came to know whence each of the gods originated, whether all of them existed always, and what they were like in their visible forms. For I reckon that Homer and Hesiod lived no more than four hundred years before my time. They are the poets who composed a theogony for the Greeks and gave the gods their epithets, assigned them their honors and special skills, and described their visible forms" (2.53).

Herodotus has a point. The Greek gods do indeed come to life for us in Homer and Hesiod; before that, in the Bronze Age, they are mere names attested in Linear B. Over the centuries, Homer attained the status of a Panhellenic teacher, sage, and even cult figure. His poetry was performed and recited at major religious festivals; countless copies of his poems circulated throughout the ancient world; his texts were subjected to massive scholarly scrutiny. A long tradition of allegorical interpretation discovered hidden physical, moral, and philosophical (especially Stoic and Neoplatonic) tenets in both epics. By late antiquity, Homer had been deified, his epics canonized, and their meaning sublimated. In some quarters, the *Iliad* and *Odyssey* had indeed achieved a status similar to that of a sacred text.

The only other text in Western civilization that has received comparable treatment is the Bible. The Old and New Testaments are sacred scripture because, like the Qur'an, they claim to be inspired by divine revelation and represent God's own voice. Their authority is based on that claim. By contrast, in Greek polytheism numerous divine voices competed for the ears of the faithful, and the boundaries between the sacred and the nonsacred were more fluid. Greek attitudes toward oracles are a case in point. Oracles were believed to emanate directly from a divinity. For that reason alone they carried considerable authority. Purportedly oral, the oracular responses of the Dodonian Zeus and the Delphic, Clarian, or Didymean Apollo were recorded, collected, and interpreted. Outside Greece, divine origin and religious authority are two of the qualities that characterize sacred texts. Yet there is no evidence that oracles were treated as sacred texts in Greece, for good reason. Oracles were not identified with particular religious constituencies, and many were concerned with mundane matters.

If cult regulations, Homeric epics, and Delphic oracles do not qualify as sacred texts, which texts do? Whether a given text should be considered sacred depends as much on our own understanding of what makes a text sacred as on whether that text was considered sacred in antiquity. It is easy to see why a Greek temple or a divine image should be sacred, why things dedicated to a divinity are sacred, or why some degree of sanctity should attach to seers, prophets, and "holy men." It is much more difficult to recognize a sacred text. Does its sacredness lie in (a) its content, (b) its ritual use, or (c) any reverence accorded to copies of the text? Categories a and b are more relevant for Greece than c. The philosopher Heraclitus reportedly deposited a copy of his work in the temple of Artemis at Ephesus. The dedication made that particular copy the sacred property of the goddess, but it did not make Heraclitus's work a sacred text.

The Greek term that corresponds literally to "sacred text" is *hieros logos* (sacred utterance or sacred story).

In Herodotus and Pausanias, it characterizes myths that explain the secret rites of various mystery cults. In a royal decree, Ptolemy IV (221–205 BCE) orders all persons "performing initiation rites for Dionysus" in Egypt to bring "a sealed copy of the sacred text [*hieros logos*]" to Alexandria. In a cult hymn from Andros, Isis claims to have "engraved the awe-inspiring *hieros logos* for the initiates." Invariably, *hieroi logoi* tend to be associated with foreign countries such as Egypt, Persia, or Phoenicia; with legendary figures such as Orpheus, Pythagoras, and Zarathustra; or with great antiquity—Plato mentions "ancient *hieroi logoi*" about the immortality of the soul (*Letters* 7.335a). Doubtless the majority of *hieroi logoi* circulated in oral form; of those that made it into writing, none survives. Equally lost are secret and potentially "sacred" texts or books attested for various mystery cults.

Without the guidance of extant texts explicitly identified as sacred by the Greeks, sacred texts remain hard to pinpoint. There is no lack of suitable candidates, all of which are the products of marginal groups outside the mainstream of Greek religion. If a specific religious identity, a distinct message, and a ritual connection are among the criteria for inclusion, the following texts have the strongest claims:

1. Three bone tablets from Olbia inscribed with the words *Dionysus, Orphics,* and pairs of opposites such as life/death, peace/war, truth/falsehood, and body/soul (*SEG* 28.659–61; ca. 450 BCE). Associated with a religious group and reflecting a particular worldview, these tablets meet two of the criteria that define sacred texts.

2. A series of so-called Orphic gold tablets with afterlife texts found in multiple copies in different parts of the Greek-speaking world and ranging in date from approximately 400 BCE to 250 CE. Most of them instruct the deceased where to go and what to say in the underworld: "I am the son of Earth and starry Heaven. I am dying from parching thirst. Quickly, give me cold water to drink from the Lake of Memory." Others make more esoteric claims that suggest rites of rebirth: "You have become a god from a human." "Now you have died and now you have come into being, thrice-blessed, on this very day. Tell Persephone that it was Bacchios himself who set you free." Several tablets contain enigmatic references to an (initiatory?) immersion in milk: "A bull you jumped into milk. A ram you fell into milk." Profoundly esoteric and eschatological, these texts clearly reflect deeply held beliefs that made them sacred for the Dionysiac initiates in whose tombs they were found (see also Mysteries).

3. Papyrus Gurob 1, a fragmentary papyrus from the end of the 3rd century BCE that mentions Eleusinian and Orphic divinities such as Demeter, Rhea, Brimo, Dionysus, Erikepaios, and Eubuleus; refers to sacrifices of a ram and a goat and to the consumption of sacrificial meat; quotes bits and pieces of hexameters from what is clearly an Orphic poem; enumerates the toys of Dionysus Zagreus (a pinecone, spinning top, knucklebones,

and mirror); and offers an esoteric medley of mysterious words and phrases reminiscent of the mystery cults of Dionysus and Sabazius: "save me," "one Dionysus," "god through bosom," "ox-herd," and "put into the basket." Was this text recited during some ritual? Its mysterious content puts it in a very special category.

4. The extant corpus of magical papyri, including love charms, cures against diseases, ritual scenarios for gaining power and control. Taken singly these texts were hardly sacred. But magical handbooks from late antiquity refer to magical recipes copied or quoted from a "sacred book" *(hiera biblos)*. It is tempting to interpret this designation self-referentially as evidence for the special status and high esteem in which collections of magical texts were held in certain circles.

If sacred texts are hard to find in ancient Greece, it is because they were rare and confined to the esoteric margins of Greek religion. More importantly, however, the concept of sacred texts reflects conditions and presuppositions more suitable to the monotheistic book religions than to the brand of polytheism peculiar to the Greeks.

BIBL.: Carsten Colpe, "Heilige Schriften," *Reallexikon für Antike und Christentum* 14 (1987): 184–223. Albert Henrichs, "*Hieroi Logoi* and *Hierai Bibloi*: The (Un)written Margins of the Sacred in Ancient Greece," *Harvard Studies in Classical Philology* 101 (2002): 1–59. Idem, "Writing Religion: Inscribed Texts, Ritual Authority, and the Religious Discourse of the Polis," in *Written Texts and the Rise of Literate Culture in Ancient Greece* (ed. Harvey Yunis; Cambridge, 2003), 38–58. R. C. T. Parker, *Athenian Religion: A History* (Oxford, 1996), esp. 43–55.   A.H.

Etruria

Sacred writings in the Etruscan language are known mainly from short inscriptions recording dedications to the gods and a few longer texts that contain religious calendars or other ritual information. The bilingual Etruscan/Phoenician gold tablets found at Pyrgi and dating around 500 BCE are brief and reveal only that the goddess Uni/Astarte was worshiped at the site and that a king of Caere, Thefarie Velianas, recognized her support by his dedications. The longest text is a real Etruscan book, the astonishing linen wrappings taken off an Egyptian mummy of the Hellenistic period (Zagreb, National Museum) and found to have a fairly lengthy text of approximately twelve hundred words, containing a fragmentary liturgical calendar of sacrifices and prayers to various Etruscan gods: Nethuns (= Neptune), Uni (= Juno), Luth, Cath, Mother Cel, Veive, and others. The writing runs from right to left, as is normal in Etruscan. This is a unique example of a type of sacred book mentioned by Latin authors, the *liber linteus* (linen book; Livy 4.7, 13, 20, 23), preserved by chance when the book was cut into strips to be used for the mummy wrappings.

Equally unusual is the bronze lifesize model of a sheep's liver found at Piacenza in northern Italy, divided

into forty-two "cells" inscribed with the names of gods. Also Hellenistic, the Piacenza liver is not a continuous text, but may be "read" by a priest to determine which region of a sacrificial liver is sacred to which gods. Included are Etruscan deities who may be equated with Latin ones, such as Tin (= Jupiter), Uni, Fufluns (= Bacchus), and Maris (= Mars?), and elusive ones such as Cilens, Thuflthas, Lethns, and many others.

From Latin and Greek sources we have references to a substantial body of Etruscan prophetic literature that provided a guide to the "Etruscan discipline" *(disciplina Etrusca)*, the principles of Etruscan religion. The Etruscan prophet Tages sang out these revelations, written down in the *Libri Tagetici*, by which priests knew how to interpret lightning, earthquakes, and other signs from the gods. His books included *Libri haruspicini*, telling how to scrutinize the organs of a sacrificed animal, and *Libri Acherontici*, pertaining to the underworld and afterlife. We also have evidence that he discussed the spheres of habitation of the gods, a doctrine echoed in an elaborate passage of Martianus Capella (*De Nuptiis Mercuriae et Philologiae* 1.41–61), and that he described the *ritus Etruscus*, the ritual for the founding of cities. A remarkable brontoscopic calendar (a calendar interpreting the occurrence of thunder on certain days), preserved by the Byzantine scholar Johannes Lydus (*De ostentis* 27–38) and attributed to the Roman savant Nigidius Figulus, may reflect his predictions.

Another noted prophet was the Nymph Vegoia (Etruscan *Lasa Vecuvia*), revealer of the material in the *Libri Vegontici*, including books on lightning kept in the temple of Apollo in Rome. An important fragment of the writings of Vegoia exists in the *Corpus Agrimensorum romanorum* (Lachmann 1848: 350), referring to creation, the division of lands, and events at the end of the eighth *saeculum* of Etruscan history.

BIBL.: Karl Lachmann, *Gromatici veteres* (Corpus Agrimensorum Romanorum 1; Berlin: Reimer, 1848).   N.T.DEG.

Rome

Religious texts at Rome do not define religious doctrine; nor is there any record of a book supposedly written by a traditional divinity of Rome. In this sense Roman religion is not a "religion of the book." Nonetheless there existed—or came to exist—a variety of religious writing, from priestly books of religious procedure to texts that were the product of divine inspiration. The latter, it seems, were always of "foreign" origin. And although they were recognized as being divinely inspired, there remained, at least within the governing class, a dissonance between a desire to learn what these books contained and a suspicion of their possibly subversive content.

The use of writing as a record of procedure is reflected on inscribed documents that may be taken as representative of the products of Roman and other Italic priests. The most important of these are the Iguvine Tables, the Acts of the Arval Brethren, and the inscriptions recording the celebration of the Secular Games. The Iguvine Tables, our earliest example, lay out the procedures to be employed by a local priestly college in the Umbrian city of Gubbio probably in the 2nd century BCE. The Acts of the Arval Brethren describe the procedures that were employed in the celebration of Dea Dia at her shrine, and the various records of the Secular Games describe the way in which those ceremonies were conducted. The inscriptions of both these groups begin in the Augustan age (31 BCE–14 CE), reflecting, it seems, Augustus's interest in publicizing his connection with traditional rituals. In fact, the great majority of the surviving inscribed calendars of festivals date to the reign of Augustus.

The appearance of cultic information on inscriptions may suggest a gradual change in the way that these writings were treated. Certainly the traditional books of the priestly colleges were not for circulation to the general public. In 56 BCE Cicero could refer to books containing the opinions (responsa) of pontifices as being "secret" (On His House 36). A second group of books that Cicero mentions in the same context are the libri reconditi (secret books) of the augurs. Thus when Tiberius Sempronius Gracchus consulted his books of augural law to review the results of the consular election he had conducted in 163, he appears to have used books to which only he had access (Cicero, On the Nature of the Gods 2.11).

There has been a considerable debate about what kind of information these books and other priestly records contained. The pontifices were traditionally associated with the early records of legal formulas and the calendar, as well as with some (now much disputed) form of historical record keeping. Their responsa presumably formed a body of precedent that the pontifices, and no others, were accustomed to use—although even they were probably not bound by them. Likewise the libri reconditi would have contained precedent collected by individual augurs for their use and the use of their college. How far the books of these and other priestly colleges contained further systematic religious rules is unclear; and we are little helped by the surviving quotations that claim to be drawn from them.

The case of Gracchus, however, illustrates important features of the intersection between text and action. Gracchus used his priestly books to review a ruling that he had made. He then transmitted this information to the senate, which in turn decided that he was correct and so invalidated the results of the consular election months after the consuls of 162 BCE had taken office. The senate did not agree with him because of what was written in the book, rather it agreed with him because it decided that what he had done in the conduct of the elections was a violation of practice. Gracchus did not have the authority to make a final decision on the matter. That pontifical or augural books were not endowed

with any inherent authority concentrated religious authority first in the hands of the priestly colleges, which were endowed with the power to interpret their contests as they saw fit, and then in the hands of the senate, which had the power to agree or disagree with their interpretation. The senate's decisions in such cases appear to have been based on the quality of the argument rather than fixed doctrine.

A rather different type of sacred text was the collection known as the Sibylline Oracles (after the prophetic Sibyl of Cumae, with whose authority they came to be associated). Significantly, they were placed in the care of the priestly college concerned with "foreign" religious practice, the college of quindecimviri. According to legend, they had been acquired by the Roman state toward the end of the regal period (one version of the story has them sold to King Tarquin by a mysterious elderly woman). Their arrival may be seen as a feature of the Hellenization of some aspects of Roman cult. It is also quite likely that the books were originally kept by the kings on the model of other collections of oracular books that were retained by Greek tyrants in this same period. Throughout the republican and imperial periods (until the collection was destroyed in the 5th century CE), access to the books was restricted to the members of the board, who could consult them only when ordered to do so by the senate. Likewise, although members of the college could make recommendations to the senate about the addition of new books to the collection, they could not add these books without prior approval by the senate. In the republic, the approved books were kept inside the temple of Jupiter Optimus Maximus (when that temple burnt down—with the oracles—in the 1st century BCE, the senate authorized the quindecimviri to assemble a new collection). With the beginning of the principate, in the reign of Augustus, they were moved to the temple of Apollo on the Palatine (Suetonius, Augustus 31).

The official Sibylline Oracles were in Greek hexameter verse (a supposed extract is preserved in the 2nd-century CE Greek writer, Phlegon, On Wonders 10). In form they appear to have consisted of a list of prodigies (e.g., the birth of an hermaphroditic child) followed by an extensive series of instructions on the form that a cult should take to expiate the prodigy in question. We do not know what religious authority was claimed for the earliest collection of oracles. It may be (as some scholars suggest) that the Sibyl was seen as divinely inspired; but it is more likely that the Sibyl spoke on the basis of her own special knowledge of the future. This is an important distinction, as divinely inspired prophecy does not seem to have had a place within Italic systems of prognostication, while we do have some evidence for writings of prophets who appear also to have spoken on their own authority. Thus two oracular texts that came to light in the course of the Hannibalic war were attributed to a seer named Marcius (Livy 25.12). These books appear to have been in Latin verse (they are called the *carmina Marciana*), and they caused enough of a stir that the urban praetor of 212 BCE asked for a consultation of the Sibylline Oracles to test their authenticity. A Sibylline Oracle was found that ordered the founding of games to Apollo just as the second of the two *carmina Marciana* had recommended. Perhaps the most interesting feature of the Marcian episode was the way that the second oracle was tested against the authority of the official collection. There was no other way that the Roman state could officially accommodate prophetic books outside the existing system.

The lengths to which the Roman state went to control access to the Sibylline Oracles may be taken as a sign of the inherent discomfort that the state felt with texts that were created outside the structure of the state religion. So, too, that the Roman state felt it necessary to recognize that some such books could offer guidance suggests that what we see in the Sibylline Books was but the tip of an oracular and prognostic iceberg. By acknowledging one set of books that could be tightly controlled, the state arrogated the right to declare other works to be either legitimate or illegitimate. This was all the more important as Roman power expanded into parts of Italy where other peoples had traditions that were different from Rome's. The most important of these (aside from the Greeks) were the Etruscans, who appear to have acknowledged both inspired prophecy—a fragment of an Etruscan-inspired prophecy attributed to a nymph named Vegoia is preserved in the collection of Latin land surveyors (Lachmann 1848: 350–51)—and haruspicy, which is a form of inductive divination based on books.

We know that other books of divine wisdom were available, which competed for attention with the Roman audience. From time to time, the Roman state took action to halt the circulation of such material for fear that it would cause unrest. Augustus, for instance, is said to have ordered the destruction of two thousand volumes of prophecy that he, acting with his quindecimviral colleagues, declared to be false, and Tiberius (ruled 14–37 CE), ordered astrologers to turn their books over to the senate for destruction after a scandal involving a member of the senate. These incidents were, however, the exceptions rather than the rule, and sacred books were allowed to circulate if they were not used for what appeared to be subversive purposes.

Perhaps the most significant feature of the imperial period was the admission that sacred writings of other peoples were of great interest. As Roman society grew more cosmopolitan, so, too, did its reading matter, and it appears to have been tacitly admitted that the gods may have spoken to other peoples in ways that they did not speak to Romans of the republic. Roman emperors tended to advertise their personal connections with individual divinities, and they often did so through the media offered by non-Roman religious systems, possibly because the offerings of the indigenous Roman tradition were so poor. The rise in the status of inspired writings of other cultures, be they Egyptian, Greek, or Persian, was a significant feature of religious life in the first three centuries CE. As such it may also have been a factor that facilitated the rise of the most bookish of all Mediterranean religions, Christianity.

BIBL.: M. Beard, J. North, and S. Price, *Religions of Rome*, vol. 1 (Cambridge, 1998). Karl Lachmann, *Gromatici veteres* (*Corpus Agrimensorum Romanorum* 1; Berlin, 1848). J. Linderski, *Roman Questions: Selected Papers* (Stuttgart, 1995). C. Moatti (ed.), *La mémoire perdue: recherches sur l'administration romaine* (Collections de l'école française de Rome 243; Rome, 1998). D. S. Potter, *Prophets and Emperors: Human and Divine Authority from Augustus to Theodosius* (Cambridge, Mass., 1994). D.S.P.

Christianity

The Greek word for "canon," a Semitic loanword, means a "straight rod," "reed," "rule," "standard," "formulation," or "rule of faith." From the 1st to the 3rd centuries CE, Christians insisted on the word's fundamental meaning—as a criterion for faith preserved in the preaching, confession, or gospel. Only in the 4th century did the term refer to a formally recognized collection of books (see Athanasius's *Decrees of the Synod of Nicea* 18 [soon after 350] and the Council of Laodicea, canon 60 [date uncertain]).

The "early church" was not a unified religious and social entity in the 1st century. Accounts of Jesus's ministry, passion, and resurrection were products of different groups, including the Twelve, the seven Hellenists, the Johannine community, the first Galilean Christians, the family of Jesus, and the transmitters of the sayings source (Q) and of the *Gospel of Thomas*. Each group had a view of authority and its expression in rituals, ministry, or writing. Unity prevailed, however, in the case of holy scripture: like fellow Jews, Christians accepted the Torah—in Hebrew or in Greek. As a prophetic and apocalyptic movement, most Christians also revered the prophets, particularly Isaiah. The Psalms, composed by the king and prophet David, enjoyed great favor. The third part of the scriptural canon was not fixed, as it still was not for contemporary Jews. Paul and the Letter of Jude cited texts later excluded from the Jewish canon (see 1 Cor. 2.9; Jude 14–16). With respect to the sacred books, one of the Pastoral Epistles speaks for all: "All scripture is inspired by God and profitable for teaching, for reproof, for correction, and for training in righteousness" (2 Tim. 3.16).

Common among "Christian" movements was respect for Jesus Christ, and his name became an authority alongside scripture. His ministry was remembered; he was present in Christians' missionary or liturgical activity. Citing Papias, Eusebius highlights the importance of oral traditions among early Christians (*Church His-*

tory 3.39.4). This companionship of oral and written word is not surprising, given the parallel of tractate *Avot* in the Mishnah, with its two channels of revelation, the written and the oral Torah.

As time passed, respect for the words of Jesus did not prevent new compositions: Passion narratives, collections of sayings, and miracle stories, often preserved in writing (see Luke 1.1). The Gospels written at the end of the 1st century corresponded initially to different communities, including texts that did not achieve canonical status, such as the *Gospel of Peter* (probably not only a passion narrative, but a general account of Jesus's ministry) or the *Gospel of Thomas* (a collection of Jesus's sayings; Nag Hammadi II.2).

Early Christian groups, despite tense relations, strove for unity. Matthew and Luke readily adapted texts from Mark, the sayings source (Q), and other documents. Somewhat later the *Gospel of the Ebionites* tried to harmonize the three Synoptic Gospels (Matthew, Mark, and Luke). Evidencing a strong preference for one account, Tatian, a late-2nd-century Syrian theologian, composed in Greek a single work developed out of the four Gospels, the so-called *Diatessaron* (lit., [one] through four). Such was its success that its Syriac form was canonical for centuries. Only in the 4th century was it replaced by the four Gospels, called the "gospel of the separated" (see Theodoret of Cyrrhus, *Compendium of Heretical Tales* 1.20). Without any official decision, the increasingly collaborative early Christian movements became the majority church in the 2nd century and accepted the Gospels of various communities. The collection of four Gospels is presupposed by the 2nd-century figures Papias (in Eusebius, *Church History* 3.39.14–17) and Hegesippus (4.22.3). Yet in 180 Irenaeus (*Against the Heresies* 3.11.8) had to legitimate the "weakness" of having four Gospels. Defenders of the fourfold canon also had to explain the contradictions between the Gospels, particularly the divergent beginnings.

Jesus's words and ministry would have fallen into oblivion without human transmitters, both male and female "apostles" (cf. 2 Cor. 5.18). Many of the early Christian communities had a special bond to an apostolic figure considered their founder. When disputes arose, they relied on the teachings of their apostle. In a 2nd-century controversy over the date of Easter, the Roman church, claiming the privilege of the tombs of Peter and Paul, tried to impose its practice. But the churches of Asia Minor defended their system based on the authority of John and Philip, interred respectively in Ephesus and Hierapolis (Eusebius, *Church History* 3.24.2–4; 5.24.1–3).

Widespread interest in apostles led to the perpetuation of two forms: the preservation of their message in letters and of their lives in narratives. Paul himself contributed to the preservation of his image (first as persecutor, second as church leader; see Gal. 1.13–17). He and his disciples eagerly disseminated his letters to a wide audience (see Col. 4.16). Not long after his death, disciples gathered a collection of his letters, authentic or pseudepigraphic, probably organized according to length. Polycarp, bishop of Smyrna, worked to preserve Paul's heritage (*Letter to the Philippians* 3), and 2 Peter knew the corpus (see 2 Pet. 3.15–17). As with the four Gospels, the problem of justifying multiple documents again emerges. A solution surfaces in a fragmentary document discovered by the Italian librarian Muratori, now variously dated to the 2nd or 4th century. Paul's letters are organized so as to represent a group of seven letters sent to seven churches. Because seven symbolizes totality, seven letters is as good as having only one (Muratorian Fragment 39–63)!

The theological bipolarity of Gospel-Apostle encouraged the creation of a corpus of the major documents of the new covenant in the mid-2nd century, in which the four Gospels and the Pauline Epistles appear side by side. Luke's two volumes were both accepted, but Acts was detached from the Gospel of Luke to become the beginning of a companion series. To this category belong also some Catholic Epistles (e.g., 1 Peter and 1 John) and the Book of Revelation. Since then, these texts (Gospels, Epistles, Book of Acts, and Book of Revelation) were considered to be holy books and thus served as liturgical readings, reservoirs of knowledge, and arsenals of arguments.

One theologian, Marcion, dismissed oral tradition. For theological reasons, he refused the revelation preserved in the Hebrew Bible and decided to "purify" the Christian message. He resolved to build his teaching only on written texts—one Gospel (a drastically revised Luke) and a collection of Pauline letters. Marcion removed from these any trace of Jewish influence and contrasted the unknown God revealed in Jesus to the tyrannical and vengeful demiurge of the Hebrew Bible. His rejection of the Old Testament forced Christians to decide whether it should be preserved. The various authoritative texts of groups marginalized as "gnostic" also elicited a reaction. Therefore, in the second half of the 2nd century a canon of Christian scripture emerged. Christians in various places accepted a tripartite scripture consisting of Gospels, Epistles, and the "rest." Evidence for this development includes the Muratorian Fragment for Rome; the writings of Tertullian for North Africa; Irenaeus for Asia Minor, where he was born, and for Gaul, where he later moved; and Clement of Alexandria for Egypt.

Ultimately the readers of the books were as important as the books themselves. The four Gospels were assembled because the groups who respected individual texts were in contact and accepted the validity of other communities' texts. In that light the situation of the Johannine community becomes clear. It long comprised an independent branch of Christianity, but around 100 an internal dispute concerning Christology occurred—was Jesus a fully human person or, as divine, did he only appear to be human? The Johannine Epistles took a stand and became, with the Gospel of John, the canon of the "orthodox" wing of the Johannine community. After the schism of the Johannine community (see 1 John 2.19), the orthodox group must have joined mainstream Christian communities, taking their books along. This development explains the presence of both the Gospel of John and 1 John, an orthodox explanation of the Gospel, in the New Testament canon. That the Gospel of John was a latecomer is clear from its very position as the fourth and last of the canonical Gospels. The *Acts of John* and other Johannine documents are vestiges of the "heterodox" Johannine community.

A problem arose in the West: everybody knew that no apostle had written Hebrews, an epistle accepted from the beginning in the East. Out of respect for the East, the West finally acknowledged this epistle but claimed that Paul himself wrote it. The East believed that, if the content was Pauline, the form was due to a follower of Paul such as Luke.

A parallel problem arose in the East: after an initial period of favor (shared with the *Apocalypse of Peter*, another apocalypse mentioned in the Muratorian Fragment), the Book of Revelation was widely disregarded. Some still accepted it but allegorically eliminated its subversive orientation and never read it liturgically. Others, particularly in Alexandria, rejected the book, as well as its millennarist and Montanist appropriations.

One must distinguish a collection's birth from its formal canonization. The creation of the corpus of four Gospels or of Pauline letters was a work of 2nd-century piety, recognizing the authority of these documents. Not yet a formal canon validated by official decision, its existence was a common opinion shared by those who considered themselves to be the orthodox church. Around 200 the reality of a New Testament, a companion volume for Christians to the First Testament, came into existence. Unity, however, long remained an abstraction, for in practice it was still a collection of several manuscripts. Even the name New Testament was slow in coming. Christian authors still used the old terms *Lord* or *Gospel* for the Gospels and *Apostle* for the Epistles.

One would have to wait until the 4th century for official decisions and authoritative lists: in the East the *Thirty-Ninth Festal Epistle* by Athanasius of Alexandria (367), in the West the African synods of Hippo (393) and Carthage (397 and 419). Christian communities had delineated criteria of canonicity since the 2nd century. Canonical writings must be of apostolic origin, used in the liturgy, and must conform to the truth venerated by the church. The 4th century further specified that a book must be apostolic to be part of the canonical Christian scriptures, and if so, it is also inspired by the Holy Spirit.

Without being part of the Holy Scripture, many other texts nevertheless still possessed authority. When in the 3rd century Origen reflected on the matter, he delineated undisputed books, rejected books, and disputed books (Eusebius, *Church History* 6.25). Origen deemed the third category needed (a) because some books were accepted by some and rejected by others and (b) because in addition to the canonical books, others were useful for personal devotion or theological inquiry.

In his *Against Marcion* 4.2 Tertullian chose a Latin term applied to legal documents *(instrumentum)* to define the scriptures of the literary collection of the new covenant *(instrumentum evangelicum)*. In the *Passion of Perpetua and Felicitas* 1.4 the author, probably Tertullian, used the same term *(instrumentum ecclesiae)* for the acts of the two martyrs. Both types of documents, the canonical and the hagiographical, are useful "tools" for Christian believers. Two centuries later, realizing the miraculous power of relics, Augustine invited his miraculously cured parishioners to record their stories (in the so-called *libelli*; see *City of God* 22.8; *Sermons* 320–24 in *Patrologia latina* 38.1443–45). He deemed it important to have, in addition to the wonders of the New Testament, witnesses of contemporary miracles, evidencing the Spirit's continued work. There was therefore space between the canonical and the apocryphal documents for a third category: inspired narratives and hagiographies. The so-called *Protevangelium of James*, a life of Mary, was never part of the canon, but the Eastern church, considering it useful, never rejected it as apocryphal. When Eusebius of Caesarea revisited Origen's New Testament canon, he also respected this division in three categories (*Church History* 3.25). The Byzantine period and the Middle Ages confirmed the importance of this tripartition. Christian art amply demonstrates how deeply these texts enriched its iconographic program. One of innumerable expressions of this influence occurs in a group of mosaics of Monreale in Sicily that include scenes of the apostles' lives inspired by noncanonical texts. A focus on these texts, uninhibited by a canonical bias, reveals the rich details of a vital religiosity.

BIBL.: Hans von Campenhausen, *The Formation of the Christian Bible* (trans. J. A. Baker; Philadelphia, 1972). Shaye J. D. Cohen, *From the Maccabees to the Mishnah* (Library of Early Christianity 7; Philadelphia, 1987), 174–213. Jean-Daniel Kaestli, "Histoire du canon du Nouveau Testament," in *Introduction au Nouveau Testament: Son histoire, son écriture, sa théologie* (ed. Daniel Marguerat; Geneva, 2000), 449–74. Lee M. McDonald and James A. Sanders (eds.), *The Canon Debate* (Peabody, Mass., 2002). Bruce M. Metzger, *The Canon of the New Testament: Its Origin, Development, and Significance* (Oxford, 1987). F.B.

Esotericism and Mysticism

Introduction

This chapter, entitled "Esotericism and Mysticism," two terms famously hard to define, includes a wide range of disparate topics. The sections on ancient Babylonian and Egyptian religion associate esotericism—which David Frankfurter aptly characterizes as the "cultivation of secrecy" involving "religious activities and . . . a distinctively secret body of knowledge"—with claims to divine kingship, as a means of protecting the rulers' prerogatives and claiming a royal monopoly on divine power. In his discussion of Mesopotamian religion, for example, Eckhart Frahm notes traditions relating how certain kings and groups of priests received esoteric knowledge, often protected not only by sacred writing but also by cryptography. Simo Parpola, discussing what he calls "Mesopotamian mysticism," similarly locates its origin in the institution of divine kingship. Edward Wente, discussing the early traditions in Egypt, points out that "the most restricted knowledge was that said to be possessed by the king as priest of the sun-god."

Several sections show how sources that originated in royal and priestly circles later came to be translated, often reformulated, and popularized. For example, Frankfurter, who takes up the discussion of Greco-Roman Egypt, points out how secrets originally restricted to priests, who were "strongly conscious of the intrinsic efficacy of writing, names, and images," later were presented in the Greek and Demotic magical papyri: "A preponderance of revelation spells across the *PGM/PDM* corpus suggests that the priestly owners of these manuals may have been selling experiences once reserved for priests now to Greek and Roman outsiders." Frankfurter goes on to observe that by the time of Damascius, as well as in the Hermetica, "esotericism is closely linked with the achievement of self-transcendence, divine visions, and even union with the divine—that is, a sort of mysticism." Such lore, once practiced only by kings and priests, now became the basis of man-

uals of "spiritual practice" of various sorts. Frankfurter closes by observing that it was not only magical practices and rituals effecting union with the divine that came into more widespread use in Roman Egypt; Egyptian mortuary practices, too, came to be revised and popularized in a variety of works that ranged from the Amduat to the *Books of Jeu* and the *Apocalypse of Paul.*

The chapter also includes discussion of theurgy, Heikhalot tradition, Gnosticism, Hermeticism, and Manicheism. Sarah Iles Johnston characterizes theurgy as one of "many mystic religious movements that combined elements of Platonic philosophy, practices drawn from traditional cult, and newer doctrines" that allegedly drew from direct access to divine revelation. Diverse in its manifestations during the first few centuries CE, theurgy involves ritual intended to align the practitioner with the divine power, offer access to that power, or to effect forms of transformation. Philip Alexander contributes a discussion of Heikhalot mysticism during the talmudic period (ca. 200–700 CE), which he calls "the first clear instance of esotericism within Judaism." Alexander summarizes the wide range of beliefs and rituals that, in his view, reflect not only literary traditions but mystical and theurgical practice as well. Although he qualifies Gershom Scholem's characterization of Heikhalot traditions as "Jewish Gnosticism," he does point out affinities between these sources and, for example, the Nag Hammadi treatises. Karen King's discussion of Gnosticism suggests that Alexander's cautious approach to the term is well founded. King opens by arguing that the term *gnosticism* is a modern misnomer for a wide range of tendencies in early Christian circles. Following this, she shows that the Nag Hammadi sources, other Coptic and Greek texts, and the writings of such teachers as Valentinus and his disciples demonstrate a wide range of teachings and practices, most of them Christian, but far too diverse to justify the traditional classification. Guy Stroumsa discusses Manicheism, a strongly dualistic world religion established by Mani (216–77 CE) and widespread for over a thousand years. While Mani, regarding himself as an apostle of Jesus, claimed to offer a perfected Christian teaching, the "complex mythology" of his teachings was treated as heresy by the Christian emperors of the West. As is evident, the extraordinary variety of traditions included in this chapter demonstrates the difficulty of generalizing about esotericism and mysticism, and invites the reader instead to investigate each of these traditions through the bibliography included at the end of each section. E.P.

Egypt

Early period. Egyptian religious texts, particularly those deriving from a mortuary context, frequently allude to their own secret nature and occasionally mention the exclusivity of those having access to such esoteric material. Perhaps the most restricted knowledge was that said to be possessed by the king as priest of the sun-god, which even enabled him to speak the mysterious language of baboons while adoring the rising sun-god Re. Because of the pharaoh's divine status, both as the falcon Horus and as son of Re, it was believed possible for him to consort with the gods. Thus, for example, Thutmose III recounted in mystical terms how upon entering the temple holy of holies at his coronation he ascended to heaven as a divine falcon and received the diadems of his father Re. But since the king deputized his priestly function, his recondite knowledge was actually shared by higher clergy and elite officials. Over time, mysteries associated with the divine kingship became available to deceased mortals as royal esoteric texts and myths were incorporated in the mortuary literature of commoners.

The Middle Kingdom Coffin Texts and the New Kingdom Book of the Dead contain interrogatory spells that derived from the initiation rites of various professional guilds whose members possessed restricted knowledge. Certain occupations, such as net-maker, fowler, fisherman, carpenter, embalmer, and priest, required some sort of initiation involving questions and answers whereby the novice not only demonstrated familiarity with technical aspects of the trade but also provided secret, mythical names of the many, often highly specialized, objects peculiar to the profession. Within the Book of the Dead are included spells derived from priestly initiation rites, such as chapter 17, a dramatic initiatory interrogation, and chapter 125, containing the so-called Negative Confession.

Arguments for the existence of pharaonic mysticism revolve largely around mortuary texts: principally the Coffin Texts, Book of the Dead, and cosmographic compositions from the New Kingdom royal tombs. Although such documents obviously formed part of the funerary equipment of a dead person, there are indications that certain spells contained in these texts were also used upon earth, either by a ritualist acting on behalf of the deceased or by a living person for his or her own benefit. Particularly relevant to the issue of mysticism are spells designed to transform an individual into a divine entity and those containing statements baldly identifying the speaker with a high deity such as Re or Atum. While it is generally maintained that the transformation spells, even when known or recited upon earth, were entirely postmortem in their application and did not involve a *unio mystica* through meditation, occasional statements in texts pertaining to the sun-god's nightly passage through the underworld indicate that they were as equally efficacious upon earth for a living person as in the netherworld for a dead person.

Although the Book of Amduat, probably composed in the Middle Kingdom but first attested in New Kingdom royal tombs and a vizier's tomb, has been regarded as having its origins in the royal solar cult, it is clear from statements in the text that a limited number of commoners had access to it. Included are references to its efficaciousness on earth for the living person who knows its contents, and it is stated that such an individual is the likeness of the great god. Amduat describes the sun-god's progress through the twelve hours of the night and fusion with the inert Osiris in the underworld, enabling the sun's daily rebirth, and this paradigm operated for the living person, whose life cycle was homologous to the daily death and rebirth of the sun-god in the underworld. The occurrence of enigmatic writing in portions of the Amduat suggests that it served as a means of testing an initiate's mastery of the mysteries.

While Amduat stresses gnosis, the Book of Gates, also from the royal tombs, deals more with praxis. A living person, participating in the sun-god's nightly course through the netherworld, at various points makes offerings to groups of beings in the beyond and thereby becomes a member of each group. In the Book of the Heavenly Cow, another nonroyal composition from the royal tombs, there is the comment that the living person who recites the text is said by people to be like Re on the day of his birth. Certain board games of secular origin were apparently played on a religious level with the intention of participating in the sun-god's journey through the underworld and achieving apotheosis with the god at his rising.

While it may be pushing the evidence too far to state that a genuine *unio mystica* with an absolutely transcendent deity was achievable through meditation in pharaonic Egypt, certainly identification with high deities such as Re allowed the individual to share in divine processes of renewal even before death. The panontistic nature of Egyptian religion and the cyclic nature of time, in which life and death and day and night were homologues, allowed for mystical participation in the divine otherworldly realm. Such interaction between seemingly opposed realms of existence is consonant with other ancient Egyptian paranormal practices: incubation of dreams, banqueting with the dead in tombs, and letters to the dead. The very language used to describe mysterious processes in the beyond suggests that mysticism was not inherently alien to Egyptian religious experience.   E.F.W.

Greco-Roman period. To the extent that esotericism involves the cultivation of secrecy around religious activities and of a distinctively secret body of knowledge, esotericism in Egyptian religion was fundamentally the provenance of the temple priesthoods. Esotericism arose as a natural outgrowth of priestly writing (theological, mortuary, and ritual compositions) and ritual gesture (oracular incubation). Although these literary and ritual pursuits were conducted as part of priestly duties, rather than to fulfill spiritual longings, they gave rise to a more self-conscious piety whose greatest flowering took place during the Greco-Roman period.

A self-conscious secrecy surrounds the lore and productions of the House of Life, or temple scriptorium, at least as early as the Middle Kingdom, when the Admonitions of Ipuwer lament that "books are stolen, the secrets [of the scriptorium] laid bare. Lo, magic spells are divulged, spells are made worthless through being repeated by people" (6.7), while the Harris Magical Papyrus instructs "not to reveal [this spell] to the common man—[it is] a mystery of the House of Life" (6.10). The spells and ritual utterances in manuals such as the Harris Papyrus display a world of mythological recombination and synthesis, based in the reuse of archaic written materials and the reapplication of kingship ritual, that is indeed altogether removed from the popular religious culture. Such esoteric priestly innovations included the development of "pantheistic" forms of popular gods (Brooklyn Magical Papyrus) and locally protective forms of royal gods (Horus *cippi*; see Illness). The priestly composers were strongly conscious of the intrinsic efficacy of writing, names, and images, so that their very literary pursuits (and indeed, the full range of temple rituals) were imbued with magical power. The preservation and ongoing reinterpretation of ancient oracles in the Demotic Chronicle, Oracle of the Lamb, and Oracle of the Potter (Ptolemaic era) likewise show priests' devotion to discerning the ongoing truth in ancient divine pronouncements, somewhat in the manner of sectarian Jewish biblical interpretation.

These esoteric forms of normative priestly work emerge as dominant motifs in Greco-Egyptian materials of the Roman period: the Greek and Demotic magical papyri *(PGM/PDM)* and the Hermetica. Despite their being written in Greek and incorporating the names of Greek gods, the *PGM/PDM* continue many of the essential motifs, deities, functions, and assumptions of earlier Egyptian ritual manuals while incorporating a veritable bricolage of Mediterranean myths, deities, and formulas. They also show a concern for secrecy and privacy exceeding the earlier texts, a development no doubt attributable to imperial pressures on priestly authority and infrastructure. Arcane substances of dubious nature (semen of Heracles, eyes of a bat) are listed for mundane rites, as if to preserve these rites as the priests' unique domain: temple scribes concealed their true equivalents behind encoded names, one text explains, "so that [the masses], since they do not take care, might not bother themselves [with ritual spells, being prevented] by the consequence of their failures" (PGM XII.401–6). The Hermetica similarly advertise themselves as illegitimate translations of an arcane priestly wisdom: the Egyptian language, one text insists, is fundamentally "obscure and conceals the significance of the words" and, if rendered in Greek, would be completely garbled (*Corpus Hermeticum* 16.1; see further Hermeticism). Thus, manifestly syncretic ideas about the soul and divinity, some of which were certainly rooted in Egyptian temple traditions, are cast as secret revelations, the provenance of the House of Life.

Even in the late 5th century CE, priestly traditions are preserved and cultivated among some families as an esoteric repository of power. A philosopher named Damascius describes the priestly dedication and secret clairvoyant talents of the brothers Heraiscus and Asclepiades (floruit 480s), who could—alone in a world under Christian control—discern divinity in sacred images and had intimate connections with Egyptian gods (*Philosophical History*, frags. 72, 76). They seem to have considered themselves guardians of a secret tradition, linked to the dwindling temples of Egypt, in which basic priestly devotions, theurgy, ritual gesture, and mantic claims are all combined.

By Damascius's time, and even in the Hermetica, esotericism is closely linked with the achievement of self-transcendence, divine visions, and even union with the divine—that is, a sort of mysticism. But we should not expect to find mysticism in the earlier stages of priestly esotericism. Instead, one finds normative priestly activities, such as divination and mortuary preparation, that eventually become expanded into more concerted "spiritual" pursuits.

A cache of 2nd-century BCE documents found in the priestly center of Saqqara describes the peregrinations of Hor of Sebennytos, priest of Thoth, as he seeks professional guidance from Isis and other gods by incubating in various shrines. These texts show an individual's pursuit of divine presence and guidance, but for professional purposes: in which temple should he serve? which deities will be beneficial? While of clearly personal value, Hor pursues divine visions and messages as a function of his priestly role. Other priests' votive graffiti on major Egyptian temples (Karnak, Philae) suggest that priests often circulated among principal shrines for purposes of professional incubation. The intrapriestly traditions that grew up around these pursuits concerning the "god's appearance" *(ph ntr),* and its ritual acquisition led, over the course of the Greco-Roman period, both to the literary idealization of the provoked epiphany and to its commodification for paying outsiders. Papyrus Oxyrhynchus 11.1381 includes a dramatic scene of the god Imouthes' appearance; while spell manuals such as the "Mithras Liturgy" (*PGM* IV.475–829), commemorative inscriptions such as the anonymous paean to a vision of the god Mandulis at the temple of Kalabsha, and even the allusive depiction of otherworldly vision in Apuleius's *The Golden Ass* 11.23 all promise momentous divine visions out of Egyptian ritual procedure. Meanwhile, a preponderance of revelation spells across the *PGM/PDM* corpus suggests that the priestly owners of these manuals may have been selling experiences once reserved for priests now to Greek and Roman outsiders, much like the Theban "old men" who initiate the author Thessalus of Tralles (1st century CE; *On the Virtues of Plants* 12–13).

Another kind of Egyptian mystical procedure derives from mortuary symbolism: the geography of the afterlife, its obstructing demons, and the theme of the soul's judgment and transformation. The evolution of mortuary literature such as the Amduat and Book of Gates over the Greco-Roman period shows a progressive interest in revealing otherworldly details and in discussing the soul's transformation through death in ways that reflect this-worldly spiritual ambitions, not just mortuary ritual (see Wente 1982 and Podemann Sørensen 1992). Egyptian "fiction" of the same period (e.g., Setna Khaemwasct II) cultivates the theme of revelatory descents to the underworld by living heroes; and the priest Hor himself may have practiced such descents (##8, 13; Ray 1976: 43–44, 57, 131). Gnostic literature of Roman Egyptian provenance, such as the *Books of Jeu* and the *Apocalypse of Paul* (Nag Hammadi Codex 5.2), maintains the legacy of these trends in the mortuary literature by depicting the horrific guardians through whom the rising soul must pass to transcend this world and achieve divinity. It is possible that the Egyptian "mysteries" imported to Rome and other cities incorporated a version of this mortuary mythology for the purposes of initiation.

BIBL.: Jan Assmann, "Death and Initiation in the Funerary Religion of Ancient Egypt," in James P. Allen et al., *Religion and Philosophy in Ancient Egypt* (New Haven, Conn., 1989), 135–59. Gertie Englund, "The Border and the Yonder Side," in *Gold of Praise* (ed. Emily Teeter and John A. Larson; Chicago, 1999), 101–9. A. D. Nock, "The Vision of Mandulis Aion," in Nock, *Essays on Religion and the Ancient World* (ed. Zeph Stewart; Oxford, 1972), 2.566–74. J. Podemann Sørensen, "Native Reactions to Foreign Rule and Culture in Religious Literature," in *Ethnicity in Hellenistic Egypt* (ed. Per Bilde et al.; Aarhus, 1992), 164–81. J. D. Ray, *The Archive of Hor* (London, 1976). Edward F. Wente, "Mysticism in Pharaonic Egypt?" *Journal of Near Eastern Studies* 41 (1982): 161–79. D.F.

Mesopotamia

Mysticism

The roots of Mesopotamian mysticism are to be found in the institution of divine kingship. To explain the paradoxical divinity of a mortal king, he was presented as son of the goddess of love, Inanna/Ishtar, the divine spirit capable of crossing the boundary of heaven and earth. In due course, the arguments backing up this central dogma expanded into a complex system of mystical thought, pervading the entire Mesopotamian civilization. The relevant ideas and practices are best known from Neo-Assyrian and Neo-Babylonian sources (first half of the 1st millennium BCE), but they have a long prehistory extending back to the 3rd millennium, if not earlier.

The divinity of the king resided in his spiritual perfection, which made him consubstantial with god. This notion was expressed and propagated by means of a plethora of verbal and visual images, symbols, and allegories, such as "sacred marriage," which symbolized the king's mystical union with god. The most important of these was the so-called sacred tree, which symbolized a person's spiritual growth toward god. Its crown and base stood for heaven and earth, its trunk for the power of love, and its fruits for virtues equated with divine powers. Perfecting the latter according to the esoteric doctrine of the tree opened the way to immortality. Important myths such as the Epic of Gilgamesh and the Descent of Ishtar explicate this way of salvation in allegoric terms keyed to the tree. The spiritual meanings of the myths and symbols were, however, never put into writing but kept as secrets to be discovered only through initiation and contemplation.

In Mesopotamian texts and iconography, the king is often portrayed as a personification of the sacred tree, to emphasize his status as the "perfect man." However, this does not mean that the possibility of attaining spiritual perfection was limited to the king alone. In the Descent of Ishtar, the goddess plays the role of a fallen but resurrected soul, thus opening the possibility of spiritual rebirth and salvation to anybody ready to tread her path.

Emulating the sufferings of the goddess, her devotees practiced ascetic denial of the flesh, the world with its temptations being visualized in terms of prostitution. Accordingly, sexual abstinence was considered virtuous, and self-emasculation was common among the devotees, who saw themselves as brides adorning themselves for a final union with god in heavenly weddings. The ascetic practices of the cult frequently led to visionary experiences and altered states, including prophecy. Initiates into the secrets of the goddess were pledged not to divulge them to others, under penalty of death.

Another path of salvation lay in the practice of wisdom, figuratively referred to as descent to the ABZU/ *apsû*, the transcendental "ocean of enlightenment." It was believed that gods communicated with humans in riddles sent in dreams and hidden in sacred scripture and that only those precious few who could decode these secret messages would be saved. Accordingly, salvation was sought in intensive study of canonical scripture for hidden mystical meanings, the discovery of which could result in ecstatic experiences.

Mesopotamian mysticism exerted considerable influence on Gnosticism and primitive Judaism and Christianity.

BIBL.: Alasdair Livingstone, *Mystical and Mythological Explanatory Works of Assyrian and Babylonian Scholars* (Oxford, 1986). Simo Parpola, *Assyrian Prophecies* (Helsinki, 1997).   S.P.

Esotericism

The concept of secrecy was well established in Mesopotamia; many Sumerian and Akkadian words refer to it. Sumerian AD-ḪAL (secret), with the Akkadian equivalent *pirištu*, is the most common one; etymologically, both terms are related, like the Latin word *secretus*, to the notion of dividing something off. Other Sumero-Akkadian word pairs referring to the realm of esoteric knowledge are NÌ-DUL = *katimtu* (hidden, covered) and (KI)-ÙRU = *niṣirtu* (guarded).

The notion of secrecy was especially important in the sphere of the divine. Several Mesopotamian gods bear epithets that identify them as keepers of heavenly and earthly secrets, among them Enki/Ea, the god of wisdom, Nabu, patron of the scribes, and the Assyrian goddess Ishtar, whose cult was shrouded in mystery. Ninshubur kept the secrets of the sky-god Anu, Nusku those of Enlil, king of the gods. According to Mesopotamian tradition, the gods transmitted their secret lore to selected royal figures who in turn passed it on to certain groups of scholars and scribes. Shamash and Adad taught oil and liver divination to the legendary antediluvian King Enmeduranki, who instructed the people of Nippur, Sippar, and Babylon in it; later in the chain of transmission, the respective art was passed down from "the scholar, the knowledgeable one, who guards the secrets of the great gods," to his own son. Another king considered to be well versed in secret lore was the Ur III ruler Shulgi (2094–2047 BCE). King Assurbanipal (669–630 BCE) of Assyria reports that he became acquainted with esoteric knowledge by reading cuneiform signs written on "stones from before the flood." Several groups of priests (e.g., *ramku, nêšakku,* and *surmaḫḫu*) and bookkeepers *(šassukku)* were renowned for dealing with esoteric wisdom. The secret lore of ancient Mesopotamia was thought to procure, to those who were acquainted with it, both a deeper understanding of the world (here, divination was of particular importance) and the power of manipulating it

(especially by rituals and incantations). Therefore, Mesopotamian rulers tried to control such knowledge, and it had to be kept apart from those who might misuse it.

In prehistoric times, secret lore may have been handed down orally in Mesopotamia. It is, however, only in written texts that the esoteric tradition becomes tangible for us. Remarkably, there are hints that already some of the earliest lexical lists from the end of the 4th millennium BCE were considered to be "secret knowledge of the sage." These lists, apart from their practical purpose as a repertoire of cuneiform signs, give a taxonomy of the world that might well have been regarded as esoteric.

Writing, theoretically, made the secret lore available to people from whom it should be kept apart. Therefore, access to written texts that contained esoteric knowledge had to be restricted. This was achieved, on the one hand, by considering the art of writing *(tupšarrūtu)* in general, or at least its more sophisticated forms, as a secret, a conception explicitly articulated in a Sumerian school text from the early 2nd millennium BCE. The academy where writing was taught was compared, in a Sumerian riddle, to a (sealed) tablet-box (cf. *arcana,* derived from Latin *arca* [box]). On the other hand, cryptography was used. Already in the middle of the 3rd millennium, the esoteric UD-GAL-NUN orthography, a most erudite system based on various etymologies and Akkadian equivalents of Sumerian words, was invented to write texts containing mythical narratives, which were obviously considered to be secret.

Different forms of cryptography, including cipher writing and the employment of newly invented pictorial signs, remained in use in Mesopotamia until Hellenistic times. In some cases, they may have been employed in order to conceal the meaning of certain texts from those not belonging to the inner circle. In other cases, however, especially when used in colophons, the cryptographic sections were probably nothing but a playful show of erudition by the scribe who produced the respective text.

From the end of the 2nd millennium BCE onward, many texts contained clauses that identified their contents as secret lore and claimed that the knowledgeable one should reveal them only to another knowledgeable one; spreading the respective knowledge to someone uninitiated would be "a taboo of ―― god." Among the texts in question are lists of gods and stars, omens, magico-medical and astronomical treatises, rituals, incantations, and cultic commentaries. The exclusive character of the respective knowledge is apparent not only from these clauses but also from an anonymous letter from the reign of Esarhaddon (681–669 BCE) in which a goldsmith is accused of having hired a Babylonian to teach to his son the arts of divination and exorcism, an activity that was obviously regarded as an offense against the attempt of the king and his scholars to monopolize these fields of knowledge. A Babylonian document, not from the palace but from the temple sphere and dated to 541 BCE, accuses a temple functionary from Uruk of having revealed the knowledge written down on certain tablets to a temple slave; the functionary is to bear "the punishment of the king." The letter and the document show that the secrecy clauses of the texts have to be taken seriously.

During recent years, attempts have been made to show that a systematic esoteric doctrine that can be grasped only by comparison with later Jewish traditions was at the base of all aspects of Assyrian religion. This idea is highly speculative. It is not, however, improbable that there were esoteric teachings regarding individual features of Mesopotamian religion that were never put into writing. For example, the scarcity of written information on Mesopotamian temple towers might hint at their function being deliberately shrouded in mystery by Assyrian and Babylonian priests.

BIBL.: R. Borger, "Geheimwissen," in *Reallexikon der Assyriologie und vorderasiatischen Archäologie* (ed. Erich Ebeling; Berlin, 1957–71), 3.188–91. J.-J. Glassner, "Savoirs secrets et écritures secrètes des scribes mésopotamiens," *Politica Hermetica* 13 (1999): 15–30. J. G. Westenholz, "Thoughts on Esoteric Knowledge and Secret Lore," in *Intellectual Life of the Ancient Near East: Papers Presented at the 43rd Rencontre assyriologique international, Prague, July 1–5, 1996* (ed. J. Prosecký; Prague, 1998), 451–62.   E.F.

Israel

The earliest clearly documented mystical movement within Judaism is the Heikhalot (Heavenly Palaces) mysticism of the talmudic period (2nd–7th centuries CE). The literature of the movement, which is written for the most part in rabbinic Hebrew, although in a very distinctive style, is preserved in many medieval manuscripts. It is highly amorphous and never seems to have reached definitive closure. Indeed, because Heikhalot ideas continued to be used creatively by later Jewish mystics, additions and changes were being made to the texts as late as the 12th and 13th centuries (by the Rhineland Jewish pietists, the Hasidei Ashkenaz) and the 17th century (by the Sabbateans). However, there seems to be no reason to doubt that the bulk of the surviving material goes back to late antiquity. The most noteworthy treatises are the Greater Treatise on the Heavenly Palaces (*Heikhalot rabbati*), the Lesser Treatise on the Heavenly Palaces (*Heikhalot zutarti*), and the Book of the Heavenly Palaces (*Sefer heikhalot*, also known as *3 Enoch*).

Heikhalot mysticism, like other forms of mysticism, is shot through with a desire for communion with a transcendent, divine world. Normally in the literature, this takes place through an ascent to the Merkavah (the Chariot), God's heavenly throne, to be found in the innermost of seven concentric palaces (*heikhalot*), which

are located in the seventh heaven. The ascent, which is paradoxically called a "descent" (the mystics being known as "descenders to the Chariot" [*yoredei Merkavah*]), appears to be an "out-of-body" experience—a soul excursion of some kind. The psychological condition described cannot now be determined precisely, but clearly some sort of trance or hypnotic state is indicated. Interestingly, in the most famous account of an ascent, in *Heikhalot rabbati,* the adept is said to continue speaking while in trance and to describe what he is seeing as he journeys through the celestial regions. The ascent is represented as highly difficult and dangerous: the adept has to traverse vast distances, he is opposed by hosts of fearsome angels, and he finds himself in a bewildering fiery realm in which the physical laws of this world are suspended or turned inside out. At the climax of his journey he sees the Divine Glory seated on the Merkavah and joins the highest angels in chanting the celestial praise.

This is the form that communion with the divine takes for these mystics. There seems to be no suggestion of absorption into the divine: the ontological distance between God and the adept is strictly preserved. Indeed, it is stressed that even at the height of his ecstasy all that the mystic sees is simply a representation of God: God, in himself, dwells in impenetrable regions beyond the seventh heaven. However, one tradition (found in *3 Enoch*) does hint at the possibility of union with the godhead. It records how one human being, the biblical patriarch Enoch, bodily ascended into heaven and was physically transformed into the highest of the archangels, Metatron, who is called "the Lesser YHWH" and depicted as the ruler of the cosmos. Later mystics may be correct in seeing this tradition as implying the identity of Metatron and the "manifest" God. If the ascent of Enoch is taken as a paradigm of the mystical ascent, then the possibility seems to be contemplated that the ontological gap between humanity and God may be bridged and the adept ultimately become divine.

The dominant form of the *unio/communio mystica* in the Heikhalot texts involves an upward movement of the "soul" to "God," but they also contain a minor tradition of a contrary movement in which the adept stays where he is and "God" comes down to earth in the person of an archangel (usually called the Prince of Torah [*Sar Torah*]) to commune with him. Significantly, in both traditions it is the adept who takes the initiative and "compels" the contact through theurgical praxis and magical invocation.

The dating of this literature is a problem. In the 19th century, Heinrich Graetz dated it to the early Islamic period (9th century CE). In the 20th century, however, following the lead of Gershom Scholem (1965), the tendency was to push it back into the talmudic period. Scholem suggested that some elements could be carried back as early as the 2nd century CE. The Babylonian Talmud contains clear allusions to Heikhalot ideas (tractate

Hagigah 11b–16a and elsewhere), although it does not elaborate on these because it regards them as esoteric knowledge. There are two ways of explaining this relationship. One is to suppose that the Heikhalot texts are a kind of commentary or midrash on the talmudic allusions—an attempt by later scholars to reconstruct the esoteric doctrine at which the Talmud hints. The other is to suppose that the Heikhalot texts genuinely contain in fuller form the ideas alluded to in the Talmud. The second alternative is more plausible. The first seems to require us to postulate a discontinuity between the talmudic and post-talmudic periods that it is hard to justify. Moreover there are highly convincing details in the Heikhalot texts that cannot by any stretch of the imagination have been derived midrashically from the Talmud. Although some of the Heikhalot texts as we now have them are post-talmudic and clearly allude to the Talmud, the bulk of the literature and the doctrine goes back to the talmudic era.

Another problem is whether the Heikhalot texts represent a purely literary movement or reflect genuine mystical and theurgical praxis. There can be little doubt that literary artifice is present in the tradition, particularly in its later phases. However, it seems equally clear that the texts point to real mysticism. Heikhalot mysticism fits rather well into the religious ethos of the eastern Mediterranean world in late antiquity. It shows significant parallels with the theurgy of the Chaldean Oracles and with certain forms of Gnosticism. The similarities with Gnosticism seemed so strong to Scholem that he claimed Heikhalot mysticism could be classified as "Jewish Gnosticism." This is probably overstating the case. Although Heikhalot mysticism shares a similar cosmology with the gnostic texts, it lacks a strong dualism (the "hidden" God and the "manifest" God are not opposed powers). However, given that, on the one hand, some gnostics were certainly acquainted with postbiblical Jewish tradition (note, e.g., the Nag Hammadi treatises *The Hypostasis of the Archons* and *On the Creation of the World*) and that, on the other hand, the talmudic rabbis were aware of certain gnostic ideas, an indirect relationship between Gnosticism and Heikhalot mysticism is highly probable.

The Heikhalot movement cannot be traced back any earlier than the 2nd century CE. However, as is becoming increasingly apparent, it drew on much earlier ideas. Its general cosmology, broad picture of the heavenly world, angelology, and doctrine of ascent to heaven can be closely paralleled in the apocalyptic writings of the Second Temple period. Indeed some of the Heikhalot writings, such as *3 Enoch,* can be classified as late apocalypses. There are also close parallels with some of the Dead Sea Scrolls. Particularly important here is the work known as the Songs of the Sabbath Sacrifice. This work seems to describe the celestial temple and the worship that the angels perform there. It moves inward through a series of increasingly holy domains, until it finally reaches in the holy of holies the immediate presence of God. The text does not explain how this detailed knowledge of the heavenly world was acquired, whether through ascent, or vision, or some other mode of revelation. However, its parallelism with the later Heikhalot texts, both in general terms and in specific detail, is striking. The basic doctrine of the Songs of the Sabbath Sacrifice was probably elaborated by priests in Jerusalem in Second Temple times as part of an attempt to provide a more spiritual understanding of the temple cult. The outward rituals of sacrifice were given meaning because they reflected heavenly realities and assisted communion with that heavenly world.

There also are possible antecedents to the Heikhalot ideas earlier still in the biblical period. The Heikhalot mystics themselves claimed to be replicating the visionary experiences of the great biblical prophets, particularly Ezekiel's vision of the Chariot of God, the Merkavah (Ezek. 1). Unlike the oracles of the prophets, however, Heikhalot teaching was open only to initiates: it was not proclaimed to all Israel. In prophecy and apocalypticism the throne-vision is instrumental, a means to an end. In Heikhalot literature it has become an end in itself. The Heikhalot visionaries were mystics; the prophets and apocalyptists were not. It is very hard to find mysticism in Judaism in any precise sense of the term before the 2nd century CE. Glimmerings of mysticism begin to appear in the late Second Temple period at Qumran in the doctrine of the communion of the earthly and heavenly communities in the worship of God. There are also arguably mystical ideas in the writings of the Jewish Platonic philosopher Philo of Alexandria. His treatise *On the Contemplative Life* describes an idealized, protomonastic community dedicated to communion with God. But the first clearly mystical program in Judaism does not emerge until the Heikhalot mystics of the talmudic period.

The rabbinic authorities of the talmudic period regarded the teachings of Heikhalot mystics with considerable suspicion. This is hardly surprising since on the face of it they challenged some of the fundamental beliefs of rabbinic Judaism: they reopened channels of direct communication with God that rabbinic Judaism held to have been firmly closed since prophecy had ceased in Israel; and, with their interest in high archangels such as Metatron (the Lesser YHWH), they ran the serious risk of compromising monotheism. The authorities declared esoteric the teachings of the Heikhalot mystics (which they called the "Account of the Chariot"), along with speculation on cosmology and cosmogony (the "Account of Creation"; Mishnah, tractate *Hagigah* 2.1). Although the study of these matters was not in itself banned, it was forbidden to expound and discuss them in public. The mystical circles themselves concurred with this view. Their writings are full of warnings about the dangers of their doctrine and praxis, about how these should be confined to the select circles of the initiated. This is the first clear instance of esotericism within Judaism. It is true that the apocalyptic movement of the Second Temple period speaks a lot about "mysteries" (mysteries regarding the future, the structure of the cosmos, and the heavenly world). Some of the texts imply that their ideas had been around for generations in Israel, known only to the few. But the precise purpose of these texts is to reveal the mysteries, to make them known to all Jews. It is also true that certain teachings (e.g., about physiognomy and the phases of the moon) seem to have been reserved for an inner circle within the Qumran Community (the community reflected in the Dead Sea Scrolls): this is suggested by their being written in code. Early Jewish thinkers were well aware that there were more things in heaven and earth than were dreamed of in their philosophy, but they were on the whole content not to try to inquire into these, but to concentrate on what had been clearly revealed to Israel (Deut. 29.29 [= 29.28 Hebrew]). It was not until the talmudic period that we first get the idea of an esoteric doctrine within Judaism that can be made known only to the initiated.

BIBL.: Philip S. Alexander, "3 (Hebrew Apocalypse of) Enoch," in *The Old Testament Pseudepigrapha*, vol. 1: *Apocalyptic Literature and Testaments* (ed. James H. Charlesworth; London, 1983), 223–315. David J. Halperin, *The Faces of the Chariot: Early Jewish Responses to Ezekiel's Vision* (Tübingen, 1988). Peter Schäfer, *The Hidden and Manifest God: Some Major Themes in Early Jewish Mysticism* (Albany, N.Y., 1992). Gershom Scholem, *Jewish Gnosticism, Merkabah Mysticism, and the Talmudic Tradition* (2nd ed.; New York, 1965).   P.S.A.

Manicheism

Manicheism, a strongly dualistic world religion established by Mani (216–77 CE) during the Sasanian Empire, soon reached distant lands and cultures, east and west, from North Africa to central Asia and China. Marco Polo, toward the end of the 13th century, could still meet a group of Manicheans in China.

Mani, who was born near Ctesiphon, in a milieu open to various religious trends, grew up among the Elkasaites, a Jewish-Christian baptist community in southern Mesopotamia. As a boy and young man, he went through a series of religious experiences, losing his faith in the salvific power of baptism and developing a close contact with his "heavenly twin," source of his prophetic powers. Mani eventually left the Elkasaites and began preaching his own doctrine, which was directly rooted in his deep cosmological and anthropological dualism. For Mani, the created, material world (including the human body) was the source of all evil. Hence, his soteriology was based upon the soul freeing itself from the body and the eventual destruction of the created universe.

In 241 CE, Mani went to India, or more precisely to Sind (Bactriana), at the time the Buddhist kingdom of the Kushan. A Buddhist prince was so impressed by Mani that he saw in him an avatar of the Buddha. Mani's missionary instincts must have been much strengthened by his Indian experience. Moreover, his strongly dualistic conception of the religious community, a core of monks, the *perfecti*, surrounded by the larger group of the *auditores*, is structurally similar to that of the Buddhist *samgha* (community).

The next year, he was offered the opportunity of an audience with Shapur I, the new Sasanian king, to whom he presented himself as a man of god and an inspired prophet, a doctor of the soul as well as of the body. Mani dedicated to Shapur his only work written in Middle Persian, the *Shapuragan,* which deals mainly with eschatology. Using Sasanian support, Mani soon sent missionaries to Syria, Palestine, Egypt, Armenia, and along the Silk Road. After the death of Shapur in 272, however, his son Bahram, now on the throne, sought to reestablish the preeminence of traditional Zoroastrian cult and turned his back on Mani (as well as on the Christians). In 276, Mani, who had dared to confront the king in Gondeshapur, was condemned to death by a Mazdean religious tribunal, but died in prison before the sentence could be carried out.

Mani's immediate Jewish-Christian background strongly points to a gnostic source for his dualism. One should not exclude, however, a Zoroastrian influence. Mani's teachings, indeed, bear a strong mark of eclecticism, and his immediate followers, who served as missionaries for the new religion in different lands, harbored a religious and cultural syncretism of ecumenical dimensions. Manicheism, indeed, is the first religion consciously established as a world religion, meant to incorporate the main teachings of all previous religions (except Judaism). Mani insists mainly upon the Christian dimension of his teaching, which he claims to represent a perfected Christian doctrine, considering himself to be not only the apostle of Jesus Christ, but also "the last prophet" and the paraclete announced by Jesus. (It is in Manichean doctrine that one must look for the source of the Qur'anic metaphor of "the seal of prophecy.") Although the idea of the last prophet is originally Jewish-Christian, Mani erased from the list all the biblical prophets, retaining only Adam, Seth, and Noah as predecessors of Jesus. But early Manichean doctrine also makes place for Zarathustra and Buddha, considering them as prophets sent, respectively, to the lands of the "center" (Iran, Babylonia) and of the East (India, China), while Jesus had been sent to the Western lands (Palestine, Egypt, Greece, Rome).

After Mani's "passion," the Manichean church grew quickly, thanks to a highly organized pyramidal structure: under the "Guide" were twelve "masters," seventy-two "bishops" (or "deacons"), and a series of cells, from Carthage to Samarkand. This growth took place despite relentless persecution from all sides. The

Romans perceived the Manicheans as a "fifth column" from an enemy realm. With the Christianization of the empire, in the West as well as in the East, they were considered heretics of a particularly vicious brand. Except for a short period, from 762 to 840, when the Uighur king converted with his court to "the religion of light," Manicheism remained everywhere a *religio illicita*—in the Roman Empire, under the Islamic caliphate (where they were accused of *zandaka,* or dualist heresy), or in Tang China. Platonist philosophers, Christian and Muslim theologians—all polemicized against the Manichean dualist beliefs and myths, while the state authorities persecuted them (in 527 CE, for the first time, an edict of Justinian punished Manicheans with death). Under such conditions, it is understandable that the Manicheans soon found various ways to keep a low profile, hide their true beliefs, and masquerade as Christians or Muslims. The oasis of Kellis, in the western desert in Egypt, for instance, became the hiding place of a Manichean community, while the Cologne Mani Codex, which tells us about Mani's youth among the Elkasaites, is the smallest codex known from the ancient world. This imperious need to hide does much to explain the dearth of archeological or iconographical material, although we know that the Manicheans were famous for the illustrations that accompanied their sacred texts.

Until the end of the 19th century, the only sources for the study of Manicheism were anti-Manichean polemics written in Greek, Syriac, Latin, and Arabic. Throughout the 20th century, however, a succession of impressive discoveries brought to light extremely important Manichean documents, including texts of Mani himself and others written by his disciples and in the first generation of Manichean theologians. These documents, which are often translations from the lost Syriac originals, are written in Middle Iranian, Parthian, Sogdian, Uighur, Chinese (documents found at the oasis of Turpan in the beginning of the 20th century), Coptic (the texts discovered in the late 1920s at Medinet Madi in upper Egypt and toward the end of the 20th century at Kellis), or Greek (the Cologne Mani Codex, discovered in the 1970s). The Manichean texts represent various literary genres: a biography of the prophet, historical documents, theological and doctrinal tractates, homilies, hymns, prayers and other liturgical texts, at least one manual of confession of sins, myths, and stories. Thanks to these discoveries, and despite the great difficulty raised by the breadth of their linguistic spectrum, the study of Manicheism has made dramatic progress, and both the history and the tenets of that religion are now incomparably better understood than earlier on.

In the first modern study of Manicheism, published in 1734–39, the Huguenot Isaac de Beausobre argued that Jewish apocalyptic literature of the second Commonwealth, in particular the Ethiopian Book of Enoch, reflected Mani's intellectual and religious background. This intuition, more than two centuries before the discovery of the Dead Sea Scrolls at Qumran and the Cologne Mani Codex, where this literature is shown to have been of primary importance among Mani's baptists, is quite remarkable. Indeed, to a great extent, Mani built his new and highly complex mythology upon the basis offered by such ancient Jewish works as the Enochic Book of Giants. Manicheism is a religion of the book *par excellence*. For Mani, one of the reasons for the failure of previous prophets, such as Zarathustra, Jesus, or Buddha, was that they did not take care to write their own books. Mani himself was a prolific writer: besides his *Shapuragan,* which has been reconstituted, he wrote a "Gospel" (of which a few fragments and a summary are preserved), a "Treasure," a book of "Mysteries," "Legends," "The Image" (perhaps an illustrated catechism), "The Giants," and a series of letters. Of all these, only some fragments and testimonies are extant (Mani's letters were found—in Coptic translation—at Medinet Madi, but disappeared during the bombing of Berlin at the end of the Second World War).

The complex mythology (it is unclear to what extent Mani himself believed in all the details of his system) was established upon a few simple principles: the dualism of good and evil, light and darkness, and the three cosmic epochs: the initial time of their separation, the middle time (in which human history is situated) of their mixing, and the end time of their final dissociation, that is, when the salvation of all particles of light and the destruction of material darkness will take place. Throughout this cosmic drama, a series of gods, divinities, and demons play a role.

Before the existence of the cosmos, the two natures lived completely separated from one another. The Father of Greatness lived in the land of light, together with his five "homes": intelligence, science, thought, reflection, and conscience; while the King of Darkness lived in the dark land in his five worlds: smoke, fire, wind, water, and darkness. The middle time began with the first war between the two principles, when the King of Darkness attacked the Father of Greatness. The latter "called" (i.e., evoked as) the Mother of the Living, who in her turn called the Primordial Man, who then called his five sons. The Primordial Man offered himself and his sons to be eaten by the King of Darkness. The Father of Greatness then called the Living Spirit, the Friend of the Lights, and the Great Architect to rescue the Primordial Man, the very type of a *salvator salvandus*. The Living Spirit killed the archons, or sons of darkness, and used their skins to make the heavens. He then "showed his forms" to them, and the sun and the moon were created. The Third Messenger manifested himself, accompanied by twelve naked virgins, in order to provoke the ejaculation of the archons, which in its turn provoked the creation of land and sea, and then hid in order to begin the process of separation of light from darkness.

The second war began when the demons Nebroel and Ashaklun created Adam and Eve in order to prolong the exile of the lights. As a response, the Father of Greatness sent Jesus the Splendor (Yeshu Ziwa) to awaken Adam from his sleep. The final or eschatological time will also be the time of the third and final, or "great," war. In the end, all the light particles will escape, from the moon and the sun, through the Milky Way, and from the material world, which will be transformed into a *bolos* (a ball; the *globus horribilis* referred to by Augustine) of damned darkness. While the roots of Manichean mythology lie in Jewish apocalyptic literature, one must recognize that they underwent a radical transformation.

Mani's system is the most strongly dualistic one ever devised. In ways much more radical than in Zoroastrianism or in the various gnostic mythologies, the opposition between the realms of spirit and matter is absolute—and identical to that between good and evil. Even there, however, the balance of power between the Father of Greatness and the King of Darkness is heavily tipped in favor of the former: the final separation of the two principles and the dissolution of the mixing between them will only emphasize the ontological chasm between them. The eventual victory of the powers of Light is never questioned.

The Manichean elects lived in urban monastic communities, led in prayer and instruction by the higher grades of the hierarchy, until they were sent forth as missionaries. These monks and nuns were asked to observe five "commandments": (1) telling the truth, (2) nonviolence (which includes violence against the vegetal world, hence prohibiting agricultural work), (3) chastity, (4) food taboos (in particular vegetarianism) and fasts, and (5) poverty. The five main duties of the laypersons were (1) the ten commandments of Manicheism, (2) prayer, (3) almsgiving, (4) fasting, and (5) confession of sins. One can clearly detect here a Manichean influence on the five "pillars" of Islam.

The Manichean liturgical year was modeled along the main events of Mani's life: his birth, his call, his passion. Its most solemn festival, the Bema, celebrated the founder of the church, his passion, and the salvation he brought. In many ways, the Bema (preceded by a cycle of fasts) is strongly reminiscent of Christian Easter.

We may find it difficult to appreciate the appeal of such odd doctrines and practices. Yet, we must recall the seductive powers that they held over many of the best minds in the ancient and medieval worlds. Augustine, for instance, was for nine years a Manichean auditor and remains one of our most important sources of information. The evocative power of Manicheism survived the religion itself—in medieval Europe, in the West as well as in Byzantium. "Manicheism" became a term of opprobrium, used to designate various dualistic Christian heresies, such as the Paulicians, the Bogomils, and the Cathars.

BIBL.: Jes P. Asmussen, *Manichaean Literature* (Delmar, N.Y., 1975). S. N. C. Lieu, *Manichaeism in the Later Roman Empire and Medieval China* (2nd ed.; Tübingen, 1992). Aldo Magris (ed.), *Il Manicheismo: Antologia dei Testi* (Brescia, 2000). G. G. Stroumsa, *Savoir et salut* (Paris, 1992). M. Tardieu, *Le manichéisme* (Paris, 1981). G.G.S.

Theurgy

During the first few centuries CE, there arose many mystic religious movements that combined elements of Platonic philosophy, practices drawn from traditional cult, and newer doctrines that adherents claimed were revealed to them directly by the gods. One of the earliest and most influential of these movements was theurgy, which particularly emphasized the importance of worshiping the gods through ritual; the word *theurgy*, in fact, derives from Greek words meaning "divine" and "work" and thus could be translated as "divinely oriented actions." In insisting on the importance of ritual, theurgists set themselves in opposition to other, contemporary mystics such as Plotinus (205–69), who held that humans should worship the gods and improve their own souls through contemplation and the study of philosophy alone. Below the surface of this debate lay other vital issues of the time. The belief that contemplation and philosophy alone were adequate aligned with the premise that human souls did not completely descend from the divine sphere into incarnation, whereas the theurgists' belief that ritual was a necessary adjunct aligned with the assumption that souls did descend into human bodies—and thus, that rituals performed in the material world, using material objects, were psychically therapeutic. Those who espoused only contemplation and philosophy portrayed the material world as a source of pollution; those who also embraced ritual believed that even its lowliest parts were charged with potentially salvific divine power.

Theurgy's sacred texts were dactylic-hexameter Greek poems known as the *Chaldean Oracles*, allegedly recited by Apollo and Hecate either during epiphanies or through the mouths of possessed mediums. Their style and content suggest that they were composed during the latter half of the 2nd century. We now possess only fragments of these *Oracles*, which were quoted by later exegetes and critics of theurgy, but a substantial body of longer texts once circulated widely, attracting interest among philosophers and mystics throughout later antiquity. Iamblichus (245–325) and other late antique writers composed commentaries on the *Chaldean Oracles*, seeking to interpret them both in their own right and in comparison to other sacred writings such as those attributed to Orpheus and Hermes.

Theurgy was said to have been founded by a man named Julian, who came to be known as "the Chaldean," and his son Julian, known as "the Theurgist." The *Chaldean Oracles* supposedly were delivered to the two Julians. (The application of the adjective *Chaldean* to the elder Julian and the *Oracles* probably reflects an attempt to lend exotic authority to what were essentially

Greek and Roman practices and beliefs, as ancient Chaldea was regarded as a source of arcane religious knowledge.) Whether these men actually existed is open to debate, but ancient sources describe the younger Julian accompanying Marcus Aurelius on campaign and aiding him in battle by creating masks that threw thunderbolts, by splitting rocks in half with magical commands, and by bringing on a rainstorm that saved the army from dying of thirst. He also was credited with ending a plague in the city of Rome. Like most mystic and esoteric religious systems, theurgy passed its doctrines and rites from individual to individual. Theurgy's most famous follower was the emperor Julian (331–63), who was initiated into its mysteries by Maximus of Ephesus.

Theurgy adopted Middle Platonic metaphysical and cosmological doctrines, including transcendence of the highest god, who is often referred to in theurgy as the Father. The Father was characterized as pure Intellect (Nous) and understood to consist of pure, fiery light. Out of the Father sprang various nontranscendent emanations, all of whom had cosmogonic and salvific roles; these entities were also made of light, although of lesser purity. Most important to the daily life of the theurgist was an emanation called the Cosmic Soul (Psyche), whom they identified with the Greek goddess Hecate. She was imagined to dwell between the earthly and divine realms, dividing the two and yet facilitating the passage between them of both the individual mortal soul as it ascended into the heavenly realm and various divine benefits as they descended into the earthly realm. She was also credited with teaching the theurgist many rituals. As in many other Middle Platonic systems, matter (hylē) lay at the bottom of the ontological scale and reflected the divine Ideas or Forms only imperfectly. Because of this, matter might induce corporeal passions that would lead the theurgist astray. Both philosophical training and rituals helped the theurgist to overcome them.

In terms of ritual, theurgy bore many resemblances to mainstream Greek and Roman religions insofar as it included purifications, initiations, and various "magical" rites such as the invocation of gods by their secret names and the manipulation of natural materials such as plants and stones. But it also developed special rituals designed to bring about an encounter (systasis) between a theurgist and a god. Many of these focused on the theurgist receiving divine light and then incorporating it into his body and soul. During a systasis, the theurgist might receive further information about how to perform rituals, might simply improve his soul through its encounter with divine light, or might, through incorporation of this light, cause his soul to ascend temporarily into the divine realm (anagōgē), where it could benefit from gazing upon divine beauty. Iamblichus's treatise On the Mysteries gives general information about how such rituals were supposed to work; specific instructions for some of the rituals are found in fragments of the Chaldean Oracles and comments of their exegetes. The most notable anagogic technique was the ritualized inhalation of sunlight, understood to be the material manifestation of divine light (a detailed description of a very similar process is found in a slightly later document commonly known as the Mithras Liturgy, which may have been influenced by theurgy; see PGM IV.475–829). But Iamblichus and others emphasized that, in addition to everything that the theurgist himself was to do, divinity itself had to be present and cooperative before anagōgē could occur. Given this, the term theurgy can also be interpreted to mean the work of the gods upon mortals. Our texts hint that, after bodily death, the purified soul of the theurgist had the right to remain in the angelic realm, but was expected selflessly to descend once again into incarnation, in order to help the souls of others reach perfection.

BIBL.: Sarah Iles Johnston, "Rising to the Occasion: Theurgic Ascent in Its Cultural Milieu," in Envisioning Magic: A Princeton Seminar and Symposium (ed. P. Schaefer and H. Kippenberg; Studies in the History of Religions 75; Leiden: Brill, 1997), 165–94. C. van Liefferinge, La théurgie, des Oracles Chaldaïques à Proclus (Kernos Supplément 9; Liège, 1999). Gregory Shaw, Theurgy and the Soul: The Neoplatonism of Iamblichus (University Park: Pennsylvania State University Press, 1995).   S.I.J.

Hermeticism

Between the 1st and 3rd centuries CE, a set of texts emerged in Hellenized Roman Egypt under the name of the god Hermes Trismegistus, an amalgam of the Egyptian Thoth and the Greek Hermes. (The epithet Trismegistus [Thrice greatest] grows from the Egyptian habit of forming superlative adjectives through repetition; see the description of Hermes on the Rosetta Stone, Greek line 19.) With a reputation and wisdom that dwarfs anything attested for his classical Greek counterpart, the Egyptian Hermes had a special insight into the hidden workings of the universe as well as wide-ranging expertise in techniques of harnessing the cosmos through magical rites. He spoke in a language familiar with many of the major intellectual currents flowing through Roman Alexandria, including Middle Platonism as well as gnostic, Jewish, and Egyptian theologies.

The chief surviving tracts are seventeen short Greek texts from the Corpus Hermeticum (1–14 and 16–18) and the longer Latin Asclepius. These are to be supplemented by the Coptic Nag Hammadi Codex 6.6–8 (mid-4th century CE); Greek excerpts from Stobaeus (5th century CE); the surviving Armenian translation (6th century CE) of the Definitions of Hermes Trismegistus; the smaller Fragmenta Hermetica, quoted in Greek, Latin, and Syriac authors from the 3rd to 13th centuries CE (Nock and Festugière 1945–54: vol. 4); and two small pieces of the Vienna papyrus, *Papyri Graecae Vindobonenses* 29456 recto and 29828 recto. In addition to these texts, often called the "philosophical" Hermetica, we find fragments elsewhere of less systematic "technical" Hermetica that cover the arcane subjects of astrology, astrological medicine, alchemy, and the magical properties of various substances (Festugière 1944–54: vol. 1). Although we have no evidence that the technical tracts were assembled into formal collections before Byzantine times, Zosimus of Panopolis (*Fragmenta Graeca* 245) suggests that at least some pieces of what we know as the *Corpus Hermeticum* circulated together as early as the end of the 3rd century CE. The split between philosophical and technical texts is not absolute. Although the more speculative philosophical texts aim at a salvific gnosis and the more practically oriented technical texts seek after narrower results, the two genres share certain features, and late antique figures such as Iamblichus seem to confound the separation altogether (see Fowden 1986: 116–41).

Contents and contexts. The range of interests revealed in these texts defies easy description. There is no shortage of relevant contexts for understanding the corpus, but it is surely the case that the Hermetica are to be understood as one among several late antique traditions, including Gnosticism and Neoplatonism, that refashioned Mediterranean religious traditions and the philosophical insights of Platonists into intensely personal soteriological disciplines. While the form of the philosophical tracts is often dialogic, their tone is more often revelatory. Pupils gather around masters to hear of the divine, the basic ontological structures of the cosmos, and the place of humans within it. The truth learned in these contexts was not a dry abstraction but rather, in Fowden's apt phrase, a "catalytic force" in individuals' lives (1986: xxiii). The wisdom promised not merely enlightenment but spiritual ascent as well. As the initiate learns of the hierarchical orders of heaven, the soul becomes buoyant—it leaves behind attachments to the material world, takes on ethereal qualities, and comes not just to know god, but to be like god.

The texts present themselves as authentic and ancient Egyptian wisdom translated into Greek. *Corpus Hermeticum* 16 warns presciently that when the Greeks one day attempt to translate the texts, the Greek language will fail because it cannot match the Egyptian language's power to carry inside its words the very presence of things (compare Iamblichus, *On the Mysteries* 7.4–5). Assessing other, less fanciful possibilities for the origins of the texts has been the subject of no little scholarly debate and discussion. While treatments of the Hermetica early in the 20th century were likely to argue strongly for influence from one tradition or the other (whether Greek, Iranian, or Egyptian), recent work has tended to take a more inclusive approach and explore the notion that many, apparently contradictory, traditions lived together in these documents.

Jewish influences are likely in some texts, including the genres of apocalypse (*Corpus Hermeticum* 1.1–5) and prophecy (*Asclepius* 24). The creation story of Genesis is used as an apparent proof text at *Corpus Hermeticum* 1.4–5, 12, 18 and 3.1–3. In addition, the two *Papyri Graecae Vindobonenses* show the discourse of Hermes and Tat on the front side, but on the verso an apocryphal text of the Hebrew Bible, the Book of Jannes and Jambres. Gnostic views of the material world are clear in *Corpus Hermeticum* 1.20, 4, and 6.3, and more extensively at *Corpus Hermeticum* 13 and Nag Hammadi Codex 6.6. Also the notion that one might "know" god is much more common in Jewish and Christian circles than in classical and Hellenistic Greek ones (Fowden 1986: 112). Plato's legacy is also easy to find. God is equated with the Good (*Corpus Hermeticum* 6), the mechanics of Hades bear a resemblance to those seen in Plato's *Myth of Er* (Nag Hammadi Codex 6.8), and the anthropogony of the *Timaeus* shows through at *Asclepius* 8. Egyptian influence shows most obviously in the form of the texts, for which Platonic dialogues offer less satisfying parallels. More likely models are Egyptian wisdom sayings which, mirroring the inherited nature of the scribal office, cast a "father" passing down scribal wisdom to his "son." The bisexual divinity that produces the cosmos (*Corpus Hermeticum* 1.9; 5.7; and *Asclepius* 20–21) is likely Egyptian in origin (Mahé 1978–82: 2.292). The careful divine hand making the human body (*Corpus Hermeticum* 5.6–7) is reminiscent of the Egyptian Hymn to Khnum (Mahé 1978–82: 2.292–95). The traditional Egyptian ritual practice of statue animation appears (*Corpus Hermeticum* 17; *Asclepius* 19, 22–24, 37–38; Copenhaver 1992: 238), as does the broad notion of the Egyptian land as a manifestation of heaven (*Asclepius* 24; compare *Corpus Hermeticum* 5; 11.22; see Mahé 1978–82: 2.94–95). The Hermetic texts speak of a cosmos built on the distinctive cosmological complications of Middle Platonism. At *Corpus Hermeticum* 1.9 the highest order of the divine being (the pure mind [Nous]) remains aloof from creation by producing a demiurgic double of itself. The demiurgic Nous is actually responsible for the creative act and serves the double function of securing divine proximity to the world and shielding the transcendent god from being sullied by contact with the material. Such a doubling of the divine is also observable in the distinction at *Asclepius* 3 and 8 between the cosmic god and the higher unknown god. Also characteristic of Middle Platonism is the prominence of Nous and soul conceived as the ontological strata, bookended by god and matter, in which dwell various classes of divine and lower beings (*Corpus Hermeticum* 1, 10, 12).

Legacies. The marriage of Platonic philosophy to Egyptian theology makes a decisive contribution to the history of Platonism. Plato's successors had perennially to struggle with the master's view that the material world is no more than an image, which in Plato's understanding always veers toward a shadow and phantom of the world's higher orders. But the traditional Egyptian view that the land of Egypt is an imitation of heaven itself, and the temple of the gods, offered a near perfect solution to the pernicious Platonic problems of ontological and epistemological corruption implicit in the material world. It recasts imitation in a strongly positive light and opens up the possibility of reinterpreting the material world no longer as always a potentially misleading phantom, but instead as a divine manifestation. Such a view had always been an option for the Platonist, but it was rarely exercised. Among the many late antique texts that show the influence of Platonists, one can see this view emerging most fully in the Hermetica. They offer a crucial pivot in the turn from Middle Platonist ambivalence toward the material world to the post-Iamblichean Neoplatonists' growing attentiveness to it as always potentially a theophany. The well-established Egyptian practice of statue animation offered a solution on a smaller scale, but one with no less a profound influence. The Hermetica follow a traditional Egyptian view that humans have the power to create gods in the cultic images they fabricate, which through proper techniques of consecration become vehicles for the real presence of the gods themselves. No more powerful answer to Plato could be imagined, and such practices soon become the central component of the ritualized version of Platonism that would hold sway, after Iamblichus, all the way down to Ficino's day (15th century).

The Hermetic texts lived long after late antiquity, with their fortunes waxing and waning in rough congruence to those the Neoplatonists. The text of the *Corpus Hermeticum* as we know it is the product of Byzantine editors, and in the 11th century Michael Psellus produced a commentary on *Corpus Hermeticum* 1 and perhaps other Hermetic writings. In the Latin West, interest in Hermes was minimal until the 12th century. As the school of Chartres rediscovered Plato in the distinctive dress of Calcidius's Neoplatonic translation and commentary, they also found new interest in the Hermetic materials, both the *Asclepius* and Latin paraphrases from Arabic compilations. Hermes was admired by no less a figure than Albertus Magnus, who mentions him in twenty-three of his works, as an ancient pagan who closely mirrored the Christian truth (Copenhaver 1992: xlvii). The Hermetica, along with other works of late antique Platonist inspiration such as the *Book on Causes*, the *Theology of Aristotle*, and the corpus of the Pseudo-Dionysius presented a tantalizing, marginally doctrinal spiritualism in a Platonic mode that church officials were unable to resist. Ficino's translation of *Corpus Hermeticum* 1–14 (1471) secured Hermes' status for the Renaissance. The work saw dozens of editions and translations into vernacular languages and spurred a small industry of commentators of all intellectual inclinations well into the 17th century, including Giordano Bruno and Robert Fludd.

History of scholarship. Where the legacy of lived Hermeticism ends, the history of scholarship on the corpus begins. The ruse of authorship of the texts survived until Isaac Casaubon at the request of James I of England scrutinized the pagan prophecies of Christ. In 1614 he published his finding that the Hermetica date from roughly the period on which the scholarly consensus still rests. The opinion wore away Hermes' reputation and consigned him to obscurity for centuries. The German philologist Richard Reitzenstein in his 1904 *Poimandres* argued for an Egyptian context of religious praxis for understanding the texts; he later suggested a strong Iranian element in his 1921 *Das iranische Erlösungsmysterium*. Festugière's massive four-volume work *La révélation d'Hermès Trismégiste* (1944–54) examined with extreme erudition the place of the corpus in Greek intellectual tradition and stifled other forms of inquiry until Garth Fowden's reawakening of the Egyptian social and historical questions first opened by Reitzenstein. It is a testimony to the rich complexities of the late antique era that these texts prove so difficult to sound out with precision. Despite the rather large body of modern scholarship, the study of Hermeticism remains best characterized by sets of binaries rather than consensus. Scholarly debate is structured around poles such as Greek vs. Egyptian, philosophical vs. practical, religion vs. magic, history of ideas vs. social history. The Hermetica present too many facets to be finally delimited by the usually useful categories of classical, Egyptian, or Near Eastern religions, and it is safe to say that no consensus of new categories has yet emerged.

BIBL.: Brian P. Copenhaver, *Hermetica* (Cambridge, 1992). A.-J. Festugière, *La révélation d'Hermès Trismégiste* (4 vols.; Paris, 1944–54). Garth Fowden, *The Egyptian Hermes* (Cambridge, 1986). Jean-Pierre Mahé, *Hermès en Haute Égypte* (2 vols.; Quebec, 1978–82). Arthur Darby Nock and A.-J. Festugière (eds.), *Corpus Hermeticum* (4 vols.; Paris, 1944–54).   P.T.S.

Gnosticism

The term *Gnosticism* was first used by Henry More in 1669, in the context of Protestant anti-Catholic polemics. He characterized Catholicism as "a spice of the old abhorred Gnosticism," a kind of false prophecy that seduces true Christians to idolatry. It is likely that he coined the term, based on the title of the 2nd-century CE work by Irenaeus of Lyon, *Exposé and Overthrow of What Is Falsely Called Gnosis* (commonly known as *Against the Heresies*). The Greek word *gnōsis* is usually translated as "knowledge," but its derivative "Gnosticism" has come to stand for false knowledge, in short for heresy.

Gnosticism is, however, heresy of a particular kind. In the 2nd and 3rd centuries CE, theologians such as Irenaeus and Tertullian had developed a discourse that distinguished heresy from true belief. In the 18th to 20th centuries, church historians reproduced many elements of this discourse in their discussions of Gnosticism. Particularly prominent are the following views. Orthodoxy is both chronologically prior and theologically superior to heresy, which results from a contamination of the original, pure gospel of Christ by the addition of non-Christian ("pagan") elements. Orthodoxy is typified by unity and unanimity; heresy, by division and dissention. Heresy is characterized by theological error due to the erroneous interpretation of scriptures (such as mistaken views of creation and the creator or a too-literal hermeneutics) and an improper understanding of the dual nature of Christ as human and divine. This error can lead only to immorality, whether ascetic hatred of creation or libertinism. Following this pattern, modern scholars characterize Gnosticism as a contamination of Christianity, either by Greek philosophy, oriental myth, or Jewish heterodoxy. Although some scholars have argued that Gnosticism was a pre-Christian religion (a view with few current supporters), most see it as a religion arising about the same time as Christianity and in competition with it. The influence of this religion on Christianity in the 2nd century produced the so-called gnostic heresy, which led to division within the church. Following the lead of their early Christian opponents, scholars claimed that these heretics held the view that the creator-god of Genesis is not the true Deity of spiritual goodness and perfection, but only a flawed purveyor of mere justice or even a malicious agent of evil. Christ taught humanity that they belong to the spiritual realm above, not to this lower world of matter and flesh. The true Deity sent Christ into the world to bring the truth and show the way back to the transcendent realm above. Christ was a divine being who never became truly human, nor did he suffer or die; he only appeared to take on flesh in order to mislead the rulers of the lower world (a view called Docetism). Irenaeus insisted that such views so disparaged the created world that they could lead only to a false ascetic rejection of life or a libertine flaunting of traditional mores. This picture of Gnosticism is largely derived from the portrait of early intra-Christian controversy, but modern scholars have modified that portrait in important ways.

Modern scholars have generally divided the earliest types of Christian error into two types, Jewish Christianity and Gnosticism. Jewish Christianity represents those varieties of early Christianity whose beliefs and practices were characterized by too much or too positive an attitude toward Judaism; Gnosticism, by too little or too negative an attitude. Orthodoxy apparently sailed between this Scylla and Charybdis, safe from both dangers. This division illustrates two crucial points. Determining the correct relationship of Judaism to Christianity was and is the single most important factor in defining authentic Christianity. Gnosticism functions largely as part and parcel of the practices of determining normative Christian identity; it came into being as a rhetorical term used to label the opponents (usually the losers) in intra-Christian controversies.

This normative, rhetorical function has had some unfortunate consequences. First, a wide variety of ideas, textual remains, individuals, and groups have been classified as "gnostic," often with little in common theologically or sociologically. Second, scholars have tended to reify Gnosticism into an independently existing historical entity in its own right, exerting much effort in searching for its origin, tracing its development, and defining its essential characteristics. The enormous variety of materials that are classified under this single nomenclature have made it impossible to define a single set of essential characteristics (phenomenological typology) or locate a single point of origin and trace a linear genealogy of the historical development of Gnosticism. Yet such problems are irresolvable, not because of the lack of evidence or even because of the variety of the materials categorized as gnostic, but because a rhetorical term has been confused with a historical entity. Third, modern historiography of Gnosticism has become entangled in normative enterprises, involving ancient and modern discourses of orthodoxy and heresy, progress, reason, and orientalism. In these discourses Gnosticism is classified as a marginal "sectarian," "primitive," "esoteric," or "syncretistic" religion with its roots in oriental myth, in contrast to authentic "ethnic," "developed," "historical," or "universal" religions, exemplified by Western Christendom. All too often, characterizations of the primary texts are drawn uncritically from their Christian or Neoplatonist detractors, leading to inaccurate and caricatured portraits of gnostic beliefs and practices. Not only "dualism" and "elitism" have been named as essential characteristics of Gnosticism, but also "impiety" and nonrational "myth." Such characterizations are more useful for the politics of religious polemic than for historical inquiry.

To sum up: Gnosticism is a term that belongs to the discourse of normative Christian identity formation. In current usage, it refers to (1) all varieties of early Christianity that are characterized by this discourse as having too little or too negative an appropriation of Judaism; (2) any outside, non-Jewish contamination of pure Christianity (such as the "acute Hellenization of Christianity" or the pre-Christian, oriental root of Christian heresy); or (3) any tradition said to be closely related to this contaminated Christianity, whether or not they contain explicitly Christian elements, such as Hermeticism, Platonizing Sethianism, Mandeism, Manicheism, the Albigensian heresy, or the medieval Cathars.

Yet despite this broad usage, there was and is no such thing as Gnosticism, if we mean by that some kind of ancient religious entity with a single origin and distinct set of characteristics. What existed were a variety of mostly unrelated individuals and groups living in or near urban centers around the eastern Mediterranean in the 1st to 5th centuries CE. Since antiquity, they have been known from descriptions written by their detractors, mostly 2nd- to 4th-century Christian polemicists such as Irenaeus of Lyon, Clement of Alexandria,

Hippolytus of Rome, Origen of Alexandria, Tertullian of Carthage, and Epiphanius of Salamis. The Neoplatonist Plotinus also wrote extensively "Against the Gnostics" (*Ennead* 2.9). These works mention groups and individuals, some of whom belonged to Christian churches, taught or studied in philosophical schools, or formed their own more or less ephemeral groups. They relate that these groups variously practiced baptism, ascent rituals, theurgy, healing magic, or the mysterious rite of the bridal chamber.

In addition to this polemical literature from antiquity, ancient manuscripts stemming from these groups have come to light since the 8th century. Chief among them are a set of treatises written in the Coptic language: the 5th-century Bruce Codex containing the *Books of Jeu* and the so-called *Untitled Text;* the 4th-century Askew Codex containing a revelation dialogue between Jesus and his disciples called the *Pistis Sophia;* the 5th-century Berlin Codex containing the *Gospel of Mary,* the *Apocryphon of John,* the *Sophia of Jesus Christ,* and an *Act of Peter;* a collection of 4th-century codices, popularly titled the Nag Hammadi Library, which contain a total of forty-six different works, almost all of which were previously unknown; and most recently, the *Gospel of the Savior* from a 4th-century manuscript in the Egyptian Museum in Berlin. These works represent a broad range of literary genres, including cosmological treatises, hymns, revelation dialogues, gospels, apostolic acts, wisdom sayings, and prophetic oracles. They evince a wide variety of theological and philosophical perspectives and show clear connections with almost every stream of ancient religious thought and practice, giving a remarkable glimpse into the cultural hybridity of ancient urban pluralism. At the same time, however, most are ascetic in their ethics, and a majority have direct ties to Christianity. The Nag Hammadi collection, for example, was found buried in a jar near the site of an ancient Pachomian monastery and appears to have belonged to the monks. Why these works were hidden remains a mystery, but it is plausible that they were buried to protect them from destruction at the hands of increasingly suppressive, 5th-century orthodox bishops.

The Coptic treatises provide a wealth of new information about Christian diversity and controversy during the formative centuries of Christian beginnings. They illustrate the range of issues that were under debate and offer new insights into the development of Christian thought and practice. For example, the *Gospel of Thomas,* a 1st- or 2nd-century collection of sayings of Jesus, presents Jesus as a teacher of wisdom and indeed as divine Wisdom herself. Although it contains more than forty parallels with the Synoptic Gospels, it presents many new sayings that give an alternative interpretation of Jesus and his words. It is his teaching, not his death and resurrection, that gives life; he reveals what is hidden in creation yet beyond human ability to perceive. The sayings of the *Gospel of Thomas* are meant to encourage people to seek the kingdom of God within themselves, to uncover the hidden wisdom of God in creation, and to reject all worldly pursuits that lead one away from God. When they do, they will come to realize their true identity as the children of God, created in the divine image, and will have eternal life.

Another 2nd-century work, the *Gospel of Mary,* presents a dialogue between the Savior and his disciples after the resurrection. He tells them to seek after the Son of Man within and to recognize that there is no sin beyond their own love of the deceptive material nature, which leads to suffering and death. They are to receive his peace and go forth to preach the gospel of the kingdom, not laying down any law beyond what he taught, lest it encumber them. Then the Savior departs. But rather than be at peace, the disciples weep, fearing persecution—all but Mary. She comforts them and reveals hidden teaching from the Savior about the ascent of the soul to God. Andrew and Peter, however, reject her words, jealous that a woman has knowledge that is superior to their own. But Levi defends her and assures them that the Savior loved her more than the other disciples. As they go out to preach, the gospel ends. This brief story presupposes a Platonizing dualism of the flesh and the spirit, asking humans to recognize that their true selves are spiritual; they should reject the world and the false powers who seek to entrap them by accepting the teaching of the Savior. The gospel presents Mary (probably the Magdalene) as a leader among the disciples and affirms that authority to teach and preach should be based on spiritual maturity, not gender.

Other post-revelation dialogues present alternative views of Jesus's teaching, death, and resurrection. Texts such as the *First Apocalypse of James* (Nag Hammadi V.3) and the *Letter of Peter to Philip* (Nag Hammadi VIII.2) affirm that Jesus truly became flesh, suffered, and died, but they argue that his resurrection proves that the body is not the true self. The true self is spiritual and cannot be destroyed by the death of the body; this is the message that the Savior came to teach. A quite different perspective is offered by the 3rd-century *Apocalypse of Peter,* in which the Savior reveals that he had stood by laughing in scorn as a fleshly substitute was put to death. He assures Peter that those people who call themselves bishops and deacons are only "dry canals" (79.31); such people "blaspheme the truth and proclaim evil teaching" (74.23–25) by "cleav[ing] to the name of a dead man" (74.13–14). The true Savior is "the intellectual Spirit filled with radiant light" who comes to unite the perfect light in humanity with his Holy Spirit (83.9–15). The *Apocalypse of Peter* illustrates clearly how heated intra-Christian polemics had become by the 3rd century (see also *Testimony of Truth;* Nag Hammadi IX.3).

Another set of literature is associated with the name of Valentinus and his followers. Valentinus was born in Egypt, but later taught in Rome in the mid-2nd century.

The *Gospel of Truth,* from the Nag Hammadi collection (I.3, XII.2), was probably written by him. It presents a radical monism, stating that the transcendent Father of Truth is the source of all things that exist, including the material world. His transcendence, however, led to error because his creatures were unable to perceive his divine fullness. So Jesus Christ came to enlighten them and show them the way and the truth. His crucifixion on the cross (tree) is interpreted as the proclamation of the knowledge of the Father, bringing eternal life to those who "ate" from its fruit—an apparent allegory of the Genesis trees of paradise. Again and again, the *Gospel of Truth* offers allegorical and spiritualizing interpretations of familiar gospel materials, especially from the Gospel of John. The author of the *Gospel of Truth* argues that God is neither harsh nor wrathful, but is totally without evil, imperturbably sweet, and omniscient (42.4–10), a view in sharp contrast to Christian apocalyptic images of God as a vengeful judge. Instead, those who receive the knowledge of Christ become perfect in unity with the Father, being set at rest and refreshed in the Spirit. In a similar mode, another Valentinian work from Nag Hammadi, the *Treatise on the Resurrection* (I.4), states that those who believe the gospel attain the resurrection here and now; it is not the resurrection of the body, but "the transformation of things and a transition into newness," in which "the light flows down upon the darkness" (48.35–49.6). The author employs Pauline images and seems to take seriously Paul's statement that "flesh and blood cannot inherit the kingdom of God" (1 Cor. 15.50).

Later teachers, said to be students of Valentinus, apparently pursued quite a different direction, as far as information from Christian detractors shows. These tendencies are now partially illustrated in an early-3rd-century treatise from Nag Hammadi, *Tripartite Tractate* (I.5). This lengthy work describes the devolution of divine beings from the primordial, monadic godhead. One of these, the Logos (word) ruptures the spiritual unity of the divine fullness when, out of love, he produces lower material and psychic (soul) beings. From these are generated the lower world and humanity, ruled by a lower creator-god and his angels. Although the Logos's motive had been love, the consequences of his action led him to repent of his action. From his repentance, the Savior is generated; he brings salvation to humanity by drawing them back into unity with the Father through the Holy Spirit, baptism, and the rite of the bridal chamber. We see here early Christian attempts to elaborate an expansive theological cosmology out of Jewish scripture, Platonizing philosophy, and developing Christian literary and ritual traditions.

Schenke (1974) identified yet another set of related literature from this corpus, which he dubbed "Sethian." This literature, too, is quite varied but it evinces a common set of mythological themes: the primordial Deity is composed of a triad—the Father (Invisible Spirit), the Mother (Barbelo), and the Son (Autogenes-Christ). Autogenes produced four aeons and illuminators, named Harmozel, Oroiael, Daveithe, and Eleleth; these aeons constitute the final place of rest for Adam, Seth, the seed of Seth (gnostics), and those who repent late. Beneath the divine realm lies the realm of the lower creator-god Yaldabaoth. He creates humanity in the image of the divine Adam, but traps him in the lower material body. Sethian myth divides history into four periods: the age of Adam, the age of Seth, the age of the original Sethians, and the present time (see especially the *Gospel of the Egyptians;* Nag Hammadi III.2). Increasingly, scholars refer to this literature as classical Gnosticism.

One of the most important Sethian works is the *Apocryphon of John.* It presents the typical elements of Sethian myth as a revelation of the Savior to his disciple John and contains a version of the famous Sophia myth. Sophia (Wisdom), the last and least of the divine beings, desires to create a likeness out of herself; the result is the ignorant and malformed Yaldabaoth, the creator and despot of the lower world. Like other Sethian works (notably *Hypostasis of the Archons* [Nag Hammadi II.4] and *On the Origin of the World* [II.5, XIII.2]), the *Apocryphon of John* (II.1, III.1, IV.1) retells the story of Genesis with a novel twist. In this version, the creator is an arrogant and malicious pretender who claims to be the only true God, but who in fact creates humanity in order to dominate the spiritual light of the heavenly Adam. He creates the lower world as a parodic imitation of the divine world, thus making it difficult to discern what is counterfeit from what is true. He tries to keep humanity from the knowledge of good and evil and from eternal life; he attempts to destroy them all with a flood; he and his angels rape Eve and other women in order to raise up children for themselves; and he condemns humanity to the body of suffering and death. But in everything he is thwarted by divine emissaries from the world of light who aid humanity, speaking through the snake in the garden, Eve, Christ, and others in order to bring knowledge and salvation. Although often interpreted as a story of human alienation and revolt, this myth actually evinces a strong, almost utopian commitment to the values of its day. It figures the divine realm as the place of true goodness, knowledge, justice, and peace; the lower world as its opposite. In so doing, the *Apocryphon of John* provides a searing critique of the way that power is illegitimately exercised in the world below and a vision of hope that keeps the ideals of divinity and goodness alive in the midst of lived violence and domination.

Many other works defy categorization altogether. Among these is *Thunder: Perfect Mind* (Nag Hammadi VI.2), a collection of oracles that probably stem from a female prophet. It contains no overtly Jewish or Christian themes nor does it fit neatly into any established Greek or Roman religion or philosophy. Rather it is composed of an extensive set of paradoxical and prescriptive oracles: "Do not be ignorant of me!" "I am the whore and the holy one." "I am strength and I am fear. I am war and peace." "In my weakness, do not forsake me, and do not be afraid of my power." "Come forward to childhood, and do not despise it because it is small and little" (13.15, 18; 14.30–32; 15.19–21; 17.24–27). This use of paradox seems almost compellingly postmodern in its affirmation that identity is neither fixed nor stable—whether of gender, social role, ethnicity, honor status, divine and human, age, or economic status; there is no unity except in "displacing the duality of apparent opposites" (McGuire 1994: 104).

These examples merely begin to illustrate the wealth and variety of the literature that has been classified as Gnosticism, but they do demonstrate the incapacity of a single term, let alone a set of stereotyping derogations, to describe these works adequately.

BIBL.: Karen L. King, *What Is Gnosticism?* (Cambridge, Mass., 2003). Bentley Layton, *The Gnostic Scriptures* (Garden City, N.Y., 1987). Alain Le Boulluec, *Le notion d'hérésie dans la littérature grecque, IIe–IIIe siècles* (Paris, 1985). Anne McGuire, "Thunder, Perfect Mind," in *Searching the Scriptures: A Feminist Commentary* (ed. Elisabeth Schüssler Fiorenza; New York, 1994), 2.39–54. Elaine Pagels, *The Gnostic Gospels* (New York, 1979). James M. Robinson and Richard Smith (eds.), *The Nag Hammadi Library in English* (3rd ed.; San Francisco, 1988). Kurt Rudolph, *Gnosis: The Nature and History of Gnosticism* (trans. R. M. Wilson; San Francisco, 1983). Hans-Martin Schenke, "Das sethianische System nach Nag-Hammadi-Handschriften," in *Studia Coptica* (ed. Peter Nagel; Berlin, 1974), 165–74.   K.L.K

Epilogue

Bruce Lincoln

Acertain tension is manifest in the preceding articles of this volume, in which extremely knowledgeable specialists address issues of enormous complexity with a maximum of efficiency and economy. Being both learned and scrupulous, they struggle to select a few choice examples from the countless possibilities available to them, after which they are forced to abbreviate and simplify even these. Toward the end of their articles, as they move to summarize, generalize, and distill, they suffer once more as they sacrifice diversity, nuance, complexity, and prudent qualifications on the conjoined altars of the Big Picture and the Short Article. *Sic semper est* with encyclopedias, even the sainted Pauly-Wissowa. The problem is more acute still for one charged (or cursed) with writing the final article: summary of summaries, epitome of epitomes, thinnest, blandest, most superficial, most simplistic, and therefore inevitably—also, quite rightly—most open to objection.

Admittedly insuperable difficulties can be liberating, however, since one is free to err in the manner of one's choosing, all possible approaches being wrong. Accordingly, I will frame the following discussion with two broad sets of questions. First, what do we mean by "the ancient world"? What constitutes the ancient and separates it from that which follows (a category I will, for the sake of convenience and provocation, call the "post-ancient")? Second, what forms does religion take and what roles does it play in the ancient? In the post-ancient? And how do changes in the religious contribute to the change from one era to the other?

As an initial attempt to engage these questions—one that is admittedly inadequate and destined for further refinement—let me advance the proposition that "the ancient" is that situation in which religion is not one system of culture coexisting among many others, but occupies the central position and plays a unique role—informing, inflecting, integrating, stabilizing, even at times controlling and determining all others (a position that has had some currency at least since Fustel de Coulanges 1864). Such a formulation carries a Hegelian danger, of course, threatening to turn into its opposite. For were religion to be found everywhere, there would be no borders to delimit and define it. Indeed, its very ubiquity might render it unrecognizable, rather like "culture" or life itself. That many, perhaps most ancient languages have no term to match the semantics of English "religion" (Latin is only a partial exception) lends support to this suspicion. It also raises the possibility that the emergence of the term and category "religion" is itself a product of the cultural transformation effected by the Reformation and Enlightenment, making this concept a particularly anachronistic instrument for understanding the situation of the premodern (compare the discussions of W. C. Smith 1963 and Asad 1993).

Although this argument has the merit of making us cautious, it errs by way of overstatement. To say that nothing in antiquity was free of religion—not war, disease, erotic love, science, the arts, poetry, or the state; not the landscape, the family, the meat on the table, or the fire on the hearth—is to say not that everything "was" religious, only that religious concerns were a part of all else, and a part that remains—to us, at least—analytically recognizable. Proceeding thus, we might theorize "the ancient" as that situation where, to cite just a few examples, one treats toothache by reciting the account of creation, reads the organs of sacrificial victims before waging battle, secures the verity of speech acts with sacred oaths, and conducts international diplomacy through appeals to mythic genealogy (Pritchard 1969, 100–101; Cicero, *On Divination* 1.95; Hesiod, *Theogony* 782–806; Herodotus 7.150, e.g.).

Scholars have often worked with such a model, although often it remains subtextual and implicit (Loew 1967, Eliade 1954, Frankfort 1948). Correlated with this model (whether as consequence or motive is hard to tell) is an understanding that "the ancient" ended with a "Greek miracle" that anticipated the Enlightenment by breaking with myth, tradition, and puerile superstition to achieve a critical view of religion (Nestle 1940, Cornford 1912, Vernant 1982). Xenophanes, Heraclitus, and Socrates are often singled out in this respect and accorded particular credit. Closer reading, however, makes clear that these thinkers were hardly critics of religion as such, but only critics of specific forms. Thus, for all that Xenophanes chided Homer and Hesiod for telling scandalous tales about the gods, and notwithstanding his sly suggestion that cattle imagined gods in bovine form, he also maintained, apropos of proper etiquette at drinking parties: "It is fitting, above all, for men of good cheer to hymn the god with well-spoken *mythoi* and pure *logoi,* having poured libations and prayed to be able to accomplish just things" (Xenophanes, DK 21B11 and 21B112; 21B15, cf. 21B16; 21B1, ll. 13–16). He made clear in the same passage, which represents the longest excerpt we have of his work, his concern that religion should promote decorum, well-being, grace, and harmony. As a negative complement, he did maintain "there is nothing useful" in beliefs that promote violent disorders *(stasias sphedanas),* but this is hardly a critique of religion *per se* (ll. 21–23).

Similarly, Socrates claimed to have grounded his incessant critical activity on an oracle received from the Delphic Pythia, and he took pains to assure the jury that tried him for impiety *(asebēia)* that he was incapable of this offense, since a personal *daimōn* supervised his conduct and he always heeded this deity's advice (Plato, *Apology* 20e–23c, 40a–c). Plato's valuation of reasoned knowledge *(epistēmē)* over faith *(pistis)* and opinion *(doxa)* also involved less criticism of religion than is normally supposed. Thus, he maintained that the philosophical disposition which makes it possible for a very small elite to acquire such knowledge is itself the product of postmortem experiences before the soul's reincarnation. In that heavenly realm, ultimate reality is revealed to all, but its true nature is remembered only by those who have cultivated exceptional powers of self-control by their prior training and *askēsis* (Plato, *Phaedrus* 246d–249d, *Republic* 614b–621d). Ultimately, Plato's epistemology is inseparable from his theory of the soul and its fate (psychology in the most literal sense and eschatology), also his metaphysics and soteriology. In a word, his philosophy incorporates and depends on religion, albeit a form of religion that eschews civic cult, while drawing on dissident strains of speculation current among Orphics, Pythagoreans, and others.

"The ancient" does break down, of course, but it does so gradually, not through any "miracle" (itself a surprisingly religious trope, as is that of "genius," which often attends it). Earlier, to characterize "the ancient," I cited a set of examples that gestured toward medicine (the Babylonian toothache charm), warfare (Roman divination before battle), law (Greek oaths), and diplomacy (Persian use of genealogies to court potential allies). Change, however, can be seen in all these domains, as when epilepsy ("the sacred disease") is said to derive from natural causes and when generals repeat divinatory consultations until they get the results they want or proceed in defiance of the readings (Hippocratic corpus, *On the Sacred Disease*; Cicero, *On Divination* 2.52). The same shift toward a "post-ancient" less thoroughly encompassed by religion can be perceived when statements are secured by signing a contract, rather than swearing an oath; or when threats and bribes, rather than invocations of shared ancestors, are used to enlist allies (Thucydides 5.89). Such changes come piecemeal, however, so that antiquity ends—if the model we are currently entertaining permits us to conclude that it ends at all—only in fits and starts. Indeed, the model allows the view that "the ancient" reasserts itself (or simply persists) whenever oaths are sworn in a court of law, wherever prayers are said for the sick or for soldiers in battle, and whenever nations make common cause on the basis of shared beliefs.

Our first attempt sought to resolve all problems at once by identifying "the ancient" with the omnipresence of religion, while paying no attention to complexities internal to the latter term. The result was a critical instrument too blunt for the Gordian knot. It is time to back up and seek a sharper blade.

Elsewhere, in quite a different context, I have sought to define religion as a polythetic entity involving at least four domains: (1) a discourse whose concerns transcend the human, temporal, and contingent, and that claims for itself a similarly transcendent status; (2) a set of practices whose goal is to produce a proper world and/or proper human subjects, as defined by the religious discourse to which these practices are connected; (3) a community whose members construct their identity with reference to a religious discourse and its attendant practices; (4) an institution that regulates discourse, practices, and community, reproducing them over time and modifying them as necessary, while asserting their eternal validity and transcendent value (Lincoln 2003: 5–7). Accordingly, I would suggest that the transition from ancient to post-ancient might better be studied with reference to these four variables, rather than to the one that is their sum and product, "religion" *tout court*.

As a starting point, one might observe that the most authoritative discourses of antiquity tended to be acts of speech that understood—and represented—themselves to be inspired. Not simply human utterances, these were pronouncements in which some divine agency was felt to be at work, speaking through select human instruments and channels. Mantic, oracular, and prophetic speech regularly enjoyed such status, as did royal proclamations and poetic performance. Poetry was extraordinarily important, and the reasons for this must be assessed from two complementary perspectives, technological and ideological. Prior to the emergence of alphabetic script and the consequent spread of literacy, poetry was the most effective technique of memory. Any proposition or narrative that could be put in poetic language was thereby rendered more memorable than in any other linguistic form and therefore more likely to be transmitted across space and time. Such encoding was reserved for those cultural contents that were (or better: were judged and became, as a result of this judgment) most important. Reflecting and compounding this practical advantage was the claim of divine status that poets regularly made for themselves and their art. As Hesiod put it, the very breath with which he spoke—the material substance of his speech—was placed in his lungs by the Muses themselves, who were daughters of Zeus and Memory (Mnemosynē) (Hesiod, *Theogony* 31–32: *enepneusan de moi audēn thespin*). The Delphic Pythia, by contrast, gave oracles only in trance, when possessed by Apollo. The proof that the god spoke through her came not only from the state of her body and visage, but also because she spoke in perfect hexameters (Plutarch, *On the Obsolescence of Oracles*). Similar constructions of poetic discourse as sacred and of poets as "masters of truth" (Detienne 1996) are to be found among the Hebrew prophets, Vedic seers, Roman sibyls, and the hymns attributed to Zarathustra (Kugel 1990).

With the spread of literacy and alphabetic script, written prose gradually displaced oral poetry as the most effective mnemonic technique, and widespread cultural changes followed (Havelock 1963, Goody 1987, Ong 1982). In the realm of religion, sacred books came to enjoy higher status than did inspired utterances. Growing awareness that the latter might not be what they claimed and were open to manipulation by their human agents also served to undercut their authority. This authority might be preserved, however, when the utterances in question were textualized and reconstituted as revealed scripture, as in the case of the biblical prophets and the Sibylline books.

So bibliocentric (initially in the broad, and later in the narrow sense) did religious discourse become that the danger emerged of excess production and oversupply. To control this danger, priestly bodies assumed the power to impose limits through canon formation and the closure of prophecy, sometimes with the backing of state power, as when Augustus had the Sibylline Books collected, purged of suspicious content, and placed in the temple of his patron deity, where they were kept under lock and key, accessible only to authorized priests (Suetonius, *Augustus* 31.1). Similar processes, if less dramatic and under less direct state control, elsewhere produced restricted bodies of scripture that were invested with authoritative status. Energies were directed toward the interpretation of these texts rather than the production of new ones. Reading rather than speaking became the privileged moment of religious discourse, and innovation no longer came through the claim of inspiration, but through the practice of shrewd hermeneutics. To put it in slightly different terms, as Jeremiah yielded to the rabbis, John the Baptist to the Church Fathers, Muhammad to the *qadis* and *ulama,* one can see not only Weber's routinization of charisma, but also the historic shift from a prophetic ethos associated with orality to the scholarly ethos of the text.

Religious practices also changed significantly from the ancient to the post-ancient. Two sorts of practice fell into relative desuetude, both of which purported to mediate between the sacred and profane in direct, material fashion. The first of these was a whole complex of behaviors involving the statues of deities. Most commonly, the presence of such statues in temples constituted the sanctuaries as the site of a god's residence on earth, thereby cementing the relation of a specific city and people to a specific deity. Thus, to cite but one example, the statue of Marduk in the temple Esagila at Babylon marked the city as this god's special domain and the god as this city's patron, also as the dominant member of the pantheon when the city's power expanded. For as was true with other Mesopotamian cities, when the Babylonians were victorious in warfare, they often captured (the statues of) other cities' deities as tokens of subordination and risked similar capture of their own god should they in turn be conquered. The priests of this temple were charged with the care, feeding, decoration, and worship of Marduk's resident statue, which is to say his virtual, palpable presence. This was not mere servitude, however, since deity and people were engaged in an ongoing mutually beneficial exchange. The flow of benefits to humanity was particularly dramatized at the *Akitu* (New Year) festival, when the king clasped the hands of Marduk's image and thereby had his legitimacy and power renewed by the god himself, with consequences for the prosperity of the land and people:

> [Marduk], exalted among the gods,
> [Who dwells in the temple Esag]il, who creates the laws,
> [Who . . .] to the great gods,
> [. . .] I praise your heroism.

[May] your heart [be sympathetic] to whoever seizes your hands.
"Temple Program for the New Year's Festival at Babylon," ll. 396–400, trans. A.
Sachs, in Pritchard, *Ancient Near Eastern Texts*, p. 334

Other peoples developed different practices. Sometimes access to the statues was restricted to the priesthood or its high-ranking members. Sometimes worshippers were permitted to make contact by entering an inner sanctum of the temple where the statue/deity was housed. In other cases, images were brought forth to outer chambers on festal occasions or even paraded through the streets of the city. Some of the statues represented benevolent, nurturing deities who brought blessings to their people; others were demanding and jealous figures, who threatened those they found inadequately devoted or attentive. But in all instances, these blocks of material substance were the site where relations between the human and the divine were transacted, the point of conjuncture between sacred and profane.

At least equal in importance was the practice of sacrifice, the most common and also the most significant form of ritual among virtually all ancient peoples. Countless theories of sacrifice have been offered (W. R. Smith 1889, Hubert and Mauss 1964, Burkert 1983, Thieme 1957, Detienne and Vernant 1989, Girard 1977, Grottanelli 1999) and the practice itself could be infinitely varied in its performance. Ordinarily, it involved the immolation of an animal or vegetable offering (much more rarely a human victim), the spiritual portion of which was believed to pass to the divine, while the material portion became the basis of a feast enjoyed by the human performers, with the gods as their honored guests, thereby restoring a commensality lost in the mythic primordium. All details of the performance could be invested with symbolic content—for instance, the division of the victim's body might provide analysis of the categoric distinctions between divine, human, and animal levels of existence (Vernant 1989, Grottanelli and Parise 1988)—or the ritual might replicate events recounted in cosmogonic myth that homologize the body to the world as microcosm to macrocosm (Lincoln 1986). Sacrifice also provided a means to invest bloody and violent acts with sacral significance and avoid the charge that one killed just to obtain food. Rather, one assumed the burden and awesome responsibility of caring for the gods and the cosmos, which meant performing each minute part of the action in perfectly controlled, symbolically appropriate fashion. Preparation of the feast and disposal of the remains, no less than actual dispatch of the victim, were subject to the same regulation and scrutiny, since all aspects of sacrificial ritual were "good to think" and therefore subject to symbolic elaboration.

Destruction of the Second Temple in 70 CE made it impossible for the priests of Israel to continue their performance of sacrifice. The resulting reorganization of cult and thought led to the emergence of that which we know as Judaism(s). In other traditions, no such dramatic events were responsible, but over time sacrifice and the use of statues ceased to form the center of ritual practice, and material mediations of every sort diminished in their import. They were displaced—although never completely—by practices that relocated the prime site of interest and action inside the human subject. Prayer; the cultivation of certain valorized dispositions, sentiments, and states of being; the habit of monitoring one's progress toward these ethical and existential ideals; and reporting flaws and slips to spiritual advisors, while submitting to their guidance and discipline, became privileged aspects of religious practice with the move toward the post-ancient.

Clearly, these developments correlated with shifts in the nature of religious community. In the ancient, religion was a shared concern of groups existing at familial, civic, ethnic, and national levels of integration. The collective identity of such groups was strongly overdetermined, being based simultaneously on territory, language, polity, kinship, and laws, as well as the religion that members held in common and that, in turn, held them. One's neighbors were thus one's fellow citizens and also one's co-religionists, who spoke the same language, shared the same norms, celebrated the same festivals, and worshiped at the same altars, seeking favor of the same gods for the group of which they were all a part. The post-ancient, by contrast, saw the emergence of communities based primarily—and also most explicitly and emphatically—on religious considerations, integrating persons who might be divided by geography, language, culture, or citizenship.

This development had begun as early as the 6th century BCE with the Pythagoreans. Among its contributing factors was the formation of great empires that brought disparate populations into a single political entity and tax structure, but left subject peoples only very imperfectly integrated by religion and culture. At the same time, expanded trade and improved communications permitted relatively wide circulation of religious tenets, texts, and teachers, all of which gradually refashioned themselves in broader, less localized idioms as they engaged—and absorbed feedback from—a disparate international audience (Grottanelli 1982). At times, imperial powers sought to introduce aspects of their native religion to the provinces, or at least to the elite strata therein (e.g., Seleucid policy at the time of the Maccabean revolt). At other times, the imperial center imported religious forms from the periphery as a conscious policy (e.g., the Roman *evocatio* ritual that appropriated gods of conquered enemies); as a means to indulge growing taste for the exotic (e.g., the introduction of Isis and Cybele at Rome); or as part of the backwash that inevitably accompanies conquest (e.g., Mithraism). The diaspora of various groups (such as the Magi and the Jews) and the proselytizing activities of others (the missions recounted in the Acts of the Apostles and related apocrypha) also contributed to the de-territorialization of religious community characteristic of the post-ancient.

In contrast to older groups focused on a specific temple, city, cult place, or sacred locale, which they served and from which they took their identity, the increasingly international, multiethnic, and geographically dispersed population of post-ancient religious communities was held together not only by shared symbols, beliefs, and practices, but also by itinerant leaders and mobile texts such as the epistles of the New Testament, the polemic exchanges among Church Fathers, the corpora assembled at Qumran and Nag Hammadi, or the rabbinic responsa. Inclusion or exclusion in such amorphous communities was not ascribed by birth in a given place, lineage, or social stratum, but was elective. One joined by conversion, that is, by accepting the beliefs, practices, texts, and leadership that constituted the group and were central to their self-understanding. The promise of salvation provided a prime inducement to convert and the conviction that one's faith offered salvation to others (whose contributions would sustain and renew the group) provided a prime motive to proselytize. Soteriological concerns thus figured prominently in the life of post-ancient religions, whose members sought—and promised others—escape from a world they experienced as hostile, bewildering, and finite to an alternative realm of eternal bliss. Such escape was prefigured by the move from one social group, identity, and set of loyalties to another: abandoning one's family, for instance, to join one's new brothers-and-sisters-in-Christ (Matthew 10.37, Luke 14.26). This shift further correlates to a change from "locative" worldviews concerned with the proper emplacement of all things and persons (since being-in-place is what renders them sacred) to "utopian" orientations that valorize mobility as transcendence and liberation (J. Z. Smith 1978).

One final point about religious community in the post-ancient context: In groups that made shared beliefs and practices their chief criteria of inclusion, deviation from these had serious consequences and could provoke not only debate and discussion, but also power struggles and schism. Accordingly, issues of heterodoxy and orthodoxy, heteropraxy and orthopraxy, heresy and heresiology all rose to prominence, along with the institutional means to frame and resolve them—and also to enforce the hierarchic elevation of victors over vanquished.

This brings us to institutions. In the ancient, specifically religious institutions—priesthoods, temples, cult sites, and so on—were typically subordinate to institutions of the state, be these civic, national, or imperial, democratic, oligarchic, or royal. Smaller and weaker than their political counterparts, religious institutions served and were dependent on them for protection, financial support, and personnel. As examples, consider Athenian interest in Eleusis, the temples of the Acropolis, and the Panathenaea; the haoma sacrifices at Persepolis (Bowman 1970); or the integration of priestly and magisterial offices in the Roman *cursus honorum*. Only in a very few cases, where religious institutions possessed extraordinary prestige and authority such that they attracted an international clientele and rich contributions, were they able to sustain themselves and achieve a situation of relative autonomy. Delphi is the paradigmatic case, alongside only a handful of others.

In the post-ancient, some religious institutions such as the rabbinate attained a certain measure of autonomy from the states to which they were subject, but from which they maintained a cautious distance. In other situations—Byzantium and the Islamic caliphate, in particular—religious and political organizations and concerns interpenetrated each other so thoroughly as practically to merge. The most dramatic development, however, occurred in the West, where events beginning with the conversion of Constantine and the Edict of Milan (313 CE) produced a centralized, well-staffed and well-funded, hierarchic religious establishment that became the senior partner in the collaborations of church and state subsequent to the fall of Rome (476 CE). In all these forms and locales, however, religious bodies secured considerable control over such vital arenas of activity as education (general and professional), social welfare (charity and counseling), record keeping, rites of passage (the crucial moments of subject and family formation), and moral scrutiny and control (through preaching, confession, absolution, and pastoral care). Gradually, they perfected the ability to extract revenue from the faithful through a variety of mechanisms. Thus, in addition to contributions (tithing, *zakkat*) that were often voluntary in name only, bequests intended to secure salvation were also an important source of income, as was commerce in spiritual goods and services of varied sorts: blessings, indulgences, relics, charms, mystic knowledge, magic formulas, and so forth.

As ancient religion gave way to post-ancient, a discourse based on canonic corpora of sacred texts displaced inspired performances of sacred verse; practices of prayer, contemplation, and self-perfection displaced mediations through sacrifice and statues of the deity; de-territorialized elective communities constructed on the basis of religious adherence displaced multi-stranded groups within which ties of geography, politics, kinship, culture, and religion were all isomorphic and mutually reinforcing; and institutions that, with some exceptions, had better funding, a wider range of activities, and more autonomy from the state displaced their weaker, more localized predecessors.

Although these sweeping generalizations call for extended treatment that would attend to the nuances and particularities of a thousand specific cases, the constraints of a concluding article point in the opposite direction, toward a summation whose oversimplifications serve chiefly to prompt objections, further inquiry, and debate. And so, here it is: The transition yields Christianity. Or, to put it a bit more cautiously, the ancient ends and the post-ancient begins with Christianity(ies), Judaism(s), and Islam(s), with the westernmost form of Christianity as the extreme case.

Bibliography

Asad, Talal. *Genealogies of Religion: Discipline and Reasons of Power in Christianity and Islam.* Baltimore: Johns Hopkins University Press, 1993.

Assmann, Jan, ed. *Die Erfindung des inneren Menschen: Studien zur religiösen Anthropologie.* Gütersloh: G. Mohn, 1993.

Bianchi, Ugo, and Martin Vermaseren, eds. *La soteriologia dei culti orientali nell'Impero romano*. Leiden: Brill, 1982.

Bowman, Raymond. *Aramaic Ritual Texts from Persepolis*. Chicago: University of Chicago Press, 1970.

Brown, Peter. *Society and the Holy in Late Antiquity*. Berkeley: University of California Press, 1982.

Burkert, Walter. *Homo necans: The Anthropology of Ancient Greek Sacrificial Ritual and Myth*, trans. Peter Bing. Berkeley: University of California Press, 1983. [German original 1972.]

Cornford, Francis Macdonald. *From Religion to Philosophy: A Study in the Origins of Western Speculation*. London: E. Arnold, 1912.

Detienne, Marcel. *The Masters of Truth in Archaic Greece*, trans. Janet Lloyd. New York: Zone Books, 1996. [French original 1967.]

Detienne, Marcel, and Jean-Pierre Vernant. *The Cuisine of Sacrifice among the Greeks*, trans. Paula Wissing. Chicago: University of Chicago Press, 1989. [French original 1979.]

Dodds, E. R. *Pagan and Christian in an Age of Anxiety: Some Aspects of Religious Experience from Marcus Aurelius to Constantine*. Cambridge: Cambridge University Press, 1965.

Eliade, Mircea. *The Myth of the Eternal Return*, trans. Willard R. Trask. Princeton: Princeton University Press, 1954. [French original 1949.]

Frankfort, Henri. *Kingship and the Gods: A Study of Ancient Near Eastern Religion as the Integration of Society and Nature*. Chicago: University of Chicago Press, 1948.

Fustel de Coulanges, Numa Denis. *The Ancient City: A Study on the Religion, Laws, and Institutions of Greece and Rome*. Baltimore: Johns Hopkins University Press, 1980. [French original 1864.]

Girard, René. *Violence and the Sacred*, trans. Patrick Gregory. Baltimore: Johns Hopkins University Press, 1977. [French original 1972.]

Goody, Jack. *The Interface between the Written and the Oral*. Cambridge: Cambridge University Press, 1987.

Grottanelli, Cristiano. "Healers and Saviors of the Eastern Mediterranean," in Bianchi and Vermaseren 1982.

———. *Il sacrificio*. Rome: Laterza, 1999.

Grottanelli, Cristiano, and Nicola Parise. *Sacrificio e società nel mondo antico*. Rome: Laterza, 1988.

Havelock, Eric Alfred. *Preface to Plato*. Cambridge, Mass.: Harvard University Press, 1963.

Hubert, Henri, and Marcel Mauss. *Sacrifice: Its Nature and Function*. Chicago: University of Chicago Press, 1964. [French original 1899.]

Kippenberg, Hans, ed. *Die vorderasiatischen Erlösungsreligionen in ihrem Zusammenhang mit der antiken Stadtherrschaft*. Frankfurt am Main: Suhrkamp, 1991.

Kugel, James, ed. *Poetry and Prophecy: The Beginnings of a Literary Tradition*. Ithaca: Cornell University Press, 1990.

Lincoln, Bruce. *Holy Terrors: Thinking about Religion after September 11*. Chicago: University of Chicago Press, 2003.

———. *Myth, Cosmos, and Society: Indo-European Themes of Creation and Destruction*. Cambridge, Mass.: Harvard University Press, 1986.

Loew, Cornelius. *Myth, Sacred History, and Philosophy: The Pre-Christian Religious Heritage of the West*. New York: Harcourt, Brace & World, 1967.

Momigliano, Arnaldo. *Alien Wisdom: The Limits of Hellenization*. Cambridge: Cambridge University Press, 1975.

———. *On Pagans, Jews, and Christians*. Middletown, Conn.: Wesleyan University Press, 1987.

Nestle, Wilhelm. *Vom Mythos zum Logos: Die Selbstentfaltung des griechischen Denkens von Homer bis auf die Sophistik und Sokrates.* Stuttgart: A. Kröner, 1940.

Ong, Walter. *Orality and Literacy: The Technologizing of the Word.* London: Methuen, 1982.

Pritchard, James, ed. *Ancient Near Eastern Texts Relating to the Old Testament,* 3rd ed. Princeton: Princeton University Press, 1969. "A Cosmological Incantation: The Worm and the Toothache," trans. E. A. Speiser, pp. 100–101.

Smith, Jonathan Z. *Drudgery Divine: On the Comparison of Early Christianities and the Religions of Late Antiquity.* Chicago: University of Chicago Press, 1990.

———. *Map Is Not Territory: Studies in the History of Religions.* Leiden: Brill, 1978.

Smith, Wilfred Cantwell. *The Meaning and End of Religion: A New Approach to the Religious Traditions of Mankind.* New York: Macmillan, 1963.

Smith, William Robertson. *Lectures on the Religion of the Semites: First series, The Fundamental Institutions.* New York: Appleton, 1889.

Stroumsa, Guy. "Les mutations religieuses de l'antiquité tardive," lectures given at the Collège de France, Spring 2004 (publication forthcoming).

Thieme, Paul 1957. "Vorzarathustrisches bei den Zarathustriern und bei Zarathustra," *Zeitschrift der Deutschen Morgenländischen Gesellschaft* 107 (1957): 67–104.

Vernant, Jean-Pierre. "At Man's Table: Hesiod's Foundation Myth of Sacrifice," in Detienne and Vernant 1989, pp. 21–86. [French original 1979.]

———. *The Origins of Greek Thought.* Ithaca, N.Y.: Cornell University Press, 1982. [French original 1962.]

Illustrations

Acknowledgments

The publishers thank the following sources for permission to reproduce the color illustrations following p. 172:

Sety I gazes upon Osiris: Courtesy of the Oriental Institute at the University of Chicago and the Egypt Exploration Society

Shrine with Isis and Osiris: © The British Museum

Painted figure of the goddess Maat: Photograph © 1991 by David Silverman

Lion from the Ishtar Gate: Hirmer Fotoarchiv

Silver bull calf: Courtesy of Ashkelon Excavations, The Leon Levy Excavation

Reconstruction of Solomon's Temple: © Lawrence E. Stager. Artist: Catherine S. Alexander

Ezekiel in the Valley of the Bones: The Jewish Museum/Art Resource, New York

Mosaic from Hammath-Tiberias: Photo by Z. Radovan, Jerusalem

Hittite gold pendant of a god: Erich Lessing/Art Resource, New York

Sphinx gate: Borromeo/Art Resource, New York

Zoroastrian fire temple: SEF/Art Resource, New York

Minoan ritual: Hirmer Fotoarchiv

Krater depicting Dionysus and Hades: The Darius Painter (Greek, South Italian, Apulian), Volute Krater, detail, main scene, Side A, about 335–325 BCE. Toledo Museum of Art, Gift of Edward Drummond Libbey, Florence Scott Libbey, and the Egypt Exploration Society

Statue of Artemis of Ephesus: Scala/Art Resource, New York

The Campana Panel: Réunion des Musées Nationaux/Art Resource, New York

Etruscan Tomb of the Reliefs: Scala/Art Resource, New York

Roman cameo of Livia with Tiberius: Erich Lessing/Art Resource, New York

Shrine of household gods: Werner Forman/Art Resource, New York

Wall painting of Isis ceremonies: Scala/Art Resource, New York

The Last Supper: Scala/Art Resource, New York

Good Shepherd fresco: Courtesy Harold Attridge

Contributors

A.B.McG.	Andrew McGowan, Trinity College, University of Melbourne
A.C.	Angelos Chaniotis, Seminar für Alte Geschichte, University of Heidelberg
A.J.S.	Anthony Spalinger, Department of Classics and Ancient History, Aukland University
A.K.G.	Ann Guinan, University of Pennsylvania
A.H.	Anders Hultgård, Teologiska institutionen, Uppsala University
A.M.H.	Albert Henrichs, Department of the Classics, Harvard University
A.Y.C.	Adela Yarbro Collins, Divinity School, Yale University
B.A.	Bendt Alster, Helsingør, Denmark
B.D.S.	Bryan Spinks, Divinity School, Yale University
B.E.D.	Brian E. Daley, Department of Theology, University of Notre Dame
B.J.C.	Billie Jean Collins, Department of Middle Eastern and South Asian Studies, Emory University
B.L.	Bruce Lincoln, Divinity School, University of Chicago
B.L.E.	Barry Eichler, University of Pennsylvania Museum of Archaeology and Anthropology
B.P.-L.	Beate Pongratz-Leisten, Princeton University
C.A.B.	Charles A. Bobertz, School of Theology, St. John's University
C.A.F.	Christopher A. Faraone, Department of Classics, University of Chicago
C.E.N.	Carole Newlands, Department of Classics, University of Wisconsin, Madison
C.J.G.	Christopher Gill, Department of Classics and Ancient History, Univesity of Exeter
Chr.L.	Christian Leitz, Ägyptologisches Institut, University of Tübingen
C.O.	Carolyn Osiek, Brite Divinity School, Texas Christian University
C.U.	Christoph Uehlinger, University of Zurich
D.A.S.M.	Dominic Montserrat, Department of Classical Studies, The Open University
D.B.	David Brakke, Department of Religious Studies, Indiana University
D.Br.	Dominique Briquel, University of Paris, Sorbonne
D.E.A.	David Aune, Department of Theology, University of Notre Dame
D.E.H.	David Hahm, Department of Greek and Latin, The Ohio State University
D.F.	David Frankfurter, Religious Studies Program, Department of History, University of New Hampshire
D.K.	Dina Katz, Leiden, The Netherlands
D.Kr.	Derek Krueger, Department of Religious Studies, Univesity of North Carolina at Greensboro
D.L.	David Lorton, Baltimore, Maryland
D.P.S.	David Silverman, Department of Asian and Middle Eastern Studies, University of Pennsylvania
D.P.W.	David P. Wright, Department of Near Eastern and Judaic Studies, Brandeis University
D.S.P.	David Potter, Department of Classics, University of Michigan
E.F.	Eckhart Frahm, Seminar für Sprachen und Kulturen des Vorderen Orient, University of Heidelberg

E.F.W.	Edward F. Wente, Oriental Institute, University of Chicago
E.O.	Eckart Otto, Institut für Alttestamentliche Theologie, University of Munich
E.P.	Elaine Pagels, Princeton University
E.S.	Eileen Schuller, Department of Religious Studies, McMaster University
F.A.M.W.	Frans Wiggermann, Department of Semitic Languages, Free University, Amsterdam
F.B.	François Bovon, Divinity School, Harvard University
F.G.	Fritz Graf, Department of Greek and Latin, The Ohio State University
F.M.K.	F. M. Kotwal, Bombay, India
G.G.S.	Guy Stroumsa, Department of Comparative Religion, The Hebrew University of Jerusalem
G.L.W.	Gernot L. Windfuhr, Department of Near Eastern Studies, University of Michigan
G.M.B.	Gary Beckman, Department of Near Eastern Studies, University of Michigan
G.O.L.	Gregorio del Olmo Lete, Departamento de Filología Semítica, Barcelona University
G.R.	Gil Renberg, Department of Greek and Latin, The Ohio State University
H.A.	Hector Avalos, Department of Philosophy and Religious Studies, Iowa State University
H.G.K.	Hans G. Kippenberg, Max-Weber-Kolleg, Erfurt
H.H.	Hripsime Haroutunian, Oriental Institute, University of Chicago
H.K.	Helen King, Department of Classics, University of Reading
H.St.	Heike Sternberg, Institute of Egyptology, University of Göttingen
H.O.W.	Harco Willems, Department of Egyptology, University of Leuven
H.W.A.	Harold Attridge, Divinity School, Yale University
I.C.	Izak Cornelius, Department of Ancient Studies, University of Stellenbosch
I.E.-B.	Ingrid Edlund-Berry, Department of Classics, University of Texas at Austin
I.K.	Israel Knohl, Bible Department, Hebrew University
J.A.	Jan Assmann, University of Heidelberg
J.A.S.	James A. Sanders, Ancient Biblical Manuscript Center, Claremont, California
J.B.	John Bodel, Department of Classics, Brown University
J.B.R.	James Rives, York University
J.D.M.	Jon Mikalson, Department of Classics, University of Virginia
J.E.G.	James E. Goehring, Department of Classics, Philosophy, and Religion, University of Mary Washington
J.F.Q.	Joachim Friedrich Quack, Ägyptologisches Seminar, Free University Berlin
J.G.W.	Joan Westenholz, Oriental Institute, University of Chicago
J.J.C.	John J. Collins, Divinity School, Yale University
J.-J.G.	J.-J. Glassner, Centre national de la recherche scientifique, Paris
J.J.P.	John J. Pilch, Theology Department, Georgetown University
J.K.C.	Jamsheed K. Choksy, Departments of Central Eurasian Studies, History, and Religious Studies, Indiana University
J.L.C.	James L. Crenshaw, Divinity School, Duke University
J.M.T.	Jean MacIntosh Turfa, University of Pennsylvania Museum of Archaeology and Anthropology
J.N.	John North, Department of Ancient History, University College London
J.N.B.	Jan N. Bremmer, Faculty of Theology and Religious Studies, University of Groningen
J.P.A.	James P. Allen, Department of Egyptian Art, Metropolitan Museum of Art
J.P.S.	Jørgen Podemann Sørensen, Department of History of Religions, University of Copenhagen
J.R.B.	John Baines, Faculty of Oriental Studies, University of Oxford
J.S.	John Scheid, Collège de France, Paris
J.T.	John Taylor, Department of Ancient Egypt and Sudan, The British Museum
J.T.F.	John T. Fitzgerald, Department of Religious Studies, University of Miami
J.W.B.	James W. Boyd, Department of Philosophy, Colorado State University
J.Z.	Jürgen Zangenberg, University of Wuppertal, Germany

674

K.D.   Ken Dowden, Institute of Archaeology and Antiquity, University of Birmingham
†K.H.   Keith Hopkins, Kings College, University of Cambridge
K.L.K.   Karen L. King, Harvard Divinity School, Harvard University
K.v.d.T.   Karel van der Toorn, University of Amsterdam
L.B.v.d.M.   L. B. van der Meer, Faculteit der Archeologie, Leiden University
L.B.Z.   Louise Bruit Zaidman, University of Paris 7 – Dénis Diderot
L.E.P.   Laurie Pearce, University of California, Berkeley
†L.K.   László Kákosy, Department of Egyptology, Eötvös University
L.K.H.   Lowell K. Handy, American Theological Library Association, Chicago
M.B.   Mary Beard, Faculty of Classics and Newnham College, Cambridge University
M.F.   Michael Fishbane, Divinity School, University of Chicago
M.S.   Marcel Sigrist, École Biblique et Archéologique Française, Jerusalem
M.S.S.   Mark S. Smith, Department of Hebrew and Judaic Studies, New York University
M.St.   Michael Stausberg, Department of the History of Religions, The University of Bergen
M.T.   Mario Torelli, Dipartimento Uomo e Territorio, sezione Studi Comparati sulle Società Antiche,
              University of Perugia
N.K.G.   Norman Gottwald, Pacific School of Religion, Berkeley, California
N.M.   Nanno Marinatos, Department of Classics and Mediterranean Studies, University of Illinois at
              Chicago
N.T.de G.   Nancy de Grummond, Classics Department, Florida State University
N.W.   Neal Walls, Divinity School, Wake Forest University
O.C.   Olivier de Cazanove, Department of Ancient History, University of Paris 1
O.M.D.   Olga M. Davidson, Department of Near Eastern and Judaic Studies, Brandeis University
P.-A.B.   Paul-Alain Beaulieu, Department of Near Eastern Languages and Civilizations, Harvard University
P.F.B.   Paul F. Bradshaw, University of Notre Dame
Ph.B.   Philippe Borgeaud, Département des sciences de l'antiquité, University of Geneva
P.G.   Philippe Gignoux, Section des Sciences Religieuses, École Pratique des Hautes Études, Paris
P.J.F.   Paul John Frandsen, The Carsten Niebuhr Institute of Ancient Near East Studies, Copenhagen
P.S.A.   Philip Alexander, University of Manchester
P.T.S.   Peter T. Struck, Department of Classical Studies, University of Pennsylvania
R.A.   Rainer Albertz, Alttestamentliches Seminar der Evangelisch-Theologischen Fakultät, University of
              Münster
R.C.T.P.   Robert Parker, New College, Oxford University
R.I.P.   Richard I. Pervo, St. Paul, Minnesota
R.J.C.   Richard J. Clifford, Weston Jesuit School of Theology
R.H.B.   Richard Beal, Oriental Institute, University of Chicago
R.L.   René Lebrun, Catholic University of Louvain, Louvain-la-Neuve
R.L.B.   Roger Beck, Department of Classics, University of Toronto
R.L.G.   Richard Gordon, Ilmminster, Germany
R.M.   Robert Meyer, Aegyptologisches Institut, University of Heidelberg
R.R.W.   Robert Wilson, Divinity School, Yale University
S.A.   Susan Ackerman, Department of Religion, Dartmouth College
S.B.   Susanne Bickel, Département des sciences de l'antiquité, University of Fribourg
S.B.P.   Simon B. Parker, School of Theology, Boston University
S.F.   Steven J. Friesen, University of Missouri, Columbia
S.I.J.   Sarah Iles Johnston, Department of Greek and Latin, The Ohio State University
S.M.O.   Saul M. Olyan, Program in Judaic Studies and Department of Religious Studies, Brown University
S.P.   Simo Parpola, Institute for Asian and African Studies, University of Helsinki
S.R.F.P.   Simon R. F. Price, Lady Margaret Hall, Oxford University

CONTRIBUTORS

S.S.   Suzanne Said, Department of Classics, Columbia University

T.A.   Tzvi Abusch, Department of Near Eastern and Judaic Studies, Brandeis University

T.L.H.   Tawny L. Holm, Department of Religious Studies, Indiana University of Pennsylvania

T.M.F.   Thomas M. Finn, Department of Religion, College of William and Mary

T.v.d.H.   Theo van den Hout, Oriental Institute, University of Chicago

V.B.   Virginia Burrus, Theological School, Drew University

V.E.I.   Vedia Izzet, Christ's College, University of Cambridge

W.B.   Walter Burkert, University of Zürich

Wa.Sa.   Walther Sallaberger, Institut für Assyriologie und Hethitologie, University of Munich

W.W.M.   William Malandra, Department of Asian Studies, University of Texas

† Deceased

Index

Juno (Roman deity), 286, 420. *See also* Hera (Greek deity)

Juno Caelestis (Carthaginian deity), 116, 123

Juno Regina, 277

Juno Sospita, 117, 121

Jupiter (Roman deity), 4, 18, 276, 286, 420. *See also* Zeus (Greek deity)

Jupiter Dolichenus, 279, 322

Justice, 30–31, 84, 86, 532; Egyptian, 30, 91–92, 155, 351, 352, 372; Greek, 525, 541–542; Hittite, 540; Jewish, 30–31, 155, 183, 503; Mesopotamian, 86, 499; in Plato, 96. *See also* Theodicy

Justinian, *Digests*, 311

Justin Martyr, 279, 323, 545, 595

Kamrusepa (Hittite deity), 419, 588

Karnak, 159

Karnak temple, 256, 290, 313

Karnea (Greek festival), 285

Keret, story of, 53, 54

Kesh, 166

Khattushili, 521

Khnum (Egyptian deity), 579

Khnum Festival of Esna, 282

Khoyak rites, 244

Khwarnah (Iranian deity), 362

KI.LAM festival (Hittite), 193, 283

King: Aramean, 178; Assyrian, 171; divinity of, 549–550; Egyptian, 88, 92, 93, 94, 155, 156, 157, 244, 247, 248, 289–290, 328, 329, 515, 534, 549–550, 578, 641; Hittite, 192, 193, 194, 195, 259, 260, 299, 317, 336, 339, 539–540, 553–554, 569; Iranian, 589; in Judaism, 35, 181, 298, 551; Mesopotamian, 88, 93, 94, 165, 167, 250, 252–253, 283, 330, 331, 516, 518, 587, 627, 628, 643; in New Year festival, 37, 39; Persian, 318; Phoenician, 177; in polytheism, 18; as priest, 288; Roman, 230, 306, 559; Syro-Canaanite, 175, 295, 296, 550–551; Ugaritic, 175

Kingdom in Heaven (Hittite myth), 588

Kirder, 198, 202, 301, 302, 318, 556

Kirta Epic, 174, 356, 377, 519, 584

Kittum (Mesopotamian goddess), 292

Kom, temple of, 248

Kom Ombo, 159

Kore, 99, 100, 268, 285

Kronia (Greek festival), 38, 42, 52, 268, 282, 285

Kubaba, 7–8, 8

Kuhn, Adalbert, 46

Kumarbi (Hittite deity), 8, 47, 190, 191, 419

Kumarbi Cycle, 47, 48, 49, 53, 55, 61, 191

Kumidi, temple of, 256

Kybebe, 7, 8

Kysis, 159

Lactantius, 67, 69

Lamentation, 358

Lane-Fox, Robin, 134

Laran (Etrurian deity), 421

Lares (Roman deities), 366

Larsa, 166, 168

Lasa (Etrurian deity), 421

Latin League, 113

Law, 85, 86, 87, 94–95; Egyptian, 88; Hittite, 521–522; Iranian, 94, 522, 523, 524; Jewish, 316, 519–521; Mesopotamian, 516; Roman, 527; written, 127

Leibniz, Wilhelm Gottfried, 540

Lelwani (Hittite deity), 299

Lent (Christian feast), 287

Lentulus Marcellinus, 559

Leonidas, 268

Lesses, Rebecca, 150

Letter of Aristeas, 521

Letter of Peter to Philip, 654

Levites, 297, 298, 310

Libation: and Eleusinian mysteries, 100; Greek, 341, 342; Mesopotamian, 293, 331; Roman, 346; Syro-Canaanite, 332; and transfer and assimilation, 12–13. *See also* Ritual

Linear A, 206

Linear B, 208, 211, 267, 591

Literacy, 128–129, 131, 134, 136, 166, 660; Egyptian, 351. *See also* Writing

Livius Andronicus, 55

Livy, 36, 118, 127, 343, 592

Logos, 422

Lucan: *Civil War*, 365

Lucian: *Alexander or the False Prophet*, 304; *Philopseudes*, 145; *On the Syrian Goddess*, 377

Lucretius, 365, 527

Ludi Romani, Ludi Magni (Roman festival), 285

Ludi saeculares (Roman festival), 286

Lugulbanda, 54

Luhmann, Niklaus, 15

Lupercalia (Roman festival), 274, 275, 286

Luxor, temple of, 247

Lycurgus, *Lament of Leocrates*, 85

Ma'at, concept of. *See* Egypt

Maat (Egyptian deity), 60, 85, 329, 534, 538

Maccabean revolt, 186, 187, 553

Macedonian kings, 218, 219

Macrobius, *Saturnalia*, 27, 274

Magi, 202, 301, 318, 555

Magic, 139–152; Anatolian, 150; and Bible (Hebrew), 140; and Christianity, 140, 141, 149, 369; definitions of, 139–142; Egyptian, 142, 147, 149, 150, 157, 160, 162, 290, 350–351, 454–456, 579, 601, 625–626; Greek, 140, 141, 145, 146, 147, 149, 150, 467, 635; Hittite, 300, 336–337, 461–463, 631–632; Hurrian, 146; and Jesus, 140; in Judaism, 139–140, 141, 144, 146, 150, 460; Mesopotamian, 144, 250, 292, 295, 353, 354, 355, 457–458; in New Testament, 140; in Plato, 142–143; Roman, 150, 367, 368; Syro-Canaanite, 356, 376; and YHWH, 139, 140; Zoroastrian, 361. *See also* Witchcraft

Magical papyri, 635, 642, 643

Magna Mater. *See* Cybele/Magna Mater

Malinowski, Bronislaw, 51, 142

Maltomini, Franco, 151

Mandulis (Egyptian deity), 160

Mani, 464, 556, 641, 647

Manicheism, 82, 198, 231, 432–433, 556; Bayle on, 540; and Christianity, 647; cosmos in, 648–649; development of, 647–649; disorder in, 507; dualism in, 648, 649; evil in, 507, 648, 649; and heresy, 632–633; illness in, 464; and Judaism, 647; and Kirder, 318; legal protection for, 523–524; matter in, 506, 507; medicine in, 464; morality in, 523; pollution in, 506; purity in, 506, 507; and Romans, 647–648; and Zoroastrianism, 647

Marathon, 268–269

Marcion, 236, 546, 623, 638

Marcionites, 82

Marcius, 636–637

Marcus Aurelius, *Meditations*, 527

Zoroastrianism *(continued)*
individual in, 431–432; initiation in, 445; judgment after death in, 204, 506; and Kirder, 318, 556; laity in, 360; lies in, 339, 340, 570; magi in, 318; magic in, 361; and Manicheism, 647; marriage in, 445; material world in, 265; medicine in, 463, 464; monotheism in, 201, 203, 204; morality in, 201, 203, 204, 265, 522–523, 524; netherworld in, 506; New Year in, 266; offerings in, 339–340; order in, 361, 505, 506; physical world in, 339; and politics, 301, 555, 556; pollution in, 265, 340, 505, 506, 509; polytheism of, 204; prayer in, 266, 360–362; pregnancy in, 444; priests in, 266, 360; prophecy in, 383; purification in, 339, 506; purity in, 265; religious control in, 570; rites of passage in, 444–445; ritual in, 204, 265–266, 632; sacred time and space in, 264–266; sacrifice in, 360, 382; shamanism in, 302; sin in, 80, 505, 506; spiritual world in, 339; temples in, 202, 265–266, 318, 382, 612–613; theodicy of, 540, 541; vision in, 382–383; visual representations in, 612–613; and women, 301, 302; women in, 204. *See also* Iran; Zarathustra (Zoroaster)

Zukru (Syro-Canaanite festival), 255, 283

Zurwan (Iranian deity), 420